Lecture Notes in Computer Science 4421

Lecture Notes in Computer Science 4421

Commenced Publication in 1973
Founding and Former Series Editors:
Gerhard Goos, Juris Hartmanis, and Jan van Leeuwen

Rocco De Nicola (Ed.)

Programming Languages and Systems

16th European Symposium on Programming, ESOP 2007
Held as Part of the Joint European Conferences
on Theory and Practics of Software, ETAPS 2007
Braga, Portugal, March 24 - April 1, 2007
Proceedings

Volume Editor

Rocco De Nicola
Dipartimento di Sistemi e Informatica
Università di Firenze
Viale Morgagni 65
50134 Firenze, Italy
E-mail: denicola@dsi.unifi.it

Library of Congress Control Number: 2007922404

CR Subject Classification (1998): D.3, D.1, D.2, F.3, F.4, E.1

LNCS Sublibrary: SL 1 – Theoretical Computer Science and General Issues

ISSN 0302-9743
ISBN-10 3-540-71314-X Springer Berlin Heidelberg New York
ISBN-13 978-3-540-71314-2 Springer Berlin Heidelberg New York

Springer is a part of Springer Science+Business Media

springer.com

Printed in Germany

Typesetting: Camera-ready by author, data conversion by Scientific Publishing Services, Chennai, India
Printed on acid-free paper SPIN: 12032907 06/3142 5 4 3 2 1 0

Foreword

ETAPS 2007 is the tenth instance of the European Joint Conferences on Theory and Practice of Software, and thus a cause for celebration.

The events that comprise ETAPS address various aspects of the system development process, including specification, design, implementation, analysis and improvement. The languages, methodologies and tools which support these activities are all well within its scope. Different blends of theory and practice are represented, with an inclination towards theory with a practical motivation on the one hand and soundly based practice on the other. Many of the issues involved in software design apply to systems in general, including hardware systems, and the emphasis on software is not intended to be exclusive.

History and Prehistory of ETAPS

ETAPS as we know it is an annual federated conference that was established in 1998 by combining five conferences [Compiler Construction (CC), European Symposium on Programming (ESOP), Fundamental Approaches to Software Engineering (FASE), Foundations of Software Science and Computation Structures (FOSSACS), Tools and Algorithms for Construction and Analysis of Systems (TACAS)] with satellite events.

All five conferences had previously existed in some form and in various colocated combinations: accordingly, the prehistory of ETAPS is complex. FOSSACS was earlier known as the Colloquium on Trees in Algebra and Programming (CAAP), being renamed for inclusion in ETAPS as its historical name no longer reflected its contents. Indeed CAAP's history goes back a long way; prior to 1981, it was known as the Colleque de Lille sur les Arbres en Algebre et en Programmation. FASE was the indirect successor of a 1985 event known as Colloquium on Software Engineering (CSE), which together with CAAP formed a joint event called TAPSOFT in odd-numbered years. Instances of TAPSOFT, all including CAAP plus at least one software engineering event, took place every two years from 1985 to 1997 inclusive. In the alternate years, CAAP took place separately from TAPSOFT.

Meanwhile, ESOP and CC were each taking place every two years from 1986. From 1988, CAAP was colocated with ESOP in even years. In 1994, CC became a "conference" rather than a "workshop" and CAAP, CC and ESOP were thereafter all colocated in even years.

TACAS, the youngest of the ETAPS conferences, was founded as an international workshop in 1995; in its first year, it was colocated with TAPSOFT. It took place each year, and became a "conference" when it formed part of ETAPS 1998. It is a telling indication of the importance of tools in the modern field of informatics that TACAS today is the largest of the ETAPS conferences.

The coming together of these five conferences was due to the vision of a small group of people who saw the potential of a combined event to be more than the sum of its parts. Under the leadership of Don Sannella, who became the first ETAPS steering committee chair, they included: Andre Arnold, Egidio Astesiano, Hartmut Ehrig, Peter Fritzson, Marie-Claude Gaudel, Tibor Gyimothy, Paul Klint, Kim Guldstrand Larsen, Peter Mosses, Alan Mycroft, Hanne Riis Nielson, Maurice Nivat, Fernando Orejas, Bernhard Steffen, Wolfgang Thomas and (alphabetically last but in fact one of the ringleaders) Reinhard Wilhelm.

ETAPS today is a loose confederation in which each event retains its own identity, with a separate programme committee and proceedings. Its format is open-ended, allowing it to grow and evolve as time goes by. Contributed talks and system demonstrations are in synchronized parallel sessions, with invited lectures in plenary sessions. Two of the invited lectures are reserved for "unifying" talks on topics of interest to the whole range of ETAPS attendees. The aim of cramming all this activity into a single one-week meeting is to create a strong magnet for academic and industrial researchers working on topics within its scope, giving them the opportunity to learn about research in related areas, and thereby to foster new and existing links between work in areas that were formerly addressed in separate meetings.

ETAPS 1998–2006

The first ETAPS took place in Lisbon in 1998. Subsequently it visited Amsterdam, Berlin, Genova, Grenoble, Warsaw, Barcelona, Edinburgh and Vienna before arriving in Braga this year. During that time it has become established as the major conference in its field, attracting participants and authors from all over the world. The number of submissions has more than doubled, and the numbers of satellite events and attendees have also increased dramatically.

ETAPS 2007

ETAPS 2007 comprises five conferences (CC, ESOP, FASE, FOSSACS, TACAS), 18 satellite workshops (ACCAT, AVIS, Bytecode, COCV, FESCA, FinCo, GT-VMT, HAV, HFL, LDTA, MBT, MOMPES, OpenCert, QAPL, SC, SLA++P, TERMGRAPH and WITS), three tutorials, and seven invited lectures (not including those that were specific to the satellite events). We received around 630 submissions to the five conferences this year, giving an overall acceptance rate of 25%. To accommodate the unprecedented quantity and quality of submissions, we have four-way parallelism between the main conferences on Wednesday for the first time. Congratulations to all the authors who made it to the final programme! I hope that most of the other authors still found a way of participating in this exciting event and I hope you will continue submitting.

ETAPS 2007 was organized by the Departamento de Informática of the Universidade do Minho, in cooperation with

- European Association for Theoretical Computer Science (EATCS)
- European Association for Programming Languages and Systems (EAPLS)
- European Association of Software Science and Technology (EASST)
- The Computer Science and Technology Center (CCTC, Universidade do Minho)
- Camara Municipal de Braga
- CeSIUM/GEMCC (Student Groups)

The organizing team comprised:

- João Saraiva (Chair)
- José Bacelar Almeida (Web site)
- José João Almeida (Publicity)
- Luís Soares Barbosa (Satellite Events, Finances)
- Victor Francisco Fonte (Web site)
- Pedro Henriques (Local Arrangements)
- José Nuno Oliveira (Industrial Liaison)
- Jorge Sousa Pinto (Publicity)
- António Nestor Ribeiro (Fundraising)
- Joost Visser (Satellite Events)

ETAPS 2007 received generous sponsorship from Fundação para a Ciência e a Tecnologia (FCT), Enabler (a Wipro Company), Cisco and TAP Air Portugal.

Overall planning for ETAPS conferences is the responsibility of its Steering Committee, whose current membership is:

Perdita Stevens (Edinburgh, Chair), Roberto Amadio (Paris), Luciano Baresi (Milan), Sophia Drossopoulou (London), Matt Dwyer (Nebraska), Hartmut Ehrig (Berlin), José Fiadeiro (Leicester), Chris Hankin (London), Laurie Hendren (McGill), Mike Hinchey (NASA Goddard), Michael Huth (London), Anna Ingólfsdóttir (Aalborg), Paola Inverardi (L'Aquila), Joost-Pieter Katoen (Aachen), Paul Klint (Amsterdam), Jens Knoop (Vienna), Shriram Krishnamurthi (Brown), Kim Larsen (Aalborg), Tiziana Margaria (Göttingen), Ugo Montanari (Pisa), Rocco de Nicola (Florence), Jakob Rehof (Dortmund), Don Sannella (Edinburgh), João Saraiva (Minho), Vladimiro Sassone (Southampton), Helmut Seidl (Munich), Daniel Varro (Budapest), Andreas Zeller (Saarbrücken).

I would like to express my sincere gratitude to all of these people and organizations, the programme committee chairs and PC members of the ETAPS conferences, the organizers of the satellite events, the speakers themselves, the many reviewers, and Springer for agreeing to publish the ETAPS proceedings. Finally, I would like to thank the organizing chair of ETAPS 2007, João Saraiva, for arranging for us to have ETAPS in the ancient city of Braga.

Edinburgh, January 2007

Perdita Stevens
ETAPS Steering Committee Chair

Preface

This volume contains 34 papers presented at ESOP 2007, the annual European Symposium on Programming, held in Braga, Portugual, in March 2007. The goal of ESOP has always been to bridge the gap between theory and practice of programming, and the conferences continue to be devoted to addressing fundamental issues in the specification, analysis, and implementation of programming languages and systems.

The volume begins with a summary of the invited talk by Andy Pitts and continues with the contributed ESOP papers. The papers deal with important issues such as models and languages for services, logics, type theories and other verification techniques, language-based security, static analysis and abstract interpretation, semantic theories for object-oriented languages, process algebraic techniques for proving systems properties, and term-rewriting theories.

The 34 papers contained in this volume were selected by the Program Committee out of 136 submissions, each reviewed by at least three researchers. The reviews were made by the Program Committee and by 181 additional referees, listed below. The accepted papers were selected during a two-week electronic discussion by the Program Committee.

Thanks go to the authors, the members of the Program Committee, and the external referees for their excellent work, to the ETAPS Steering Committee Chair Perdita Stevens and the ETAPS 2007 Local Organization chaired by João Saraiva for providing infrastructure and gentle reminders, and finally to Andrei Voronkov and the maintainers of the Easychair Conference Management Systems that was very useful in all the phases of paper handling.

January 2007 Rocco De Nicola

Organization

Program Chair

Rocco De Nicola
Dipartimento di Sistemi e Informatica
Università di Firenze, Italy

Program Committee

Steve Brookes	CMU Pittsburgh, USA
Gerard Boudol	INRIA Sophia Antipolis, France
Giuseppe Castagna	ENS Paris, France
Patrick Cousot	ENS Paris, France
Mads Dam	KTH Stockolm, Sweden
Pierpaolo Degano	Univ. Pisa, Italy
Sophia Drossopoulou	Imperial College, UK
Cedric Fournet	Microsoft Cambridge, UK
Stefania Gnesi	ISTI CNR, Italy
Joshua Guttman	MITRE, USA
Chris Hankin	Imperial College, UK
Matthew Hennessy	Univ. Sussex, UK
Alan Jeffrey	Bell Labs, USA
John Mitchell	Stanford Univ., USA
Fleming Nielson	IMM Copenhagen, Denmark
Catuscia Palamidessi	INRIA Paris, France
Benjamin Pierce	U. Pennsylvania, USA
Andrei Sabelfeld	Chalmers Univ., Sweden
Don Sannella	Univ. Edinburgh, UK
Bernhard Steffen	Univ. Dortmund, Germany
Walid Taha	Rice Univ. , USA
Jan Vitek	Purdue Univ., USA
Martin Wirsing	LMU Munich, Germany
Xavier Leroy	INRIA Paris, France
Gianluigi Zavattaro	Univ. Bologna, Italy

Additional Referees

Andreas Abel
Pedro Adao
Irem Aktug
Tristan Allwood
Davide Ancona
Jesus Aranda
Zena Ariola
Aslan Askarov
Robert Atkey

Roberto Bagnara
Adam Barker
Massimo Bartoletti
Joerg Bauer
Hubert Baumeister
Maurice ter Beek
Lennart Beringer
Clara Bertolissi
Lorenzo Bettini
Hariolf Betz
Karthik Bhargavan
Nicole Bidoit
Gavin Bierman
Chiara Bodei
Viviana Bono
Marcello Bonsangue
Michele Boreale
Gilles Brassard
Mario Bravetti
Roberto Bruni
Cristiano Calcagno
Nick Cameron
Brian Campbell
Luca Cardelli
Magnus Carlsson
K. Chatzikokolakis
James Cheney
Antonio Cisternino
Ricardo Corin
Andrea Corradini
Antonio Cunei
David Cunningham
Mika Cohen
Ferruccio Damiani
Vincent Danos
Olivier Danvy
Pierre-Malo Deniélou
Moshe Deutsch
Alessandra Di Pierro
Dino Distefano
Kevin Donnelly
Stephan Ellner
Moreno Falaschi
Alessandro Fantechi
Jérôme Feret
Gianluigi Ferrari
Gian-Luigi Ferrari
Jean-Christ. Filliatre
Robby Findler
Andrea Flexeder
Nate Foster
Alain Frisch
Thom Frhwirth
Rachele Fuzzati
Fabio Gadducci
Han Gao
Stéphane Gaubert
Thomas Gawlitza
Stephen Gilmore
Sabine Glesner
Johan Glimming
Jens C. Godskesen
Ulla Goltz
Dilian Gurov
Rene Rydhof Hansen
Fritz Henglein
Rolf Hennicker
Stephan Herrmann
Mike Hicks
Thomas Hildebrandt
Tom Hirschowitz
Matthias Hölzl
Suresh Jagannathan
Johan Jeuring
Stefan Kahrs
Gerwin Klein
Alexander Knapp
Naoki Kobayashi
Ivan Lanese
Cosimo Laneve
Diego Latella
Christopher League
Jooyong Lee
James Leifer
Francesca Levi
Ruy Ley-Wild
Cedric Lhoussaine
Michele Loreti
Markus Müller-Olm
Kenneth MacKenzie
Patrick Maier
Luc Maranget
Luca Martini
Franco Mazzanti
Hernan Melgratti
Dale Miller
Antoine Miné
David Monniaux
Anders Møller
Ralf Nagel
Sebastian Nanz
Joachim Niehren
Christoffer R. Nielsen
Peter O'Hearn
Chris Okasaki
Carlos Olarte
Peter Olvecki
Karol Ostrovsky
Luca Padovani
Catuscia Palamidessi
Matthew Parkinson
Emir Pasalic
Marius Petria
Andrew Phillips
Henrik Pilegaard
Andrew Pitts
Randy Pollack
Christian W. Probst
Riccardo Pucella
Rosario Pugliese
Harald Raffelt
Julian Rathke
Axel Rauschmayer
Yann Regis-Gianas
Bernhard Reus
Tamara Rezk
M. Birna van Riemsdijk
Xavier Rival
Alessandro Romanel
Mads Rosendahl
Claudio Russo
Alejandro Russo
Didier Remy
Oliver Rüthing
Matthew Sackman

Jens-Wolfhard Schicke
Andreas Schroeder
Peter Sewell
Vitaly Shmatikov
Jeremy Siek
Julien Signoles
Sam Staton
Martin Sulzmann
Hans Svensson
Deian Tabakov
Javier Thayer
Stephan Thesing
Alwen Tiu
Jacques Thomas
Simon Thompson
Alwen Tiu
Andrew Tolmach
Terkel K. Tolstrup
Angelo Troina
Frank D. Valencia
Wim Vanhoof
Daniele Varacca
Betti Venneri
Cristian Versari
Eelco Visser
Jan Vitek
David Walker
Herbert Wiklicky
Verena Wolf
Hongwei Xi
Zhe Yang
Steve Zdancewic
Noam Zeilberger
Gefei Zhang
Ye Zhang
Elena Zucca
Roberto Zunino

Table of Contents

Invited Talk

Models and Languages for Web Services

Verification

Term Rewriting

Language Based Security

Logics and Correctness Proofs

Static Analysis and Abstract Interpretation I

Static Analysis and Abstract Interpretation II

Semantic Theories for Object Oriented Languages

Process Algebraic Techniques

Applicative Programming

Types for Systems Properties

Techniques for Contextual Equivalence in Higher-Order, Typed Languages

Andrew Pitts

University of Cambridge

Abstract. Two phrases in a programming language are said to be contextually equivalent if, roughly speaking, they are interchangeable in any complete program without affecting the observable behaviour of the program. I will discuss precise formalisations of this fundamental notion of semantic equivalence for the case of higher-order, typed (HOT) languages, such as ML and Haskell. How does the structure of a type affect properties of contextual equivalence of expressions of that type? It can be very difficult to answer this question when working directly from the definition of contextual equivalence—mainly because HOT programs can make use of their constituent sub-expressions in dynamically complicated ways. This talk will survey some of the semantic techniques (both denotational and operational) that have been devised for proving properties of HOT contextual equivalence.

R. De Nicola (Ed.): ESOP 2007, LNCS 4421, p. 1, 2007.

Structured Communication-Centred Programming for Web Services

Marco Carbone[1], Kohei Honda[2], and Nobuko Yoshida[1]

[1] Department of Computing, Imperial College London
[2] Department of Computer Science, Queen Mary University of London

Abstract. This paper relates two different paradigms of descriptions of communication behaviour, one focussing on global message flows and another on end-point behaviours, using formal calculi based on session types. The global calculus, which originates from a web service description language (W3C WS-CDL), describes an interaction scenario from a vantage viewpoint; the end-point calculus, an applied typed π-calculus, precisely identifies a local behaviour of each participant. We explore a theory of end-point projection, by which we can map a global description to its end-point counterpart preserving types and dynamics. Three principles of well-structured description and the type structures play a fundamental role in the theory.

1 Introduction

Communication-Centred Programming. The explosive growth of Internet in the last decades has led to the de facto, global standards for naming scheme (URI, Domain Names), communication protocols (SOAP, HTTP, TCP/IP) and message format (XML). These elements offer a useful basis for building applications centring on communication among distributed agents through these standards. Such communication-centred applications are sometimes called *web services*. Web services are an active area of infrastructural development, involving the major standardisation bodies such as W3C and OASIS.

A concrete application area of communication-centred applications is *business protocol*. A business protocol is a series of structured and automated interactions among business entities. It is predominantly inter-domain, is often regulation-bound, and demands clear shared understanding about its meaning. Some protocols such as industry standards will remain unchanged for a long time once specified; others may undergo frequent updates. Because of its inherent inter-organisational nature, there is a strong demand for a common standard for specifying business protocols on a sound technical basis.

Global Description of Interaction. One of the standardisation efforts for a language to specify business protocols is the Web Services Choreography Description Language (WS-CDL) [26], developed by W3C WS-CDL Working Group since 2004 in collaboration with π-calculus experts including the present authors. WS-CDL offers a fully expressive global description language for channel-based

R. De Nicola (Ed.): ESOP 2007, LNCS 4421, pp. 2–17, 2007.

communication equipped with general control constructs (e.g. sequencing, conditionals and recursion), and is conceived with potential usage of type-based formal validation from the outset. The intuition behind the term *choreography* may be summarised thus:

"Dancers dance following a global scenario without a single point of control"

WS-CDL is conceived as a language for describing such a "global scenario": once specified, this scenario is to be executed by individual distributed processes without a single point of control.[1] Another significant feature is WS-CDL's informal use of *sessions* for communication: at the outset of each run of a protocol, a session is established between communication parties so that involved communications can be distinguished from different runs of the same or other protocols.

End-Point Projection. The global description of a communication behaviour is useful since, among others, it offers a clear view of dynamics of the whole interactions. Real execution of the description, however, is always through communication among distributed end-points which (as the notion of choreography dictates) may as well involve no centralised control. Thus we ask:

How can we project a global description to end-point processes so that their interactions precisely realise the original global description?

Such a projection may be called *end-point projection (EPP)*, a terminology from WS-CDL Working Group. Having a universally agreed and well-founded EPP is fundamental for the engineering use of global descriptions, from design to implementations to validations/verifications to run-time monitoring (see § 5).

This paper establishes a formal theory of EPP by introducing the two typed calculi for interaction, a distilled version of WS-CDL (a global calculus) and an applied π-calculus (an end-point calculus), and defining a mapping from the former to the latter. This mapping is highly non-trivial due to the different nature of descriptions: a global calculus directly describes interactions among multiple participants involving sequencing, branching and recursion, which differs from the end-point-based description given in the π-calculus. A central contribution of this work is the identification of three basic principles for global descriptions under which we can define a *sound* and *complete* EPP, in the sense that, through a given EPP, all and only globally described behaviour is realised as communication among end-points. The three principles are: *connectedness* (a basic local causality principle), *well-threadedness* (a stronger locality principle based on session types [23,16,12,25,13,6]) and *coherence* (a consistency principle for description of each participant in a global description). Schematically, the EPP mapping has the following shape:

$$I \quad \mapsto \quad A[P] \mid B[Q] \mid C[R] \mid \cdots$$

[1] A related idea is *orchestration* where one master component, "conductor", directly controls activity of one or more slave components, which is useful when communicating parties can be placed under a common administrative domain, see [1].

where I is a global description, A, B and C are *participants* of the protocol and P, Q and R are projections of I onto A, B and C respectively. We shall show that, when applied to well-typed interactions following the three principles, the EPP mapping thus defined satisfies *type preservation*, *soundness* and *completeness.*

The EPP theory opens a conduit between global descriptions and accumulated studies on process calculi, allowing the use of the latter's rich theories for engineering aims. The EPP theory will be published as an associated document of WS-CDL 1.0 [11] (which contains many examples and full technical details), and will form part of its open-source implementation [19].

Related Work. Global methods for describing communication have been practiced in many different forms, including MSCs, UML diagrams and Petri-Nets [24]. In the context of security study, Strand Space [15] is a model for analysing security protocols based on their global representation; while Briais and Nestmann [7] present a notation for representing protocol narrations and relate it to the π-calculus (which is a form of end-point projection in our sense). These notations and models offer a useful basis for design/specification/analysis, but are not intended as full-fledged programming languages, so that they lack in e.g. general control structures and constructs for value passing and state change.

DiCons is a global notation for programming Internet applications [2] whose primitives include web server invocation, email, and web form filing. A formal notion of end-point projection has not been studied in [2].

The present work shares with many recent works its use of types of the mobile processes, including, but not limited to, Pict [20], Polyphonic C♯ [3] and the preceding studies on session type disciplines [6,12,13,16,23,25]. In the context of session types, our work extends their usage to global descriptions and intra-session parallel communications. These preceding works are based on end-point languages and calculi. The EPP theory offers a passage through which these and other related studies can be reflected onto global descriptions.

Fournet, Gordon, Bhargavan and Corin studied security-related aspects of web services. In [5], they have implemented part of WS-Security libraries, and analyse them through a translation into the π-calculus. The benefits of such a tool may be reflected onto global descriptions through the theory of EPP.

Laneve and Padovani [17] give a model of orchestrations using an extensions of π-calculus to join patterns. Busi et al. [8] study a bisimulation-based correspondence between choreography and orchestration. In [14], they further studied a calculus for web services of end-point descriptions based on predicate-driven communication. A formal theory of end-point projection is the main difference of our work from these preceding works.

2 The Global Calculus

2.1 Buyer-Seller Protocol

We outline the key technical ideas using an example from [21], the "Buyer-Seller Protocol". The participants involved are a Buyer, a Seller and a Shipper. We describe the protocol with both text and a sequence diagram.

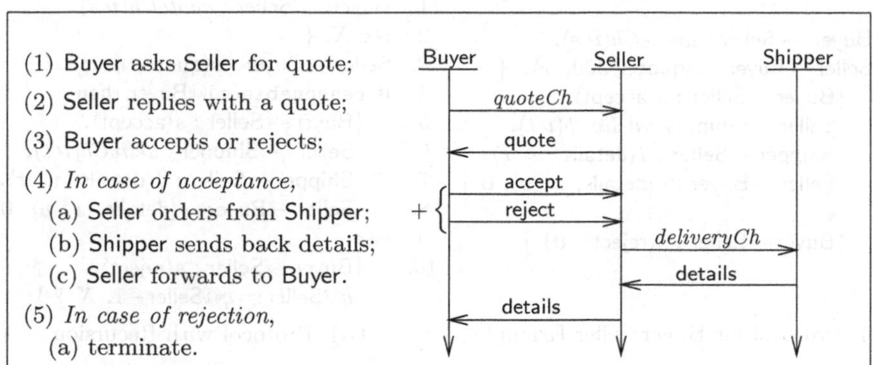

(1) Buyer asks Seller for quote;
(2) Seller replies with a quote;
(3) Buyer accepts or rejects;
(4) In case of acceptance,
(a) Seller orders from Shipper;
(b) Shipper sends back details;
(c) Seller forwards to Buyer.
(5) In case of rejection,
(a) terminate.
Buyer
Seller
Shipper
quoteCh
quote
accept
reject
+
deliveryCh
details
details

The diagram is ambiguous at the branching (+) actions in (4) and (5): the purpose of such diagrams is to offer an informal overview: they naturally omit detailed control structures (choices, loops, etc.) and manipulation of values/states. The reason why such global descriptions are practised in engineering is because they enable a clear grasp of the whole interaction structure, lessening synchronisation and other errors at the design stage.

WS-CDL is intended to extend these virtues of global notations to a full fledged description language. We find, through our involvement in its design process, that it is based on two engineering principles: the **Service Channel Principle (SCP)** where invocation channels (e.g. a channel at which Buyer first communicates to Seller, or Seller to Shipper) can be shared and invoked repeatedly; and the **Session Principle (SP)** where a sequence of conversations belonging to a protocol should not be confused with other concurrent runs of this or other protocols by the participants i.e. each such sequence should form a logical unit of a conversation, or a *session*.

(**SCP**) corresponds to the repeated availability of replicated input channels in the π-calculus (called *uniformly receptive* [22] and *server channels* in [4]), or, in practice, of public URLs. (**SP**) is a basic principle in many communication-centred programs, and can be given simple type abstraction with decidable type checking [12,16,25].[2] The global calculus is built from formalisation of these two principles, as well as combinators for composing descriptions. Before introducing the syntax formally, we first outline its basic ideas using an example.

Figure 1 (a) gives a description of the Buyer-Seller Protocol in the global calculus. In (a), Line 1 describes Action (1) in the protocol. The *quoteCh* is a *service channel*, which may be considered as a public URL for a specific service. The invocation marks the start of a session between the buyer and the seller: the $\boldsymbol{\nu}$-bound s is a *session channel*, a fresh name to be used for later communication in this session. Unlike standard process calculi, *the syntax no longer describes input and output actions separately: the information exchange between two parties is directly described as one interaction.*

[2] In implementations of web services, sessions are implemented using so-called *correlation identities* (which may be considered as nonces in cryptographic protocols).

```
1. Buyer → Seller : quoteCh(ν s).
2. Seller → Buyer : s⟨quote, 300, x⟩. {
3.    {Buyer → Seller : s⟨accept⟩.
4.      Seller → Shipper : delivCh(ν t).
5.      Shipper → Seller : t⟨details, v, x⟩.
6.      Seller → Buyer : s⟨details, x, y⟩. 0 }
7.    +
8.    {Buyer → Seller : s⟨reject⟩. 0} }
```

(a) Protocol for Buyer-Seller Example

```
1.  Buyer → Seller : quoteCh(ν s).
2.  rec X. {
3.  Seller → Buyer : s⟨quote, q, x⟩.
4.  if reasonable(x)@Buyer then
5.     {Buyer → Seller : s⟨accept⟩.
6.       Seller → Shipper : delivCh(ν t).
7.       Shipper → Seller : t⟨details, v, x⟩.
8.       Seller → Buyer : s⟨details, x, y⟩. 0 }
9.  else
10.    {Buyer → Seller : s⟨reject⟩.
       q@Seller := q@Seller − 1. X } }
```

(b) Protocol with Recursion

Fig. 1. Business Protocols in the Global Calculus

Line 2 describes Action (2), Seller's reply to Buyer. The session has already been started and now the two participants communicate using the session channel s. In addition, three factors involved: quote identifies the particular operation used in this communication (i.e. request for quote), 300 is the quote sent by Seller; x is a variable located at Buyer where the communicated value will be stored.

Lines 3/8 describe Action (3), where Buyer communicates its choice (accept or reject) to Seller through s. Two series of actions which follow these choices are combined by + in Line 7. If accept is chosen, Seller sends Shipper the Buyer's details via the service channel *delivCh* of Shipper, creating a fresh session channel t (Line 4). Then in Line 5, Shipper sends back the shipping details through t. Finally in Line 6, Seller forwards the details to Buyer by sending the value stored in variable x: here the protocol terminates. In Line 8, Buyer communicates reject, in which case the protocol immediately terminates.

In (a), we can observe the distinction between service channels and session channels implements (**SCP**) and (**SP**); sessions offer logical grouping of threads of interactions, where each thread starts with a procedure-call-like service invocation at a service channel and carry out in-session communications at associated session channels. This point can be seen more clearly in Fig. 1 (b), a refinement of (a). In (b), if Buyer chooses reject, the protocol recurs to Line 3, after decrementing the quote. In Line 4, a unary predicate `reasonable`(x) is evaluated at Seller's site ("@" indicates a location, similarly in Line 10). The session notation makes it clear that all quote-messages from Seller to Buyer in the recursion are done within a single session. §4 shall show that such session information plays a crucial role in tractable end-point projection.

2.2 Syntax and Dynamics

The syntax of the global calculus [9] is given by BNF. $I, I', \ldots$ denote *terms* of the calculus, also called *interactions*. $ch, ch' \ldots$ range over *service channels*; $s, t, \ldots$ range over *session channels*; $\tilde{s}$ indicates a vector of session channels; A, B, $C, \ldots$ range over *participants*; $x, y, z, \ldots$ over variables local to each participant; $X, X', \ldots$ over *term variables*; and $e, e', \ldots$ over arithmetic and other first-order expressions.

$I ::=$	$A \to B : ch(\nu\, \tilde{s}).\, I$	(init)	$\mid$	$(\nu s)\, I$	(new)
$\mid$	$A \to B : s\langle \mathsf{op},\ e,\ y\rangle.\, I$	(comm)	$\mid$	X	(recvar)
$\mid$	$x@A := e.\, I$	(assign)	$\mid$	$I_1 + I_2$	(sum)
$\mid$	$I_1 \mid I_2$	(par)	$\mid$	$\mu X.\, I$	(rec)
$\mid$	$\mathsf{if}\ e@A\ \mathsf{then}\ I_1\ \mathsf{else}\ I_2$	(cond)	$\mid$	$\mathbf{0}$	(inaction)

(init) denotes a session initiation by A via B's service channel ch, with fresh session channels $\tilde{s}$ and continuation I. (comm) denotes an in-session communication over a session channel s, where op is an operator name. Note that y does not bind in I. "|" and "+" denote respectively parallel and choice. $(\nu s)\, I$ is the π-calculus-like name restriction, binding s in I. Since such a hiding is only generated by session initiation, we stipulate that a hiding never occurs inside a prefix, sum or conditional. (cond) and (assign) are standard conditional and assignment ($e@A$ indicates e is located at A). $\mu X.\, I$ is recursion, where the variable X is bound in I. $\mathbf{0}$ denotes termination. The free and bound session channels and term variables are defined in the usual way. We often omit $\mathbf{0}$ and empty vectors.

The reduction of the global calculus is close to that of imperative languages. A *state* σ assigns a value to the variables located at each participant. We shall write $\sigma@A$ to denote the portion of σ local to A, and $\sigma[y@A \mapsto v]$ to denote a new state σ' which is identical to σ except that $\sigma'@A(y)$ is equal to v. A reduction "$(\sigma,\ I) \to (\sigma',\ I')$" says that I in the state σ performs one-step computation and becomes I' with the new state σ'. Below we list some of the rules generating the reduction (a complete set of rules can be found in [11]).

$$\text{(G-INIT)}\ (\sigma,\ A \to B : ch(\nu\, \tilde{s}).\, I) \to (\sigma, (\nu \tilde{s})\, I)$$

$$\text{(G-COM)}\quad \frac{\sigma' = \sigma[x@B \mapsto v] \quad \sigma \vdash e@A \Downarrow v}{(\sigma,\ A \to B : s\langle \mathsf{op},\ e,\ x\rangle.\, I) \to (\sigma',\ I)} \qquad \text{(G-ASGN)}\quad \frac{\sigma \vdash e@A \Downarrow v \quad \sigma' = \sigma[x@A \mapsto v]}{(\sigma, x@A := e.\, I) \to (\sigma',\ I)}$$

(G-INIT) is for session initiation: after A initiates a session with B on service channel ch, A and B share $\tilde{s}$ locally (indicated by $(\nu\tilde{s})$), and the next I is unfolded. The initiation channel ch will play an important role for typing and the end-point projection later. (G-COM) is a key rule: the expression e is evaluated into v in the A-portion of the state σ and then assigned to the variable x located at B resulting in the new state $\sigma[x@B \mapsto v]$. The same variable (say x) located at different participants are distinct (hence $\sigma@A(x)$ and $\sigma@B(x)$ may differ). Other rules for parallel, summation, recursion and restriction are omitted.

As an example of reduction, consider, for instance:

$$\mathsf{Buyer} \to \mathsf{Seller} : quoteCh(\nu\, s).\ \mathsf{Seller} \to \mathsf{Buyer} : s\langle \mathsf{quote},\ 300,\ x\rangle.\ I'$$

with state σ. By (G-INIT), we get $(\sigma, (\nu s)\ \mathsf{Seller} \to \mathsf{Buyer} : s\langle \mathsf{quote},\ 300,\ x\rangle.\ I')$. Now, by rule (G-COM), this evolves into $(\sigma[x@\mathsf{Buyer} \mapsto 300], (\nu s)\ I')$.

2.3 Session Types for Global Descriptions

We use a generalisation of session types [16]. The grammar of types follows.

$$\alpha ::= s \blacktriangleright \Sigma_i \mathsf{op}_i(\theta_i).\ \alpha_i \mid s \blacktriangleleft \Sigma_i \mathsf{op}_i(\theta_i).\ \alpha_i \mid \alpha_1 \,|\, \alpha_2 \mid \mathsf{end} \mid \mu\mathbf{t}.\ \alpha \mid \mathbf{t}$$

where $\theta, \theta', \ldots$ range over *value types*. $\alpha, \alpha', \ldots$ are *session types*. $s \blacktriangleright \Sigma_i \mathsf{op}_i(\theta_i).\ \alpha_i$ is a *branching input type* at session channel s, indicating a process is ready to receive any of the (pairwise distinct) operators $\{\mathsf{op}_i\}$, each with a value of type θ_i; $s \blacktriangleleft \Sigma_i \mathsf{op}_i(\theta_i).\ \alpha_i$, a *branching output type* at s, is its exact dual. The type $\alpha_1 \,|\, \alpha_2$ is a *parallel composition of* α_1 *and* α_2, abstracting parallel composition of two sessions. We take $|$ to be commutative and associative, with end, the *inaction type* indicating session termination, being the identity. We demand session channels in α_1 and α_2 to be disjoint: this guarantees a linear use of session channels. $\mathbf{t}$ is a *type variable*, while $\mu\mathbf{t}.\alpha$ is a *recursive type*, where $\mu\mathbf{t}$ binds free occurrences of $\mathbf{t}$ in α. In recursive types, we assume each recursion is guarded, i.e., in $\mu\mathbf{t}.\alpha$, α is an n-ary parallel composition of input/output types. Recursive types are regarded as regular trees in the standard way [13].

Note that session channels occur free in session types: this is necessary to allow multiple session channels to be used in parallel in a single session; with this, we can faithfully capture use cases of web services which exchange different data simultaneously, leading to a generalisation of session types in the literature. Let us show a simple example:

$$s \blacktriangleleft \mathsf{quote}(\mathtt{int}).\ \mathsf{end} \mid s' \blacktriangleleft \mathsf{extra}(\mathtt{string}).\ \mathsf{end}$$

Here a participant is sending a quote (integer) at s and extra information about the product at s' in a single session: without using distinct session channels, two communications can get confused and result in a type error.

A *typing judgment* has the form $\Gamma \vdash I : \Delta$ where Γ is *service typing* and Δ *session typing*. The grammar of typings follows where $A \neq B$ in $\tilde{s}[A, B]$:

$$\begin{aligned} \Gamma &::= \emptyset \mid \Gamma, ch@A\!:\!(\tilde{s})\alpha \mid \Gamma, x@A\!:\!\theta \mid \Gamma, X\!:\!\Delta \\ \Delta &::= \emptyset \mid \Delta,\ \tilde{s}[A, B]\!:\!\alpha \mid \Delta,\ \tilde{s}\!:\!\bot \end{aligned}$$

Each time a session is initiated, session channels need be freshly generated. Thus, the type of a service channel indicates a vector of session channels to be initially exchanged, in addition to how they are used. This is formulated by *service type* $(\tilde{s})\alpha$ where $\tilde{s}$ is a vector of pairwise distinct session channels covering all session channels in α, and α does not contain free type variables. In a service typing, $ch@A : (\tilde{s})\alpha$ says that ch is located at A and offers a service interface $(\tilde{s})\alpha$; $x@A : \theta$ says that a variable x located at A may store values of type θ; finally, $X : \Delta$ says that when the interaction recurs to X, it should have the typing Δ.

The typing uses a primary type assignment $\tilde{s}[A, B] : \alpha$, which says that a vector of session channels $\tilde{s}$, all belonging to a same session between A and B, has the session type α when seen from the viewpoint of A. We write Γ_1, Γ_2 (resp. Δ_1, Δ_2) if there is no overlap between the free variables/names in Γ_1 and Γ_2 (resp. Δ_1 and Δ_2). The notation $\mathsf{fsc}(\Delta)$ denotes the set of free service/session channels in Δ. In the following, we present the main typing rules:

$$\text{(G-TCOM)}\ \frac{\Gamma \vdash I \triangleright \Delta, \tilde{s}\,[A,B]\!:\!\alpha_j \quad \Gamma \vdash e@A\!:\!\theta_j \quad \Gamma \vdash x@B\!:\!\theta_j \quad s \in \{\tilde{s}\} \quad j \in J}{\Gamma \ \vdash A \!\rightarrow\! B : s\langle \mathsf{op_j},\ e,\ x\rangle.\ I \ \triangleright\ \Delta, \tilde{s}\,[A,B]\!:\! s \blacktriangleleft \Sigma_{i\in J}\mathsf{op_i}(\theta_i).\ \alpha_i}$$

$$\text{(G-TCOM}_2\text{)}\ \frac{\Gamma \vdash I \triangleright \Delta, \tilde{s}\,[B,A]\!:\!\alpha_j \quad \Gamma \vdash e@A\!:\!\theta_j \quad \Gamma \vdash x@B\!:\!\theta_j \quad s \in \{\tilde{s}\} \quad j \in J}{\Gamma \ \vdash A \!\rightarrow\! B : s\langle \mathsf{op_j},\ e,\ x\rangle.\ I \ \triangleright\ \Delta, \tilde{s}\,[B,A]\!:\! s \blacktriangleright \Sigma_{i\in J}\mathsf{op_i}(\theta_i).\ \alpha_i}$$

$$\text{(G-TPAR)}\ \frac{\Gamma \vdash I_1 \triangleright \Delta_1 \quad \Gamma \vdash I_2 \triangleright \Delta_2}{\Gamma \vdash I_1 \mid I_2 \triangleright \Delta_1 \bullet \Delta_2} \qquad \text{(G-TINIT)}\ \frac{\Gamma,\ ch@B\!:\!(\tilde{s})\alpha \vdash I \triangleright \Delta, \tilde{s}\,[B,A]\!:\!\alpha}{\Gamma,\ ch@B\!:\!(\tilde{s})\alpha \vdash A \rightarrow B : ch(\nu\,\tilde{s}).\ I \triangleright \Delta}$$

Rule (G-TCOM) states that, for typing an in-session communication of e from A to B at s with the choice op_j, (1) the body I should assign α_j to $\tilde{s}$ containing s; (2) the value e should be typed in the source (A) with θ_j; and (3) the variable (parameter) x should be typed in the target (B) with the same type. Then, in the conclusion, a branching type is formed whose j-th branch consists of op_j, θ_j and α_i. In (G-TCOM), the session type in focus is considered direction from the viewpoint of A. We may also regard it from the receiver's viewpoint (B), which is its symmetric variant (G-TCOM$_2$). Rule (G-TPAR) uses the linearity condition found in [16]. The the operator $\bullet$ is well-defined whenever the linearity condition is satisfied and is such that $\tilde{s}[A,B] : \alpha \in \Delta_1 \bullet \Delta_2$ iff either $\tilde{s}[A,B] : \alpha_1 \in \Delta_1$, $\tilde{s}[A,B] : \alpha_2 \in \Delta_2$ and $\alpha = \alpha_1 \mid \alpha_2$; or $\tilde{s}[A,B] : \alpha \in \Delta_1$ and $\{\tilde{s}\} \cap \mathsf{fsc}(\Delta_2) = \emptyset$; or its symmetric case. The other rules are standard [11].

As a simple example, we type the Buyer-Seller interaction I in Fig. 1 (a). Service channel *quoteCh* is assigned with the following service type:

$$(s)\ s \blacktriangleleft \mathsf{quote}(\mathtt{integer}).\ s \blacktriangleright (\ \mathsf{accept}(\mathtt{null}).\ s \blacktriangleleft \mathsf{details}(\mathtt{string}).\ \mathsf{end}\ + \\ \mathsf{reject}(\mathtt{null}).\ \mathsf{end}\ )$$

Service channel *deliveryCh* has type $(t)\ t \blacktriangleleft \mathsf{details}(\mathtt{string}).\ \mathsf{end}$. Denoting two types by $(s)\alpha_1$ and $(t)\alpha_2$, we have: $\mathit{quoteCh}\!:\!(s)\,\alpha_1,\ \mathit{deliveryCh}\!:\!(t)\,\alpha_2 \vdash I \triangleright \emptyset$.

Similarly, we can type the interaction in Figure 1 (b) where we have recursion. The typing of the service channel *quoteCh* will differ in the "rejection" branch, given as: $(s)\ \mu\mathbf{t}.\ s \blacktriangleleft \mathsf{quote}(\mathtt{integer}).\ s \blacktriangleright (\ldots + \mathsf{reject}(\mathtt{null}).\ \mathbf{t})$.

The typing system also incorporates subtyping based on an inclusion ordering on each type (formalised using simulation like in [13]).

Theorem 1 (Subject Reduction). *Assume* $\Gamma \vdash \sigma$. *Then* $\Gamma \vdash I \triangleright \Delta$ *and* $(\sigma, I) \rightarrow (\sigma', I')$ *imply* $\Gamma \vdash \sigma'$ *and* $\Gamma \vdash I' \triangleright \Delta'$ *for some* Δ' *s.t.* $\mathsf{fsc}(\Delta') \subset \mathsf{fsc}(\Delta)$.

3 The End-Point Calculus

3.1 Syntax and Dynamics

The end-point calculus is the π-calculus [18] extended with sessions [16] as well as locations and store [10]. $P, Q, \ldots$ denote *processes*, $M, N, \ldots$ *networks*.

$$P ::= \ !\,ch(\tilde{s}).\ P \mid \overline{ch}(\nu\tilde{s}).\ P \mid s \rhd \Sigma_i \mathsf{op}_i(y_i).\ P_i \mid \overline{s} \lhd \mathsf{op}\langle e\rangle.\ P \mid x := e.\ P \\ \mid \mathsf{if}\ e\ \mathsf{then}\ P_1\ \mathsf{else}\ P_2 \mid P_1 \oplus P_2 \mid P_1 \mid P_2 \mid (\nu s)\ P \mid X \mid \mu X.\ P \mid \mathbf{0}$$

$$N ::= \ A[\,P\,]_\sigma \ \mid\ N_1 \mid N_2 \ \mid\ (\nu s)\ N \ \mid\ \epsilon$$

The first two processes describe session initiations; the next two, in-session communications (where y_i in the first construct, branching input, is *not* bound in P_i, and $\{\mathsf{op}_i\}$ should be pairwise distinct). Next, $x := e.\ P$ assigns a value v to x in its store then continues as P. The rest is standard. Networks are parallel composition of participants, where a *participant* is of the shape $A[\ P\ ]_\sigma$, with A being the name of the participant, P its behaviour, and σ its local state. We often omit σ when irrelevant.

The reduction semantics for the end-point calculus follows the π-calculus. Below we list the three key rules (other rules are found in [11]).

$$\begin{array}{lll}
\text{(E-INIT)} & A[\ !\,ch(\tilde{s}).\ P \mid P'\ ]_\sigma \mid B[\ \overline{ch}(\nu\tilde{s}).\ Q \mid Q'\ ]_{\sigma'} & \\
& \quad \rightarrow\ (\nu\tilde{s})\ (A[\ !\,ch(\tilde{s}).\ P \mid P \mid P'\ ]_\sigma \mid B[\ Q \mid Q'\ ]_{\sigma'}) & \\
\text{(E-COM)} & A[\ s \rhd \Sigma_i \mathsf{op}_i(x_i).\ P_i \mid P'\ ]_\sigma \mid B[\ \overline{s} \lhd \mathsf{op_j}\langle e\rangle.\ Q \mid Q'\ ]_{\sigma'} & \\
& \quad \rightarrow\ A[\ P_j \mid P'\ ]_{\sigma[x_j \mapsto v]} \mid B[\ Q \mid Q'\ ]_{\sigma'} & (\sigma \vdash e \Downarrow v) \\
\text{(E-ASGN)} & A[\ x := e.\ P \mid P'\ ]_\sigma\ \rightarrow\ A[\ P \mid P'\ ]_{\sigma[x \mapsto v]} & (\sigma \vdash e \Downarrow v)
\end{array}$$

(E-INIT) defines the session initiation: two participants A and B will synchronise to start a session, $!\,ch(\tilde{s}).\ P$ denoting a service and $\overline{ch}(\nu\tilde{s}).\ Q$ a request. It will result in sharing fresh session names $\tilde{s}$ local to A and B. These session names are then used in (E-COM) for communication. In (E-COM), communicated values are assigned to local variables, rather than substituted, for having the correspondence with the global calculus. (E-ASGN) updates a local store.

3.2 Session Typing of End-Point Calculus

In the end-point calculus, we use two typing judgements, $\Gamma \vdash_A P \rhd \Delta$ (where P is typed as a behaviour for A) and $\Gamma \vdash M \rhd \Delta$. Γ (service typing) and Δ (session typing) are given as before except (1) Γ adds $\overline{ch}@A : (\tilde{s})\alpha$; and (2) we replace $\tilde{s}[A, B] : \alpha$ by $\tilde{s}@A : \alpha$. The selected typing rules are given below.

$$\text{(E-TB)}\ \frac{j \in J \quad K \subseteq J \quad s \in \tilde{s} \quad \Gamma \vdash x_j : \theta_j \quad \Gamma \vdash_A P_j \rhd \Delta \cdot \tilde{s}@A : \alpha_j}{\Gamma \vdash s \rhd \Sigma_{i \in J} \mathsf{op}_i(x_i).P_i \rhd \Delta \cdot \tilde{s}@A : s \blacktriangleright \Sigma_{i \in K} \mathsf{op}_i(\theta_i).\ \alpha_i}$$

$$\text{(E-TS)}\ \frac{j \in J \subseteq K \quad \Gamma \vdash e : \theta_j \quad \Gamma \vdash_A P \rhd \Delta \cdot \tilde{s}@A : \alpha_j}{\Gamma \vdash_A \overline{s} \lhd \mathsf{op_j}\langle e\rangle.P \rhd \Delta \cdot \tilde{s}@A : s \blacktriangleleft \Sigma_{i \in K} \mathsf{op}_i(\theta_i).\ \alpha_i}$$

$$\text{(E-TSERV)}\ \frac{\Gamma \vdash_A P \rhd \tilde{s}@A : \alpha}{\Gamma, ch@A : (\tilde{s})\alpha \vdash_A\ !\,ch(\tilde{s}).\ P \rhd \emptyset} \qquad \text{(E-TREQ)}\ \frac{\Gamma, \overline{ch}@B : (\tilde{s})\alpha \vdash_A P \rhd \Delta \cdot \tilde{s}@A : \alpha}{\Gamma, \overline{ch}@B : (\tilde{s})\alpha \vdash_A \overline{ch}(\nu\tilde{s}).P \rhd \Delta}$$

(E-TB) is for branching input. The resulting typing can have less branches than the real process, so that the process is prepared to receive any operator specified in the type. (E-TS) is its dual: the typing can have more branches than the real process, so that the process invokes at most those operators specified in the typing. Combining (E-TB) and (E-TS), an output never invokes a non-existent option in the input. (E-TSERV) is for the server side of initialisation. In the premise, the session typing should not have session channels other than the target of initialisation: this prevents *free* session channels from occurring under the replicated input, thus guaranteeing their linear usage. By our convention, neither ch nor $\overline{ch}$ occurs in Γ in the conclusion. The output side of initialisation (E-TREQ) is analogous, except it does not need the linearity constraint. The remaining rules are standard [16]: for example, with parallel composition, we ensure that an input of type α is composed with an output of its dual.

We recall our running example, Figure 1 (a) in § 2.1. An end-point representation of this example for Buyer may be written:

$$\mathsf{Buyer}[\ \overline{quoteCh}(\boldsymbol{\nu} s).\ s \rhd \mathsf{quote}(x).\ (\overline{s} \lhd \mathsf{accept}.\ s \rhd \mathsf{details}(y).\ \mathbf{0} \oplus \overline{s} \lhd \mathsf{reject}.\ \mathbf{0})\ ]$$

Above $\mathsf{Buyer}[P]$ indicates a participant (a named agent) whose behaviour is given by the process P. The Seller's code is given as:

$$\begin{array}{l}\mathsf{Seller}[!\ quoteCh(s).\ \overline{s} \lhd \mathsf{quote}\langle 300\rangle.\ s \rhd \\ \quad (\mathsf{accept}.\ \overline{deliveryCh}(\boldsymbol{\nu} t).\ t \rhd \mathsf{delivery}(x).\ \overline{s} \lhd \mathsf{delivery}\langle x\rangle.\ \mathbf{0}\ +\ \mathsf{reject}.\ \mathbf{0})]\end{array}$$

The end-point representation for Shipper is given similarly. These end-point descriptions do not directly and explicitly describe how interaction proceeds globally, which may often be the central concern of communication-centred applications designers/users. However, they precisely represent local communication behaviours which give rise to global interactions. The two service channels *quoteCh* and *deliveryCh* are replicated and ready to be invoked, following (**SCP**).

We can type these processes using the service types $(s)\alpha_1$ and $(t)\alpha_2$ from § 3.3. The type of the seller becomes (writing P for its process):

$$quoteCh\colon (s)\,\alpha_1,\ \overline{deliveryCh}\colon (t)\,\overline{\alpha}_2 \vdash \mathsf{Seller}[\ P\ ]_\sigma \rhd \emptyset.$$

Note that the service channel *deliveryCh* is overlined, indicating the direction: this is because the input channel is located at the shipper's. In the global calculus, a channel is always used for both input and output, so there is no such need. Similarly we may type the end-point processes for Buyer and Seller with recursion as in Figure 1 (b), as:

$$\begin{array}{l}\mathsf{Buyer}[\ \mu X.\ \overline{quoteCh}(\boldsymbol{\nu} s).\ s \rhd \mathsf{quote}(x). \\ \quad \mathsf{if\ reasonable}(x)\ \mathsf{then}\ \overline{s} \lhd \mathsf{accept}.\ s \rhd \mathsf{details}(y).\ \mathbf{0}\ \mathsf{else}\ \overline{s} \lhd \mathsf{reject}.\ X\ ] \quad | \\ \mathsf{Seller}[\ !\ quoteCh(s).\ \mu X.\ \overline{s} \lhd \mathsf{quote}\langle 300\rangle.\ s \rhd \\ \quad (\mathsf{accept}.\ \overline{deliveryCh}(\boldsymbol{\nu} t).\ t \rhd \mathsf{delivery}(x).\ \overline{s} \lhd \mathsf{delivery}\langle x\rangle.\ \mathbf{0} + \mathsf{reject}.\ X)]\end{array}$$

We may also note, both in its term and in its typing, the end-point process for Shipper in Figure 1 (b) does not involve recursion, since its session is self-contained inside a recursion.

Theorem 2 (subject reduction). *If* $\Gamma \vdash N \rhd \Delta$ *and* $N \to N'$ *then* $\Gamma \vdash N' \rhd \Delta$.

A significant corollary of this result is the lack of communication error in the sense that typed processes never invoke missing operations and never communicate ill-typed values. This is fundamental for end-point processes since they describe inputs and outputs separately, unlike global descriptions.

4 The End-Point Projection

4.1 Three Principles for End-Point Projections

A theory of EPP assigns to global descriptions the precise and transparent operational content as communicating processes. This task becomes subtle because a *global calculus allows descriptions that do not make sense at end-points, i.e. as distributed communicating processes.* Below we discuss three issues in this regard one by one, together with the corresponding disciplines which disallow them.

Connectedness. Consider the following code snippet for global description.

$$\mathsf{Buyer} \to \mathsf{Seller} : ch_1(\boldsymbol{\nu}\, s).\ \ \mathsf{Shipper} \to \mathsf{Depot} : ch_2(\boldsymbol{\nu}\, t)$$

Remembering "." indicates sequencing, Shipper is described as contacting Depot only after Buyer has performed a request to Seller in the description above. Implementing this behaviour as distributed processes demands that Shipper be notified once the first communication is performed by message passing, for instance in:

$$\mathsf{Buyer} \to \mathsf{Seller} : ch_1(\boldsymbol{\nu}\, s).\ \mathsf{Seller} \to \mathsf{Shipper} : ch(\boldsymbol{\nu}\, s').\ \mathsf{Shipper} \to \mathsf{Depot} : ch_2(\boldsymbol{\nu}\, t)$$

Observe the second description is directly realisable as end-point processes, while the first one is not. Even if one may informally write down the first description, it is the second one which can have a precise correspondence with end-point behaviour. Thus we preclude descriptions like the first one, by demanding each participant acts only as a result of its local event. We call this principle *connectedness.* Connectedness is simply defined by tracking active/passive participants of each action, as formally given in [11]. Informally, for each A, A's sending action or its self-contained action (e.g. assignment and evaluation of a conditional guard) should always be immediately preceded by A's receiving action or its another self-contained action. Connectedness is closed under reductions.

Well-threadedness. The next condition is also about causality, but a slightly more subtle one. Consider the following connected interaction:

$$\begin{array}{l}\mathsf{Buyer} \to \mathsf{Seller} : ch_1(\boldsymbol{\nu}\, s).\ \mathsf{Seller} \to \mathsf{Shipper} : ch_2(\boldsymbol{\nu}\, t).\\ \quad \mathsf{Shipper} \to \mathsf{Buyer} : ch_3(\boldsymbol{\nu}\, u).\ \mathsf{Buyer} \to \mathsf{Seller} : s\langle \mathsf{op},\ v,\ x\rangle.\ I\end{array}$$

We claim that this global code (regardless of I) is unrealisable at end-points. In fact, the first action tells us that there is a thread in Buyer which invokes Seller. This thread becomes inactive in the second line where a service at ch_3 in Buyer is invoked. In the final line, Buyer communicates to Seller via s opened in the initial action. Written in the end-point calculus:

$$\begin{array}{rlll}\mathsf{Buyer}[& \overline{ch_1}(\boldsymbol{\nu} s).\ \overline{s} \lhd \mathsf{op}\langle v\rangle.\ P \ \ \mid\ \ !\, ch_3(t).\ Q &]_{\sigma_1} & \mid\\ \mathsf{Seller}[& !\, ch_1(s).\ \overline{ch_2}(\boldsymbol{\nu} t).\ s \rhd \mathsf{op}(x).\ Q' &]_{\sigma_2} & \mid\\ \mathsf{Shipper}[& !\, ch_2(t).\ \overline{ch_3}(\boldsymbol{\nu} u).\ R &]_{\sigma_2} & \end{array}$$

The first process of Buyer invokes ch_1 and sends v with operation op in the same session, while the second is a service at ch_3 (by **SCP** this channel should be ready to receive invocations). $\overline{s} \lhd \mathsf{op}\langle v\rangle$ cannot be located under ch_3, as it belongs to a session s. When the three processes interact, first, Buyer invokes ch_1, then Seller invokes ch_2 of Shipper: up to here the interaction follows the original global scenario. However, at this point, the action $s \rhd \mathsf{op}(x)$ is free to react with its dual action $\overline{s} \lhd \mathsf{op}\langle v\rangle$, *before* Shipper *invokes* Seller*'s other component*, the service at ch_3. Thus the sequencing in the global description gets violated.

The fundamental issue in the example above is that the given global code assumes a false, or unrealisable, dependency among actions: the last action belongs to a thread which started from the invocation of ch_1, while the description says it should take place as a direct result of the third action at a distinct thread which has been opened by the invocation at ch_3. If a global description is free from such false dependency, we say it is *well-threaded.* For the formal definition, we first annotate a global interaction with identifiers for threads. *Annotated interactions*, denoted by $\mathcal{A}, \mathcal{A}', \ldots$, are given by the following grammar.

$$\begin{array}{rl}\mathcal{A} ::= & A^{\tau_1} \to B^{\tau_2} : ch(\nu\, \tilde{s}).\mathcal{A} \mid x@A^{\tau} := e.\,\mathcal{A} \mid \mathcal{A}_1 \mid^{\tau} \mathcal{A}_2 \mid \mu^{\tau} X^{A}.\,\mathcal{A} \mid X^{A}_{\tau} \\ & \mid A^{\tau_1} \to B^{\tau_2} : s\langle \mathsf{op},\ e,\ y\rangle.\,\mathcal{A} \mid \mathcal{A}_1 +^{\tau} \mathcal{A}_2 \mid \mathsf{if}\ e@A^{\tau}\ \mathsf{then}\ \mathcal{A}_1\ \mathsf{else}\ \mathcal{A}_2 \mid \mathbf{0}\end{array}$$

where $\tau_i \in \mathbb{N}$ (called *thread*) and $\tau_1 \neq \tau_2$ in the first two lines. Our task is to find a notion of "consistent annotation" so that causality specified globally is precisely realisable locally. We demand: if an input is annotated by τ then its directly succeeding output is annotated by τ again, similarly for self-contained actions; that two actions by $\mathcal{A}$ in the same session are annotated by the same thread; and that the input of session initiation is always given a fresh thread. We say I is *well-threaded* when it is connected and has a consistent annotation. If I is well-threaded and has no free session channels, it has a primary annotation from which all of its consistent annotations are derivable [11, §14, Prop. 11]. As an example, consider the following annotated interaction.

$$\begin{array}{l}\mathsf{Buyer}^{\tau_1} \to \mathsf{Seller}^{\tau_2} : ch_1(\nu\, s).\ \mathsf{Seller}^{\tau_3} \to \mathsf{Shipper}^{\tau_4} : ch_2(\nu\, t). \\ \quad \mathsf{Shipper}^{\tau_5} \to \mathsf{Buyer}^{\tau_6} : ch_3(\nu\, u).\ \mathsf{Buyer}^{\tau_7} \to \mathsf{Seller}^{\tau_8} : s\langle \mathsf{op},\ v,\ x\rangle.\ I\end{array}$$

By the first two conditions, we have $\tau_1 = \tau_7$ and $\tau_6 = \tau_7$, hence $\tau_6 = \tau_1$, which violates the third condition. So this is *not* well-threaded. But the following annotated interaction is well-threaded:

$$\begin{array}{l}\mathsf{Buyer}^{1} \to \mathsf{Seller}^{2} : ch_1(\nu\, s).\ \ \mathsf{Seller}^{2} \to \mathsf{Buyer}^{3} : ch_2(\nu\, t). \\ \quad \mathsf{Buyer}^{3} \to \mathsf{Seller}^{2} : t\langle \mathsf{op}_1,\ v_1,\ x\rangle.\ \mathsf{Seller}^{2} \to \mathsf{Buyer}^{1} : s\langle \mathsf{op}_2,\ v_2,\ y\rangle.\ \mathbf{0}\end{array}$$

and in fact gives rise to the following correct end-points.

$$\begin{array}{lll}\mathsf{Buyer}[& \overline{ch_1}(\nu s).\ \overline{s} \lhd \mathsf{op}_2\langle v_2\rangle.\mathbf{0} \ \mid\ !\,ch_2(t).\ t \rhd \mathsf{op}_1(x).\ \mathbf{0} &] \ \mid \\ \mathsf{Seller}[& !\,ch_1(s).\ \overline{ch_2}(\nu t).\ \overline{t} \lhd \mathsf{op}_1\langle v_1\rangle.s \rhd \mathsf{op}(y).\ \mathbf{0} &]\end{array}$$

There is a type discipline accepting all and only well-threaded interactions, from which we can derive a sound and complete algorithm for checking well-threadedness and for calculating, if any, (primary) consistent annotations [11].

Coherence. The final principle concerns consistency of descriptions of a behaviour belonging to the same service. We first note that it is often necessary to *merge* threads to obtain the final end-point behaviour of a single service. Consider the parallel composition:

$$\begin{array}{l}\mathsf{Buyer} \rightarrow \mathsf{Seller} : ch(\boldsymbol{\nu}\, s).\ \mathsf{Seller} \rightarrow \mathsf{Buyer} : s\langle \mathsf{op}_1,\ e,\ x_1\rangle.\ I_1 \ \ | \\ \mathsf{Buyer} \rightarrow \mathsf{Seller} : ch(\boldsymbol{\nu}\, t).\ \mathsf{Seller} \rightarrow \mathsf{Buyer} : t\langle \mathsf{op}_2,\ e,\ x_2\rangle.\ I_2\end{array}$$

where $\mathsf{op}_1 \neq \mathsf{op}_2$. Above, Buyer invokes Seller's service at *ch* twice in parallel. Now consider constructing the code for this service at channel *ch*: we need to merge these two threads into one end-point behaviour. But the global description is contradictory, since in one invocation the service reacts with op_1, while in the other the service reacts with op_2. As can be observed from this example, in a global description, the description of the behaviour of a single end-point can be *scattered in different portions of the code.* Hence we need to guarantee, in EPP, that these scattered descriptions are mergeable. This mergeablity condition is called *coherence.* Let $\mathcal{A}$ be consistently annotated. We list the key rules defining the partial operation $\mathsf{TP}(\mathcal{A}, \tau)$ (see [11] for a full definition):

$$\mathsf{TP}(A^{\tau_1} \rightarrow B^{\tau_2} : b(\boldsymbol{\nu}\, \tilde{s}).\ \mathcal{A}, \tau) \stackrel{\text{def}}{=} \begin{cases} \overline{b}(\boldsymbol{\nu}\tilde{s}).\ \mathsf{TP}(\mathcal{A}, \tau_1) & \text{if } \tau = \tau_1 \\ !\, b(\tilde{s}).\ \mathsf{TP}(\mathcal{A}, \tau_2) & \text{if } \tau = \tau_2 \\ \mathsf{TP}(\mathcal{A}, \tau) & \text{otherwise} \end{cases}$$

$$\mathsf{TP}(A^{\tau_1} \rightarrow B^{\tau_2} : s\langle \mathsf{op_i},\ e_i,\ x_i\rangle.\ \mathcal{A}, \tau) \stackrel{\text{def}}{=} \begin{cases} \overline{s} \lhd \mathsf{op}\langle e\rangle.\ \mathsf{TP}(\mathcal{A}, \tau) & \text{if } \tau = \tau_1 \\ s \rhd \mathsf{op_i}(x_i).\ \mathsf{TP}(\mathcal{A}, \tau) & \text{if } \tau = \tau_2 \\ \mathsf{TP}(\mathcal{A}, \tau) & \text{otherwise} \end{cases}$$

$$\mathsf{TP}(\mathcal{A}_1 +^{\tau'} \mathcal{A}_2, \tau) \stackrel{\text{def}}{=} \begin{cases} \mathsf{TP}(\mathcal{A}_1, \tau') \oplus \mathsf{TP}(\mathcal{A}_2, \tau') & \text{if } \tau = \tau' \\ \mathsf{TP}(\mathcal{A}_1, \tau) \sqcup \mathsf{TP}(\mathcal{A}_2, \tau) & \text{otherwise} \end{cases}$$

In the third rule, $\sqcup$ is a partial commutative binary operator on processes such that: (1) if P is a prefixed process with a service channel as its subject, then $P \sqcup \mathbf{0} = \mathbf{0} \sqcup P = P$; and (2) $s \rhd \Sigma_{i\in J}\mathsf{op}_i(y_i).\ P_i \sqcup s \rhd \Sigma_{i\in K}\mathsf{op}_i(y_i).\ Q_i \stackrel{\text{def}}{=} \Sigma_{i\in J\cap K}\mathsf{op}_i(y_i).\ (P_i \sqcup Q_i) + \Sigma_{i\in J\setminus K}\mathsf{op}_i(y_i).\ P_i + \Sigma_{i\in K\setminus J}\mathsf{op}_i(y_i).\ Q_i$ with $P_i \bowtie Q_i$, where $P \bowtie Q$ says that the operation $P \sqcup Q$ is defined (thus we demand overlapping branches be mutually consistent); and (3) otherwise $P \sqcup Q$ is defined congruently up to $\equiv$. The partial operation $P \sqcup Q$ is called *merging operation.*

Given an annotated interaction $\mathcal{A}$, we write $\tau_1 \equiv_{\mathcal{A}} \tau_2$ whenever τ_1 and τ_2 in $\mathcal{A}$ belong to the same service channel. We say that $\mathcal{A}$ is *coherent* if it is consistently annotated (hence well-threaded) and $\mathsf{TP}(\mathcal{A}, \tau)$ is well-defined for each τ, and moreover satisfies: for each pair of threads τ_1, τ_2 in $\mathcal{A}$ such that $\tau_1 \equiv_{\mathcal{A}} \tau_2$, it holds that $\mathsf{TP}(\mathcal{A}, \tau_1) \sqcup \mathsf{TP}(\mathcal{A}, \tau_2)$ is defined. Coherence of a well-typed interaction is decidable [11, §15, Prop.13].

With coherence as the final principle, we can now project a well-structured global description to end-point processes that precisely realise the original global scenario (the projection is essentially invariant under different consistent annotations [11, §16.1, Prop.14]). Formally, let I be a restriction-free and coherent interaction with free session names $\tilde{s}$ and let $\mathcal{A}$ be one of its consistent annotations. Then the end point projection of $(\boldsymbol{\nu}\tilde{s})\ \mathcal{A}$ under σ is defined as:

$$\mathsf{EPP}((\boldsymbol{\nu}\tilde{s})\ \mathcal{A}, \sigma) \stackrel{\text{def}}{=} (\boldsymbol{\nu}\tilde{s})\ \Pi_{A\in \mathsf{part}(\mathcal{A})}\ A[\ \Pi_{[\tau]} \sqcup_{\tau'\in[\tau]} \mathsf{TP}(\mathcal{A}, \tau')\ ]_{\sigma}$$

where ΠP_i denotes the parallel composition, $\mathsf{part}(\mathcal{A})$ denotes the set of participants mentioned in $\mathcal{A}$ and $[\tau]$ denotes the equivalence class ($\equiv_{\mathcal{A}}$) of τ.

4.2 Pruning and Main Theorem

Consider an interaction which is composed from two branches whose first two interactions are $\mathsf{Buyer} \to \mathsf{Seller} : ch(\nu\, s)$. $\mathsf{Seller} \to \mathsf{Buyer} : s\langle\mathsf{ack}\rangle$ and then in one branch we have $\mathsf{Buyer} \to \mathsf{Seller} : s\langle\mathsf{go}\rangle$ and in the other $\mathsf{Buyer} \to \mathsf{Seller} : s\langle\mathsf{stop}\rangle$. We then obtain its EPP:

$$\mathsf{Buyer}[\overline{ch}(\nu s).s\rhd \mathsf{ack}.s\lhd \mathsf{go} \oplus \overline{ch}(\nu s).s\rhd \mathsf{ack}.s\lhd \mathsf{stop}] \mid \mathsf{Seller}[!\, ch(s).\overline{s}\lhd \mathsf{ack}.s\rhd (\mathsf{go}+\mathsf{stop})]$$

Let us reduce the original global description, which, by dropping one branch, leads to $\mathsf{Seller} \to \mathsf{Buyer} : s\langle\mathsf{ack}\rangle$. $\mathsf{Buyer} \to \mathsf{Seller} : s\langle\mathsf{go}\rangle$. This EPP is:

$$\mathsf{Buyer}[\overline{ch}(\nu s).s \rhd \mathsf{ack}.s \lhd \mathsf{go}] \mid \mathsf{Seller}[!\, ch(s).\overline{s} \lhd \mathsf{ack}.s \rhd \mathsf{go})]$$

Now we compare this end-point process with the reductum of the original EPP before, which is $\mathsf{Buyer}[\overline{ch}(\nu s).s\rhd \mathsf{ack}.s\lhd \mathsf{go}] \mid \mathsf{Seller}[!\, ch(s).\overline{s}\lhd \mathsf{ack}.s\rhd (\mathsf{go}+\mathsf{stop})]$, where Seller has a redundant, useless branch "stop". This example shows that reduction in a global description can lose information which is still kept in the corresponding reduction in its EPP. This motivates the asymmetric relation of *pruning* $P \prec Q$, which indicates that if we cut off such unnecessary branches and replication from Q then we obtain P (see [11] for a formal definition). If $P \prec Q$, then P and Q are strong bisimilar under the minimal typing of P.

The main result of the paper follows. Below, by abuse of notation, I denotes consistently annotated interaction. $\equiv_\mu$ is the extension of $\equiv$ with the folding/unfolding of recursion. The proof is found in [11, §16.2–5]. (1) implies the lack of communication errors for the result of EPP.

Theorem 3 (end-point projection). *Let I be coherent, $\Gamma \vdash I \rhd \Delta$ and $\Gamma \vdash \sigma$:*

(1) (type preservation) *If $\Gamma \vdash I \rhd \emptyset$ and $\Gamma \vdash \sigma$, then $\Gamma \vdash \mathsf{EPP}(I,\sigma) \rhd \emptyset$.*
(2) (soundness) *If $\mathsf{EPP}(I,\sigma) \to N$ then there exists (I',σ') such that $(\sigma,\ I) \to (\sigma',\ I')$ and $\mathsf{EPP}(I',\sigma') \prec \equiv_\mu N$.*
(3) (completeness) *If $(\sigma,\ I) \to (\sigma',\ I')$ then $\mathsf{EPP}(I,\sigma) \to N$ s.t. $\mathsf{EPP}(I',\sigma') \prec N$.*

5 Extensions and Future Work

Channel passing is a practically useful extension for business protocols, for example in the scenarios where participants need to send links to other participants. A typical example is when Buyer wants to buy from Seller, but Buyer does not know Seller's address (service channel) on the net. The only information Buyer has is a service channel of DirectoryService, which will send back the address of Seller to Buyer which in turn interacts with Seller through the obtained channel. Can we have a consistent EPP theory with unknown participants and channels? This has been an open problem left in WS-CDL's current specification (which allows channel passing only for fixed participants). A possible extension of the EPP theory to channel passing, together with the treatment of other useful additional constructs, is discussed in [11]. Another interesting future topic is relaxations of the well-formedness principles while maintaining a sound EPP theory, on which some ideas are also discussed in [11].

The EPP theory has been developed with practical use in mind. There are several engineering scenes where the theory and its extensions may be useful.

- *Code generation.* We can create a complete distributed application by projecting a detailed global description to each of its end-points.
- *Prototype generation.* Projection can also be used for generating a *skeleton code* for each end-point which only contains basic communication behaviour, to be elaborated to full code. This is already used in [19].
- *Use of conformance.* A team of programmers initially agree on a shared global specification for communications among end-points: during/after programming, each programmer can check if her/his code conforms to the specification by conformance checking against projection. The conformance scheme is useful in other scenes, for example when we wish to check the usability of an existing service/library in a given global description.
- *Runtime monitoring, testing and debugging.* At runtime, each end-point can check if ongoing communications at his/her site conform to the global description by checking against its projection to that end-point. The monitoring can also be used for debugging and testing existing code.

Further, many static analyses/logical validation methods would become available for a global description from their well-developed end-point counterpart. The present work is intended as an initial trial towards a well-founded framework for communication-centred programming based on two distinct, and mutually complementary, descriptive paradigms, underpinned by a theory of EPP.

Acknowledgements. We thank Robin Milner for instigating and setting up the directions of our ongoing collaboration with W3C WS-CDL WG; the WG members, in particular Gary Brown, Steve Ross-Talbot and Nickolas Kavantzas for collaboration; and Joshua Guttman for his comments on an early version of the paper. This work is supported by EPSRC GR/T04236, GR/S55545, GR/S55538, GR/T04724, GR/T03208, GR/T03258 and IST2005-015905 MOBIUS.

References

1. Conversation with Steve Ross-Talbot. *ACM Queue*, 4(2), 2006.
2. Jos Baeten, Harm van Beek, and Sjouke Mauw. Specifying internet applications with DiCons. In *SAC'01*, pages 576–584. ACM Press, 2001.
3. Nick Benton, Luca Cardelli, and Cedric Fournet. Modern concurrency abstractions for C#. *ACM Trans. Program. Lang. Syst.*, 26(5):769–804, 2004.
4. Martin Berger, Kohei Honda, and Nobuko Yoshida. Sequentiality and the π-calculus. In *TLCA'01*, volume 2044 of *LNCS*, pages 29–45, 2001.

5. K. Bhargavan, C. Fournet, and A. Gordon. Verified reference implementations of WS-Security protocols. In *WS-FN'06*, LNCS, 2006.
6. Eduardo Bonelli, Adriana B. Compagnoni, and Elsa L. Gunter. Correspondence assertions for process synchronization in concurrent communications. *JFP*, 15(2):219–247, 2005.
7. Sébastien Briais and Uwe Nestmann. A formal semantics for protocol narrations. In *TGC*, volume 3705, pages 163–181, 2005.
8. Nadia Busi, Roberto Gorrieri, Claudio Guidi, Roberto Lucchi, and Gianluigi Zavattaro. Choreography and orchestration conformance for system design. In *Coordination*, volume 4038 of *LNCS*, pages 63–81, 2006.
9. M. Carbone, K. Honda, and N. Yoshida. A calculus of global interaction based on session types. In *DCM '06*, ENTCS, 2006.
10. M. Carbone, M. Nielsen, and V. Sassone. A calculus for trust management. In *FSTTCS '04*, volume 3328 of *LNCS*, pages 161–173. Springer, 2004.
11. Marco Carbone, Kohei Honda, Nobuko Yoshida, Robin Milner, Gary Brown, and Steve Ross-Talbot. A theoretical basis of communication-centred concurrent programming. To be published by W3C. Available at www.dcs.qmul.ac.uk/~carbonem/cdlpaper, 2006.
12. Mariangiola Dezani-Ciancaglini, Dimitris Mostrous, Nobuko Yoshida, and Sophia Drossopoulou. Session Types for Object-Oriented Languages. In *ECOOP'06*, volume 4067 of *LNCS*, pages 328–352, 2006.
13. Simon Gay and Malco Hole. Subtyping for session types in the pi calculus. *Acta Informatica*, 42(2-3):191–225, November 2005.
14. Claudio Guidi, Roberto Lucchi, Gianluigi Zavattaro, Nadia Busi, and Roberto Gorrieri. SOCK: a calculus for service oriented computing. In *ICSOC'06*, volume 4294 of *LNCS*, 2006.
15. J. D. Guttman, F. J. Thayer, and L. D. Zuck. The faithfulness of abstract protocol analysis: message authentication. In *CCS '01*, pages 186–195. ACM Press, 2001.
16. Kohei Honda, Vasco Vasconcelos, and Makoto Kubo. Language primitives and type disciplines for structured communication-based programming. In *ESOP'98*, volume 1381 of *LNCS*, pages 22–138, 1998.
17. Cosimo Laneve and Luca Padovani. Smooth orchestrators. In *FoSSaCS'06*, volume 3921 of *LNCS*, pages 32–46, 2006.
18. R. Milner, J. Parrow, and D. Walker. A calculus of mobile processes, I and II. *Information and Computation*, 100(1):1–40,41–77, September 1992.
19. PI4SOA. http://www.pi4soa.org.
20. Benjamin C. Pierce and David N. Turner. Pict: A programming language based on the pi-calculus. In *Proof, Language and Interaction: Essays in Honour of Robin Milner*. MIT Press, 2000.
21. S. Ross-Talbot and T. Fletcher. WS-CDL Primer. To be published by W3C, 2006.
22. D. Sangiorgi. The name discipline of uniform receptiveness. In *ICALP'97*, volume 1256 of *LNCS*, pages 303–313. Springer, 1997.
23. Kaku Takeuchi, Kohei Honda, and Makoto Kubo. An interaction-based language and its typing system. In *PARLE'94*, volume 817 of *LNCS*, pages 398–413, 1994.
24. W.M.P. van der Aalst. Inheritance of interorganizational workflows: How to agree to disagree without loosing control? *Info. Tech. and Management*, 2(3):195–231, 2002.
25. Vasco Vasconcelos, António Ravara, and Simon J. Gay. Session types for functional multithreading. In *CONCUR'04*, volume 3170 of *LNCS*, pages 497–511, 2004.
26. W3C WS-CDL Working Group. Web services choreography description language version 1.0. http://www.w3.org/TR/2004/WD-ws-cdl-10-20040427/.

CC-Pi: A Constraint-Based Language for Specifying Service Level Agreements*

Maria Grazia Buscemi[1] and Ugo Montanari[2]

[1] IMT Lucca Institute for Advanced Studies, Italy
marzia.buscemi@imtlucca.it
[2] Dipartimento di Informatica, University of Pisa, Italy
ugo@di.unipi.it

Abstract. Service Level Agreements are a key issue in Service Oriented Computing. SLA contracts specify client requirements and service guarantees, with emphasis on Quality of Service (cost, performance, availability, etc.). In this work we propose a simple model of contracts for QoS and SLAs that also allows to study mechanisms for resource allocation and for joining different SLA requirements. Our language combines two basic programming paradigms: name-passing calculi and concurrent constraint programming (cc programming). Specifically, we extend cc programming by adding synchronous communication and by providing a treatment of names in terms of restriction and structural axioms closer to nominal calculi than to variables with existential quantification. In the resulting framework, SLA requirements are constraints that can be generated either by a single party or by the synchronisation of two agents. Moreover, restricting the scope of names allows for local stores of constraints, which may become global as a consequence of synchronisations. Our approach relies on a system of *named* constraints that equip classical constraints with a suitable algebraic structure providing a richer mechanism of constraint combination. We give reduction-preserving translations of both cc programming and the calculus of explicit fusions.

1 Introduction

An important aspect of web services concerns client requirements and service guarantees with emphasis on Quality of Service, such as cost, performance, availability. These are commonly referred to as Service Level Agreements. SLAs between organisations are used in several areas of IT services, like hosting and communication services. The terms and conditions appearing in a SLA contract can be negotiated among the contracting parties prior to service execution.

In this paper we present a simple calculus, called *cc-pi calculus*, for modeling processes able to specify QoS requirements and to conclude SLA contracts. The proposed language is also equipped with mechanisms for resource allocation and for joining different SLA requirements. Our approach combines basic features of name-passing calculi and of concurrent constraint (cc) programming.

* Research supported by the EU IST-FP6 16004 Integrated Project SENSORIA.

R. De Nicola (Ed.): ESOP 2007, LNCS 4421, pp. 18–32, 2007.

Name-passing calculi, such as the pi-calculus [7], are a key paradigm of computation whose interaction mechanism may dynamically change the communication topology. Since the introduction of name-passing calculi, the notion of *names* has been recognised as crucial in theories for concurrency and mobility.

The name-passing calculus we start with is the pi-F calculus [19]. The pi-F calculus is a variant of the pi-calculus [7], whose synchronisation mechanism is global and, instead of binding formal names to actual names, it yields *explicit fusions*, i.e. simple constraints expressing name equalities. For example, consider two processes $\overline{u}\langle v\rangle.P$ and $u\langle x\rangle.Q$, that are ready to make an output and an input on u, respectively. The interaction between these processes results in the explicit fusion of v and x. This fusion will also affect any further process R running in parallel: $R\,|\,\overline{u}\langle v\rangle.P\,|\,u\langle x\rangle.Q \rightarrow R\,|\,P\,|\,Q\,|\,x=v$. The restriction operator (x) can be used to limit the scope of a fusion, e.g.: $R\,|\,(x)(\overline{u}\langle v\rangle.P\,|\,u\langle x\rangle.Q) \rightarrow R\,|(x)(P\,|\,Q\,|\,x=v)$.

The cc-pi calculus extends the pi-F calculus by generalising explicit fusions like $x=v$ to *named constraints* and by adding primitives for handling such constraints. While the informal concept of constraint is widely used in a variety of different fields, a very general, formal notion of constraint system has been introduced in the cc programming paradigm [15]. Actually, cc programming is a simple and powerful computing model based on a shared store of constraints that provides partial information about possible values that variables can take. Concurrent agents can act on this store by performing either a `tell` action (for adding a constraint, if the resulting store is *consistent*) or an `ask` action (for checking if a constraint is *entailed* by the store). As computation proceeds, more and more information are accumulated, thus the store is *monotonically refined*.

Of the classical cc programming paradigm we keep the `ask` and `tell` constructs, but we extend/modify several other aspects. Maybe the most radical change is to give up the monotonicity requirement. While non-monotonicity was already present in the so-called *linear* cc programming [14], the introduction in our calculus of a `retract` construct, whose effect is to erase a previously told constraint, is strongly suggested by the need of allocating a resource and of deallocating *the same* resource. Of course monotonicity is the basis of several properties of cc programming, which thus do not hold in our framework. However whenever retracts are forbidden, or their usage is limited, some of the useful properties could be reinstated. We also introduce a `check` operation for verifying if a constraint is consistent with the store of constraints.

Another important difference with respect to [15] is that we adopt a different concept of general, abstract constraint system. While the classical notion is equipped with an operation of entailment and a predicate of consistency, being based on Dana Scott's information systems, we employ constraints forming c-semirings [2]. Roughly, a c-semiring consists of a set equipped with two binary operations, the sum $+$ and the product $\times$, such that $+$ is associative, commutative and idempotent, $\times$ is associative and commutative and $\times$ distributes over $+$. A c-semiring is automatically equipped with a partial ordering $a \leq b$, which means that a is more constrained than b, or, more interestingly, that a entails b, $a \vdash b$. The sum $a+b$ chooses the worst constraint better than a and b, while the product $a \times b$ combines two constraints. The simplest c-semiring consists of the booleans with $\vee$ as $+$ and $\wedge$ as $\times$.

Our c-semirings enjoy two kinds of nice properties. On the one hand they are very stable, since cartesian products, functional spaces and powerdomains of c-semirings are c-semirings. On the other hand c-semirings are quite adequate for modeling the so-called *soft* constraints, i.e. constraints which do not return only true or false, but more informative values instead. In fact it is easy to define c-semirings expressing fuzzy, hierarchical, or probabilistic values. Also, optimization algorithms work on the c-semiring consisting of the reals plus infinity with the operations of sum as $\times$ and min as $+$. Several efficient algorithms defined for ordinary, crisp constraints, like local propagation or dynamic programming, can be generalized to c-semirings.

The former kind of properties is used in the paper to model networks of constraints for defining constraint satisfaction problems (CSPs) [8]. In fact, a single constraint, or even a network of constraints, is a function which, given an assignment of the variables to some domain D, returns a boolean, or rather a value in a generic c-semiring in the soft case. CSPs are a well-established formalism, especially studied in the artificial intelligence area, adequate to specify many kinds of real-life problems. In this paper we do not fully explore the latter aspect of c-semirings. However we consider it as extremely valuable and we plan to further exploit it in the future. In fact, we believe that a lot of non-functional requirements of QoS can be adequately modeled using c-semirings.

The last, important difference with respect to [15] is that we handle variables, or rather names, in a very different way. In ordinary `cc` programming, constraints involving variables are seen as relations, in the style of Tarski's cylindrical algebras. This interpretation is particularly visible in the axioms for hiding (written as $\exists$) and variable equality. Instead, in our *named* constraints we regard variables as ordinary names in the pi-calculus style. More precisely, names are introduced, as for pi-calculus agents [9], by means of permutation algebras. Operations of permutation algebras are permutations of names. A key concept of permutation algebras is the *support* of a value, that specifies the set of names such that the permutations which do not affect them do not modify the value. Thus, equipping a c-semiring with a permutation algebra structure allows to characterise the set of relevant, i.e. *free*, names of a constraint c as the support of c. Since the treatment of names is the same, we can handle constraints as processes, making both syntax and semantics of our calculus simpler and more natural.

Besides `ask`, `tell`, `retract` and `check` there is another way in which agents can interact with the constraints existing in the system. In fact, synchronization of processes works like a global `ask` and `tell` construct. Two agents trying to perform an output $\overline{x}\langle y \rangle$ and an input $x'\langle y' \rangle$ action can synchronize only if the constraint $x = x'$ is entailed by the store. The result of the synchronization is a new constraint $y = y'$ which is told to the store. Fusion $y = y'$ can modify deeply the store, depending on the actual constraint system. For instance it can allow two local constraints to interact, establishing a SLA between the two partners. However, if the resulting constraint is inconsistent, the synchronization is forbidden. It can become possible at some later time if some other agent performs a `retract` action which makes the store less constrained.

The special role of fusions in the control mechanisms of our calculus requires their presence in all constraint systems. Thus, we propose named c-semirings with name fusions, or equalities, as the underlying data model of cc-pi calculus.

In the paper, we show the generality of our approach by proposing three examples of named c-semirings, i.e. name equalities, Herbrand constraint systems, and soft CSPs, and we prove that they are effectively named c-semirings. We also show how our model can be applied in specifying and monitoring SLAs. Finally, we explore the expressiveness of our calculus by giving reduction-preserving translations of Pi-F and cc programming into cc-pi.

A motivating example. Consider a service offering computing resources (e.g. units of CPUs of a given power) and suppose the service provider and a client want to reach a SLA. The provider P_{N}, with N available resources and the client C_{n} requiring at least n resources can be specified in our framework as follows, being max the maximum number of resources that can be allocated to each client:

$$\begin{aligned} P_{\mathsf{N}} &= (x_0)\,(\mathtt{tell}\;(x_0 = \mathsf{N}).Q(x_0))\\ Q(x) &= (v)\,(x')\,(\mathtt{tell}\;(x' = x - v).\mathtt{tell}\;(v \le \mathsf{max}).c\langle v\rangle.Q(x')).\\ C_{\mathsf{n}} &= (y)\,(\mathtt{tell}\;(y \ge n).\overline{c}\langle y\rangle.\tau.\mathtt{retract}\;(y \ge n).\mathtt{tell}\;(y = 0)). \end{aligned}$$

In words, P_{N} first sets the initial number of resources to N and evolves to Q. Process Q creates a name v representing the resources available to a client and a non-negative name x' counting the resources left after concluding a contract with the client; Q then adds the constraints $x' = x - v$ for setting the value of x' and $v \le \mathsf{max}$ for imposing the bound max on v. Finally, Q signs the contract, i.e. it synchronises on a channel c with a client and, if the synchronisation succeeds, Q becomes ready to accept a new request. On the other side, C_{n} initially creates a local name y and places the constraint $y \ge n$. Next, C_{n} tries to synchronise on a public port c with a server. In case of success, C_{n} makes some calculation involving the obtained resources, which is modelled as a silent action τ. Then, C_{n} releases the allocated resources by removing the above constraint on y ($\mathtt{retract}\;(y \ge n)$). Hence, a negotiation between P_{N} and C_{n} begins with the two parties placing their constraints. P_{N} and C_{n} can then synchronise (thus yielding the fusion of names v and y), if the resulting constraint system is consistent, i.e. if $\mathsf{n} \le min(N, \mathsf{max})$, as shown by the graph representation below.

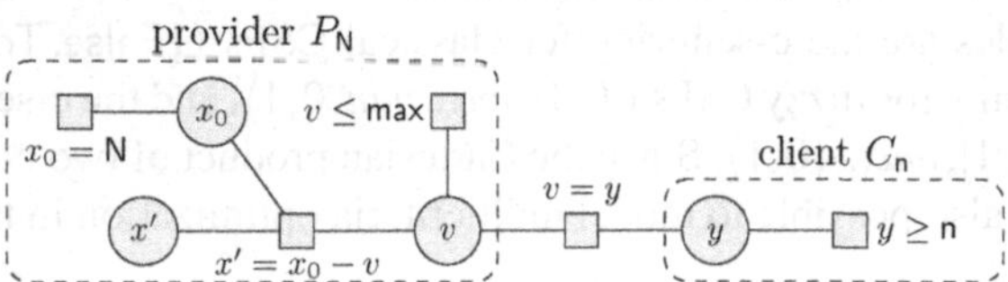

Related work. Bacciu *et al.* [1] also propose a framework for specifying client requirements and provider guarantees on the offered services, along with negotiation mechanisms. Unlike our model, their approach relies on fuzzy sets rather than on c-semirings. The process calculus introduced in [4] focuses on controlling and coordinating distributed process interactions respecting QoS parameters expressed as c-semiring values, but the model does not cover negotiations. The ρ-calculus [11] is a concurrent calculus with first-order constraints and high-order procedural abstraction. Akin to our approach, the ρ-calculus is parametric to a certain constraint system. In [18] the ρ-calculus has been encoded into the Fusion Calculus [13]. Thus, we expect that ρ can also be encoded into cc-pi. The pi$^+$-calculus [5] is an extension of the pi-calculus with constraint agents that can perform `tell` and `ask` actions. In contrast to our model, the constraint systems are first-order theories rather than algebraic structures and they do not support local stores. However, to our knowledge, none of the above languages has been applied for specifying SLA contracts. SLAng [17] and WSLA [6] are XML-based languages for defining SLAs at a lower level of abstractions. The elements of SLAng are also constraints on the behaviour of associated services and service clients, but their are specified in OCL. WSLA provides the ability to create new SLAs as functions over existing metrics. This is useful to formalise requirements that are expressed in terms of multiple QoS parameters. The semantics for expressions over metrics is not formally defined, though.

2 Background

2.1 C-Semirings

We give here the basic definitions and properties concerning c-semirings. We refer to [2] for a more detailed treatment.

Definition 1 (c-semiring). *A* constraint semiring (c-semiring) *is a tuple* $\langle A, +, \times, 0, 1\rangle$ *such that: (i) A is a set and* $0, 1 \in A$*; (ii)* $+$ *is commutative, associative, idempotent,* 0 *is its unit element and* 1 *is its absorbing element; (iii)* $\times$ *is associative, commutative and distributes over* $+$.

Let us consider the relation $\leq$ over A such that $a \leq b$ iff $a+b=b$. Then, it is possible to prove that (see [2]): (i) $\leq$ is a partial order; (ii) $+$ and $\times$ are monotone on $\leq$; (iii) $\times$ is intensive on $\leq$: $a \times b \leq a, b$; (iv) 0 is its minimum and 1 its maximum; (v) $\langle A, \leq\rangle$ is a complete lattice and, for all $a, b \in A$, $+$ is the least upper bound operator, that is, $a+b = lub(a,b)$. Moreover, if $\times$ is idempotent, then: $+$ distributes over $\times$; $\langle A, \leq\rangle$ is a distributive lattice and $\times$ is its greatest lower bound. Informally, the relation $\leq$ gives us a way to compare semiring values and constraints.

Typical examples are the c-semiring for classical CSPs $\langle\{\mathsf{False}, \mathsf{True}\}, \vee, \wedge, \mathsf{False}, \mathsf{True}\rangle$, the c-semiring for fuzzy CSPs $\langle [0,1], max, min, 0, 1\rangle$, and the c-semiring for probabilistic CSPs $\langle [0,1], max, \cdot, 0, 1\rangle$. Since the Cartesian product of two c-semirings is still a c-semiring, it is also possible to model multicriteria optimization in this framework.

2.2 Permutation Algebras

We denote by $\mathcal{N}$ the infinite, countable, totally ordered set of *names* and we use $x, y, z \ldots$ to denote names. We write $\widetilde{x}$ for the tuple of names $\langle x_1, \ldots, x_n\rangle$. A *substitution* is a function $\sigma : \mathcal{N} \to \mathcal{N}$. We denote by $[y_1/x_1, \cdots, y_n/x_n]$ the substitution that maps x_i into y_i for $i = 1, \ldots, n$ and which is the identity on the other names. The *identity substitution* is denoted by id. A *permutation* is a bijective name substitution. We let ρ range over permutations. The *kernel*, $K(\rho)$ of a permutation ρ is the set of the names that are changed by the permutation. A *permutation algebra* is defined by a carrier set and by a function defining how states are transformed by the finite-kernel permutations.

An interesting example is given by the permutation algebra for the pi-calculus [9]. In that case, the carrier contains all the processes, up to structural congruence, and the interpretation of a permutation is the associated name substitution.

The carrier of a permutation algebra can be partitioned into *orbits*, where two elements are in the same orbit if one can be obtained from the other by applying some permutation. To every element a a *symmetry* $\mathrm{sym}(a)$ can be associated, i.e. the group of all permutations ρ such that $a = \rho(a)$. The *support* $\mathrm{supp}(a)$ of an element a is the smallest set of names such that all the permutations that do not modify them are in $\mathrm{sym}(a)$. Intuitively, the names in $\mathrm{supp}(a)$ are the free names of a, the permutations which do not modify them are obviously not influent on a. Indeed, the permutations exchanging names in $\mathrm{supp}(a)$ with names not in $\mathrm{supp}(a)$ are renamings of the free names and do not belong to $\mathrm{sym}(a)$, while the permutations in $\mathrm{sym}(a)$ which modify only names in the support are genuine self-transformations of the element. A permutation algebra is *finite-support* if each element of its carrier has finite support.

3 Named Constraints

In this section, we propose a definition of *named constraints* that relies on the notion of *named c-semirings*. Essentially, a named c-semiring is a c-semiring enriched with a notion of name fusions, a permutation algebra A and a hiding operator $(\nu x.)$. In particular, A allows to characterise the finite set of *relevant names* of each element of the c-semiring as the support $\mathrm{supp}(c)$ of c in A, and $\nu x.c$ makes a name x local in c, in the style of process calculi. A named constraint is an element of a named c-semiring with an associated support.

Definition 2. *We define* (name) fusions *as total equivalence relations on $\mathcal{N}$ with only finitely many non-singular equivalence classes. By $x{=}y$ we denote the fusion with a unique non-singular equivalence class containing x and y.*

Definition 3. *A* named c-semiring $\mathcal{C} = \langle C, +, \times, \nu x., \rho, 0, 1\rangle$ *is a tuple where: (i) $x{=}y \in C$ for all x and y in $\mathcal{N}$; (ii) $\langle C, +, \times, 0, 1\rangle$ is a c-semiring; (iii) $\langle C, \rho\rangle$ is a finite-support permutation algebra; (iv) $\nu x. : C \to C$, for each name x, is a unary operation; (v) for all $c, d \in C$ and for all ρ the following axioms hold.*

$$
\begin{array}{ll}
(\text{FUSE}) & x{=}y \times c \;=\; x{=}y \times [y/x]c \\
(\text{HIDE}) & \nu x.\,1 = 1 \quad \nu x.\nu y.c = \nu y.\nu x.c \quad \nu x.(c \times d) = c \times \nu x.d \text{ if } x \notin \mathrm{supp}(c) \\
 & \nu x.(c+d) = c + \nu x.d \text{ if } x \notin \mathrm{supp}(c) \quad \nu x.\,c = \nu y.\,[y/x]c \text{ if } y \notin \mathrm{supp}(c) \\
(\text{PERM}) & \rho 0 = 0 \quad \rho 1 = 1 \quad \rho(c \times d) = \rho c \times \rho d \quad \rho(c+d) = \rho c + \rho d \\
 & \rho\,(\nu x.c) = \nu x.\,(\rho c) \text{ if } x \notin K(\rho)
\end{array}
$$

The (FUS) axiom accounts for combining fusions and generic elements of c-semirings: $x{=}y \times c$ is equivalent to the product $x{=}y \times [y/x]c$ where y is replaced by x in c. The (HIDE) and (PERM) axioms rule how the ν and ρ operations, respectively, interact with the operations of the c-semiring. The axioms (HIDE) are inspired by the analogous structural congruence axioms for restriction in process calculi. Roughly, the c-semiring product $\times$ corresponds to the parallel composition of processes and constraint hiding is the counterpart of restriction on processes. The notion of support supp(c) associated with permutation algebras recalls the concept of free names in process calculi. According to the (PERM) axioms, ρ distributes with respect to $\times$ and $+$, and ρ is inactive on 0 and 1. Finally, the order of ρ and ν can be changed if x is not affected by ρ.

We propose below three examples of named c-semirings aimed at showing the generality of our approach. Specifically, we consider c-semirings for name equalities, for Herbrand constraint systems and for soft CSPs. Note that these named c-semirings can be suitably composed to model more complex constraint systems.

Example 1 (Name Equalitites). Let $\mathcal{R}$ be the set of all equivalence relation on $\mathcal{N}$. We define C_E as the tuple $C_E = \langle C, +, \times, \nu x., \rho, 0, 1\rangle$ such that: (i) $C = \mathcal{R}$; (ii) $R_1 + R_2 = R_1 \cap R_2$; (iii) $R_1 \times R_2 = (R_1 \cup R_2)^\star$, i.e. $R_1 \times R_2$ is the reflexive, transitive, and symmetric closure of $R_1 \cup R_2$; (iv) $\nu x.R = R + \{(y,z) \mid y,z \neq x \text{ or } y = z = x\}$, i.e. $\nu x.R$ is obtained from R by replacing the equivalence class of x with the singleton $\{x\}$; (v) $\rho R = \{(\rho(x), \rho(y)) \mid (x,y) \in R\}$; (vi) $0 = (\mathcal{N} \times \mathcal{N})$ and $1 = \{(x,x) \mid x \in \mathcal{N}\}$.

Proposition 1. *C_E is a named c-semiring with idempotent product $\times$.*

Example 2 (Herbrand Constraint System). Given a signature Σ, let $=_E$ be an equational theory on $T_\Sigma(\mathcal{N})$, plus the additional axioms:

$$\frac{f(t_1,\ldots,t_n) =_E f(t'_1,\ldots,t'_n)}{t_i =_E t'_i}\; i = 1,\ldots,n \qquad\qquad \frac{x =_E t \quad t_1 =_E t_2}{[t/x]t_1 =_E [t/x]t_2}$$

and with the restrictions: $x \neq_E t(x)$ and $f(t_1,\ldots,t_n) \neq_E g(t_1,\ldots,t_m)$, where $t(x)$ is any term different than x which contains x and $f \neq g$. We define C_H as the tuple $C_H = \langle C, +, \times, \nu x., \rho, 0, 1\rangle$ where: (i) C is the set of the above-defined equational theories plus a bottom element $\bot$; (ii) $E_1 + E_2 = E_1 \cap E_2$; (iii) $E_1 \times E_2$ is the unification of E_1 and E_2, i.e. it is the smallest equational theory largest than or equal to $E_1 \cup E_2$, if it exists, otherwise $\bot$; (iv) $\nu x.\, E = E \cap \bar{E}$, where $t_1 =_{\bar{E}} t_2$ iff $t_1 = t_2$ or x does not occur in t_1, t_2; (v) $\rho t_1 =_{\rho E} \rho t_2$ iff $t_1 =_E t_2$; (vi) $0 = \bot$ and $1 = \{(t,t) \mid t \in T_\Sigma(\mathcal{N})\}$.

Proposition 2. *C_H is a named c-semiring with idempotent product $\times$.*

Example 3 (soft CSPs). Given a domain D of interpretation for $\mathcal{N}$, and a c-semiring $S = \langle A, +, \times, 0, 1\rangle$, a *soft* constraint c can be represented as a function $c = (\mathcal{N} \to D) \to A$ associating to each variable assignment $\eta = \mathcal{N} \to D$ a value of A. We define C_{soft} as the tuple $C_{\text{soft}} = \langle C, +', \times', \nu x., \rho, 0', 1'\rangle$ such that: (i) C is the set of all soft constraints over $\mathcal{N}$, D and S; (ii) fusions $x{=}y$ are defined as $(x = y)\eta = 1$ if $\eta(x) = \eta(y)$, $(x = y)\eta = 0$ otherwise; (iii) $(c_1 +' c_2)\eta = c_1\eta + c_2\eta$; (iv) $(c_1 \times' c_2)\eta = c_1\eta \times c_2\eta$; (v) $(\nu x.c)\eta = \sum_{d \in D}(c\eta[^d/_x])$, where the assignment $\eta[^d/_x]$ is defined, as usual, as $\eta[^d/_x](y) = d$ if $x = y$, $\eta(y)$ otherwise; (vi) $(\rho c)\eta = c\overline{\eta}$ with $\overline{\eta}(x) = \eta(\rho(x))$; (vii) $0'\eta = 0$ and $1'\eta = 1$ for all η.

Proposition 3. *C_{soft} is a named c-semiring with idempotent product $\times$.*

Note that the support supp(c) of an element of C_{soft} coincides with the support of a functional constraint c as defined in [3].

Definition 4 ((named) constraint). *Given a named c-semiring with equalities* $\langle A, +, \times, \rho, \nu x., 0, 1\rangle$, *a* (named) constraint *c is an element of A.*

We define here the notions of *consistency* and *entailment* of constraints. They are analogous to the corresponding definitions given by Saraswat and Rinard [15]. Below we abbreviate by $(\times C)$ the product $c_1 \times \ldots \times c_n$ with $C = \{c_1, \ldots, c_n\}$.

Definition 5. *Let* $\langle A, +, \times, \rho, \nu x., 0, 1\rangle$ *be a named c-semiring and* $C \subseteq A$ *be a set of constraints. C is* consistent *if* $(\times C) \neq 0$. *Moreover, given a constraint* $c \in A$, *we say that C entails c, written* $C \vdash c$, *if* $(\times C) \leq c$.

4 The cc-pi Calculus

4.1 Syntax

We assume the countable set of names $\mathcal{N}$ and a set of process identifiers, ranged over by D. We let c range over constraints of an arbitrary named c-semiring $\mathcal{C}$.

Definition 6. *The sets of* prefixes *and* cc-pi processes *are defined as follows:*

PREFIXES	$\pi ::= \tau \mid \bar{x}\langle\tilde{y}\rangle \mid x\langle\tilde{y}\rangle \mid \texttt{tell}\ c \mid \texttt{ask}\ c \mid \texttt{retract}\ c \mid \texttt{check}\ c$
UNCONSTRAINED PROCESSES	$U ::= \mathbf{0} \mid U \vert U \mid \sum_i \pi_i.U_i \mid (x)U \mid D(\tilde{y})$
CONSTRAINED PROCESSES	$P ::= U \mid c \mid P \vert P \mid (x)P$

The τ prefix stands for a silent action, the output prefix $\bar{x}\langle\tilde{y}\rangle$ for emitting over the port x the message $\tilde{y}$ and the input prefix $x\langle\tilde{y}\rangle$ for receiving over x a message and binding it to $\tilde{y}$. Prefix `tell` c generates a constraint c and puts it in parallel with the other constraints, if the resulting parallel composition of constraints is consistent; `tell` c is not enabled otherwise. Prefix `ask` c is enabled if c is entailed by the set of constraints in parallel. Prefix `retract` c removes a constraint c, if c is present. Prefix `check` c is enabled if c is consistent with the set of constraints in parallel. *Unconstrained processes U* are essentially processes that can only contain constraints c in prefixes `tell` c, `ask` c, `retract` c, and `check` c. As usual, 0 stands for the inert process and $U \mid U$ for the parallel composition. $\sum_i \pi_i.U_i$ denotes an external choice in which some guarded unconstrained process U_i is chosen when the corresponding guard π_i is enabled. Restriction $(x)U$ makes the name x local in U. A defining equation for a process identifier D is of the form $D(\tilde{x}) \stackrel{\text{def}}{=} U$ with $|\tilde{x}| = |\tilde{y}|$. *Constrained processes P* are defined like unconstrained processes U but for the fact that P may have constraints c in parallel with processes. We simply write processes to refer to constrained processes.

We extend the usual notion of *free names* of a process by stating that the set of free names of a constraint c is the support $\text{supp}(c)$ defined in the previous section. Formally, the set $\text{fn}(P)$ is inductively defined as follows:

$$\mathrm{fn}(\mathbf{0}) = \emptyset \;\; \mathrm{fn}(\tau.U) = \mathrm{fn}(U) \;\; \mathrm{fn}(\bar{x}\langle\tilde{y}\rangle.U) = \{x,y\} \cup \mathrm{fn}(U) \;\; \mathrm{fn}(x\langle\tilde{y}\rangle.U) = \{x,y\} \cup \mathrm{fn}(U)$$
$$\mathrm{fn}(\pi.U) = \mathrm{supp}(c) \cup \mathrm{fn}(U) \quad \text{if } \pi = \texttt{tell}\ c, \texttt{ask}\ c, \texttt{retract}\ c, \texttt{check}\ c$$
$$\mathrm{fn}(\textstyle\sum_i \pi_i.U_i) = \cup_i \mathrm{fn}(\pi_i.U_i) \quad \mathrm{fn}(D(\tilde{x})) = \mathrm{fn}(U) \quad \text{if } D(\tilde{x}) \stackrel{\mathrm{def}}{=} U$$
$$\mathrm{fn}(c) = \mathrm{supp}(c) \quad \mathrm{fn}(P\,|\,Q) = \mathrm{fn}(P) \cup \mathrm{fn}(Q) \quad \mathrm{fn}((x)P) = \mathrm{fn}(P) \setminus \{x\}$$

We write $\mathrm{n}(P)$ for the set of *names* of a process P and $\mathrm{bn}(P) = \mathrm{n}(P) \setminus \mathrm{fn}(P)$ for the set of *bound names*; the usual notion of α-conversion on bound names holds. By σP we denote the process obtained from P by simultaneously substituting each free occurrence of z in P by $\sigma(z)$, possibly α-converting bound names.

4.2 Operational Semantics

The reduction semantics, as usual, is given in two steps: the definition of a *structural congruence*, which rearranges processes into adjacent positions, and a notion of *reduction relation* that captures computations.

Definition 7. *We let* structural congruence, $\equiv$, *be the least congruence over processes closed with respect to α-conversion and satisfying the following rules.*

$$(\text{AX-PAR}) \quad P|0 \equiv P \qquad P|Q \equiv Q|P \qquad (P|Q)|R \equiv P|(Q|R)$$
$$(\text{AX-RES}) \quad (x)0 \equiv 0 \quad (x)(y)P \equiv (y)(x)P \quad P|(x)Q \equiv (x)(P|Q) \quad \textit{if } x \notin \mathrm{fn}(P)$$
$$(\text{AX-REC}) \quad D(\tilde{y}) \equiv [\tilde{y}/\tilde{x}]U \quad \textit{if } D(\tilde{x}) \stackrel{\mathrm{def}}{=} U$$

These axioms can be applied for reducing every process P into a normal form $(x_1)\ldots(x_n)(C\,|\,U)$, where C is a parallel composition of constraints and U is an unconstrained process. Specifically, the axioms are applied from left to right in the following order: (AX-RES) for moving forward restrictions, and (AX-PAR) for grouping constraints together, and (AX-REC).

Definition 8. *The* reduction relation *over processes $\rightarrow$ is the least relation satisfying the following inference rules. We use the following notations: C stands for the parallel composition of constraints $c_1\,|\ldots|\,c_n$; C* consistent *means $(c_1 \times \ldots \times c_n) \neq 0$; $C \vdash c$ if $(c_1 \times \ldots \times c_n) \leq c$; $C - c$ stands for $c_1\,|\ldots|\,c_{i-1}\,|\,c_{i+1}\,|\ldots|\,c_n$ if $c = c_i$ for some i, while $C - c = C$ otherwise.*

$$(\text{TAU})\ C\,|\,\tau.U \rightarrow C\,|\,U \qquad (\text{TELL})\ C\,|\,\texttt{tell}\ c.U \rightarrow C\,|\,c\,|\,U \ \textit{ if } C\,|\,c \textit{ consistent}$$

$$(\text{ASK})\ C\,|\,\texttt{ask}\ c.U \rightarrow C\,|\,U \quad \textit{if } C \vdash c \quad (\text{RETRACT})\ C\,|\,\texttt{retract}\ c.U \rightarrow (C - c)\,|\,U$$

$$(\text{CHECK})\ C\,|\,\texttt{tell}\ c.U \rightarrow C\,|\,U \ \textit{ if } C\,|\,c \textit{ consistent}$$

$$(\text{COM})\ C\,|\,\bar{x}\langle\tilde{y}\rangle.U + \textstyle\sum \pi_i.U_i\,|\,z\langle\tilde{w}\rangle.V + \sum \pi'_j.V_j \;\longrightarrow\; C \cup \{\tilde{y} = \tilde{w}\}\,|\,U\,|\,V$$
$$\textit{if } |\tilde{y}| = |\tilde{w}|,\ C\,|\,\tilde{y} = \tilde{w} \textit{ consistent and } C \vdash x = z$$

$$(\text{SUM})\ \frac{C\,|\,\pi_i.U_i \rightarrow P}{C\,|\,\sum \pi_i.U_i \rightarrow P} \qquad (\text{PAR})\ \frac{P \rightarrow P'}{P\,|\,U \rightarrow P'\,|\,U}$$

$$(\text{RES })\ \frac{P \rightarrow P'}{(x)P \rightarrow (x)P'} \qquad (\text{STRUCT})\ \frac{P \equiv P' \quad P' \rightarrow Q' \quad Q' \equiv Q}{P \rightarrow Q}$$

The idea behind this reduction relation is to proceed as follows. First, rearranging processes into the normal form $(x_1) \dots (x_n)(C \mid U)$ by means of rule (STRUCT). Next, applying the rules (TELL), (ASK), (RETRACT), and (CHECK) for primitives on constraints and the rule (COM) for synchronising processes. Finally, closing with respect to parallel composition and restriction ((PAR), (RES)). More in detail, rule (TELL) states that if $C \mid c$ is consistent then a process can place c in parallel with C, the process is stuck otherwise. Rules (ASK) and (CHECK) specify that a process starting with an $\mathtt{ask}\ c$ or, respectively, $\mathtt{check}\ c$ prefix evolves to its continuation if c is entailed by C or, respectively, if $c \mid C$ is consistent, and that the process is stuck otherwise. By rule (RETRACT) a process can remove c if c is among the syntactic constraints in C; e.g., the process $x{=}y \mid y = z \mid \mathtt{retract}\ x = z.U$ does not affect $x{=}y \mid y = z$. In rules (COM), we write $\widetilde{y} = \widetilde{w}$ to denote the parallel composition of fusions $y_1 = w_1 \mid \dots, \mid y_n = w_n$. Intuitively, two processes $\overline{x}\langle\widetilde{y}\rangle.P$ and $z\langle\widetilde{w}\rangle.Q$ can synchronise if the equality of the names x and z is entailed by C and if the parallel composition $C \mid \widetilde{y} = \widetilde{w}$ is consistent. Note that it is legal to treat fusions as constraints c over C, because we only consider named c-semiring with fusions, as noted in § 3. Rule (PAR) allows for closure with respect to unconstrained processes in parallel. This rule imposes to take into account all constraints in parallel when applying the rules for constraints and synchronisation.

The present semantics does not specify how to solve at each step the constraint system given by the parallel composition of constraints C. However, in [10] it is shown how to apply dynamic programming to solve a CSP by solving its subproblems and then by combining solutions to obtain the solution of the whole problem. A visual representation of the problem is given by considering a graph where names are represented as nodes and constraints as arcs connecting the names involved in each constraint.

Example 4. Let P and Q be the following two processes (we write $c(x_1,\dots,x_n)$ for a constraint c with support $\mathrm{supp}(c) = \{x_1,\dots,x_n\}$):

$$P \equiv (x)\,(z)\,\mathtt{tell}\ c(x).\overline{y}\langle x\rangle.x\langle z\rangle.\mathbf{0} \qquad Q \equiv (w)\,\mathtt{tell}\ c'(w,v).y\langle w\rangle.\overline{w}\langle v\rangle.\mathbf{0}$$

First, P and Q make their respective $\mathtt{tell}$ actions, which necessarily succeed as the constraint system is initially empty and the constraints c and c' have different support. The graph representation of the resulting store of constraints is depicted in Fig. (a) below. Next, the two processes try to synchronise on port y and, according to rule (COM), the synchronisation takes place if the constraint combination $c \times c' \times x = w$ has a solution (Fig. (b)). Finally, the processes synchronise on port x, which is identified to w, thus yielding the fusion $z = v$ (Fig. (c)).

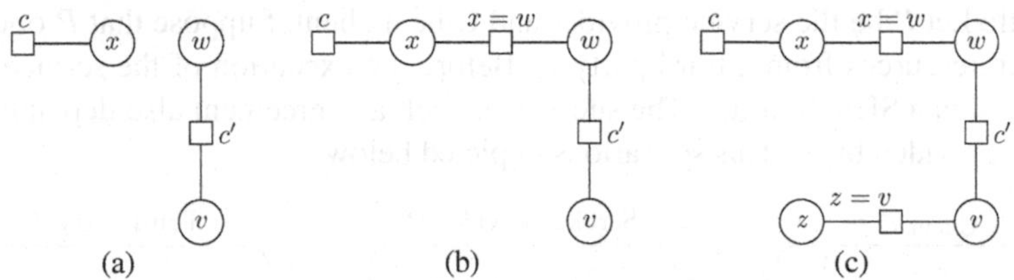

Remark on `retract`. We have chosen to introduce the `retract` operation in the calculus in order to model non-monotonic constraint systems. For instance, an agent can perform a `retract` action for removing from a store a constraint that it had previously placed, thus enabling a `tell` operation which would be stuck otherwise or for releasing some resources after using them. Nevertheless, we can consider a version of the cc-pi calculus not including the `retract` primitive. For this fragment of the calculus the following additional axioms for relating parallel composition with product and restriction with hiding hold: $c_1 \,|\, c_2 \equiv c_1 \times c_2$ and $(x)c \equiv \nu x.c$. These axioms cannot be included in the original cc-pi calculus. In fact, a constraint c can be removed only if c is syntactically present in the store of constraints, while by applying product or hiding we generate new syntactic constraints. Note that the axioms for structural congruence in Def. 7 along with the above ones lead to processes into a normal form $(\tilde{x})\,(c\,|\,U)$, where U does not contain restrictions.

5 Specifying Service Level Agreements

In this section we show how to model within our framework SLA contracts. The idea is to specify each SLA parameter as a variable and each SLA requirement or guarantee as a constraint that connects the involved variables. The parties are modelled as communicating processes. A constraint can be generated either by a single process or by the synchronisation of two processes that induces the identification of the communicated values. Note that our constraint-based approach allows to specify not only negotiations to reach a SLA contract, but also run-time checks that the contracts is not violated by the involved parties.

Here we consider two examples that show how to apply our approach in modelling the SLA management system. The first example is centered around the basic mechanism for reaching and validating a contract. The second example extends the example given in the introduction with three clients. For simplicity, in both examples we take the constraint system to be a CSP by instantiating cc-pi with the named c-semiring $\mathcal{C}_{\text{soft}}$, defined in Example 3, over the c-semiring $S = \langle\{\mathsf{False}, \mathsf{True}\}, \vee, \wedge, \mathsf{False}, \mathsf{True}\rangle$. This choice leads to solutions consisting of the set of tuples of legal domain values. We could generalise such constraint system with soft constraints by replacing S with an arbitrary c-semiring.

5.1 A Web Hosting Service

Consider a service that offers different web hosting solutions, varying in cost and in bandwidth. Let P be the service provider and C be a client. Suppose that P obtains its bandwidth resources from a third party T. Before the execution of the service, P and C want to sign a SLA contract. The success of such an agreement also depends on the resources provided by T. This scenario is depicted below.

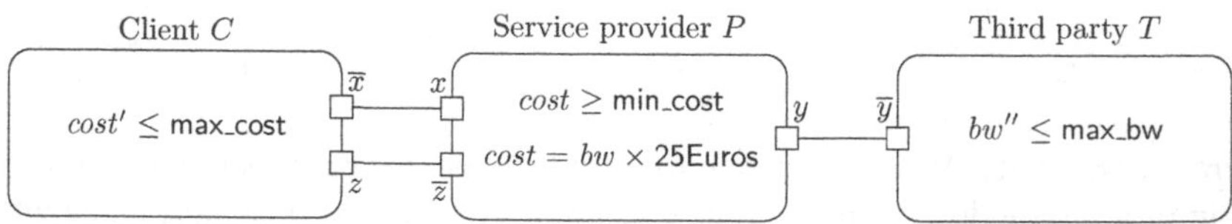

The interaction protocol is as follows. Each party imposes its SLA requirements or guarantees: P specifies the minimum cost $\mathsf{min\_cost}$ for the service and the cost per unit of bandwidth $cost = bw \cdot \mathsf{25\_Euros}$, C imposes a maximum cost $\mathsf{max\_cost}$ it can pay for the service, and T fixes the maximum bandwidth $\mathsf{max\_bw}$ that it can supply. Next, P communicates with C and with T on ports x and y, respectively. If the above constraints are consistent with each other, i.e. if $c = ((\mathsf{min\_cost} \leq cost \leq \mathsf{max\_cost}) \times (bw \leq \mathsf{max\_bw}) \times (cost = bw \cdot \mathsf{25\_Euros}) \times (cost = cost') \times (bw = bw' = bw'')) \neq 0$, P and C can sign this contract c, by synchronising on z. Then, the service is executed and, assuming P provides C with a certain bandwidth $\mathsf{act\_bw}$ and the corresponding cost, the two parties validate the contract by performing `check` operations on their respective parameters. Note that the semantics of `check` enables this validation while not modifying the constraints of the contract. The specification of P, C, and T in cc-pi is as below and the whole system is represented by the parallel composition of the three parties.

$$\begin{aligned}
P_{\mathsf{min_cost}} &\equiv (bw)(cost)(\mathtt{tell}\,((cost \geq \mathsf{min_cost}) \times (cost = bw \cdot \mathsf{25_Euros})\,).\\
&\quad x\langle bw, cost\rangle.\overline{y}\langle bw\rangle.\overline{z}\langle\rangle.P'_{\mathsf{act_bw}})\\
P'_{\mathsf{act_bw}} &\equiv \overline{x}\langle \mathsf{act_bw}, \mathsf{act_bw} \cdot \mathsf{25_Euros}\rangle.\mathtt{check}((\mathsf{act_bw} \cdot \mathsf{25_Euros} = cost) \times\\
&\quad (\mathsf{act_bw} = bw)).z\langle\rangle\\
C_{\mathsf{max_cost}} &\equiv (bw')(cost')(\mathtt{tell}\,(cost' \leq \mathsf{max_cost}).\overline{x}\langle bw', cost'\rangle.z\langle\rangle.C')\\
C' &\equiv (b', c')(x\langle b', c'\rangle.\mathtt{check}((b' = bw') \times (c' = cost')).\overline{z}\langle\rangle)\\
T_{\mathsf{max_bw}} &\equiv (bw'')(\mathtt{tell}\,(bw'' \leq \mathsf{max_bw}).y\langle bw''\rangle)
\end{aligned}$$

5.2 Resource Allocation

We consider a slightly more complex scenario of the example given in the introduction with one provider P_{N} and three clients C_{n_1}, C_{n_2}, and C_{n_3}. The graph representation of the constraint system resulting from the negotiation among the parties is depicted below. Each node represents a variable, and each constraint is modelled by a hyperedge connecting the variables involved in the constraint.

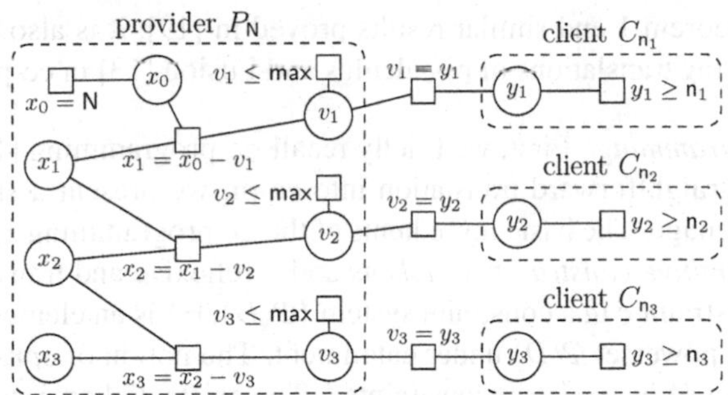

Suppose that P_{N} has allocated the resources y_1 and y_2, with $y_i \geq n_i$ for $i = 1, 2$, to C_{n_1} and C_{n_2}, respectively. If C_{n_3} makes a request $y_3 \geq n_3$ that P_{N} is not able to satisfy because $n_1 + n_2 + n_3 \geq \mathsf{N}$, the synchronisation between P_{N} and C_{n_3} cannot take place until some resources y_i, with $y_i \geq n_3$, are released.

6 Expressiveness Results

Encoding Pi-F calculus. We start by recalling the Pi-F calculus. For better relating the calculus with cc-pi, we present the Pi-F in the standard pi-calculus fashion rather than in the 'commitment' style [19].

Definition 9. *The syntax of Pi-F processes is the same as the one given in Definition 6 minus summation,* `tell`, `ask`, `retract`, *and* `check` *and where constraints c are taken over the named c-semiring of equalities C_E defined in Example 1. The structural congruence $\equiv_F$ is as in Def. 7 plus the axioms below:*

$$x{=}x \equiv_F \mathbf{0} \qquad x{=}y \equiv_F y{=}x \qquad x{=}y \,|\, y{=}z \equiv_F x{=}z \,|\, y{=}z \qquad (x)\,(x{=}y) \equiv_F \mathbf{0}$$

$$x{=}y \,|\, x\langle z\rangle.P \equiv_F x{=}y \,|\, y\langle z\rangle.P \qquad x{=}y \,|\, \overline{x}\langle z\rangle.P \equiv_F x{=}y \,|\, \overline{y}\langle z\rangle.P$$

$$z{=}y \,|\, x\langle z\rangle.P \equiv_F z{=}y \,|\, z\langle y\rangle.P \qquad z{=}y \,|\, \overline{x}\langle z\rangle.P \equiv_F z{=}y \,|\, \overline{x}\langle y\rangle.P$$

The reduction relation $\rightarrow_F$ between processes is the smallest relation closed with respect to $\_\,|\,\_$, $(x)\,\_$ and $\_ \equiv_F \_$, which satisfies:

$$\overline{x}\langle\widetilde{z}\rangle.P \,|\, x\langle\widetilde{w}\rangle.Q \rightarrow_F P \,|\, Q \,|\, \{\widetilde{z} = \widetilde{w}\} \quad \text{if } |\widetilde{z}| = |\widetilde{w}|$$

Note that this syntax rules out processes containing name fusions under prefixes. This choice follows the analogous restriction applied in cc-pi, which avoids that two processes synchronise and, simultaneously, add some constrains to the store, thus possibly yielding an inconsistency.

Definition 10. *The translation $[\![\_]\!]_F$ of pi-F processes into cc-pi processes is trivial: it maps pi-F constructs on their homonymous versions in cc-pi.*

Theorem 1. *1. If $P \rightarrow_F Q$ then $[\![P]\!]_F \rightarrow [\![Q]\!]_F$. 2. If $[\![P]\!]_F \rightarrow Q'$ then $P \rightarrow_F Q$ and $Q' \equiv [\![Q]\!]_F$.*

By exploiting Theorem 1 and similar results proved in [19], it is also possible to give reduction-preserving translations of pi-calculus and Fusion [13] in cc-pi.

Encoding cc *programming.* First, we briefly recall cc programming [15]. For the purpose of a more straightforward translation into cc-pi, we present a slightly modified version of the language. The basic ingredients of the cc programming constraint system are a set D of *primitive constraints* or *tokens* and a reflexive and transitive *entailment* relation $\vdash$. A constraint c in a constraint system $\langle \mathcal{P}(D), \vdash\rangle$ is an element of $\mathcal{P}(D)^\star$, i.e. the closure of the powerset $\mathcal{P}(D)$ under entailment. The notion of *consistency* is given by identifying a set of *inconsistent* constraints I. The existential operator on constraints $\exists x c$ is formalised in terms of cylindric algebras.

Definition 11. *The syntax of* cc *programming is defined as follows:*

$$\begin{array}{lll} \text{PREFIXES} & \pi ::= & \texttt{tell}\ c \;\big|\; \texttt{ask}\ c \\ \text{PROCESSES} & A ::= & \texttt{success} \;\big|\; \pi.A \;\big|\; A|A \;\big|\; \sum_i \pi_i.A_i \;\big|\; \exists_{x,c} A \;\big|\; p(\widetilde{y}) \end{array}$$

Following standard lines [16,12], we replace the classical hiding operator $\exists_x A$ with $\exists_{x,c} A$ that represents the evolution of a process of the form $\exists_x A'$, where c is the local constraint produced during the evolution. Moreover, $p(\tilde{y})$ is a *procedure call*, where p is the name of the procedure and $\tilde{y}$ is the tuple of actual parameters. The meaning of a process is given with respect to a set of procedure declarations of the form $p(\tilde{x}) := A$. An *instantiation* of $p(\tilde{x}) := A$ is an object of the form $p(\tilde{y}) := [\tilde{y}/\tilde{x}]A$. A *configuration* is a pair $\langle c, A \rangle$ with a constraint c representing the store and a process A. The reduction relation $\rightarrow_C$ over configurations is the smallest relation given by the following rules.

$$(\text{TELL})\ \langle c, \texttt{tell}\ c'.A \rangle \mapsto \langle (c \cup c')^\star, A \rangle \qquad \text{if } (c \cup c')^\star \text{ consistent}$$

$$(\text{ASK})\ \langle c, \texttt{ask}\ c'.A \rangle \mapsto \langle c, A \rangle \qquad \text{if } c \vdash c'$$

$$(\text{SUM})\ \frac{\langle c, \pi_i.A_i \rangle \mapsto \langle c', A' \rangle}{\langle c, \Sigma_i \pi_i.A_i \rangle \mapsto \langle c', A' \rangle} \qquad (\text{PAR})\ \frac{\langle c, A \rangle \mapsto \langle c', A' \rangle}{\langle c, A \,|\, B \rangle \mapsto \langle c', A' \,|\, B \rangle}$$

$$(\text{PAR}')\ \frac{\langle c, A \rangle \mapsto \langle c', A' \rangle}{\langle c, B \,|\, A \rangle \mapsto \langle c', B \,|\, A' \rangle} \qquad (\text{HIDE})\ \frac{\langle c \cup \exists x d, A \rangle \mapsto \langle c' \cup \exists x d, A' \rangle}{\langle d, \exists_{x,c} A \rangle \mapsto \langle d, \exists_{x,c'} A' \rangle}$$

$$(\text{PROC})\ \frac{\langle c, [\tilde{y}/\tilde{x}]A \rangle \mapsto \langle c', A' \rangle \quad \text{and} \quad p(\tilde{x}) := A}{\langle c, p(\tilde{y}) \rangle \mapsto \langle c', A' \rangle}$$

Definition 12. *The translation* $[\![\_]\!]_F$ *of* cc *processes in cc-pi is trivial:*

$$[\![\texttt{success}]\!]_C = \mathbf{0} \quad [\![\texttt{ask}\ c.A]\!]_C = \texttt{ask}\ c.[\![A]\!]_C \quad [\![\texttt{tell}\ c.A]\!]_C = \texttt{tell}\ c.[\![A]\!]_C$$
$$[\![A \,|\, B]\!]_C = [\![A]\!]_C \,|\, [\![B]\!]_C \quad [\![\exists_{x,c} A]\!]_C = (x)\,(c \,|\, [\![A]\!]_C) \quad [\![\Sigma \pi_i.A_i]\!]_C = \Sigma [\![\pi_i.A_i]\!]_C$$
$$[\![p(\tilde{y})]\!]_C = D_p(\tilde{y})$$

where for each cc *procedure declaration* $p(\tilde{x}) := A$ *we give a defining equation* $D_p(\tilde{x}) = Q$ *with* $[\![A]\!]_C = Q$.

Lemma 1. *A constraint system* $\langle \underline{\mathcal{P}(D)}, \vdash \rangle$ *can be represented as a named c-semiring* $\langle C, +, \times, \nu x., \rho, 0, 1 \rangle$ *with: (i)* $C = \mathcal{P}(D) \cup \bot$*, where* $\bot$ *corresponds to the set I; (ii)* $c_1 + c_2 = (c_1 \cap c_2)$*; (iii)* $c_1 \times c_2 = (c_1 \cup c_2)^\star$*; (iv)* $\nu x.c = \exists x c$ *and* $\rho c = \rho c$*; (v)* $0 = \bot$ *and* $1 = C$.

Theorem 2. *1. If* $\langle c, A \rangle \mapsto \langle c', A' \rangle$ *then* $c \,|\, [\![A]\!]_C \rightarrow c' \,|\, [\![A']\!]_C$*. 2. If* $c \,|\, [\![A]\!]_C \rightarrow P$ *then* $\langle c, A \rangle \mapsto \langle c', A' \rangle$ *and* $P \equiv c' \,|\, [\![A']\!]_C$.

Note that cc programming handles the evolution of local stores of constraints through the rule (HIDE), while cc-pi (without `retract`) obtains the same effect by reducing processes into a normal form in which names are conveniently α-converted. This fact plays a crucial role in the proof of Theorem 2.

7 Concluding Remarks

This paper is mainly focused on presenting the cc-pi calculus and on showing its flexibility as a constrained-based model for specifying SLA contracts and resource allocation. We foresee several directions for future work. We plan to consider a distributed version of the calculus by equipping, e.g., processes with locations and by limiting the synchronous behavior of processes and constraints to a single locality. It would also be interesting to study suitable mechanisms for assuring transactional and security properties of process executions, e.g. by enforcing that only the process which has told a constraint can retract it. We also intend to further study the ability of c-semirings to model soft constraints to express nonfunctional properties of SLAs.

Acknowledgments. We thank the anonymous referees for helpful comments.

References

1. A. Bacciu, A. Botta, and H. Melgratti. A fuzzy approach for negotiating quality of services. In *Proc. TGC '06*. To appear.
2. S. Bistarelli, U. Montanari, and F. Rossi. Semiring-based constraint satisfaction and optimization. *Journal of the ACM*, 44(2):201–236, 1997.
3. S. Bistarelli, U. Montanari, and F. Rossi. Soft concurrent constraint programming. *ACM Trans. Comput. Logic*, 7(3):563–589, 2006.
4. R. De Nicola, G. Ferrari, U. Montanari, R. Pugliese, and E. Tuosto. A process calculus for QoS-aware applications. In *Proc. COORDINATION'05*, volume 3454 of *Lect. Notes in Comput. Sci.* Springer, 2005.
5. J. F. Diaz, C. Rueda, and F. Valencia. A calculus for concurrent processes with constraints. *CLEI Electronic Journal*, 1(2), 1998.
6. A. Keller and H. Ludwig. The WSLA framework: Specifying and monitoring service level agreements for web services. *Jour. Net. and Sys. Manag.*, 11(1):57–81, 2003.
7. R. Milner, J. Parrow, and J. Walker. A calculus of mobile processes, I and II. *Inform. and Comput*, 100(1):1–40,41–77, 1992.
8. U. Montanari. Networks of constraints: fundamental properties and application to picture processing. *Information Science*, 7:95–132, 1974.
9. U. Montanari and Pistore M. Structured coalgebras and minimal hd-automata for the pi-calculus. *Theoret. Comput. Sci*, 340(3):539–576, 2005.
10. U. Montanari and F. Rossi. Constraint relaxation may be perfect. *Artif. Intell.*, 48(2):143–170, 1991.
11. J. Niehren and M. Mueller. Constraints for free in concurrent computation. In *Proc. Asian '95*, volume 1023 of *Lect. Notes in Comput. Sci.* Springer, 1995.
12. M. Nielsen, C. Palamidessi, and F. Valencia. On the expressive power of temporal concurrent constraint programming languages. In *Proc. PPDP'02*. ACM, 2002.
13. J. Parrow and B. Victor. The fusion calculus: Expressiveness and symmetry in mobile processes. In *Proc. LICS'98*. IEEE, Computer Society Press, 1998.
14. V. Saraswat and P. Lincoln. Higher-order linear concurrent constraint programming, 1992. Technical Report, Xerox Parc.
15. V. Saraswat and M. Rinard. Concurrent constraint programming. In *Proc. POPL'90*. ACM Press, 1990.
16. V. Saraswat, M. Rinard, and P. Panangaden. Semantic foundations of concurrent constraint programming. In *Proc. POPL'91*. ACM Press, 1991.
17. J. Skene, D. Lamanna, and W. Emmerich. Precise service level agreements. In *Proc. ICSE'04*, 2004.
18. B. Victor and J. Parrow. Constraints as processes. In *Proc. CONCUR'96*, volume 1119 of *Lect. Notes in Comput. Sci.* Springer, 1996.
19. L. Wischik and P. Gardner. Explicit fusions. *Theoret. Comput. Sci*, 340(3):606–630, 2005.

A Calculus for Orchestration of Web Services*

Alessandro Lapadula, Rosario Pugliese, and Francesco Tiezzi

Dipartimento di Sistemi e Informatica Università degli Studi di Firenze

Abstract. We introduce COWS (*Calculus for Orchestration of Web Services*), a new foundational language for SOC whose design has been influenced by WS-BPEL, the *de facto* standard language for orchestration of web services. COWS combines in an original way a number of ingredients borrowed from well-known process calculi, e.g. asynchronous communication, polyadic synchronization, pattern matching, protection, delimited receiving and killing activities, while resulting different from any of them. Several examples illustrates COWS peculiarities and show its expressiveness both for modelling imperative and orchestration constructs, e.g. web services, flow graphs, fault and compensation handlers, and for encoding other process and orchestration languages.

1 Introduction

Web services are a successful instantiation of service-oriented computing (SOC), an emerging paradigm for developing loosely coupled, interoperable, evolvable systems and applications which exploits the pervasiveness of the Internet and its related technologies. Web services are autonomous, stateless, platform-independent and composable computational entities that can be published, located and invoked through the Web via XML messages. These very features foster a programming style based on service composition and reusability: new customized service-based applications can be developed on demand by appropriately assembling other existing, heterogeneous services.

Service definitions are used as templates for creating service instances that deliver application functionality to either end-user applications or other instances. The loosely coupled nature of SOC implies that the connection between communicating instances cannot be assumed to persist for the duration of a whole business activity. Therefore, there is no intrinsic mechanism for associating messages exchanged under a common context or as part of a common activity. Even the execution of a simple request-response message exchange pattern provides no built-in means of automatically associating the response message with the original request. It is up to each single message to provide a form of context thus enabling services to associate the message with others. This is achieved by embedding values in the message which, once located, can be used to correlate the message with others logically forming a same stateful interaction 'session'.

To support the web service approach, many new languages, most of which based on XML, have been designed, like e.g. business coordination languages (such as WS-BPEL, WSFL, WSCI, WS-CDL and XLANG), contract languages (such as WSDL and SWS), and query languages (such as XPath and XQuery). However, current software engineering technologies for development and composition of web services remain at

* This work has been supported by the EU project SENSORIA, IST-2 005-016004.

R. De Nicola (Ed.): ESOP 2007, LNCS 4421, pp. 33–47, 2007.

the descriptive level and do not integrate such techniques as, e.g., those developed for component-based software development. Formal reasoning mechanisms and analytical tools are still lacking for checking that the web services resulting from a composition meet desirable correctness properties and do not manifest unexpected behaviors. The task of developing such verification methods is hindered also by the very nature of the languages used to program the services, which usually provide many redundant constructs and support quite liberal programming styles.

Recently, many researchers have exploited the studies on *process calculi* as a starting point to define a clean semantic model and lay rigorous methodological foundations for service-based applications and their composition. Process calculi, being defined algebraically, are inherently compositional and, therefore, convey in a distilled form the paradigm at the heart of SOC. This trend is witnessed by the many process calculi-like formalisms for orchestration and choreography, the two more common forms of web services composition. Most of these formalisms, however, do not suit for the analysis of currently available SOC technologies in their completeness because they only consider a few specific features separately, possibly by embedding *ad hoc* constructs within some well-studied process calculus (see, e.g., the variants of π-calculus with transactions [2,19,20] and of CSP with compensation [9]).

Here, we follow a different approach and exploit WS-BPEL [1], the *de facto* standard language for orchestration of web services, to drive the design of a new process calculus that we call COWS (*Calculus for Orchestration of Web Services*). Similarly to WS-BPEL, COWS supports shared states among service instances, allows a same process to play more than one partner role and permits programming stateful sessions by correlating different service interactions. However, COWS intends to be a foundational model not specifically tight to web services' current technology. Thus, some WS-BPEL constructs, such as e.g. fault and compensation handlers and flow graphs, do not have a precise counterpart in COWS, rather they are expressed in terms of more primitive operators (see Section 3). Of course, COWS has taken advantage of previous work on process calculi. Its design combines in an original way a number of constructs and features borrowed from well-known process calculi, e.g. asynchronous communication, polyadic synchronization, pattern matching, protection, delimited receiving and killing activities, while however resulting different from any of them.

The rest of the paper is organized as follows. Syntax and operational semantics of COWS are defined in Section 2 where we also show many illustrative examples. Section 3 presents the encodings of several imperative and orchestration constructs, while Section 4 presents the encoding of the orchestration language Orc [28]. Finally, Section 5 touches upon comparisons with related work and directions for future work.

2 COWS: Calculus for Orchestration of Web Services

The basic elements of COWS are *partners* and *operations*. Alike channels in [10], a *communication endpoint* is not atomic but results from the composition of a partner name p and of an operation name o, which can also be interpreted as a specific implementation of o provided by p. This results in a very flexible naming mechanism that allows a same service to be identified by means of different logic names (i.e. to play more than one partner role as in WS-BPEL). Additionally, it allows the names composing an endpoint to be dealt with separately, as in a request-response interaction, where usually the service provider knows the name of the response operation, but not the partner name of the service it has to reply to. This mechanisms is also sufficiently expressive to support implementation of explicit locations: a located service can be represented by using a same partner for all its receiving endpoints. Partner and operation names can be exchanged in communication, thus enabling many different interaction patterns among service instances. However, as in [25], dynamically received names cannot form the communication endpoints used to receive further invocations.

COWS computational entities are called *services*. Typically, a service creates one specific instance to serve each received request. An instance is composed of concurrent threads that may offer a choice among alternative receive activities. Services could be able to receive multiple messages in a statically unpredictable order and in such a way that the first incoming message triggers creation of a service instance which subsequent messages are routed to. Pattern-matching is the mechanism for correlating messages logically forming a same interaction 'session' by means of their same contents. It permits locating those data that are important to identify service instances for the routing of messages and is flexible enough for allowing a single message to participate in multiple interaction sessions, each identified by separate correlation values.

To model and update the shared state of concurrent threads within each service instance, receive activities in COWS bind neither names nor variables. This is different from most process calculi and somewhat similar to [29,30]. In COWS, however, inter-service communication give rise to substitutions of variables with values (alike [29]), rather than to fusions of names (as in [30]). The range of application of the substitution generated by a communication is regulated by the *delimitation* operator, that is the only binder of the calculus. Additionally, this operator permits to generate fresh names (as the restriction operator of the π-calculus [27]) and to delimit the field of action of the *kill* activity, that can be used to force termination of whole service instances. Sensitive code can however be protected from the effect of a forced termination by using the *protection* operator (inspired by [8]).

Syntax. The syntax of COWS, given in Table 1, is parameterized by three countable and pairwise disjoint sets: the set of *(killer) labels* (ranged over by $k, k', \ldots$), the set of *values* (ranged over by $v, v', \ldots$) and the set of 'write once' *variables* (ranged over by x, $y, \ldots$). The set of values is left unspecified; however, we assume that it includes the set of *names*, ranged over by $n, m, \ldots$, mainly used to represent partners and operations. The language is also parameterized by a set of *expressions*, ranged over by e, whose exact syntax is deliberately omitted; we just assume that expressions contain, at least, values and variables. Notably, killer labels are *not* (communicable) values. Notationally, we prefer letters $p, p', \ldots$ when we want to stress the use of a name as a partner, $o, o', \ldots$ when we want to stress the use of a name as an operation. We will use w to range over values and variables, u to range over names and variables, and d to range over killer labels, names and variables.

Services are structured activities built from basic activities, i.e. the empty activity **0**, the kill activity **kill**$(\_)$, the invoke activity $\_\cdot\_!\_$ and the receive activity $\_\cdot\_?\_$, by means of prefixing $\_.\_$, choice $\_ + \_$, parallel composition $\_ \mid \_$, protection $\{\!|\_|\!\}$, delimitation $[\_]\,\_$ and replication $*\,\_$. Notably, as in the Lπ [25], communication endpoints of receive

Table 1. COWS syntax

$s ::= \mathbf{kill}(k) \mid u \cdot u'!\bar{e} \mid g \mid s \mid s \mid \{\!|s|\!\} \mid [d]\, s \mid *\, s$	(services)
$g ::= \mathbf{0} \mid p \cdot o?\bar{w}.s \mid g + g$	(input-guarded choice)

Table 2. COWS structural congruence (excerpt of laws)

$*\mathbf{0} \equiv \mathbf{0}$	$*\, s \equiv s \mid *\, s$	$\{\!|\mathbf{0}|\!\} \equiv \mathbf{0}$
$\{\!|\{\!|s|\!\}|\!\} \equiv \{\!|s|\!\}$	$\{\!|[d]\, s|\!\} \equiv [d]\, \{\!|s|\!\}$	$[d]\, \mathbf{0} \equiv \mathbf{0}$
$[d_1]\, [d_2]\, s \equiv [d_2]\, [d_1]\, s$	$s_1 \mid [d]\, s_2 \equiv [d]\, (s_1 \mid s_2)$	if $d \notin \mathrm{fd}(s_1) \cup \mathrm{fk}(s_2)$

activities are identified statically because their syntax only allows using names and not variables. The decreasing order of precedence among the operators is as follows: monadic operators, choice and parallel composition.

Notation $\bar{\cdot}$ stands for tuples of objects, e.g. $\bar{x}$ is a compact notation for denoting the tuple of variables $\langle x_1, \ldots, x_n \rangle$ (with $n \geq 0$). We assume that variables in the same tuple are pairwise distinct. All notations shall extend to tuples component-wise. In the sequel, we shall omit trailing occurrences of $\mathbf{0}$, writing e.g. $p \cdot o?\bar{w}$ instead of $p \cdot o?\bar{w}.\mathbf{0}$, and use $[d_1, \ldots, d_n]\, s$ in place of $[d_1] \ldots [d_n]\, s$.

The only *binding* construct is delimitation: $[d]\, s$ binds d in the scope s. The occurrence of a name/variable/label is *free* if it is not under the scope of a binder. We denote by $\mathrm{fd}(t)$ the set of names, variables and killer labels that occur free in a term t, and by $\mathrm{fk}(t)$ the set of free killer labels in t. Two terms are *alpha-equivalent* if one can be obtained from the other by consistently renaming bound names/variables/labels. As usual, we identify terms up to alpha-equivalence.

Operational Semantics. COWS operational semantics is defined only for *closed* services, i.e. services without free variables/labels (similarly to many real compilers, we consider terms with free variables/labels as programming errors), but of course the rules also involve non-closed services (see e.g. the premises of rules *(del_)*). Formally, the semantics is given in terms of a structural congruence and of a labelled transition relation.

The structural congruence $\equiv$ identifies syntactically different services that intuitively represent the same service. It is defined as the least congruence relation induced by a given set of equational laws. We explicitly show in Table 2 the laws for replication, protection and delimitation, while omit the (standard) laws for the other operators stating that parallel composition is commutative, associative and has $\mathbf{0}$ as identity element, and that guarded choice enjoys the same properties and, additionally, is idempotent. All the presented laws are straightforward. In particular, commutativity of consecutive delimitations implies that the order among the d_i in $[\langle d_1, \ldots, d_n \rangle]\, s$ is irrelevant, thus in the sequel we may use the simpler notation $[d_1, \ldots, d_n]\, s$. Notably, the last law can be used to extend the scope of names (like a similar law in the π-calculus), thus enabling communication of restricted names, except when the argument d of the delimitation is a free killer label of s_2 (this avoids involving s_1 in the effect of a kill activity inside s_2).

Table 3. Matching rules

$$\mathcal{M}(x,v)=\{x\mapsto v\} \qquad \mathcal{M}(v,v)=\emptyset \qquad \frac{\mathcal{M}(w_1,v_1)=\sigma_1 \qquad \mathcal{M}(\bar{w}_2,\bar{v}_2)=\sigma_2}{\mathcal{M}((w_1,\bar{w}_2),(v_1,\bar{v}_2))=\sigma_1\uplus\sigma_2}$$

To define the labelled transition relation, we need a few auxiliary functions. First, we exploit a function $[\![\_]\!]$ for evaluating *closed* expressions (i.e. expressions without variables): it takes a closed expression and returns a value. However, $[\![\_]\!]$ cannot be explicitly defined because the exact syntax of expressions is deliberately not specified.

Then, through the rules in Table 3, we define the partial function $\mathcal{M}(\_,\_)$ that permits performing *pattern-matching* on semi-structured data thus determining if a receive and an invoke over the same endpoint can synchronize. The rules state that two tuples match if they have the same number of fields and corresponding fields have matching values/variables. Variables match any value, and two values match only if they are identical. When tuples $\bar{w}$ and $\bar{v}$ do match, $\mathcal{M}(\bar{w},\bar{v})$ returns a substitution for the variables in $\bar{w}$; otherwise, it is undefined. *Substitutions* (ranged over by σ) are functions mapping variables to values and are written as collections of pairs of the form $x\mapsto v$. Application of substitution σ to s, written $s\cdot\sigma$, has the effect of replacing every free occurrence of x in s with v, for each $x\mapsto v\in\sigma$, by possibly using alpha conversion for avoiding v to be captured by name delimitations within s. We use $|\sigma|$ to denote the number of pairs in σ and $\sigma_1\uplus\sigma_2$ to denote the union of σ_1 and σ_2 when they have disjoint domains.

We also define a function, named *halt*(_), that takes a service s as an argument and returns the service obtained by only retaining the protected activities inside s. *halt*(_) is defined inductively on the syntax of services. The most significant case is $halt(\{\!|s|\!\}) = \{\!|s|\!\}$. In the other cases, *halt*(_) returns $\mathbf{0}$, except for parallel composition, delimitation and replication operators, for which it acts as an homomorphism.

Finally, we define a predicate, *noc*(_, _, _, _), that takes a service s, an endpoint $p\cdot o$, a tuple of receive parameters $\bar{w}$ and a matching tuple of values $\bar{v}$ as arguments and holds true if either there are no conflicting receives within s (namely, s cannot immediately perform a receive activity matching $\bar{v}$ over the endpoint $p\cdot o$), or $p\cdot o?\bar{w}$ is the most defined conflicting receive. The predicate exploits the notion of *active context*, namely a service $\mathbb{A}$ with a 'hole' $[\![\cdot]\!]$ such that, once the hole is filled with a service s, if the resulting term $\mathbb{A}[\![s]\!]$ is a COWS service then it is capable of immediately performing an activity of s. Formally, active contexts are generated by the grammar:

$$\mathbb{A} ::= [\![\cdot]\!] \mid \mathbb{A}+g \mid g+\mathbb{A} \mid \mathbb{A}\,|\,s \mid s\,|\,\mathbb{A} \mid \{\!|\mathbb{A}|\!\} \mid [d]\,\mathbb{A} \mid *\,\mathbb{A}$$

Now, predicate $noc(s,p\cdot o,\bar{w},\bar{v})$ can be defined as follows:

$$(\,s=\mathbb{A}[\![p\cdot o?\bar{w}'.s']\!]\;\wedge\;\mathcal{M}(\bar{w}',\bar{v})=\sigma\,)\Rightarrow|\mathcal{M}(\bar{w},\bar{v})|\leqslant|\sigma|$$

where $s=\mathbb{A}[\![p\cdot o?\bar{w}'.s']\!]$ means that s can be written as $p\cdot o?\bar{w}'.s'$ filling the hole of some active context $\mathbb{A}$.

The labelled transition relation $\xrightarrow{\alpha}$ is the least relation over services induced by the rules in Table 4, where label α is generated by the following grammar:

$$\alpha ::= \dagger k \mid (p\cdot o)\lhd\bar{v} \mid (p\cdot o)\rhd\bar{w} \mid p\cdot o\lfloor\sigma\rfloor\bar{w}\,\bar{v} \mid \dagger$$

Table 4. COWS operational semantics

$$\mathbf{kill}(k) \xrightarrow{\dagger k} \mathbf{0} \ \ (kill) \qquad\qquad p \cdot o?\bar{w}.s \xrightarrow{(p\cdot o)\rhd\bar{w}} s \ \ (rec)$$

$$\frac{[\![\bar{e}]\!] = \bar{v}}{p \cdot o!\bar{e} \xrightarrow{(p\cdot o)\lhd\bar{v}} \mathbf{0}} \ (inv) \qquad\qquad \frac{g_1 \xrightarrow{\alpha} s}{g_1 + g_2 \xrightarrow{\alpha} s} \ (choice)$$

$$\frac{s \xrightarrow{p\cdot o\lfloor\sigma\uplus\{x\mapsto v'\}\rfloor\,\bar{w}\,\bar{v}} s'}{[x]\,s \xrightarrow{p\cdot o\lfloor\sigma\rfloor\,\bar{w}\,\bar{v}} s'\cdot\{x\mapsto v'\}} \ (del_{sub}) \qquad\qquad \frac{s \xrightarrow{\dagger k} s'}{[k]\,s \xrightarrow{\dagger} [k]\,s'} \ (del_{kill})$$

$$\frac{s \xrightarrow{\alpha} s' \quad d \notin \mathrm{d}(\alpha) \quad s = \mathbb{A}[\![\mathbf{kill}(d)]\!] \Rightarrow \alpha = \dagger, \dagger k}{[d]\,s \xrightarrow{\alpha} [d]\,s'} \ (del_{pass}) \qquad\qquad \frac{s \xrightarrow{\alpha} s'}{\{\!|s|\!\} \xrightarrow{\alpha} \{\!|s'|\!\}} \ (prot)$$

$$\frac{s_1 \xrightarrow{(p\cdot o)\rhd\bar{w}} s_1' \qquad s_2 \xrightarrow{(p\cdot o)\lhd\bar{v}} s_2' \qquad \mathcal{M}(\bar{w},\bar{v}) = \sigma \qquad noc(s_1 \mid s_2, p\cdot o, \bar{w}, \bar{v})}{s_1 \mid s_2 \xrightarrow{p\cdot o\lfloor\sigma\rfloor\,\bar{w}\,\bar{v}} s_1' \mid s_2'} \ (com)$$

$$\frac{s_1 \xrightarrow{p\cdot o\lfloor\sigma\rfloor\,\bar{w}\,\bar{v}} s_1' \qquad noc(s_2, p\cdot o, \bar{w}, \bar{v})}{s_1 \mid s_2 \xrightarrow{p\cdot o\lfloor\sigma\rfloor\,\bar{w}\,\bar{v}} s_1' \mid s_2} \ (par_{conf}) \qquad\qquad \frac{s_1 \xrightarrow{\dagger k} s_1'}{s_1 \mid s_2 \xrightarrow{\dagger k} s_1' \mid halt(s_2)} \ (par_{kill})$$

$$\frac{s_1 \xrightarrow{\alpha} s_1' \qquad \alpha \neq (p\cdot o\lfloor\sigma\rfloor\,\bar{w}\,\bar{v}), \dagger k}{s_1 \mid s_2 \xrightarrow{\alpha} s_1' \mid s_2} \ (par_{pass}) \qquad\qquad \frac{s \equiv s_1 \quad s_1 \xrightarrow{\alpha} s_2 \quad s_2 \equiv s'}{s \xrightarrow{\alpha} s'} \ (cong)$$

In the sequel, we use $\mathrm{d}(\alpha)$ to denote the set of names, variables and killer labels occurring in α, except for $\alpha = p \cdot o\lfloor\sigma\rfloor\,\bar{w}\,\bar{v}$ for which we let $\mathrm{d}(p \cdot o\lfloor\sigma\rfloor\,\bar{w}\,\bar{v}) = \mathrm{d}(\sigma)$, where $\mathrm{d}(\{x \mapsto v\}) = \{x, v\}$ and $\mathrm{d}(\sigma_1 \uplus \sigma_2) = \mathrm{d}(\sigma_1) \cup \mathrm{d}(\sigma_2)$. The meaning of labels is as follows: $\dagger k$ denotes execution of a request for terminating a term from within the delimitation $[k]$, $(p \cdot o) \lhd \bar{v}$ and $(p \cdot o) \rhd \bar{w}$ denote execution of invoke and receive activities over the endpoint $p \cdot o$, respectively, $p \cdot o\lfloor\sigma\rfloor\,\bar{w}\,\bar{v}$ (if $\sigma \neq \emptyset$) denotes execution of a communication over $p \cdot o$ with receive parameters $\bar{w}$ and matching values $\bar{v}$ and with substitution σ to be still applied, $\dagger$ and $p \cdot o\lfloor\emptyset\rfloor\,\bar{w}\,\bar{v}$ denote *computational steps* corresponding to taking place of forced termination and communication (without pending substitutions), respectively. Hence, a *computation* from a closed service s_0 is a sequence of connected transitions of the form

$$s_0 \xrightarrow{\alpha_1} s_1 \xrightarrow{\alpha_2} s_2 \xrightarrow{\alpha_3} s_3 \ldots$$

where, for each i, α_i is either $\dagger$ or $p \cdot o\lfloor\emptyset\rfloor\,\bar{w}\,\bar{v}$ (for some $p, o, \bar{w}$ and $\bar{v}$); services s_i, for each i, will be called *reducts* of s_0.

We comment on salient points. Activity $\mathbf{kill}(k)$ forces termination of all unprotected parallel activities (rules *(kill)* and *(par$_{kill}$)*) inside an enclosing $[k]$, that stops the killing effect by turning the transition label $\dagger k$ into $\dagger$ (rule *(del$_{kill}$)*). Existence of such delimitation is ensured by the assumption that the semantics is only defined for closed services.

Sensitive code can be protected from killing by putting it into a protection $\{\!|\_|\!\}$; this way, $\{\!|s|\!\}$ behaves like s (rule *(prot)*). Similarly, $[d]\,s$ behaves like s, except when the transition label α contains d or when a kill activity for d is active in s and α does not correspond to a kill activity (rule *(del$_{pass}$)*): in such cases the transition should be derived by using rules *(del$_{kill}$)* or *(del$_{sub}$)*. In other words, kill activities are executed *eagerly*. A service invocation can proceed only if the expressions in the argument can be evaluated (rule *(inv)*). Receive activities can always proceed (rule *(rec)*) and can resolve choices (rule *(choice)*). Communication can take place when two parallel services perform matching receive and invoke activities (rule *(com)*). Communication generates a substitution that is recorded in the transition label (for subsequent application), rather than a silent transition as in most process calculi. If more than one matching receive activity is ready to process a given invoke, then only the more defined one (i.e. the receive that generates the 'smaller' substitution) progresses (rules *(com)* and *(par$_{conf}$)*). This mechanism permits to correlate different service communications thus implicitly creating interaction sessions and can be exploited to model the precedence of a service instance over the corresponding service specification when both can process the same request. When the delimitation of a variable x argument of a receive is encountered, i.e. the whole scope of the variable is determined, the delimitation is removed and the substitution for x is applied to the term (rule *(del$_{sub}$)*). Variable x disappears from the term and cannot be reassigned a value. Execution of parallel services is interleaved (rule *(par$_{pass}$)*), but when a kill activity or a communication is performed. Indeed, the former must trigger termination of all parallel services (according to rule *(par$_{kill}$)*), while the latter must ensure that the receive activity with greater priority progresses (rules *(com)* and *(par$_{conf}$)*). The last rule states that structurally congruent services have the same transitions.

Examples. We end this section with a few observations and examples aimed at clarifying the peculiarities of our formalism.

Communication of private names. Communication of private names is standard and exploits scope extension as in π-calculus.[1] Receive and invoke activities can interact only if both are in the scopes of the delimitations that bind the variables argument of the receive. Thus, to enable communication of private names, besides their scopes, we must possibly extend the scopes of some variables, as in the following example:

$$\begin{array}{ll} [x]\,(p\cdot o?\langle x\rangle.s \mid s') \mid [n]\,p\cdot o!\langle n\rangle \quad \equiv & (n \text{ fresh}) \\ [n]\,[x]\,(p\cdot o?\langle x\rangle.s \mid s' \mid p\cdot o!\langle n\rangle) \xrightarrow{p\cdot o\,\lfloor\emptyset\rfloor\,\langle x\rangle\,\langle n\rangle} & \\ [n]\,(s \mid s')\cdot\{x\mapsto n\} & \end{array}$$

Notice that the substitution $\{x \mapsto n\}$ is applied to all terms delimited by $[x]$, not only to the continuation s of the service performing the receive. This accounts for the global scope of variables and permits to easily model the *delayed input* of fusion calculus [30].

Protected kill activity. The following simple example illustrates the effect of executing a kill activity within a protection block:

$$[k]\,(\{\!|s_1 \mid \{\!|s_2|\!\} \mid \mathbf{kill}(k)|\!\} \mid s_3) \mid s_4 \xrightarrow{\dagger} [k]\,\{\!|\,\{\!|s_2|\!\}\,|\!\} \mid s_4$$

[1] The variant of π-calculus closest to COWS is localised π-calculus [25] and, indeed, in [21] we define an encoding that enjoys *operational correspondence*.

where, for simplicity, we assume that $halt(s_1) = halt(s_3) = \mathbf{0}$. In essence, $\mathbf{kill}(k)$ terminates all parallel services inside delimitation $[k]$ (i.e. s_1 and s_3), except those that are protected at the same nesting level of the kill activity (i.e. s_2).

Conflicting receive activities. This example shows a *persistent service* (implemented by mean of replication), that, once instantiated, enables two conflicting receives:

$$\begin{array}{l} *\,[x]\,(\,p_1 \cdot o?\langle x\rangle.s_1 \mid p_2 \cdot o?\langle x\rangle.s_2\,) \mid p_1 \cdot o!\langle v\rangle \mid p_2 \cdot o!\langle v\rangle \xrightarrow{p_1 \cdot o\,\lfloor\emptyset\rfloor\,\langle x\rangle\,\langle v\rangle} \\ *\,[x]\,(\,p_1 \cdot o?\langle x\rangle.s_1 \mid p_2 \cdot o?\langle x\rangle.s_2\,) \mid s_1 \cdot \{x \mapsto v\} \mid p_2 \cdot o?\langle v\rangle.s_2 \cdot \{x \mapsto v\} \mid p_2 \cdot o!\langle v\rangle \end{array}$$

Now, the persistent service and the created instance, being both able to receive the same tuple $\langle v\rangle$ along the endpoint $p_2 \cdot o$, compete for the request $p_2 \cdot o!\langle v\rangle$. However, our (prioritized) semantics, in particular rule *(com)* in combination with rule *(par$_{conf}$)*, allows only the existing instance to evolve (and, thus, prevents creation of a new instance):

$$*\,[x]\,(\,p_1 \cdot o?\langle x\rangle.s_1 \mid p_2 \cdot o?\langle x\rangle.s_2\,) \mid s_1 \cdot \{x \mapsto v\} \mid s_2 \cdot \{x \mapsto v\}$$

Message correlation. Consider now uncorrelated receive activities executed by a same instance, like in the following service:

$$*\,[x]\,p_1 \cdot o_1?\langle x\rangle.[y]\,p_2 \cdot o_2?\langle y\rangle.s$$

The fact that the messages for operations o_1 and o_2 are uncorrelated implies that, e.g., if there are concurrent instances then successive invocations for a same instance can mix up and be delivered to different instances. If one thinks it right, this behaviour can be avoided simply by correlating successive messages by means of some correlation data, e.g. the first received value as in the following service:

$$*\,[x]\,p_1 \cdot o_1?\langle x\rangle.[y]\,p_2 \cdot o_2?\langle y, x\rangle.s$$

3 Modelling Imperative and Orchestration Constructs

In this section, we present the encoding of some higher level imperative and orchestration constructs (mainly inspired by WS-BPEL). The encodings illustrate flexibility of COWS and somehow demonstrate expressiveness of the chosen set of primitives.

In the sequel, we will write $Z_{\bar{v}} \triangleq W$ to assign a symbolic name $Z_{\bar{v}}$ to the term W and to indicate the values $\bar{v}$ occurring within W. Thus, $Z_{\bar{v}}$ is a family of names, one for each tuple of values $\bar{v}$. We use $\hat{n}$ to stand for the endpoint $n_p \cdot n_o$. Sometimes, we write $\hat{n}$ for the tuple $\langle n_p, n_o\rangle$ and rely on the context to resolve any ambiguity.

Imperative constructs. Due to lack of space, we only present the encodings of those constructs that will be further exploited in the rest of the section. We refer the interested reader to [21] for deeper explanations and additional encodings.

We start adding *matching with assignment* $[\bar{w} = \bar{e}]$ to COWS basic activities. If $\bar{w}$ and $\bar{e}$ do match, service $[\bar{w} = \bar{e}].s$ returns a substitution that will eventually assign to the variables in $\bar{w}$ the corresponding values of $\bar{e}$, and service s can proceed. In COWS, this meaning can be rendered through the following encoding (for $\hat{m}$ fresh)

$$\langle\!\langle [\bar{w} = \bar{e}].s \rangle\!\rangle \;=\; [\hat{m}]\,(\hat{m}!\bar{e} \mid \hat{m}?\bar{w}.\langle\!\langle s \rangle\!\rangle)$$

Notably, the new construct differs from standard assignment both because values can occur on the left of =, in which case it behaves as a matching mechanism, and because, like the receive activity, it does not bind the variables on the left of =, thus it cannot reassign a value to them if a value has already been assigned (more details are in [21]).

Conditional choice is encoded similarly:

$$\langle\!\langle \textbf{if } (e) \textbf{ then } \{s_1\} \textbf{ else } \{s_2\} \rangle\!\rangle \;=\; [\hat{m}]\,(\hat{m}!\langle e\rangle \mid (\hat{m}?\langle \textbf{true}\rangle.\langle\!\langle s_1\rangle\!\rangle + \hat{m}?\langle \textbf{false}\rangle.\langle\!\langle s_2\rangle\!\rangle))$$

where **true** and **false** are the values that can result from evaluation of e.

Sequential composition can be encoded alike in CCS [26, Chapter 8] however, due to the asynchrony of invoke and kill activities, the notion of well-termination must be relaxed wrt CCS. Firstly, we settle that services may indicate their termination by exploiting the invoke activity $x_{done} \cdot o_{done}!\langle\rangle$, where x_{done} is a distinguished variable and o_{done} is a distinguished name. Secondly, we say that a service s is *well-terminating* if, for every reduct s' of s and partner p, $s' \cdot \{x_{done} \mapsto p\} \xrightarrow{(p \cdot o_{done}) \lhd \langle\rangle}$ implies that

- either $s' \xrightarrow{\alpha} s''$ for some $\alpha = \dagger$ or $\alpha = \dagger k$ and s'' is well-terminating
- or $s' \xrightarrow{\alpha} s''$ implies $\alpha = (p \cdot o) \lhd \bar{v}$, for some s'', p, o and $\bar{v}$.

Notably, well-termination does not demand a service to terminate, but only that whenever the service can perform activity $p \cdot o_{done}!\langle\rangle$ and cannot perform any kill activities, then it terminates except for, possibly, some parallel pending invoke activities. As usual, the encoding relies on the assumption that all calculus operators themselves (in particular, parallel composition) can be rendered as to preserve well-termination. Finally, if we only consider well-terminating services, then, for a fresh p, we can let:

$$\langle\!\langle s_1 ; s_2 \rangle\!\rangle \;=\; [p]\,(\langle\!\langle s_1 \cdot \{x_{done} \mapsto p\}\rangle\!\rangle \mid p \cdot o_{done}?\langle\rangle.\langle\!\langle s_2\rangle\!\rangle)$$

Fault and compensation handlers. Fault handling is strictly related to the notion of *compensation*, namely the execution of specific activities (attempting) to reverse the effects of previously executed activities. We consider here a minor variant of the WS-BPEL compensation protocol. To begin with, we extend COWS syntax as shown in the upper part of Table 5. The *scope* activity $[s : \textbf{catch}(\phi_1)\{s_1\} : \ldots : \textbf{catch}(\phi_n)\{s_n\} : s_c]_\iota$ permits explicitly grouping activities together. The declaration of a scope activity contains a unique scope identifier ι, a service s representing the normal behaviour, an optional list of fault handlers, and a compensation handler s_c. The *fault generator* activity $\textbf{throw}(\phi)$ can be used by a service to rise a fault signal ϕ. This signal will trigger execution of activity s', if a construct of the form $\textbf{catch}(\phi)\{s'\}$ exists within the same scope. The *compensate* activity $\textbf{undo}(\iota)$ can be used to invoke a compensation handler of an inner scope named ι that has already completed normally (i.e. without faulting). Compensation can only be invoked from within a fault or a compensation handler. As in WS-BPEL, we fix two syntactic constraints: handlers do not contain scope activities and for each $\textbf{undo}(\iota)$ occurring in a service there exists at least an inner scope ι.

In fact, it is not necessary to extend COWS syntax because fault and compensation handling can be easily encoded. The most interesting cases of the encoding are shown in the lower part of Table 5 (in the remaining cases, the encoding acts as an homomorphism), where the killer labels used to identify scopes and the introduced partner

Table 5. Syntax and encoding of fault and compensation handling

$s ::= \ \ldots$	(services)
$\mid\ \mathbf{throw}(\phi)$	(fault generator)
$\mid\ \mathbf{undo}(\imath)$	(compensate)
$\mid\ [s : \mathbf{catch}(\phi_1)\{s_1\} : \ldots : \mathbf{catch}(\phi_n)\{s_n\} : s_c]_\imath$	(scope)

$$\langle\!\langle [s : \mathbf{catch}(\phi_1)\{s_1\} : \ldots : \mathbf{catch}(\phi_n)\{s_n\} : s_c]_\imath \rangle\!\rangle_k = [p_{\phi_1}, \ldots, p_{\phi_n}]\ (\ \langle\!\langle \mathbf{catch}(\phi_1)\{s_1\}\rangle\!\rangle_k \mid \ \ldots \ \mid \langle\!\langle \mathbf{catch}(\phi_n)\{s_n\}\rangle\!\rangle_k \mid [k_\imath]\,(\ \langle\!\langle s\rangle\!\rangle_{k_\imath}\ ;\ (\ x_{done}\cdot o_{done}!\langle\rangle \mid \{\!|p_\imath \cdot o_{comp}?\langle\rangle.\langle\!\langle s_c\rangle\!\rangle_{k_\imath}|\!\}\ )\ )\ )$$

$$\langle\!\langle \mathbf{catch}(\phi)\{s\}\rangle\!\rangle_k = p_\phi \cdot o_{fault}?\langle\rangle.[k']\ \langle\!\langle s\rangle\!\rangle_{k'}$$

$$\langle\!\langle \mathbf{undo}(\imath)\rangle\!\rangle_k = p_\imath \cdot o_{comp}!\langle\rangle \mid x_{done}\cdot o_{done}!\langle\rangle$$

$$\langle\!\langle \mathbf{throw}(\phi)\rangle\!\rangle_k = \{\!|p_\phi \cdot o_{fault}!\langle\rangle \mid x_{done}\cdot o_{done}!\langle\rangle|\!\} \mid \mathbf{kill}(k)$$

names are taken fresh for s, s_1, ..., s_n and s_c. The two distinguished names o_{fault} and o_{comp} denote the operations for receiving fault and compensation signals, respectively. We are assuming that for each scope identifier or fault signal named n, the partner used to activate scope compensation or fault handling, respectively, is p_n.

The encoding $\langle\!\langle\cdot\rangle\!\rangle_k$ is parameterized by the identifier k of the closest enclosing scope, if any. The parameter is used when encoding a fault generator, to launch a kill activity that forces termination of all the remaining activities of the enclosing scope, and when encoding a scope, to delimit the field of action of inner kill activities. The compensation handler s_c of scope $\imath$ is installed when the normal behaviour s successfully completes, but it is activated only when signal $p_\imath \cdot o_{comp}!\langle\rangle$ occurs. Similarly, if during normal execution a fault ϕ occurs, a signal $p_\phi \cdot o_{fault}!\langle\rangle$ triggers execution of the corresponding fault handler (if any). Installed compensation handlers are protected from killing by means of $\{\!|\_|\!\}$. Notably, both the compensate activity and the fault generator activity can immediately terminate (thus enabling possible sequential compositions); this, of course, does not mean that the corresponding handler is terminated.

Flow graphs. Flow graphs provide a direct and intuitive way to structure workflow processes, where activities executed in parallel can be synchronized by settling dependencies, called (flow) links, among them. At the beginning of a parallel execution, all involved links are inactive and only those activities with no synchronization dependencies can execute. Once all incoming links of an activity are active (i.e., they have been assigned either a positive or negative state), a guard, called *join condition*, is evaluated. When an activity terminates, the status of the outgoing links, which can be positive, negative or undefined, is determined through evaluation of a *transition condition*. When an activity in the flow graph cannot execute (i.e., the join condition fails), a *join failure* fault is emitted to signal that some activities have not completed. An attribute called 'suppress join failure' can be set to *yes* to ensure that join condition failures do not throw the join failure fault (this effect is called *Dead-Path Elimination* [1]).

To express the constructs above, we extend the syntax of COWS as illustrated in the upper part of Table 6. A *flow graph activity* $[\overline{fl}]\ ls$ is a delimited *linked service*, where

Table 6. Syntax and encoding of flow graphs

s ::=	$\ldots \mid [\overline{fl}]\, ls \mid \sum_{i\in I} p_i \cdot o_i?\bar{w}_i.s_i$	(services)
ls ::=	$(jc) \overset{sjf}{\Rightarrow} s \Rightarrow (\overline{fl},\bar{e}) \mid s \Rightarrow (\overline{fl},\bar{e}) \mid ls \mid ls$	(linked services)
jc ::=	$\mathbf{true} \mid \mathbf{false} \mid fl \mid \neg jc \mid jc \vee jc \mid jc \wedge jc$	(join conditions)
sjf ::=	$yes \mid no$	(supp. join failure)

$$\langle\!\langle [\overline{fl}]\, ls \rangle\!\rangle = [\overline{fl}]\, \langle\!\langle ls \rangle\!\rangle \qquad \langle\!\langle ls_1 \mid ls_2 \rangle\!\rangle = \langle\!\langle ls_1 \rangle\!\rangle \mid \langle\!\langle ls_2 \rangle\!\rangle \qquad \langle\!\langle s \Rightarrow (\overline{fl},\bar{e}) \rangle\!\rangle = \langle\!\langle s \rangle\!\rangle; [\overline{fl} = \bar{e}]$$

$$\langle\!\langle (jc) \overset{yes}{\Rightarrow} s \Rightarrow (\overline{fl},\bar{e}) \rangle\!\rangle = \mathbf{if}\ (jc)\ \mathbf{then}\ \{\langle\!\langle s \rangle\!\rangle; [\overline{fl} = \bar{e}]\}\ \mathbf{else}\ \{[outLinkOf(s) = \overline{\mathbf{false}}]\}$$

$$\langle\!\langle (jc) \overset{no}{\Rightarrow} s \Rightarrow (\overline{fl},\bar{e}) \rangle\!\rangle = \mathbf{if}\ (jc)\ \mathbf{then}\ \{\langle\!\langle s \rangle\!\rangle; [\overline{fl} = \bar{e}]\}\ \mathbf{else}\ \{\mathbf{throw}(\phi_{join\_f})\}$$

$$\begin{aligned}\langle\!\langle \textstyle\sum_{i\in\{1..n\}} p_i \cdot o_i?\bar{w}_i.s_i \rangle\!\rangle = {} & p_1 \cdot o_1?\bar{w}_1.[\textstyle\bigcup_{j\in\{2..n\}} outLinkOf(s_j) = \overline{\mathbf{false}}].\langle\!\langle s_1 \rangle\!\rangle \\ & + \ldots + p_n \cdot o_n?\bar{w}_n.[\textstyle\bigcup_{j\in\{1..n-1\}} outLinkOf(s_j) = \overline{\mathbf{false}}].\langle\!\langle s_n \rangle\!\rangle\end{aligned}$$

the activities within ls can synchronize by means of the flow links in $\overline{fl}$, rendered as (boolean) variables. A linked service is a service equipped with a set of incoming flow links that forms the *join condition*, and a set of outgoing flow links that represents the *transition condition*. Incoming flow links and join condition are denoted by $(jc) \overset{sjf}{\Rightarrow}$. Outgoing links are represented by $\Rightarrow (\overline{fl_{i\in I}}, \bar{e}_{i\in I})$ where each pair (fl_i, e_i) is composed of a flow link fl_i and the corresponding transition (boolean) condition e_i. Attribute sjf permits suppressing possible join failures. Input-guarded summation replaces binary choice, because we want all the branches of a multiple choice to be considered at once.

Again, we show that in fact it is not necessary to extend the syntax because flow graphs can be easily encoded by relying on the capability of COWS of modelling a state shared among a group of activities. The most interesting cases of the encoding are shown in the lower part of Table 6. The encoding exploits the auxiliary function $outLinkOf(s)$, that returns the tuple of outgoing links in s. Flow graphs are rendered as delimited services, while flow links are rendered as variables. A join condition is encoded as a boolean condition within a conditional construct, where the transition conditions are rendered as the assignment $[\overline{fl} = \bar{e}]$. In case attribute 'suppress join failure' is set to *no*, a join condition failure produces a fault signal that can be caught by a proper fault handler. Choice among (linked) services is implemented in such a way that, when a branch is selected, the links outgoing from the activities of the discarded branches are set to *false* (the encoding of conditional choice can be modified similarly).

4 Encoding the Orchestration Language Orc

We present here the encoding of Orc [28], a recently proposed task orchestration language with applications in workflow, business process management, and web service orchestration. Orc *expressions* are generated by the following grammar:

$$f, g \ ::= \ \mathbf{0} \mid S(w) \mid E(w) \mid f > x > g \mid f \mid g \mid g\ \mathbf{where}\ x :\in f$$

where S ranges over *site names*, E over *expression names*, x over variables, and w over *parameters*, i.e. variables or values (ranged over by v). Each expression name E has a unique declaration of the form $E(x) \triangleq f$. Expressions $f > x > g$ and g **where** $x :\in f$ bind variable x in g.

We now briefly describe the semantics of Orc expressions (and refer the interested reader to [21] for a formal account). Evaluation of expressions may call a number of sites and returns a (possibly empty) stream of values. In [28], this is formalized through a labelled transition relation, where label τ indicates an internal event while label $!v$ indicates publication of the value v resulting from evaluating an expression. A *site call* can progress only when the actual parameter is a value; it elicits one response. While site calls use a call-by-value mechanism, *expression calls* use a call-by-name mechanism, namely the actual parameter replaces the formal one and then the corresponding expression is evaluated. *Symmetric parallel composition* $f \mid g$ consists of concurrent evaluations of f and g. *Sequential composition* $f > x > g$ activates a concurrent copy of g with x replaced by v, for each value v returned by f. *Asymmetric parallel composition* g **where** $x :\in f$ starts in parallel both f and the part of g that does not need x. The first value returned by f is assigned to x and the continuation of f and all its descendants are then terminated.

The encoding of Orc expressions in COWS exploits function $\langle\!\langle\cdot\rangle\!\rangle_{\hat{r}}$ shown in Table 7. The function is defined by induction on the syntax of expressions and is parameterized by the communication endpoint $\hat{r}$ used to return the result of expressions evaluation. Thus, a site call is rendered as an invoke activity that sends a pair made of the parameter of the invocation and the endpoint for the reply along the endpoint $\hat{S}$ corresponding to site name S. Expression call is rendered similarly, but we need two invoke activities: $\hat{E}!\langle \hat{r}, \hat{r}' \rangle$ activates a new instance of the body of the declaration, while $z!\langle w \rangle$ sends the value of the actual parameter (when this value will be available) to the created instance, by means of a private endpoint stored in z received from the encoding of the corresponding expression declaration along the private endpoint $\hat{r}'$ previously sent. Sequential composition is encoded as the parallel composition of the two components sharing a delimited endpoint, where a new instance of the component on the right is created every time that on the left returns a value along the shared endpoint. Symmetric parallel composition is encoded as parallel composition, where the values produced by the two components are sent along the same return endpoint. Finally, asymmetric parallel composition is encoded in terms of parallel composition in such a way that, whenever the encoding of f returns its first value, this is passed to the encoding of g and a kill activity is enabled. Due to its eager semantics, the kill will terminate what remains of the term corresponding to the encoding of f.

Moreover, for each site S, we define the service:

$$* [x, y]\, \hat{S}?\langle x, y \rangle.y!\langle e^S_x \rangle \tag{1}$$

that receives along the endpoint $\hat{S}$ a value (stored in x) and an endpoint (stored in y) to be used to send back the result, and returns the evaluation of e^S_x, an unspecified expression corresponding to S and depending on x.

Similarly, for each expression declaration $E(x) \triangleq f$ we define the service:

$$* [y, z]\, \hat{E}?\langle y, z \rangle.[\hat{r}]\, (z!\langle \hat{r} \rangle \mid [x]\, (\hat{r}?\langle x \rangle \mid \langle\!\langle f \rangle\!\rangle_y)) \tag{2}$$

Table 7. Orc encoding

$\langle\!\langle \mathbf{0} \rangle\!\rangle_{\hat{r}} = \mathbf{0}$ $\quad$ $\langle\!\langle S\,(w) \rangle\!\rangle_{\hat{r}} = \hat{S}\,!\langle w, \hat{r}\rangle$ $\quad$ $\langle\!\langle E(w) \rangle\!\rangle_{\hat{r}} = [\hat{r}']\,(\hat{E}!\langle \hat{r}, \hat{r}'\rangle \mid [z]\,\hat{r}'?\langle z\rangle.z!\langle w\rangle)$

$\langle\!\langle f > x > g \rangle\!\rangle_{\hat{r}} = [\hat{r}_f]\,(\langle\!\langle f \rangle\!\rangle_{\hat{r}_f} \mid *\,[x]\,\hat{r}_f?\langle x\rangle.\langle\!\langle g \rangle\!\rangle_{\hat{r}})$ $\quad$ $\langle\!\langle f \mid g \rangle\!\rangle_{\hat{r}} = \langle\!\langle f \rangle\!\rangle_{\hat{r}} \mid \langle\!\langle g \rangle\!\rangle_{\hat{r}}$

$\langle\!\langle g\ \mathbf{where}\ x :\in f \rangle\!\rangle_{\hat{r}} = [\hat{r}_f, x]\ (\ \langle\!\langle g \rangle\!\rangle_{\hat{r}} \mid [k]\,(\ \langle\!\langle f \rangle\!\rangle_{\hat{r}_f} \mid \hat{r}_f?\langle x\rangle.\mathbf{kill}(k)\ )\ )$

Here, the received value (stored in x) is processed by the encoding of the body of the declaration, that is activated as soon as the expression is called.

Finally, the encoding of an Orc expression f, written $[\![f]\!]_{\hat{r}}$, is the parallel composition of $\langle\!\langle f \rangle\!\rangle_{\hat{r}}$, of a service of the form (1) or (2) for each site or expression called in f, in any of the expressions called in f, and so on recursively.

In [21], we prove that there is a formal correspondence, based on the operational semantics, between Orc expressions and the COWS services resulting from their encoding. This is another sign of COWS expressiveness because it is known that Orc can express the most common workflow patterns identified in [31]. By letting $s \overset{\alpha}{\Longrightarrow} s'$ to mean that there exist two services, s_1 and s_2, such that s_1 is a reduct of s, $s_1 \overset{\alpha}{\longrightarrow} s_2$ and s' is a reduct of s_2, the above property can be stated as follows

Theorem 1. *Given an Orc expression f and an endpoint $\hat{r}$, $f \overset{l}{\hookrightarrow} f'$ implies* $[\![f]\!]_{\hat{r}} \equiv \langle\!\langle f \rangle\!\rangle_{\hat{r}} \mid s \overset{\alpha}{\Longrightarrow} \langle\!\langle f' \rangle\!\rangle_{\hat{r}} \mid s$, *where* $\alpha = \hat{r} \lhd \langle v\rangle$ *if* $l = !v$, *and* $\alpha = (p \cdot o \lfloor \emptyset \rfloor \bar{w}\,\bar{v})$ *if* $l = \tau$.

The proof (see [21]) proceeds by induction on the length of the inference of $f \overset{l}{\hookrightarrow} f'$.

5 Concluding Remarks

We have introduced COWS, a formalism for specifying and combining services, while modelling their dynamic behaviour (i.e. it deals with service orchestration rather than choreography). COWS borrows many constructs from well-known process calculi, e.g. π-calculus, update calculus, StAC$_i$, and Lπ, but combines them in an original way, thus being different from all existing calculi. COWS permits modelling different and typical aspects of (web) services technologies, such as multiple start activities, receive conflicts, routing of correlated messages, service instances and interactions among them.

The correlation mechanism was first exploited in [32], that, however, only considers interaction among different instances of a single business process. Instead, to connect the interaction protocols of clients and of the respective service instances, the calculus introduced in [3], and called SCC, relies on explicit modelling of sessions and their dynamic creation (that exploits the mechanism of private names of π-calculus). Interaction sessions are not explicitly modelled in COWS, instead they can be identified by tracing all those exchanged messages that are correlated each other through their same contents (as in [14]). We believe that the mechanism based on correlation sets (also used by WS-BPEL), that exploits business data and communication protocol headers to correlate different interactions, is more robust and fits the loosely coupled world of Web

Services better than that based on explicit session references. Another notable difference with SCC is that in COWS services are not necessarily persistent.

Many works put forward enrichments of some well-known process calculus with constructs inspired by those of WS-BPEL. The most of them deal with issues of web transactions such as interruptible processes, failure handlers and time. This is, for example, the case of [19,20,23,24] that present timed and untimed extensions of the π-calculus, called $\mathtt{web}\pi$ and $\mathtt{web}\pi_\infty$, tailored to study a simplified version of the scope construct of WS-BPEL. Other proposals on the formalization of flow compensation are [5,4] that give a more compact and closer description of the *Sagas* mechanism [13] for dealing with long running transactions.

We have focused on service orchestration rather than on service choreography. In [6,7] both aspects are studied. Other approaches are based on the use of schema languages [11] and Petri nets [15]. In [18] a sort of distributed input-guarded choice of join patterns, called *smooth orchestrators*, gives a simple and effective representation of synchronization constructs. The work closest to ours is [22], where WS-CALCULUS is introduced to formalize the semantics of WS-BPEL. COWS represents a more foundational formalism than WS-CALCULUS in that it does not rely on explicit notions of location and state, it is more manageable (e.g. has a simpler operational semantics) and, at least, equally expressive (as the encoding of WS-CALCULUS in COWS shows, [21]).

This paper has focussed on showing the descriptive power of COWS. We leave as a future work the task of developing a formal account of its expressiveness. We also plan to develop analytical tools, such as e.g. behavioural equivalences and type systems, supporting services verification. Behavioural equivalences could provide a means to establish formal correspondences between different views (abstraction levels) of a service, e.g. the contract it has to honour and its true implementation. Type systems, possibly based on behavioural types (see e.g. [12,16,17]), could permit to express and enforce policies of interest for (web) services for, e.g., disciplining resources usage, constraining the sequences of messages accepted by services, ensuring service interoperability and compositionality, guaranteeing absence of deadlock in service composition, checking that interaction obeys a given protocol.

Acknowledgements. We thank the anonymous referees for their useful comments.

References

1. A. Alves et al. Web Services Business Process Execution Language Version 2.0. Technical report, WS-BPEL TC OASIS, August 2006. `http://www.oasis-open.org/`.
2. L. Bocchi, C. Laneve, and G. Zavattaro. A calculus for long-running transactions. In *FMOODS*, *LNCS* 2884, pp. 124–138, 2003.
3. M. Boreale, R. Bruni, L. Caires, R. De Nicola, I. Lanese, M. Loreti, F. Martins, U. Montanari, A. Ravara, D. Sangiorgi, V. T. Vasconcelos, and G. Zavattaro. SCC: a Service Centered Calculus. In *WS-FM*, *LNCS* 4184 , pp. 38–57, 2006.
4. R. Bruni, M. Butler, C. Ferreira, T. Hoare, H. Melgratti, and U. Montanari. Comparing two approaches to compensable flow composition. In *CONCUR*, *LNCS* 3653, pp. 383–397, 2005.
5. R. Bruni, H.C. Melgratti, and U. Montanari. Theoretical foundations for compensations in flow composition languages. In *POPL*, pp. 209–220. ACM, 2005.

6. N. Busi, R. Gorrieri, C. Guidi, R. Lucchi, and G. Zavattaro. Choreography and orchestration: A synergic approach for system design. In *ICSOC*, *LNCS* 3826, pp. 228–240, 2005.
7. N. Busi, R. Gorrieri, C. Guidi, R. Lucchi, and G. Zavattaro. Choreography and orchestration conformance for system design. In *COORDINATION*, *LNCS* 4038, pp. 63–81, 2006.
8. M.J. Butler and C. Ferreira. An operational semantics for StAC, a language for modelling long-running business transactions. In *COORDINATION*, *LNCS* 2949, pp. 87–104, 2004.
9. M.J. Butler, C.A.R. Hoare, and C. Ferreira. A trace semantics for long-running transactions. In *25 Years Communicating Sequential Processes*, *LNCS* 3525, pp. 133–150, 2005.
10. M. Carbone and S. Maffeis. On the expressive power of polyadic synchronisation in π- calculus. *Nordic J. of Computing*, 10(2):70–98, 2003.
11. S. Carpineti and C. Laneve. A basic contract language for web services. In *ESOP*, *LNCS* 3924, pp. 197–213, 2006.
12. S. Chaki, S. K. Rajamani, and J. Rehof. Types as models: model checking message-passing programs. In *POPL*, pp. 45–57, 2002.
13. H. Garcia-Molina and K. Salem. Sagas. In *SIGMOD*, pp. 249–259. ACM Press, 1987.
14. C. Guidi, R. Lucchi, R. Gorrieri, N. Busi, and G. Zavattaro. SOCK: a calculus for service oriented computing. In *ICSOC*, *LNCS* 4294, pp. 327–338, 2006.
15. S. Hinz, K. Schmidt, and C. Stahl. Transforming BPEL to petri nets. In *Business Process Management* 3649, pp. 220–235, 2005.
16. A. Igarashi and N. Kobayashi. A generic type system for the pi-calculus. *Theor. Comput. Sci.*, 311(1-3):121–163, 2004.
17. N. Kobayashi, K. Suenaga, and L. Wischik. Resource usage analysis for the π-calculus. In *VMCAI*, *LNCS* 3855, pp. 298–312, 2006.
18. C. Laneve and L. Padovani. Smooth orchestrators. In *FoSSaCS*, *LNCS* 3921, pp. 32–46, 2006.
19. C. Laneve and G. Zavattaro. Foundations of web transactions. In *FoSSaCS*, *LNCS* 3441, pp. 282–298, 2005.
20. C. Laneve and G. Zavattaro. web-pi at work. In *TGC*, *LNCS* 3705, pp. 182–194, 2005.
21. A. Lapadula, R. Pugliese, and F. Tiezzi. A calculus for orchestration of web services (full version). Technical report, Dipartimento di Sistemi e Informatica, Univ. Firenze, 2006. `http://rap.dsi.unifi.it/cows`
22. A. Lapadula, R. Pugliese, and F. Tiezzi. A WSDL-based type system for WS-BPEL. In *COORDINATION*, *LNCS* 4038, pp. 145–163, 2006.
23. M. Mazzara and I. Lanese. Towards a unifying theory for web services composition. In *WS-FM*, *LNCS* 4184, pp. 257–272, 2006.
24. M. Mazzara and R. Lucchi. A pi-calculus based semantics for WS-BPEL. *Journal of Logic and Algebraic Programming*, 70(1):96–118, 2006.
25. M. Merro and D. Sangiorgi. On asynchrony in name-passing calculi. *Mathematical Structures in Computer Science*, 14(5):715–767, 2004.
26. R. Milner. *Communication and concurrency.* Prentice-Hall, 1989.
27. R. Milner, J. Parrow, and D. Walker. A calculus of mobile processes, I and II. *Inf. Comput.*, 100(1):1–40, 41–77, 1992.
28. J. Misra and W. R. Cook. Computation orchestration: A basis for wide-area computing. *Journal of Software and Systems Modeling*. Springer, May 2006.
29. J. Parrow and B. Victor. The update calculus. In *AMAST*, *LNCS* 1349, pp. 409–423, 1997.
30. J. Parrow and B. Victor. The fusion calculus: Expressiveness and symmetry in mobile processes. In *Logic in Computer Science*, pp. 176–185, 1998.
31. W.M.P. van der Aalst, A.H.M. ter Hofstede, B. Kiepuszewski, and A.P. Barros. Workflow patterns. *Distributed and Parallel Databases*, 14(1):5–51. Springer, 2003.
32. M. Viroli. Towards a formal foundational to orchestration languages. *ENTCS*, 105:51–71. Elsevier, 2004.

A Concurrent Calculus with Atomic Transactions*

Lucia Acciai[1], Michele Boreale[2], and Silvano Dal Zilio[1]

[1] LIF, CNRS and Université de Provence, France
[2] Dipartimento di Sistemi e Informatica, Università di Firenze, Italy

Abstract. The *Software Transactional Memory* (STM) model is an original approach for controlling concurrent accesses to resources without the need for explicit lock-based synchronization mechanisms. A key feature of STM is to provide a way to group sequences of read and write actions inside *atomic blocks*, similar to database transactions, whose whole effect should occur atomically.

In this paper, we investigate STM from a process algebra perspective and define an extension of asynchronous CCS with atomic blocks of actions. We show that the addition of atomic transactions results in a very expressive calculus, enough to easily encode other concurrent primitives such as guarded choice and multiset-synchronization (à la join-calculus). The correctness of our encodings is proved using a suitable notion of bisimulation equivalence. The equivalence is then applied to prove interesting "laws of transactions" and to obtain a simple normal form for transactions.

1 Introduction

The craft of programming concurrent applications is about mastering the strains between two key factors: getting hold of results as quickly as possible, while ensuring that only correct results (and behaviors) are observed. To this end, it is vital to avoid unwarranted access to shared resources. The *Software Transactional Memory* (STM) [18] model is an original approach for controlling concurrent accesses to resources without using explicit lock-based synchronization mechanisms. Similarly to database transactions, the STM approach provides a way to group sequences of read and write actions inside *atomic blocks* whose whole effect should occur atomically. The STM model has several advantages. Most notably, it dispenses the programmer from the need to explicitly manipulate locks, a task widely recognized as difficult and error-prone. Moreover, atomic transactions provide a clean conceptual basis for concurrency control, which should ease the verification of concurrent programs. Finally, the model is effective: there exist several STM implementations for designing software for multiprocessor systems; these applications exhibit good performances in practice (compared to equivalent, hand-crafted, code using locks).

We investigate the STM model from a process algebra perspective and define an extension of asynchronous CCS [20] with atomic blocks of actions. We call this calculus ATCCS. The choice of a dialect of CCS is motivated by an attention to economy: to focus on STM primitives, we study a calculus as simple as possible and dispense with

* This work was partially supported by the French ANR ARASSIA project COPS and the EU FET-GC2 initiative, project SENSORIA.

R. De Nicola (Ed.): ESOP 2007, LNCS 4421, pp. 48–63, 2007.

orthogonal issues such as values, mobility of names or processes, *etc*. We believe that our work could be easily transferred to a richer setting. Our goal is not only to set a formal ground for reasoning on STM implementations but also to understand how this model fits with other concurrency control mechanisms. We also view this calculus as a test bed for extending process calculi with atomic transactions. This is an interesting direction for investigation since, for the most part, works that mix transactions with process calculi consider *compensating transactions*, see e.g. [3,5,7,8,9,11,19].

The idea of providing hardware support for software transactions originated from works by Herlihy and Moss [18] and was later extended by Shavit and Touitou [22] to software-only transactional memory. Transactions are used to protect the execution of an atomic block. Intuitively, each thread that enters a transaction takes a snapshot of the shared memory (the global state). The evaluation is optimistic and all actions are performed on a copy of the memory (the local state). When the transaction ends, the snapshot is compared with the current state of the memory. There are two possible outcomes: if the check indicates that concurrent writes have occurred, the transaction aborts and is rescheduled; otherwise, the transaction is committed and its effects are propagated instantaneously. Very recently, Harris et al. [17] have proposed a (combinator style) language of transactions that enables arbitrary atomic operations to be composed into larger *atomic expressions*. We base the syntax of ATCCS on the operators defined in [17].

The main contributions of this work are: (1) the definition of a process calculus with atomic transactions; and (2) the definition of an asynchronous bisimulation equivalence $\approx_a$ that allows compositional reasoning on transactions. We also have a number of more specific technical results. We show that ATCCS is expressive enough to easily encode interesting concurrent primitives, such as (preemptive versions of) guarded choice and multiset-synchronization, and the leader election problem (Section 3). Next, we define an equivalence between atomic expressions $\simeq$ and prove that $\approx_a$ and $\simeq$ are congruences (Section 4). These equivalences are used to prove the correctness of our encodings, to prove interesting "behavioral laws of transactions" and to define a simple normal form for transactions. We also show that transactions (modulo $\simeq$) have an algebraic structure close to that of a bound semilattice, an observation that could help improve the design of the transaction language. The proofs of the main theorems can be found in a long version of this paper [1].

2 The Calculus

We define the syntax and operational semantics of ATCCS, which is essentially a cut down version of asynchronous CCS, without choice and relabeling operators, equipped with atomic blocks and constructs for composing (transactional) sequences of actions.

Syntax of Processes and Atomic Expressions. The syntax of ATCCS, given in Table 1, is divided into syntactical categories that define a stratification of terms. The definition of the calculus depends on a set of names, ranged over by $a, b, \ldots$. As in CCS, names model communication channels used in process synchronization, but they also occur as objects of read and write actions in atomic transactions.

Atomic expressions, ranged over by $M, N, \ldots$, are used to define sequences of actions whose effect should happen atomically. Actions $\texttt{rd}\,a$ and $\texttt{wt}\,a$ represent attempts to input and output to the channel a. Instead of using snapshots of the state for managing transaction, we use a log-based approach. During the evaluation of an atomic block, actions are recorded in a private log δ (a sequence $\alpha_1 \ldots \alpha_n$) and have no effects outside the scope of the transaction until it is committed. The action `retry` aborts an atomic expression unconditionally and starts its execution afresh, with an empty log ε. The termination action `end` signals that an expression is finished and should be committed. If the transaction can be committed, all actions in the log are performed at the same time and the transaction is closed, otherwise the transaction aborts. Finally, transactions can be composed using the operator `orElse`, which implements (preemptive) alternatives between expressions. In M `orElse` N, the expression N is executed if M aborts and has the behavior of M otherwise.

Processes, ranged over by $P, Q, R, \ldots$, model concurrent systems of communicating agents. We have the usual operators of CCS: the empty process, $\mathbf{0}$, the parallel composition $P \mid Q$, and the input prefix $a.P$. There are some differences though. The calculus is asynchronous, meaning that a process cannot block on output actions. Also, we use *replicated input* $*\,a\,.P$ instead of recursion (this does not change the expressiveness of the calculus) and we lack the choice and relabeling operators of CCS. The hiding operator $P \setminus^n a$ bounds the scope of name a to P (we consider processes up-to α-renaming of bound names; we discuss the meaning of the annotation n in page 53). Finally, the main addition is the presence of the operator $\texttt{atom}(M)$, which models a transaction that safeguards the expression M. The process $\{\!|A|\!\}_M$ represents the ongoing evaluation of an atomic block M: the subscript is used to keep the initial code of the transaction, in case it is aborted and executed afresh, while A holds the remaining actions that should be performed.

An *ongoing atomic block*, $A, B, \ldots$, is essentially an atomic expression enriched with an *evaluation state* σ and a *log* δ of the currently recorded actions. A state σ is a multiset of names that represents the output actions visible to the transaction when it was initiated. (This notion of state bears some resemblance with tuples space in coordination calculi, such as Linda [10].) When a transaction ends, the state σ recorded in the block $(M)_{\sigma;\delta}$ (the state at the initiation of the transaction) can be compared with the current state (the state when the transaction ends) to check if other processes have concurrently made changes to the global state, in which case the transaction should be aborted.

Notation. In the following, we write $\sigma \uplus \{a\}$ for the multiset σ enriched with the name a and $\sigma \setminus \sigma'$ for the multiset obtained from σ by removing elements found in σ', that is the smallest multiset σ'' such that $\sigma \subseteq \sigma' \uplus \sigma''$. The symbol $\emptyset$ stands for the empty multiset while $\{a^n\}$ is the multiset composed of exactly n copies of a, where $\{a^0\} = \emptyset$.

Given a log δ, we use the notation $\mathrm{WT}\,(\delta)$ for the multiset of names which appear as objects of a write action in δ. Similarly, we use the notation $\mathrm{RD}(\delta)$ for the multiset of names that are objects of read actions. The functions WT and RD may be inductively defined as follows: $\mathrm{WT}\,(\texttt{wt}\,a.\delta) = \mathrm{WT}\,(\delta) \uplus \{a\}$; $\mathrm{RD}(\texttt{rd}\,a.\delta) = \mathrm{RD}(\delta) \uplus \{a\}$; $\mathrm{WT}\,(\texttt{rd}\,a.\delta) = \mathrm{WT}\,(\delta)$; $\mathrm{RD}(\texttt{wt}\,a.\delta) = \mathrm{RD}(\delta)$ and $\mathrm{WT}\,(\varepsilon) = \mathrm{RD}(\varepsilon) = \varepsilon$.

Table 1. Syntax of ATCCS: Processes and Atomic Expressions

Actions	$\alpha, \beta ::= \mathtt{rd}\, a$	(tentative) read access to a
	$\mid\ \mathtt{wt}\, a$	(tentative) write access to a
(Atomic) Expressions	$M, N ::= \mathtt{end}$	termination
	$\mid\ \mathtt{retry}$	abort and retry the current atomic block
	$\mid\ \alpha.M$	action prefix
	$\mid\ M\ \mathtt{orElse}\ N$	alternative
Ongoing expressions	$A, B ::= (M)_{\sigma;\delta}$	execution of M with state σ and log δ
	$\mid\ A\ \mathtt{orElse}\ B$	ongoing alternative
Processes	$P, Q ::= \mathbf{0}$	nil
	$\mid\ \overline{a}$	(asynchronous) output
	$\mid\ a.P$	input
	$\mid\ *a.P$	replicated input
	$\mid\ P \mid Q$	parallel composition
	$\mid\ P \backslash^n a$	hiding
	$\mid\ \mathtt{atom}(M)$	atomic block
	$\mid\ \{\!\!\{A\}\!\!\}_M$	ongoing atomic block

Example: Composing Synchronization. Before we describe the meaning of processes, we try to convey the semantics of ATCCS (and the usefulness of the atomic block operator) using a simple example. We take the example of a concurrent system with two memory cells, M_1 and M_2, used to store integers. We consider here a straightforward extension of the calculus with "value-passing." In this setting, we can model a cell with value v by an output $\overline{m_i}!v$ and model an update by a process of the form $m_i?x.(\overline{m_i}!v' \mid \ldots)$. With this encoding, the channel name m_i acts as a lock protecting the shared resource M_i.

Assume now that the values of the cells should be synchronized to preserve a global invariant on the system. For instance, we model a flying aircraft, each cell store the pitch of an aileron and we need to ensure that the aileron stay aligned (that the values of the cells are equal). A process testing the validity of the invariant is for example P_1 below (we suppose that a message on the reserved channel *err* triggers an alarm). There are multiple design choices for resetting the value of both cells to 0, e.g. P_2 and P_3.

$$P_1 \triangleq m_1?x.m_2?y.\text{if } x\,!{=}\,y \text{ then } \overline{err}!$$

$$P_2 \triangleq m_2?x.m_1?y.(\overline{m_1}!0 \mid \overline{m_2}!0) \qquad P_3 \triangleq m_1?x.(\overline{m_1}!0 \mid m_2?y.\overline{m_2}!0)$$

Table 2. Operational Semantics: Processes

$$(\text{OUT})\ \overline{a};\sigma \to \mathbf{0};\sigma \uplus \{a\} \qquad (\text{REP})\ *a.P;\sigma \uplus \{a\} \to P \mid *a.P;\sigma$$

$$(\text{IN})\ a.P;\sigma \uplus \{a\} \to P;\sigma \qquad (\text{COM})\ \frac{P;\sigma \to P';\sigma \uplus \{a\} \quad Q;\sigma \uplus \{a\} \to Q';\sigma}{P|Q \to P' \mid Q'}$$

$$(\text{PARL})\ \frac{P;\sigma \to P';\sigma'}{P \mid Q;\sigma \to P' \mid Q;\sigma'} \qquad (\text{HID})\ \frac{P;\sigma \uplus \{a^n\} \to P';\sigma' \uplus \{a^m\} \qquad a \notin \sigma,\sigma'}{P\backslash^n a;\sigma \to P'\backslash^m a;\sigma'}$$

$$(\text{PARR})\ \frac{Q;\sigma \to Q';\sigma'}{P \mid Q;\sigma \to P \mid Q';\sigma'} \qquad (\text{ATST})\ \mathtt{atom}(M);\sigma \to \{\!|(M)_{\sigma;\varepsilon}|\!\}_M;\sigma$$

$$(\text{ATPASS})\ \frac{A \to A'}{\{\!|A|\!\}_M;\sigma \to \{\!|A'|\!\}_M;\sigma} \qquad (\text{ATRE})\ \{\!|(\mathtt{retry})_{\sigma';\delta}|\!\}_M;\sigma \to \mathtt{atom}(M);\sigma$$

$$(\text{ATFAIL})\ \frac{\text{RD}(\delta) \not\subseteq \sigma}{\{\!|(\mathtt{end})_{\sigma';\delta}|\!\}_M;\sigma \to \mathtt{atom}(M);\sigma}$$

$$(\text{ATOK})\ \frac{\text{RD}(\delta) \subseteq \sigma \quad \sigma = \sigma'' \uplus \text{RD}(\delta) \quad \text{WT}(\delta) = \{a_1,\ldots,a_n\}}{\{\!|(\mathtt{end})_{\sigma';\delta}|\!\}_M;\sigma \to \overline{a_1} \mid \cdots \mid \overline{a_n};\sigma''}$$

Each choice exemplifies a problem with lock-based programming. The composition of P_1 with P_2 leads to a race condition where P_1 acquire the lock on M_1, P_2 on M_2 and each process gets stuck. The composition of P_1 and P_3 may break the invariant (the value of M_1 is updated too quickly). A solution in the first case is to strengthen the invariant and enforce an order for acquiring locks, but this solution is not viable in general and opens the door to *priority inversion* problems. Another solution is to use an additional (master) lock to protect both cells, but this approach obfuscate the code and significantly decreases the concurrency of the system.

Overall, this simple example shows that synchronization constraints do not compose well when using locks. This situation is consistently observed (and bears a resemblance to the inheritance anomaly problem found in concurrent object-oriented languages). The approach advocated in this paper is to use atomic transactions. In our example, the problem is solved by simply wrapping the two operations in a transaction, like in the process $\mathtt{atom}\big(\mathtt{rd}\,(m_2?y).\mathtt{wt}\,(m_2!0).\mathtt{rd}\,(m_1?x).\mathtt{wt}\,(m_1!0)\big)$, which ensures that all cell updates are effected atomically. More examples may be found on the paper on composable memory transactions [17], which makes a compelling case that "even correctly-implemented concurrency abstractions cannot be composed together to form larger abstractions."

Operational Semantics. Like for the syntax, the semantics of ATCCS is stratified in two levels: there is one reduction relation for processes and a second for atomic expressions. With a slight abuse of notation, we use the same symbol ($\to$) for both relations.

Table 3. Operational Semantics: Ongoing Atomic Expression

$$(\text{ARDOK})\ \frac{\text{RD}(\delta) \uplus \{a\} \subseteq \sigma}{(\texttt{rd}\,a.M)_{\sigma;\delta} \to (M)_{\sigma;\delta.\texttt{rd}\,a}} \qquad (\text{ARDF})\ \frac{\text{RD}(\delta) \uplus \{a\} \not\subseteq \sigma}{(\texttt{rd}\,a.M)_{\sigma;\delta} \to (\texttt{retry})_{\sigma;\delta}}$$

$$(\text{AWR})\quad (\texttt{wt}\,a.M)_{\sigma;\delta} \to (M)_{\sigma;\delta.\texttt{wt}\,a}$$

$$(\text{AOI})\quad (M_1\ \texttt{orElse}\ M_2)_{\sigma;\delta} \to (M_1)_{\sigma;\delta}\ \texttt{orElse}\ (M_2)_{\sigma;\delta}$$

$$(\text{AOF})\ (\texttt{retry})_{\sigma;\delta}\ \texttt{orElse}\ B \to B \qquad (\text{AOE})\ (\texttt{end})_{\sigma;\delta}\ \texttt{orElse}\ B \to (\texttt{end})_{\sigma;\delta}$$

$$(\text{AOL})\ \frac{A \to A'}{A\ \texttt{orElse}\ B \to A'\ \texttt{orElse}\ B} \qquad (\text{AOR})\ \frac{B \to B'}{A\ \texttt{orElse}\ B \to A\ \texttt{orElse}\ B'}$$

Reduction for Processes. Table 2 gives the semantics of processes. A reduction is of the form $P;\sigma \to P';\sigma'$ where σ is the state of P. The state σ records the names of all output actions visible to P when reduction happens. It grows when an output is reduced, (OUT), and shrinks in the case of inputs, (IN) and (REP). A parallel composition evolves if one of the component evolves or if both can synchronize, rules (PARL), (PARR) and (COM). In a hiding $P \setminus^n a$, the annotation n is an integer denoting the number of outputs on a that are visible to P. Intuitively, in a "configuration" $P \setminus^n a;\sigma$, the outputs visible to P are those in $\sigma \uplus \{a^n\}$. This extra annotation is necessary because the scope of a is restricted to P, hence it is not possible to have outputs on a in the global state. Rule (HID) allows synchronization on the name a to happen inside a hiding. For instance, we have $(P \mid \overline{a}) \setminus^n a;\sigma \to P \setminus^{n+1} a;\sigma$.

The remaining reduction rules govern the evolution of atomic transactions. Like in the case of (COM), all those rules, but (ATOK), leave the global state unchanged. Rule (ATST) deals with the initiation of an atomic block $\texttt{atom}(M)$: an ongoing block $\{\!|(M)_{\sigma;\varepsilon}|\!\}_M$ is created which holds the current evaluation state σ and an empty log ε. An atomic block $\{\!|A|\!\}_M$ reduces when its expression A reduces, rule (ATPASS). (The reduction relation for ongoing expressions is defined by the rules in Table 3.) Rules (ATRE), (ATFAIL) and (ATOK) deal with the completion of a transaction. After a finite number of transitions, the evaluation of an ongoing expression will necessarily result in a fail state, $(\texttt{retry})_{\sigma;\delta}$, or a success, $(\texttt{end})_{\sigma;\delta}$. In the first case, rule (ATRE), the transaction is aborted and started again from scratch. In the second case, we need to check if the log is consistent with the current evaluation state. A log is consistent if the read actions of δ can be performed on the current state. If the check fails, rule (ATFAIL), the transaction aborts. Otherwise, rule (ATOK), we commit the transaction: the names in $\text{RD}(\delta)$ are taken from the current state and a bunch of outputs on the names in $\text{WT}(\delta)$ are generated.

Reduction for Ongoing Expressions. Table 3 gives the semantics of ongoing atomic expressions. We recall that, in an expression $(\texttt{rd}\,a.M)_{\sigma;\delta}$, the subscript σ is the *initial state*, that is a copy of the state at the time the block has been created and δ is the log of actions performed since the initiation of the transaction.

Rule (ARDOK) states that a read action $\mathtt{rd}\,a$ is recorded in the log δ if all the read actions in $\delta.\mathtt{rd}\,a$ can be performed in the initial state. If it is not the case, the ongoing expression fails, rule (ARDF). This test may be interpreted as a kind of optimization: if a transaction cannot commit in the initial state then, should it commit at the end of the atomic block, it would mean that the global state has been concurrently modified during the execution of the transaction. Note that we consider the initial state σ and not $\sigma \uplus \mathrm{WT}(\delta)$, which means that, in an atomic block, write actions are not directly visible (they cannot be consumed by a read action). This is coherent with the fact that outputs on $\mathrm{WT}(\delta)$ only take place after commit of the block. Rule (AWR) states that a write action always succeeds and is recorded in the current log.

The remaining rules govern the semantics of the `retry`, `end` and `orElse` constructs. These constructs are borrowed from the STM combinators used in the implementation of an STM system in Concurrent Haskell [17]. We define these operators with an equivalent semantics, with the difference that, in our case, a state is not a snapshot of the (shared) memory but a multiset of visible outputs. A composition M `orElse` N corresponds to the interleaving of the behaviors of M and N, which are independently evaluated with respect to the same evaluation state (but have distinct logs). The `orElse` operator is preemptive: the ongoing block M `orElse` N ends if and only M ends or M aborts and N ends.

3 Encoding Concurrency Primitives

Our first example is a simple solution to the celebrated *leader election* problem that does not yield to deadlock. Consider a system composed by n processes and a token, named t, that is modeled by an output $\bar{t}$. A process becomes a leader by getting (making an input on) t. As usual, all participants run the same process (except for the value of their identity). We suppose that there is only one copy of the token in the system and that leadership of process i is communicated to the other processes by outputting on a reserved name win_i. A participant that is not a leader outputs on $lose_i$. The protocol followed by the participants is defined by the following process:

$$L_i \triangleq \big(\mathtt{atom}\big(\mathtt{rd}\,t.\mathtt{wt}\,k.\mathtt{end}\ \mathtt{orElse}\ \mathtt{wt}\,k'.\mathtt{end}\big) \mid k.\overline{win_i} \mid k'.\overline{lose_i}\big) \backslash^0 k \backslash^0 k'$$

In this encoding, the atomic block is used to protect the concurrent accesses to t. If the process L_i commits its transaction and grabs the token, it immediately release an output on its private channel k. The transactions of the other participants may either fail or commit while releasing an output on their private channel k'. Then, the elected process L_i may proceed with a synchronization on k that triggers the output $\overline{win_i}$. The semantics of `atom()` ensures that only one transaction can acquire the lock and commit the atomic block, then no other process have acquired the token in the same round and we are guaranteed that there could be at most one leader.

This expressivity result is mixed blessing. Indeed, it means that any implementation of the atomic operator should be able to solve the leader election problem, which is known to be very expensive in the case of loosely-coupled systems or in presence of failures (see e.g. [21] for a discussion on the expressivity of process calculi and electoral systems). On the other hand, atomic transactions are optimistic and are compatible with the use of probabilistic approaches. Therefore it is still reasonable to expect a practical implementation of ATCCS.

In the following, we show how to encode two fundamental concurrency patterns, namely (preemptive versions of) the choice and join-pattern operators.

Guarded choice. We consider an operator for choice, $\mu_1.P_1 + \cdots + \mu_n.P_n$, such that every process is prefixed by an action μ_i that is either an output $\overline{a}_i$ or an input a_i. The semantics of choice is characterized by the following three reduction rules (we assume that Q is also a choice):

$$\text{(C-INP)}\ a.P+Q;\sigma\uplus\{a\}\to P;\sigma \qquad \text{(C-OUT)}\ \overline{a}.P+Q;\sigma\to P;\sigma\uplus\{a\}$$

$$\text{(C-PASS)}\ \frac{a\notin\sigma\quad Q;\sigma\to Q';\sigma'}{a.P+Q;\sigma\to Q';\sigma'}$$

A minor difference with the behavior of the choice operator found in CCS is that our semantics gives precedence to the leftmost process (this is reminiscent of the preemptive behavior of `orElse`). Another characteristic is related to the asynchronous nature of the calculus, see rule (C-OUT): since an output action can always interact with the environment, a choice $\overline{a}.P+Q$ may react at once and release the process $\overline{a} \mid P$.

Like in the example of the leader election problem, we can encode a choice $\mu_1.P_1 + \cdots + \mu_n.P_n$ using an atomic block that will mediate the interaction with the actions $\mu_1,\ldots,\mu_n$. We start by defining a straightforward encoding of input/output actions into atomic actions: $[\![\overline{a}]\!] = \mathtt{wt}\,a$ and $[\![a]\!] = \mathtt{rd}\,a$. Then the encoding of choice is the process

$$[\![\mu_1.P_1+\cdots+\mu_n.P_n]\!] \triangleq \big(\mathtt{atom}([\![\mu_1]\!].[\![\overline{k_1}]\!].\mathtt{end}\ \mathtt{orElse}\ \cdots\ \mathtt{orElse}\ [\![\mu_n]\!].[\![\overline{k_n}]\!].\mathtt{end}) \\ \mid k_1.[\![P_1]\!] \mid \cdots \mid k_n.[\![P_n]\!]\big) \setminus^0 k_1 \ldots \setminus^0 k_n$$

The principle of the encoding is essentially the same that in our solution to the leader election problem. Actually, using the encoding for choice, we can rewrite our solution in the following form: $L_i \triangleq t.\overline{win_i} + \overline{lose_i}.\mathbf{0}$. Using the rules in Table 2, it is easy to see that our encoding of choice is compatible with rule (C-INP), meaning that:

$$\begin{aligned}[\![a.P+Q]\!];\sigma\uplus\{a\} &\to^* \big(\{\!|(\mathtt{end})_{\sigma\uplus\{a\};\mathtt{rd}\,a.\mathtt{wt}\,k_1}|\!\}_M \mid k_1.[\![P]\!] \mid \ldots\big)\setminus^0 k_1 \setminus \ldots;\sigma\uplus\{a\}\\ &\to \big(\overline{k_1} \mid k_1.[\![P]\!] \mid \ldots\big)\setminus^0 k_1\setminus\ldots;\sigma\\ &\to \big([\![P]\!] \mid \ldots\big)\setminus^0 k_1\setminus\ldots;\sigma\end{aligned}$$

where the processes in parallel with $[\![P]\!]$ are harmless. In the next section, we define a weak bisimulation equivalence $\approx_{\mathsf{a}}$ that can be used to garbage collect harmless processes in the sense that, e.g. $(P \mid k.Q)\setminus^0 k \approx_{\mathsf{a}} P$ if P has no occurrences of k. Hence, we could prove that $[\![a.P+Q]\!];\sigma\uplus\{a\} \to^*\approx_{\mathsf{a}} [\![P]\!];\sigma$, which is enough to show that our encoding is correct with respect to rule (C-INP). The same is true for rules (C-OUT) and (C-PASS).

Join Patterns. A multi-synchronization $(a_1 \times \cdots \times a_n).P$ may be viewed as an extension of input prefix in which communication requires a synchronization with the n outputs $\overline{a_1}, \ldots, \overline{a_n}$ at once. that is, we have the reduction:

$$\text{(J-INP)} \quad (a_1 \times \cdots \times a_n).P;\sigma \uplus \{a_1,\ldots,a_n\} \rightarrow P;\sigma$$

This synchronization primitive is fundamental to the definition of the Gamma calculus of Banâtre and Le Métayer and of the Join calculus of Fournet and Gonthier. It is easy to see that the encoding of a multi-synchronization (input) is a simple transaction:

$$[\![(a_1 \times \cdots \times a_n).P]\!] \triangleq \big(\mathtt{atom}([\![a_1]\!].\cdots.[\![a_n]\!].[\![\overline{k}]\!].\mathtt{end}) \mid k.[\![P]\!]\big) \setminus^0 k \quad \text{(where } k \text{ is fresh)}$$

and that we have $[\![(a_1 \times \cdots \times a_n).P]\!];\sigma \uplus \{a_1,\ldots,a_n\} \rightarrow^* (\mathbf{0} \mid [\![P]\!]) \setminus^0 k;\sigma$, where the process $(\mathbf{0} \mid [\![P]\!]) \setminus^0 k$ is behaviorally equivalent to $[\![P]\!]$, that is:

$$[\![(a_1 \times \cdots \times a_n).P]\!];\sigma \uplus \{a_1,\ldots,a_n\} \rightarrow^* \approx_{\mathsf{a}} [\![P]\!];\sigma$$

Based on this encoding, we can define two interesting derived operators: a mixed version of multi-synchronization, $(\mu_1 \times \cdots \times \mu_n).P$, that mixes input and output actions; and a replicated version, that is analogous to replicated input.

$$[\![(\mu_1 \times \cdots \times \mu_n).P]\!] \triangleq \big(\mathtt{atom}([\![\mu_1]\!].\cdots.[\![\mu_n]\!].[\![\overline{k}]\!].\mathtt{end}) \mid k.[\![P]\!]\big) \setminus^0 k$$

$$[\![*(\mu_1 \times \cdots \times \mu_n).P]\!] \triangleq \big(\overline{r} \mid *r.\mathtt{atom}([\![\mu_1]\!].\cdots.[\![\mu_n]\!].[\![\overline{r}]\!].[\![\overline{k}]\!].\mathtt{end}) \mid *k.[\![P]\!]\big) \setminus^0 r \setminus^0 k$$

By looking at the possible reductions of these (derived) operators, we can define derived reduction rules. Assume δ is the log $[\![\mu_1]\!].\cdots.[\![\mu_n]\!]$, we have a simulation result comparable to the case for multi-synchronization, namely:

$$[\![(\mu_1 \times \cdots \times \mu_n).P]\!];\sigma \uplus \mathrm{RD}(\delta) \rightarrow^* \approx_{\mathsf{a}} [\![P]\!];\sigma \uplus \mathrm{WT}(\delta)$$

$$[\![*(\mu_1 \times \cdots \times \mu_n).P]\!];\sigma \uplus \mathrm{RD}(\delta) \rightarrow^* \approx_{\mathsf{a}} [\![*(\mu_1 \times \cdots \times \mu_n).P]\!] \mid [\![P]\!];\sigma \uplus \mathrm{WT}(\delta)$$

To obtain join-definitions, we only need to combine a sequence of replicated multi-synchronizations using the choice composition defined precedently. (We also need hiding to close the scope of the definition.) Actually, we can encode even more flexible constructs mixing choice and join-patterns. For the sake of simplicity, we only study examples of such operations. The first example is the (linear) join-pattern $(a \times b).P \wedge (a \times c).Q$, that may fire P if the outputs $\{a,b\}$ are in the global state σ and otherwise fire Q if $\{a,c\}$ is in σ (actually, real implementations of join-calculus have a preemptive semantics for pattern synchronization). The second example is the derived operator $(a \times b) + (b \times c \times \overline{a}).P$, such that P is fired if outputs on $\{a,b\}$ are available or if outputs on $\{b,c\}$ are available (in which case an output on a is also generated). These examples can be easily interpreted using atomic transactions:

$$\begin{aligned}[\![(a \times b).P \wedge (a \times c).Q]\!] \triangleq \big(\mathtt{atom}(\ & [\![a]\!].[\![b]\!].[\![\overline{k_1}]\!].\mathtt{end}\ \mathtt{orElse} \\ & [\![a]\!].[\![c]\!].[\![\overline{k_2}]\!].\mathtt{end}) \mid k_1.P \mid k_2.Q\big) \setminus^0 k_1 \setminus^0 k_2\end{aligned}$$

$$\begin{aligned}[\![(a \times b + b \times c \times \overline{a}).P]\!] \triangleq \big(\mathtt{atom}(\ & [\![a]\!].[\![b]\!].[\![\overline{k}]\!].\mathtt{end}\ \mathtt{orElse} \\ & [\![b]\!].[\![c]\!].[\![\overline{a}]\!].[\![\overline{k}]\!].\mathtt{end}) \mid k.P\big) \setminus^0 k\end{aligned}$$

In the next section we define the notion of bisimulation used for reasoning on the soundness of our encodings. We also define an equivalence relation for atomic expressions that is useful for reasoning on the behavior of atomic blocks.

4 Bisimulation Semantics

A first phase before obtaining a bisimulation equivalence is to define a Labeled Transition System (LTS) for ATCCS processes related to the reduction semantics.

Labeled Semantics of ATCCS. It is easy to derive labels from the reduction semantics given in Table 2. For instance, a reduction of the form $P;\sigma \rightarrow P';\sigma \uplus \{a\}$ is clearly an *output transition* and we could denote it using the transition $P \xrightarrow{\overline{a}} P'$, meaning that the effect of the transition is to add a message on a to the global state σ. We formalize the notion of label and transition. Besides output actions $\overline{a}$, which corresponds to an application of rule (OUT), we also need *block actions*, which are multisets of the form $\{a_1,\ldots,a_n\}$ corresponding to the commit of an atomic block, that is to the deletion of a bunch of names from the global state in rule (ATOK). Block actions include the usual labels found in LTS for CCS and are used for labeling input and communication transitions: an input action a, which intuitively corresponds to rules (IN) and (REP), is a shorthand for the (singleton) block action $\{a\}$; the silent action τ, which corresponds to rule (COM), is a shorthand for the empty block action $\emptyset$. In the following, we use the symbols $\theta,\gamma,\ldots$ to range over block actions and $\mu,\mu',\ldots$ to range over labels, $\mu ::= \overline{a} \mid \theta \mid \tau \mid a$.

The labeled semantics for ATCCS is the smallest relation $P \xrightarrow{\mu} P'$ satisfying the two following clauses:

1. we have $P \xrightarrow{\overline{a}} P'$ if there is a state σ such that $P;\sigma \rightarrow P';\sigma \uplus \{a\}$;
2. we have $P \xrightarrow{\theta} P'$ if there is a state σ such that $P;\sigma \uplus \theta \rightarrow P';\sigma$.

Note that, in the case of the (derived) action τ, we obtain from clause 2 that $P \xrightarrow{\tau} P'$ if there is a state σ such that $P;\sigma \rightarrow P';\sigma$. As usual, silent actions label transitions that do not modify the environment (in our case the global state) and so are invisible to an outside observer. Unlike CCS, the calculus has more examples of silent transition than mere internal synchronization, e.g. the initiation and evolution of an atomic block, see e.g. rules (ATST) and (ATPASS). Consequently, a suitable (weak) equivalence for ATCCS should not distinguish e.g. the processes `atom(retry)`, `atom(end)`, $(a.\overline{a})$ and $\mathbf{0}$. The same is true with input transitions. For instance, we expect to equate the processes $a.\mathbf{0}$ and `atom(rd`a`.end)`.

Our labeled semantics for ATCCS is not based on a set of transition rules, as it is usually the case. Nonetheless, we can recover an axiomatic presentation of the semantics using the tight correspondence between labeled transitions and reductions characterized by Proposition 1.

Proposition 1. *Consider two processes P and Q. The following implications are true:*

(COM) *if* $P \xrightarrow{a} P'$ *and* $Q \xrightarrow{\overline{a}} Q'$ *then* $P \mid Q \xrightarrow{\tau} P' \mid Q'$;
(PAR) *if* $P \xrightarrow{\mu} P'$ *then* $P \mid Q \xrightarrow{\mu} P' \mid Q$ *and* $Q \mid P \xrightarrow{\mu} Q \mid P'$;

(HID) *if* $P \xrightarrow{\mu} P'$ *and the name* a *does not appear in* μ *then* $P \setminus^n a \xrightarrow{\mu} P' \setminus^n a$;
(HIDOUT) *if* $P \xrightarrow{\overline{a}} P'$ *then* $P \setminus^n a \xrightarrow{\tau} P' \setminus^{n+1} a$;
(HIDAT) *if* $P \xrightarrow{\mu} P'$ *and* $\mu = \theta \uplus \{a^m\}$, *where* a *is a name that does not appear in the label* θ, *then* $P \setminus^{n+m} a \xrightarrow{\theta} P' \setminus^n a$.

Proof. In each case, we have a transition of the form $P \xrightarrow{\mu} P'$. By definition, there are states σ and σ' such that $P;\sigma \rightarrow P';\sigma'$. The property is obtained by a simple induction on this reduction (a case analysis on the last reduction rule is enough). □

We define additional transition relations used in the remainder of the paper. As usual, we denote by $\Rightarrow$ the *weak transition relation*, that is the reflexive and transitive closure of $\xrightarrow{\tau}$. We denote by $\xRightarrow{\mu}$ the relation $\Rightarrow$ if $\mu = \tau$ and $\Rightarrow \xrightarrow{\mu} \Rightarrow$ otherwise. If s is a sequence of labels $\mu_0 \ldots \mu_n$, we denote $\xrightarrow{s}$ the relation such that $P \xrightarrow{s} P'$ if and only if there is a process Q such that $P \xrightarrow{\mu_0} Q$ and $Q \xrightarrow{\mu_1 \ldots \mu_n} P'$ (and $\xrightarrow{s}$ is the identity relation when s is the empty sequence ε). We also define a weak version $\xRightarrow{s}$ of this relation in the same way. Lastly, we denote $\xrightarrow{a^n}$ the relation $\xrightarrow{a} \ldots \xrightarrow{a}$, the composition of n copies of $\xrightarrow{a}$.

Asynchronous Bisimulation for Processes and Expressions. Equipped with a labeled transition system, we can define a weak *asynchronous bisimulation* relation, denoted $\approx_{\mathsf{a}}$, in the style of [2].

Definition 1 (weak asynchronous bisimulation). *A symmetric relation* $\mathcal{R}$ *is a weak asynchronous bisimulation if whenever* $P\mathcal{R}Q$ *then the following holds:*

1. *if* $P \xrightarrow{\overline{a}} P'$ *then there is* Q' *such that* $Q \xRightarrow{\overline{a}} Q'$ *and* $P'\mathcal{R}Q'$;
2. *if* $P \xrightarrow{\theta} P'$ *then there is a process* Q' *and a block action* γ *such that* $Q \xRightarrow{\gamma} Q'$ *and* $(P' \mid \prod_{a \in (\gamma \setminus \theta)} \overline{a}) \,\mathcal{R}\, (Q' \mid \prod_{a \in (\theta \setminus \gamma)} \overline{a})$.

We denote with $\approx_{\mathsf{a}}$ *the largest weak asynchronous bisimulation.*

Assume $P \approx_{\mathsf{a}} Q$ and $P \xrightarrow{\tau} P'$, the (derived) case for silent action entails that there is Q' and θ such that $Q \xRightarrow{\theta} Q'$ and $P' \mid \prod_{a \in \theta} \overline{a} \approx_{\mathsf{a}} Q'$. If θ is the silent action, $\theta = \{\,\}$, we recover the usual condition for bisimulation, that is $Q \Rightarrow Q'$ and $P' \approx_{\mathsf{a}} Q'$. If θ is an input action, $\theta = \{a\}$, we recover the definition of asynchronous bisimulation of [2]. Due to the presence of block actions γ, the definition of $\approx_{\mathsf{a}}$ is slightly more complicated than in [2], but it is also more compact (we only have two cases) and more symmetric. Hence, we expect to be able to reuse known methods and tools for proving the equivalence of ATCCS processes. Another indication that $\approx_{\mathsf{a}}$ is a good choice for reasoning about processes is that it is a congruence.

Theorem 1. *Weak asynchronous bisimulation* $\approx_{\mathsf{a}}$ *is a congruence.*

Proof. It suffices to prove that $\approx_{\mathsf{a}}$ is preserved by every operator of the calculus [1]. □

We need to define a specific equivalence relation to reason on transactions. Indeed, the obvious choice that equates two expressions M and N if $\mathtt{atom}(M) \approx_{\mathsf{a}} \mathtt{atom}(N)$ does not lead to a congruence. For instance, we have $(\mathtt{rd}\,a.\mathtt{wt}\,a.\mathtt{end})$ equivalent to $\mathtt{end}$ while $\mathtt{atom}(\mathtt{rd}\,a.\mathtt{wt}\,a.\mathtt{end}\ \mathtt{orElse}\ \mathtt{wt}\,b.\mathtt{end}) \not\approx_{\mathsf{a}} \mathtt{atom}(\mathtt{end}\ \mathtt{orElse}\ \mathtt{wt}\,b.\mathtt{end})$. The first transaction may output a message on b while the second always end silently.

Table 4. Algebraic Laws of Transactions

Laws for atomic expressions:

(COMM)	$\alpha.\beta.M$	$\simeq$	$\beta.\alpha.M$
(DIST)	$\alpha.(M$ orElse $N)$	$\simeq$	$(\alpha.M)$ orElse $(\alpha.N)$
(ASS)	M_1 orElse $(M_2$ orElse $M_3)$	$\simeq$	$(M_1$ orElse $M_2)$ orElse M_3
(IDEM)	M orElse M	$\simeq$	M
(ABSRT1)	α.retry	$\simeq$	retry
(ABSRT2)	retry orElse M	$\simeq$	$M \simeq M$ orElse retry
(ABSEND)	end orElse M	$\simeq$	end

Laws for processes:

(ASY)	$a.\overline{a}$	$\approx_a$	$\mathbf{0}$
(A-ASY)	atom(rd a.wt a.end)	$\approx_a$	$\mathbf{0}$
(A-1)	atom(rd a.end)	$\approx_a$	$a.\mathbf{0}$

We define an equivalence relation between atomic expressions $\simeq$, and a *weak atomic preorder* $\sqsupseteq$, that relates two expressions if they end (or abort) for the same states. We also ask that equivalent expressions should perform the same changes on the global state when they end. We say that two logs δ, δ' have same effects, denoted $\delta =_\sigma \delta'$ if $\sigma \setminus \mathrm{RD}(\delta) \uplus \mathrm{WT}(\delta) = \sigma \setminus \mathrm{RD}(\delta') \uplus \mathrm{WT}(\delta')$. We say that $M \sqsupseteq_\sigma N$ if and only if either (1) $(N)_{\sigma;\varepsilon} \Rightarrow (\texttt{retry})_{\sigma,\delta}$; or (2) $(N)_{\sigma;\varepsilon} \Rightarrow (\texttt{end})_{\sigma,\delta}$ and $(M)_{\sigma;\varepsilon} \Rightarrow (\texttt{end})_{\sigma;\delta'}$. Similarly, we have $M \simeq_\sigma N$ if and only if either (1) $(M)_{\sigma;\varepsilon} \Rightarrow (\texttt{retry})_{\sigma,\delta}$ and $(N)_{\sigma;\varepsilon} \Rightarrow (\texttt{retry})_{\sigma,\delta'}$; or (2) $(M)_{\sigma;\varepsilon} \Rightarrow (\texttt{end})_{\sigma;\delta}$ and $(N)_{\sigma;\varepsilon} \Rightarrow (\texttt{end})_{\sigma,\delta'}$ with $\delta =_\sigma \delta'$.

Definition 2 (weak atomic equivalence). *Two atomic expressions M, N are equivalent, denoted $M \simeq N$, if and only if $M \simeq_\sigma N$ for every state σ. Similarly, we have $M \sqsupseteq N$ if and only if $M \sqsupseteq_\sigma N$ for every state σ.*

While the definition of $\sqsupseteq$ and $\simeq$ depend on a universal quantification over states, testing the equivalence of two expressions is not expensive. First, we can rely on a monotonicity property of reduction: if $\sigma \subseteq \sigma'$ then for all M the effect of $(M)_{\sigma,\delta}$ is included in those of $(M)_{\sigma',\delta}$. Moreover, we define a normal form for expressions later in this section (see Proposition 2) that greatly simplifies the comparison of expressions. Another indication that $\simeq$ is a good choice of equivalence for atomic expressions is that it is a congruence.

Theorem 2. *Weak atomic equivalence $\simeq$ is a congruence.*

On the Algebraic Structure of Transactions. The equivalence relations $\simeq$ and $\approx_a$ can be used to prove interesting laws of atomic expressions and processes. We list some of these laws in Table 4. Let $\mathcal{M}$ denotes the set of all atomic expressions. The behavioral rules for atomic expressions are particularly interesting since they exhibit a rich algebraic structure for $\mathcal{M}$. For instance, rules (COMM) and (DIST) state that action prefix $\alpha.M$ is a commutative operation that distribute over `orElse`. We also have that $(\mathcal{M}, \texttt{orElse}, \texttt{retry})$ is an idempotent semigroup with left identity `retry`, rules (ASS), (ABSRT2) and (IDEM), and that `end` annihilates $\mathcal{M}$, rule (ABSEND). Most of these laws appear in [17] but are not formally proved.

Actually, we can show that the structure of $\mathcal{M}$ is close to that of a bound join-semilattice. We assume unary function symbols $a()$ and $\overline{a}()$ for every name a (a term $\overline{a}(M)$ is intended to represent a prefix $\texttt{wt}\, a.M$) and use the symbols $\sqcup, \texttt{1}, \texttt{0}$ instead of `orElse`, `end`, `retry`. With this presentation, the behavioral laws for atomic expression are almost those of a semilattice. By definition of $\sqsupseteq$, we have that $M \sqcup M' \simeq M$ if and only if $M \sqsupseteq M'$ and for all M, N we have $\texttt{1} \sqsupseteq M \sqcup N \sqsupseteq M \sqsupseteq \texttt{0}$.

$$\mu(\mu'(M)) \simeq \mu'(\mu(M)) \qquad \mu(M \sqcup N) \simeq \mu(M) \sqcup \mu(N) \qquad \mu(\texttt{0}) \simeq \texttt{0}$$

$$\texttt{0} \sqcup M \simeq M \simeq M \sqcup \texttt{0} \qquad \texttt{1} \sqcup M \simeq \texttt{1}$$

It is possible to prove other behavioral laws to support our interpretation of `orElse` as a join. However some important properties are missing, most notably, while $\sqcup$ is associative, it is not commutative. For instance, $a(\overline{b}(\texttt{1})) \sqcup \texttt{1} \not\simeq \texttt{1}$ while $\texttt{1} \simeq \texttt{1} \sqcup a(\overline{b}(\texttt{1}))$, rule (ABSEND). This observation could help improve the design of the transaction language: it will be interesting to enrich the language so that we obtain a real lattice.

Normal Form for Transactions. Next, we show that it is possible to rearrange an atomic expression (using behavioral laws) to put it into a simple *normal form*. This procedure can be understood as a kind of compilation that transform an expression M into a simpler form.

Informally, an atomic expression M is said to be in *normal form* if it does not contain nested `orElse` (all occurrences are at top level) and if there are no redundant branches. A redundant branch is a sequence of actions that will never be executed. For instance, the read actions in $\texttt{rd}\,a.\texttt{end}$ are included in $\texttt{rd}\,a.\texttt{rd}\,b.\texttt{end}$, then the second branch in the composition $(\texttt{rd}\,a.\texttt{end})$ `orElse` $(\texttt{rd}\,a.\texttt{rd}\,b.\texttt{end})$ is redundant: obviously, if $\texttt{rd}\,a.\texttt{end}$ fails then $\texttt{rd}\,a.\texttt{rd}\,b.\texttt{end}$ cannot succeed. We overload the functions defined on logs and write $\text{RD}(M)$ for the (multiset of) names occurring in read actions in M. We define $\text{WT}(M)$ similarly. In what follows, we abbreviate $(M_1\ \texttt{orElse}\ \ldots\ \texttt{orElse}\ M_n)$ with the expression $\bigsqcup_{i \in 1..n} M_i$. We say that an expression M is in *normal form* if it is of the form $\bigsqcup_{i \in 1..n} K_i$ where for all indexes $i, j \in 1..n$ we have: (1) K_i is a sequence of action prefixes $\alpha_{j_1}.\ldots.\alpha_{j_{n_i}}.\texttt{end}$; and (2) $\text{RD}(K_i) \not\subseteq \text{RD}(K_j)$ for all $i < j$. Condition (1) requires the absence of nested `orElse` and condition (2) prohibits redundant branches (it also means that all branches, but the last one, has a read action).

Proposition 2. *For every expression M there is a normal form M' such that $M \simeq M'$.*

Proof. Laws (COMM), (DIST) and (ASS) in Table 4 can be applied for eliminating nested `orElse`. Next, we use the fact that if K is a redundant branch of M then $M \sqsupseteq K$. □

Our choice of using bisimulation for reasoning about atomic transactions may appear arbitrary. In the long version [1], we study a testing equivalence for ATCCS, more particularly an asynchronous may testing semantics [15].

5 Future and Related Works

There is a long history of works that try to formalize the notions of transactions and atomicity, and a variety of approaches to tackle this problem. We review some of these works that are the most related to ours.

We can list several works that combine ACID transactions with process calculi. Gorrieri et al [16] have modeled concurrent systems with atomic behaviors using an extension of CCS. They use a two-level transition systems (a high and a low level) where high actions are decomposed into atomic sequences of low actions. To enforce isolation, atomic sequences must go into a special invisible state during all their execution. Contrary to our model, this work does not follow an optimistic approach: sequences are executed sequentially, without interleaving with other actions, as though in a critical section. Another related calculus is RCCS, a reversible version of CCS [13,14] based on an earlier notion of process calculus with backtracking [4]. In RCCS, each process has access to a log of its synchronization's history and may always wind back to a previous state. This calculus guarantees the ACD properties of transactions (isolation is meaningless since RCCS do not use a shared memory model). Finally, a framework for specifying the semantics of transactions in an object calculus is given in [23]. The framework is parametrized by the definition of a transactional mechanism and allows the study of multiple models, such as the usual lock-based approach. In this work, STM is close to a model called *versioning semantics*. Like in our approach, this model is based on the use of logs and is characterized by an optimistic approach where log consistency is checked at commit time. Fewer works consider behavioral equivalences for transactions. A foundational work is [6], that gives a theory of transactions specifying atomicity, isolation and durability in the form of an equivalence relation on processes, but it provides no formal proof system.

Linked to the upsurge of works on Web Services (and on long running Web transactions), a larger body of works is concerned with formalizing *compensating transactions*. In this context, each transactive block of actions is associated with a compensation (code) that has to be run if a failure is detected. The purpose of compensation is to undo most of the visible actions that have been performed and, in this case, atomicity, isolation and durability are obviously violated. We give a brief survey of works that formalize compensable processes using process calculi. These works are of two types: (1) *interaction based compensation* [7,8,19], which are extensions of process calculi (like π or join-calculus) for describing transactional choreographies where composition take place dynamically and where each service describes its possible interactions and compensations; (2) *compensable flow composition* [9,11], where ad hoc process algebras are designed from scratch to describe the possible flow of control among services. These calculi are oriented towards the orchestration of services and service failures. This second approach is also followed in [3,5] where two frameworks for composing transactional services are presented.

The study of ATCCS is motivated by our objective to better understand the semantics of the STM model. Obtaining a suitable behavioral equivalence for atomic expression is a progress for the verification of concurrent applications that use STM. However, we can imagine using our calculus for other purposes. An interesting problem is to develop an approach merging atomic and compensating transactions. A first step in this direction is to enrich our language and allow the parallel composition of atomic expressions and the nesting of transactions. We are currently working on this problem. Another area for research stems from our observation (see Section 4) that the algebraic structure of atomic expressions is lacking interesting property. Indeed, it will be interesting to enrich the language of expressions in order to obtain a real lattice. The addition of a symmetric choice operator for atomic expressions may be a solution, but it could introduce unwanted nondeterminism in the evaluation of transactions.

References

1. L. Acciai, M. Boreale and S. Dal Zilio. A Concurrent Calculus with Atomic Transactions (long version). `http://arxiv.org/abs/cs.LO/0610137`.
2. R. Amadio, I. Castellani and D. Sangiorgi. On Bisimulations for the Asynchronous π-Calculus. *Th. Comp. Sci.*, 195(2):291–324, 1998.
3. D. Berardi, D. Calvanese, G. De Giacomo, R. Hull and M. Mecella. Automatic Composition of Transition-Based Web Services with Messaging. In *Proc. of VLDB*, 2005.
4. J.A. Bergstra, A. Ponse and J.J. van Wamel. Process Algebra with Backtracking. In *Proc. of REX Workshop*, LNCS 803, 1994.
5. S. Bhiri, O. Perrin and C. Godart. Ensuring Required Failure Atomicity of Composite Web Services. In *Proc. of WWW*, ACM Press, 2005.
6. A.P. Black, V. Cremet, R. Guerraoui and M. Odersky. An Equational Theory for Transactions. In *Proc. of FSTTCS*, LNCS 2914, 2003.
7. L. Bocchi, C. Laneve and G. Zavattaro. A Calculus for Long Running Transactions. In *Proc. of FMOODS*, LNCS 2884, 2003.
8. R. Bruni, H.C. Melgratti and U. Montanari. Nested Commits for Mobile Calculi: extending Join. In *Proc. of IFIP TCS*, 563–576, 2004.
9. R. Bruni, H.C. Melgratti and U. Montanari. Theoretical Foundations for Compensations in Flow Composition Languages. In *Proc. of POPL*, ACM Press, 209–220, 2005.
10. N. Busi, R. Gorrieri, G. Zavattaro. A Process Algebraic View of Linda Coordination Primitives. *Th. Comp. Sci.*, 192(2):167–199, 1998.
11. M.J. Butler, C. Ferreira and M.Y. Ng. Precise Modeling of Compensating Business Transactions and its Application to BPEL. In *J. UCS*, 11:712–743, 2005.
12. T. Chothia and D. Duggan. Abstractions for Fault-Tolerant Global Computing. *Th. Comp. Sci.*, 322(3):567–613, 2004.
13. V. Danos and J. Krivine. Reversible Communicating System. In *Proc. of CONCUR*, LNCS 3170, 2004.
14. V. Danos and J. Krivine. Transactions in RCCS. In *Proc. of CONCUR*, LNCS 3653, 2005.
15. R. De Nicola and M.C.B. Hennessy. Testing Equivalence for Processes. *Th. Comp. Sci.*, 34:83–133, 1984.
16. R. Gorrieri, S. Marchetti and U. Montanari. A^2CCS: Atomic Actions for CCS. *Th. Comp. Sci.*, 72(2-3):203–223, 1990.
17. T. Harris, S. Marlow, S.P. Jones and M. Herlihy. Composable Memory Transactions. In *Proc. of PPOPP*, ACM Press, 48–60, 2005.
18. M. Herlihy, J.E. Moss. Transactional Memory: Architectural Support for Lock-Free Data Structures In *Proc. of International Symposium on Computer Architecture*, 1993.

19. C. Laneve and G. Zavattaro. Foundations of Web Transactions. In *Proc. of FoSSaCS*, LNCS 3441, 2005.
20. R. Milner. Calculi for Synchrony and Asynchrony. *Th. Comp. Sci.*, 25:267–310, 1983.
21. C. Palamidessi. Comparing the Expressive Power of the Synchronous and the Asynchronous pi-calculus. *Math. Struct. in Comp. Sci.*, 13(5), 2003.
22. N. Shavit and D. Touitou. Software Transactional Memory. In *Proc. of Principles of Distributed Computing*, ACM Press, 1995.
23. J. Vitek, S. Jagannathan, A. Welc and A.L. Hosking. A semantic Framework for Designer Transactions. In *Proc. of ESOP*, LNCS 2986, 2004.

Modal I/O Automata for Interface and Product Line Theories

Kim G. Larsen[1], Ulrik Nyman[1], and Andrzej Wąsowski[1,2]

[1] Department of Computer Science, Aalborg University
[2] Computational Logic and Algorithms Group, IT University of Copenhagen
{kgl,ulrik,wasowski}@cs.aau.dk

Abstract. Alfaro and Henzinger use alternating simulation in a two player game as a refinement for interface automata [1]. We show that interface automata correspond to a subset of modal transition systems of Larsen and Thomsen [2], on which alternating simulation coincides with modal refinement. As a consequence a more expressive interface theory may be built, by a simple generalization from interface automata to modal automata. We define modal I/O automata, an extension of interface automata with modality. Our interface theory that follows can express liveness properties, disallowing trivial implementations of interfaces, a problem that exists for theories build around simulation preorders. In order to further exemplify the usefulness of modal I/O automata, we construct a behavioral variability theory for product line development.

1 Introduction

An interface theory [1,3,4,5,6,7] is a type-system-like theory for component languages, where types (*interfaces*) describe components (*implementations*) with *composition* being the only operator available. A type error proves that either a component does not *conform* to its interface, or that two composed components are *incompatible*. Since the overall structure of these type systems is so simple, it is often accepted not to give typing rules explicitly when describing interface theories (for example [1,3,4,5,6]), focusing instead on the essential ingredients of conformance, compatibility and composition.

Regular, non-component types are only applied to existing objects in program code. In contrast for interface theories it makes sense to discuss interfaces as specifications of application's architecture in isolation from actual source code. An interface abstracts the component in terms of the assumptions made by the component and the guarantees that it provides. One reasons about possible connections between component implementations (*compositions*) by using properties of composition of interfaces; most importantly *independent implementability* (that any implementations conforming to compatible interfaces are compatible) and generality properties (that the composition of interfaces produces an interface with the weakest assumptions and strongest guarantees).

R. De Nicola (Ed.): ESOP 2007, LNCS 4421, pp. 64–79, 2007.

We consider behavioral interface theories suitable for specification of communication protocols between components (web services or embedded systems). Such theories typically require a *contravariant* treatment of inputs and outputs to ensure deadlock-free implementations: inputs guaranteed by the specification are always offered by the implementation and that the implementation never produces more outputs than the specification. This observation led de Alfaro, Henzinger and colleagues [1,3,4] to a conclusion that game theoretical models of interaction are most suitable as building blocks for behavioral interface theories. While we do appreciate the values of the game theoretical formulations, we disagree with some claims in the above cited work and argue that game formulations are insufficient in themselves: there is a genuine value in combining the game theoretical approach with more traditional formulations based on transition systems, or more precisely on modal transition systems.

The two worlds of game models and modal transition systems convey largely orthogonal information about the moves of a system. Game models specify who has *control* over transitions, while modal transition systems focus on requirements, *modality*: which moves are allowed and which are required. In this paper we try to relate the two worlds, explain their weaknesses and their qualities. Eventually we combine them into a unified interface theory.

Game theoretical notions of conformance are often based on alternating simulation [8]. We show that alternating simulation in a two player setting, as used in interface automata [1,9], is just a special case of modal transition systems refinement developed by Larsen and Thomsen [2] in the late eighties. This suggests that the real value of the game theoretic approach to component theories does not lie in the use of alternating simulation, but in the use of *control* information in the composition synthesis algorithms.

Not surprisingly then, modal transition systems themselves cannot be used to build an interface theory, without adding control information. We build a new interface theory around *modal I/O automata,* which combine features of both game theoretic models and modal transition systems. Thanks to this new combination, our interfaces are now able to express liveness properties, which was impossible in existing interface theories (after this work has been completed we have learned about [10], which achieves a similar effect in a different setting).

In order to further demonstrate the usefulness of our modal I/O automata, we construct a *product line* [11,12,13] *theory.* In simple words a product line is a set of similar products built by combining *assets* from a common platform available in the development process. The differences between the products are referred to as *variability.* Our theory is a behavioral formalism for describing the variability of components. The theory supports deciding whether given requirements can be satisfied by choosing concrete instances from the set of available assets. This theory, though very small, is to the best of our knowledge one of the very few attempts at describing software product lines in a behavioral fashion, and unlike the previous work [14], which takes a top-down approach to describing product families, it facilitates a bottom up construction of products, which is how product line development is more typically understood in the software engineering community. This contribution is not meant to be comprehensive, highly developed and well set in the tradition of the product line development. It should be understood as a simple example that emphasizes the semantic difference between modeling components in component based development and modeling assets for product family development. We do hope to extend this theory soon and report about it separately in detail.

The paper proceeds as follows. In the next section we shall explain the main results of the paper in nontechnical terms. Our main results concentrate in sections 3, 5 and 6. In Section 3 we draw a correspondence between the alternating simulation and observational modal refinement. In Section 4 modal I/O automata are defined, which are then used to construct an interface theory in Section 5 and a product line theory in Section 6. Sections 5 and 6 are largely independent, though they share a lot of intuitions. We conclude in Section 7.

2 Interface Automata vs Modal Automata: An Example

Consider an example interface automaton for a *Client* component (Fig. 1 (left), originally presented in [1]). This simple model describes a component that occasionally may want to send a package, and once it has made the request it is ready to receive an acknowledgment. The signature of the interface also mentions a fail input, but the component is never able to receive it. This means that *Client* is only capable of interacting with network links that never fail.

In interface automata, due to a game theoretic semantics, all outputs are controlled by the component itself (called the *Output* player), while all inputs to such components are controlled by the environment player (called the *Input* player). An implementation conforms to the interface iff whenever some input is offered by the interface, then it is also offered by the implementation, and whenever an implementation produces any output, this output is also present in the interface (conformance formalized as alternating simulation [8]).

Such a notion of conformance implies that compatibility can be passed from interfaces to components: if there is no winning strategy for the input player that leads to a deadlock in the interface automaton, then there won't be such a strategy for the same player that interacts directly with any implementation. Similarly if there is no strategy for the output player that leads to an output that cannot be accepted by the environment, then there is also no such strategy for any of the implementations.

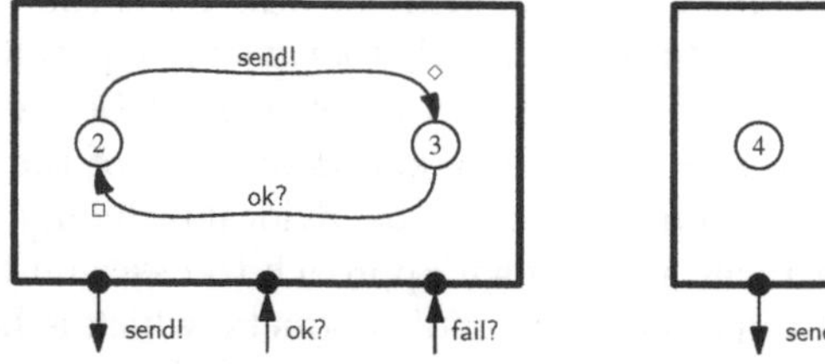

Fig. 1. The *Client* interface (left) and a trivial implementation of it (right)

Unfortunately this notion of conformance, though very much safety oriented, does not enforce that the implementations take on any useful activities at all. Consider for example the diagram on the right side of Fig. 1. It presents a model of an implementation that does not perform any actions ever. In other words this is a network application that does not use the network at all. Still this new model conforms to its interface on the left, as in its initial state it does not add any illegal outputs and it offers all the inputs that were offered by the interface.

If we turn this into the terminology used in modal transition systems it means that all the inputs are *required*, which is indicated by the $\Box$ (must) modality on the corresponding transition, and the outputs are *allowed*, which is indicated by the $\Diamond$ (may) modality on the transitions. In a modal transition systems perspective, conformance is based on modal refinement [2]. This refinement requires that whenever an implementation makes a step, then it must be possible to mimic it by an allowed transition of the specification; whenever the specification makes a required step it must be possible to match it with some required step of the corresponding state in the implementation. With the assignment of *may* to output transitions and *must* to input transitions this sounds nearly like the alternating simulation described above. In Section 3 we prove that indeed the two relations coincide if we require that the may transition relation is input-enabled.

Consequently modality gives strictly more modeling power than alternating refinement. Various modalities can be assigned to actions regardless of whom controls them. Instead of allowing all possible extensions on inputs, as in interface automata, the designer is able to control what extensions are allowed. For example we can change the *Client* model of Fig. 1 to have a must modality ($\Box$) on the *send!* transition, which will have the effect that now all the implementations must be able to proceed producing an output. This would rule out trivial implementations as the one presented on the right side of Fig. 1.

The game theoretic formulation of conformance gives a certain interpretation to inputs and outputs. Namely that inputs are *incoming requests* for service (for example remote procedure calls), while outputs are *outgoing requests* for service (also remote procedure calls, albeit in the other direction). With such an interpretation it becomes clear that removing services from the promised list should be illegal, while removing calls to external services is perfectly fine. This is exactly what alternating simulation achieves. What it misses is a more complex structure of communication.

In asynchronous systems some messages indeed convey calls for service, however many other return feedback from the services (return a value). When a given output models returning a value from a component, then clearly it should never be removed, as then the whole component becomes useless. Fig. 2 illustrates another interface modeling a data link layer, which exploits the interplay between control and modality. The *must* modality is placed on transmt! transitions, as the data link layer would be useless if the implementation was permitted not to forward packets down the stack. Similarly the transition sending back the error message cannot legally be removed. At the same time the call for linkStatus! is a may transition as some implementations are allowed not to consult the hardware

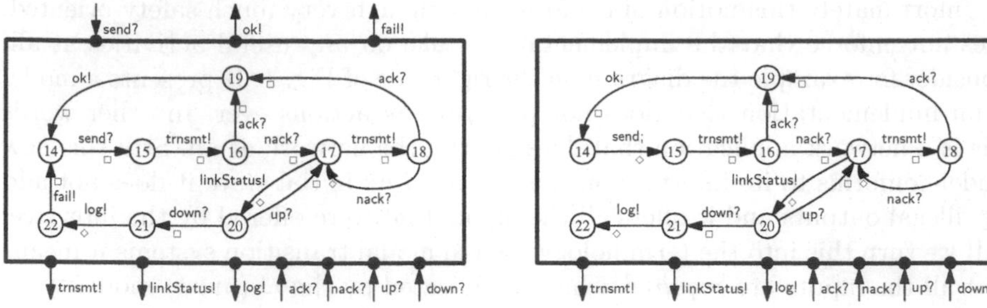

Fig. 2. *DataLink* layer with nontrivial modalities (left). Composition *DataLink* ⊗ *Client* (right). State 22 is an error state, where *DataLink* can produce the fail action, not accepted by *Client*.

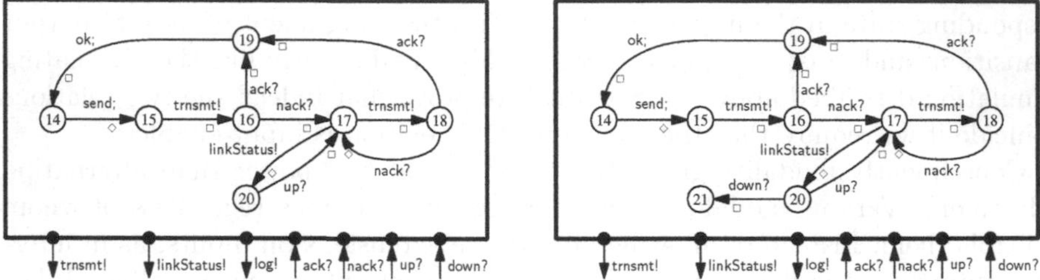

Fig. 3. Composed interfaces *LinkLayer* | *Client* and variability models *LinkLayer* · *Client*

link explicitly to detect errors. Finally not all implementations are forced to be able to work with links that fail twice in a row, which is modeled by the second nack! transition being a may transition.

Now consider how the two interfaces of Fig. 1 (left) and Fig. 2 (left) should be composed. The composition resembles a product computation (taken separately for the may transition relation and the must transition relation). As a result we obtain the interface presented on the right side of Fig. 2. Because the client component was so weak, the ultimate interface shows a system that possibly may never do anything. However if *Client* will send some packets, these packets will certainly be processed by the composition, unless the hardware link is broken. In such a case it might be that the implementation will produce a fail! message which will cause a deadlock with the current version of the *Client* (this can happen when the composition is in state 22). Since we cannot modify the composed system we instead synthesize a new interface which restricts the use of the composition in order to guarantee error freeness. States of the composition that can experience deadlocks are called *error states*. We follow Alfaro and Henzinger in removing error states, and transitively all states from which error states can be reached by following *internally controllable transitions* of the component (outputs and internal actions). This leads to the interface on Fig. 3

(left), expressing the fact that this component works well as long as the physical link never goes down.

The pruning mechanism described above would not be possible without the information describing which transitions are internally controllable being explicitly present in the model. It does not seem possible to compute the safe fragment of the product automaton, by just investigating the modalities of transitions. While we have said that modal refinement is strictly more expressive than alternating simulation, the control information of interface automata has its unique qualities too: it enables valuable synthesis algorithms not otherwise possible.

Let us now revisit the model of Fig. 2 (left) giving it a different interpretation than previously. Instead of perceiving it as an abstraction of a component, we should now see it as a description of a set of components. A modal automaton describes in fact a whole, often infinite, set of possible implementation automata[1]. One can think of them as all possible configurations of the model. This feature of modal automata suggests the possibility of using them as a behavioral formalism in describing variability in product lines.

A product line is a collection of products that are similar in that they offer overlapping functionality, and in that they are built from assets selected from a common platform. In here we want to describe both assets and the whole product line by modal I/O automata. If each of the assets is modeled as a modal I/O automaton we can model the capabilities of the family by composing these descriptions. However this time we would not be interested in a composition that guarantees compatible behavior of any selection of assets. It is normally expected that not all the assets in a product line platform are mutually compatible. Some of them will deadlock (for example a failing link layer and our *Client* component). The requirement for composing the variability descriptions is not to synthesize an interface that guarantees correctness of composition of all possible combination of assets, but to precisely describes what the correct combinations are: i.e. what are the deadlock free behaviors respecting the modalities that can be constructed with the available automata.

It turns out that a composition like that exists and it resembles the pruning of the product automaton for interface automata. The only difference is that now error states are the states where the error must be possible to realize (so one party must be required to produce an output that the other party must not be allowed to receive) and that we prune all the states from which reaching an error state is unavoidable (in our interface theory we have pruned states from which reaching errors might be possible).

The result of composing *Client* and *LinkLayer* using the variability model semantics is presented on the right side of Figure 3. This result contains a slightly bigger model than the interface automaton composition on the left. It states that there exists a pair of assets (implementations of *Client* and *LinkLayer*) such that it is able to accept a link down message without an error message. The transition

[1] This is also true for interface automata, though to a much lesser extent. Due to the lack of modality the set of implementations for an interface automaton is much simpler than it can be for a modal automaton.

with the down message was removed in the interface compositions as, for some pairs of implementations, it would lead to a deadlock.

Can a given specification be implemented by choosing components from available assets? Is the result of the composition the most general possible, containing all possible legal products? Can we find what the configuration of these elements should be? We address some of these questions in section 6, with an intention of elaborating more in upcoming work.

3 Alternating Simulation vs Modal Refinement

Let us begin with defining modal automata, a version of modal transition systems [2] extended with signatures. A modal automaton has two transition relations indicating respectively allowed (*may*) and required (*must*) behavior.

Definition 1 (Modal Automaton). *A modal automaton S is a six tuple: $S = (states_S, start_S, ext_S, int_S, \longrightarrow_\Diamond, \longrightarrow_\Box)$ where $states_S$ is a finite set of states, $start_S \in states_S$ is the initial state, ext_S and int_S are disjoint sets of external and internal actions and $act_S = ext_S \cup int_S$, $\longrightarrow_\Diamond S \subseteq states_S \times act_S \times states_S$ is the may transition relation describing allowed behavior, and $\longrightarrow_\Box S \subseteq states_S \times act_S \times states_S$ is the must transition relation describing required behavior.*

Throughout the paper we sometimes use the symbols "!", "?" and ";" after an action. This is done in order to increase the readers intuition of whether the action is respectively an output, input or internal action. No symbol is used when the action can be of more than one type. These symbols could be left out completely as it is the identity of the action that is significant.

In the following we write $s \xrightarrow{\tau}{}^*_\Box s'$ meaning that there exists a sequence of internal *must* actions leading from s to s'. The same is defined for *may* transitions.

A modal automaton is *syntactically consistent* if everything that is required is also allowed, such that $\longrightarrow_\Box \subseteq \longrightarrow_\Diamond$. In the following we only consider syntactically consistent modal automata. A modal automaton is an *implementation* if the two transition relations coincide.

A modal automaton describes a set of possible implementations. Simplistically when refining a modal automaton specification into an implementation one can remove a *may* transition, that does not have a corresponding *must* transitions or strengthen it into a *must* transition. In general this refinement is not syntactic, but behavioral, so it is not the syntactic transitions that are refined but the actual steps taken by the transition system. The same transition can be refined differently each time it is taken.

Definition 2 (Modal Refinement). *For a pair of modal automata S and T with the same signature, a binary relation $R \subseteq states_S \times states_T$ is a modal refinement if whenever sRt and $a \in act_S$ it holds that*

if $t \xrightarrow{a}_\Box t'$ then $\exists s'. s \xrightarrow{a}_\Box s'$ and $(s', t') \in R$.
if $s \xrightarrow{a}_\Diamond s'$ then $\exists t'. t \xrightarrow{a}_\Diamond t'$ and $(s', t') \in R$.

Modal refinement $\leq_{\mathrm{m}}$ *is defined as the largest such relation. We say that a modal automaton S modally refines a modal automaton T, written* $S \leq_{\mathrm{m}} T$*, iff there exists a modal refinement containing* $(start_S, start_T)$.

Observational modal refinement is a weaker refinement in which the two modal automata can take internal transitions, that cannot be directly observed by the other automaton. In absence of internal actions the observational refinement coincides with the non-observational one.

Definition 3 (Observational Modal Refinement). *For a pair of modal automata S and T with the same signature, a binary relation* $R \subseteq states_S \times states_T$ *is an observational modal refinement if whenever sRt and* $a \in acts_S$ *it holds that*

$$\text{if } t \xrightarrow{a}_{\Box} t' \text{ and } a \in ext_T \text{ then } \exists s'. s \xrightarrow{a}_{\Box} s' \wedge (s', t') \in R.$$
$$\text{if } s \xrightarrow{a}_{\Diamond} s' \text{ and } a \in ext_S \text{ then } \exists t'. t \xrightarrow{\tau}{}^{*}_{\Diamond} t'. \exists t''. t' \xrightarrow{a}_{\Diamond} t'' \wedge (s', t'') \in R.$$
$$\text{if } s \xrightarrow{a}_{\Diamond} s' \text{ and } a \in int_S \text{ then } \exists t'. t \xrightarrow{\tau}{}^{*}_{\Diamond} t'. (s', t') \in R$$

Observational modal refinement $\leq^{*}_{\mathrm{m}}$ *is defined as the largest such relation. We say that a modal automaton S observationally refines a modal automaton T if there exists an observational modal refinement containing* $(start_S, start_T)$.

Interface Automata [1] can be considered a subset of modal automata in which the external actions ext_S are partitioned into inputs in_S and outputs out_S.

Definition 4 (Interface Automaton). *An* interface automaton *P is a tuple* $P = (states_P, start_P, in_P, int_P, out_P, \longrightarrow_P)$ *where* $states_P$ *is a finite set of states,* $start_P \in states_P$ *is the initial state,* in_P*,* out_P *and* int_P *are three pairwise disjoint sets of input, output and hidden (internal) actions respectively, and* $\longrightarrow_P \subseteq states_P \times act_P \times states_P$ *is the set of transitions where* $act_P = in_P \cup out_P \cup int_P$.

We require that the transition relation is input-deterministic such that for all $s, s', s'' \in states_P$ *and all input actions* $a \in in_P$ *if* $s \xrightarrow{a?} s'$ *and* $s \xrightarrow{a?} s''$ *then* $s' = s''$.

Similarly as for Modal Automata we define $s \xrightarrow{\tau}{}^{*} s'$ for Interface Automata to mean that there exists a sequence of internal transitions leading from s to s'. We define *alternating simulation* for interface automata as commonly used in software specification [9], which is slightly less general than the original [1]:

Definition 5 (Alternating Simulation). *For a pair of interface automata S and T with the same signature, a binary relation* $R \subseteq states_S \times states_T$ *is an alternating simulation if whenever sRt and* $a \in acts_S$ *it holds that:*

$$\text{if } t \xrightarrow{a?} t' \text{ and } a \in in_T \text{ then } \exists s'. s \xrightarrow{a?} s' \text{ and } (s', t') \in R$$
$$\text{if } s \xrightarrow{a!} s' \text{ and } a \in out_S \text{ then } \exists t'. t \xrightarrow{\tau}{}^{*} t'. \exists t''. t' \xrightarrow{a} t'' \text{ and } (s, t'') \in R$$
$$\text{if } s \xrightarrow{a;} s' \text{ and } a \in int_S \text{ then } \exists t'. t \xrightarrow{\tau}{}^{*} t' \text{ and } (s', t') \in R$$

Alternating simulation $\leq_{\mathrm{a}}$ *is defined as the largest such relation. We say that S simulates T, written* $S \leq_{\mathrm{a}} T$*, if there exists an alternating simulation containing* $(start_S, start_T)$.

In order to compare interface automata with modal automata, we construct a translation function $\mathcal{T}$ mapping from the former to the latter. The result of the translation always fulfills the conditions listed below. It is easy to see that for modal automata that fulfill these conditions a reversed mapping can be constructed, too.

1. The may transition relation is input enabled, meaning that for each state $s \in states_S$ and each input action $a \in ins_S$ there exists a state s' and a may transition $s \xrightarrow{a?}_{\Diamond} s'$
2. The constructed modal automaton is syntactically consistent: $\longrightarrow_{\Box} \subseteq \longrightarrow_{\Diamond}$
3. Must transitions are only labeled by inputs: $\longrightarrow_{\Box S} \subseteq states_S \times ins_S \times states_S$

Let s_{mayall} be a fresh state that allows all behavior but does not require any behavior. If U denotes the universe of all inputs, such that for all interface automata P, $in_P \in U$, then we define the translation function as follows:

$$\mathcal{T}(states_P, start_P, in_P, out_P, int_P, \rightarrow_P) = (states_S, start_S, ext_S, int_S, \longrightarrow_{\Diamond}, \longrightarrow_{\Box})$$

where $states_S = states_P \cup \{s_{mayall}\}$, $start_S = start_P$, $ext_S = U \cup out_P$, $int_S = int_P$
and $s_1 \xrightarrow{a}{}^{S}_{\Diamond} s_2$ if $s_1 \xrightarrow{a}{}^{P} s_2$ and $a \in out_P \cup int_P$
and $s_3 \xrightarrow{a}{}^{S}_{\Box} s_4$ and $s_3 \xrightarrow{a}{}^{S}_{\Diamond} s_4$ if $s_3 \xrightarrow{a}{}^{P} s_4$ and $a \in in_P$
and $s_3 \xrightarrow{a}{}^{S}_{\Diamond} s_{mayall}$ if $\forall s' \in states_P (s_3, a, s') \notin \longrightarrow^P$ and $a \in U$,
and s_{mayall} is a fresh state such that $\forall a \in act_S . s_{mayall} \xrightarrow{a}{}^{S}_{\Diamond} s_{mayall}$.

Theorem 6. *Alternating simulation and observational modal refinement coincide for interface automata in the following sense:*

$$\textit{for any two interface automata } S, T\text{: } S \leq_{\mathrm{a}} T \textit{ iff } \mathcal{T}(S) \leq^{*}_{\mathrm{m}} \mathcal{T}(T) \qquad (1)$$

Theorem 6 suggests that the usefulness of game theoretical models for component theories does not lie in its conformance relation. The crux is the use of control information in synthesis algorithms, when paths to error states are pruned. If this is the case we can construct an interface theory based on modal refinement and modal automata augmented with control information. Since modal refinement is richer and we can use a generalization of the synthesis algorithm used for interface automata, we will obtain a more expressive interface theory.

The fact that alternating simulation coincides with the *observational* version of modal refinement is expected, because Definition 5 embeds a closure on internal transitions. In fact in the absence of internal actions alternating simulation coincides with the regular modal refinement, as described in Definition 2, which is easy to prove. In order to simplify the developments we use the regular modal refinement ($\leq_{\mathrm{m}}$) from now on, even though most of our theorems can reasonably be considered for the observational refinement ($\leq^{*}_{\mathrm{m}}$), too.

4 Modal I/O Automata

Let us now define modal I/O automata, an extension of modal automata with control information, that will be the main ingredients of our interface theory and the product line theory coming in the next sections.

Definition 7. *A modal I/O automaton S is a tuple $S = (states_S, start_S, ins_S, outs_S, ints_S, \longrightarrow_\Diamond, \longrightarrow_\Box)$, where $states_S$ is a set of states, $start_S \in states_S$ is an initial state, ins_S, $outs_S$ and $ints_S$ are pairwise disjoint sets of inputs, outputs and internal actions respectively ($acts_S = ins_S \cup outs_S \cup ints_S$), $\longrightarrow_\Diamond S \subseteq states_S \times acts_S \times states_S$ is a may-transition relation, and $\longrightarrow_\Box S \subseteq states_S \times acts_S \times states_S$ is a must-transition relation. Like previously we only consider syntactically consistent modal I/O automata here, so $\longrightarrow_\Box \subseteq \longrightarrow_\Diamond$.*

The composition for modal I/O automata combines both the modal aspects and the communications aspects. Two modal I/O automata S_1,S_2 are *composeable* iff their actions only overlap on complementary types: $(ins_{S_1} \cup ints_{S_1}) \cap (ins_{S_2} \cup ints_{S_2}) = \emptyset$ and $(outs_{S_1} \cup ints_{S_1}) \cap (outs_{S_2} \cup ints_{S_2}) = \emptyset$. The composition $S_1 \otimes S_2$ gives rise to a modal I/O automaton S such that $states_S = states_{S_1} \times states_{S_2}$, $start_S = (start_{S_1}, start_{S_2})$, $ins_S = (ins_{S_1} \setminus outs_{S_2}) \cup (ins_{S_2} \setminus outs_{S_1})$, $outs_S = (outs_{S_1} \setminus ins_{S_2}) \cup (outs_{S_2} \setminus ins_{S_1})$, $ints_S = ints_{S_1} \cup ints_{S_2} \cup (ins_{S_1} \cap outs_{S_2}) \cup (outs_{S_1} \cap ins_{S_2})$. The transition relations are given by the following rules (see Fig. 2 for an example):

$$\frac{s_1 \xrightarrow{a!}_\gamma s_1' \quad s_2 \xrightarrow{a?}_\gamma s_2'}{s_1 \otimes s_2 \xrightarrow{a}_\gamma s_1' \otimes s_2'} \ \gamma \in \{\Box, \Diamond\} \qquad \frac{s_1 \xrightarrow{a?}_\gamma s_1' \quad s_2 \xrightarrow{a!}_\gamma s_2'}{s_1 \otimes s_2 \xrightarrow{a}_\gamma s_1' \otimes s_2'} \ \gamma \in \{\Box, \Diamond\}$$

$$\frac{s_1 \xrightarrow{a}_\gamma s_1' \quad a \notin acts_{S_2}}{s_1 \otimes s_2 \xrightarrow{a}_\gamma s_1' \otimes s_2} \ \gamma \in \{\Box, \Diamond\} \qquad \frac{s_2 \xrightarrow{a}_\gamma s_2' \quad a \notin acts_{S_1}}{s_1 \otimes s_2 \xrightarrow{a}_\gamma s_1 \otimes s_2'} \ \gamma \in \{\Box, \Diamond\}$$

For technical reasons (efficiency and simplicity) we always assume that unreachable states are removed after computing a composition (both here and in later sections). The following theorem is a simple corollary from the general fact that the modal refinement is a precongruence [15,16]:

Theorem 8. *Modal refinement is a precongruence with respect to the above composition operator: for any four modal I/O automata T_1, T_2, S_1, S_2 such that $T_1 \leq_m S_1$ and $T_2 \leq_m S_2$ it holds that $T_1 \otimes T_2 \leq_m S_1 \otimes S_2$.*

The composition operator ($\otimes$) defined above corresponds to a usual composition of software (hardware) *components*. Whenever we use it below we mean an unrestricted connection of components, which does not preclude deadlocks or other kinds of errors. We shall soon introduce two seemingly similar composition operators, ($|$) and ($\cdot$) having a very different use. In fact they are algorithms synthesizing *specifications* of how a result of simple composition ($\otimes$) should be used in order to guarantee the absence of certain errors.

5 A Modal Interface Theory

Interface theories support component based development. The aim is to specify component interfaces and from these interfaces to derive the interfaces of composite components. The novel aspect of the interface theory presented here is that the components can specify both required and allowed behavior, consequently it is suitable for expressing liveness properties.

In our specific interface theory an interface is given by a modal I/O automaton. A given interface specifies a set of potential implementations (concrete implementations have identical transition relations $\longrightarrow_\Diamond = \longrightarrow_\Box$). The goal of our interface theory is to be able to use interface descriptions to describe legal implementations of components in a component based system. The implementation relation, the relation that specifies which implementations conform to a given interface description is modal refinement $\leq_{\mathrm{m}}$. From the interface descriptions of two components it should be possible to derive the interface of the combined component. This is done without knowing more about the implementations, than the fact that they conform to their individual interface specification.

The result of composing two interfaces is a subset of the result of composing two modal I/O automata, in which all possible internally controllable paths leading to error states are removed. An *error state* is a state in which one component can output something that the other component might be unable to receive:

$$\begin{aligned} &err^{\mathrm{i}}_{S_1,S_2} = \{(s_1,s_2) \in states_{S_1 \otimes S_2} \mid \text{there exists } a \in int_{S_1 \otimes S_2} \text{ and states } s_1',\, s_2' \\ &\text{such that } (s_1 \xrightarrow{a!}{}^{S_1}_{\Diamond}\, s_1' \text{ and } s_2 \not\xrightarrow{a?}{}^{S_2}_{\Box}) \text{ or } (s_2 \xrightarrow{a!}{}^{S_2}_{\Diamond}\, s_2' \text{ and } s_1 \not\xrightarrow{a?}{}^{S_1}_{\Box})\} \end{aligned} \tag{2}$$

State 22 on Fig. 2 is an error state, witnessed by the fail action.

We are now ready to define the set of states of the composition:

$$states_{S_1|S_2} = \bigcap_{n=0}^{\infty} prune^n_{\mathrm{i}}(states_{S_1 \otimes S_2} \setminus err^{\mathrm{i}}_{S_1,S_2}) \ , \tag{3}$$

where $prune_{\mathrm{i}}(S) = \{s \in S \mid \forall s' \forall a \in int_{S_1 \otimes S_2}.\, s \xrightarrow{a}_{\Diamond} s' \text{ implies } s' \in S\}$, which is a monotonic function that removes, from the set of states S, all those states that in one internally controllable step may reach a state that is not in S.

See Figure 3 (left) for an example of how pruning works. State 22 has been removed as an error state, then state 21 was pruned as an error state can be reached from it by the internally controllable transition log!. Then all transitions involving states 21 and 22 were removed. State 20 remains in the result as the must transition labeled down is externally controllable.

Definition 9 (Composition). *The composition of two interfaces S_1 and S_2 is defined if S_1 and S_2 are composable modal I/O automata and $start_{S_1 \otimes S_2} \in states_{S_1|S_2}$ (see above). The composition results in a modal I/O automaton $S_1|S_2$ such that $S_1|S_2 = (states_{S_1|S_2}, start_{S_1 \otimes S_2}, ins_{S_1 \otimes S_2}, outs_{S_1 \otimes S_2}, int_{S_1 \otimes S_2}, \longrightarrow^{S_1 \otimes S_2}_{\Diamond} \cap (states_{S_1|S_2} \times acts_{S_1 \otimes S_2} \times states_{S_1|S_2}), \longrightarrow^{S_1 \otimes S_2}_{\Box} \cap (states_{S_1|S_2} \times acts_{S_1 \otimes S_2} \times states_{S_1|S_2}))$.*

Two interfaces are compatible if the set of states resulting from composition, $states_{S_1|S_2}$, contains the initial state $(start_{S_1}, start_{S_2})$.

A desirable property of an interface theory is that components can be implemented independently of each other once the specifications are known. The following theorem formally states that this theory satisfies the property.

Theorem 10 (Independent Implementability). *For any two compatible interfaces S_1, S_2 and for any two implementations I_1, I_2, $I_1 \leq_m S_1$ and $I_2 \leq_m S_2$, it holds that $I_1 \otimes I_2 \leq_m S_1|S_2$.*

This has three implications. First, $I_1 \otimes I_2$ would deliver all the required behavior promised by $S_1|S_2$ as long as it interacts with an environment obeying $S_1|S_2$. Second, $I_1 \otimes I_2$ will not do anything that $S_1|S_2$ would not allow in such an environment. Third, since $S_1|S_2$ does not contain error states then $I_1 \otimes I_2$ will not deadlock.

Theorem 11 (Deadlock Freeness Preservation). *For any two compatible interfaces S_1, S_2, any two implementations I_1, I_2, so $I_1 \leq_m S_1$ and $I_2 \leq_m S_2$, and any interface T compatible with $S_1|S_2$, if $T \otimes (S_1|S_2)$ has no reachable error states then $T \otimes (I_1 \otimes I_2)$ has no reachable error states.*

Finally the composition operator ($|$) is commutative and associative up to graph isomorphism.

6 A Product Line Theory

In product line development one typically maintains a family of existing *assets* that are composed in a bottom-up fashion in order to build a product. Here we assume that existing assets are sufficient to build the product and no genuinely new programming is required. Assets are organized in small subfamilies, that can be thought of as configurable components. Choosing an asset from a subfamily is a configuration process. We model subfamilies as modal I/O automata, and call them *variability models*, to distinguish them from interfaces. The configuration process amounts to finding a suitable modal refinement of a variability model.

There is a need for a mechanism for composing variability models, to enable reasoning about the products that can be constructed using available assets. As in the interface theory we are interested in computing the legal uses for the composition of two models, without reaching error states. However we weaken the requirement this time: we do not require that *all* possible pairs of implementations give an error free composition, but only that there *exists* a pair of implementations that can avoid errors under a suitable use.

Two variability models are composable if their input, output and hidden actions do not overlap (the general rule for modal I/O automata). Two composable families can be composed, resulting in a description of a higher level component family. The signature of this variability model is found in the same way as for modal I/O automata. The requirement for the description of this more abstract family is that a specification that refines its description can be realized by choosing some concrete implementations from both lower level families involved. So that in effect one can configure the final product by configuring the abstract composed variability model, being sure that the selected configuration can be refined to configurations of each of the smaller components, available in the collection of assets. We give a sufficient condition for a refinement of a variability model to be decomposable.

The ultimate composition closely resembles the composition ($|$) for interface automata: it uses the regular modal I/O automata composition ($\otimes$) first and then removes error states. However now only internally controllable *required transitions* are pruned, while in the interface theory we had also removed states reachable by *allowed executions* of the same kind. The very existence of allowed internally controlled execution to an error state was considered dangerous in the interface theory—it is not in the product line theory. This is because we are not interested in eliminating errors by all means, but only in making sure that there exist error-free realizations of the specification. For two syntactically composable variability models we define the set of error states, $err^{\mathrm{v}}_{S_1,S_2}$, to be:

$$err^{\mathrm{v}}_{S_1,S_2} = \{(s_1, s_2) \in states_{S_1 \otimes S_2} \mid \text{there exists } a \in ints_{S_1 \otimes S_2} \text{ and states } s_1', s_2' \\ \text{such that } (s_1 \xrightarrow{a!}_{\Box} s_1' \text{ and } s_2 \not\xrightarrow{a?}_{\Diamond}) \text{ or } (s_1 \not\xrightarrow{a?}_{\Diamond} \text{ and } s_2 \xrightarrow{a!}_{\Box} s_2')\} \quad (4)$$

In Figure 2 (right) state 22 is still an error state, though for a different reason than previously: in state 22 the *LinkLayer must* be able to produce fail, but the *Client* is *not allowed* to receive it. If a product of two variability models contains an error state it means that there exist configurations of composed assets that cannot safely work together. However, in the same spirit as in the interface theory, we can compute the set of legal uses that guarantee that there *exist* pairs of compatible configurations to interact with them. We remove from the product $S_1 \otimes S_2$ all the states that according to the variability specification *must* be able to reach an error state. If there is no states left then the two variability models are *incompatible*. Otherwise we arrive at a specification of states and transitions among the compatible states that constraint possible legal implementations obtained from these two families. Formally:

$$states_{S_1 \cdot S_2} = \bigcap_{n=0}^{\infty} prune^n_{\mathrm{v}}(states_{S_1 \otimes S_2} \setminus err^{\mathrm{v}}_{S_1,S_2}) \ , \quad (5)$$

where $prune_{\mathrm{v}}(S) = \{s \in S \mid \forall s'. \forall a \in ints_{S_1 \otimes S_2} \cup outs_{S_1 \otimes S_2}.\ s \xrightarrow{a}_{\Box} s' \text{ and } s' \in S\}$. We compute the two transition relations for the composition, by projecting the transition relations of the parallel composition $S_1 \otimes S_2$ onto the new set of states:

$$\longrightarrow_{\Diamond}^{S_1 \cdot S_2} = \longrightarrow_{\Diamond}^{S_1 \otimes S_2} \cap (states_{S_1 \cdot S_2} \times acts_{S_1 \otimes S_2} \times states_{S_1 \cdot S_2}) \quad (6)$$

$$\longrightarrow_{\Box}^{S_1 \cdot S_2} = \longrightarrow_{\Box}^{S_1 \otimes S_2} \cap (states_{S_1 \cdot S_2} \times acts_{S_1 \otimes S_2} \times states_{S_1 \cdot S_2}) \ . \quad (7)$$

Finally we can state the complete result of the composition: a modal I/O automaton $S_1 \cdot S_2$ such that $S_1 \cdot S_2 = (states_{S_1 \cdot S_2}, (start_{S_1}, start_{S_2}), ins_{S_1 \otimes S_2}, outs_{S_1 \otimes S_2}, ints_{S_1 \otimes S_2}, \longrightarrow_{\Diamond}^{S_1 \cdot S_2}, \longrightarrow_{\Box}^{S_1 \cdot S_2})$ and all the components are defined above.

Definition 12. *Two variability models are compatible if they are composable and their composition is nonempty.*

It turns out that *observationally consistent* refinements of compositions of variability models are realizable with existing assets. We define observational consistency for states of a single automaton. Let $t \xrightarrow{A}_{\Box}{}^{*} t'$ mean that t' is reachable from t via a possible empty sequence of required transitions labeled by possibly different actions from a set A.

Definition 13. *Let T be a modal automaton and let $A \subseteq act_T$ be a set of actions. A relation $C \subseteq states_T \times states_T$ is an observational consistency relation with respect to A if for any pair of states $(t_1, t_2) \in C$ the following two properties hold:*

1. $\forall t_1'.$ *if* $t_1 \xrightarrow{A}{}_{\square}^{*} t_1'$ *then* $\forall a \notin A. \forall t_1''. t_1' \xrightarrow{a}{}_{\square} t_1''$ *implies* $\exists t_2'. t_2 \xrightarrow{a}{}_{\diamond} t_2' \wedge (t_1'', t_2') \in C.$
2. $\forall t_2'.$ *if* $t_2 \xrightarrow{A}{}_{\square}^{*} t_2'$ *then* $\forall a \notin A. \forall t_2''. t_2' \xrightarrow{a}{}_{\square} t_2''$ *implies* $\exists t_1'. t_1 \xrightarrow{a}{}_{\diamond} t_1' \wedge (t_1', t_2'') \in C.$

Two states are observationally consistent if there exists an observational consistency relation relating them. A set of states is said to be observationally consistent with respect to A if all possible pairs of states from the set are observationally consistent with respect to A. An automaton T is observationally consistent with respect to A iff the set $\{start_T\}$ is an observationally consistent set.

The following theorem states the existence of decomposition formally:

Theorem 14 (Decomposability). *Let T_1, T_2 be deterministic composable variability models, and S be a configuration (a deterministic variability model itself) such that $S \leq_{\mathrm{m}} T_1 \cdot T_2$, and T_1, S are observationally consistent with respect to $act_{T_1} \setminus act_{T_2}$ and T_2, S are observationally consistent with respect to $act_{T_2} \setminus act_{T_1}$. Then there exist S_1 and S_2 such that $S_1 \leq_{\mathrm{m}} T_1$ and $S_2 \leq_{\mathrm{m}} T_2$ and $S_1 \otimes S_2 \leq_{\mathrm{m}} S$.*

A version of the theorem, not requiring observational consistency, does not hold, which can be demonstrated with a counter-example, not included here.

An important corollary is that the decomposition can be carried over down to precise configurations: if a concrete configuration of a product is required, then there exist concrete configurations of assets to realize it. The question whether a specification is realizable with given assets is reduced to establishing observational consistency and a modal refinement between the postulated requirement and the variability model. Consequently the abstract variability model can be communicated to configuration engineers and used to configure final products.

Let us close our discussion with a statement that the $(\cdot)$ operator is general enough to describe all implementations safely realizable with existing assets.

Theorem 15 (Completeness). *For any two compatible variability models T_1, T_2 and any two compatible concrete implementation specifications I_1, I_2, where $I_1 \leq_{\mathrm{m}} T_1$ and $I_2 \leq_{\mathrm{m}} T_2$ it holds that $I_1 \cdot I_2 \leq_{\mathrm{m}} T_1 \cdot T_2$.*

7 Conclusion and Future Work

We have investigated the relation between alternating simulation as used in interface automata and observational modal refinement, concluding that former is a case of the latter. We have argued that the strength of the game theoretic approach to interface theories does not lie in alternating refinement itself, but in the labeling of transitions with control information; in partitioning the actions into internally and externally controllable. We have extended modal transition systems with this information and demonstrated that in this way interface theories tracking liveness properties, can be built. Finally we have presented a product line theory describing variability in behavior of component families.

In the future we would like to extend the product line theory of Section 6 to a full featured theory based on observational modal refinement and study its properties in depth. Also it appears interesting to investigate the relation between the general notion of alternating refinement [8] and (modal) transition systems, lifting the restrictions accepted in Section 3 after the interface automata model.

References

1. Alfaro, L., Henzinger, T.A.: Interface automata. In: Proceedings of the Ninth Annual Symposium on Foundations of Software Engineering (FSE), Vienna, Austria, ACM Press (2001) 109–120
2. Larsen, K.G., Thomsen, B.: A modal process logic. In: LICS, IEEE Computer Society (1988)
3. Chakabarti, A., de Alfaro, L., Henzinger, T.A., Stoelinga, M.I.A.: Resource interfaces. In Alur, R., Lee, I., eds.: EMSOFT 03: 3rd Intl. Workshop on Embedded Software. LNCS, Springer (2003)
4. Alfaro, L., Henzinger, T., Stoelinga, M.I.A.: Timed interfaces. In Sangiovanni-Vincentelli, A., Sifakis, J., eds.: EMSOFT 02: 2nd Intl. Workshop on Embedded Software. LNCS, Springer (2002)
5. Larsen, K.G., Nyman, U., Wąsowski, A.: Interface input/output automata. In Misra, J., Nipkow, T., Sekerinski, E., eds.: 14th International Symposium on Formal Methods (FM) Hamilton, Canada, August 21–27, 2006 Proceedings. Volume 4085 of LNCS., Springer (2006) 82–97
6. Černá, I., Vařeková, P., Zimmerová, B.: Component substitutability via equivalencies of component-interaction automata. In: FACS'06. (2006) 115–130 To be published in ENTCS.
7. Hermanns, H., Rehof, J., Stoelinga, M.I.A., eds.: Workshop Procedings FIT 2005: Foundations of Interface Technologies. ENTCS, Elsevier Science Publishers (2005)
8. Alur, R., Henzinger, T.A., Kupferman, O., Vardi, M.: Alternating refinement relations. In Sangiorgi, D., de Simone, R., eds.: Proceedings of the Ninth International Conference on Concurrency Theory (CONCUR'98). Volume 1466 of LNCS., Springer (1998) 163–178
9. Alfaro, L., Henzinger, T.A.: Interface-based design. In: In Engineering Theories of Software Intensive Systems, Marktoberdorf Summer School, Kluwer Academic Publishers (2004)
10. Carrez, C., Fantechi, A., Najm, E.: Assembling components with behavioral contracts. Annales del Télécommunications **60** (2005)
11. Parnas, D.L.: On the design and development of program families. IEEE Transactions on Software Engineering **Vol. SE-2** (1976) 1–9
12. Czarnecki, K., Eisenecker, U.W.: Generative Programming: Methods, Tools, and Applications. Addison-Wesley (2000)

13. Pohl, K., Böckle, G., van der Linden, F.: Software Product Line Engineering—Foundations, Principles, and Techniques. Springer (2005)
14. Larsen, K.G., Larsen, U., Wąsowski, A.: Color-blind specifications for transformations of reactive synchronous programs. In Cerioli, M., ed.: FASE, Edinburgh, April 2005. LNCS, Springer (2005)
15. Boudol, G., Larsen, K.G.: Graphical versus logical specifications. In Arnold, A., ed.: CAAP. Volume 431 of Lecture Notes in Computer Science., Springer (1990) 57–71
16. Larsen, K.G.: Modal specifications. In Sifakis, J., ed.: Automatic Verification Methods for Finite State Systems. Volume 407 of Lecture Notes in Computer Science., Springer (1989) 232–246

Using History Invariants to Verify Observers

K. Rustan M. Leino and Wolfram Schulte

Microsoft Research, Redmond, WA, USA
{leino,schulte}@microsoft.com

Abstract. This paper contributes a technique that expands the set of object invariants that one can reason about in modular verification. The technique uses *history invariants*, two-state invariants that describe the evolution of data values. The technique enables a flexible new way to specify and verify variations of the observer pattern, including iterators. The paper details history invariants and the new kind of object invariants, and proves a soundness theorem.

1 Introduction

The *observer* pattern is an important and common programming idiom [13]. For example, it is a foundation of the model-view-controller paradigm on which all modern graphical user interfaces rely. The observer pattern consists of a *subject* object, which contains some data that may change over time, and a number of *observer* objects. An observer *depends on* the data of the subject in some way. For example, an observer may display the current data values of the subject in a graphical user interface. For efficiency, such an observer may keep a local copy of the data to be displayed, so that it can redraw the display without needing to consult the subject. A variation of the observer pattern is the *iterator* pattern [13], where the subject is a collection and the observers are iterators. An observer may iterate through the items of the collection, providing clients with one data item at a time. These two patterns are different mainly in that the collection does not have references to its iterators. In this paper, we focus on the one-to-many dependency between the subject and observers, which the two patterns have in common, so we will simply refer to both of them as the observer pattern.

To verify the correctness of a program that uses the observer pattern, it is necessary to be able to write specifications for both subject and observers. We are interested in *modular verification* of programs, which allows a program's modules (or classes) to be verified separately. In order for the verification process to be *sound*, the separately verified correctness of each module should imply the correctness of the whole program. For the observer pattern, this means we want to be able to specify and verify the subject separately from the observers.

Verifying the observer pattern is a challenge. The difficulty is that the data consistency of an observer, which is expressed as an *object invariant*, depends on the data of the subject. Updates of the subject and the maintenance of these invariants must therefore be coordinated. The situation is further complicated by the fact that the subject may not be able to reach (through object references in the heap) all the observers, and the observer invariants, let alone the observer classes, may not be available in the separate-verification context of the subject. A partial solution, which works when the observers are known by the subject, has been given by Barnett and Naumann [5].

R. De Nicola (Ed.): ESOP 2007, LNCS 4421, pp. 80–94, 2007.

In this paper, we introduce a specification and verification methodology that is well-suited for supporting the kinds of object invariants one wants to write in observer classes. In a nutshell, the subject advertises how its data values evolve over time, and this allows observers to declare object invariants that depend on the subject's data, provided the object invariants are insensitive to the evolution of the subject. In more detail, our solution consists of the following ingredients:

1. We use *history invariants* to specify how an object may evolve. A history invariant is a reflexive and transitive *two-state predicate* that relates any earlier state to any later state in a program's execution. In our solution, subjects have history invariants.
2. We allow an object invariant of an observer to access the fields of the subject, provided the dereference goes via a field annotated with a new field modifier, **subject**. If an object invariant dereferences a **subject** field, we call it an *observer invariant*.
3. We explicitly keep track of whether an object invariant is known to hold, in which case we say that the object is *consistent*.
4. An observer invariant can be assumed if the observer and its subject are *both* in the consistent state.
5. For the soundness of modular verification, each observer invariant gives rise to an additional proof obligation, which is that it be maintained under the history invariant of the subject.

Our main contributions in this paper are 2, 4, and 5, which together give a methodology to specify and verify observer patterns, including its iterator variation. Ingredient 3 comes from the Boogie methodology, which we explain in Section 2. For ingredient 1, history invariants were introduced by Liskov and Wing [22] under the name of *constraints*, and are supported by the Java Modeling Language (JML) [18]; our paper contributes a formalization of history invariants in the presence of reentrancy and representation objects.

Example. Figure 1 shows our solution to specifying a verifiable observer pattern. An observer's cache depends on the state of the subject. When a subject's state is updated, it notifies all of its observers, so that they can synchronize their caches.

We use a field *vers* (for "version") in both the subject and observers, so that an observer can detect whether it is currently synchronized with the subject. We have found this specification idiom useful for all of our observer-pattern examples, though our methodology does not depend on it. (The *vers* field is in fact used in the implementation of the iterator pattern in both .NET [1] and Java [14], where it is used to detect modifications of the underlying collection when there is still an active iterator.)

Note that between the update of *state* and *vers* in method *Update*, the observer's invariant is broken. Our methodology handles this on account of ingredient 4. At the end of the **expose** block, the observer's invariant holds again, on account of the specification idiom used in the observer invariant.

The program is correct and satisfies the proof obligations of our methodology: the history invariants are admissible, because they are reflexive and transitive; the updates performed by the *Subject* methods are allowed, because they maintain the history invariants; and the observer invariants are admissible, because they are maintained under the subject's history invariants.

```
interface IObserver {
  void Notify();
}

class Subject {
  rep Set⟨peer IObserver⟩ obs;
  int state; int vers;

  history invariant old(vers) ⩽ vers;
  history invariant vers = old(vers) ⇒
      state = old(state);

  Subject()
  { initialize (this) {
      state = 0; vers = 0;
      obs = new Set⟨peer IObserver⟩();
    }
  }

  void Register(IObserver o)
    requires o ≠ null ∧ o.owner = owner;
  { expose (this)
      { obs.Add(o); }
    o.Notify();
  }

  void Update(int y)
  { expose (this)
      { state = y; vers = vers + 1; }
    foreach (IObserver o in obs)
      { o.Notify(); }
  }

  int Get()
    ensures result = state;
  { return state; }
}
```

```
class MyObserver : IObserver {
  readonly subject Subject subj;
  int cache; int vers;

  invariant vers ⩽ subj.vers;
  invariant
    subj ≠ null ∧ subj.vers = vers ⇒
      cache = subj.state;

  MyObserver(Subject s)
    requires s ≠ null;
    ensures owner = s.owner;
  { initialize (this) {
      cache = s.Get(); vers = s.vers;
      sub = s; owner = s.owner;
    }
  }

  void Notify()
  { expose (this) {
      cache = s.Get();
      vers = s.vers;
    }
  }

  void DisplayData()
  { ... }
}

class Program {
  void Main() {
    Subject s = new Subject();
    MyObserver o =
        new MyObserver(s);
    s.Register(o);
    s.Update(57);
  }
}
```

Fig. 1. An example of the observer pattern, where class *Subject* uses objects of type *IObserver* as its observers. Each of the two columns in this figure is a separately verifiable module. The details of the constructs used in this example are explained in the paper. As details that make the verification go through, we have assumed that each object has a reference valued *owner* and a boolean *inv* field. Further, we assumed that the condition $PeerConsistent(x) \land \neg x.owner.inv$ is implicitly added as a postcondition to all constructors (with **this** for x), as a precondition to all methods (with **this** for x), and as a precondition to all constructors and methods (for each reference parameter x). On entry to a constructor body, we also assume that the new object starts off with some arbitrary, unshared, and exposed owner. Finally, we assume that all methods are implicitly allowed to modify the fields of **this** and of any parameter x, and also the fields of the peers of **this** and x.

Outline. In the next section, we describe the foundations of our work, as well as a body of previous work that tackles the problem of specifying and verifying the observer pattern. In Section 3, we define history invariants and their associated proof obligations. In Section 4, we define the additional machinery needed to support observer invariants, culminating in a soundness theorem about them. The paper wraps up with additional examples (Section 5), more related work (Section 6), future work (Section 7), and conclusions (Section 8).

2 Methodologies for Object Invariants

In this section, we review how a modular-verification system deals with objects invariants. We also look at how previous work has tackled the problem of specifying and verifying the observer pattern. In this section and throughout most of the paper, we ignore the issue of subclassing.

Visible-state semantics. The first question to address when designing a methodology for object invariants is: when does the invariant of an object hold? A simple answer is: whenever no constructor or method of the object is active. This simple methodology is called *visible-state semantics* [25,18], because an object's invariant holds in all states visible to public clients of the object.

Because of the possibility of reentrancy in object-oriented programs, we need to be concerned about the situation where an object a breaks its invariant, calls a method on an object b, and then b calls back into some method of a that assumes the invariant to hold. Visible-state semantics prevents this situation by using alias control, as with the *universe type system* [25,26]: a can be used only as a read-only object while the method on b is invoked, restricting b's use of a to read-only methods, and visible-state semantics does not allow read-only methods to rely on the invariant.

Boogie methodology. A richer methodology is the *Boogie methodology* supported by Spec# [4]. The basic Boogie methodology [2] adds a bit inv to every object. If $inv = true$, the object is said to be *consistent*, its invariant holds, and its fields are not allowed to be updated. If $inv = false$, the object is said to be *mutable*, its invariant may be violated, and the fields are allowed to be updated. This guarantees the following *program invariant* (a condition that holds in all reachable states of the program):

$$(\forall\, o \bullet\ o.inv \Rightarrow Inv(o)\,) \tag{1}$$

where, here and throughout, the quantification ranges over non-null, allocated objects and $Inv(o)$ denotes the declared object invariant of o. For the moment, we assume $Inv(o)$ to be an *intra-object invariant*, that is, that it depends only on the fields declared in the class of o.

By mentioning inv explicitly in preconditions, methods can indicate whether or not they expect the object invariant to hold on entry.

The Boogie methodology controls changes to the inv field by introducing two special program statements. The statement **unpack** o changes $o.inv$ from $true$ to $false$, and the statement **pack** o changes $o.inv$ from $false$ to $true$, after first checking that $Inv(o)$ holds. (This check can be done either by static verification or by run-time checking. In this paper, we focus on static verification.)

Use of **unpack** and **pack** is typically stylized, so in this paper we instead use a block statement **initialize** (o) $\{S\}$, which abbreviates:

S; **pack** o

and a block statement **expose** (o) $\{S\}$, which abbreviates:

unpack o; S; **pack** o

The former typically wraps the body of a constructor and the latter wraps the bodies of other methods, as we have seen in Fig. 1.

Owners and representation objects. Going beyond intra-object invariants, we now consider invariants that span several objects. To meet preconditions involving inv, it becomes necessary for an object o to know the state of its *representation objects* (or *rep objects*), that is, the objects that o uses in its implementation. The Boogie methodology lets a class declare a field with the **rep** modifier to say that the field references a rep object (*cf.* [8,6,7,25,10]).

We introduce another field for every object, $owner$, which determines an ownership hierarchy among objects [19]. The $owner$ field points in the inverse direction of **rep** fields; in fact, declaring a field f to be **rep** induces the object invariant:

$$\mathbf{this}.f = \mathbf{null} \lor \mathbf{this}.f.owner = \mathbf{this}$$

The methodology guarantees the following program invariant [2,19]:

$$(\forall\, o \bullet\; o.inv \Rightarrow (\forall\, r \bullet\; r.owner = o \Rightarrow r.inv\,)) \tag{2}$$

To achieve this guarantee, the methodology restricts assignments to $owner$. For our purposes, it suffices to set $owner$ upon creation of objects (see [19] for a treatment of ownership transfer) and to add the following precondition to the **unpack** o statement: $\neg o.owner.inv$.

Using ownership, we can allow object invariants to dereference **rep** fields. That is, if f is a **rep** field, then we can now allow $Inv(o)$ to depend on $o.f.x$ for any field x. Nevertheless, this is not sufficient for the observer pattern: an observer can mention fields of its subject (like $\mathbf{this}.subj.x$) in its object invariant only if $subj$ is a **rep** field, which implies the observer is the unique owner of the subject. Not only does this disallow the existence of more than one observer, but it also seems odd for an observer to consider its subject to be part of its implementation.

Peers. As another possible field modifier, the Boogie methodology allows **peer** [25,19,10]. Declaring a reference-valued field f to be **peer** induces the following object invariant:

$$\mathbf{this}.f = \mathbf{null} \lor \mathbf{this}.owner = \mathbf{this}.f.owner$$

Unlike **rep** fields, **peer** fields are not allowed to be freely dereferenced in object invariants. However, **peer** modifiers lead us to the useful concept of an object o being *peer consistent*, which says that o and all its peers are consistent:

$$PeerConsistent(o) \;=\; (\forall\, p \bullet\; p.owner = o.owner \Rightarrow p.inv\,)$$

A subject and its observers are better suited as peers rather than that one owns the other, because if both use $PeerConsistent(\mathbf{this})$ in their method preconditions, then the subject methods can invoke methods on any observer, and vice versa.

Visibility-based invariants. To specify and verify the observer pattern, we need a methodology that allows us to mention $\mathbf{this}.subj.x$ in the invariant of observers, where $subj$ is a field that references the subject object and x is a field of the subject. This is allowed under the two restrictions of *scope visibility* [19].

The first restriction of scope visibility says that an observer can mention $\mathbf{this}.subj.x$ in its invariant if the invariant is visible to every verification context that can contain an update of the x field. This works out fine for the iterator pattern, but forbids the development of observer classes separate from the development of the subject class.

The second restriction is that updating a subject's field $s.x$ requires not only that the subject s be in the mutable state ($inv = false$), but also that every observer o for which $o.subj = s$ be in the mutable state. This restriction is hard to live with if the number of such observers o is unbounded. It is especially hard to live with if the observers are not reachable from the subject, which is the case in the iterator pattern.

Update guards. Barnett and Naumann relax the second restriction for visibility-based invariants [5]. Instead of requiring observers whose invariants mention $\mathbf{this}.subj.x$ to be in the mutable state when x is updated, Barnett and Naumann propose checking that the imminent update of x maintains the actual invariant of these observers. To provide some way to abstract over an observer's invariant, they also introduce the declaration of an *update guard* in the observer classes. The update guard is a condition on the update of the subject's x field that is sufficient to maintain the observer's invariant. The update guard is declared as a two-state predicate. For example, an update guard

$$\mathbf{this}.subj.x : \quad \mathbf{old}(\mathbf{this}.subj.x) \leqslant \mathbf{this}.subj.x$$

says that increasing the subject's x field maintains the observer's invariant.

Update guards can be used to specify the observer pattern, as long as the first restriction for visibility-based invariants holds: observer classes must be visible to the subject when it is verified.

Monotonicity. Another situation where we can allow an object invariant to mention $\mathbf{this}.f.x$ is when x is a read-only field. This situation is almost like for intra-object invariants, because if x is immutable, then the only way to change the value of $\mathbf{this}.f.x$ is to change $\mathbf{this}.f$. Immutability is a special case of monotonicity. If the value of a field x only changes monotonically, by some metric, then it is unproblematic to allow an invariant $Inv(o)$ to mention $o.f.x$, provided $Inv(o)$ is maintained under such monotonic changes (*cf.* [11]). Monotonicity conditions can be specified as reflexive and transitive history invariants, which is in fact what we do.

Our solution. Let us briefly compare our solution to the previous work we have discussed in this section. Rather than declaring update guards in the observer classes, which requires these observer classes to be known when the subject's data are updated, we propose declaring *in the subject class* how the subject's data may evolve. This means that the subject need not be aware of how many observers and observer classes there are—such an observer is allowed to declare an invariant that *depends on* the subject's data, provided the invariant has the property that it is automatically maintained when the subject's data evolve as advertised.

3 History Invariants

History invariants (or *constraints*, as Liskov and Wing called them [22]) are two-state predicates. In this section, we first discuss intra-object history invariants in the context of a visible-state semantics, and then look into inter-object history invariants in the context of the Boogie methodology.

Visible-state semantics. In the visible-state semantics, an object invariant for object o is a property that should hold of all visible states of o. A history invariant for o is a property that should hold for any earlier-later pair of visible states of o. History invariants can therefore be used to constrain the way that values change over time.

The history invariant in the following example says that the value of *size* will only ever increase:

```
class Histogram⟨K⟩ {                          Histogram(int size)
  int size;                                     requires 0 ⩽ size;  {...}
  invariant 0 ⩽ size;
  history invariant old(size) ⩽ size;        void Resize(int size)
  ...                                           requires this.size ⩽ size;
                                             ...
```

Let's see how the *Histogram* class maintains its history invariant. The object's first visible state is defined at the time the *Histogram* constructor finishes. Different, subsequent visible states can be created only by mutating methods, like *Resize*. The pre- and post-states of *Resize* are visible states. Consequently, a visible-state semantics for *Histogram* has to guarantee that the history invariant for **this** also holds between pre- and post-states of *Resize*.

For visible-state semantics, history invariants are thus added as proof obligations to post-conditions of public methods. But note that their verification only guarantees that each pair of method pre- and post-states obeys the history invariant. However, history invariants for an object o have to hold between any two visible states that result from a computation on o. By requiring history invariants to be reflexive and transitive, we guarantee that the history invariant holds between any earlier and later visible states.

Boogie methodology. We now describe how to incorporate history invariants into the Boogie methodology. Continuing our example, we could implement the *Histogram* class using a **rep** field of type *Hashtable*, where we assume that the class *Hashtable* has a *size* field:

```
class Histogram⟨K⟩ {                Histogram(int size)
  rep Hashtable⟨K, int⟩ ht;           requires 0 ⩽ size;  {...}
  invariant 0 ⩽ ht.size;
  history invariant                 Resize(int size)
    old(ht.size) ⩽ ht.size;           requires ht.size ⩽ size;
  ...                               ...
```

In the visible-state semantics above, a history invariant of an object holds for pairs of its visible states. In the Boogie methodology, a history invariant of an object holds for pairs of its consistent states.

In the following formulas, we adorn state-dependent predicates with stores as indices. One-state predicates have one state, two-state predicates have two states as indices, *i.e.*, $q_{\sigma,\tau}$ denotes q evaluated in the two states σ, τ where **old** expressions in q refer to state σ and the non-old expressions refer to state τ. We use $Hist(o)$ to denote the declared history invariant of o; $[Hist(o)]_{\sigma,\tau}$ is $Hist(o)$ evaluated in the two states σ, τ. We use $\sigma \leqslant \tau$ to denote that state σ occurs earlier than state τ in a program run.

For the rest of the paper, we only allow ownership-based invariants with **rep** fields. These give rise to the program invariants (1) and (2). The methodology extended with history invariants also needs to establish the following program invariant:

$$(\forall\, o, \sigma, \tau \bullet\ \sigma \leqslant \tau \wedge [o.inv]_\sigma \wedge [o.inv]_\tau \Rightarrow [Hist(o)]_{\sigma,\tau}) \qquad (3)$$

This important condition says that if σ and τ are two states that occur in that execution order and $o.inv$ holds in both of those states, then the history invariant for o relates those two states.

We define a history invariant to be *admissible* if (a) it is reflexive, (b) it is transitive, and (c) it depends only on the fields of **this** and the fields of transitive rep objects of **this**. While property (c) is just a syntactical check, properties (a) and (b) give rise to the proof obligations:

$$(\forall\, o, \sigma \bullet\ [Hist(o)]_{\sigma,\sigma}) \qquad (4)$$

$$(\forall\, o, \sigma, \tau, \upsilon \bullet\ [Hist(o)]_{\sigma,\tau} \wedge [Hist(o)]_{\tau,\upsilon} \Rightarrow [Hist(o)]_{\sigma,\upsilon}) \qquad (5)$$

which are checked by a theorem prover.

In addition to the proof obligations stemming from admissibility, a history invariant also needs to be verified at various points in the program. Since the Boogie methodology enforces that a field $t.f$ can be changed only if t and all its transitive owners are mutable, the only way to violate the condition (3) in a program is when an object o changes (in τ) from mutable to consistent and there was a previous time (namely σ) when o was consistent. Therefore, we check history invariants at the end of **expose** blocks. That is, we redefine **expose** (o) $\{S\}$ to stand for:

let $\rho = \sigma$ in **unpack** o; S; **assert** $[Hist(o)]_{\rho,\sigma}$; **pack** o

where we use σ to denote the current program state.

We can now prove that our methodology for history invariants is *sound*, that is, that (3) follows from the admissibility checks and the added check in the **expose** statement.

Proof (3). Consider the (possibly infinite) sequence of states in any execution of the program, and consider a particular object o. Consider any two states σ and τ in this sequence, such that $o.inv$ holds in both of those states. The proof now proceeds by induction over the length of the sequence from σ to τ. We consider four cases.

- If σ and τ are the same state, then $[Hist(o)]_{\sigma,\tau}$ follows directly from reflexivity (4).
- If σ and τ are different states and there is some intervening state ρ in which $o.inv$ also holds, then by the induction hypothesis on the two shorter sequences, $[Hist(o)]_{\sigma,\rho}$ and $[Hist(o)]_{\rho,\tau}$ hold, so $[Hist(o)]_{\sigma,\tau}$ holds by transitivity (5).

– If σ and τ are consecutive states, then σ and τ bracket some primitive statement. We argue that this primitive statement does not affect any field $x.f$, where x is o or a transitive rep object of o, because the methodology allows a field update of $x.f$ only if x and its transitive owners are mutable (see (1) and (2)).
– If σ and τ are different, non-consecutive states and they have no intervening state in which $o.inv$ holds, then σ and τ bracket the execution of an **expose** (o) statement. The added check in the **expose** statement guarantees that $[\mathit{Hist}(o)]_{\sigma,\tau}$ holds. □

4 Observer Invariants

Object invariants of observers often depend on the stability of subjects. A prime example for this dependency is given by the observer pattern, as implemented in Figure 1. Its observer invariant says: if the version of the observer coincides with the version of the collection, then the cache of the state of the observer coincides with the state held in the subject. This property can now be used, for example, by the observer's *DisplayData* method: without reading the subject's entire state, it can now guarantee that it displays the current value of the subject, provided the versions of subject and observer still agree.

Observers make the dependency on their subject explicit by annotating a field with the **subject** modifier. Declaring a field *subj* to be **subject** induces the object invariant:

$$\mathbf{this}.subj = \mathbf{null} \lor \mathbf{this}.subj.owner = \mathbf{this}.owner$$

This is the same as the object invariant induced by **peer** fields, but **subject** fields will be used differently in defining the admissibility condition for object invariants.

We define an object invariant to be *admissible* if (a) it depends only on fields of **this**, fields of transitive rep objects of **this** (that is, fields like $\mathbf{this}.f_0.f_1.\cdots.x$ where the f_i are **rep** fields), and fields of subject objects of **this** (that is, fields like $\mathbf{this}.subj.x$, where *subj* is a **subject** field), and (b) it is stable under the history invariant of any subject object dereferenced in the invariant. While property (a) is just a syntactic check, property (b) gives rise to the following proof obligation, for every **subject** field *subj* that is dereferenced in the invariant:

$$\begin{array}{l}(\forall\, o,\sigma,\tau \bullet \\ \quad \sigma \leqslant \tau \land [o.inv]_\sigma \land (\forall f \bullet [o.f]_\sigma = [o.f]_\tau\ ) \land \\ \quad [o.subj.inv]_\sigma \land [o.subj.inv]_\tau \land [\mathit{Hist}(o.subj)]_{\sigma,\tau} \\ \quad \Rightarrow [\mathit{Inv}(o)]_\tau\ )\end{array} \tag{6}$$

This condition is checked by the theorem prover.

In the presence of **subject** fields, the object invariant doesn't necessarily hold when the object is consistent (as we saw at the program point between the updates of *state* and *vers* in method *Update* in Fig. 1). However, it does hold if the object's subject objects are consistent as well. So, in our methodology, the program invariant (1) is replaced by the following program invariant:

$$\begin{array}{l}(\forall\, o \bullet\ o.inv \land \\ \quad (\forall\, \mathbf{subject}\ \text{field}\ f\ \text{of}\ o\ \text{dereferenced in}\ \mathit{Inv}(o) \bullet\ o.f = \mathbf{null} \lor o.f.inv\ ) \\ \quad\quad \Rightarrow \mathit{Inv}(o)\ )\end{array} \tag{7}$$

(To receive the benefit of a stronger program invariant, one can think of $\mathit{Inv}(o)$ as denoting just one conjunct of the object invariant, which reduces the number of f's that the antecedent says need to be consistent, and then repeat the program invariant for each conjunct of the object invariant.)

In order for (7) to hold, we need to add an additional check as part of the **pack** statement, namely: for every subject field f of o, **pack** (o) also imposes the precondition $o.f = \mathbf{null} \vee o.f.inv$.

We can now prove that our revised methodology is *sound*, that is, that (7) follows from the admissibility checks and the added preconditions of the **pack** statement. For brevity, we will give the proof for an object invariant $Inv(o)$ that mentions exactly one **subject** field, $subj$.

Proof (7). The proof runs by induction over the sequence of states in any execution of the program. The induction base is trivial: Program execution starts in a state where no objects are allocated. In the induction step, we consider the different ways in which a state change could violate (7):

case o is allocated: A newly allocated object o start with $\neg o.inv$.
case a heap location $t.x$ that is referred to by a term $o.f_0.f_1.\cdots.x$ in $Inv(o)$ is changed: According to the methodology, a field $t.x$ is allowed to be updated only if t and its transitive owners are mutable, so $\neg o.inv$.
case $o.inv$ is changed from *false* to *true* (which happens in **pack** (o)): The precondition of the pack statement checks that $Inv(o)$ holds.
case $o.inv$ holds and $s.inv$ is changed from *false* to *true* (which happens in **pack** (s)), for an s such that $o.subj = s$: We distinguish two cases:

- If this **pack** (s) was part of an **initialize** (s), then $\neg s.inv$ always held before this time. But since $o.inv$ holds, there must have been an earlier **pack** (o), $o.subj$ would have been unchanged since the most recent such **pack** (o), and that **pack** (o) would have checked that $o.subj.inv$ held. So this case does not exist.
- If this **pack** (s) was part of an **expose** (s), then let σ denote the state immediately before the **expose** (s) and let τ denote the state immediately after $s.inv$ has been set to true, *i.e.*, after the **pack** (s). Due to the block structure of expose statements, we know that the condition $\neg s.inv$ is stable throughout the execution after state σ and before state τ. Moreover, $o.inv$ is stable between these states, because any change to $o.inv$ would mean there was a **pack** (o) inside the **expose** (s), and that **pack** (o) would have checked $s.inv$, which doesn't hold. Because $o.inv$ is stable, then so is $o.f$ for every field f of o. In summary, we now have:

$$\sigma \leqslant \tau \wedge [o.inv]_\sigma \wedge (\forall f \bullet \ [o.f]_\sigma = [o.f]_\tau\ ) \wedge \\ [o.subj.inv]_\sigma \wedge [o.subj.inv]_\tau$$

By the last two conjuncts and (3), we also have $[Hist(o.subj)]_{\sigma,\tau}$. Altogether, we then have the antecedent of (6), from which we conclude $[Inv(o)]_\tau$. □

5 Further Examples

We show two more examples of how to use history invariants to prove observer patterns.

Collection Iterator Pattern [13]. Figure 2 shows an application of our methodology to the class of a *Collection* (the subject) and its associated class of *Iterator* objects

```
class Collection⟨T⟩ {
  rep T[] elems;
  int ct; int vers;

  invariant elems ≠ null ∧
    0 ⩽ ct ⩽ elems.Length;
  history invariant
    old(vers) ⩽ vers;
  history invariant
    vers = old(vers) ⇒
      ct = old(ct) ∧
      elems[0 : ct] = old(elems[0 : ct]);

  Collection(int capacity)
    requires 0 ⩽ capacity;
  { initialize (this) {
      elems = new T[capacity];
      ct = 0; vers = 0;
    }
  }

  void Add(T t)
  { expose (this) {
      if (ct = elems.Length) { ... }
      elems[ct] = t;
      ct++; vers++;
    }
  }

  T Remove(int i)
    requires 0 ⩽ i < ct;
  { T t = elems[i];
    expose (this) {
      elems[i: ct − 1] = elems[i + 1: ct];
      ct−−; vers++;
    }
    return t;
  }
}
```

```
class Iterator⟨T⟩ {
  readonly subject Collection⟨T⟩ coll;
  readonly int vers;
  int n; bool inRange;

  invariant coll ≠ null ∧
    −1 ⩽ n ∧ vers ⩽ coll.vers;
  invariant
    vers = coll.vers ⇒
      inRange = (0 ⩽ n < coll.ct);

  Iterator(Collection⟨T⟩ c)
    requires c ≠ null;
    ensures owner = c.owner;
  { initialize (this) {
      coll = c; vers = c.vers;
      n = −1; inRange = false;
      owner = c.owner;
    }
  }

  bool MoveNext()
    requires vers = coll.vers
      otherwise InvalidOperation;
    ensures result = inRange;
  { expose (this) {
      if (n < coll.ct) { n++; }
      inRange = n < coll.ct;
    }
    return inRange;
  }

  T Current()
    requires vers = coll.vers
      otherwise InvalidOperation;
    requires inRange;
  { return coll.elems[n]; }
}
```

Fig. 2. Class *Collection*$\langle T \rangle$ represents a list of items of type T that can be retrieved by an *Iterator*$\langle T \rangle$. These classes exhibit a variation of the observer pattern and their specifications are handled by our methodology.

(the observers). Each *Collection* object contains a *vers* field that is increased with each update of the collection. The iterator's methods require as a precondition that the versions of the iterator and collection match up. If they don't match up, the caller is in error, a situation that is caught when trying to statically verify the caller.

```
class Master {
  int tm;  int vers;

  invariant 0 ⩽ tm;
  history invariant old(vers) ⩽ vers;
  history invariant vers = old(vers) ⇒
      old(tm) ⩽ tm;

  Master()
    ensures tm = 0 ∧ vers = 0;
  { initialize (this)
        { tm = 0;  vers = 0; }
  }

  void Tick(int n)
    requires 0 ⩽ n;
    ensures old(tm) ⩽ tm;
  { expose (this)
        { tm = tm + n; }
  }

  void Reset()
    ensures tm = 0;
  { expose (this)
        { vers = vers + 1;  tm = 0; }
  }
}
```

```
class Clock {
  readonly subject Master ms;
  int tm;  int vers;

  invariant ms ≠ null ∧ 0 ⩽ tm;
  invariant vers ⩽ ms.vers;
  invariant vers = ms.vers ⇒
        tm ⩽ ms.tm;

  Clock(Master m)
    requires m ≠ null;
    ensures owner = m.owner;
  { initialize (this) {
        ms = m;  Synch();
        owner = m.owner;
    }
  }

  private void Synch()
  { tm = ms.tm;  vers = ms.vers; }

  int GetTime()
    ensures 0 ⩽ result ⩽ ms.tm;
  { if (vers ≠ ms.vers)
        { expose (this) { Synch(); } }
    return tm;
  }
}
```

Fig. 3. Our rendition of Barnett and Naumann's master and slave clock example [5]. For verification, we assume the private method *Synch* to be inlined at its call sites.

For compatibility with existing non-verified clients, the iterator methods will throw an *InvalidOperation* exception in case the *Iterator* client is in error.

Note that the observer invariant is necessary for verifying the definedness of the method *Current*: The implicit precondition says that the iterator is peer consistent. The collection is a peer of the iterator, since *coll* is declared with `subject`, so peer consistency of the iterator implies peer consistency of the collection. Because the iterator and collection are both consistent, the observer invariant can be assumed on entry to *Current*. Together with the explicit preconditions of the method, we conclude that the array index n in *Current*'s implementation is in range.

Master and Slave Clocks [5]. A master clock has two timer functions, *Tick*, which increases the time, and *Reset*, which resets the time to zero. A slave clock's time never exceeds its master's time. Slaves have a *GetTime* method that returns the time at which the slave clock most recently synchronized its time with the master. The number of necessary synchronizations of a slave clock with a master clock should be minimal. This means that as long as *Tick* is called on the master, a slave doesn't have to synchronize.

But as soon as the master's clock is reset, a slave's clock must be synchronized to fulfill its contract. Figure 3 shows our solution.

6 Related Work

Automated program verification has a long history, *cf.* [23]. Only much more recently did it become feasible to do large-scale automatic reasoning as automatic theorem provers made great progress and are now optimized for proving software checking (*e.g.*, [9]), verification-condition generation became optimized for those theorem provers (*e.g.*, [12]), and programming methodology progressed (*e.g.*, [2,19,5,15]).

History invariants were introduced by Liskov and Wing [22] to constrain the behavior of possible subtypes. Their paper did not explore the possibility of using them for verifying object invariants. History invariants are also supported by the Java Modeling Language (JML) [18], which uses visible-state semantics. To the best of our knowledge, static verification tools for JML do not yet support history invariants.

Our use of history invariants is similar to Rely/Guarantee style reasoning as introduced by Jones [16]. It enables a compositional reasoning about concurrent programs. Rely/Guarantee conditions are also two-state predicates. In our setting, Rely/Guarantee conditions would mean that a subject guarantees the stability of a property on which the invariants of the observers rely.

Verifying observers is a form of verifying heap properties. This area has recently gotten a lot of attention (*e.g.*, [21]). In the sequel, we focus only on traditional program verification work for modern languages.

Another approach to specifying the update-notify idiom of the observer pattern is proposed by Middelkoop *et al.* [24]. They use a mix between the visible-state semantics and the Boogie methodology where all objects are consistent on method boundaries unless explicitly stated otherwise. The approach does not yet address representation objects.

Inspector methods [15] are pure methods that can depend on owned state. They elegantly address the existing data abstraction problem in ownership systems, but do not help in verifying observers independent from subjects.

Kassios's dynamic frames [17] abstractly specify the effect of mutator methods using abstraction functions and dependency relations (and without needing a built-in ownership system). The work is formulated in the context of an idealized logical framework; it was not developed to address maintaining observer invariants, but rather to delineate change. We look forward to seeing an implementation of the approach in an automatic program verifier.

Like observers and subjects, the classes of a program can depend on each other in a one-to-many way. For example, many classes depend on the *String* class. A different approach exists for handling this situation [20].

An important recent strand in verifying heap structures is separation logic [27]. It is an extension of Hoare logic for programs that use pointers or references into a heap. However, its assertion language is not first order; instead, it uses a powerful spatial conjunction that is integral for partitioning the heap. While proof system for separation logic have been started, they are still somewhat primitive and tool support is not yet there for a full object-oriented language.

7 Future Work

We are currently investigating the best way to incorporate history invariants into Spec# [4] and the Boogie program verifier [3]. We want to further develop the presented methodology to support subtyping, which we believe to be an orthogonal issue, just like in the basic Boogie methodology [2]. With subtyping, one might have a situation where a subclass acts like an observer to a field declared in a superclass. Another area of interest is to understand how the verification of history invariants fits in with other methodologies, like monotonic type states [11] and visibility-based invariants. Last but not least, we want to explore whether history invariants can be used to verify more design patterns, like invariants over static fields.

8 Conclusion

This paper extends the limits of sound modular verification for inter-object invariants. In most previous approaches for one-to-many dependencies, all classes had to be developed together. Our approach allows one object (the subject) to export a history invariant, which other objects (the observers) can depend on. A history invariant typically describes some stability of the subject's state space. Introducing those properties has two benefits: it allows observers to make their validity dependent on the stability of the subject, and subjects do not have to know anything about the existence of observers. This fosters modular development and verification.

Acknowledgments. We are grateful to the anonymous referees for their thoughtful and helpful suggestions.

References

1. Brad Abrams. *.NET Framework Standard Library Annotated Reference, Volume 1*. Addison Wesley Longman Publishing, 2004.
2. Mike Barnett, Robert DeLine, Manuel Fähndrich, K. Rustan M. Leino, and Wolfram Schulte. Verification of object-oriented programs with invariants. *JOT*, volume 3, number 6, pages 27–56, 2004.
3. Mike Barnett, Robert DeLine, Bart Jacobs, Bor-Yuh Evan Chang, and K. Rustan M. Leino. Boogie: A modular reusable verifier for object-oriented programs. In *FMCO 2005*, volume 4111 of *LNCS*, pages 364–387. Springer, September 2006.
4. Mike Barnett, K. Rustan M. Leino, and Wolfram Schulte. The Spec# programming system: An overview. In *CASSIS 2004*, volume 3362 of *LNCS*, pages 49–69. Springer, 2005.
5. Mike Barnett and David A. Naumann. Friends need a bit more: Maintaining invariants over shared state. In *MPC 2004*, LNCS, pages 54–84. Springer, July 2004.
6. Chandrasekhar Boyapati, Robert Lee, and Martin C. Rinard. Ownership types for safe programming: Preventing data races and deadlocks. In *OOPSLA 2002*, volume 37, number 11 in *SIGPLAN Notices*, pages 211–230. ACM, November 2002.
7. Dave G. Clarke and Sophia Drossopoulou. Ownership, encapsulation and the disjointness of type and effect. In *OOPSLA 2002*, volume 37, number 11 in *SIGPLAN Notices*, pages 292–310. ACM, November 2002.

8. Dave G. Clarke, John. M. Potter, and James Noble. Ownership types for flexible alias protection. In *OOPSLA '98*, volume 33, number 10 in *SIGPLAN Notices*, pages 48–64. ACM, October 1998.
9. David Detlefs, Greg Nelson, and James B. Saxe. Simplify: A theorem prover for program checking. Technical Report HPL-2003-148, HP Labs, July 2003.
10. Werner Dietl, Sophia Drossopoulou, and Peter Müller. Generic universe types. In *FOOL/WOOD '07*. ACM SIGPLAN, January 2007. 13 pages.
11. Manuel Fähndrich and K. Rustan M. Leino. Heap monotonic typestates. In *Proceedings of International Workshop on Aliasing, Confinement and Ownership in object-oriented programming (IWACO)*, July 2003.
12. Cormac Flanagan and James B. Saxe. Avoiding exponential explosion: Generating compact verification conditions. In *POPL 2001*, pages 193–205. ACM, January 2001.
13. Erich Gamma, Richard Helm, Ralph Johnson, and John Vlissides. *Design Patterns*. Addison-Wesley Professional, January 1995.
14. James Gosling, Bill Joy, and Guy Steele. *The Java™ Language Specification*. Addison-Wesley, 1996.
15. Bart Jacobs and Frank Piessens. Verification of programs with inspector methods. In *FTfJP 2006*, July 2006.
16. Cliff B. Jones. Development methods for computer programs including a notion of interference. Technical report, Oxford University, PhD thesis, 1981.
17. Ioannis T. Kassios. Dynamic frames: Support for framing, dependencies and sharing without restrictions. In *FM 2006*, volume 4085 of *LNCS*, pages 268–283. Springer, August 2006.
18. Gary T. Leavens, Albert L. Baker, and Clyde Ruby. JML: A notation for detailed design. In *Behavioral Specifications of Businesses and Systems*, pages 175–188. Kluwer Academic Publishers, 1999.
19. K. Rustan M. Leino and Peter Müller. Object invariants in dynamic contexts. In *ECOOP 2004*, volume 3086 of *LNCS*, pages 491–516. Springer, June 2004.
20. K. Rustan M. Leino and Peter Müller. Modular verification of static class invariants. In John Fitzgerald, Ian J. Hayes, and Andrzej Tarlecki, editors, *FM*, volume 3582 of *LNCS*, pages 26–42. Springer, 2005.
21. Tal Lev-Ami and Shmuel Sagiv. TVLA: A system for implementing static analyses. In *SAS 2000*, pages 280–301, 2000.
22. Barbara H. Liskov and Jeannette M. Wing. A behavioral notion of subtyping. *ACM Transactions on Programming Languages and Systems*, 16(6):1811–1841, November 1994.
23. D. C. Luckham, S. M. German, F. W. von Henke, R. A. Karp, P. W. Milne, D. C. Oppen, W. Polak, and W. L. Scherlis. Stanford Pascal Verifier user manual. Technical Report STAN-CS-79-731, Stanford University, 1979.
24. Ronald Middelkoop, Cornelis Huizing, Ruurd Kuiper, and Erik Luit. Invariants for non-hierarchical object structures. In *Brazilian Symposium on Formal Methods, SBMF 2006*, pages 233–248. SBC, September 2006.
25. Peter Müller. *Modular Specification and Verification of Object-Oriented Programs*, volume 2262 of *LNCS*. Springer, 2002. PhD thesis, FernUniversität Hagen.
26. Peter Müller, Arnd Poetzsch-Heffter, and Gary T. Leavens. Modular invariants for layered object structures. *Science of Computer Programming*, 2006. To appear.
27. Matthew J. Parkinson and Gavin M. Bierman. Separation logic and abstraction. In *POPL 2005*, pages 247–258. ACM, January 2005.

On the Implementation of Construction Functions for Non-free Concrete Data Types

Frédéric Blanqui[1], Thérèse Hardin[2], and Pierre Weis[3]

[1] INRIA & LORIA, BP 239, 54506 Villers-lès-Nancy Cedex, France
[2] UPMC, LIP6, 104, Av. du Pr. Kennedy, 75016 Paris, France
[3] INRIA, Domaine de Voluceau, BP 105, 78153 Le Chesnay Cedex, France

Abstract. Many algorithms use concrete data types with some additional invariants. The set of values satisfying the invariants is often a set of representatives for the equivalence classes of some equational theory. For instance, a sorted list is a particular representative wrt commutativity. Theories like associativity, neutral element, idempotence, etc. are also very common. Now, when one wants to combine various invariants, it may be difficult to find the suitable representatives and to efficiently implement the invariants. The preservation of invariants throughout the whole program is even more difficult and error prone. Classically, the programmer solves this problem using a combination of two techniques: the definition of appropriate construction functions for the representatives and the consistent usage of these functions ensured via compiler verifications. The common way of ensuring consistency is to use an abstract data type for the representatives; unfortunately, pattern matching on representatives is lost. A more appealing alternative is to define a concrete data type with private constructors so that both compiler verification and pattern matching on representatives are granted. In this paper, we detail the notion of private data type and study the existence of construction functions. We also describe a prototype, called Moca, that addresses the entire problem of defining concrete data types with invariants: it generates efficient construction functions for the combination of common invariants and builds representatives that belong to a concrete data type with private constructors.

1 Introduction

Many algorithms use data types with some additional invariants. Every function creating a new value from old ones must be defined so that the newly created value satisfy the invariants whenever the old ones so do.

One way to easily maintain invariants is to use abstract data types (ADT): the implementation of an ADT is hidden and construction and observation functions are provided. A value of an ADT can only be obtained by recursively using the construction functions. Hence, an invariant can be ensured by using appropriate construction functions. Unfortunately, abstract data types preclude pattern matching, a very useful feature of modern programming languages [10,11,16,15]. There have been various attempts to combine both features in some way.

R. De Nicola (Ed.): ESOP 2007, LNCS 4421, pp. 95–109, 2007.

In [23], P. Wadler proposed the mechanisms of *views*. A view on an ADT α is given by providing a concrete data type (CDT) γ and two functions $in : \alpha \rightarrow \gamma$ and $out : \gamma \rightarrow \alpha$ such that $in \circ out = id_\gamma$ and $out \circ in = id_\alpha$. Then, a function on α can be defined by matching on γ (by implicitly using in) and the values of type γ obtained by matching can be injected back into α (by implicitly using out). However, by leaving the applications of in and out implicit, we can easily get inconsistencies whenever in and out are not inverses of each other. Since it may be difficult to satisfy this condition (consider for instance the translations between cartesian and polar coordinates), these views have never been implemented. Following the suggestion of W. Burton and R. Cameron to use the in function only [3], some propositions have been made for various programming languages but none has been implemented yet [4,17].

In [3], W. Burton and R. Cameron proposed another very interesting idea which seems to have attracted very little attention. An ADT must provide construction and observation functions. When an ADT is implemented by a CDT, they propose to also export the constructors of the CDT but only for using them as patterns in pattern matching clauses. Hence, the constructors of the underlying CDT can be used for pattern matching but not for building values: only the construction functions can be used for that purpose. Therefore, one can both ensure some invariants and offer pattern matching. These types have been introduced in OCaml by the third author [24] under the name of *concrete data type with private constructors*, or *private data type* (PDT) for short.

Now, many invariants on concrete data types can be related to some equational theory. Take for instance the type of *list* with the constructors [] and ::. Given some elements $v_1..v_n$, the sorted list which elements are $v_1..v_n$ is a particular representative of the equivalence class of $v_1::..::v_n::[]$ modulo the equation $x::y::l=y::x::l$. Requiring that, in addition, the list does not contain the same element twice is a particular representative modulo the equation $x::x::l=x::l$.

Consider now the type of join lists with the constructors *empty*, *singleton* and *append*, for which concatenation is of constant complexity. Sorting corresponds to associativity and commutativity of *append*. Requiring that no argument of *append* is *empty* corresponds to neutrality of *empty* wrt *append*. We have a structure of commutative monoid.

More generally, given some equational theory on a concrete data type, one may wonder whether there exists a representative for each equivalence class and, if so, whether a representative of $C(t_1 \dots t_n)$ can be efficiently computed knowing that $t_1 \dots t_n$ are themselves representatives.

In [21,22], S. Thompson describes a mechanism introduced in the Miranda functional programming language for implementing such non-free concrete data types without precluding pattern matching. The idea is to provide conditional rewrite rules, called *laws*, that are implicitly applied as long as possible on every newly created value. This can also be achieved by using a PDT which construction functions (primed constructors in [21]) apply as long as possible each of the laws. Then, S. Thompson studies how to prove the correctness of functions defined by pattern matching on such *lawful types*. However, few hints are given on how to check whether the laws indeed implement the invariants one has in mind. For this reason and because reasoning on lawful types is difficult, the law mechanism was removed from Miranda.

In this paper, we propose to specify the invariants by unoriented equations (instead of rules). We will call such a type a *relational data type* (RDT). Sections 2 and 3 introduce private and relational data types. Then, we study when an RDT can be implemented by a PDT, that is, when there exist construction functions computing some representative for each equivalence class. Section 4 provides some general existence theorem based on rewriting theory. But rewriting may be inefficient. Section 5 provides, for some common equational theories, construction functions more efficient than the ones based on rewriting. Section 6 presents Moca, an extension of OCaml with relational data types whose construction functions are automatically generated. Finally, Section 7 discusses some possible extensions.

2 Concrete Data Types with Private Constructors

We first recall the definition of a first-order term algebra. It will be useful for defining the values of concrete and private data types.

Definition 1 (First-order term algebra). A *sorted term algebra definition* is a triplet $\mathcal{A} = (\mathcal{S}, \mathcal{C}, \Sigma)$ where $\mathcal{S}$ is a non-empty set of *sorts*, $\mathcal{C}$ is a non-empty set of *constructor symbols* and $\Sigma : \mathcal{C} \to \mathcal{S}^+$ is a *signature* mapping a non-empty sequence of sorts to every constructor symbol. We write $C : \sigma_1 \dots \sigma_n \sigma_{n+1} \in \Sigma$ to denote the fact that $\Sigma(C) = \sigma_1 \dots \sigma_n \sigma_{n+1}$. Let $\mathcal{X} = (\mathcal{X}_\sigma)_{\sigma \in \mathcal{S}}$ be a family of pairwise disjoint sets of *variables*. The sets $\mathcal{T}_\sigma(\mathcal{A}, \mathcal{X})$ of *terms of sort* σ are inductively defined as follows:

- If $x \in \mathcal{X}_\sigma$, then $x \in \mathcal{T}_\sigma(\mathcal{A}, \mathcal{X})$.
- If $C : \sigma_1 \dots \sigma_{n+1} \in \Sigma$ and $t_i \in \mathcal{T}_{\sigma_i}(\mathcal{A}, \mathcal{X})$, then $C(t_1, \dots, t_n) \in \mathcal{T}_{\sigma_{n+1}}(\mathcal{A}, \mathcal{X})$.

Let $\mathcal{T}_\sigma(\mathcal{A})$ be the set of terms of sort σ containing no variable.

In the following, we assume given a set $\mathcal{S}_0$ of primitive types like `int`, `string`, ... and a set $\mathcal{C}_0$ of primitive constants `0`, `1`, `"foo"`, ... Let Σ_0 be the corresponding signature ($\Sigma_0(0) = \texttt{int}, \dots$).

In this paper, we call *concrete data type* (CDT) an inductive type *à la* ML defined by a set of *constructors*. More formally:

Definition 2 (Concrete data type). A *concrete data type definition* is a triplet $\Gamma = (\gamma, \mathcal{C}, \Sigma)$ where γ is a sort, $\mathcal{C}$ is a non-empty set of *constructor symbols* and $\Sigma : \mathcal{C} \to (\mathcal{S}_0 \cup \{\gamma\})^+$ is a *signature* such that, for all $C \in \mathcal{C}$, $\Sigma(C) = \sigma_1 .. \sigma_n \gamma$. The set $Val(\gamma)$ of *values of type* γ is the set of terms $\mathcal{T}_\gamma(\mathcal{A}_\Gamma)$ where $\mathcal{A}_\Gamma = (\mathcal{S}_0 \cup \{\gamma\}, \mathcal{C}_0 \cup \mathcal{C}, \Sigma_0 \cup \Sigma)$.

This definition of CDTs corresponds to a small but very useful subset of all the possible types definable in ML-like programming languages. For the purpose of this paper, it is not necessary to use a more complex definition.

Example 1. The following type[1] `cexp` is a CDT definition with two constant constructors of sort `cexp` and a binary operator of sort `cexp cexp cexp`.

```
type cexp =  Zero | One | Opp of cexp | Plus of cexp * cexp
```

Now, a private data type definition is like a CDT definition together with construction functions as in abstract data types. Constructors can be used as patterns as in concrete data types but they *cannot* be used for value creation (except in the definition of construction functions). For building values, one must use construction functions as in abstract data types. Formally:

Definition 3 (Private data type). A *private data type definition* is a pair $\Pi = (\Gamma, \mathcal{F})$ where $\Gamma = (\pi, \mathcal{C}, \Sigma)$ is a CDT definition and $\mathcal{F}$ is a family of *construction functions* $(f_C)_{C \in \mathcal{C}}$ such that, for all $C : \sigma_1..\sigma_n\pi \in \Sigma$, $f_C : \mathcal{T}_{\sigma_1}(\mathcal{A}_\Gamma) \times \ldots \times \mathcal{T}_{\sigma_n}(\mathcal{A}_\Gamma) \to \mathcal{T}_\pi(\mathcal{A}_\Gamma)$. Let $Val(\pi)$ be the set of the *values of type* π, that is, the set of terms that one can build by using the construction functions only. The function $f : \mathcal{T}_\pi(\mathcal{A}_\Gamma) \to \mathcal{T}_\pi(\mathcal{A}_\Gamma)$ such that, for all $C : \sigma_1..\sigma_n\pi \in \Sigma$ and $t_i \in \mathcal{T}_{\sigma_i}(\mathcal{A}_\Gamma)$, $f(C(t_1..t_n)) = f_C(f(t_1)..f(t_n))$, is called the *normalization function associated to* $\mathcal{F}$.

This is quite immediate to see that:

Lemma 1. *$Val(\pi)$ is the image of f.*

PDTs have been implemented in OCaml by the third author [24]. Extending a programming language with PDTs is not very difficult: one only needs to modify the compiler to parse the PDT definitions and check that the conditions on the use of constructors are fulfilled.

Note that construction functions have no constraint in general: the full power of the underlying programming language is available to define them.

It should also be noted that, because the set of values of type π is a subset of the set of values of the underlying CDT γ, a function on π defined by pattern matching may be a total function even though it is not defined on all the possible cases of γ. Defining a function with patterns that match no value of type π does not harm since the corresponding code will never be run. It however reveals that the developer is not aware of the distinction between the values of the PDT and those of the underlying CDT, and thus can be considered as a programming error. To avoid this kind of errors, it is important that a PDT comes with a clear identification of its set of possible values. To go one step further, one could provide a tool for checking the completeness and usefulness of patterns that takes into account the invariants, when it is possible. We leave this for future work.

Example 2. Let us now start our running example with the type `exp` describing operations on arithmetic expressions.

```
type exp = private Zero | One | Opp of exp | Plus of exp * exp
```

[1] Examples are written with OCaml [10], they can be readily translated in any programming language offering pattern-matching with textual priority, as Haskell, SML, etc.

This type exp is indeed a PDT built upon the CDT cexp. Prompted by the keyword private, the OCaml compiler forbids the use of exp constructors (outside the module my_exp.ml containing the definition of exp) except in patterns. If Zero is supposed to be neutral by the writer of my_exp.ml, then he/she will provide construction functions as follows:

```
let rec zero = Zero and one = One and opp x = Opp x
and plus = function
| (Zero,y) -> y
| (y,Zero) -> y
| (x,y)-> Plus(x,y)
```

3 Relational Data Types

We mentioned in the introduction that, often, the invariants upon concrete data types are such that the set of values satisfying them is indeed a set of representatives for the equivalence classes of some equational theory. We therefore propose to specify invariants by a set of unoriented equations and study to which extent such a specification can be realized with an abstract or private data type. In case of a private data type however, it is important to be able to describe the set of possible values.

Definition 4 (Relational data type). A *relational data type (RDT) definition* is a pair $(\Gamma, \mathcal{E})$ where $\Gamma = (\pi, \mathcal{C}, \Sigma)$ is a CDT definition and $\mathcal{E}$ is a finite set of equations on $\mathcal{T}_\pi(\mathcal{A}_\Gamma, \mathcal{X})$. Let $=_\mathcal{E}$ be the smallest congruence relation containing $\mathcal{E}$. Such an RDT is *implementable* by a PDT $(\Gamma, \mathcal{F})$ if the family of construction functions $\mathcal{F} = (f_C)_{C \in \mathcal{C}}$ is *valid wrt* $\mathcal{E}$:

(Correctness): For all $C : \sigma_1..\sigma_n\pi$ and $v_i \in Val(\sigma_i)$, $f_C(v_1..v_n) =_\mathcal{E} C(v_1..v_n)$.
(Completeness): For all $C : \sigma_1..\sigma_n\sigma$, $v_i \in Val(\sigma_i)$, $D : \tau_1..\tau_p\sigma \in \Sigma$ and $w_i \in Val(\tau_i)$, $f_C(v_1..v_n) = f_D(w_1..w_p)$ whenever $C(v_1..v_n) =_\mathcal{E} D(w_1..w_p)$.

We are going to see that the existence of a valid family of construction functions is equivalent to the existence of a valid normalization function:

Definition 5 (Valid normalization function). A map $f : \mathcal{T}_\pi(\mathcal{A}_\Gamma) \to \mathcal{T}_\pi(\mathcal{A}_\Gamma)$ is a *valid normalization function* for an RDT $(\Gamma, \mathcal{E})$ with $\Gamma = (\pi, \mathcal{C}, \Sigma)$ if:
(Correctness): For all $t \in \mathcal{T}_\pi(\mathcal{A}_\Gamma)$, $f(t) =_\mathcal{E} t$.
(Completeness): For all $t, u \in \mathcal{T}_\pi(\mathcal{A}_\Gamma)$, $f(t) = f(u)$ whenever $t =_\mathcal{E} u$.

Note that a valid normalization function is idempotent ($f \circ f = f$) and provides a decision procedure for $=_\mathcal{E}$ (the boolean function $\lambda xy.f(x) = f(y)$).

Theorem 6. The normalization function associated to a valid family is a valid normalization function.

Proof

- Correctness. We proceed by induction on the size of $t \in \mathcal{T}_\pi$. We have $C : \sigma_1..\sigma_n\pi \in \Sigma$ and t_i such that $t = C(t_1..t_n)$. By definition, $f(t) = f_C(f(t_1)..f(t_n))$. By induction hypothesis, $f(t_i) =_\mathcal{E} t_i$. Since the family is valid and $f(t_1)..f(t_n)$ are values, $f_C(f(t_1)..f(t_n)) =_\mathcal{E} C(f(t_1)..f(t_n))$. Thus, $f(t) =_\mathcal{E} t$.

- Completeness. Let $t, u \in \mathcal{T}_\pi$ such that $t =_\mathcal{E} u$. We have $t = C(t_1..t_n)$ and $u = D(u_1..u_p)$. By definition, $f(t) = f_C(f(t_1)..f(t_n))$ and $f(u) = f_D(f(u_1)..f(u_p))$. By correctness, $f(t_i) =_\mathcal{E} t_i$ and $f(u_j) =_\mathcal{E} u_j$. Hence, $C(f(t_1)..f(t_n)) =_\mathcal{E} D(f(u_1)..f(u_p))$. Since the family is valid and $f(t_1)..f(t_n)$ are values, $f_C(f(t_1)..f(t_n)) = f_D(f(t_1)..f(t_n))$. Thus, $f(t) = f(u)$. ∎

Conversely, given $f : \mathcal{T}_\pi(\mathcal{A}_\Gamma) \to \mathcal{T}_\pi(\mathcal{A}_\Gamma)$, one can easily define a family of construction functions that is valid whenever f is a valid normalization function.

Definition 7 (Associated family of constr. functions). Given a CDT $\Gamma = (\pi, \mathcal{C}, \Sigma)$ and a function $f : \mathcal{T}_\pi(\mathcal{A}_\Gamma) \to \mathcal{T}_\pi(\mathcal{A}_\Gamma)$, the *family of construction functions associated to* f is the family $(f_C)_{C \in \mathcal{C}}$ such that, for all $C : \sigma_1..\sigma_n\pi \in \Sigma$ and $t_i \in \mathcal{T}_{\sigma_1}(\mathcal{A}_\Gamma)$, $f_C(t_1, \ldots, t_n) = f(C(t_1, \ldots, t_n))$.

Theorem 8. The family of construction functions associated to a valid normalization function is valid.

Example 3. We can choose `cexp` as the underlying CDT and $\mathcal{E} = \{$ `Plus x Zero = x`$\}$ to define a RDT implementable by the PDT `exp`, with the valid family of construction functions `zero`, `one`, `opp`, `plus`.

4 On the Existence of Construction Functions

In this section, we provide a general theorem for the existence of valid families of construction functions based on rewriting theory. We recall the notions of rewriting and completion. The interested reader may find more details in [8].

Standard rewriting. A *rewrite rule* is an ordered pair of terms (l, r) written $l \to r$. A rule is *left-linear* if no variable occurs twice in its left hand side l.

As usual, the set $\mathrm{Pos}(t)$ of *positions in* t is defined as a set of words on positive integers. Given $p \in \mathrm{Pos}(t)$, let $t|_p$ be the subterm of t at position p and $t[u]_p$ be the term t with $t|_p$ replaced by u.

Given a finite set $\mathcal{R}$ of rewrite rules, the *rewriting relation* is defined as follows: $t \to_\mathcal{R} u$ iff there are $p \in \mathrm{Pos}(t)$, $l \to r \in \mathcal{R}$ and a substitution θ such that $t|_p = l\theta$ and $u = t[r\theta]_p$. A term t is an $\mathcal{R}$-*normal form* if there is no u such that $t \to_\mathcal{R} u$. Let $=_\mathcal{R}$ be the symmetric, reflexive and transitive closure of $\to_\mathcal{R}$.

A *reduction ordering* $\succ$ is a well-founded ordering (there is no infinitely decreasing sequence $t_0 \succ t_1 \succ \ldots$) stable by context ($C(..t..) \succ C(..u..)$ whenever $t \succ u$) and substitution ($t\theta \succ u\theta$ whenever $t \succ u$). If $\mathcal{R}$ is included in a reduction ordering, then $\to_\mathcal{R}$ is well-founded (terminating, strongly normalizing).

We say that $\to_\mathcal{R}$ is *confluent* if, for all terms t, u, v such that $u \leftarrow^*_\mathcal{R} t \to^*_\mathcal{R} v$, there exists a term w such that $u \to^*_\mathcal{R} w \leftarrow^*_\mathcal{R} v$. This means that the relation $\leftarrow^*_\mathcal{R}\to^*_\mathcal{R}$ is included in the relation $\to^*_\mathcal{R}\leftarrow^*_\mathcal{R}$ (composition of relations is written by juxtaposition).

If $\to_\mathcal{R}$ is confluent, then every term has at most one normal form. If $\to_\mathcal{R}$ is well-founded, then every term has at least one normal form. Therefore, if $\to_\mathcal{R}$ is confluent and terminating, then every term has a unique normal form.

Standard completion. Given a finite set $\mathcal{E}$ of equations and a reduction ordering $\succ$, the standard Knuth-Bendix completion procedure [2] tries to find a finite set $\mathcal{R}$ of rewrite rules such that:

- $\mathcal{R}$ is included in $\succ$,
- $\to_\mathcal{R}$ is confluent,
- $\mathcal{R}$ and $\mathcal{E}$ have same theory: $=_\mathcal{E}\ =\ =_\mathcal{R}$.

Note that completion may fail or not terminate but, in case of successful termination, $\mathcal{R}$-normalization provides a decision procedure for $=_\mathcal{E}$ since $t =_\mathcal{E} u$ iff the $\mathcal{R}$-normal forms of t and u are syntactically equal.

However, since permutation theories like commutativity or associativity and commutativity together (written AC for short) are included in no reduction ordering, dealing with them requires to consider rewriting with pattern matching modulo these theories and completion modulo these theories. In this paper, we restrict our attention to AC.

Definition 9 (Associative-commutative equations). Let *Com* be the set of commutative constructors, *i.e.* the set of constructors C such that $\mathcal{E}$ contains an equation of the form $C(x,y) = C(y,x)$. Then, let $\mathcal{E}_{AC}$ be the subset of $\mathcal{E}$ made of the commutativity and associativity equations for the commutative constructors, $=_{AC}$ be the smallest congruence relation containing $\mathcal{E}_{AC}$ and $\mathcal{E}_{\neg AC} = \mathcal{E} \setminus \mathcal{E}_{AC}$.

Rewriting modulo AC. Given a set $\mathcal{R}$ of rewrite rules, *rewriting with pattern matching modulo AC* is defined as follows: $t \to_{\mathcal{R},AC} u$ iff there are $p \in \mathrm{Pos}(t)$, $l \to r \in \mathcal{R}$ and a substitution θ such that $t|_p =_{AC} l\theta$ and $u = t[r\theta]_p$. A reduction ordering $\succ$ is *AC-compatible* if, for all terms t, t', u, u' such that $t =_{AC} t'$ and $u =_{AC} u'$, $t' \succ u'$ iff $t \succ u$. The relation $\to_{\mathcal{R},AC}$ is *confluent modulo AC* if $(\leftarrow^*_{\mathcal{R},AC}{=_{AC}}\to^*_{\mathcal{R},AC}) \subseteq (\to^*_{\mathcal{R},AC}{=_{AC}}\leftarrow^*_{\mathcal{R},AC})$.

Completion modulo AC. Given a finite set $\mathcal{E}$ of equations and an *AC*-compatible reduction ordering $\succ$, completion modulo *AC* [18] tries to find a finite set $\mathcal{R}$ of rules such that:

- $\mathcal{R}$ is included in $\succ$,
- $\to_{\mathcal{R},AC}$ is confluent modulo *AC*,
- $\mathcal{E}$ and $\mathcal{R} \cup \mathcal{E}_{AC}$ have same theory: $=_\mathcal{E}\ =\ =_{\mathcal{R}\cup\mathcal{E}_{AC}}$.

Definition 10. A theory $\mathcal{E}$ has a *complete presentation* if there is an AC-compatible reduction ordering for which the *AC*-completion of $\mathcal{E}_{\neg AC}$ successfully terminates.

Many interesting systems have a complete presentation: (commutative) monoids, (abelian) groups, rings, etc. See [13,5] for a catalog. Moreover, there are automated tools implementing completion modulo AC. See for instance [6,12].

A term may have distinct $\mathcal{R}, AC$-normal forms but, by confluence modulo AC, all normal forms are AC-equivalent and one can easily define a notion of normal form for AC-equivalent terms [13]:

Definition 11 (AC-normal form). Given an associative and commutative constructor C, *C-left-combs* (resp. *C-right-combs*) and their *leaves* are inductively defined as follows:

- If t is not headed by C, then t is both a C-left-comb and a C-right-comb. The *leaves* of t is the one-element list $leaves(t) = [t]$.
- If t is not headed by C and u is a C-right-comb, then $C(t, u)$ is a C-right-comb. The *leaves* of $C(t, u)$ is the list $t :: leaves(u)$.
- If t is not headed by C and u is a C-left-comb, then $C(u, t)$ is a C-left-comb. The *leaves* of $C(u, t)$ is the list $leaves(u)@[t]$, where @ is the concatenation.

Let *orient* be a function associating a kind of combs (left or right) to every AC-constructor. Let $\leq$ be a total ordering on terms. Then, a term t is in *AC-normal form wrt orient and* $\leq$ if:

- Every subterm of t headed by an AC-constructor C is an $orient(C)$-comb whose leaves are in increasing order wrt $\leq$.
- For every subterm of t of the form $C(u, v)$ with C commutative but non-associative, we have $u \leq v$.

As it is well-known, one can put any term in AC-normal form:

Theorem 12. Whatever the function *orient* and the ordering $\leq$ are, every term t has an AC-normal form $t\downarrow_{AC}$ wrt *orient* and $\leq$, and $t =_{AC} t\downarrow_{AC}$.

Proof. Let $\mathcal{A}$ be the set of rules obtained by choosing an orientation for the associativity equations of $\mathcal{E}_{AC}$ according to *orient*:

- If $orient(C)$ is "left", then take $C(x, C(y, z)) \rightarrow C(C(x, y), z)$.
- If $orient(C)$ is "right", then take $C(C(x, y), z) \rightarrow C(x, C(y, z))$.

$\rightarrow_{\mathcal{A}}$ is a confluent and terminating relation putting every subterm headed by an AC-constructor into a comb form according to *orient*. Let *comb* be a function computing the $\mathcal{A}$-normal form of a term. Let now *sort* be a function permuting the leaves of combs and the arguments of commutative but non-associative constructors to put them in increasing order wrt $\leq$. Then, the function $sort \circ comb$ computes the AC-normal form of any term and $sort(comb(t)) =_{AC} t$. ∎

This naturally provides a decision procedure for AC-equivalence: the function $\lambda xy.sort(comb(x)) = sort(comb(y))$. It follows that $\mathcal{R}, AC$-normalization together with AC-normalization provides a valid normalization function, hence the existence of a valid family of construction functions:

Theorem 13. If $\mathcal{E}$ has a complete presentation, then there exists a valid family of construction functions.

Proof. Assume that $\mathcal{E}$ has a complete presentation $\mathcal{R}$. We define the computation of normal forms as it is generally implemented in rewriting tools. Let *step* be a function making an $\mathcal{R}, AC$-rewrite step if there is one, or failing if the term is in normal form. Let *norm* be the function applying *step* until a normal form is reached. Since $\mathcal{R}$ is a complete presentation of $\mathcal{E}$, by definition of the completion procedure, $sort \circ comb \circ norm$ is a valid normalization function. Thus, by Theorem 8, the associated family of construction functions is valid. ■

The construction functions described in the proof are not very efficient since they are based on rewriting with pattern matching modulo AC, which is NP-complete [1], and do not take advantage of the fact that, by definition of PDTs, they are only applied to terms already in normal form. We can therefore wonder whether they can be defined in a more efficient way for some common equational theories like the ones of Figure 1.

Name	**Abbrev**	**Definition**	**Example**
associativity	$Assoc(C)$	$C(C(x,y),z) = C(x,C(y,z))$	$(x+y)+z = x+(y+z)$
commutativity	$Com(C)$	$C(x,y) = C(y,x)$	$x+y = y+x$
neutrality	$Neu(C,E)$	$C(x,E) = x$	$x+0 = x$
inverse	$Inv(C,I,E)$	$C(x,I(x)) = E$	$x+(-x) = 0$
idempotence	$Idem(C)$	$C(x,x) = x$	$x \wedge x = x$
nilpotence	$Nil(C,A)$	$C(x,x) = A$	$x \oplus x = \bot$ (exclusive or)

Fig. 1. Some common equations on binary constructors

Rewriting provides also a way to check the validity of construction functions:

Theorem 14. If $\mathcal{E}$ has a complete presentation $\mathcal{R}$ and $\mathcal{F} = (f_C)_{C \in \mathcal{C}}$ is a family such that, for all $C : \sigma_1..\sigma_n\pi \in \Sigma$ and terms $v_i \in Val(\sigma_i)$, $f_C(v_1..v_n)$ is an $\mathcal{R}, AC$-normal form of $C(v_1..v_n)$ in AC-normal form, then $\mathcal{F}$ is valid.

Proof

- Correctness. Let $C : \sigma_1..\sigma_n\pi \in \Sigma$ and $v_i \in Val(\sigma_i)$. Since $f_C(v_1..v_n)$ is an $\mathcal{R}, AC$-normal form of $C(v_1..v_n)$, we clearly have $f_C(v_1..v_n) =_\mathcal{E} C(v_1..v_n)$.
- Completeness. Let $C : \sigma_1..\sigma_n\pi \in \Sigma$, $v_i \in Val_\mathcal{F}(\sigma_i)$, $D : \tau_1..\tau_p\pi \in \Sigma$, and $w_i \in Val_\mathcal{F}(\tau_i)$ such that $C(v_1..v_n) =_\mathcal{E} D(w_1..w_p)$. Since $\mathcal{R}$ is a complete presentation of $\mathcal{E}$, $norm(C(v_1..v_n)) =_{AC} norm(D(w_1..w_p))$. Thus, $f_C(v_1..v_n) = f_D(w_1..w_p)$. ■

It follows that rewriting provides a natural way to explain what are the possible values of an RDT: values are AC-normal forms matching no left hand side of a rule of $\mathcal{R}$.

5 Towards Efficient Construction Functions

When there is no commutative symbol, construction functions can be easily implemented by simulating innermost rewriting as follows:

Definition 15 (Linearization). Let VPos(t) be the set of positions $p \in \text{Pos}(t)$ such that $t|_p$ is a variable $x \in \mathcal{X}$. Let $\rho : \text{VPos}(t) \to \mathcal{X}$ be an injective mapping and $lin(t)$ be the term obtained by replacing in t every subterm at position $p \in \text{VPos}(t)$ by $\rho(p)$. Let now $Eq(t)$ be the conjunction of `true` and of the equations $\rho(p) = \rho(q)$ such that $t|_p = t|_q$ and $p, q \in \text{VPos}(t)$.

Definition 16. Given a set $\mathcal{R}$ of rewrite rules, let $\mathcal{F}(\mathcal{R})$ be the family of construction functions $(f_C)_{C \in \mathcal{C}}$ defined as follows:

- For every rule $l \to r \in \mathcal{R}$ with $l = C(l_1, \ldots, l_n)$, add to the definition of f_C the clause $lin(l_1), \ldots, lin(l_n)$ `when` $Eq(l)$ `->` $\widehat{lin(r)}$, where $\widehat{t}$ is the term obtained by replacing in t every occurrence of a constructor C by a call to its construction function f_C.
- Terminate the definition of f_C by the *default clause* `x -> C(x)`.

Theorem 17. Assume that $\mathcal{E}_{AC} = \emptyset$ and $\mathcal{E}$ has a complete presentation $\mathcal{R}$. Then, $\mathcal{F}(\mathcal{R})$ is valid wrt $\mathcal{E}$ (whatever the order of the non-default clauses is).

We now consider the case of commutative symbols. We are going to describe a modular way of defining the construction functions by pursuing our running example, with the type `exp`. Assume that `Plus` is declared to be associative and commutative only. The construction functions can then be defined as follows:

```
let zero = Zero and one = One and opp x = Opp x

and plus = function
| Plus(x,y), z -> plus (x, plus (y,z))
| x, y -> insert_plus x y

and insert_plus x = function
| Plus(y,_) as u when x <= y -> Plus(x,u)
| Plus(y,t) -> Plus (y, insert_plus x t)
| u when x > u -> Plus(u,x)
| u -> Plus(x,u)
```

One can easily see that `plus` does the same job as the function *sort* ∘ *comb* used in Theorem 12 but in a slightly more efficient way since $\mathcal{A}$-normalization and sorting are interleaved.

Assume moreover that `Zero` is neutral. The AC-completion of { `Plus`(`Zero`, x) $= x$} gives { `Plus`(`Zero`, x) $\to x$}. Hence, if x and y are terms in normal form, then `Plus`(x, y) can be rewritten modulo AC only if $x =$ `Zero` or $y =$ `Zero`. Thus, the function `plus` needs to be extended with two new clauses only:

```
and plus = function
| Zero, y -> y
| x, Zero -> x
| Plus(x,y), z -> plus (x, plus (y,z))
| x, y -> insert_plus x y
```

Assume now that Plus is declared to have Opp as inverse. Then, the completion modulo AC of { $\texttt{Plus(Zero},x) = x$, $\texttt{Plus(Opp(}x),x) = \texttt{Zero}$} gives the following well known rules for abelian groups [13]: { $\texttt{Plus(Zero},x) \to x$, $\texttt{Plus(Opp(}x),x) \to \texttt{Zero}$, $\texttt{Plus(Plus(Opp(}x),x),y) \to y$, $\texttt{Opp(Zero)} \to \texttt{Zero}$, $\texttt{Opp(Opp(}x)) \to x$, $\texttt{Opp(Plus(}x,y)) \to \texttt{Plus(Opp(}y),\texttt{Opp(}x))$ }.

The rules for Opp are easily translated as follows:

```
and opp = function
| Zero -> Zero
| Opp(x) -> x
| Plus(x,y) -> plus (opp y, opp x)
| _ -> Opp(x)
```

The third rule of abelian groups is called an *extension* of the second one since it is obtained by first adding the context $Plus([],y)$ on both sides of this second rule,then normalizing the right hand side. Take now two terms x and y in normal form and assume that (x, y) matches none of the three clauses previously defining plus, that is, x and y are distinct from Zero, and x is not of the form $\texttt{Plus}(x_1, x_2)$. To get the normal form of $\texttt{Plus}(x, y)$, we need to check that x and the normal form of its opposite $\texttt{Opp}(x)$ do not occur in y. The last clause defining plus needs therefore to be modified as follows:

```
and plus = function
| Zero, y -> y
| x, Zero -> x
| Plus(x,y), z -> plus (x, plus (y,z))
| x, y -> insert_opp_plus (opp x) y

and insert_opp_plus x y =
  try delete_plus x y
  with Not_found -> insert_plus (opp x) y

and delete_plus x = function
| Plus(y,_) when x < y -> raise Not_found
| Plus(y,t) when x = y -> t
| Plus(y,t) -> Plus (y, delete_plus x t)
| y when y = x -> Zero
| _ -> raise Not_found
```

Forgetting about Zero and Opp, suppose now that Plus is declared associative, commutative and idempotent. The function plus is kept but the insert function is modified as follows:

```
and insert_plus x = function
| Plus(y,_) as u when x = y -> u
| Plus(y,_) as u when x < y -> Plus(x,u)
| Plus(y,t) -> Plus (y,insert_plus x t)
| u when x > u -> Plus(u,x)
| u when x = u -> u
| u -> Plus(x,u)
```

Nilpotence can be dealt with in a similar way.

In conclusion, for various combinations of the equations of Figure 1, we can define in a nice modular way construction functions that are more efficient than the ones based on rewriting modulo AC. We summarize this as follows:

Definition 18. A set of equations $\mathcal{E}$ is a theory of type:
(1) if $\mathcal{E}_{AC} = \emptyset$ and $\mathcal{E}$ has a complete presentation,
(2) if $\mathcal{E}$ is the union of $\{Assoc(C), Com(C)\}$ with either $\{Neu(C,E), Inv(C,I,E)\}$, $\{Idem(C)\}$, $\{Neu(C,E), Idem(C)\}$ $\{Nil(C,A)\}$ or $\{Neu(C,E), Nil(C,A)\}$.

Two theories are disjoint if they share no symbol.

Let us give schemes for construction functions for theories of type 2. A clause is generated only if the conditions `Neu(C,E)`, `Inv(C,I,E)`, etc. are satisfied. These conditions are not part of the generated code.

```
let f_C = function
| E, x when Neu(C,E) -> x
| x, E when Neu(C,E) -> x
| C(x,y), z when Assoc(C) -> f_C(x,f_C(y,z))
| x, y when Inv(C,I,E) -> insert_inv_C (f_I x) y
| x, y -> insert_C x y

and f_I = function
| E -> E
| I(x) -> x
| C(x,y) -> f_C(f_I y, f_I x)
| x -> I x

and insert_inv_C x y =
  try delete_C x y
  with Not_found -> insert_C (f_I x) y

and delete_C x = function
| Plus(y,_) when x < y -> raise Not_found
| Plus(y,t) when x = y -> t
| Plus(y,t) -> C(y, delete_C x t)
| y when y = x -> E
| _ -> raise Not_found

and insert_C x = function
| C(y,_) as u when x = y & idem -> u
| C(y,t) when x = y & nil -> f_C(A,t)
| C(y,_) as u when x <= y & com -> C(x,u)
| C(y,t) when Com(C) -> C(y, insert_C x t)
| u when x > u & Com(C) -> C(u,x)
| u when x = u & Idem(C) -> u
| u when x = u & Nil(C,A) -> A
| u -> C(x,u)
```

Theorem 19. Let $\mathcal{E}$ be the union of pairwise disjoint theories of type 1 or 2. Assume that, for all constructor C which theory is of type k, f_C is defined as in Definition 16 if $k = 1$, and as above if $k = 2$. Then, $(f_C)_{C \in \mathcal{C}}$ is valid wrt $\mathcal{E}$.

Proof. Assume that $\mathcal{E} = \bigcup_{i=1}^{n} \mathcal{E}_i$ where $\mathcal{E}_1, \ldots, \mathcal{E}_n$ are pairwise disjoint theories of type 1 or 2. Whatever the type of $\mathcal{E}_i$ is, we saw that $\mathcal{E}_i$ has a complete presentation $\mathcal{R}_i$. Therefore, since $\mathcal{E}_1, \ldots, \mathcal{E}_n$ share no symbol, by definition of completion, the AC-completion of $\mathcal{E}$ successfully terminates with $\mathcal{R} = \bigcup_{i=1}^{n} \mathcal{R}_i$. Thus, $\rightarrow_{\mathcal{R},AC}$ is terminating and AC-confluent. Since $\mathcal{F} = (f_C)_{C \in \mathcal{C}}$ computes $\mathcal{R}, AC$-normal forms in AC-normal forms, by Theorem 14, $\mathcal{F}$ is valid. ■

The construction functions of type 2 can be easily extended to deal with ring or lattice structures (distributivity and absorbance equations).

More general results can be expected by using or extending results on the modularity of completeness for the combination of rewrite systems. The completeness of hierarchical combinations of non-AC-rewrite systems is studied in [19]. Note however that the modularity of confluence for AC-rewrite systems has been formally established only recently in [14].

Note that the construction function definitions of type 1 or 2 provide the same results with call-by-value, call-by-name or lazy evaluation strategy.

The detailed study of the complexity of theses definitions (compared to AC-rewriting) is left for future work.

6 The Moca System

We now describe the Moca prototype, a program generator that implements an extension of OCaml with RDTs. Moca parses a special ".mlm" file containing the RDT definition and produces a regular OCaml module (interface and implementation) which provides the construction functions for the RDT. Moca provides a set of keywords for specifying the equations described in Figure 1.

For instance, the RDT `exp` can be defined in Moca as follows:

```
type exp = private Zero | One | Opp of exp | Plus of exp * exp
  begin associative commutative neutral(Zero) opposite(Opp) end
```

Moca also features user's arbitrary rules with the construction: `rule` *pattern* `->` *pattern*. These rules add extra clauses in the definitions of construction functions generated by Moca: the LHS *pattern* is copied verbatim as the pattern of a clause which returns the RHS *pattern* considered as an expression where constructors are replaced by calls to the corresponding construction functions. Of course, in the presence of such arbitrary rules, we cannot guarantee the termination or completeness of the generated code. This construction is thus provided for expert users that can prove termination and completeness of the corresponding set of rules. That way, the programmer can describe complex RDTs, even those which cannot be described with the set of predefined equational invariants.

Moca also accepts polymorphic RDTs and RDTs mutually defined with record types (but equations between record fields are not yet available).

The equations of Figure 1 also support n-ary constructor, implemented as unary constructors of type `t list -> t`. In this case, `Plus` gets a single argument of type `exp list`. Normal forms are modified accordingly and use lists instead of combs. For instance, associative normal forms get flat lists of arguments: in a `Plus`(l) expression, no element of l is a `Plus`(l') expression. The corresponding data structure is widely used in rewriting.

Finally, Moca offers an important additional feature: it can generate construction functions that provide maximally shared representatives. To fire maximal sharing, just add the `-sharing` option when compiling the ".mlm" file. In this case, the generated type is slightly modified, since every functional constructor gets an extra argument to keep the hash code of the term. Maximally shared representatives have a lot of good properties: not only data size is minimal and user's memoized functions can be light speed, but comparison between representatives is turned from a complex recursive term comparison to a pointer comparison – a single machine instruction. Moca heavily uses this property for the generation of construction functions: when dealing with non-linear equations, the maximal sharing property allows Moca to replace term equality by pointer equality.

7 Future Work

We plan to integrate Moca to the development environment Focal [20]. Focal units contain declarations and definitions of functions, statements and proofs as first-class citizens. Their compilation produces both a file checkable by the theorem prover Coq [7] and a OCaml source code. Proofs are done either within Coq or via the automatic theorem prover Zenon [9], which issues a Coq file when it successes. Every Focal unit has a special field, giving the type of the data manipulated in this unit. Thus, it would be very interesting to do a full integration of private/relational data types in Focal, the proof of correctness of construction functions being done with Zenon or Coq and then recorded as a theorem to be used for further proofs. This should be completed by the integration of a tool on rewriting and equational theories able to complete equational presentations, to generate and prove the corresponding lemmas and to show some termination properties. Some experiments already done within Focal on coupling CiME [6] and Zenon give a serious hope of success.

Acknowledgments. The authors thank Claude Kirchner for his comments on a previous version of the paper.

References

1. D. Benanav, D. Kapur, and P. Narendran. Complexity of matching problems. *J. of Symbolic Computation*, 3(1-2):203–216, 1987.
2. P. Bendix and D. Knuth. *Computational problems in abstract algebra*, chapter Simple word problems in universal algebra. Pergamon Press, 1970.
3. F. Burton and R. Cameron. Pattern matching with abstract data types. *J. of Functional Programming*, 3(2):171–190, 1993.

4. W. Burton, E. Meijer, P. Sansom, S. Thompson, and P. Wadler. Views: An extension to Haskell pattern matching. `http://www.haskell.org/extensions/views.html`, 1996.
5. P. Le Chenadec. *Canonical forms in finitely presented algebras*. Research notes in theoretical computer science. Pitman, 1986.
6. E. Contejean, C. Marché, B. Monate, and X. Urbain. *CiME version 2.02*. LRI, CNRS UMR 8623, Université Paris-Sud, France, 2004. `http://cime.lri.fr/`.
7. Coq Development Team. *The Coq Proof Assistant Reference Manual, Version 8.0*. INRIA, France, 2006. `http://coq.inria.fr/`.
8. N. Dershowitz and J.-P. Jouannaud. Rewrite systems. In J. van Leeuwen, editor, *Handbook of Theoretical Computer Science*, volume B, chapter 6. North Holland, 1990.
9. D. Doligez. Zenon, version 0.4.1. `http://focal.inria.fr/zenon/`, 2006.
10. D. Doligez, J. Garrigue, X. Leroy, D. Rémy, and J. Vouillon. *The Objective Caml system release 3.09, Documentation and user's manual*. INRIA, France, 2005. `http://caml.inria.fr/`.
11. S. P. Jones (editor). *Haskell 98 Language and Libraries, The revised report*. Cambridge University Press, 2003.
12. J.-M. Gaillourdet, T. Hillenbrand, B. Löchner, and H. Spies. The new Waldmeister loop at work. In *Proc. of CADE'03*, LNCS 2741. `http://www.waldmeister.org/`.
13. J.-M. Hullot. *Compilation de formes canoniques dans les théories équationnelles*. PhD thesis, Université Paris 11, France, 1980.
14. J.-P. Jouannaud. Modular church-rosser modulo. In *Proc. of RTA'06*, LNCS 4098.
15. P.-E. Moreau, E. Balland, P. Brauner, R. Kopetz, and A. Reilles. *Tom Manual version 2.3*. INRIA & LORIA, Nancy, France, 2006. `http://tom.loria.fr/`.
16. P.-E. Moreau, C. Ringeissen, and M. Vittek. A pattern matching compiler for multiple target languages. In *Proc. of CC'03*, LNCS 2622.
17. C. Okasaki. Views for standard ML. In *Proc. of ML'98*.
18. G. Peterson and M. Stickel. Complete sets of reductions for some equational theories. *J. of the ACM*, 28(2):233–264, 1981.
19. K. Rao. Completeness of hierarchical combinations of term rewriting systems. In *Proc. of FSTTCS'93*, LNCS 761.
20. R. Rioboo, D. Doligez, T. Hardin, and all. *FoCal Reference Manual, version 0.3.1*. Université Paris 6, CNAM & INRIA, 2005. `http://focal.inria.fr/`.
21. S. Thompson. Laws in Miranda. In *Proc. of LFP'86*.
22. S. Thompson. Lawful functions and program verification in Miranda. *Science of Computer Programming*, 13(2-3):181–218, 1990.
23. P. Wadler. Views: a way for pattern matching to cohabit with data abstraction. In *Proc. of POPL'87*.
24. P. Weis. Private constructors in OCaml. `http://alan.petitepomme.net/cwn/2003.07.01.html#5`, 2003.

Anti-pattern Matching*

Claude Kirchner, Radu Kopetz, and Pierre-Etienne Moreau

INRIA & LORIA, Nancy, France
{Claude.Kirchner,Radu.Kopetz,Pierre-Etienne.Moreau}@loria.fr

Abstract. It is quite appealing to base the description of pattern-based searches on positive as well as negative conditions. We would like for example to specify that we search for white cars that are not station wagons.

To this end, we define the notion of anti-patterns and their semantics along with some of their properties. We then extend the classical notion of matching between patterns and ground terms to matching between anti-patterns and ground terms. We provide a rule-based algorithm that finds the solutions to such problems and prove its correctness and completeness. Anti-pattern matching is by nature different from disunification and quite interestingly the anti-pattern matching problem is unitary. Therefore the concept is appropriate to ground a powerful extension to pattern-based programming languages and we show how this is used to extend the expressiveness and usability of the Tom language.

1 Introduction

Pattern matching is a widely spread concept both in the computer science community and in everyday life. Whenever we search for something, we build a structured object, a pattern, that specifies the features we are interested in. But we are often in the case where we want to exclude certain characteristics: typically we would like to specify that we search for white cars that are not station wagons.

We call *anti-patterns* the patterns that may contain complement symbols, denoted by $\urcorner$. For example, the web search engine from Google has an option where we can specify what specific words we do *not* want the result pages to contain. But it is not possible to express a search that has nested negations. What are the nested negations used for? Consider the following situation: using a search engine for cars, we want to search for a car that is not white; but in the case the car is ecological, we do not care about the color. This kind of search can be expressed in the following manner: $\urcorner car(white, \_) \vee car(\_, ecological)$ which could be equivalently expressed by the anti-pattern $\urcorner car(white, \urcorner ecological)$.

Another of our motivations comes from the popular "Business rules" management systems (BRMS for short) that provide a restricted anti-pattern capability. For example, although it is possible to use nested negations in Ilog JRules, one

* UMR 7503 CNRS-INPL-INRIA-Nancy2-UHP.

R. De Nicola (Ed.): ESOP 2007, LNCS 4421, pp. 110–124, 2007.

of the most representative business rule language on the market[1], they are not handled in full generality. A BRMS consists mainly of three components: a set of facts representing the current state of the system called Working Memory (WM), a set of *IF-THEN* rules that test and alter the WM, and a rule interpreter that applies the rules on the WM. A BRMS uses pattern matching to find out if an object is in the WM or not. If we put in the working memory the following fact: *car(white, ecological)*, and we insert the following rules:

1. if *there is no car that has the color white and the type ecological* then $action_1$,
2. if *there is no car that has the color white and the type not ecological* then $action_2$,
3. if *there is no car that has the color white and the type not diesel* then $action_3$.

none of the actions are fired. When we look at the three rules, we can see that basically the rule engine ignores the second negation. We consider that for the second rule, the action should have been fired.

A further issue that is not addressed in current pattern matching based languages, is the problem of non-linearity inside a negative context. We are not aware of the existence of a language where we can express in a single pattern the following search: look for a car that does not have both interior and exterior color the same. This should give all the cars with different interior-exterior colors.

In this rich context, our first contribution is to define in the next section the concept of anti-pattern and its semantics. Indeed as a term t represents the set of all its ground instances, the anti-pattern $\urcorner t$ represents the complement of the representation of t in the set of ground terms and this definition is extended recursively. Of course, many frameworks and results have already contributed to the use of negation in logic based languages. Having in particular in mind negation by failure in Prolog [8], the explicit use of counter-examples [16], disunification [11], feature constraints [3], inclusion constraints [20] and negation in iRho [17], we will motivate and explain the usefulness of anti-patterns.

Our second contribution concerns the definition of the notion of matching anti-patterns against terms in Section 3. In Section 4 we present a rule based algorithm for transforming anti-pattern matching problems into classical equational ones. The latter ones can be further solved using a subset of the disunification rules. In Section 5, such problems are shown to be unitary, which is a nice property in particular when using anti-patterns for programming purposes. We finally report in the Section 6 on the implementation of this algorithm in Tom — a programming language that extends C and Java by offering algebraic data-types and pattern matching facilities [19,15] — and discuss how anti-patterns could be used to extend the expressiveness of this language.

Although we will make precise our main notations, we assume that the reader is familiar with the standard notions of algebraic rewrite systems, for example presented in [5,14].

[1] `http://www.ilog.com/products/jrules`

2 Terms and Anti-terms

We briefly recall or introduce the notations for a few concepts that will be used along this paper.

A signature $\mathcal{F}$ is a set of function symbols, each one having a fixed arity. $\mathcal{T}(\mathcal{F},\mathcal{X})$ is the set of *terms* built from a given finite set $\mathcal{F}$ of function symbols and a denumerable set $\mathcal{X}$ of variables. A term t is said to be *linear* if no variable occurs more than once in t. The set of variables occurring in a term t is denoted by $\mathcal{V}ar(t)$. If $\mathcal{V}ar(t)$ is empty, t is called a *ground term* and $\mathcal{T}(\mathcal{F})$ is the set of ground terms.

A *substitution* σ is an assignment from $\mathcal{X}$ to $\mathcal{T}(\mathcal{F},\mathcal{X})$, denoted $\sigma = \{x_1 \mapsto t_1, \ldots, x_k \mapsto t_k\}$ when its domain $\mathsf{Dom}(\sigma)$ is finite. Its application, written $\sigma(t)$, is defined by $\sigma(x_i) = t_i$, $\sigma(f(t_1,\ldots,t_n)) = f(\sigma(t_1),\ldots,\sigma(t_n))$ for $f \in \mathcal{F}_n$, and $\sigma(y) = y$ if $y \notin \mathcal{D}om(\sigma)$. Given a term t, σ is called a *grounding substitution* when $\sigma(t) \in \mathcal{T}(\mathcal{F})$. The set of substitutions is denoted Σ. The set of grounding substitutions for a term t is denoted $\mathcal{GS}(t)$.

The ground semantics of a term $t \in \mathcal{T}(\mathcal{F},\mathcal{X})$ is the set of all its ground instances: $[\![t]\!]_g = \{\sigma(t) \mid \sigma \in \mathcal{GS}(t)\}$. In particular, when $x \in \mathcal{X}$, we have $[\![x]\!]_g = \mathcal{T}(\mathcal{F})$.

2.1 Anti-terms

Definition 2.1 (Syntax of anti-terms). *Given $\mathcal{F}$ and $\mathcal{X}$, the syntax of an anti-term is defined as follows:*

$$\mathcal{AT} ::= x \mid \urcorner\mathcal{AT} \mid f(\mathcal{AT},\ldots,\mathcal{AT})$$

where $x \in \mathcal{X}$, $f \in \mathcal{F}$ and the arity is respected. The set of anti-terms is denoted $\mathcal{AT}(\mathcal{F},\mathcal{X})$ (resp. $\mathcal{AT}(\mathcal{F})$ for ground anti-terms). Any term is an anti-term, i.e. $\mathcal{T}(\mathcal{F},\mathcal{X}) \subseteq \mathcal{AT}(\mathcal{F},\mathcal{X})$.

For example, if x, y, z denote variables, a, b, c constants, f, g two function symbols of arity 2 and 1, the following expressions are anti-terms: $\urcorner x$, $\urcorner a$, $\urcorner f(\urcorner a, g(\urcorner x))$, $f(x,y)$, $f(\urcorner a, b)$, $f(x, \urcorner x)$.

Definition 2.2 (Free variables). *The free variables of an anti-term q are defined inductively by:*

1. $\mathcal{FV}ar(x) = \{x\}$,
2. $\mathcal{FV}ar(\urcorner q) = \emptyset$,
3. $\mathcal{FV}ar(f(q_1,\ldots,q_n)) = \cup_{i=1..n}\mathcal{FV}ar(q_i)$, *with the arity of f equal to n.*

Example 2.1. Assuming that a is a constant and f is binary, we have: $\mathcal{FV}ar(a) = \emptyset$, $\mathcal{FV}ar(\urcorner x) = \emptyset$, $\mathcal{FV}ar(f(x, \urcorner x)) = \{x\}$, $\mathcal{FV}ar(\urcorner f(x, \urcorner x)) = \emptyset$.

Definition 2.3 (Substitutions on anti-terms). *A substitution σ uniquely extends to an endomorphism σ' of $\mathcal{AT}(\mathcal{F},\mathcal{X})$: if x is a free variable, $\sigma'(x) = \sigma(x)$, otherwise $\sigma'(x) = x$. For $q, q_1, \ldots, q_n \in \mathcal{AT}(\mathcal{F},\mathcal{X})$, we have $\sigma'(f(q_1,\ldots,q_n)) = f(\sigma'(q_1),\ldots,\sigma'(q_n))$, and $\sigma'(\urcorner q) = \urcorner\sigma'(q)$.*

Example 2.2. Note that substitutions are active only on the free variables: $\sigma(f(x, \neg x)) = f(\sigma(x), \neg\sigma(x))$, $\sigma(f(x, \neg y)) = f(\sigma(x), \neg y)$.

The notion of grounding substitutions is also extended to anti-terms (e.g. t) as substitutions (e.g. σ) such that $\mathcal{FV}ar(\sigma(t)) = \emptyset$.

Intuitively, the semantics of the complement of a term represents the complement of its semantics in $\mathcal{T}(\mathcal{F})$. Therefore, the complement of a variable $\neg x$ denotes $\mathcal{T}(\mathcal{F})\backslash[\![x]\!]_g = \mathcal{T}(\mathcal{F})\backslash\mathcal{T}(\mathcal{F}) = \emptyset$. Similarly, $\neg f(x)$ denotes $\mathcal{T}(\mathcal{F})\backslash\{f(t) \mid t \in \mathcal{T}(\mathcal{F})\}$. In the following we extend this intuition to complements of complements, as well as complements which occur in subterms, and we formally define the semantics of an anti-term.

As usual, a *position* is a finite sequence of natural numbers. The subterm u of a term t at position ω is denoted $t_{|\omega}$, where ω describes the path from the root of t to the root of u. $t(\omega)$ denotes the root symbol of $t_{|\omega}$.

By $t[s]_\omega$ we express that the term t contains s as subterm at position ω. Positions are ordered in the classical way: $\omega_1 < \omega_2$ if ω_1 is the prefix of ω_2 [14].

The ground semantics extends to anti-terms:

Definition 2.4 (Ground semantics of anti-terms). *The ground semantics of any anti-term $q \in \mathcal{AT}(\mathcal{F}, \mathcal{X})$ is defined recursively in the following way:*

$$[\![q[\neg q']_\omega]\!]_g = [\![q[z]_\omega]\!]_g \backslash [\![q[q']_\omega]\!]_g$$

where z is a fresh variable and for all $\omega' < \omega$, $q(\omega') \neq \neg$.

Example 2.3

1. $[\![\neg a]\!]_g = [\![z]\!]_g \backslash [\![a]\!]_g = \mathcal{T}(\mathcal{F})\backslash\{a\}$,
2. $[\![\neg x]\!]_g = [\![z]\!]_g \backslash [\![x]\!]_g = \mathcal{T}(\mathcal{F})\backslash\mathcal{T}(\mathcal{F}) = \emptyset$, for any variable x,
3. $[\![\neg\neg x]\!]_g = [\![z]\!]_g \backslash [\![\neg x]\!]_g = [\![z]\!]_g \backslash([\![z']\!]_g \backslash [\![x]\!]_g) = \mathcal{T}(\mathcal{F})\backslash(\mathcal{T}(\mathcal{F})\backslash\mathcal{T}(\mathcal{F})) = \mathcal{T}(\mathcal{F})$,
4. $[\![\neg g(x)]\!]_g = [\![z]\!]_g \backslash [\![g(x)]\!]_g = \mathcal{T}(\mathcal{F})\backslash\{g(\sigma(x)) \mid \sigma \in \mathcal{GS}(g(x))\}$,
5. $[\![g(\neg x)]\!]_g = [\![g(z)]\!]_g \backslash [\![g(x)]\!]_g = \emptyset$,
6. $[\![\neg g(\neg x)]\!]_g = [\![z]\!]_g \backslash [\![g(\neg x)]\!]_g = \mathcal{T}(\mathcal{F})\backslash\emptyset = \mathcal{T}(\mathcal{F})$,
7. we can also express that we are looking for something that is either not rooted by g, or it is $g(a)$:
$$\begin{aligned}[\![\neg g(\neg a)]\!]_g &= [\![z]\!]_g \backslash [\![g(\neg a)]\!]_g = [\![z]\!]_g \backslash([\![g(z')]\!]_g \backslash [\![g(a)]\!]_g)\\ &= \mathcal{T}(\mathcal{F})\backslash([\![g(z')]\!]_g \backslash \{g(a)\})\\ &= \mathcal{T}(\mathcal{F})\backslash(\{g(\sigma(z')) \mid \sigma \in \mathcal{GS}(g(z'))\}\backslash\{g(a)\})\\ &= \mathcal{T}(\mathcal{F})\backslash\{g(z) \mid z \in \mathcal{T}(\mathcal{F}, \mathcal{X})\} \cup \{g(a)\},\end{aligned}$$
8. $[\![f(a, \neg b)]\!]_g = [\![f(a, z)]\!]_g \backslash [\![f(a, b)]\!]_g = \{f(a, \sigma(z)) \mid \sigma \in \mathcal{GS}(f(a, z))\}\backslash\{f(a, b)\}$,
9. $[\![\neg f(x, x)]\!]_g = [\![z]\!]_g \backslash [\![f(x, x)]\!]_g = \mathcal{T}(\mathcal{F})\backslash\{f(\sigma(x), \sigma(x)) \mid \sigma \in \mathcal{GS}(f(x, x))\}$
note the crucial use of non-linearity to denote any term except those rooted by f with identical subterms,
10. $$\begin{aligned}[\![f(x, \neg x)]\!]_g &= [\![f(x, z)]\!]_g \backslash [\![f(x, x)]\!]_g\\ &= \{f(\sigma(x), \sigma(z)) \mid \sigma \in \mathcal{GS}(f(x, z))\}\backslash\{f(\sigma(x), \sigma(x)) \mid \sigma \in \mathcal{GS}(f(x, x))\}\\ &= f(a, b), f(a, c), f(b, c), \ldots\end{aligned}$$

The second condition of Definition 2.4 is essential. It prevents from replacing a subterm by a fresh variable inside a complemented context (i.e. below a $\neg$). Otherwise, for $\neg g(\neg a)$ we would have had $[\![\neg g(\neg a)]\!]_g = [\![\neg g(z)]\!]_g \backslash [\![\neg g(a)]\!]_g = \emptyset$.

These simple examples show that anti-terms provide a compact and expressive representation for the sets of terms. A nice property can be easily derived from them:

Proposition 2.1. *For any* $t \in \mathcal{AT}(\mathcal{F}, \mathcal{X})$*, we have* $[\![\neg\neg t]\!]_g = [\![t]\!]_g$

Proof. Using the Definition 2.4, $[\![\neg\neg t]\!]_g = [\![z]\!]_g \setminus [\![\neg t]\!]_g = [\![z]\!]_g \setminus ([\![z']\!]_g \setminus [\![t]\!]_g)$ $= [\![t]\!]_g$. □

3 Matching Anti-patterns

Before showing how anti-terms can be used for matching ground terms, we recall the standard definitions and results for the classical terms, as they are presented in [5,14] for example.

3.1 Pattern Matching

Definition 3.1 (Matching)

1. *a* pattern *is a term,*
2. *a* matching equation *is a problem* $p \prec\!\!\prec t$ *with* p *a pattern and* t *a term,*
3. *a substitution* σ *is a* solution of the matching equation $p \prec\!\!\prec t$ *if* $\sigma(p) = t$,
4. *a* matching system S *is a conjunction of matching equations,*
5. *a substitution* σ *is a* solution of a matching system S *if it is solution of all the matching equations in* S*. The set of solutions of* S *is denoted by* $\mathcal{S}ol(\mathsf{S})$,
6. *we denote by Fail a matching system without solution.*

In this paper, without loss of generality, we only consider matching equations of the form $p \prec\!\!\prec t$ where t is a *ground term.* The solution of a matching system S, when it exists, is unique and is computed by a simple recursive algorithm [13]. This algorithm can be expressed by the set of *rewrite rules* Match, given below. The symbol $\wedge$ is assumed to be associative, commutative and idempotent, S is any conjunction of matching equations, p_i are patterns, and t_i are ground terms:

Decompose	$f(p_1,\ldots,p_n) \prec\!\!\prec f(t_1,\ldots,t_n)$	$\mapsto\!\!\!\!\rightarrow$	$\bigwedge_{i=1,\ldots,n} p_i \prec\!\!\prec t_i$
SymbolClash	$f(p_1,\ldots,p_n) \prec\!\!\prec g(t_1,\ldots,t_m)$	$\mapsto\!\!\!\!\rightarrow$	*Fail* if $f \neq g$
MergingClash	$x \prec\!\!\prec t_1 \wedge x \prec\!\!\prec t_2$	$\mapsto\!\!\!\!\rightarrow$	*Fail* if $t_1 \neq t_2$
Delete	$p \prec\!\!\prec p$	$\mapsto\!\!\!\!\rightarrow$	*True*
PropagateClash	$\mathsf{S} \wedge$ *Fail*	$\mapsto\!\!\!\!\rightarrow$	*Fail*
PropagateSuccess	$\mathsf{S} \wedge$ *True*	$\mapsto\!\!\!\!\rightarrow$	S

The soundness and the completeness of Match is expressed as follows:

Theorem 3.1 ([14]). *The normal form by the rules in* Match *of any matching problem* $p \prec\!\!\prec t$ *such that* $t \in \mathcal{T}(\mathcal{F})$*, exists and is unique.*

1. *if it is of the form* $\bigwedge_{i \in I} x_i \prec\!\!\prec t_i$ *with* $I \neq \emptyset$*, then the substitution* $\sigma = \{x_i \mapsto t_i\}_{i \in I}$ *is the unique match from* p *to* t,
2. *if it is True then* p *and* t *are identical, i.e.* $p = t$,
3. *if it is Fail, then there is no match from* p *to* t.

3.2 Anti-pattern Matching

We now extend the classical notion of matching equation by allowing anti-terms on the left side. We will further call them anti-patterns.

When considering classical patterns, a matching equation $p \ll t$ has a solution when there exists a substitution σ such that $\sigma(p) = t$, that is when $t \in [\![p]\!]_g$. Indeed more precisely $\sigma \in \mathcal{GS}(p)$ is a solution if $\{t\} = [\![\sigma(p)]\!]_g$. This extends naturally to the anti-patterns.

Definition 3.2 (Solutions of anti-pattern matching). *For all $q \in \mathcal{AT}(\mathcal{F}, \mathcal{X})$ and $t \in \mathcal{T}(\mathcal{F})$, the solutions of the anti-pattern matching problem $q \ll t$ are:*

$$Sol(q \ll t) = \{\sigma \mid t \in [\![\sigma(q)]\!]_g, \text{ with } \sigma \in \mathcal{GS}(q)\}$$

Remember that by Definition 2.3, the substitutions apply only on free variables. Also note that for $p \in \mathcal{T}(\mathcal{F}, \mathcal{X})$, we have $[\![\sigma(p)]\!]_g = \{\sigma(p)\}$; this is not always true for the anti-patterns. Take for example $f(x, \neg b)$, and $\sigma = \{x \mapsto a\}$: the set $[\![\sigma(f(x, \neg b))]\!]_g = [\![f(a, \neg b))]\!]_g$ has more than one element, as we saw in Example 2.3. Here are some examples for the solutions of anti-pattern matching problems:

Example 3.1

1. $Sol(f(a, \neg b) \ll f(a, a)) = \Sigma$,
2. $Sol(\neg g(x) \ll g(a)) = \{\sigma \mid g(a) \in \mathcal{T}(\mathcal{F}) \backslash \{g(\sigma(x)) \mid \sigma \in \mathcal{GS}(g(x))\}\} = \emptyset$,
3. $Sol(f(\neg a, x) \ll f(b, c)) = \{x \mapsto c\}$,
4. $Sol(f(x, \neg x) \ll f(a, b)) = \{x \mapsto a\}$,
5. $Sol(f(x, \neg g(x)) \ll f(a, g(b))) = \{x \mapsto a\}$,
6. $Sol(f(x, \neg g(x)) \ll f(a, g(a))) = \emptyset$.

4 Anti-pattern Matching and Equational Problems

The relation between anti-pattern matching and equational problems is not trivial. For instance, the interpretation of $\neg q \ll t$ should not be $q \neq t$. Although this may be correct in the case of ground terms, like $\neg a \ll b$, it is not true in the general case. Take for example $\neg g(x) \ll g(a)$, which according to Definition 3.2 has no solution. But the solutions of $g(x) \neq g(a)$ are the solutions of $x \neq a$. In this section we provide a way of transforming any anti-pattern matching problem into a corresponding equational one that has the same set of solutions. We extend the notion of an equation between terms [11] to the notion of an equation containing anti-patterns:

Definition 4.1 (Solutions of equations with anti-patterns). *For any anti-pattern q and ground term t, σ is a solution of the equational problem $\exists w_1, \ldots, w_n, \forall y_1, \ldots, y_m : q = t$ if:*

1. *the domain of σ is $\mathcal{FV}ar(q) \backslash \{w_1, \ldots, w_n, y_1, \ldots, y_m\}$,*
2. *there exists a substitution ρ whose domain is $\{w_1, \ldots, w_n\} \backslash (\mathcal{FV}ar(q) \cup \{y_1, \ldots, y_m\})$ such that for all substitutions θ whose domain is $\{y_1, \ldots, y_m\} \backslash (\mathcal{FV}ar(q) \cup \{w_1, \ldots, w_n\})$ we have: $t \in [\![\theta\rho\sigma(q)]\!]_g$.*

We denote by $Sol(\exists w_1, \ldots, w_n, \forall y_1, \ldots, y_m : q = t)$ the set of all substitutions that are solutions of $\exists w_1, \ldots, w_n, \forall y_1, \ldots, y_m : q = t$. We have the following properties:

1. $Sol(q = t) = Sol(q \ll t)$, since t is a ground term,
2. $Sol(\exists w_1, \ldots, w_n, \forall y_1, \ldots, y_m : not(q = t)) = \{\sigma \mid t \notin [\![\theta\rho\sigma(q)]\!]_g\}$, with the same conditions on θ, ρ, σ as in Definition 4.1, and *not* being the classical logic negation. One may notice that the substitutions ρ and σ do not have the variables $\{y_1, \ldots, y_m\}$ in their domains, and therefore we can safely eliminate θ in $Sol(\exists w_1, \ldots, w_n, \forall y_1, \ldots, y_m : not(q = t)) = \{\sigma \mid t \notin [\![\rho\sigma(q)]\!]_g\}$, because the ground semantics will instantiate anyway $\{y_1, \ldots, y_m\}$ with all their possible values.

Given an anti-pattern q and a ground term t, we consider the following rewrite system AP-Elim. This transforms an anti-pattern matching problem into an equational one:

$$
\begin{array}{lll}
\mathsf{ElimMatch}\ q \ll t & \mapsto\!\!\!\rightarrow & q = t \\
\mathsf{ElimAnti}\quad q[\urcorner q']_\omega = t & \mapsto\!\!\!\rightarrow & \exists z\ q[z]_\omega = t \ \wedge\ \forall x \in \mathcal{FV}ar(q')\ not(q[q']_\omega = t) \\
 & & \text{if } \forall\ \omega' < \omega,\ q(\omega') \neq \urcorner \text{ and } z \text{ a fresh variable}
\end{array}
$$

Clearly, these rules are terminating and the normal form does not contain anymore the $\urcorner$ symbol. If we apply these rules on the example we provided earlier, $\urcorner g(x) \ll g(a)$, we obtain $\exists z\ z = g(a) \ \wedge\ \forall x\ not(g(x) = g(a))$ which is equivalent with $\forall x\ g(x) \neq g(a)$, that has no solution. Thus, for this example these transformations are valid. As shown below they are also valid in the general case:

Proposition 4.1. *The rules are sound and preserving: they do not introduce unexpected solutions, and no solution is lost in the application of the rules.*

Proof. By Definition 4.1, this is clear for the rule ElimMatch. For ElimAnti, we consider ω a position such that $q[\urcorner q']_\omega$ and $\forall\ \omega' < \omega,\ q(\omega') \neq \urcorner$.

Considering as usual that $Sol(A \wedge B) = Sol(A) \cap Sol(B)$ we have the following result for the right hand side of the rule:

$$
\begin{array}{l}
Sol(\exists z\ q[z]_\omega = t \ \wedge\ \forall x \in \mathcal{FV}ar(q')\ not(q[q']_\omega = t)) \\
= Sol(\exists z\ q[z]_\omega = t\ ) \cap\ Sol(\forall x \in \mathcal{FV}ar(q')\ not(q[q']_\omega = t))
\end{array}
$$

From Definition 4.1, $Sol(\exists z\ q[z]_\omega = t) = \{\sigma \mid \exists \rho \text{ such that } \mathsf{Dom}(\rho) = \{z\}, t \in [\![\rho\sigma(q[z]_\omega)]\!]_g, \text{ and } \mathsf{Dom}(\sigma) = \mathcal{FV}ar(q[z]) \backslash \{z\}\}$.

To have $t \in [\![\rho\sigma(q[z]_\omega)]\!]_g$ the only possible value for $\rho(z)$ is $t_{|\omega}$. So we can further rewrite the above solutions in:

$$\{\sigma \mid t \in [\![\sigma(q[t_{|\omega}]_\omega)]\!]_g,\ \textit{with}\ \mathsf{Dom}(\sigma) = \mathcal{FV}ar(q[z]) \backslash \{z\}\} \tag{1}$$

Applying also the Definition 4.1, $Sol(\forall x \in \mathcal{FV}ar(q')\ not(q[q']_\omega = t))$ is equal to:

$$\{\sigma \mid t \notin [\![\sigma(q[q']_\omega)]\!]_g\ \textit{with}\ \mathsf{Dom}(\sigma) = \mathcal{FV}ar(q[q']) \setminus \mathcal{FV}ar(q')\} \tag{2}$$

On the other hand, for the left part of the rule ElimAnti, by Definition 4.1 we have:

$$\begin{aligned} Sol\ (q[\urcorner q']_\omega = t) &= \{\sigma \mid t \in [\![\sigma(q[\urcorner q']_\omega)]\!]_g,\ with\ \mathsf{Dom}(\sigma) = \mathcal{FV}ar(q[\urcorner q'])\} \\ &= \{\sigma \mid t \in ([\![\sigma(q[z]_\omega)]\!]_g \backslash [\![\sigma(q[q']_\omega)]\!]_g),\ with \ldots\},\ \text{since } \forall \omega' < \omega, q(\omega') \neq \urcorner \\ &= \{\sigma \mid t \in [\![\sigma(q[z]_\omega)]\!]_g\ and\ t \notin [\![\sigma(q[q']_\omega)]\!]_g,\ with\ \mathsf{Dom}(\sigma) = \mathcal{FV}ar(q[\urcorner q'])\} \\ &= \{\sigma \mid t \in [\![\sigma(q[z]_\omega)]\!]_g,\ with \ldots\} \cap\ \{\sigma \mid t \notin [\![\sigma(q[q']_\omega)]\!]_g\ with \ldots\} \end{aligned} \tag{3}$$

Now it remains to check the equivalence of (3) with the intersection of (1) and (2). First of all, $\mathcal{FV}ar(q[z]) \backslash \{z\} = \mathcal{FV}ar(q[q']) \setminus \mathcal{FV}ar(q') = \mathcal{FV}ar(q[\urcorner q'])$ which means that we have the same domain for σ in (3), (1), and (2). Therefore, we have to prove: $\{\sigma \mid t \in [\![\sigma(q[z]_\omega)]\!]_g\} = \{\sigma \mid t \in [\![\sigma(q[t_{|\omega}]_\omega)]\!]_g\}$.

But σ does not instantiate z, and for the inclusion $t \in [\![\sigma(q[z]_\omega)]\!]_g$ to be true, the only possible value of z is $t_{|\omega}$. As we considered an arbitrary $\urcorner$, we can conclude that the rule is sound and preserving, wherever it is applied on a term. □

Using the rewrite system AP-Elim, we can eliminate all $\urcorner$ symbols from any anti-pattern matching problem. The normal forms have the following structure: $\exists z\ q = t\ \wedge\ \forall x\ not(\exists z'\ q' = t\ \wedge\ \forall x'\ not(\ldots))$.

We consider a set of boolean simplification rules, called DeMorgan, that is applied on these normal forms: $not(\exists z\ P) \Rightarrow\!\!\!\!\!\rightarrow \forall z\ not(P), not(\forall z\ P) \Rightarrow\!\!\!\!\!\rightarrow \exists z\ not(P)$, $not(a \wedge b) \Rightarrow\!\!\!\!\!\rightarrow not(a) \vee not(b), not(a \vee b) \Rightarrow\!\!\!\!\!\rightarrow not(a) \wedge not(b), not(not(a)) \Rightarrow\!\!\!\!\!\rightarrow a$, $not(a = b) \Rightarrow\!\!\!\!\!\rightarrow a \neq b$, $not(a \neq b) \Rightarrow\!\!\!\!\!\rightarrow a = b$. The resulting expression no longer contains any *not*, and thus is a classical equational problem. We call it an *anti-pattern disunification problem.*

5 Solving Anti-pattern Matching Via Disunification

As presented previously, an anti-pattern matching problem can be translated into an equivalent equational problem. A natural way to solve this type of problem is to use a disunification algorithm such as described in [11]. Due to lack of space, we cannot present disunification in detail. Instead we give in Figure 1 the set of rules we consider. The interested reader can refer to [11] for a detailed presentation of disunification.

5.1 Disunification Rules

[11] presents a set of disunification rules that is proved to be sound and preserving. Moreover, irreducible problems for these rules are definitions with constraints, i.e. either $\top$, $\perp$ or a conjunction of equalities and disequalities. In Figure 1 we present this set of rules, but tailored for anti-pattern matching problems. It is still sound and preserving, but also ensures (thanks to Theorem 5.1) that for each problem a normal form exists and is unique. We will further call it AP-Match.

Universality_1	$\forall z:\ z = t \wedge \mathsf{S}$	$\mapsto\!\!\!\!\rightarrow$	$\perp$
Universality_2	$\forall z:\ z \neq t \wedge \mathsf{S}$	$\mapsto\!\!\!\!\rightarrow$	$\perp$
Universality_3	$\forall z:\ \mathsf{S}$	$\mapsto\!\!\!\!\rightarrow$	S if $z \notin \mathcal{V}ar(\mathsf{S})$
Universality_4	$\forall z:\ \mathsf{S} \wedge (z \neq t \vee \mathsf{S}')$	$\mapsto\!\!\!\!\rightarrow$	$\forall z:\ \mathsf{S} \wedge \mathsf{S}'(z \leftarrow t)$
Universality_5	$\forall z:\ \mathsf{S} \wedge (z = t \vee \mathsf{S}')$	$\mapsto\!\!\!\!\rightarrow$	$\forall z:\ \mathsf{S} \wedge \mathsf{S}'$ if $z \notin \mathcal{V}ar(\mathsf{S}')$
Replacement	$z = t \wedge \mathsf{S}$	$\mapsto\!\!\!\!\rightarrow$	$z = t \wedge \mathsf{S}(z \leftarrow t)$
Elimination_1	$a = a$	$\mapsto\!\!\!\!\rightarrow$	$\top$
Elimination_2	$a \neq a$	$\mapsto\!\!\!\!\rightarrow$	$\perp$
PropagateClash_1	$\mathsf{S} \wedge \perp$	$\mapsto\!\!\!\!\rightarrow$	$\perp$
PropagateClash_2	$\mathsf{S} \vee \perp$	$\mapsto\!\!\!\!\rightarrow$	S
$\text{PropagateSuccess}_1$	$\mathsf{S} \wedge \top$	$\mapsto\!\!\!\!\rightarrow$	S
$\text{PropagateSuccess}_2$	$\mathsf{S} \vee \top$	$\mapsto\!\!\!\!\rightarrow$	$\top$
Clean_1	$a \wedge a$	$\mapsto\!\!\!\!\rightarrow$	a
Clean_2	$a \vee a$	$\mapsto\!\!\!\!\rightarrow$	a
Clash_1	$f(p_1 \dots p_n) = g(t_1 \dots t_n)$	$\mapsto\!\!\!\!\rightarrow$	$\perp$ if $f \not\equiv g$
Clash_2	$f(p_1 \dots p_n) \neq g(t_1 \dots t_n)$	$\mapsto\!\!\!\!\rightarrow$	$\top$ if $f \not\equiv g$
Decompose_1	$f(p_1 \dots p_n) = f(t_1 \dots t_n)$	$\mapsto\!\!\!\!\rightarrow$	$\bigwedge_{i=1,\dots,n} p_i = t_i$
Decompose_2	$f(P_1 \dots P_n) \neq f(t_1 \dots t_n)$	$\mapsto\!\!\!\!\rightarrow$	$\bigvee_{i=1,\dots,n} p_i \neq t_i$
Merging_1	$z = t \wedge z = u$	$\mapsto\!\!\!\!\rightarrow$	$z = t \wedge t = u$
Merging_2	$z \neq t \vee z \neq u$	$\mapsto\!\!\!\!\rightarrow$	$z \neq t \vee t \neq u$
Merging_3	$z = t \wedge z \neq u$	$\mapsto\!\!\!\!\rightarrow$	$z = t \wedge t \neq u$
Merging_4	$z = t \vee z \neq u$	$\mapsto\!\!\!\!\rightarrow$	$t = u \vee z \neq u$
Removed rules:	OccurCheck, Explosion, Elimination of disjunctions		
New rules:			
Exists_1	$\exists z:\ \mathsf{S}$	$\mapsto\!\!\!\!\rightarrow$	S if $z \notin \mathcal{V}ar(\mathsf{S})$
Exists_2	$\exists z:\ \mathsf{S} \wedge (z \neq t \vee \mathsf{S}')$	$\mapsto\!\!\!\!\rightarrow$	S if $z \notin \mathcal{V}ar(\mathsf{S})$
Exists_3	$\exists z:\ \mathsf{S} \wedge (z = t \vee \mathsf{S}')$	$\mapsto\!\!\!\!\rightarrow$	S if $z \notin \mathcal{V}ar(\mathsf{S})$

Fig. 1. Simplified presentation of the disunification rules: AP-Match

From the classical presentation of disunification rules, three rules have been removed. They were no longer necessary in the restricted case of the anti-patterns, as their application conditions are never fulfilled. Three new rules that are proved to be sound and preserving [9] have been added. They ensure the elimination of all variables that are existentially quantified. The justification is simple, and consists in showing that any problem containing an occurrence of an existentially quantified variable is reducible: if there is such a variable, one of the three introduced rules is tried. The condition $z \notin \mathcal{V}ar(\mathsf{S})$ may prevent from applying a rule. In that case, we have $z \in \mathcal{V}ar(\mathsf{S})$ and therefore one of the following rules can be applied: Replacement (or Merging), Decompose (or Clash) — if the variable z is inside a term.

In [11] there is a clear separation between the elimination of parameters and the rules that reach definitions with constraints. But, as affirmed both in [11] and [9], such a strict control is only for presentation purposes. In our algorithm, we use a single step approach.

5.2 Solved Forms

In the following we show that an *anti-pattern disunification problem* (resulting from the application of AP-Elim, followed by DeMorgan can be simplified by the rewrite system AP-Match, given in Figure 1, such that it does not contain any disjunction or disequality.

Example 5.1. If we consider $f(x, \urcorner y) \prec\!\!\prec f(a, b)$, the corresponding anti-pattern disunification problem is computed in the following way:

$$\begin{aligned} f(x, \urcorner y) \prec\!\!\prec f(a, b) &\mapsto\!\!\!\!\rightarrow f(x, \urcorner y) = f(a, b) \\ &\mapsto\!\!\!\!\rightarrow \exists z\ f(x, z) = f(a, b) \wedge \forall y\ not(f(x, y) = f(a, b)) \\ &\mapsto\!\!\!\!\rightarrow \exists z\ f(x, z) = f(a, b) \wedge \forall y\ f(x, y) \neq f(a, b) \end{aligned}$$

Proposition 5.1. *Given an* anti-pattern disunification problem, *the normal form wrt. the rewrite system* AP-Match *does not contain disjunctions or disequalities.*

Proof. We consider an anti-pattern $q \in \mathcal{AT}(\mathcal{F}, \mathcal{X})$, and an arbitrary application of ElimAnti:

$$q[\urcorner q']_\omega = t \mapsto\!\!\!\!\rightarrow \exists z\ q[z]_\omega = t\ \wedge\ \forall x \in \mathcal{FV}ar(q')\ not(q[q']_\omega = t)$$

If a disequality or a disjunction is produced, it comes from the $not(q[q']_\omega = t)$. We now consider the variables that occur in this expression. Each of them belongs to one of the following classes:

1. the free variables of q',
2. the free variables of $q[q']_\omega$ — excepting the free variables of q',
3. the variables of $q[q']_\omega$ that are not free.

In the following we show that the normal form cannot contain such a variable. Therefore, the normalization of $\forall x \in \mathcal{FV}ar(q'), not(q[q']_\omega = t)$ leads to either $\top$ or $\bot$:

1. these are universally quantified variables, and they will be eliminated by Universality rules,
2. let us consider $y \in \mathcal{FV}ar(q[q']_\omega)\backslash\mathcal{FV}ar(q')$, and let us suppose that the reduction of $not(q[q']_\omega = t)$ generates the disequality $y \neq t_{|\omega_1}$, then the reduction of the first part $\exists z\ q[z]_\omega = t$ will generate $y = t_{|\omega_2}$, with $\omega_2 = \omega_1$ because t and the skeleton of q are the same in both parts. By applying the Replacement rule, all the occurrences of $y \neq t_{|\omega_1}$ are transformed in $t_{|\omega_1} \neq t_{|\omega_1}$ and later eliminated,
3. any variable that is not free (i.e. is under a $\urcorner$) will be universally quantified by a further application of the rule ElimAnti, therefore later eliminated by Universality$_1$ or Universality$_2$. □

Theorem 5.1. *Given an* anti-pattern disunification problem, *its normal form wrt. the rewrite system* AP-Match *exists and is unique.*

1. *when it is of the form* $\bigwedge_{i\in I} x_i = t_i$ *with* $I \neq \emptyset$ *and* $x_i \neq x_j$ *for all* $i \neq j$, *the substitution* $\sigma = \{x_i \mapsto t_i\}_{i\in I}$ *is the solution of the matching problem,*
2. *when it is* $\top$, *any substitution* σ *is a solution of the matching problem,*
3. *when it is* $\bot$, *the matching problem has no solution.*

Proof. By applying Proposition 5.1. □

5.3 Simple Examples

Let us show on a few examples how the rules behave. First with one complement:

$$\begin{aligned}
& f(a, \urcorner b) \prec\!\!\prec f(a,a) \\
& \mapsto\!\!\!\rightarrow f(a, \urcorner b) = f(a,a) \mapsto\!\!\!\rightarrow \exists z f(a,z) = f(a,a) \wedge not(f(a,b) = f(a,a)) \\
& \mapsto\!\!\!\rightarrow \exists z f(a,z) = f(a,a) \wedge f(a,b) \neq f(a,a) \\
& \mapsto\!\!\!\rightarrow \exists z(a = a \wedge z = a) \wedge (a \neq a \vee b \neq a) \mapsto\!\!\!\rightarrow \exists z(z = a) \wedge (\bot \vee \top) \\
& \mapsto\!\!\!\rightarrow \top \wedge \top \mapsto\!\!\!\rightarrow \top.
\end{aligned}$$

Of course complements can be nested as illustrated below:

$$\begin{aligned}
& \urcorner f(a, \urcorner b) \prec\!\!\prec f(a,b) \\
& \mapsto\!\!\!\rightarrow \urcorner f(a, \urcorner b) = f(a,b) \mapsto\!\!\!\rightarrow \exists z\ z = f(a,b) \wedge not(f(a, \urcorner b) = f(a,b)) \\
& \mapsto\!\!\!\rightarrow \exists z\ z = f(a,b) \wedge not(\ \exists z' f(a,z') = f(a,b) \wedge not(f(a,b) = f(a,b))) \\
& \mapsto\!\!\!\rightarrow \exists z\ z = f(a,b) \wedge (\forall z' f(a,z') = f(a,b) \vee f(a,b) = f(a,b)) \\
& \mapsto\!\!\!\rightarrow \top \wedge (\forall z'(a = a \wedge z' = b) \vee (a = a \wedge b = b)) \\
& \mapsto\!\!\!\rightarrow \forall z'(z' = b) \vee \top \mapsto\!\!\!\rightarrow \top.
\end{aligned}$$

We can also consider anti-pattern problems with variables, such as $f(\urcorner a, x) \prec\!\!\prec f(b,c)$, whose solution is $\{x \mapsto c\}$. The pattern can be non-linear: $f(x, \urcorner x) \prec\!\!\prec f(a,b)$, leading to $\{x \mapsto a\}$. Nested negation and non-linearity can be combined:

$$\begin{aligned}
& \urcorner f(x, \urcorner g(x)) \prec\!\!\prec f(a, g(b)) \\
& \mapsto\!\!\!\rightarrow \urcorner f(x, \urcorner g(x)) = f(a, g(b)) \\
& \mapsto\!\!\!\rightarrow \exists z\ z = f(a,g(b)) \wedge \forall x\ not(f(x, \urcorner g(x)) = f(a,g(b))) \\
& \mapsto\!\!\!\rightarrow \exists z\ z = f(a,g(b)) \wedge \forall x\ not(\exists z'\ f(x,z') = f(a,g(b)) \\
& \qquad\qquad\qquad\qquad \wedge \forall x\ not(f(x,g(x)) = f(a,g(b)))) \\
& \mapsto\!\!\!\rightarrow \exists z\ z = f(a,g(b)) \wedge \forall x(\forall z'\ f(x,z') = f(a,g(b)) \vee \exists x\ f(x,g(x)) = f(a,g(b))) \\
& \mapsto\!\!\!\rightarrow \top \wedge \forall x\ (\forall z'\ (x = a \wedge z' = g(b)) \vee \exists x\ (x = a \wedge g(x) = g(b))) \\
& \mapsto\!\!\!\rightarrow \forall x\ (x = a \wedge \forall z'\ (z' = g(b)) \vee \exists x\ (x = a \wedge x = b)) \\
& \mapsto\!\!\!\rightarrow \forall x\ (x = a \wedge \bot \vee \exists x\ (x = a \wedge a = b)) \\
& \mapsto\!\!\!\rightarrow \forall x\ (\bot \vee \exists x\ (x = a \wedge \bot)) \mapsto\!\!\!\rightarrow \forall x\ (\bot \vee \bot) \mapsto\!\!\!\rightarrow \bot.
\end{aligned}$$

5.4 Summing Up the Relations with Disunification

When comparing anti-pattern problems with general disunification ones, there are many similarities, but some important differences also. In the anti-pattern case, a solved form does not contain any quantifier whereas disunification allows existential ones. Another important difference is the unitary property (Theorem 5.1) which is obviously not true for disunification: $x \neq a$ has many solutions in general. Disunification contains rules (called *globally preserving*) that return an equational problem whose solutions are a subset of the given problem. The Explosion and the Elimination of disjunctions rules are such examples. In our case, the complexity is dramatically reduced since these rules are unnecessary.

6 Implementation

We do not have enough space to present the implementation in detail but the reader should know that the presented anti-pattern matching algorithm has been fully implemented and integrated in Tom.[2] With the purpose of also supporting anti-patterns, we enriched the syntax of the Tom patterns to allow the use the operator '!' (representing '⌝'). Therefore, constructs as the following one are now valid in this language:

```
%match(s) {
  f(a(),g(b()))   -> { /* action 1: executed when f(a,g(b))<<s   */ }
  f(!a(),g(b()))  -> { /* action 2: when f(x,g(b))<<s with x!=a */ }
  !f(x,!g(x))     -> { /* action 3: when not f(x,y)<<s or ...   */ }
  !f(x,g(y))      -> { /* action 4 */ }
}
```

Similarly to `switch/case`, an action part is executed when its corresponding pattern matches the subject `s`. Note that non-linear patterns are allowed.

Without the use of anti-patterns, one would be forced to verify additional conditions in the action part. For example, the previous `%match` should have been written:

```
%match(s) {
  f(a(),g(b()))   -> { /* action 1 */ }
  f(x,g(b)) -> { if(x != a) { /* action 2 */ } }
  y -> { if(symb(y) != f) { /* action 3 */ }
         else { %match(y) { f(x,g(x)) -> { /* action 3 */ } } } }
  z -> {
    if(symb(z) != f) { /* action 4 */}
    else { %match(z) {
                f(x,g(y)) -> { break; /* do not perform action 4 */ }
                _ -> { /* action 4 */ } } } }
}
```

This example clearly shows that anti-pattern semantics cannot be easily obtained in a standard setting. Note also that method extraction would be necessary to avoid duplicating actions. This would make the code even more complex.

7 Related Work

There has been a huge amount of work that can be related in a way or another with the content of this paper. In spite of this, the anti-patterns are quite a novelty for pattern matching languages. It is important to stress that we introduced

[2] `http://tom.loria.fr`

the anti-patterns with the purpose of having a compact and permissive representation to match *ground terms*: the use of nested negations replaces the use of conjunctions and/or disjunctions and there is no restriction to linear terms for example. It is also a useful representation which is both intuitive and easy to compile in an efficient way. In the context of Tom, general algorithms such as disunification [10,11,9] could have been used. But since pattern-matching is the main execution mechanism, we were interested in a specialized approach that is both simpler and more efficient.

Lassez [16] presented a way of expressing exclusion by the means of counter-examples: typically, the expression $f(x,y)/\{f(a,u) \vee f(u,a)\}$ represents all the ground instances of $f(x,y)$, different from $f(a,u)$ and $f(u,a)$. Even though this is a useful and close approach, it is more restrictive than the anti-patterns. Consider for example the anti-pattern $\urcorner f(a, \urcorner b)$, that cannot be represented by terms with counter-examples, unless we allow the counter-examples to also have counter-examples, i.e. $z/\{f(a,y/\{b\})\}$ — an issue not addressed in [16]. Moreover, the application domain of terms with counter-examples was rather machine learning than efficient term rewriting. This may explain why they restricted to linear terms and studied if these types of expressions have an equivalent representation using disjunctions. Actually, complementing non-linear terms was not very much addressed (except for disunification) and standard algorithms that computes complements are incorrect for non-linear terms, as mentioned in [18]. Complementing higher order patterns is also considered only in the linear case.

Although the syntax of set constraints [2,20,1,7] allows the use of complement without any restriction of linearity or level of complement, we are not aware of any good semantics for the general case. Moreover, despite the fact that theoretically it is possible to have a constraint of the form $f(a,b) \subseteq \neg f(a, \neg b)$, existing implementations do not allow the complement in its fully generality. For example the CLP(Set) language in B-Prolog[3] allows the use of the symbol '\' as a unary operator representing the complement. However, it is only defined for variables, and not for constants. Another example is CLP(SC) [12], where we are restricted to use only predicates of arity 0 and 1, which obviously cannot have the same expressiveness as anti-patterns. Besides that, it does not provide variable assignments. Constraints over features trees [4,3,6] include the *exclusion constraint* which is a formula of the form $\neg\exists y(xfy)$, which says that the feature f is undefined for x, i.e. there is no edge that starts from x labeled with f. A more complex semantics of nested negations is not provided, for example to express that *there is no 'a' in relation with x, unless x is in relation with 'b'*.

CDuce[4] allows for the use of complement when declaring types but it restricts it to be used on types alone, and do not deal with variables complements.

The constrained terms, as defined in [9], can be used to obtain the semantics of some anti-patterns. They may have constraints — conjunction of disequalities — attached to their variables. Considering for example $f(a, \urcorner b)$, this is semantically

[3] `http://www.probp.com/`
[4] `http://www.cduce.org/`

equivalent to $f(a, z)$, *constrained by* $z \neq b$. But for a more complex expression, like $f(a, \urcorner g(b, \urcorner c))$, this approach is not expressive enough because the use of disjunctions in the constraints is not allowed.

8 Conclusion and Future Work

In this paper we have defined the notion of *anti-patterns* along with their semantics. We have shown how anti-pattern matching problems can be transformed in specific disunification problems. Therefore, most of the properties (confluence, termination) that hold for the disunification rules are still true for the anti-pattern matching ones. Moreover, we proved that anti-pattern matching is unitary, that the rules are sound and fully preserving, and that the computed solved forms do not contain any disequality — properties that are not true for general disunification problems. Finally, the anti-pattern matching algorithm has been implemented and is available in the Tom system.

We are currently working on two questions. The first one is about the precise complexity of the anti-pattern matching problem. For instance, the satisfiability in $\mathcal{T}(\mathcal{F})$ of equational problems is known to be NP-complete. However, solving anti-pattern matching being a more restricted disunification problem, we conjecture that solving an anti-pattern matching problem is polynomial.

The second one concerns the study of anti-pattern matching in presence of associative operators. This is quite appealing because of the nice expressiveness that such a feature will provide. For instance in Tom the pattern $(*, !a, *)$ would denote a list which contains at least one element different from a, whereas $!(*, a, *)$ would denote a list which does not contain any a. This will be more generally useful for theories like associativity and commutativity and anti-pattern matching should therefore be investigated for appropriate equational theories.

Acknowledgments. We sincerely thank Luigi Liquori for stimulating discussions and suggestions, Emilie Balland for her comments on the preliminary version of this paper and the anonymous referees for their valuable remarks and suggestions.

References

1. A. Aiken, D. Kozen, and E. Wimmers. Decidability of systems of set constraints with negative constraints. *Information and Computation*, 122(1):30–44, 1995.
2. A. Aiken and E. L. Wimmers. Solving systems of set constraints (extended abstract). In *LICS*, pages 329–340. IEEE Computer Society, 1992.
3. H. Ait-Kaci, A. Podelski, and G. Smolka. A feature constraint system for logic programming with entailment. *Theoretical Computer Science*, 122(1–2):263–283, 1994.
4. F. Baader, H.-J. Bürckert, B. Nebel, W. Nutt, and G. Smolka. On the expressivity of feature logics with negation, functional uncertainty, and sort equations. *Journal of Logic, Language and Information*, 2:1–18, 1993.

5. F. Baader and T. Nipkow. *Term Rewriting and all That*. Cambridge University Press, 1998.
6. R. Backofen and G. Smolka. A complete and recursive feature theory. *Theoretical Computer Science*, 146(1–2):243–268, July 1995.
7. W. Charatonik and L. Pacholski. Negative set constraints with equality. In *LICS*, pages 128–136. IEEE Computer Society, 1994.
8. K. L. Clark. *Logic and databases*, chapter Negation as Failure, pages 293–322. Plenum Press, New York, 1978.
9. H. Comon. *Unification et disunification. Théories et applications.* Thèse de Doctorat d'Université, Institut Polytechnique de Grenoble (France), 1988.
10. H. Comon. Disunification: a survey. In J.-L. Lassez and G. Plotkin, editors, *Computational Logic. Essays in honor of Alan Robinson*, chapter 9, pages 322–359. The MIT press, Cambridge (MA, USA), 1991.
11. H. Comon and P. Lescanne. Equational problems and disunification. In C. Kirchner, editor, *Unification*, pages 297–352. Academic Press inc., London, 1990.
12. J. S. Foster. CLP(SC): Implementation and efficiency considerations. In *Proceedings Workshop on Set Constraints, held in Conjunction with CP'96, Boston, Massachusetts*, 1996.
13. G. Huet. *Résolution d'equations dans les langages d'ordre 1, 2, ..., ω.* Thèse de Doctorat d'Etat, Université de Paris 7 (France), 1976.
14. C. Kirchner and H. Kirchner. Rewriting, solving, proving. A preliminary version of a book available at `http://www.loria.fr/~ckirchne/rsp.ps.gz`, 1999.
15. C. Kirchner, P.-E. Moreau, and A. Reilles. Formal validation of pattern matching code. In P. Barahona and A. Felty, editors, *Proceedings of the 7th ACM SIGPLAN PPDP*, pages 187–197. ACM, July 2005.
16. J.-L. Lassez and K. Marriott. Explicit representation of terms defined by counter examples. *Journal of Automated Reasoning*, 3(3):301–317, 1987.
17. L. Liquori. iRho: the software [system description]. *DCM: International Workshop on Development in Computational Models. Electr. Notes Theor. Comput. Sci.*, 135(3):85–94, 2006.
18. A. Momigliano. Elimination of negation in a logical framework. In *Proceedings of the 14th Annual Conference of the EACSL on Computer Science Logic*, volume 1862 of *LNCS*, pages 411–426, London, UK, 2000. Springer Verlag.
19. P.-E. Moreau, C. Ringeissen, and M. Vittek. A Pattern Matching Compiler for Multiple Target Languages. In G. Hedin, editor, *12th Conference on Compiler Construction, Warsaw (Poland)*, volume 2622 of *LNCS*, pages 61–76. Springer-Verlag, May 2003.
20. M. Müller, J. Niehren, and A. Podelski. Inclusion constraints over non-empty sets of trees. In M. Dauchet, editor, *Theory and Practice of Software Development, International Joint Conference CAAP/FASE/TOOLS*, volume 1214 of *LNCS*, pages 217–231. Springer Verlag, Apr. 1997.

A Certified Lightweight Non-interference Java Bytecode Verifier*

Gilles Barthe[1], David Pichardie[2,**], and Tamara Rezk[1]

[1] INRIA Sophia Antipolis, France
[2] IRISA/INRIA Rennes, France

Abstract. Non-interference is a semantical condition on programs that guarantees the absence of illicit information flow throughout their execution, and that can be enforced by appropriate information flow type systems. Much of previous work on type systems for non-interference has focused on calculi or high-level programming languages, and existing type systems for low-level languages typically omit objects, exceptions, and method calls, and/or do not prove formally the soundness of the type system. We define an information flow type system for a sequential JVM-like language that includes classes, objects, arrays, exceptions and method calls, and prove that it guarantees non-interference. For increased confidence, we have formalized the proof in the proof assistant Coq; an additional benefit of the formalization is that we have extracted from our proof a certified lightweight bytecode verifier for information flow. Our work provides, to our best knowledge, the first sound and implemented information flow type system for such an expressive fragment of the JVM.

1 Introduction

Starting from the work of Volpano and Smith [21], type systems have become a popular means to enforce information flow policies in programming languages [19]. It is striking to notice that, although mobile code security is one central motivation behind those works, there has been very little effort to study information flow in low-level languages such as Java bytecode. While focusing on source languages is useful to provide developers with assurance that their code does not leak information unduly, users need to be provided with enforcement mechanisms that operate at bytecode level, because Java applets are downloaded as JVM bytecode programs.

Contribution. We define and prove the soundness of an information flow type system for a sequential fragment of the Java Virtual Machine (JVM) with objects, arrays, methods, and exceptions; the type system follows the principles of bytecode verification and thus can be integrated in a standard Java security architecture.

* Work partially supported by IST Project MOBIUS, by the RNTL Castles and by the ACI Sécurité SPOPS.

** Most of this work was performed while at INRIA Sophia Antipolis.

R. De Nicola (Ed.): ESOP 2007, LNCS 4421, pp. 125–140, 2007.

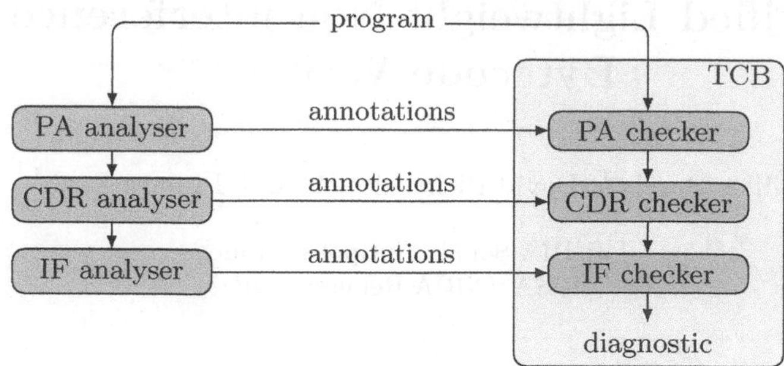

Fig. 1. Information flow analyser and checker

In order to deal with the unstructured nature of bytecode programs, and in particular jumps and exceptions, the analysis is performed in three successive phases, described in the left part of Figure 1:

1. the PA (pre-analyse) analyser computes information that can be used to reduce the control flow graph and to detect branches that will never be taken. The PA analyser performs analyses of null pointers (to predict unthrowable null pointer exceptions), classes (to predict target of `throws` instructions), array accesses (to predict unthrowable out-of-bounds exceptions), and exceptions (to over-approximate the set of throwable exceptions for each method).
2. the CDR analyser computes control dependence regions (cdr), using the results of the PA analyser to minimise the size of regions. The computations are based on well-known techniques based on post-dominators (see the companion report [5] for details).
3. the IF (Information Flow) analyser uses lightweight bytecode verification techniques, which adapt Kildall's algorithm to compute efficiently for each program point its security environment (i.e. the upper bound of the guards under which it executes) and a stack type that records the security levels of elements of the stack at this program point.

Checking, described on the right part of Figure 1, assumes that programs are annotated with (part of) the results of the PA, CDR, and IF analysers:

1. the PA checker verifies that annotations provided by the PA analyser are correct. Correctness is expressed as as an equivalence between the JVM semantics and an instrumented semantics that manipulate programs annotated with the results of the PA analyser;
2. the CDR checker verifies that regions provided by the CDR analyser verify the safe over-approximation properties (SOAP) of Section 4. Its correctness relies on the correctness of the PA checker;
3. the IF checker verifies type correctness in the style of lightweight bytecode verification. Correctness is proved by showing that typable programs are non-interfering. Its correctness relies on the correctness of the CDR checker and by transitivity on the correctness of the PA checker.

We have formally defined the CDR and IF checkers, and proved their correctness in the Coq proof assistant. The correctness proof assumes that the PA checker is correct; defining and proving the correctness of (parts of) the PA checker in Coq has been done elsewhere [7], and integrating this development in our framework is left for future work.

Related Work. We refer to the survey article of Sabelfeld and Myers [19] for a more complete account of recent developments in language-based security, and only focus on most relevant work.

Java. Jif [15] is an information-flow typed extension of Java that builds upon the decentralised label model to support flexible and expressive information flow policies. Jif offers developers a practical tool for ensuring that applications meet their information flow policies, but lacks a soundness proof. However, Banerjee and Naumann [3,16] have shown the soundness of a simpler information flow type system for a fragment of Java with objects and methods.

Hedin and Sands [12] have observed that most implementations of the Java API invalidate the assumption, common to our work and to [3,15], that references are opaque, i.e. the only observations that an attacker can make about a reference are those about the object to which it points, and exhibited a typable Jif program that unintentionally leaks information through invoking API methods. There are several ways to address this issue, but we leave it for future work.

JVM. The paper improves substantially on our earlier work [6]: the language of this paper is more realistic (it includes methods and arrays and provides an accurate treatment of exceptions), the security policies are more expressive (we adopt arbitrary lattices of security levels instead of two-element lattices), the enforcement mechanism is more accurate (thanks to the PA checker) and simpler (some redundant typing constraints have been removed), and the soundness proof has been machine checked using the proof assistant Coq.

Lanet *et al.* [8] report on a successful use of model-checking techniques to detect illicit information flows in a case study involving Java smart cards. Genaim and Spoto [10] propose another automatic method to check information flow policies for Java bytecode using boolean functions and binary decision diagrams.

Type-preserving compilation. Generalising the results of earlier work with Naumann [4], we have shown that programs typable into an fragment of Jif are compiled into bytecode programs that are accepted by our information flow checker [17]. These results show that (a fragment of) Jif can be used to develop information-flow aware applications that are accepted by our type system. Conversely, they show that applications written in (a fragment of) Jif can be verified automatically at the consumer side by an enhanced bytecode verifier. Zanardini [23] has shown for a fragment of Java including objects and method calls that the compiled counterpart of a source Java program that is accepted by an analyser for abstract non-interference (ANY) [11], also satisfies ANY. This issue has also been studied in the context of typed assembly languages [9,22].

2 Language: Syntax and Semantics

Our information flow type checker is checked correct against Bicolano[1], which formalises the semantics of the JVM in Coq. Bicolano consists of a small step semantics, which captures one-step execution of the JVM and a big step semantics, a small step semantics where method calls are big step (which dispenses from dealing with stack frames and is useful for reasoning); all semantics are proved equivalent in the usual sense. For the purpose of this paper, we have also defined a non-standard semantics on annotated programs, using annotations to eliminate some impossible transitions.

Programs. A program in the JVM is composed of a set of classes. Each class includes a set of fields and a set of methods, including a distinguished method **main** that is the first one to be executed. Each method description includes a method identifier, its code (set of labelled bytecode instructions), a table of exception handlers, and a signature that gives the type of its arguments and of its result.[2] We note $\mathsf{Handler}(i, C) = t$ when there is a handler at program point t for exception of class C thrown at program point i, and $\mathsf{Handler}(i, C) \uparrow$ otherwise. A method identifier may correspond to several methods in the class hierarchy according to overriding of methods. We assume there is a function lookup attached to each program that takes a method identifier and a class name and returns the method to be executed.

Memory Model. The memory model is summarised in Figure 2. During the execution of a method values manipulated by the JVM are either numerical values (taken in a set $\mathcal{N}$), locations (taken in an infinite set $\mathcal{L}$), or simply the *null* constant. Method computation is done on states of the form $\langle h, pc, \rho, s\rangle$ where h is the heap of objects and arrays, pc is the current program point, ρ is the set of local variables and s the operand stack. Heaps are modelled as a partial function $h : \mathcal{L} \rightharpoonup (\mathcal{O} + \mathcal{A})$ from location to objects or arrays. The set $\mathcal{O}$ of objects is modelled as $\mathcal{C} \times (\mathcal{F} \rightharpoonup \mathcal{V})$, i.e. a class name and a partial function from fields to values. The set $\mathcal{A}$ of arrays is modelled as $\mathcal{N} \times \mathcal{S} \times (\mathcal{N} \rightharpoonup \mathcal{V})$, i.e. each array a handles a length number (noted $a.length$), a security level (noted $at(a)$) and a partial function from index to values (whose accesses are noted $a[i]$). The array security level is a proof artifact useful to keep track of the level attached to every element of an array during allocation. It is straightforward to prove equivalence between executions which manipulate this extra information and those who do not. A set of local variables is a mapping $\rho \in \mathcal{X} \to \mathcal{V}$ from local variables to values. Operand stacks are lists of values. A method execution terminates on *final states.* A final state is either a pair $(v, h) \in \mathcal{V} \times \text{Heap}$ (normal termination), or a pair $(\langle l\rangle, h) \in \mathcal{L} \times \text{Heap}$ (the method execution terminates because of an exception thrown on an object pointed by a location l, but not caught in this method).

---

[1] `http://mobius.inria.fr/bicolano`

[2] In this abstract, we assume that all methods return a value upon normal termination; however our formalisation also considers void methods.

$\mathcal{N}$: numerical values $\mathcal{L}$: locations $\mathcal{X}$: variable names
$\mathcal{C}$: class names $\mathcal{F}$: field names $\mathcal{P}$: program points

$\mathcal{V} = \mathcal{N} + \mathcal{L} + \{null\}$	values
$\text{LocalVar} = \mathcal{X} \rightarrow \mathcal{V}$	local variables
$\text{OpStack} = \mathcal{V}^*$	operand stacks
$\mathcal{O} = \mathcal{C} \times (\mathcal{F} \rightharpoonup \mathcal{V})$	objects
$\mathcal{A} = \mathcal{N} \times \mathcal{S} \times (\mathcal{N} \rightharpoonup \mathcal{V})$	arrays
$\text{Heap} = \mathcal{L} \rightharpoonup (\mathcal{O} + \mathcal{A})$	heap
$\text{State} = \text{Heap} \times \mathcal{P} \times \text{LocalVar} \times \text{OpStack}$	states
$\text{FinalState} = (\mathcal{V} + \mathcal{L}) \times \text{Heap}$	final states

Fig. 2. Memory model of the JVM

Operational Semantics. Semantic transitions between consecutive states are modelled by a relation $\leadsto_m^\tau$, parameterised by a tag $\tau \in \{\emptyset\} + \mathcal{C}$ (set noted Tag in the sequel) to describe the nature of the transition ($c \in \mathcal{C}$ for a transition which throws an exception of class c and $\emptyset$ for any other transition). We note $\rho, h \Downarrow_m r, h$ the transitive closure $\langle 1, \rho, \varepsilon, h\rangle (\leadsto_m)^\star r, h$ between an initial state and a final result.

We give in Figure 3 the semantics[3] of some instructions. There are four rules for the virtual call instruction. The first models the case where execution of the callee terminates normally. The location l is used to resolve the virtual call. Thanks to the class of l and the identifier m_{ID}, a method m' is found in the class hierarchy (through the lookup operator). The transitive closure of $\leadsto_m$ is then used to obtain the result of the execution of m'. Execution of m' is initialised with location l for the reserved variable *this* and the elements of the operand stack os_1 for the other variables. The second and the third rules model the cases where execution of the called method terminates by an uncaught exception. In the former rule the thrown exception is caught in method m while in the latter rule it is uncaught and m then terminates abnormally. In both cases, we impose that thrown exception has been statically predicted by the result excAnalysis(m_{ID}) of the exception analysis. The fourth rule corresponds to a null pointer exception thrown because the virtual call was made on a null reference. We note **np** the Java class associated to the null pointer exception. When a native exception **np** is thrown the catching mechanism is model by the function RuntimeExceptionHandling. Each instruction which performs accesses references (like getfield f, putfield f and throw) has similar semantics rules. The fifth rule corresponds to the array store instruction (xastore) where the value v is stored in the array pointed by the location l, at the index number i. The last two rules concern the instruction throw which throws the exception pointed by the reference on top of the stack.

[3] For every function $f \in A \rightarrow B$, $x \in A$ and $v \in B$, we let $f[x \mapsto v]$ denote the unique function f' s.t. $f'(y) = f(y)$ if $y \neq x$ and $f'(x) = v$. Further, we let $A^\star$ denote the set of A-stacks for every set A. We use:: to denote the cons and concatenation operations on stacks.

$$\frac{P_m[i] = \mathsf{invokevirtual}\ m_{\mathrm{ID}} \qquad m' = \mathsf{lookup}_P(m_{\mathrm{ID}}, \mathsf{class}(h(l))) \qquad \{this \mapsto l, \boldsymbol{x} \mapsto os_1\}, h \Downarrow_{m'} v, h'}{\langle i, \rho, os_1 :: l :: os_2, h\rangle \leadsto^{\emptyset}_m \langle i+1, \rho, v :: os_2, h'\rangle}$$

$$\frac{\begin{array}{ccc} P_m[i] = \mathsf{invokevirtual}\ m_{\mathrm{ID}} & m' = \mathsf{lookup}_P(m_{\mathrm{ID}}, \mathsf{class}(h(l))) & e = \mathsf{class}(h'(l')) \\ \{this \mapsto l, \boldsymbol{x} \mapsto os_1\}, h \Downarrow_{m'} \langle l'\rangle, h' & \mathsf{Handler}_m(i, e) = t & \boxed{e \in \mathsf{excAnalysis}(m_{\mathrm{ID}})} \end{array}}{\langle i, \rho, os_1 :: l :: os_2, h\rangle \leadsto^{e}_m \langle t, \rho, l' :: \epsilon, h'\rangle}$$

$$\frac{\begin{array}{ccc} P_m[i] = \mathsf{invokevirtual}\ m_{\mathrm{ID}} & m' = \mathsf{lookup}_P(m_{\mathrm{ID}}, \mathsf{class}(h(l))) & e = \mathsf{class}(h'(l')) \\ \{this \mapsto l, \boldsymbol{x} \mapsto os_1\}, h \Downarrow_{m'} \langle l'\rangle, h' & \mathsf{Handler}_m(i, e) \uparrow & \boxed{e \in \mathsf{excAnalysis}(m_{\mathrm{ID}})} \end{array}}{\langle i, \rho, os_1 :: l :: os_2, h\rangle \leadsto^{e}_m \langle l'\rangle, h'}$$

$$\frac{P_m[i] = \mathsf{invokevirtual}\ m_{\mathrm{ID}} \qquad l' = \mathrm{fresh}(h) \qquad \boxed{\mathsf{nullAnalysis}(m, i) \neq safe}}{\langle i, \rho, os_1 :: null :: os_2, h\rangle \leadsto^{\mathbf{np}}_m \mathsf{RuntimeExceptionHandling}(h, l', \mathbf{np}, i, \rho)}$$

$$\frac{P_m[i] = \mathsf{xastore} \qquad 0 \leq i < h(l).length}{\langle i, \rho, v :: i :: l :: os, h\rangle \leadsto^{\emptyset}_m \langle i+1, \rho, os, h[l \mapsto h(l)[i \mapsto v]]\rangle}$$

$$\frac{P_m[i] = \mathsf{throw} \qquad e = \mathsf{class}(h(l)) \qquad \mathsf{Handler}_m(i, e) = t \qquad \boxed{e \in \mathsf{classAnalysis}(m, i)}}{\langle i, \rho, l :: os, h\rangle \leadsto^{e}_m \langle t, \rho, l :: \epsilon, h\rangle}$$

$$\frac{P_m[i] = \mathsf{throw} \qquad e = \mathsf{class}(h(l)) \qquad \mathsf{Handler}_m(i, e) \uparrow \qquad \boxed{e \in \mathsf{classAnalysis}(m, i)}}{\langle i, \rho, l :: os, h\rangle \leadsto^{e}_m \langle l\rangle, h}$$

with $\mathsf{RuntimeExceptionHandling} : \mathrm{Heap} \times \mathcal{L} \times \mathcal{C} \times \mathcal{PP} \times (\mathcal{X} \rightharpoonup \mathcal{V}) \to \mathrm{State} + (\mathcal{L} \times \mathrm{Heap})$ defined by

$$\mathsf{RuntimeExceptionHandling}(h, l', C, i, \rho) = \begin{cases} \langle t, \rho, l' :: \epsilon, h[l' \mapsto \mathsf{default}(C)]\rangle & \text{if } \mathsf{Handler}_m(i, C) = t \\ \langle l'\rangle, h[l' \mapsto \mathsf{default}(C)] & \text{if } \mathsf{Handler}_m(i, C) \uparrow \end{cases}$$

Fig. 3. Selected semantics rules

In several rules boxed premises represent extra-hypotheses added to the standard JVM semantics thanks to the PA analyser, in the same way that only well-typed states are considered when assuming a program is byte-code verified. It is possible to show that our instrumented semantics coincides with the standard semantics if the PA analysis is safe.

3 Policies

The security policy is expressed at the level of methods and based on the assumption that the attacker can only draw observations on the input/output behaviour of methods. We do not consider the case of executions that hang, nor of "wrong" executions that get stuck—such executions are eliminated by bytecode verification.

The policy is given by a lattice $(\mathcal{S}, \leq, \sqcup, \sqcap)$ of security levels, and:

- a security level k_{obs} that determines the observational capabilities of the attacker. More precisely, the attacker can observe fields, local variables, and return values whose level is at or below k_{obs};
- a global policy $ft : \mathcal{F} \to \mathcal{S}$ that attaches security levels to fields. The global policy is used to determine a notion of equivalence $\sim$ between heaps. Intuitively, two heaps h_1 and h_2 are equivalent if $h_1(l).f = h_2(l).f$ for all locations l and fields f s.t. $ft(f) \leq k_{\mathrm{obs}}$;

– a table of method signatures, that associates to each method identifier[4] and security level (corresponding to the object called) a security signature of the form $\boldsymbol{k_v} \xrightarrow{k_h} \boldsymbol{k_r}$, where $\boldsymbol{k_v}$ provides the security level of the method local variables, including its arguments[5], k_h is the heap effect of the method, i.e. the lower bound for security levels of fields that are affected during execution of the method, and $\boldsymbol{k_r}$ is a record of security levels of the form $\{n : k_n, e_1 : k_{e_1}, \ldots e_n : k_{e_n}\}$, where k_n is the security level of the return value (normal termination) and each e_i is an exception class that might be propagated by the method, associated with a security level k_i.[6] It indicates the level of information than can be learnt by observing if the method terminates by an uncaught exception e_i or by a normal return.

A method is safe w.r.t. a signature $\boldsymbol{k_v} \xrightarrow{k_h} \boldsymbol{k_r}$ if:

1. two terminating runs of the method with $\sim_{\boldsymbol{k_v}}$-equivalent inputs and equivalent heaps, yield $\sim_{\boldsymbol{k_r}}$-equivalent results and equivalent heaps;
2. the heap effect of the method is greater than k_h, i.e. the method does not perform field updates on fields whose security level is below k_h.

Note that the heap effect does not appear in the statement of non-interference proper but is needed to make a modular analysis. We use the heap effect for virtual calls that occur in a high context in order to enforce that no modification is done on low information during the execution of the called method.

Formally, the observational power of the attacker is defined by various *indistinguishability* relations $\sim^D$ on each different semantic sub-domains D of the JVM memory, see Figure 4; these relations are parameterised by a bijection $\beta \in \mathcal{L} \rightharpoonup \mathcal{L}$ on (a partial set of) locations in order to model the difference between the allocation history between two states (following Banerjee and Naumann's approach [3]): after a high branching where allocations may occur, objects might be indistinguishable, even if their locations are different during execution. Figure 5 presents the notion of output indistinguishability. In all cases, heaps must be indistinguishable. This definition implies that if indistinguishability outputs are of different nature (like normal value/exception or two exceptions from different classes) the security level of the corresponding exception must be high in the output signature $\boldsymbol{k_r}$. When outputs are of similar nature (two normal values or two exceptions of the same class) they are indistinguishable as soon as the corresponding security level in $\boldsymbol{k_r}$ is low.

Definition 1 (Safe method and program). *A method m is* safe *w.r.t. a policy $\boldsymbol{k_v} \xrightarrow{k_h} \boldsymbol{k_r}$, if for every partial function $\beta \in \mathcal{L} \rightharpoonup \mathcal{L}$ and every $\rho_1, \rho_2 \in$*

[4] Associating signatures with method identifier instead of method allows to enforce that overriding of a method preserves its declared security signatures.

[5] I.e. local variables have a fixed security level. Leroy [14] defines a transformation that ensures this property, and shows it enables on-device bytecode verification. Hunt and Sands [13] propose an alternative approach.

[6] In the rest of the paper, we will write $\boldsymbol{k_r}[n]$ instead of k_n and $\boldsymbol{k_r}[e_i]$ instead of k_{e_i}.

relation	definition
$v_1 \sim_\beta^{\mathcal{V}} v_2$ where $v_1, v_2 \in \mathcal{V}$	$null \sim_\beta^{\mathcal{V}} null \quad \dfrac{v \in \mathcal{N}}{v \sim_\beta^{\mathcal{V}} v} \quad \dfrac{v_1, v_2 \in \mathcal{L} \quad \beta(v_1) = v_2}{v_1 \sim_\beta^{\mathcal{V}} v_2}$
$\rho_1 \sim_{\beta,\boldsymbol{k_v}}^{\text{LocalVar}} \rho_2$ where $\rho_1, \rho_2 \in$ LocalVar	$\forall x \in \mathcal{X},\ \boldsymbol{k_v}(x) \leq k_{\text{obs}} \Rightarrow \rho_1(x) \sim_\beta^{\mathcal{V}} \rho_2(x)$
$o_1 \sim_\beta^{\mathcal{O}} o_2$ where $o_1, o_2 \in \mathcal{O}$	– $\mathsf{class}(o_1) = \mathsf{class}(o_2)$ – $\forall f \in dom(o_1),\ ft(f) \leq k_{\text{obs}} \Rightarrow o_1(f) \sim_\beta^{\mathcal{V}} o_2(f)$
$a_1 \sim_\beta^{\mathcal{A}} a_2$ where $a_1, a_2 \in \mathcal{A}$	– $a_1.length = a_2.length$ and $at(a_1) = at(a_2)$ – $\forall i \in [0, a_1.length[,\ at(a_1) \leq k_{\text{obs}} \Rightarrow a_1[i] \sim_\beta^{\mathcal{V}} a_2[i]$
$h_1 \sim_\beta^{\text{Heap}} h_2$ where $h_1, h_2 \in$ Heap	– β is a bijection between $dom(\beta)$ and $rng(\beta)$ – $dom(\beta) \subseteq dom(h_1)$ and $rng(\beta) \subseteq dom(h_2)$ – $\forall l \in dom(\beta),\ h_1(l) \sim_\beta^{\mathcal{O}} h_2(\beta(l))$ or $h_1(l) \sim_\beta^{\mathcal{A}} h_2(\beta(l))$

Fig. 4. Indistinguishability relations

$$\frac{h_1 \sim_\beta h_2 \quad \boldsymbol{k_r}[n] \leq k_{\text{obs}} \Rightarrow v_1 \sim_\beta v_2}{(v_1, h_1) \sim_{\beta,\boldsymbol{k_r}} (v_2, h_2)}$$

$$\frac{h_1 \sim_\beta h_2 \quad \boldsymbol{k_r}[\mathsf{class}(h_1(l_1))] \leq k_{\text{obs}} \quad l_1 \sim_\beta l_2}{(\langle l_1 \rangle, h_1) \sim_{\beta,\boldsymbol{k_r}} (\langle l_2 \rangle, h_2)}$$

$$\frac{h_1 \sim_\beta h_2 \quad \boldsymbol{k_r}[\mathsf{class}(h_1(l_1))] \not\leq k_{\text{obs}}}{(\langle l_1 \rangle, h_1) \sim_{\beta,\boldsymbol{k_r}} (v_2, h_2)} \qquad \frac{h_1 \sim_\beta h_2 \quad \boldsymbol{k_r}[\mathsf{class}(h_2(l_2))] \not\leq k_{\text{obs}}}{(v_1, h_1) \sim_{\beta,\boldsymbol{k_r}} (\langle l_2 \rangle, h_2)}$$

$$\frac{h_1 \sim_\beta h_2 \quad \boldsymbol{k_r}[\mathsf{class}(h_1(l_1))] \not\leq k_{\text{obs}} \quad \boldsymbol{k_r}[\mathsf{class}(h_1(l_1))] \not\leq k_{\text{obs}}}{(\langle l_1 \rangle, h_1) \sim_{\beta,\boldsymbol{k_r}} (\langle l_2 \rangle, h_2)}$$

Fig. 5. Output indistinguishability

$\mathcal{X} \rightharpoonup \mathcal{V}$, $h_1, h_2, h_1', h_2' \in$ Heap, $r_1, r_2 \in \mathcal{V}+\mathcal{L}$ *such that* $\rho_1, h_1 \Downarrow_m r_1, h_1'$, $\rho_2, h_2 \Downarrow_m r_2, h_2'$ *and* $h_1 \sim_\beta h_2$, $\rho_1 \sim_{\boldsymbol{k_v},\beta} \rho_2$*:*

- non-interference *there exists a partial function* $\beta' \in \mathcal{L} \rightharpoonup \mathcal{L}$ *such that* $\beta \subseteq \beta'$ *and* $(r_1, h_1) \sim_{\beta',\boldsymbol{k_r}} (r_2, h_2)$*;*
- heap effect safety *for each location* $l \in dom(h_1)$ *and each fields* $f \in \mathcal{F}$ *such that* $k_h \not\leq ft(f)$, $h_1(l).f = h_1'(l).f$.

A program is safe *with respect to a table of method signature* Γ *if for all its method* m, m *is safe with respect to all policies in* $\{\ \Gamma_m[k] \mid k \in \mathcal{S}\ \}$.

4 Verification of Control Dependence Regions

The CDR checker begins by computing the static flow graph of all methods. In order to treat methods accurately, the flow graph of method m is represented by an indexed successor relation $(\mapsto_m^\tau)_{\tau \in \text{Tag}} \subseteq (\mathcal{PP} \times \mathcal{PP}) + \mathcal{PP}$, where Tag is either an exception class (exceptional flow) or $\emptyset$ (normal flow). We write $i \mapsto_m^\tau j$ (resp. $i \mapsto_m^\tau$) if $(i, j) \in \mapsto_m^\tau$ (resp. $i \in \mapsto_m^\tau$). Furthermore, we say that i is a return point if $i \mapsto^\tau$ for some τ and note $i \mapsto_m j$ for $\exists \tau,\ i \mapsto_m^\tau j$.

The CDR checker retrieves the functions provided by the CDR analyser:

$$region_m : \mathcal{PP} \times \text{Tag} \to \wp(\mathcal{PP}) \qquad jun_m : \mathcal{PP} \times \text{Tag} \rightharpoonup \mathcal{PP}$$

and checks the SOAP[7] properties below in order to guarantee the correctness of the information that they provide:

SOAP1: for all program points i, j, k and tag τ such that $i \mapsto_m j$, $i \mapsto_m^\tau k$ and $j \neq k$ (i is hence a branching point), $k \in region_m(i, \tau)$ or $k = jun_m(i, \tau)$;

SOAP2: for all program points i, j, k and tag τ, if $j \in region_m(i, \tau)$ and $j \mapsto_m k$, then either $k \in region_m(i, \tau)$ or $k = jun_m(i, \tau)$;

SOAP3: for all program points i, j and tag τ, if $j \in region(i, \tau)$ (or $i = j$) and j is a return point then $jun_m(i, \tau)$ is undefined;

SOAP4: for all program points i and tags τ_1, τ_2, if $jun_m(i, \tau_1)$ and $jun_m(i, \tau_2)$ are defined and $jun_m(i, \tau_1) \neq jun_m(i, \tau_2)$ then $jun_m(i, \tau_1) \in region_m(i, \tau_2)$ or $jun_m(i, \tau_2) \in region_m(i, \tau_1)$;

SOAP5: for all program points i, j and tag τ, if $j \in region(i, \tau)$ (or $i = j$) and j is a return point then for all tag τ' such that $jun_m(i, \tau')$ is defined, $jun_m(i, \tau') \in region_m(i, \tau)$.

Junction points uniquely delimit ends of regions. SOAP1 expresses that successors of branching points belongs (or ends) the region associated with the same kind as their successor relation. SOAP2 says that a successor of a point in a region is either still in the same region or at this end. SOAP3 forbids junction points for a region which contains (or start with) a return point. SOAP4 and SOAP5 express properties between regions of a same program point but with different tags. SOAP4 says that if two differently tagged regions end in distinct points, the junction point of one must belong to the region of the other. SOAP5 imposes that the junction point of a region must be within every region which contains (or starts with) a return point and is decorated with a different tag.

5 Type System

The information flow type system is defined as a modular (i.e. method-wise) data flow analysis of an abstract transition relation. Typing is defined relative to the table Γ of method signatures (used to handle method calls) and to the global policy *ft*, to the CDR annotations, to a security environment *se* that assigns security levels to program points (used to avoid implicit flows) and to a current method signature *sgn*.

Typing Rules. The typing rules are designed to prevent information leakage through imposing appropriate constraints; Figure 6 presents some selected typing rules which are commented below. Typing rules are of one of the two forms below,

[7] Safe Over Approximation Property.

$$\frac{\begin{array}{c} P_m[i] = \mathsf{invokevirtual}\ m_{\mathrm{ID}} \qquad \Gamma_{m_{\mathrm{ID}}}[k] = \boldsymbol{k}'_a \xrightarrow{k'_h} \boldsymbol{k}'_r \\ k \sqcup k_h \sqcup se(i) \leq k'_h \qquad k \leq \boldsymbol{k}'_a[0] \qquad \forall i \in [0, \mathsf{length}(st_1) - 1],\ st_1[i] \leq \boldsymbol{k}'_a[i+1] \\ k_e = \bigsqcup_{e \in \mathsf{excAnalysis}(m_{\mathrm{ID}})} \boldsymbol{k}'_r[e] \qquad \forall j \in region(i, \emptyset),\ k \sqcup k_e \leq se(j) \end{array}}{\Gamma, region, se, \boldsymbol{k_a} \xrightarrow{k_h} \boldsymbol{k_r}, i \vdash^{\emptyset} st_1 :: k :: st_2 \Rightarrow \mathsf{lift}_{k \sqcup k_e}\left((\boldsymbol{k}'_r[n] \sqcup se(i)) :: st_2\right)}$$

$$\frac{\begin{array}{c} P_m[i] = \mathsf{invokevirtual}\ m_{\mathrm{ID}} \qquad \Gamma_{m_{\mathrm{ID}}}[k] = \boldsymbol{k}'_a \xrightarrow{k'_h} \boldsymbol{k}'_r \\ k \sqcup k_h \sqcup se(i) \leq k'_h \qquad k \leq \boldsymbol{k}'_a[0] \qquad \forall i \in [0, \mathsf{length}(st_1) - 1],\ st_1[i] \leq \boldsymbol{k}'_a[i+1] \\ e \in \mathsf{excAnalysis}(m_{\mathrm{ID}}) \qquad \forall j \in region(i, e),\ k \sqcup \boldsymbol{k}'_r[e] \leq se(j) \qquad \mathsf{Handler}(i, e) = t \end{array}}{\Gamma, region, se, \boldsymbol{k_a} \xrightarrow{k_h} \boldsymbol{k_r}, i \vdash^{e} st_1 :: k :: st_2 \Rightarrow (k \sqcup \boldsymbol{k}'_r[e]) :: \varepsilon}$$

$$\frac{\begin{array}{c} P_m[i] = \mathsf{invokevirtual}\ m_{\mathrm{ID}} \qquad \Gamma_{m_{\mathrm{ID}}}[k] = \boldsymbol{k}'_a \xrightarrow{k'_h} \boldsymbol{k}'_r \\ k \sqcup k_h \sqcup se(i) \leq k'_h \qquad k \leq \boldsymbol{k}'_a[0] \qquad \forall i \in [0, \mathsf{length}(st_1) - 1],\ st_1[i] \leq \boldsymbol{k}'_a[i+1] \\ e \in \mathsf{excAnalysis}(m_{\mathrm{ID}}) \quad k \sqcup \boldsymbol{k}'_r[e] \leq \boldsymbol{k}_r[e] \quad \forall j \in region(i, e),\ k \sqcup \boldsymbol{k}'_r[e] \leq se(j) \quad \mathsf{Handler}(i, e) \uparrow \end{array}}{\Gamma, region, se, \boldsymbol{k_a} \xrightarrow{k_h} \boldsymbol{k_r}, i \vdash^{e} st_1 :: k :: st_2 \Rightarrow}$$

$$\frac{P[i] = \mathsf{xastore} \qquad k_1 \sqcup k_2 \sqcup k_3 \leq k_e \qquad \forall j \in region(i, \emptyset),\ k_e \leq se(j)}{\Gamma, region, se, \boldsymbol{k_a} \xrightarrow{k_h} \boldsymbol{k_r}, i \vdash^{\emptyset} k_1 :: k_2 :: k_3[k_e] :: st \Rightarrow \mathsf{lift}_{k_e}(st)}$$

Fig. 6. Selected typing rules

where the rule on the left is used for normal intra-method execution, and the rule on the right is used for return instructions:

$$\frac{P[i] = ins \quad constraints}{\Gamma, ft, region, se, sgn, i \vdash^{\tau} st \Rightarrow st'} \qquad \frac{P[i] = ins \quad constraints}{\Gamma, ft, region, se, sgn, i \vdash^{\tau} st \Rightarrow}$$

where $st, st' \in \overline{\mathcal{S}}^{\star}$ are stacks of *extended security levels*, ins is an instruction found at point i in program P, and τ is a tag. An *extended security level* is either a standard level $k \in \mathcal{S}$ or a pair of level (k, k_e) (noted $k[k_e]$) to type array references. Here k represents the level of the reference while k_e is the level of the elements in the array. Such a distinction is mandatory to be able to have low arrays of high elements. Tags are useful when several rules deal with a same instruction. Depending on the nature of the rule ($st \Rightarrow st'$ or $st \Rightarrow$) and the tag ($\tau = \emptyset$ or $\tau = e \in \mathcal{C}$) we make a non-ambiguous correspondence between semantic and typing rules.

Virtual call. There are several constraints common to all rules for virtual calls. The constraint $k \leq k'_h$ avoids invocation of methods with low heap effect on high target objects, as invoking two different target objects (in two executions) may lead to different method bodies to be executed (due to method lookup) and thus if the method identifier has a low heap effect ($k_h \leq k_{\mathrm{obs}}$), then the low memory may be modified differently in both executions. The constraint $se(i) \leq k'_h$ prevents implicit flows (low assignment in high regions) during execution of the called method. The constraint $k_h \leq k'_h$ prevents the called method to update fields with a level lower that k_h. It allows to avoid invocation of methods with low effect on the heap by a method with high effect. Finally, constraints $k \leq \boldsymbol{k}'_a[0]$

and $\forall i \in [0, \mathsf{length}(st_1) - 1],\ st_1[i] \le \boldsymbol{k'_a}[i+1]$ link argument levels with formal parameter levels.

In the first typing rule, the next stack type is lifted[8] with level $k \sqcup k_e$ to avoid indirect flows because of null a pointer exception on the current object. The level k_e is greater than all levels of the exceptions that may escape from the called method. If abnormal termination of the called method reveals secret information then k_e is high and the next stack type must be high too. The security level of the return value is $(k'_r[n] \sqcup se(i))$. The level $k'_r[n]$ corresponds to the level of the return value in the context of the called method. $se(i)$ prevents implicit flow on the result after the virtual call.

The second and the third typing rule are parameterised by an exception e that may be caught by the called method. In the second rule, this exception is caught in the current method while in the third it is not. In both rules $k \sqcup \boldsymbol{k'_r}[e]$ gives an upper bound on the information that can be gained by observing if the called method reached the point $i+1$. This level is hence used to constrain $region(i, e)$, the top of the stack when e is caught and the security level $\boldsymbol{k_r}[e]$ when it is not.

Arrays. We only give the rule concerning normal execution of the array store instruction. We require the stored value to have a lower level than those of the array content ($k_1 \le k_e$). The level k_2 of the index should be lower than k_e to prevent attacker to learn information by observing which part of the array has been modified. In a similar way, the level k_3 of the reference should be lower than k_e to avoid modifying two distinct arrays with observable contents. Several exceptions can occur when performing an array store (due to null pointer reference, out-of-bound access or wrong type assignment) so we lift the stack type with the level k_e and impose a similar constraint on the current region.

Typing Method and Program. The definition of typable method is stated to ensure that runs of typable programs (i.e. programs whose methods are typable against their signatures) verify at each step the constraints imposed by the typing rules, provided they are called with parameters that respect the signature of their main method.

Definition 2 (Typable method and program). *A method m is typable w.r.t. a method signature table Γ, a global field policy ft, a signature sgn and a cdr $region_m$ if there exists a security environment $se : \mathcal{PP} \to \mathcal{S}$ and a function $S : \mathcal{PP} \to \overline{\mathcal{S}}^{\star}$ such that $S_1 = \varepsilon$ and for all $i, j \in \mathcal{PP}$, $\tau \in$ Tag:*

1. *$i \mapsto^{\tau} j$ implies there exists $st \in \overline{\mathcal{S}}^{\star}$ such that $\Gamma, ft, region, se, sgn, i \vdash^{\tau} S_i \Rightarrow st$ and $st \sqsubseteq S_j$;*
2. *$i \mapsto^{\tau}$ implies $\Gamma, ft, region, se, sgn, i \vdash^{\tau} S_i \Rightarrow$*

where $\sqsubseteq$ denotes the point-wise extension of $\le$ on stack types.

[8] Lifting a stack type with a level k correspond to a map of $\lambda x.k \sqcup x$ on the whole stack. This technique was initially proposed in [6].

```
int m(boolean x,C y) throws C
{
  if (x) {throw new C();}
  else {y.f = 3;};
  return 1;
}
```

0 : load x
1 : ifeq 4
2 : new C
3 : throw
4 : load y
5 : push 3
6 : putfield f
7 : const 1
8 : return

i	$S(i)$	$se(i)$
0	ε	L
1	$L :: \varepsilon$	L
2	ε	L
3	$L :: \varepsilon$	L
4	ε	L
5	$H :: \varepsilon$	L
6	$L :: H :: \varepsilon$	L
7	ε	H
8	$H :: \varepsilon$	H

$region(1, \emptyset) = \{2, 3, 4, 5, 6, 7, 8\}$ $jun(1, \emptyset)$ undef.

$region(6, \emptyset) = \emptyset$ $jun(6, \emptyset) = 7$ $region(6, \mathbf{np}) = \{7, 8\}$ $jun(6, \mathbf{np})$ undef.

Fig. 7. Typable methods at source and bytecode level

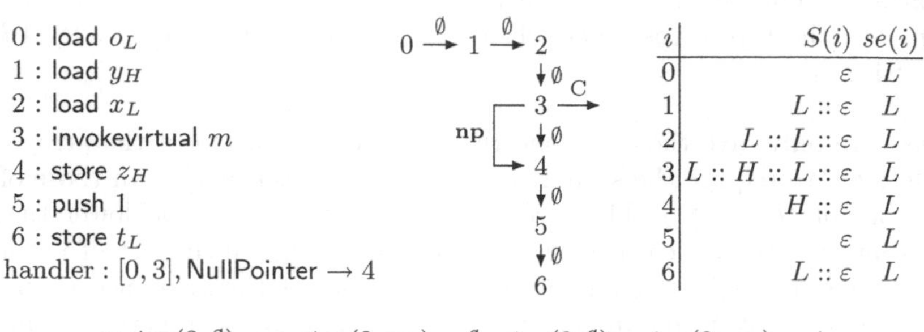

0 : load o_L
1 : load y_H
2 : load x_L
3 : invokevirtual m
4 : store z_H
5 : push 1
6 : store t_L
handler : [0, 3], NullPointer → 4
np
C
i | $S(i)$ | $se(i)$
0 | ε | L
1 | $L :: \varepsilon$ | L
2 | $L :: L :: \varepsilon$ | L
3 | $L :: H :: L :: \varepsilon$ | L
4 | $H :: \varepsilon$ | L
5 | ε | L
6 | $L :: \varepsilon$ | L

$region(3, \emptyset) = region(3, \mathbf{np}) = \emptyset$ $jun(3, \emptyset) = jun(3, \mathbf{np}) = 4$
$region(3, C) = \{4, 5, 6, \ldots\}$ $jun(3, C)$ undef.

Fig. 8. Typable fragment with virtual call

A program is typable with respect to a table of method signature Γ, a global field policy ft and a family of cdr $(region_m)_m$ if for all its method m, m is typable with respect to Γ, ft, $region_m$ and all signature in $\{ \Gamma_m[k] \mid k \in \mathcal{S} \}$.

In contrast to [6], types are monovariant, i.e. there is a single stack type per program point. Monovariant analyses are less precise, but remain sufficiently precise for showing type-preserving compilation. Monovariant analyses are more efficient, but harder to prove correct, as several monotonicity results are needed.

Typable Examples. We now give two examples of typable methods. For simplicity, we take as lattice of security levels $\mathcal{S} = \{L, H\}$ with $L \leq H$, where H is the high level for confidential data, and L is the low level for observable data. We note x_k a local variable x whose security level is k.

Figure 7 presents an example of a typable method `m`, giving the corresponding source code and the tagged flow graph. `m` may throw two kinds of exceptions: an exception of class `C` depending on the value of `x`, and an exception of class **np** depending on the values of `x` and `y`. Normal return depends on `y` because execution terminates normally only if it is not *null*. The method `m` is typable with the signature $m : (\mathit{this} : L,\ x : L,\ y : H) \xrightarrow{H} \{n : H,\ C : L,\ \mathbf{np} : H\}$ with the cdr (given only for branching points), the type stacks and the security environment given in Figure 7.

Figure 8 gives another example[9] where fine grain exception handling is necessary for the code to be typable. Here the update $t_L = 1$ at point 6 is accepted if and only if $se(6)$ is low. This fragment is accepted by our type system since, thanks to the fine grain regions, typing rule for virtual call only propagates exception levels $\boldsymbol{k_r}[\mathbf{np}] = H$ in the region $\mathit{region}(3, \mathbf{np})$ (instead of $\mathit{region}(3, C)$).

6 Main Result

We have formalised in Coq several predicates: i) the security condition as SAFE[10]; ii) the correctness of program annotations as PA; iii) the SOAP properties as CDR (given in Section 4); iv) the information flow type checker as IF based on the notion of typable program (Definition 2).

We have machine-checked the following theorem.

Theorem 1. CDR *and* IF *are decidable predicates. Furthermore for every annotated program P,*

$$\mathsf{PA}(P) \wedge \mathsf{CDR}(P) \wedge \mathsf{IF}(P) \Longrightarrow \mathsf{SAFE}(P)$$

The first item is proved by formalising boolean-valued functions $\mathsf{check}_{\mathrm{CDR}}$ and $\mathsf{check}_{\mathrm{IF}}$ that characterise the predicates CDR and IF respectively. The function $\mathsf{check}_{\mathrm{CDR}}$ performs a direct verification of the SOAP properties for each method, and the function $\mathsf{check}_{\mathrm{IF}}$ uses lightweight bytecode verification techniques : typability of each method of a program is achieved by traversing the static flow graph and checking for all edges the corresponding typing condition. What is left for future work is to define a decidable predicate $\mathsf{check}_{\mathrm{PA}}$ that entails PA.

The second item is proved in two steps: first, we prove unwinding lemmas and lemmas about security environments. The unwinding lemmas show that one-step execution of typable programs does not reveal secret information. This is formalised using state indistinguishability; indistinguishability between operand stacks is defined relative to stack types S and T, and hence we had to define state indistinguishability relative to stack types. In the sequel, we write $s \sim_{S,T} t$ whenever s and t are equivalent w.r.t. S and T. The unwinding lemmas are of the form (we omit partial bijections and transition tags):

- *locally respects:* if $s \sim_{S,T} t$, and $\mathsf{pc}(s) = \mathsf{pc}(t) = i$, and $s \leadsto s'$, $t \leadsto t'$, $i \vdash S \Rightarrow S'$, and $i \vdash T \Rightarrow T'$, then $s' \sim_{S',T'} t'$.
- *step consistent:* if $s \sim_{S,T} t$ and $s \leadsto s'$ and $\mathsf{pc}(s) \vdash S \Rightarrow S'$, and security environment at program point $\mathsf{pc}(s)$ is high, and S is high, then $s' \sim_{S',T} t$.

[9] To keep the example short here we give compressed version of a compiled code.

[10] Note that SAFE is based on the small-step semantics which acts as reference in Bicolano (without any instrumentation) as defined in Definition 1.

In addition to the unwinding lemmas, we need two lemmas about security environments:

- *high branching:* if $s \sim_{S,T} t$ with $\mathsf{pc}(s) = \mathsf{pc}(t) = i$ and $\mathsf{pc}(s') \neq \mathsf{pc}(t')$, if $s \leadsto^{\tau} s'$, $t \leadsto^{\tau'} t'$, $i \vdash^{\tau} S \Rightarrow S'$ and $i \vdash^{\tau'} T \Rightarrow T'$, then S' and T' are high and se is high in both region $region(i, \tau)$ and $region(i, \tau')$.
- *high step:* if $s \leadsto s'$, and $\mathsf{pc}(s) \vdash S \Rightarrow S'$, and security environment at program point $\mathsf{pc}(s)$ is high, and S is high, then S' is high.

We then provide a high-level reasoning establishing that a typable program is safe. This part of the proof is not dedicated to a specific fragment of the JVM but applies instead for cdr-based non-interference proofs on low level languages.

7 Remarks on Formal Proofs

The whole Coq development[11] is about 20,000 lines of definitions and proofs; the most important details of the proofs are given in a companion report [5].

The IF checker, and to a lesser extent the CDR checker are complex programs that form the cornerstone of the security architectures that we propose. It is therefore fundamental that their implementation is correct, and therefore their soundness proof should be machine checked. The need for machine-checked proofs is accentuated by the fact that non-interference proofs are particularly involved (w.r.t. say standard type safety proofs discussed in [2]), and that some lemmas as *locally respects* involve two parallel executions leading to an explosion of cases. For example, the JVM virtual call has 5 different transitions (call on a null reference which generates a null pointer exception caught or not, normal termination of the callee, termination by an exception caught or not in the caller context) which required 15 distinct proofs to be exhaustively confronted.

Another motivation for formal proofs is *foundational proof carrying code* or FPCC [1] since the Trusted Computed Base is here relegated to the Coq type checker and the formal definition of non-interference. However, we depart from FPCC in our strategy to prove programs: whereas FPCC uses deductive reasoning to encode proof rules or typing rules, we provide a computational encoding that enables the use of reflective tactics and yields compact certificates. Once we have defined a boolean-valued function $\mathsf{check}_{\mathrm{PA}}$ that entails PA, one can rewrite the main theorem as

$$\mathsf{check}_{\mathrm{PA}}(P) = \mathrm{True} \wedge \mathsf{check}_{\mathrm{CDR}}(P) = \mathrm{True} \wedge \mathsf{check}_{\mathrm{IF}}(P) = \mathrm{True} \Longrightarrow \mathsf{SAFE}(P)$$

Thus the certificate for an annotated program shall be of the form

$$\langle \mathsf{refleq}\ \mathrm{True}, \mathsf{refleq}\ \mathrm{True}, \mathsf{refleq}\ \mathrm{True} \rangle$$

where refleq True is a proof of True = True.

[11] Available on-line at `http://www.irisa.fr/lande/pichardie/iflow`

Agreeingly, much of the certificate is already in the annotations (that are in P), but in comparison with FPCC, we do not have a part of the certificate that encodes deductively the type derivation for P.

Following the approach of *proof carrying proof checkers* [7], it is also possible to extract certified checkers from Coq proofs, which opens up the possibility of safely downloading proof checkers, adding flexibility to the PCC infrastructure.

8 Conclusion

We have developed an information flow type system for a fragment of the JVM that includes objects, methods, exceptions, and arrays, and machine checked its soundness in Coq.

An important goal for future work is to experiment with our type system, by running our verifier on Jif case studies. Unfortunately, most case studies make an intensive use of declassification, which is not provisioned by our type system. Therefore, it seems important to design and machine check type systems that support information release [20]. Another important goal is to extend our results to multi-threaded Java, in order to broaden the scope of applications of our type system; the proposal of Russo and Sabelfeld [18] to control the interactions between threads and the schedulers seems a suitable starting point.

References

1. A.W. Appel and A.P. Felty. A semantic model of types and machine instuctions for proof-carrying code. In *Proceedings of POPL'00*, pages 243–253. ACM Press, 2000.
2. B.E. Aydemir, A. Bohannon, M. Fairbairn, J.N. Foster, B.C. Pierce, P. Sewell, D. Vytiniotis, G. Washburn, S. Weirich, and S. Zdancewic. Mechanized Metatheory for the Masses: The PoplMark Challenge. In *Proceedings of TPHOLs'05*, volume 3603 of *Lecture Notes in Computer Science*, pages 50–65. Springer-Verlag, 2005.
3. A. Banerjee and D. Naumann. Stack-based access control for secure information flow. *Journal of Functional Programming*, 15:131–177, March 2005.
4. G. Barthe, D. Naumann, and T. Rezk. Deriving an Information Flow Checker and Certifying Compiler for Java. In *Symposium on Security and Privacy, 2006*. IEEE Press, 2006.
5. G. Barthe, D. Pichardie, and T. Rezk. Non-interference for low level languages. Technical report, INRIA, 2006. `http://hal.inria.fr/inria-00106182`.
6. G. Barthe and T. Rezk. Non-interference for a JVM-like language. In M. Fähndrich, editor, *Proceedings of TLDI'05*, pages 103–112. ACM Press, 2005.
7. F. Besson, T. Jensen, and D Pichardie. Proof-Carrying Code from Certified Abstract Interpretation and Fixpoint Compression. *Theoretical Computer Science*, 364(3):273-291, 2006.
8. P. Bieber, J. Cazin, V. Wiels, G. Zanon, P. Girard, and J.-L. Lanet. Checking Secure Interactions of Smart Card Applets: Extended version. *Journal of Computer Security*, 10:369–398, 2002.
9. E. Bonelli, A.B. Compagnoni, and R. Medel. Information flow analysis for a typed assembly language with polymorphic stacks. In *Proceedings of CASSIS'05*, volume 3956 of *Lecture Notes in Computer Science*, pages 37–56. Springer-Verlag, 2005.

10. S. Genaim and F. Spoto. Information Flow Analysis for Java Bytecode. In *Proceedings of VMCAI'05*, volume 3385 of *Lecture Notes in Computer Science*, pages 346–362. Springer-Verlag, 2005.
11. R. Giacobazzi and I. Mastroeni. Abstract non-interference: Parameterizing non-interference by abstract interpretation. In *Proceedings of POPL'04*, pages 186–197. ACM Press, 2004.
12. D. Hedin and D. Sands. Noninterference in the presence of non-opaque pointers. In *Proceedings of CSFW'06*, pages 255–269. IEEE Computer Society Press, 2006.
13. S. Hunt and D. Sands. On Flow-Sensitive Security Types. In *Proceedings of POPL'06*, pages 79–90. ACM Press, 2006.
14. X. Leroy. Bytecode verification on Java smart cards. *Software–practice and experience*, 32(4):319–340, April 2002.
15. A.C. Myers. Jflow: Practical mostly-static information flow control. In *Proceedings of POPL'99*, pages 228–241. ACM Press, 1999.
16. D. Naumann. Verifying a secure information flow analyzer. In *Proceedings of TPHOLs'05*, volume 3603 of *Lecture Notes in Computer Science*, pages 211–226. Springer-Verlag, 2005.
17. T. Rezk. *Verification of confidentiality policies for mobile code.* PhD thesis, Université de Nice Sophia-Antipolis, 2006.
18. A. Russo and A. Sabelfeld. Securing interaction between threads and the scheduler. In *Proceedings of CSFW'06*, 2006.
19. A. Sabelfeld and A. Myers. Language-Based Information-Flow Security. *IEEE Journal on Selected Areas in Comunications*, 21:5–19, January 2003.
20. A. Sabelfeld and D. Sands. Dimensions and principles of declassification. In *Proceedings of CSFW'05*. IEEE Press, 2005.
21. D. Volpano and G. Smith. A Type-Based Approach to Program Security. In M. Bidoit and M. Dauchet, editors, *Proceedings of TAPSOFT'97*, volume 1214 of *Lecture Notes in Computer Science*, pages 607–621. Springer-Verlag, 1997.
22. D. Yu and N. Islam. A typed assembly language for confidentiality. In P. Sestoft, editor, *Proceedings of ESOP'06*, volume 3924 of *Lecture Notes in Computer Science*, pages 162–179. Springer-Verlag, 2006.
23. D. Zanardini. *Certified Abstract Non-Interference: Object-Oriented Code Validation for Information Flow Security.* PhD thesis, Università di Verona, April 2006.

Controlling the What and Where of Declassification in Language-Based Security

Heiko Mantel and Alexander Reinhard

Security Engineering Group, RWTH Aachen University, Germany
mantel@cs.rwth-aachen.de, reinhard@i4.informatik.rwth-aachen.de

Abstract. While a rigorous information flow analysis is a key step in obtaining meaningful end-to-end confidentiality guarantees, one must also permit possibilities for declassification. Sabelfeld and Sands categorized the existing approaches to controlling declassification in their overview along four dimensions and according to four prudent principles [16].

In this article, we propose three novel security conditions for controlling the dimensions *where* and *what*, and we explain why these conditions constitute improvements over prior approaches. Moreover, we present a type-based security analysis and, as another novelty, prove a soundness result that considers more than one dimension of declassification.

1 Introduction

Research on information flow security aims at finding better ways to characterizing and analyzing security requirements concerning aspects of confidentiality and integrity. Regarding confidentiality, the aim of an information flow analysis is to answer: "Can a given program be trusted to operate in an environment where it has read access to secret data and write access to untrusted information sinks?" There is a variety of approaches to information flow security on the level of concrete programs (see [12] for an overview). In the simplest case, one has a two-level policy demanding that information cannot flow from *high* to *low*. Secure information flow can then be characterized using the idea underlying *noninterference* [6]: If *low* outputs of the program do not depend on *high* inputs then there is no danger that secret data is leaked to untrusted sinks.

Noninterference provides an intuitively convincing, declarative characterization of information flow security. However, there are security mechanisms and application scenarios that need some information to flow from *high* to *low*. For instance, a password-based authentication mechanism necessarily reveals some information about the secret password, decryption relies on a dependence between a cipher-text and the secret plain-text that it encodes, and electronic commerce requires secret data to be released after it has been paid for. For making information flow security compatible with such requirements, one must permit exceptions in the security policy. But, this raises the question how to control that one does not introduce possibilities for unintended information leakage.

R. De Nicola (Ed.): ESOP 2007, LNCS 4421, pp. 141–156, 2007.

For clarifying the intentions underlying the various approaches to controlling information release, three dimensions were introduced in [9]: *what* information is declassified, *who* can control whether declassification occurs, and *where* can declassification happen. In [16], Sabelfeld and Sands develop a taxonomy that categorizes the existing approaches along these dimensions[1] and propose four prudent principles of controlling declassification. The taxonomy clarified the relationship between the various approaches, and it revealed some anomalies and misconceptions that had previously gone unnoticed. Another interesting outcome is that each approach mainly aims at a single dimension and does not provide adequate control for any of the respective other dimensions.

In this article, our scope is controlling the *what* and *where* of declassification in a type-based security analysis. In summary, our research contributions are:

- A novel security characterization for controlling *where* declassification occurs. Our property WHERE is similar to *intransitive noninterference* [9], but WHERE satisfies the prudent principles of declassification from [16], including monotonicity, which is not satisfied by intransitive noninterference.
- Two novel security characterizations for controlling *what* is declassified. Our properties WHAT_1 and WHAT_2 are similar to selective dependency [3] and its descendants (e.g., [13]), but, unlike these properties, WHAT_1 and WHAT_2 are applicable to concurrent programs. Lifting a security characterization from a sequential to a concurrent setting is often not straightforward, in particular, one must address the danger of internal timing leaks [15].
- A security type system for analyzing the information flow in concurrent programs under policies that permit controlled exceptions. Our type system localizes *where* declassification occurs and controls *what* is declassified. We prove soundness results with respect to each of our properties WHERE, WHAT_1, and WHAT_2. To our knowledge, the only other formal soundness result for an information flow type system that considers *where* and *what* is the one by Li and Zdancewic [7]. However, they aim at sequential programs and mainly at controlling the *what* dimension [16].

In our project, we gained some further insights on controlling declassification. For instance, our property WHAT_1 is compositional but does not satisfy the monotonicity principle, while our property WHAT_2 is not compositional but satisfies monotonicity. We found that, when controlling the *what* dimension of declassification, one faces a fundamental difficulty when attempting to satisfy compositionality as well as monotonicity (see Sect. 3.2). While using the prudent principles of declassification as a sanity check for our security characterizations, we found that formalizing the informal descriptions of the principles from [16] is not always completely straightforward, and in some cases more than one formalization is sensible. As an example, we provide two alternative formalizations of the conservativity principle for WHERE (see Theorem 2).

[1] The taxonomy distinguishes localization of declassification with respect to aspects of time during program execution (*when*) from other aspects of localization (*where*) and categorizes according to the four dimensions: *what*, *who*, *where*, and *when*.

2 Controlling Declassification in Dimension *where*

We propose a novel characterization of information flow security that controls *where* declassification can occur. It is ensured that declassification is localized to specific parts of the security policy as well as to specific parts of the computation.

Definition 1. *A* multi-level security policy *(brief:* MLS policy*) is a pair* $(\mathcal{D}, \leq)$, *where* $\mathcal{D}$ *is a set of security domains and* $\leq \subseteq \mathcal{D}\times\mathcal{D}$ *is a partial order. The triple* $(\mathcal{D}, \leq, \rightsquigarrow)$ *is an* MLS policy with exceptions *where* $\rightsquigarrow \subseteq \mathcal{D}\times\mathcal{D}$. *The minimal and the maximal domain in* $(\mathcal{D}, \leq)$ *are called low and high, respectively, if they exist.*

Computation steps are modeled by labeled transitions between configurations of the form $\langle\!| \langle C_1 \dots C_n\rangle, s |\!\rangle$. Here, the state s is a mapping from program variables to values, and the vector models a pool of n threads that concurrently execute the commands $C_1, \dots, C_n \in Com$, respectively. For simplicity, we do not distinguish between commands and command vectors of length one in the notation and use the term *program* for referring to commands as well as to command vectors.

We distinguish ordinary computation steps, which are modeled by a transition relation $\twoheadrightarrow_o$, from declassification steps, which are modeled by a family of relations $(\twoheadrightarrow_d^{\mathcal{D}_1 \to D_2})_{\mathcal{D}_1, \{D_2\} \subseteq \mathcal{D}}$. Given a policy $(\mathcal{D}, \leq, \rightsquigarrow)$, the intuition is that an ordinary transition must strictly obey the ordering $\leq$ (which means that information may only flow upwards according to $\leq$), while declassification steps may violate this ordering by downgrading information from the domains in $\mathcal{D}_1$ to the domain D_2. However, such violations must comply with the relation $\rightsquigarrow$.

2.1 Preliminaries

Given a set *Var* of program variables, a *domain assignment* is a function $dom : Var \to \mathcal{D}$. By assigning a security domain $dom(Id)$ to each variable, it creates a connection between the configurations in a computation and the security policy. Taking the perspective of an observer in a security domain D, two states s, t are indistinguishable if all variables at or below this domain have the same value.

Definition 2. *For a given domain* $D \in \mathcal{D}$, *two states* s *and* t *are* D-equal *(denoted by* $s =_D t$*) if* $\forall Id \in Var : dom(Id) \leq D \implies s(Id) = t(Id)$.

In the following, let $(\mathcal{D}, \leq, \rightsquigarrow)$ be a policy and *dom* be a domain assignment. We adopt the naming conventions used above: D denotes a security domain, s and t denote states, C denotes a command, and V and W denote command vectors.

The PER approach [14] characterizes information flow security based on indistinguishability relations on programs. Two programs are indistinguishable for a security domain D if running them in two D-equal states reveals no secrets to an observer in D, unless this is explicitly permitted by the given security policy. The D-indistinguishability relation is not reflexive. It only relates programs to themselves if they have secure information flow.

Definition 3 ([15]). *A* strong D-bisimulation *is a symmetric relation* R *on command vectors of equal size that satisfies the formula in Fig. 1 where the part with dark-gray background is deleted. The relation* $\approxeq_D$ *is the union of all strong* D*-bisimulations. A program* V *is* strongly secure *if* $V \approxeq_D V$ *holds for all* $D \in \mathcal{D}$.

$$
\begin{array}{l}
\forall s, s', t : \forall i \in \{1 \dots n\} : \forall W : \\
(V \; R \; V' \wedge \langle C_i, s \rangle \twoheadrightarrow \langle W, t \rangle \wedge s =_D s') \\
\Rightarrow \exists W', t' : W \; R \; W' \wedge \langle C'_i, s' \rangle \twoheadrightarrow \langle W', t' \rangle \\
\qquad \wedge \left[t =_D t' \vee \left[\begin{array}{l} \exists \mathcal{D}_1, \{D_2\} \subseteq \mathcal{D} : \\ \left[\begin{array}{l} \langle C_i, s \rangle \twoheadrightarrow_d^{\mathcal{D}_1 \to D_2} \langle W, t \rangle \\ \wedge \forall D' \in \mathcal{D}_1 : (D' \rightsquigarrow D_2 \vee D' \leq D_2) \\ \wedge D_2 \leq D \wedge \exists D' \in \mathcal{D}_1 : s \neq_{D'} s' \end{array} \right] \end{array} \right] \right]
\end{array}
$$

Fig. 1. Characterization of Strong $(D, \rightsquigarrow)$-Bisimulation Relations (see Definition 4) where $V = \langle C_1, \dots, C_n \rangle$, $V' = \langle C'_1, \dots, C'_n \rangle$, and $\twoheadrightarrow \; = \; \twoheadrightarrow_o \cup (\bigcup_{\mathcal{D}_1, \{D_2\} \subseteq \mathcal{D}} \twoheadrightarrow_d^{\mathcal{D}_1 \to D_2})$

For two commands $C, C' \in Com$, being strongly D-bisimilar ($C \approxeq_D C'$) means that each computation step that is possible for C in a state s can be simulated in each D-equal state s' by a computation step of C', where the resulting programs W and W' are strongly D-bisimilar and the resulting states t and t' are D-equal. As a consequence, strong security enforces the flow of information to comply with the ordering $\leq$ without permitting any exceptions. The strong security condition is the weakest security definition that is scheduler independent and is preserved under parallel and sequential composition [11]. Technically, the former is a consequence of requiring strongly D-bisimilar programs to execute in lock-step.

2.2 A Novel Characterization of Flow Security

In this article, we propose several characterizations of information flow security that permit declassification while controlling it in a particular dimension. Our security conditions are derived using the PER approach, and each of them is presented as a variant of the strong security condition. We use the terms *what-security* and *where-security* to indicate in which dimension declassification is controlled and distinguish different variants for the same dimension with indices.

Definition 4 (WHERE). *A* strong $(D, \rightsquigarrow)$-bisimulation *is a symmetric relation R on command vectors of equal size that satisfies the entire formula in Fig. 1. The relation $\approxeq_D^{\rightsquigarrow}$ is the union of all strong $(D, \rightsquigarrow)$-bisimulations. A program V has secure information flow while complying with the restrictions where declassification can occur if $V \approxeq_D^{\rightsquigarrow} V$ holds for all $D \in \mathcal{D}$ (brief: V is* where-*secure or $V \in$ WHERE).*

Declassification is possible as t and t' in Fig. 1 need not be D-equal. However, such exceptions are constrained by the formula with dark-gray background:

- steps causing declassification must be declassification transitions $\twoheadrightarrow_d^{\mathcal{D}_1 \to D_2}$;
- information flow must be permitted from each $D' \in \mathcal{D}_1$ to D_2 (by $\rightsquigarrow$ or $\leq$);
- declassification may only affect D if D_2 is observable, and it may only reveal differences between s and s' that can be observed from domains in $\mathcal{D}_1$.

That is, *where*-security localizes exceptions, within a computation, to the declassification steps and, within an MLS policy, to where $\rightsquigarrow$ permits it. In this respect, our condition is similar to intransitive noninterference [9], but the two security conditions are not identical. Most importantly, *where*-security satisfies all prudent principles of declassification (see Sect. 2.3), unlike intransitive noninterference [16]. Technically, the differences become apparent in the definition of the respectively underlying notion of a strong D-bisimulation. In [9], firstly, declassification steps downgrade information from a single domain D_1 (rather than from a set of domains $\mathcal{D}_1$), secondly, declassification steps may only make information flow according to the relation $\rightsquigarrow$ (rather than according to $\rightsquigarrow \cup \leq$), and thirdly, each transition must be simulated by a transition with the identical annotation (while Fig. 1 requires nothing about the labels of the transition $\langle\!| C'_i, s' |\!\rangle \twoheadrightarrow \langle\!| W', t' |\!\rangle$). The first two relaxations are helpful for a flexible combination with a control of *what* is downgraded. The third relaxation is crucial for satisfying the principle *monotonicity of release* (see Sect. 2.3).

2.3 Prudent Principles and Compositionality

To investigate our security definition more concretely, we augment the multi-threaded while language MWL from [15] with a declassifying assignment:

$$\begin{aligned} C ::= &\ \mathsf{skip} \mid Id{:=}Exp \mid C_1; C_2 \mid \mathsf{if}\ B\ \mathsf{then}\ C_1\ \mathsf{else}\ C_2\ \mathsf{fi} \mid \mathsf{while}\ B\ \mathsf{do}\ C\ \mathsf{od} \\ &\mid \mathsf{fork}(CV) \mid [Id{:=}Exp] \end{aligned}$$

We use B and Exp for denoting Boolean-valued and integer-valued expressions, respectively. The language $\mathcal{E}$ for expressions shall not be specified here. We only assume that the evaluation of expressions is atomic and deterministic. That expression Exp evaluates to value n in state s is denoted by $\langle\!| Exp, s |\!\rangle \downarrow n$. We assume a function *sources* that returns for an expression the set of security domains on which the value of the expression possibly depends or, more formally, $\forall s, t : (((\forall D \in sources(Exp) : s =_D t) \wedge \langle\!| Exp, s |\!\rangle \downarrow n \wedge \langle\!| Exp, t |\!\rangle \downarrow m) \implies n = m)$.

The semantics of MWL instantiate the transition relations $\twoheadrightarrow_o$ and $\twoheadrightarrow_d^{\mathcal{D}_1 \rightarrow D_2}$. A command $[Id{:=}Exp]$ causes a $\twoheadrightarrow_d^{\mathcal{D}_1 \rightarrow D_2}$ transition where $\mathcal{D}_1 = sources(Exp)$ and $D_2 = dom(Id)$. Assignments, skip, conditionals, loops, and fork cause ordinary transitions. The statement $\mathsf{fork}(CV)$ spawns the threads $\langle C \rangle V$ where C is the designated *main thread*. If threads are created within the sub-command C_1 of a sequential composition $C_1; C_2$ then C_2 is executed after the main thread has terminated. A formal definition of the semantics is provided in Appendix A.

Sabelfeld and Sands propose the following principles of declassification [16]:

Semantic consistency: The (in)security of a program is invariant under semantics-preserving transformations of declassification-free subprograms.

Conservativity: The security of a program with no declassifications is equivalent to noninterference.

Monotonicity of release: Adding further declassifications to a secure program cannot render it insecure.

Non-occlusion: The presence of a declassification operation cannot mask other covert information leaks.

We now validate our security characterization against these prudent principles.

As suggested in [16], we define semantic equivalence between programs by $\approxeq = \approxeq_{high}$, where $\approxeq_{high}$ is the strong *high*-bisimulation for the single-domain policy $(\{high\}, \{(high, high)\})$. A *context* $\mathcal{C}$ is a program where the hole $\bullet$ may occur as an atomic sub-command. We use $\mathcal{C}[C]$ to denote the program that one obtains by replacing each occurrence of $\bullet$ with C. The proof of the following and all other theorems in this article will be provided in an extended version.

Theorem 1 (Semantic consistency). *Let C, C' be programs without declassification commands. Then $C' \approxeq C$ and $\mathcal{C}[C] \in WHERE$ imply $\mathcal{C}[C'] \in WHERE$.*[2]

Strong security follows from *where*-security not only if there are no declassification operations in a program, but also if the policy does not permit any exceptions. In the other direction, *where*-security is a weakening of strong security.

Theorem 2 (Conservativity)

1. *If $\rightsquigarrow = \emptyset$ and $V \in WHERE$ then V is strongly secure.*
2. *If no declassification occurs in V and $V \in WHERE$ then V is strongly secure.*
3. *If V is strongly secure then $V \in WHERE$.*

Monotonicity holds with respect to the exceptions permitted by the policy and also with respect to the declassification operations in the program.

Theorem 3 (Monotonicity). *Let $\rightsquigarrow \subseteq \rightsquigarrow'$.*

1. *If $V \in WHERE$ for $(\mathcal{D}, \leq, \rightsquigarrow)$ then $V \in WHERE$ for $(\mathcal{D}, \leq, \rightsquigarrow')$.*
2. *If $\mathcal{C}[Id{:=}Exp] \in WHERE$ then $\mathcal{C}[\,[Id{:=}Exp]\,] \in WHERE$.*

Theorems 1–3 demonstrate that our novel security characterization satisfies the first three principles of declassification from [16]. A formal proof of the fourth prudent principle is impossible. Such a proof would require a formal characterization of secure information flow as a reference point, which we do not have a priori as Definition 4 *defines* a characterization based on an intuitive understanding.

The following compositionality results hold for WHERE. We define expressions Exp, Exp' to be D*-indistinguishable* (denoted by $Exp \equiv_D Exp'$) if $\forall s, t : ((s =_D t \wedge \langle Exp, s \rangle \downarrow n \wedge \langle Exp', t \rangle \downarrow m) \Rightarrow n = m)$.

Theorem 4. *If $C_1 \approxeq_D^{\rightsquigarrow} C_1'$, $C_2 \approxeq_D^{\rightsquigarrow} C_2'$ and $V \approxeq_D^{\rightsquigarrow} V'$ then*

1. $C_1; C_2 \approxeq_D^{\rightsquigarrow} C_1'; C_2'$;
2. $\mathsf{fork}(C_1 V) \approxeq_D^{\rightsquigarrow} \mathsf{fork}(C_1' V')$;
3. $B \equiv_D B' \Rightarrow (\mathsf{while}\ B\ \mathsf{do}\ C_1\ \mathsf{od} \approxeq_D^{\rightsquigarrow} \mathsf{while}\ B'\ \mathsf{do}\ C_1'\ \mathsf{od})$;
4. $(B \equiv_D B' \vee C_1 \approxeq_D^{\rightsquigarrow} C_2) \Rightarrow (\mathsf{if}\ B\ \mathsf{then}\ C_1\ \mathsf{else}\ C_2\ \mathsf{fi} \approxeq_D^{\rightsquigarrow} \mathsf{if}\ B'\ \mathsf{then}\ C_1'\ \mathsf{else}\ C_2'\ \mathsf{fi})$.

3 Controlling Declassification in the Dimension *what*

We propose two characterizations of information flow security that control what is declassified. Each of them is a natural adaptation of the idea underlying Cohen's *selective dependency* [3] (and its descendants like, e.g., *delimited release* [13] or *abstract noninterference* [5]) to a multi-threaded language.

[2] As usual, the proposition does not hold if one replaces sub-commands with declassification commands. For instance, consider $\mathcal{C} = \bullet$, $C = [l{:=}h]$, and $C' = l{:=}h$ for the two-domain policy where $dom(h) = high$, $dom(l) = low$, and $high \rightsquigarrow low$.

Definition 5. *An* MLS policy with escape hatches *is a triple* $(\mathcal{D}, \leq, \mathcal{H})$*, where* $(\mathcal{D}, \leq)$ *is an MLS policy, and* $\mathcal{H} \subseteq \mathcal{D} \times \mathcal{E}$ *is a set of escape hatches.*

From now, we assume that $(\mathcal{D}, \leq, \mathcal{H})$ denotes an MLS policy with escape hatches. Given a policy $(\mathcal{D}, \leq, \mathcal{H})$ the intuition is that, for any D, the visible behavior of secure programs may depend on the initial value of identifiers visible to D and also on the initial values of expressions Exp if $(D', Exp) \in \mathcal{H}$ and $D' \leq D$. Formally, an observer in a domain D may be able to determine which equivalence class of the relation $=_D^{\mathcal{H}}$ contains the initial state, but no further information.

Definition 6. *Two states s and t are* $(D, \mathcal{H})$-equal *($s =_D^{\mathcal{H}} t$) if*
1. $s =_D t$ *and*
2. $\forall (D', Exp) \in \mathcal{H} : (D' \leq D \implies ((\langle\!| Exp, s |\!\rangle \downarrow n \wedge \langle\!| Exp, t |\!\rangle \downarrow m) \Rightarrow n = m))$

That is, an escape hatch $(D', Exp) \in \mathcal{H}$ indicates that observers in domain $D \geq D'$ may learn the initial value of expression Exp during a program's execution. The following lemma shows that $(D, \mathcal{H})$-equality is a subset of D-equality.

Lemma 1. $\forall D : \forall s, t : [(\forall \mathcal{H} : (s =_D^{\mathcal{H}} t \implies s =_D t)) \wedge (s =_D t \implies s =_D^{\emptyset} t)]$

3.1 Two Novel Characterizations of Flow Security

Our conditions WHAT$_1$ and WHAT$_2$ constitute adaptations of strong security (Definition 3) that permit declassification while controlling *what* is declassified.

Definition 7 (WHAT$_1$). *A* strong $(D, \mathcal{H})$-bisimulation *is a symmetric relation R on command vectors of equal size that satisfies the formula in Fig. 2. The relation $\approx_D^{\mathcal{H}}$ is the union of all strong $(D, \mathcal{H})$-bisimulations. A program V has secure information flow while complying with the restrictions what can be declassified if $\forall D : V \approx_D^{\mathcal{H}} V$ (brief: V is what$_1$-*secure *or $V \in WHAT_1$).*

The difference between Definition 7 and the definition of strong D-bisimulations (see Definition 3) is that $=_D^{\mathcal{H}}$ occurs instead of $=_D$ on both sides of the implication. In the premise, $s =_D^{\mathcal{H}} s'$ occurs instead of $s =_D s'$. This modification leads to a *relaxation* of the security condition (see Lemma 1): differences in the values of an expression Exp that occurs in an escape hatch (D', Exp) may be revealed to an observer in domain D if $D' \leq D$. In the consequence, using $t =_D^{\mathcal{H}} t'$ instead of $t =_D t'$ leads to a *strengthening* of the security condition: the states t and t' must not differ in the values of expressions Exp that occur in an escape hatch $(D', Exp) \in \mathcal{H}$ with $D' \leq D$. The intention is to prevent unintended information leakage via subsequent declassifications that involve escape hatches.

Example 1. In this and the following examples we assume the two-level policy.

For illustrating the first modification, let $\mathcal{H} = \{(low, \mathsf{h1{+}h2})\}$, $C_1 =$ l:=h1+h2, and $C_2 =$ [l:=h1+h2]. Neither C_1 nor C_2 is strongly secure (take *low*-equal states that differ in the value of h1+h2), but both are *what*$_1$-secure. Recall that *what*$_1$-security does not aim at localizing *where* declassification occurs and, hence, declassifying assignments are treated like usual assignments (unlike in Sect. 2).

For illustrating the second modification, let $C_3 =$ h1:=0; [l:=h1+h2]. This program leaks the initial value of h2 and, hence, does not comply with the security policy. In fact, this program is not *what*$_1$-secure due to the requirement $t =_D^{\mathcal{H}} t'$.

$$\forall s, s', t : \forall i \in \{1 \dots n\} : \forall W : \\ (V\, R\, V' \wedge \langle C_i, s \rangle \twoheadrightarrow \langle W, t \rangle \wedge s =_D^{\mathcal{H}} s') \\ \Rightarrow \exists W', t' : \langle C_i', s' \rangle \twoheadrightarrow \langle W', t' \rangle \wedge t =_D^{\mathcal{H}} t' \wedge W\, R\, W'$$

Fig. 2. Characterization of Strong $(D, \mathcal{H})$-Bisimulation Relations (see Definition 7) where $V = \langle C_1, \dots, C_n \rangle$, $V' = \langle C_1', \dots, C_n' \rangle$, and $\twoheadrightarrow \; = \; \twoheadrightarrow_o \cup (\bigcup_{\mathcal{D}_1, \{D_2\} \subseteq \mathcal{D}} \twoheadrightarrow_d^{\mathcal{D}_1 \to D_2})$

Unfortunately, $what_1$-security does not satisfy the monotonicity principle (see Sect. 3.2). As a solution, we propose another security characterization.

Definition 8 (WHAT$_2$). *A program V has secure information flow while complying with the restrictions what can be declassified if $\forall D : \exists \mathcal{H}' \subseteq \mathcal{H} : V \approxeq_D^{\mathcal{H}'} V$ (brief: V is* $what_2$-secure *or $V \in WHAT_2$).*

Note that Definition 8 is also based on the notion of a strong $(D, \mathcal{H})$-bisimulation. The difference from Definition 7 is the existential quantification over $\mathcal{H}'$. This relaxation could be exploited in a security analysis by treating expressions in escape hatches like usual expressions if they are not used for declassification. Another effect of the relaxation is that the monotonicity principle is satisfied.

3.2 Prudent Principles and Compositionality

We now validate the security characterizations of this section against the prudent principles (see Sect. 2.3) and use the results to compare the characterizations.

Interestingly, WHAT$_1$ and WHAT$_2$ are preserved even if one replaces arbitrary sub-programs with semantically equivalent ones.

Theorem 5 (Strong semantic consistency). *Let C, C' be programs (possibly containing declassification commands).*
1. *If $C' \approxeq C$ and $\mathcal{C}[C] \in WHAT_1$ then $\mathcal{C}[C'] \in WHAT_1$.*
2. *If $C' \approxeq C$ and $\mathcal{C}[C] \in WHAT_2$ then $\mathcal{C}[C'] \in WHAT_2$.*

Both security conditions satisfy the conservativity principle. Additionally, $what_2$-security is a relaxation of strong security. Due to the strict handling of variables in escape hatches, $what_1$-security is not a relaxation of strong security if $\mathcal{H} \neq \emptyset$.

Theorem 6 (Conservativity)
1. *(a) If $\mathcal{H} = \emptyset$ and $V \in WHAT_1$ then V is strongly secure.*
   (b) If $\mathcal{H} = \emptyset$ and $V \in WHAT_2$ then V is strongly secure.
2. *(a) If $\mathcal{H} = \emptyset$ and V is strongly secure then $V \in WHAT_1$.*
   (b) If V is strongly secure, then $V \in WHAT_2$.

Theorem 7 (Monotonicity of Release)
Let $\mathcal{H} \subseteq \mathcal{H}'$. If $V \in WHAT_2$ for $(\mathcal{D}, \leq, \mathcal{H})$ then $V \in WHAT_2$ for $(\mathcal{D}, \leq, \mathcal{H}')$.

Example 2. Consider C_4 = h1:=0. Intuitively, this program has secure information flow for the two-domain policy (where dom(h1) = $high$), and it also satisfies the strong security condition. For any set $\mathcal{H}$, we obtain $C_4 \in$ WHAT$_2$ from $C_4 \approxeq_{low}^{\emptyset} C_4$ (take $\mathcal{H}' = \emptyset$). However, C_4 is not $what_1$-secure for $\mathcal{H} = \{(low, \texttt{h1+h2})\}$ as it updates the variable h1, which occurs in the escape hatch.

Example 2 demonstrates that WHAT_1 does not satisfy monotonicity. The problem is that the condition $V \approx_D^{\mathcal{H}} V$ does not permit the updating of variables that occur in some escape hatch in $\mathcal{H}$. While such updates might lead to an information leak in subsequent assignments, they are harmless given that the variable only occurs in escape hatches that are never used for declassification. This problem does not arise with WHAT_2 as one can choose $\mathcal{H}'$ such that it only contains escape hatches that are used.

While we are confident that our characterizations WHAT_1 and WHAT_2 are adequate, a formal proof of the *non-occlusion* principle is not possible as we are defining what security means (as already explained for WHERE in Sect. 2.3).

However, we can analyze the compositionality of our security characterizations. We define expressions Exp, Exp' to be $(D, \mathcal{H})$-*indistinguishable* (denoted by $Exp \equiv_D^{\mathcal{H}} Exp'$) if $\forall s,t : ((s =_D^{\mathcal{H}} t \wedge \langle\!| Exp, s |\!\rangle \downarrow n \wedge \langle\!| Exp', t |\!\rangle \downarrow m) \Rightarrow n = m)$.

Theorem 8. *If $C_1 \approx_D^{\mathcal{H}} C_1'$, $C_2 \approx_D^{\mathcal{H}} C_2'$, and $V \approx_D^{\mathcal{H}} V'$ then*
1. $C_1;\, C_2 \approx_D^{\mathcal{H}} C_1';\, C_2'$;
2. $\mathsf{fork}(C_1 V) \approx_D^{\mathcal{H}} \mathsf{fork}(C_1' V')$;
3. $B \equiv_D^{\mathcal{H}} B' \Rightarrow (\mathsf{while}\ B\ \mathsf{do}\ C_1\ \mathsf{od} \approx_D^{\mathcal{H}} \mathsf{while}\ B'\ \mathsf{do}\ C_1'\ \mathsf{od})$;
4. $(B \equiv_D^{\mathcal{H}} B' \vee C_1 \approx_D^{\mathcal{H}} C_2) \Rightarrow (\mathsf{if}\ B\ \mathsf{then}\ C_1\ \mathsf{else}\ C_2\ \mathsf{fi} \approx_D^{\mathcal{H}} \mathsf{if}\ B'\ \mathsf{then}\ C_1'\ \mathsf{else}\ C_2'\ \mathsf{fi})$.

Corollary 1. *If $C_1, C_2, V \in WHAT_1$ then*
1. $C_1;\, C_2 \in WHAT_1$;
2. $\mathsf{fork}(C_1 V) \in WHAT_1$;
3. *if the policy has a domain low and* $B \equiv_{low}^{\mathcal{H}} B$ *then* $\mathsf{while}\ B\ \mathsf{do}\ C_1\ \mathsf{od} \in WHAT_1$;
4. $[\forall D \in \mathcal{D} : (B \not\equiv_D^{\mathcal{H}} B \Longrightarrow C_1 \approx_D^{\mathcal{H}} C_2)] \Longrightarrow \mathsf{if}\ B\ \mathsf{then}\ C_1\ \mathsf{else}\ C_2\ \mathsf{fi} \in WHAT_1$.

Due to the existential quantification of $\mathcal{H}'$ in Definition 8, WHAT_2 is not compositional. This is illustrated by the following example.

Example 3. The programs $C_2 = [\mathsf{l{:=}h1{+}h2}]$ and $C_4 = \mathsf{h1{:=}0}$ (from Examples 1 and 2) are both *what*$_2$-secure for the set $\mathcal{H} = \{(low, \mathsf{h1{+}h2})\}$. However, neither $C_3 = C_4; C_2$ nor $C_5 = \mathsf{fork}(C_4\langle C_2\rangle)$ is *what*$_2$-secure.

In summary, none of our two characterizations WHAT_1 and WHAT_2 is superior to the respective other characterization. While WHAT_1 is compositional (see Corollary 1) but does not satisfy the monotonicity principle (see Example 2), WHAT_2 satisfies monotonicity (see Theorem 7) but is not compositional (see Example 3). It would be desirable to obtain a security characterization that is compositional and that satisfies the monotonicity principle. Unfortunately, one faces a fundamental difficulty when one also wants to control the *what* dimension of declassification. As discussed in Example 3, $C_3 = C_4; C_2$ and $C_5 = \mathsf{fork}(C_4\langle C_2\rangle)$ both violate the two-level policy for the set $\mathcal{H} = \{(low, \mathsf{h1{+}h2})\}$ and, hence, these programs should not be considered as *what*-secure. However, being able to declassify the expression $\mathsf{h1{+}h2}$ is the very purpose of the escape hatch $(low, \mathsf{h1{+}h2})$ and, hence, the program $C_2 = [\mathsf{l{:=}h1{+}h2}]$ should be considered as *what*-secure. The inherent trade-off becomes apparent when considering $C_4 = \mathsf{h1{:=}0}$. If one classifies this program as *what*-secure then one arrives at a security condition that is not compositional (as, e.g., C_3 and C_5 are not *what*-secure). However, if one classifies C_4 as not *what*-secure then one arrives at a security condition that does not satisfy monotonicity because C_4 is *what*-secure for $\mathcal{H} = \emptyset$.[3]

4 A Sound Type System for Information Flow Security

We present a security type system that can be used as a basis for automating the information flow analysis. The type system provides an integrated control of the *where* dimension and of the *what* dimension of declassification.

Definition 9. *If* $(\mathcal{D}, \leq, \rightsquigarrow)$ *is an* MLS policy with exceptions *and* $(\mathcal{D}, \leq, \mathcal{H})$ *is an* MLS policy with escape hatches *then the tuple* $(\mathcal{D}, \leq, \rightsquigarrow, \mathcal{H})$ *is an* MLS policy controlling the where and what of declassification.

In the following, let $(\mathcal{D}, \leq, \rightsquigarrow, \mathcal{H})$ be a policy and *dom* be a domain assignment.

The core of the type system is the rule for declassification commands as this is where declassification actually occurs. Our security characterizations in Sections 2 and 3 provide some guidance for developing such a rule, but there are still some pitfalls that one must avoid. As an example, consider the rule below, where *Var*(*Exp*) denotes the set of identifiers occurring in the expression *Exp*:

$$\frac{\begin{array}{c} dom(Id) = D \qquad \forall D' \in sources(Exp) : D' \ (\leq \cup \rightsquigarrow) \ D \qquad Exp \equiv_D^{\mathcal{H}} Exp \\ \forall (D', Exp') \in \mathcal{H} : ((D' \leq D \wedge Id \in Var(Exp')) \implies Exp \equiv_{D'}^{\mathcal{H}} Exp) \end{array}}{[Id{:=}Exp]} \quad (1)$$

In the above rule, the second premise ensures that declassification complies with $\rightsquigarrow$ or, in other words, that the *where* of declassification is localized according to the policy. The third premise ensures that executing the declassification command in $(D, \mathcal{H})$-equal states leads to D-equal states. Finally, the fourth premise controls the information flow into variables that occur in escape hatches.

Nevertheless, the above typing rule is not sound in a compositional security analysis. For instance, Rule (1) allows one to derive [h1:=0] as well as [l:=h1+h2], but the sequential composition of these commands leaks the initial value of h2 and, hence, does not comply with the two-level policy for $\mathcal{H} = \{(low, \mathsf{h1{+}h2})\}$. In order to avoid such problems, the rule also needs to ensure that a declassification does not enable information leakage in assignments that are executed subsequently.[4] A solution would be to forbid assignments to variables that occur in escape hatches that contain complex expressions (i.e., expressions that are not identifiers). This solution can be implemented by adding the following condition as another premise to Rule (1):

$$\forall (D', Exp') \in \mathcal{H} : (Id \in Var(Exp') \implies Exp' = Id)$$

[3] It is not an option to classify C_4 as not *what*-secure for $\mathcal{H} = \emptyset$ because then one would essentially have to classify *all* assignments as not *what*-secure.

[4] Note that, in a concurrent program, such assignment may occur *after* the given declassification (sequential composition), *before* the declassification (backwards jumps due to loops), and also in a program executed by a concurrent thread.

$$\frac{}{\vdash Const : \emptyset} \qquad \frac{dom(Id) = D}{\vdash Id : \{D\}} \qquad \frac{\vdash Exp_1 : \mathcal{D}_1 \quad \dots \quad \vdash Exp_m : \mathcal{D}_m}{\vdash Op(Exp_1, \dots, Exp_m) : \bigcup_{i\in\{1,\dots,m\}} \mathcal{D}_i}$$

Fig. 3. Type rules for expressions

$$\frac{}{\vdash \mathsf{skip}} \qquad \frac{\vdash Exp : \mathcal{D}' \quad \forall D \in \mathcal{D}' : D \leq dom(Id) \quad Id \leftarrow Exp}{\vdash Id{:=}Exp}$$

$$\frac{\vdash C \quad \vdash V}{\vdash \mathsf{fork}(CV)} \qquad \frac{\vdash Exp : \mathcal{D}' \quad \forall D \in \mathcal{D}' : D(\rightsquigarrow \cup \leq) dom(Id) \quad Id \leftarrow Exp}{\vdash [Id{:=}Exp]}$$

$$\frac{\vdash C_0 \quad \dots \vdash C_{n-1}}{\vdash \langle C_0, \dots C_{n-1}\rangle} \quad \frac{\vdash C_1 \quad \vdash C_2}{\vdash C_1 \,;\, C_2} \quad \frac{\vdash B : \{low\} \quad \vdash C}{\vdash \mathsf{while}\, B \,\mathsf{do}\, C \,\mathsf{od}}$$

$$\frac{\vdash C_1 \quad \vdash C_2 \quad \forall D : B \equiv_D B \Rightarrow C_1 \approxeq_D^{\rightarrow} C_2 \quad \forall D : B \equiv_D^{\mathcal{H}} B \Rightarrow C_1 \approxeq_D^{\mathcal{H}} C_2}{\vdash \mathsf{if}\, B \,\mathsf{then}\, C_1 \,\mathsf{else}\, C_2 \,\mathsf{fi}}$$

Fig. 4. Rules of the Integrated Security Type System

In the type system, we use the judgment $\vdash Exp : \mathcal{D}'$ instead of the function *sources*. Intuitively, $\vdash Exp : \mathcal{D}'$ means that if $Id \in Var(Exp)$ then $dom(Id) \in \mathcal{D}'$ and that if $D \in \mathcal{D}'$ then there is a variable $Id \in Var(Exp)$ with $dom(Id) = D$. The judgment is defined formally by the rules in Fig. 3, and it fulfills the requirements for the function *sources* as the following theorem shows.

Theorem 9. *If* $\vdash Exp : \mathcal{D}'$ *and* $\forall D' \in \mathcal{D}' : D' \leq D$ *then* $Exp \equiv_D Exp$.

To improve the readability of the typing rules, we introduce a judgment $Id \leftarrow Exp$. Intuitively, this judgment captures that *Exp* may be assigned to *Id* in a declassifying assignment. The following formal definition is based on the conditions that we have motivated earlier in this section.

Definition 10. *We define the judgment* $Id \leftarrow Exp$ *by*

$$\begin{aligned} Id \leftarrow Exp \equiv \forall D \in \mathcal{D} : ((D = dom(Id) \vee (D, Id) \in \mathcal{H}) \Rightarrow Exp \equiv_D^{\mathcal{H}} Exp) \\ \wedge \forall (D', Exp') \in \mathcal{H} : (Id \in Var(Exp') \implies Exp' = Id). \end{aligned}$$

The integrated security type system for commands is presented in Fig. 4. Recall that we implicitly assume $(\mathcal{D}, \leq, \rightsquigarrow, \mathcal{H})$ to be an *MLS policy controlling the where and what of declassification*. To make the policy explicit, we use the notation $\vdash_{\mathcal{D},\leq,\rightsquigarrow,\mathcal{H}} V$ for denoting that $\vdash V$ is derivable with the typing rules.

Note that the rule for conditionals has two semantic side conditions. In this respect our presentation of the typing rules is similar to the one of the typing rules for intransitive noninterference in [9]. In that article, it is demonstrated how such semantic side conditions can be syntactically approximated by safe approximation relations in a sound way, and similar constructions are possible for our side conditions. Moreover, the premises of the typing rules for assignments and declassification involve the judgment $Id \leftarrow Exp$. Due to space limitations, we also omit the fairly straightforward syntactic approximation of Definition 10.

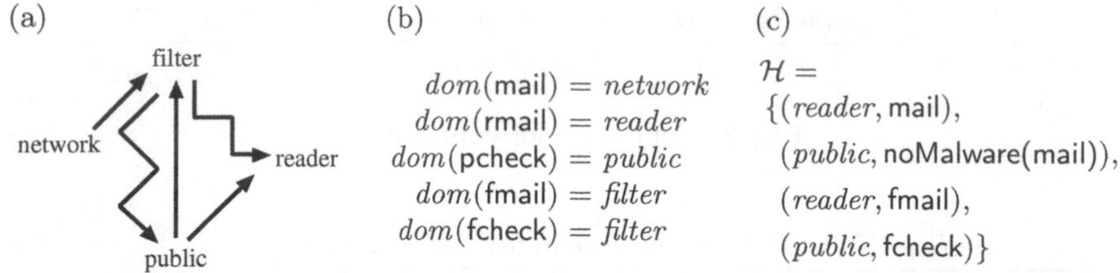

Fig. 5. (a) MLS policy with exceptions, (b) domain assignment, (c) escape hatches

```
fcheck:=noMalware(mail); % check that the mail contains no malware
[pcheck:=fcheck];        % make check result public
if check then fmail:=mail % copy the mail into an auxiliary variable
         else fmail:=0 fi; % set the auxiliary variable to a dummy value
[rmail:=fmail]           % forward mail to reader
```

Fig. 6. An example for a filter program

Theorem 10 (Soundness of Security Type System)

1. *If* $\vdash_{\mathcal{D},\leq,\rightsquigarrow,\mathcal{H}} V$ *then* V *is* where*-secure.*
2. *If* $\vdash_{\mathcal{D},\leq,\rightsquigarrow,\mathcal{H}} V$ *then* V *is* what$_1$*-secure.*
3. *If* $\vdash_{\mathcal{D},\leq,\rightsquigarrow,\mathcal{H}} V$ *then* V *is* what$_2$*-secure for all* $(\mathcal{D}, \leq, \rightsquigarrow, \mathcal{H}')$ *with* $\mathcal{H} \subseteq \mathcal{H}'$.

That is, the type system is sound with respect to the security characterizations introduced in Sect. 2 and 3. In particular, the *what* and *where* of declassification in type-correct programs complies with the respectively given policy.

5 An Exemplary Security Analysis

In our application scenario, an e-mail arrives via a network and is forwarded to a user. Before the user reads an e-mail in the mail reader, the e-mail must pass a filter. The filter shall check whether the e-mail is infected by malware and shall also make the result of the check publicly available, e.g., to permit the computation of statistics about the infection rate of incoming e-mail. For this scenario, we can distinguish four security domains, a domain for the network, a domain for the filter, a domain for the mail reader, and a domain for public information. The main security requirements are that all e-mail from the network passes the filter before reaching the reader and that no e-mails are made public.

The resulting security policy is depicted in Fig. 5. The first security requirement is captured by this policy as the only path from domain *network* to domain *reader* is via domain *filter*. The second requirement is captured by the set of escape hatches as the only escape hatch with variable mail as expression has *reader* as target domain. The first requirement concerns the *where* dimension while the second requirement concerns the *what* dimension of declassification. A simple example for a filter program is depicted in Fig. 6. Note that declassifying assignments are used to declassify the result of the malware check (which depends on the variable mail) to domain *public* and to declassify an incoming mail to domain *reader*. The filter program forwards mail only if the malware check was negative. While this *what* aspect of declassification is not captured in our security policy, it would also be possible to define an MLS policy that captures this aspect. We refrain from pursuing such possibilities here.

An analysis of the filter program with the typing rules from Fig. 4 yields that the program is type correct (three applications of the rule for sequential composition, one application of the rule for conditionals, three applications of the rule for assignments, and two applications of the rule for declassifying assignments). Theorem 10 allows us to conclude that the program in Fig. 6 is *where*-secure, $what_1$-secure, and $what_2$-secure for the MLS policy in Fig. 5.

6 Related Work

Declassification is a current topic in language-based information flow security and there already is a variety of approaches to controlling declassification [16]. In the *what* dimension this survey lists, for instance, [8,13], and in the *where/when* dimension, for instance, [4,10,9]. *Non-disclosure* is a recent approach in the *where* dimension that aims at multi-threaded programs [2,1]. The idea is to expand the flow relation $\leq$ according to annotations at the executing sub-programs. A given expansion of $\leq$ localizes *where* declassification can occur in the program. The construction of expansions implicitly assumes that the exceptions that are permitted correspond to a transitive relation, an assumption that we do not need to make for WHERE.

Very few approaches limit declassification in more than one dimension.

According to [16], *relaxed noninterference* [7] mainly addresses the *what* dimensions, but it also addresses some aspects of the *where* dimension. Relaxed noninterference has a syntactic flavor as declassification may only involve syntactically equivalent λ-terms.[5] While this approach appears quite restrictive, the benefit is that one obtains some localization in the program as declassification can only happen *where* a particular syntactic expression occurs. Since *relaxed noninterference* only considers a two-level policy, there is no notion of limiting *where* declassification can occur in the flow policy.

According to [16], *abstract noninterference* [5] mainly addresses the *what*-dimension. In fact, it is a generalization of selective dependency like *delimited release* [13], WHAT_1, and WHAT_2. However, abstract noninterference also has similarities to robust declassification [17], which is a prominent representative for controlling the *who* dimension.

Another aspect, in which our work differs from many other approaches, is that we address concurrent programs. Lifting a security analysis from a sequential to a concurrent setting is often nontrivial as one must consider the possibility of races

[5] In [7] Li and Zdancewic use a $\beta-\eta$-equivalence. But they already point out, that it is not clear if this is an useful choice or what would be more useful.

and address the danger of internal timing leaks. For an overview on approaches addressing concurrency, we can only refer to [12] due to space restrictions.

7 Conclusion

While a number of approaches to controlling declassification in a language-based security analysis has been proposed in recent years, little work has addressed controlling multiple dimensions of declassification in an integrated fashion.

The aim of our investigation was to more adequately control the *where* and *what* of declassification. For controlling the *where* dimension, we proposed the condition WHERE, and we proved that it is compositional and satisfies the prudent principles of declassification (unlike, e.g., intransitive noninterference). For controlling *what*, we proposed the conditions WHAT_1 and WHAT_2, and we identified an inherent trade-off between the monotonicity principle and compositionality. To our knowledge, the soundness result for our type system is the first such result that clearly identifies which aspects of *where* and *what* are controlled.

The starting point for deriving our novel security characterizations was the strong security condition. The advantages of this condition include that it is compositional and robust with respect to choices of the scheduler (see [15] for a more detailed analysis). The strong security condition also rules out dangers of internal leaks in concurrent programming without making any assumptions about the possibilities of race conditions in a program. As a consequence, this condition is somewhat restrictive, which is technically due to the use of a strong bisimulation relation that requires a lock-step execution of related programs. While a less restrictive baseline characterization would be desirable, we do not know of any convincing solutions for controlling the *where* dimension in multi-threaded programs based on a less restrictive security condition.

Acknowledgments. We thank Henning Sudbrock for helpful comments. We also thank the anonymous reviewers for their suggestions.

This work was funded by the DFG in the Computer Science Action Program and by the Information Society Technologies program of the European Commission, Future and Emerging Technologies under the IST-2005-015905 MOBIUS project. This article reflects only the authors' views, and the Commission, the DFG, and the authors are not liable for any use that may be made of the information contained therein.

References

1. A. Almeida Matos. *Typing secure information flow: declassification and mobility.* PhD thesis, École Nationale Supérieure des Mines de Paris, 2006.
2. A. Almeida Matos and G. Boudol. On declassification and the non-disclosure policy. In *In Proc. IEEE Computer Security Foundations Workshop*, 2005.
3. E. Cohen. Information transmission in sequential programs. In *Foundations of Secure Computation*, pages 297–335. Academic Press, 1978.

4. M. Dam and P. Giambiagi. Information flow control for cryptographic applets, 2003. Presentation at Dagstuhl Seminar on Language-Based Security, http://kathrin.dagstuhl.de/03411/Materials2/.
5. R. Giacobazzi and I. Mastroeni. Abstract non-interference: Parameterizing non-interference by abstract interpretation. In *Proc. of the 31st Annual ACM SIGPLAN-SIGACT Symposium on Principles of Programming Languages*, pages 186–197, 2004.
6. J. A. Goguen and J. Meseguer. Security Policies and Security Models. In *Proceedings of the IEEE Symposium on Security and Privacy*, pages 11–20, Oakland, CA, USA, 1982.
7. P. Li and S. Zdancewic. Downgrading policies and relaxed noninterference. In *Proc. of the 32nd ACM SIGPLAN-SIGACT symposium on Principles of programming languages*, pages 158–170, New York, NY, USA, 2005.
8. G. Lowe. Quantifying information flow. In *Proc. of the 15th IEEE Computer Security Foundations Workshop*, page 18, Washington, DC, USA, 2002.
9. H. Mantel and D. Sands. Controlled Declassification based on Intransitive Noninterference. In *Proceedings of the 2nd ASIAN Symposium on Programming Languages and Systems, APLAS 2004*, LNCS 3303, pages 129–145, Taipei, Taiwan, 2004.
10. A. Di Pierro, C. Hankin, and H. Wiklicky. Approximate Non-Interference. *Journal of Computer Security*, 12(1):37–81, 2004.
11. A. Sabelfeld. Confidentiality for Multithreaded Programs via Bisimulation. In *Proceedings of Andrei Ershov 5th International Conference on Perspectives of System Informatics*, number 2890 in LNCS, pages 260–274, 2003.
12. A. Sabelfeld and A. C. Myers. Language-based Information-Flow Security. *IEEE Journal on Selected Areas in Communication*, 21(1):5–19, 2003.
13. A. Sabelfeld and A. C. Myers. A model for delimited information release. In *Proceedings of the International Symposium on Software Security*, 2004.
14. A. Sabelfeld and D. Sands. A Per Model of Secure Information Flow in Sequential Programs. In *Proceedings of the 8th European Symposium on Programming*, LNCS, pages 50–59, 1999.
15. A. Sabelfeld and D. Sands. Probabilistic Noninterference for Multi-threaded Programs. In *Proceedings of the 13th IEEE Computer Security Foundations Workshop*, pages 200–215, Cambridge, UK, 2000.
16. A. Sabelfeld and D. Sands. Dimensions and Principles of Declassification. In *Proceedings of the 18th IEEE Computer Security Foundations Workshop*, pages 255–269. IEEE Computer Society, 2005.
17. S. Zdancewic and A. Myers. Robust declassification. In *14th IEEE Computer Security Foundations Workshop (CSFW '01)*, pages 15–26, Washington - Brussels - Tokyo, 2001.

A Operational Semantics of MWL

The intuition of a *deterministic judgment* of the form $\langle\!| C, s |\!\rangle \twoheadrightarrow \langle\!| W, t |\!\rangle$ is that command C performs a computation step in state s, yielding a state t and a vector of commands W, which has length zero if C terminated, length one if it has neither terminated nor spawned any threads, and length greater than one if new threads were spawned. The transition arrow is labeled to distinguish

$$\frac{}{\langle\!| \mathsf{skip}, s |\!\rangle \twoheadrightarrow_o \langle\!| \langle\rangle, s |\!\rangle} \quad \frac{\langle\!| Exp, s |\!\rangle \downarrow n}{\langle\!| Id{:=}Exp, s |\!\rangle \twoheadrightarrow_o \langle\!| \langle\rangle, [Id = n]s |\!\rangle} \quad \frac{}{\langle\!| \mathsf{fork}(CV), s |\!\rangle \twoheadrightarrow_o \langle\!| \langle C\rangle V, s |\!\rangle}$$

$$\frac{\langle\!| B, s |\!\rangle \downarrow \mathsf{True}}{\langle\!| \mathsf{if}\ B\ \mathsf{then}\ C_1\ \mathsf{else}\ C_2\ \mathsf{fi}, s |\!\rangle \twoheadrightarrow_o \langle\!| C_1, s |\!\rangle} \quad \frac{\langle\!| B, s |\!\rangle \downarrow \mathsf{False}}{\langle\!| \mathsf{if}\ B\ \mathsf{then}\ C_1\ \mathsf{else}\ C_2\ \mathsf{fi}, s |\!\rangle \twoheadrightarrow_o \langle\!| C_2, s |\!\rangle}$$

$$\frac{\langle\!| B, s |\!\rangle \downarrow \mathsf{True}}{\langle\!| \mathsf{while}\ B\ \mathsf{do}\ C\ \mathsf{od}, s |\!\rangle \twoheadrightarrow_o \langle\!| C; \mathsf{while}\ B\ \mathsf{do}\ C\ \mathsf{od}, s |\!\rangle} \quad \frac{\langle\!| B, s |\!\rangle \downarrow \mathsf{False}}{\langle\!| \mathsf{while}\ B\ \mathsf{do}\ C\ \mathsf{od}, s |\!\rangle \twoheadrightarrow_o \langle\!| \langle\rangle, s |\!\rangle}$$

$$\frac{\langle\!| C_1, s |\!\rangle \twoheadrightarrow_o \langle\!| \langle\rangle, s' |\!\rangle}{\langle\!| C_1; C_2, s |\!\rangle \twoheadrightarrow_o \langle\!| C_2, s' |\!\rangle} \quad \frac{\langle\!| C_1, s |\!\rangle \twoheadrightarrow_o \langle\!| C_1' V, s' |\!\rangle}{\langle\!| C_1; C_2, s |\!\rangle \twoheadrightarrow_o \langle\!| \langle C_1'; C_2\rangle V, s' |\!\rangle}$$

$$\frac{\langle\!| Exp, s |\!\rangle \downarrow n \quad sources(Exp) = \mathcal{D}_1 \quad dom(Id) = D_2}{\langle\!| [Id{:=}Exp], s |\!\rangle \twoheadrightarrow_d^{\mathcal{D}_1 \to D_2} \langle\!| \langle\rangle, [Id = n]s |\!\rangle} \quad \frac{\langle\!| C_1, s |\!\rangle \twoheadrightarrow_d^{\mathcal{D}_1 \to D_2} \langle\!| \langle\rangle, s' |\!\rangle}{\langle\!| C_1; C_2, s |\!\rangle \twoheadrightarrow_d^{\mathcal{D}_1 \to D_2} \langle\!| C_2, s' |\!\rangle}$$

Fig. 7. Deterministic operational semantics of MWL

ordinary computation steps (labeling: $\twoheadrightarrow_o$) from declassification steps (labeling: $\twoheadrightarrow_d^{\mathcal{D}_1 \to D_2}$). An inductive definition of the semantics is given by the rules in Fig. 7.

To model concurrent computations, the deterministic judgment is lifted to a *nondeterministic judgment* of the form $\langle\!| V, s |\!\rangle \to \langle\!| V', t |\!\rangle$. The intuitive meaning is that some thread C_i in V performs a step in state s resulting in the state t and some thread pool W'. The global thread pool V' results then by replacing C_i with W'. This is formalized by the rules in Fig. 8.

$$\frac{\langle\!| C_i, s |\!\rangle \twoheadrightarrow_o \langle\!| W', s' |\!\rangle}{\langle\!| \langle C_0 \ldots C_{n-1}\rangle, s |\!\rangle \to \langle\!| \langle C_0 \ldots C_{i-1}\rangle W' \langle C_{i+1} \ldots C_{n-1}\rangle, s' |\!\rangle}$$

$$\frac{\langle\!| C_i, s |\!\rangle \twoheadrightarrow \langle\!| W', s' |\!\rangle}{\langle\!| \langle C_0 \ldots C_{n-1}\rangle, s |\!\rangle \to \langle\!| \langle C_0 \ldots C_{i-1}\rangle W' \langle C_{i+1} \ldots C_{n-1}\rangle, s' |\!\rangle}$$

Fig. 8. Non-deterministic operational semantics of MWL

Cost Analysis of Java Bytecode

E. Albert[1], P. Arenas[1], S. Genaim[2], G. Puebla[2], and D. Zanardini[2]

[1] DSIC, Complutense University of Madrid, E-28040 Madrid, Spain
[2] CLIP, Technical University of Madrid, E-28660 Boadilla del Monte, Madrid, Spain

Abstract. Cost analysis of Java bytecode is complicated by its unstructured control flow, the use of an operand stack and its object-oriented programming features (like dynamic dispatching). This paper addresses these problems and develops a generic framework for the automatic cost analysis of sequential Java bytecode. Our method generates *cost relations* which define at compile-time the cost of programs as a function of their input data size. To the best of our knowledge, this is the first approach to the automatic cost analysis of Java bytecode.

1 Introduction

Cost analysis has been intensively studied in the context of declarative (see, e.g., [17,16,18,12,5] for functional programming and [10,11] for logic programming) and *high-level* imperative programming languages (mainly focused on the estimation of worst case execution times and the design of cost models [23]). Traditionally, cost analysis has been formulated at the source level. However, there are situations where we do not have access to the source code, but only to compiled code. An example of this is *mobile code*, where the *code consumer* receives code to be executed. In this context, Java bytecode [13] is widely used, mainly due to its security features and the fact that it is *platform-independent*. Automatic cost analysis has interesting applications in this context. For instance, the receiver of the code may want to infer cost information in order to decide whether to reject code which has too large cost requirements in terms of computing resources (in time and/or space), and to accept code which meets the established requirements [8,2,3]. In fact, this is the main motivation for the *Mobile Resource Guarantees* (MRG) research project [3], which establishes a *Proof-Carrying Code* [15] framework for guaranteeing resource consumption. Furthermore, the *Mobility, Ubiquity and Security* (MOBIUS) research project [4], also considers resource consumption as one of the central properties of interest for proof-carrying code. Also, in parallel systems, knowledge about the cost of different procedures can be used in order to guide the partitioning, allocation and scheduling of parallel processes.

The aim of this work is to develop an automatic approach to the cost analysis of Java bytecode which statically generates *cost relations*. These relations define the cost of a program as a function of its input data size. This approach was proposed by Debray and Lin [10] for logic programs, and by Rabhi and Manson [16] for functional programs. In these approaches, cost functions are expressed by means of *recurrence equations* generated by abstracting the recursive

R. De Nicola (Ed.): ESOP 2007, LNCS 4421, pp. 157–172, 2007.

structure of the program and by inferring size relations between arguments. A low-level object-oriented language such as Java bytecode introduces novel challenges, mainly due to: 1) its unstructured control flow, e.g., the use of goto statements rather than recursive structures; 2) its object-oriented features, like virtual method invocation, which may influence the cost; and 3) its stack-based model, in which stack cells store intermediate values. This paper addresses these difficulties and develops a generic framework for the automatic cost analysis of Java bytecode programs. The process takes as input the bytecode corresponding to a method and yields a cost relation after performing these steps:

1. The input bytecode is first transformed into a *control flow graph* (CFG). This allows making the unstructured control flow of the bytecode explicit (challenge 1 above). Advanced features like virtual invocation and exceptions are simply dealt as additional nodes in the graph (challenge 2).
2. The CFG is then represented as a set of rules by using an *intermediate recursive representation* in which we *flatten* the local stack by converting its contents into a series of additional local variables (challenge 3).[1]
3. In the third step, we infer *size relations* among the input variables for all calls in the rules by means of static analysis. These size relations are constraints on the possible values of variables (for integers) and constraints on the length of the longest reachable path (for references).
4. The fourth phase provides, for each rule of the recursive representation, a safe approximation of the set of input arguments which are "relevant" to the cost. This is performed using a simple static analysis.
5. From the recursive representation, its relevant arguments, and the size relations, the fifth step automatically yields as output the *cost relation* which expresses the cost of the method as a function of its input arguments.

We point out that computed cost relations, in many cases, can be simplified to the point of deriving statically an *upper and lower* threshold cost for the input size arguments and/or obtaining a *closed form* solution. Such simplifications have been well-studied in the field of algorithmic complexity (see e.g. [22]).

2 The Java Bytecode Language

Java bytecode [13] is a low-level object-oriented programming language with unstructured control and an *operand stack* to hold intermediate computational results. Moreover, objects are stored in dynamic memory (the *heap*). A Java bytecode program consists of a set of *class files*, one for each class or interface. A class file contains information about its *name* $c \in \mathit{Class\_Name}$, the class it extends, the interfaces it implements, and the fields and methods it defines. In particular, for each method, the class file contains: a method signature $m \in \mathit{Meth\_Sig}$ which consists of its name $\mathit{name}(m) \in \mathit{Meth\_Name}$ and its

[1] Note that this is possible since in every *valid* bytecode program the height of the local stack at each program point is fixed and therefore can be computed statically.

type $type(m) = \tau_1, \ldots, \tau_n \to \tau \in \mathit{Meth\_Type}$ where $\tau, \tau_i \in \mathit{Type}$; its bytecode $bc_m = \langle pc_0{:}b_0, \ldots, pc_{n_m}{:}b_{n_m} \rangle$, where each b_i is a *bytecode instruction* and pc_i is its address; and the method's exceptions table. When it is clear from the context, we omit bytecode addresses and refer to a *method signature* as *method*.

In this work we consider a subset of the JVM [13] language which is able to handle operations on integers, object creation and manipulation (by accessing fields and calling methods) and exceptions (either generated by abnormal execution or explicitly thrown by the program). We omit interfaces, static fields and methods and primitive types different from integers. Methods are assumed to return an integer value. Thus, our bytecode instruction set (*bcInst*) is:

bcInst ::= push x | istore v | astore v | iload v | aload v | iconst a | iadd | isub | imul
| idiv | if$\diamond$ pc | goto pc | new *Class_Name* | invokevirtual *Class_Name.Meth_Sig*
| invokespecial *Class_Name.Meth_Sig* | athrow | ireturn
| getfield *Class_Name.Field_Sig* | putfield *Class_Name.Field_Sig*

where $\diamond$ is a comparison operator (ne,le,_icmpgt, etc.), v a local variable, a an integer, pc an instruction address, and x an integer or the special value NULL.

3 From Bytecode to Control Flow Graphs

This section describes the generation of a *control flow graph* (CFG) from the bytecode of a method. This will allow transforming the unstructured control flow of bytecode into recursion. The technique we use follows well-established ideas in compilers [1], already applied in Java bytecode analysis [19].

Given a method m, we denote by G_m its CFG, which is a directed graph whose nodes are referred to as *blocks*. Each block $Block_{id}$ is a tuple of the form $\langle id, G, B, D \rangle$ where: id is the block's unique identifier; G is the *guard* of the block which indicates under which conditions the block is executed; B is a sequence of contiguous bytecode instructions which are guaranteed to be executed unconditionally (i.e., if G succeeds then all instructions in B are executed before control moves to another block); and D is the *adjacency list* for $Block_{id}$, i.e., D contains the identifiers of all blocks which are possible successors of $Block_{id}$, i.e., $id' \in D$ iff there is an arc from $Block_{id}$ to $Block_{id'}$. Guards originate from bytecodes where the execution might take different paths depending on the runtime values. This is the case of bytecodes for conditional jumps, method invocation, and exceptions manipulation. In the CFG this will be expressed by *branching* from the corresponding block. The successive blocks will have mutually exclusive guards since only one of them will be executed. Guards take the form guard(cond), where cond is a Boolean condition on the local variables and stack elements of the method. It is important to point out that guards in the successive blocks will not be taken into account when computing the cost of a program.

A large part of the bytecode instruction set has only one successor. However, there are three types of branching statements:

Conditional jumps: of the form "pc_i : if$\diamond$ pc_j". Depending on the truth value of the condition, the execution can jump to pc_j or continue, as usual, with pc_{i+1}.

The graph describes this behavior by means of two arcs from the block containing the instruction of pc_i to those starting respectively with instructions of pc_j and pc_{i+1}. Each one of these new blocks begins by a `guard` expressing the condition under which such block is to be executed.

Dynamic dispatch: of the form "pc_i : invokevirtual $c.m$". The type of the object o whose method is being invoked is not known statically (it could be c or any subclass of c); therefore, we cannot determine statically which method is going to be invoked. Hence, we need to make all possible choices explicit in the graph. We deal with dynamic dispatching by using the function `resolve_virtual`(c, m), which returns the set *ResolvedMethods* of pairs $\langle d, \{c_1, \ldots, c_k\}\rangle$, where d is a class that defines a method with signature m and each c_i is either c or a subclass of c which inherits that specific method from d. For each $\langle d, \{c_1, \ldots, c_k\}\rangle \in$ *ResolvedMethods*, a new block $Block_d^{pc_i}$ is generated with a unique instruction `invoke`$(d{:}m)$ which stands for the *non-virtual* invocation of the method m that is defined in the class d. In addition, the block has a guard of the form `instanceof`$(o, \{c_1, \ldots, c_k\})$ (o is a stack element) to indicate that the block is applicable only when o is an instance of one of the classes $c_1, \ldots, c_k$. An arc from the block containing pc_i to $Block_d^{pc_i}$ is added, together with an arc from $Block_d^{pc_i}$ to the block containing the next instruction at pc_{i+1} (which describes the rest of the execution after invoking m). Note that the `invokevirtual` is no longer needed in the CFG since it was split into several `invoke` instructions which cover all the possible runtime scenarios. Yet, in order to take into account the cost of dynamic dispatching, we replace the `invokevirtual` by a corresponding call to `resolve_virtual`. Fields are treated in a similar way.

Exceptions: As regards the structure of the CFG, exceptions are not dealt with in a special way. Instead, the possibility of an exception being raised while executing a bytecode statement b is simply treated as an additional branching after b. Let $Block_b$ be the block ending with b; arcs exiting from $Block_b$ are those originated by its *normal behavior* control flow, together with those reaching the sub-graphs which correspond to exception handlers.

Describing dynamic dispatching and exceptions as additional blocks simplifies program analysis. After building the CFG, we do not need to distinguish how and why blocks were generated. Instead, all blocks can be dealt with uniformly.

Example 1 (running example). The execution of the method `add(n, o)` shown in Fig. 1 computes: $\Sigma_{i=0}^{n} i$ if `o` is an instance of A; $\Sigma_{i=0}^{\lfloor n/2 \rfloor} 2i$ if `o` is an instance of B; and $\Sigma_{i=0}^{\lfloor n/3 \rfloor} 3i$ if `o` is an instance of C. The CFG of the method `add` is depicted at the bottom of the figure. The fact that the successor of `6: if_icmpgt 16` can be either the instruction at address `7` or `16` is expressed by means of two arcs from $Block_1$, one to $Block_2$ and another one to $Block_3$, and by adding the guards icmpgt and icmple to $Block_2$ and $Block_3$, respectively. The invocation `13: invokevirtual A.incr : (I)I` is split into 3 possible runtime scenarios described in blocks $Block_4$, $Block_5$ and $Block_6$. Depending on the type of the object `o` (the second stack element from top, denoted `s(top(1))` in the guards),

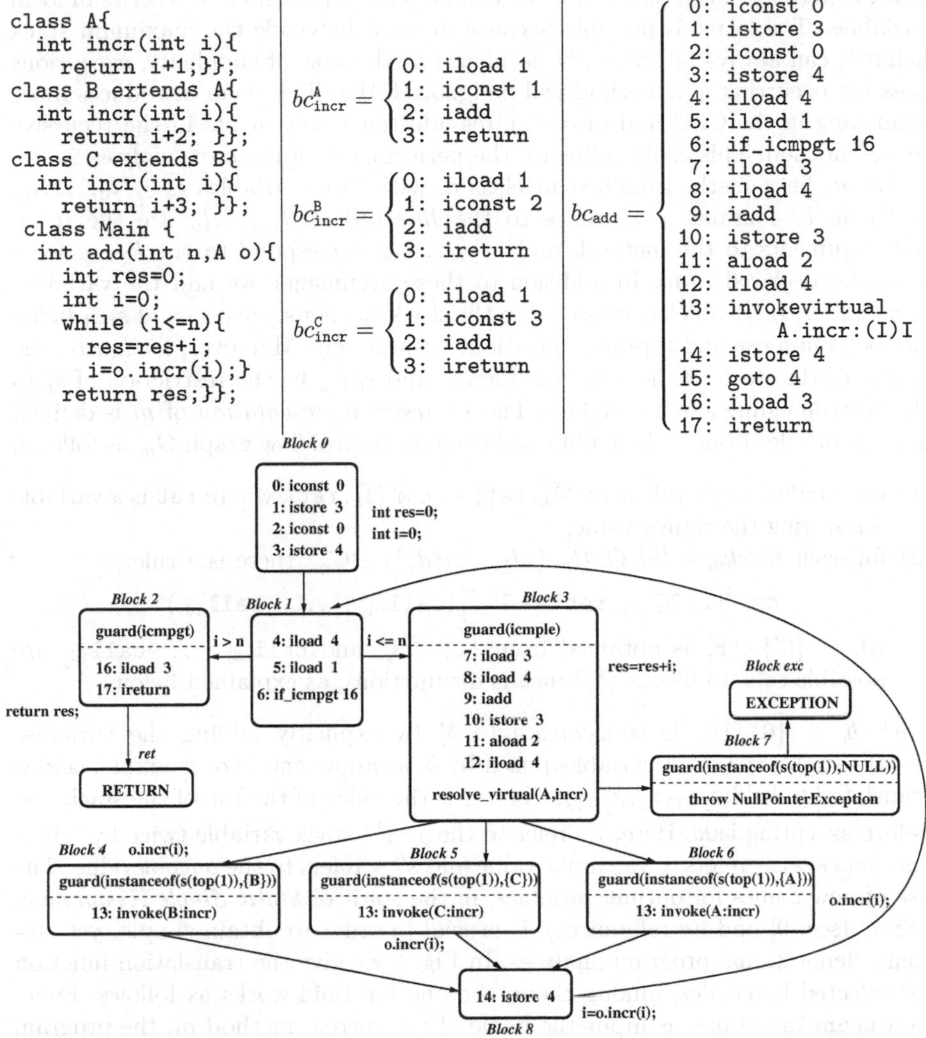

Fig. 1. The running example in source code, bytecode, and control flow graph

only one of these blocks will be executed and hence one of the definitions for `incr` will be invoked. Note that the `invokevirtual` bytecode is replaced by `resolve_virtual`. The exception behavior when `o` is a `NULL` object is described in blocks $Block_7$ and $Block_{exc}$. □

4 Recursive Representation with Flattened Stack

In this section, we present a method for obtaining a representation of the code of a method where 1) iteration is transformed into recursion and 2) the operand stack is *flattened* in the sense that its contents are represented as a series of local variables. The latter is possible because in valid bytecode the maximum stack height t can always be statically decided. For the sake of simplicity, exceptions possibly occurring in a method will be ignored. Handling them introduces more branching in the CFG and also requires additional arguments in the recursive representation. This could influence the performance of the cost analysis.

Let m be a method defined in class c, with *local* variables $\overline{l_k} = l_0, \ldots, l_k$; of them, l_0 contains a reference to the *this* object, $l_1, \ldots, l_n$ are the n input arguments to the method, and $l_{n+1}, \ldots, l_k$ correspond to the $k - n$ local variables declared in m. In addition to these arguments, we add the variables $\overline{s_t} = s_0, \ldots, s_{t-1}$, which correspond to the stack elements, with s_0 and s_{t-1} being the bottom-most and top-most positions respectively. Moreover, let h_{id} be the height of the stack at the entry of $Block_{id}$, and $\overline{s_t}|_{h_{id}}$ be the restriction of $\overline{s_t}$ to the corresponding stack variables. The *recursive representation* of m is defined as a set of rules *head* $\leftarrow$ *body* obtained from its control flow graph G_m as follows:

(1) the *method entry* rule is $\mathtt{c{:}m}(\overline{\mathtt{l_n}}, \mathtt{ret}) \leftarrow \mathtt{c{:}m}^0(\overline{\mathtt{l_k}}, \mathtt{ret})$, where $\mathtt{ret}$ is a variable for storing the return value,
(2) for each $Block_{id} = \langle id, G, \overline{B}_p, \{id_1, \ldots, id_j\}\rangle \in G_m$, there is a rule:

$$\mathtt{c{:}m}^{id}(\overline{\mathtt{l_k}}, \overline{\mathtt{s_t}}|_{\mathtt{h_{id}}}, \mathtt{ret}) \leftarrow \mathtt{G}', \overline{\mathtt{B}}'_{\mathtt{p}}(\mathtt{call_{id_1}}\ ;\ \ldots\ ;\ \mathtt{call_{id_j}})$$

where $\{\mathtt{G}'\} \cup \overline{\mathtt{B}}'_{\mathtt{p}}$ is obtained from $\{\mathtt{G}\} \cup \overline{\mathtt{B}}_{\mathtt{p}}$, and $\mathtt{call_{id_1}}\ ;\ldots;\ \mathtt{call_{id_j}}$ are possible calls to blocks (";" means disjunction), as explained below.

Each $b_i \in \{\mathtt{G}\} \cup \overline{\mathtt{B}}_{\mathtt{p}}$ is *translated* into b'_i by explicitly adding the variables (local variables or stack variables) used by b_i as arguments. For example, iadd is translated to $\mathsf{iadd}(s_{j-1}, s_j, s'_{j-1})$, where j is the index of the top of the stack just before executing iadd. Here, we refer to the $j{-}1^{th}$ stack variable twice by different names: s_{j-1} refers to the input value and s'_{j-1} refers to the output value. The use of new names for output variables, in the spirit of *Static Single Assignment (SSA)* (see [9] and its references), is crucial in order to obtain simple, yet efficient, denotational program analyses. In Fig. 2 we give the translation function for selected bytecodes; among them, the one for `iadd` works as follows. Function `translate` takes as input the name of the current method m, the program counter pc of the bytecode, the bytecode (in this case iadd), the current local variable *names* $\overline{\mathtt{l_k}}$, and the current stack variable *names* $\overline{\mathtt{s_t}}$. In line 1, we retrieve the index of the top stack element before executing the current bytecode. In line 2, we generate new stack variable *names* $\overline{\mathtt{s'}}_{\mathtt{t}}$ by renaming the output variable of iadd in $\overline{\mathtt{s}}_{\mathtt{t}}$. As notation, given a sequence $\overline{a}_n$ of elements, $\overline{a}_n[i \mapsto b]$ denotes the replacement in $\overline{a}_n$ of the element a_i by b. In line 3, we return ($\mathtt{ret}\langle\_\rangle$) the translated bytecode together with the new stack variable *names*. Assume that $\mathtt{G}{=}pc_0{:}b_0$ and $\overline{\mathtt{B}}_{\mathtt{p}}{=}\langle pc_1{:}b_1, \ldots, pc_p{:}b_p\rangle$. The translation of all bytecodes is done iteratively as follows:

$$\mathtt{for\ i = 0\ to\ p}\ \ \{\langle b'_i, \overline{\mathtt{l}}_{\mathtt{k}}^{\mathtt{i+1}}, \overline{\mathtt{s}}_{\mathtt{t}}^{\mathtt{i+1}}\rangle = \mathtt{translate}(\mathtt{m}, pc_i, b_i, \overline{\mathtt{l}}_{\mathtt{k}}^{\mathtt{i}}, \overline{\mathtt{s}}_{\mathtt{t}}^{\mathtt{i}})\}$$

We start from an initial set of local and stack variables, $\overline{\mathtt{l}}_{\mathtt{k}}^0{=}\overline{\mathtt{l}}_{\mathtt{k}}$ and $\overline{\mathtt{s}}_{\mathtt{t}}^0{=}\overline{\mathtt{s}}_{\mathtt{t}}$; in each step, `translate` takes as input the local and stack variable names which

$\mathtt{translate(m, pc, iadd, \overline{l_k}, \overline{s_t}) :=}$ $\quad\mathtt{let\ j = top\_stack\_index(pc, m)\ in}$ $\quad\quad\mathtt{\overline{s'_t} = \overline{s_t}[j{-}1 \mapsto s'_{j-1}]}$ $\quad\quad\mathtt{ret\langle iadd(s_{j-1}, s_j, s'_{j-1}), \overline{l_k}, \overline{s'_t}\rangle}$	$\mathtt{translate(m, pc, iload(v), \overline{l_k}, \overline{s_t}) :=}$ $\quad\mathtt{let\ j = top\_stack\_index(pc, m)\ in}$ $\quad\quad\mathtt{\overline{s'_t} = \overline{s_t}[j{+}1 \mapsto s'_{j+1}]}$ $\quad\quad\mathtt{ret\ \langle iload(l_v, s'_{j+1}), \overline{l_k}, \overline{s'_t}\rangle}$
$\mathtt{translate(m, pc, guard(icmpgt), \overline{l_k}, \overline{s_t}) :=}$ $\quad\mathtt{let\ j = top\_stack\_index(pc, m)\ in}$ $\quad\mathtt{ret\ \langle guard(icmpgt(s_{j-1}, s_j)), \overline{l_k}, \overline{s_t}\rangle}$ $\mathtt{translate(m, pc, ireturn(v), \overline{l_k}, \overline{s_t}) :=}$ $\quad\mathtt{ret\langle ireturn(s_0, ret), \overline{l_k}, \overline{s_t}\rangle}$	$\mathtt{translate(m, pc, invoke(b{:}m'), \overline{l_k}, \overline{s_t}) :=}$ $\quad\mathtt{let\ j = top\_stack\_index(pc, m),}$ $\quad\quad\mathtt{n = number\_of\_arguments(b, m')\ in}$ $\quad\quad\mathtt{\overline{s'_t} = \overline{s_t}[j{-}n \mapsto s'_{j-n}]}$ $\quad\quad\mathtt{ret\ \langle b : m'(s_{j-n}, \ldots, s_j, s'_{j-n}), \overline{l_k}, \overline{s'_t}\rangle}$

Fig. 2. Translation of selected bytecode instructions

were generated by translating the previous bytecode. At the end of this loop, we can define each $\mathtt{call}_{id_i}$, $1 \leq i \leq j$, as $\mathtt{c{:}m}^{id_i}(\overline{\mathtt{l}}_k^{p+1}, \overline{\mathtt{s}}_t^{p+1}|_{h_{id_i}}, \mathtt{ret})$, meaning that we call the next block with the last local and (restricted) stack variable *names*.

Example 2. Consider the CFG in Fig. 1. The translation of *Block*$_3$ and *Block*$_4$ works as shown below. For clarity, in the block identifiers we have not included the class name for the add method. Also, we ignore the exception branch from *Block*$_3$ to *Block*$_7$.

$\mathtt{add^3(\overline{l_4}, s_0, s_1, ret) \leftarrow}$ $\quad\mathbf{guard}(\mathbf{icmple}(\mathtt{s_0, s_1})),$ $\quad\mathtt{iload(l_3, s'_0),\quad iload(l_4, s'_1), iadd(s'_0, s'_1, s''_0),}$ $\quad\mathtt{istore(s''_0, l'_3), aload(l_2, s'''_0), iload(l_4, s''_1),}$ $\quad\mathtt{resolve\_virtual(A, incr),}$ $\quad\mathtt{(\ add^4(l_0, l_1, l_2, l'_3, l_4, s'''_0, s''_1, ret)\ ;}$ $\quad\quad\mathtt{add^5(l_0, l_1, l_2, l'_3, l_4, s'''_0, s''_1, ret);}$ $\quad\quad\mathtt{add^6(l_0, l_1, l_2, l'_3, l_4, s'''_0, s''_1, ret)\ )}$	$\mathtt{add^4(\overline{l_4}, s_0, s_1, ret) \leftarrow}$ $\quad\mathbf{guard}(\mathbf{instanceof}(\mathtt{s_0}, \{\mathbf{B}\})),$ $\quad\mathtt{B{:}incr(s_0, s_1, s'_0),}$ $\quad\mathtt{add^8(\overline{l_4}, s'_0, ret).}$

In the $\mathtt{add^3}$ rule, dynamic dispatch is represented as a disjunction of calls to $\mathtt{add^4}$, $\mathtt{add^5}$ or $\mathtt{add^6}$. Thus, in the rule for $\mathtt{add^4}$, we find a call to (the translation of) `incr` from class `B` which corresponds to the translation of `invoke(B:incr)`; arguments passed to `incr` are the two top-most stack elements; the return value (the last argument) goes also to the stack. Note the change in the superscript when a variable is updated. □

Several optimizations are applied to the above translation. An important one is to replace (redundant) stack variables corresponding to intermediate states by local variables whenever possible. This can be done by tracking dependencies between variables, which stem from instructions like `iload` and `istore`. The fact that the program is in SSA form makes this transformation relatively straightforward. However, note that, in order to eliminate stack variables from the head of a block, we need to consider all calling patterns to the block.

Example 3. After eliminating redundant variables, the optimized version of rules 3 and 4 from Ex. 2 is as follows:

$\mathtt{add}^3(\overline{\mathtt{l}}_4, \mathtt{ret}) \leftarrow$ $\mathbf{guard}(\mathbf{icmple}(\mathbf{l}_4, \mathbf{l}_1))$, $\underline{\mathtt{iload}(\mathtt{l}_3, \mathtt{s}'_0), \mathtt{iload}(\mathtt{l}_4, \mathtt{s}'_1), \mathtt{iadd}(\mathtt{l}_3, \mathtt{l}_4, \mathtt{l}'_3)}$, $\underline{\mathtt{istore}(\mathtt{s}''_0, \mathtt{l}'_3), \mathtt{aload}(\mathtt{l}_2, \mathtt{s}'''_0), \mathtt{iload}(\mathtt{l}_4, \mathtt{s}''_1)}$, $\mathtt{resolve\_virtual}(\mathtt{A}, \mathtt{incr})$, $(\mathtt{add}^4(\mathtt{l}_0, \mathtt{l}_1, \mathtt{l}_2, \mathtt{l}'_3, \mathtt{l}_4, \mathtt{ret})$; $\mathtt{add}^5(\mathtt{l}_0, \mathtt{l}_1, \mathtt{l}_2, \mathtt{l}'_3, \mathtt{l}_4, \mathtt{ret})$; $\mathtt{add}^6(\mathtt{l}_0, \mathtt{l}_1, \mathtt{l}_2, \mathtt{l}'_3, \mathtt{l}_4, \mathtt{ret})$)	$\mathtt{add}^4(\overline{\mathtt{l}}_4, \mathtt{ret}) \leftarrow$ $\mathbf{guard}(\mathbf{instanceof}(\mathbf{l}_2, \{\mathbf{B}\}))$, $\mathtt{B{:}incr}(\mathtt{l}_2, \mathtt{l}_4, \mathtt{s}'_0)$, $\mathtt{add}^8(\overline{\mathtt{l}}_4, \mathtt{s}'_0, \mathtt{ret})$.

The underlined instructions have been used to discover equivalences among stack elements and local variables. For example, all the arguments of `iadd` have been replaced by local variables. However, eliminating stack variables is not always possible. This is the case of $\mathtt{s}'_0$ in the rule $\mathtt{add}^4$, as it corresponds to the return value of `B:incr`. After these optimizations, the underlined instructions become redundant and could be removed. However, we do not remove them in order to take their cost into account in the next sections. □

5 Size Relations for Cost Analysis

Obtaining *size-relations* between the states at different program points is indispensable for setting up cost relations. In particular, they are essential for defining the cost of one block in terms of the cost of its successors. In general, various *measures* can be used to determine the *size* of an input. For instance, in symbolic languages (see, e.g., [10]), term-depth, list-length, etc. are used as term sizes. In Java bytecode, we consider two cases: for integer variables, *size-relations* are constraints on the possible values of variables; for reference variables, they are constraints on the length of the longest reachable paths.

Example 4. Consider the two loops below, written in Java for simplicity:

```
while( i>0 ) { i--; }            while( l != null ) { l = l.next; }
```

A useful *size-relation* for cost analysis is that the value of `i` is always greater than `0` and decreases by `1` in each iteration, and that the longest path reachable from `l` is decreasing by `1` in each iteration. □

Inferring *size-relations* is not straightforward: such relations might be the result of executing several statements, calling methods or loops. For instance, in our running example, the size relation for variable `i` is the result of executing the method `incr` and is propagated through the loop in the procedure `add`. Fixpoint computation is often required. Fortunately, there are several abstract interpretation based approaches for inferring *size-relations* between integer variables [7], as well as between reference variables (in terms of longest path length) [20].

5.1 The Notion of *Size Relation*

In order to set up cost relations, we need, for each rule in the recursive representation, the *calls-to size-relations* between the variables in the head of the rule and the variables used in the calls (to rules) which occur in the body. Note that, given a rule $\mathtt{p}(\bar{\mathtt{x}}) \leftarrow \mathtt{G}, \bar{\mathtt{B}}_\mathtt{k}, (\mathtt{q}_1; \ldots; \mathtt{q}_\mathtt{n})$, each $\mathtt{b_i} \in \bar{\mathtt{B}}_\mathtt{k}$ is either a bytecode or a call to another rule (which stems from the translation of a method invocation). We denote by $\mathtt{calls}(\bar{\mathtt{B}}_\mathtt{k})$ the set of all $\mathtt{b_i}$ corresponding to a method call, and by $\mathtt{bytecode}(\bar{\mathtt{B}}_\mathtt{k})$ the set of all $\mathtt{b_i}$ corresponding to other bytecodes.

Definition 1 (calls-to size-relations). *Let $\mathcal{R}_m$ be the recursive representation of a method m, where each rule takes the form $\mathtt{p}(\bar{\mathtt{x}}) \leftarrow \mathtt{G}, \bar{\mathtt{B}}_\mathtt{k}, (\mathtt{q}_1(\bar{\mathtt{y}}); \cdots; \mathtt{q}_\mathtt{n}(\bar{\mathtt{y}}))$. The calls-to* size-relations *of $\mathcal{R}_m$ are triples of the form*

$$\langle \mathtt{p}(\bar{\mathtt{x}}), \mathtt{p}'(\bar{\mathtt{z}}), \varphi \rangle \quad \textit{where} \quad \mathtt{p}'(\bar{\mathtt{z}}) \in \mathtt{calls}(\bar{\mathtt{B}}_\mathtt{k}) \cup \{\mathtt{p\_cont}(\bar{\mathtt{y}})\}$$

describing, for all rules, the size-relation *between $\bar{\mathtt{x}}$ and $\bar{\mathtt{z}}$ when $\mathtt{p}'(\bar{\mathtt{z}})$ is called, where $\mathtt{p\_cont}(\bar{\mathtt{y}})$ refers to the program point immediately after $\bar{\mathtt{B}}_\mathtt{k}$. The* size-relation *$\varphi$ is given as a conjunction of linear constraints $\mathtt{a}_0+\mathtt{a}_1\mathtt{v}_1+\cdots+\mathtt{a}_\mathtt{n}\mathtt{v}_\mathtt{n}\ \mathtt{op}\ 0$, where $\mathtt{op} \in \{=, \leq, <\}$, each $\mathtt{a_i}$ is a constant and $\mathtt{v_k} \in \bar{\mathtt{x}} \cup \bar{\mathtt{z}}$ for each $\mathtt{k}$.*

Note that in the definition above there is no need to have separate relations for each $\mathtt{q_i}(\bar{\mathtt{y}})$ as, in the absence of exceptions, size relations are exactly the same for all of them, since they correspond to the same program point.

5.2 Inferring Size Relations

A simple, yet quite precise and efficient, *size-relation* analysis for the recursive representation of methods can be done in two steps: 1) compiling the bytecodes into the linear constraints they impose on variables; and 2) computing a bottom-up fixpoint on the compiled rules using standard bottom-up fixpoint algorithms. Compilation into linear constraints is done by an abstraction function α_{size} which basically replaces guards and bytecodes by the constraints they impose on the corresponding variables. In general, each bytecode performing (linear) arithmetic operations is replaced by a corresponding linear constraint, and each bytecode which manipulates objects is compiled to linear constraints on the length of the longest reachable path from the corresponding variable [20]. Here are some examples of abstracting guards and bytecodes into linear constraints:

$\alpha_{\mathtt{size}}(\mathtt{iload}(\mathtt{l}_1, \mathtt{s}_0)) := (\mathtt{l}_1 = \mathtt{s}_0)$	$\alpha_{\mathtt{size}}(\mathtt{guard}(\mathtt{icmpgt}(\mathtt{s}_1, \mathtt{s}_0))) := (\mathtt{s}_1 > \mathtt{s}_0)$
$\alpha_{\mathtt{size}}(\mathtt{iadd}(\mathtt{s}_1, \mathtt{s}_0, \mathtt{s}_0')) := (\mathtt{s}_0' = \mathtt{s}_0 + \mathtt{s}_1)$	$\alpha_{\mathtt{size}}(\mathtt{getfield}(\mathtt{s}_1, \mathtt{f}, \mathtt{s}_1')) := (\mathtt{s}_1' < \mathtt{s}_1)$

It is important to note that $\alpha_{\mathtt{size}}$ uses the same name for the original variables in order to refer to their sizes. Compiling the rules of Ex. 3 results in:

$\mathtt{add}^3(\bar{\mathtt{l}}_4, \mathtt{ret}) \leftarrow \mathtt{l}_4 \leq \mathtt{l}_1, \mathtt{l}_3' = \mathtt{l}_3 + \mathtt{l}_4,$ $\mathtt{resolve\_virtual}(\mathtt{A}, \mathtt{incr}),$ $(\mathtt{add}^4(\bar{\mathtt{l}}_2, \mathtt{l}_3', \mathtt{l}_4, \mathtt{ret}); \mathtt{add}^5(\bar{\mathtt{l}}_2, \mathtt{l}_3', \mathtt{l}_4, \mathtt{ret}); \mathtt{add}^6(\bar{\mathtt{l}}_2, \mathtt{l}_3', \mathtt{l}_4, \mathtt{ret}))$	$\mathtt{add}^4(\bar{\mathtt{l}}_4, \mathtt{ret}) \leftarrow$ $\mathtt{B{:}incr}(\mathtt{l}_2, \mathtt{l}_4, \mathtt{s}_0'),$ $\mathtt{add}^8(\bar{\mathtt{l}}_4, \mathtt{s}_0', \mathtt{ret}).$

Example 5. Compiling all the rules corresponding to the program in Fig. 1 and computing a bottom-up fixpoint over an appropriate abstract domain [7] would result in the following calls-to *size-relations* for rules from Ex. 2:

$\langle \mathtt{add}^3(\mathtt{l_0,l_1,l_2,l_3,l_4,ret}), \mathtt{add}^3\_\mathtt{cont}(\mathtt{l_0,l_1,l_2,l_3',l_4,ret}), \{\mathtt{l_4 \le l_1, l_3' = l_3 + l_4}\}\rangle$
$\langle \mathtt{add}^4(\mathtt{l_0,l_1,l_2,l_3,l_4,ret}), \mathtt{B{:}incr}(\mathtt{l_2,l_4,ret}), \{\}\rangle$
$\langle \mathtt{add}^4(\mathtt{l_0,l_1,l_2,l_3,l_4,ret}), \mathtt{add}^4\_\mathtt{cont}(\mathtt{l_0,l_1,l_2,l_3,l_4,s_0',ret}), \{\mathtt{s_0' = l_4 + 2}\}\rangle$

□

6 Cost Relations for Java Bytecode

We now present our approach to the automatic generation of *cost relations* which define the computational cost of the execution of a bytecode method. They are generated from the recursive representation of the method (Sec. 4) and by using the information inferred by the size analysis (Sec. 5). An important issue in order to obtain optimal cost relations is to find out the arguments which can be safely ignored in cost relations.

6.1 Restricting Cost Relations to (Subsets of) Input Arguments

Let us consider $Block_{id}$ in a CFG, represented by the rule $\mathtt{c{:}m}^{id}(\overline{\mathtt{l_k}}, \mathtt{ret}) \leftarrow \mathtt{G}, \overline{\mathtt{B}}_\mathtt{h}$, $(\mathtt{call}_{\mathtt{id}_1} ; \ldots ; \mathtt{call}_{\mathtt{id}_j})$ in which local and stack variables are no longer distinguishable. The cost function for $Block_{id}$ takes the form $C_{id} : (\mathbb{Z})^n \to \mathbb{N}_\infty$, with $n \le k$ argument positions, and where $\mathbb{Z}$ is the set of integers and $\mathbb{N}_\infty$ is the set of natural numbers augmented with a special symbol ∞, denoting *unbounded.*

Our aim here is to minimize the number n of arguments which need to be taken into account in cost functions. As usual in cost analysis, we consider that the output argument `ret` cannot influence the cost of any block, so that it can be ignored in cost functions. Furthermore, it is sometimes possible to disregard some input arguments. For instance, in our running example, $\mathtt{l_3}$ is an *accumulating* parameter whose value does not affect the control flow nor the cost of the program: it merely keeps the value of the temporary result.

Given a rule, the arguments which can have an impact on the cost of the program are those which may affect directly or indirectly the program guards (i.e., they can affect the control flow of the program), or are used as input arguments to external methods whose cost, in turn, may depend on the input size. Computing a safe approximation of the set of variables affecting a series of statements is a well studied problem in static analysis. To do this, we need to follow data dependencies against the control flow, and this involves computing a fixpoint. Our problem is slightly simpler than *program slicing* [21], since we do not need to delete redundant program statements; instead, we only need to detect relevant arguments. Given a rule $p(\overline{\mathtt{x}}) \leftarrow body$ (p for short), $\hat{\mathtt{l}}_p \subseteq \overline{\mathtt{x}}$ is the sub-sequence of *relevant variables* for p. The sequence $\hat{\mathtt{l}}_P$, obtained by union of sequences $\{\hat{\mathtt{l}}_p\}_{p \in P}$ for a set P of rules, keeps the ordering on variables.

Example 6. Given p_i, corresponding to $Block_i$ in the graph of the running example, we are interested in computing which variables in this rule are relevant to program guards or external methods. For example, 1) when the execution flow reaches p_2, we execute the unconditional bytecode instructions in p_2 and move to the final block. As a result, there are no relevant variables for p_2, since none can have any impact on its cost, and p_2 does not *reach* any guards nor methods. 2) On the other hand, p_3 can reach the guards in p_4, p_5 and p_6, which take the form `instanceof(_)` and involve $\mathtt{l}_2$. Also, the guard in p_3 itself, involving $\mathtt{l}_1$ and $\mathtt{l}_4$, can be recursively reached via the loop. Moreover, the call to the external method `incr` involves $\mathtt{l}_2$ and $\mathtt{l}_4$. After computing a fixpoint, we conclude that $\hat{\mathtt{l}}_{p_3} = \{\mathtt{l}_1, \mathtt{l}_2, \mathtt{l}_4\}$. 3) We have $\hat{\mathtt{l}}_{p_8} = \{\mathtt{l}_1, \mathtt{l}_2, \mathtt{s}_0\}$; here, $\mathtt{s}_0$ is also relevant since it affects $\mathtt{l}_4$ (which in turn is involved in the guard of p_3, reachable from p_8). □

6.2 The Cost Relation

Herein, we define the cost function $C_{id} : (\mathbb{Z})^n \rightarrow \mathbb{N}_\infty$ for a $Block_{id}$ by means of a *cost relation* which consists of a set of *cost equations*. It will allow us to reason about the computational cost of the execution of the block *id*. The intuitive idea is that, given the rule $\mathtt{p}(\bar{\mathtt{x}}) \leftarrow \mathtt{G}, \mathtt{B}, (\mathtt{q}_1; \ldots; \mathtt{q}_n)$ associated to $Block_{id}$, we generate:

- one cost equation which defines the cost of `p` as the cost of the statements in `B`, plus the cost of its *continuation*, denoted `p_cont`;
- another cost equation which defines the cost of `p_cont` as either the cost of $\mathtt{q}_1$ (if its guard is satisfied), …, or the cost of $\mathtt{q}_n$ (if its guard is satisfied).

We specify the cost of the *continuation* in a separate equation because the conditions for determining the alternative path $\mathtt{q}_i$ that the execution will take (with $i = 1, \ldots, n$) are only known at the end of the execution of `B`; thus, they cannot be evaluated before `B` is executed. In the definition below, we use the function α_{guard} to replace those guards which indicate the type of an object by the appropriate test (e.g., $\alpha_{guard}(\mathtt{guard}(\mathtt{instanceof}(\mathtt{s}_0, \{\mathtt{B}\}))) := \mathtt{s}_0 \in \mathtt{B}$). For guards on size relations, it is equivalent to α_{size}.

Definition 2 (cost relation). *Let $\mathcal{R}_m$ be the recursive representation of a method m where each block takes the form $\mathtt{p}(\bar{\mathtt{x}}) \leftarrow \mathtt{G}_\mathtt{p}, \mathtt{B}, (\mathtt{q}_1(\bar{\mathtt{y}}); \cdots; \mathtt{q}_n(\bar{\mathtt{y}}))$ and $\hat{\mathtt{l}}_\mathtt{p}$ be its sequence of relevant variables. Let φ be the calls-to size relation for $\mathcal{R}_m$ where each size relation is of the form $\langle \mathtt{p}(\bar{\mathtt{x}}), \mathtt{p}'(\bar{\mathtt{z}}), \varphi^{\mathtt{p}(\bar{\mathtt{x}})}_{\mathtt{p}'(\bar{\mathtt{z}})} \rangle$ for all $\mathtt{p}'(\bar{\mathtt{z}}) \in \mathtt{calls}(\mathtt{B})$ $\cup \{\mathtt{q}(\bar{\mathtt{y}})\}$ such that $\mathtt{q}(\bar{\mathtt{y}})$ refers to the program point immediately after `B`. Then, we generate the cost equations for each block of the above form in $\mathcal{R}_m$ as follows:*

$$C_p(\hat{\mathtt{l}}_p) = \sum_{b \in bytecode(B)} T_b + \sum_{r(\bar{z}) \in calls(B)} C_r(\hat{\mathtt{l}}_r) + C_{p\_cont}(\cup_{i=1}^{n} \hat{\mathtt{l}}_{q_i}) \qquad \bigwedge_{r(\bar{z}) \in calls(B)} (\varphi^{p(\bar{x})}_{r(\bar{z})}) \wedge \varphi^{p(\bar{x})}_{q(\bar{y})}$$

$$C_{p\_cont}(\cup_{i=1}^{n} \hat{\mathtt{l}}_{q_i}) = \begin{cases} C_{q_1}(\hat{\mathtt{l}}_{q_1}) & \alpha_{guard}(G_{q_1}) \\ \ldots & \\ C_{q_n}(\hat{\mathtt{l}}_{q_n}) & \alpha_{guard}(G_{q_n}) \end{cases}$$

where T_b is the cost unit associated to the bytecode b. The cost relation associated to $\mathcal{R}_m$ and φ is defined as the set of cost equations of its blocks.

Let us notice four points about the above definition. 1) The size relationships between the input variables provided by the size analysis are *attached* to the cost equation for p (in Sect. 7 we discuss how to apply them). 2) Guards do not affect the cost: they are simply used to define the applicability conditions of the equations. 3) Arguments of the cost equations are only the relevant arguments to the block. In the equation for the continuation, we need to include the union of all relevant arguments to each of the subsequent blocks $\mathtt{q_i}$.

The cost T_b of an instruction b depends on the chosen *cost model*. If our interest is merely on finding out the complexity or on approximating the number of bytecode statements which will be executed, then T_b can be the same for all instructions. On the other hand, we may use more refined cost models in order to estimate the execution time of methods. Such models may assign different costs to different instructions. One approach might be based on the use of a *profiling* tool which estimates the value of each T_b on a particular platform. (see, e.g., an application [14] for Prolog). It should be noted that, since we are not dealing with the problem of choosing a realistic cost model, a direct comparison between the result of our analysis and the actual measured run time (e.g., in milliseconds) cannot be done; instead, in this paper we focus only on the number of instructions to be executed.

Example 7. Consider the recursive representation in Ex. 2 (without irrelevant variables, as explained in Ex. 6). Consider the size relations derived in Ex. 5; by applying Def. 2, we obtain the following cost relations:

$$
\begin{array}{lcll}
C_{\mathsf{add}}(\mathtt{l_1},\mathtt{l_2}) & = & C_{\mathsf{add^0}}(\mathtt{l_1},\mathtt{l_2}) & \\
C_{\mathsf{add^0}}(\mathtt{l_1},\mathtt{l_2}) & = & \mathtt{T_0} + C_{\mathsf{add^1}}(\mathtt{l_1},\mathtt{l_2},\mathtt{l_4'}) & \mathtt{l_4'} = \mathtt{0} \\
C_{\mathsf{add^1}}(\mathtt{l_1},\mathtt{l_2},\mathtt{l_4}) & = & \mathtt{T_1} + C_{\mathsf{add^1\_cont}}(\mathtt{l_1},\mathtt{l_2},\mathtt{l_4}) & \\
C_{\mathsf{add^1\_cont}}(\mathtt{l_1},\mathtt{l_2},\mathtt{l_4}) & = & \begin{cases} C_{\mathsf{add^2}}() \\ C_{\mathsf{add^3}}(\mathtt{l_1},\mathtt{l_2},\mathtt{l_4}) \end{cases} & \begin{array}{l} \mathtt{l_4} > \mathtt{l_1} \\ \mathtt{l_4} \leq \mathtt{l_1} \end{array} \\
C_{\mathsf{add^2}}() & = & \mathtt{T_2} & \\
C_{\mathsf{add^3}}(\mathtt{l_1},\mathtt{l_2},\mathtt{l_4}) & = & \mathtt{T_3} + C_{\mathsf{add^3\_cont}}(\mathtt{l_1},\mathtt{l_2},\mathtt{l_4}) & \\
C_{\mathsf{add^3\_cont}}(\mathtt{l_1},\mathtt{l_2},\mathtt{l_4}) & = & \begin{cases} C_{\mathsf{add^4}}(\mathtt{l_1},\mathtt{l_2},\mathtt{l_4}) \\ C_{\mathsf{add^5}}(\mathtt{l_1},\mathtt{l_2},\mathtt{l_4}) \\ C_{\mathsf{add^6}}(\mathtt{l_1},\mathtt{l_2},\mathtt{l_4}) \end{cases} & \begin{array}{l} \mathtt{l_2} \in \mathtt{B} \\ \mathtt{l_2} \in \mathtt{C} \\ \mathtt{l_2} \in \mathtt{A} \end{array} \\
C_{\mathsf{add^4}}(\mathtt{l_1},\mathtt{l_2},\mathtt{l_4}) & = & \mathtt{T_4} + C_{\mathtt{B:incr}}(\mathtt{l_2},\mathtt{l_4}) + C_{\mathsf{add^8}}(\mathtt{l_1},\mathtt{l_2},\mathtt{s_0}) & \mathtt{s_0} = \mathtt{l_4} + \mathtt{2} \\
C_{\mathsf{add^5}}(\mathtt{l_1},\mathtt{l_2},\mathtt{l_4}) & = & \mathtt{T_5} + C_{\mathtt{C:incr}}(\mathtt{l_2},\mathtt{l_4}) + C_{\mathsf{add^8}}(\mathtt{l_1},\mathtt{l_2},\mathtt{s_0}) & \mathtt{s_0} = \mathtt{l_4} + \mathtt{3} \\
C_{\mathsf{add^6}}(\mathtt{l_1},\mathtt{l_2},\mathtt{l_4}) & = & \mathtt{T_6} + C_{\mathtt{A:incr}}(\mathtt{l_2},\mathtt{l_4}) + C_{\mathsf{add^8}}(\mathtt{l_1},\mathtt{l_2},\mathtt{s_0}) & \mathtt{s_0} = \mathtt{l_4} + \mathtt{1} \\
C_{\mathsf{add^8}}(\mathtt{l_1},\mathtt{l_2},\mathtt{s_0}) & = & \mathtt{T_8} + C_{\mathsf{add^1}}(\mathtt{l_1},\mathtt{l_2},\mathtt{s_0}) &
\end{array}
$$

$\mathtt{T_{B_i}}$ denotes the sum of the costs of all bytecode instructions contained in $Block_i$. For brevity, as the blocks 0, 2, 4, 5, 6, and 8 have a single-branched continuation, we merge their two equations. Note that the cost relation for the external method `incr` does not include the third argument since it is an output argument. □

Demonstrating the correctness of our approach to cost analysis requires: (1) Defining the meaning of cost in terms of the Java bytecode operational semantics; (2) Inheriting that definition to a corresponding (equivalent) operational a semantics of the recursive representation. (3) Demonstrating that the cost relations describe the cost as defined in step 2. The first two steps are straightforward as the CFG and the recursive representation describe the behavior of the original program, in particular at each branching point we have several possibilities from which *only* one will be executed. The correctness of the third step stems from the facts that the cost relations are obtained from the recursive representation by replacing each bytecode by its cost, and that the size analysis provides us with information that can be used to compute (or approximate) the number of times we visit in each program point during the execution.

7 Solving and Approximating Cost Functions

The cost relations we presented in Sect. 6 allow reasoning about the computational cost of methods, provided that size analysis was effective. However, such cost relations generally depend on the cost of other calls (i.e., they are often recursive). It is thus convenient to obtain a *closed form solution* for the function which corresponds to the cost of the method. This can be done in two steps. The first one involves eliminating existential variables, i.e., those which do not occur in the left hand side, thus obtaining *recurrence equations.* The second step involves using existing tools for solving recurrence equations and/or computing upper or lower bounds for them.

7.1 Obtaining Recurrence Equations

First, we consider size relations which only contain *equalities.* Given an existential variable y, a size relation φ and a sequence of (input) variables $\overline{x}$, we denote by $\mathsf{solve}(y, \varphi, \overline{x})$ the operation which returns an expression e, with $Vars(e) \subseteq \overline{x}$, such that $\varphi \models (y = e)$. The result can be possibly y itself if no other e is found. For instance, for φ_2 in Ex. 5, the operation $\mathsf{solve}(s_0', \varphi_2, \langle l_1, l_2, l_4\rangle)$ returns $l_4 + 2$. This allows replacing equation (1) by equation (2):

$$C_{\mathsf{add}^4}(\mathtt{l}_1, \mathtt{l}_2, \mathtt{l}_4) = \mathtt{T}_4 + C_{\mathtt{B:incr}}(\mathtt{l}_2, \mathtt{l}_4) + C_{\mathsf{add}^8}(\mathtt{l}_1, \mathtt{l}_2, \mathtt{s}_0) \quad (1)$$
$$C_{\mathsf{add}^4}(\mathtt{l}_1, \mathtt{l}_2, \mathtt{l}_4) = \mathtt{T}_4 + C_{\mathtt{B:incr}}(\mathtt{l}_2, \mathtt{l}_4) + C_{\mathsf{add}^8}(\mathtt{l}_1, \mathtt{l}_2, \mathtt{l}_4 + 2) \quad (2)$$

where $\mathtt{s}_0$ is replaced by its solved form $\mathtt{l}_4 + 2$. Similarly, we can obtain recurrence equations for the cost of blocks add^5, add^6, and add^0. This way, all cost equations in Ex. 7 are converted into recurrence equations.

There exist morc complicated situations, in which size analysis needs to approximate information and it is only able to provide *intervals* in which the values of a variable may range, rather than equalities. Given a variable y, a size relation φ and a sequence of variables $\overline{x}$, the operation $\mathsf{interval}(\varphi, y, \overline{x})$ returns:

- An interval $[e_1, e_2]$ with $(Vars(e_1) \cup Vars(e_2)) \subseteq \overline{x}$, s.t. $\varphi \models (e_1 \leq y \leq e_2)$.
- Otherwise, the same variable y.

For instance, consider the cost relation $C_p(\overline{x}) = \sum T_b + C_q(y) \quad \varphi$, where $[e_1, e_2] = \mathsf{interval}(\varphi, y, \overline{x})$. As y can vary within an interval, we can only now estimate upper and lower bounds for $C_p(\overline{x})$. To do so, we have to cover all possible variations of y (i.e., the situation in which the value of y *moves faster* and the one in which it *moves slower*). For this purpose, we can generate the following relation:

$$C_p(\overline{x}) = \begin{cases} \sum T_b + C_q(e_1) \\ \sum T_b + C_q(e_2) \end{cases}$$

and then *maximize* or *minimize* the cost relation, depending on whether we want to approximate the upper or lower bound, respectively, as we explain below. In a more complicated case, the cost of q might depend on a sequence of variables $\overline{y}$ rather than a single y, and the size analysis might provide intervals (not only equalities) for several of them. This leads to a more complex formalization not included due to lack of space.

7.2 Approximating Recurrence Equations

Algorithms for approximating recurrence equations have been studied by a number of researchers (see, e.g., [22]) and there are several systems available (e.g., Mathematica, Maxima, Maple, Matlab, CASLog). As already mentioned, it is not always possible to find closed form solutions for a set of recurrence equations. However, it turns out that it is quite often possible to find a closed form which is not a solution to the set of equations, but is guaranteed to be an upper (or lower) bound of the cost function. In many cases, finding an upper (or lower) bound can be sufficient. In particular, in the cost relations presented in Sect. 6, it is interesting to compute upper or lower bounds in two situations:

- when we have alternative branches corresponding to the second cost equation in Def. 2 (which represent a dynamic dispatch or a conditional branching),
- when we have intervals (rather than equalities) for the size relations of some variables, as explained in Sect. 7.1.

For the estimation of upper and lower bounds in such cases, we provide a modified version of the second equation in Def. 2 (the first one remains identical):

$$C_{\mathtt{p}}(\overline{x}) = \begin{cases} C_{\mathtt{q_1}}(\overline{x}) & G_{\mathtt{q_1}} \\ \quad \ldots & \\ C_{\mathtt{q_n}}(\overline{x}) & G_{\mathtt{q_n}} \end{cases} \qquad C^{up}_{\mathtt{p}}(\overline{x}) = max \begin{cases} C^{up}_{\mathtt{q_1}}(\overline{x}) & G_{\mathtt{q_1}} \\ \quad \ldots & \\ C^{up}_{\mathtt{q_n}}(\overline{x}) & G_{\mathtt{q_n}} \end{cases}$$

(a) *Cost recurrence equation* $C_{\mathtt{p}}$ (b) *Upper bound of recurrence equation*

Similarly, the lower bound $C^{low}_{\mathtt{p}}(\overline{x})$ of $C_{\mathtt{p}}(\overline{x})$ is defined as $C^{up}_{\mathtt{p}}(\overline{x})$ but computing mins rather than maxs.

Example 8. Consider the upper bound $C^{up}_{\mathtt{add}}(\mathtt{l_1}, \mathtt{l_2})$, obtained from the cost relation $C_{\mathtt{add}}(\mathtt{l_1}, \mathtt{l_2})$ in Ex. 7. We only show the cost equations for $C_{\mathtt{add^3}}$:

$$C^{up}_{\mathtt{add^3}}(\mathtt{l_1}, \mathtt{l_2}, \mathtt{l_4}) = \mathtt{T_3} + C^{up}_{\mathtt{add^3\_cont}}(\mathtt{l_1}, \mathtt{l_2}, \mathtt{l_4})$$

$$C^{up}_{\mathtt{add^3\_cont}}(\mathtt{l_1}, \mathtt{l_2}, \mathtt{l_4}) = \mathtt{max} \begin{cases} C^{up}_{\mathtt{add^4}}(\mathtt{l_1}, \mathtt{l_2}, \mathtt{l_4}) & \mathtt{l_2} \in \mathtt{B} \\ C^{up}_{\mathtt{add^5}}(\mathtt{l_1}, \mathtt{l_2}, \mathtt{l_4}) & \mathtt{l_2} \in \mathtt{C} \\ C^{up}_{\mathtt{add^6}}(\mathtt{l_1}, \mathtt{l_2}, \mathtt{l_4}) & \mathtt{l_2} \in \mathtt{A} \end{cases}$$

In this case, we can easily find the following closed form solution by isolating each of the different branches in $C^{up}_{\mathtt{add^3\_cont}}$.

(*a*) if $\mathtt{l_2} \in \mathtt{A}$ $\quad C^{up}_{\mathtt{add}}(\mathtt{l_1}, \mathtt{l_2}) = (\mathtt{l_1} + 1)(\mathtt{T_1} + \mathtt{T_3} + \mathtt{T_4} + \mathtt{T_{A:incr}} + \mathtt{T_8}) + \mathtt{T_0} + \mathtt{T_1} + \mathtt{T_2}$
(*b*) if $\mathtt{l_2} \in \mathtt{B}$ $\quad C^{up}_{\mathtt{add}}(\mathtt{l_1}, \mathtt{l_2}) = (\mathtt{l_1}/2 + 1)(\mathtt{T_1} + \mathtt{T_3} + \mathtt{T_4} + \mathtt{T_{B:incr}} + \mathtt{T_8}) + \mathtt{T_0} + \mathtt{T_1} + \mathtt{T_2}$
(*c*) if $\mathtt{l_2} \in \mathtt{C}$ $\quad C^{up}_{\mathtt{add}}(\mathtt{l_1}, \mathtt{l_2}) = (\mathtt{l_1}/3 + 1)(\mathtt{T_1} + \mathtt{T_3} + \mathtt{T_4} + \mathtt{T_{C:incr}} + \mathtt{T_8}) + \mathtt{T_0} + \mathtt{T_1} + \mathtt{T_2}$

We use $T_{A:incr}$ to denote the constant cost `A:incr`. The upper bound is $max(a, b, c)$ and the lower bound is $min(a, b, c)$. In any case, the cost is linear with the size of l_1. If $T_{A:incr}=T_{B:incr}=T_{C:incr}$ then a is the upper bound and c the lower bound. □

Unfortunately, it is rather difficult to syntactically characterize the class of programs whose cost relations can be expressed in a closed form.

8 Conclusion

We have presented an automatic approach to the cost analysis of Java bytecode, based on generating at compile-time cost relations for an input bytecode program. Such relations are functions of input data which are informative by themselves about the computational cost, provided an accurate size analysis is used to establish relationships between the input arguments. Essentially, the sources of inaccuracy in size analysis are: 1) guards depending (directly of indirectly) on values which are not handled in the abstraction, e.g., non-integer values, numeric fields or multidimensional arrays, cyclic data-structures; 2) loss of precision due to the abstraction of (non-linear) arithmetic instructions and domain operations like widening. In such cases, we can still set up cost relations; however, they might not be useful if the size relationships are not precise enough.

To the best of our knowledge, our work presents the first approach to the automatic cost analysis of Java bytecode. Related work in the context of Java bytecode includes the work in the MRG project [3], which can be considered complementary to ours. MRG focuses on building a proof-carrying code [15] architecture for ensuring that bytecode programs are free from run-time violations of resource bounds. Also, the resource which has been studied in more depth is heap consumption, since applications to be deployed on devices with a limited amount of memory, such as smartcards, must be rejected if they require more memory than that available. Another related work is [6], where a resource usage analysis is presented. Again, this work focuses on memory consumption and it aims at verifying that the program executes in bounded memory by making sure that the program does not create new objects inside loops. The analysis has been certified by proving its correctness using the Coq proof assistant.

Acknowledgments. This work was funded in part by the Information Society Technologies program of the European Commission, Future and Emerging Technologies under the IST-15905 *MOBIUS* project, by the Spanish Ministry of Education (MEC) under the TIN-2005-09207 *MERIT* project, and the Madrid Regional Government under the S-0505/TIC/0407 *PROMESAS* project. S. Genaim was supported by a *Juan de la Cierva* Fellowship awarded by MEC.

References

1. A. V. Aho, R. Sethi, and J. D. Ullman. *Compilers - Principles, Techniques and Tools.* Addison-Wesley, 1986.
2. E. Albert, G. Puebla, and M. Hermenegildo. Abstraction-Carrying Code. In *Proc. of LPAR'04*, number 3452 in LNAI, pages 380–397. Springer-Verlag, 2005.

3. D. Aspinall, S. Gilmore, M. Hofmann, D. Sannella, and I. Stark. Mobile Resource Guarantees for Smart Devices. In *CASSIS'04*, number 3362 in LNCS. Springer, 2005.
4. G. Barthe, L. Beringer, P. Crégut, B. Grégoire, M. Hofmann, P. Müller, E. Poll, G. Puebla, I. Stark, and E. Vétillard. Mobius: Mobility, ubiquity, security: Objectives and progress report. In *Trustworthy Global Computing'06*, LNCS, 2007.
5. R. Benzinger. Automated higher-order complexity analysis. *Theor. Comput. Sci.*, 318(1-2), 2004.
6. D. Cachera, D. Pichardie T. Jensen, and G. Schneider. Certified memory usage analysis. In *FM'05*, number 3582 in LNCS. Springer, 2005.
7. P. Cousot and N. Halbwachs. Automatic discovery of linear restraints among variables of a program. In *Proc. POPL*. ACM, 1978.
8. K. Crary and S. Weirich. Resource bound certification. In *POPL*. ACM, 2000.
9. R. Cytron, J. Ferrante, B. K. Rosen, M. N. Wegman, and F. K. Zadeck. Efficiently computing static single assignment form and the control dependence graph. *TOPLAS*, 13(4), 1991.
10. S. K. Debray and N. W. Lin. Cost analysis of logic programs. *TOPLAS*, 15(5), 1993.
11. S. K. Debray, P. López-García, M. Hermenegildo, and N.-W. Lin. Lower Bound Cost Estimation for Logic Programs. In *Proc. ILPS'97*. MIT Press, 1997.
12. G. Gomez and Y. A. Liu. Automatic time-bound analysis for a higher-order language. In *Proc. of PEPM*. ACM Press, 2002.
13. T. Lindholm and F. Yellin. *The Java Virtual Machine Specification*. Addison-Wesley, 1996.
14. E. Mera, P. López-García, G. Puebla, M. Carro, and M. Hermenegildo. Combining Static Analysis and Profiling for Estimating Execution Times. In *PADL'07*, LNCS. Springer-Verlag, 2007. To appear.
15. G. Necula. Proof-Carrying Code. In *POPL'97*. ACM Press, 1997.
16. F. A. Rabhi and G. A. Manson. Using Complexity Functions to Control Parallelism in Functional Programs. TR. CS-90-1, Dept. of C.S., Univ. of Sheffield, UK, 1990.
17. M. Rosendhal. Automatic Complexity Analysis. In *Proc. FPCA*. ACM, 1989.
18. D. Sands. A naïve time analysis and its theory of cost equivalence. *J. Log. Comput.*, 5(4), 1995.
19. F. Spoto. JULIA: A Generic Static Analyser for the Java Bytecode. In *Proc. of the 7th Workshop on Formal Techniques for Java-like Programs, FTfJP'2005*, Glasgow, Scotland, July 2005. Available at `www.sci.univr.it/~spoto/papers.html`.
20. F. Spoto, P. M. Hill, and E. Payet. Path-length analysis for object-oriented programs. In *Proc. EAAI*, 2006.
21. F. Tip. A Survey of Program Slicing Techniques. *J. of Prog. Lang.*, 3, 1995.
22. H. S. Wilf. *Algorithms and Complexity*. A.K. Peters Ltd, 2002.
23. R. Wilhelm. Timing analysis and timing predictability. In *Proc. FMCO*, LNCS. Springer-Verlag, 2004.

On the Relationship Between Concurrent Separation Logic and Assume-Guarantee Reasoning*

Xinyu Feng, Rodrigo Ferreira, and Zhong Shao

Department of Computer Science, Yale University
New Haven, CT 06520-8285, U.S.A.
{feng,rodrigo,shao}@cs.yale.edu

Abstract. We study the relationship between Concurrent Separation Logic (CSL) and the assume-guarantee (A-G) method (a.k.a. rely-guarantee method). We show in three steps that CSL can be treated as a specialization of the A-G method for well-synchronized concurrent programs. First, we present an A-G based program logic for a low-level language with built-in locking primitives. Then we extend the program logic with explicit separation of "private data" and "shared data", which provides better memory modularity. Finally, we show that CSL (adapted for the low-level language) can be viewed as a specialization of the extended A-G logic by enforcing the invariant that "*shared resources are well-formed outside of critical regions*". This work can also be viewed as a different approach (from Brookes') to proving the soundness of CSL: our CSL inference rules are proved as lemmas in the A-G based logic, whose soundness is established following the syntactic approach to proving soundness of type systems.

1 Introduction

It is hard to prove non-interference and correctness of shared-state concurrent programs because of the exponential state space. Memory aliasing makes concurrency verification even harder. Therefore a program logic supporting both thread modularity and memory modularity is the key to practical concurrency verification.

Peter O'Hearn [11, 10] proposed concurrent separation logic (CSL), which applies the local-reasoning idea from separation logic [7, 14] to verify shared-state concurrent programs with memory pointers. Separation logic assertions are used to capture ownerships of resources. Separating conjunction enforces the partition of resources. Verification of sequential threads in CSL is no different from verification of sequential programs. Memory modularity is supported by using separating conjunction and frame rules. However, following Owicki and Gries [12], CSL works only for *well-synchronized programs* in the sense that transfer of resource ownerships can only occur at entry and exit points of critical regions. It is unclear how to apply CSL to support general concurrent programs with ad-hoc synchronizations.

* This research is based on work supported in part by gifts from Intel and Microsoft, and NSF grants CCR-0524545. Any opinions, findings, and conclusions contained in this document are those of the authors and do not reflect the views of these agencies.

R. De Nicola (Ed.): ESOP 2007, LNCS 4421, pp. 173–188, 2007.

Another approach to modular verification of shared-state concurrent programs is the assume-guarantee method (a.k.a. rely-guarantee method) [8]. In this approach, invariants of state transitions are specified using assumptions and guarantees. Each thread ensures that its atomic transitions satisfy its guarantee to the environment (*i.e.,* the collection of all other threads) as long as its assumption is satisfied by the environment. Non-interference is guaranteed as long as threads have compatible specifications, *i.e.,* the guarantee of each thread satisfies the assumptions of all other threads. The A-G method supports thread modular verification in the sense that each thread is verified with regard to its own specifications, and without looking into code of other threads. It is very general and does not require language constructs for synchronizations. However, in each individual step of the verification, we need to prove that the state transition satisfies the guarantee. This makes proofs more complicated in A-G reasoning than in CSL. Also, assumptions and guarantees are usually complicated and hard to define, because they specify global invariants for all shared resources during the program execution.

In this paper we study the relationship between CSL and A-G reasoning. We propose the Separated A-G Logic (SAGL), which extends A-G reasoning with the local-reasoning idea in separation logic. Instead of treating all resources as shared, SAGL partitions resources into shared and private. Like in CSL, each thread has full access to its private resources, which are invisible to its environments. Shared resources can be accessed in two ways in SAGL: they can be accessed directly, or be converted into private first and then accessed. Conversions between shared and private can occur at any program point, instead of being coupled with critical regions. Both direct accesses and conversions are governed by guarantees, so that non-interference is ensured following A-G reasoning. Private resources are not specified in assumptions and guarantees, therefore specifications in SAGL are simpler and more modular than A-G reasoning.

We then show that CSL can be viewed as a specialization of SAGL with the invariant that *shared resources are well-formed outside of critical regions*. The specialization is pinned down by formalizing the CSL invariant as a specific assumption and guarantee in SAGL. Our formulation can also be viewed as a novel approach to proving the soundness of CSL. Different from Brookes' proof based on an action-trace semantics [2], we prove that CSL inference rules are lemmas in SAGL with the specific assumption and guarantee. The soundness of SAGL is then proved following the syntactic approach to type soundness [18]. The proofs are formalized in the Coq proof assistant [16].

Our study is based on an assembly language with RISC-style instructions and built-in lock/unlock and memory allocation/free primitives. Instead of using the high-level parallel language proposed by Hoare [6], we use the assembly language because it has cleaner semantics, which makes our formulation much simpler. For instance, we do not use variables, instead we only use register files and memory. Therefore we can have a quick formulation [4] in Coq without worrying about variable renaming issues. Also we do not have to formalize the complicated syntactic constraints enforced in CSL over shared variables. Another important reason is that our work at low level can be easily applied to generate proof-carrying code [9]. CSL and the A-G method studied in this paper are all adapted to this low-level language. The relationship between the low-level CSL and the original logic by O'Hearn [11, 10] is discussed in Sect. 7.

In the rest of this paper, we first present our low-level language in Sect. 2. We then present an A-G based logic (AGL) for this language in Sect. 3. We extend AGL with local reasoning and propose SAGL in Sect. 4. In Sect. 5, we adapt the original CSL to the low-level language and formalize the relationship between CSL and SAGL. We use two examples to illustrate the use of SAGL in Sect. 6. Finally, we discuss related work and conclude in Sect. 7.

2 The Language

Figure 1 defines the model of an abstract machine and the syntax of the assembly language. The whole program state $\mathbb{P}$ contains a shared memory $\mathbb{M}$, a lock mapping $\mathbb{L}$ which maps a lock to the id of its owner thread, and n threads $[\mathbb{T}_1,\ldots,\mathbb{T}_n]$. The memory is modeled as a finite partial mapping from memory locations $\mathtt{l}$ (natural numbers) to word values (natural numbers). Each thread $\mathbb{T}_i$ contains its own code heap $\mathbb{C}$, register file $\mathbb{R}$, the instruction sequence $\mathbb{I}$ that is currently being executed, and its thread id i.

The code heap $\mathbb{C}$ maps code labels to instruction sequences, which is a list of assembly instructions ending with a jump instruction. The set of instructions we present here are the commonly used subsets in RISC machines. We also use lock/unlock primitives to do synchronization, and use alloc/free to do dynamic memory allocation and free.

The step relation ($\longmapsto$) of program states ($\mathbb{P}$) is defined in Fig. 2. We use the auxiliary relation $(\mathbb{M},\mathbb{T},\mathbb{L}) \stackrel{\mathsf{t}}{\longmapsto} (\mathbb{M}',\mathbb{T}',\mathbb{L}')$ to define the effects of the execution of the thread $\mathbb{T}$. Here we follow the preemptive thread model where execution of threads can be preempted at any program point, but execution of individual instructions is *atomic*. In Fig. 2 we show operational semantics of representative instructions, which are mostly standard. Note that we do not support reentrant-locks. If the lock l has been acquired, execution of the "lock l" instruction will be blocked even if the lock is owned by the current thread. The relation Next_ι defines the effects of the sequential instruction ι over memory and register files.

$$
\begin{array}{rlcl}
(\mathit{Program}) & \mathbb{P} & ::= & (\mathbb{M},[\mathbb{T}_1,\ldots,\mathbb{T}_n],\mathbb{L}) \\
(\mathit{Thread}) & \mathbb{T}_i & ::= & (\mathbb{C},\mathbb{R},\mathbb{I},i) \\
(\mathit{CodeHeap}) & \mathbb{C} & \in & \mathit{Labels} \rightharpoonup \mathit{InstrSeq} \\
(\mathit{Memory}) & \mathbb{M} & \in & \mathit{Labels} \rightharpoonup \mathit{Word} \\
(\mathit{RegFile}) & \mathbb{R} & \in & \mathit{Register} \rightarrow \mathit{Word} \\
(\mathit{LockMap}) & \mathbb{L} & ::= & \mathit{Locks} \rightharpoonup \{1,\ldots,n\} \\
(\mathit{Register}) & \mathtt{r} & ::= & \mathtt{r}_0 \mid \ldots \mid \mathtt{r}_{31} \\
(\mathit{Labels}) & \mathtt{f},\mathtt{l} & ::= & i \ (\mathit{nat\ nums}) \\
(\mathit{Locks}) & l & ::= & i \ (\mathit{nat\ nums}) \\
(\mathit{Word}) & \mathtt{w} & ::= & i \ (\mathit{nat\ nums}) \\
(\mathit{InstrSeq}) & \mathbb{I} & ::= & \mathsf{j}\ \mathtt{f} \mid \mathsf{jr}\ \mathtt{r}_s \mid \iota;\mathbb{I} \\
(\mathit{Instr}) & \iota & ::= & \mathsf{add}\ \mathtt{r}_d,\mathtt{r}_s,\mathtt{r}_t \mid \mathsf{addi}\ \mathtt{r}_d,\mathtt{r}_s,i \mid \mathsf{alloc}\ \mathtt{r}_d,\mathtt{r}_s \mid \mathsf{beq}\ \mathtt{r}_s,\mathtt{r}_t,\mathtt{f} \mid \mathsf{bgt}\ \mathtt{r}_s,\mathtt{r}_t,\mathtt{f} \\
& & & \mid \mathsf{free}\ \mathtt{r}_s \mid \mathsf{lock}\ l \mid \mathsf{ld}\ \mathtt{r}_t,i(\mathtt{r}_s) \mid \mathsf{sub}\ \mathtt{r}_d,\mathtt{r}_s,\mathtt{r}_t \mid \mathsf{st}\ \mathtt{r}_t,i(\mathtt{r}_s) \mid \mathsf{unlock}\ l
\end{array}
$$

Fig. 1. The Abstract Machine

$$(\mathbb{M},[\mathbb{T}_1,\ldots,\mathbb{T}_n],\mathbb{L}) \longmapsto (\mathbb{M}',[\mathbb{T}_1,\ldots,\mathbb{T}_{k-1},\mathbb{T}'_k,\mathbb{T}_{k+1},\ldots,\mathbb{T}_n],\mathbb{L}')$$
$$\text{if } (\mathbb{M},\mathbb{T}_k,\mathbb{L}) \overset{\mathsf{t}}{\longmapsto} (\mathbb{M}',\mathbb{T}'_k,\mathbb{L}') \text{ for any } k;$$
where

$(\mathbb{M},(\mathbb{C},\mathbb{R},\mathbb{I},k),\mathbb{L}) \overset{\mathsf{t}}{\longmapsto} (\mathbb{M}',\mathbb{T}',\mathbb{L}')$		
if $\mathbb{I} =$	then $(\mathbb{M}',\mathbb{T}',\mathbb{L}') =$	
j $\mathtt{f}$	$(\mathbb{M},(\mathbb{C},\mathbb{R},\mathbb{I}',k),\mathbb{L})$	where $\mathbb{I}' = \mathbb{C}(\mathtt{f})$
jr $\mathtt{r}_s$	$(\mathbb{M},(\mathbb{C},\mathbb{R},\mathbb{I}',k),\mathbb{L})$	where $\mathbb{I}' = \mathbb{C}(\mathbb{R}(\mathtt{r}_s))$
beq $\mathtt{r}_s,\mathtt{r}_t,\mathtt{f};\mathbb{I}'$	$(\mathbb{M},(\mathbb{C},\mathbb{R},\mathbb{I}',k),\mathbb{L})$ $(\mathbb{M},(\mathbb{C},\mathbb{R},\mathbb{I}'',k),\mathbb{L})$	if $\mathbb{R}(\mathtt{r}_s) \neq \mathbb{R}(\mathtt{r}_t)$ if $\mathbb{R}(\mathtt{r}_s) = \mathbb{R}(\mathtt{r}_t)$ and $\mathbb{I}'' = \mathbb{C}(\mathtt{f})$
lock $l;\mathbb{I}'$	$(\mathbb{M},(\mathbb{C},\mathbb{R},\mathbb{I}',k),\mathbb{L}\{l\rightsquigarrow k\})$ $(\mathbb{M},(\mathbb{C},\mathbb{R},\mathbb{I},k),\mathbb{L})$	if $l \notin dom(\mathbb{L})$ if $l \in dom(\mathbb{L})$
unlock $l;\mathbb{I}'$	$(\mathbb{M},(\mathbb{C},\mathbb{R},\mathbb{I}',k),\mathbb{L}\setminus\{l\})$	if $\mathbb{L}(l) = k$
$\iota;\mathbb{I}'$ for other ι	$(\mathbb{M}',(\mathbb{C},\mathbb{R}',\mathbb{I}',k),\mathbb{L})$	where $(\mathbb{M}',\mathbb{R}') = \mathsf{Next}_\iota\,(\mathbb{M},\mathbb{R})$

and

if $\iota =$	then $\mathsf{Next}_\iota\,(\mathbb{M},\mathbb{R}) =$	
addi $\mathtt{r}_d,\mathtt{r}_s,i$	$(\mathbb{M},\mathbb{R}\{\mathtt{r}_d\rightsquigarrow\mathbb{R}(\mathtt{r}_s)+i\})$	
ld $\mathtt{r}_t,i(\mathtt{r}_s)$	$(\mathbb{M},\mathbb{R}\{\mathtt{r}_t\rightsquigarrow\mathbb{M}(\mathbb{R}(\mathtt{r}_s)+i)\})$	when $\mathbb{R}(\mathtt{r}_s)+i \in dom(\mathbb{M})$
st $\mathtt{r}_t,i(\mathtt{r}_s)$	$(\mathbb{M}\{\mathbb{R}(\mathtt{r}_s)+i\rightsquigarrow\mathbb{R}(\mathtt{r}_t)\},\mathbb{R})$	when $\mathbb{R}(\mathtt{r}_s)+i \in dom(\mathbb{M})$
alloc $\mathtt{r}_d,\mathtt{r}_s$	$(\mathbb{M}\{\mathtt{l},\ldots,\mathtt{l}+\mathbb{R}(\mathtt{r}_s)-1\rightsquigarrow\_\},\mathbb{R}\{\mathtt{r}_d\rightsquigarrow\mathtt{l}\})$	where $\mathtt{l},\ldots,\mathtt{l}+\mathbb{R}(\mathtt{r}_s)-1 \notin dom(\mathbb{M})$
free $\mathtt{r}_s$	$(\mathbb{M}\setminus\{\mathbb{R}(\mathtt{r}_s)\},\mathbb{R})$	when $\mathbb{R}(\mathtt{r}_s) \in dom(\mathbb{M})$

Fig. 2. Operational Semantics of the Machine

Note the way we distinguish "blocking" states from "stuck" states caused by unsafe operations, *e.g.*, freeing dangling pointers. If an unsafe operation is made, there is no resulting state satisfying the step relation ($\overset{\mathsf{t}}{\longmapsto}$) for the current thread. If a thread tries to acquire a lock which has been taken, it stutters: the resulting state will be the same as the current one (therefore the lock instruction will be executed again).

3 AGL: An A-G Based Program Logic

In this section we present an A-G based program logic (AGL) for our assembly language. AGL is a variation of the CCAP logic [19] which applies the A-G method for assembly code verification. Different from CCAP, AGL works for the preemptive thread model instead of the non-preemptive model.

Figure 3 shows the specification constructs for AGL. For each thread in the program, its specification contains three parts: the specification Ψ for the code heap, the assumption A and the guarantee G. The specification Φ of the whole program just groups specifications for each thread. We use CiC, our *meta-logic* mechanized by Coq [16], as the assertion language for assertions and program specifications. CiC corresponds to the higher-order predicate logic with inductive definitions via Curry-Howard isomorphism.

$$\begin{array}{rrcl}
(\mathit{XState}) & \mathbb{X} & ::= & (\mathbb{M},(\mathbb{R},i),\mathbb{L}) \\
(\mathit{ProgSpec}) & \Phi & ::= & ([\Psi_1,\ldots,\Psi_n],[(\mathsf{A}_1,\mathsf{G}_1),\ldots,(\mathsf{A}_n,\mathsf{G}_n)]) \\
(\mathit{CdHpSpec}) & \Psi & ::= & \{\mathtt{f} \leadsto \mathtt{a}\}^* \\
(\mathit{Assertion}) & \mathtt{a} & \in & \mathit{XState} \rightarrow \mathit{Prop} \\
(\mathit{Assume}) & \mathsf{A} & \in & \mathit{XState} \rightarrow \mathit{XState} \rightarrow \mathit{Prop} \\
(\mathit{Guarantee}) & \mathsf{G} & \in & \mathit{XState} \rightarrow \mathit{XState} \rightarrow \mathit{Prop}
\end{array}$$

Fig. 3. Specification Constructs for AGL

$\boxed{\Phi,[\mathtt{a}_1,\ldots,\mathtt{a}_n] \vdash \mathbb{P}}$ ***(Well-formed program)***

$$\frac{\Phi=([\Psi_1,\ldots,\Psi_n],[(\mathsf{A}_1,\mathsf{G}_1),\ldots,(\mathsf{A}_n,\mathsf{G}_n)]) \qquad \mathsf{NI}([(\mathsf{A}_1,\mathsf{G}_1),\ldots,(\mathsf{A}_n,\mathsf{G}_n)]) \qquad \Psi_k,\mathsf{A}_k,\mathsf{G}_k \vdash \{\mathtt{a}_k\}(\mathbb{M},\mathbb{T}_k,\mathbb{L}) \text{ for all } k}{\Phi,[\mathtt{a}_1,\ldots,\mathtt{a}_n] \vdash (\mathbb{M},[\mathbb{T}_1,\ldots,\mathbb{T}_n],\mathbb{L})} \text{ (PROG)}$$

$\boxed{\Psi,\mathsf{A},\mathsf{G} \vdash \{\mathtt{a}\}(\mathbb{M},\mathbb{T},\mathbb{L})}$ ***(Well-formed thread)***

$$\frac{\mathtt{a}\,(\mathbb{M},(\mathbb{R},k),\mathbb{L}) \qquad \Psi,\mathsf{A},\mathsf{G} \vdash \mathbb{C}:\Psi \qquad \Psi,\mathsf{A},\mathsf{G} \vdash \{\mathtt{a}\}\mathbb{I}}{\Psi,\mathsf{A},\mathsf{G} \vdash \{\mathtt{a}\}(\mathbb{M},(\mathbb{C},\mathbb{R},\mathbb{I},k),\mathbb{L})} \text{ (THRD)}$$

$\boxed{\Psi,\mathsf{A},\mathsf{G} \vdash \mathbb{C}:\Psi'}$ ***(Well-formed code heap)***

$$\frac{\forall \mathtt{f} \in dom(\Psi'): \quad \Psi,\mathsf{A},\mathsf{G} \vdash \{\Psi'(\mathtt{f})\}\mathbb{C}(\mathtt{f})}{\Psi,\mathsf{A},\mathsf{G} \vdash \mathbb{C}:\Psi'} \text{ (CDHP)}$$

Fig. 4. AGL Inference Rules

Assumptions and guarantees are meta-logic predicates over a pair of extended thread states $\mathbb{X}$, which contains the shared memory $\mathbb{M}$, the thread's register file $\mathbb{R}$ and id k, and the global lock mapping $\mathbb{L}$. The assumption A for a thread specifies the expected invariant of state transitions made by the environment. The arguments it takes are states before and after a transition, respectively. The guarantee G of a thread specifies the invariant of state transitions made by the thread.

The code heap specification Ψ assigns a precondition $\mathtt{a}$ to each instruction sequence in the code heap $\mathbb{C}$.The assertion $\mathtt{a}$ is a meta-logic predicate over the extended thread state $\mathbb{X}$. It ensures the safe execution of the corresponding instruction sequence. We do not assign postconditions to instruction sequences. Since each instruction sequence ends with a jump instruction, we use the assertion at the target address as the postcondition.

Inference rules. Inference rules of AGL are presented in Figs. 4 and 5. The PROG rule defines the well-formedness of the program $\mathbb{P}$ with respect to the program specification Φ and the set of preconditions $([\mathtt{a}_1,\ldots,\mathtt{a}_n])$ for the instruction sequences that are currently executed by all the threads. Checking the well-formedness of $\mathbb{P}$ involves two steps. First we check the compatibility of assumptions and guarantees for all the threads. The predicate NI is defined as follows:

$$\begin{array}{l}\mathsf{NI}([(\mathsf{A}_1,\mathsf{G}_1),\ldots,(\mathsf{A}_n,\mathsf{G}_n)]) \stackrel{\text{def}}{=} \forall i,j,\mathbb{M},\mathbb{M}',\mathbb{R}_i,\mathbb{R}'_i,\mathbb{R}_j,\mathbb{L},\mathbb{L}'. \\ \quad i \neq j \rightarrow \mathsf{G}_i\,(\mathbb{M},(\mathbb{R}_i,i),\mathbb{L})\,(\mathbb{M}',(\mathbb{R}'_i,i),\mathbb{L}') \rightarrow \mathsf{A}_j\,(\mathbb{M},(\mathbb{R}_j,j),\mathbb{L})\,(\mathbb{M}',(\mathbb{R}_j,j),\mathbb{L}'),\end{array} \quad (1)$$

$\boxed{\Psi, \mathsf{A}, \mathsf{G} \vdash \{\mathsf{a}\}\mathbb{I}}$ ***(Well-formed instr. sequences)***

$$\frac{\Psi, \mathsf{A}, \mathsf{G} \vdash \{\mathsf{a}\}\iota\{\mathsf{a}'\} \quad \Psi, \mathsf{A}, \mathsf{G} \vdash \{\mathsf{a}'\}\mathbb{I} \quad (\mathsf{a} \circ \mathsf{A}) \Rightarrow \mathsf{a}}{\Psi, \mathsf{A}, \mathsf{G} \vdash \{\mathsf{a}\}\iota;\mathbb{I}} \text{ (SEQ)}$$

$$\frac{\forall \mathbb{X}@(\mathbb{M}, (\mathbb{R}, k), \mathbb{L}).\, \mathsf{a}\,\mathbb{X} \rightarrow \Psi(\mathbb{R}(\mathtt{r}_s))\,\mathbb{X} \quad (\mathsf{a} \circ \mathsf{A}) \Rightarrow \mathsf{a}}{\Psi, \mathsf{A}, \mathsf{G} \vdash \{\mathsf{a}\}\mathsf{jr}\ \mathtt{r}_s} \text{ (JR)}$$

$\boxed{\Psi, \mathsf{A}, \mathsf{G} \vdash \{\mathsf{a}\}\iota\{\mathsf{a}'\}}$ ***(Well-formed instructions)***

$$\frac{\begin{array}{l}\forall \mathbb{X}@(\mathbb{M}, (\mathbb{R}, k), \mathbb{L}).\, \mathsf{a}\,\mathbb{X} \wedge l \notin dom(\mathbb{L}) \rightarrow \mathsf{a}'\,\mathbb{X}' \wedge \mathsf{G}\,\mathbb{X}\,\mathbb{X}' \\ \qquad \text{where } \mathbb{X}' = (\mathbb{M}, (\mathbb{R}, k), \mathbb{L}\{l \rightsquigarrow k\}).\end{array}}{\Psi, \mathsf{A}, \mathsf{G} \vdash \{\mathsf{a}\}\mathsf{lock}\ l\,\{\mathsf{a}'\}} \text{ (LOCK)}$$

$$\frac{\begin{array}{l}\forall \mathbb{X}@(\mathbb{M}, (\mathbb{R}, k), \mathbb{L}).\, \mathsf{a}\,\mathbb{X} \rightarrow \mathbb{L}(l) = k \wedge \mathsf{a}'\,\mathbb{X}' \wedge \mathsf{G}\,\mathbb{X}\,\mathbb{X}' \\ \qquad \text{where } \mathbb{X}' = (\mathbb{M}, (\mathbb{R}, k), \mathbb{L} \setminus \{l\}).\end{array}}{\Psi, \mathsf{A}, \mathsf{G} \vdash \{\mathsf{a}\}\mathsf{unlock}\ l\,\{\mathsf{a}'\}} \text{ (UNLOCK)}$$

$$\frac{\begin{array}{l}\forall \mathbb{X}@(\mathbb{M}, (\mathbb{R}, k), \mathbb{L}).\forall \mathtt{l}.\, \mathsf{a}\,\mathbb{X} \wedge \{\mathtt{l}, \ldots, \mathtt{l}+\mathbb{R}(\mathtt{r}_s)-1\} \notin dom(\mathbb{M}) \rightarrow \\ \qquad \mathbb{R}(\mathtt{r}_s) > 0 \wedge \mathsf{a}'\,\mathbb{X}' \wedge \mathsf{G}\,\mathbb{X}\,\mathbb{X}' \\ \quad \text{where } \mathbb{X}' = (\mathbb{M}\{\mathtt{l}, \ldots, \mathtt{l}+\mathbb{R}(\mathtt{r}_s)-1 \rightsquigarrow \_\}, (\mathbb{R}\{\mathtt{r}_d \rightsquigarrow \mathtt{l}\}, k), \mathbb{L})\end{array}}{\Psi, \mathsf{A}, \mathsf{G} \vdash \{\mathsf{a}\}\mathsf{alloc}\ \mathtt{r}_d, \mathtt{r}_s\,\{\mathsf{a}'\}} \text{ (ALLOC)}$$

Fig. 5. AGL Inference Rules (cont'd)

which simply says that the guarantee of each thread should satisfy assumptions of all other threads. Then we apply the THRD rule to check that implementation of each thread actually satisfies the specification. Each thread $\mathbb{T}_i$ is verified separately. therefore thread modularity is supported.

In the THRD rule, we require that the precondition a be satisfied by the current extended thread state $(\mathbb{M}, (\mathbb{R}, k), \mathbb{L})$; that the thread code heap satisfy its specification Ψ, A and G; and that it be safe to execute the current instruction sequence $\mathbb{I}$ under the precondition a and the thread specification.

The CDHP rule checks the well-formedness of thread code heaps. It requires that each instruction sequence specified in Ψ' be well-formed with respect to the imported interfaces specified in Ψ, the assumption A and the guarantee G.

The SEQ rule and the JR rule ensure that it is safe to execute the instruction sequence if the precondition is satisfied. If the instruction sequence starts with a normal sequential instruction ι, we need to come up with an assertion a' which serves both as the postcondition of ι and as the precondition of the remaining instruction sequence. Also we need to ensure that, if the current thread is preempted at a state satisfying a, a must be preserved by any state transitions (by other threads) satisfying the assumption A. This is enforced by $(\mathsf{a} \circ \mathsf{A}) \Rightarrow \mathsf{a}$:

$$(\mathsf{a} \circ \mathsf{A}) \Rightarrow \mathsf{a} \quad \stackrel{\text{def}}{=} \quad \forall \mathbb{X}, \mathbb{X}'.\, \mathsf{a}\,\mathbb{X} \wedge \mathsf{A}\,\mathbb{X}\,\mathbb{X}' \rightarrow \mathsf{a}\,\mathbb{X}'.$$

If we reach the last jump instruction of the instruction sequence, the JR rule requires that the assertion assigned to the target address in Ψ be satisfied after the jump. It also requires that a be preserved by state transitions satisfying A. Here we use the syntactic sugar $\forall X @ (x_1,\ldots,x_n).\, P(X,x_1,\ldots,x_n)$ to mean that, for all tuple X containing elements $x_1,\ldots,x_n$, the predicate P holds. It is formally defined as:

$$\forall X, x_1,\ldots,x_n.(X = (x_1,\ldots,x_n)) \to P(X,x_1,\ldots,x_n)\,.$$

The notation $\lambda X @ (x_1,\ldots,x_n).\, f(X,x_1,\ldots,x_n)$ that we use later is defined similarly. The rule for direct jumps (j f) is similar to the JR rule and is not presented here.

Instruction rules require that the precondition ensure the safe execution of the instruction; and that the resulting state satisfy the postcondition. Also, if shared states ($\mathbb{M}$ and $\mathbb{L}$) are updated by the instruction, we need to ensure that the update satisfies the guarantee G. For the lock instruction, if the control falls through, we know that the lock is not held by any thread. This extra knowledge can be used together with the precondition a to show the postcondition is satisfied by the resulting state. The rest of instruction rules are straightforward and will not be explained here. Interested readers can refer to the companion technical report [4] for a complete presentation of instruction rules.

The soundness of AGL is also formalized in the technical report [4], which is similar to the soundness theorem of SAGL presented in Sect. 4.

4 SAGL: Separated A-G Logic

AGL is a general program logic supporting thread modular verification of concurrent code. However, because it treats all memory as shared resources, it does not have good memory modularity, and assumptions and guarantees are hard to define and use. During program verification, we have to prove for each individual instruction that the guarantee is not broken, even if there is no memory sharing. Moreover, if each thread dynamically allocates memory and uses allocated memory as private resources (see the example in Sect. 6), the domain of memory becomes dynamic and nondeterministic, which makes it very hard to specify the assumption and guarantee.

In this section, we extend AGL with explicit partition of private resources and shared resources. The extended logic, which we call Separated A-G Logic (SAGL), has much better support of memory modularity than AGL without sacrificing any expressiveness. Borrowing the local-reasoning idea in separation logic, private resources of one thread are not visible to other threads, therefore will not be touched by others. Assumptions and guarantees in SAGL only specify shared resources. The dynamic domain of private memory caused by memory allocation is no longer a challenge to define assumptions and guarantees because private memory does not have to be specified.

Figure 6 shows our extensions of AGL specifications for SAGL. In the specification Ψ of each thread code heap, the precondition assigned to each code label now becomes a pair of assertions $(\mathtt{a},\nu)$. The assertion a plays the same role as in AGL. It specifies the shared resources (all memory are treated as shared in AGL). The assertion ν specifies the private resources of the thread. Other threads' private resources are not specified.

$$\begin{array}{lrcl} (\mathit{CdHpSpec}) & \Psi & ::= & \{\mathtt{f} \leadsto (\mathtt{a},\nu)\}^* \\ (\mathit{Assertion}) & \mathtt{a},\nu & \in & \mathit{XState} \to \mathit{Prop} \end{array}$$

Fig. 6. Extension of AGL Specification Constructs in SAGL

$\boxed{\Phi, [(\mathsf{a}_1, \nu_1), \ldots, (\mathsf{a}_n, \nu_n)] \vdash \mathbb{P}}$ ***(Well-formed program)***

$$\frac{\Phi = ([\Psi_1, \ldots, \Psi_n], [(\mathsf{A}_1, \mathsf{G}_1), \ldots, (\mathsf{A}_n, \mathsf{G}_n)]) \quad \mathsf{NI}([(\mathsf{A}_1, \mathsf{G}_1), \ldots, (\mathsf{A}_n, \mathsf{G}_n)]) \\ \mathbb{M}_s \uplus \mathbb{M}_1 \uplus \cdots \uplus \mathbb{M}_n = \mathbb{M} \quad \Psi_k, \mathsf{A}_k, \mathsf{G}_k \vdash \{(\mathsf{a}_k, \nu_k)\}\, (\mathbb{M}_s, \mathbb{M}_k, \mathbb{T}_k, \mathbb{L}) \text{ for all } k}{\Phi, [(\mathsf{a}_1, \nu_1), \ldots, (\mathsf{a}_n, \nu_n)] \vdash (\mathbb{M}, [\mathbb{T}_1, \ldots, \mathbb{T}_n], \mathbb{L})} \text{ (PROG)}$$

$\boxed{\Psi, \mathsf{A}, \mathsf{G} \vdash \{(\mathsf{a}, \nu)\}\, (\mathbb{M}_s, \mathbb{M}_\nu, \mathbb{T}, \mathbb{L})}$ ***(Well-formed thread)***

$$\frac{\mathsf{a}\, (\mathbb{M}_s, (\mathbb{R}, k), \mathbb{L}) \quad \nu\, (\mathbb{M}_\nu, (\mathbb{R}, k), \mathbb{L}|_k) \quad \Psi, \mathsf{A}, \mathsf{G} \vdash \mathbb{C} : \Psi \quad \Psi, \mathsf{A}, \mathsf{G} \vdash \{(\mathsf{a}, \nu)\}\, \mathbb{I}}{\Psi, \mathsf{A}, \mathsf{G} \vdash \{(\mathsf{a}, \nu)\}\, (\mathbb{M}_s, \mathbb{M}_\nu, (\mathbb{C}, \mathbb{R}, \mathbb{I}, k), \mathbb{L})} \text{ (THRD)}$$

$\boxed{\Psi, \mathsf{A}, \mathsf{G} \vdash \mathbb{C} : \Psi'}$ ***(Well-formed code heap)***

$$\frac{\forall \mathtt{f} \in dom(\Psi') : \quad \Psi, \mathsf{A}, \mathsf{G} \vdash \{\Psi'(\mathtt{f})\}\, \mathbb{C}(\mathtt{f})}{\Psi, \mathsf{A}, \mathsf{G} \vdash \mathbb{C} : \Psi'} \text{ (CDHP)}$$

Fig. 7. SAGL Inference Rules

Inference rules. The inference rules of SAGL are shown in Figs. 7 and 8. They look very similar to AGL rules. In the PROG rule, as in AGL, we check the compatibility of assumptions and guarantees, and check the well-formedness of each thread. However, here we require that there be a partition of memory into $n+1$ parts: one part $\mathbb{M}_s$ is shared and other parts $\mathbb{M}_1, \ldots, \mathbb{M}_n$ are privately owned by the threads $\mathbb{T}_1, \ldots, \mathbb{T}_n$, respectively. When we check the well-formedness of thread $\mathbb{T}_k$, the memory in the extended thread state is not the global memory. It just contains $\mathbb{M}_s$ and $\mathbb{M}_k$.

The THRD rule in SAGL is similar to the one in AGL, except that the memory visible by each thread is separated into two parts: the shared $\mathbb{M}_s$ and the private $\mathbb{M}_\nu$. We require that assertions a and ν hold over $\mathbb{M}_s$ and $\mathbb{M}_\nu$ respectively. Since ν only specifies the private resource, we use the "filter" operator $\mathbb{L}|_k$ to prevent ν from having access to the ownership information of locks not owned by the current thread:

$$(\mathbb{L}|_k)(l) \stackrel{\text{def}}{=} \begin{cases} k & \mathbb{L}(l) = k \\ \textit{undefined} & \text{otherwise} \end{cases} \tag{2}$$

i.e., $\mathbb{L}|_k$ is a subset of $\mathbb{L}$ which maps locks to k.

Instruction rules are shown in Fig. 8. In the SEQ rule, we use (a, ν) as the precondition. However, to ensure that the precondition is preserved by state transitions satisfying A, we only check a (*i.e.*, we check $(\mathsf{a} \circ \mathsf{A}) \Rightarrow \mathsf{a}$) because A only specifies shared resources. We know that the private resources will not be touched by the environment. We require a to be precise to enforce the unique boundary between shared and private resources. Following the definition in CSL [11], an assertion a is precise if and only if for any memory $\mathbb{M}$, there is at most one subset $\mathbb{M}'$ that satisfies a, *i.e.*,

$$\begin{aligned} \mathsf{Precise}(\mathsf{a}) \stackrel{\text{def}}{=} \forall \mathbb{M}, \mathbb{R}, k, \mathbb{L}, \mathbb{M}_1, \mathbb{M}_2.\ & (\mathbb{M}_1 \subseteq \mathbb{M}) \wedge (\mathbb{M}_2 \subseteq \mathbb{M}) \wedge \\ & \mathsf{a}\, (\mathbb{M}_1, (\mathbb{R}, k), \mathbb{L}) \wedge \mathsf{a}\, (\mathbb{M}_2, (\mathbb{R}, k), \mathbb{L}) \rightarrow \mathbb{M}_1 = \mathbb{M}_2 . \end{aligned} \tag{3}$$

The JR rule requires a be precise and it be preserved by state transitions satisfying the assumption. Also, the specification assigned to the target address needs to be satisfied

$\boxed{\Psi, \mathsf{A}, \mathsf{G} \vdash \{(\mathsf{a}, \nu)\}\mathbb{I}}$ ***(Well-formed instr. sequences)***

$$\frac{\Psi, \mathsf{A}, \mathsf{G} \vdash \{(\mathsf{a}, \nu)\}\iota\{(\mathsf{a}', \nu')\} \quad \Psi, \mathsf{A}, \mathsf{G} \vdash \{(\mathsf{a}', \nu')\}\mathbb{I} \quad (\mathsf{a} \circ \mathsf{A}) \Rightarrow \mathsf{a} \quad \mathsf{Precise}(\mathsf{a})}{\Psi, \mathsf{A}, \mathsf{G} \vdash \{(\mathsf{a}, \nu)\}\iota; \mathbb{I}} \text{ (SEQ)}$$

$$\frac{\mathsf{Precise}(\mathsf{a}) \quad (\mathsf{a} \circ \mathsf{A}) \Rightarrow \mathsf{a} \quad \forall \mathbb{X}@(\mathbb{M}, (\mathbb{R}, k), \mathbb{L}).\ (\mathsf{a} * \nu)\ \mathbb{X} \rightarrow (\mathsf{a}' * \nu')\ \mathbb{X} \wedge (\lfloor \mathsf{G} \rfloor_{(\mathsf{a}, \mathsf{a}')}\ \mathbb{X}\ \mathbb{X}) \quad \text{where } (\mathsf{a}', \nu') = \Psi(\mathbb{R}(\mathtt{r}_s))}{\Psi, \mathsf{A}, \mathsf{G} \vdash \{(\mathsf{a}, \nu)\}\mathsf{jr}\ \mathtt{r}_s} \text{ (JR)}$$

$\boxed{\Psi, \mathsf{A}, \mathsf{G} \vdash \{(\mathsf{a}, \nu)\}\iota\{(\mathsf{a}', \nu')\}}$ ***(Well-formed instructions)***

$$\frac{\forall \mathbb{X}@(\mathbb{M}, (\mathbb{R}, k), \mathbb{L}).\ (\mathsf{a} * \nu)\ \mathbb{X} \wedge l \notin dom(\mathbb{L}) \rightarrow (\mathsf{a}' * \nu')\ \mathbb{X}' \wedge (\lfloor \mathsf{G} \rfloor_{(\mathsf{a}, \mathsf{a}')}\ \mathbb{X}\ \mathbb{X}') \quad \text{where } \mathbb{X}' = (\mathbb{M}, (\mathbb{R}, k), \mathbb{L}\{l \rightsquigarrow k\})}{\Psi, \mathsf{A}, \mathsf{G} \vdash \{(\mathsf{a}, \nu)\}\mathsf{lock}\ l\{(\mathsf{a}', \nu')\}} \text{ (LOCK)}$$

$$\frac{\forall \mathbb{X}@(\mathbb{M}, (\mathbb{R}, k), \mathbb{L}).\ (\mathsf{a} * \nu)\ \mathbb{X} \rightarrow \mathbb{L}(l) = k \wedge (\mathsf{a}' * \nu')\ \mathbb{X}' \wedge (\lfloor \mathsf{G} \rfloor_{(\mathsf{a}, \mathsf{a}')}\ \mathbb{X}\ \mathbb{X}') \quad \text{where } \mathbb{X}' = (\mathbb{M}, (\mathbb{R}, k), \mathbb{L} \setminus \{l\})}{\Psi, \mathsf{A}, \mathsf{G} \vdash \{(\mathsf{a}, \nu)\}\mathsf{unlock}\ l\{(\mathsf{a}', \nu')\}} \text{ (UNLOCK)}$$

Fig. 8. SAGL Inference Rules (cont'd)

by the resulting state of the jump, and the identity state transition made by the jump satisfies the guarantee G. We use the separating conjunction of the shared and private predicates as the pre- and post-condition. We define $\mathsf{a} * \nu$ as:

$$\begin{aligned} \mathsf{a} * \nu \stackrel{\text{def}}{=}\ & \lambda(\mathbb{M}, (\mathbb{R}, k), \mathbb{L}). \\ & \exists \mathbb{M}_1, \mathbb{M}_2.(\mathbb{M}_1 \uplus \mathbb{M}_2 = \mathbb{M}) \wedge \mathsf{a}\ (\mathbb{M}_1, (\mathbb{R}, k), \mathbb{L}) \wedge \nu\ (\mathbb{M}_2, (\mathbb{R}, k), \mathbb{L}|_k)\,. \end{aligned} \tag{4}$$

Again, the use of $\mathbb{L}|_k$ prevents ν from having access to the ownership information of locks not owned by the current thread. We use $f_1 \uplus f_2$ to represent the union of finite partial mappings with disjoint domains.

To ensure G is satisfied over shared resources, we lift G to $\lfloor \mathsf{G} \rfloor_{(\mathsf{a}, \mathsf{a}')}$:

$$\begin{aligned} \lfloor \mathsf{G} \rfloor_{(\mathsf{a}, \mathsf{a}')} \stackrel{\text{def}}{=}\ & \lambda \mathbb{X}@(\mathbb{M}, (\mathbb{R}, k), \mathbb{L}), \mathbb{X}'@(\mathbb{M}', (\mathbb{R}', k'), \mathbb{L}'). \\ & \exists \mathbb{M}_1, \mathbb{M}_2, \mathbb{M}'_1, \mathbb{M}'_2.\ (\mathbb{M}_1 \uplus \mathbb{M}_2 = \mathbb{M}) \wedge (\mathbb{M}'_1 \uplus \mathbb{M}'_2 = \mathbb{M}') \\ & \wedge \mathsf{a}\ (\mathbb{M}_1, (\mathbb{R}, k), \mathbb{L}) \wedge \mathsf{a}'\ (\mathbb{M}'_1, (\mathbb{R}', k'), \mathbb{L}') \\ & \wedge \mathsf{G}\ (\mathbb{M}_1, (\mathbb{R}, k), \mathbb{L})\ (\mathbb{M}'_1, (\mathbb{R}', k'), \mathbb{L}'), \end{aligned} \tag{5}$$

Here we use precise predicates a and a' to enforce the unique boundary between shared and private resources.

As expected, the SAGL rule for each individual instruction is almost the same as its counterpart in AGL, except that we always use the separating conjunction of predicates for shared and private resources. Each instruction rule requires that memory in states before and after the transition can be partitioned to private and shared; private parts satisfy private predicates and shared parts satisfy shared predicates and G.

It is important that we always combine shared predicates with private predicates instead of checking separately the relationship between a and a' and between ν and

ν'. This gives us the ability to support *dynamic redistribution* of private and shared memory. Instead of enforcing static partition, we allow that part of private memory becomes shared under certain conditions and vice versa. As we will show in the next section, this ability makes our SAGL very expressive and is the enabling feature that makes the embedding of CSL into SAGL possible.

AGL can be viewed as a specialized version of SAGL where all the ν's are set to emp (emp is an assertion which can only be satisfied by memory with empty domain).

Soundness. The soundness of SAGL is formulated in Theorem 1. In addition to the safety of well-formed programs, it also characterizes partial correctness: assertions assigned to labels in Ψ will hold whenever the labels are reached. Theorem 1 is proved following the syntactic approach to type soundness [18]. Here we only present the main theorem. The proof is given in our technical report and is formalized in Coq [4].

Theorem 1 (SAGL-Soundness). *For any program* $\mathbb{P}$ *with specification* $\Phi = ([\Psi_1,\ldots,\Psi_n],[(\mathsf{A}_1,\mathsf{G}_1),\ldots,(\mathsf{A}_n,\mathsf{G}_n)])$*, if* $\Phi,[(a_1,\nu_1)\ldots,(a_n,\nu_n)] \vdash \mathbb{P}$*, then,*

- *for any natural number m, there exists* $\mathbb{P}'$ *such that* $(\mathbb{P} \longmapsto^m \mathbb{P}')$*;*
- *for any m and* $\mathbb{P}' = (\mathbb{M}',[\mathbb{T}'_1,\ldots,\mathbb{T}'_n],\mathbb{L}')$*, if* $(\mathbb{P} \longmapsto^m \mathbb{P}')$*, then,*
  - $\Phi,[(a'_1,\nu'_1),\ldots,(a'_n,\nu'_n)] \vdash \mathbb{P}'$ *for some* $a'_1,\ldots,a'_n$ *and* $\nu'_1,\ldots,\nu'_n$*;*
  - *for any k, there exist* $\mathbb{M}''$*,* $\mathbb{T}''_k$ *and* $\mathbb{L}''$ *such that* $(\mathbb{M}',\mathbb{T}'_k,\mathbb{L}') \overset{\mathsf{t}}{\longmapsto} (\mathbb{M}'',\mathbb{T}''_k,\mathbb{L}'')$*;*
  - *for any k, if* $\mathbb{T}'_k = (\mathbb{C}_k,\mathbb{R}'_k,\mathsf{jr}\ r_s,k)$*, then* $(a''_k * \nu''_k)\ (\mathbb{M}',(\mathbb{R}'_k,k),\mathbb{L}')$ *holds, where* $(a''_k,\nu''_k) = \Psi_k(\mathbb{R}'_k(r_s))$*;*
  - *for any k, if* $\mathbb{T}'_k = (\mathbb{C}_k,\mathbb{R}'_k,\mathsf{bgt}\ r_s,r_t,f;\mathbb{I},k)$ *and* $\mathbb{R}'_k(r_s) > \mathbb{R}'_k(r_t)$*, then* $(a''_k * \nu''_k)\ (\mathbb{M}',(\mathbb{R}'_k,k),\mathbb{L}')$ *holds, where* $(a''_k,\nu''_k) = \Psi_k(f)$*;*

5 Concurrent Separation Logic (CSL)

Both AGL and SAGL treat lock/unlock primitives as normal instructions. They do not require that shared memory be protected by locks. This shows the generality of the A-G method, which makes no assumption about language constructs for synchronizations. Any ad-hoc synchronizations can be verified using the A-G method.

If we focus on a special class of programs following Hoare [6] where accesses of shared resources are protected by critical regions (implemented by locks in our language), we can further simplify our SAGL logic and derive a variation of CSL (CSL adapted to our assembly language).

5.1 CSL Specifications and Rules

In CSL, shared memory is partitioned and each part is protected by a unique lock. For each part of the partition, an invariant is assigned to specify its well-formedness.

$$
\begin{array}{rrcl}
(\mathit{ProgSpec}) & \phi & ::= & ([\psi_1,\ldots,\psi_n],\Gamma) \\
(\mathit{CdHpSpec}) & \psi & ::= & \{\mathtt{f} \leadsto \nu\}^* \\
(\mathit{ResourceINV}) & \Gamma & \in & \mathit{Locks} \rightarrow \mathit{MemPred} \\
(\mathit{MemPred}) & \mathtt{m} & \in & \mathit{Memory} \rightarrow \mathit{Prop}
\end{array}
$$

Fig. 9. Specification Constructs for CSL

$$\begin{array}{l}
\mathtt{m} * \mathtt{m}' \stackrel{\mathrm{def}}{=} \lambda \mathbb{M}.\exists \mathbb{M}_1, \mathbb{M}_2.\ (\mathbb{M}_1 \uplus \mathbb{M}_2 = \mathbb{M}) \wedge \mathtt{m}\ \mathbb{M}_1 \wedge \mathtt{m}'\ \mathbb{M}_2 \\
\nu * \mathtt{m} \stackrel{\mathrm{def}}{=} \lambda \mathbb{X} @ (\mathbb{M}, (\mathbb{R}, k), \mathbb{L}).\exists \mathbb{M}_1, \mathbb{M}_2.\ (\mathbb{M}_1 \uplus \mathbb{M}_2 = \mathbb{M}) \wedge \nu\ (\mathbb{M}_1, (\mathbb{R}, k), \mathbb{L}) \wedge \mathtt{m}\ \mathbb{M}_2 \\
\forall_* x \in S.\ P(x) \stackrel{\mathrm{def}}{=} \begin{cases} \mathsf{emp} & \text{if } S = \emptyset \\ P(x_i) * \forall_* x \in S'.\ P(x) & \text{if } S = S' \uplus \{x_i\} \end{cases} \\
\mathsf{acq}\ l\ \nu \stackrel{\mathrm{def}}{=} \lambda(\mathbb{M}, (\mathbb{R}, k), \mathbb{L}).\ \nu\ (\mathbb{M}, (\mathbb{R}, k), \mathbb{L}\{l \leadsto k\}) \\
\mathsf{rel}\ l\ \nu \stackrel{\mathrm{def}}{=} \lambda(\mathbb{M}, (\mathbb{R}, k), \mathbb{L}).\ \mathbb{L}(l) = k \wedge \nu\ (\mathbb{M}, (\mathbb{R}, k), \mathbb{L} \setminus \{l\})
\end{array}$$

Fig. 10. Definitions of Notations in CSL

A thread cannot access shared memory unless it has acquired the corresponding lock. After the lock is acquired, the thread takes advantage of mutual-exclusion provided by locks and treats the part of memory as private. When the thread releases the lock, it must ensure that the part of memory is well-formed with regard to the corresponding invariant. In this way the following global invariant is enforced:

Shared resources are well-formed outside critical regions.

Figure 9 shows the specification constructs for CSL. The program specification ϕ contains a collection of code heap specifications for each thread and the specification Γ for lock-protected memory. Code heap specification ψ maps a code label to an assertion ν as the precondition of the corresponding instruction sequence. Here ν plays similar role of the private predicate in SAGL. Since each thread privately owns the lock protected memory if it owns the lock, all memory accessible by a thread is viewed as private memory. Therefore we do not need an assertion a to specify the shared memory as we did in SAGL. This also explains why we do not need assumptions and guarantees in CSL. The specification Γ of lock-protected memory maps a lock to an invariant $\mathtt{m}$, which specifies the corresponding part of memory. The invariant $\mathtt{m}$ is simply a predicate over memory because the register file is private to each thread.

Inference rules. The inference rules for CSL are presented in Fig. 11. The PROG rule requires that there be a partition of the global memory into $n+1$ parts. Each $\mathbb{M}_k$ is privately owned by thread $\mathbb{T}_k$. The well-formedness of $\mathbb{T}_k$ is checked by applying the THRD rule. $\mathbb{M}_s$ is the part of memory protected by free locks (locks not owned by any threads). It must satisfy the invariants specified in Γ. Here a_Γ is the separating conjunction of invariants assigned to free locks in Γ, which is defined as:

$$\mathsf{a}_\Gamma \stackrel{\mathrm{def}}{=} \lambda(\mathbb{M}, (\mathbb{R}, k), \mathbb{L}).\ (\forall_* l \in (\mathit{dom}(\Gamma) - \mathit{dom}(\mathbb{L})).\ \Gamma(l))\ \mathbb{M}, \qquad (6)$$

that is, *shared resources are well-formed outside of critical regions*. Here $\forall_*$ is an indexed, finitely iterated separating conjunction, which is formalized in Fig. 10. Separating conjunctions with memory predicates ($\nu * \mathtt{m}$ and $\mathtt{m} * \mathtt{m}'$) are also defined in Fig. 10. As in O'Hearn's original work on CSL [11], we also require all invariants specified in Γ to be precise, *i.e.*, $\mathsf{Precise}(\Gamma)$.

The THRD rule checks the well-formedness of threads. It requires that the current extended thread state satisfies the precondition ν. Since ν only cares about the resource privately owned by the thread, it takes $\mathbb{L}|_k$ instead of complete $\mathbb{L}$ as argument. Recall that $\mathbb{L}|_k$ is defined in (2) in Section 4 to represent the subset of $\mathbb{L}$ which maps locks to

$\boxed{\phi, [\nu_1, \ldots, \nu_n] \vdash \mathbb{P}}$ ***(Well-formed program)***

$$\frac{\phi = ([\psi_1, \ldots, \psi_n], \Gamma) \qquad \mathbb{M}_s \uplus \mathbb{M}_1 \uplus \cdots \uplus \mathbb{M}_n = \mathbb{M} \quad \mathsf{a}_\Gamma\ (\mathbb{M}_s, \_, \mathbb{L}) \quad \mathsf{Precise}(\Gamma) \quad \psi_k, \Gamma \vdash \{\nu_k\}\,(\mathbb{M}_k, \mathbb{T}_k, \mathbb{L}) \text{ for all } k}{\phi, [\nu_1, \ldots, \nu_n] \vdash (\mathbb{M}, [\mathbb{T}_1, \ldots, \mathbb{T}_n], \mathbb{L})} \text{ (PROG)}$$

$\boxed{\psi, \Gamma \vdash \{\nu\}\,(\mathbb{M}, \mathbb{T}, \mathbb{L})}$ ***(Well-formed thread)***

$$\frac{\nu\ (\mathbb{M}, (\mathbb{R}, k), \mathbb{L}|_k) \quad \psi, \Gamma \vdash \mathbb{C} : \psi \quad \psi, \Gamma \vdash \{\nu\}\,\mathbb{I}}{\psi, \Gamma \vdash \{\nu\}\,(\mathbb{M}, (\mathbb{C}, \mathbb{R}, \mathbb{I}, k), \mathbb{L})} \text{ (THRD)}$$

$\boxed{\psi, \Gamma \vdash \mathbb{C} : \psi'}$ ***(Well-formed code heap)***

$$\frac{\forall \mathtt{f} \in dom(\psi') : \quad \psi, \Gamma \vdash \{\psi'(\mathtt{f})\}\,\mathbb{C}(\mathtt{f})}{\psi, \Gamma \vdash \mathbb{C} : \psi'} \text{ (CDHP)}$$

$\boxed{\psi, \Gamma \vdash \{\nu\}\,\mathbb{I}}$ ***(Well-formed instr. sequences)***

$$\frac{\psi, \Gamma \vdash \{\nu\}\,\iota\,\{\nu'\} \quad \psi, \Gamma \vdash \{\nu'\}\,\mathbb{I}}{\psi, \Gamma \vdash \{\nu\}\,\iota; \mathbb{I}} \text{ (SEQ)} \qquad \frac{\forall \mathbb{X} @ (\mathbb{M}, (\mathbb{R}, k), \mathbb{L}).\ \nu\ \mathbb{X} \to \psi(\mathbb{R}(\mathtt{r}_s))\ \mathbb{X}}{\psi, \Gamma \vdash \{\nu\}\,\mathsf{jr}\ \mathtt{r}_s} \text{ (JR)}$$

$\boxed{\psi, \Gamma \vdash \{\nu\}\,\iota\,\{\nu'\}}$ ***(Well-formed instructions)***

$$\frac{\nu * \mathtt{m} \Rightarrow \mathsf{acq}\ l\ \nu'}{\psi, \Gamma\{l \rightsquigarrow \mathtt{m}\} \vdash \{\nu\}\,\mathsf{lock}\ l\,\{\nu'\}} \text{ (LOCK)} \qquad \frac{\nu \Rightarrow (\mathsf{rel}\ l\ \nu') * \mathtt{m}}{\psi, \Gamma\{l \rightsquigarrow \mathtt{m}\} \vdash \{\nu\}\,\mathsf{unlock}\ l\,\{\nu'\}} \text{ (UNLOCK)}$$

Fig. 11. CSL Inference Rules

k. The CDHP rule and rules for instruction sequences are similar to their counterparts in AGL and SAGL and require no more explanation.

In the LOCK rule, we use "acq l ν'" to represent the weakest precondition of ν'; and "$\nu \Rightarrow \nu'$" for logical implication lifted for state predicates. They are formalized in Fig. 10. If the lock l instruction successfully acquires the lock l, we know by our global invariant that the part of memory protected by l satisfies the invariant $\Gamma(l)$ (*i.e.*, $\mathtt{m}$), because l is a free lock before lock l is executed. Therefore, we can carry the knowledge $\mathtt{m}$ in the postcondition ν'. Also, carrying $\mathtt{m}$ in ν' allows subsequent instructions to access that part of memory, since separation logic predicates capture ownerships of memory.

In the UNLOCK rule, "rel l ν'" is the weakest precondition for ν' (see Fig. 10). At the time the lock l is released, the memory protected by l must be well formed with respect to $\mathtt{m} = \Gamma(l)$. The separating conjunction here ensures that ν' does not specify this part of memory. Therefore the following instructions cannot use the part of memory unless the lock is acquired again.

The complete set of rules are presented in the technical report [4]. The frame rule, conjunction rule and consequence rule are admissible in our CSL. These rules and the proof of their admissibility can be found in the report [4] too.

5.2 Interpretation of CSL in SAGL

We prove the soundness of CSL by giving it an interpretation in SAGL, and proving CSL rules as derivable lemmas. This interpretation also formalizes the specialization made for CSL to achieve the simplicity.

From SAGL's point of view, each thread has two parts of memory: the private and the shared. In CSL, the private memory of a thread includes the memory protected by locks held by the thread and the memory that will never be shared. The shared memory are the parts protected by free locks. Therefore, we can use the following interpretation to translate a CSL specification to a SAGL specification:

$$[\![\nu]\!]_\Gamma \stackrel{\text{def}}{=} (\mathsf{a}_\Gamma, \nu) \tag{7}$$

$$[\![\psi]\!]_\Gamma \stackrel{\text{def}}{=} \lambda \mathtt{f}.[\![\psi(\mathtt{f})]\!]_\Gamma \text{ if } \mathtt{f} \in dom(\psi), \tag{8}$$

where a_Γ formalizes the CSL invariant and is defined by (6). We just reuse CSL specification ν as the specification of private memory, and use the separating conjunction a_Γ of invariants assigned to free locks as the specification for shared memory.

Since the assumption and guarantee in SAGL only specifies shared memory, we can define A_Γ and G_Γ for CSL threads:

$$\mathsf{A}_\Gamma \stackrel{\text{def}}{=} \lambda \mathbb{X}@(\mathbb{M},(\mathbb{R},k),\mathbb{L}),\mathbb{X}'@(\mathbb{M}',(\mathbb{R}',k'),\mathbb{L}').\mathbb{R}=\mathbb{R}' \wedge k=k' \wedge (\mathsf{a}_\Gamma\,\mathbb{X} \rightarrow \mathsf{a}_\Gamma\,\mathbb{X}') \tag{9}$$

$$\mathsf{G}_\Gamma \stackrel{\text{def}}{=} \lambda \mathbb{X}@(\mathbb{M},(\mathbb{R},k),\mathbb{L}),\mathbb{X}'@(\mathbb{M}',(\mathbb{R}',k'),\mathbb{L}').\, k=k' \wedge \mathsf{a}_\Gamma\,\mathbb{X} \wedge \mathsf{a}_\Gamma\,\mathbb{X}' \tag{10}$$

which enforces the invariant a_Γ of shared memory.

With above interpretations, we can prove the following soundness theorem.

Theorem 2 (CSL-Soundness)

1. *If* $\psi,\Gamma \vdash \{\nu\}\iota\{\nu'\}$ *in CSL, then* $[\![\psi]\!]_\Gamma,\mathsf{A}_\Gamma,\mathsf{G}_\Gamma \vdash \{[\![\nu]\!]_\Gamma\}\iota\{[\![\nu']\!]_\Gamma\}$ *in SAGL;*
2. *If* $\psi,\Gamma \vdash \{\nu\}\mathbb{I}$ *in CSL and* $\mathsf{Precise}(\Gamma)$, *then* $[\![\psi]\!]_\Gamma,\mathsf{A}_\Gamma,\mathsf{G}_\Gamma \vdash \{[\![\nu]\!]_\Gamma\}\mathbb{I}$ *in SAGL;*
3. *If* $\psi,\Gamma \vdash \mathbb{C}:\psi'$ *in CSL and* $\mathsf{Precise}(\Gamma)$, *then* $[\![\psi]\!]_\Gamma,\mathsf{A}_\Gamma,\mathsf{G}_\Gamma \vdash \mathbb{C}:[\![\psi']\!]_\Gamma$ *in SAGL;*
4. *If* $\psi,\Gamma \vdash \{\nu\}(\mathbb{M}_k,\mathbb{T}_k,\mathbb{L})$ *in CSL,* $\mathsf{Precise}(\Gamma)$, *and* $\mathsf{a}_\Gamma\,(\mathbb{M}_s,\_,\mathbb{L})$, *then* $[\![\psi]\!]_\Gamma,\mathsf{A}_\Gamma,\mathsf{G}_\Gamma \vdash \{[\![\nu]\!]_\Gamma\}(\mathbb{M}_s,\mathbb{M}_k,\mathbb{T}_k,\mathbb{L})$ *in SAGL;*
5. *If* $([\psi_1,\ldots,\psi_n],\Gamma),[\nu_1,\ldots,\nu_n] \vdash \mathbb{P}$ *in CSL, then* $\Phi,[[\![\nu_1]\!]_\Gamma,\ldots,[\![\nu_n]\!]_\Gamma] \vdash \mathbb{P}$ *in SAGL, where* $\Phi = ([[\![\psi_1]\!]_\Gamma,\ldots,[\![\psi_n]\!]_\Gamma],[(\mathsf{A}_\Gamma,\mathsf{G}_\Gamma),\ldots,(\mathsf{A}_\Gamma,\mathsf{G}_\Gamma)])$.

6 SAGL Examples

We use two complementary examples to demonstrate how SAGL combines merits of AGL and CSL. Figure 12 shows a simple program, which allocates a fresh memory cell and then writes into and reads from it. Following the MIPS convention, we assume the register $\mathtt{r}_0$ always contains 0. The corresponding high-level pseudo code is given as comments (followed by "; ;"). It is obvious that two threads executing the same code (but may use different m) will never interfere with each other, therefore the test in line (7) is always True and the program never reaches the unsafe branch.

It is trivial to certify the code in CSL since there is no memory-sharing at all. However, due to the nondeterministic operation of the alloc instruction, it is challenging to

```
start:   -{(emp, emp)}
         addi  r1, r0, 1                ;; local int x, y;
         alloc r2, r1                   ;; x := alloc(1);
         -{(emp, r2 ↦ _)}
         addi  r1, r0, m
         st    r1, 0(r2)                ;; [x] := m;
         -{(emp, (r2 ↦ m) ∧ r1 = m)}
         ld    r3, 0(r2)                ;; y := [x];
         -{(emp, (r2 ↦ m) ∧ r1 = m ∧ r3 = m)}
         beq   r1, r3, safe             ;; while(y == m){}
unsafe:  -{(emp, False)}
         free  r0                       ;; free(0);   (* unsafe! *)
safe:    -{(emp, r2 ↦ _)}
         j     safe
```

Fig. 12. Example 1: Memory Allocation

$$
\begin{aligned}
\mathsf{a}_1 &\stackrel{\text{def}}{=} \exists p,q.\ (\mathtt{m} \mapsto p) * (\mathtt{n} \mapsto q) \wedge gcd(p,q) = gcd(\alpha,\beta)\\
\mathsf{a}_2 &\stackrel{\text{def}}{=} \exists p,q.\ (\mathtt{m} \mapsto p) * (\mathtt{n} \mapsto q) \wedge gcd(p,q) = gcd(\alpha,\beta) \wedge \mathtt{x} = p \wedge \mathtt{y} \geq q \wedge (p \geq q \rightarrow \mathtt{y} = q)\\
\mathsf{a}_3 &\stackrel{\text{def}}{=} \exists p,q.\ (\mathtt{m} \mapsto p) * (\mathtt{n} \mapsto q) \wedge gcd(p,q) = gcd(\alpha,\beta) \wedge \mathtt{x} = p \wedge \mathtt{y} = q \wedge p > q\\
\mathsf{a}_4 &\stackrel{\text{def}}{=} \exists p.\ (\mathtt{m} \mapsto p) * (\mathtt{n} \mapsto p) \wedge p = gcd(\alpha,\beta)\\
\mathsf{A}_1 &\stackrel{\text{def}}{=} ([\mathtt{m}] = [\mathtt{m}]') \wedge ([\mathtt{n}] \geq [\mathtt{n}]') \wedge ([\mathtt{m}] \geq [\mathtt{n}] \rightarrow [\mathtt{n}] = [\mathtt{n}]') \wedge (gcd([\mathtt{m}],[\mathtt{n}]) = gcd([\mathtt{m}]',[\mathtt{n}]'))\\
\mathsf{G}_1 &\stackrel{\text{def}}{=} ([\mathtt{n}] = [\mathtt{n}]') \wedge ([\mathtt{m}] \geq [\mathtt{m}]') \wedge ([\mathtt{n}] \geq [\mathtt{m}] \rightarrow [\mathtt{m}] = [\mathtt{m}]') \wedge (gcd([\mathtt{m}],[\mathtt{n}]) = gcd([\mathtt{m}]',[\mathtt{n}]'))
\end{aligned}
$$

```
local int x, y;                        local int x, y;
while(true){                           while(true){
  -{(a1, emp)}
  x := [m];                              x := [n];
  y := [n];                              y := [m];
  -{(a2, emp)}
  if(x > y)                  ||          if(x > y)
    -{(a3, emp)}
    [m] := x-y;                            [n] := x-y;
  if(x == y) { break;}                   if(x == y) { break;}
}                                      }
-{(a4, emp)}
```

Fig. 13. Example 2: Parallel GCD

certify the code in AGL because the specification of A and G requires global knowledge of memory. We certify the code in SAGL. Assertions are shown as annotations enclosed in "-{}". Recall that in SAGL the first assertion in the pair specifies shared resources and the second one specifies private resources. We treat all the resources as private, therefore the shared predicate is simply emp. The corresponding A and G are trivial. The whole verification is as simple as in CSL.

Our second example is adapted from Yu and Shao [19], which computes the greatest common divisor (GCD) of α and β, stored at locations m and n initially. The high-level pseudo code is shown in Fig. 13. Each thread's local variables are allocated in its private registers in the assembly code, which is similar to the high-level code and is shown in the technical report [4].

In this example, synchronization is achieved without using locks. To certify the code in CSL, we have to rewrite it by wrapping each memory-access command using lock and unlock commands and by introducing auxiliary variables. This time we use the "AGL part" of SAGL to certify the code: private predicates are simply emp. Assertions for the first thread are shown as annotations. In A_1 and G_1, we use primed values (*e.g.*, $[\mathtt{m}]'$ and $[\mathtt{n}]'$) to represent memory values in the resulting state of each action.

We give more examples in the technical report [4], which illustrate the support of dynamic redistribution of shared and private memory in SAGL.

7 Related Work and Conclusion

O'Hearn [11] proposed CSL for a high-level parallel language following Hoare [6]. Synchronization in the language is achieved by the conditional critical region (CCR) in the form of "with *r* when *b* do *c*". Semantics of CCRs is as follows: the statement *c* can be executed only if the resource *r* has not been acquired by others and the Boolean expression *b* is true; otherwise the thread will be blocked. We adapt CSL to an assembly language. The CCR can be implemented using our lock/unlock primitives. Each lock in our language corresponds to a resource name at the high-level. Atomic instructions in our assembly language are very similar to actions in Brookes Semantics [2], where semantic functions are defined for statements and expressions. These semantic functions can be viewed as a translation from the high-level language to a low-level language similar to ours. Recently, Reynolds [15] and Brookes [3] have studied grainless semantics for concurrency. Brookes also gives a grainless semantics to CSL [3].

The PROG rule of our CSL corresponds to O'Hearn's parallel composition rule [11]. The number of threads in our machine is fixed, therefore the nested parallel composition statement supported by Brookes [2] is not supported in our language. We studied verification of assembly code with dynamic thread creation in an earlier paper [5].

CSL is still evolving. Bornat *et al.* [1] proposed a refinement of CSL with fine-grained resource accounting. Parkinson *et al.* [13] applied CSL to verify a non-blocking implementation of stacks. As in the original CSL, these works also assume language constructs for synchronizations. We suspect that there exist reductions from these variations to SAGL-like logics. We leave this as our future work.

Concurrently with our work on SAGL, Vafeiadis and Parkinson [17] proposed another approach to combining rely/guarantee and separation logic, which we refer to here as RGSep. Both RGSep and SAGL partition memory into shared and private parts. However, shared memory cannot be accessed directly in RGSep. It has to be converted into private first to be accessed. Conversions can only occur at boundaries of critical regions, which is a built-in language construct required by RGSep to achieve atomicity. RGSep, in principle, does not assume smallest granularity of transitions. In SAGL, shared memory can be accessed directly, or be converted into private first and then accessed. Conversions can be made dynamically at any program point, instead of being coupled with critical regions. However, like A-G reasoning, SAGL assumes smallest granularity. We suspect that RGSep can be compiled into a specialized version of SAGL, following the way we translate CSL. On the other hand, if our instructions are wrapped using critical regions, SAGL might be derived from RGSep too.

We also use SAGL as the basis to formalize the relationship between CSL and A-G reasoning. We encode the CSL invariant as an assumption and guarantee in SAGL, and prove that CSL rules are derivable from corresponding SAGL rules with the specific assumption and guarantee. Soundness of SAGL is proved following the syntactic approach to type soundness. Our work has been formalized in Coq [4].

References

[1] R. Bornat, C. Calcagno, P. O'Hearn, and M. Parkinson. Permission accounting in separation logic. In *Proc. 32nd ACM Symp. on Principles of Prog. Lang.*, pages 259–270, 2005.

[2] S. Brookes. A semantics for concurrent separation logic. In *Proc. 15th International Conference on Concurrency Theory (CONCUR'04)*, volume 3170 of *LNCS*, pages 16–34, 2004.

[3] S. Brookes. A grainless semantics for parallel programs with shared mutable data. In *Proc. MFPS XXI*, volume 155 of *Electr. Notes Theor. Comput. Sci.*, pages 277–307, 2006.

[4] X. Feng, R. Ferreira, and Z. Shao. On the relationship between concurrent separation logic and assume-guarantee reasoning. Technical Report YALEU/DCS/TR-1374 and Formulation in Coq, Dept. of Computer Science, Yale University, New Haven, CT, January 2007.

[5] X. Feng and Z. Shao. Modular verification of concurrent assembly code with dynamic thread creation and termination. In *Proc. ICFP'05*, pages 254–267, 2005.

[6] C. A. R. Hoare. Towards a theory of parallel programming. In C. A. R. Hoare and R. H. Perrott, editors, *Operating Systems Techniques*, pages 61–71. Academic Press, 1972.

[7] S. S. Ishtiaq and P. W. O'Hearn. BI as an assertion language for mutable data structures. In *Proc. 28th ACM Symp. on Principles of Prog. Lang.*, pages 14–26, 2001.

[8] C. B. Jones. Tentative steps toward a development method for interfering programs. *ACM Trans. on Programming Languages and Systems*, 5(4):596–619, 1983.

[9] G. Necula. Proof-carrying code. In *Proc. 24th ACM Symp. on Principles of Prog. Lang.*, pages 106–119. ACM Press, Jan. 1997.

[10] P. W. O'Hearn. Resources, concurrency and local reasoning. *Theoretical Computer Science (to appear)*. Journal version of [11].

[11] P. W. O'Hearn. Resources, concurrency and local reasoning. In *Proc. 15th Int'l Conf. on Concurrency Theory (CONCUR'04)*, volume 3170 of *LNCS*, pages 49–67, 2004.

[12] S. Owicki and D. Gries. Verifying properties of parallel programs: an axiomatic approach. *Commun. ACM*, 19(5):279–285, 1976.

[13] M. Parkinson, R. Bornat, and P. O'Hearn. Modular verification of a non-blocking stack. In *Proc. 34th ACM Symp. on Principles of Prog. Lang.*, page to appear. ACM Press, Jan. 2007.

[14] J. C. Reynolds. Separation logic: A logic for shared mutable data structures. In *Proc. LICS'02*, pages 55–74, July 2002.

[15] J. C. Reynolds. Toward a grainless semantics for shared-variable concurrency. In *Proc. FSTTCS'04*, volume 3328 of *LNCS*, pages 35–48, 2004.

[16] The Coq Development Team. The Coq proof assistant reference manual. The Coq release v8.0, Oct. 2004.

[17] V. Vafeiadis and M. Parkinson. A marriage of rely/guarantee and separation logic. Available at `http://www.cl.cam.ac.uk/~mjp41/RGSep.pdf`, 2007.

[18] A. K. Wright and M. Felleisen. A syntactic approach to type soundness. *Information and Computation*, 115(1):38–94, 1994.

[19] D. Yu and Z. Shao. Verification of safety properties for concurrent assembly code. In *Proc. 2004 ACM SIGPLAN Int'l Conf. on Functional Prog.*, pages 175–188, September 2004.

Abstract Predicates and Mutable ADTs in Hoare Type Theory

Aleksandar Nanevski[1], Amal Ahmed[2], Greg Morrisett[1], and Lars Birkedal[3]

[1] Harvard University
{aleks,greg}@eecs.harvard.edu
[2] Toyota Technological Institute at Chicago
amal@tti-c.org
[3] IT University of Copenhagen
birkedal@itu.dk

Abstract. *Hoare Type Theory* (HTT) combines a dependently typed, higher-order language with monadically-encapsulated, stateful computations. The type system incorporates pre- and post-conditions, in a fashion similar to Hoare and Separation Logic, so that programmers can modularly specify the requirements and effects of computations within types.

This paper extends HTT with quantification over abstract predicates (i.e., higher-order logic), thus embedding into HTT the Extended Calculus of Constructions. When combined with the Hoare-like specifications, abstract predicates provide a powerful way to define and encapsulate the invariants of private state that may be shared by several functions, but is not accessible to their clients. We demonstrate this power by sketching a number of abstract data types that demand ownership of mutable memory, including an idealized custom memory manager.

1 Background

Dependent types provide a powerful form of specification for higher-order, functional languages. For example, using dependency, we can specify the signature of an array subscript operation as $\mathtt{sub} : \forall\alpha.\Pi x{:}\mathtt{array}\,\alpha.\Pi y{:}\{i{:}\mathtt{nat} \mid i < x.\mathtt{size}\}.\alpha$, where the type of the second argument, y, refines the underlying type nat using a predicate that ensures that y is a valid index for the array x.

Dependent types have long been used in the development of formal mathematics, but their use in practical programming languages has proven challenging. One of the main reasons is that the presence of any computational effects, including non-termination, exceptions, access to store, or I/O – all of which are indispensable in practical programming – can quickly render a dependent type system unsound.

The problem can be addressed by severely restricting dependencies to only effect-free terms (as in for instance DML [30]). But the goal of our work is to try to realize the full power of dependent types for specification of effectful programs. To that end, we have been developing the foundations of a language that we call *Hoare Type Theory* or HTT [22], which we intend to be an expressive and explicitly annotated internal language, providing a semantic framework for elaborating more practical external languages.

R. De Nicola (Ed.): ESOP 2007, LNCS 4421, pp. 189–204, 2007.

HTT starts with a pure, dependently typed core language and augments it with an indexed monadic type of the form $\{P\}x{:}A\{Q\}$. This type encapsulates and describes effectful computations that may diverge or access a mutable store. The type can be read as a Hoare-like partial correctness specification, asserting that if the computation is run in a world satisfying the pre-condition P, then if it terminates, it will return a value x of type A and be in a world described by Q. Through Hoare types, the system can enforce soundness in the presence of effects. The Hoare type admits small footprints as in Separation Logic [26,24], where the pre- and postconditions only describe the part of the store that the program actually uses; the unspecified part is automatically assumed invariant.

Recently, several variants of Hoare Logic for higher-order, effectful languages have appeared. Yoshida, Honda and Berger [31,4] define a logic for PCF with references, Krishnaswami [13] defines a Separation Logic for core ML extended with a monad, and Birkedal et al. [5] define a Higher-Order Separation Logic for reasoning about ADTs in first-order programs. However, we believe that HTT has several key advantages over these and other proposed logics. First, HTT supports *strong* (i.e., type-varying) updates of mutable locations, while the above program logics require that the types of memory locations are *invariant.* This restriction makes it difficult to model stateful protocols as in the Vault language [7], or low-level languages such as TAL [20] and Cyclone [12] where memory management is intended to be coded within the language. Second, none of these logics considers pointer arithmetic, nor source language features like type abstraction, modules, or dependent types, which we consider here. Third, and most significant, Hoare logics cannot really interact with the type systems of the underlying language, unlike HTT where specifications are *integrated with types.* In Hoare Logic, it is not possible to abstract over specifications in the source programs, aggregate the logical invariants of the data structures with the data itself, compute with such invariants, or nest the specifications into larger specifications or types. These features are essential ingredients for data abstraction and information hiding, and, in fact, a number of works have been proposed towards integrating Hoare-like reasoning with type checking. Examples include tools and languages like Spec# [1], SPLint [9], ESC/Java [8], and JML [6].

There are several important outstanding problems in the design of such languages for integrated programming and verification. As discussed in [6], for example: (1) It is desirable to use effectful code in the specifications, but most languages insist that specifications must be pure, in order to preserve soundness. Such a restriction frequently leads to implementing the same functionality twice – once purely for specification, and once impurely for execution. (2) Specifications should be able to describe and control pointer aliasing. (3) It is tricky to define a useful notion of object or module invariant, primarily because of local state owned by the object. Most definitions end up beeing too restrictive to support some important programming patterns [2].

Our prior work on HTT [22] addresses the first two problems: (1) we allow effectful code in specifications by granting such code first-class status, via the monad for Hoare triples, and (2) we control pointer aliasing, by employing the small footprint approach of Separation Logic. Both of these properties were discussed at the beginning of this section. The focus of this paper are extensions to HTT that enable us to also address problem (3), among others.

In a language like HTT that integrates programming and verification, truly reusable program components (e.g., libraries of data types and first-class objects) require that their *internal invariants* are appropriately abstracted. The component interfaces need to include not only abstract types, but also abstract specifications. Thus it is natural to extend HTT with support for abstraction over predicates (i.e., higher-order logic). More specifically, we describe a variant of HTT that includes the Extended Calculus of Constructions (ECC) [14], modulo minor differences described in Section 5. This allows terms, types, and predicates to all be abstracted within terms, types, and predicates respectively.

There are several benefits of this extension. First, higher-order logic can formulate almost any predicate that may be encountered during program verification, including predicates defined by induction and coinduction. Second, we can reason *within* the system, about the equality of terms, types and predicates, *including abstract types and abstract predicates.* In the previous version of HTT [22], we could only reason about the equality of terms, whereas equality on types and predicates was a judgment (accessible to the typechecker), but *not* a proposition (accessible to the programmer). Internalized reasoning on types endows HTT with a form of *first-class* modules that can contain types, terms, *and axioms.* It is also important in order to fully support strong updates of locations. Third, higher-order logic can *define* many constructs that, in the previous version, had to be primitive. For instance, the definition of heaps can now be encoded within the language, thus simplifying some aspects of the meta theory.

Most importantly, however, *abstraction over predicates suffices to represent the private state of functions or ADTs within the type system.* Private state can be hidden from the clients by existentially abstracting over the state invariant. Thus, libraries for mutable state can provide precise specifications, yet have sufficient abstraction mechanisms that different implementations can share a common interface. Moreover, specifications may choose to reveal certain aspects of private state to the client, thus granting the client partial or complete access to, or even ownership of portions of the private state.

We demonstrate these ideas with a few idealized examples including a module for memory allocation and deallocation.

2 Overview

Similar to the modern monadic functional languages [19], HTT syntax splits into the pure and the impure fragment. The pure fragment contains higher-order functions and pairs, and the impure fragment contains the effectful commands for memory lookup and strong update (memory allocation and deallocation can be defined), as well as conditionals and recursion. The expressions from the effectful fragment can be coerced into the pure one by monadic encapsulation.

The type constructors include the primitive types of booleans, natural numbers and the unit type, the standard constructors Π and Σ for dependent products and sums, as well as Hoare types $\{P\}x{:}A\{Q\}$, and subset types $\{x{:}A.\,P\}$. The Hoare type $\{P\}x{:}A\{Q\}$ is the *monadic type* which classifies effectful computations that may execute in any initial heap satisfying the assertion P, and either diverge, or terminate returning a value $x{:}A$ and a final heap satisfying the assertion Q. The subset type $\{x{:}A.\,P\}$ classifies all the elements of A that satisfy the predicate P. We adopt the standard convention and write $A{\rightarrow}B$ and $A{\times}B$ instead of $\Pi x{:}A.\,B$ and $\Sigma x{:}A.\,B$ when B does not depend on x.

The syntax of our extended HTT is presented in the following table.

$$\begin{array}{llcl}
\textit{Types} & A,B,C & ::= & K \mid \mathsf{nat} \mid \mathsf{bool} \mid 1 \mid \mathsf{prop} \mid \mathsf{mono} \mid \Pi x{:}A.\,B \mid \\
 & & & \Sigma x{:}A.\,B \mid \{P\}x{:}A\{Q\} \mid \{x{:}A.\,P\} \\
\textit{Elim terms} & K,L & ::= & x \mid K\ N \mid \mathsf{fst}\ K \mid \mathsf{snd}\ K \mid \mathsf{out}\ K \mid M : A \\
\textit{Intro terms} & M,N,O & ::= & K \mid () \mid \lambda x.\,M \mid (M,N) \mid \mathsf{do}\,E \mid \mathsf{in}\ M \mid \\
 & & & \mathsf{true} \mid \mathsf{false} \mid \mathsf{z} \mid \mathsf{s}\ M \mid M+N \mid M \times N \mid \mathsf{eq_{nat}}(M,N) \mid \\
\textit{(Assertions)} & P,Q,R & & \top \mid \bot \mid \mathsf{xid}_{A,B}(M,N) \mid \neg P \mid P \wedge Q \mid \\
 & & & P \vee Q \mid P \supset Q \mid \forall x{:}A.\,P \mid \exists x{:}A.\,P \mid \\
\textit{(Small types)} & \tau,\sigma & & \mathsf{nat} \mid \mathsf{bool} \mid 1 \mid \mathsf{prop} \mid \Pi x{:}\tau.\,\sigma \mid \Sigma x{:}\tau.\,\sigma \mid \{P\}x{:}\tau\{Q\} \mid \{x{:}\tau.\,P\} \\
\textit{Commands} & c & ::= & !_\tau\ M \mid M :=_\tau N \mid \mathsf{if}_A\ M\ \mathsf{then}\ E_1\ \mathsf{else}\ E_2 \mid \\
 & & & \mathsf{case}_A\ M\ \mathsf{of}\ \mathsf{z} \Rightarrow E_1\ \mathsf{or}\ \mathsf{s}\ x \Rightarrow E_2 \mid \\
 & & & \mathsf{fix}\ f(y{:}A){:}B = \mathsf{do}\,E\ \mathsf{in}\ \mathsf{eval}\ f\ M \\
\textit{Computations} & E,F & ::= & \mathsf{return}\,M \mid x \leftarrow K; E \mid x \Leftarrow c; E \mid x =_A M; E \\
\textit{Context} & \Delta & ::= & \cdot \mid \Delta, x{:}A \mid \Delta, P
\end{array}$$

HTT supports predicative type polymorphism [18], by differentiating *small types*, which do not admit type quantification, from *large types* (or just types for short), which can quantify over small types only. For example, the polymorphic identity function can be written as $\lambda\alpha.\lambda y.y : \Pi\alpha{:}\mathsf{mono}.\Pi y{:}\alpha.\alpha$, but α ranges over only small types. The restriction to predicative polymorphism is crucial for ensuring that during type-checking, normalization of terms, types, and predicates terminates [22]. Note that "small" Hoare triples $\{P\}x{:}\tau\{Q\}$ and subset types $\{x{:}\tau.\,P\}$, where P and Q (but not τ) may contain type quantification are considered small. This is because P and Q are *refinements*, i.e. they do not influence the underlying semantics and the equational reasoning about terms: If two terms of some Hoare or subset types are semantically equal, then they remain equal even if P and Q are replaced by some other assertions.

To support abstraction over types and predicates, HTT introduces types mono and prop which classify small types and assertions respectively. With the type mono, HTT can *compute* with small types as if they were data. For example, if $x{:}\mathsf{mono}{\times}(\mathsf{nat}{\rightarrow}\mathsf{nat})$, then the variable x may be seen as a module declaring a small type and a function on nats. The expression $\mathsf{fst}\ x$ extracts the small type.

Terms. The terms are classified as introduction or elimination terms, according to their standard logical properties. The split facilitates equational reasoning and bidirectional typechecking [25]. The terms are not annotated with types, as the typechecker can infer most of them. When this is not the case, the construct $M : A$ may supply the type explicitly. This construct also switches the direction in the bidirectional typechecking.

HTT features the usual terms for lambda abstraction and applications, pairs and the projections, as well as natural numbers, booleans and the unit element. The introduction form for the Hoare types is $\mathsf{do}\, E$, which encapsulates the effectful computation E, and suspends its evaluation. The notation is intended to closely resemble the familiar Haskell-style do-notation for writing effectful computations. The constructor in is a coercion from A into a subset type $\{x{:}A.\, P\}$, and out is the opposite coercion.

Terms also include small types τ and assertions P, which are the elements of mono and prop respectively. HTT does not currently have any constructors to inspect the structure of such elements. They are used solely during typechecking, and can be safely erased before program execution.

We illustrate the HTT syntax using the following example. Consider an ML-like function $f = \lambda y{:}\mathsf{unit}.\, x := !x + 1;\ \mathsf{if}\ (!x = 1)\ \mathsf{then}\ 0\ \mathsf{else}\ 1$, where we assume a free variable $x{:}\mathsf{nat\ ref}$. A computation in HTT that defines this function and then immediately applies it, may be written as follows.

$$\begin{array}{l} f = \lambda y.\, \mathsf{do}\, (u \Leftarrow !_{\mathsf{nat}}\, x; v \Leftarrow (x :=_{\mathsf{nat}} u + \mathsf{s\ z}); t \Leftarrow !_{\mathsf{nat}}\, x; \\ \qquad\qquad\qquad s \Leftarrow \mathsf{if}_{\mathsf{nat}}\ (\mathsf{eq}_{\mathsf{nat}}(t, \mathsf{s\ z}))\ \mathsf{then\ z\ else\ s\ z}; \mathsf{return}\, s); \\ x \leftarrow f\ (); \mathsf{return}\, (x) \end{array}$$

We point out some characteristic properties. This program, and all its stateful subcomponents belong to the syntactic domain of computations. Each computation can intuitively be described as a semi-colon-separated list of commands, which usually perform some imperative operation, and then bind to a variable. For example $x \Leftarrow c$ executes the primitive command c, and binds the return result to x. $x \leftarrow K$ executes the computation encapsulated in K, thus performing all the side effects that may have been suspended in K. $x =_A M$ does not perform any side-effects, but is simply the syntactic sugar for the usual let-binding of $M{:}A$ to x. In all these cases, the variable x is immutable, as is customary in functional programming, and its scope extends to the right, until the end of the block enclosed by the nearest do. Associated with these commands, is the construct $\mathsf{return}\, M$. It creates the trivial computation that immediately returns the value M. $\mathsf{return}\, M$ and $x \leftarrow K; E$ correspond to the standard monadic *unit* and *bind*, respectively.

The commands $!_\tau\, M$ and $M :=_\tau N$ are used to read and write memory respectively. The index τ is the type of the value being read or written. Note that unlike ML and most statically-typed languages, HTT supports *strong updates.* That is, if x is a location holding a nat, then we can update the contents of x with a value of an arbitrary (small) type, not just another nat. (Here, we make the simplifying assumption that locations can hold a value of any type (e.g., values are boxed).) Type-safety is ensured by the pre-condition for memory reads which captures the requirement that to read a τ value out of location M, we must be able to prove that M currently holds such a value.

In the if and case commands, the index type A is the type of the branches. The fixpoint command $\mathsf{fix}\ f(y{:}A){:}B = \mathsf{do}\, E\ \mathsf{in\ eval}\ f\, M$, first obtains the function $f{:}\Pi y{:}A.\, B$ such that $f(y) = \mathsf{do}(E)$, then evaluates the computation $f(M)$, and returns the result.

In the subsequent text we adopt a number of syntactic conventions for terms. First, we will represent natural numbers in their usual decimal form. Second, we omit the variable x in $x \Leftarrow (M :=_\tau N); E$, as x is of unit type. Third, we abbreviate the computation of the form $x \Leftarrow c; \mathsf{return}\, x$ simply as c, in order to avoid introducing a spurious variable x. For the same reason, we abbreviate $x \leftarrow K; \mathsf{return}\, x$ as $\mathsf{eval}\ K$.

Returning to the example above, the type of f in the translated HTT program is $1 \rightarrow \{P\}s{:}\mathsf{nat}\{Q\}$ where, intuitively, the precondition P requires that the location x points to some value $v{:}\mathsf{nat}$, and the postcondition Q states that if v was zero, then the result s is 0, otherwise the result is 1, and regardless x now points to $v+1$. Furthermore, in HTT, the specifications capture the *small footprint* of f, reflecting that x is the only location accessed when the computation is run. Technically, realizing such a specification using the predicates we provide requires a number of auxiliary definitions and conventions which are explained below. For instance, we must define the relation $x \mapsto v$ stating that x points to v, the equalities, and how v can be scoped across both the pre- and post-condition.

Assertions. The assertion logic is classical and includes the standard propositional connectives and quantifiers over all types of HTT. Since prop is a type, we can quantify over propositions, and more generally over propositional functions, giving us the power of higher-order logic. The primitive proposition $\mathsf{xid}_{A,B}(M, N)$ implements *heterogeneous equality* (aka. *John Major equality* [17]), and is true only if the types A and B, as well as the terms $M{:}A$ and $N{:}B$ are propositionally equal. We will use this proposition to express that if two heap locations x_1 (pointing to value $M_1{:}\tau_1$) and x_2 (pointing to value $M_2{:}\tau_2$) are equal, then $\tau_1 = \tau_2$ and $M_1 = M_2$. When the index types are equal in the heterogeneous equality $\mathsf{xid}_{A,A}(M, N)$, we abbreviate that as $\mathsf{id}_A(M, N)$, and often also write $M =_A N$ or just $M = N$. We denote by $\mathsf{lfp}_A(Q)$ the least fixed point of the monotone predicate $Q{:}(A \rightarrow \mathsf{prop}) \rightarrow A \rightarrow \mathsf{prop}$ (Q is monotone if it uses the argument only in positive positions). It is well-known that this construct is definable in higher-order logic [11]. Heaps in which HTT computations are evaluated can be defined as a simple subset type $\mathsf{heap} = \{h{:}(\mathsf{nat} \times \Sigma\alpha{:}\mathsf{mono}.\alpha) \rightarrow \mathsf{prop}.\ \mathsf{Finite}(h) \wedge \mathsf{Functional}(h)\}$. The underlying type $\mathsf{nat} \times \Sigma\alpha{:}\mathsf{mono}.\,\alpha$ implies that a heap is a ternary relation which takes $M{:}\mathsf{nat}$, $\alpha{:}\mathsf{mono}$ and $N{:}\alpha$ and decides if the location M points to $N{:}\alpha$. The predicates Finite and $\mathsf{Functional}$ are easily definable to state that a heap assigns to at most finitely many locations, and at most one value to every location. In HTT, heap locations are natural numbers, rather than elements of an abstract type. This simplifies the semantics somewhat, and also enables pointer arithmetic. Note that heaps in HTT can store only values of small types. This is sufficient for modeling languages with predicative polymorphism like SML, but is too weak for modeling Java, or the impredicative polymorphism of Haskell.

We also adopt the usual predicates from Separation Logic [26,24]: emp, $(n \mapsto_\tau x)$ and $(n \hookrightarrow_\tau x)$ all have type $\mathsf{heap} \rightarrow \mathsf{prop}$. $\mathsf{emp}\ h$ holds iff h is the empty relation; $(n \mapsto_\tau x)(h)$ holds if h contains *only one* location n pointing to a value $x{:}\tau$. Similarly, $(n \hookrightarrow_\tau x)(h)$ states that h contains *at least* the location n pointing to $x{:}\tau$. Finally, given $P, Q{:}\mathsf{heap} \rightarrow \mathsf{prop}$, the spatial conjunction

$P * Q$:heap→prop is defined so that $(P * Q)(h)$ holds iff P and Q hold on disjoint subheaps of h. All of these predicates are easily definable using higher-order assertion logic.

3 Examples

Small footprints. HTT supports small-footprint specifications, as in Separation Logic [22]. If do E has type $\{P\}x{:}A\{Q\}$ — note that here P : heap→prop and Q : heap→heap→prop — then P and Q need only describe the properties of the heap fragment that E actually requires in order to run. The actual heap in which E will run may be much larger, but the unspecified portion will automatically be assumed invariant. To illustrate this idea, let us consider a simple program that reads from the location x and increases its contents.

$$\begin{aligned}\mathsf{incx}\ :\ & \{\lambda i.\, \exists n{:}\mathsf{nat}.\, (x \mapsto_{\mathsf{nat}} n)(i)\}\, r{:}1\\ & \{\lambda i.\, \lambda m.\, \forall n{:}\mathsf{nat}.\, (x \mapsto_{\mathsf{nat}} n)(i) \supset (x \mapsto_{\mathsf{nat}} n{+}1)(m)\}\\ & = \mathsf{do}(u \Leftarrow !_{\mathsf{nat}}\, x; x :=_{\mathsf{nat}} u + 1; \mathsf{return}\,(\,))\end{aligned}$$

Notice that the precondition states that the initial heap i contains *exactly one* location x, while the postcondition relates i with the heap m obtained after the evaluation (and states that m contains exactly one location too). This does not mean that incx can evaluate only in singleton heaps. Rather, incx requires a heap from which it can carve out a fragment that satisfies the precondition, i.e. a fragment containing a location x pointing to a nat. For example, we may execute incx against a larger heap, which contains the location y as well, and the contents of y is guaranteed to remain unchanged.

$$\begin{aligned}\mathsf{incxy}\ :\ & \{\lambda i.\, \exists n.\, \exists k{:}\mathsf{nat}.\, (x \mapsto_{\mathsf{nat}} n * y \mapsto_{\mathsf{nat}} k)(i)\}\, r{:}1\\ & \{\lambda i.\, \lambda m.\, \forall n.\, \forall k{:}\mathsf{nat}.\, (x \mapsto_{\mathsf{nat}} n * y \mapsto_{\mathsf{nat}} k)(i) \supset (x \mapsto_{\mathsf{nat}} n{+}1 * y \mapsto_{\mathsf{nat}} k)(m)\}\\ & = \mathsf{do}(\mathsf{eval}\ \mathsf{incx})\end{aligned}$$

To avoid clutter in specifications, we introduce a convention: if P, Q:heap→prop are predicates that may depend on the free variable $x{:}A$, we write $x{:}A.\,\{P\}y{:}B\{Q\}$ instead of $\{\lambda i.\, \exists x{:}A.\, P(i)\}y{:}B\{\lambda i.\, \lambda m.\, \forall x{:}A.\, P(i) \supset Q(m)\}$. This notation lets x seem to scope over both the pre- and post-condition. For example the type of incx can now be written $n{:}\mathsf{nat}.\,\{x \mapsto_{\mathsf{nat}} n\}r{:}1\{x \mapsto_{\mathsf{nat}} n{+}1\}$. The convention is easily generalized to a finite context of variables, so that we can also abbreviate the type of incxy as $n{:}\mathsf{nat}, k{:}\mathsf{nat}.\,\{x \mapsto_{\mathsf{nat}} n {*} y \mapsto_{\mathsf{nat}} k\}r{:}1\{x \mapsto_{\mathsf{nat}} n{+}1 * y \mapsto_{\mathsf{nat}} k\}$. Following the terminology of Hoare Logic, we call the variables abstracted outside of the Hoare triple, like n and k above, *logic variables* or *ghost variables*.

Nontermination. The following is a computation of an arbitrary monadic type that diverges upon forcing.

$$\begin{aligned}\mathsf{diverge}\ :\ & \{P\}x{:}A\{Q\}\\ & = \mathsf{do}\,(\mathsf{fix}\ f(y : 1) : \{P\}x{:}A\{Q\} = \mathsf{do}\,(\mathsf{eval}\ (f\ y))\\ & \qquad \mathsf{in}\ \mathsf{eval}\ f\ (\,))\end{aligned}$$

diverge sets up a recursive function $f(y : 1) = \mathsf{do}\,(\mathsf{eval}\,(f\, y))$; then applies it to $(\,)$ to obtain another suspended computation $\mathsf{do}\,(\mathsf{eval}\, f\,(\,))$, which is immediately forced by eval to trigger another application to $(\,)$, and so on.

Allocation and Deallocation. The reader may be surprised that we provide no primitives for allocating (or deallocating) locations within the heap. This is because we can encode such primitives *within* the language in a style similar to Benton's recent semantic framework for specification of machine code [3]. We can encode a number of memory management implementations and give them a uniform interface, so that clients can choose from among different allocators.

We assume that upon start up, the memory module already "owns" all of the free memory of the program. It exports two functions, alloc and dealloc, which can transfer the ownership of locations between the allocator module and its clients. The functions share the memory owned by the module, but this memory will not be accessible to the clients (except via direct calls to alloc and dealloc).

The definitions of the allocator module will use two essential features of HTT. First, there is a mechanism in HTT to abstract the local state of the module and thus protect it from access from other parts of the program. Second, HTT supports strong updates, and thus it is possible for the memory module to recycle locations to hold values of different type at different times throughout the course of the program execution.

The interface for the allocator can be captured with the type:

$$\begin{aligned}\mathsf{Alloc} = [\,&I : \mathsf{heap}{\rightarrow}\mathsf{prop},\\ &\mathsf{alloc} : \Pi\alpha{:}\mathsf{mono}.\, \Pi x{:}\alpha.\, \{I\}r{:}\mathsf{nat}\{\lambda i.\, (I * r \mapsto_\alpha x)\},\\ &\mathsf{dealloc} : \Pi n{:}\mathsf{nat}.\, \{I * n \mapsto -\}r{:}1\{\lambda i.\, I\}\ ]\end{aligned}$$

where the notation $[x_1{:}A_1, \ldots, x_n{:}A_n]$ abbreviates a sum $\Sigma x_1{:}A_1 \cdots \Sigma x_n{:}A_n.1$. In English, the interface says that there is some abstract invariant I, reflecting the internal invariant of the module, paired with two functions. Both functions require that the invariant I holds before and after calls to the functions. In addition, a call $\mathsf{alloc}\,\tau\,x$ will yield a location r and a guarantee that r points to x. Furthermore, we know from the use of the spatial conjunction that r is disjoint from the internal invariant I. Thus, updates by the client to r will not break the invariant I. On the other hand, accessing locations hidden by I becomes impossible. As will be apparent from the typing rules in Section 4, each location access requires proving that the location exists. But, when I is abstracted, the knowledge needed to construct this proof, is hidden as well. Dually, dealloc requires that we are given a location n, pointing to some value and disjoint from the memory covered by the invariant I. Upon return, the invariant is restored and the location consumed.

If M is a module with this signature, then a program fragment that wishes to use this module will have to start with a pre-condition $\mathsf{fst}\ M$. That is, clients will generally have the type $\Pi M{:}\mathsf{Alloc}.\{(\mathsf{fst}\ M) * P\}r{:}A\{\lambda i.\,(\mathsf{fst}\ M) * Q(i)\}$ where Alloc is the signature given above.

Allocator Module 1. Our first implementation of the allocator module assumes that there is a location r such that all the locations $n \geq r$ are free. The value of r is recorded in the location 0. All the free locations are initialized with the unit value ( ). Upon a call to alloc, the module returns the location r and sets $0 \mapsto_{\mathsf{nat}} r{+}1$, thus removing r from the set of free locations. Upon a call $\mathsf{dealloc}\,n$, the value of r is decreased by one if $r = n$ and otherwise, nothing happens. Obviously, this kind of implementation is very naive. For instance, it assumes unbounded memory and will leak memory if a deallocated cell was not the most recently allocated. However, the example is still interesting to illustrate the features of HTT. First, we define a predicate that describes the free memory as a list of consecutive locations initialized with $() : 1$.

$$\begin{aligned}\mathsf{free} \;&:\; (\mathsf{nat} \times \mathsf{heap}) \to \mathsf{prop}\\ &=\; \mathsf{lfp}\,(\lambda F.\, \lambda(r,h).\, (r \mapsto_1 () * \lambda h'.\, F\,(r{+}1, h'))(h))\end{aligned}$$

Then we can implement the allocator module as follows:

$$\begin{aligned}[\,I \;&=\; \lambda h.\, \exists r{:}\mathsf{nat}.\, (0 \mapsto_{\mathsf{nat}} r * \lambda h'.\, \mathsf{free}(r,h') * \lambda h''.\, \top)(h),\\ \mathsf{alloc} \;&=\; \lambda\alpha.\, \lambda x.\, \mathsf{do}\,(u \Leftarrow\, !_{\mathsf{nat}}\, 0;\, u :=_\alpha x;\, 0 :=_{\mathsf{nat}} u{+}1;\, \mathsf{return}\, u),\\ \mathsf{dealloc} \;&=\; \lambda n.\, \mathsf{do}\,(u \Leftarrow\, !_{\mathsf{nat}}\, 0;\\ &\qquad \mathsf{if}\ \mathsf{eq}_{\mathsf{nat}}(u, n{+}1)\ \mathsf{then}\ n :=_1 ();\, 0 :=_{\mathsf{nat}} n;\, \mathsf{return}\,()\ \mathsf{else}\ \mathsf{return}\,())\,]\end{aligned}$$

Allocator Module 2. In this example we present a (slightly) more sophisticated allocator module. The module will have the same Alloc signature as in the previous example, but the implementation does not leak memory upon deallocation. We take some liberties and assume as primitive a standard set of definitions and operations for the inductive type of lists.

$$\begin{aligned}\mathsf{list} \;&:\; \mathsf{mono}{\to}\mathsf{mono}\\ \mathsf{nil} \;&:\; \Pi\alpha{:}\mathsf{mono}.\, \mathsf{list}\ \alpha\\ \mathsf{cons} \;&:\; \Pi\alpha{:}\mathsf{mono}.\, \alpha{\to}\mathsf{list}\ \alpha{\to}\mathsf{list}\ \alpha\\ \mathsf{snoc} \;&:\; \Pi\alpha{:}\mathsf{mono}.\, \Pi x{:}\{y{:}\mathsf{list}\ \alpha.\, y {\neq_{\mathsf{list}\ \alpha}} \mathsf{nil}\ \alpha\}.\, \{z{:}\alpha \times \mathsf{list}\ \alpha.\, x = \mathsf{in}\ (\mathsf{cons}(\mathsf{fst}\ z)(\mathsf{snd}\ z))\}\\ \mathsf{nil?} \;&:\; \Pi\alpha{:}\mathsf{mono}.\, \Pi x{:}\mathsf{list}\ \alpha.\, \{y{:}\mathsf{bool}.(y =_{\mathsf{bool}} \mathsf{true}) \subset\supset (x =_{\mathsf{list}\ \alpha} \mathsf{nil}\ \alpha)\}\end{aligned}$$

The operation snoc maps non-empty lists back to pairs so that the head and tail can be extracted (without losing equality information regarding the components.) The operation nil? tests a list, and returns a bool which is true iff the list is nil.

As before, we define the predicate free that describes the free memory, but this time, we collect the (finitely many) addresses of the free locations into a list.

$$\begin{aligned}\mathsf{free} \;&:\; ((\mathsf{list}\ \mathsf{nat}){\times}\mathsf{heap}){\to}\mathsf{prop}\\ &=\; \mathsf{lfp}\,(\lambda F.\, \lambda(l,h).\, (l = \mathsf{nil}\ \mathsf{nat}) \vee \exists x'{:}\mathsf{nat}.\, \exists l'{:}\mathsf{list}\ \mathsf{nat}.\\ &\qquad l = \mathsf{cons}\ \mathsf{nat}\ x'\ l' \wedge (x' \mapsto_1 () * \lambda h'.\, F(l',h'))(h))\end{aligned}$$

The intended invariant now is that the list of free locations is stored at address 0, so that the module is implemented as follows:

$$\begin{aligned}[\,I \;&=\; \lambda h.\, \exists l{:}\mathsf{list}\ \mathsf{nat}.\, (0 \mapsto_{\mathsf{list}\ \mathsf{nat}} l * \lambda h'.\, \mathsf{free}(l,h'))(h),\\ \mathsf{alloc} \;&=\; \lambda\alpha.\, \lambda x.\, \mathsf{do}\,(l \Leftarrow\, !_{\mathsf{list}\ \mathsf{nat}}\, 0;\ \mathsf{if}\ (\mathsf{out}\ (\mathsf{nil?}\ \mathsf{nat}\ l))\ \mathsf{then}\ \mathsf{eval}\ (\mathsf{diverge})\\ &\qquad \mathsf{else}\ p \Leftarrow \mathsf{out}\ (\mathsf{snoc}\ \mathsf{nat}\ (\mathsf{in}\ l));\ 0 :=_{\mathsf{list}\ \mathsf{nat}} \mathsf{snd}\ p;\\ &\qquad \mathsf{fst}\ p :=_\alpha x;\ \mathsf{return}\,(\mathsf{fst}\ p)),\\ \mathsf{dealloc} \;&=\; \lambda x.\, \mathsf{do}\,(l \Leftarrow\, !_{\mathsf{list}\ \mathsf{nat}}\, 0;\, x :=_1 ();\, 0 :=_{\mathsf{list}\ \mathsf{nat}} \mathsf{cons}\ \mathsf{nat}\ x\ l;\, \mathsf{return}\,())\,]\end{aligned}$$

This version of alloc reads the free list out of location 0. If it is empty, then the function diverges. Otherwise, it extracts the first free location z, writes the rest of the free list back into 0, and returns z. The dealloc simply adds its argument back to the free list.

Functions with local state. Now, we consider examples that illustrate various modes of use of the invariants on local state. We assume the allocator from the previous example, and admit the free variables I and alloc, with types as in Alloc. These can be instantiated with either of the two implementations above.

Let us consider an HTT computation that allocates a location x with integer content, and then returns a computation for incrementing x. The first attempt at writing this computation may be as:

$$E = \mathsf{do}\,(x \leftarrow \mathsf{alloc\ nat}\ 0;\ \mathsf{do}\,(z \Leftarrow !_{\mathsf{nat}}\, x; x :=_{\mathsf{nat}} z{+}1; \mathsf{return}\,(z{+}1))).$$

E can be given several different types that describe its behavior with various levels of precision. But, here, we are interested in a type for E that describes it "fully". In other words, we would like to specify that the return value of E is a computation whose successive executions return an increasing sequence of natural numbers. The computation remembers the last computed natural number in its local store (here, the location x) which persists between successive calls. But the details of this store should be hidden from the clients of E, precisely to preserve its locality.

In HTT we can use the ability to combine terms, propositions and Hoare triples, and abstract x away, while exposing only the invariant that the computation increases the content of x.

$$\begin{array}{rcl} E_1 & = & \mathsf{do}\,(x \leftarrow \mathsf{alloc\ nat}\ 0\ \mathsf{in}\ (\lambda v.\, x \mapsto_{\mathsf{nat}} v, \mathsf{do}\,(z \Leftarrow !_{\mathsf{nat}}\, x; x :=_{\mathsf{nat}} z{+}1; \mathsf{return}\,(z{+}1)))) \\ & : & \{I\} \\ & & \quad t{:}\Sigma_{inv:\mathsf{nat}\to\mathsf{heap}\to\mathsf{prop}}.\, v{:}\mathsf{nat}.\ \{inv\ v\}r{:}\mathsf{nat}\{\lambda h.\,(inv\ (v{+}1)\ h) \wedge r = v{+}1\} \\ & & \{\lambda i.\, I * (\mathsf{fst}\ t\ 0)\} \end{array}$$

E_1 differs from E in that it also defines the invariant $inv = \lambda v.\, x \mapsto_{\mathsf{nat}} v$. When used in the specifications, inv brings out the important aspects of the local store, which are the last computed natural number v, and the fact that initially $v = 0$ (as the separating conjunct $(\mathsf{fst}\ t\ 0)$ in the postcondition formally states because $\mathsf{fst}\ t = inv$). However, the type of E_1 hides the existence of the local reference x which stores v. In fact, from the outside, there is no reason to believe that the local store of E_1 consists of only one location. We could imagine a similar program E_2 that maintains two different locations x and y, increases them at every call, and returns their mean. Such a program will have a different invariant $inv = \lambda v.\, x \mapsto_{\mathsf{nat}} v * y \mapsto_{\mathsf{nat}} v$ for its local store. However, because the type abstracts over the invariant, E_1 and E_2 would have the same type. The equal types hint that the two programs would be observationally equivalent, i.e. they could freely be interchanged in any context. We do not prove this property here, but it is intriguing future work, related to the recent result of Yoshida, Honda and Berger [31,4] on observational completeness of Hoare Logic.

In the next example, we consider an HTT equivalent of the following SML program $\lambda f{:}(\mathsf{unit}\to\mathsf{unit})\to\mathsf{unit}.\ \mathsf{let\ val}\ x = \mathsf{ref}\ 0\ \mathsf{val}\ g = \lambda y.\, x := !x + 1; ()\ \mathsf{in}\ f\ g$. The HTT specification should bring out the property that the argument function f can only access the local reference x by invoking g. Part of the problem is similar to that with E; the local state of g must be abstracted in order to make the dependence on x invisible to f. However, this is not sufficient. Because we evaluate $f\ g$ at the end, we need to know how f uses g, in order to describe the postcondition for the whole program. In other words, we also need to provide an invariant for f, *which is a higher-order predicate, because it depends on the invariant of* g.

One possible HTT implementation is as follows.

$$\begin{array}{rcl} F & = & \lambda f.\,\mathsf{do}\,(x \leftarrow \mathsf{alloc\ nat}\ 0; \\ & & \qquad g = (\lambda v.\, x \mapsto_{\mathsf{nat}} v, \mathsf{do}\,(z \Leftarrow !_{\mathsf{nat}}\, x; x :=_{\mathsf{nat}} z{+}1; \mathsf{return}\,(\,))); \\ & & \qquad \mathsf{eval}\,((\mathsf{snd}\ f)\ g)) \\ & : & \Pi f{:}\Sigma p{:}\mathsf{nat}{\rightarrow}(\mathsf{nat}{\rightarrow}\mathsf{heap}{\rightarrow}\mathsf{prop}){\rightarrow}\mathsf{heap}{\rightarrow}\mathsf{prop}. \\ & & \qquad \Pi g{:}\Sigma inv{:}\mathsf{nat}{\rightarrow}\mathsf{heap}{\rightarrow}\mathsf{prop}.\ v{:}\mathsf{nat}.\ \{inv\ v\}r{:}1\{inv\ (v+1)\}. \\ & & \qquad w{:}\mathsf{nat}.\ \{\mathsf{fst}\ g\ w\}s{:}1\{p\ w\ (\mathsf{fst}\ g)\}. \\ & & \qquad \{I\}t{:}1\{\lambda i.\, I * \lambda h.\, \exists x{:}\mathsf{nat}.\ (\mathsf{fst}\ f)\ 0\ (\lambda v.\, x \mapsto_{\mathsf{nat}} v)\ h\} \end{array}$$

In this program, f and g carry the invariants of their local states (e.g., $p = \mathsf{fst}\ f$ is the invariant of $\mathsf{snd}\ f$ and $inv = \mathsf{fst}\ g = \lambda v.\, x \mapsto_{\mathsf{nat}} v$ is the invariant of $\mathsf{snd}\ g$). The predicate p takes a natural number n and an argument inv, and returns a description of the state obtained after applying f to g in a state where $inv(n)$ holds. The postcondition for F describes the ending heap as $p\ 0\ inv$ thus revealing that initially the local reference x stores the value 0. The last two examples show that HTT can hide, but also reveal information about local state when needed.

4 Type System

The type system presented in this paper extends our previous work [22] with several features associated with the ECC [14]. The extensions include dependent sums and subset types, as well as the type prop of assertions, the type mono of small types, and the ability to compute with elements of both of these types. The additions introduce non-trivial changes in the equational reasoning of HTT. This involves the algorithms for computing canonical forms (a canonical form of an expression is its beta-reduced and eta-long version), as well as the corresponding proof of soundness. The type system of HTT consists of the following judgments: (1) $\Delta \vdash K \Rightarrow A\,[N']$ *infers* that K is an elim term of type A, and N' is its canonical form. A and N' are synthesized as outputs of the judgment. (2) $\Delta \vdash M \Leftarrow A\,[M']$ *checks* that M is an intro term of type A, and computes the canonical form M'. (3) $\Delta; P \vdash E \Rightarrow x{:}A.\,Q\,[E']$ *infers* that E is a computation with result $x{:}A$, precondition P, *strongest* postcondition Q, and canonical form E'. Q and E' are synthesized as outputs. (4) $\Delta; P \vdash E \Leftarrow x{:}A.\,Q\,[E']$ *checks* that E is a computation with result $x{:}A$, precondition P and postcondition (not necessarily strongest) Q. The canonical form E' is the output. (5) $\Delta \Longrightarrow P$ defines when the assertion P is true. It implements classical higher-order logic. (6) $\vdash \Delta\ \mathsf{ctx}\,[\Delta']$ states that Δ is a well-formed variable context, with canonical form Δ'. (7) $\Delta \vdash A \Leftarrow \mathsf{type}\,[A']$ states that A is a well-formed type, with canonical form A'. As can be noticed, the computation of canonical forms is hard-wired into the judgments, so that it becomes part of type checking. However, space precludes us from presenting the full details about canonical forms here. In the following text, we illustrate the typing rules of HTT, but we ignore the canonical forms and other aspects of equational reasoning (i.e., we omit from the judgments the information enclosed in [brackets]). The complete details can be found in the technical report [21].

The type system implements bidirectional typechecking [25,28], to automatically compute a significant portion of omitted types. A fragment of the rules is given in the figure below.

$$\frac{}{\Delta, x{:}A, \Delta_1 \vdash x \Rightarrow A}\,\mathsf{var} \qquad \frac{\Delta, x{:}A \vdash M \Leftarrow B}{\Delta \vdash \lambda x.\, M \Leftarrow \Pi x{:}A.\, B}\,\Pi\mathsf{I}$$

$$\frac{\Delta \vdash K \Rightarrow \Pi x{:}A.\, B \qquad \Delta \vdash M \Leftarrow A}{\Delta \vdash K\ M \Rightarrow [M/x]B}\,\Pi\mathsf{E} \qquad \frac{\Delta \vdash M \Leftarrow A \qquad \Delta \vdash N \Leftarrow [M/x]B}{\Delta \vdash (M, N) \Leftarrow \Sigma x{:}A.\, B}\,\Sigma\mathsf{I}$$

$$\frac{\Delta \vdash K \Rightarrow \Sigma x{:}A.\, B}{\Delta \vdash \mathsf{fst}\ K \Rightarrow A}\,\Sigma\mathsf{E1} \qquad \frac{\Delta \vdash K \Rightarrow \Sigma x{:}A.\, B}{\Delta \vdash \mathsf{snd}\ K \Rightarrow [\mathsf{fst}\ K/x]B}\,\Sigma\mathsf{E2}$$

$$\frac{\Delta \vdash M \Leftarrow A \qquad \Delta \Longrightarrow [M/x]P}{\Delta \vdash \mathsf{in}\ M \Leftarrow \{x{:}A.\, P\}}\,\{\}\mathsf{I} \qquad \frac{\Delta \vdash K \Rightarrow \{x{:}A.\, P\}}{\Delta \vdash \mathsf{out}\ K \Rightarrow A}\,\{\}\mathsf{E1}$$

$$\frac{\Delta \vdash K \Rightarrow \{x{:}A.\, P\}}{\Delta \Longrightarrow [\mathsf{out}\ K/x]P}\,\{\}\mathsf{E2} \qquad \frac{\Delta \vdash K \Rightarrow A \qquad A = B}{\Delta \vdash K \Leftarrow B}\,\Rightarrow\Leftarrow$$

$$\frac{\Delta \vdash A \Leftarrow \mathsf{type} \qquad \Delta \vdash M \Leftarrow A}{\Delta \vdash M : A \Rightarrow A}\,\Leftarrow\Rightarrow$$

In general, the typing rules for elim terms break down the type when read from premise to the conclusion. In the base case, the type of a variable can always be read off from the context, and therefore, elim terms can always synthesize their types. Dually, the typing rules for intro terms break down a type when read from the conclusion to the premise. If the conclusion type is given, the types for the premises can be computed and need not be provided.

When considering an elim term that happens to be intro (i.e. has the form $M{:}A$), the rule $\Leftarrow\Rightarrow$ synthesizes the type A, assuming that M checks against it. Conversely, when checking an intro term that happens to be be elim (i.e. has form K) against a type B, the rule $\Rightarrow\Leftarrow$ synthesizes the type A for K and explicitly compares if $A = B$. This comparison invokes the equational reasoning, which we do not explain here. It suffices to say that the equations used in this reasoning are derived from the usual alpha, beta and eta laws for pure functions and pairs, and the generic monadic laws [19] for the Hoare types (i.e., the unit laws and associativity).

We next describe the typing judgments for the impure fragment. The main intuition here is that a computation E may be seen as a heap transformer, because its execution turns the input heap into the output heap. The judgment $\Delta; P \vdash E \Rightarrow x{:}A.\, Q\,[E']$ essentially converts E into the equivalent binary relation on heaps, so that the assertion logic can reason about E using standard mathematical machinery for relations. The predicates $P, Q{:}\mathsf{heap}{\rightarrow}\mathsf{heap}{\rightarrow}\mathsf{prop}$ represent binary heap relations. P is the starting relation onto which the typing rules build as they convert E one command at a time. The generated strongest postcondition

Q is the relation that most precisely captures the semantics of E. The judgment $\Delta; P \vdash E \Leftarrow x{:}A.\, Q\,[E']$ checks if Q is a postcondition for E, by generating the strongest postcondition S and then trying to prove the implication $S \Longrightarrow Q$ in the assertion logic.

Given $P, Q, S{:}\mathsf{heap}{\to}\mathsf{heap}{\to}\mathsf{prop}$, and $R, R_1, R_2{:}\mathsf{heap}{\to}\mathsf{prop}$ we define the following predicates of type $\mathsf{heap}{\to}\mathsf{heap}{\to}\mathsf{prop}$.

$$\begin{array}{lcl} P \circ Q & = & \lambda i.\, \lambda m.\, \exists h{:}\mathsf{heap}.\, (P\ i\ h) \wedge (Q\ h\ m) \\ R_1 \multimap R_2 & = & \lambda i.\, \lambda m.\, \forall h{:}\mathsf{heap}.\, (R_1 * \lambda h'.\, h' = h)\ (i) \supset (R_2 * \lambda h'.\, h' = h)\ (m) \\ R \gg Q & = & \lambda i.\, \lambda m.\, \forall h{:}\mathsf{heap}.\, (\lambda h'.\, R(h') \wedge h = h') \multimap Q(h) \end{array}$$

$P \circ Q$ is standard relational composition. $R_1 \multimap R_2$ is the relation that selects a fragment R_1 from the input heap, and *replaces* it with some fragment R_2 in the output heap. We will use this relation to describe the action of memory update, where the old value stored into the memory must be replaced with the new value. The relation $R \gg Q$ selects a fragment R of the input heap, and then behaves like Q on that fragment. This captures precisely the semantics of the "most general" computation of Hoare type $\{R\}x{:}A\{Q\}$, in the small footprint semantics, leading to the following typing rules.

$$\frac{\Delta; \lambda i.\, \lambda m.\, i = m \wedge (R * \lambda h'.\, \top)(m) \vdash E \Leftarrow x{:}A.\, (R \gg Q)}{\Delta \vdash \mathsf{do}\, E \Leftarrow \{R\}x{:}A\{Q\}}$$

$$\frac{\Delta \vdash K \Rightarrow \{R\}x{:}A\{S\} \qquad \Delta, i{:}\mathsf{heap}, m{:}\mathsf{heap}, (P\ i\ m) \Longrightarrow (R * \lambda h'.\, \top)(m) \qquad \Delta, x{:}A; P \circ (R \gg S) \vdash E \Rightarrow y{:}B.\, Q}{\Delta; P \vdash x \leftarrow K; E \Rightarrow y{:}B.\, (\lambda i.\, \lambda m.\, \exists x{:}A.\, (Q\ i\ m))}$$

To check if $\mathsf{do}\, E$ has type $\{R\}x{:}A\{Q\}$, we verify that E has a postcondition $R \gg Q$. The checking is initialized with a relation stating that the initial heap $i = m$ contains a sub-fragment satisfying R (c.f., the conjunct $(R * \lambda h'.\, \top)(m)$).

To check $x \leftarrow K; E$, where K has type $\{R\}x{:}A\{S\}$, we must first prove that the beginning heap contains a sub-fragment satisfying R so that K can be executed at all (c.f. $(P\ i\ m) \Longrightarrow (R * \lambda h'.\, \top)(m)$). The strongest postcondition for K, is $P \circ (R \gg S)$, which is taken as the precondition for checking E.

$$\frac{\Delta \vdash M \Leftarrow A}{\Delta; P \vdash \mathsf{return}\, M \Rightarrow x{:}A.\, (\lambda i.\, \lambda m.\, (P\ i\ m) \wedge x =_A M)}$$

$$\frac{\Delta \vdash \tau \Leftarrow \mathsf{mono} \qquad \Delta \vdash M \Leftarrow \mathsf{nat} \qquad \Delta, i{:}\mathsf{heap}, m{:}\mathsf{heap}, (P\ i\ m) \Longrightarrow (M \hookrightarrow_\tau -)(m) \qquad \Delta, x{:}\tau; \lambda i.\, \lambda m.\, (P\ i\ m) \wedge (M \hookrightarrow_\tau x)(m) \vdash E \Rightarrow y{:}B.\, Q}{\Delta; P \vdash x \Leftarrow\, !_\tau\, M; E \Rightarrow y{:}B.\, (\lambda i.\, \lambda m.\, \exists x{:}\tau.\, (Q\ i\ m))}$$

$$\frac{\Delta \vdash \tau \Leftarrow \mathsf{mono} \qquad \Delta \vdash M \Leftarrow \mathsf{nat} \qquad \Delta \vdash N \Leftarrow \tau \qquad \Delta, i{:}\mathsf{heap}, m{:}\mathsf{heap}, (P\ i\ m) \Longrightarrow (M \hookrightarrow -)(m) \qquad \Delta; P \circ ((M \mapsto -) \multimap (M \mapsto_\tau N)) \vdash E \Rightarrow y{:}B.\, Q}{\Delta; P \vdash M :=_\tau N; E \Rightarrow y{:}B.\, Q}$$

The postcondition for the trivial, pure, computation $\mathsf{return}\, M$ includes the precondition (as M does not change the heap) but must also state that M is the return value. Before the lookup $x = !_\tau\, M$, we must prove that M points to a value of type τ at the beginning (c.f., $(P\ i\ m) \Longrightarrow (M \hookrightarrow_\tau -)(m)$). After the lookup, the heap looks exactly as before $(P\ i\ m)$ but we also know that x equals the content of M, that is, $(M \hookrightarrow_\tau x)(m)$. Before the update $M :=_\tau N$, we must prove that M is allocated and initialized with some value *with an arbitrary type* (i.e., $(M \hookrightarrow -)(m)$). After the lookup, the old value is removed from the heap, and replaced with N, that is $(P \circ ((M \mapsto -) \multimap (M \mapsto_\tau N)))$.

Finally, we briefly illustrate the judgment $\Delta \Longrightarrow P$, which defines the assertion logic of HTT in the style of natural deduction. The assertion logic contains the rules for introduction and elimination of implication and the universal quantifier, and the rest of the propositional constructs are formalized using axiom schemas that encode the standard introduction and elimination rules. We present here the axioms for conjunction and heterogeneous equality.

$$\begin{array}{llll} \mathsf{andi} & : \forall p, q{:}\mathsf{prop}.\, p \supset q \supset p \wedge q & \mathsf{ande} & : \forall p, q, r{:}\mathsf{prop}.\, p \wedge q \supset (p \supset q \supset r) \supset r \\ \mathsf{xidi}_A & : \forall x{:}A.\, \mathsf{xid}_{A,A}(x, x) & \mathsf{xide}_A & : \forall p{:}A {\to} \mathsf{prop}.\, \forall x, y{:}A.\, \mathsf{xid}_{A,A}(x, y) \supset p\ x \supset p\ y \end{array}$$

For each index type A, the axiom xidi_A asserts the reflexivity of the equality relation, and the axiom xide_A asserts that equal values are not distinguishable by any arbitrary propositional contexts. The logic includes axioms for extensionality of functions and pairs, Peano arithmetic, booleans and excluded middle.

We conclude this section with an informal description of the main theoretical result of the paper, which relates typechecking with evaluation.

Theorem 1 (Soundness). *The type system of HTT is sound, in the following sense: if $\Delta; P \vdash E \Leftarrow x{:}A.\, Q\, [E']$, and E terminates when evaluated in a heap i satisfying $P\ i\ i$, then the resulting heap m satisfies $Q\ i\ m$.*

Obviously, to establish this theorem, we must first define formally the operational semantics for HTT. Then the theorem follows from the Preservation and Progress lemmas, which take the customary form, but are much harder to prove than in the usual simply-typed setting. For example, Preservation must establish not only that evaluation preserves types, but also postconditions of effectful computations, as well as the canonical forms of pure terms. On the other hand, the Progress lemma first requires showing that the assertion logic of HTT is sound. This assertion logic is a higher-order logic over heaps, and its soundness basically implies that our axiomatization indeed correctly captures the properties of the real heaps encountered during evaluation. In particular, if we have proved that a certain location exists at a given program point, then when that program point is reached, we can safely take an operational step and dereference the location. We establish the soundness of the assertion logic, by developing a crude set-theoretic model based on the standard approach to modeling ECC. The interested reader is referred to the accompanying technical report [21] for full details of the proofs.

5 Conclusions and Related Work

In this paper we present an extension of our Hoare Type Theory (HTT) [22], with higher-order predicates, and allow quantification over abstract predicates at the level of terms, types and assertions. This significantly increases the power of the system to encompass definition of inductive predicates, abstraction of program invariants, and even first-class modules that can contain not only types and terms, but also axioms over types and terms. The novel application of this type system is to express sharing of local state between functions and/or datatypes, and transfer of state ownership between datatypes and the memory manager.

We have already discussed related work on program logics for higher-order, effectful programs in Section 1, as well as work on verification tools and languages (e.g., Spec#, ESC/Java, JML, and so on) aimed at integrating Hoare-like reasoning with type checking. The work on dependently typed systems with stateful features, has mostly focused on how to appropriately restrict the language so that effects do not pollute the types. Such systems have mostly employed singleton types to enforce purity. Examples include Dependent ML by Xi and Pfenning [30], Applied Type Systems by Xi et al. [29,32], a type system for certified binaries by Shao et al. [27], and the theory of refinements by Mandelbaum et al. [15]. HTT differs from all these approaches, because types are allowed to depend on monadically encapsulated effectful computations.

We mention that HTT may be obtained by adding effects and the Hoare type to the Extended Calculus of Constructions (ECC) [14]. There are some differences between ECC and the pure fragment of HTT, but they are largely inessential. For example, HTT uses classical assertion logic, whereas ECC is intuitionistic, but consistent with classical extensions. The latter has been demonstrated in Coq [16] which implements and subsumes ECC. Also, HTT contains only two type universes (small and large types), while ECC is more general, and contains the whole infinite tower. However, we expect that it should be simple to extend HTT to the full tower of universes.

Finally, we mention here the representative work of Ni and Shao [23] and Filliâtre [10] who implement Hoare-style reasoning in Coq. Ni and Shao use Coq to verify properties of assembly code, while Filliâtre exploits Coq tactics and decision procedures to partially automate the verification of imperative programs. We note that these two approaches are fundamentally different from ours, as they impose an additional level of indirection. Where they use type theory to axiomatize Hoare-style reasoning, we integrate Hoare logic within the type system of the underlying language, so that specifications become an integral part of programming.

References

1. M. Barnett, K. R. M. Leino, and W. Schulte. The Spec# programming system: An overview. In *CASSIS 2004*. LNCS. Springer, 2004.
2. M. Barnett and D. Naumann. Friends need a bit more: Maintaining invariants over shared state. In *Mathematics of Program Construction*, LNCS 3125, 2004.
3. N. Benton. Abstracting Allocation: The New new Thing. In CSL'06.
4. M. Berger, K. Honda, and N. Yoshida. A logical analysis of aliasing in imperative higher-order functions. In ICFP'05, pages 280–293.
5. B. Biering, L. Birkedal, and N. Torp-Smith. BI hyperdoctrines, Higher-Order Separation Logic, and Abstraction. ITU-TR-2005-69, IT University, Copenhagen.

6. L. Burdy, Y. Cheon, D. Cok, M. Ernst, J. Kiniry, G. T. Leavens, K. R. M. Leino, and E. Poll. An overview of JML tools and applications. *International Journal on Software Tools for Technology Transfer*, 7(3):212–232, June 2005.
7. R. DeLine and M. Fahndrich. Enforcing high-level protocols in low-level software. In PLDI'01, pages 59–69, 2001.
8. D. L. Detlefs, K. R. M. Leino, G. Nelson, and J. B. Saxe. Extended static checking. Compaq Systems Research Center, Research Report 159, December 1998.
9. D. Evans and D. Larochelle. Improving security using extensible lightweight static analysis. *IEEE Software*, 19(1):42–51, 2002.
10. J.-C. Filliâtre. Verification of non-functional programs using interpretations in type theory. *Journal of Functional Programming*, 13(4):709–745, July 2003.
11. J. Harrison. Inductive definitions: automation and application. In *Higher Order Logic Theorem Proving and Its Applications*, LNCS 971, Springer, 1995.
12. T. Jim, G. Morrisett, D. Grossman, M. Hicks, J. Cheney, and Y. Wang. Cyclone: A safe dialect of C. *USENIX Annual Technical Conference*, 2002.
13. N. Krishnaswami. Separation logic for a higher-order typed language. SPACE'06.
14. Z. Luo. *An Extended Calculus of Constructions.* PhD thesis, U of Edinburgh, 1990.
15. Y. Mandelbaum, D. Walker, and R. Harper. An effective theory of type refinements. In ICFP'03, pages 213–226.
16. The Coq development team. *The Coq proof assistant reference manual.* LogiCal Project, 2004. Version 8.0.
17. C. McBride. *Dependently Typed Functional Programs and their Proofs.* PhD thesis, University of Edinburgh, 1999.
18. J. C. Mitchell. *Foundations for Programming Languages.* MIT Press, 1996.
19. E. Moggi. Notions of computation and monads. *Information and Computation*, 93(1):55–92, 1991.
20. G. Morrisett, D. Walker, K. Crary, and N. Glew. From System F to typed assembly language. *TOPLAS*, 21(3):527–568, 1999.
21. A. Nanevski, A. Ahmed, G. Morrisett, and L. Birkedal. Abstract predicates and mutable ADTs in Hoare Type Theory. TR-14-06, Harvard University. Available at `http://www.eecs.harvard.edu/~aleks/papers/hoarelogic/htthol.pdf`.
22. A. Nanevski, G. Morrisett, and L. Birkedal. Polymorphism and separation in Hoare Type Theory. In ICFP'06, pages 62–73.
23. Z. Ni and Z. Shao. Certified assembly programming with embedded code pointers. In POPL'06, pages 320–333.
24. P. W. O'Hearn, H. Yang, and J. C. Reynolds. Separation and information hiding. In POPL'04, pages 268–280.
25. B. C. Pierce and D. N. Turner. Local type inference. *TOPLAS*, 22(1):1–44, 2000.
26. J. C. Reynolds. Separation logic: A logic for shared mutable data structures. In LICS'02, pages 55–74.
27. Z. Shao, V. Trifonov, B. Saha, and N. Papaspyrou. A type system for certified binaries. *TOPLAS*, 27(1):1–45, January 2005.
28. K. Watkins, I. Cervesato, F. Pfenning, and D. Walker. A concurrent logical framework: The propositional fragment. LNCS 3085, Springer 2004.
29. H. Xi. Applied Type System (extended abstract). LNCS 3085, 2004.
30. H. Xi and F. Pfenning. Dependent types in practical programming. POPL'99.
31. N. Yoshida, K. Honda, and M. Berger. Logical reasoning for higher-order functions with local state. Personal communication, August 2006.
32. D. Zhu and H. Xi. Safe programming with pointers through stateful views. In PADL'05, pages 83–97.

Structure of a Proof-Producing Compiler for a Subset of Higher Order Logic

Guodong Li, Scott Owens, and Konrad Slind

School of Computing, University of Utah

Abstract. We give an overview of a proof-producing compiler which translates recursion equations, defined in higher order logic, to assembly language. The compiler is implemented and validated with a mix of translation validation and compiler verification techniques. Both the design of the compiler and its mechanical verification are implemented in the same logic framework.

1 Introduction

Most compilers are used to compile programs. However, it also makes sense to execute logic [1], and thus to compile logic. This is the basis for logic programming, where search for solutions to problems phrased as logic formulas is the dominant paradigm [12]. In this paper we address another—hitherto unexploited—opportunity for logic compilation; namely, the term language that dwells within higher order logic [16,17]. This language comprises, roughly speaking, ML-style pure terminating functional programs, *i.e.*, those (computable) functions that can be expressed by well-founded recursion in higher order logic [21]. Features like type inference, polymorphism, and pattern matching make this subset a comfortable setting in which to program. Although this language does not contain all computable functions, it does express a very wide range of algorithms and, of course, the logic provides a setting for correctness proofs of such programs.

Compilation techniques developed for functional programming may be applied to translate these programs to machine code. However, since we are in a formal setting, it is natural to ask for more, namely the formal correctness of compilation. There are two main approaches to achieving this high level of assurance: compiler verification and translation validation. Compiler verification proceeds by formally specifying, in the object logic, the source and target languages, along with the compilation algorithm. Then the correctness of the compiler is proven once and forall: a single object logic theorem establishes that all successful runs of the compiler generate correct code. In contrast, translation validation [18] does a per-run correctness proof. Its main advantage is that only the results of compilation steps need to be verified, which can at times be far simpler than verifying the algorithms performing the compilation.

We have built a proof-producing compiler for a simple subset of higher order logic terms in the HOL-4 proof system [17]. The compiler is mainly based on translation validation, but compiler verification techniques such as those found in

R. De Nicola (Ed.): ESOP 2007, LNCS 4421, pp. 205–219, 2007.

[9,11,14] are also used. A run of the compiler returns an (automatically proved) theorem expressing the correctness of the compilation run; from this theorem the generated code, for an ARM-like machine, can be directly read-off.

The task of compiling the term language of a logic using the logic itself poses a couple of novel challenges: first, the source language is not visible in the logic; second, there is no notion of evaluation for the logic. Source functions have a set-theoretic semantics which has to be reconciled with the operational semantics of the target machine.

In the remainder of the paper, we give an overview of the structure of the compiler, and summarize our experiences to date.[1]

2 Overview

One immediate advantage of taking logic terms as the source language is that many front end tasks are already provided by the HOL-4 system: lexical analysis, parsing, type inference, overloading resolution, function definition, and termination proof (needed to admit recursive functions, since HOL is a logic of total functions). The result of all this activity is a valid HOL function definition, embodied in a possibly recursive equation. From this starting point, a sequence of proof-based transformations pass through intermediate languages, ending in assembly. We will describe four intermediate languages: *HOL-* (HOL Minor), *ANF/ACF* (Administrative Normal Form / A Combinator Form), *HSL* (Heap and Stack Level), and *CFL* (Control Flow Level). HOL-, ANF and ACF programs are simply HOL functions, with no attached operational semantics. It is this feature that enables us to use standard mathematics to prove properties of HOL- and ANF programs directly in HOL. HSL and CFL, on the other hand, are imperative languages represented with syntax trees and operational semantics.

The translation from a source function to HOL- is performed and validated in the front-end in an *ad hoc* manner; in fact there may be multiple source languages that target HOL-. The translation from HOL- to ANF/ACF is mainly expressed as a collection of verified rewrite rules. Currently, the translation from HOL- to ANF/ACF includes performing closure conversion, CPS conversion, and register allocation in that order. ANF is used for the compilation to HSL, while ACF is for the validation of such compilation. ACF is obtained from ANF through verified rewriting. The result is a theorem equating the original function with the ACF translation of its body.

An ANF-format program is converted (not by proof) to a corresponding HSL program, which is in turn converted to its CFL by laying out the heap and the stacks. Finally, the CFL is translated to ARM-like object code by linearizing the control-flow structures. Roughly speaking, the path from HOL- to HSL proceeds by translation validation, while the other steps rely on compiler verification techniques.

[1] Source code along with examples is included in the '`examples/dev/sw`' directory in the HOL-4 distribution (`http://hol.sourceforge.net`).

Since we do not have an evaluation semantics for HOL- or ACF, widely-used techniques for proving semantics preservation for the translation, *e.g.*, simulation arguments based on rule-induction over the evaluation relation, are not applied to validate the translation from ACF to HSL. Instead, we derive a collection of Hoare rules from the operational semantics of HSL and show that this semantics agrees with the ACF level function by bottom-up reasoning. Thus, for an ACF function g with inputs $\boldsymbol{i}$ and outputs $\boldsymbol{o}$, and the HSL program S_{hsl} obtained from g, the following statement must be proved (where $\sigma[[v]]$ reads the value of variable v from state σ):

$$\vdash_{thm} \forall \sigma_{\text{hsl}}.\ (\mathsf{run}_{\text{hsl}}\ S_{hsl}\ \sigma_{\text{hsl}})\ [[\boldsymbol{o}]] = g\ (\sigma_{\text{hsl}}\ [[\boldsymbol{i}]])$$

HSL states are defined over virtual registers, heap variables and stack variables, while CFL states range over machine registers and machine memory locations. The correctness of the translation from HSL to CFL is phrased by relating the states of these two languages by a relation $\backsimeq$. The correctness statement asserts that the execution of a HSL statement S_{hsl} has the same effect on a HSL state as the execution of its corresponding CFL statement S_{cfl}:

$$\vdash_{def} (\sigma_{\text{hsl}} \backsimeq \sigma_{\text{cfl}}) \doteq (\forall v \in \sigma_{\text{hsl}}.\sigma_{\text{hsl}}[[v]] = \sigma_{\text{cfl}}[[v']]) \text{ where } v' \text{ is } v\text{'s injection into } \sigma_{\text{cfl}}$$
$$\vdash_{thm} \sigma_{\text{hsl}} \backsimeq \sigma_{\text{cfl}} \Rightarrow (\mathsf{run}_{\text{hsl}}\ S_{\text{hsl}}\ \sigma_{\text{hsl}} \backsimeq \mathsf{run}_{\text{cfl}}\ S_{\text{cfl}}\ \sigma_{\text{cfl}})$$

The runtime state σ_{arm} for the machine is a tuple of a program counter (pc), a process status register ($cpsr$), physical registers and physical memory (ω). If a CFL program S_{cfl} is correctly translated to an ARM program S_{arm}, then the execution of S_{cfl} and S_{arm} should result in the same status of registers and memory, thus any property proved at the CFL level can be pushed down to the ARM level:

$$\vdash_{thm} \mathsf{run}_{\text{cfl}}\ S_{\text{cfl}}\ \sigma_{\text{cfl}} = (\mathsf{run}_{\text{arm}}\ S_{\text{arm}}\ (pc, pcsr, \sigma_{\text{cfl}})).\omega$$

Collecting all correctness statements together gives the validation proof for the translation from HOL- to ARM: for a HOL- function g with inputs $\boldsymbol{i}$ and outputs $\boldsymbol{o}$, and the final flat code S_{arm} obtained from g, in the state after the execution of S_{arm}, the values left in outputs $\boldsymbol{o}$ are equal to applying the function g to the initial values of inputs $\boldsymbol{i}$ in σ_{arm}

$$\vdash_{thm} \forall \sigma_{\text{arm}}.(\mathsf{run}_{\text{arm}}\ S_{\text{arm}}\ \sigma_{\text{arm}})[[\boldsymbol{o}]] = g\ (\sigma_{\text{arm}}[[\boldsymbol{i}]])$$

3 Language Syntax and Semantics

In Figures 1-3 we give the syntax of the intermediate languages. HOL- is a simple polymorphically-typed functional language handling tail-recursive equations where variables range over tuples of elements from types that can be directly represented in machine words for the ARM, *e.g.*, booleans and 32-bit words. 'Let'-binding, λ expression and function call are also supported.

ANF is obtained from HOL- by performing closure conversion to eliminate higher order functions, and a CPS (continuation-passing style) transformation so that all expressions are flattened and the control flow is pinned down into a sequence of elementary steps. Register allocation is performed on a data structure obtained by analyzing the ANF program. This ANF program is also rewritten to its ACF form that is a 'constructor'-like semantic function.

$op_b ::= + \mid - \mid * \mid \ggg \mid \gg \mid \gtrdot \mid \ll \mid \& \mid \shortmid \mid \#$	arithmetic / bitwise operator
$op_r ::= = \mid \neq \mid < \mid > \mid \leq \mid \geq$	relational operator
$op_l ::= \wedge \mid \vee \mid \neg$	logic operator
$e ::= w \mid v$	word and variable identifier
$\mid \overrightarrow{e}$	tuple, i.e.$(\ldots, e, \ldots)$
$\mid e\ op_b\ e \mid e\ op_r\ e \mid e\ op_l\ e$	binary operation
$\mid \lambda v.\, e$	anonymous function
$\mid \mathsf{if}\ e\ \mathsf{then}\ e\ \mathsf{else}\ e$	conditional
$\mid \mathsf{let}\ \overrightarrow{v}\ = e\ \mathsf{in}\ e$	let definition
$\mid e\ e$	application
$\mid f$	named function
$f ::= f_{id}\ \overrightarrow{v} = e$	function definition

$x ::= w \mid v$	word and variable identifier
$e ::= \overrightarrow{x}$	tuple
$\mid (\mathsf{op}\ op_b)\ x\ x \mid (\mathsf{op}\ op_r)\ x\ x$	binary operation
$\mid \mathsf{if}\ v\ \mathsf{then}\ e\ \mathsf{else}\ e$	conditional on single variable
$\mid \mathsf{let}\ v\ = e\ \mathsf{in}\ e$	let assignment to single variable
$\mid \mathsf{let}\ \overrightarrow{v}\ = f\ e\ \mathsf{in}\ e$	function call
$f ::= f_{id}\ \overrightarrow{v} = e$	function definition

$x, f ::=$ similar to x, f in ANF	
$y ::= \overrightarrow{x} \mid y\ op_b\ y$	data processing operation
$z ::= \lambda \overrightarrow{v}.\, y \mid \lambda \overrightarrow{v}.f\ \overrightarrow{x}$	data processing function
$c ::= \lambda \overrightarrow{v}.\, (x, op_r, x)$	conditional function
$e ::= z \mid \mathsf{sc}\ e\ e \mid \mathsf{cj}\ c\ e\ e \mid \mathsf{tr}\ c\ e\ e$	compositional function

Fig. 1. Syntax of HOL- (top), ANF (middle) and ACF (bottom)

As mentioned, HOL-, ANF, and ACF programs are mathematical functions with no associated evaluation semantics. They can be understood as λ expressions, and the order of reductions is not specified on them.

HSL is a simple imperative language that supports various structured control statements including blocks (BLK), sequential composition (SC), conditionals (CJ) and tail recursion (TR), plus an important structure for function call—FC. Variables are divided into register variables, heap (global) variables, and stack (local) variables. A BLK structure is just a list of atomic instructions. An FC structure consists of an argument passing pair (the first component is for the caller, the second component for is the callee), a body statement, and a result passing pair. Heap variables are not allowed in parameters or results since their values are not transferred through the stack. A HSL program will never contain any comparison or jump instructions. Variables are divided into register variables, heap variables and stack variables. Variables in ANF format have been mapped to either register, heap or stack variables by register allocation and inter-procedural analysis. In our current implementation, heap (global) variables are replaced with stack variables during closure conversion, thus actually no heap variable appears in the HSL.

CFL explicitly lays outs the heap and stacks for function calls. It specifies machine registers and memory locations for the variables in HSL. A function call in HSL is implemented by dividing the processing into three phases: pre-call processing, function body execution and post-call processing. Pointer registers `hp` (heap pointer), `fp` (frame pointer), `ip` (intra-procedure register pointer), `sp` (stack pointer) and `lr` (link register) are used to control the layout of the heap and stack frames for functions. CFL works over machine registers and memory, thus a (one-to-one) mapping from HSL variables to them is required.

The translation from CFL to the object code simply performs the linearization of control-flow structures. The format of an ARM instruction is: $op\{cond\}\ d_1\ d_2$. The *cond* field controls conditional execution of the instruction, it is omitted for unconditional execution; d_1 and d_2 are the destination operand and source operands respectively.

op^b	$::= add \mid sub \mid mul \mid ror \mid lsr \mid asr \mid$	
	$\mid lsl \mid and \mid orr \mid eor \mid rsb \mid mla, \ldots$	arithmetic and bitwise operators
r	$::= r_0 \mid r_1 \mid \ldots \mid r_8$	register variable
v	$::= r \mid sk[.]$	register and stack variable
y	$::= w \mid r$	word constant and register
x	$::= w \mid v$	constant and variable
$inst$	$::= \mathsf{op}^b\ r\ y\ y$	arithmetic and bitwise operation
	$\mid ldr\ r\ (hp[i] \mid sk[.]) \mid str\ (hp[i] \mid sk[.])\ r$	access to heap and stack
s	$::= \mathsf{BLK}\ \widetilde{inst}$	basic block containing an instr. list
	$\mid \mathsf{CJ}\ (x, op_r, x)\ s\ s$	conditional jump
	$\mid \mathsf{TR}\ (x, op_r, x)\ s$	tail recursion (loop)
	$\mid \mathsf{FC}\ (\widetilde{x}, \widetilde{v})\ s\ (\widetilde{v}, \widetilde{x})$	function call
p	$::= (\overrightarrow{v}, s, \overrightarrow{x})$	programs

r_d	$::= \mathsf{HSL}.r$	data register
r_b	$::= hp \mid fp \mid ip \mid sp \mid lr$	base (pointer) register
r	$::= r_d \mid r_b$	register
m	$::= m[r_b, +i] \mid m[r_b, -i]$	memory location
v, y, x, p	$::=$ similar to v, y, x, p in HSL	
$inst$	$::= \mathsf{op}^b\ r\ y\ y \mid ldr\ r\ m \mid str\ m\ r \mid push\ \widetilde{r} \mid pop\ \widetilde{r}$	single instruction
s	$::= \mathsf{BLK}\ \widetilde{inst} \mid \mathsf{CJ}\ (x, op_r, x)\ s\ s \mid \mathsf{TR}\ (x, op_r, x)\ s$	control flow structures

$$\frac{}{\mathsf{BLK}\ [\,] \vdash \sigma \rightarrowtail \sigma} \qquad \frac{\texttt{eval\_inst}\ inst\ \sigma = \sigma_1 \quad \mathsf{BLK}\ instL \vdash \sigma_1 \rightarrowtail \sigma_2}{\mathsf{BLK}\ (inst::instL) \vdash \sigma \rightarrowtail \sigma_2}$$

$$\frac{S_1 \vdash \sigma \rightarrowtail \sigma_1 \quad S_2 \vdash \sigma_1 \rightarrowtail \sigma_2}{\mathsf{SC}\ S_1\ S_2 \vdash \sigma \rightarrowtail \sigma_2} \qquad \frac{S_1 \vdash \sigma \rightarrowtail \sigma_1 \quad \texttt{is\_true (eval\_cond}\ cond\ \sigma\texttt{)}}{\mathsf{CJ}\ cond\ S_1\ S_2 \vdash \sigma \rightarrowtail \sigma_1}$$

$$\frac{S_2 \vdash \sigma \rightarrowtail \sigma_1 \quad \texttt{is\_false (eval\_cond}\ cond\ \sigma\texttt{)}}{\mathsf{CJ}\ cond\ S_1\ S_2 \vdash \sigma \rightarrowtail \sigma_1} \qquad \frac{\texttt{is\_true (eval\_cond}\ cond\ \sigma\texttt{)}}{\mathsf{TR}\ cond\ S \vdash \sigma \rightarrowtail \sigma}$$

$$\frac{S \vdash \sigma \rightarrowtail \sigma_1 \quad \texttt{is\_false(eval\_cond}\ cond\ \sigma\texttt{)} \quad \mathsf{TR}\ cond\ S \vdash \sigma_1 \rightarrowtail \sigma_2}{\mathsf{TR}\ cond\ S \vdash \sigma \rightarrowtail \sigma_2}$$

$$\frac{\texttt{copy}\ (\sigma_\epsilon,\sigma)\ (callee.\boldsymbol{i},caller.\boldsymbol{i}) = \sigma_1 \quad S \vdash \sigma_1 \rightarrowtail \sigma_2 \quad \texttt{copy}\ (\sigma,\sigma_2)\ (caller.o,callee.i) = \sigma_3}{\mathsf{FC}\ (caller.\boldsymbol{i},callee.\boldsymbol{i})\ S\ (caller.\boldsymbol{o},callee.\boldsymbol{o}) \vdash \sigma \rightarrowtail \sigma_3}$$

Fig. 2. Syntax for HSL (top) and CFL (middle), and evaluation rules (bottom) (Note: FC structures only appear in HSL)

In our machine model, the data memory is separated from instruction memory (also known as the *instruction buffer*, which is modeled as a function mapping an address to an instruction). At each step the instruction pointed to by the *pc* is executed. A program is executed until the first position beyond the code area is reached.

r	$::=$	$\mathsf{CFL}.r \mid pc$	machine register
m, v, y, x	$::=$	similar to m, v, y, x in CFL	
$inst$	$::=$	$b\{op_r\} + k \mid b\{op_r\} - k$	branch instruction
		$\mid \texttt{cmp}\ y\ y \mid \texttt{tst}\ y\ y$	comparison instruction
		$\mid \mathsf{CFL}.inst$	operation instruction
p	$::=$	$(\overrightarrow{v}, \widetilde{inst}, \overrightarrow{x})$	programs

$$\frac{\texttt{eval\_op}\ (op\ y\ \boldsymbol{x})\ \omega = \omega_1}{op\ y\ \boldsymbol{x} \vdash (pc, cpsr, \omega) \rightarrowtail (pc+1, cpsr, \omega_1)} \qquad \frac{\texttt{update\_cpsr}\ cpsr\ d_1\ d_2 = cpsr_1}{cmp\ d_1\ d_2 \vdash (pc, cpsr, \omega) \rightarrowtail (pc+1, cpsr_1, \omega)}$$

$$\frac{\texttt{is\_true}\ (\texttt{eval\_cpsr}\ cpsr\ rop)}{b\{rop\}\ (+/-)\ k \vdash (pc,\ cpsr,\ \omega) \rightarrowtail (pc\ (+/-)\ k,\ cpsr,\ \omega)}$$

$$\frac{\texttt{is\_false}\ (\texttt{eval\_cpsr}\ cpsr\ rop)}{b\{rop\}\ (+/-)\ k \vdash (pc,\ cpsr,\ \omega) \rightarrowtail (pc + 1,\ cpsr,\ \omega)}$$

Fig. 3. Syntax and evaluation rules of the machine language

Since expressions in HOL-, ANF and ACF are simply HOL functions, no explicit definitions for either the syntax or the semantics of them are required. In contrast, the abstract syntax for HSL and CFL is presented as inductive data types, and the operational semantics of them are defined over these data types (note that in our definition the body of a TR structure keeps running when the condition does not hold).

4 Translation and Verification

In this section we discuss the stages of compilation, focusing on how the proofs are organized.

4.1 From HOL- to ANF/ACF

Various well-known source-to-source translations are employed at this level: the input is first transformed to a first order function, then to ANF by performing a CPS transformation. And then a standard graph-colouring register allocation phase is invoked to produce a data structure for generating HSL programs. Finally, ANF is rewritten to ACF, an equivalent combinatory format.

Closure Conversion. Higher order and local functions in HOL- are eliminated by closure conversion, where the free variables for local functions are captured in an environment as passed to the function as an extra argument.

Combinator format. Although we do not have syntax trees for functions at this level, we can define and use 'constructor'-like semantic functions, and use them to implement translation steps. The recursion equation is translated to an equivalent combinatory format based on combinators for sequential composition (Seq), parallel composition (Par), conditionals (Ite), and tail-recursion (Rec). Note that the Seq and Par combinators are sufficient to express `let`-expressions.

$$
\begin{array}{ll}
\vdash_{def} \mathsf{Seq}\ f_1\ f_2 \doteq \lambda x. f_2(f_1\ x) & \vdash_{def} \mathsf{Par}\ f_1\ f_2 \doteq \lambda x.(f_1\ x, f_2\ x) \\
\vdash_{def} \mathsf{Ite}\ f_1\ f_2\ f_3 & \doteq \lambda x.\mathsf{if}\ f_1\ x\ \mathsf{then}\ f_2\ x\ \mathsf{else}\ f_3\ x \\
\vdash_{def} \mathsf{Rec}\ f_1\ f_2\ f_3 & \doteq \lambda x.\mathsf{if}\ f_1\ x\ \mathsf{then}\ f_2\ x\ \mathsf{else}\ \mathsf{Rec}\ (f_3\ x) \\
\vdash_{thm} (\lambda x.\mathsf{let}\ v = f_1(x)\ \mathsf{in}\ f_2(x,v)) & \doteq \mathsf{Seq}\ (\mathsf{Par}(\lambda x.x)\ f_1)\ f_2
\end{array}
$$

CPS Conversion. Once the program is in combinator format, a CPS translation is applied. CPS is defined semantically: $\mathsf{CPS}\ f \doteq \lambda k\ x. k\ (f\ x)$ specifies the CPS interface to a function. From this definition, it is easy to prove the theorem relating ordinary function application to CPS function application: $\vdash \forall f\ x. f\ x = (\mathsf{CPS}\ f)\ (\lambda x.x)\ x$. The CPS transformation phase repeatedly rewrites with the following theorems to push the CPS function down through the combinators:

$$
\begin{array}{ll}
\vdash_{thm} \mathsf{CPS}\ (\mathsf{Seq}\ f_1\ f_2) & = \mathsf{CPS\_SEQ}\ (\mathsf{CPS}\ f_1)\ (\mathsf{CPS}\ f_2) \\
\vdash_{thm} \mathsf{CPS}\ (\mathsf{Par}\ f_1\ f_2) & = \mathsf{CPS\_PAR}\ (\mathsf{CPS}\ f_1)\ (\mathsf{CPS}\ f_2) \\
\vdash_{thm} \mathsf{CPS}\ (\mathsf{Ite}\ e\ f_1\ f_2) & = \mathsf{CPS\_ITE}\ (\mathsf{CPS}\ e)\ (\mathsf{CPS}\ f_1)\ (\mathsf{CPS}\ f_2) \\
\vdash_{thm} \mathsf{CPS}\ (\mathsf{Rec}\ e\ f_1\ f_2) & = \mathsf{CPS\_REC}\ (\mathsf{CPS}\ e)\ (\mathsf{CPS}\ f_1)\ (\mathsf{CPS}\ f_2)
\end{array}
$$

where

$$
\begin{array}{ll}
\vdash_{def} \mathsf{CPS\_SEQ}\ f_1\ f_2 & \doteq \lambda k\ x.f_1\ (\lambda r.f_2\ k\ r)\ x \\
\vdash_{def} \mathsf{CPS\_PAR}\ f_1\ f_2 & \doteq \lambda k\ x.f_1\ (\lambda r_2.f_2\ (\lambda r_1.k\ (r_2, r_1))\ x)\ x \\
\vdash_{def} \mathsf{CPS\_ITE}\ e\ f_1\ f_2 & \doteq \lambda k\ x.e\ (\lambda r.\mathsf{let}\ k_1 = k\ \mathsf{in}\ \mathsf{if}\ r\ \mathsf{then}\ f_1\ k_1\ x\ \mathsf{else}\ f_2\ k_1\ x)\ x \\
\vdash_{def} \mathsf{CPS\_REC}\ e\ f_1\ f_2 & \doteq \lambda k\ x.k\ (\mathsf{Rec}\ (e\ (\lambda x.x))\ (f_1\ (\lambda x.x))\ (f_2\ (\lambda x.x))\ x)
\end{array}
$$

Then the CPS interface from the expression is removed by rewriting with the theorem $\vdash \mathsf{CPS}\ f\ k = \lambda x.\,\mathsf{let}\ z = f\ x\ \mathsf{in}\ k\ z$ to obtain a readable, let-based A-normal form. There is also a pass to remove all the β-redexes introduced in the CPS translation. The quality of the ANF expression is improved by removing as many tuples as possible, and by removing redundant let expressions that simply rename variables. All phases of transformations are term rewriting with theorems that establish equality for the input and result of each rewriting step.

Register Allocation. This phase converts the ANF form to a data structure suitable for performing register allocation. Interestingly, the graph colouring register allocation algorithm does not have to be verified; instead, the computed colouring can be taken and used to build a term incorporating the required spilling. To formally prove that this new term is equivalent to the original is very simple, amounting to not much more than checking that the two expressions are α-equivalent. In our implementation this task is fulfilled implicitly when we verify the translation from ACF to HSL by comparing the ACF with the synthesized function. This nice trick was first noticed by Hickey and Nogin [8] and is also used by Leroy [11]. It allows the results of standard register allocation algorithms to be used, without having to verify their correctness. The following example shows the HOL- (left) and an ANF (right) of the TEA block cipher [23] (names of variables spilled begin with m and those in registers begin with r):

$$\begin{array}{l} \mathsf{DELTA} = 0x9e3779b9w \\ \mathsf{ShiftXor}(x, s, k_0, k_1) = \\ \quad ((x \ll 4) + k_0) \mathbin{\#} (x + s) \mathbin{\#} \\ \quad ((x \gg 5) + k_1) \\ \mathsf{Round}\ ((y, z), (k_0, k_1, k_2, k_3), s) = \\ \quad \mathtt{let}\ s' = s + \mathsf{DELTA}\ \mathtt{in} \\ \quad \mathtt{let}\ y' = y + \mathsf{ShiftXor}\ (z, s', k_0, k_1) \\ \quad \mathtt{in}\ \ ((y', z + \mathsf{ShiftXor}\ (y', s', \\ \qquad k_2, k_3)), (k_0, k_1, k_2, k_3), s') \\ \mathsf{Rounds}\ (n, s : \mathit{state}) = \\ \quad \mathtt{if}\ n = 0w\ \mathtt{then}\ s \\ \quad \mathtt{else}\ \mathsf{Rounds}\ (n - 1w, \mathsf{Round}\ s) \end{array}$$

$$\begin{array}{l} \mathsf{Rounds}(r_0, (r_8, r_5), (r_4, r_3, r_2, r_6), r_7) = \\ \mathtt{let}\ v_9 = (\mathsf{op}\ =)\ (r_0, 0w)\mathtt{in} \\ \mathtt{if}\ v_9\ \mathtt{then}\ ((r_8, r_5), (r_4, r_3, r_2, r_6), r_7) \\ \mathtt{else}\ \mathtt{let}\ m_2 = (\mathsf{op}\ -)\ (r_0, 1w)\ \mathtt{in} \\ \qquad \mathtt{let}\ m_4 = (\mathsf{op}\ +)\ (r_7, 2654435769w)\ \mathtt{in} \\ \qquad \mathtt{let}\ r_1 = \mathsf{ShiftXor}\ (r_5, m_4, r_4, r_3)\ \mathtt{in} \\ \qquad \mathtt{let}\ r_9 = (\mathsf{op}\ +)\ (r_8, r_1)\ \mathtt{in} \\ \qquad \mathtt{let}\ r_1 = \mathsf{ShiftXor}\ (r_9, m_4, r_2, r_6)\ \mathtt{in} \\ \qquad \mathtt{let}\ r_1 = (\mathsf{op}\ +)\ (r_5, r_1)\ \mathtt{in} \\ \qquad \mathtt{let}\ ((m_5, m_3), (m_1, m_0, m_6, r_1), r_0) = \\ \qquad \quad \mathsf{Rounds}\ (m_2, (r_9, r_1), (r_4, r_3, r_2, r_6), m_4) \\ \qquad \mathtt{in}\ ((m_5, m_3), (m_1, m_0, m_6, r_1), r_0) \end{array}$$

ACF. The ANF is again converted to an equivalent 'constructor'-like semantic function (*i.e.*, ACF) based on combinators for sequential composition (sc), conditionals (cj) and tail-recursion (tr). By definition sc = Seq and cj = Ite; however, tr is a little different from Rec.

$$\vdash_{def}\ \mathsf{tr}\ f_1\ f_2 \doteq \lambda x.\mathsf{if}\ f_1\ x\ \mathsf{then}\ x\ \mathsf{else}\ \mathsf{tr}\ (f_2\ x)$$
$$\vdash_{thm}\ (f\ x = \mathsf{if}\ f_1\ x\ \mathsf{then}\ f_2\ x\ \mathsf{else}\ f\ (f_3\ x)) \Leftrightarrow (f = \mathsf{sc}\ (\mathsf{tr}\ f_1\ f_3)\ f_2)$$

4.2 From ACF to HSL

To support reasoning about HSL programs, we use the following Hoare triples:

$$\{P\}\ S\ \{Q\} \doteq \forall \sigma_{\mathrm{hsl}}.P\ \sigma_{\mathrm{hsl}} \Rightarrow Q(\mathsf{run}_{\mathrm{hsl}}\ S\ \sigma_{\mathrm{hsl}})$$

We first derive standard Hoare rules. Then, to bridge the semantic gap between an ACF function g with inputs $\boldsymbol{i}$ and outputs $\boldsymbol{o}$, and the HSL structure S built from g's ANF, we specialize the axiomatic semantics to obtain a refined set of Hoare rules—dubbed the *projective* Hoare rules. A projective Hoare rule says: provided that inputs $\boldsymbol{i}$ have initial values $\boldsymbol{v}$, and any variable x in the live variable set ξ has value k, then in the state σ' after the execution of S, the values left in outputs $\boldsymbol{o}$ are equal to applying the function f to the initial values $\boldsymbol{v}$, and x's value is still k:

$$\begin{array}{l} S \vdash \xi\ \uparrow\ (\boldsymbol{i}, f, \boldsymbol{o}) \doteq \\ \forall x \in \xi\, \forall \boldsymbol{v} \forall k \forall \sigma_{\mathrm{hsl}}.(\boldsymbol{i}_f\ \sigma_{\mathrm{hsl}} = \boldsymbol{v}) \wedge (\sigma_{\mathrm{hsl}}[[x]] = k) \Rightarrow \\ \mathtt{let}\ \sigma'_{\mathrm{hsl}} = \mathsf{run}_{\mathrm{hsl}}\ S\ \sigma_{\mathrm{hsl}}\ \mathtt{in}\ \wedge (\boldsymbol{o}_f\ \sigma'_{\mathrm{hsl}} = f\ \boldsymbol{v}) \wedge (\sigma'_{\mathrm{hsl}}[[x]] = k) \end{array}$$

where functions i_f and o_f project from a data state the values of vector $\boldsymbol{i}$ and $\boldsymbol{o}$. If the judgement embodied by a projective Hoare rule holds on the S derived from g, then the synthesized function f should be equivalent to g and, indeed this is easy to prove automatically since they are quite similar.

The projective Hoare rules utilize the following definitions. Operator mk_cnd turns a condition into a condition function. Suppose $\overrightarrow{\xi}$ turns a set ξ into a vector, and $\overleftarrow{\boldsymbol{v}}$ turns a vector $\boldsymbol{v}$ into a set, then the product of a vector and a set makes a new vector that comprises $\boldsymbol{v_1}$ and all elements in ξ, $\boldsymbol{v_1} \times \xi \doteq (\boldsymbol{v_1}, \overrightarrow{\xi})$. The dot product of a function and a set gives a new function: $(\lambda \boldsymbol{x}.f\ \boldsymbol{x}) \odot \xi \doteq \lambda(\boldsymbol{x}, \overrightarrow{\xi}).(f\ \boldsymbol{x}, \overrightarrow{\xi})$. A vector and a projective function are interchangeable.

$$\frac{s_1 \vdash \xi_1 \uparrow (\boldsymbol{i_1}, f_1, \boldsymbol{o_1}) \quad s_2 \vdash \xi_2 \uparrow (\boldsymbol{o_1}, f_2, \boldsymbol{o_2})}{\mathsf{SC}\ s_1\ s_2 \vdash \xi_1 \cap \xi_2 \uparrow (\boldsymbol{i_1}, \mathsf{sc}\ f_1\ f_2, \boldsymbol{o_2})}\ \text{sc\_rule}$$

$$\frac{s_1 \vdash \xi_1 \uparrow (\boldsymbol{i}, f_1, \boldsymbol{o}) \quad s_2 \vdash \xi_2 \uparrow (\boldsymbol{i}, f_2, \boldsymbol{o})}{\mathsf{CJ}\ cnd\ s_1\ s_2 \vdash \xi_1 \cap \xi_2 \uparrow (\boldsymbol{i}, (\mathsf{cj}\ (\texttt{mk\_cnd}\ cnd)\ f_1\ f_2), \boldsymbol{o})}\ \text{cj\_rule}$$

$$\frac{s \vdash \xi \uparrow (\boldsymbol{i}, f, \boldsymbol{i})}{\mathsf{TR}\ cnd\ s \vdash \xi \uparrow (\boldsymbol{i}, (\mathsf{tr}\ (\texttt{mk\_cnd}\ cnd)\ f), \boldsymbol{i})}\ \text{tr\_rule} \qquad \frac{s \vdash \xi \uparrow (\boldsymbol{i}, f, \boldsymbol{o}) \quad g\ \boldsymbol{i'} = f\ \boldsymbol{i}}{s \vdash \xi \uparrow (\boldsymbol{i'}, g, \boldsymbol{o})}\ \text{shuffle\_rule}$$

$$\frac{s \vdash \xi \uparrow (\boldsymbol{i}, f, \boldsymbol{o}) \quad \xi' \subseteq \xi}{s \vdash \xi \uparrow (\boldsymbol{i} \times \xi', f \odot \xi', \boldsymbol{o} \times \xi')}\ \text{pick\_rule} \qquad \frac{s \vdash \xi \uparrow (\boldsymbol{i}, f, \boldsymbol{o}) \quad \xi' \subseteq \xi}{s \vdash \xi' \uparrow (\boldsymbol{i}, f, \boldsymbol{o})}\ \text{shrink\_rule}$$

$$\frac{s \vdash \xi \uparrow (callee.\boldsymbol{i}, f, callee.\boldsymbol{o}) \quad \overleftarrow{caller.\boldsymbol{o}} \cap \xi' = \phi}{\mathsf{FC}\ (caller.\boldsymbol{i}, f, callee.\boldsymbol{i})\ s\ (caller.\boldsymbol{o}, f, callee.\boldsymbol{o}) \vdash \xi' \uparrow (caller.\boldsymbol{i}, f, caller.\boldsymbol{o})}\ \text{fc\_rule}$$

These rules are used to keep track of how the relation between specific inputs and outputs change during the execution. Rules sc_rule, cj_rule and tr_rule are control flow rules and their meaning is self-explanatory. The live variable set ξ stores the variables that are still live but not modified by the current statement. In other words, when the value of a live variable is not altered by the current statement, it is stored in ξ for future use. A live variable is either in ξ, or in the outputs $\boldsymbol{o}$. When it becomes not live any more, it should be removed from ξ. Maintaining a ξ helps to reduce the number of variables in the inputs and outputs. Rule pick_rule is for extracting variables from the live variable set, while shrink_rule is used to discard variables not live any more from the set. Rule shuffle_rule is to restructure the input vector. Restructuring the ouput vector is accomplished by appending an empty block and applying the shuffle_rule to it. A basic block is simulated as a whole as it is a macro instruction, thus there exists no rule for it.

Application of projective rules is controlled by an annotated structure with inputs, outputs and context information, which guides the symbolic simulation and the application of rules. Control flow rules `sc_rule`, `cj_rule` and `tr_rule` are applied on structures SC, CJ and TR respectively. For instance, when reasoning about a (CJ *cond* S_1 S_2) structure, we first reason about S_1 and S_2 separately, then apply the `cj_rule` rule. The application of data flow rules `pick_rule`, `shrink_rule` and `shuffle_rule` are guided by the "use" and "def" information of a structure maintained by the compiler.

4.3 From HSL to CFL

The main task for this translation is to implement function calls and map heap variables and stack variables to memory (for wider application we handle heap variables here although they are replaced with stack variables during closure conversion). Obviously the mapping function, $\searrow$, shall be a one-to-one function.

The storage for local (stack) variables is allocated on function entry and released on function exit. In particular, local variables are held in a stack frame that will be "destroyed" on function exit, and the storage for its stack can be "collected" and reused for other function calls. The memory is modelled as a finite map with addresses ranging from 0 to $2^{32} - 1$.

We introduce an injection relation $\leftrightharpoons^{\searrow}$ to relate the states occurring during the execution of HSL code and that of the translated CFL code, where $\searrow$ consists of three injective functions $\searrow_{rg}$, $\searrow_{hp}$ and $\searrow_{sk}$ that map logical registers, heap variables and stack variables to machine registers and memory locations respectively. Of course all procedures use the same $\searrow_{hp}$ as they share the global heap. The correctness statement amounts to showing that the execution of a HSL statement S_{hsl} has the same effect on a HSL state as the execution of its corresponding CFL statement S_{cfl} (notation D_σ and D_S return the domains of the finite maps in σ and the variables accessed by the instruction in S).

$$\begin{array}{l}
\vdash_{def} \mathsf{one_one_inj}\ \sigma_{\text{hsl}}\ \searrow\ \sigma_{\text{cfl}} \doteq \forall v_1, v_2 \in D_{\sigma_{\text{hsl}}}.\ \mathsf{addr}\ \sigma_{\text{cfl}}\ v_1^{\searrow} \neq \mathsf{addr}\ \sigma_{\text{cfl}}\ v_2^{\searrow} \\
\vdash_{def} \sigma_{\text{hsl}} \leftrightharpoons^{\searrow} \sigma_{\text{cfl}} \doteq \forall v \in D_{\sigma_{\text{hsl}}}.\ \sigma_{\text{hsl}}[[v]] = \sigma_{\text{cfl}}[[v^{\searrow}]] \\
\vdash_{def} (S_{\text{hsl}} \equiv^{\searrow} S_{\text{cfl}}) \doteq \\
\quad \forall \sigma_{\text{hsl}} \forall \sigma_{\text{cfl}}.\ (D_{S_{\text{hsl}}} = D_{\sigma_{\text{hsl}}} \wedge \sigma_{\text{hsl}} \leftrightharpoons^{\searrow} \sigma_{\text{cfl}}) \Rightarrow (\mathsf{run}_{\text{hsl}}\ S_{\text{hsl}}\ \sigma_{\text{hsl}} \leftrightharpoons^{\searrow} \mathsf{run}_{\text{cfl}}\ S_{\text{cfl}}\ \sigma_{\text{cfl}})
\end{array}$$

The function addr returns the address of a mapped variable. An address is parameterized by a state containing the values of base registers (e.g. fp and sp). Given an injection $\searrow$, the translation from HSL to CFL for most structures is simple and we just need to replace HSL variables with their mapped machine registers and memory locations. A FC structure will be converted to the sequential composition of pre-call processing, callee's body and post-call processing:

$$\begin{array}{l}
r_i^{\searrow} \doteq \searrow_{rg}\ r_i \quad hp[i]^{\searrow} \doteq m[\searrow_{hp}\ i] \quad sk[i]^{\searrow} \doteq m[\searrow_{sk}\ i] \quad S^{\searrow} \doteq \forall v \in D_S.\ S[v \leftarrow v^{\searrow}] \\
\Gamma_{\text{hsl}}\ S \doteq S^{\searrow} \quad \text{when } S \text{ is a } \mathsf{BLK,SC,CJ} \text{ or } \mathsf{TR} \text{ structure} \\
\Gamma_{\text{hsl}}\ (\mathsf{FC}\ (caller.\boldsymbol{i}, callee.\boldsymbol{i})\ S\ (caller.\boldsymbol{o}, callee.\boldsymbol{o})) \doteq \\
\quad \mathsf{SC}\ (\mathsf{SC}\ pre\ (\Gamma_{\text{hsl}}\ S))\ post \quad \text{for valid } pre,\ post \text{ and } \searrow' \text{ described below}
\end{array}$$

When $\searrow_{sk}$ maps different stack variables to different memory locations, the translation for BLK, SC, CJ and TR structures guarantees semantics preservation. The translation for FC is more complicated: we require that the pre-call processing and post-call processing fulfill the parameter passing and result returning task; and the execution of the pre-call processing, function body and post-call processing should not modify the values of the caller's register and stack variables except for those set to receive results (we name this the *value recovering* property). Assuming that $\searrow$ is an one-to-one injection, we have:

$$\frac{}{(\mathsf{BLK}\ S) \equiv^{\searrow} (\mathsf{BLK}\ S^{\searrow})} \qquad \frac{S_{\text{hsl\_1}} \equiv^{\searrow} S_{\text{cfl\_1}} \quad S_{\text{hsl\_2}} \equiv^{\searrow} S_{\text{cfl\_2}}}{\mathsf{SC}\ S_{\text{hsl\_1}}\ S_{\text{hsl\_2}} \equiv^{\searrow} \mathsf{SC}\ S_{\text{cfl\_1}}\ S_{\text{cfl\_2}}}$$

$$\frac{S_{\text{hsl\_1}} \equiv^{\searrow} S_{\text{cfl\_1}} \quad S_{\text{hsl\_2}} \equiv^{\searrow} S_{\text{cfl\_2}}}{\mathsf{CJ}\ cond\ S_{\text{hsl\_1}}\ S_{\text{hsl\_2}} \equiv^{\searrow} \mathsf{CJ}\ cond^{\searrow}\ S_{\text{cfl\_1}}\ S_{\text{cfl\_2}}} \qquad \frac{S_{\text{hsl}} \equiv^{\searrow} S_{\text{cfl}}}{\mathsf{TR}\ cond\ S_{\text{hsl}} \equiv^{\searrow} \mathsf{TR}\ cond^{\searrow}\ S_{\text{cfl}}}$$

$$\frac{\begin{array}{c}\forall \sigma.\sigma[[caller.\boldsymbol{i}^{\searrow}]] = (\mathsf{run}_{\text{cfl}}\ pre\ \sigma)[[callee.\boldsymbol{i}^{\searrow'}]] \quad S_{\text{hsl}} \equiv^{\searrow'} S_{\text{cfl}} \\ \forall \sigma.\sigma[[\overleftarrow{callee.\boldsymbol{o}}^{\searrow'}]] = (\mathsf{run}_{\text{cfl}}\ post\ \sigma)[[caller.\boldsymbol{o}^{\searrow}]] \\ \forall \sigma.\forall v \in (D^{rg,sk}_{S_{caller}} \setminus caller.\boldsymbol{o}).\ \sigma[[v^{\searrow}]] = (\mathsf{run}_{\text{cfl}}\ (\mathsf{SC}\ (\mathsf{SC}\ pre\ S_{\text{cfl}})\ post)\ \sigma)[[v^{\searrow}]]\end{array}}{\mathsf{FC}\ (caller.\boldsymbol{i}, callee.\boldsymbol{i})\ S_{hsl}\ (caller.\boldsymbol{o}, callee.\boldsymbol{o}) \equiv^{\searrow} \mathsf{SC}\ (\mathsf{SC}\ pre\ S_{\text{cfl}})\ post}$$

There are many ways to guarantee that the value recovering property holds. One of them is to layout the frames of the caller and callee in such a way that their domains do not intersect with each other; and the values of register variables modified by the callee's execution are recovered on the function entry. This leads to a valid implementation of a frame layout and a function call procedure. The areas in the memory devoted to stack frames (i.e. the activation record) are marked by the ip, fp and sp. When the callee is called, space for results are reserved by growing the stack, then the caller pushes all parameters into the stack; and then the frame for the callee is created. Specifically, when a callee is called, its stack frames shall not be overlapped with the callee's frame.

As indicated by the following rule, an implementation is valid if it ensures that: (1) the parameter/result passing and the body execution do not change the values of stack variables in the caller's frame except those for receiving results (*i.e.*, $caller.\boldsymbol{o}$); (2) all register variables are pushed into memory before parameter passing on function entry and then popped from memory before result passing on function exit. In the following rule, $\sigma\langle v\rangle$ represents reading the value at concrete address v from state σ, and D_r is the abbreviation of $D_{S_{caller}}$.

$$\frac{\begin{array}{c}\sigma_1 = \mathsf{run}_{\mathrm{cfl}}\ pre\ \sigma \quad \sigma_2 = \mathsf{run}_{\mathrm{cfl}}\ S_{\mathrm{cfl}}\ \sigma_1 \quad \sigma_3 = \mathsf{run}_{\mathrm{cfl}}\ post\ \sigma_2 \\ \forall v \in (D_r^{sk})^{\searrow}.\sigma\langle v\rangle = \sigma_1\langle v\rangle \quad \exists x_i.\,\sigma_1\langle x_i\rangle = \sigma[[r_i]] \text{ for } i \in D^{rg}_{S_{callee}} \\ \forall v \in (D_r^{sk})^{\searrow} \cup \{x_i \mid i \in D^{rg}_{S_{callee}}\}.\sigma_2\langle v\rangle = \sigma_1\langle v\rangle \\ \forall v \in (D_r^{sk} \setminus \overleftarrow{caller}.\boldsymbol{o})^{\searrow}.\,\sigma_3\langle v\rangle = \sigma_2\langle v\rangle \quad \forall r_i \in (D_r^{rg} \setminus \overleftarrow{caller}.\boldsymbol{o}).\,\sigma_3[[r_i]] = \sigma_2\langle x_i\rangle\end{array}}{\forall\sigma.\forall v{\in}(D_r^{rg,sk}\setminus\overleftarrow{caller}.\boldsymbol{o}).\,\sigma[[v^{\searrow}]]{=}(\mathbf{run}_{\mathrm{cfl}}\ (\mathsf{SC}\ (\mathsf{SC}\ pre\ S_{\mathrm{cfl}})\ post)\ \sigma)[[v^{\searrow}]]}$$

Complying with these requirements, our implementation compiles function calls into a callee-save style calling convention. Specifically, $\searrow_{sk}{=}\searrow'_{sk}{=}\ \lambda i.(fp, -(i+12))$, $\searrow_{rg}{=}\searrow'_{rg}{=}\ \lambda r.r$ and $\searrow_{hp}{=}\searrow'_{hp}{=}\ \lambda i.(hp, -i)$. By carefully moving the pointers fp, ip and sp we keep the caller's frame and callee's frame located in separate areas in the memory. All parameters and results are passed through the stack, and the callee saves all data registers (*i.e.*, $r_0 - r_8$) in all cases. This solution is suboptimal but easier to verify. In particular, it allows us, while performing colouring register allocation, not to add interferences between caller-save registers and temporaries that are live across a call.

higher address (32-bit word based address) lower address

$\leftarrow \ldots$	global heap	previous frame	current frame	next frame	$\ldots \rightarrow$

	`Memory`	`Addr`		`Memory`	`Addr`
caller's ip	reserved for pc	i		...	.
caller's fp	saved lr	i-1		stack variable n	j
	save ip	i-2	caller's sp	parameter/result k	j-1
	save fp	i-3		...	.
	stored reg 8	i-4		parameter/result 0	k
	...	.	callee's ip	reserved for pc	k-1
	stored reg 0	i-12	callee's fp	saved lr	k-2
	stack variable 0	i-13		...	.

$$\begin{aligned} pre = {} & \mathsf{BLK}\ [sub\ sp\ sp\ (max(\#caller.\boldsymbol{i}, \#caller.\boldsymbol{o}) - \#caller.\boldsymbol{i});\ push\ caller.\boldsymbol{i}; \\ & mov\ ip\ sp;\ sub\ fp\ ip\ 1;\ sub\ sp\ sp\ 1;\ push\ \{r_0, \ldots, r_8, fp, ip, lr\}; \\ & add\ sp\ sp\ 12;\ pop\ callee.\boldsymbol{i};\ sub\ sp\ fp\ (12 + \#stack\_variables)] \\ post = {} & \mathsf{BLK}\ [add\ sp\ ip\ \#callee.\boldsymbol{o};\ push\ callee.\boldsymbol{o};\ sub\ sp\ fp\ 12; \\ & pop\ \{r_0, \ldots, r_8, fp, ip, lr\};\ mov\ sp\ ip;\ pop\ caller.\boldsymbol{o}; \\ & sub\ sp\ fp\ (12 + \#stack\_variables)] \end{aligned}$$

One subtlety appearing in proofs is that the initial values of hp, sp, ip and fp must be greater than specific values so that the memory can accomodate all stack frames and the areas consumed by pre/post processing.

Both the heap and the stacks are simply finite maps, thus we do not formalize and rely on any heap management and stack property. In [3] a block-base memory model between a machine memory and a high-level view is introduced to manage frame stacks. As in our method, separation is enforced between stack blocks belonging to different function activation records.

4.4 From CFL to ARM

The translation from CFL to ARM proceeds by linearizing the SC, CJ and TR structures. The instructions in basic blocks are already in the right format. Our translation always generates flat code satisfying good properties including: (1) any execution of the translated code will not access beyond its own area in the instruction buffer; (2) the data state after an execution is independent of the initial values of pc and $cpsr$; (3) all executions terminate.

The translation verification for CJ proceeds by case analysis on the condition; while that for TR by the induction on the number of rounds the body is executed. This linearization scheme turns out to be most succinct in terms of the length of generated code. One optimization is performed at the flat code level for function calls: all occurrences of a callee are moved to the same area in the code so that only one copy is left. Unconditional jumps are inserted appropriately. The correctness proof for this relocation is straight forward because the adjusted code runs in the same way as its old version.

$$\begin{array}{rl}
\Gamma_{\text{cfl}}\ (\mathsf{BLK}\ (inst :: instL)) \doteq & inst :: \Gamma_{\text{cfl}}(\mathsf{BLK}\ instL) \\
\Gamma_{\text{cfl}}\ (\mathsf{BLK}\ [\,]) \doteq & [\,] \\
\Gamma_{\text{cfl}}\ (\mathsf{SC}\ s_1\ s_2) \doteq & (\Gamma_{\text{cfl}}\ s_1)\ \uplus\ (\Gamma_{\text{cfl}}\ s_2) \\
\Gamma_{\text{cfl}}\ (\mathsf{CJ}\ (v_1, rop, v_2)\ s_t\ s_f) \doteq & \mathsf{let}\ (\rho_t\ \rho_f) = (\Gamma_{\text{cfl}}\ s_t, \Gamma_{\text{cfl}}\ s_f)\ \mathsf{in} \\
& \quad (\mathsf{cmp}\ v_1\ v_2) :: (\mathsf{b}\{rop\}\ +\ \|\rho_f\| + 2) :: \\
& \quad \rho_f \uplus [\mathsf{bal}\ +\ \|\rho_t\| + 1] \uplus \rho_t \\
\Gamma_{\text{cfl}}\ (\mathsf{TR}\ (v_1, rop, v_2)\ s) \doteq & \mathsf{let}\ \rho = \Gamma_{\text{cfl}}\ s\ \mathsf{in} \\
& \quad (\mathsf{cmp}\ v_1\ v_2) :: (\mathsf{b}\{rop\} + \|\rho\| + 2) :: \rho\ \uplus [\mathsf{bal} - (|\rho| + 2)]
\end{array}$$

Note that $\|\rho\|$ returns the number of instructions in ρ, and $\rho_1 \uplus \rho_2$ appends ρ_2 to ρ_1.

Example. With the following abbreviations,

$$\begin{array}{l}
body \doteq \mathsf{BLK}\ [msub\ r_3\ r_0\ 1w;\ mmul\ r_2\ r_0\ r_1;\ mmov\ r_0\ r_3;\ mmov\ r_1\ r_2] \\
blk_1 \doteq \mathsf{BLK}\ [mmov\ r_2\ r_1] \quad snd \doteq \lambda(v_0, v_1).v_1 \\
f_1 \doteq \lambda(v_0, v_1).(v_0 - 1w, v_0 + v_1) \quad f_2 \doteq \mathsf{tr}\ (\lambda(v_0, v_1).v_0 = 0w)))\ f_1
\end{array}$$

the intermediate forms of the factorial function and the derivation of the specification connecting the $fact_{hsl}$ and $fact_{acf}$ (where $Axiom_1 = blk_1\ \vdash\ \{\}\ \uparrow ((r_0, r_1), snd, r_2))$ are

HOL-: $fact\ (x, a) \doteq \texttt{if}\ x = 0w\ \texttt{then}\ a\ \texttt{else}\ fact\ (x - 1w, x \times a)$
ACF: $fact_{acf} \doteq \mathsf{sc}\ (\mathsf{tr}\ (\lambda(v_0, v_1).v_0 = 0w)\ f_1)\ snd$
HSL: $fact_{hsl} \doteq \mathsf{SC}\ (\mathsf{TR}\ (r_0, eq, 0w)\ body)\ blk_1$
CFL: $fact_{cfl} \doteq \Gamma_{hsl}\ fact_{hsl} = fact_{hsl}$
ARM: $fact_{arm} \doteq \Gamma_{cfl}\ fact_{cfl} = [cmp\ r_0\ r_1;\ beq\ +\ 6;\ sub\ r_3\ r_0\ 1w;\ mul\ r_2\ r_0\ r_1;\ mov\ r_0\ r_3;\ mov\ r_1,\ r_2;\ bal\ -\ 6;\ mov\ r_2,\ r_1]$

$$\dfrac{\dfrac{body\ \vdash\ \{\}\ \uparrow\ ((r_0, r_1), f_1, (r_0, r_1))}{\mathsf{TR}\ (r_0, ne, 0w)\ body\ \vdash\ \{\}\ \uparrow\ ((r_0, r_1), f_2, (r_0, r_1))}\ \text{tr\_rule} \qquad Axiom_1}{\mathsf{SC}\ (\mathsf{TR}\ (r_0, ne, 0w)\ body)\ blk_1\ \vdash\ \{\}\ \uparrow\ ((r_0, r_1), fact_{acf}, r_2)}\ \text{sc\_rule}$$

5 Related Work

We have also developed a hardware compiler for a similar source language [7]: it takes in HOL function definitions and emits FPGA-level netlists. Compilation proceeds essentially by refinement steps: control structures in logic are refined by formulas representing unclocked circuits implementing those structures, and those circuit-formulas are further refined to be formulas for clocked circuits.

Hickey and Nogin [8] constructed a compiler from a higher order, untyped, functional language to Intel x86 code, based entirely on higher-order rewrite rules. The compiler is written in the MetaPRL logical framework. A set of rewrite rules are used to convert a higher level program to a lower level program. However, verification of the rules remains to be done. Since their source languages and intermediate representations are similar to ours, we may apply their rules during the translation from HOL to HOL- and then ANF, *e.g.*, the closure conversion and CPS conversion rules; yet our existing verification techniques for these translations are still valid. Similarly, Watson [22] proposes a refinement calculus for the compilation from high-level language to .NET assembly; Sampaio [20] uses term rewriting to convert source programs to their normal forms representing object code. These latter works are not machine automated.

Leroy [2,11] has verified a compiler from a subset of C, Clight, to PowerPC assembly code in the Coq system. The semantics of Clight is completely deterministic and specified as big-step operational semantics. Several intermediate languages are introduced and translations between them are verified. The proof of semantics preservation for the translation proceeds by induction over the Clight evaluation derivation and case analysis on the last evaluation rule used; in contrast, our proofs proceed by verifying that the rewrite rules used are semantics preserving and the execution of programs at different phases has the same effect on the corresponding states. Leroy also uses translation validation to sidestep the difficult correctness proof for register allocation. He relies on an outside verifier to check *a posteriori* the graph colouring register allocator.

A purely operational semantics based development is that of Klein and Nipkow [9] which gives a thorough formalization of a Java-like language. A compiler from this language to a subset of Java Virtual Machine is verified using Isabelle/HOL. However, that compiler targets high-level code than our assembly, for example it assumes an unbounded number of registers. Compilation from a type-safe subset of C to DLX assembly code has been verified using the Isabelle/HOL theorem prover [10]. A big step semantics and a small step semantics for this language are related by the proof.

There has recently been a large amount of work on verifying low-level languages, originally prompted by the ideas of proof carrying code and typed assembly language [15]. We are currently investigating links with recent work on Hoare Logics for assembly language, *e.g.*, [5,13] and also extensions such as Separation Logic [19]. Of course, compiler verification itself is a venerable topic, with far too many publications to survey (see Dave's bibliography [4]). Restricting to assembler verification, one of the most relevant works for us is by Moore [14].

6 Conclusions and Future Work

We have presented the design of a compiler for a subset of higher order logic which operates by running proofs. The fact that the source language is not associated with any evaluation semantics makes the translation validation somewhat novel. Our end-to-end, fully automatic compiler successfully bridges the large gap between programs in logic and low level assembly programs.

Currently, the validation of the translation from an ACF program to its HSL program requires the HSL program to inherit ACF's structure, thus restricting the degree of optimizations at the HSL level. In spite of this restriction, many optimizations can be performed in the other levels. For example, optimizations on basic blocks are easy since their validation simply requires symbolic simulation.

Currently, we are strengthening the front end translation to support ML-style datatypes and non-tail recursive functions. We are also augumenting the back end to tackle dynamic memory allocation, as well as changing the current ARM-like target language to the detailed ARM model developed by Fox [6].

Acknowledgements. We thank Thomas Tuerk for his help in refining the definition of the ARM model. We also appreciate the advice from the anonymous reviewers.

References

1. Stefan Berghofer and Tobias Nipkow, *Executing higher order logic*, P. Callaghan, Z. Luo, J. McKinna, R. Pollack, editors, Types for Proofs and Programs, International Workshop (TYPES 2000), 2000.
2. Sandrine Blazy, Zaynah Dargaye, and Xavier Leroy, *Formal verification of a C compiler front-end*, 14th International Symposium on Formal Methods (FM 2006), Hamilton, Canada, 2006.
3. Sandrine Blazy and Xavier Leroy, *Formal verification of a memory model for C-like imperative languages*, International Conference on Formal Engineering Methods (ICFEM 2005), Manchester, UK, 2005.
4. Maulik A. Dave, *Compiler verification: a bibliography*, ACM SIGSOFT Software Engineering Notes **28** (2003), no. 6, 2–2.

5. Xinyu Feng, Zhong Shao, Alexander Vaynberg, Sen Xiang, and Zhaozhong Ni, *Modular verification of assembly code with stack-based control abstractions*, ACM SIGPLAN 2006 Conference on Programming Language Design and Implementation (PLDI'06), 2006, pp. 401–414.
6. Anthony Fox, *Formal verification of the ARM6 micro-architecture*, Tech. Report 548, University of Cambridge Computer Laboratory, November 2002.
7. M. Gordon, J. Iyoda, S. Owens, and K. Slind, *Automatic formal synthesis of hardware from higher order logic*, Proceedings of Fifth International Workshop on Automated Verification of Critical Systems (AVoCS 2005), ENTCS, vol. 145, 2005.
8. Jason Hickey and Aleksey Nogin, *Formal compiler construction in a logical framework*, Journal of Higher-Order and Symbolic Computation **19** (2006), no. 2-3, 197–230.
9. Gerwin Klein and Tobias Nipkow, *A machine-checked model for a Java-like language, virtual machine and compiler*, TOPLAS **28** (2006), no. 4, 619–695.
10. Dirk Leinenbach, Wolfgang Paul, and Elena Petrova, *Towards the formal verification of a C0 compiler: Code generation and implementation correctnes*, 4th IEEE International Conference on Software Engineering and Formal Methods (SEFM 2006), 2005.
11. Xavier Leroy, *Formal certification of a compiler backend, or: programming a compiler with a proof assistant*, Symposium on the Principles of Programming Languages (POPL 2006), ACM Press, 2006.
12. Kim Marriott and Peter J. Stuckey, *Programming with constraints, an introduction*, MIT Press, 1998.
13. John Matthews, J Strother Moore, Sandip Ray, and Daron Vroon, *Verification condition generation via theorem proving*, LPAR 2006 (LNCS 4246), Springer Verlag, 2006.
14. J Strother Moore, *Piton: A mechanically verified assembly-level language*, Automated Reasoning Series, Kluwer Academic Publishers, 1996.
15. Greg Morrisett, David Walker, Karl Crary, and Neal Glew, *From System F to typed assembly language*, ACM Transactions on Programming Languages and Systems **21** (1999), no. 3, 527–568.
16. Tobias Nipkow, Lawrence C. Paulson, and Markus Wenzel, *Isabelle/HOL — a proof assistant for higher-order logic*, LNCS, vol. 2283, Springer, 2002.
17. Michael Norrish and Konrad Slind, *HOL-4 manuals*, 1998-2006, Available at `http://hol.sourceforge.net/`.
18. A. Pnueli, M. Siegel, and E. Singerman, *Translation validation*, 4th International Conference on Tools and Algorithms for Construction and Analysis of Systems (TACAS '98), 1998.
19. John C. Reynolds, *Separation logic: A logic for shared mutable data structures*, IEEE Symposium on Logic in Computer Science (LICS'02), 2002, pp. 55–74.
20. Augusto Sampaio, *An algebraic approach to compiler design, volume 4 of AMAST series in computing*, World Scientific, 1997.
21. Konrad Slind, *Reasoning about terminating functional programs*, Ph.D. thesis, Institut für Informatik, Technische Universität München, 1999.
22. Geoffrey Watson, *Compilation by refinement for a practical assembly language*, International Conference on Formal Engineering Methods (ICFEM 2003), 2003.
23. David Wheeler and Roger Needham, *TEA, a tiny encryption algorithm*, Fast Software Encryption: Second International Workshop, 1999.

Modular Shape Analysis for Dynamically Encapsulated Programs

N. Rinetzky[1,⋆], A. Poetzsch-Heffter[2], G. Ramalingam[3,⋆⋆], M. Sagiv[1], and E. Yahav[4]

[1] Tel Aviv University
{maon,msagiv}@tau.ac.il
[2] University of Kaiserlautern
poetzsch@informatik.uni-kl.de
[3] Microsoft Research India
grama@microsoft.com
[4] IBM T.J. Watson Research Center
eyahav@us.ibm.com

Abstract. We present a *modular* static analysis which identifies structural (shape) invariants for a subset of heap-manipulating programs. The subset is defined by means of a non-standard operational semantics which places certain restrictions on aliasing and sharing across modules. More specifically, we assume that live references (*i.e.*, used before set) between subheaps manipulated by different modules form a tree. We develop a conservative static analysis algorithm by abstract interpretation of our non-standard semantics. Our *modular* algorithm also ensures that the program obeys the above mentioned restrictions.

1 Introduction

Modern programs rely significantly on the use of heap-allocated linked data structures. In this paper, we present a novel method for automatically verifying properties of such programs in a modular fashion. We consider a program to be a collection of modules. We develop a shape (heap) analysis which treats each module separately. Modular analyses are attractive because they promise scalability and reuse.

Modular analysis [1], however, is particularly difficult in the presence of aliasing. The behavior of a module can depend on the aliasing created by clients of the module and vice versa. Analyzing a module making worst-case assumptions about the aliasing created by clients (or vice versa) can complicate the analysis and lead to imprecise results. Instead of analyzing arbitrary programs, we restrict our attention to certain "well-behaved" programs. The main idea behind our approach is to assume a modularly-checkable program-invariant concerning aliases of live intermodule references.

Motivating Example. Fig. 1 shows the code of a module, m_{RP}, which serves as our running example. The code is written in a Java-like language. Module m_{RP} contains two classes: Class `R` is a class of resources to be used by clients of the module. A resource has a recursive field, `n`, which is used to link resources in an internal list. Class `RPool`

⋆ Supported in part by the IBM Ph.D. Fellowship Program, and in part by a grant from the Israeli Academy of Science.

⋆⋆ Work done partly when the author was at IBM Research.

R. De Nicola (Ed.): ESOP 2007, LNCS 4421, pp. 220–236, 2007.

is a pool of resources which stores resources using their internal list. We assume that the n-field is read or written only by `RPool`'s methods: `acquire`, which gets a resource out of the pool, and `release`, which stores a resource in the pool.

Typical properties we want to verify modularly are that for *any well behaved* program that uses m_{RP}, the methods of `RPool` never leak resources and never issue an acquired resource before it is released.[1] Note that these properties do not hold for arbitrary programs because of possible aliasing in the module induced by the client behavior: Consider an invocation of `p.release(r)` in a memory state in which `p` points to a non-empty resource pool. If `r` points to the head of a resource list containing more than one resource, then the tail of the list might be leaked. If, after being released into the pool that `p` points to, `r` is released into other pools, then these pools, along with the one pointed-to by `p` share (parts) of their resource lists. Note that after a shared resource is acquired from one pool, it can still be acquired from the other pools. Finally, if the resource that `r` points to is already in `p`'s pool, then `p`'s resource list becomes cyclic. A resource which is acquired from a pool whose list is cyclic, stays in the pool.

```
public class RPool {
  private R rs;
  // transferred: { e }
  public
  void release(R e){
    e.n=this.rs;
    this.rs=e;
  }
  // transferred: { }
  public R acquire(){
    R r = this.rs;
    if (r!=null) {
      this.rs=r.n;
      r.n = null; }
    else
      r = new R();
    return r;
  }}

public class R {
  R n; ... }
```

Fig. 1. Module m_{RP}

Given a module, and the user specification for the other modules it uses, our analysis tries to verify that the given module is "well-behaved". If this verification is unsuccessful, the analysis gives up and reports that the module may not adhere to our constraints. Otherwise, the analysis computes invariants of the given module that hold in any "well-behaved" program containing the module. A program comprised only of successfully verified modules is guaranteed to be "well-behaved".

1.1 Overview

Non-standard semantics. The basis for our approach is a *non-standard semantics* that captures the aliasing constraints mentioned above. In this paper, a module is a collection of type-definitions and procedures, and a component is a subheap. Our semantics represents the heap as an (evolving and changing) collection of (heap) *components*. Every component is comprised of objects whose types are defined in the same module. (We say that a component *belongs to* that module.) Note that multiple components belonging to the same module may co-exist. References between components belonging to different modules are allowed, however, the *internal structure* of a component can be accessed or modified only by the (procedures in the) module to which it belongs.[2] Components can be in two different states: *sealed* and *unsealed*. Sealed components represent encapsulated data returned by a module to its callers (and, hence, are expected to satisfy certain *module invariants*). In contrast, unsealed components are components that are currently being modified and may be in an unstable state.

---

[1] Similarly, in the analysis of a client of m_{RP}, we would like to verify that the client does not use a dangling reference to a released resource. Our analysis can establish this property.

[2] A module m can manipulate a component of a module m' by an intermodule procedure call.

At any point during program execution, the internal structure of only one component is "visible" and can be accessed or mutated, *i.e.*, only one unsealed component is "visible". We refer to this component as the *current component*. The only way a sealed component can be *unsealed* (permitting its internal structure to be examined and modified) is to pass it as a parameter of an appropriate intermodule procedure call so that the component becomes part of the current component for the called procedure. Our semantics requires that all parameters and the return value(s) of intermodule procedure calls must be sealed components. For brevity, we do not consider primitive values here.

Constraints. So far we have not really placed any constraints on the program. The above are standard "good modularity principles" and most programs will fit this model with minor adjustments. Before we describe the constraints we place on sharing across modules, we describe the two key issues that motivate these constraints:

1. How can we analyze a module M without using any information about the clients of M (*i.e.*, without using information about the usage context of M)?
2. When analyzing a client module C that makes use of another module M, how do we handle *intermodule* calls from C to M using only the analysis results for module M (*i.e.*, without analyzing module M again)?

We say that a component *owns* another component if it has a *live* reference (*i.e.*, used before set) to the other component. The most important constraint we place is that a component cannot be owned by two or more components. As a result, the heap (or the program state) may be seen as, effectively, a tree of components. Informally, this ensures that distinct components do not share (live) state. Furthermore, we require that all references to a component from its owner have the same target object. We call this object the component's *header*.[3] We refer to a program which satisfies these constraints as a *dynamically encapsulated* program. Recall that our analysis also verifies that a program is *dynamically encapsulated*.

In this paper, we require that the module dependency relation (see Sec. 2) be acyclic. This constraint simplifies our semantics (and analysis) as module reentrancy does not need to be considered: When a module is invoked *all* of its components are guaranteed to be sealed. We note that our techniques can be generalized to handle cyclic dependencies, provided that the ownership relation is required to be acyclic.

Benefits. The above constraints let us deal with the two issues mentioned above in a tractable way. The restriction on sharing between components simplifies dealing with intermodule calls as they cannot have unexpected side-effects: *e.g.*, an intermodule call on one component C_1 cannot affect the state of another component C_2 that is accessible to the caller. As for the first issue, *we conservatively identify all possible input states for an intermodule call by iteratively identifying all possible sealed components that can be generated by a module.*

Specification. We now describe the extra specification a user must provide for the modular analysis. This specification consists of: (i) a *module specification* that partitions a

[3] Note the slight difference in terminology: In ownership type systems, owners are objects and do not belong to their ownership contexts. In our approach, components are the owners; the component header belongs to the component that is dominated by the header.

program's types and procedures into modules; (ii) an annotation for every (public) procedure that indicates for every parameter whether it is intended to be "transferred" to the callee or not; these annotations are only considered in intermodule procedure calls. A sealed component that is passed as a *transferred* parameter of an intermodule call cannot be subsequently used by the calling module (*e.g.*, to be passed as a parameter for a subsequent intermodule call). This constraint serves to directly enforce the requirement that the heap be a tree of components. For example, for `release` we specify that the caller transfer ownership only of the resource parameter.

Given the above specification, our modular analysis can automatically detect the boundaries of the heap-components and (conservatively) determine whether the program satisfies the constraints described above

Abstraction. Our modular analysis is obtained as an abstract interpretation of our non-standard semantics. We use a 2-step successive abstraction. We first apply a novel *trimming abstraction* which abstracts away the contents of sealed components when analyzing a module. (Loosely speaking, only the heap structure of the current component, and the aliasing relationships between intermodule references leaving the current component, are tracked.) We then apply a *bounded* conservative abstraction of trimmed memory states. Rather than providing a new intraprocedural abstraction, we show how to *lift* existing *intra*procedural shape analyses, *e.g.*, [2, 3, 4], to obtain a modular shape abstraction (see Sec. 4). Our analysis is parametric in the abstraction of trimmed memory states and can use different (bounded) abstractions when analyzing different modules.

Analysis. Our static analysis is conducted in an assume-guarantee manner allowing each module to be analyzed separately. The analysis, computes a conservative representation of every possible sealed components of the analyzed module in dynamically encapsulated programs. This process, in effect, identifies structural invariants of the sealed components of the analyzed module, *i.e.*, it infers module invariants (for dynamically encapsulated programs). Technically, the module is analyzed together with its *most-general-client* using a framework for interprocedural shape analysis, *e.g.*, [5, 6].

Extensions. In this paper, we use a very conservative abstraction of sealed components and inter-component references (for simplicity). The abstraction, in effect, retains no information about the state of a sealed component (which typically belongs to other modules used by the analyzed module). This can lead to an undesirable loss in precision in the analysis (in general). We can refine the abstraction by using *component-digests* [7], which encode (hierarchical) properties of whole *components* in a typestate-like manner [8]. This, *e.g.*, can allow our analysis to distinguish between a reference to a pool of closed socket components from a reference to a pool of connected socket components.

1.2 Main Contributions

(i) We introduce an interesting class of dynamically encapsulated programs; (ii) We define a natural notion of *module invariant for dynamically encapsulated programs*; (iii) We show how to utilize dynamic encapsulation to enable modular shape analysis; and (iv) We present a modular shape analysis algorithm which (conservatively) verifies that a program is dynamically encapsulated and identifies its module invariants.

Due to space restrictions, many formal details and the possible extensions of our techniques are omitted and can be found in [9].

2 Program Model and Specification Language

Program model. We analyze imperative object-based (*i.e.*, without subtyping) programs. A program consists of a collection of procedures and a distinguished `main` procedure. The programmer can also define her own types (à la `C` structs).

Syntactic domains. We assume the syntactic domains $x \in \mathcal{V}$ of variable identifiers, $f \in \mathcal{F}$ of field identifiers, $T \in \mathcal{T}$ of type identifiers, $p \in \mathcal{PID}$ of procedure identifiers, and $m \in \mathcal{M}$ of module identifiers. We assume that types, procedures, and modules have unique identifiers in every program.

Modules. We denote the module that a procedure p belongs to by $m(p)$ and the module that a type identifier T belongs to by $m(T)$. A module m_1 *depends* on module m_2 if $m_1 \neq m_2$ and one of the following holds: (i) a procedure of m_1 invokes a procedure of m_2; (ii) a procedure of m_1 has a local variable whose type belongs to m_2; or (iii) a type of m_1 has a field whose type belongs to m_2.

Procedures. A procedure p has local variables (V_p) and formal parameters (F_p), which are considered to be local variables, *i.e.*, $F_p \subseteq V_p$. Only local variables are allowed.

Specification language. We expect to be given a partitioning of the program types and procedures into modules. Every procedure should have an ownership transfer specification given by a set $F_p^t \subseteq F_p$ of *transferred (formal) parameters*. (A formal parameter is a transferred parameter if it points to a transferred component in an intermodule call.) For example, `e` is `release`'s only transferred parameter, and `acquire` has none.

Simplifying assumptions. We assume that procedure invocations should be *cutpoint-free* [5]. (We explain this assumption, and a possible relaxation, in Sec. 3.2.) In addition, to simplify the presentation, we make the following assumptions: (a) A program manipulates only pointer-valued fields and variables; (b) Formal parameters *cannot* be assigned to; (c) Objects of type T can be allocated and references to such objects can be *used as l-values* by a procedure p only if $m(p) = m(T)$; (d) Actual parameters to an intermodule procedure call should not be aliased and should point to a component owned by the caller. In particular, they should have a non-*null* value; and (e) The caller always becomes the owner of the return value of an intermodule procedure call.

3 Concrete Dynamic-Ownership Semantics

In this section, we define $\mathcal{DOS}$, a non-standard semantics which checks whether a program executes in conformance with the constraints imposed by the dynamic encapsulation model. ($\mathcal{DOS}$ stands for *dynamic-ownership semantics*.) $\mathcal{DOS}$ provides the execution traces that are the foundation of our analysis. For space reasons, we only discuss key aspects of the operational semantics, formally defined in [9].

$\mathcal{DOS}$ is a *store-based* semantics (see, *e.g.*, [10]). A traditional aspect of a store-based semantics is that a memory state represents a heap comprised of all the allocated objects. $\mathcal{DOS}$, on the other hand, is a *local heap* semantics [11]: A memory state which occurs during the execution of a procedure does not represent objects which, at the time of the invocation, were not reachable from the actual parameters.

$\mathcal{DOS}$ is a small-step operational semantics [12]. Instead of encoding a stack of activation records inside the memory state, as traditionally done, $\mathcal{DOS}$ maintains a *stack of program states* [9, 13]: Every program state contains a program point and a memory state. The program state of the *current procedure* is stored at the top of the stack, and it is the only one which can be manipulated by intraprocedural statements. When a procedure is invoked, the *entry memory state* of the callee is computed by a $Call$ operation according to the caller's current memory state, and pushed into the stack. When a procedure returns, the stack is popped, and the caller's *return memory state* is updated using a Ret operation according to its memory state before the invocation (the *call memory state*) and the callee's (popped) *exit memory state*.

The use of a stack of program states allows us to represent in every memory state the (values of) local variables and the local heap of just one procedure. An execution trace of a program P always begins with P's `main` procedure starts executing on an *initial memory state* in which all variables have a *null* value and the heap is empty. We say that a memory state is *reachable* in a program P if it occurs as the current memory state in an execution trace of P.

3.1 Memory States

Fig. 2 defines the concrete semantic domains and the meta-variables ranging over them. We assume *Loc* to be an unbounded set of locations. A value $v \in$ *Val* is either a location, *null*, or $\ominus$, the inaccessible value used to represent references which should not be accessed.

A memory state in the $\mathcal{DOS}$ semantics is a 5-tuple $\sigma = \langle \rho, L, h, t, m \rangle$. The first four components comprise, essentially, a 2-level store: $\rho \in \mathcal{E}$ is an environment assigning values for the variables of the *current* procedure. $L \subset Loc$ contains the locations of allocated objects. (An object is identified by its location. We interchangeably use the terms object and location.) $h \in \mathcal{H}$ assigns values to fields of allocated objects. $t \in \mathcal{TM}$ maps every allocated object to the type-identifier of its (immutable) type. Implicitly, t associates every allocated location to a module: The module that a location $l \in L$ *belongs to in memory state* σ, denoted by $m(t(l))$, is $m(t(l))$. The additional component, $m \in \mathcal{M}$, is the module of the current procedure. We refer to m as the *current module* of σ. (We denote the current module of a state σ by $m(\sigma)$.)

$l \in Loc$
$v \in Val = Loc \cup \{null\} \cup \{\ominus\}$
$\rho \in \mathcal{E} = \mathcal{V} \hookrightarrow Val$
$h \in \mathcal{H} = Loc \hookrightarrow \mathcal{F} \hookrightarrow Val$
$t \in \mathcal{TM} = Loc \hookrightarrow \mathcal{T}$
$\sigma \in \Sigma = \mathcal{E} \times 2^{Loc} \times \mathcal{H} \times \mathcal{TM} \times \mathcal{M}$

Fig. 2. Semantic domains

Note that in $\mathcal{DOS}$, reachability, and thus domination,[4] are defined with respect to the *accessible heap*, *i.e.*, $\ominus$-valued references do not lead to any object.

[4] An object l_2 is *reachable from* (resp. *connected to*) an object l_1 in a memory state σ if there is a directed (resp. undirected) path in the heap of σ from l_1 to l_2. An object l is *reachable* in σ if it is reachable from a location which is pointed-to by some variable. An object l is a *dominator* if every access path pointing to an object reachable from l, must traverse through l.

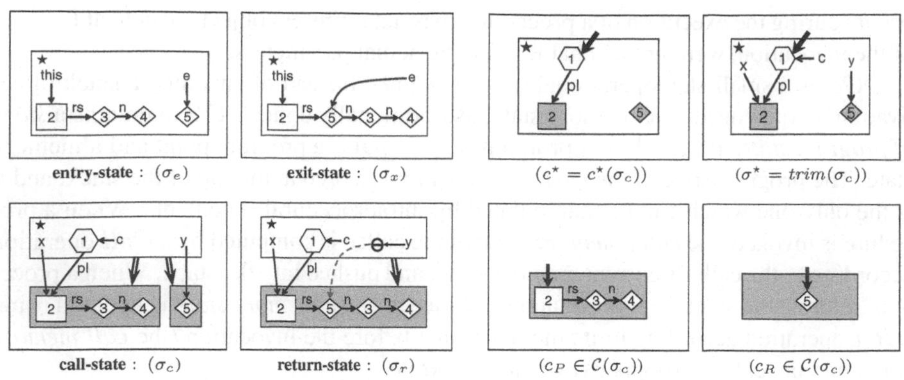

Fig. 3. $(\sigma_c, \sigma_e, \sigma_x, \sigma_r)$: $\mathcal{DOS}$ memory states occurring in an invocation of `x.release(y)` on σ_c. $(c^\star, c_P, c_R)$: The implicit components of σ_c. $(\sigma^\star)$: The trimmed memory state induced by σ_c.

Example 1. Fig. 3 (σ_c) depicts a possible $\mathcal{DOS}$ memory state that may arise in the execution of a program using the module m_{RP}. The state contains a *client* object (shown as an hexagon) pointed-to by variable `c` and having a `pl`-field pointing to a resource pool (shown as a rectangle). The resource pool, containing two resources (shown as diamonds) is also pointed-to by a variable `x`. In addition, a local variable `y` points to a resource outside the pool. (The numbers attached to nodes indicate the location of objects. The value of a (non-null) pointer variable is shown as an edge from a label consisting of the variable name to the object pointed-to by the variable. The value of a (non-null) field f of an object is shown as an f-labeled edge emanating from the object. Other graphical elements can be ignored for now.) The states σ_c and σ_e (also shown in Fig. 3), depict, respectively, the call- and the entry-memory states of an invocation of `x.release(y)` which we use as an example throughout this section. Note that σ_e represents only the values of the local variables of `release` and does not represent the (unreachable) client-object. In the return memory state of the invocation, depicted in Fig. 3 (σ_r), the dangling reference `y` has the $\ominus$-value, and the resource pool dominates the resources in its list. (The return state *does not* represent the value of `y` before the call, indicated by the dashed arrow.)

Components. Intuitively, a component provides a partial view of a $\mathcal{DOS}$ memory state σ. A component of σ consists of a set of reachable objects in σ, which all belong to the same module, and records their types, their link structure, and their *spatial interface i.e.*, references to and from immediately connected objects and variables.

More formally, a component $c \in \mathcal{C} = 2^{Loc} \times 2^{Loc} \times 2^{Loc} \times \mathcal{H} \times \mathcal{TM} \times \mathcal{M}$ is a 6-tuple. A *component* $c = \langle I, L, R, h, t, m \rangle$ is a *component of* a $\mathcal{DOS}$ memory state σ if the following holds: L, the set of c's *internal objects*, contains only reachable objects in σ. $I \subseteq L$ and $R \subseteq Loc \setminus L$ constitute c's spatial interface: I records the *entry locations* into c. An object inside c is an *entry location* if it is pointed-to by a variable or by a field of a *reachable* object outside c. R is c's *rim*. An object outside c is in c's rim if it is pointed-to by a field of an object inside c. h defines the values of fields for objects inside c. We refer to a field pointing to an internal resp. rim object as an intra- resp. inter-component reference. h should be the restriction of σ's heap on L. t defines the types of the objects inside c and in its rim. t should be the restriction of σ's type map on $L \cup R$. m is c's *component module*. We say that component c belongs to m. The type of every object inside c must belong to m. (If L is empty then m must be the current module of σ.) Note that a component c records (among other things) all the aliasing information available in σ pertaining to fields of c's internal objects. For reasons explained below, we treat a variable pointing to a location outside the current component as an inter-component reference leaving the current component, and add that location to its rim (and relax the definition of a component accordingly).

Example 2. Memory state $\sigma_c = \langle \rho_c, L_c, h_c, t_c, m_c \rangle$, depicted in Fig. 3, is comprised of three components. A rectangular frame encompasses the internal objects of every component. The current component, marked with a star, belongs to m_c, the client's module. The sealed components, drawn shaded, belong to module m_{RP}. Fig. 3 ($c^\star$) depicts $c^\star = \langle I^\star, L^\star, R^\star, h^\star, t^\star, m_c \rangle$, the current component of σ_c, separately from σ_c. The client-object is the only object inside $c^\star$. It is also an entry location, *i.e.*, $I^\star = L^\star = \{1\}$. An entry location is drawn with a wide arrow pointing to it. The resource pool and the resource are rim objects, *i.e.*, $R^\star = \{2, 5\}$. Rim objects are drawn opaque. The `pl`-labeled edge depicts the only (inter-component) reference in $c^\star$. Note that $h^\star = h_c|_{\{1\}}$ and $t^\star = t_c|_{\{1,2,5\}}$. Fig. 3 ($c_P$) and ($c_R$) depict σ_c's sealed components.

The types of the reachable objects in a memory state σ induce a (unique) *implicit component decomposition* of σ: (i) a single *implicit current component*, denoted by $c^\star(\sigma)$, containing all the *reachable* objects in σ that belong to σ's current module and (ii) a set of *implicit sealed components*, denoted by $\mathcal{C}(\sigma)$, containing (disjoint subsets of) all the *other* reachable objects. Two objects *reside within* the same implicit sealed component if they belong to the same module $m_s \neq m(\sigma)$ and are connected in σ's heap via an *undirected heap path* which only goes through objects that belong to module m_s.

The component decomposition of a memory state σ induces an *implicit component (directed) graph*. The nodes of the graph are the implicit components of σ. The graph has an edge from c_1 to c_2 if there is a rim object in c_1 which is an entry location in c_2, *i.e.*, if there is a reference from an object in c_1 to an object in c_2. For simplicity, we assume that the graph is connected, and treat local variables in a way that ensures that.

Example 3. Component $c^\star$, c_P, and c_R are the implicit components of σ_c, *i.e.*, $c^\star = c^\star(\sigma_c)$ and $\{c_P, c_R\} = \mathcal{C}(\sigma_c)$. Double-line arrows depict the edges of the component graph. This graph is connected because $c^\star$'s rim contains the resource pointed-to by y.

From now on, whenever we refer to a component of a memory state σ, we mean an implicit component of σ, and use the term *implicit component* only for emphasis. (For formal definitions of components and of component graphs, see [9].)

Dynamically encapsulated memory state. We define the constraints imposed on memory states by the dynamic encapsulation model by placing certain restrictions on the allowed implicit components and induced implicit component graphs.

Definition 1 (Dynamic encapsulation). *A $\mathcal{DOS}$ memory state $\sigma \in \Sigma$ is said to be* ***dynamically encapsulated****, if (i) the implicit component graph of σ is a directed tree and (ii) every (implicit) sealed component in σ has exactly one entry location.*

We refer to the parent (resp. child) of a component c in the component tree as the *owner* of c (resp. a subcomponent of c). We refer to the single entry location of a sealed component c in a dynamically encapsulated memory state σ as c's *header*, and denote it by $hdr(c)$. We denote the module of a component c by $m(c)$.

Invariant 1. *The following properties hold in every dynamically encapsulated $\mathcal{DOS}$ memory state $\sigma \in \Sigma$ and its implicit decomposition: (i) A local variable can only point to a location inside $c^\star(\sigma)$, the current component of σ, or to the header of one of $c^\star(\sigma)$'s subcomponents. (ii) For every component, every rim object is the header of a sealed component of σ. (iii) A field of an object in a component of σ can only point to an object inside c, or to the header of one of c's subcomponents. (iv) All the objects in a sealed component are reachable from the component's header. (v) A header dominates its reachable heap.*[4] *(vi) Every reachable object is inside exactly one component. (vii) If $c_1 \in \mathcal{C}(\sigma)$ owns $c_2 \in \mathcal{C}(\sigma)$ then $m(c_1)$* depends *on $m(c_2)$.*

$\mathcal{DOS}$ preserves dynamic encapsulation. Thus, from now on, whenever we refer to a $\mathcal{DOS}$ memory state, we mean a *dynamically encapsulated $\mathcal{DOS}$* memory state. As a consequence of our simplifying assumptions and the acyclicity of the module dependency relation, the following holds for every $\mathcal{DOS}$ memory state σ: (i) The internal objects of $c^\star(\sigma)$ are exactly those that the current procedure can manipulate without an (indirect) intermodule procedure call. (ii) The rim of $c^\star(\sigma)$ contains all the objects which the current procedure can pass as parameters to an intermodule procedure call.

3.2 Operational Semantics

Intraprocedural Statements. Intraprocedural statements are handled as usual in a two-level store semantics for pointer programs (see, *e.g.*, [10]). The only unique aspect of $\mathcal{DOS}$, formalized in [9], is that it aborts if an inaccessible-valued pointer is accessed.

Interprocedural Statements. $\mathcal{DOS}$ is a local-heap semantics [11]: when a procedure is invoked, it starts executing on an *input heap* containing only the set of *available objects for the invocation*. An object is *available for an invocation* if it is a *parameter object*, *i.e.*, pointed-to by an actual parameter, or if it is reachable from one. We refer to a component whose header is a parameter object as a *parameter component*.

A local-heap semantics and its abstractions benefit from not having to represent unavailable objects. However, in general, the semantics needs to take special care of available objects that are pointed-to by an access path which bypasses the parameters (*cutpoints* [11]). In this paper, we do not wish to handle the problem of analyzing programs with an unbounded number of cutpoints [11], which we consider a separate research problem. Thus, for simplicity, we require that *intramodule* procedure calls should be *cutpoint-free* [5], *i.e.*, the parameter objects should dominate[4] the available objects for the invocation. (In general, we can handle a *bounded* number of cutpoints.[5])

[5] We can treat a bounded number of cutpoints as additional parameters: Every procedure is modified to have k additional (hidden) formal parameters (where k is the bound on the number of allowed cutpoints). When a procedure is invoked, the (modified) *semantics* binds the additional parameters with references to the cutpoints. This is the essence of [6]'s treatment of cutpoints.

$$
\begin{array}{ll}
\langle Call_{y=p(x_1,\ldots,x_k)}, \sigma_c \rangle \overset{D}{\rightsquigarrow} \sigma_e & m_c = m(p) \Rightarrow \textsc{cpf}\ \ D_{\rho_c,h_c}(dom(\rho_c), F_p) \\
\quad \sigma_e = \langle \rho_e, L_c, h_c|_{L_{rel}}, t_c|_{L_{rel}}, m(p) \rangle & m_c \neq m(p) \Rightarrow \textsc{dif}\ \ \forall 1 \leq i < j \leq k : \rho_c(x_i) \neq \rho_c(x_j) \\
\quad \rho_e = [z_i \mapsto \rho_c(x_i) \mid 1 \leq i \leq k] & \qquad\qquad\qquad\ \ \textsc{loc}\ \ \forall 1 \leq i \leq k : \rho_c(x_i) \in Loc \\
\quad \text{where: } L_{rel} = R_{h_c}(\{\rho_c(x_i) \in Loc \mid 1 \leq i \leq k\}) & \\
\langle Ret_{y=p(x_1,\ldots,x_k)}, \sigma_c, \sigma_x \rangle \overset{D}{\rightsquigarrow} \sigma_r & m_c \neq m(p) \Rightarrow \textsc{own}\ \forall z \in F_p^{nt} : \rho_x(z) \in Loc \\
\quad \sigma_r = \langle \rho_r, L_x, h_r, t_r, m_c \rangle & \qquad\qquad\qquad\ \ \textsc{dom}\ \forall z \in F_p^{nt} : D_{\rho_x^{\ominus}, h_x}(F_p^{nt}, \{z\}) \\
\quad \rho_r = (block \circ \rho_c)[y \mapsto \rho_x(ret)] & \\
\quad h_r = (block \circ h_c|_{L_c \setminus L_{rel}}) \cup h_x & \\
\quad t_r = t_c|_{L_c \setminus L_{rel}} \cup t_x & \\
\quad \text{where: } L_{rel} = R_{h_c}(\{\rho_c(x_i) \in Loc \mid 1 \leq i \leq k\}) & \\
\qquad\qquad \rho_x^{\ominus} = \rho_x[z \mapsto \ominus \mid m_c \neq m(p), z \in F_p^t] & \\
\qquad\qquad block = \lambda v \in Val. \begin{cases} \rho_x^{\ominus}(z_i) & v = \rho_c(x_i), 1 \leq i \leq k \\ v & \text{otherwise} \end{cases} &
\end{array}
$$

Fig. 4. *Call* an *Ret* operations for an arbitrary procedure call $y = p(x_1, \ldots, x_k)$ assuming p's formal variables are $z_1, \ldots, z_k$. $\sigma_c = \langle \rho_c, L_c, h_c, t_c, m_c \rangle$. $\sigma_x = \langle \rho_x, L_x, h_x, t_x, m_x \rangle$. $F_p^{nt} = \{ret\} \cup (F_p \setminus F_p^t)$. Variable `ret` is used to communicate the return value. We use the following functions and relations, formally defined in [9]: $R_h(L)$ computes the locations which are reachable in heap h from the set of locations L. The auxiliary relation $D_{\rho,h}(V_I, V_D)$ holds if the set of objects pointed-to by a variable in V_D, according to environment ρ, dominates the part of heap h reachable from them, with respect to the objects pointed-to by the variables in V_I.

Fig. 4 defines the meaning of the *Call* and *Ret* operations pertaining to an arbitrary procedure call $y = p(x_1, \ldots, x_k)$.

Procedure calls. The *Call* operation computes the callee's *entry memory state* (σ_e). First, it checks whether the call satisfies our *simplifying* assumptions. In case of an intramodule procedure invocation, the caller's memory state (σ_c) is required to satisfy the domination condition (CPF) ensuring cutpoint-freedom. Intermodule procedure calls are invoked under even stricter conditions which are fundamental to our approach: Every parameter object must dominate the subheap reachable from it. This ensures that distinct components are unshared. However, there is no need to check these conditions as they are invariants in our semantics: Inv. 1(i,iv,v) ensures that every parameter object to an intermodule procedure call is a header which dominates its reachable heap. (Note that Inv. 1(iv) can be exploited to check whether an object is a dominator by only inspecting access paths traversing through its component.) Thus, only our simplifying assumptions pertaining to non-nullness (LOC) and non-aliasing of parameters (DIF) need to be checked.

The entry memory state is computed by binding the values of the formal parameters in the callee's environment to the values of the corresponding actual parameters; projecting the caller's heap and type map on the available objects for the invocation; and setting the module of the entry memory state to be the module of the invoked procedure.

Note that in intermodule procedure calls, the change of the current module implicitly changes the component tree: all the available objects for the invocation which belong to the callee's module constitute the callee's current component. By Inv. 1 (vi,vii), these objects must come from parameter components.

Example 4. Fig. 3 (σ_e) shows the entry memory state resulting from applying the *Call* operation pertaining to the procedure call `x.release(y)` on the call memory state σ_c, also shown in Fig. 3. All the objects in σ_e belong to m_{RP}, and thus, to its current component. Note that the latter is, essentially, a fusion of c_P and c_R, the sealed components in σ_c.

Note: The current component of a $\mathcal{DOS}$ memory state $\sigma \in \Sigma$ is the root of the component tree induced by the *local heap* represented in σ. In a *global heap*, this current component might have been one or more non-root subcomponents of a larger component-tree which is only partially visible to the current procedure. For example, the current component of the client procedure is not visible during the execution of `release`.

Procedure returns. The caller's return memory state (σ_r) is computed by a *Ret* operation. When an *intermodule* procedure invocation returns, *Ret* first checks that in the exit memory state (σ_x) every non-transferred formal parameter points to an object (OWN) which dominates its reachable subheap (DOM). This ensures that returned components are disjoint and, in particular, that the procedure's execution respected its ownership transfer specification. (Here we exploit simplifying assumption (b) of Sec. 2.)

Ret updates the caller's memory state (which reflects the program's state at the time of the call) by carving out the input heap passed to the callee from the caller's heap and replacing it instead with the callee's (possibly) mutated heap. In $\mathcal{DOS}$, an object never changes its location and locations are never reallocated. Thus, any pointer to an available object in the caller's memory state (either by a field of an unavailable object or a variable) points after the replacement to an up-to-date version of the object.

Most importantly, the semantics ensures that any future attempt by the caller to access a transferred component is foiled: We say that a local variable of the caller is *dangling* if, at the time of the invocation, it points to (the header of) a component transferred to the callee. A pointer field of an object in the caller's memory state which was unavailable for the invocation is considered to be *dangling* under the same condition. The semantics enforces the transfer of ownership by *blocking*: assigning the special value $\ominus$ to every dangling reference in the caller's memory state. (Blocking also occurs when an *intra*module procedure invocation returns to propagate ownership transfers done by the callee.) Note that cutpoint-freedom ensures that the only object that separate the callee's heap from the caller's heap are parameter objects. Thus, in particular, the only references that might be blocked point to parameter objects.

When an intermodule call returns, and the current module changes, the component tree is changed too: The callee's current component may be split into different components whose headers are the parameter objects pointed-to by non-transferred parameters. These components may be different from the (input) parameter components.

Example 5. Fig. 3 (σ_r) depicts the memory state resulting from applying the *Ret* operation pertaining to the procedure call `x.release(y)` on the memory state σ_c and σ_x, also shown in Fig. 3. The insertion of the resource pointed-to by `y` at the call-site into the pool has (implicitly) fused the two m_{RP}-components. By the standard semantics, `y` should point to the first resource in the list (as indicated by the dashed arrow). This would violate dynamic encapsulation. $\mathcal{DOS}$, however, utilizes the *ownership specification* to block `y` thus preserving dynamic encapsulation.

3.3 Observational Soundness

We say that two values are *comparable* in $\mathcal{DOS}$ if neither one is $\ominus$. We say that a $\mathcal{DOS}$ memory state σ is *observationally sound* with respect to a standard semantics σ_G if every pair of access paths that have comparable values in σ, has equal values in σ iff they have equal values in σ_G. $\mathcal{DOS}$ *simulates* the standard 2-level store semantics: Executing the same sequence of statements in the $\mathcal{DOS}$ semantics and in the standard semantics either results in a $\mathcal{DOS}$ memory states which is observationally sound with respect to the resulting standard memory state, or the $\mathcal{DOS}$ execution gets *stuck* due to a constraint breach (detected by $\mathcal{DOS}$). A program is *dynamically encapsulated* if it does not have have an execution trace which gets stuck. (Note that the initial state of an execution in $\mathcal{DOS}$ is observationally sound with respect to its standard counterpart).

Our goal is to detect structural invariants that are true according to the *standard semantics*. $\mathcal{DOS}$ acts like the standard semantics as long as the program's execution satisfies certain constraints. $\mathcal{DOS}$ enforces these restrictions by blocking references that a program should not access. Similarly, our analysis reports an invariant concerning equality of access paths only when these access paths have comparable values.

An invariant concerning equality of access paths in $\mathcal{DOS}$ for a dynamically encapsulated program is also an invariant in the standard semantics. This makes abstract interpretation algorithms of $\mathcal{DOS}$ suitable for verifying data structure invariants, for detecting memory error violations, and for performing compile-time garbage collection.

4 Modular Analysis

This section presents a conservative static analysis which identifies conservative *module invariants*. These invariants are true in *any* program according to the $\mathcal{DOS}$ semantics and in *any dynamically encapsulated* programs according to the standard semantics.

The analysis is derived by two (successive) abstractions of the $\mathcal{DOS}$ semantics: The *trimming semantics* provides the basis of our *modular* analysis by representing only components of the analyzed module. The *abstract trimming semantics* allows for an effective analysis by providing a *bounded* abstraction of trimmed memory states (utilizing existing *intra*procedural abstractions).

Module Invariants. A *module invariant* of a module m is a property that holds for all the components that belong to m when they are not being used (*i.e.*, for sealed components). Our analysis finds module invariants by computing a conservative description of the set of all possible sealed components of the module. More formally, the *module invariant of module m for type T*, denoted by $[\![Inv_m\, T]\!] \subseteq 2^{\mathcal{C}}$, is a set of sealed components of module m whose header is of type T: a sealed component c is in $[\![Inv_m\, T]\!]$ iff there exists a reachable $\mathcal{DOS}$ memory state σ in some program such that $c \in \mathcal{C}(\sigma)$.

For example, the module invariant of module m_{RP} for type `RPoll` in our running example is the set containing all resource pools with a (possibly empty) *acyclic* finite list of resources. The module invariant of module m_{RP} for type `R` is the singleton set containing a single resource with a *nullified* `n`-field: An acquired resource always has a *null*-valued `n`-field and a released resource is inaccessible.

Trimming semantics. The trimming semantics represents only the parts of the heap which belong to the current module. In particular, it abstracts away all information contained in sealed components and the shape of the component tree.

More formally, the *domain of trimmed states* is $\Sigma^\star = \mathcal{E} \times \mathcal{C}$. The *trimmed state induced by a $\mathcal{DOS}$ memory state $\sigma \in \Sigma$*, denoted by $trim(\sigma)$, is $\langle \rho, c^\star(\sigma) \rangle$. (For example, Fig. 3 ($\sigma^\star$) depicts the trimmed memory state induced by the $\mathcal{DOS}$ memory state shown in Fig. 3 (σ_c).) We say that two trimmed memory states are *isomorphic*, denoted by $\sigma_1^\star \sim \sigma_2^\star$, if $\sigma_1^\star$ can be obtained from $\sigma_2^\star$ by a consistent location renaming. A trimmed memory state $\sigma^\star$ *abstracts* a $\mathcal{DOS}$ memory state σ if $\sigma^\star \sim trim(\sigma)$.

A trimmed memory state contains enough information to determine the induced effect [14] under the trimming abstraction of intraprocedural statements and intramodule $Call$ and Ret operations by applying the statement to *any* memory state it represents. Intuitively, the reason for this uniform behavior is that the aforementioned statements are indifferent to the *contents* of sealed components: They only consider the values of fields of objects inside the current component (inter-component references included).

Analyzing intermodule procedure calls. The main challenge lies in the handling of intermodule procedure calls: Applying the induced effect of $Call$ is challenging because the *most important* information required to determine the input heap of an intermodule call is the contents of parameter components. However, this is exactly the information lost under the *trimming abstraction* of the call memory state. Applying the induced effect of Ret operations pertaining to intermodule procedure calls is challenging as it considers information about the contents of heap parts manipulated by *different* modules.

We overcome the challenge pertaining to $Call$ operations by utilizing the fact that $\mathcal{DOS}$ always changes components as a whole, *i.e.*, there is no sharing between components, thus changes to one component cannot affect *a part* of the internal structure of another component. In particular, we are *anticipating the possible entry memory states of an intermodule procedure call*: In the $\mathcal{DOS}$ semantics, the current component of an entry memory state to an intermodule procedure call is comprised, essentially, as a *necessarily* disjoint union of parameter components. Note that components are sealed only when an intermodule procedure call returns. Furthermore, the only way a sealed component can be mutated is to pass it back as a parameter to a procedure of its own module. Thus, a partial view of the execution trace, which considers only the executions of procedures that belong to the analyzed module, and collects the sealed components generated when an intermodule procedure invocation returns, can (conservatively) anticipate the possible input states for the next intermodule invocations. Specifically, *only* a combination of *already generated sealed components* of the module can be the component parameters in an intermodule procedure invocation.

We resolve Ret's need to consider components belonging to different modules utilizing the ownership transfer specification and the limited effect of intermodule procedure invocations on the caller's current component: The only effect an intermodule procedure call has on the current component of the caller is that (i) dangling references are blocked and (ii) the return value is assigned to a local variable. (By our simplifying assumptions, the return value must point either to a parameter object or to a component not previously owned by the caller. The latter case amounts to a new object in the rim of the caller's current component). Given a sound ownership specification for the invoked procedures we can apply this effect directly to the caller's memory state. This approach can be generalized (and made more precise) to handle richer specifications concerning, *e.g.*, nullness of parameters, aliasing of parameters (and return values), and digests.

Abstract trimming semantics. We provide an effective conservative abstract interpretation [14] algorithm which determines module invariants by devising a bounded abstraction of trimmed memory states. Rather than providing a new intraprocedural abstraction and analyses, we show how to *lift* existing *intra*procedural shape analyses to obtain a modular shape abstraction. An abstraction of a trimmed memory state, being comprised of an environment of a single procedure and a subheap, is very similar to an abstraction of a standard two-level store. The additional elements that the abstraction needs to track is a bounded number of entry-locations and a distinction between internal objects and rim objects. In addition, the abstract domain, expected to support operations pertaining to basic pointer manipulating statements, should be extended to allow for: checking if a $\ominus$-valued reference is accessed; the operations required for cutpoint-free local-heap analysis: carving out subheaps reachable from variables and combining disjoint subheaps; and the ability to answer queries regarding domination by variables. The only additional operation required to implement our analysis is of *blocking*, *i.e.*, setting the values of all reference pointing to a given variable-pointed object to $\ominus$. The abstract domains of [2, 3, 4], which already support the operations required for performing standard local-heap cutpoint-free analysis, can be extended with these operations.

Modular analysis. We conduct our modular static analysis by performing an interprocedural analysis of a module together with its *most-general-client*. The most-general-client simulates the behavior of an arbitrary dynamically encapsulated (*well behaved*) client. Essentially, it is a collection of non-deterministic procedures that execute arbitrary sequences of procedure calls to the analyzed module. The parameters passed to these calls also result from an arbitrary (possibly recursive) sequence of procedure calls. The most-general client exploits the fact that *different components are effectively disjoint* to separately create the value of every parameter passed to an intermodule procedure call. Thus, any conservative interprocedural analysis of the most-general client (which uses an extended abstract domain, as discussed above, and utilizes ownership specification to determine the effect of intermodule procedure calls made by the analyzed module) can modularly detect module invariants. In particular, the analysis can be performed by extending existing interprocedural frameworks for interprocedural shape analysis, *e.g.*, [5, 6]. Note that during the analysis process we also find conservative *module implementation invariants*: Properties that hold for all possible current components at different program points inside the component in every possible execution. [9] provides a scheme for constructing the most-general-client of a module. ([9] also provides a characterization of the module invariants based on a fixpoint equation system).

5 Related Work

A distinguishing aspect of our work is that we integrate a shape analysis with encapsulation constraints. Our work presents a nice interplay between encapsulation and modular shape analysis: it uses dynamic encapsulation to enable modular shape analysis, and uses shape analysis to determine that the program is dynamically encapsulated. In this section, we review some closely related work to both aspects of our approach. More discussion on related work can be found in [9].

Modular static analysis. [1] describes the fundamental techniques for modular static program analysis. These techniques allow to compose separate analyses of different program parts. We use their techniques, in particular, we use simple *user provided interfaces* to communicate the (limited) effect of mutations done by different modules.

Modular heap analysis. [15] presents a modular analysis which infers class invariants based on an abstraction of program traces. [16] is an extension which handles subtyping. The determined invariants concern values of atomic fields of objects of the analyzed class and of subobjects, provided that they are never leaked to the context, *e.g.*, passed as return values. [17] modularly determines invariants regarding the value of an integer field and the length of an array field of the *same* object. Our analysis, computes shape invariants of subheaps comprised of objects that may be passed as parameters.

Interprocedural shape analysis. [18, 19] utilize user-specified pre- and post- conditions to achieve modular shape analysis which can handle a bounded number of flat set-like data structures. It allows objects to be placed in multiple sets. In our approach, an object can be placed only in a single separately-analyzed but arbitrarily-nested set. Other interprocedural shape analysis algorithms *e.g.*, [5, 6, 11, 20, 21, 22], compute procedure summaries, but are not modular. [22] tracks properties of single objects. The other algorithms abstract whole local heaps. Our abstraction, on the other hand, represent only a part of the local heap (*i.e.*, only the current component). We note that the aforementioned approaches do not require a user specification, which we require.

Encapsulation. Deep ownership models structure the heap into a tree of so-called *owner contexts* (see [23] for a survey). Our module-induced decomposition of a memory state into a tree of components is similar to the package-induced partitioning of a memory state into a tree of memory-regions in [24]. Our constraints are similar to external uniqueness [25], which requires that there be a *unique* reference pointing to an object from outside its (transitively) owned context. Our ownership specification is also in the spirit of [25]'s destructive reads and borrowing. [26] uses shape analysis to modularly verify (specified) uniqueness of a *live* reference to an *object*. Our use of sealed and unsealed components is close to the use of packed and unpacked owner contexts in Boogie [27, 28]. The latter, however, can handle reentrancy. The central difference between the approaches is that our techniques infer module invariants whereas Boogie verifies class invariants provided by the programmer.

Local reasoning. [29] and [30] allow to modularly conduct local reasoning [10] about abstract data structures and abstract data types with inheritance, respectively. The reasoning requires user-specified resource invariants and loop invariants. Our analysis automatically infers these invariants based on an ownership transfer specification (and an instance of the bounded parametric abstraction). [30], however, allows for more sharing than in our model. Our use of rim-objects (resp. abstract sealed components) is analogous to [30]'s use of *abstract predicates*' names (resp. resource invariants).

6 Conclusion

Our long term research goal is to devise precise and efficient static shape analysis algorithms which are applicable to realistic programs. We see this work as an important step towards a modular shape analysis. While the ownership model is fairly restrictive with respect to the coupling between separate components, it is very permissive about what can happen inside a single component. This model is also sufficient to express several, natural, usage constraints that arise in practice. (In particular, when accompanied with digests.) We believe that our restrictions can be relaxed to help address a larger class of programs. We plan to pursue this line of research in future work.

Acknowledgments. We are grateful for the helpful comments of T. Lev-Ami, R. Manevich, S. Rajamani, J. Reineke, G. Yorsh, and the anonymous referees.

References

1. Cousot, P., Cousot, R.: Modular static program analysis, invited paper. In: CC. (2002)
2. Lev-Ami, T., Immerman, N., Sagiv, M.: Abstraction for shape analysis with fast and precise transformers. In: CAV. (2006)
3. Manevich, R., Yahav, E., Ramalingam, G., Sagiv, M.: Predicate abstraction and canonical abstraction for singly-linked lists. In: VMCAI. (2005)
4. Distefano, D., O'Hearn, P.W., Yang, H.: A local shape analysis based on separation logic. In: TACAS. (2006)
5. Rinetzky, N., Sagiv, M., Yahav, E.: Interprocedural shape analysis for cutpoint-free programs. In: SAS. (2005)
6. Gotsman, A., Berdine, J., Cook., B.: Interprocedural shape analysis with separated heap abstractions. In: SAS. (2006)
7. Rinetzky, N., Ramalingam, G., Sagiv, M., Yahav, E.: Componentized heap abstractions. Tech. Rep. 164, Tel Aviv University (2006)
8. Strom, R.E., Yemini, S.: Typestate: A programming language concept for enhancing software reliability. IEEE Trans. Software Eng. **12**(1) (1986) 157–171
9. Rinetzky, N., Poetzsch-Heffter, A., Ramalingam, G., Sagiv, M., Yahav, E.: Modular shape analysis for dynamically encapsulated programs. Tech. Rep. 107, Tel Aviv University (2006)
10. Reynolds, J.: Separation logic: a logic for shared mutable data structures. In: LICS. (2002)
11. Rinetzky, N., Bauer, J., Reps, T., Sagiv, M., Wilhelm, R.: A semantics for procedure local heaps and its abstractions. In: POPL. (2005)
12. Plotkin, G.D.: A Structural Approach to Operational Semantics. Technical Report DAIMI FN-19, University of Aarhus (1981)
13. Knoop, J., Steffen, B.: The interprocedural coincidence theorem. In: CC. (1992)
14. Cousot, P., Cousot, R.: Abstract interpretation: A unified lattice model for static analysis of programs by construction of approximation of fixed points. In: POPL. (1977)
15. Logozzo, F.: Class-level modular analysis for object oriented languages. In: SAS. (2003)
16. Logozzo, F.: Automatic inference of class invariants. In: VMCAI. (2004)
17. Aggarwal, A., Randall, K.: Related field analysis. In: PLDI. (2001)
18. Lam, P., Kuncak, V., Rinard, M.: Hob: A tool for verifying data structure consistency. In: CC (tool demo). (2005)
19. Wies, T., Kuncak, V., Lam, P., Podelski, A., Rinard, M.: Field constraint analysis. In: VMCAI. (2006)

20. Jeannet, B., Loginov, A., Reps, T., Sagiv, M.: A relational approach to interprocedural shape analysis. In: SAS. (2004)
21. Chong, S., Rugina, R.: Static analysis of accessed regions in recursive data structures. In: SAS. (2003)
22. Hackett, B., Rugina, R.: Region-based shape analysis with tracked locations. In: POPL. (2005)
23. Noble, J., Biddle, R., Tempero, E., Potanin, A., Clarke, D.: Towards a model of encapsulation. In: IWACO. (2003)
24. Zhao, T., Noble, J., Vitek, J.: Scoped types for real-time java. In: RTSS. (2004)
25. Clarke, D., Wrigstad, T.: External uniqueness is unique enough. In: ECOOP. (2003)
26. Boyland, J.: Alias burying: unique variables without destructive reads. Softw. Pract. Exper. **31**(6) (2001) 533–553
27. Barnett, M., DeLine, R., Fähndrich, M., Leino, K.R.M., Schulte, W.: Verification of object-oriented programs with invariants. Journal of Object Technology **3**(6) (2004) 27–56
28. Leino, K.R.M., Müller, P.: A verification methodology for model fields. In: ESOP. (2006)
29. O'Hearn, P., Yang, H., Reynolds, J.: Separation and information hiding. In: POPL. (2004)
30. Bierman, G., Parkinson, M.: Separation logic and abstractions. In: POPL. (2005)

Static Analysis by Policy Iteration on Relational Domains

Stephane Gaubert[1], Eric Goubault[2], Ankur Taly[3], and Sarah Zennou[2]

[1] INRIA Rocquencourt
stephane.gaubert@inria.fr
[2] CEA-LIST, MeASI
{eric.goubault,sarah.zennou}@cea.fr
[3] IIT Bombay
ankurtaly@iitb.ac.in

Abstract. We give a new practical algorithm to compute, in finite time, a fixpoint (and often the least fixpoint) of a system of equations in the abstract numerical domains of zones and templates used for static analysis of programs by abstract interpretation. This paper extends previous work on the non-relational domain of intervals to relational domains. The algorithm is based on policy iteration techniques– rather than Kleene iterations as used classically in static analysis– and generates from the system of equations a finite set of simpler systems that we call *policies*. This set of policies satisfies a *selection property* which ensures that the minimal fixpoint of the original system of equations is the minimum of the fixpoints of the policies. Computing a fixpoint of a policy is done by linear programming. It is shown, through experiments made on a prototype analyzer, compared in particular to analyzers such as LPInv or the Octagon Analyzer, to be in general more precise and faster than the usual Kleene iteration combined with widening and narrowing techniques.

1 Introduction

One of the crucial steps of static analysis by abstract interpretation [CC76] is the precise and efficient solving of the system of equations representing the abstraction of the program properties we want to find out. This is generally done by iteration solvers, based on Kleene's theorem, improved using extrapolation methods such as widening and narrowing operators [CC91]. These methods are quite efficient in practice, but are not always very precise and are difficult to tune as the quality and efficiency might depend a lot on the code under analysis.

In [CGG+05], some of the authors proposed a new method for solving these abstract semantic equations, which is based on policy iteration. The idea of policy iteration was introduced by Howard in the setting of Markov decision processes (one player stochastic games), see [How60]. It reduces a fixpoint problem to a sequence of simpler fixpoints problems, which are obtained by fixing policies (strategies of one player). This method was extended to a subclass of (zero-sum) two player stochastic games by Hoffman and Karp [HK66]. However,

R. De Nicola (Ed.): ESOP 2007, LNCS 4421, pp. 237–252, 2007.

static analysis problems lead to more general fixed point equations, which may be degenerate, as in the case of deterministic games [GG98]. The algorithm introduced in [CGG+05] works in a general setting, it always terminates with a fixpoint, the minimality of which can be guaranteed for the important subclass of sup-norm nonexpansive maps, see theorem 3 and remark 5 of [CGG+05]. The experiments showed that in general, policy iteration on intervals was faster and more precise than Kleene iteration plus (standard) widenings and narrowings. In this paper, we extend the framework of [CGG+05] to deal with policy iteration in relational domains, such as zones [Min01a], octagons [Min01b] and TCMs (Template Constraint Matrices [SSM05b]). We describe a general finite time algorithm that computes a fixpoint of functionals in such domains, and often a least fixpoint. We did not treat polyhedral analyses [CH78], as general polyhedra are in general not scalable.

There are two key novelties by comparison with [CGG+05]. The first one is that the computation of closures (canonical representatives of a set of constraints), which was trivial in the case of intervals, must now be expressed in terms of policies, in such a way that the selection property on which policy iteration relies is satisfied. We solve this problem by means of linear programming duality: we show in particular that every policy arising in a closure operation can be identified to an extreme point of a polyhedron. Secondly, for each policy, we have to solve a (simpler) set of equations, for which we use linear programming [Chv83], and not Kleene iteration as in [CGG+05]. We have developped a prototype; first benchmarks show that we gain in efficiency and in general in precision with respect to Kleene iteration solvers, in zones (comparison was made possible thanks to a prototype on the more refined domain of octagons of A. Miné [Min05]), and in simple TCMs (using LPInv [SSM05a]). This is conjecturally true for general TCMs too, a claim which is not yet substantiated by experimental results as we have not yet implemented general TCMs in our analyzer.

The paper is organized as follows: In section 2, we recap some of the basics of abstract interpretation and recall the main operations on the zone and TCMs abstract domains. We then introduce our policy iteration technique for both domains in section 3. Algorithmic and implementation issues are treated in section 4. We end up in section 5 by showing that policy iteration exhibits very good results in practice.

2 Basics

2.1 Abstract Interpretation by Static Analysis

Invariants, that can be obtained by abstract interpretation based static analysis, provide sound overapproximations of the set of values that program variables can take at each control point of the program. They are obtained by computing the *least fixpoint* of a system of abstract equations derived from the program to analyze. The correctness of the approximation is in general[1] guaranteed by the

[1] See [CC92] for more general frameworks.

theory of *Galois Connections* between the *concrete domain* (the set of variable values of the program) and the *abstract domain* (more easily tractable representatives of possible sets of values that the program can take).

For a complete lattice $(\mathcal{L}_e, \sqsubseteq_e)$, we write $\bot_e$ for its lowest element, $\top_e$ for its greatest element, $\sqcup_e$ and $\sqcap_e$ for the meet and join operations, respectively. We say that a self-map f of $(\mathcal{L}_e, \sqsubseteq_e)$ is *monotone* if $x \sqsubseteq_e y \Rightarrow f(x) \sqsubseteq_e f(y)$. Existence of fixpoints is ensured by the *Knaster-Tarski theorem* which states that every monotone self-map on a complete lattice has a fixpoint and indeed a least fixpoint. The least fixpoint of a monotone self-map f on a complete lattice will be denoted f^-.

Let $(\mathcal{L}_c, \sqsubseteq_c)$ be the complete lattice representing the concrete domain and $(\mathcal{L}_a, \sqsubseteq_a)$ the one representing the abstract domain. In most cases, the link between the two domains is expressed by a *Galois connection* [CC77], that is a pair (α, γ) of maps with the following properties : $\alpha : \mathcal{L}_c \to \mathcal{L}_a$ and $\gamma : \mathcal{L}_a \to \mathcal{L}_c$ are both monotone, and $\alpha(v_c) \sqsubseteq_a v_a$ iff $v_c \sqsubseteq_c \gamma(v_a)$. The map α is the *abstraction function*, γ, the *concretization function*. These properties guarantee that α gives the best upper approximation of a concrete property, in the abstract domain.

Figure 1 gives a C program (`test2`, left part) together with the semantic equations (right part) for both zones and TCMs domain where M_i is the abstract local invariant to be found at program line i. This would be our running example throughout the paper.

The function *context_initialization* creates an initial local invariant: typically by initializing the known variables to the top element of the abstract lattice of properties, or to some known value. The function $Assignment(var \leftarrow val)(M_j)$ is the (forward) abstract transformer which computes the new local invariant after assignment of value val to variable var from local invariant M_i. Finally, $(\cdot)^*$ is the normalization, or closure, of an abstract value, see section 2.2.

```
0   i = 150;
1   j = 175;
2   while (j >= 100){
3     i++;
4     if (j<= i){
5         i = i - 1;
6         j = j - 2;
7     }
8   }
9
```

$$M_0 = context\_initialization$$
$$M_2 = (Assignment\ (i \leftarrow 150,\ \ j \leftarrow 175)(M_0))^*$$
$$M_3 = ((M_2 \sqcup M_8) \sqcap (j \geq 100))^*$$
$$M_4 = (Assignment\ (i \leftarrow i+1)(M_3))^*$$
$$M_5 = (M_4 \sqcap (j \leq i))^*$$
$$M_7 = (Assignment\ (i \leftarrow i-1,\ \ j \leftarrow j-2)(M_5))^*$$
$$M_8 = ((M_4 \sqcap (j > i))^* \sqcup M_7$$
$$M_9 = ((M_2 \sqcup M_8) \sqcap (j < 100))^*$$

Fig. 1. A program (left part) and its representation by equations

Abstract versions f_a of the concrete primitives f_c such as *assignment*, *context_initialization* etc. are defined as $f_a(v) = \alpha(f_c(\gamma(v)))$, but in general we use a computable approximation $f_a(v)$ such that $\alpha(f_c(\gamma(v))) \sqsubseteq_a f_a(v)$. In particular invariants are preserved: if x is a (resp. the least) fixpoint of f_a then $\gamma(x)$ is a (resp. the least) (post) fixpoint of f_c.

Kleene iteration. It is well-known since Kleene that the least fixpoint of a continuous function on a complete lattice is $\bigsqcup_{n\in\mathbb{N}} f^n(\bot)$. This result gives an immediate algorithm for computing the fixpoint : starting from the value $x_0 = \bot$, the k-th iteration computes $x_k = x_{k-1} \sqcup f(x_{k-1})$. The algorithm finishes when $x_k = x_{k-1}$. For (only) monotonic functions, one may need more general ordinal iterations. In practice though, as these iterations might not stabilize in finite time, it is customary to use acceleration techniques, such as widening and narrowing operators [CC91] in place of the union in the equation above: for instance, on intervals, we can use the following widening ∇ and narrowing Δ operators:

$$[a,b]\nabla[c,d] = [e,f] \text{ with } e = \begin{cases} a & \text{if } a \le c \\ -\infty & \text{otherwise} \end{cases} \quad \text{and } f = \begin{cases} b & \text{if } d \le b \\ \infty & \text{otherwise,} \end{cases}$$

$$[a,b]\Delta[c,d] = [e,f] \text{ with } e = \begin{cases} c \text{ if } a = -\infty \\ a \text{ otherwise} \end{cases} \quad \text{and } f = \begin{cases} d \text{ if } b = \infty \\ b \text{ otherwise,} \end{cases}$$

These ensure finite time convergence to a fixpoint, which is not necessarily the least fixpoint: widening returns a post fixpoint while narrowing computes a fixpoint from a post fixpoint. On intervals, and for our running example, figure 1, if these widening and narrowing operators are applied after 10 iterations (as was done in [CGG+05] for matter of comparisons), we get the following iteration sequence, where we only indicate what happens at control points 3, 7, 8 and 9. We write (i_l^k, j_l^k) for the abstract values at line l and iteration k (describing the concrete values of variables i and j). Widening takes place between iteration 9 and 10 and narrowing between 11 and 12.

$(i_3^1, j_3^1) = ([150,150],[175,175])$
$(i_7^1, j_7^1) = \bot$
$(i_8^1, j_8^1) = ([151,151],[175,175])$
$(i_9^1, j_9^1) = \bot$
...
$(i_3^9, j_3^9) = ([150,158],[175,175])$
$(i_7^9, j_7^9) = \bot$
$(i_8^9, j_8^9) = ([151,159],[175,175])$
$(i_9^9, j_9^9) = \bot$
(widening)
$(i_3^{10}, j_3^{10}) = ([150,+\infty[,[175,175])$
$(i_7^{10}, j_7^{10}) = ([149,+\infty[,[173,173])$
$(i_8^{10}, j_8^{10}) = ([151,+\infty[,[173,175])$
$(i_9^{10}, j_9^{10}) = \bot$
$(i_3^{11}, j_3^{11}) = ([150,+\infty[,]-\infty,175])$
$(i_7^{11}, j_7^{11}) = ([150,+\infty[,]-\infty,149])$
$(i_8^{11}, j_8^{11}) = ([150,+\infty[,]-\infty,175])$
$(i_9^{11}, j_9^{11}) = ([150,+\infty[,]-\infty,99])$
(narrowing)
$(i_3^{12}, j_3^{12}) = ([150,+\infty[,[100,175])$
$(i_7^{12}, j_7^{12}) = ([150,+\infty[,[98,149])$
$(i_8^{12}, j_8^{12}) = ([150,+\infty[,[98,175])$
$(i_9^{12}, j_9^{12}) = ([150,+\infty[,[98,99])$

2.2 Two Existing Relational Abstract Domains

In this section we present some basics on the *zone* and *TCM* domains. In particular the loss of precision due to widenings is discussed. For an exhaustive treatment see respectively the references [Min01a] and [SSM05b,SCSM06]. These domains enable one to express linear relations between variables, all sub-polyhedral ([CH78]): in zones, linear relations involve only differences between variables, whereas in TCM, they involve finitely many linear combinations of the variables. Unlike in the case of polyhedral domains, these linear combinations are given *a priori*.

In the sequel we consider a finite set $V = \{v_1, \ldots, v_n\}$ of real valued variables. Let $\mathbb{I} = \mathbb{R} \cup \{-\infty, \infty\}$ be the extension of the set $\mathbb{R}$ of real values with two special values $-\infty$ (will be used to model a linear relation without solution in $\mathbb{R}$) and ∞ (linear relation will be satisfied by any value). The operators $\leq, \geq, min, max$ are extended as usual to deal with these values.

Zone Abstract Domain. To represent constraints like $v \leq c$ we extend V by a virtual fresh variable v_0 whose value is always zero so that $v \leq c$ becomes equivalent to $v_i - v_0 \leq c$. Let us denote $V_0 = V \cup \{v_0\}$. A *zone* is then a vector $c = (c_{0,0}, c_{0,1}, c_{0,2}, \ldots c_{n,n})$ where $c_{i,j} \in \mathbb{I}$ stands for the constraint $v_i - v_j \leq c_{i,j}$ for $v_i, v_j \in V_0$. The *concretization* of c is the set of real values of variables in V whose pairwise differences $v_i - v_j$ are bounded by the coordinates $c_{i,j}$ of c. Formally, $\gamma(c) = \{(x_1, \ldots, x_n) \in \mathbb{R}^n \mid x_i - x_j \leq c_{i,j},\ -c_{0,i} \leq x_i \leq c_{i,0}\}$.

TCM Abstract Domain. A *Template Constraint Matrix* T (TCM) is an ordered set $T = \{e_1, \ldots, e_m\}$ of linear relations $e_i(x) = a_{i,1}x_1 + \ldots + a_{i,n}x_n$ where $(a_{i,1}, \ldots, a_{i,n})$ and $x = (x_1, \ldots, x_n)$ are real valued vectors of length $n = |V|$. In practice this TCM T can be represented by a matrix M of dimension $m \times n$ and such that its entry (i, j) is $a_{i,j}$. Hence the ith line of this matrix is the vector $(a_{i,1}, \ldots, a_{i,n})$. For the sake of simplicy, we sometimes identify a TCM T with its representation by matrix in the sequel where T_i will denote its ith row.

The *TCM Abstract Domain* consists of the set of all possible m-dimensional vectors $c = (c_1, \ldots, c_m)$ with $c_i \in \mathbb{I}$. The concretization of an element c in the domain is the set of real values $x = (x_1, \ldots, x_n)$ that satisfy $e_i(x) + c_i \geq 0$ with $c_i \neq +\infty$ for all i. Thus, $\gamma(c) = \{(x_1, \ldots, x_n) \in \mathbb{R}^n \mid e_i(x) + c_i \geq 0 \wedge c_i \neq +\infty\}$. In particular, $\gamma(c) = \emptyset$ if $c_i = -\infty$ for some i. Thus the TCM domain keeps track of the bounds for a fixed set of pre-defined linear constraints. A linear assertion (a conjunction of linear relations) of the form $e_i(x) + c_i \geq 0$ will be denoted $e(x) + c \geq 0$ with $e = (e_1, \ldots, e_m)$ and $c = (c_1, \ldots, e_m)$.

A precise fixpoint detection in static analysis can be made by use of one TCM per control point in the program to analyse. As it complicates the presentation but does not change our theoretical results, we present operations in the case of one TCM. In the case of several TCMs, operation results or operands have to be expressed in the same TCM. This operation is called *projection*.

Linear Programming. The emptiness of the concretization can be checked using *Linear Programming* (see [Chv83] for an systematic treatment).

Let $e(x) + c \geq 0$ be a linear assertion. A linear programming (LP) problem consists in minimizing a linear relation $f(x)$, called the *objective function*, subject to the constraint of $e(x) + c \geq 0$. The concretization emptiness problem corresponds to the case where $f(x)$ is the constant map 0. A LP problem may have three answers: the problem is *infeasible*, or there is *one optimal solution*, or the problem is *unbounded* ($f(x)$ can be decreased down to $-\infty$). A linear programming problem can be solved either by the simplex algorithm (whose theoretical complexity is exponential, but which is efficient in practice) or by modern interior point methods, which are polynomial time and practically efficient.

Order and extrema. To get a lattice structure, the zone and TCM domains are extended with a supremum $\top = (\top, \dots, \top)$ (whose concretization is $\mathbb{I}^n$ itself) and an infimum $\bot$ which is any vector with at least one coordinate whose value is $-\infty$ (its concretization is empty). If $\gamma(c)$ of a zone or TCM c is not empty, c is said to be *consistent* otherwise it is *inconsistent*. The *order* $\sqsubseteq$ is the vector order: $c_1 \sqsubseteq c_2$ iff $c_1(i) \leq c_2(i)$ for every $i = 1, .., |c_1| = |c_2|$. We have $c_1 \sqsubseteq c_2 \Longrightarrow \gamma_1(c_1) \subseteq \gamma_2(c_2)$ but the converse is not true. This problem is addressed by the *closure* operation.

Closure. Several zones or TCMs vectors may have the same concrete domain. As a canonical representative, the *closed* one is chosen. The *closure* c^* of a *consistent* zone or TCM vector c is the $\sqsubseteq$-minimal zone or TCM vector such that $\gamma(c^*) = \gamma(c)$.

Closure on zones. If $c = (c_{0,1}, \dots, c_{n,n})$ is a consistent zone then $c^* = (c^*_{0,0}, \cdots c^*_{n,n})$ is such that $c^*_{i,j} = min_{1 \leq k \leq n-1}\{c_{ii_1} + \ldots + c_{i_{k-1}j} | \forall i_1, \dots, i_{k-1} \in \{1, \dots, n\}\}$. A zone c is consistent iff every diagonal coordinate of c^* is zero. It follows that the consistency and closure problems reduce to an all pairs shortest path problem.

Closure on TCMs. Let $c = (c_1, \dots, c_m)$ be a consistent vector on the TCM T seen as a matrix of dimension $m \times n$. Let us denote $c_{|\mathbb{R}}$ the subvector of c in which ∞ coordinates are deleted. Let $T_{|\mathbb{R}}$ be the corresponding submatrix of lines T_i of T such that $c_i \neq \infty$. Closure c^* of c is the vector $(c^*_1, \dots, c^*_m)$ such that c^*_i is the solution of the LP problem "*minimize* $c_{|\mathbb{R}}\lambda$ *subject to* $T_{|\mathbb{R}}\lambda = T_i$, $\lambda \geq 0$". It has been shown in [SSM05b] that as c is consistent no LP problem may be unbounded[2]. Hence as $\gamma(c^*) = \gamma(c) \neq \emptyset$ we conclude all these m LP problems have an optimal solution or an infeasible solution. An infeasible solution would just mean that the bound c^*_i for the constraint is ∞, in otherwords the constraint is unbounded.

Meet and Join. The $\sqcup$ operation is a pointwise maximum between the vector coordinates: $c_1 \sqcup c_2 = (max\{c_1(1), c_2(1)\}, \dots, max\{c_1(k), c_2(k)\})$. This operation is the best approximation for the union in the TCM domain (*lub*) and preserves closure. In the context of polyhedra this definition corresponds to the so called *weak join* of polyhedra [SCSM06] as it does not involve addition of any new constraints.

The $\sqcap$ operation is a pointwise mimimum operation between the vector coordinates: $c_1 \sqcap c_2 = (min\{c_1(1), c_2(1)\}, \dots, min\{c_1(k)), c_2(k)\})$. This operation is exact but *does not* preserve closure.

[2] If it were not the case, this would contradict $\gamma(c) = \gamma(c^*)$ as we would have $\gamma(c^*) = \emptyset$ and $\gamma(c) \neq \emptyset$ by hypothesis.

Widening on zones. $c_1 \nabla c_2 = c$ with $c_i = c_1(i)$ if $c_2(i) \leq c_1(i)$ otherwise $c_i = \infty$. An important remark about the widening is that its use forbids to close the left operand otherwise termination is not guaranteed. The consequence when computing a fixpoint with a Kleene iteration is as follows. After a widening, closure is forbidden so that for a pair $v_i - v_j$ whose bound becomes $+\infty$, this difference will remain unbounded until the end of the Kleene iteration. This situation occurs on the left part of the computation table below, where the triple $(i_9^3, j_9^3, i_9^3 - j_9^3)$ stands for the zone $\{150 \leq x_1 - x_0 \leq 158 \wedge 175 \leq x_2 - x_0 \leq 175 \wedge -25 \leq x_1 - x_2 \leq -17\} \cup \{x - x \leq 0\}$. At iteration [10] a widening iteration is computed. It can be seen that the result on every constraint involving the upper bound of i from control point [3] remains unbounded (this is a special case where zones computing a widening gives a closed zone but it is not true in general as shown in A. Mine's thesis [Min04]). In the worst case, every pair is concerned by the widening so that the constraint set becomes a set of intervals. This drawback does not exist with the policy iteration as we do not use the widening operator.

$$\begin{array}{rcl}
(i_3^1, j_3^1, i_3^1 - j_3^1) & = & ([150,150],[175,175], \\
 & & [-25,25]) \\
(i_7^1, j_7^1, i_7^1 - j_7^1) & = & \bot \\
(i_8^1, j_8^1, i_8^1 - j_8^1) & = & ([151,151],[175,175], \\
 & & [-24,24]) \\
(i_9^1, j_9^1, i_9^1 - j_9^1) & = & \bot \\
 & \ldots & \\
(i_3^9, j_3^9, i_3^9 - j_3^9) & = & ([150,158],[175,175], \\
 & & [-25,-17]) \\
(i_7^9, j_7^9, i_7^9 - j_7^9) & = & \bot \\
(i_8^9, j_8^9, i_8^9 - j_8^9) & = & ([151,159],[175,175], \\
 & & [-24,-16]) \\
(i_9^9, j_9^9, i_9^9 - j_9^9) & = & \bot \\
\text{(widening)} & & \\
(i_3^{10}, j_3^{10}, i_3^{10} - j_3^{10}) & = & ([150,\infty],[175,175], \\
 & & [-\infty,-25] \\
(i_4^{10}, j_4^{10}, i_4^{10} - j_4^{10}) & = & ([149,\infty],[173,173], \\
 & & [-\infty,-24]
\end{array}
\qquad
\begin{array}{rcl}
 & \ldots & \\
c_3^1 & = & (-150,150,-175,175, \\
 & & -25,25) \\
c_7^1 & = & \bot \\
c_8^1 & = & (-151,151,-175,175, \\
 & & -24,24) \\
c_9^1 & = & \bot \\
 & \ldots & \\
c_3^9 & = & (-150,158,-175,175, \\
 & & -17,25) \\
c_7^9 & = & \bot \\
c_8^9 & = & (-151,158,-175,175, \\
 & & -16,24) \\
c_9^9 & = & \bot \\
\text{(widening)} & & \\
c_3^{10} & = & (-150,-175,175,25) \\
c_4^{10} & = & (-149,-173,175,24) \\
 & \ldots &
\end{array}$$

Widening on TCMs. It corresponds to the computation of a vector c', $|c'| \leq |c_1|$ from c_1's coordinates such that $\gamma(c') \subseteq \gamma(c_2)$. There are two cases to consider: either c_1 or c_2 is inconsistent and $c_1 \nabla c_2$ is simply $c_1 \sqcup c_2$. Otherwise let us denote b_i to be the solution of the LP problem "*minimize* $e_i(x) + c_1(i)$ *subject to* $e(x) + c_2 \geq 0$". If b_i is positive then $c(i) = b_i$ otherwise the linear expression e_i *is deleted from* T. Deleting a linear expression avoids the problem described on zones which is that after a widening, closures are no more allowed in a Kleene iteration. Nevertheless deleting a linear expression in a TCM impoverishes the expressiness of the abstract domain. The major drawback of the widening operator when used with Kleene iteration is not solved. For instance on the program of Figure 1, Kleene iterations with TCM $T = \{x_1, -x_1, x_2, -x_2, x_1 - x_2, x_2 - x_1\}$ (which models zones) are shown on the right part of the computation table above. Results are identical to those in the case of zones, when widening occurs: from iteration [10] on, the TCM reduces to $T' = T \backslash \{-x_1, x_2 - x_1\}$ so that further vectors have only four coordinates.

3 Policy Iteration for Relational Abstract Domains

The aim of policy iteration is to compute a fixpoint of some monotonic function F which is a combination of "simpler" monotonic maps g, for which we can hope for fast algorithms to compute their least fixpoints. For complete lattices such as the interval domain [CGG+05], the maps g do not contain the intersection operator. F is the intersection of a certain number of such g maps, and the goal of policy iteration techniques is to ensure (and find) the simpler g which has as least fixpoint, a fixpoint of F (not the least one in general). We will prove that if we have a "selection property", definition 1, then we can compute the least fixpoint of F from the least fixpoints of the maps g, theorem 2. The policy iteration algorithm will traverse in a clever manner the space of these g maps to find efficiently a fixpoint of F.

To present policy iteration in a uniform manner for zone and TCM we use notion of *closed domains.* A closed domain $(\overline{\mathcal{L}}, \overline{\bot}, \overline{\top}, \overline{\sqsubseteq}, \overline{\sqcup}, \overline{\sqcap})$ is such that $\mathcal{L}$ is an abstract domain and $\overline{\mathcal{L}}$ contains only closed elements of $\mathcal{L}$. As closure is only defined for consistent elements, we introduce the bottom element $\overline{\bot}$ representing all inconsistent elements to equip $\overline{\mathcal{L}}$ with a lattice structure. Top element is $\overline{\top}$. The order $\overline{\sqsubseteq}$ is $\overline{\bot}\overline{\sqsubseteq}\overline{c}\overline{\sqsubseteq}\overline{\top}$ for every c and for $c_1, c_2 \neq \overline{\bot}$ $c_1 \overline{\sqsubseteq} c_2$ iff $c_1 \sqsubseteq c_2$. Operators are as follows:

$x \overline{\sqcap} y = z$ with $z = \overline{\bot}$ if $x = \overline{\bot}$ or $y = \overline{\bot}$; $z = (x \sqcap y)^*$ otherwise.
$x \overline{\sqcup} y = z$ with $z = x$ if $y = \overline{\bot}$; $z = y$ if $x = \overline{\bot}$; $z = x \sqcup y$ otherwise.

Note that both zone and TCM closure closure satisfy that $x^* = x^{**} \sqsubseteq x$ and they are monotonic.

3.1 Selection Property

Remember (see [CGG+05]), that in intervals, policies are of four types ll, rr, lr and rl defined below. When $I = [-a, b]$ and $J = [-c, d]$, $ll(I, J) = I$ (l is for "left"), $rr(I, J) = J$ (r for "right"), $lr(I, J) = [-a, d]$ and $rl(I, J) = [-c, b]$. The maps g are derived from F by replacing the operator $\cap$ (intersection) by any of these four operators.

Thus, $F([a, b]) = ([1, 2] \cap [a, b]) \cup ([3, 4] \cap [a, b])$, where $[a, b]$ is an interval of real values, will have 16 policies as there are 4 options for each intersection; $\mathcal{G}$ is composed of: $llll([a, b]) = [1, 2] \cup [3, 4]$, $lrll([a, b]) = [1, b] \cup [3, 4]$, $rlll([a, b]) = [2, b] \cup [3, 4]$, $rrll([a, b]) = [a, b] \cup [3, 4]$, $lllr([a, b]) = [1, 2] \cup [3, b]$, $lrlr([a, b]) = [1, b] \cup [3, b]$, $rllr([a, b]) = [a, 2] \cup [3, b]$, $rrlr([a, b]) = [a, b] \cup [3, b]$, $llrl([a, b]) = [1, 2] \cup [a, 4]$, $lrrl([a, b]) = [1, b] \cup [a, 4]$, $rlrl([a, b]) = [a, 2] \cup [a, 4]$, $rrrl([a, b]) = [a, b] \cup [a, 4]$, $llrr([a, b]) = [1, 2] \cup [a, b]$, $lrrr([a, b]) = [1, b] \cup [a, b]$, $rlrr([a, b]) = [a, 2] \cup [a, b]$, $rrrr([a, b]) = [a, b] \cup [a, b]$

We then say that F satisfies the *selection property* since F is such that for all intervals x $F(x) = min\{g(x) \mid g \in \mathcal{G}\}$. We extend this definition to deal with relational domains:

Definition 1. *Let $\mathcal{G}$ denote a finite or infinite set of monotone self maps on the complete lattice $\overline{\mathcal{L}}$, we say that a monotone self map F satisfies the selection property if the two following properties are satisfied:*

(1) $F = F^* = (inf\{g \mid g \in \mathcal{G}\})$
(2) for all $x \in \overline{\mathcal{L}}$, there exists $h \in \mathcal{G}$ (a policy) such that $F(x) = h(x)$.

In condition (1), $F = F^*$ holds as $g(x)$ are closed and we have property that $x^* = x^{**}$. Hence the least fixpoint of F is a least fixpoint of some policy:

Theorem 2. *Let F be a monotone self map on a complete lattice $\overline{\mathcal{L}}$, satisfying the selection property for a set of monotone self maps $\mathcal{G}$. Then the least fixpoint of F is reached by the least fixpoint of some policy:*

$$F^- = inf\{(g^-)^* \mid g \in \mathcal{G}\}$$

Proof. To prove this theorem we need to show that

(1) $F^- \sqsubseteq (g^-)^*$ for all $g \in \mathcal{G}$
(2) F^- is a fixed point of some policy

(1) Let g be a policy. By definition 1, we have $F(x) \sqsubseteq g^*(x)$ for all x. By Tarski's theorem, the least fixed point of a monotone self map h on $\overline{\mathcal{L}}$ is given by $h^- = inf\{x \in \overline{\mathcal{L}} \mid h(x) \sqsubseteq x\}$. Since $F(x) \sqsubseteq g^*(x)$, we can deduce that every post fixed point of $g^*(x)$ is also a post fixed point of F. Therefore by Tarski's theorem, we conclude that that

$$F^- \sqsubseteq (g^*)^-$$

Since the * and g are monotonic, we have $g^*((g^-)^*) \sqsubseteq g^*((g^-)) = (g(g^-))^* = (g^-)^*$. Therefore $(g^-)^*$ is a post fixed point of g^*. So by Tarskis's theorem we have

$$(g^*)^- \sqsubseteq (g^-)^*$$

From this relation and $F^- \sqsubseteq (g^*)^-$ we get $F^- \sqsubseteq (g^-)^*$ Since this relation is true for all g, we get the desired relation

$$F^- \sqsubseteq (inf\{g^- \mid g \in \mathcal{G}\})^*$$

(2) By the selection property there exists a policy h such that $F^- = F(F^-) = h(F^-)$. So F^- is a fixed point of h hence is greater than h^- which implies $h^- \sqsubseteq F^-$. By definition of $*$, we have $(h^-)^* \sqsubseteq h^- \sqsubseteq F^-$. Therefore,

$$(inf\{(g^-) \mid g \in \mathcal{G}\})^* \sqsubseteq F^-$$

. □

This theorem proves that algorithm 1 computes a fixpoint of an application F that satisfies the selection property. Starting from an initial policy provided by a function *initial_policy* this algorithm computes iteratively the least fixpoint x of some policy g_k (done at iteration k). If x is a fixpoint of F then algorithm terminates otherwise a new policy g_{k+1} is selected for iteration $k+1$ in such a way that $g_{k+1}^* = x$ (this is always possible as F has the selection property).

Algorithm 1. Policy iteration algorithm

```
k ← 1 ; g_1 ← initial_policy(𝒢)
while true do
  x_k ← (g_k^-)^*
  if x_k = F(x_k) then
    return x_k
  else
    find g such that F(x_k) = g^*(x_k)
    k ← k + 1 ; g_k ← g
  end if
end while
```

Algorithm 1 may not return the least fixpoint. However, for some classes of monotone maps, including sup-norm non-expansive maps, an extension of algorithm 1 does provide the least fixpoint, see theorem 3 and remark 5 in [CGG+05]: when a fixpoint for F is detected at iteration n it is possible to scan all the remaining policies g that belong to $\mathcal{G}\backslash\{g_1,\ldots,g_n\}$ and to compute their least fixpoint and finally returning the least one between all of them.

The following theorem states that algorithm 1 is correct and computes a decreasing chain of post fixpoints of an application satisfying the selection porperty:

Theorem 3. *Let F be a monotone self map on the complete lattice $\overline{\mathcal{L}}$ satisfying the selection property for a set of maps $\mathcal{G}$. We have the two following properties:*

(i) If algorithm 1 finishes then the returned value is a fixpoint of F

(ii) The sequence of least fixpoints of maps $g_k \in \mathcal{G}$ generated by the algorithm 1 is a strictly decreasing chain, that is

$$(g_{k+1}^-)^* \sqsubset (g_k^-)^*$$

Proof. Correctness of the algorithm (property (i)) is trivial as it terminates only if the test $x_k = F(x_k)$ is satisfied.

We prove the property (ii) by induction on the number n of iterations of the algorithm that is the length of the sequence of successive g_k. The basis case, $n = 0$, is trivial. For the induction case, we suppose that the algorithm has been iterated n times and that the sequence is such that $(g_{k+1}^-)^* \sqsubseteq (g_k^-)^*$ for $k < n$.

If $F((g_n^-)^*) = (g_n^-)^*$ then algorithm terminates and the property is true. Otherwise the map g_{n+1} is such that

$$F((g_n^-)^*) = g_{n+1}((g_n^-)^*) \tag{1}$$

Moreover, by condition (1) of F we get $F((g_n^-)^*) \sqsubseteq g_n((g_n^-)^*)$ so that $g_{n+1}((g_n^-)^*) \sqsubseteq g_n((g_n^-)^*)$. Since $*$ is monotonic we have $g_{n+1}((g_n^-)^*) \sqsubseteq g_n((g_n^-)^*) \sqsubseteq g_n((g_n^-)) = g_n^-$. Therefore

$$g_{n+1}((g_n^-)^*) \sqsubseteq g_n^- \qquad (2)$$

Now as $F = (inf_{g\in\mathcal{G}}\ g)^*$ we have $F^* = (inf_{g\in\mathcal{G}}\ g)^{**}$ and since for all x $x^* = x^{**}$ we deduce $F^* = F$. So from (1) we get $g_{n+1}((g_n^-)^*) = (g_{n+1}((g_n^-)^*))^*$.

By monotonicity of $*$ and from (2) we have $g_{n+1}((g_n^-)^*) = (g_{n+1}((g_n^-)^*))^* \sqsubseteq (g_n^-)^*$ that is $(g_n^-)^*$ is a post fixed point of g_{n+1}. And as it not a fixed point of g_{n+1}, by Tarski's theorem we conclude that

$$(g_{n+1}^-)^* \sqsubseteq g_{n+1}^- \sqsubset (g_n^-)^* \qquad \square$$

If $\mathcal{G}$ is finite and has n policies then algorithm 1 finishes within at most n iterations:

Corollary 4. *If the set $\mathcal{G}$ is finite then algorithm 1 returns a fixpoint of F and the number of iterations of algorithm 1 is bounded by the height of $\{g^-|g \in \mathcal{G}\}$ which in turn is bounded by the cardinality of $\mathcal{G}$.*

3.2 Operations with Policy

We show that the meet and closure operations of any map can be expressed as an infimum of simpler maps.

Meet policies. The meet $c = c_1 \sqcap c_2$ of two vectors (zones or TCM vectors) c_1 and c_2 of length k is obtained by taking the pointwise minimum between each pair of coordinates. That is the ith coordinate of the result comes either from the left or right operand coordinate.

We use this remark to build a family of meet policies in the following way: Let $L \sqsubseteq \{1,\ldots,k\}$ be a set of coordinates whose corresponding policy will be denoted $\sqcap_L$. The set L contains every index i for which we take the ith coordinate of the left operand: if $i \in L$ then $c(i) = c_1(i)$ otherwise $c(i) = c_2(i)$.

We have trivially $c_1 \sqcap c_2 = \bigcap_{L\subseteq\{1,..,k\}} c_1 \sqcap_L c_2$ that is $\sqcap$ satisfies the selection property for the set of $\sqcap_L$ policies.

Closure policies. Remember that the closure of a consistent zone or TCM c is the minimal c^* such that $\gamma(c) \sqsubseteq \gamma(c^*)$.

Closure policies for zones. For a consistent zone c let $c_{ij}^p = c_{i,i_1} + c_{i_2,i_3} + \ldots + c_{i_{k-1},i_k} + c_{i_k,j}$ with $c_{i_p i_{p+1}}$ a coordinate of c and $p = i, i_1, ..., i_k, j$ and a sequence of variable indices called a *path from i to j*.

By definition, $c_{i,j}^*$ is the minimal c_{ij}^p amongst all pathes p from i to j. As mentioned in Section 2.2 the minimal c_{ij}^p can be obtained for a path length $|p|$ less than the number of variables. Hence $c_{i,j}^* = \bigcap_{p,|p|\leq n} c_{i,j}^p$ which satisfies the selection property.

Example. Take the example of figure 1. Our policy analyzer finds (in one policy iteration) the loop invariant at control point [9] left below, whereas a a typical static analyzer using Kleene iteration finds a less precise invariant (right below, using A. Mine's octagon analyzer).

$$\begin{cases} 150 \leq i \leq 174 \\ 98 \leq j \leq 99 \\ -76 \leq j - i \leq -51 \end{cases} \qquad \begin{cases} 150 \leq i \\ 98 \leq j \leq 99 \\ j - i \leq -51 \\ 248 \leq j + i \end{cases}$$

Consider now the program shown left below. The fixpoint found by our method (after two unfoldings) is given right below. This is incomparable to the fixpoint found in octogons (below), but its concretisation is smaller in width. This example needs two policies to converge.

```
0  void main() {
1   i = 1; j = 10;
2   while (i <= j){
3     i = i + 2;
4     j = j - 1; }
5  }
```

Policy iteration:

$$5 \leq i \leq 10,\ 4 \leq j \leq 8,\ -3 \leq j - i \leq -1$$

Kleene on octagons:

$$6 \leq i \leq 12,\ \frac{9}{2} \leq j \leq 10,\ -3 \leq j - i \leq -1$$

At [5] the initial policy chosen (see section 4.2) gives the invariant of the right part below. The value of the functional on the invariant found using this initial policy (and this is the only control point at which we have not reached the least fixpoint) is on the left below:

$$\begin{cases} 5 \leq i \leq 11,\ 2 \leq j \leq 8 \\ -3 \leq j - i \leq -1 \end{cases} \qquad \begin{cases} 5 \leq i \leq 10,\ 4 \leq j \leq 8 \\ -3 \leq j - i \leq -1 \end{cases}$$

It is easy to see that the entry describing the maximum of i has to be changed to a length two closure, and the minimum of the entry describing the minimum of j has to be changed to a length two closure, the rest of the equations being unchanged.

Closure policies for TCM. Let $c = (c_1, \ldots, c_m)$ be a consistent TCM vector on T seen as a matrix of dimension $m \times n$. Closure c^* of c is the vector $(c_1^*, \ldots, c_m^*)$ such that c_i^* is the solution of the LP problem "*minimize* $c_{|\mathbb{R}}\lambda$ *subject to* $T_{|\mathbb{R}}\lambda = T_i$, $\lambda \geq 0$". As we had mentioned before, this LP problem has an optimal solution or an infeasible solution. An infeasible solution means that the constraint e_i is unbounded and so we set c_i^* to ∞. Otherwise, it has been shown that the optimal solution is reached at a vertex of the polyhedron $T_{|\mathbb{R}}^* = T_i$, $\lambda \geq 0$ (no of vertices or extreme points will be finite). Call this polyhedron P_i. Hence we have $c^*(i) = inf\{x \in \mathbb{R} \mid x \textit{ is a vertex of } P_i\}$. A policy map is then any map that returns any vector whose ith coordinate is a vertex of polyhedron P_i so that $c^* = inf\{(\lambda c \mid \lambda \textit{ is a vertex of } P_i\}$.

In this paper we only deal with two operations - meet and closure. However in general we can deal with all transfer functions involved in Linear relation analysis. The basic idea is to express the transfer function as a Linear minimization problem and then take the policies corresponding to the vertices of the polyhedron, as we did for the closure operation.

4 Algorithmic Issues

Algorithm 1 gives a general method to compute a fixpoint of some map F that satifies the selection property (Definition 1). In this section we give a method (based on linear programming rather than Kleene iteration as in [CGG$^+$05]) to compute least fixpoints of the policies. We give also some heuristics for the choice of intial policies on zone and TCM domain.

4.1 Least Fixpoint Computation, for a Given Policy

Each iteration k of algorithm 1 needs to compute the least fixpoint of a policy g_k, where every entry of g_k is a finite supremum of affine maps. By Tarski's theorem, this least fixpoint is the minimal vector x such that $g_k(x) \leq x$. If this least fixed point is finite, it can be found by solving a linear program: we minimize the linear form $\sum_{1\leq i\leq p} x_i$ over the constraints $g_k(x) \leq x$, where $x_1, \ldots, x_p$ are the variables composing the vector x. If the value of the latter linear program is unbounded, some entries of the least fixpoint x of g_k must be equal to $-\infty$. Note that the simplex method provides at least one of these entries, because, when a linear program is unbounded, the simplex method returns a half-line included in the feasible set, on which the objective function is still unbounded. Hence, the least fixed point can be found by solving a sequence of linear programs. The method we use takes into account the "block upper triangular form" of the system $g_k(x) \leq x$ to reduce the execution time. In fact, the size of "blocks" turns out to be small, in practice, so the linear programs that we call only involve small subsets of variables.

Each block C_i is solved in order. The result of the linear program corresponding to any C_i would either be a *finite* solution, *infeasible* solution or an *unbounded* solution. These are handled as follows:

(i) *Finite* solution: In this case we set the values of x_j, for all $j \in C_i$ to those at the extreme point where the least solution was obtained. Next we propagate these values in the other subblocks.

(ii) *Infeasible* solution: In this case we set each x_j to $+\infty$ for all $j \in C_i$. These values are then propagated as the above.

(iii) *Unbounded* solution: This is a very rare case. Unboundedness means that one or more variables $x_j (j \in C_i)$ are not bounded from below i.e. their minimum value is -∞. In order to find a value for these variables, we solve the linear program again with the same constraints but with the objective function being just x_j (this is done for all $j \in C_i$). If the corresponding linear program returns *unbounded*, x_j is set to -∞. As in the above cases the value of each x_j is then.

4.2 Initial Policy for Zones and TCM

For meet policy, we do as for intervals in [CGG+05]: we choose the left coordinate (respectively the right constraint) if the right coordinate (respectively the left entry) does not bring any information on a constraint between variables, i.e. is $+\infty$. We also give priority to constant entries. In case of a tie, we choose first the left coordinate. In the case of zone closure, we begin by paths of length one that is the zone itself. Initial closure policy on TCM chooses any vertex. The choice may sometimes depend on the LP programming method. For instance with a simplex algorithm that enumerates vertices in an order that decreases the objective function the first considered vertex may be taken as an initial policy.

5 Experiments

A prototype has been developped for experiments. It takes C programs, constructs abstract semantic equations on the zone domain, solves them by the policy iteration algorithm of this article, and outputs the local invariants in text format. The front end is based on CIL [CIL], the equations are solve using the GLPK library [GLP] through its OCAML binding [Mim].

In this section, we show some experiments on simple programs, which can be found at `http://www.di.ens.fr/~goubault/GOUBAULTpapers.html`. These programs are briefly described below. We write in the columns from left to right, the number of lines, of variables, of while loops, the maximum depth of nested loops. Then we give the number of "elementary operations"/policy iteration that our analyzer used, the number of elementary operations/Kleene iterations in the case of the octagon analyzer, and the number of elementary operations/Kleene iterations for LPInv. These elementary operations are estimated, as follows: we indicate below columns "compl./#pols" (resp. compl./iter.oct., compl./iter. LPInv) the number of calls to the simplex solver: s/the average dimension: d (number of variables involved)/the average simplex iteration number: k (resp. the number of closure operations: c/assignment operations: a, and the same format as for our analyzer for the LPInv analyzer). These operations account for the main complexity in the three analyzers: the number of operations is of the order sd^2k for our analyzer and LPInv, and $cn^3 + an$, where n is the number of variables, for the octagon analyzer. We can see that the complexity is far less for our analyzer. The octagon analyzer spends a lot of operations doing closure operations, that we do not have to do. LPInv needs to solve the same order or even more linear programming problems, but more complex (i.e. needing more iterations to converge) and with a much higher dimensionality. Our method needs very few policies to converge, hence has few linear programming problems, which are very simple (very low dimensionality in particular) because of the SCC algorithm of Section 4.1.

Program	lines	vars	loops	depth	compl./#pols.	compl./iters.oct.	compl./iters.LPInv
test1	11	2	1	1	20/2 113/1.02/0.17	1132/7 138/14	14014/6 88/11.14/1.28
test1b	15	2	1	1	20/2 113/1.02/0.17	548/6 130/14	12952/6 78/11.6/1.23
test2	15	2	1	1	40/1 86/1.03/0.43	1268/12 309/16	31828/16 267/10.5/1.08
test3	14	2	1	1	34/1 96/1.03/0.33	1364/12 333/16	62348/16 282/14/1.12766
test4	13	2	2	2	68/3 124/1.27/0.34	906/4 220/13	50940/16 302/11.75/1.20
ex3	20	5	1	1	49/1 212/1.56/0.09	56250/8 225/13	22599614/16 1251/67.9/3.92
ex5	23	5	5	1	392/1 659/1.49/0.27	49370/23 394/24	33133177/20 3007/67.96/2.38

The results that our analyzer, A. Miné's octagon analyzer and LPInv (which uses octagons in our case) obtain are shown in the longer version of the paper available at `http://www.di.ens.fr/~goubault/GOUBAULTpapers.html`. We can see that although our analyzer is much faster, and computes in a less precise domain (zones) than octagons, it provides very similar invariants than both analyzers. It is even far more precise for `test2` and `test3` as already explained in section 2.2. It provides in general better results than LPInv. The Octagon analyzer is better for programs of the style of `test1` since in that case, constraints on forms of the type $i + j$ (in zones, but not in octagons) are useful for getting invariants. Still, it suffices to unroll two times the main loop (`test1b`) to have comparable or even better results, with our analyzer.

6 Conclusion

We have described in this paper a new algorithm to compute efficiently and precisely, fixed points in relational abstract domains such as zones and TCMs, thus applicable to a large variety of situations.

There are two directions in which we would like to go from here. The first one is to extend this work to other domains, like the relational ones of [GP06], or domains dealing with pointers and general aliasing properties. The second direction of interest is the use of policy iteration algorithms to have better "incremental" analyzes [CDEN06]. As a matter of fact, one can hope that given a program P (identified with the abstract functionnal giving its semantics), a policy π giving the least fixpoint of P, light perturbations P' of P will only perturbate very little policy π. Hence π will be a very good initial policy guess for the policy iteration algorithm run on P'.

References

[CC76] P. Cousot and R. Cousot, *Static determination of dynamic properties of programs*, 2nd International Symposium on Programming, Paris, France, 1976.

[CC77] P. Cousot and R. Cousot, *Abstract interpretation: A unified lattice model for static analysis of programs by construction of approximations of fixed points*, Principles of Programming Languages 4 (1977), 238–252.

[CC91] P. Cousot and R. Cousot, *Comparison of the Galois connection and widening/narrowing approaches to abstract interpretation. JTASPEFL '91, Bordeaux*, BIGRE **74** (1991), 107–110.

[CC92] P. Cousot and R. Cousot, *Abstract interpretation frameworks*, Journal of Logic and Computation **2** (1992), no. 4, 511–547.

[CDEN06] C. Conway, D. Dams, S. A. Edwards, and K. Namjoshi, *Incremental algorithms for inter-procedural automaton-based program analysis*, Computer Aided Verification, Springer-Verlag, LNCS, 2006.

[CGG+05] A. Costan, S. Gaubert, E. Goubault, M. Martel, and S. Putot, *A policy iteration algorithm for computing fixed points in static analysis of programs*, CAV, LNCS, vol. 3576, 2005, pp. 462–475.

[CH78] P. Cousot and N. Halbwachs, *Automatic discovery of linear restraints among variables of a program*, Conference Record of the Fifth Annual ACM SIGPLAN-SIGACT Symposium on Principles of Programming Languages, 1978, pp. 84–97.

[Chv83] V. Chvátal, *Linear programming*, Freeman and Co., 1983.

[CIL] *CIL*, Tech. report, Berkeley University, http://manju.cs.berkeley.edu/cil/.

[GG98] S. Gaubert and J. Gunawardena, *The duality theorem for min-max functions*, C.R. Acad. Sci. **326** (1998), no. 1, 43–48.

[GLP] *GLPK*, Tech. report, Gnu, http://www.gnu.org/software/glpk/.

[GP06] E. Goubault and S. Putot, *Static analysis of numerical algorithms*, Static Analysis Symposium, Springer-Verlag, LNCS, 2006.

[HK66] A. J. Hoffman and R. M. Karp, *On nonterminating stochastic games*, Management sciences **12** (1966), no. 5, 359–370.

[How60] R. Howard, *Dynamic programming and markov processes*, Wiley, 1960.

[Mim] S. Mimram, *OcamlGLPK*, Tech. report, Gnu, http://ocaml-glpk.sourceforge.net/.

[Min01a] A. Miné, *A new numerical abstract domain based on difference-bound matrices*, PADO II, LNCS, vol. 2053, 2001, pp. 155–172.

[Min01b] A. Miné, *The octagon abstract domain*, AST 2001 in WCRE 2001, IEEE, 2001, pp. 310–319.

[Min04] A. Miné, *Weakly relational numerical abstract domains*, Ph.D. thesis, Ecole Nationale Supérieure, France, 2004.

[Min05] A. Miné, *The octagon domain library*, 2005.

[SCSM06] S. Sankaranarayanan, M. Colon, H. Sipma, and Z. Manna, *Efficient strongly relational polyhedral analysis*, VMCAI, LNCS, 2006, to appear.

[SSM05a] H. Sipma S. Sankaranarayanan and Z. Manna, *Lpinv: Linear programming invariant generator*, 2005.

[SSM05b] S. Sankaranarayanan, H. Sipma, and Z. Manna, *Scalable analysis of linear systems using mathematical programming*, VMCAI, LNCS, vol. 3385, 2005.

Computing Procedure Summaries for Interprocedural Analysis*

Sumit Gulwani[1] and Ashish Tiwari[2]

[1] Microsoft Research, Redmond, WA 98052
sumitg@microsoft.com
[2] SRI International, Menlo Park, CA 94025
tiwari@csl.sri.com

Abstract. We describe a new technique for computing procedure summaries for performing an interprocedural analysis on programs. Procedure summaries are computed by performing a backward analysis of procedures, but there are two key new features: (i) information is propagated using "generic" assertions (rather than regular assertions that are used in intraprocedural analysis); and (ii) unification is used to simplify these generic assertions. We illustrate this general technique by applying it to two abstractions: unary uninterpreted functions and linear arithmetic. In the first case, we get a PTIME algorithm for a special case of the long-standing open problem of interprocedural global value numbering (the special case being that we consider unary uninterpreted functions instead of binary). This also requires developing efficient algorithms for manipulating singleton context-free grammars, and builds on an earlier work by Plandowski [13]. In linear arithmetic case, we get new algorithms for precise interprocedural analysis of linear arithmetic programs with complexity matching that of the best known deterministic algorithm [11].

1 Introduction

Precise interprocedural analysis (also referred to as full context-sensitive analysis) is provably harder than intraprocedural analysis [14]. One way to do precise interprocedural analysis is to do procedure-inlining followed by an intra-procedural analysis. There are two potential problems with this approach. First, in presence of recursive procedures, procedure-inlining may not be possible. Second, even if there are no recursive procedures, procedure-inlining may result in an exponential blow-up of the program. For example, if procedure P_1 calls procedure P_2 two times, which in turn calls procedure P_3 two times, then procedure inlining will result in 4 copies of procedure P_3 inside procedure P_1. In general, leaf procedures can be replicated an exponential number of times.

A more standard way to do interprocedural analysis is by means of computing procedure summaries [20]. Each procedure is analyzed once (or a few times in

* Second author supported in part by the National Science Foundation under grant CCR-0326540.

R. De Nicola (Ed.): ESOP 2007, LNCS 4421, pp. 253–267, 2007.

```
main(){                                          P(){
  x := 0; y := 1; a := 2; b := 4;                  if (*) {
  P(); Assert(y = 2x + 1);                             x := x + a;
  x := 0; y := 0; a := ?; b := 2a;                     y := y + b;
  P(); Assert(y = 2x);                             }
  y := x + 3; a := ?; b := a;                      else P()
  P(); Assert(y = x + 3);                        }
}
```

Fig. 1. An example program

case of recursive procedures) to build its summary. A procedure summary can be thought of as some succinct representation of the behavior of the procedure that is also parametrized by any information about its input variables. However, there is no automatic recipe to efficiently construct or even represent these procedure summaries, and abstraction specific techniques are required.

The original formalism proposed by Sharir and Pnueli [20] for computing procedure summaries was limited to finite lattices of dataflow facts. Sagiv, Reps and Horwitz generalized the Sharir-Pnueli framework to build procedure summaries using context-free graph reachability [15], even for some kind of infinite domains. They successfully applied their technique to detect linear constants interprocedurally [17]. However, their generalized framework requires appropriate distributive transfer functions as input - and such transfer functions are not known for any natural abstract domain more powerful than linear constants.

In this paper (Section 3), we describe a general technique for constructing precise procedure summaries. This technique can be effectively used for a useful class of program abstractions (over infinite domains). We apply this technique to obtain precise interprocedural analyses for two useful abstractions - unary uninterpreted functions, and linear arithmetic (which is more powerful than the domain of linear constants used by Sagiv, Reps and Horwitz). The former (described in Section 4) gives a polynomial-time algorithm for a special case of the long-standing open problem of interprocedural global value numbering, while the latter (described in Section 5) yields a new algorithm for interprocedural linear arithmetic analysis with the same complexity as that of the best known deterministic algorithm [11].

Our procedure summaries are in the form of constraints (on the input variables of the procedure) that must be satisfied to guarantee that some appropriate generic assertion (involving output variables of the procedure) holds at the end of the procedure. A generic assertion is an assertion that involves some *context* variables that can be instantiated by symbols (or more formally, by terms with holes) of the underlying abstraction. For example, consider procedure P shown in Figure 1 with input variables x, y, a, b and output variables x, y. $\alpha x + \beta y = \gamma$ is a generic assertion in the theory of linear arithmetic involving variables x, y (and context variables α, β, γ, which denote unknown constants). Using the technique described in this paper, we compute the summary of procedure P as "$\alpha x + \beta y = \gamma$

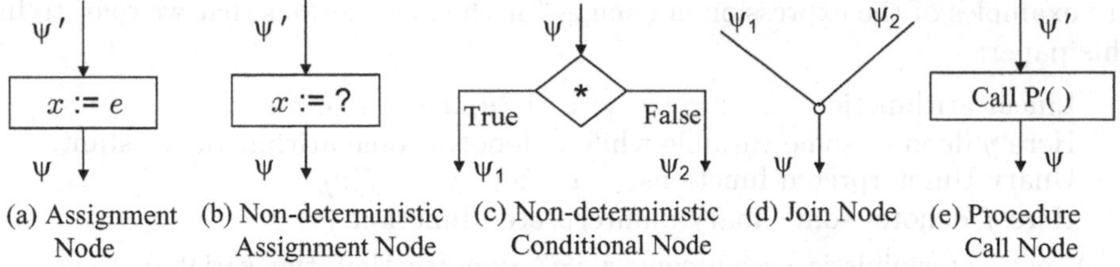

(a) Assignment Node (b) Non-deterministic Assignment Node (c) Non-deterministic Conditional Node (d) Join Node (e) Procedure Call Node

Fig. 2. Flowchart nodes in our abstracted program model

holds at the end of procedure P iff $\alpha a + \beta b = 0 \wedge \alpha x + \beta y = \gamma$ holds at the beginning of procedure P". After computing such a procedure summary for P, we can use it to verify the assertions in the `Main` procedure. To verify the first assertion $y = 2x + 1$, we first match it with the generic assertion $\alpha x + \beta y = \gamma$ to obtain the substitution $\alpha \mapsto -2, \beta \mapsto 1$ and $\gamma \mapsto 1$ for the context variables. We then instantiate the procedure summary with this substitution to obtain the precondition $b - 2a = 0 \wedge y - 2x = 1$. We then check that this precondition is satisfied in procedure `Main` immediately before the first call to procedure P. Similarly, we can verify the other two assertions.

The key idea in computing such procedure summaries is to compute weakest preconditions of generic assertions. However, a naive weakest precondition computation may be exponential in the number of operations performed (each conditional node can double the size of the precondition), and may not even terminate (in presence of loops). Hence we use some techniques for strengthening and simplifying the weakest preconditions (without any loss of precision). This simplification is based on recent connections between unification and assertion checking (described in Section 2.2). For example, consider computing the weakest precondition of the generic assertion $x = \beta y$ in the theory of unary uninterpreted functions for the procedure Q in Figure 3. (Here β represents some unknown sequence of uninterpreted functions.) The naive weakest precondition computation will not terminate and will yield $x = \beta y \wedge fx = \beta f y \wedge ffx = \beta ffy \wedge \ldots$. However, our simplification procedure will simply (and strengthen) the first two conjuncts to $x = \beta y \wedge \beta f = f \beta$, denoting that the relationship $x = \beta y$ holds at the end of procedure only if (β is of the form such that) $\beta f = f \beta$ and $x = \beta y$ holds at the beginning of the procedure. It turns out that the constraints thus obtained $\beta f = f \beta \wedge x = \beta y$ form a fixed-point, and hence our weakest precondition computation terminates immediately.

2 Preliminaries

2.1 Program Model

We assume that each procedure in a program is abstracted using the flowchart nodes shown in Figure 2. In the assignment node, x refers to a program variable while e denotes some expression in the underlying abstraction. We refer to the language of such expressions as *expression language of the program*. Following are examples of the expression languages for the abstractions that we refer to in this paper:

- Linear arithmetic. $e ::= y \mid c \mid e_1 \pm e_2 \mid c \times e$
  Here y denotes some variable while c denotes some arithmetic constant.
- Unary Uninterpreted functions. $e ::= y \mid f(e)$
  Here f denotes some unary uninterpreted function.

A non-deterministic assignment $x :=?$ denotes that the variable x can be assigned any value. Such non-deterministic assignments are used as a safe abstraction of statements (in the original source program) that our abstraction cannot handle precisely.

A join node has two incoming edges. Note that a join node with more incoming edges can be reduced to multiple join nodes with two incoming edges.

Non-deterministic conditionals, represented by $*$, denote that the control can flow to either branch irrespective of the program state before the conditional. They are used as a safe abstraction of guarded conditionals, which our abstraction cannot handle precisely. We abstract away the guards in conditionals because otherwise the problem of assertion checking can be easily shown to be undecidable even when the program expressions involves operators from simple theories like linear arithmetic [10] or uninterpreted functions [9]. This is a very commonly used restriction for a program model while proving preciseness of a program analysis for that model.

For simplicity, we assume that the inputs and outputs of a procedure are passed as global variables. Hence, the procedure call node simply denotes the name of the procedure to be called. Also, we assume that we are given the whole program with a special entry procedure called `Main`.

2.2 Unification and Assertion Checking

A *regular* assertion is a conjunction of equalities $e = e'$ between two expressions. A substitution σ is a mapping from variables to expressions. A substitution σ is applied to an expression e (or assertion ψ), by replacing all variables x by $\sigma(x)$ in the expression (assertion). The result is denoted in postfix notation by $e\sigma$ (or $\psi[\sigma]$). A program state is a substitution on program variables. A regular assertion ψ is said to hold at a program point π if $\psi[\sigma]$ is valid (in the underlying theory) for every program state σ reached at π (along any path).

A substitution σ is a *unifier* for ψ if $\psi[\sigma]$ is valid. A substitution σ_1 is *more-general* than a substitution σ_2 if there is a substitution σ_3 s.t. $x\sigma_2 = x\sigma_1\sigma_3$ for all x. A theory is *unitary* if for all equalities $e = e'$ in that theory, there exists a unifier that is more-general than any other unifier of $e = e'$. A substitution σ can be treated as the formula $\bigwedge_x x = \sigma(x)$. For a unitary theory $\mathbb{T}$, we denote the conjunction representing the most-general unifier for ψ by $\mathtt{Unif}_{\mathbb{T}}(\psi)$.

The formula $\mathtt{Unif}(\psi)$ logically implies ψ, but it is, in general, not equivalent to ψ. Since it is often "simpler" than ψ, we may wish to replace ψ by $\mathtt{Unif}(\psi)$. The basic result formally stated in Property 1 is that, *in many useful abstractions*, the formulas ψ and $\mathtt{Unif}(\psi)$ are "equivalent" as far as invariance of assertions is concerned.

Property 1 ([5]). Let π be any location in a program that is specified using the flowchart nodes in Figure 2 and expressions from some unitary theory $\mathbb{T}$. An equality $e = e'$ holds at π iff $\texttt{Unif}_{\mathbb{T}}(e = e')$ holds at π.

The above property is stated and proved in [5]. The key insight is that *runs* of a program are just substitutions and if every run validates an assertion, then every run should also validate a more-general unifier of that assertion. Property 1 is used at two places in our generic weakest-precondition computation based technique for interprocedural analysis: (a) for simplification of formulas for efficiency purpose (Section 3.2), (b) for detecting fixed-point computation (Section 3.2).

Note that we present our results in the context of unitary theories for efficiency reasons; otherwise both Property 1 and our general approach of Section 3 can be generalized.

3 General Technique for Interprocedural Analysis

Our technique for interprocedural analysis uses the standard two phase summary-based approach. The two phases are described in Section 3.2 and Section 3.3.

3.1 Generic Assertions

A *generic* assertion is an assertion that involves context-variables apart from regular program variables. A context-variable represents some unknown term with holes, with the constraint that this unknown term does not involve any program variables (i.e., it only involves symbols from the underlying theory or abstraction). An important consequence of this constraint is that generic assertions are closed under weakest precondition computation across assignments to program variables.

We say that a generic assertion A_1 is more general than another generic assertion A_2 if there exists an instantiation σ of the context variables of A_1 such that $A_2 = A_1[\sigma]$. We define a set of generic assertions to be *complete* w.r.t. a given set of program variables V if for any generic assertion A_1 in the underlying theory involving program variables V, there exists a generic assertion A_2 in the set such that A_2 is more general than A_1.

For the theory of linear arithmetic, the singleton set $\{\sum_i \alpha_i x_i = \alpha\}$ constitutes a complete set of generic assertions with respect to the set of variables $\{x_i\}_i$. Here α, α_i denote unknown constants. For the theory of unary uninterpreted functions, the set $\{\alpha x_1 = \beta x_2 \mid x_1, x_2 \in V,\ x_1 \not\equiv x_2\}$ is a complete set of generic assertions with respect to the set of variables V. Here α, β represent unknown strings (applications) of unary uninterpreted functions.

3.2 Phase 1: Computing Procedure Summaries

Let P be a procedure with V as the set of its output variables. Let G be some complete set of generic assertions with respect to V for the underlying abstraction. The summary of procedure P is a collection of formulas ψ_i, one for each generic assertion A_i in G. The formula ψ_i is the weakest precondition of the generic assertion A_i denoting that the generic assertion A_i holds at the end of procedure P only if the formula ψ_i holds at the beginning of procedure P. Each formula ψ_i itself is a conjunction of generic assertions. (Observe that weakest precondition computation involves substitution of regular variables by program expressions and performing conjunctions of formulas. Hence, conjunctions of generic assertions are closed under weakest precondition computation.)

Computing summary for procedure P requires computing the weakest precondition of each generic assertion in G one by one. The weakest precondition of a given generic assertion A across a procedure is computed by computing a formula ψ at each procedure point using the following transfer functions across flowchart nodes. The correctness of the following transfer functions is immediate.

Initialization: The formula at all procedure points except the procedure exit point is initialized to *true*. The formula at the exit is initialized to the generic assertion A.

Assignment Node: See Figure 2(a). The formula ψ' before an assignment node $x := e$ is obtained from the formula ψ after the assignment node by substituting x by e in ψ, i.e. $\psi' = \psi[x \mapsto e]$.

Non-deterministic Assignment Node: See Figure 2(b). The formula ψ' before a non-deterministic assignment node $x :=?$ is obtained from the formula ψ after the non-deterministic assignment node by universally quantifying out the variable x. However, for the case when program expressions come from a unitary theory, we can simplify $\forall x(\psi)$ to $\psi[x \mapsto c_1] \wedge \psi[x \mapsto c_2]$, where c_1 and c_2 are two distinct constants (or provably unequal terms) in the underlying theory.

Non-deterministic Conditional Node: See Figure 2(c). The formula ψ before a non-deterministic conditional node is obtained by taking the conjunction of the formulas ψ_1 and ψ_2 on the two branches of the conditional, i.e., $\psi = \psi_1 \wedge \psi_2$.

Join Node: See Figure 2(d). The formulas ψ_1 and ψ_2 on the two predecessors of a join node are same as the formula ψ after the join node, i.e., $\psi_1 = \psi$ and $\psi_2 = \psi$.

Procedure Call Node: See Figure 2(e). Let $\psi \equiv \bigwedge_{i=1}^{k} A_i'$. Let $A_i \in G$ be such that A_i is more general than A_i' and let σ_i be the instantiation such that $A_i' = A_i[\sigma_i]$. Let ψ_i' be the formula in the summary of procedure P' that represents the weakest precondition of A_i before procedure P'. Then, $\psi' = \bigwedge_{i=1}^{k} \psi_i'[\sigma_i]$.

Simplification

Property 1 says that we do not need to distinguish between two regular assertions that have the same set of unifiers. We can generalize this to generic assertions. We say two formulas (conjunctions of generic assertions) ψ and ψ' are *essentially equivalent*, denoted by $\psi \rightleftharpoons \psi'$, if $\psi\sigma$ and $\psi'\sigma$ have the same set of unifiers for *every* substitution σ that assigns every context variable in ψ, ψ' to a term with a hole (in the signature of the underlying theory). We denote by $\psi \rightharpoonup \psi'$ the fact that every unifier of $\psi\sigma$ is also a unifier of $\psi'\sigma$ (for every σ).

We can simplify ψ at any program point by replacing it by another essentially equivalent formula ψ'. The soundness and completeness of this transformation follows from Property 1. This simplification is needed to bound the size of the formula ψ because otherwise a naive computation of weakest precondition may lead to an exponential blowup in the number of operations performed. In case of linear arithmetic, this simplification simply involves removing linearly dependent equations. In case of unary uninterpreted functions, this simplification involves strengthening the formula.

Observe that the number of conjuncts in the formula computed before any node (in particular the procedure call node) is at most quadratic in the maximum number of conjuncts in any simplified formula. Hence, the time required to simplify any such formula can be bounded by $T_{\mathbb{T}}(k)$, which is as defined below.

Definition 1 (Simplification Cost $T_{\mathbb{T}}(k)$). *For any theory $\mathbb{T}$, let $S_{\mathbb{T}}(k)$ denote the maximum number of conjunctions (of generic assertions) in any simplified formula over k program variables. Let $T_{\mathbb{T}}(k)$ denote the time required to simplify a formula over k program variables with at most $(S_{\mathbb{T}}(k))^2$ generic assertions.*

Fixed-Point Computation

In presence of loops (inside procedures as well as in call-graphs), we iterate until fixed-point is reached. The standard way to perform such an iteration is to maintain a worklist that stores all program points whose formulas have changed with respect to the formulas in the previous iteration, but whose change has not yet been propagated to its predecessors.

Let ψ be the formula computed at some program point π, and let ψ' be the formula at π in the previous iteration. If ψ and ψ' are logically equivalent, then it is intuitive that the formula at π has not changed from the previous iteration (and hence does not require any further propagation to the predecessors of π). However, it follows from Property 1 that we can strengthen this notion to conclude that the formula at π has not changed even if $\psi \rightleftharpoons \psi'$. This observation is important because it allows to detect fixed-point faster. In case of unary uninterpreted functions, this makes significant difference (E.g., for the loop in procedure Q in Figure 3, fixed-point is not even reached with the former intuitive notion of change, while it is reached in 2 steps with the latter stronger notion of change, as explained on Page 255). The number of times the formula ψ at each point inside a procedure gets updated is bounded by the *maximum unifier chain length* of the underlying theory as defined below.

Definition 2 (Maximum Unifier Chain Length $M_{\mathbb{T}}(k)$). *We define the* maximum unifier chain length *of any theory $\mathbb{T}$ for k variables, denoted by $M_{\mathbb{T}}(k)$, to be the maximum length of any chain $\psi_1, \psi_2, \ldots$ (where each ψ_i is a conjunction of generic assertions over k variables) such that $\psi_i \rightharpoonup \psi_{i+1}$ but $\psi_{i+1} \not\rightharpoonup \psi_i$.*

Computational Complexity

The number of updates performed during phase 1 is bounded above by $n \times M_{\mathbb{T}}(k)$, where n is the total number of program points and k is the maximum number of program variables that are live at any program point (This follows from Definition 2). The cost of each update is bounded above by $T_{\mathbb{T}}(k)$. Hence, the cost of Phase 1 is $O(n \times M_{\mathbb{T}}(k) \times T_{\mathbb{T}}(k))$.

3.3 Phase 2: Using Procedure Summaries

We now show how to use the procedure summaries computed in phase 1 to verify and discover assertions at different program points. The correctness of this phase is easy to observe, while its computational complexity is bounded above by that of phase 1.

Verifying a given assertion at a given program point. For this purpose, we can perform the weakest precondition computation of the given assertion as in Phase 1. However, there are two main differences. The formula computed at each program point is a regular assertion instead of a generic assertion. Secondly, the preconditions computed at the beginning of the procedures are copied before the call sites of those procedures. When the process reaches a fixed-point, we declare the assertion to be true iff the precondition computed at the beginning of `Main` procedure is `true`.

Computing all invariants at a given program point. Instead of computing the weakest precondition of a given assertion at a program point π (as described above), we can also compute the weakest preconditions of a complete set of generic assertions. The preconditions obtained at the beginning of `Main` procedure for each of these generic assertions will be in the form of constraints on the context variables. These constraints exactly characterize the invariants that hold at π.

Computing all invariants at all program points. We can repeat the above process for all program points to compute all invariants at all program points. However, when the expression language of the program comes from a unitary theory (e.g., linear arithmetic and uninterpreted functions), we can perform a more efficient analysis based on a forward intraprocedural analysis for that abstract domain. For this purpose, we simply run a forward intraprocedural analysis on each procedure. The invariant at the entry point of `Main` procedure is initialized to `true`, while for all other procedures, it is obtained as the join of the invariants before all call sites of that procedure. We only need to describe the transfer function for the procedure call node. Let F be the invariants computed before the procedure call node. Let $\sigma = \texttt{Unif}(F)$ be the substitution representing the most-general unifier of F. (Note that unitary theories have a single most-general unifier). Let V be the set of variables that do not have a definition in σ, but are the inputs to procedure P. Let the summary of procedure P be: "the assertion ψ_i holds at the end of procedure iff the constraints ψ_i' hold at the beginning of procedure" (for all generic assertions ψ_i from some complete set G). The transfer function for the procedure call node then is: $F_i' = \bigwedge_i \texttt{Normalize}(\forall V \psi_i'[\sigma], \psi_i)$.

The key idea here is to instantiate each of the constraints ψ_i' with σ and universally quantify out the remaining input variables V (by using the same technique described in weakest precondition computation across non-deterministic assignment nodes). There is no precision loss in quantifying out V since, by assumption, there are no invariants on V. The resulting constraints on context variables describe all relationships of the form ψ_i that hold among the output variables of procedure P after the procedure call node. The function `Normalize` translates these constraints into the desired invariants. `Normalize`(C, ψ_i) takes as input some constraints C on the context variables corresponding to some generic assertion ψ_i and returns the assertions obtained by eliminating the context variables. (Eg., `Normalize`$(a + b = 0 \wedge c - d = 0, ax + by + cz = d)$ returns $x = y \wedge z = 1$, which is obtained by eliminating a, b, c, d from $\forall a, b, c, d(a + b = 0 \wedge c - d = 0 \Rightarrow ax + by + cz = d))$.

4 Unary Uninterpreted Functions

In this section, we instantiate the above general framework for performing interprocedural analysis over the abstraction of unary uninterpreted functions. As a result, we obtain a PTIME algorithm for computing all equality invariants when the program is specified using the flowchart nodes described in Figure 2, and the expression language of the program involves unary uninterpreted functions.

Unary uninterpreted functions can be used to model fields of structures and objects in programs, as well as deterministic function calls with one argument–this is useful when the function body is unavailable or is too complicated to analyze. Yet another motivation for studying the unary uninterpreted abstraction comes from the long-standing open problem of interprocedural global value numbering. This problem seeks to analyze programs whose expression language contains uninterpreted functions of *any* arity. A brief history of this problem is given in Section 6. The results in this section, thus, make progress toward solving this open problem.

Apart from the general ideas mentioned in Section 3, our results in this section also rely on another key idea of representing large strings succinctly via singleton context-free grammars [13].

Notation. Terms constructed using unary function symbols can be represented as strings. For example, the term $f(g(x))$ can be treated as the string fgx. The expressions $f(\_)$ and $f(g(\_))$, (respectively strings f and fg) are terms with a hole $\_$. Variables that take terms with a hole as values, or equivalently context variables, will be denoted by α, β, etc. The concrete terms with holes are denoted by C, D, E, F with suitable annotations.

4.1 Simplification

We compute procedure summaries by backward propagation of all the generic assertions in the set $\{\alpha x_1 = \beta x_2 \mid x_1, x_2 \in V,\ x_1 \not\equiv x_2\}$, where V is the set of output variables of the corresponding procedure. The assertions generated in the process are simplified to one of the following forms:

$$(1)\ \alpha C x_i = \beta C' x_j \qquad (2)\ \alpha C \alpha^{-1} = \beta C' \beta^{-1} \qquad (3)\ \alpha = \beta C$$

```
P(){
  x := fgx;
  y := gfy;
  if (*) { Q(); }
  else { P(); }
}
```

```
Q(){
  while (*) {
     x := fx;
     y := fy;
  }
}
```

```
main(){
  y := a;
  x := fa;
  P();
  assert(x = fy);
}
```

Fig. 3. Program

Thus, every ψ is simply a conjunction of assertions of these forms. The *inverse* operator, $^{-1}$, satisfies the intuitive axioms: $(\alpha\beta)^{-1} = \beta^{-1}\alpha^{-1}$, $\alpha\alpha^{-1} = \epsilon$, and $(\alpha^{-1})^{-1} = \alpha$.[1] The strings C, C' in Form 2 are allowed to contain the inverse operator, whereas strings C, C' in Form 1 and Form 3 do not contain the inverse operator. Equations of Form 2 are an elegant way of encoding constraints on the context-variables α and β that are generated by the backward analysis.

We show now that weakest precondition computation across the various program nodes maintains assertions in one of these forms. We consider the case of a Procedure Call node "Call P()" (the other cases are easy to verify). At any stage of the fixpoint computation, the (partially computed) summary of a procedure P will be given as: "$\alpha' x_i = \beta' x_j$ holds at the end of procedure P if ψ''_{ij} holds at the beginning" for each pair $x_i, x_j \in V$. Equations of Form 2 and Form 3 are unchanged in the weakest precondition computation. The weakest precondition of an equation $\alpha C x_i = \beta C' x_j$ is obtained by instantiating ψ''_{ij} by $\{\alpha' \mapsto \alpha C, \beta' \mapsto \beta C'\}$. Applying this replacement in equations of Form 1 or Form 2 in ψ''_{ij} gives back equations of the same form. When applied on equations of Form 3, we get equations of the form $\alpha C = \beta C'$. We remove the largest common suffix of C, C' and if the equation does not reduce to Form 3, then the weakest precondition is *false*.

Bounding the size of ψ. We will show that any conjunction of equations of Form 1, Form 2, and Form 3 over k variables can be simplified to contain *at most* $k(k-1)/2 + 1$ equations. Specifically,

- for each pair x_i, x_j of variables, there is at most one equation of Form 1; and
- either there is at most one equation of Form 2, or there is at most one equation of Form 3.[2]

The Simplification procedure uses unification to simplify the equations and keeps the result *essentially equivalent* to the original set. It performs two main steps. For a fixed pair x, y of variables, let ψ_{xy} denote the set containing all equations of Form 1 in ψ. First, by repeated use of Lemma 1 ψ_{xy} is simplified to a set containing at most one equation of Form 1 and either one equation of Form 3 or

[1] Note that the inverse operator implicitly builds in simplification using unification. For instance, while $fx = fy$ does not logically imply $x = y$, using the inverse axioms we have $fx = fy \Rightarrow f^{-1}fx = f^{-1}fy \Rightarrow x = y$.

[2] Note that an equation of Form 3 essentially gives a concrete solution, since we can assume, by Property 1, that one of α, β is ϵ.

Ite	Proc	Current Summary for $\alpha x = \beta y$	Comment
0	P, Q	*true*	Init
1	Q	$\text{Simp}(\alpha x = \beta y, \alpha f x = \beta f y) = (\alpha x = \beta y, \alpha f \alpha^{-1} = \beta f \beta^{-1})$	
2	P	$\alpha f g x = \beta g f y, \alpha f \alpha^{-1} = \beta f \beta^{-1}$	Use Q's summary
3	Q	$\alpha x = \beta y, \alpha f \alpha^{-1} = \beta f \beta^{-1}$	fixpoint for Q
4	P	$\text{Simp}(\alpha f g f g x = \beta g f g f y, \alpha f g x = \beta g f y, \alpha f \alpha^{-1} = \beta f \beta^{-1})$	Use P's summary
5	P	$\alpha f = \beta, \alpha f g x = \beta g f y$	fixpoint for P

Fig. 4. This figure illustrates summary computation for interprocedural analysis over the unary abstraction. In Column 3, the summary consists of the constraints that must hold at the beginning of the procedure P/Q for $\alpha x = \beta y$ to be an invariant at the end of the procedure.

finitely many equations of Form 2. For example, in iteration 2 of Figure 4, the set of equations $\{\alpha x = \beta y, \alpha f x = \beta f y\}$ is simplified to $\{\alpha x = \beta y, \alpha f \alpha^{-1} = \beta f \beta^{-1}\}$.

Lemma 1. *The equation set* $\{\alpha C_i x = \beta C'_i y : i = 1, 2\}$ *either has no solutions, or it has the same solutions as a set containing either one of these two equations and at most one equation of Form 2 or Form 3.*

Next, if there is an equation of Form 3 then it can be used to simplify an equation of Form 2 to either *false* or *true*. Otherwise, a set $\{\alpha C_i \alpha^{-1} = \beta C'_i \beta^{-1}, i = 2, \ldots, k\}$ containing multiple equations of Form 2 is simplified by repeated use of Lemma 2.

Lemma 2. *The equation set* $\{\alpha C_i \alpha^{-1} = \beta C'_i \beta^{-1}, i = 1, 2\}$ *is either unsatisfiable, or has the same solutions as a set containing at most one equation of either Form 2 or Form 3.*

For example, in iteration 4-5 of Figure 4, $\{\alpha f \alpha^{-1} = \beta f \beta^{-1}, \alpha f g \alpha^{-1} = \beta g f \beta^{-1}\}$ is simplified to $\{\alpha f = \beta\}$. In this way, any conjunction ψ of equations of Form 1, Form 2, and Form 3 is simplified to a conjunction with at most $k(k-1)/2+1$ equations.[3]

The algorithms used in the proof of Lemma 1 and Lemma 2 use a constant number of string operations. Assuming the basic string operations take time T_{base}, the time taken to simplify $S_{\text{uu}}(k)^2 = O(k^4)$ assertions is $O(k^4 T_{\text{base}})$.

Maximum Unifier Chain Length. It is easy to see that the maximum unifier chain length for k variables is bounded by $k(k-1)/2+2$. This is because the number of equations in ψ can increase only $k(k-1)/2+1$ times, and beyond that the formula either becomes unsatisfiable, or it is forced to have a unique solution for its variables. Note that it is not possible for the number of equations to remain the same and the formula to get stronger. This is a consequence of Lemma 1.

[3] The observation that we need to keep only a small number of equations $Cx_i = \alpha C' x_j$ intuitively means that we keep only a few runs. However, these runs in the *simplified* formula may not correspond to any real runs, but some equivalent hypothetical runs.

Hence, for the case of unary uninterpreted (uu) abstraction, we have:

$$S_{\text{uu}}(k) = \frac{k(k-1)}{2} + 1 \qquad T_{\text{uu}}(k) = O(k^4 T_{\text{base}}) \qquad M_{\text{uu}}(k) = \frac{k(k-1)}{2} + 2$$

4.2 Computational Complexity: Efficient Representations

We note that the time complexity of interprocedural analysis for the unary uninterpreted abstraction is polynomial *assuming* that the string operations can be performed efficiently. However, the length of strings can be *exponential* in the size of the program, as the following example shows.

Example 1. Consider the n procedures $P_0, \ldots, P_{n-1}$ defined as

$$P_i(x_i)\ \{\ t := P_{i-1}(x_i);\ y_i := P_{i-1}(t);\ \mathit{return}(y_i); \}$$
$$P_0(x_0)\ \{\ y_0 := f x_0;\ \mathit{return}(y_0); \}$$

The summary of procedure P_i is: $y_i = \alpha x_i$ iff $\alpha = f^{2^i}$.

Hence, if we use a naive (explicit) representation, the size of ψ can grow exponentially (when we apply substitutions during transfer function computation across procedure call nodes). Instead we appeal to shared representation of strings using *singleton context-free grammars* (SCFG). An SCFG is a context-free grammar where each nonterminal represents *exactly* one (terminal) string. An SCFG can represent strings in an exponentially succinct way. The strings C_i's that arise in the equations can be represented succinctly using SCFGs in size that is linear in the size of the program (because the program itself is an implicit succinct representation of these strings using SCFGs).

Example 2. Following up on Example 1, we note that the string f^{2^n} can be represented by the SCFG with start symbol A_n and productions $\{A_{i+1} \to A_i A_i \mid 1 \le i \le n\} \cup \{A_0 \to f\}$. In particular, the summaries of the procedures can be represented as: $y_i = \alpha x_i$ iff $\alpha = A_i$.

A classic result by Plandowski [13] shows that equality of two strings represented as SCFGs can be checked in polynomial time. Apart from this, the simplification procedure implicit in the proofs of Lemma 1 and Lemma 2 require largest common prefix/suffix computation and substring extraction. It is an easy exercise to see that these string operations can also be performed on SCFG representations in polynomial time. Hence, the computational procedure outlined above can be implemented in polynomial time using the SCFG representation of strings. In conclusion, this shows that summaries can be computed in PTIME on the abstraction of unary symbols. We remark here that Plandowski's result has been generalized to trees [19] suggesting that it may be possible to generalize our result to the interprocedural global value numbering problem (over binary uninterpreted functions).

5 Linear Arithmetic

The technique described in Section 3.2 can also be used effectively to compute procedure summaries for the abstraction of linear arithmetic. We compute the weakest precondition of the generic assertion $\alpha_1 x_1 + \cdots + \alpha_k x_k = \alpha$ (which constitutes a complete set by itself) where $x_1, \ldots, x_k$ are the output variables of the corresponding procedure.

The conjunction ψ of equations thus obtained at any point in the procedure during the weakest precondition computation can be seen as *linear* equations *over* the $k^2 + k + 1$ variables: k^2 variables representing the products $\alpha_i x_j$ and the $k + 1$ variables α_i and α. We can simplify the equations thus obtained by maintaining only the linearly independent (non-redundant) equations. We know that there can not be more than $k^2 + k + 1$ linearly independent equations and hence ψ can have at most $k^2 + k + 1$ equations. This shows that for the linear arithmetic (la) abstraction,

$$S_{\text{la}}(k) = k^2 + k + 1 \qquad T_{\text{la}}(k) = O(T_{\text{base}} k^8) \qquad M_{\text{la}}(k) = k^2 + k + 1,$$

where T_{base} denotes the time to perform an arithmetic operation. Since constants can become large (programs can encode large numbers succinctly), we use modulo arithmetic and randomization to get a true PTIME procedure, as in [11].

Müller-Olm and Seidl also gave a precise interprocedural algorithm for linear arithmetic of similar complexity [11]. However, their algorithm is different and is based on the the observation that *runs* of a procedure correspond to linear transformations and there can be only quadratic many linearly-independent transformations. In a certain sense, this is the *dual* of our approach.

6 Related Work and Discussion

Forward vs. Backward Analysis. The approach presented in this paper for computing procedure summaries is based on backward propagation of generic assertions. It is presently unclear how the dual approach, namely forward propagation of a complete set of generic assertions, can be effectively used. A forward propagation involves developing context-sensitive or distributive transfer functions for assignment nodes (usually involves existential quantifier elimination) and join nodes. Giving a general procedure for such operations appears to be hard for regular assertions (intraprocedural case) and would be significantly more difficult for generic assertions.

Nevertheless, these difficulties may be overcome for very specific abstractions, such as linear arithmetic [11,8]. In this case, the authors essentially look at a procedure as a linear transformation and compute in the $(k+1)^2$-dimensional vector space of these linear transformations. This allows them to perform abstract interpretation using either backward or forward analysis [11,8]. However, this general approach of developing interprocedural analysis by describing program behaviors as transformations (in a finite dimensional vector space) is applicable only on arithmetic abstractions. In contrast, our approach promises to be simpler, and more generally applicable.

Weakest Precondition of Generic Assertions vs. Regular Assertions. To ensure termination of weakest precondition computation over generic assertions, we used some connections between unification and assertion checking. Similar connections have been used earlier for weakest precondition computation for regular assertions in the intraprocedural case [5,6]. However, in the intraprocedural case, we just need to solve unification problems over regular assertions. These problems are well-studied and efficient algorithms are known for several theories. In the interprocedural case, we now have to solve unification problems over *generic* assertions. In the theorem proving community, these are studied under the name of "second-order unification" and "context unification". These problems are known to be more difficult than their first-order counterparts. Thus, while our approach of backward analysis based on generic assertions provides a uniform framework for developing interprocedural analyses, it also helps to ascertain the difficulty of interprocedural analysis over intraprocedural analysis by drawing connections with the complexity of second-order unification vs. standard unification in theorem proving. Templates, which are similar to generic assertions, have been used to generate invariants, but only in the context of intraprocedural analysis and without any completeness guarantees [18].

History of Global Value Numbering. Since checking equivalence of program expressions is an undecidable problem, in general, program operators are commonly abstracted as uninterpreted functions to detect expression equivalences. This form of equivalence is also called *Herbrand equivalence* [16] and the process of discovering it is often referred to as *value numbering.* Kildall [7] gave the first intraprocedural algorithm for this problem based on performing abstract interpretation [2] over the lattice of Herbrand equivalences in exponential time. This was followed by several PTIME, but imprecise, intraprocedural algorithms [1,16,3]. The first PTIME intraprocedural algorithm was given by Gulwani & Necula [4], and then by Müller-Olm, Rüthing, & Seidl [9]. However, PTIME interprocedural global value numbering algorithm has been elusive. There are some new results, but only under severe restrictions that functions are side-effect free and one side of the assertion is a constant [12]. Neither of these assumptions is satisfied by the program in Figure 3. The technique described in this paper yields a PTIME algorithm for the special case of unary uninterpreted functions.

7 Conclusion

Proving non-trivial properties of programs requires analyzing programs over rich abstractions. The scalability of such program analyses depends upon the possibility of constructing efficient and precise summaries of procedures over such abstractions. In this paper, we have described a new technique for computing procedure summaries for a class of program abstractions over infinite domains, thereby adding to some limited piece of work known in this area.

In the description of our technique, we assume at some places that conditionals are non-deterministic and expression language of the program comes from a unitary theory. These assumptions are needed to prove that our technique computes the most precise procedure summary in an efficient manner. We believe that the general ideas in our technique can be extended to reason about predicates in conditionals and handle expressions that are not from a unitary theory (e.g., as suggested in [6]), albeit with some (unavoidable) precision loss because the problem is undecidable in general.

References

1. B. Alpern, M. N. Wegman, and F. K. Zadeck. Detecting equality of variables in programs. In *15th Annual ACM Symposium on POPL*, pages 1–11, 1988.
2. P. Cousot and R. Cousot. Abstract interpretation: A unified lattice model for static analysis of programs by construction or approximation of fixpoints. In *4th Annual ACM Symposium on POPL*, pages 234–252, 1977.
3. K. Gargi. A sparse algorithm for predicated global value numbering. In *PLDI*, volume 37, 5, pages 45–56. ACM Press, June 17–19 2002.
4. S. Gulwani and G. C. Necula. A polynomial-time algorithm for global value numbering. In *Static Analysis Symposium*, volume 3148 of *LNCS*, pages 212–227, 2004.
5. S. Gulwani and A. Tiwari. Assertion checking over combined abstraction of linear arithmetic & uninterpreted functions. In *ESOP*, volume 3924 of *LNCS*, Mar. 2006.
6. S. Gulwani and A. Tiwari. Assertion checking unified. In *Proc. VMCAI*, LNCS 4349. Springer, 2007. See also Microsoft Research Tech. Report MSR-TR-2006-98.
7. G. A. Kildall. A unified approach to global program optimization. In *1st ACM Symposium on POPL*, pages 194–206, Oct. 1973.
8. M. Müller-Olm, M. Petter, and H. Seidl. Interprocedurally analyzing polynomial identities. In *STACS*, volume 3884 of *LNCS*, pages 50–67. Springer, 2006.
9. M. Müller-Olm, O. Rüthing, and H. Seidl. Checking Herbrand equalities and beyond. In *VMCAI*, volume 3385 of *LNCS*, pages 79–96. Springer, Jan. 2005.
10. M. Müller-Olm and H. Seidl. A note on Karr's algorithm. In *31st International Colloquium on Automata, Languages and Programming*, pages 1016–1028, 2004.
11. M. Müller-Olm and H. Seidl. Precise interprocedural analysis through linear algebra. In *31st ACM Symposium on POPL*, pages 330–341, Jan. 2004.
12. M. Müller-Olm, H. Seidl, and B. Steffen. Interprocedural Herbrand equalities. In *ESOP*, volume 3444 of *LNCS*, pages 31–45. Springer, 2005.
13. W. Plandowski. Testing equivalence of morphisms on context-free languages. In *Algorithms - ESA '94*, volume 855 of *LNCS*, pages 460–470. Springer, 1994.
14. T. Reps. On the sequential nature of interprocedural program-analysis problems. *Acta Informatica*, 33(8):739–757, Nov. 1996.
15. T. Reps, S. Horwitz, and M. Sagiv. Precise interprocedural dataflow analysis via graph reachability. In *22nd ACM Symposium on POPL*, pages 49–61, 1995.
16. O. Rüthing, J. Knoop, and B. Steffen. Detecting equalities of variables: Combining efficiency with precision. In *SAS*, volume 1694 of *LNCS*, pages 232–247, 1999.
17. M. Sagiv, T. Reps, and S. Horwitz. Precise interprocedural dataflow analysis with applications to constant propagation. *TCS*, 167(1–2):131–170, 30 Oct. 1996.
18. S. Sankaranarayanan, H. Sipma, and Z. Manna. Non-linear loop invariant generation using grbner bases. In *POPL*, pages 318–329, 2004.
19. M. Schmidt-Schauß. Polynomial equality testing for terms with shared substructures. Technical Report 21, Institut für Informatik, November 2005.
20. M. Sharir and A. Pnueli. Two approaches to interprocedural data flow analysis. In *Program Flow Analysis: Theory and Applications*. Prentice-Hall, 1981.

Small Witnesses for Abstract Interpretation-Based Proofs

Frédéric Besson, Thomas Jensen, and Tiphaine Turpin

IRISA/{Inria, CNRS, Université de Rennes 1}
Campus de Beaulieu, F-35042 Rennes, France

Abstract. Abstract interpretation-based proof carrying code uses post-fixpoints of abstract interpretations to witness that a program respects a safety policy. Some witnesses carry more information than needed and are therefore unnecessarily large. We introduce a notion of size of a witness and propose techniques for reducing the size of such certificates. For distributive analyses, we show that a smallest witness exist and we give an iterative algorithm for computing it. For non-distributive analyes we propose a technique for pruning a witness and illustrate this pruning on a relational, polyhedra-based analysis. Finally, only the existence of a witness is needed to assure the code consumer of the safety of a given program. This makes possible a compression technique of witnesses where only part of a witness is sent together with an encoding of the iterative steps necessary to prove that it is part of a post-fixpoint.

1 Introduction

Proof-carrying code (PCC) is a software security infrastructure in which programs come equipped with certificates that allow a code consumer to check that the program respects a given safety policy. There are several requirements to the structure of such certificates which at the same time must be easy to produce for the code producer, small relative to the code size, and simple to check by the code consumer. Initial PCC works used as certificates a lambda-term encoding of proofs [Nec97] to be type-checked by the Logical Framework (LF). To optimise the size of these proofs, Necula and Lee proposed LF_i a compressed proof format for LF terms [NL98]. For a weaker logic, Necula and Rahul transmit as certificate an oracle (a stream of bits) that guides a higher-order logic interpreter in its proof search [NR01]. Wu, Appel, Stump [WAS03] show how to combine these ideas with dedicated program logics in order to obtain foundational proof checkers with small witnesses. Albert *et al.*, [AAPH06] propose abstract interpretation as a way to fully automate the generation of certificates. In this approach, fixpoints (invariants) play the role of certificates and a checker will have to verify *a)* that a proposed certificate is indeed a fixpoint of an abstract interpretation of the program and *b)* that this fixpoint entails the safety policy.

An important issue is how to encode such certificates in a manner that keeps the certificate small while still allowing efficient checking. This paper propose a theory based on abstract interpretation for studying this issue. Given an abstract

R. De Nicola (Ed.): ESOP 2007, LNCS 4421, pp. 268–283, 2007.

interpretation F of program p over an abstract domain D of program properties, and a safety policy expressed as a property ϕ in D, we study the set of *witnesses* of ϕ with respect to p, *i.e.*, the elements $w \in D$ satisfying $F(w) \sqsubseteq w \sqcap \phi$. Section 2 formalises the notion of witness and discuss how to optimise the *size* of a witness.

For certain kinds of abstract interpretations it is possible to guarantee the existence of a smallest witness for any abstract property. This is the case *e.g.*, for distributive data flow analyses [MJ81, MR90] and disjunctive-complete abstract interpretations. In Section 3 we provide a fixpoint characterisation of the smallest witness of a given abstract property for any distributive analysis and illustrate how to obtain an effective algorithm for a class of set-based analyses. In the general case, it is impossible to compute a smallest witness without resorting to an exhaustive search. Instead we propose in Section 4 a technique for *pruning* a witness to obtain a witness that is smaller relative to the initial witness. We illustrate this by showing how to prune the result of a relational, polyhedra-based abstract interpretation.

For the PCC application of fixpoint compression it is important to note that it is the *existence* of a witness that matters. This makes further optimisations possible because a code certificate now only have to convey the code consumer with sufficient information to convince him that he is able to build a witness. To make this idea concrete, we define in Section 5 certificates as *strategies* that encode the steps that an iterative fixpoint solver will take in order to reconstruct a complete fixpoint given the values at selected program points. This can be seen as a generalisation of the Lighwteight Java Byte Code using stack maps defined by Rose [Ros03] and used in the KVM Java virtual machine for embedded devices. Section 6 discusses related work, notably the recent proposal by Albert *et al.* [AAPH06] for reducing fixpoints produced by a generic fixpoint algorithm.

2 Obtaining Witness from Abstract Interpretation

Central to PCC is the ability to generate checkable proofs of programs. Previous works have shown how to obtain a proof from abstract interpretations. The key insight is that abstract interpretation does not return a yes/no answer but a property which over-approximates the program behaviour. In abstract interpretation terms, the notion of approximation is formalised by a Galois insertion between the semantic (concrete) domain of the program and the abstract domain of properties. A correct over-approximation of the program behaviour is a post-fixpoint of the abstraction of the program. As a result, proving that a program verifies a property, say ϕ, amounts to proving that there exists a post-fixpoint of the abstraction of the program semantics, say ψ, which entails ϕ. Under these conditions, this is a basic result from the theory of abstract interpretation [CC77] that the least fixpoint of the program semantics satisfies the property.

$$(\exists \psi, [\![p]\!]^\sharp(\psi) \sqsubseteq \psi \wedge \psi \sqsubseteq \phi) \Rightarrow \mathrm{lfp}([\![p]\!]) \models \phi$$

In a static analysis context, the abstract semantics ($[\![.]\!]^\sharp$) and the ordering of properties ($\sqsubseteq$) are computable functions. Therefore, given the property ψ, checking that a program verifies a property ϕ is a straightforward computation.

2.1 Witnesses

This motivates the definition of a proof witness for abstract interpretation.

Definition 1 (Direct witness). *A* direct *witness for a property $\phi \in D$ and a (monotone) abstract operator $F : D \to D$ is an abstract property $w \in D$ such that w is a post-fixpoint of F ($F(w) \sqsubseteq w$); and w entails ϕ ($w \sqsubseteq \phi$).*

This definition of a witness is the naive instantiation of PCC in the context of abstract interpretation. We propose to study a larger class of witnesses that are compact to encode and as fast to check. The key observation here is that verifying a witness involves some unavoidable computation of F, the results of which need not appear explicitly in the witness. To this end, Definition 2 relaxes the notion of direct witness while preserving its role (the existence of a witness entails the satisfaction of ϕ) and keeping the same verification cost.

Definition 2 (Witness). *An abstract interpretation witness proof for a property $\phi \in D$ and a (monotone) abstract operator $F : D \to D$ is an abstract property $w \in D$ such that $F(w) \sqsubseteq w \sqcap \phi$.*

The following Lemmas affirms that witnesses are as good as direct ones for proving ϕ, and that there are more of them than direct witnesses.

Lemma 1

1. *If w is a witness then $F(w)$ is a direct witness.*
2. *If w is a direct witness then w is a witness.*

Proof Sketch. Follows directly from the monotonicity of F, the definition of the greatest lower bound operator ($\sqcap$) and the transitivity of the ordering $\sqsubseteq$. □

We focus on optimising the latter, more general version of witnesses.

2.2 On the Size of Witnesses

When choosing a witness, there are two criteria of interest: its size and its verification cost. In this paper we focus on the size of witnesses, but the results in Sections 3 and 4 should be a good starting point for reducing the verification cost, at least in terms of memory.

In the theory of abstract interpretation, the least fixpoint ($\mathrm{lfp}(F)$) is the strongest property that can be proved of a program and is therefore a poor choice for a witness, because it contains information that is not needed for proving a particular property. *E.g.*, to prove a property at a specific program point (such as absence of array accesses out of bounds or the absence division by zero) only a few program variables and a few program points are relevant. For the others, no information is needed. So, we will rather search for weaker witnesses which are usually smaller because they encode the minimal amount of information needed to prove the property. Notice that the program property to be proved is usually not a witness because it is not a post-fixpoint of F.

To make this argument more precise, consider standard data flow analyses that compute a property for each program point. These analyses operate on a product lattice D^n where n is the number of program points, or even (if we further refine the decomposition) the number of pairs (pp, v) where pp is a program point and v is a variable. Lattice elements are n-tuples for which the ith projection is, for example, a formula characterizing the property of the ith program point. The ordering is point-wise

$$(\psi_1, \ldots, \psi_n) \sqsubseteq (\psi'_1, \ldots, \psi'_n) \text{ iff } \psi_1 \sqsubseteq \psi'_1 \wedge \ldots \wedge \psi_n \sqsubseteq \psi'_n$$

and the size of the property of the whole program is the sum of the size of the atomic formulae.

$$\mid (\psi_1, \ldots, \psi_n) \mid = \mid \psi_1 \mid + \ldots + \mid \psi_n \mid$$

As argued above, for a number of program points these ψ's can be set to $\top$ (and hence left out) because they are not needed for proving the particular property. This suggests that as a general rule, smaller witnesses are those that are weaker (higher up) in the lattice ordering $\sqsubseteq$. While not universally true, this is valid for all analyses based on lattices obtained as meet-completions of sets of unordered atomic properties and, for the present paper, we will adopt the principle that the smaller witnesses are those that are higher in the lattice ordering.

3 Optimal Witnesses for Distributive Analyses

In this section, we show that for distributive analyses it is possible to compute the *weakest* witness which, as soon as our size assumptions are verified, is also the smallest. We also provide an algorithm for computing such optimal witnesses for a class of set-based distributive analyses which includes classical data flow problems such as live variables and reaching definitions [MJ81, MR90].

3.1 Lattice of Witnesses

We show that for distributive analyses, witnesses form a lattice. As a consequence, there exists a weakest witness (provided the set of witnesses is not empty). In the following, we consider a lattice of abstract properties D and a distributive function F (i.e., such that $\forall X \neq \emptyset, F\left(\bigsqcup_{x \in X} x\right) = \bigsqcup_{x \in X} F(x)$).

Theorem 1. *Let W be the set of witnesses for a distributive function F and a property ϕ. If W is not empty then $(W, lfp(F), \sqcup, \sqsubseteq)$ is a complete lattice.*

Proof. Because $\text{lfp}(F)$ is the least fixpoint of F it is also the least post-fixpoint. As a result, as the set of witnesses is not empty, it is also the least witness.

It remains to show that the least upper bound operators is well-defined *i.e.,* the least upper bounds of witnesses is also a witness: $\forall S \subseteq W, \sqcup S \in W$. By definition of a witness, we have that for all $w \in S$, $F(w) \sqsubseteq w \sqcap \phi$. Since F is distributive, we have that $F(\bigsqcup_{w \in S} w) = \bigsqcup_{w \in S} F(w) \sqsubseteq \bigsqcup_{w \in S}(w \sqcap \phi) = \sqcup S \sqcap \phi$. It follows that $\sqcup S$ is a witness. □

As a result, the weakest witness ww is the least upper bound of all witnesses and is given by $\text{ww} = \bigsqcup W$.

3.2 Weakest Witnesses as Greatest Fixpoints

In this section, we show that the weakest witness is the greatest fixpoint of the function $\widetilde{F}$ which given a x computes the weakest precondition wp such that $F(wp) \sqsubseteq x \sqcap \phi$.

Definition 3. *Let F be a distributive function and ϕ a property. $\widetilde{F} : D \to D$ is the function defined by: $\widetilde{F}(x) = \bigsqcup\{y \mid F(y) \sqsubseteq x \sqcap \phi\}$.*

Theorem 2 states that ww, if it exists, is the greatest fixpoint of $\widetilde{F}$.

Theorem 2. *Let F be a distributive function and ϕ be an abstract property. If the greatest fixpoint of $\widetilde{F}$ is not undefined ($gfp(\widetilde{F}) \neq \bot$) then it is the weakest witness of ϕ ($ww = gfp(\widetilde{F})$).*

Proof. We show that the witnesses of ϕ are exactly the pre-fixpoints of $\widetilde{F}$ *i.e.*, $W = \{x \mid x \sqsubseteq \widetilde{F}(x)\}$.

- $\subseteq$: Assume that $w \in W$. By definition of a witness, we have $F(w) \sqsubseteq w \sqcap \phi$. It follows that $w \in \{y \mid F(y) \sqsubseteq w \sqcap \phi\}$. By definition of the least upper-bound operator, we obtain that $w \sqsubseteq \bigsqcup\{y \mid F(y) \sqsubseteq w \sqcap \phi\} = \widetilde{F}(w)$. Therefore, $w \in \{x \mid x \sqsubseteq \widetilde{F}(x)\}$.
- $\supseteq$: Assume that w is a pre-fixpoint of $\widetilde{F}$: $w \sqsubseteq \bigsqcup\{y \mid F(y) \sqsubseteq w \sqcap \phi\}$. By monotony and distributivity of F, we get $F(w) \sqsubseteq F\left(\bigsqcup\{y \mid F(y) \sqsubseteq w \sqcap \phi\}\right) = \bigsqcup\{F(y) \mid F(y) \sqsubseteq w \sqcap \phi\}$. By definition of $\sqcup$, we also have $\bigsqcup\{F(y) \mid F(y) \sqsubseteq w \sqcap \phi\} \sqsubseteq w \sqcap \phi$. By transitivity, we obtain that $F(w) \sqsubseteq w \sqcap \phi$ *i.e.*, $w \in W$.

We conclude, since ww is defined as the greatest witness, that it is the greatest pre-fixpoint of $\widetilde{F}$ and therefore its greatest fixpoint. □

As a result, if the lattice of properties satisfies the *finite descending chain condition*, the weakest witness can be computed by fixpoint iteration: ww $= \widetilde{F}^{\infty}(\top)$.

3.3 Weakest Witnesses for Set-Based Analyses

The specification of the function $\widetilde{F}$ is not directly executable. However, for set-based distributive analyses, $\widetilde{F}$ can be derived symbolically without resorting to a naive tabulation. Canonical set-based distributive analyses are data-flow analyses such as available expressions, busy expressions and live variables analyses [MJ81, MR90]. We illustrate the symbolic computation of $\widetilde{F}$ for data flow problems which solution is expressed as the solution of a distributive function F defined component-wise $F(x_1, \ldots, x_n) = (F_1(x_1, \ldots, x_n), \ldots, F_n(x_1, \ldots, x_n))$ such that each F_i is defined by a set expression se of the following form

$$se ::= y \mid c \mid se_1 \cap c \mid se_1 \cup se_2$$

where y is a variable, c is a constant set, $\cap$ is set intersection and $\cup$ is set union.

To compute $\widetilde{F}$ symbolically, the key insight is the definition of a *weakest precondition* operator wp. Given a set expression e and a upper-bound b for this expression, it computes the greatest n-tuple $(v_1, \ldots, v_n)$ so that $e(v_1, \ldots, v_n) \sqsubseteq b$. In other words, it computes the weakest precondition over the variables such that the set expression is dominated by the upper-bound b.

Definition 4. *The weakest precondition operator wp is inductively defined by*

$$\begin{array}{ll} wp(x_j)(b) & = \top^n[j \mapsto b] \\ wp(c)(b) & = \textit{if } c \subseteq b \textit{ then } \top^n \textit{ else } \bot^n \\ wp(e \cap c)(b) & = wp(e)(b \cup \bar{c}) \\ wp(e \cup e')(b) & = wp(e)(b) \sqcap wp(e')(b) \end{array}$$

where $\bar{c}$ is the complement of c and $\sqcap$ is point-wise intersection of n-tuples.

Lemma 2 states formally that wp is a weakest precondition operator.

Lemma 2. *Given a set expression e and a set bound b, the following holds:*

$$wp(e)(b) = \bigsqcup\{(x_1, \ldots, x_n) \mid e(x_1, \ldots, x_n) \subseteq b\}.$$

Proof Sketch. The proof is by induction over the set expression e. The cases $e = x_j$ and $e = c$ are proved by definition of wp and $\subseteq$. The remaining cases $e = e_1 \cap c$ and $e = e_1 \cup e_2$ are proved by induction hypothesis using the facts that $e_1 \cap c \subseteq b$ iff $e_1 \subseteq b \cup \bar{c}$ and that $e_1 \cup e_2 \subseteq b$ iff $e_1 \subseteq b \wedge e_2 \subseteq b$. □

Theorem 3 states that $\widetilde{F}$ can be computed using wp.

Theorem 3. *Let F be a function defined by $F(x) = (F_1(x), \ldots, F_n(x))$ and $\phi = (\phi_1, \ldots, \phi_n)$ be a tuple of set properties. We have that the* inverse *of F with respect to ϕ ($\widetilde{F}$) is alternatively defined by:*

$$\widetilde{F}(x) = \bigsqcap_{i \in [1,n]} wp(F_i)(x_i \cap \phi_i).$$

Proof. By definition, we have $\widetilde{F}(x) = \bigsqcup\{y \mid F(y) \sqsubseteq x \sqcap \phi\}$. Because F and ϕ are tuples, this can be rewritten as: $\widetilde{F}(x_1, \ldots, x_n) = \bigsqcup\{y \mid \bigwedge_{i \in [1,n]} F_i(y) \subseteq x_i \sqcap \phi_i\} = \bigsqcup \bigcap_{i \in [1,n]}\{y \mid F_i(y) \subseteq x_i \cap \phi_i\} = \bigsqcap_{i \in [1,n]} \bigsqcup\{y \mid F_i(y) \subseteq x_i \cap \phi_i\}$ (the last equality holds because the sets are downward closed and because the F_i are monotone). By Lemma 2, we finally obtain $\widetilde{F}(x) = \bigsqcap_{i \in [1,n]} wp(F_i)(x_i \cap \phi_i)$. □

4 Fixpoint Pruning

In theory, for analyses that are not distributive, it would be possible to make them distributive by disjunctive completion. However, this approach generally leads to analyses of forbidding complexity. In this section, we develop a method for *pruning* a computed (post-)fixpoint into a small witness of a given property, by computing a sort of disjunctive completion relative to the initial post-fixpoint. We will first develop the general pruning technique and then show how its workings for a relational polyhedra analysis.

4.1 General Algorithm

Let $w \in D$ be a witness of the property ϕ. Our only assumption is that the property is expressed as a set of constraints (*e.g.*, $\{x + y \geq 0, x \leq 42\}$ for a polyhedral analysis). In that case, we have that the powerset $\mathcal{P}(w)$ of w is a sublattice of D when ordered by set inclusion. The idea of pruning is now simply to look for smaller witnesses in this powerset. For flow-sensitive analyses, the number of constraints is at least proportional to the size of the program and can increase quickly if there are many variables. Therefore, a global minimization of the witness by a direct search in the power set is not feasible. It is however possible to adapt the algorithm from the previous section to minimize a witness.

The disjunctive completion $D^{\vee}$ of $\mathcal{P}(w)$ is the lattice that contains every disjunction of elements of $\mathcal{P}(w)$. As a unique representation, we choose to represent its elements as sets of maximal disjuncts (sometimes called "crowns" [DP90]).

Lemma 3. *Let F be a function and ϕ a property on a domain D of constraints sets. Let $D^{\vee} = \{X \subseteq \mathcal{P}(w) \mid \forall x, y \in X, x \sqsubseteq y \implies x = y\}$, and define $X \sqsubseteq^{\vee} Y$ by $\forall x \in X, \exists y \in Y\ x \sqsubseteq y$. The disjunctive completion $(D^{\vee}, \sqsubseteq^{\vee})$ of $\mathcal{P}(D)$ is a complete lattice whose least upper bound operator satisfies $X \sqcup^{\vee} Y = \{x \in X \cup Y \mid \forall y \in X \cup Y\ x \sqsubseteq y \implies x = y\}$. Furthermore, letting $F^{\vee}(X) = \bigsqcup^{\vee}_{x \in X} \{\bigsqcap\{y \in \mathcal{P}(w) \mid y \sqsupseteq F(x)\}\}$, the existence of witnesses for $F^{\vee}$ with respect to the property $\{\phi\}$ ensures the safety of the program.*

These are standard results. The second part follows from the existence of a Galois connection between the concrete domain and $D^{\vee}$ that makes $F^{\vee}$ an over-approximation of the semantics. □

$F^{\vee}$ is distributive, so we can use $\widetilde{F^{\vee}}$ (Definition 3) to compute an optimal witness.

The problem is that this weakest witness is in $D^{\vee}$ and therefore its minimality doesn't implies that it is small. Intuitively, it contains all possible minimal proofs of the security property and hence can be very large, if there are many disjuncts. We thus take a slightly different way in order to keep witnesses in $\mathcal{P}(w)$. While $\widetilde{F^{\vee}} : D^{\vee} \to D^{\vee}$ is defined by

$$\widetilde{F^{\vee}}(X) = \bigsqcup^{\vee} \{Y \in D^{\vee} \mid F^{\vee}(Y) \sqsubseteq^{\vee} X \sqcap^{\vee} \{\phi\}\}$$

we define on the same lattice $D^{\vee}$ a variant $\widehat{F}$ whose result is further constrained.

Definition 5. *Let F be a function and ϕ a property on a domain D of constraints sets. The function $\widehat{F} : D^{\vee} \to D^{\vee}$ for pruning w is defined by*

$$\widehat{F}(X) = \bigsqcup^{\vee} \{\{y\} \mid y \in \mathcal{P}(w) \wedge \exists x \in \mathcal{P}(w)\ \{x\} \sqsubseteq^{\vee} X \wedge F(y) \sqsubseteq x \sqcap \phi \wedge y \sqsubseteq x\}.$$

We remark that $\widehat{F}$ is monotone and let $\widehat{W}$ be its greatest (pre-)fixpoint.

In this definition, the quantification $\exists x \in \mathcal{P}(w)\ \{x\} \sqsubseteq^{\vee} X\ \wedge \ldots$ can be replaced equivalently by the more direct formula: $\exists x \in X \ldots$. Since $D^{\vee}$ is of finite height,

$\widehat{W}$ can be computed as $\widehat{W} = \widehat{F}^{\infty}(\top^{\vee})$. The following theorem establishes how $\widehat{F}$ and $\widehat{W}$ are used for pruning.

Theorem 4. *$\widehat{W}$ is the set of maximal witnesses in $\mathcal{P}(w)$.*

Proof. We proceed in three steps.

- We first prove that every $w' \in \widehat{W}$ is a witness. As $\widehat{W} = \widehat{F}(\widehat{W})$, by definition of $\widehat{F}$ and the property of $\sqcup^{\vee}$ (Lemma 3), there exists an $x \in \mathcal{P}(w)$ such that $\{x\} \sqsubseteq^{\vee} \widehat{W} \wedge F(w') \sqsubseteq x \sqcap \phi \wedge w' \sqsubseteq x$. Since $w' \in \widehat{W}$ we also know that $\{w'\} \sqsubseteq^{\vee} \widehat{W}$ and that w' is maximal with respect to this property. Thus, from $\{x\} \sqsubseteq^{\vee} \widehat{W}$ and $w' \sqsubseteq x$, we deduce that $x = w'$. Therefore, $F(w') \sqsubseteq x \sqcap \phi$, i. e., w' is a witness.
- $\supseteq$: Let w' be a maximal witness. We have that $F(w') \sqsubseteq w' \sqcap \phi \wedge w' \sqsubseteq w'$. So, $\{w'\}$ is a pre-fixpoint of $\widehat{F}$. We conclude by definition of $\widehat{W}$ that $\{w'\} \sqsubseteq^{\vee} \widehat{W}$, that is, $w' \sqsubseteq w''$ for some $w'' \in \widehat{W}$ As shown before, w'' is a witness, therefore $w' = w''$ (because w' is a maximal witness) and $w' \in \widehat{W}$.
- $\subseteq$: We can now finish the proof of the first inclusion. Let $w' \in \widehat{W}$, w' is therefore a witness. Let w'' be a maximal witness greater than w'. From the second inclusion, $w'' \in \widehat{W}$, which implies that $w' = w''$ by definition of $D^{\vee}$ as a set of crowns. Thus w' is a *maximal* witness. □

The actual computation of the greatest fixpoint of $\widehat{F}$ is feasible if the disjunctions have a reasonable number of disjuncts, but this might not always be the case (theoretically, this number can be exponential in the number of constraints). In this case, we can further approximate the optimal solution. We start with the following remark: a disjunction can be under-approximated by any of its disjuncts. Therefore, we can make the pruning feasible by just choosing one disjunct at each step, rather than keeping them all. This leads to the the definition of $\hat{F}$ that is an (non-deterministic) under-approximation of $\widehat{F}$.

Definition 6. *The partial (non-deterministic) function $\hat{F} : \mathcal{P}(D) \to \mathcal{P}(D)$ for approximatively pruning w is defined by*

$$\hat{F}(x) = \textit{choose a weakest } y \sqsubseteq x \textit{ s.t. } F(y) \sqsubseteq x \sqcap \phi.$$

It is easy to see that every pre-fixpoint of $\hat{F}$ (formally, every x such that $x \sqsubseteq \hat{F}(x)$ for some choice) is a witness. We get a small one by computing $\hat{F}^{\infty}(\top)$. Also, every optimal witness can be reached by applying the approximated pruning.

4.2 Polyhedra Analysis

We illustrate the pruning algorithm on a convex polyhedra analysis. This analysis infers linear invariants that can be used to prove among other properties the absence of integer overflows and illegal array accesses. The domain of convex polyhedra has been used in various contexts, notably to analyse imperative programs [CH78] and synchronous programs [Hal93]. To focus the presentation, we consider the case of linear transition systems.

Definition 7. *A linear transition system is defined by:*

- *a finite set* S *of locations*
- *a finite set* V *of integer variables*
- *a finite set* E *of edges of the form* $s \xrightarrow{p} s'$ *where* $s, s' \in S$ *and* p *is a convex polyhedron of* $\mathbb{R}^{V \cup V'}$ *(with* $V' = \{v' \mid v \in V\}$ *a primed copy of* V*)*
- *a function* I *that maps every location to a convex polyhedron of* $\mathbb{R}^V$.

The operational semantics is as follows: if there is an edge $s \xrightarrow{p} s'$ then the system performs a transition from the location s with a valuation $\sigma \in \mathbb{R}^V$ of the variables to the location s' with valuation $\tau \in \mathbb{R}^V$ iff $\sigma + \tau' \subseteq p$ where $\sigma + \tau'(v) = \sigma(v)$ and $\sigma + \tau'(v') = \tau(v)$. p can describe assignments and guards with linear expressions. $I(l)$ represents the possible valuations of the initial states whose location is l, and is typically false for all but one location.

The abstract semantics of a linear system is defined over the product lattice $D = \text{Pol}(V)^S$ (where $\text{Pol}(V)$ is the lattice of convex polyhedra of $\mathbb{R}^V$) as the least fixpoint of the function $F : D \to D$ defined by:

$$F(x) = \left[s' \mapsto I(s') \sqcup^{\text{Pol}(V)} \bigsqcup_{s \xrightarrow{p} s' \in E}^{\text{Pol}(V)} [\![p]\!](x(s)) \right]$$

where the abstract semantics $[\![p]\!] : \text{Pol}(V) \to \text{Pol}(V)$ of a particular transition polyhedron p is defined by

$$[\![p]\!](x) = \mathbf{proj}_{V'} \left(x \times \mathbb{R}^{V'} \sqcap^{\text{Pol}(V \cup V')} p \right) [\forall v \; v/v'] .$$

Here, $\text{proj}_{V'} : \text{Pol}(V \cup V') \to \text{Pol}(V')$ is the polyhedra projection on the $\mathbb{R}^{V'}$ subspace, and $[\forall v \; v/v']$ is the substitution that "unprimes" every variable.

If we consider that the elements of $\text{Pol}(V)$ are represented as sets of constraints then the whole abstract domain can be defined as a sets of constraints by the coding $x \leftrightarrows \bigcup_{s \in S} \{s\} \times x(s)$.

So, given an abstract property $w \in \text{Pol}(V)^S$ we can compute the weakest precondition operator $\widehat{F} : \widetilde{\mathcal{P}(w)} \to \widetilde{\mathcal{P}(w)}$ as described above. This can be formulated in terms of basics operations on sets and polyhedra.

$$\widehat{F}(X) = \bigsqcup_{\substack{x \in X \\ I \sqsubseteq x}}^{\widetilde{\mathcal{P}(w)}} \bigsqcap_{s \in S}^{\widetilde{\mathcal{P}(w)}} \bigsqcap_{s \xrightarrow{p} s'}^{\widetilde{\mathcal{P}(w)}} \bigsqcup_{\substack{C \subseteq w(s) \\ [\![p]\!](C) \sqsubseteq x(s')}}^{\widetilde{\mathcal{P}(w)}} \{\{s\} \times C\}$$

The meaning of this formula is that, starting from a set of witness candidates, we keep those that are satisfied by the initial condition, compute the set of weakest preconditions in one step for each of them, merge the result and keep only the weakest of the computed properties, i.e., those that do not imply any other such precondition (outermost $\sqcup$). For each candidate, the computation of maximal preconditions can be done state by state (outer $\sqcap$), taking the cross-product:

note that this $\sqcap$ can be implemented as a kind of product (a cartesian product where (a, b) is replaced by $a \cup b$) because the terms are independent (they operate on different states). Finally, for every state we take the set of maximal properties that are preconditions of every successor ($\sqcap\sqcup$).

The non-optimal version of pruning can also be applied to polyhedra analysis: instead of keeping a set of maximal witness candidates, we only keep one. The outer $\sqcup$ thus disappears. For every transition, only one weakest precondition of the constraints in its successor state is choosen, removing the innermost $\sqcup$. Therefore, no disjunctions are created anymore, and every gratest lower bound $\{a\} \sqcap \{b\}$ can be replaced by $\{a \cup b\}$. We obtain the simplified partial operator $\hat{F} : D \rightarrow D$ with the following inplementation:

$$\hat{F}(x) = \begin{cases} \bigcup_{s \in S} \{s\} \times \bigcup_{s \xrightarrow{p} s'} \begin{array}{l} \textit{choose a weakest } C \subseteq w(s) \\ \textit{s.t. } [\![p]\!](C) \sqsubseteq x(s') \end{array} & \textit{if } I \sqsubseteq x \\ \textit{undefined} & \textit{otherwise} \end{cases}$$

We have tested this algorithm to reduce linear invariants produced by the linear systems analyser StInG [SSM04]. For a given property, we iterate the witness optimisation function $\hat{F}$ until a fixpoint is reached. For the choice function, we use a greedy heuristics which minimises (locally) the constraints to be added to the witness.

As a first example we consider a simple version of bubble sort whose code is shown in Figure 1. We want to prove that array accesses are safe. Therefore,

```
for i = 0 to |t| - 2
  for j = 0 to |t| - 2
    exchange t[j] and t[j+1] if needed
```

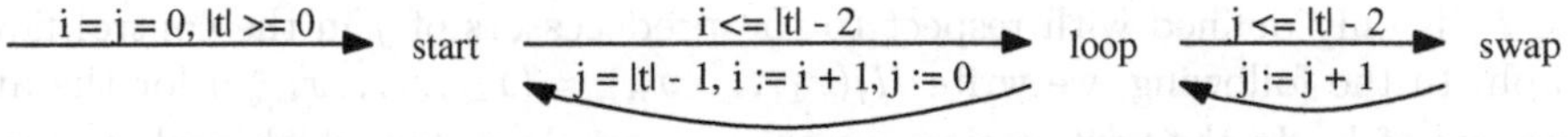

i = j = 0, |t| >= 0 → start; start — i <= |t| - 2 → loop; loop — j = |t| - 1, i := i + 1, j := 0 → start; loop — j <= |t| - 2 → swap; swap — j := j + 1 → loop

Fig. 1. Linear transition system for a simple bubble sort

the property is that $0 \leq j \leq |t| - 1$ must hold in the body of the inner loop: $\phi = \{(swap, 0 \leq j), (swap, j \leq |t| - 1)\}$. The program is represented by the linear transition system of Figure 1. The effect of pruning is shown in Table 1. Basically, we find that the upper bound of j is unnecessary to keep because it is implied by the guards. On the other hand, the lower bound can only be proved by induction.

Other examples have been processed in the same way. For instance, for a variant of the classic "train beacon" [Hal98], our witness for proving that trains cannot collide only keeps 7 of the 18 linear invariants generated by StInG. Not all the programs we have tested show a dramatic reduction of the number of constraints. However, these examples are very abstract and only model aspects relevant to the property. For more realistic applications, we expect that more pruning would be possible.

Table 1. Pruning a witness for bubble sort

Location	Initial polyhedron	Remaining constraints
start	$j = 0, \|t\| \geq 0$	$j = 0$
loop	$j \geq 0, \|t\| - j \geq 0$	$j \geq 0$
swap	$j \geq 0, \|t\| - j - 2 \geq 0$	$j \geq 0$

5 Certificates

As stated in the introduction, it is the *existence* of a witness that matters, not its actual content. Based on this observation, we propose to define a *certificate* and an algorithm for checking such certificates such that if the algorithm accepts the certificate then the existence of a witness is guaranteed. We propose a format of certificates, define the algorithm for decoding such certificates and prove the correctness of the algorithm. Then we show how to generate those certificates from a witness, whose reconstruction costs no more than aplying F once, checking $\sqsubseteq$ once and checking ϕ on an abstract property.

Recall that static analyses which attach a property per program point operate over a product lattice D^n where D is the domain of properties and n the number of program points. Note that we could also have a product of diferent domains, which is equivalent to taking a "sum" lattice for D. The abstract semantics function $F : D^n \to D^n$ exhibits static dependencies between program points and if we note $x = (x_1, \ldots, x_n)$ then F has the form:

$$F(x) = (F_1(x_{i_{1,1}}, \ldots, x_{i_{1,k_1}}), \ldots, F_n(x_{i_{n,1}}, \ldots, x_{i_{n,k_n}})).$$

Intuitively, properties attached to a particular program point only depends on a subset of the other program points. Typically, for intra-procedural analyses, F_j is only defined with respect to the predecessors of j in the control flow graph. In the following, we write $\Pi_j(x_1, \ldots, x_n) = (x_{i_{j,1}}, \ldots, x_{i_{j,k_j}})$ for the arguments of F_j. In the next section, we propose an algorithm which exploits such dependencies to rebuild a witness from sparse certificates.

5.1 Certificate Format and Checking Algorithm

Existing witness reconstruction algorithms [Ros03, BJP06, AAPH06] are using as certificate a sparse *direct* witness (Definition 1). The current algorithm is more flexible: it relies on a more relaxed definition of witness (see Definition 2) and allows to iterate the F_js more than once. Together, these properties can be exploited to obtain smaller certificates. Definition 8 presents the format of certificates for a product domain D^n.

Definition 8. *A certificate is a pair (K, S) where $K : [1, n] \mapsto D$ is a* partial *mapping from program points to properties and $S \in [1, n]^*$ is a sequence of program points.*

The meaning of a certificate (K, S) is that, starting from an abstract state defined by K (with all undefined program points interpreted as $\top$), and recomputing the program points in S using the F_js should result in a direct witness.

The algorithm for checking a certificate (K, S) is formally defined in Figure 2. We first prove an invariant that entails the correctness and allows for an optimization of the algorithm.

check(K, S) =
  check that every j defined in K appears at least once in S (1)
  let $w \in D^n$ be defined as $w = \left[j \mapsto \begin{cases} K(j) \text{ if } K(j) \text{ is defined} \\ \top \text{ otherwise} \end{cases} \right]$
  for each j in S in sequence do
    compute $w'_j = F_j(\Pi_j(w))$
    check that $w'_j \sqsubseteq w_j$ (2)
    $w_j \leftarrow w'_j$
  done
  check that $w \sqsubseteq \phi$ (3)

Fig. 2. Checking algorithm

Lemma 4. *Let (K, S) be a certificate. When computing check(K, S), at each iteration of the loop, $F_j(\Pi_j(w)) \sqsubseteq w_j$ holds for every j that has already been visited once.*

Proof. We show that this property is an inductive invariant. Let $w^k \in D^n$ be the content of the variable w after the k-th iteration of the loop.

- The property is obvious at the beginning, since no j has been visited.
- Assume the invariant just before the k-th iteration. We need to prove that it holds just after. Let $j \in [1, n]$ such that j has been visited during iterations $[1, k]$. First we remark that $w^k \sqsubseteq w^{k-1}$, because of the test $w'_j \sqsubseteq w_j$ in line (2). Thus, as F_j is monotone we have $F_j(\Pi_j(w^k)) \sqsubseteq F_j(\Pi_j(w^{k-1}))$ and to show $F_j(\Pi_j(w^k)) \sqsubseteq w^k_j$ it is enough to prove $F_j(\Pi_j(w^{k-1})) \sqsubseteq w^k_j$. We consider two cases.
  - If j was visited during the k-th iteration then the assignment in the loop implies that $w^k_j = F_j(\Pi_j(w^{k-1}))$ and we conclude.
  - Otherwise j had been visited before. The invariant before iteration k thus implies that $F_j(\Pi_j(w^{k-1})) \sqsubseteq w^{k-1}_j$ and we also know that $w^k_j = w^{k-1}_j$ because j was not visited at this iteration. □

This suggests the following optimization: the test $w'_j \sqsubseteq w_j$ in the loop only needs to be done for the first occurence of j in S.

The following theorem establishes the correctness of the algorithm.

Theorem 5. *Let (K, S) be a certificate. If check(K, S) succeeds then the program satisfies the associated security property ϕ.*

Proof. We prove that when exiting from the loop, $F_j(\Pi_j(w)) \sqsubseteq w_j$ holds for every $j \in [1, n]$.

- If j appears in S, Lemma 4 applies.
- Otherwise, the line (1) of the algorithm ensures that j is not defined in K. Therefore, the initial value of w_j was $\top$. As w_j was never updated, the constraint is trivially satisfied.

This proves that the tuple w obtained at the end of the reconstruction is a post-fixpoint of F. Line (3) ensures that this is also a direct witness for ϕ. □

This verification scheme has the following benefits, compared to the naive solution of sending/verifying the whole witness:

- Abstract states need to be sent only for a subset of the program points.
- Some program points may not need to be evaluated, if they are not necessary to prove the property.
- Comparisons between abstract states are only needed for the program points for which an abstract state is sent.

5.2 Certificate Generation

For a witness w, we are looking for a good certificate for the verification algorithm described above. The simplest one is (w, S) where S can be any strategy that evaluates every program point once (in any order). But, if for example F is a forward analysis and S follows the control flow graph, then most of the w_j will be overwritten before being used and therefore can be omitted. Keeping only the loop headers allows for much smaller certificates, with simple strategies. This is the core idea of the compression technique proposed in [BJP06].

We slightly generalize this setting in two ways: First, the control flow graph is more than we really need: what is required is the dependencies between the w_j which may form a sparser graph. We opt for an intermediate solution: the "static" dependency that are induced by the projections Π_j, restricted to the program points for which w has a non-$\top$ value. Second, rather than anottating loop headers, what we really want to do is to break every cycle of this dependency graph with at least one program point for which K is defined, which for some loop nestings requires stricly less of them. While it does not exploit all the generality of the checker, this strategy is optimal for generating certificates that evaluate every w_j at most once.

Definition 9. *The dependency graph of w is the directed graph $DP_w = (J_w, \rightarrow)$ whose set of vertices is $J_w = \{j \in [1, n] \mid w_j \neq \top\}$ and such that $i \rightarrow j$ iff "$i \in \Pi_j(w)$", formally $\Pi_j(x_1, \ldots, x_n) = (x_{i_{j,1}}, \ldots, x_{i_{j,k_j}})$ with $i_{j,l} = i$ for some l.* The following theorem (whose proof is omitted) formalizes the intuition that it is sufficient to break the cycles in DP_w to obtain a certificate.

Theorem 6. *Let (K, S) be a certificate such that*

- $\forall j \in Dom(K) \quad K(j) = w_j$ *and*
- $\forall i, j \quad i, j \in S \wedge j \rightarrow i \implies j$ *first appears before* i *in* $S \vee K(j) = w_j$ *and*
- $\forall j \quad K(j)$ *is defined* $\implies j \in S$.

Then check(K, S) succeeds.

Therefore, generating a smallest certificate for w amounts to finding a minimal subset K of $[1, n]$ that "breaks the cycles". This is known as the feedback node set problem. While it is NP-complete in the general case, some polynomial algorithms [LL88, Koe05] exists for the particular case of *reducible* graphs, which is the case of structured control flow graphs. They run in $O(m \log(n))$ where m is the number of edges and n the number of vertices. Note that this applies to weighted graphs as well, so that it would be possible to take into account the concrete coding size needed by each program point for a particular witness.

The graph obtained from DP_w by removing the exiting arcs of every vertex in some feedback node set K naturally forms a partial order, and it is easy to see that every total order S on J_w satisfying this order meets the necessary conditions for Theorem 6 to apply, thus implying the validity of the certificate (K, S). We haven't explored the possible representation of the order S. A possible solution is to let the code consumer deduce such an order from the K part, which is trivial as soon as the user has sufficient ressources to build the reverse dependency graph.

Applying this principle to the bubble sort example of the previous section, we take the *loop* state that split the whole graph, ending with the certificate $(\{loop \rightarrow j \geq 0\}, [loop, swap])$, compared to the initial polyhedron and pruned witness that are shown in Table 1.

Finally we can justify the choice for the definition of witnesses that we tried to optimize in the previous sections. As we are sending parts of this abstract property, it is best if its size is already minimized, hence the weakened condition $F(w) \sqsubseteq \phi$ rather than $w \sqsubseteq \phi$ in the (relaxed) definition of witnesses. But we remark that the condition can be further generalized in, say $F^k(w) \sqsubseteq \phi, k \geq 0$, the limit being given by our certificate generation and verification algorithms: as the checker permits to iterate more than once, valid certificates could be obtained with the condition $F^k(w) \sqsubseteq \phi, k \geq 0$ for witnesses. However, letting $k = 1$ ensures a very simple certificate generation (Theorem 6). Note that the other constraint that w must be a post-fixpoint is crucial for the verification to succeed and cannot be weakened.

6 Related Work

Albert *et al.* [AAPH06] describe a technique for reducing fixpoints produced by a generic fixpoint algorithm. The fixpoint algorithm is presented in the setting of logic program analysis but the underlying algorithmics of queues and dependence graph is common to workset-based analyses. The reduction technique monitors the fixpoint iteration to detect which program points improves other program points. The reduced certificate then consists of the fixpoint value at these program points plus data to start the fixpoint iteration. The checker takes as argument a reduced abstract property and an iteration strategy for the fixpoint algorithm and use the generic algorithm for generating the full fix-point.

Thus, the certificates have the same structure as ours. The main difference is that their certificates are obtained by observing the behavior of an iterative fixpoint solving while our algorithm works by using the dependencies in the post-fixpoint once it has been produced. This means that our algorithm also allows us to compress a witness that is already much smaller than the least fixpoint whereas their approach only allows to compress the least fixpoint.

Rose [Ros03] proposes a fixpoint reconstruction algorithm for lightweight data flow graphs. The Java byte code verifier of the KVM is using this approach to check sparse certificates. The lightweight bytecode verifier is an instance of our algorithm for which the S part of the certificate specifies that the program points have to be processed in increasing order. This specialisation has the disadvantage that the number of program point in the K part of the certificate might be larger than needed. Also, the least fixpoint (i.e., the stronger one) is rebuilt, while there could be a much smaller witness that ensure the same property.

Besson, Jensen and Pichardie [BJP06] show how to certify checkers for abstract interpretation-based analyses. They propose a fixpoint reconstruction algorithm using the notion of *direct* witnesses *i.e.,* post-fixpoints that verify the property. Because our current algorithm is based on a more relaxed definition of witnesses (Definition 2), our certificates can be sparser. Moreover, Besson *et al.,* do not investigate how to optimise witnesses.

7 Conclusion

We have developed a general theory showning how invariants, issued as post-fixpoints of abstract interpretations, can be compressed to provide witnesses of particular program properties, as required *e.g.*, in proof-carrying code. In the case of distributive analyses, we have shown how an optimal (smallest) witness can be computed. For the non-distributive case (notably convex polyhedra analysis) we have shown how to compute a good approximation of minimal witnesses.

It is important to note that we are essentialy changing (pruning) the proof that we send to the code consumer, while the other compression mechanisms proposed so far keep all the informations produced by the original analysis.

The witnesses can be further compressed by only sending enough information to enable their reconstruction and hence verify their existence, as in [BJP06]. It would be interesting to apply lower level compression techniques to this setting, for example, sending only enough bits of information to resolve the "choices" that a checker has to make when rebuilding a witness, in the spirit of [NR01].

The pruning technique has been tested on invariants issued by a convex polyhedra analysis for proving simple security properties, namely the safety of array accesses in small programs and the absence of colisions in a system for controling trains. Even for those simple case studies, there is an improvement in the size of certificates.

References

[AAPH06] E. Albert, P. Arenas, G. Puebla, and M. Hermenegildo. Reduced certificates for abstraction-carrying code. In *Proc. of the 22nd Int. Conf. on Logic Programming*, pages 163–178. Springer LNCS vol. 4079, 2006.

[BJP06] F. Besson, T. Jensen, and D. Pichardie. Proof-Carrying Code from Certified Abstract Interpretation and Fixpoint Compression. *Theoretical Computer Science*, 364:273–291, 2006.

[CC77] P. Cousot and R. Cousot. Abstract interpretation: A unified lattice model for static analysis of programs by construction of approximations of fixpoints. In *Proc. of the 4th ACM Symp. on Principles of Programming Languages*, pages 238–252. ACM Press, 1977.

[CH78] P. Cousot and N. Halbwachs. Automatic discovery of linear restraints among variables of a program. In *Proc. of the 5th ACM Symp. on Principles of programming languages*, pages 84–96. ACM Press, 1978.

[DP90] B.A. Davey and H.A. Priestley. *Introduction to Lattices and Order*. Cambridge University Press, 1990.

[Hal93] N. Halbwachs. Delay analysis in synchronous programs. In *Proc. of 5th Int. Conf. on Computer Aided Verification*, volume 697 of *LNCS*, pages 333–346. Springer-Verlag, 1993.

[Hal98] N. Halbwachs. About synchronous programming and abstract interpretation. *Science of Computer Programming*, 31(1):75–89, May 1998.

[Koe05] H. Koehler. A contraction algorithm for finding minimal feedback sets. In *Proc. of the 28th Australasian Conf. on Computer Science*, pages 165–173. Australian Computer Society, Inc., 2005.

[LL88] H. Levy and D. W. Low. A contraction algorithm for finding small cycle cutsets. *J. Algorithms*, 9(4):470–493, 1988.

[MJ81] S.S. Muchnick and N.D. Jones. *Program Flow Analysis: Theory and Application.* Prentice Hall Professional Technical Reference, 1981.

[MR90] T. Marlowe and B. Ryder. Properties of data flow frameworks. *Acta Informatica*, 28:121–163, 1990.

[Nec97] G. Necula. Proof-carrying code. In *Proc. of the 24th ACM Symp. on Principles of programming languages*, pages 106–119. ACM Press, 1997.

[NL98] G. Necula and P. Lee. Efficient representation and validation of proofs. In *Proc. of the 13th IEEE Symp. on Logic in Computer Science*, pages 93–104. IEEE Computer Society, 1998.

[NR01] G. C. Necula and S. P. Rahul. Oracle-based checking of untrusted software. In *Proc. of the 28th ACM Symp. on Principles of programming languages*, pages 142–154. ACM Press, 2001.

[Ros03] E. Rose. Lightweight bytecode verification. *J. Automated Reasoning*, 31(3-4):303–334, 2003.

[SSM04] S. Sankaranarayanan, H. Sipma, and Z. Manna. Constraint-based linear-relations analysis. In *Proc. of the 11th Static Analysis Symposium*, volume 3148 of *LNCS*, pages 53 – 68. Springer-Verlag, 2004.

[WAS03] D. Wu, A. W. Appel, and A. Stump. Foundational proof checkers with small witnesses. In *Proc. of the 5th ACM Int. Conf. on Principles and Practice of Declarative Programming*, pages 264–274. ACM Press, 2003.

Interprocedurally Analysing Linear Inequality Relations

Helmut Seidl, Andrea Flexeder, and Michael Petter

Technische Universität München, Boltzmannstrasse 3, 85748 Garching, Germany
{seidl,flexeder,petter}@cs.tum.edu
http://www2.cs.tum.edu/~{seidl,flexeder,petter}

Abstract. In this paper we present an alternative approach to interprocedurally inferring linear inequality relations. We propose an abstraction of the effects of procedures through *convex sets* of transition matrices. In the absence of conditional branching, this abstraction can be characterised precisely by means of the least solution of a constraint system. In order to handle conditionals, we introduce auxiliary variables and postpone checking them until after the procedure calls. In order to obtain an effective analysis, we approximate convex sets by means of *polyhedra*. Since our implementation of function composition uses the frame representation of polyhedra, we rely on the subclass of *simplices* to obtain an efficient implementation. We show that for this abstraction the basic operations can be implemented in polynomial time. First practical experiments indicate that the resulting analysis is quite efficient and provides reasonably precise results.

1 Introduction

In [5], Cousot and Halbwachs present an *intraprocedural* analysis of linear inequalities based on an abstraction of the collecting semantics [4] by means of convex polyhedra. They draw upon both the frame and the constraint representation of polyhedra to perform the subsumption test and widening [5] on polyhedra. More precise widening strategies on convex polyhedra are provided in [1]. Based on this approach an *interprocedural* analysis can be obtained by relating input and output states of a procedure call by means of linear inequalities. This leads to convex *transition invariants* on program variables before and after the procedure call.

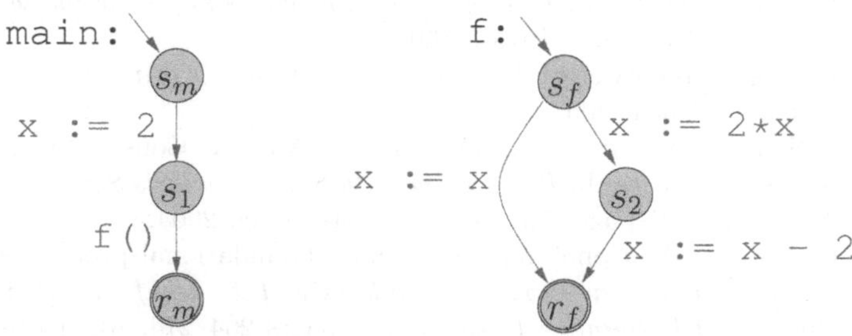

Fig. 1. An example program for transition invariants

R. De Nicola (Ed.): ESOP 2007, LNCS 4421, pp. 284–299, 2007.

In the example in figure 1 (from [8]), the procedure call `f()` at program state 2 can be described by the transition invariant $x = x' \vee x = 2 \cdot x' - 2$. The approximation of this invariant by polyhedra leads to a complete loss of information. Although transition invariants work in several practical cases (e.g., the `McCarthy91` function [6]), they seem too restrictive for a precise interprocedural analysis.

Instead, we propose an interprocedural alternative to transition invariants. Our approach is based on convex sets of *transition matrices* to capture the effects of procedures. For our intraprocedural reachability analysis, the program states are abstracted by convex sets of vectors, describing the values of the program variables. The transformation of program states is described by linear *transition matrices*, similar to [8]. Within our approach we compute a finite representation for the effect of procedures [9] (i.e. convex sets of transition matrices) which can be embedded into the reachability analysis. In the absence of conditionals, this abstraction can be characterised precisely by means of the least solution of a suitable constraint system. Since conditional branching cannot be represented by linear transformations, conditionals can obviously not be evaluated on convex sets of transition matrices. Therefore, we introduce *auxiliary variables* for each condition and postpone checking them until after the procedure call. In order to obtain an effective analysis, we follow the standard approach of approximating convex sets by means of *convex polyhedra* [5]. Our composition operation for polyhedra relies on the *frame representation* of polyhedra, represented by sets of points, rays and lines. In order to avoid the expensive continual conversion between the two polyhedral representation forms [5], we resort to the frame representation alone. Testing for *subsumption* as well as computing the *union* of two convex polyhedra is reduced to linear programming problems [5]. In order to infer the linear inequalities for a program point, the conversion to the constraint representation is deferred to the end of the computation of the procedure effects or the very end of the analysis. However, polyhedra tend to be complex. Consequently, operations on polyhedra are expensive [10]. This induces the demand for perhaps more efficient representations of convex sets. In [7], *octagons*, an efficient subclass of polyhedra, are introduced. Within this approach at most two program variables per inequality are allowed with restrictions on the coefficients, permitting only inequalities of the form $\pm x \pm y \leq c$. *Simon* et al. abandon all restrictions on the coefficients for the considered pair of occurring program variables in [13]. In contrast, *Clarisó* et al. propose in [3] to approximate polyhedra with *octahedra*. In contrast to the former approaches, they allow any number of program variables but the coefficients of the inequalities are restricted to ± 1 or 0. A quite general approach is introduced by *Sankaranarayanan* et al., who introduce generic inequality templates and solve systems of inequalities on the coefficients of the templates [11]. All these approaches consist in restricted classes of constraint systems, though their frame representation can easily become exponential.

This does not hold for *simplices*. Simplices are convex polyhedra which are restricted in the number of frame elements to at most n *linearly independent elements* and a base point, if n is the dimension of the underlying vector space. Thus, simplices form a subclass of polyhedra and their frame representation has approximately the same size as the constraint representation. This is the reason why we started to experiment with approximations of convex sets by means of simplices. Based on this approximation, we achieve that subsumption testing reduces to solving $n+1$ systems of at most n linear equations. Thus, our subsumption test can be performed in polynomial time.

Our approach for interprocedurally identifying linear inequality relations among the variables of a program is subsequently described in detail. In section 2 we introduce control flow graphs, representing our inspected program class. Furthermore, the collecting semantics of our program class is described. In section 3 we turn to the abstraction of the concrete semantics based on convex sets. In addition, we present a method for interprocedurally dealing with conditionals. Effective approximations of convex sets are discussed in section 5, where we also present simplices and the basic operations on simplices. Finally, first experimental results and comparisons of our various approaches are reported in section 6.

2 The General Set-Up

This section introduces the programs to be analysed together with their collecting semantics. We assume that a program is represented by a finite set of disjoint *control flow graphs* $\mathbf{G}$, as illustrated in figure 1.

Each graph $G_f \in \mathbf{G}$ corresponds to a *procedure* f from a finite set $Proc$ of procedures. Each control flow graph $G_f \in \mathbf{G}$ consists of:

- a finite set N_f of *program points* of the procedure f,
- a finite set $E_f \subseteq (N_f \times Label \times N_f)$ of labelled control-flow *edges*,
- the start point $s_f \in N_f$ for the procedure f, as well as the
- return point $r_f \in N_f$ of f.

Labels at control-flow edges either are linear assignments (e.g. $\texttt{x}_1\texttt{:=x}_2\texttt{+5}$), procedure calls (e.g. h()), non-deterministic assignments ($\texttt{x}_1\texttt{:= ?}$) or linear conditions (e.g. $\texttt{x}_1\texttt{-x}_2\texttt{-3} \geq \texttt{0}$). For simplicity, we only consider conditionals of the form $t \geq 0$.

We suppose that the program operates on the n global program variables $\mathbf{x}_1, \ldots, \mathbf{x}_n$. We assume the variables to take values on an ordered field $\mathbb{F}$. In the following we consider the field $\mathbb{Q}$. Then a program state can be modelled by a $(n+1)$-dimensional column *vector* $x = (1, x_1, \ldots, x_n)^T \in \{1\} \times \mathbb{Q}^n$. Each component x_i, $i > 0$, of the vector x represents the value assigned to the program variable $\mathbf{x}_i$. Note that we use an extra 0-th component 1. This extra component allows modelling the semantic effects of affine assignments through linear transformations, e.g. as considered in [8].

The set of all state vectors attained at a program point through program execution forms the *collecting semantics* of the program at this program point. Every assignment $\mathbf{x}_i := t$ of a linear term $t = t_0 + \sum_{j=1}^{n} t_j \cdot \mathbf{x}_j$ causes a *linear transformation* $[\![\mathbf{x}_i := t]\!] : 2^{\mathbb{Q}^{n+1}} \to 2^{\mathbb{Q}^{n+1}}$ on the underlying set of program states. Its effect onto a single program state can be described by multiplication of x with the following matrix:

$$[\![\mathbf{x}_i := t_0 + \sum_{j=1}^{n} t_j \cdot \mathbf{x}_j]\!] = \left(\begin{array}{c|c} \mathbf{I}_i & \mathbf{0} \\ \hline \multicolumn{2}{c}{t_0 \;\ldots\; t_n} \\ \hline \mathbf{0} & \mathbf{I}_{n-i} \end{array}\right)$$

with $\mathbf{I}_i$: $(i \times i)$-dimensional identity matrix in $\mathbb{Q}^{i \times i}$. As we consider extended program states, the matrix of this definition is from $\mathbb{Q}^{(n+1)^2}$. We only consider matrices where the entry at position $(0,0)$ is equal to 1 and the remaining entries in the 0th row are 0.

For the beginning, we assume that the program does not contain conditional branching, i.e. edges labelled with inequalities. Since linear transformations are closed under composition, we realise that the effects of procedures can be represented by *sets* of linear transformations of the extended program state. These sets of transformations can be characterised by the least solution of the following constraint system $\mathbf{T}$:

$$
\begin{array}{lll}
[\text{T0}]\ \mathbf{T}(s_f) \supseteq \{\mathbf{Id}\} & & \\
[\text{T1}]\ \mathbf{T}(v) & \supseteq \{[\![\mathbf{x}_i := t]\!]\} \circ \mathbf{T}(u) & \text{for } (u,\ \mathtt{x_i\ :=\ t}\ ,\ v) \in E_f \\
[\text{T2}]\ \mathbf{T}(v) & \supseteq \{[\![\mathbf{x}_i := c]\!] \mid c \in \mathbb{Q}\} \circ \mathbf{T}(u) & \text{for } (u,\ \mathtt{x_i\ :=?}\ ,\ v) \in E_f \\
[\text{T3}]\ \mathbf{T}(v) & \supseteq \mathbf{T}(r_h) \circ \mathbf{T}(u) & \text{for } (u,\ \mathtt{h()}\ ,\ v) \in E_f
\end{array}
$$

Here, the operator $\circ$ denotes the element-wise function composition of two sets of transformations. Thus, the effect of a whole procedure is the effect accumulated at the return point of the procedure.

Constraint [T0] expresses that no initialisation of the program variables is performed at the start point s_f of any procedure $f \in Proc$. This results in the identity mapping **Id**. [T1] describes the accumulation of the effect of a linear assignment. It is obtained by the composition of the linear transformation corresponding to the assignment with the effect already accumulated for the start point u of the edge. If the edge is labelled with a non-deterministic assignment, each value $c \in \mathbb{Q}$ can be assigned to the program variable $\mathbf{x}_i$. This is described by the constraint [T2]. Constraint [T3] describes the handling of edges, which are labelled with a procedure call. We simply compose all transformations of the called procedure with the transformations accumulated before the procedure call. Since all right-hand sides in the constraint system $\mathbf{T}$ represent monotonic functions, a least solution for this system exists. We denote the components of this least solution by $\mathbf{T}(u)$ (u a program point).

Given the effects of procedures, we can characterise the sets of program states reaching program points by the least solution of the constraint system $\mathbf{A}$:

$$
\begin{array}{lll}
[\text{A0}]\ \mathbf{A}(s_{main}) \supseteq \{1\} \times \mathbb{Q}^n & & \\
[\text{A1}]\ \mathbf{A}(s_h) & \supseteq \mathbf{A}(u) & \text{if } (u,\ \mathtt{h()}\ ,\ \_) \text{ calls } h \in Proc \\
[\text{A2}]\ \mathbf{A}(v) & \supseteq [\![\mathbf{x}_i := t]\!]\ \mathbf{A}(u) & \text{for } (u,\ \mathtt{x_i\ :=\ t}\ ,\ v) \in E_f \\
[\text{A3}]\ \mathbf{A}(v) & \supseteq \bigcup_{c \in \mathbb{Q}} [\![\mathbf{x}_i := c]\!]\ \mathbf{A}(u) & \text{for } (u,\ \mathtt{x_i\ :=?}\ ,\ v) \in E_f \\
[\text{A4}]\ \mathbf{A}(v) & \supseteq \mathbf{T}(r_h)\ \mathbf{A}(u) & \text{for } (u,\ \mathtt{h()}\ ,\ v) \in E_f
\end{array}
$$

The first constraint [A0] expresses that program execution starts with a call to the specific procedure `main`. At this point, no assumptions on the set of program states can be made. Constraint [A1] describes that the start point of a procedure h is dependent of all the program points where h is called. Linear and non-deterministic assignments, as defined in [A2] and [A3], result in applying the transformation functions corresponding to the edges element-wise to the sets of vectors reaching the start point of the edge. The same does also hold for procedure calls where the effect of a call to h is given by the set of transformations $\mathbf{T}(r_h)$, provided by the least solution of the constraint system $\mathbf{T}$. This is formalised in the constraint [A4], where the function application is performed element-wise to the sets of vectors. Again, the least solution for this constraint system exists according to the fixpoint theorem of Knaster-Tarski and we denote its components by $\mathbf{A}(u)$ (u a program point).

3 Convex Abstraction

In order to interprocedurally infer linear inequality relations, we want to construct a precise abstraction for our collecting semantics. The abstraction should provide for every program point u (hopefully all) linear inequalities, which are valid for all program states reaching u. Geometrically, a linear inequality specifies a half space. The conjunctive combination of these half spaces results in a *convex set of vectors*. This may serve as a justification of an abstraction of the concrete semantics by means of convex sets, the *convex abstraction*.

Formally, let $\mathcal{C}(\mathbb{Q}^{n+1})$ denote the set of all convex subsets of vectors over $\mathbb{Q}^{n+1}$. On convex sets, the greatest lower bound $\sqcap$ is given by the set theoretical intersection, while the least upper bound $\sqcup$ is given by the convex hull of the set theoretical union: $\langle X_1 \rangle \sqcup \langle X_2 \rangle = \langle X_1 \cup X_2 \rangle$ with $X_i \subseteq \{1\} \times \mathbb{Q}^n, i = 1, 2$. The set $\mathcal{C}(\mathbb{Q}^{n+1})$ of all convex subsets of vectors together with the subset relation $\subseteq$ as partial ordering relation (denoted by $\sqsubseteq$ here) forms a complete lattice.

Now, we define the abstraction $\alpha : 2^{\mathbb{Q}^{n+1}} \to \mathcal{C}(\mathbb{Q}^{n+1})$ by: $\alpha(X) = \langle X \rangle$ where $\langle X \rangle$ denotes the least convex set containing $X \subseteq \{1\} \times \mathbb{Q}^n$. The convex set $\langle X \rangle$ can be obtained from X by applying the convex hull operation to X:

$$\langle X \rangle = \left\{ \sum_{i=1}^{n} \lambda_i z_i \mid n \in \mathbb{N} \wedge 0 \leq \lambda_i \wedge \sum_{i=1}^{n} \lambda_i = 1 \wedge z_i \in X \right\}$$

Clearly, α commutes with arbitrary unions and therefore is an abstraction.

Within our interprocedural approach the effect of assignments is modelled by a set of linear transformations. Each of these transformations can be represented by a matrix, similar to [8]. As a matrix corresponds to a $(n+1)^2$-dimensional vector, the abstraction α is also applicable to sets of matrices. Thus, the abstract effect $[\![\mathbf{x}_i := t]\!]^\sharp$ of a linear assignment $\mathbf{x}_i := t$ results in the convex hull of the single $(n+1)^2$ vector obtained from $[\![\mathbf{x}_i := t]\!]$. In the case of a non-deterministic assignment, all possible constant values of $\mathbb{Q}$ could be assigned to the program variable. This effect is described by the following convex set of transition matrices:

$$[\![\mathbf{x}_i :=?]\!]^\sharp = \left\langle \left\{ \left(\begin{array}{c|c} \mathbf{I}_i & \mathbf{0} \\ \hline \lambda\, 0 \;\ldots\; 0 & \\ \hline \mathbf{0} & \mathbf{I}_{n-i} \end{array} \right) \mid \lambda \in \mathbb{Q} \right\} \right\rangle$$

In order to approximate the convex abstraction of the effect of procedure calls, we apply the abstraction to the constraint system $\mathbf{T}$. The resulting system $\mathbf{T}^\sharp$ is given by:

$[\mathrm{T0}^\sharp]\ \mathbf{T}^\sharp(s_f) \sqsupseteq \{\mathbf{I}\}$	$\mathbf{I} \in \mathbb{Q}^{(n+1)^2}$
$[\mathrm{T1}^\sharp]\ \mathbf{T}^\sharp(v) \sqsupseteq [\![\mathbf{x}_i := t]\!]^\sharp \circ^\sharp \mathbf{T}^\sharp(u)$	for $(u,\ \mathtt{x_i := t}\ ,\ v) \in E_f$
$[\mathrm{T2}^\sharp]\ \mathbf{T}^\sharp(v) \sqsupseteq [\![\mathbf{x}_i :=?]\!]^\sharp \circ^\sharp \mathbf{T}^\sharp(u)$	for $(u,\ \mathtt{x_i :=?}\ ,\ v) \in E_f$
$[\mathrm{T3}^\sharp]\ \mathbf{T}^\sharp(v) \sqsupseteq \mathbf{T}(r_h)^\sharp \circ^\sharp \mathbf{T}^\sharp(u)$	for $(u,\ \mathtt{h()}\ ,\ v) \in E_f$

In the abstraction, we have used the convex composition $\circ^\sharp$ on convex sets of linear transformations, which is defined by an element-wise matrix-multiplication composed with the convex hull operation:

$$\langle \mathbf{C}_1 \rangle \circ^\sharp \langle \mathbf{C}_2 \rangle = \langle C_1 C_2 \mid C_i \in \mathbf{C}_i \rangle \text{ with } \mathbf{C}_i \subseteq \mathbb{Q}^{(n+1)^2}$$

The least solution of $\mathbf{T}^\sharp$ provides an abstract effect of a procedure represented as a convex set of transformation matrices. We only consider those matrices where the entry at position $(0, 0)$ is equal to 1 and the remaining entries at the 0th row are all 0. We denote the components of this least solution by $\mathbf{T}^\sharp(u)$ (u a program point).

Accordingly, we can describe the reachability analysis in the convex abstraction by the constraint system $\mathbf{A}^\sharp$ obtained from the concrete constraint system $\mathbf{A}$ by applying the abstraction α:

$$\begin{array}{lll}
[\mathrm{A0}^\sharp]\ \mathbf{A}^\sharp(s_{main}) & \sqsupseteq \{1\} \times \mathbb{Q}^n & \\
[\mathrm{A1}^\sharp]\ \mathbf{A}^\sharp(s_g) & \sqsupseteq \mathbf{A}^\sharp(u) & \text{if } (u, \mathtt{h}()\ ,\ _) \text{ calls } h \in Proc \\
[\mathrm{A2}^\sharp]\ \mathbf{A}^\sharp(v) & \sqsupseteq [\![\mathbf{x}_i := t]\!]^\sharp \cdot^\sharp \mathbf{A}^\sharp(u) & \text{for } (u, \mathtt{x_i := t}\ ,\ v) \in E_f \\
[\mathrm{A3}^\sharp]\ \mathbf{A}^\sharp(v) & \sqsupseteq [\![\mathbf{x}_i := ?]\!]^\sharp \cdot^\sharp \mathbf{A}^\sharp(u) & \text{for } (u, \mathtt{x_i := ?}\ ,\ v) \in E_f \\
[\mathrm{A4}^\sharp]\ \mathbf{A}^\sharp(v) & \sqsupseteq \mathbf{T}^\sharp(r_h) \cdot^\sharp \mathbf{A}^\sharp(u) & \text{for } (u, \mathtt{h}()\ ,\ v) \in E_f
\end{array}$$

Analogously to the abstract composition operator $\circ^\sharp$, the abstract application operator $\cdot^\sharp$ is defined by element-wise application composed with the convex hull operation. The least solution of the system $\mathbf{A}^\sharp$ again exists and provides us with a convex set of vectors for every program point u. For convenience, we denote the components of this least solution by $\mathbf{A}^\sharp(u)$ (u a program point).

First we want to show the safety and precision of the convex abstraction. For this purpose we verify that the abstraction commutes with function application and composition of the linear transformations.

Proposition 1. *For every set of vectors $X \subseteq \{1\} \times \mathbb{Q}^n$ and all sets of transformation matrices $\mathbf{C}, \mathbf{C}_1, \mathbf{C}_2 \subseteq \mathbb{Q}^{(n+1)^2}$, the following equalities hold:*

1. $\langle \{Cx \mid x \in X\ ,\ C \in \mathbf{C}\ \} \rangle = \langle \{Cx \mid x \in \langle X \rangle\ ,\ C \in \langle \mathbf{C} \rangle\ \} \rangle$
2. $\langle \{C_1 C_2 \mid\ C_i \in \mathbf{C}_i\ \} \rangle = \langle \{C_1 C_2 \mid\ C_i \in \langle \mathbf{C}_i \rangle\ \} \rangle$

For the constraint systems $\mathbf{A}^\sharp$ and $\mathbf{T}^\sharp$ we therefore obtain from proposition 1 with the fixpoint transfer lemma:

Theorem 1. *For every program point u and every procedure f of the program with return point r_f, the following holds:*

1. $\mathbf{A}^\sharp(u) = \alpha(\mathbf{A}(u)) = \langle \mathbf{A}(u) \rangle$
2. $\mathbf{T}^\sharp(r_f) = \alpha(\mathbf{T}(r_f)) = \langle \mathbf{T}(r_f) \rangle$

This theorem means that the smallest fixpoints of the constraint systems $\mathbf{T}^\sharp$ and $\mathbf{A}^\sharp$ precisely characterise the convex abstraction α applied to the smallest fixpoints of the constraint systems $\mathbf{T}$ and $\mathbf{A}$ for the collecting semantics.

In general, the least solutions of the abstract constraint systems will not be reached after finitely many fixpoint iterations. In order to arrive at practical algorithms for computing safe (over-) approximations of the least solutions of these constraint systems, we therefore must rely on effective representations of convex sets together with effective abstract *composition* and *application* operations as well as effective implementations of *subsumption* and *union*. In order to speed up fixpoint iteration, a *widening* operator must be provided.

By now, we have specified the convex abstraction and verified its *correctness and precision*. However, our abstraction of the effects of procedures only works for non-deterministic branching, i.e. in the absence of inequality guards. Linear inequality analysis is not yet very significant without the handling of conditionals. The next section therefore provides a technique to enhance the base framework to handle linear inequality guards.

4 Linear Inequality Guards

Clearly, the reachability analysis can be enhanced to deal with linear inequality guards $(\mathbf{b} \geq 0)$. As in [5], the effect of such a guard is interpreted as the intersection with the corresponding half-space of state vectors, which satisfy the guard:

$$[\![\mathbf{b} \geq 0]\!]\, X \;=\; \{x \in X \mid \mathbf{b}x \geq 0\}$$

where for $\mathbf{b} = b_0 + b_1\mathbf{x}_1 + \ldots + b_n\mathbf{x}_n$ and $x = (1, x_1, \ldots, x_n)^T$,

$$\mathbf{b}x = b_0 + b_1x_1 + \ldots + b_nx_n$$

When analysing programs with conditional branching, the effects of procedures can no longer be described by sets of linear transformations. Since the constraint system $\mathbf{T}$ only speaks about linear transformations, conditionals cannot be easily integrated into our concrete semantics. The constraint system $\mathbf{A}$ for the reachability analysis, however, can be extended to conditionals by introducing the following constraint:

$$[\text{A5}]\;\mathbf{A}(v) \supseteq \{x \in \mathbf{A}(u) \mid \mathbf{b}x \geq 0\}\;\; \text{for } (u,\; (\mathbf{b} \geq 0),\; v) \in E_f$$

Within the convex abstraction, the idea for interprocedurally handling conditionals therefore is to *postpone* their evaluation during the computation of procedure effects until the reachability analysis. Up to this time, we suggest to store the value of each condition in an *auxiliary variable*, which then can be checked for non-negativity.

Thus, we extend the original semantics by introducing new "program variables", one for each guard. Assuming that the guards are numbered $n+1, \ldots, n+g$, the auxiliary variables are denoted by $\mathbf{x}_{n+1} \ldots \mathbf{x}_{n+g}$. This leads to an extension of every program state by g extra components. All the auxiliary variables are initially set to 0. During the effect computation we replace the jth conditional $(\mathbf{b} \geq 0)$ with the assignment $\mathbf{x}_{n+j} := \mathbf{b}$. As the value of each condition is just stored in an auxiliary variable, conditionals now can be treated within our effect computation. Accordingly, we modify the constraint system $\mathbf{T}^\sharp$ as follows:

$$[\text{T4}^\sharp]\;\mathbf{T}^\sharp(v) \sqsupseteq [\![\mathbf{x}_{n+j} := \mathbf{b}]\!]^\sharp \circ^\sharp \mathbf{T}^\sharp(u)\;\; \text{for } (u,\; (\mathbf{b} \geq 0),\; v) \in E_f$$

where $(\mathbf{b} \geq 0)$ denotes the jth conditional.

Clearly, every feasible program execution path of the original program will also be a feasible execution path of the transformed program – but not necessarily vice versa. Thus, our postponed evaluation of guards introduces a safe over-approximation of the concrete semantics. Due to the extension of every program state the constraint [A0$^\sharp$] must be adapted to handle conditionals:

$$[\text{A0}^\sharp]\ \mathbf{A}^\sharp(s_{main}) \sqsupseteq 1 \times \mathbb{Q}^n \times 0^g$$

This constraint shows that at the start point of procedure $main$ every program state is possible, in which all auxiliary variables are 0.

There are two natural choices for scheduling the evaluation of the postponed guards $(\mathbf{x}_{n+j} \geq 0)$ during the reachability analysis. The first alternative is to schedule their evaluation *directly after* each procedure call. Then the constraint system $\mathbf{A}^\sharp$ is modified as follows:

$$[\text{A4}^\sharp]\ \mathbf{A}^\sharp(v) \sqsupseteq \mathbf{T}^\sharp(r_h) \circ^\sharp \mathbf{A}^\sharp(u) \cap \{(1, x_1, \ldots, x_{n+g}) \mid x_{n+j} \geq 0 \text{ for all } j\} \quad \text{for } (u,\ h(),\ v) \in E_f$$

$$[\text{A5}^\sharp]\ \mathbf{A}^\sharp(v) \sqsupseteq \{x \in \mathbf{A}^\sharp(u) \mid \mathbf{b}x \geq 0\} \ \text{ for } (u,\ (\mathbf{b} \geq 0),\ v) \in E_f$$

The modified constraint [A4$^\sharp$] describes the postponed evaluation of guards after each procedure call, whereas the additional constraint [A5$^\sharp$] illustrates the direct evaluation when a conditional has been visited.

As a second alternative, we may postpone the evaluation of guards even during the reachability analysis – in order to perform a *single* check for every program point u just before the valid linear inequalities for u are inferred. To this end, we use the original constraint [A4$^\sharp$]. Furthermore, we replace the constraint [A5$^\sharp$] with corresponding assignments to the auxiliary variables:

$$[\text{A5}^\sharp]\ \mathbf{A}^\sharp(v) \sqsupseteq [\![\mathbf{x}_{n+j} := \mathbf{b}]\!]^\sharp(\mathbf{A}^\sharp(u)) \ \text{ for } (u,\ (\mathbf{b} \geq 0),\ v) \in E_f$$

where $(\mathbf{b} \geq 0)$ denotes the jth conditional. Finally, we introduce extra unknowns $\mathbf{A}^\sharp(u)'$ for each program point u which are meant to receive the final analysis results. For these, we have the extra constraint:

$$[\text{A}']\ \mathbf{A}^\sharp(u)' \sqsupseteq \mathbf{A}^\sharp(u) \cap \{(1, x_1, \ldots, x_{n+g}) \mid x_{n+j} \geq 0 \text{ for all } j\} \ \text{ for } u \in N_f$$

The latter alternative may lose more precision in comparision to an analysis based on immediate evaluation of guards, because more execution paths are admitted. A first comparison between the two alternatives is shown in section 6. In case of an analysis over integer variables, however, all of the second analysis can be performed within the field $\mathbb{Q}$ – up to the final condition evaluation. Thus, we obtain a tight integer solution already if the final round of intersections is performed by an ILP solver.

5 Representing Convex Sets

So far, we have introduced a framework for an interprocedural analysis for inferring linear inequalities. In order to arrive at practical analysis algorithms, it remains to choose suitable effective representations for convex sets, which support the necessary operations as well as a widening operation to enforce termination of the fixpoint iteration.

Convex Polyhedra

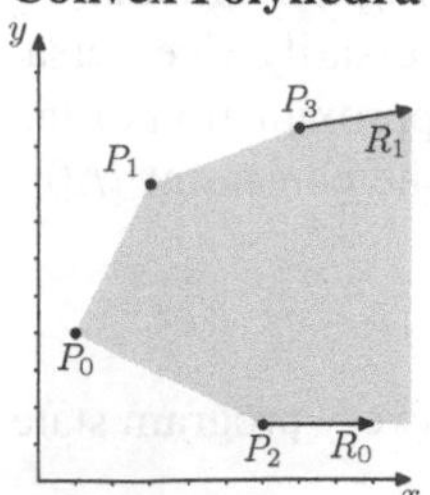

For this purpose we focus on the subset of $\mathcal{C}(\mathbb{Q}^{n+1})$ of *convex polyhedra* [5], denoted by $\mathcal{P}$. For our approach, we find it convenient to use the *frame representation* of polyhedra. This means that a polyhedron $\mathbf{F}$ is represented as a triple $\mathbf{F} = \langle \mathbf{P}, \mathbf{R}, \mathbf{L} \rangle$ where $\mathbf{P}$ denotes a finite set of points, $\mathbf{R}$ is a finite set of rays and $\mathbf{L}$ is a finite set of lines. The figure on the left-hand side illustrates a polyhedron in $\mathbb{Q}^2$, which consists of a point set and a ray set, forming the polyhedron $\langle \{P_0, P_1, P_2, P_3\}, \{R_0, R_1\}, \emptyset \rangle$.

Every element of $\mathbf{R}$, respectively $\mathbf{L}$, is a vector, which can be considered as the difference of two points in the considered vector space. As mentioned in 2, we use projective space within our vectors. Thus, the extra 0-th component of a vector is always 1 for points and 0 for rays or lines. The set of points, represented by $\langle \mathbf{P}, \mathbf{R}, \mathbf{L} \rangle$, is given by:

$$[\![\langle \mathbf{P}, \mathbf{R}, \mathbf{L} \rangle]\!] = \{\sum_{i=0}^{q} \lambda_i P_i + \sum_{i=0}^{r} \mu_i R_i + \sum_{i=0}^{s} \eta_i L_i \mid q, r, s \geq 0 \wedge \lambda_i, \mu_i \geq 0 \wedge \sum_{i} \lambda_i = 1\}$$

with $\mathbf{P} = \{P_0, \ldots, P_q\}$, $\mathbf{R} = \{R_0, \ldots, R_r\}$, $\mathbf{L} = \{L_0, \ldots, L_s\}$. In order to use polyhedra as effective representation of convex sets of transition matrices in the constraint system $\mathbf{T}^\sharp$, we must provide algorithms for composition, union, widening as well as an effective test for subsumption on polyhedra. We introduce the polyhedral composition $\circ^{\mathcal{P}}$ as an abstraction of $\circ^{\#}$, in order to easily express the composition on the frame representation of polyhedra.

Composition. Let $\mathbf{F}_i = \langle \mathbf{P}_i, \mathbf{R}_i, \mathbf{L}_i \rangle$, $i = 1, 2$, denote the frame representation of two polyhedra of transition matrices. The polyhedral composition $\mathbf{F} = \mathbf{F}_1 \circ^{\mathcal{P}} \mathbf{F}_2$ results in the frame $\mathbf{F}$ defined by the triple $\langle \mathbf{P}, \mathbf{R}, \mathbf{L} \rangle$, where

$$\begin{aligned} \mathbf{P} &= \{\mathbf{P}_1 \circ \mathbf{P}_2\} \\ \mathbf{R} &= \{\mathbf{P}_1 \circ \mathbf{R}_2 \ \cup \ \mathbf{R}_1 \circ \mathbf{R}_2 \ \cup \ \mathbf{R}_1 \circ \mathbf{P}_2\} \\ \mathbf{L} &= \{\mathbf{L}_1 \circ \mathbf{P}_2 \ \cup \ \mathbf{L}_1 \circ \mathbf{R}_2 \ \cup \ \mathbf{L}_1 \circ \mathbf{L}_2 \ \cup \ \mathbf{P}_1 \circ \mathbf{L}_2 \ \cup \ \mathbf{R}_1 \circ \mathbf{L}_2\} \end{aligned}$$

Here, $\circ$ denotes the element-wise multiplication of two sets of matrices.
By construction we obtain:

Proposition 2. *The result of the polyhedral composition is a superset of the convex composition:* $[\![\mathbf{F}_1 \circ^{\mathcal{P}} \mathbf{F}_2]\!] \sqsupseteq [\![\mathbf{F}_1]\!] \circ^\sharp [\![\mathbf{F}_2]\!]$

The other direction $\sqsubseteq$ is not necessarily valid in presence of rays and lines. If the frame consists of points only, the polyhedral composition $\circ^{\mathcal{P}}$ is equivalent to the convex composition $\circ^\sharp$.

Widening. In order to compute effectively some (hopefully non-trivial) solution of the constraint system $\mathbf{T}^\sharp$ by means of convex polyhedra, we should avoid infinite ascending chains during fixpoint iteration. This can be achieved by the use of widening for polyhedra, e.g. the *standard widening* introduced by Cousot and Halbwachs [5]. Here, we rely on those more precise widening strategies of Bagnara et.al. [1], which are restricted to the frame representation of a convex polyhedron.

Union and Subsumption. In every step of the fixpoint iteration we must check if the next polyhedron $\mathbf{F}$ for a constraint variable is already subsumed by the old value $\mathbf{F}'$, i.e. whether $[\![\mathbf{F}]\!] \sqsubseteq [\![\mathbf{F}']\!]$. This subsumption test can be implemented by successively testing for all frame elements of polyhedron $\mathbf{F}$ whether they can be represented by the elements of the polyhedron $\mathbf{F}'$ or not. Thus, subsumption testing reduces to checking the feasibility of a *linear program* [12]. Union for two polyhedra (following referred to as *polyhedral union*) on the other hand is implemented readily using set theoretical union on each of the three components of the frame representation. Subsequent subsumption testing may be used to remove redundant elements from the result.

Linear Guards. According to the extended constraint system for the reachability analysis, as presented in section 4, both alternatives for evaluating conditionals can be applied to convex polyhedra. For performing intersections on polyhedra we apply the techniques from [5].

In practice, program analysis using polyhedra is quite expensive [10]. Thus, in recent approaches special subclasses of polyhedra have been proposed, e.g. octagons [7] or octahedra [3]. These subclasses rely on restricted forms of constraint systems to specify polyhedra, which then can be handled efficiently. Since the frame representation of these polyhedra can be easily exponential in the number of constraints, they cannot be applied here.

This is the reason why we will turn our attention to *simplices*, a particular subclass of polyhedra, whose frame representation has almost the same size as the constraint representation.

Simplices

The idea is to *restrict the number of frame elements* in the frame representation $\langle \mathbf{P}, \mathbf{R}, \mathbf{L} \rangle$ of a non-empty polyhedron to n frame elements and a base point $P_0 \in \mathbf{P}$, whereas the differences $P - P_0, P_0 \neq P \in \mathbf{P}$ together with the rays and lines are *all linearly independent*. In the following this fact is referred to as the linear independence of frame elements.

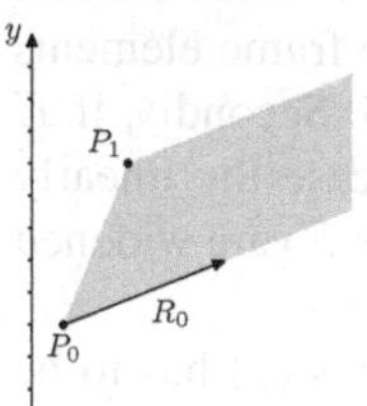

The figure on the left-hand side illustrates the simplex $\langle \{P_0, P_1\}, \{R_0\}, \emptyset \rangle \subseteq \mathbb{Q}^2$. Two-dimensional simplices may consist of at most three frame elements. Obviously, in this example the difference $P_1 - P_0$ is linearly independent from the ray R_0. For simplices, we need again an appropriate *subsumption test*, *union* as well as an effective *composition*. Furthermore, *widening* on simplices must be introduced to assure the linear independence of frame elements. Union and composition for simplices can be readily implemented by using the corresponding polyhedral operations and subsequently determining a preferably small simplex (referred to as *enclosing simplex*) which encloses the polyhedron.

Enclosing Simplex. Given a polyhedron $\mathbf{F}$, a simplex $\mathbf{S}$ is called *enclosing simplex* for $\mathbf{F}$ iff $[\![\mathbf{F}]\!] \sqsubseteq [\![\mathbf{S}]\!]$. This enclosing simplex is realised by successively building up the simplex. Starting with an empty simplex, which is successively widened with all the frame elements of the polyhedron $\mathbf{F}$.

Subsumption. As for polyhedra the subsumption test for simplices $[\![\mathbf{S}]\!] \sqsubseteq [\![\mathbf{S}']\!]$ is performed by successively checking the points, rays and lines of $\mathbf{S}$ whether they can be expressed through the points, rays and lines of $\mathbf{S}'$ or not. However, for simplices each such test can be performed through solving an appropriate *system of linear equations*. Because of the linear independence of frame elements, this system has a unique solution. In order to determine whether a point P, a ray R or a line L is subsumed by the simplex $\langle \mathbf{P}, \mathbf{R}, \mathbf{L} \rangle$, the corresponding system of linear equations has to be solved:

$$P = P_0 + \sum_{i=1}^{q} \lambda_i (P_i - P_0) + \sum_{i=0}^{r} \mu_i R_i + \sum_{i=0}^{s} \eta_i L_i \tag{1}$$

$$R = \sum_{i=0}^{r} \mu_i R_i + \sum_{i=0}^{s} \eta_i L_i \tag{2}$$

$$L = \sum_{i=0}^{s} \eta_i L_i \tag{3}$$

where $\sum_{i=1}^{q} \lambda_i \leq 1 \wedge \lambda_i, \mu_i \geq 0$ holds, $P_i \in \mathbf{P}, R_i \in \mathbf{R}, L_i \in \mathbf{L}$ and P_0 as base point. The complexity of solving such a system of linear equations is *cubic* in the number of frame elements. If the system of linear equations is feasible and the restrictions for the coefficients λ_i, μ_i hold, the point P, the ray R or the line L is considered as subsumed.

Composition. The composition of two simplices (referred to as simplicial composition) is reduced to the polyhedral composition $\circ^{\mathcal{P}}$ and subsequently determining the enclosing simplex.

Union. Union for two simplices $\mathbf{S}_1, \mathbf{S}_2$ (simplicial union) is implemented using the polyhedral union of the simplices and subsequently determining the enclosing simplex for this polyhedron. This can be efficiently realised by successively widening of simplex $\mathbf{S}_1$ with all the frame elements of $\mathbf{S}_2$.

Widening. Widening of a simplex $\mathbf{S}$ with a frame element E results in three distinct cases: First, if the frame element E is linearly independent of all the frame elements of $\mathbf{S}$, E can be directly added to the corresponding element set of $\mathbf{S}$. Secondly, if E is already subsumed, $\mathbf{S}$ does not have to be widened. In the third case the linearly dependent frame elements of $\mathbf{S}$ (i.e. their linear combination represents E) are widened according to one of the algorithms presented in figure 2, 3, 4.

When widening the simplex with a *point* P, the system of equations (1) has to be solved to determine the coefficients for the frame elements, who contribute to the linear combination of P (v. line 4 of the algorithm in figure 2). The frame elements, more precisely the points and rays of the simplex, whose restrictions on the coefficients do not hold, have to be widened.

If the restriction of a ray R_j does not hold, i.e. $\mu_j < 0$, the ray R_j is removed from the ray set of the simplex and added to its line set, as line 5 of the algorithm in figure 2 demonstrates. Furthermore, if the restriction on the coefficient of a point P_i does not hold there are two cases: if $\lambda_i < 0$ then P_i is removed from the point set and the difference $P_0 - P_i$ is added to the line set, whereas if $\lambda_i > 1$ the difference $P_i - P_0$ is

```
1  widen(⟨P,R,L⟩, P){
2    choose some base point P_0 ∈ P;
3    determine λ_i, μ_j with 1 ≤ i ≤ q, 0 ≤ j ≤ r
4    P = P_0 + Σ_{i=1}^{q} λ_i(P_i − P_0) + Σ_{j=0}^{r} μ_j R_j + Σ_{i=0}^{s} η_i L_i
5    for all j s.t. μ_j < 0: L ← L ∪ R_j; R ← R \ R_j;
6    for all i s.t. λ_i ≠ 0:
7      if (λ_i < 0) {L ← L ∪ (P_0 − P_i); P ← P \ P_i;}
8      if (λ_i > 1) {R ← R ∪ (P_i − P_0); P ← P \ P_i; }
9    while (Σ_{j=1}^{q} λ_j > 1) {R ← R ∪ (P_q − P_0); P ← P \ P_q; q ← q − 1; }
10   return ⟨P,R,L⟩;
11 }
```

Fig. 2. Widening of a simplex with a *point* P

```
1  widen(⟨P,R,L⟩, R){
2    choose some base point P_0 ∈ P;
3    determine λ_i, μ_j with 1 ≤ i ≤ q, 0 ≤ j ≤ r
4    R = Σ_{i=1}^{q} λ_i(P_i − P_0) + Σ_{j=0}^{r} μ_j R_j + Σ_{i=0}^{s} η_i L_i
5    for all j s.t. μ_j < 0: L ← L ∪ R_j; R ← R \ R_j;
6    for all i s.t. λ_i ≠ 0:
7      if (λ_i < 0) {L ← L ∪ (P_0 − P_i); P ← P \ P_i;}
8      if (λ_i > 0) {R ← R ∪ (P_i − P_0); P ← P \ P_i; }
9    return ⟨P,R,L⟩;
10 }
```

Fig. 3. Widening of a simplex with a *ray* R

added to the ray set. Additionally, the restriction on the sum of the points' coefficients $\sum_{i=1}^{q} \lambda_i \leq 1$ must be preserved. As long as this restriction does not hold, the ray set is augmented with the differences $P_i - P_0$ (v. line 9 of the algorithm in figure 2). The resulting simplex subsumes P and does only consist of linearly independent frame elements. Note that the precision of the widening presented here strongly depends on the choice of the *base point* P_0, but can be implemented in such a way, the choice of P_0 becomes irrelevant for the precision of the resulting simplex.

In the case of widening a simplex with a *ray* R, we determine the coefficients for the differences $P_i - P_0, P_0 \neq P_i \in \mathbf{P}$ and the rays $\mathbf{R}$ (v. line 4 of the algorithm in figure 3). Analogously to the algorithm widening with a point (v. 2), all the points and rays, whose coefficients do not hold, are widened i.e. they are added to the ray set, respectively line set (v. line 5/6 of the algorithm in figure 3).

```
widen(⟨P,R,L⟩, L){
  choose some base point P_0 ∈ P;
  determine λ_i, μ_j with 1 ≤ i ≤ q, 0 ≤ j ≤ r
  L = Σ_{i=1}^{q} λ_i(P_i − P_0) + Σ_{j=0}^{r} μ_j R_j + Σ_{i=0}^{s} η_i L_i
  for all j s.t. μ_j ≠ 0 do L ← L ∪ R_j; R ← R \ R_j; od
  for all i s.t. λ_i ≠ 0 do L ← L ∪ (P_0 − P_i); P ← P \ P_i; od
  return ⟨P,R,L⟩;
}
```

Fig. 4. Widening of a simplex with a *line* L

Considering widening a simplex with a *line* L, all the rays and point differences with non-zero coefficient, i.e. contributing to represent L, are widened to new lines, as described in detail in the algorithm in figure 4.

When using simplices, termination of the fixpoint algorithm over the constraint system $\mathbf{T}^\sharp$ need not be ensured by introducing additional widening. Since in $\mathbb{Q}^k$, $k = \mathcal{O}(n^2)$, a non-empty simplex can be enlarged at most $3k$-times, no infinite ascending chains may occur. However, note that due to the frequent computation of the enclosing simplex, the fixpoint iteration over the constraint system $\mathbf{T}^\sharp$ based on simplices leads to a less precise approximation of convex sets than convex polyhedra.

Linear Guards. Since the class of simplices has been introduced in order to efficiently approximate convex polyhedra when computing the effects of procedures, it is not required to evaluate linear guards on simplices within our approach. Our reachability analysis relies on polyhedra, on which the conditions can be directly evaluated, v. section 4. When using simplices for the reachablity analysis, the evaluation of conditionals on simplices cannot be performed directly after each procedure call or when a condition is passed, because the result of an intersection is not necessarily again a simplex. Since the creation of an enclosing simplex after the condition evaluation will cause too much imprecision, checking the condition must be postponed until the end of the analysis. Thus, it is preferable to transform the simplex into a convex polyhedron and additionally perform the condition evaluation.

Moreover, operations on simplices have a better runtime complexity than on polyhedra:

Theorem 2. *All the simplicial operations (subsumption, union, widening and composition) can be performed in a time, polynomial in the number of variables n.*

Proof. Assume that the simplices considered here describe subsets of $\mathbb{Q}^k$, where $k = \mathcal{O}(n^2)$. The simplicial operations of *inclusion* testing and *widening* are reduced to solving a system of at most $k+1$ linear equations, which can be performed in $\mathcal{O}(k^3)$ for a simplex with $k+1$ frame elements. *Union* is reduced to $(k+1)$-times successive widening, *subsumption* to $(k+1)$-times inclusion testing. Thus, each operation can be performed in time $\mathcal{O}(k^4)$. The simplicial *composition* is given by the element-wise composition of the frame elements (i.e. $\mathcal{O}(k^2)$ matrix multiplications) and subsequently determining its enclosing simplex, leading to a total complexity of $\mathcal{O}(k^5)$. □

6 Preliminary Experimental Results

So far, we have introduced two different representations for convex sets – convex polyhedra and simplices. Even more, we have presented two alternatives for evaluating conditionals within the reachability analysis – directly after each procedure call or once at the end of the analysis. To get a general idea of the performance of these different options in practical application, we have examined the behaviour of our interprocedural approach on a collection of example programs. Here, we concentrate on three characteristic examples, *recursive add, array bounds* and *nested loops*.

The example program *recursive add* contains a procedure, that recursively calls itself, computing the addition of two numbers. Furthermore, in *array bounds* array bound checking, as done by Java programs, is simulated. Finally, we consider the iteration variables in the program *nested loops*, containing four nested `for`-loops. This program also covers the case that a loop is bounded by the iteration variable of an outer loop.

The analysis set-up consists of approximating convex sets either by convex polyhedra or simplices and trying either direct condition evaluation or a single evaluation at the end of the analysis. Our prototypical implementation is more complex than the theoretical analysis described in this paper, as it deals with local variables, passing of parameters and return values in procedures.

The following chart compares the effect analysis by means of convex polyhedra and with simplices for each example program:

Table 1. Simplex compared to polyhedra

Program	LOC	# Procedures	Increase in efficiency	Precision
recursive add	26	4	62 %	100 %
array bounds	25	2	97 %	100 %
nested loops	28	2	98 %	75 %

The *runtime* of the reachability analysis by means of convex polyhedra does not differ significantly from the reachability analysis by means of simplices. However, the effect analysis by means of simplices is *dramatically faster* than the effect analysis by means of convex polyhedra, as the column *Increase in efficiency* of table 1 illustrates. Effect analysis with simplices has terminated in few seconds for all benchmarks.

Concerning the *precision* of the inferred inequalities, we have discovered that both the approach via simplices and that via convex polyhedra is able to infer the exact result for the recursive function in the case of *recursive add* and the dependence of the iteration variable from the variable upper bound for *array bounds*. Yet for the example program *nested loops* both approaches have returned quite precise results. However, in this case the analysis by means of simplices has missed some lower loop bounds and thus has not reached the full precision of the analysis with polyhedra, cf. table 1.

Since the analysis using simplices is rather fast and the quality of the inferred inequalities is not too imprecise, we conclude that it might be a good compromise to rely on simplices for the effect analysis and to resort to convex polyhedra or other approximations of convex polyhedra (e.g. octahedra from [3]) for the reachability analysis. Contrary to our theoretical expectations from section 4, no advantage could be observed of immediate condition evaluation over single evaluation at the very end of the analysis – but this may just be due to the perhaps not very representative selection of benchmark programs.

7 Conclusion

We have introduced a general framework for interprocedurally identifying linear inequality relations between the variables of a program for each program point. This can be achieved by representing the effects of procedures with convex sets of transition matrices. Within our approach we accumulate the single edge effects in order to describe the effect of a whole procedure. These procedure effects can be simply embedded into a reachability analysis by means of arbitrary approximations of convex polyhedra.

In the absence of conditional branching the convex abstraction can be characterised precisely by the least solution of a constraint system. In order to handle conditional branching within our framework, we propose to store the value of each conditional in an auxiliary variable during effect analysis and postpone the evaluation up to the reachability analysis. This postponement is safe, merely leading to an over-approximation.

In order to finitely represent and compute with convex sets, we approximate them by means of convex polyhedra. We resort to the frame representation of polyhedra, thus avoiding the expensive continual conversion between the two representations. The frame representation of convex polyhedra, on the other hand, can be exponentially larger than their constraint representation. For this reason, we propose the subclass of *simplices* as an abstract domain. Since for simplices the number of frame elements is restricted, we obtain a small representation for convex sets. Moreover, the basic operations on simplices can be performed in polynomial time. Thus, our effect analysis by means of simplices runs in polynomial time, more precisely, the analysis is linear in the program size and polynomial in the number of program variables and guards.

First practical experiments indicate that this approach is quite efficient and provides reasonably precise results. In contrast to convex transition invariants, our interprocedural analysis is able to yield the exact invariant $x = 2$ for program point r_m in figure 1. It remains for future work to examine the scalability of our approach for larger and more realistic benchmark programs. However, if the complexity for larger programs prevents a practical application of our approach, *clustering*, as introduced in Astrée [2], could be included.

References

1. R. Bagnara, E. Zaffanella, P. M. Hill, and E. Ricci. Precise widening operators for convex polyhedra. In *10th International Static Analysis Symposium (SAS)*, pages 337–354, 2003.
2. B. Blanchet, P. Cousot, R. Cousot, J. Feret, L. Mauborgne, A. Miné, D. Monniaux, and X. Rival. A static analyzer for large safety-critical software. In *Proceedings of the ACM SIGPLAN Conference on Programming Language Design and Implementation (PLDI)*, pages 196–207, 2003.
3. R. Clarisó and J. Cortadella. The Octahedron abstract domain. In *11th International Static Analysis Symposium (SAS)*, pages 312–327, 2004.
4. P. Cousot and R. Cousot. Abstract interpretation frameworks. *Journal of Logic and Computation*, 2(4):511–547, 1992.
5. P. Cousot and N. Halbwachs. Automatic discovery of linear restraints among variables of a program. In *5th Ann. ACM Symposium on Principles of Programming Languages (POPL)*, pages 84–97, 1978.
6. Z. Manna and J. McCarthy. Properties of programs and partial function logic. 1970.
7. A. Miné. The Octagon abstract domain. In *Analysis, Slicing, and Transformation (AST)*, pages 310–319, 2001.
8. M. Müller-Olm and H. Seidl. Program analysis through linear algebra. In *31th Ann. ACM Symposium on Principles of Programming Languages (POPL)*, 2004.

9. M. Müller-Olm and H. Seidl. A generic framework for interprocedural analysis of numerical properties. In *12th Static Analysis Symposium (SAS)*, pages 235–250, 2005.
10. S. Sankaranarayanan, M. Colon, H. Sipma, and Z. Manna. Efficient strongly relational polyhedral analysis. In *7th International Conference, Verification, Model Checking and Abstract Interpretation (VMCAI)*, 2006.
11. S. Sankaranarayanan, H. Sipma, and Z. Manna. Constraint based linear relations analysis. In *11th International Static Analysis Symposium (SAS)*, pages 53–68, 2004.
12. A. Schrijver. *Theory of linear and integer programming*. 1986.
13. A. Simon, A. King, and J. M. Howe. Two Variables per Linear Inequality as an Abstract Domain. In *Logic Based Program Development and Transformation (LOPSTR)*, pages 71–89, 2002.

Precise Fixpoint Computation Through Strategy Iteration

Thomas Gawlitza and Helmut Seidl

TU München, Institut für Informatik, I2
85748 München, Germany
{gawlitza,seidl}@in.tum.de

Abstract. We present a practical algorithm for computing least solutions of systems of equations over the integers with addition, multiplication with positive constants, maximum and minimum. The algorithm is based on strategy iteration. Its run-time (w.r.t. the uniform cost measure) is independent of the sizes of occurring numbers. We apply our technique to solve systems of interval equations. In particular, we show how arbitrary intersections as well as full interval multiplication in interval equations can be dealt with precisely.

1 Introduction

In this paper we are interested in computing the precise least solutions of systems of interval equations using addition, multiplication, intersection and union [4,11,12]. Instead of doing so directly, we first consider the simpler problem of solving systems of equations over the integers using the operations addition, multiplication with positive constants, minimum and maximum. In fact, this computational problem can be considered as "one half" of precisely solving systems of equations over the interval domain: we simply may represent the value a by the interval $[-\infty, a]$. Thus, every method for computing precise least solutions of interval equations can be used to determine least solutions of integer equations. At least in absence of full multiplication, there is also a reduction in the opposite direction: solving interval equations precisely can be reduced to solving systems of integer equations as well.

Precise interval analysis has recently been considered by Su and Wagner [16] who propose a polynomial-time algorithm in case that one argument of every multiplication and intersection is constant. A clarified and improved version of this algorithm is presented in [6]. Since the linear ordering of integers has infinite ascending chains, ordinary fixpoint iteration will not result in terminating algorithms. For the lucky case where all numbers are non-negative, polynomial fixpoint algorithms are provided in [15]. In presence of general minima as well as negative numbers, no practical precise methods have been suggested so far. Clearly, we could apply general techniques such as the widening and narrowing approach of Cousot and Cousot [5]. While often returning amazingly good results, widening and narrowing is not guaranteed to compute the *least* solution of an equation system. Recently, *strategy iteration* has been proposed as an alternative method for approximative abstract interpretation in [3] where also conditions are derived under which least solutions can be obtained. Strategy iteration has been introduced by Howard for solving stochastic control problems [8,14] and is also applied to

R. De Nicola (Ed.): ESOP 2007, LNCS 4421, pp. 300–315, 2007.

zero-sum two player games [7,13,17] or fixpoints of min-max-plus systems [2]. In general, strategy iteration will find *some* fixpoint which in the context of program analysis thus provides a safe over-approximation. For *expanding systems* the returned solution, though, is not always guaranteed to be the least possible [3]. Given that strategy iteration finds some fixpoint, we can be sure to have reached the *least* one if fixpoints are *unique*. One instance of this principle are fixpoint equations over Banach spaces where the transformation induced by right-hand sides is *contracting*. This is the reason why strategy iteration is nicely applicable to *discounted* mean-payoff games. Discounting, however, relies on exact arithmetic on potentially large numbers [18].

Here, we propose an approach based on an *instrumentation* of the underlying lattice. We first consider the simpler case of equation systems over the complete lattice of integers (extended with $\pm\infty$) where right-hand sides use addition, multiplication with positive constants as well as minimum and maximum. The instrumentation is meant to count the number of accesses to variables during fixpoint iteration. By itself, this instrumentation is not sufficient to guarantee uniqueness of fixpoints. It is sufficient, though, to guarantee for systems without maximum operators to admit at most one solution which maps all variables to values exceeding $-\infty$. This observation allows us to apply the generalization of the Bellman-Ford algorithm from [6] to compute this unique solution efficiently. Together with a suitable strategy iteration, we thus obtain an exact method for solving integer equations. This method vastly generalizes the results from [9,15] which are only applicable to systems of equations without negative numbers. Along the lines of [6], our technique for systems of integer equations provides us with a *precise* algorithm for interval equations. This basic approach, however, can only handle equations where multiplication is always with constant intervals. Beyond that, we also provide a technically non-trivial extension resulting in a precise method also for systems of interval equations where arbitrary multiplication is allowed.

All our algorithms are *uniform*, i.e., their numbers of arithmetic operations do not depend on the numbers occurring in the systems. Also, they return *precise* answers and thus do not rely on widening or narrowing. Our implementation also indicates that the algorithm is decently efficient even on rather large systems of interval equations. The rest of the paper is organized as follows. In section 2, we introduce basic notions for systems of equations over the integers. In section 3, we present our instrumentation technique for integers and show how to construct a strategy iteration algorithm based on max strategies to compute the precise least solution of a system of integer equations containing multiplication with positive constants, addition, minimum and maximum. In section 4, we apply and generalize these methods to obtain algorithms for computing precise least solutions of interval equations. This section presents our novel techniques for precisely dealing with full multiplication in interval equations.

2 Notation and Basic Concepts

In the beginning, we are interested in solving systems of equations over the complete lattice of integers $\mathcal{Z} = \mathbb{Z} \cup \{-\infty, \infty\}$ equipped with the natural ordering

$$-\infty < \ldots < -2 < -1 < 0 < 1 < 2 < \ldots < \infty.$$

On $\mathcal{Z}$, we consider the operations addition, multiplication with positive constants, minimum "$\wedge$" and maximum "$\vee$" extended to operands "$-\infty$" and "∞". As usual, addition and multiplication are extended as follows:

$$\begin{array}{llll} x+(-\infty) = (-\infty)+x = -\infty, & 0{\cdot}x = x{\cdot}0 = 0 & \text{for all } x \\ x{\cdot}(-\infty) = (-\infty){\cdot}x = -\infty, & x{\cdot}\infty = \infty{\cdot}x = \infty & \text{for all } x > 0 \\ x{\cdot}(-\infty) = (-\infty){\cdot}x = \infty, & x{\cdot}\infty = \infty{\cdot}x = -\infty & \text{for all } x < 0 \\ x+\infty = \infty+x = \infty & & \text{for all } x \neq -\infty \end{array}$$

A system of integer equations is a sequence of equations $\mathbf{x}_i = e_i$ for $i = 1, \ldots, n$, where the variables $\mathbf{x}_i$ on the left-hand sides are pairwise distinct and and the right-hand sides e_i are expressions e built up from constants and variables by means of our operations, i.e., adhere to the following grammar:

$$e ::= a \mid \mathbf{x}_i \mid e_1' + e_2' \mid b \cdot e \mid e_1' \vee e_2' \mid e_1' \wedge e_2'$$

where $a \in \mathcal{Z}$ and $b > 0$. The set of variables of the system under consideration will be denoted by $\mathbf{X}$ in the following. In [15] polynomial algorithms for computing least solutions are presented for similar systems — but only when computing least solutions over nonnegative integers. In [6], also negative integers are allowed. Minima, however, are only considered when one argument is constant. Here, we lift the latter restriction. For a *variable assignment* $\mu : \mathbf{X} \to \mathcal{Z}$ an expression e is mapped to a value $[\![e]\!]\mu \in \mathcal{Z}$:

$$\begin{array}{ll} [\![a]\!]\mu = a & [\![\mathbf{x}_j]\!]\mu = \mu(\mathbf{x}_j) \\ [\![e_1' + e_2']\!]\mu = [\![e_1']\!]\mu + [\![e_2']\!]\mu & [\![b \cdot e_2']\!]\mu = b \cdot [\![e_2']\!]\mu \\ [\![e_1' \wedge e_2']\!]\mu = [\![e_1']\!]\mu \wedge [\![e_2']\!]\mu & \end{array}$$

where $a \in \mathcal{Z}$ and $b > 0$. As usual, a *solution* is a variable assignment μ which satisfies all equations of a system $\mathcal{E}$, i.e. $\mu(\mathbf{x}_i) = [\![e_i]\!]\mu$ for all i. Since every right-hand side e_i induces a monotonic function $[\![e_i]\!]$, every system $\mathcal{E}$ has a unique least solution.

This least solution can be computed by performing ordinary fixpoint iteration over the finite lattice $\{-\infty < a < \ldots < b < \infty\}$ for suitable bounds $a \leq b$. This results in practical algorithms only if reasonably small bounds a, b to the values of variables can be revealed. Here, our goal is to exhibit practical algorithms whose run-time[1] is *independent* of the sizes of involved numbers. We call such algorithms *uniform*. The uniform run-time therefore only depends on structural properties of the equation system. In particular, we define the *size* $|\mathcal{E}|$ of $\mathcal{E}$ as the number of variables plus the sum of expression sizes of right-hand sides.

3 Computing Least Solutions

An interesting approach for constructing uniform fixpoint algorithms is *strategy iteration* as proposed by Costan et al. [3]. Rephrased for a system $\mathcal{E}$ of integer equations, they let a min strategy π select one of the e_i in every occurring minimum expression

[1] w.r.t. a uniform cost measure which counts every arithmetic operation as well as comparisons on integers as $\mathcal{O}(1)$.

$e_1 \wedge e_2$. The least solution μ_π of the resulting system then is guaranteed to be an *upper* bound to the least solution of $\mathcal{E}$. If μ_π is not a solution of $\mathcal{E}$, the strategy can be *improved*. If on the other hand, μ_π is a solution of $\mathcal{E}$, the iteration terminates.

Example 1 (From [3]). Consider the system consisting of $\mathbf{x} = \mathbf{y} \wedge 1$ and $\mathbf{y} = 2\mathbf{x} \vee -1$. A min strategy might select the expression 1 in the first equation resulting in:

$$\mathbf{x} = 1 \qquad\qquad \mathbf{y} = 2\mathbf{x} \vee -1$$

whose least solution maps $\mathbf{x}$ to 1 and $\mathbf{y}$ to 2, which is a solution of the original system. Note, however, that the *least* solution of the original system maps $\mathbf{x}$ and $\mathbf{y}$ to -1. □

As indicated by example 1, strategy iteration based on min strategies may not necessarily result in least solutions. Our idea therefore is to rely on *max* strategies instead which select one of the arguments of every maximum expression in the equation system. This alone, however, is not a meaningful approach since least solutions of equation systems with minimum alone will often have just trivial least solutions.

Example 2. Consider the system: $\mathbf{x} = 0 \vee \mathbf{x}+1$. A (max) strategy might either select the expression 0 or the expression $\mathbf{x} + 1$ in the right-hand side. In the first case, the least solution of the resulting system maps $\mathbf{x}$ to 0, whereas in the second case, the least solution maps $\mathbf{x}$ to $-\infty$. The least solution of the original system, however, is given by $\mu^* = \{\mathbf{x} \mapsto \infty\}$. □

Our extra idea here therefore is to *instrument* the underlying lattice in such a way that we can rely on *particular* solutions of conjunctive systems for approximating the least solution of the original system, namely those which do not map variables to $-\infty$. Due to our instrumentation, these solutions happen to be *unique* and thus are computable by *greatest* fixpoint iteration. The idea of the instrumentation is to provide an extra component which, besides the reached value in $\mathbb{Z}$, additionally records the minimal (nonnegative) depth of recursive descents into variables necessary to produce this value. Accordingly, the instrumented domain is given by $\mathcal{D} = \mathbb{D} \cup \{-\infty, \infty\}$ where $\mathbb{D} = \mathbb{Z} \times \mathbb{N}$ is the set of *finite* elements of $\mathcal{D}$ and $-\infty$ and ∞ are the least and greatest elements, respectively. The ordering on $\mathbb{D}$ is given by:

$$(a_1, j_1) \leq (a_2, j_2) \quad \text{iff} \quad a_1 < a_2 \vee (a_1 = a_2 \wedge j_1 \geq j_2)$$

This ordering is again linear. The operators "+" and "$b\cdot$" over $\mathcal{D}$ behave similar to the corresponding operators over $\mathcal{Z}$ when applied to $-\infty$ or ∞. For finite elements, we define:

$$(a_1, j_1) + (a_2, j_2) = (a_1 + a_2, j_1 \vee j_2)$$

$$b \cdot (a, j) = \begin{cases} -\infty & \text{if } b = \infty \text{ and } a < 0 \\ (a, j) & \text{if } b = \infty \text{ and } a = 0 \\ \infty & \text{if } b = \infty \text{ and } a > 0 \\ (b \cdot a, j) & \text{if } \infty > b > 0 \end{cases}$$

Furthermore we introduce a function inc defined by $\mathsf{inc}(-\infty) = -\infty$, $\mathsf{inc}(\infty) = \infty$ and $\mathsf{inc}((a, j)) = (a, j + 1)$. The function inc distributes over $+, \cdot, \wedge$ and $\vee$, i.e.:

$$\mathsf{inc}(x + y) = \mathsf{inc}(x) + \mathsf{inc}(y) \qquad \mathsf{inc}(b \cdot x) = b \cdot \mathsf{inc}(y)$$
$$\mathsf{inc}(x \wedge y) = \mathsf{inc}(x) \wedge \mathsf{inc}(y) \qquad \mathsf{inc}(x \vee y) = \mathsf{inc}(x) \vee \mathsf{inc}(y)$$

Algorithm 1. Generalized Bellman-Ford algorithm

for $i = 1$ **to** n **do** $\mu(\mathbf{x}_i) \leftarrow \infty$;
for $j = 1$ **to** n **do**
  for $i = 1$ **to** n **do** $\mu(\mathbf{x}_i) \leftarrow [\![e_i]\!]^\sharp \mu$;
for $j = 1$ **to** n **do**
  for $i = 1$ **to** n **do if** $[\![e_i]\!]^\sharp \mu < \mu(\mathbf{x}_i)$ **then** $\mu(\mathbf{x}_i) \leftarrow -\infty$;
return μ;

The evaluation of an expression e (possibly containing applications of inc) over $\mathcal{D}$ will be denoted by $[\![e]\!]^\sharp$. In order to instrument the equation system $\mathcal{E}$ to additionally record accesses to variables, we define a lifting operation as follows. For every expression e over $\mathcal{Z}$, the corresponding *lifted* expression $[e]^\sharp$ is obtained from e by replacing every constant $a \in \mathbb{Z}$ with $(a, 0)$ and every variable $\mathbf{x}_j$ with $\mathsf{inc}(\mathbf{x}_j)$. Let $\mathcal{E}^\sharp$ denote the corresponding lifted system over $\mathcal{D}$ where every equation $\mathbf{x}_i = e_i$ is replaced with $\mathbf{x}_i = [e_i]^\sharp$ for $i = 1, \ldots, n$. Thus, in a lifted system, every occurrence of a variable in a right-hand side is guarded by a call to the function inc. We verify:

Theorem 1. *Assume that $\mathcal{E}$ is a system of integer equations with least solution μ^*. Let $\mu^\sharp$ denote the least solution of the corresponding lifted system $\mathcal{E}^\sharp$. Then for every variable $\mathbf{x}_i$ the following holds:*

1. $\mu^*(\mathbf{x}_i) = \mu^\sharp(\mathbf{x}_i)$ *whenever* $\mu^*(\mathbf{x}_i) \in \{-\infty, \infty\}$;
2. $\mu^\sharp(\mathbf{x}_i) = (\mu^*(\mathbf{x}_i), j)$ *for some* $j \in \mathbb{N}$ *whenever* $\mu^*(\mathbf{x}_i) \in \mathbb{Z}$. □

Given the above theorem, our goal is to compute the least solution of the lifted equation system $\mathcal{E}^\sharp$ over the instrumented lattice $\mathcal{D}$. Thereby, we first consider the case, in which no right-hand side of $\mathcal{E}^\sharp$ contains a maximum. We call such systems *conjunctive*. The *greatest* solution of a conjunctive equation system turns out to be easily computable.

Theorem 2. *Let $\mathcal{E}^\sharp$ denote a conjunctive lifted system of integer equations with n variables and greatest solution $\mu^\sharp$. Then*

1. $\mu^\sharp$ *can be computed in time* $\mathcal{O}(n \cdot |\mathcal{E}^\sharp|)$;
2. *If* $\mu^\sharp(\mathbf{x}_i) \in \mathbb{D}$, *then* $\mu^\sharp(\mathbf{x}_i) = (a, j)$ *for some* $0 \leq j \leq n$.

Proof. Here, we rely on alg. 1, which is an adaption of the Bellman-Ford algorithm. In particular, if the greatest solution $\mu^\sharp$ does not map variables to $-\infty$, then just n rounds of Round Robin iterations suffice to determine $\mu^\sharp$. For a correctness proof, we refer to [6] where a similar result is shown for least solutions of *disjunctive* systems, i.e., systems having no occurrences of minimum operators. The use of Gaussian elimination to determine $\mu^\sharp$, also reveals the second statement. □

We call a variable assignment μ *feasible* iff $\mu(\mathbf{x}_i) > -\infty$ for all variables $\mathbf{x}_i$. Our key result for conjunctive lifted systems is:

Theorem 3. *Let $\mathcal{E}^\sharp$ denote a conjunctive lifted system of integer equations with greatest solution $\mu^\sharp$. If $\mathcal{E}^\sharp$ has a feasible solution μ, then $\mu = \mu^\sharp$.*

Proof. Obviously, if there exists a feasible solution μ, then the greatest solution $\mu^\sharp$ is also feasible. To show, that $\mu^\sharp$ is *the only* feasible solution, we first consider a system $\mathcal{E}^\sharp$ which consists of a single equation:

$$\mathbf{x}_1 = a_0 \wedge b_1 \cdot \mathsf{inc}^{k_1}(\mathbf{x}_1) + a_1 \wedge \ldots \wedge b_r \cdot \mathsf{inc}^{k_r}(\mathbf{x}_1) + a_r$$

where $b_j > 0$, $k_j > 0$ and $a_0, a_j \in \mathcal{Z}$. Note that a_0 can also equal ∞. If $b_1 \cdot \mathsf{inc}^{k_1}(a_0) + a_1 \wedge \ldots \wedge b_r \cdot \mathsf{inc}^{k_r}(a_0) + a_r \geq a_0$, then a_0 is the greatest solution and the only one exceeding $-\infty$. For a contradiction, assume $z > -\infty$ were another solution, i.e., $-\infty < z < a_0$. Then $b_1 \cdot \mathsf{inc}^{k_1}(z) + a_1 \wedge \ldots \wedge b_r \cdot \mathsf{inc}^{k_r}(z) + a_r < a_0$. Since the second component of $b_1 \cdot \mathsf{inc}^{k_1}(z) + a_1 \wedge \ldots \wedge b_r \cdot \mathsf{inc}^{k_r}(z) + a_r$ exceeds the second component of z, z cannot be a solution. If on the other hand, $b_1 \cdot \mathsf{inc}^{k_1}(a_0) + a_1 \wedge \ldots \wedge b_r \cdot \mathsf{inc}^{k_r}(a_0) + a_r < a_0$, the equation has $-\infty$ as only solution.

Now consider an arbitrary conjunctive equation system $\mathcal{E}^\sharp$ with feasible solutions. We proceed by induction on the number n of variables in right-hand sides. If $n = 0$, the statement trivially holds. So let $n > 0$, and let $\mathbf{x}_i$ be a variable that occurs in a right-hand side of $\mathcal{E}^\sharp$. Consider the equation $\mathbf{x}_i = e_i$ of $\mathcal{E}^\sharp$. Our goal is to construct an expression e' without occurrences of $\mathbf{x}_i$ which is equivalent to e_i. Then we replace all occurrences of $\mathbf{x}_i$ in right-hand sides with e'. By using distributivity, we have:

$$e_i = e'_0 \wedge b_1 \cdot \mathsf{inc}^{k_1}(\mathbf{x}_i) + e'_1 \wedge \ldots \wedge b_r \cdot \mathsf{inc}^{k_r}(\mathbf{x}_i) + e'_r$$

for suitable constants $b_j > 0$, $k_j > 0$ and expressions e'_0, e'_j not containing $\mathbf{x}_i$. Then we choose e' as e'_0. For an arbitrary feasible solution μ' of $\mathcal{E}^\sharp$, let ρ denote the substitution $\rho(\mathbf{x}_i) = \mathbf{x}_i$ and $\rho(\mathbf{x}_j) = \mu'(\mathbf{x}_j)$ for $j \neq i$. According to the single equation case, the single equation $\mathbf{x}_i = e_i\,\rho$ has a unique feasible solution which is given by $\mathbf{x}_i = e'\,\rho$. Thus, we can substitute every occurrence of $\mathbf{x}_i$ in right-hand sides of $\mathcal{E}^\sharp$ with e' to obtain a system of equations which has a superset of feasible solutions of $\mathcal{E}^\sharp$ — but one variable less in right-hand sides. Then the assertion follows with the induction hypothesis. □

Since conjunctive lifted systems with a feasible solution have exactly one feasible solution which thus is equal to the greatest solution[2], we can apply alg. 1 to compute it. Next, we show how conjunctive systems with feasible solutions can be used to determine the least solution of a lifted system $\mathcal{E}^\sharp$. For that, let $M(\mathcal{E}^\sharp)$ denote the set of all maximum expressions in $\mathcal{E}^\sharp$. A (max) *strategy* π is a function mapping every expression $e_1 \vee e_2$ in $M(\mathcal{E}^\sharp)$ to one of the subexpressions e_1, e_2. Let $\mathcal{E}^\sharp(\pi)$ denote the conjunctive system obtained from $\mathcal{E}^\sharp$ by recursively replacing every maximum expression with the respective subexpression selected by π.

Now assume that we are given a strategy π such that the greatest solution μ_π of $\mathcal{E}^\sharp(\pi)$ is feasible and a lower bound to the least solution of $\mathcal{E}^\sharp$, i.e., $\mu_\pi \leq \mu^\sharp$. As a consequence $\mu^\sharp$ must also be feasible. If μ_π is a solution of $\mathcal{E}^\sharp$, then we have already found the least solution of $\mathcal{E}^\sharp$ and are done. Otherwise, some expression $e_1 \vee e_2$ in $M(\mathcal{E}^\sharp)$ exists where π does not select the expression e_i with $[\![e_i]\!]^\sharp \mu_\pi > [\![e_{3-i}]\!]^\sharp \mu_\pi$. In

[2] Their least solution still might not be feasible.

order to *improve* the strategy, we may, e.g., pursue the policy to modify π at all such expressions simultaneously. Thus, we define the improved strategy $P(\mu_\pi)$ by:

$$P(\mu_\pi)(e_1 \vee e_2) = \begin{cases} e_1 & \text{if } [\![e_1]\!]^\sharp \mu_\pi \geq [\![e_2]\!]^\sharp \mu_\pi \\ e_2 & \text{if } [\![e_1]\!]^\sharp \mu_\pi < [\![e_2]\!]^\sharp \mu_\pi \end{cases}$$

Proposition 1. *Let $\mu^\sharp$ denote the least solution of the system $\mathcal{E}^\sharp$, and assume that $\mu < \mu^\sharp$ is a feasible variable assignment. Let π be the strategy $\pi = P(\mu)$ and μ' denote the greatest solution of $\mathcal{E}^\sharp(\pi)$. Then $\mu < \mu' \leq \mu^\sharp$.* □

Algorithm 2. Strategy Improvement Algorithm

```
μ ← μ0;
while (μ not solution of E♯){
    π ← P(μ); μ ← greatest solution of E♯(π);
}
return μ;
```

Proof. Let μ_1 denote the variable assignment defined by $\mu_1(\mathbf{x}_i) = [\![e_i]\!]^\sharp \mu$ for every equation $\mathbf{x}_i = e_i$ of $\mathcal{E}^\sharp$. By construction, $\mu < \mu_1 \leq \mu^\sharp$. We claim that $\mu_1 \leq \mu'$. By monotonicity, we have for every equation $\mathbf{x}_i = e'_i$ of $\mathcal{E}^\sharp(\pi)$, $[\![e'_i]\!]^\sharp \mu_1 \geq [\![e'_i]\!]^\sharp \mu = [\![e_i]\!]^\sharp \mu = \mu_1(\mathbf{x}_i)$. Thus, μ_1 is a pre-fixpoint of $\mathcal{E}^\sharp(\pi)$. Since, by the fixpoint theorem of Knaster-Tarski, the greatest solution of a system is an upper bound for all pre-fixpoints, $\mu_1 \leq \mu'$ which is the claim above. Since $\mathcal{E}^\sharp(\pi)$ has just one feasible solution, μ' is also the least solution of $\mathcal{E}^\sharp(\pi)$ exceeding μ. Therefore, μ' is bounded by the least solution of $\mathcal{E}^\sharp$ exceeding μ. Since μ is bounded by $\mu^\sharp$, the latter equals $\mu^\sharp$. Thus $\mu' \leq \mu^\sharp$. □

Assume that $\mathcal{E}^\sharp$ is an equation system for which we are given an initial feasible variable assignment $\mu_0 \leq \mu^\sharp$. We propose strategy improvement algorithm 2, that, given $\mathcal{E}^\sharp$ and μ_0 returns the least solution of $\mathcal{E}^\sharp$. By proposition 1, the sequence of variable assignments μ constructed by alg. 2 forms a strictly increasing chain. Since every variable assignment in this strictly increasing chain is the greatest solution of $\mathcal{E}^\sharp(\pi)$ for some strategy π, every strategy occurs at most once. Since algorithm 2 terminates with a solution of the system, proposition 1 also implies that it returns the least solution.

Our approach is remarkable in that it does not rely on discounting as, e.g., the related algorithms in [13,2] for computing game values of mean-payoff games. Instead, we use ordinary arithmetic on numbers of length $\mathcal{O}(n \cdot \log(B))$ where B is the maximal absolute value of a finite constant occurring in $\mathcal{E}$.

So far we have assumed that the least solution of $\mathcal{E}^\sharp$ is feasible and that we have an initial feasible variable assignment $\mu_0 \leq \mu^\sharp$ at hand. We have not yet revealed how to arrive at such a variable assignment. Note that we cannot ignore this problem and start with any strategy instead.

Example 3. Consider the lifted system $\mathbf{x} = (\mathsf{inc}(\mathbf{x}) \wedge (0,0)) \vee (0,0)$. The strategy π which replaces the maximum-expression with $\mathsf{inc}(\mathbf{x}) \wedge (0,0)$ leads to the conjunctive system $\mathbf{x} = \mathsf{inc}(\mathbf{x}) \wedge (0,0)$ with a unique solution which maps $\mathbf{x}$ to $-\infty$. □

Our problem therefore is to come up with a first lower approximation to the least solution which is feasible. For that, consider again a lifted system $\mathcal{E}^\sharp$ with n variables and least solution $\mu^\sharp$. Our solution is to initially perform n rounds of Round-Robin iteration. A related idea seems also implicit in section 5 of [3] in order to speed up strategy iteration in general. Let μ_0 denote the variable assignment resulting from the initial iteration. By construction, $\mu_0 \leq \mu^\sharp$. A closer look also reveals that $\mu_0(\mathbf{x}_i) = -\infty$ iff $\mu^\sharp(\mathbf{x}_i) = -\infty$. Thus, we can use the variable assignment μ_0 to remove all variables from $\mathcal{E}^\sharp$ that are mapped to $-\infty$ by the least solution. This means, that we replace every expression e where $[\![e]\!]\mu_0 = -\infty$ with $-\infty$ and remove every equation $\mathbf{x}_i = e_i$ where $\mu_0(\mathbf{x}_i) = -\infty$. For the resulting system we then can use μ_0 as an initial feasible variable assignment. We remark that we also can use a work-list-based approach to determine an initial variable assignment $\mu_0 \leq \mu^\sharp$ s.t. $\mu_0(\mathbf{x}_i) = -\infty$ iff $\mu^\sharp(\mathbf{x}_i) = -\infty$.

Example 4. Consider the lifted system

$$\mathbf{x} = (\mathsf{inc}(\mathbf{x}) + \mathsf{inc}(\mathbf{y})) \vee (0,0) \qquad \mathbf{y} = (\mathsf{inc}(\mathbf{x}) + (1,0)) \wedge (10,0).$$

Two rounds of Round-Robin iteration results in the feasible variable assignment μ_0 that maps $\mathbf{x}$ to $(2,2)$ and $\mathbf{y}$ to $(3,3)$. Also, μ_0 results in a strategy which selects the first argument expression of the max expression. This results in the conjunctive system

$$\mathbf{x} = \mathsf{inc}(\mathbf{x}) + \mathsf{inc}(\mathbf{y}) \qquad \mathbf{y} = \mathsf{inc}(\mathbf{x}) + (1,0) \wedge (10,0)$$

with greatest solution μ_1 that maps $\mathbf{x}$ to ∞ and $\mathbf{y}$ to $(10,0)$: which corresponds to the least solution of the original system. □

For a precise characterization of the run-time, let $\Pi(m)$ denote the maximal number of updates of strategies necessary for systems with m maximum expressions. We have:

Theorem 4. *The least solution of a system $\mathcal{E}$ of integer equations with n variables and m maximum expressions can be computed uniformally in time $\mathcal{O}(n \cdot |\mathcal{E}| \cdot \Pi(m))$.* □

The factor $n \cdot |\mathcal{E}|$ accounts for computing greatest solutions of conjunctive systems through n rounds of Round Robin iteration. Practical implementations, though, might use variants of work-list-based fixpoint iteration instead which at least practically will terminate much earlier. Finally, there is the factor $\Pi(m)$. At every maximum which has at least one constant argument, the strategy can be improved at most once. At general maximum subexpressions, the situation is less clear. The preliminary experience with our implementation as well as all practical experiments with strategy iteration we know of seem to indicate that the number of strategy improvements $\Pi(m)$ (at least practically) grows quite slowly in the number m of maxima. The systems up to 100.000 variables, e.g., which we tried used less than 20 iterations! Interestingly, though, it is still open whether (or: under which circumstances) the trivial upper bound of 2^m for $\Pi(m)$ can be significantly improved [17,1]. Concerning the complexity, strategy iteration algorithms thus can be compared with the simplex method for linear programming: many known variants of the latter method work very well in practice even for large scale applications with thousands of variables. We are better off, though, with strategy iteration: while for many variants of the simplex algorithm, inputs are known on which the algorithm needs exponentially many pivot operations (see, e.g., [10] for a nice overview), no inputs are known for strategy iteration using more than a *linear* number of iterations.

4 Interval Analysis

In this section, we explain how the fixpoint methods from section 3 can be used to compute precise least solutions of systems of interval equations. Let $\mathcal{I}$ denote the complete lattice of intervals partially ordered by the subset relation (here denoted by "$\sqsubseteq$"). Thus,

$$\mathcal{I} = \{\emptyset\} \cup \{[l,u] \in (\mathbb{Z} \cup \{-\infty\}) \times (\mathbb{Z} \cup \{\infty\}) \mid l \leq u\}$$

where $[l,u]$ represents the interval $\{z \in \mathbb{Z} \mid l \leq z \leq u\}$. As usual, the empty interval $\emptyset$ is the least element of $\mathcal{I}$, the greatest lower bound "$\sqcap$" of intervals is given by their intersection while the least upper bound "$\sqcup$" for non-empty intervals is defined by $[l_1,u_1] \sqcup [l_1,u_2] = [l_1 \wedge l_2, u_1 \vee u_2]$. Addition and multiplication are given by:

$$\begin{aligned} [l_1,u_1] + [l_2,u_2] &= [l_1 + l_2, u_1 + u_2] \\ [l_1,u_1]\cdot[l_2,u_2] &= [u_1\cdot u_2 \wedge l_1\cdot l_2 \wedge l_1\cdot u_2 \wedge u_1\cdot l_2,\; u_1\cdot u_2 \vee l_1\cdot l_2 \vee l_1\cdot u_2 \vee u_1\cdot l_2] \end{aligned}$$

We consider systems of equations $\mathbf{x}_i = e_i$ for $i = 1,\ldots,n$ over intervals similar to the ones we have considered over $\mathcal{Z}$. Thus, we allow right-hand sides e_i of the form

$$e \quad ::= \quad I \mid \mathbf{x}_j \mid e_1' \sqcup e_2' \mid e_1' \sqcap e_2' \mid e_1' + e_2' \mid e_1' \cdot e_2'$$

where $I \in \mathcal{I}$ denotes constant intervals. In [3], also postfix operators "$\uparrow$" and "$\downarrow$" are provided which preserve empty intervals and, when applied to a non-empty interval $[l,u]$ return $[l,u]\uparrow = [l,\infty]$ and $[l,u]\downarrow = [-\infty,u]$, respectively. We also could introduce an operator ";" defined by $I_1 ; I_2 = \emptyset$ if $I_1 = \emptyset$ and $I_1 ; I_2 = I_2$ otherwise. This operator is useful for expressing reachability assumptions. We have omitted all three operators, since these can be defined by: $I\uparrow = I + [0,\infty]$, $I\downarrow = I + [-\infty,0]$ and $I_1 ; I_2 = [0,0] \cdot I_1 + I_2$. Since all right-hand sides of equations are monotonic, every system of interval equations has a unique least solution. Such systems can be used for determining safe ranges for the values of integer variables. Instead of formally introducing interval analysis, we illustrate this application by an example.

Example 5. Consider the following control-flow graph for which we want to infer the information, that program point 5 is unreachable:

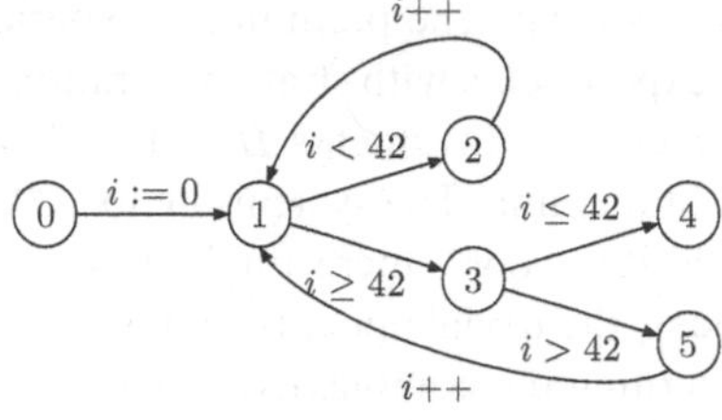

Let i_k denote the interval approximations for the sets of values of variable i at program point $k = 0,\ldots,5$. This leads to the system :

$$\begin{aligned} i_1 &= [0,0] \sqcup i_5 + [1,1] \sqcup i_2 + [1,1] & i_2 &= i_1 \sqcap [-\infty,41] \\ i_3 &= i_1 \sqcap [42,\infty] & i_4 &= i_3 \sqcap [-\infty,42] \\ i_5 &= i_3 \sqcap [43,\infty] \end{aligned}$$

It is not obvious how the usual widening and narrowing approach (with program point 1 as widening point) would identify program point 5 as unreachable. The least solution of the equation system, however, identifies program point 5 as unreachable. □

Assume that $\mathcal{E}$ is an equation system over $\mathcal{I}$. Our goal is to compute the least solution by decomposing $\mathcal{E}$ into a system of integer equations for the upper and *negated* lower bounds. For every interval variable $\mathbf{x}_i$ of $\mathcal{E}$, we therefore introduce two integer variables $\mathbf{x}_i^+, \mathbf{x}_i^-$ for the upper and *negated* lower bound of $\mathbf{x}_i$, respectively. Negating the lower bounds of intervals allows us to determine the values of the variables $\mathbf{x}_i^+$ as well as the values of the variables $\mathbf{x}_i^-$ by means of *least* fixpoint iteration within the same system of equations. Note, however, that upper and lower bounds of intervals are not independent. Interaction occurs at subexpressions which evaluate to the empty interval. Therefore, our construction will depend on information about the potential emptiness of the expressions in S where S is the set of all subexpressions of right-hand sides in $\mathcal{E}$. This information is specified by a valuation σ from S into the two-element lattice $D_2 = \{\bot, \top\}$ where $\bot < \top$. $\sigma(e) = \bot$ thereby indicates that the value of e is the empty interval, and $\sigma(e) = \top$ that the value of e is non-empty. The set of valuations form a complete lattice where the maximal length of a strictly ascending chain is bounded by $|S| \in \mathcal{O}(|\mathcal{E}|)$. Given a variable assignment μ, we can determine a valuation $\Sigma(\mu) : S \to D_2$ which is compatible with μ by:

$$\Sigma(\mu)(e) = \begin{cases} \bot & \text{if } [\![e]\!]\mu = \emptyset \\ \top & \text{if } [\![e]\!]\mu \neq \emptyset \end{cases}$$

Note that the valuation $\Sigma(\mu)$ monotonically depends on μ. We introduce the system $\mathcal{E}_\sigma^\pm$ which is obtained from $\mathcal{E}$ by replacing every interval equation $\mathbf{x}_i = e_i$ with the equations $\mathbf{x}_i^+ = [e_i]_\sigma^+$ and $\mathbf{x}_i^- = [e_i]_\sigma^-$ over $\mathcal{Z}$. Thereby, $[e]_\sigma^+ = [e]_\sigma^- = -\infty$ whenever $\sigma(e) = \bot$. Otherwise:

$$\begin{array}{llll}
[\emptyset]_\sigma^+ & = -\infty & [\emptyset]_\sigma^- & = -\infty \\
[[l,u]]_\sigma^+ & = u & [[l,u]]_\sigma^- & = -l \\
[e_1 + e_2]_\sigma^+ & = [e_1]_\sigma^+ + [e_2]_\sigma^+ & [e_1 + e_2]_\sigma^- & = [e_1]_\sigma^- + [e_2]_\sigma^- \\
[e_1 \sqcup e_2]_\sigma^+ & = [e_1]_\sigma^+ \vee [e_2]_\sigma^+ & [c_1 \sqcup c_2]_\sigma^- & = [e_1]_\sigma^- \vee [e_2]_\sigma^- \\
[e_1 \sqcap e_2]_\sigma^+ & = [e_1]_\sigma^+ \wedge [e_2]_\sigma^+ & [e_1 \sqcap e_2]_\sigma^- & = [e_1]_\sigma^- \wedge [e_2]_\sigma^-
\end{array}$$

The rules of the transformation do not yet deal with multiplication. Multiplication will be considered subsequently. In absence of multiplications, the least solution $\mu_\sigma^\pm$ of $\mathcal{E}_\sigma^\pm$ can be computed with our methods from section 3. Once we are given a variable assignment μ for $\mathcal{E}_\sigma^\pm$, we obtain a variable assignment $[\mu]$ for the original system $\mathcal{E}$ by[3]:

$$[\mu](\mathbf{x}_i) = \begin{cases} \emptyset & \text{if } \mu(\mathbf{x}_i^+) = \mu(\mathbf{x}_i^-) = -\infty \\ [-\mu(\mathbf{x}_i^-), \mu(\mathbf{x}_i^+)] & \text{if } \mu(\mathbf{x}_i^+), \mu(\mathbf{x}_i^-) > -\infty \end{cases}$$

For the correctness of our algorithm the following proposition is fundamental.

[3] We do not need to define $[\mu](\mathbf{x}_i)$ for any of the remaining cases, since these will not occur in the algorithms to be presented below.

Proposition 2. *Assume that $\mathcal{E}$ is a system of interval equations without multiplication whose least solution is μ^*. Let $\sigma : S \rightarrow D_2$ be a valuation. Assume $\mathcal{E}_\sigma^\pm$ is the corresponding system of integer equations for the upper and negated lower bounds with least solution $\mu_\sigma^\pm$. Then:*

1. $[\mu_\sigma^\pm] \sqsubseteq \mu^*$ *whenever* $\sigma \leq \Sigma(\mu^*)$;
2. $[\mu_\sigma^\pm] = \mu^*$ *whenever* $\sigma = \Sigma(\mu^*)$;
3. $\Sigma([\mu_\sigma^\pm]) > \sigma$ *whenever* $\sigma < \Sigma(\mu^*)$. □

Algorithm 3. Algorithm for interval equations

$\sigma \leftarrow \bot$;
do {
  $\mu_\sigma^\pm \leftarrow$ least solution of $\mathcal{E}_\sigma^\pm$; $\mu \leftarrow [\mu_\sigma^\pm]$; $\sigma_{old} \leftarrow \sigma$; $\sigma \leftarrow \Sigma(\mu)$;
} **while** $(\sigma \neq \sigma_{old})$
return μ;

Assertion 1 of proposition 2 guarantees for a possibly too small valuation σ, that the integer system will return a lower approximation to the least solution μ^*. Assertion 2 guarantees for precise σ that the integer system in deed recovers μ^*. Finally, assertion 3 assures that, as long as $\Sigma(\mu^*)$ has not been reached, the new valuation will be strictly larger than the old one. In light of proposition 2, it is now clear how our algorithm for computing the least solution μ^* of a system $\mathcal{E}$ of interval equations should work. It starts with a valuation $\sigma = \bot$ from $S \rightarrow D_2$ that maps every subexpression e to $\bot$. Given a current valuation $\sigma \leq \Sigma(\mu^*)$, it computes the least solution of the integer system $\mathcal{E}_\sigma^\pm$. According to proposition 2, this will either reveal the least solution of $\mathcal{E}$, if σ already equals $\Sigma(\mu^*)$, or some further expressions evaluating to non-empty intervals, in the other case. In the latter case, σ is updated and the algorithm repeats. Thus, alg. 3 computes the least solution of a system of interval equations $\mathcal{E}$ after $\mathcal{O}(|\mathcal{E}|)$ iterations.

Before we consider multiplication, we illustrate alg. 3 by an example.

Example 6. Consider the following system of interval equations:

$$\mathbf{x} = (\mathbf{x} + [1,1] \sqcap [0,42]) \sqcup [10,10]$$

In the first step the algorithm considers $\mathcal{E}_\bot^\pm$ given by:

$$\mathbf{x}^+ = -\infty \vee 10 \qquad \mathbf{x}^- = -\infty \vee -10$$

Using the obvious least solution the algorithm computes a valuation σ that returns $\top$ for all expressions. Thus, we obtain $\mathcal{E}_\sigma^\pm$ as:

$$\mathbf{x}^+ = (\mathbf{x}^+ + 1 \wedge 42) \vee 10 \qquad \mathbf{x}^- = (\mathbf{x}^- + (-1) \wedge 0) \vee -10$$

Solving $\mathcal{E}_\sigma^\pm$ reveals the least solution which maps $\mathbf{x}^+$ to 42 and $\mathbf{x}^-$ to -10. This corresponds to the least solution of $\mathcal{E}$ which maps $\mathbf{x}$ to $[10, 42]$. □

We now extend the setting by multiplications where at least one argument is a constant non-empty interval $I \in \mathcal{I}$, i.e., every multiplication subexpression in right-hand sides is of the form $I \cdot e$ for $I \in \mathcal{I} \setminus \{\emptyset\}$. Therefore, we enrich the transformations $[\cdot]_\sigma^+$ and $[\cdot]_\sigma^-$ by defining $[I \cdot e]_\sigma^+$ and $[I \cdot e]_\sigma^-$ for $I = [l, u]$ and e an expression s.t. $\sigma(e) \neq \bot$ by:

$$[I \cdot e]_\sigma^+ = \begin{cases} l \cdot [e]_\sigma^+ \vee \ u \cdot [e]_\sigma^+ & \text{if } l \geq 0 \\ -l \cdot [e]_\sigma^- \vee \ u \cdot [e]_\sigma^+ & \text{if } l < 0, u \geq 0 \\ -l \cdot [e]_\sigma^- \vee -u \cdot [e]_\sigma^- & \text{if } u < 0 \end{cases}$$

$$[I \cdot e]_\sigma^- = \begin{cases} l \cdot [e]_\sigma^- \vee \ u \cdot [e]_\sigma^- & \text{if } l \geq 0 \\ -l \cdot [e]_\sigma^+ \vee \ u \cdot [e]_\sigma^- & \text{if } l < 0, u \geq 0 \\ -l \cdot [e]_\sigma^+ \vee -u \cdot [e]_\sigma^+ & \text{if } u < 0 \end{cases}$$

If $\sigma(e) = \bot$, then $[I \cdot e]_\sigma^+$ and $[I \cdot e]_\sigma^-$ are given as $-\infty$. Thus, we obtain right-hand sides in which multiplications with *nonnegative* constants occur. By simplifying expressions $0 \cdot e$ to 0, we obtain a system of integer equations as considered in section 3.

Example 7. Let $\mathcal{E}$ be the system $\mathbf{x} = [-1, 0] \cdot \mathbf{x} \sqcup [2, 4]$. Assume that σ is the valuation which maps all expressions from $\mathcal{E}$ to $\top$. Then the system $\mathcal{E}_\sigma^\pm$ is given by:

$$\mathbf{x}^+ = 1 \cdot \mathbf{x}^- \vee 0 \cdot \mathbf{x}^+ \vee 4 \qquad \mathbf{x}^- = 1 \cdot \mathbf{x}^+ \vee 0 \cdot \mathbf{x}^- \vee -2$$

The least solution of this system maps $\mathbf{x}^+$ and $\mathbf{x}^-$ to 4. This corresponds to the least solution of $\mathcal{E}$ which maps $\mathbf{x}$ to $[-4, 4]$. □

The resulting systems of integer equations for the upper and negated lower interval bounds still are of the form considered in section 3 and therefore can be solved by alg. 2. It turns out that proposition 2 still holds when multiplication with constant intervals is allowed. Thus, alg. 3 can be applied and we get the following important result:

Theorem 5. *Assume that $\mathcal{E}$ is a system of interval equations with n variables, m occurrences of "$\sqcup$" and k multiplications in which at least one argument is a constant interval. The least solution of $\mathcal{E}$ can be computed in time $\mathcal{O}(n \cdot |\mathcal{E}|^2 \cdot \Pi(2m + 2k))$.* □

According to theorem 5, the complexity for solving interval equations consists of the complexity for iteratively solving integer systems until the number of variables receiving non-empty intervals remains stable. The result of theorem 5, though, is not yet completely satisfactory since it is not able to deal with *full multiplication* of intervals — meaning that an interval analysis based on theorem 5 is bound to treat general multiplication expressions conservatively. E.g. $x \cdot y$ have to be treated as $[-\infty, \infty]$. Dealing with full multiplication of intervals is non-trivial, though. Let $(x)^+$ and $(x)^-$ denote the upper and negated lower bound of an interval x. For non-empty intervals x, y the values $(xy)^+$ and $(xy)^-$ are given as:

$$\begin{aligned} (xy)^+ &= \ \ x^+y^+ \vee \ \ x^-y^- \vee -x^+y^- \vee -x^-y^+ \\ (xy)^- &= -x^+y^+ \vee -x^-y^- \vee \ \ x^+y^- \vee \ \ x^-y^+ \end{aligned}$$

Note that, in presence of positive and negative numbers, none of the individual products is monotonic. Fortunately, the necessary multiplications are *piecewise* distributive:

	$x^+ \geq 0,\ x^- \geq 0$ $y^+ \geq 0,\ y^- \geq 0$	$x^+ > 0,\ x^- < 0$ $y^+ \geq 0,\ y^- \geq 0$	$x^+ < 0,\ x^- > 0$ $y^+ \geq 0,\ y^- \geq 0$
$(xy)^+$	$x^+y^+ \vee x^-y^-$	x^+y^+	x^-y^-
$(xy)^-$	$x^+y^- \vee x^-y^+$	x^+y^-	x^-y^+
	$x^+ \geq 0,\ x^- \geq 0$ $y^+ > 0,\ y^- < 0$	$x^+ > 0,\ x^- < 0$ $y^+ > 0,\ y^- < 0$	$x^+ < 0,\ x^- > 0$ $y^+ > 0,\ y^- < 0$
$(xy)^+$	x^+y^+	x^+y^+	$-x^+y^-$
$(xy)^-$	x^-y^+	$-x^-y^-$	x^-y^+
	$x^+ > 0,\ x^- > 0$ $y^+ < 0,\ y^- > 0$	$x^+ > 0,\ x^- < 0$ $y^+ < 0,\ y^- > 0$	$x^+ < 0,\ x^- > 0$ $y^+ < 0,\ y^- > 0$
$(xy)^+$	x^-y^-	$-x^-y^+$	x^-y^-
$(xy)^-$	x^+y^-	x^+y^-	$-x^+y^+$

Fig. 1. Simplification of bounds

Proposition 3. *Assume* $a_1, a_2, b \in \mathcal{Z}$. *Then:*

1. $(a_1 \vee a_2)b = a_1b \vee a_2b$ *as well as* $(a_1 \wedge a_2)b = a_1b \wedge a_2b$ *if* $b \geq 0$;
2. $-(a_1 \vee a_2)b = -a_1b \vee -a_2b$ *as well as* $-(a_1 \wedge a_2)b = -a_1b \wedge -a_2b$ *if* $b \leq 0$. □

Our key idea is to introduce a case distinction on whether x and y consist of negative numbers only, of positive numbers only or contain 0. Under these extra assumptions, the computations of $(xy)^+$ and $(xy)^-$ for non-empty intervals x and y can be significantly simplified as shown in figure 1. We observe that for computing $(xy)^+$ and $(xy)^-$ only two kinds of integer products occur:

non-negative products : ab for $a, b \geq 0$, or
negative products : $-ab$ for $a, b < 0$.

Proposition 3 shows that in either case, the result does not only monotonically depend on the arguments a, b but even distributively (both for "$\vee$ and "$\wedge$"). Therefore, we now consider systems of integer equations where we additionally allow in right-hand sides subexpressions e of the form $(e_1 \vee 0) \cdot (e_2 \vee 0)$ and $-((e_1 \wedge -1) \cdot (e_2 \wedge -1))$. We call such equations *extended*. It turns out that the least solution of a system of extended integer equations can be computed by means of max strategy iteration over the instrumented lattice $\mathcal{D}$ along the same lines as in section 3. To handle the occurring multiplications in the lifted systems we additionally define $(a_1, j_1) \cdot (a_2, j_2) = (a_1 \cdot a_2, j_1 \vee j_2)$ for $a_1, a_2 \neq 0$ and $(0, 0) \cdot z = (0, 0)$ for $z \in \mathcal{D}$. For a system $\mathcal{E}$ of extended integer equations, we consider the corresponding lifted system $\mathcal{E}^\sharp$ whose least solution is approximated by greatest *feasible* solutions of *feasible* max strategies π. For a conjunctive lifted system of extended integer equations [4], a variable assignment μ is called *feasible* iff

1. $\mu(\mathbf{x}_i) > -\infty$ for every variable $\mathbf{x}_i$;
2. For every subexpression $e_1 \cdot e_2$ and $i = 1, 2$: $[\![e_i]\!]^\sharp \mu > (0, 0)$ whenever $e_i \not\equiv 0$

[4] In a conjunctive system, the multiplications are of the form $e_1 \cdot e_2$ and $-((e_1 \wedge -1) \cdot (e_2 \wedge -1))$.

Assume that $\mathcal{E}^\sharp$ denotes a lifted system of extended integer equations with least solution $\mu^\sharp$ and that π denotes a strategy. As in section 3, we verify that there exists at most one feasible solution of $\mathcal{E}^\sharp(\pi)$ and that this feasible solution can be computed by n rounds of Round-Robin iteration on $\mathcal{E}^\sharp(\pi)$ whenever it exists. As for ordinary systems of integer equations, $\mathcal{E}^\sharp(P(\mu'))$ has a feasible solution if $-\infty < \mu'(\mathbf{x}_i) \leq \mu^\sharp(\mathbf{x}_i)$ for all variables $\mathbf{x}_i$. Let μ_0 denote the variable assignment obtained by n rounds of Round-Robin iteration on $\mathcal{E}^\sharp$. By construction, $\mu_0 \leq \mu^\sharp$ and w.l.o.g., $\mu_0(\mathbf{x}_i) > -\infty$ for all variables $\mathbf{x}_i$. If μ_0 does not yet equal $\mu^\sharp$, then successive strategy improvement will construct a strictly ascending chain of variable assignments approximating the least solution of $\mathcal{E}^\sharp$ along the same lines as in section 3. We have:

Theorem 6. *Let $\mathcal{E}$ be a extended integer system with n variables and m occurrences of "$\vee$". The least solution of $\mathcal{E}$ can be computed uniformally in time $\mathcal{O}(n \cdot |\mathcal{E}| \cdot \Pi(m))$.* □

The exact method for extended integer systems allows us to fully deal with multiplication in systems of interval equations. Let $\mathcal{E}$ denote a system of interval equations possibly containing arbitrary multiplications. Now we consider valuations to be functions which map the set of subexpressions S into the *four*-element lattice $D_4 = \{\bot, -, +, \top\}$ where $\bot < -, + < \top$. Thus, $\sigma(e)$ indicates whether the value e is currently only known to be empty, contained in the negative or positive numbers, respectively, or contains 0. Given a variable assignment μ, we now determine the valuation $\Sigma(\mu) : S \to D_4$ by:

$$\Sigma(\mu)(e) = \begin{cases} \bot & \text{if } [\![e]\!]\mu = \emptyset \\ - & \text{if } [\![e]\!]\mu \sqsubseteq [-\infty, -1] \\ + & \text{if } [\![e]\!]\mu \sqsubseteq [1, \infty] \\ \top & \text{if } [\![e]\!]\mu \ni 0 \end{cases}$$

The valuation $\Sigma(\mu)(e)$ monotonically depends on μ. The maximal length of a strictly ascending chain in the complete lattice of valuations over D_4 is bounded by $2 \cdot |S| \in \mathcal{O}(|\mathcal{E}|)$. Our goal is to construct a system $\mathcal{E}^\pm_\sigma$ for upper and negated lower interval bounds in presence of full multiplication, relative to a valuation σ. For that, we enrich the transformations $[\cdot]^+_\sigma$ and $[\cdot]^-_\sigma$. So far, these transformations are only defined for valuations over D_2 and expressions which are not multiplications. The corresponding rules of the new transformation for these cases are syntactically identical. Therefore, it remains to explain how subexpressions $[e_1 \cdot e_2]^+_\sigma$ and $[e_1 \cdot e_2]^-_\sigma$ should be handled. If one argument e_i of the multiplication is mapped to $\bot$, i.e., currently evaluates to $\emptyset$, we define $[e_1 \cdot e_2]^+_\sigma$ and $[e_1 \cdot e_2]^-_\sigma$ as $-\infty$. If e.g. $\sigma(e_1) = \sigma(e_2) = -$, we define

$$[e_1 \cdot e_2]^+_\sigma = ([e_1]^-_\sigma \vee 0) \cdot ([e_2]^-_\sigma \vee 0) \qquad [e_1 \cdot e_2]^-_\sigma = -(([e_1]^+_\sigma \wedge -1) \cdot ([e_2]^+_\sigma \wedge -1))$$

which corresponds to the case in the lower right corner of the table in figure 1. The rules for the remaining cases are constructed analogously corresponding to figure 1. The resulting system $\mathcal{E}^\pm_\sigma$ is extended integer. Thus, we can compute its least solution $\mu^\pm_\sigma$ through the strategy iteration algorithm from section 3. Also, we find that proposition 2 also holds for systems with full multiplication. We only need now to consider valuations $\sigma : S \to D_4$. Proposition 2 implies, that algo. 3 also works for systems with full multiplication — which proves our main result for interval analysis.

Theorem 7. *Assume that $\mathcal{E}$ is a system of interval equations with arbitrary intersections, n variables, m occurrences of "$\sqcup$" and k arbitrary multiplications. The least solution of $\mathcal{E}$ can be computed uniformally in time $\mathcal{O}(n \cdot |\mathcal{E}|^2 \cdot \Pi(2m + 6k)))$.* □

The complexity estimation is based on the corresponding estimation for extended integer equations. Additionally, we must take into account the number of updates to valuations. Note also that the number of occurrences of "$\vee$"-operators in the generated extended integer systems are now bounded only by $2m + 6k$.

5 Conclusion

We considered systems of integer equations. These are necessary for precisely solving equations over the interval domain. We used an instrumentation of the lattice $\mathcal{Z}$ with one extra component to guarantee for conjunctive systems to admit at most one feasible solution. This uniqueness allowed us to construct a strategy iteration algorithm for computing least solutions of systems of integer equations. We extended this result to construct an algorithm for precisely solving systems of interval equations — even for systems using arbitrary multiplication. In the latter case we had to take into account that multiplication of integers is not monotonic. The resulting algorithms are amazingly simple and natural. Implementations can be down-loaded from `http://www2.in.tum.de/~gawlitza/policy`. First experiments show that the efficiency is promising. It remains for future work to systematically evaluate the solvers for systems of integer and interval equations on real-world examples.

References

1. H. Bjorklund, S. Sandberg, and S. Vorobyov. Complexity of Model Checking by Iterative Improvement: the Pseudo-Boolean Framework . In *Proc. 5th Int. Andrei Ershov Memorial Conf. Perspectives of System Informatics*, pages 381–394. LNCS 2890, Springer, 2003.
2. J. Cochet-Terrasson, S. Gaubert, and J. Gunawardena. A Constructive Fixed Point Theorem for Min-Max Functions. *Dynamics and Stability of Systems*, 14(4):407–433, 1999.
3. A. Costan, S. Gaubert, E. Goubault, M. Martel, and S. Putot. A Policy Iteration Algorithm for Computing Fixed Points in Static Analysis of Programs. In *Computer Aided Verification, 17th Int. Conf. (CAV)*, pages 462–475. LNCS 3576, Springer Verlag, 2005.
4. P. Cousot and R. Cousot. Static Determination of Dynamic Properties of Programs. In *Second Int. Symp. on Programming*, pages 106–130. Dunod, Paris, France, 1976.
5. P. Cousot and R. Cousot. Comparison of the Galois Connection and Widening/Narrowing Approaches to Abstract Interpretation. JTASPEFL '91, Bordeaux. *BIGRE*, 74:107–110, Oct. 1991.
6. T. Gawlitza, J. Reineke, H. Seidl, and R. Wilhelm. Polynomial Exact Interval Analysis Revisited. Technical report, TU München, 2006.
7. A. Hoffman and R. Karp. On Nonterminating Stochastic Games. *Management Sci.*, 12:359–370, 1966.
8. R. Howard. *Dynamic Programming and Markov Processes*. Wiley, New York, 1960.
9. D. E. Knuth. A Generalization of Dijkstra's algorithm. *Information Processing Letters (IPL)*, 6(1):1–5, 1977.

10. N. Megiddo. On the Complexity of Linear Programming. In T. Bewley, editor, *Advances in Economic Theory: 5th World Congress*, pages 225–268. Cambridge University Press, 1987.
11. A. Miné. Relational Abstract Domains for the Detection of Floating-Point Run-Time Errors. In *European Symposium on Programming (ESOP)*, volume 2986 of *LNCS*, pages 3–17. Springer, 2004.
12. A. Miné. Symbolic Methods to Enhance the Precision of Numerical Abstract Domains. In *Verification, Model Checking, and Abstract Interpretation, 7th Int. Conf. (VMCAI)*, pages 348–363. LNCS 3855, Springer Verlag, 2006.
13. A. Puri. *Theory of Hybrid and Discrete Systems*. PhD thesis, University of California, Berkeley, 1995.
14. M. L. Puterman. *Markov Decision Processes: Discrete Stochastic Dynamic Programming*. Wiley, New York, 1994.
15. H. Seidl. Least and Greatest Solutions of Equations over $\mathcal{N}$. *Nordic Journal of Computing (NJC)*, 3(1):41–62, 1996.
16. Z. Su and D. Wagner. A Class of Polynomially Solvable Range Constraints for Interval Analysis Without Widenings. *Theor. Comput. Sci. (TCS)*, 345(1):122–138, 2005.
17. J. Vöge and M. Jurdzinski. A Discrete Strategy Improvement Algorithm for Solving Parity Games. In *Computer Aided Verification, 12th Int. Conf. (CAV)*, pages 202–215. LNCS 1855, Springer, 2000.
18. U. Zwick and M. Paterson. The Complexity of Mean Payoff Games on Graphs. *Theoretical Computer Science (TCS)*, 158(1&2):343–359, 1996.

A Complete Guide to the Future*

Frank S. de Boer[1], Dave Clarke[1], and Einar Broch Johnsen[2]

[1] CWI, Amsterdam, Netherlands
{frb,dave}@cwi.nl
[2] Dept. of Informatics, University of Oslo, Norway
einarj@ifi.uio.no

Abstract. We present the semantics and proof system for an object-oriented language with active objects, asynchronous method calls, and futures. The language, based on Creol, distinguishes itself in that unlike active object models, it permits more than one thread of control within an object, though, unlike Java, only one thread can be active within an object at a given time and rescheduling occurs only at specific release points. Consequently, reestablishing an object's monitor invariant is possible at specific well-defined points in the code. The resulting proof system shows that this approach to concurrency is simpler for reasoning than, say, Java's multithreaded concurrency model. From a methodological perspective, we identify constructs which admit a simple proof system and those which require, for example, interference freedom tests.

1 Introduction

The increasing importance of distributed systems demands flexible communication forms between distributed processes. While object-orientation is a natural paradigm for distributed systems [17], the tight coupling between objects traditionally enforced by method calls may be criticized. *Asynchronous method calls* have been proposed to better combine object-orientation with distributed programming, with a looser coupling between a caller and a callee than in the tightly synchronized (remote) method invocation model. Return values from asynchronous calls are managed by so-called *futures* [4,10,13,20,26]. In this paper, we develop a kernel language for distributed concurrent objects in which asynchronous method calls is the basic communication construct. The model of asynchronously communicating objects is inherently concurrent, and synchronized communication and sequential execution appear as special cases. The proposed kernel language combines the concurrency model of Creol [18], an object-oriented language for concurrent objects, with first-class futures, presented in a Java-like syntax. Futures are not transparent but may be communicated between objects, so return values from asynchronous method calls may be shared. The paper presents an operational semantics for this kernel language, and introduces a novel proof system for concurrent objects with asynchronous method calls and futures.

* This research is in the context of the EU project IST-33826 CREDO: Modeling and analysis of evolutionary structures for distributed services (http://credo.cwi.nl).

R. De Nicola (Ed.): ESOP 2007, LNCS 4421, pp. 316–330, 2007.

The adopted concurrency model is based on concurrent objects, each with its own processor. Inside an object, method activations are executed in an interleaved way. Thus execution in an object is reminiscent of monitors, but explicit signaling is avoided by introducing so-called *release points* at which control may change between different method activations competing for execution. The interleaved execution of method activations allows different activities to be pursued within the object; in particular, active and reactive object behavior are easily and dynamically combined. Whereas an active object usually relies on a preselected method to define its active behavior, we exploit asynchronous method calls as *triggers of concurrent activity*. Asynchronous method calls spawn activities in other objects while the caller proceeds with its execution. Futures extend this technique to include the forwarding and sharing of replies to method calls. Each object sharing a future may choose to either completely block or alternatively to release control while waiting for the reply associated with the future. Any method may be called both synchronously and asynchronously. In fact, synchronous calls are treated as a special case of asynchronous calls, for which execution immediately blocks while waiting for the reply. Thus, synchronous calls restrict the natural concurrency of the model by sequentializing activity.

Proof theories for multithreaded object systems are complicated by the interference problem for shared variables, which appears when threads operate concurrently in the same object. Reasoning about programs in this setting is highly complex [1]: Safety is by convention rather than by language design [3]. The simplicity of the proof system proposed in this paper, in contrast to that of, for example, multithreaded Java, is a major advantage of concurrent object models compared to multithread concurrency. The proposed proof system uses a local assertion language to describe the local state of an object in the pre- and postconditions of methods and in monitor invariants. On the other hand, a global assertion language is used for describing invariant properties of inter-object synchronization. In this paper, we present a novel view of an object as a maintainer of *multiple* local monitor invariants and a global synchronization constraint. The local invariants monitor the different release points of an object. These multiple monitor invariants require a novel proof system for their mutual dependencies to establish their invariance. This clear separation of concerns between intra- and inter-object synchronization is also reflected in the completeness proof for the proof theory. In fact, the completeness proof (only briefly discussed in this paper due to lack of space) is based on a semantic characterization of the global invariant in terms of futures and two local history variables. In addition to a local communication history, recording the externally observable behavior of each object as specified by its method calls, a local scheduling history records the internal scheduling in an object, which is completely encapsulated by its local invariants, recording snapshots of the corresponding release points.

Paper overview. Sect. 2 introduces the kernel language and its operational semantics and Sect. 3 provides an example. Sect. 4 introduces the assertion language, Sect. 5 a proof system for concurrent objects with asynchronous method calls and futures, Sect. 6 discusses related work and Sect. 7 concludes the paper.

2 The Language

A kernel language for distributed concurrent objects with asynchronous method calls and futures is now introduced, extending the syntax of Featherweight Java [16]. In contrast to Featherweight Java, each object encapsulates its state; i.e., external manipulation of the state is via the object's methods only. Furthermore different objects execute concurrently: each object has a thread dedicated to executing its processes, which correspond to activations of its methods. To preserve an object's invariants for reasoning control, execution is restricted so that only one process may be active in an object at a time; other processes in the object are *suspended*. We distinguish between *blocking* a process and *releasing* a process. Blocking suspends process execution, but does not relinquish control to a suspended process. Release stops process execution and reschedules another (suspended) process. Using release points within method bodies, an object may interleave the execution of several (non-terminating) processes.

Method calls are asynchronous and the result of a call is stored in a *future*. Rather than forcing the caller to *wait* for the call to return, which is unsatisfactory in a distributed setting where communications may disappear and permanently block the caller's process, return values are first accessed when required. Execution only blocks when attempting to read from a future without a return value. Futures may also be polled, enabling fine grained control of scheduling. In contrast to the read operation on a future, the polling operation never blocks.

The implicit control flow in an object can be influenced by means of release points expressed as Boolean guards, which may include the polling of futures. This way, processes may choose between blocking and releasing control while waiting for the reply to a method call. Release points can be used to combine active and reactive processes in an object; the object can behave both as client and server without requiring an active loop to interleave these different roles.

2.1 Syntax

The language syntax is given in Fig. 1. We emphasize the differences with Java. A program P is a list of class definitions followed by a method body. A class inherits from a superclass, which may be `Object`, extending it with additional fields f and methods M. Methods have read-only access to a variable **`destiny`** which is a reference to the future that will hold the result of the current method.

$$
\begin{array}{llll}
P ::= \overline{L}\ \{\overline{T}\ \overline{x}; sr\} & & L ::= \mathbf{class}\ C\ \mathbf{extends}\ C\ \{\overline{T}\ \overline{f}; \overline{M}\} \\
M ::= T\ m\ (\overline{T}\ \overline{x})\{\overline{T}\ \overline{x}; sr\} & & e\ ::= v \mid e.\mathbf{get} \mid e!m(\overline{e}) \mid \mathbf{new}\ C() \mid \mathbf{null} \\
v\ ::= f \mid x & & s\ ::= v := e \mid \mathbf{await}\ g \mid s \Box s \mid s \parallel s \mid \mathbf{skip} \mid s; s \\
 & & \quad\quad \mid \mathbf{if}\ g\ \mathbf{then}\ s\ \mathbf{else}\ s\ \mathbf{fi} \mid \mathbf{release} \mid s \mathbin{/\!/\!/} s \\
sr ::= s; \mathbf{return}\ e & & g\ ::= \mathbf{wait} \mid b \mid v? \mid g \wedge g \\
b\ ::= \mathbf{true} \mid \mathbf{false} \mid v & & T ::= C \mid \mathbf{bool} \mid !T
\end{array}
$$

Fig. 1. The language syntax. Variables v are fields (f) or local variables (x), and C is a class name.

$$
\begin{array}{rlrl}
\mathit{config} ::= & \epsilon \mid \mathit{object} \mid \mathit{future} \mid \mathit{config}\ \mathit{config} & o ::= & (\mathit{oid}, C) \\
\mathit{object} ::= & (o, \mathit{processQ}, \mathit{fds}, \mathit{active}) & \mathit{fds} ::= & \overline{f\ v} \\
\mathit{future} ::= & (\mathit{mid}, \mathit{mc}, \mathit{mode}, v) & \mathit{mc} ::= & \mathit{oid}.m(\overline{v}) \\
\mathit{active} ::= & \mathit{process} \mid \mathtt{idle} & \mathit{process} ::= & (\overline{T\ x\ v}, \mathit{sr} : T) \\
\mathit{processQ} ::= & \epsilon \mid \mathit{process} \mid \mathit{processQ}\ \mathit{processQ} & v ::= & \mathit{oid} \mid \mathit{mid} \mid \mathtt{null} \mid b
\end{array}
$$

Fig. 2. The syntax for runtime configurations. Here, *oid* and *mid* denote identifiers for objects, and futures. Processes include both the types of local variables and the expected return type (which we often elide for simplicity of presentation).

Expressions e are standard apart from the asynchronous method call $e!m(\overline{e})$ and the (blocking) read operation v.**get**. *Statements* s are standard apart from release points **await** g, non-deterministic choice $s_1 \Box s_2$, and merge $s_1 \||| s_2$ for the interleaved execution of branches s_1 and s_2. *Guards* g are conjunctions of **wait**, Boolean expressions b, and the polling operation $v?$ on a future v. When the guard in an **await** statement evaluates to **false**, the active process is released and another suspended process may be rescheduled. Otherwise, the process proceeds. Non-deterministic choice allows either branch to be selected. The branches of a merge are interleaved at release points, influencing the flow of control within a process without allowing other processes to execute. In addition, the intermediate statements **release** and $s_1 /\!\!/\!\!/ s_2$ appear during reduction. The **release** statement is introduced when the guard of an **await** statement reduces to **false**, and the $s_1 /\!\!/\!\!/ s_2$ statement corresponds to the activation of statement s_1 in the merge of statements s_1 and s_2, where statement s_2 is delayed.

Typing. The type system, omitted for space reasons, closely resembles that of Featherweight Java [16]. Let $!T$ denote the type of a future which will ultimately contain a value of type T. An asynchronous call to a method with return type T results in a future of type $!T$. If v has type $!T$, then v.**get** has type T and $v?$ has type **bool**. Type soundness is easily established for this type system and the reduction semantics presented in Sect. 2.2 below.

2.2 Semantics

The semantics is a small-step reduction relation on *configurations* of objects and futures (see Fig. 2). *Objects* have an identifier, a class, a queue of suspended processes, fields, and an active process. The process **idle** indicates that no method is running in the object. A *future* captures the state of a method call: initially *sleeping*, the method call later becomes *active*, and finally, when *completed*, it stores its result in the future. The value $\mathit{mode} \in \{\mathtt{s}, \mathtt{a}, \mathtt{c}\}$ represents these three future states. Types are given default values by the *default* function (e.g., $\mathit{default}(C) = \mathtt{null}$, $\mathit{default}(\mathtt{bool}) = \mathtt{false}$, and $\mathit{default}(!T) = \mathtt{null}$). The *initial configuration* of a program $\overline{L}\ \{\overline{T\ x}; \mathit{sr}\}$ has one object $(o, \emptyset, \emptyset, (\overline{T\ x\ \mathit{default}(T)}, \mathit{sr} : T))$.

Reduction takes the form of a relation $\mathit{config} \rightarrow \mathit{config}'$. Rules apply to partial configurations and may be applied in parallel. This differs from the semantics of object-oriented languages with a global store [11], but is consistent with the

Creol's [18] executable semantics in Maude [5], and allows true concurrency in the distributed setting. The main rules are given in Fig. 3. The context reduction semantics decomposes a statement into a reduction context and a redex, and reduces the redex [9]. *Reduction contexts* are method bodies M, statements S, expressions E, and guards G with a single hole denoted by $\bullet$:

$$\begin{aligned} M &::= \bullet \mid S; \mathtt{return}\ e \mid \mathtt{return}\ E \\ S &::= \bullet \mid v := E \mid S; s \mid \mathtt{if}\ G\ \mathtt{then}\ s_1\ \mathtt{else}\ s_2\ \mathtt{fi} \mid S \mathbin{/\!/\!/} s \\ E &::= \bullet \mid E.\mathtt{get} \mid E!m(\overline{e}) \mid v!m(\overline{v}, E, \overline{e}) \\ G &::= \bullet \mid E? \mid G \wedge g \mid b \wedge G \end{aligned}$$

Redexes reduce in their respective contexts; i.e., body-redexes in M, stat-redexes in S, expr-redexes in E, and guard redexes in G. Redexes are defined as follows:

$$\begin{aligned} \textit{body-redexes} &::= \mathtt{return}\ v \\ \textit{stat-redexes} &::= x := v \mid f := v \mid \mathtt{await}\ g \mid s \,\Box\, s \mid \mathtt{skip}; s \mid \mathtt{if}\ b\ \mathtt{then}\ s\ \mathtt{else}\ s \\ &\quad\mid s \| s \mid \mathtt{skip} \mathbin{/\!/\!/} s \mid \mathtt{release}; s \mathbin{/\!/\!/} s' \mid \mathtt{release} \\ \textit{expr-redexes} &::= x \mid f \mid v.\mathtt{get} \mid v.m!(\overline{v}) \mid \mathtt{new}\ C() \\ \textit{guard-redexes} &::= \mathit{mid?} \mid b \wedge g \mid \mathtt{wait} \end{aligned}$$

Filling the hole of a context M with an expression r is denoted $M[r]$. Before evaluating the expression e in the method body s; `return` e, the body will be reduced to `skip`; `return` e. For simplicity, we elide the `skip` and write just `return` e.

Expressions and guards. In (Red-Call), an asynchronous call adds a sleeping future to the configuration, returning its identifier to the caller. In (Red-Get), a read operation on a future variable blocks the active process until the future is in completed mode. Blocking does not reschedule a suspended process. Object creation in (Red-New) introduces a new instance of a class into the configuration, with default values for the new object's fields. Guards determine if a process should be released and another process rescheduled. In (Red-Poll), a future variable is polled to see if a call has been executed. In contrast to (Red-Get), polling a future at a release point (`await`) enables the release of the active process. In particular, `await wait` will always release the active process.

Statements and rescheduling. In (Red-Await), a process at a release point proceeds if its guard is true and otherwise releases. When a process is released, its guard is reused to reschedule the process. A guard with clause `wait` causes a process to release. When it becomes a candidate for rescheduling, `wait` is replaced by `true` so that the process can proceed. When an active process is released or terminates, it is replaced by the `idle` process, which allows a process from the process queue to be scheduled for execution in (Red-Reschedule).

Method invocation and return. A method call results in an activation on the callee's process queue. As the call is asynchronous, there is a delay between the call and its activation, represented by the sleeping mode of a future. Subsequent to the call, (Red-Bind) creates a process to run the method. This process is added to the

$$\frac{}{(o, pq, fds, (l, M[s \| s'])) \to (o, pq, fds, (l, M[s /\!/\!/ s']))}\ (\text{RED-MERGE1})$$

$$\frac{}{(o, pq, fds, (l, M[s \| s'])) \to (o, pq, fds, (l, M[s' /\!/\!/ s]))}\ (\text{RED-MERGE2})$$

$$\frac{}{(o, pq, fds, (l, M[\texttt{skip} /\!/\!/ s])) \to (o, pq, fds, (l, M[s]))}\ (\text{RED-MERGE-SKIP})$$

$$\frac{mid \text{ is fresh}}{(o, pq, fds, l, (M[oid!m(\overline{v})])) \to (o, pq, fds, (l, M[mid]))\ (mid, oid.m(\overline{v}), \texttt{s}, \texttt{null})}\ (\text{RED-CALL})$$

$$\frac{oid \text{ is fresh} \quad fds' = defaults(C)}{(o, pq, fds, (l, M[\texttt{new}\ C()])) \to (o, pq, fds, (l, M[oid]))\ ((oid, C), \epsilon, fds', (\epsilon, \texttt{skip}))}\ (\text{RED-NEW})$$

$$\frac{enabled(s', (fds, l), \mu)}{(o, pq, fds, (l, M[\texttt{release}; s /\!/\!/ s']))\ \mu \to (o, pq, fds, (l, M[s' /\!/\!/ s]))\ \mu}\ (\text{RED-MERGE-RELEASE1})$$

$$\frac{\neg enabled(s', (fds, l), \mu)}{(o, pq, fds, (l, M[\texttt{release}; s /\!/\!/ s']))\ \mu \to (o, pq, fds, (l, M[\texttt{release}; (s \| s')]))\ \mu}\ (\text{RED-MERGE-RELEASE2})$$

$$\frac{}{(o, pq, fds, (l, M[mid.\texttt{get}]))\ (mid, mc, \texttt{c}, v) \to (o, pq, fds, (l, M[v]))\ (mid, mc, \texttt{c}, v)}\ (\text{RED-GET})$$

$$\frac{M[\texttt{release}] \neq M'[\texttt{release}; s /\!/\!/ s']}{(o, pq, fds, (l, M[\texttt{release}])) \to (o, pq :: (l, M[\texttt{skip}], fds, \texttt{idle})}\ (\text{RED-RELEASE})$$

$$\frac{b = (mode \equiv \texttt{c})}{(o, pq, fds, (l, M[mid?]))\ (mid, mc, mode, v) \to (o, pq, fds, (l, M[b]))\ (mid, mc, mode, v)}\ (\text{RED-POLL})$$

$$\frac{}{(o, pq, fds, (l, M[\texttt{wait}])) \to (o, pq, fds, (l, M[\texttt{false}]))}\ (\text{RED-WAIT})$$

$$\frac{g' = g[\texttt{true}/\texttt{wait}]}{(o, pq, fds, (l, M[\texttt{await}\ g])) \to (o, pq, fds, (l, M[\texttt{if}\ g\ \texttt{then skip else release; await}\ g'\ \texttt{fi}]))}\ (\text{RED-AWAIT})$$

$$\frac{}{(o, p :: pq, fds, \texttt{idle}) \to (o, pq, fds, p)}\ (\text{RED-RESCHEDULE})$$

$$\frac{mbody(m, C) = (\overline{T}\ \overline{x}, \overline{U}\ \overline{y}, sr : T) \qquad l - \overline{T}\ \overline{x}\ \overline{v}, \overline{U}\ \overline{y}\ default(\overline{U}), !T\ \texttt{destiny}\ mid \quad q = (l, sr : T)}{((oid, C), pq, fds, p)\ (mid, oid.m(\overline{v}), \texttt{s}, \texttt{null}) \to ((oid, C), pq :: q, fds, p)\ (mid, oid.m(\overline{v}), \texttt{a}, \texttt{null})}\ (\text{RED-BIND})$$

$$\frac{l(\texttt{destiny}) = mid}{(o, pq, fds, (l, \texttt{return}\ v : T))\ (mid, oid.m(\overline{v}), \texttt{a}, \texttt{null}) \to (o, pq, fds, \texttt{idle})\ (mid, oid.m(\overline{v}), \texttt{c}, v)}\ (\text{RED-RETURN})$$

$$\frac{config \to config'}{config\ config'' \to config'\ config''}\ (\text{RED-CONTEXT})$$

$$\frac{config\ \mu \to config'\ \mu' \qquad config''\ \mu \to config'''\ \mu'' \qquad \mathrm{dom}(\mu) = \mathrm{dom}(\mu') = \mathrm{dom}(\mu'') \qquad \mathrm{dom}(config') \cap \mathrm{dom}(config''') = \emptyset}{config\ config''\ \mu \to config'\ config'''\ \mu' \odot \mu''}\ (\text{RED-PARALLEL})$$

Fig. 3. The context reduction semantics. μ denotes a configuration of futures.

process queue, and the future changes its mode to active, thus preventing multiple activations. When process execution is completed, the return value is stored by (RED-RETURN) in the future identified by the `destiny` variable. This future changes its mode to completed and the active process becomes `idle`.

Merge and release. Either branch of a merge may be selected for reduction, captured by (RED-MERGE1) and (RED-MERGE2). When a branch of a merge statement completes, (RED-MERGE-SKIP) schedules the other branch. If a release occurs inside a merge, the other branch of the merge is the first candidate for rescheduling — rescheduling is local to a process whenever possible. If both branches release, then the process is released. Let σ map fields and local variables to their values. Process release is based on the predicate *enabled* defined on guards, futures, and states which determines whether a guard will not directly release:

$$\begin{aligned} \mathit{enabled}(\mathtt{wait}, \sigma, \mu) &= \mathit{false} \qquad \mathit{enabled}(b, \sigma, \mu) \;=\; b \\ \mathit{enabled}(v, \sigma, \mu) &= \mathit{enabled}(\sigma(v), \sigma, \mu) \\ \mathit{enabled}(\mathit{mid}?, \sigma, \mu) &= \mathit{mode} \equiv \mathtt{c}, \text{ where } (\mathit{mid}, \_, \mathit{mode}, \_) \in \mu \\ \mathit{enabled}(g \wedge g', \sigma, \mu) &= \mathit{enabled}(g, \sigma, \mu) \wedge \mathit{enabled}(g', \sigma, \mu) \end{aligned}$$

The predicate is lifted to statements; $\mathit{enabled}(\mathtt{await}\ g, \sigma, \mu) = \mathit{enabled}(g, \sigma, \mu)$ is the crucial case. In (RED-MERGE-RELEASE1), (RED-MERGE-RELEASE2) and (RED-RELEASE), the contexts and redexes do not factor expressions involving `release` uniquely: these may be factored as both $M[\mathtt{release}]$ and $M'[\mathtt{release}; s /\!/\!/ s']$. A clause is added to (RED-RELEASE) to ensure that $\mathtt{release}; s /\!/\!/ s'$ is preferred.

Context and parallel reductions. A reduction applies to a subconfiguration by rule (RED-CONTEXT). In (RED-PARALLEL) futures may be shared between concurrent reductions, increasing the amount of concurrency expressible in the rules. As the futures witnessed by one process may be changed by another, they need to be recomposed in a consistent way. This is handled by a function $\mu \odot \mu'$ which collects futures from μ and μ' and resolves conflicting futures with the same *mid*. New futures are located in config' and config'''.

Synchronization and self-calls. Reading (`get`) a future is blocking and can introduce synchronization points in the code; for example, the statements $y = e!m(\overline{e}); y.\mathtt{get}$ model the usual notion of synchronous method call, as this code blocks the active process after making a call to y until the call has completed. A minor problem arises when we wish to perform a synchronous call to self, $\mathtt{this}.m(\overline{e})$: the statements $y = \mathtt{this}!m(\overline{e}); y.\mathtt{get}$ lead to deadlock. In order to execute a local method, the process needs to be released, as in the sequence $y = \mathtt{this}!m(\overline{e}); \mathtt{await}\ y?; z = y.\mathtt{get}$. This sequence, however, does not capture the direct transfer of control as it enables any other blocked process in the object to be activated before the call to m. This ultimately means that the language needs an extension to handle synchronous self calls. A solution is proposed in [18].

3 An Example

We present a publisher-subscriber example wherein an event observed by a sensor is published to objects subscribed to a service. To avoid bottlenecks when publishing an event, the service delegates to a chain of proxy objects, where each proxy object informs both the next proxy and up to `limit` subscribing clients. We assume these classes exist: `Sensor` with method `detectEvent`, `Client` with method `signal`, and `List<T>`, parametric in type `T`, with method `add`.

```
class Service {
  Sensor sensor;  Proxy proxy;
  Service(int val) {                              // constructor
    sensor = new Sensor; proxy = new Proxy(val);
  }
  void subscribe(Client cl) { proxy.add(cl) }  // sync. call
  void process() {
    while (true) {
      !Event fut = sensor!detectEvent();
      proxy!publish(fut);                       // async. call
      await fut?;
} } }
class Proxy {
  List<Clients> myClients;  Proxy nextProxy;
  Event ev;  int limit;
  Proxy(int k) {                                  // constructor
    limit = k; myClients = new List();  nextProxy = null;
  }
  void add(Client cl) {
    if (myClients.length < limit) { myClients.add(cl); }
    else { if (nextProxy == null) nextProxy = new Proxy(limit);
        nextProxy.add(cl); }
  }
  void publish(!Event fut) {
    await fut?;
    if (nextProxy != null) { nextProxy!publish(fut); }
    ev = fut.get();
    for (Client client : myClients) { client!signal(ev); }
} }                                                  // notify clients
```

4 The Assertion Language

Assertions are used to specify (invariant) properties of the configurations occurring during computations generated by the operational semantics defined in Sect. 2.2. Assertions are constructed from expressions e of the following form:

$$e ::= z \mid z.f \mid ops(\bar{e})$$

Here z can be `this`, a local variable, or a *logical* variable. Logical variables are implicitly universally quantified. The expression $z.f$ denotes the value of the field f of the object denoted by the variable. By *ops* we mean an operation of some given abstract data type. Assertions are Boolean combinations of Boolean expressions.

In order to reason about the invocation and return of asynchronous method calls, futures are explicitly modeled as objects. Thus reasoning relies on an encoding of method calls $oid.m(\overline{e})$. Conceptually, a class representing futures is introduced for every method in the program. For every possibly inherited method m of a class C, we associate a class `Future_C_m`, with instance variables to store the callee, the actual parameters, the mode, and the return value of a call to the method. Given this class, the future $(mid, oid.m(\overline{e}), mode, v)$ corresponding to a method call of a method m of an object oid of class C, is denoted by the instance $((mid, \texttt{Future\_C\_m}), fds)$, where $fds = \texttt{callee} \mapsto oid, \overline{\texttt{arg}} \mapsto \overline{e}, \texttt{mode} \mapsto mode, \texttt{val} \mapsto v$. Note that we assume that some encoding of an enumerated type with elements $\underline{\text{s}}$leeping, $\underline{\text{a}}$ctive, and $\underline{\text{c}}$ompleted exists.

As a simple example, the assertion $z.\texttt{mode} = \texttt{c} \rightarrow z.\texttt{v} > 0$, where z is an (implicitly) universally quantified logical variable ranging over all existing instances of `Future_C_m`, states that every completed instance of `Future_C_m` stores a positive integer, or, in other words, that every completed invocation of the method m (executed by an object of type C) has returned a positive integer. In a similar manner we can express invariant properties of the actual parameters (stored in the future objects).

5 The Proof System

The proof system consists of rules for proving that a local pre/postcondition specification $\{p\}s\{q\}$ is correct with respect to a global invariant I and a set of monitor invariants. Here p and q are *local* assertions which only use expressions that refer to the local state of an object via `this`; i.e., its fields and the local variables of one of its methods. Such assertions describe local properties of an object; i.e., properties which are invariant over the executions of the other objects. The global invariant describes invariant properties of the future objects, which form the shared data structure that models the (asynchronous) interaction between objects. The global invariant only refers to the future objects and their fields, and as such is only affected by operations on futures. Monitor invariants are local assertions associated with `await` statements that describe local properties of an object which hold whenever the (associated) `await` statement is scheduled.

In order to reason about statements involving futures, i.e., the basic statements $r := e!m(\overline{e})$, $v := r.\texttt{get}$, and $\texttt{await}\ r?$, we encode their operational semantics as described in detail below. This encoding allows the application of a (standard) weakest precondition calculus (as described by the first author [6], which takes into account aliasing and object creation).

The following proof rule derives the local specification of an asynchronous method invocation: $r := e!m(\bar{e})$:

$$\frac{\{p \wedge I\}r := \texttt{new Future\_C\_m}(e, \bar{e})\{q \wedge I\}}{\{p\}r := e!m(\bar{e})\{q\}}$$

The premise of this rule is a specification which additionally establishes invariance of the global invariant I over the statement $r := \texttt{new Future\_C\_m}(e, \bar{e})$. This statement consists of a call to the constructor method of the class `Future_C_m`, uniquely determined by the method m. This constructor method initializes the newly created future object such that $fds = \texttt{callee} \mapsto e, \overline{\texttt{arg}} \mapsto \bar{e}, \texttt{mode} \mapsto \texttt{s}, \texttt{val} \mapsto \texttt{null}$, encoding the reduction rule (Red-Call). As a simple example, the above assertion $z.\texttt{mode} = \texttt{c} \rightarrow z.\texttt{v} > 0$ is invariant because the value of `mode` of the newly created object is set to `s`.

The local specification of $v := r.\texttt{get}$ is captured by the following proof rule, corresponding to reduction rule (Red-Get):

$$\frac{\{p \wedge r.\texttt{mode} = \texttt{c} \wedge I\}v := r.\texttt{val}\{q \wedge I\}}{\{p\}v := r.\texttt{get}\{q\}}$$

The precondition of the premise additionally requires that the future r is indeed completed, and thus stores the return value. As an example, the assertion $r.\texttt{mode} = \texttt{c} \rightarrow r.\texttt{v} > 0$ can be used in conjunction with the additional information $r.\texttt{mode} = \texttt{c}$ to establish $v > 0$ as a postcondition to the `get` operation.

The following proof rule captures the specification of a statement `await` r?:

$$\frac{(i \wedge r.\texttt{mode} = \texttt{c} \wedge I) \rightarrow q}{\{i\}\texttt{await}\ r?\{q\}}$$

Here i denotes the monitor invariant (implicitly) associated with the `await` statement. The premise consists of an implication establishing the postcondition in case the return value is stored in the future object r.

The proof rule for deriving a local specification of a method definition is:

$$\frac{\begin{array}{c}\{p \wedge \texttt{this} = \texttt{d.callee} \wedge \texttt{d.mode} = \texttt{s} \wedge I\}\texttt{d.mode} := \texttt{a}; \bar{x} := \texttt{d.}\overline{\texttt{arg}}\{p' \wedge I\} \\ \{p'\}s\{q'\} \\ \{q' \wedge I\}\texttt{d.mode} := \texttt{c}; \texttt{d.val} := e\{q \wedge I\}\end{array}}{\{p\}s; \texttt{return}\ e\{q\}}$$

Here we denote by `d` the (distinguished) destiny variable of the method used to denote its future object. The rule establishes the invariance of I over the statements for retrieving the arguments to the call and for returning the value of e, encoded as $\texttt{d.mode} := \texttt{a}; \bar{x} := \texttt{d.}\overline{\texttt{arg}}$ and $\texttt{d.mode} := \texttt{c}; \texttt{d.val} := e$, encoding reduction rule (Red-Return). The additional information $\texttt{this} = \texttt{d.callee} \wedge \texttt{d.mode} = \texttt{s}$ ensures that this future object indeed records a sleeping (that is, not yet activated) method call to this callee. Note that in general the invariant I in the first premise will be used to validate the assumptions about the formal parameters expressed by the precondition p' of the method body.

The rules for the remaining statements are now briefly discussed. For example, we have the following assignment axiom $\{p[e/v]\}v := e\{q\}$. Since p and q are local assertions we do not have aliasing. Therefore the substitution $[e/v]$ simply replaces occurrences of v by e, provided e does not involve object creation. Assuming that in local assertions a variable v of type C can only be compared for equality, we can perform a simple contextual analysis of occurrences of v in the case of an assignment $v :=$ `new` $C()$. For example, the assertion $(v = e)[\mathtt{new}/v]$ is false for every expression e (other than v) because e will denote an 'old' object (for details, see [6]). The rules for sequential composition, nondeterministic choice, and the conditional are standard. The rule for the merge statement involves an adaptation of the usual interference freedom test for shared variable concurrency (with the significant simplification that in our setting this test is local to the merge statement).

The proof system is used to prove that a class C maintains a set M of monitor invariants which describe its release points. The verification of these (local) monitor invariants involves a global invariant I and consists of proving that each $i \in M$ is invariant over each method body of C.[1] Formally, for every method body s; `return` e we have to prove that the specification

$$\{i \wedge \mathtt{d}' \neq \mathtt{d}\}s; \mathtt{return}\ e\{i\}$$

is correct with respect to the global invariant I and the following extended monitor invariants of its `await` statements: $i \wedge \mathtt{d}' \neq \mathtt{d} \wedge j$, where $j \in M$ is the monitor invariant of a given `await` statement in s. The additional information $\mathtt{d}' \neq \mathtt{d}$ expresses that we are dealing with two different method invocations, each with its own future represented by their local variables $\mathtt{d}'$ and $\mathtt{d}$.

5.1 Soundness and Completeness

For completeness we need to introduce the usual notion of *auxiliary* variables to validate global synchronization constraints. Auxiliary variables extend the local state of objects in order to record certain observations about internal scheduling, sending a message, setting a return value, and about the method activations themselves. A soundness proof then consists of a straightforward but tedious induction on the length of the computation which *atomically* executes the statements and their associated updates of the auxiliary variables. Conversely, completeness amounts to showing that assertions describing reachable configurations 'follow the rules' of the proof system. These assertions describe the external observable behavior of an object by means of a so-called *communication history variable*, an auxiliary variable which denotes the sequence of generated messages and which is updated by each method call, upon each method activation, and by each return statement. Furthermore, in order to reason about the internal process queue, we introduce a so-called *scheduling history variable*, an auxiliary

[1] To avoid name clashes between the local variables of i and the method body, we assume a variable convention wherein we rename the local variables x of i (and we denote its renamed local variables by x').

variable which records the local state (i.e., the current values of the local variables and the values of the fields) whenever the guard of an `await` statement is evaluated. Together these auxiliary history variables fix the internal computation of an object. This semantic property of these auxiliary variables forms the heart of the completeness proof (due to space limitations details are omitted).

6 Related Work

Futures were devised as a simple means for expressing concurrency in a manner that reduced the dependency on latency by enabling synchronization at the latest possible time. Futures were discovered by Baker and Hewitt in the 70s [14], and later rediscovered by Liskov and Shrira as Promises [20] and by Halstead in the context of MultiLisp [13]. Futures appear in languages like Alice [23], Oz-Mozart [24], Concurrent ML [22], C++ [19] and Java [25], often as libraries. Futures in these languages are essentially the same as in our language.

All implementations associate a future with the asynchronous execution of an expression in a new thread. The future is a placeholder object which is immediately returned to the calling site. From the perspective of the calling site, this placeholder is a read-only structure [21]. In some systems, this placeholder can be explicitly manipulated by the programmer in order to write the resulting data. In many implementations of futures, the placeholder can be accessed in both modes (CML, Alice, Java, C++, etc), though typically the design is such that both interfaces are presented separately — one to the caller and one to the callee. The calculus λ(fut) [21] formalizes this distinction. Programming with promises explicitly is quite low-level, so our language ties writing the resulting value with method call return.

Futures can either be transparent or non-transparent. Transparent futures cannot be explicitly manipulated, the type of the future is the same as the expected result, and accesses made to the future transparently access the result stored in the future, possibly after waiting (e.g., in Multilisp). Non-transparent futures have a separate type to denote the future (e.g., $!T$ is a future of type T), and future objects can be manipulated (e.g., in CML, Alice, Java, C++, and our language). In addition, futures can also be dealt with lazily to give the effect of *call-by-need* computation, by delaying the invocation of the asynchronous computation until the moment when the future is accessed (e.g., in Alice).

Flanagan and Felleisen [10] present different semantic models of futures at various levels of abstraction in terms of an abstract machine. Their goal was to enable optimizations and program analyses. Their language was purely functional in contrast to ours, which is an imperative, object-oriented language.

Caromel, Henrio, and Serpett [4] present an imperative, asynchronous object calculus with transparent futures. Their active objects may have internal passive objects which can be passed between active objects by first deep copying the entire (passive) object graph. We do not provide this feature, which is orthogonal to the issue discussed in this paper. To manage the complexity of reasoning about distributed and concurrent systems, they restrict the language to ensure that reduction is confluent and deterministic, whereas our focus is on preserving object invariants. No proof theory is presented for their calculus.

Actor systems [2] are concurrent processes which communicate exclusively through asynchronous messages. An actor encapsulates its fields, procedures that manipulate the state, and a single thread of control. Our objects are similar to actors, except that our methods return values which are managed by futures, and control can be released at specific points during a method execution. Messages to actors return no result and run to completion before another message can be handled. The lack of return makes programming with actors cumbersome.

Proof systems for actor languages exist [8], but these require explicit structures in the proof rules for reasoning about message queues, which our proof theory avoids. Previous work by the third author [7] on the verification of asynchronous method calls was performed in a language without first-class futures. The paper took a transformational approach by encoding the language into a sequential language with a non-deterministic assignment operator. However, the Hoare rules described only the custom semantics. Various proof systems for monitors exist [12, 15]. Our approach is distinct as we present a novel model of an object that maintains multiple local invariants monitoring its release points and a global invariant that describes its interaction with the other objects via futures. The model is formalized and has a sound and complete proof theory.

7 Discussion and Future Work

We developed a formal model for a distributed, concurrent object-oriented language with asynchronous method calls and futures. The model allows a novel view of concurrent objects as maintainers of multiple local monitor invariants and a global synchronization constraint. Having multiple monitor invariants allows a proper treatment of local process variables. In contrast, monitor invariants in existing models only refer to an object's fields, complicating reasoning about local variables in the context of the non-deterministic scheduling.

Although our language enables polling of futures (*var*? in an `if` statement), which may be used to release the active process to allow flexible internal scheduling in an object, to control interference of local proofs, our proof system restricts polling to guards in `await` statements. We argue that this proof system is significantly simpler than for the proof system for Java, based on previous work of the first author [1]. Java's proof system requires thread variables, and a general interference freedom test due to the arbitrary interleaving of threads.

In fact, one can compare proof theories for various sublanguages of the language presented here. Let us start with a base language without polling and without release points `await`. Thus, `get` is the only operation on futures.

Adding await statements: The language without `await` does not require the two history variables introduced in the completeness of our proof system; the local scheduling history becomes superfluous. This language would have no internal rescheduling, rather it would resemble an actor-based language with futures for managing the returns of asynchronous calls. The `await` statements in our language allow a clear separation of concerns between an object as maintainer of its monitor invariants and as maintainer of the global synchronization constraint. This is clearly reflected in the completeness proof where the monitor invariance only describes the internal scheduling of the `await` statements, whereas the global synchronization constraint expresses the externally observable behavior.

Adding polling to conditionals significantly increases the complexity of the proof system. Interference freedom tests are necessary [1], because the required information about the absence of return values can be invalidated by other objects. In contrast, reasoning about `await` statement with polling only requires information about the presence of reply values, which cannot be invalidated.

This suggests that either the concurrency features of programming languages should be chosen to admit a simple proof system, or that the complexity of programming with such features should be measured in terms of the complexity of their proof system, and that this should be made known to programmers.

Futures are now a part of a programmer's toolbox: Java's `util.concurrent` library supports futures, and futures handle asynchronous calls to web services. To facilitate correct programming, it is important to guide the design of language features using proof theoretical considerations. To properly support language design, both the soundness and completeness of the proof system are paramount.

In the context of the EU IST project Credo we are currently extending the existing Creol implementation [18] with additional rewrite rules for modeling futures.

References

1. E. Ábrahám, F. S. de Boer, W. P. de Roever, and M. Steffen. An assertion-based proof system for multithreaded Java. *TCS*, 331(2-3):251–290, 2005.
2. G. Agha and C. Hewitt. Actors: A conceptual foundation for concurrent object-oriented programming. In *Research Directions in Object-Oriented Programming*, pages 49–74. MIT Press, 1987.
3. P. Brinch Hansen. Java's insecure parallelism. *ACM SIGPLAN Notices*, 34(4): 38–45, Apr. 1999.
4. D. Caromel, L. Henrio, and B. Serpette. Asynchronous and deterministic objects. In *Proceedings of the 31st ACM Symposium on Principles of Programming Languages (POPL'04)*, pages 123–134. ACM Press, 2004.
5. M. Clavel, F. Durán, S. Eker, P. Lincoln, N. Martí-Oliet, J. Meseguer, and J. F. Quesada. Maude: Specification and programming in rewriting logic. *Theoretical Computer Science*, 285:187–243, Aug. 2002.
6. F. S. de Boer. A WP-calculus for OO. In W. Thomas, editor, *Proceedings of Foundations of Software Science and Computation Structure, (FOSSACS'99)*, volume 1578 of *Lecture Notes in Computer Science*, pages 135–149. Springer, 1999.
7. J. Dovland, E. B. Johnsen, and O. Owe. Verification of concurrent objects with asynchronous method calls. In *Proceedings of the IEEE International Conference on Software Science, Technology & Engineering (SwSTE'05)*, pages 141–150. IEEE Computer Society Press, Feb. 2005.
8. C. H. C. Duarte. Proof-theoretic foundations for the design of actor systems. *Mathematical Structures in Computer Science*, 9(3):227–252, 1999.

9. M. Felleisen and R. Hieb. The revised report on the syntactic theories of sequential control and state. *Theoretical Computer Science*, 103(2):235–271, 1992.
10. C. Flanagan and M. Felleisen. The semantics of future and an application. *J. Funct. Program.*, 9(1):1–31, 1999.
11. M. Flatt, S. Krishnamurthi, and M. Felleisen. A programmer's reduction semantics for classes and mixins. In *Formal Syntax and Semantics of Java*, volume 1523 of *Lecture Notes in Computer Science*, pages 241–269. Springer, 1999.
12. R. Gerth and W. P. de Roever. A proof system for concurrent ada programs. *Sci. Comput. Program.*, 4(2):159–204, 1984.
13. R. H. Halstead Jr. Multilisp: A language for concurrent symbolic computation. *ACM Transactions on Programming Languages and Systems*, 7(4):501–538, 1985.
14. B. Henry G., Jr. and C. Hewitt. The incremental garbage collection of processes. In *Proceeding of the Symposium on Artificial Intelligence Programming Languages*, number 12 in SIGPLAN Notices, page 11, August 1977.
15. C. A. R. Hoare. Monitors: An operating system structuring concept. *Commun. ACM*, 17(10):549–557, 1974.
16. A. Igarashi, B. C. Pierce, and P. Wadler. Featherweight Java: a minimal core calculus for Java and GJ. *ACM Transactions on Programming Languages and Systems*, 23(3):396–450, 2001.
17. International Telecommunication Union. Open Distributed Processing — Reference Model parts 1–4. Technical report, ISO/IEC, Geneva, July 1995.
18. E. B. Johnsen, O. Owe, and I. C. Yu. Creol: A type-safe object-oriented model for distributed concurrent systems. *Theoretical Computer Science*, 365(1–2):23–66, Nov. 2006.
19. R. G. Lavender and D. C. Schmidt. Active object: an object behavioral pattern for concurrent programming. *Proc. Pattern Languages of Programs*, 1995.
20. B. H. Liskov and L. Shrira. Promises: Linguistic support for efficient asynchronous procedure calls in distributed systems. In D. S. Wise, editor, *Proceedings of the SIGPLAN Conference on Programming Lanugage Design and Implementation (PLDI'88)*, pages 260–267, Atlanta, GE, USA, June 1988. ACM Press.
21. J. Niehren, J. Schwinghammer, and G. Smolka. A concurrent lambda calculus with futures. *Theoretical Computer Science*, 364:338–356, 2006.
22. J. H. Reppy. *Concurrent Programming in ML*. Cambridge University Press, 1999.
23. A. Rossberg, D. L. Botlan, G. Tack, T. Brunklaus, and G. Smolka. *Alice Through the Looking Glass*, volume 5 of *Trends in Functional Programming*, pages 79–96. Intellect Books, Bristol, UK, ISBN 1-84150144-1, Munich, Germany, Feb. 2006.
24. P. Van Roy and S. Haridi. *Concepts, Techniques, and Models of Computer Programming*. MIT Press, Mar. 2004.
25. A. Welc, S. Jagannathan, and A. Hosking. Safe futures for Java. In *Proceedings of the 20th annual ACM SIGPLAN conference on Object oriented programming, systems, languages, and applications (OOPSLA'05)*, pages 439–453, New York, NY, USA, 2005. ACM Press.
26. A. Yonezawa, J.-P. Briot, and E. Shibayama. Object-oriented concurrent programming in ABCL/1. In *Conference on Object-Oriented Programming Systems, Languages and Applications (OOPSLA'86). Sigplan Notices*, 21(11):258–268, Nov. 1986.

The Java Memory Model: Operationally, Denotationally, Axiomatically

Pietro Cenciarelli[1], Alexander Knapp[2], and Eleonora Sibilio[1]

[1] Dipartimento di Informatica, Università di Roma "La Sapienza"
{cenciarelli,sibilio}@di.uniroma1.it
[2] Institut für Informatik, Ludwig-Maximilians-Universität München
knapp@pst.ifi.lmu.de

Abstract. A semantics to a small fragment of Java capturing the new memory model (JMM) described in the Language Specification is given by combining operational, denotational and axiomatic techniques in a novel semantic framework. The operational steps (specified in the form of SOS) construct denotational models (configuration structures) and are constrained by the axioms of a configuration theory. The semantics is proven correct with respect to the Language Specification and shown to capture many common examples in the JMM literature.

1 Introduction

Two processes P and Q operating in parallel compete for a lock on shared data. The structure $\mathcal{A}$ shown in Fig. 1 models the parallel composition $P \mid Q$, where P executes *lock*; ... *unlock*; and the same does Q. The identifiers *lock* and *lock*′ represent *events* occurring in computation, namely the execution of a "lock" action respectively by P and Q. Similarly for *unlock* and *unlock*′.

Sets of events, called *configurations* and depicted here as rounded squares surrounding their elements, represent consistent states of computation. The {*unlock*, *lock*} configuration, for example, represents the state reached by the system after having performed a lock action *first* and then an unlock (while Q remains dormant). We know the lock came first because we see a {*lock*} subconfiguration but not an {*unlock*}. Note that there is no configuration {*lock*, *lock*′} and this represents the *mutual exclusion* of the two processes from the shared resource.

Structures as those depicted in Fig. 1 are called *configuration structures* [1], a denotational model introduced by Winskel as an alternative presentation of (prime) *event structures* [2]. Several closure conditions have been proposed over the years to make

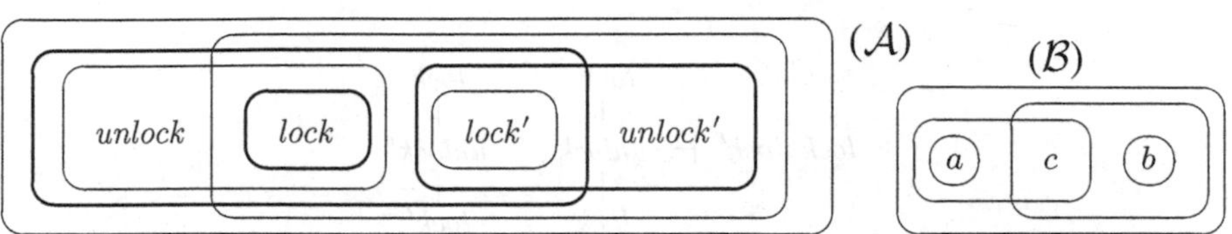

Fig. 1. Configuration structures

R. De Nicola (Ed.): ESOP 2007, LNCS 4421, pp. 331–346, 2007.

configuration structures mathematically tractable. In [3] van Glabbeek and Goltz characterise the class of configuration structures where the *causal dependency* between events can be faithfully represented by means of partial orders. Such *stable* structures are required to be closed under bounded unions and bounded intersections. Stable structures possess useful semantic properties; e.g., when a state C is part of the "history" of a state D, then D is reachable from C by a sequence of atomic steps of computation.

Unfortunately, many structures naturally arising in the semantics of concurrent systems are not stable; $\mathcal{A}$, for instance, is not. More general structures than the stable have been studied in the literature [4,5,6,7]. The *monotone* configuration structures of [6], e.g., (of which $\mathcal{A}$ is one) are those where causal dependency is preserved by inclusion of configurations, indeed a minimal requirement for monotonic reasoning about states of computation. However, consider an easy program where two threads both assign the value 42 to x (call a and b these events) while a third thread reads this value from x (event c). The corresponding structure, $\mathcal{B}$ in Fig. 1, is *not* monotone. So, a (provocative) question arises: *what are algebraically neat event-based models good for?*

The present paper advocates the usefulness of event based models by proposing a new semantic framework which combines denotational, operational and axiomatic techniques to challenge the *Java memory model.* The current definition of the Java memory model (JMM) [8] is still much driven by informal examples and, while the key ideas are understood within the community, there is a lack of rigour for mechanised reasoning. In our opinion, the reason of this is that, while the Java memory model and its run time semantics are largely independent, no formal account has been given as yet of their interplay. The notion of *execution*, introduced in the language specification as formal basis to the former, is not clearly related with the latter, in that executions may specify values being read or written which no single run of the program may be able to produce collectively. Hence, executions must be *validated* by a complicated procedure involving *tentative* executions, each validating the commitment of certain actions, but each relying on different assumptions as to the values being read or written by uncommitted actions. The connection with run time semantics is informally given by the statement that "executions should obey intra-thread consistency" [9, 4.4, clause 5].

In this paper we change perspective with respect to the language specification and propose an axiomatisation of the JMM based on the notion of *causality*, deriving from denotational semantics, rather than on the *happens-before* relation, upon which the abstract executions of [8] rely. We propose a formal framework where *structural operational semantics*, describing program evaluation, interacts with a *configuration theory*, describing the causal interplay of memory and threads.

Configuration theories were proposed in [6] as an axiomatic approach to the semantics of concurrent systems and are further developed here to capture mutual exclusion.

$$
\mathit{lock}\ \ \mathit{lock}' \vdash \begin{array}{c} \mathit{lock}' \\ | \\ \mathit{unlock} \\ | \\ \mathit{lock} \end{array} \ , \ \begin{array}{c} \mathit{lock} \\ | \\ \mathit{unlock}' \\ | \\ \mathit{lock}' \end{array}
$$

Fig. 2. Poset sequent for mutual exclusion

A configuration theory is a set of *poset sequents* which is closed under deduction. A poset sequent is made of partially ordered sets (posets) of events, where the order is interpreted as causal dependency. The sequent depicted in Fig. 2 (where order is represented by the vertical bars, with time pointing upward) spells roughly: "whenever two *lock* actions occur in a computation, they must occur sequentially, and moreover there must be an *unlock* action in between." As one would expect, this sequent is satisfied by structure $\mathcal{A}$, but not by the structure obtained by adding the configuration $\{lock, lock'\}$ to it, which violates mutual exclusion (see discussion in Sect. 3).

After developing the mathematics of configuration theories (Sect. 2 and 3), we present six poset sequents like the above axiomatising the JMM from the point of view of causal dependency (Sect. 4). The resulting configuration theory constrains the rules of a structural operational semantics for the minimal fragment of Java which is relevant for understanding the memory model (Sect. 5). Our semantics is then proven correct with respect to the Java language specification of [8, §17] (Sect. 6).

2 Stable Structures as Traces

A *set system* consists of a set E and a collection $\mathcal{A}$ of subsets of E [5]. If $A \in \mathcal{A}$ we write $sub(A)$ the set $\{B \in \mathcal{A} \mid B \subseteq A\}$. If $A, B \in sub(C)$ for some $C \in \mathcal{A}$ we say that A and B are *bound* in $\mathcal{A}$. The sets in a system $\mathcal{A}$ are called *configurations* when used for modelling a concurrent system, while the elements of the set $|\mathcal{A}| = \bigcup \mathcal{A}$ are called *events*. If $B \in \mathcal{A}$ and $A \in sub(B)$, then A is called a *subconfiguration* of B. A *labelled configuration structure* [5] is a structure $\mathcal{C}$ endowed by a labelling function $\lambda : |\mathcal{C}| \to Act$, where Act is a fixed set of labels called *actions*.

In [4] several closure conditions on the set of configurations of a structure $\mathcal{A}$ are given in order to get a precise match with *general event structures* (generalising those of [2]). They are: *finiteness* (if an event belongs to a configuration A, then it also belongs to a finite subconfiguration of A), *coincidence-freeness* (if two distinct events belong to a configuration A, then there exists a subconfiguration of A containing exactly one of them), closure under *bounded unions* and *non-emptiness* of $\mathcal{A}$. We call *configuration structures* (or just *structures*), and write them $\mathcal{C}, \mathcal{D}, \ldots$, the set systems satisfying all of the above requirements, *except* closure under bounded unions (this is not standard in literature). If $\mathcal{C} \subseteq \mathcal{D}$, we call $\mathcal{C}$ a *sub-structure* of $\mathcal{D}$, and $\mathcal{D}$ an *extension* of $\mathcal{C}$.

Coincidence-freeness endows each configuration C with a *canonical* partial order: $a \leq_C b$ iff, for all $D \in sub(C)$, $b \in D$ implies $a \in D$. This relation is called *causal dependency*. Two events $a, b \in C$ are said to be *concurrent* in C, written $a \diamond_C b$, when neither $a \leq_C b$ nor $b \leq_C a$ hold.

A structure $\mathcal{C}$ is called *connected* if, for all configurations $C \neq \emptyset$, there exists $a \in C$ such that $C \setminus \{a\} \in \mathcal{C}$. Clearly connectedness implies coincidence freeness and moreover, having assumed $\mathcal{C}$ nonempty and finitary, it also implies that $\emptyset \in \mathcal{C}$ (*rootedness*). Following [3] we call *stable* a configuration structure which is connected, closed under nonempty bounded unions and nonempty bounded intersections. Stability was introduced for *event structures* in [4]. Stable structures are precisely those where the order on a configuration determines its subconfigurations (see [3, Prop. 5.4 and Thm 5.2]). Below we establish a precise correspondence between certain stable configuration structures and *Mazurkiewicz traces*. The result motivates the use of stability as means for abstracting computations over concurrent actions.

Given a string s over a set S, we write $|s|$ the subset of elements of S occurring in s. A *path* over a set S is a string s of elements of S, none of which is repeated. If C is a configuration of a structure $\mathcal{C}$, we call *admissible* a path s over C such that $|u| \in \mathcal{C}$ for all prefixes u of s. We write $\simeq_C$ the smallest equivalence relation on the paths of C such that $uabv \simeq_C ubav$ if $a \diamond_C b$. A *trace* in C is an equivalence class of $\simeq_C$ in which all paths are admissible. The set of all traces $[s]_{\simeq_C}$ such that $|s| = C$ is denoted by $Tr(C)$. Note that the traces of all configurations in an *event structure* form a *Mazurkiewicz trace language* (see [10] for detail), and the construction can be shown to be the object map of an embedding (a *co-reflection*) of the category of event structures into that of trace languages [10, Cor. 39].

Theorem 1. *Let C be a configuration in a structure $\mathcal{C}$. There exists a one-to-one correspondence between the traces in $Tr(C)$ and the stable substructures $\mathcal{D}$ of $\mathcal{C}$ such that $C \in \mathcal{D} \subseteq sub(C)$, and moreover no other such substructure of $\mathcal{C}$ extends $\mathcal{D}$ properly.*

Proof. Let $[s]_{\simeq}$ be a trace in $Tr(C)$. We show that the set $\mathcal{D}$ of configurations of the form $|r|$, where r is a prefix of some path in $[s]_{\simeq}$, is stable. $\mathcal{D}$ is clearly rooted and connected. It is also closed under bounded unions. In fact, let $|u|$ and $|v|$ be configurations in $\mathcal{D}$, and let r_1 and r_2 be paths in $[s]_{\simeq}$, with u a prefix of r_1 and v of r_2. If v is empty the result holds trivially. Otherwise, let $v = av'$. Writing r_1 as waw', a must be independent of each event in w. Hence, $r_1 \simeq aww'$, and moreover the latter has a prefix u_1 such that $|u_1| = |u| \cup \{a\}$. By iterating the argument, all events in v can be pushed towards the front of r_1 to obtain a path in $[s]_{\simeq}$ with a prefix u_n such that $|u_n| = |u| \cup |v|$. Hence, $\mathcal{D}$ is stable, the argument for bounded intersections being similar to the above. Conversely, let $\mathcal{D}$ satisfy the stated conditions. It is easy to show that the set of paths r in C such that $|r| = C$ and $|u| \in \mathcal{D}$, for all prefixes u of r, is a trace in $Tr(C)$. This construction is inverse to the above. □

In view of the above result, we shall call *traces* of a configuration C in a structure $\mathcal{C}$ all the stable substructures of $\mathcal{C}$ satisfying the conditions of Thm. 1. The following result is used in Def. 2.

Proposition 1. *Let $\mathcal{D}$ and $\mathcal{E}$ be traces, respectively of D and E, in a structure, and let $\mathcal{D} \subseteq \mathcal{E}$. The inclusion map of D in E, written $D \hookrightarrow E$, is monotone with respect to the order induced by $\mathcal{D}$ and $\mathcal{E}$.*

Proof. Let $a \leq_D b$ and suppose $a \not\leq_E b$. There exists $A \in \mathcal{E}$ such that $b \in A \not\ni a$. Then $\mathcal{D} \not\ni D \cap A \in \mathcal{E}$. Clearly, $\{C \in \mathcal{E} \mid C \subseteq D\} \subseteq sub(D)$ is a stable substructure of $\mathcal{C}$ which includes $\mathcal{D}$ *properly* (as it contains $D \cap A$), and hence $\mathcal{D}$ is not maximal, against the assumptions. □

3 Sequents of Partial Maps

Notation. We write $f : A \rightharpoonup B$ to denote a *partial* function from A to B, and say that the expression $f(a)$ *denotes* (an element of B) when f is defined on $a \in A$. If e_1 and

e_2 are expressions as above involving partial functions, we write $e_1 = e_2$ when e_1 and e_2 denote the same element. When A and B are posets, we call $f : A \rightharpoonup B$ *monotone* if, when $f(a)$ and $f(b)$ both denote, $a \leq b$ implies $f(a) \leq f(b)$. (A different notion is usually adopted in domain theory, where the order represents approximation rather than causal dependency.) For partial maps f and g we write $f \sqsubseteq g$, if $f(x) = g(x)$ whenever $f(x)$ is defined. We use $\Gamma, \Delta, \ldots$ to denote sequences of posets, and write Γ_i the i-th component of Γ. The concatenation of two sequences Γ and Δ is written Γ, Δ. If $\Gamma = A_1, \ldots, A_m$ and $\Delta = B_1, \ldots, B_n$ are finite sequences of posets, we write $\rho : \Gamma \rightharpoonup \Delta$ to mean that ρ is an $m \times n$-matrix of monotone *injective* partial functions $\rho_{ij} : A_i \rightharpoonup B_j$. Given two matrices α and β of the form $\Gamma \rightharpoonup \Delta$, we write $\alpha \sqsubseteq \beta$ when $\alpha_{ij} \sqsubseteq \beta_{ij}$, for all i and j. Function composition is written in diagrammatical order.

Definition 1. *A poset sequent $\Gamma \vdash_\rho \Delta$ (or just* sequent*) consists of two finite sequences Γ and Δ of posets and a matrix $\rho : \Gamma \rightharpoonup \Delta$ of monotone injective partial functions.*

The posets in a sequent are meant to represent fragments of a configuration. The intuitive meaning of a sequent $\Gamma \vdash_\rho \Delta$ is that whenever a trace interprets *all* components of Γ, the interpretation extends along ρ to *at least one* component of Δ. Of course the Δ_i may include events that are not mentioned in Γ, thus specifying what is required to happen after, or must have happened before, a certain combination (Γ) of events. We write just ρ for a sequent $\Gamma \vdash_\rho \Delta$ when Γ and Δ are understood or not relevant. On the other hand, we may omit ρ when obvious from the labelling conventions.

Sequents predicate over traces. Let C be a configuration of a structure $\mathcal{C}$; by a slight abuse, we speak of a *trace* C to mean a trace $\mathcal{D}$ of C in $\mathcal{C}$. In such a case we intend C as endowed with the partial order induced by the configurations in $\mathcal{D}$. We call *interpretation* of a sequence Γ of m posets in a trace C an $m \times 1$-matrix $\Gamma \rightharpoonup C$ whose components are *total*.

Definition 2. *A structure $\mathcal{C}$ is said to* satisfy *a sequent $\Gamma \vdash_\rho \Delta$ when, for any trace C in $\mathcal{C}$ and interpretation $\pi : \Gamma \rightharpoonup C$, there exist a trace D extending C, a component $\Delta_k \in \Delta$ and a monotone injective total function $q : \Delta_k \to D$ such that $\rho_{ik} q \sqsubseteq \pi_i u$ for all i, where $u : C \hookrightarrow D$ is the inclusion.*

A *labelled sequent* ρ is one in which the elements of posets are assigned labels from Act and the maps in ρ preserve them. Definition 2 extends to labelled sequents and structures by requiring that interpretation maps preserve labels.

A pathological kind of sequent is $\vdash$, which features empty sequences as antecedent and succedent, and is decorated by the empty matrix. Under the assumption that structures are not empty, this sequents denotes the *absurd*. A sequent of the form $\vdash A$ is satisfied by structures in which every trace is bound to produce a configuration matching A. Similarly the sequent $A \vdash$ is satisfied by structures in which no configuration ever matches A.

The formal system of poset sequents introduced in [6] featured inference rules mimicking the structural rules of Gentzen's sequent calculus. The differences with the present work are in the kind of maps decorating the sequents (total in [6], partial here) and in the notion of interpretation (quantifying over configurations vs. traces). Partial maps yield a stronger system, in which the old rules are derivable. The sequent $a \vdash a\,b$, for example, is now derivable from $a \vdash \begin{smallmatrix} b \\ \mid \\ a \end{smallmatrix}$, while it was previously not, although the former holds in any structure satisfying the latter. The metatheory is also more compact, featuring four rules against ten, and a general *cut* rule, which was previously split into left and right rules. On the other hand, interpreting over traces allows us to axiomatise *mutual exclusion*, as with the lock/unlock example, which could not be captured in the old system. In fact, consider the labelled structure $\mathcal{A}$ in Fig. 1, where we assume $\lambda(lock) = \lambda(lock')$ and $\lambda(unlock) = \lambda(unlock')$, and let $\mathcal{A}'$ be the structure obtained from $\mathcal{A}$ by adding the configuration $\{lock, lock'\}$ (no mutual exclusion!). In both structures the configuration $C = \{lock, unlock, lock', unlock'\}$ is endowed with the ordering $lock \leq unlock$, $lock' \leq unlock'$. Hence, had we defined satisfaction by quantifying over configurations rather than on traces, the axiom in Fig. 2 would be satisfied by neither structures. However, while $\mathcal{A}'$ only has one trace on C (viz. $\mathcal{A}'$ itself), featuring the same order as above, $\mathcal{A}$ has two: $\{lock \leq unlock \leq lock' \leq unlock'\}$ and $\{lock' \leq unlock' \leq lock \leq unlock\}$. Hence, in the current development, $\mathcal{A}$ satisfies the axiom while $\mathcal{A}'$ does not, as expected.

The following lemmas are used to prove the soundness of our inference system of poset sequents (Fig. 3).

Let $\Gamma = \Gamma_1, \ldots, \Gamma_n$ and $\Delta = \Delta_1, \ldots, \Delta_m$ be vectors of posets; a *covariant map* from Γ to Δ consists of a function $f : \{1, \ldots, n\} \to \{1, \ldots, m\}$ on indices, and a family of (total) monos $\psi_i : \Gamma_i \rightarrowtail \Delta_{f(i)}$. We write $(f, \psi) : \Gamma \stackrel{\geq}{\longmapsto} \Delta$ such a map, shortening (f, ψ) as f when no confusion arises. A *contravariant map* $(f, \psi) : \Gamma \stackrel{\leq}{\longmapsto} \Delta$ is defined just as above, except for $f : \{1, \ldots, m\} \to \{1, \ldots, n\}$ mapping the indices of Δ to those of Γ, and the ψ_i being of the form $\Gamma_{f(i)} \rightarrowtail \Delta_i$. A matrix $\sigma : \Gamma \rightharpoonup \Sigma$ is called *right extension* of a matrix $\rho : \Gamma \rightharpoonup \Delta$ when there exists a contravariant map $(f, \psi) : \Sigma \stackrel{\leq}{\longmapsto} \Delta$ such that $\sigma_{jf(i)}\psi_i \sqsubseteq \rho_{ji}$, for all i, j; in such a case we write $\sigma \in rex(\rho)$.

Lemma 1. *Let $\sigma \in rex(\rho)$; if a structure satisfies ρ, then it satisfies σ.*

Proof. Let a structure $\mathcal{C}$ satisfy $\rho : \Gamma \rightharpoonup \Delta$, let $\sigma : \Gamma \rightharpoonup \Sigma$ be in $rex(\rho)$ by $(f, \psi) : \Sigma \stackrel{\leq}{\longmapsto} \Delta$, and let $\pi : \Gamma \to C \in \mathcal{C}$ be an interpretation of Γ in $\mathcal{C}$. Since $\mathcal{C}$ satisfies ρ there exists an inclusion $u : C \hookrightarrow D$ of C in a configuration D and, for some k, a map $q : \Delta_k \to D$ such that $\rho_{ik} q \sqsubseteq \pi_i u$, for all i. Then, $\sigma_{if(k)}\psi_k q \sqsubseteq \rho_{ik} q \sqsubseteq \pi_i u$. □

The left composition of a matrix $\sigma : \Sigma \rightharpoonup \Delta$ with a covariant map $(f, \psi) : \Gamma \stackrel{\geq}{\longmapsto} \Sigma$ is the matrix $f\sigma : \Gamma \rightharpoonup \Delta$ where $(f\sigma)_{ij}(a) = \sigma_{f(i)j}(\psi_i(a))$. A *left Kan extension* of a matrix $\rho : \Gamma \rightharpoonup \Delta$ *along a covariant map* $(f, \psi) : \Gamma \stackrel{\geq}{\longmapsto} \Sigma$ is a matrix $\hat{\rho} : \Sigma \rightharpoonup \Delta$ such that $\rho \sqsubseteq f\hat{\rho}$, and moreover $\hat{\rho} \sqsubseteq \sigma$ holds for all $\sigma : \Sigma \rightharpoonup \Delta$ such that $\rho \sqsubseteq f\sigma$. It is easy to check that, when the ψ_i are *strong*, such a $\hat{\rho}$ exists iff, whenever $f(i) = f(j)$, $\psi_i(a') = \psi_j(a'')$ iff $\rho_{ik}(a') = \rho_{jk}(a'')$. In such a case $\hat{\rho}_{hk}(a)$ is $\rho_{jk}(a')$ when j and a' exist such that $h = f(j)$ and $a = \psi_j(a')$; otherwise $\hat{\rho}_{hk}(a)$ is undefined. Note that the above definition of $\hat{\rho}$ does correspond to the categorical notion of left Kan extension [11, 10.3] in a precise sense. A matrix $\sigma : \Sigma \rightharpoonup \Delta$ is called *left extension* of a matrix $\rho : \Gamma \rightharpoonup \Delta$ when ρ has a left Kan extension $\hat{\rho}$ along some map $\Gamma \stackrel{\geq}{\longmapsto} \Sigma$ and $\sigma \sqsubseteq \hat{\rho}$; in such a case we write $\sigma \in lex(\rho)$.

$$[\text{true}]\ \frac{}{\vdash \emptyset} \qquad [\text{incl}]\ \frac{}{A \vdash_{\phi^{-1}} B}\ (\phi : B \rightarrowtail A \text{ is strong})$$

$$[\text{sub}]\ \frac{\Gamma \vdash_\rho \Delta}{\Sigma \vdash_\sigma \Pi}\ \sigma \le \rho \qquad [\text{cut}]\ \frac{\Gamma \vdash_{\tau,\rho} A, \Delta \quad \Sigma, A \vdash_{\sigma;\pi} \Pi}{\Gamma, \Sigma \vdash_{(\rho;\emptyset),(\tau\pi;\sigma)} \Delta, \Pi}$$

Fig. 3. Inference rules

Lemma 2. *Let $\sigma \in lex(\rho)$; if a structure satisfies ρ, then it satisfies σ.*

Proof. Let structure $\mathcal{C}$ satisfy $\rho : \Gamma \rightarrow \Delta$, let $\hat{\rho}$ be a Kan extension of ρ along $(f, \psi) : \Gamma \overset{>}{\longmapsto} \Sigma$, let $\sigma \sqsubseteq \hat{\rho}$ and let $\pi : \Sigma \rightarrow C \in \mathcal{C}$ be an interpretation of Σ in $\mathcal{C}$. The interpretation $f\pi$ yields a configuration $C \subseteq D \in \mathcal{C}$ and a map $q : \Delta_k \rightarrow D$ such that $\rho_{ik} q \sqsubseteq \psi_i \pi_{f(i)k} u$, where $u : C \rightarrow D$ is the inclusion. Then, $\sigma \sqsubseteq \hat{\rho}$ yields $\sigma q \sqsubseteq \pi u$. □

Figure 3 shows rule schemes for deriving poset sequents. Rule [sub] makes use of a preorder $\le$ over sequents defined to be the smallest transitive relation where $\sigma \le \rho$ when σ is either in $lex(\rho)$ or in $rex(\rho)$. In the [cut] rule two operations (comma and semi-colon) are used to compose matrices. If ρ and σ are matrices of size $m \times n$ and $r \times n$ respectively, we write $(\rho; \sigma)$ for the $(m + r) \times n$ matrix obtained by "placing ρ above σ": the ij-component of $(\rho; \sigma)$ is ρ_{ij} for $i \le m$, while it is $\sigma_{(i-m)j}$ when $i > m$. Similarly, if ρ and σ are of size $m \times n$ and $m \times r$, we write (ρ, σ) for the $m \times (n + r)$ matrix obtained by "placing ρ to the left of σ": the ij-component of (ρ, σ) is ρ_{ij} for $j \le n$, while it is $\sigma_{i(j-n)}$ when $j > n$. Finally, let τ and π be respectively a $n \times 1$ column vector and a $1 \times m$ row vector. Then, $\tau\pi$ stands for the $n \times m$ matricial *product* of the two, where $(\tau\pi)_{ij}$ is the composite map $\Gamma_i \xrightarrow{\tau_i} A \xrightarrow{\pi_j} \Pi_j$. By $\emptyset$ we mean a matrix (of suitable size) whose components are the always undefined partial functions.

Definition 3. *A* configuration theory *is a set of sequents which is closed under the rule schemes of Fig. 3.*

Theorem 2. *The rules of Fig. 3 are sound.*

The proof is almost immediate for all the rules except for [sub], where it follows from Lemmas 1 and 2. Completeness can also be obtained by adjoining to the rules of Fig. 3 the [extend] rule of [6, 5]. This is however out of the scope of the present paper.

4 A Configuration Theory of Java

We present a configuration theory specifying the rules by which events of a Java computation may depend on each other.

Let *Var*, *Mon* and *Tid* denote disjoint countable sets, respectively of program variables (ranged over by $x, y, \ldots$), monitors ($m, \ldots$) and thread identifiers ($\theta, \zeta, \xi, \ldots$). The *actions* of the theory of Java are either of the form (H, θ, x, v), where $H \in \{R, W\}$ and v is a value, or of the form (K, θ, m), with $K \in \{L, U\}$. Actions (H, θ, x, v), called *memory actions*, represent the *reading* (R) of a value v from the variable x by a thread θ, or the assignment (W for *writing*) of v to x by θ, while actions of the form (K, θ, m),

$$1)\quad a\ b \vdash \begin{array}{c} a \\ | \\ b \end{array}, \begin{array}{c} b \\ | \\ a \end{array} \qquad \begin{array}{ll} \text{1a)} & a = (\theta, x, v),\ b = (\theta, x, w) \\ \text{1b)} & a = (\theta, x, v),\ b = (\theta, m) \\ \text{1c)} & a = (\zeta, m),\ b = (\theta, m) \end{array}$$

$$2)\quad (R,\theta,x,v) \vdash \begin{array}{c} (R,\theta,x,v) \\ | \\ (W,\zeta,x,v) \end{array} \qquad 3)^{\star*}\quad \begin{array}{c} (R,\theta,x,v) \\ | \\ (W,\theta,x,w) \end{array} \vdash \begin{array}{c} (R,\theta,x,v) \\ | \\ (W,\theta,x,v) \\ | \\ (W,\theta,x,w) \end{array}, \begin{array}{c} (R,\theta,x,v) \\ | \\ (W,\zeta,x,v) \end{array}$$

$$4)^{\star*}\quad \begin{array}{ccc} (R,\theta,x,v) & & \\ | & \dots & | \\ A_1 & & A_n \end{array} \vdash B_1, \dots, B_n, \begin{array}{c} (R,\theta,x,v) \\ | \\ (W,\xi,x,v) \end{array} \text{ where } \begin{array}{c} (L,\theta,m_i) \\ | \\ A_i = (U,\zeta_i,m_i) \\ | \\ (W,\zeta_i,x,w_i) \end{array} \text{ and } \begin{array}{c} (R,\theta,x,v) \\ | \\ B_i = (W,\zeta_i,x,v) \\ | \\ (W,\zeta_i,x,w_i) \end{array}$$

$$5)\quad (U,\theta,m)^n \vdash \begin{array}{c} (U,\theta,m)^n \\ | \\ (L,\theta,m)^n \end{array} \qquad 6)^{*}\quad \begin{array}{c} (L,\theta,m) \\ | \\ (L,\zeta,m)^n \end{array} \vdash \begin{array}{c} (L,\theta,m) \\ | \\ (U,\zeta,m)^n \end{array}$$

($\star$) $v \neq w, w_i$ for all i
($*$) $\theta \neq \zeta, \zeta_i$ for all i

Fig. 4. The configuration theory of Java

called *synchronisations*, represent the *locking* (L) or the *unlocking* (U) of a monitor m by θ. When H and K are irrelevant, (H, θ, x, v) and (K, θ, m) are shortened respectively as (θ, x, v) and (θ, m). Other action component may be similarly omitted when not relevant. Events are labelled by actions. We write $e : l$ to mean that event e has label l. When no confusion arises, we use actions to denote the events of which they are labels. We do so in Fig. 4.

Figure 4 shows the axiom schemes of our configuration theory of Java. The ρ in a sequent $\Gamma \vdash_\rho \Delta$ is left implicit by convening that an event $e : A$ in Γ_i is mapped by ρ_{ij} to one with the same label A in Δ_j, in lack of which $\rho_{ij}(e)$ is undefined.

Scheme 1 describes how the different kinds of actions are to be ordered in legal program executions, according to the Java memory model [8, §17]. All memory actions of one thread over a same variable must be totally ordered (1a), while all synchronisations of a thread over a monitor must be ordered with the memory actions of that thread (1b) and with the synchronisations of other threads over the same monitor (1c).

Schemes 2, 3 and 4 specify how threads are allowed to read values from the shared memory. Any value being read by a thread θ from a variable x must have been previously assigned to x by a *possibly* different thread (2). If θ reads its own assignment, then it must be the most recent one (3), while, if it is a value assigned by another thread ζ, it must be the most recent only if θ and ζ synchronised over the same monitor (4).

Schemes 5 and 6 describe synchronisation. By a^n we mean a poset of n a-labelled events $a_1, \dots, a_n$, with the discrete ordering, while $\begin{array}{c} b^n \\ | \\ a^n \end{array}$ denotes the poset $a^n \cup b^n$ where $a_i \leq b_i$, for all i. Then, scheme 5 says that any unlock action must be paired with a preceding lock by the same thread, while 6 guarantees, in combination with 5, that locks are granted to one thread at a time.

5 An Event-Based Semantics of Java

The axioms are used to constrain the applicability of the operational rules: semantic configurations of events, labelled as in Sect. 4, are included as part of the *operational* configurations, and each time the semantics reduces a Java term an event is added to (and causal dependencies recorded in) the current semantic configuration, *provided* this complies with the specified theory. Thus, operational semantics builds a denotational model of the program (see discussion in Sect. 7). However, events may also be added to the semantic configurations *presciently* (by rule [pre] in Tab. 1), that is before the corresponding reduction is performed, and only later *fulfilled* by the execution engine. Hence, semantic configurations are also equipped with a *fulfilment predicate* $(\_)!$ on write events. Intuition is that $(W)!$ holds in η precisely when (W) has been fulfilled by program evaluation. More formally: configurations of events are called *event spaces* (and ranged over by $\eta, \zeta, \ldots$) when viewed as part of operational configurations. Mathematically an event space is just a poset equipped with a fulfilment predicate and satisfying the axioms of Fig. 4. By that we mean that it does when viewed as the (stable) structure whose configurations are its downward closed subsets.

By using prescient actions, threads may read values from the shared memory which have not yet been assigned to the corresponding variable. As predicated in the Java specification [8], this allows the language implementation to apply compiler optimisation techniques (such as swapping statements, extracting assignments from the branches of an `if...`) without violating the legal executions of a program.

Dependencies. A *syntactic dependency set* is a set of read events. Given syntactic dependency sets δ_1 and δ_2, we write $\delta_1\delta_2$ for $\delta_1 \cup \delta_2$, while $\delta\, e$ stands for $\delta \cup \{e\}$. Syntactic dependencies are attached to statements during evaluation. Intuitively, if x is assigned the value 7 by a statement $x = y + 2$, the corresponding write action must depend on some event labelled by $(R, y, 5)$. When fulfilling the assignment, the operational semantics checks that its syntactic dependencies do correspond to causal dependencies in the current event space.

An event e is adjoined to an event space η by an operation $\oplus$. More precisely, let η and η' be event spaces; we write $\eta' \in \eta \oplus e$ when:

- $|\eta'| = |\eta| \cup \{e\}$ and the order in η' extends that of η conservatively;
- fulfilment in η' extends that of η conservatively, with e unfulfilled if $e : (W)$;
- if e is labelled by (R, θ, x), then $d!$ holds for all $d : (W, \theta, x) < e$;
- if $e : (\theta) < d : (\theta)$, then d is an unfulfilled write.

We write $\eta \oplus e$ to denote *any* $\eta' \in \eta \oplus e$. If no such η' exists, then $\eta \oplus e$ is undefined. Given an event space η, a dependency set δ and a write action (W, θ, x, v), the expression $\eta \downarrow_\delta (W, \theta, x, v)$ is defined if there exists an *unfulfilled* event $e : (W, \theta, x, v)$ in η such that $d!$ holds for all $d : (W, \theta, x) < e$, and moreover $d' < e$ in η for all $d' \in \delta$. Noting that such an e is necessarily unique, we let $\eta \downarrow_\delta (W, \theta, x, v)$, when defined, denote the event space η with the new fulfilment $e!$.

Syntax. We use the following simple fragment of Java.

$$\begin{array}{rl} \textit{D-Term} ::= & \textit{D-Stm} \mid \textit{D-Expr} \\ \textit{D-Stm} ::= & \textit{Stm}\ \textit{Dep} \\ \textit{D-Expr} ::= & \textit{Expr}\ \textit{Dep} \end{array} \qquad \begin{array}{rl} \textit{Stm} ::= & \texttt{;} \mid \textit{Var} \texttt{ = } \textit{D-Expr}\ \texttt{;} \mid \textit{D-Stm}\ \textit{D-Stm} \\ & \mid \texttt{if (}\ \textit{D-Expr}\ \texttt{)}\ \textit{D-Stm}\ \texttt{else}\ \textit{D-Stm} \\ & \mid \texttt{synchronized (}\ \textit{Mon}\ \texttt{)}\ \textit{D-Stm} \\ & \mid \textit{synchronized}\ \texttt{(}\ \textit{Mon}\ \texttt{)}\ \textit{D-Stm} \\ \textit{Expr} ::= & \textit{Lit} \mid \textit{Var} \mid \textit{Expr}\ \textit{Op}\ \textit{Expr} \end{array}$$

Here, *Lit* is the syntactic domain of *literals*, which we identify with the domain of values and where we assume suitable functions $op : Lit \times Lit \rightarrow Lit$ corresponding to the syntactic binary operators $\texttt{op} \in Op$. *Dep* stands for the domain of syntactic dependency sets. A "conventional" Java term like `x = 1;` is turned into a *D-Term* (*dependent* term) by filling in empty dependency sets, i.e., $(\texttt{x} = (\texttt{1})_\emptyset\ \texttt{;})_\emptyset$, and we omit empty dependency sets in our examples.

Operational configurations. An operational configuration represents the state of execution of a multi-threaded Java program; therefore, it may include several dependent terms, one for each thread of execution. We call *multiterm* a partial map from thread identifiers to dependent terms. We let the metavariable T range over multiterms: $T : Tid \rightharpoonup D\text{-}Term$. When we assume that θ is not in the domain of T we write $T \parallel (\theta, t)$ for the multiterm T' such that $T'(\theta) = t$ and $T'(\theta') \simeq T(\theta')$ for $\theta' \neq \theta$; where $h \simeq h'$ means that if h is defined so is h', and vice versa.

An *operational configuration* is a pair (T, η) consisting of a multiterm T and an event space η. In writing operational configurations, we generally drop the parentheses and all parts that are not immediately relevant in the context of discourse; for example, we may write just "t, η" to mean some configuration $(T \parallel (\theta, t), \eta)$. Operational configurations are ranged over by γ.

Rule conventions. In writing an axiom $\gamma_1 \rightarrow \gamma_2$ we focus only on the relevant parts of the configurations involved, and understand that whatever is omitted from γ_1 remains unchanged in γ_2. For example, we understand that the axiom $\texttt{;}\ p \rightarrow p$ stands for $T \parallel (\theta, \texttt{;}\ p), \eta \rightarrow T \parallel (\theta, p), \eta$. On the other hand, rules with a premise are read by assuming that whatever changes occur in the omitted parts of the premise also occur in the conclusion. For example, we understand that:

$$\frac{e_1 \rightarrow e_2}{e_1\ \texttt{op}\ e \rightarrow e_2\ \texttt{op}\ e} \quad \text{means} \quad \frac{T_1 \parallel (\theta, (e_1)_{\delta_1}), \eta_1 \rightarrow T_2 \parallel (\theta, (e_2)_{\delta_2}), \eta_2}{T_1 \parallel (\theta, (e_1\ \texttt{op}\ e)_{\delta_1}), \eta_1 \rightarrow T_2 \parallel (\theta, (e_2\ \texttt{op}\ e)_{\delta_2}), \eta_2}\,.$$

Operational rules. The operational rules are given in Tab. 1. The metavariables used (in variously decorated form) in the rule schemes range as follows: $u, v \in Lit$, $x \in Var$, $m \in Mon$, $d, e \in Expr$, $s \in Stm$, $p, q \in D\text{-}Stm$, $\delta, \epsilon \in Dep$.

The JMM axioms (Fig. 4) constrain the operational rules. This is because the latter rely on $\oplus$ producing a legal event space. For example, an attempt by a thread θ to use [syn1] for acquiring a lock on m would fail if m is detained by a different thread in the current state η, because the expression $\eta \oplus (L, \theta, m)$ would then denote no event space satisfying the axioms for locks. Similarly, the value v read by θ in x through rule [var] is forced to comply with the model by the requirement that $\eta \oplus (R, \theta, x, v)$ be defined.

Table 1. Operational rules

$$[\text{binop1}]\quad \frac{d \to e}{d \;\mathsf{op}\; e' \to e \;\mathsf{op}\; e'} \qquad [\text{binop2}]\quad \frac{d \to e}{v \;\mathsf{op}\; d \to v \;\mathsf{op}\; e}$$

$$[\text{binop3}]\quad u \;\mathsf{op}\; v \to op(u,v) \qquad [\text{var}]\quad \theta : x, \eta \to \theta : v_{(R,\theta,x,v)}, \eta \oplus (R,\theta,x,v)$$

$$[\text{assign1}]\quad \frac{d \to e}{x = d\texttt{;} \to x = e\texttt{;}} \qquad [\text{assign2}]\quad \theta : x = v_\epsilon \,\texttt{;}_\delta, \eta \to \theta : \texttt{;}_\delta, \eta \downarrow_{\delta\epsilon} (W,\theta,x,v)$$

$$[\text{if1}]\quad \frac{d \to e}{\texttt{if (}\,d\,\texttt{)}\; p \;\texttt{else}\; q \to \texttt{if (}\,e\,\texttt{)}\; p \;\texttt{else}\; q}$$

$$[\text{if2}]\quad (\texttt{if (}\,\mathit{true}_\epsilon\,\texttt{)}\; p \;\texttt{else}\; q)_\delta \to p_{\delta\epsilon}$$

$$[\text{if3}]\quad (\texttt{if (}\,\mathit{false}_\epsilon\,\texttt{)}\; p \;\texttt{else}\; q)_\delta \to q_{\delta\epsilon}$$

$$[\text{if4}]\quad \frac{p_\delta, \eta \to p'_\delta, \eta' \qquad q_\delta, \eta \to q'_\delta, \eta'}{(\texttt{if (}\,v\,\texttt{)}\; p \;\texttt{else}\; q)_\delta, \eta \to (\texttt{if (}\,v\,\texttt{)}\; p' \;\texttt{else}\; q')_\delta, \eta'}$$

$$[\text{syn1}]\quad \theta : \texttt{synchronized (}\,m\,\texttt{)}\; p, \eta \to \theta : \mathit{synchronized}\;\texttt{(}\,m\,\texttt{)}\; p, \eta \oplus (L,\theta,m)$$

$$[\text{syn2}]\quad \frac{p_\delta \to q_\delta}{(\mathit{synchronized}\;\texttt{(}\,m\,\texttt{)}\; p)_\delta \to (\mathit{synchronized}\;\texttt{(}\,m\,\texttt{)}\; q)_\delta}$$

$$[\text{syn3}]\quad \theta : \mathit{synchronized}\;\texttt{(}\,m\,\texttt{)}\,\texttt{;}, \eta \to \theta : \texttt{;}, \eta \oplus (U,\theta,m)$$

$$[\text{skip}]\quad \texttt{;}\; p \to p \qquad [\text{seq}]\quad \frac{p_\delta \to p'_\delta}{(p\; q)_\delta \to (p'\; q)_\delta} \qquad [\text{pre}]\quad T, \eta \to T, \eta \oplus (W)$$

Examples. We show that an execution of the sample program in Fig. 5, top-left, started with all variables initialised to zero can result in `r1` and `r2` set to 1, as predicated in [9]. Using rule [pre], the operational semantics may first "guess" that `x` and `y` will eventually be set to 1 and that these settings do not causally depend on any previously read value. In fact, this will be fulfilled by execution according to the operational semantics, and thus the Java trace (writing $a \to b$ for $a \le b$) in Fig. 5, top-right, can be produced:

$$\begin{array}{ll}
\texttt{r1=x; y=1;} \parallel \texttt{r2=y; x=1;}, \emptyset & \xrightarrow{[\text{pre}]} \\
\texttt{r1=x; y=1;} \parallel \texttt{r2=y; x=1;}, \{c'\} & \xrightarrow{[\text{assign1, var}]} \\
\texttt{r1=}1_a\texttt{; y=1;} \parallel \texttt{r2=y; x=1;}, \{c' < a\} & \xrightarrow{[\text{pre}]} \\
\texttt{r1=}1_a\texttt{; y=1;} \parallel \texttt{r2=y; x=1;}, \{c' < a < b\} & \xrightarrow{[\text{assign2}]} \\
\texttt{; y=1;} \parallel \texttt{r2=y; x=1;}, \{c' < a < b!\} & \xrightarrow{[\text{skip}]} \\
\texttt{y=1;} \parallel \texttt{r2=y; x=1;}, \{c' < a < b!\} & \xrightarrow{[\text{pre}]} \\
\texttt{y=1;} \parallel \texttt{r2=y; x=1;}, \{c' < a < b!, c\} & \xrightarrow{[\text{assign2}]} \\
\texttt{;} \parallel \texttt{r2=y; x=1;}, \{c' < a < b!, c!\} & \xrightarrow{[\text{assign1, var}]} \\
\texttt{;} \parallel \texttt{r2=}1_{a'}\texttt{; x=1;}, \{c' < a < b!, c! < a'\} & \xrightarrow{[\text{pre}]} \\
\texttt{;} \parallel \texttt{r2=}1_{a'}\texttt{; x=1;}, \{c' < a < b!, c! < a' < b'\} & \xrightarrow{[\text{assign2}]} \\
\texttt{;} \parallel \texttt{; x=1;}, \{c' < a < b!, c! < a' < b'!\} & \xrightarrow{[\text{skip}]} \\
\texttt{;} \parallel \texttt{x=1;}, \{c' < a < b!, c! < a' < b'!\} & \xrightarrow{[\text{assign2}]} \\
\texttt{;} \parallel \texttt{;}, \{c'! < a < b!, c! < a' < b'!\} &
\end{array}$$

where the terms for the threads θ_1 and θ_2 are shown left and right to $\parallel$.

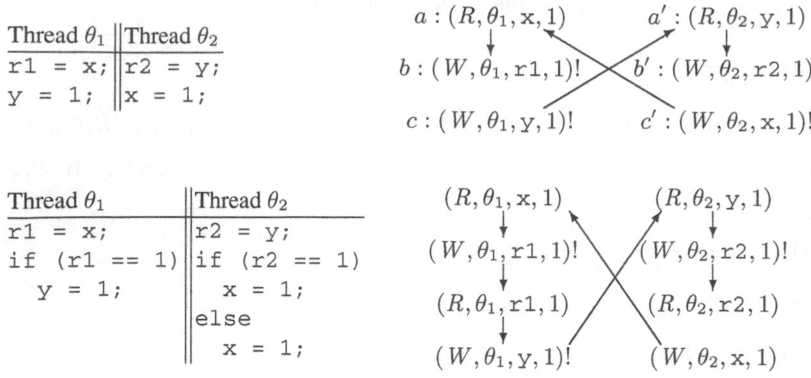

Fig. 5. Examples of Java programs and resulting Java configurations

In contrast, in the program

$$\theta_1 : \mathtt{r1 = x;\ if\ (r1 == 1)\ y = 1;} \parallel \theta_2 : \mathtt{r2 = y;\ if\ (r2 == 1)\ x = 1;}$$

the write action for y and x do depend on the values previously read from r1 and r2, respectively. Consequently, a poset like the one depicted in Fig. 5, bottom-right, in which $(W, \theta_2, \mathtt{x}, 1)$ does not extend to a fulfilled execution. But, in fact, this Java configuration with this event being fulfilled is the possible outcome of the program in Fig. 5, bottom-left, where a single write to x not depending on r2 suffices.

6 Correctness

The JMM [8, §17] is based on a notion of "happens-before". This notion subsumes on the one hand the *program order po*, a thread-wise total order of actions as dictated by sequentially executing each thread according to the Java language specification; on the other hand, it is based on the *synchronisation order so*, the total order of all lock and unlock actions in a program run. Then the *happens-before order hb*, which must be a partial order, is defined to include the transitive closure of *po* with the *synchronises-with order sw* which restricts *so* to lock and unlock actions on the same monitor.

The action description of the JMM differs from our notion of Java actions with respect to the values, which we included into the actions: In the JMM, two functions V and W are used where V gives for a write action the *value written* of this write and W references for a read action the *write seen* by this read. The write-seen function must be compatible with the happens-before order in the sense that no write can be seen by a read which actually happens after it, and no read can see a write that happened before it but has been overwritten in the happens-before order. Finally, the JMM requires that all variables of a program are properly initialised and that these initialisations can be seen by all threads. For this purpose it strengthens the synchronises-with order to include the initialising writes and the first action of each thread.

A (well-formed) *execution* of a program P with an action set A now, according to the JMM, is a tuple $(P, A, po, so, W, V, sw, hb)$ fulfilling the description above. It has to be stressed that the JMM description [8, §17] does not define the connection between the program P and the actions A and the various orderings and functions. In fact, the actions actually executed in a program run will, in general, depend on W and V, and their precise connection would be mutually recursive.

The notion of happens-before alone does not suffice to capture causally legal executions, as it would allow "out-of-thin-air" results to be produced. Thus, the JMM predicates that an execution X has to be *validated* by a sequence of other executions $(X_i)_i$ of the same program *committing* subsequently all actions of X in an increasing sequence $(C_i)_i$. The process of commitments must be such that the happens-before orders and the value-written functions of X and X_i coincide on already committed actions in C_i; the writes-seen of X_i, however, need not coincide on C_i, but only on C_{i-1}, with the additional requirement that every new read action in X_i has to see a write that happened-before in X_i and, if it is committed in C_i, then the write-seen must be in C_{i-1}. Finally, synchronisation actions immediately following each other in X_i below a committed action in C_i must persist in the validation process.

In order to prove that our semantics is correct with respect to the JMM, we have to show that a run of the operational semantics on a multiterm T such that the final Java trace is fulfilled indeed gives rise to an execution X for T that can be validated by a sequence $(X_i, C_i)_i$ of executions and commitments. We assume in the following that the operational semantics starts with an initial Java trace η_T that show initialisations for all variables of P and that η_T will be extended during computation in such a way that all subsequent events depend on the initialisations.

Let T be a multiterm and let $\vec{\gamma}$ be a computation $\gamma_0 \to \cdots \to \gamma_n$, with $\gamma_0 = (T, \eta_T)$, $\gamma_i = (T_i, \eta_i)$, and η_n totally fulfilled. For the first task, producing an execution, we observe that the computation $\vec{\gamma}$ induces a total order on the events in η_n by assigning to each $e \in |\eta_n|$ the index of the computational step in which either it was added, if $e : (R)$, or $e : (L)$, $e : (U)$, or it was fulfilled, if $e : (W)$. We construct an execution

$$exec(\vec{\gamma}) = (T, |\eta_n|, po(\vec{\gamma}), so(\vec{\gamma}), W(\vec{\gamma}), V(\vec{\gamma}), sw(\vec{\gamma}), hb(\vec{\gamma}))$$

as follows: Constraining the total order of events to each thread and to all synchronisation actions, we obtain a program order $po(\vec{\gamma})$ and a synchronisation order $so(\vec{\gamma})$, respectively; this also induces a happens-before order $hb(\vec{\gamma})$ and a synchronises-with order $sw(\vec{\gamma})$. We define the value-written function $V(\vec{\gamma})$ by setting $V(\vec{\gamma})(e) = v$ if $e : (W, v) \in \eta_n$, and a write-seen function $W(\vec{\gamma})$ by setting $W(\vec{\gamma})(e)$ to that $e' \in \eta_n$ which satisfies $e' : (W, v) \leq e : (R, v)$ in η_n and has the minimum distance of indices assigned to e and e'.

Lemma 3. *$exec(\vec{\gamma})$ is a well-formed execution of T.*

Proof. By construction, $hb(\vec{\gamma})$ is a partial order. $W(\vec{\gamma})$ conforms to the requirements of the JMM as, although there may be several writes of the desired value for a read that can be seen by the read, there will be at least one valid for $W(\vec{\gamma})$ by axioms (2–4) on Java configurations. □

For the second task, validating an execution $exec(\vec{\gamma})$, we construct a sequence of executions and commitments $(X(\vec{\gamma})_i, C(\vec{\gamma})_i)$ inductively as follows: $X(\vec{\gamma})_0$ and $C(\vec{\gamma})_0$ are empty. Assuming $X(\vec{\gamma})_k$ and $C(\vec{\gamma})_k$ to have been defined already for a $0 < k < n$, we let e_{k+1} be a minimal element of $\eta_n \setminus C_k$. Then there is a computation $\vec{\gamma}^{(k)} = \gamma_0^{(k)} \to \cdots \to \gamma_l^{(k)}$, with $\gamma_0^{(k)} = (T, \eta_T)$, $\eta_l^{(k)}$ fulfilled, $\eta_n \restriction C(\vec{\gamma})_k = \eta_l^{(k)}$, and e_{k+1} maximal in $\eta_l^{(k)}$, which uses the [pre] rule only for events in C_k. Indeed, using $exec(\vec{\gamma})$ as the guide for executing which statement and action, no rule execution can be prohibited, but it may produce a different value for the read and write actions. In fact, having chosen e_{k+1} to be minimal in $\eta_n \setminus C(\vec{\gamma})_k$ all events in the $\eta_l^{(i)}$ only depend on actions having been committed in C_k and thus, in particular, for e_{k+1} the same value as in η will be produced. As $\vec{\gamma}^{(k)}$ is a computation, it induces an execution $X(\vec{\gamma})_{k+1} = exec(\vec{\gamma}^{(k)})$ by Lem. 3; we also set $C(\vec{\gamma})_{k+1} = C(\vec{\gamma})_k \cup \{e_{k+1}\}$.

Lemma 4. *$exec(\vec{\gamma})$ is validated by the sequence $(X(\vec{\gamma})_i, C(\vec{\gamma})_i)_i$.*

Proof. By construction, the happens-before order of $exec(\vec{\gamma})$ is preserved on each $C(\vec{\gamma})_i$ and all read actions either use a happens-before value in $X(\vec{\gamma})_i$, as the [pre] rule must not be used for uncommitted actions, or see a happens-before write. □

It is worth noting that we have resolved the dilemma of the mutually dependent definitions of program actions and the values seen and written by these actions in the JMM by restricting the use of prescient write actions in our construction of a validation sequence.

7 Conclusions and Further Research

We presented a structural operational semantics of a small fragment of Java including much of what is needed to understand the JMM. The semantics was proven correct with respect to the language specification of [8]. The specification of the memory model (Fig. 4) is separate from the run time semantics (Tab. 1) and yet connected in a single formal framework which gives unambiguous account of their interplay. We believe this has been missing in the literature as yet. Moreover, the theoretical foundations of the proposed framework, combining denotational, operational and axiomatical semantics, support formal reasoning about programs, specifically for proving correctness of optimisation techniques.

There are, e.g., obvious compiler optimisations that the current JMM does *not* support. An example is the following program where threads θ_1 and θ_2 run in parallel:

θ_1 : `r1 = x; r2 = y; if (r1 == 1 && r2 == 1) z = 1;`
θ_2 : `r3 = z; if (r3 == 1) { x = 1; y = 1; } else { y = 1; x = 1; }`

After reordering the independent statements in the `else` branch, a compiler may execute assignments `x = 1;` and `y = 1;` *early*, so that `r1`, `r2`, `r3` can all be assigned `1`. However, such a behaviour is not legal according to the current JMM, as it violates the condition that the happens-before orders during validation be consistent with the final happens-before on the committed actions. In fact, the latter will have the write to `x` before the write to `y`, but during validation the write to `y` happens before the write to `x`.

This is indeed a counterexample to the claim by Manson, Pugh, and Adve [9, Thm. 1] that in the JMM all independent program statements can be reordered; it seems that the happens-before order would have to be relaxed, not requiring, e.g., the ordering of independent program actions. In our framework, such a compiler optimisation can be included by a simple editing of rule [if4]. The theory of reorderings developed by Saraswat et al. [12] takes into account also more complicated code rearrangements, but, like the JMM, is not connected to a language semantics.

On a more theoretical side, we notice that our axiomatisation of the JMM has only been used to constrain the operational rules by *local* checks on fragments of a configuration structure, the event spaces. What the *whole* structure is, which represents the full program denotationally, can also be made explicit. (The following construction extends easily to possibly infinite computations, e.g. when including `while` loops.)

Let $\eta_0, \ldots, \eta_n$ be the sequence of event spaces of a computation $\vec{\gamma}$. We write $\eta_{\vec{\gamma}}$ to denote the last event space η_n in $\vec{\gamma}$. A computation $\vec{\gamma}$ is called *accomplished* if all write actions in $\eta_{\vec{\gamma}}$ are fulfilled and moreover, if T_n is its last multiterm, then $T_n(\theta)$ is `;`, when defined, for all threads θ. We write $\underline{x}$ to denote a specific occurrence of a variable x in a program T, and similarly for monitors. Let E_T be the set whose elements are either pairs $(\underline{x}, v)$, where x is a variable and v a value, or pairs $(\underline{m}, K)$, where m is a monitor and $K \in \{L, U\}$. Viewing the elements of E_T as events, we construct a denotational model of T by assuming that operational semantics adjoins events to the current trace according to the following protocol:

- [var] adds $(\underline{x}, v) : (R, x, v)$ if v is the value read at $\underline{x}$;
- [pre] adds $(\underline{x}, v) : (W, x, v)$ if v is the value written in $\underline{x}$;
- [syn1] adds $(\underline{m}, L) : (L, m)$ when evaluating `synchronized (` $\underline{m}$ `)` p;
- [syn3] adds $(\underline{m}, U) : (U, m)$ when evaluating *synchronized* `(` $\underline{m}$ `) ;`;

Given a program T, we let $[\![T]\!]$ be the structure whose configurations are sets $C \subseteq E_T$ such that there exists an accomplished computation $\vec{\gamma}$ of T and C is a downward closed subset of $\eta_{\vec{\gamma}}$. Note that the causal dependency relation associated with such a C in $[\![T]\!]$ is included in, but may not coincide with, the partial order of $\eta_{\vec{\gamma}}$ restricted to C.

Proposition 2. $[\![T]\!]$ *satisfies the Java axioms.*

Proof. Suppose $[\![T]\!]$ does not satisfy an axiom $\Gamma \vdash_\rho \Delta$. There must exist a trace C in $[\![T]\!]$ and an interpretation $\pi : \Gamma \to C$ violating the conditions of Def. 2. By definition, $|C|$ is a downward closed subset of some $\eta_{\vec{\gamma}}$, and there exists an event space η in $\vec{\gamma}$ (hence satisfying the axioms) which contains all events in C. By an easy argument, η satisfies ρ iff so does C, against the assumptions. □

By the arguments developed in Sect. 1, we know that $[\![T]\!]$ is neither stable nor monotone. What the algebraic properties of such structures are is still under investigation, and we believe that such a denotational understanding may provide valuable tools for formal proofs of program properties.

Acknowledgements. We would like to thank Florian Lasinger for pointing us to some problems in the JMM.

References

1. Winskel, G.: Event Structure Semantics of CCS and Related Languages. In Nielsen, M., Schmidt, E.M., eds.: Proc. 9th Int. Coll. Automata, Languages and Programming (ICALP'82). Volume 140 of Lect. Notes Comp. Sci., Springer, Berlin (1982) 561–576
2. Nielsen, M., Plotkin, G.D., Winskel, G.: Petri Nets, Event Structures and Domains: Part I. Theo. Comp. Sci. **13** (1981) 85–108
3. van Glabbeek, R.J., Goltz, U.: Refinement of Actions and Equivalence Notions for Concurrent Systems. Acta Informatica **37** (2001) 229–327
4. Winskel, G.: Event Structures. In Brauer, W., Reisig, W., Rozenberg, G., eds.: Advances in Petri Nets 1986, Part II. Number 255 in Lect. Notes Comp. Sci., Springer, Berlin (1987)
5. van Glabbeek, R.J., Plotkin, G.D.: Configuration Structures. In: Proc. 10th IEEE Symp. Logics in Computer Science (LICS'95), San Diego, IEEE Press (1995) 199–209
6. Cenciarelli, P.: Configuration Theories. In Bradfield, J.C., ed.: Proc. 16th Int. Wsh. Computer Science Logic (CSL'02). Volume 2471 of Lect. Notes Comp. Sci., Springer, Berlin (2002) 200–215
7. van Glabbeek, R.J., Plotkin, G.D.: Event Structures for Resolvable Conflicts. In Fiala, J., Koubek, V., Kratochvíl, J., eds.: Proc. 29th Int. Symp. Mathematical Foundation of Computer Science (MFCS'04). Volume 3153 of Lect. Notes Comp. Sci., Springer, Berlin (2004) 550–561
8. Gosling, J., Joy, B., Steele, G., Bracha, G.: The Java Language Specification. 3rd edn. Addison-Wesley Longman, Amsterdam (2005)
9. Manson, J., Pugh, W., Adve, S.V.: The Java Memory Model. In: Proc. 32nd ACM SIGPLAN-SIGACT Symp. Principles of Programming Languages (POPL'05), ACM Press (2005) 378–391
10. Winskel, G., Nielsen, M.: Models of Concurrency. In Abramsky, S., Gabbay, D.M., Maibaum, T.S.E., eds.: Handbook of Logic in Computer Science. Vol. 4: Semantic Modelling. Oxford University Press, Oxford (1995) 1–148
11. MacLane, S.: Categories for the Working Mathematician. Springer, New York (1971)
12. Saraswat, V., Jagadeesan, R., Michael, M., von Praun, C.: A Theory of Memory Models (2006) `http://www.saraswat.org/raofull.pdf`(06/12/28).

Immutable Objects for a Java-Like Language

C. Haack[1,⋆], E. Poll[1], J. Schäfer[2,⋆⋆], and A. Schubert[1,3,⋆⋆⋆]

[1] Radboud Universiteit Nijmegen, The Netherlands
[2] Technische Universität Kaiserlautern, Germany
[3] Warsaw University, Poland

Abstract. We extend a Java-like language with immutability specifications and a static type system for verifying immutability. A class modifier `immutable` specifies that all class instances are immutable objects. Ownership types specify the depth of object states and enforce encapsulation of representation objects. The type system guarantees that the state of immutable objects does not visibly mutate during a program run. Provided immutability-annotated classes and methods are `final`, this is true even if immutable classes are composed with untrusted classes that follow Java's type system, but not our immutability type system.

1 Introduction

An object is immutable if it does not permit observable mutations of its object state. A class is immutable if all its instances are immutable objects. In this article, we present an extension of a Java-like language with immutability specifications and a static type system for verifying them.

For many reasons, favoring immutability greatly simplifies object-oriented programming [Blo01]. It is, for instance, impossible to break invariants of immutable objects, as these are established once and for all by the object constructor. This is especially pleasing in the presence of aliasing, because maintaining invariants of possibly aliased objects is difficult and causes headaches for program verification and extended static checking tools. Sharing immutable objects, on the other hand, causes no problems whatsoever. Object immutability is particularly useful in multi-threaded programs, as immutable objects are thread-safe. Race conditions on the state of immutable objects are impossible, because immutable objects do not permit writes to their object state. Even untrusted components cannot mutate immutable objects. This is why immutable objects are important in scenarios where some components (e.g. applets downloaded from the web) cannot be trusted. If a security-sensitive component checks data that it has received from an untrusted component, it typically relies on the fact that the data does not mutate after the check. A prominent example of an immutable class whose immutability is crucial for many security-sensitive applications is Java's immutable `String` class.

Unfortunately, statically enforcing object immutability for Java is not easy. The main reason for this is that an object's local state often includes more than just the object's fields. If local object states never extended beyond the object's fields, Java's `final`

⋆ Supported by the EU under the IST-2005-015905 MOBIUS project.
⋆⋆ Supported by the Deutsche Forschungsgemeinschaft (German Research Foundation).
⋆⋆⋆ Supported by an EU Marie Curie Intra-European Fellowship.

R. De Nicola (Ed.): ESOP 2007, LNCS 4421, pp. 347–362, 2007.

field modifier would be enough to enforce object immutability. However, String objects, for instance, refer to an internal character array that is considered part of the String's local state. It is crucial that this character array is encapsulated and any aliasing from outside is prevented. Java does not provide any support for specifying deep object states and enforcing encapsulation. Fortunately, ownership type systems come to rescue. Ownership type systems have been proposed to better support encapsulation in object-oriented languages, e.g., [CPN98, CD02, BLS03, MPH01, DM05]. In order to permit immutable objects with deep states, we employ a variant of ownership types. The core of our ownership type system is contained (in various disguises) in all of the ownership type systems listed above. In addition, our type system distinguishes between read-only and read-write objects. The difference between read-only objects and immutable objects is that the latter have no public mutator methods at all, whereas the former have public mutator methods that are prohibited to be called. We need read-only objects in order to support sharing mutable (but read-only) representation objects among immutable objects. Unlike read-only *references* [MPH01, BE04, TE05], our read restrictions for immutable and read-only objects are per object, not per reference.

Our type system guarantees immutability in an *open world* [PBKM00] where immutable objects are immutable even when interacting with *unchecked components* that do not follow the rules of our immutability type system. The immutability type system guarantees that unchecked components cannot break from outside the immutability of checked immutable objects. All we assume about unchecked components is that they follow the standard Java typing rules. Unchecked components could, for instance, represent legacy code or untrusted code. Our decision to support an open world has several important impacts on the design of our type system. For instance, we have to ensure that the types of public methods of immutable objects do not constrain callers beyond the restrictions imposed by Java's standard type system. Technically, this is easily achieved by restricting the ownership types of methods. Furthermore, we cannot assume that clients of immutable objects follow a read-only policy that is not already enforced by Java's standard type system. For this reason, we define read-only types in context world to be equivalent to read-write types.

A difficulty in enforcing object immutability is that even immutable objects mutate for some time, namely during their construction phase. This is problematic for several reasons. Firstly, Java does not restrict constructor bodies in any way. In particular, Java allows passing self-references from constructors to outside methods. This is undesirable for immutable objects as it would allow observing immutable objects while they are still mutating. Moreover, the rules that control aliasing for constructors should be different from the rules that control aliasing for methods. Constructors should be allowed to pass dynamic aliases to their internals to outside methods as long as these methods do not store any static aliases to the internals. Methods, on the other hand, must be disallowed to leak dynamic aliases to internals, if our goal is immutability in an open world.

2 A Java-Like Language with Immutability

In this section, we present Core Jimuva, a core language for an immutability extension of Java. We use the same syntax conventions as Featherweight Java (FJ) [IPW01]. In particular, we indicate sequences of X's by an overbar: $\bar{X}$. We assume that field declarations $\bar{F}$, constructor declarations $\bar{K}$, method declarations $\bar{M}$ and parameter declarations $\bar{ty}\,\bar{x}$ do not contain duplicate declarations. We also use some regular expression syntax: $X?$ for an optional X, $X*$ for a possibly empty list of X's, and $X \mid Y$ for an X or a Y. For any entity X (e.g., X an expression or a type), we write $\mathsf{oids}(X)$ for the set of object identifiers occurring in X and $\mathsf{vars}(X)$ for the set of variables occurring in X (including the special access variable `myaccess`). For a given class table $\bar{c}$, we write $C\,\mathtt{ext}_{\bar{c}}D$ whenever $\mathit{fm}\,\mathit{ca}\,\mathtt{class}\,C\,\mathtt{ext}\,D\{..\} \in \bar{c}$. The *subclassing relation* $<:_{\bar{c}}$ is the reflexive, transitive closure of $\mathtt{ext}_{\bar{c}}$. We omit the subscript $\bar{c}$ if it is clear from the context. Like in FJ, we assume the following sanity conditions on class tables $\bar{c}$: (1) subclassing $<:_{\bar{c}}$ is antisymmetric, (2) if C (except `Object`) occurs anywhere in $\bar{c}$ then C is declared in $\bar{c}$ and (3) $\bar{c}$ does not contain duplicate declarations or a declaration of `Object`.

Core Jimuva — a Java-like Core Language with Immutability Annotations:

$C,D,E \in \mathsf{ClassId}$	class identifiers (including `Object`)
$f,g \in \mathsf{FieldId}$	field identifiers
$m,n \in \mathsf{MethId}$	method identifiers
$k,l \in \mathsf{ConsId}$	constructor identifiers
$o,p,q,r \in \mathsf{ObjId}$	object identifiers (including `world`)
$x,y,z \in \mathsf{Var}$	variables (including `this`, `myowner`)
$ca ::= \mathtt{immutable?}$	class attributes
$ea ::= \mathtt{anon?}\ \mathtt{rdonly?}\ \mathtt{wrlocal?}$	expression attributes
$ar ::= \mathtt{rd} \mid \mathtt{rdwr} \mid \mathtt{myaccess}$	access rights for objects
$fm ::= \mathtt{final?}$	final modifier
$u,v,w \in \mathsf{Val} ::= \mathtt{null} \mid o \mid x$	values
$ty \in \mathsf{ValTy} ::= C<ar,v> \mid \mathtt{void}$	value types
$T \in \mathsf{ExpTy} ::= ea\,ty$	expression types
$c,d ::= fm\,ca\,\mathtt{class}\,C\,\mathtt{ext}\,D\{\bar{F}\ \bar{K}\ \bar{M}\}$	class declaration (where $C \neq$ `Object`)
$F ::= C<ar,v>\,f;$	field
$K ::= ea\,C.k(\bar{ty}\,\bar{x})\{e\}$	constructor (scope of $\bar{x}$ is e)
$M ::= fm<\bar{y}>T\,m(\bar{ty}\,\bar{x})\{e\}$	method (scope of $\bar{y}$ is $(T,\bar{ty},e)$, of $\bar{x}$ is e)
$e \in \mathsf{Exp} ::=$	expressions and statements
$v \mid v.f \mid v.f\mathtt{=}e \mid v.m<\bar{v}>(\bar{e}) \mid \mathtt{new}\,C<ar,v>.k(\bar{e}) \mid \mathtt{let}\,x\mathtt{=}e\,\mathtt{in}\,e \mid (C)e \mid C.k(\bar{e})$	

Derived Forms:

If $e \notin \mathsf{Val}, x \notin \mathsf{vars}(e,e',\bar{v},\bar{e})$: $\quad e.f \triangleq \mathtt{let}\,x\mathtt{=}e\,\mathtt{in}\,x.f \quad e.f\mathtt{=}e' \triangleq \mathtt{let}\,x\mathtt{=}e\,\mathtt{in}\,x.f\mathtt{=}e'$

$e.m<\bar{v}>(\bar{e}) \triangleq \mathtt{let}\,x\mathtt{=}e\,\mathtt{in}\,x.m<\bar{v}>(\bar{e}) \qquad$ If $x \notin \mathsf{vars}(e')$: $\quad e;e' \triangleq \mathtt{let}\,x\mathtt{=}e\,\mathtt{in}\,e'$

$\mathtt{skip} \triangleq \mathtt{null} \qquad e; \triangleq e;\mathtt{skip} \qquad \mathtt{let}\,x,\bar{x}\mathtt{=}e,\bar{e}\,\mathtt{in}\,e' \triangleq \mathtt{let}\,x\mathtt{=}e\,\mathtt{in}\,\mathtt{let}\,\bar{x}\mathtt{=}\bar{e}\,\mathtt{in}\,e'$

$e.m(\bar{e}) \triangleq e.m<>(\bar{e}) \qquad fm\,T\,m(\bar{ty}\,\bar{x})\{e\} \triangleq fm<>T\,m(\bar{ty}\,\bar{x})\{e\}$

$C<ar> \triangleq C<ar,\mathtt{world}> \qquad C<v> \triangleq C<\mathtt{rdwr},v> \qquad C \triangleq C<\mathtt{world}>$

Core Jimuva extends a Java core language by *immutability specifications*: the class attribute `immutable` specifies that all instances of a class are immutable objects, i.e., their object state does not visibly mutate.

The other Java extensions are auxiliary and specify constraints on objects and methods that `immutable` objects depend on: *Ownership types* are used to ensure encapsulation of representation [CPN98, CD02, BLS03]. The `rdonly`-attribute (*read-only*) is used to disallow methods of immutable objects to write to their own object state. The `wrlocal`-attribute (*write-local*) is used to constrain constructors of immutable objects not to write to the state of other immutable objects of the same class. Vitek and Bokowski's `anon` (*anonymous*) attribute [VB01] is used to constrain constructors of immutable objects not to leak references to `this`. For a given class table with `immutable`-specifications, these additional expression attributes can be automatically inferred, but we prefer to make them syntactically explicit in this paper.

Object types are of the form *C*<*ar*, *v*>, where *ar* specifies the access rights for the object and *v* specifies the object owner. Omitted access rights default to `rdwr`, omitted owners default to `world`. The expression `new`*C*<*ar*,*v*>.*k*($\bar{e}$) creates a new object of type *C*<*ar*, *v*> and then executes the body of constructor *C*.*k*() to initialize the new object. Access rights and ownership information have no effect on the dynamic behaviour of programs.

Access rights specify access constraints for *objects* (in contrast to Java's access modifiers `protected` and `private`, which specify access constraints for *classes*). The access rights are `rdwr` (*read-write, i.e., no constraints*) and `rd` (*read-only*). Read-only access to *o* forbids writes to *o*'s state and calls to *o*'s non-`rdonly` methods. Objects are implicitly parameterized by the *access variable* `myaccess`, which refers to the access rights for `this`. Consider, for instance, the following class:

```
class C ext Object {
  C<myaccess,myowner> x;
  wrlocal C.k(C<myaccess,myowner> x){ this.set(x); }
  rdonly C<myaccess,myowner> get(){ x }
  wrlocal void set(C<myaccess,myowner> x){ this.x = x; } }
```

If, for instance, *o* is an object of type `C<rd,`*p*>, then access to *o* is read-restricted. Furthermore, access to all objects in the transitive reach of *o* is read-restricted, too: *o*.`get`(), *o*.`get`().`get`(), etc., all have type *C*<`rd`, *p*> and therefore permit only `rd`-access. The following example shows how `C` can be used:

```
class D ext Object {
  C<rd,this> x;  C<myaccess,myowner> y;  C<rdwr,this> z;
  ...
  void m() {
    x = new C<rd,this>(new C<rd,this>(null)); // legal
    y = new C<myaccess,myowner>(new C<myaccess,myowner>(null)); // legal
    z = new C<rdwr,this>(new C<rdwr,this>(null)); // legal
    new C<rd,this>(new C<myaccess,myowner>(null)); // illegal
    x.get(); y.get(); z.get(); y.set(null); z.set(null); // legal
    x.set(null); // illegal call of non-rdonly method on rd-object }
  rdonly void n() {
    y.set(null); // illegal call of non-rdonly method } }
```

It may perhaps be slightly surprising that the call `y.set(null)` in `m()` is legal, although the access variable `myaccess` may possibly get instantiated to `rd`. This call is safe, because it is illegal to call the non-`rdonly` method `m()` on a `rd`-object and, hence, the call `y.set(null)` inside `m()` is never executed when `myaccess` instantiates to `rd`.

Ownership types. Objects of type *C*<*ar*,*o*> are considered *representation objects owned by o*, that is, they are not visible to the outside and can only be accessed via *o*'s interface. Objects without owners have types of the form *C*<*ar*,`world`>. The special variable `myowner` refers to the owner of `this`. Our type system restricts `myowner` and `world` to only occur inside angle brackets < · >. The `myowner` variable corresponds to the first class parameter in parametric ownership type systems [CD02, BLS03] and to the `owner` ghost field in JML's encoding of the Universe type system [DM05]. Furthermore, the Universe type system's `rep` and `peer` types [MPH01] relate to our types as follows: `rep`*C* corresponds to *C*<`rdwr`,`this`>, and `peer`*C* to *C*<`rdwr`,`myowner`>.

Owner-polymorphic methods. In a method declaration <$\bar{y}$>$T\,m(\bar{ty}\,\bar{x})\{e\}$, the scope of owner parameters $\bar{y}$ includes the types $T, \bar{ty}$ and the method body e. The type system restricts occurrences of owner parameters to inside angle brackets < · >. Owner parameters get instantiated by the values $\bar{v}$ in method call expressions *u.m*<$\bar{v}$>($\bar{e}$).

Owner-polymorphic methods permit *dynamic aliasing of representation objects*. Consider, for instance, a method of the following type:

```
<x,y> void copy(C<x> from, C<y> to)
```

A client may invoke `copy` with one or both of `x` and `y` instantiated to `this`, for instance, `copy<world,this>(o,mine)`, where `mine` refers to an internal representation object owned by the client. Dynamic aliasing of representation objects is often dangerous, but can sometimes be useful. For immutability, dynamic aliasing is useful during the object construction phase, but dangerous thereafter. For instance, the constructor `String(char[] a)` of Java's immutable `String` class passes an alias to the string's internal character array to a global `arraycopy()` method, which does the job of defensively copying `a`'s elements to the string's representation array. Our type system uses owner-polymorphic methods to permit dynamic aliasing during the construction phase of immutable objects, but prohibit it thereafter. The latter is achieved by prohibiting `rdonly`-expressions to instantiate a method's owner parameters by anything but `world`.

For `String` to be immutable, it is important that the `arraycopy()` method does not create a static alias to the representation array that is handed to it from the constructor `String(char[] a)`. Fortunately, owner-polymorphic methods prohibit the creation of dangerous static aliases! This is enforced merely by the type signature. Consider again the `copy()` method: From the owner-polymorphic type we can infer that an implementation of `copy` does not introduce an alias to the `to`-object from inside the transitive reach of the `from`-object. This is so, because all fields in `from`'s reach have types of the form *D*<*ar*,`x`> or *D*<*ar*,`from`> or *D*<*ar*,`world`> or *D*<*ar*,*o*> where *o* is in `from`'s reach. None of these are supertypes of *C*<`y`>, even if *D* is a supertype of *C*. Therefore, `copy`'s polymorphic type forbids assigning the `to`-object to fields inside `from`'s reach.

Let-bindings. Unlike FJ [IPW01] but like other languages that support ownership through dependent types [CD02, BLS03], we restrict some syntactic slots to values instead of expressions, for instance, $v.f$ instead of $e.f$. This is needed for our typing rules to meaningfully instantiate occurrences of `this` in types. We obtain an expression language similar to FJ through derived forms, see above. An automatic typechecker for full Jimuva will work on an intermediate language with `let`-bindings.

Constructors. Our language models object constructors. This is important, as object construction is a critical stage in the lifetime of immutable objects: during construction even immutable objects still mutate! For simplicity, Core Jimuva's constructors are *named*. Moreover, we have simplified explicit constructor calls: instead of calling constructors using `super()` and `this()`, constructors are called by concatenating class name C and constructor name k, i.e., $C.k()$. Constructors $C.k()$ are only visible in C's subclasses. We allow direct constructor calls $C.k()$ from constructors, and even from methods, of arbitrary subclasses of C. That is more liberal than real Java, but unproblematic for the properties we care about.

Protected fields. Jimuva's type system ensures that fields are visible in subclasses only. This is similar to Java's `protected` fields.[1] Our reason for using `protected` instead of `private` fields is proof-technical: a language with `private` fields does not satisfy the type preservation (aka subject reduction) property. On the other hand, soundness of a type system with `private` fields obviously follows from soundness of our less restrictive type system with `protected` fields.

3 Operational Semantics

Our operational semantics is small-step and similar to the semantics from Zhao et al [ZPV06]. However, in contrast to [ZPV06], we also model a mutable heap. The operational semantics is given by a state reduction relation $h :: s \rightarrow_{\bar{c}} h' :: s'$, where h is a *heap*, s a *stack* and $\bar{c}$ the underlying set of classes. We omit the subscript $\bar{c}$ if it is clear from the context. *Stack frames* are of the form $(e \,\mathsf{in}\, o)$, where e is a (partially executed) method body and o is the `this`-binding. Keeping track of the `this`-binding will be needed for defining the semantics of immutability. The `world` identifier is used as a dummy for the `this`-binding of the top-level main program. *Evaluation contexts* are expressions with a single "hole" [ ], which acts as a placeholder for the expression that is up for evaluation in left-to-right evaluation order. If $\mathscr{E}$ is an evaluation context and e an expression, then $\mathscr{E}[e]$ denotes the expression that results from replacing $\mathscr{E}$'s hole by e. Evaluation contexts are a standard data structure for operational semantics [WF94].

Runtime Structures:

$state ::= h :: s \in \mathsf{State} = \mathsf{Heap} \times \mathsf{Stack}$	states
$h ::= \overline{obj} \in \mathsf{Heap} = \mathsf{ObjId} \rightarrow (\mathsf{FieldId} \rightarrow \mathsf{Val})$	heaps
$obj ::= o\{\bar{f} = \bar{v}\} \in \mathsf{Obj} = \mathsf{ObjId} \times (\mathsf{FieldId} \rightarrow \mathsf{Val})$	objects
$s ::= \bar{fr} \in \mathsf{Stack} = \mathsf{Frame}^*$	stacks
$fr ::= e \,\mathsf{in}\, o \in \mathsf{Frame} = \mathsf{Exp} \times \mathsf{ObjId}$	stack frames
$\mathscr{E} ::= [\,] \mid v.f\texttt{=}\mathscr{E} \mid v.m\texttt{<}\bar{v}\texttt{>}(\bar{v},\mathscr{E},\bar{e}) \mid \texttt{new}\, C\texttt{<}ar,v\texttt{>}.k(\bar{v},\mathscr{E},\bar{e}) \mid$ $\texttt{let}\, x\texttt{=}\mathscr{E}\,\texttt{in}\, e \mid (C)\mathscr{E} \mid C.k(\bar{v},\mathscr{E},\bar{e})$	evaluation contexts

[1] Java's `protected` fields are slightly more permissive and package-visible, too.

We assume that every object identifier $o \neq \texttt{world}$ is associated with a unique type $\mathsf{ty}(o)$ of the form $C\texttt{<}ar,p\texttt{>}$ such that $p = \texttt{world}$ implies $ar = \texttt{rdwr}$. We define $\mathsf{rawty}(o) \triangleq C$, if $\mathsf{ty}(o) = C\texttt{<}ar,p\texttt{>}$.

We use *substitution* to model parameter passing: Substitutions are finite functions from variables, including `myaccess`, to values and access rights. We let meta-variable σ range over substitutions and write $(\bar{x}{\leftarrow}\bar{v})$ for the substitution that maps each x_i in $\bar{x}$ to the corresponding v_i in $\bar{v}$. We write id for the identity. We write $e[\sigma]$ for the expression that results from e by substituting variables x by $\sigma(x)$. Similarly for types, $T[\sigma]$. The following abbreviations are convenient:

$$\mathsf{self}(u,ar,v) \triangleq (\texttt{this},\texttt{myaccess},\texttt{myowner}{\leftarrow}u,ar,v)$$
$$\sigma,\bar{y}{\leftarrow}\bar{v} \triangleq (\bar{x},\bar{y}{\leftarrow}\bar{u},\bar{v}),\ \text{if } \sigma = (\bar{x}{\leftarrow}\bar{u}) \text{ and } \bar{x} \cap \bar{y} = \emptyset$$

We use several auxiliary functions that are essentially as in FJ [IPW01] (see also [HPSS07] for details): The function $\mathsf{mbody}_{\bar{c}}(C,m)$ looks up the method for m on C-objects in class table $\bar{c}$. Similarly, $\mathsf{cbody}_{\bar{c}}(C.k)$ for constructors. The function $\mathsf{fd}_{\bar{c}}(C)$ computes the field set for C-objects based on class table $\bar{c}$. We omit the subscript $\bar{c}$ if it is clear from the context.

State Reductions, *state* $\rightarrow_{\bar{c}}$ *state'*:

(Red Get) $h = h', o\{..f = v..\}$
$h :: s, \mathscr{E}[o.f] \,\mathsf{in}\, p \rightarrow h :: s, \mathscr{E}[v] \,\mathsf{in}\, p$

(Red Set)
$h, o\{f = u, \bar{g} = \bar{w}\} :: s, \mathscr{E}[o.f\texttt{=}v] \,\mathsf{in}\, p \rightarrow h, o\{f = v, \bar{g} = \bar{w}\} :: s, \mathscr{E}[v] \,\mathsf{in}\, p$

(Red Call) $s = s', \mathscr{E}[o.m\texttt{<}\bar{u}\texttt{>}(\bar{v})] \,\mathsf{in}\, p \quad \mathsf{ty}(o) = C\texttt{<}ar,w\texttt{>} \quad \mathsf{mbody}(C,m) = \texttt{<}\bar{y}\texttt{>}(\bar{x})(e)$
$h :: s \rightarrow h :: s, e[\mathsf{self}(o,ar,w), \bar{y}{\leftarrow}\bar{u}, \bar{x}{\leftarrow}\bar{v}] \,\mathsf{in}\, o$

(Red New) $s = s', \mathscr{E}[\texttt{new}\, C\texttt{<}ar,w\texttt{>}.k(\bar{v})] \,\mathsf{in}\, p \quad o \notin \mathsf{dom}(h) \quad \mathsf{ty}(o) = C\texttt{<}ar,w\texttt{>} \quad \mathsf{fd}(C) = \bar{t}\bar{y}\,\bar{f}$
$h :: s \rightarrow h, o\{\bar{f} = \texttt{null}\} :: s, C.k(\bar{v}) \,;\, o \,\mathsf{in}\, o$

(Red Cons) $s = s', \mathscr{E}[C.k(\bar{v})] \,\mathsf{in}\, p \quad \mathsf{cbody}(C.k) = (\bar{x})(e) \quad \mathsf{ty}(p) = D\texttt{<}ar,w\texttt{>}$
$h :: s \rightarrow h :: s, e[\mathsf{self}(p,ar,w), \bar{x}{\leftarrow}\bar{v}] \,\mathsf{in}\, p$

(Red Rtr) $e = q.m\texttt{<}\bar{u}\texttt{>}(\bar{v})$ or $e = \texttt{new}\, C\texttt{<}ar,u\texttt{>}.k(\bar{v})$ or $e = C.k(\bar{v})$
$h :: s, (\mathscr{E}[e] \,\mathsf{in}\, o), (v \,\mathsf{in}\, p) \rightarrow h :: s, \mathscr{E}[v] \,\mathsf{in}\, o$

(Red Let)
$h :: s, \mathscr{E}[\texttt{let}\, x\texttt{=}v\, \texttt{in}\, e] \,\mathsf{in}\, p \rightarrow h :: s, \mathscr{E}[e[x{\leftarrow}v]] \,\mathsf{in}\, p$

(Red Cast) $v = \texttt{null}$ or $\mathsf{rawty}(v) <: C$
$h :: s, \mathscr{E}[(C)v] \,\mathsf{in}\, p \rightarrow h :: s, \mathscr{E}[v] \,\mathsf{in}\, p$

4 Semantic Immutability

Intuitively, an object o is immutable in a given program P, if during execution of P no other object p can see two distinct states of o. A class is immutable if all its instances are immutable in all programs.

In order to formalize this definition, we have to describe the meaning of the phrase "p sees o's state". The object p can read o's fields directly or it can call o's methods and observe possible state changes that way. Thus, if o's object state is always the same on external field reads and in the prestate of external method calls on o, we can be sure that no object p ever sees mutations of o's state.

Definition 1 (Visible States). A *visible state for o* is a state of the form $(h :: s, \mathscr{E}[o.f] \,\mathsf{in}\, p)$ or $(h :: s, \mathscr{E}[o.m{<}\bar{u}{>}(\bar{v})] \,\mathsf{in}\, p)$ where $p \neq o$.

We also have to formalize what o's object state is. Just including the fields of an object is often not enough, because this only allows shallow object states. We interpret the ownership type annotations on fields as specifications of the depth of object states: if a field f's type annotation has the form $C{<}ar,\mathtt{this}{>}$ then the state of the object that f refers to is included in `this`'s state; if f's type annotation has the form $C{<}ar,\mathtt{myowner}{>}$ then the state of the object that f refers to is included in `myowner`'s state. This is formalized by the following inductive definition:

Definition 2 (Object State). For any heap h, the binary relation $\_ \in \mathsf{state}(h)(\_)$ over $\mathsf{Obj} \times \mathsf{ObjId}$ is defined inductively by the following rules:

- If $o\{\bar{f} = \bar{v}\} \in h$, then $o\{\bar{f} = \bar{v}\} \in \mathsf{state}(h)(o)$.
- If $o\{..f = q..\} \in h$ and $C{<}ar,\mathtt{this}{>}\, f \in \mathsf{fd}(\mathsf{rawty}(o))$ and $obj \in \mathsf{state}(h)(q)$, then $obj \in \mathsf{state}(h)(o)$.
- If $p \neq o$ and $p\{..f = q..\} \in \mathsf{state}(h)(o)$ and $C{<}ar,\mathtt{myowner}{>}\, f \in \mathsf{fd}(\mathsf{rawty}(p))$ and $obj \in \mathsf{state}(h)(q)$, then $obj \in \mathsf{state}(h)(o)$.

Let $\mathsf{state}(h)(o) \triangleq \{obj \mid obj \in \mathsf{state}(h)(o)\}$.

Example 1 (Object State)

```
class C ext Object { D<..,this> x; D<..,world> y; constructors methods }
class D ext Object { E<..,myowner> x; E<..,this> y; constructors methods }
class E ext Object { Object<..,myowner> x; constructors methods }
```

Let $c\{\mathtt{x} = d_1, \mathtt{y} = d_2\}$, $d_1\{\mathtt{x} = e_1, \mathtt{y} = e_2\}$, $e_1\{\mathtt{x} = o_1\}$, $e_2\{\mathtt{x} = o_2\}$ be instances of C, D, E in heap h. Then $\mathsf{state}(h)(e_1)$ consists of (the object whose identifier is) e_1; $\mathsf{state}(h)(e_2)$ consists of e_2; $\mathsf{state}(h)(d_1)$ consists of d_1, e_2, o_2; and $\mathsf{state}(h)(c)$ consists of $c, d_1, e_1, o_1, e_2, o_2$. □

Definition 3 (Immutability in a Fixed Program). Suppose $P = (\bar{c}; e_0)$ is a Jimuva-program and C is declared in $\bar{c}$. We say that *C is immutable in P* whenever the following statement holds:

If $\emptyset :: e_0 \,\mathsf{in}\, \mathtt{world} \rightarrow^*_{\bar{c}} h_1 :: s_1 \rightarrow^*_{\bar{c}} h_2 :: s_2$,
and $h_1 :: s_1$ and $h_2 :: s_2$ are visible states for o,
and $\mathsf{rawty}(o) <: C$, then $\mathsf{state}(h_1)(o) = \mathsf{state}(h_2)(o)$.

This immutability definition disallows some immutable classes that intuitively could be allowed, because the last line requires $\mathsf{state}(h_1)(o)$ and $\mathsf{state}(h_2)(o)$ to be *exactly identical.* A more liberal definition would allow object state mutations that are unobservable to the outside. For instance, immutable objects with an invisible internal mutable cache for storing results of expensive and commonly called methods could be allowed. However, standard type-based verification techniques would probably disallow unobservable object mutations. Because our primary goal is the design of a sound static type system, we do not attempt to formalize a more permissive definition of immutability up to a notion of observational equivalence of object states, but instead work with our strict definition that is based on exact equality of object states.

We are interested in immutability in an open world, where object immutability cannot be broken by unchecked components. To formally capture the open world model, we define a type erasure mapping $|\cdot|$ from Jimuva to Core Java, see [HPSS07] for details. This mapping erases ownership information, access rights, expression attributes and class attributes. The operational semantics, $\rightarrow_{\mathsf{java}}$, and typing judgment, $\vdash_{\mathsf{java}}$, for Core Java are defined in [HPSS07]. The Jimuva typing judgment, $\vdash$, will be defined in Section 6. A Java-*program* is a pair $(\bar{c};e)$ such that $(\vdash_{\mathsf{java}} \bar{c} : \mathsf{ok})$ and $(\vdash_{\mathsf{java},\bar{c}}\ e : ty)$ for some Java-type *ty*. The semantics of Jimuva and Core Java are related as follows:

- If $(\vdash \bar{c} : \mathsf{ok})$, then $(state \rightarrow_{\bar{c}} state')$ iff $(|state| \rightarrow_{\mathsf{java},|\bar{c}|} |state'|)$.
- If $(\vdash \bar{c} : \mathsf{ok})$, then $(\vdash_{\mathsf{java}} |\bar{c}| : \mathsf{ok})$.

There is also an embedding e that maps a Jimuva class table $\bar{c}$ and a Java class table $\bar{d}$ (which refers to $|\bar{c}|$) to a Jimuva class table $\mathsf{e}_{\bar{c}}(\bar{d})$ such that $|\mathsf{e}_{\bar{c}}(\bar{d})| = \bar{d}$, see [HPSS07] for details. This embedding inserts the annotations `rdwr` and `world` wherever access or ownership parameters are required. One can think of a Java-class as a Jimuva-class without any Jimuva-specific annotations. The embedding e inserts Jimuva-defaults where Jimuva-annotations are syntactically required.

Our type system is sound in an *open world with legal subclassing*. That is, we assume that unchecked classes do not extend Jimuva-annotated classes or override Jimuva-annotated methods. We could easily modify our system to guarantee immutability in an open world without this subclassing restriction, by requiring Jimuva-annotated classes and methods to be `final`. We choose not to, because we find that a bit too restrictive. Note, in this context, that Java's Extension Mechanism supports *sealed optional packages*, which prohibit subclassing from outside the package.[2]

Jimuva-annotated classes and methods: A *field declaration* $C\text{<}ar,v\text{>}f$ is *Jimuva-annotated* if $ar \neq \texttt{rdwr}$ or $v \neq \texttt{world}$. A *method* $fm\text{<}\bar{y}\text{>}ea\,ty'\,m(\bar{ty}\,\bar{x})\{e\}$ is Jimuva-*annotated* if $\bar{y}$, ea or $\mathsf{vars}(ty',\bar{ty})$ is non-empty. A *class* $fm\,ca\,\texttt{class}\,C\,\texttt{ext}\,D\{..\}$ is Jimuva-*annotated*, if it contains Jimuva-annotated field declarations or *ca* is non-empty.

Legal subclassing: A Java class table $\bar{d}$ *legally subclasses* a Jimuva class table $\bar{c}$, if no class declared in $\bar{d}$ extends a Jimuva-annotated class and no method declared in $\bar{d}$ overrides a Jimuva-annotated method.

Definition 4 (Immutability in an Open World). Suppose C is declared in Jimuva-class-table $\bar{c}$ and $(\vdash \bar{c} : \mathsf{ok})$. We say that *$C$ is immutable in $\bar{c}$* whenever C is immutable in $(\bar{c}, \mathsf{e}_{\bar{c}}(\bar{d}); \mathsf{e}_{\bar{c}}(e))$ for all Java-programs $(|\bar{c}|, \bar{d}; e)$ where $\bar{d}$ legally subclasses $\bar{c}$.

Let us say that a class table $\bar{c}$ is *correct for immutability* whenever every class that is declared `immutable` in $\bar{c}$ is in fact immutable in $\bar{c}$. Jimuva's type system is sound in the following sense:

Theorem 1 (Soundness). *If* $(\vdash \bar{c} : \mathsf{ok})$*, then $\bar{c}$ is correct for immutability.*

[2] Out-of-package subclassing results in a `SecurityException` at runtime.

5 The Immutability Type System – Informally

The simplest example of an immutable class is:[3]

```
immutable class ImmutableInt ext Object {
  int value;
  anon wrlocal ImmutableInt.k(int i) { this.value=i; }
  rdonly int get() { this.value } }
```

Here the state of an ImmutableInt object just consists of its instance field value. For more complicated immutable objects, ownership annotations are needed to specify if objects referenced by instance fields are part of the (immutable) state:

```
class Mutable ext Object {
  int value;
  anon Mutable.k(int i) { this.value=i; }
  rdonly int get() { this.value }
  void set(int i) { this.value=i; } }

immutable class EncapsulatedMutable ext Object {
  Mutable<this> m;
  anon wrlocal EncapsulatedMutable.k(Mutable m) {
      this.m = new Mutable<this>.k(m.get()); }
  rdonly int get(){ this.m.get() } }
```

Here the annotation `<this>` on the type of field `m` declares that the state of the object referenced by `m` is considered part of the state of an `EncapsulatedMutable` object. The type system enforces that constructor `EncapsulatedMutable.k(m)` makes a defensive copy of `m` to prevent representation exposure. Technically, this is achieved because `m`'s type `Mutable`, which is short for `Mutable<world>`, is not a subtype of `Mutable<this>` and, thus, a direct assignment to the field `this.m` is disallowed.

Restrictions on methods with `rdonly`. Obviously, methods of an immutable object should not modify their object state. One could try to ensure this by requiring that methods of immutable objects are side-effect free. However, ensuring side-effect freeness is not so simple, because even side-effect free methods must be allowed to call constructors that write to the heap. Limiting constructor writes for side effect freeness in a practical and safe way requires alias control [SR05]. Therefore, instead of requiring side-effect freeness, Jimuva uses a weaker restriction that is simpler to enforce on top of the ownership infrastructure.

> `rdonly`: An expression is *read-only*, if it (1) contains no field assignments, (2) all its method calls have the form $v.m$<$\bar{u}$>$(\bar{e})$ where either (a) m is `rdonly` or (b) $\bar{u} =$ `world` and v has a type C<ar,`world`>, and (3) all its `new`-calls have the form `new`C<ar,`world`>$.k(\bar{e})$.

`rdonly`-methods are guaranteed to not write to the state of immutable receivers. The `rdonly`-restriction allows important side-effecting methods. For instance, the method `getChars(int srcBegin,int srcEnd,char[] dst,int dstBegin)` from Java's

[3] For readability, keywords that could be left implicit are written in italics.

immutable `String` class writes to the array `dst` (owned by `world`). It is an example of a `rdonly` method that is not side-effect free.

Restrictions on constructors with `wrlocal` *and* `anon`. A constructor of an immutable object typically will have side-effects to initialize the object state. We have to restrict constructors of immutable objects for two reasons: (i) we have to prevent them from modifying other objects of the same class, (ii) we have to prevent them from leaking the partially constructed `this` [Goe02].

Issue (i) stems from the fact that visibility modifiers in Java constrain per-class, not per-object, visibility. So it is possible for a constructor of an immutable object to see and modify other immutable objects of the same class. For example:

```
immutable class Wrong {
    Mutable<this> m;
    rdonly int get(){ m.get() } }
    anon wrlocal Wrong.k(Wrong o) {
        this.m = new Mutable<this>.k(o.get());
        o.m.set(23); /* unwanted side-effect on other object! */ } }
```

To prevent such immutability violations, we require constructors of immutable objects to be write-local in the following sense:

`wrlocal`: An expression is *write-local*, if (1) all its field assignments have the form $v.f$=e where either $v =$ `this` or v has a type C`<rdwr,this>` and (2) all its method calls have the form $v.m$<$\bar{u}$>($\bar{e}$) where either (a) m is `rdonly` or (b) m is `wrlocal` and $v =$ `this` or (c) m is `wrlocal` and v has a type C`<rdwr,this>` or (c) v is has a type C<ar,`world`>.

To prevent constructors of immutable objects from leaking `this`, we use Vitek et al's notion of anonymity of [VB01, ZPV06]:

anon: An expression is *anonymous*, if it (1) is not `this`, (2) does not pass `this` to foreign methods, (3) does not assign `this` to fields, and (4) all its method calls have the form $v.m$<$\bar{u}$>($\bar{e}$) where either v or m is anon.

Owner-polymorphic methods. The example below uses an owner-polymorphic method to permit dynamic aliasing of the representation object `this.m` during object construction. As explained in Section 2, the polymorphic type of `copy()` prevents this method from creating a static alias to its parameter `to`. This example is a small model of Java's `String` constructor `String(char[] a)`, which gives an alias to a representation object to a global `arraycopy()` method.

```
class Utilities ext Object {
  Utilities.k(){ skip }
  <x,y> void copy(Mutable<x> from, Mutable<y> to){ to.set(from.get()); } }

immutable class EncapsulatedMutable2 ext Object {
  Mutable<this> m;
  anon wrlocal EncapsulatedMutable2.k(Mutable m) {
     this.m = new Mutable<this>.k(null);
     new Utilities.k().copy<world,this>(m,this.m); }
  rdonly int get(){ m.get() } }
```

Now is a good point to present the subtyping relation: Subtyping is defined against a type environment Γ that assigns types to variables. The following function is used in its definition:

$$\mathtt{atts(Object)} \triangleq \emptyset \qquad \mathtt{atts}(C) \triangleq ca, \text{ if } \mathit{fm}\,ca\,\mathtt{class}\,C\,\mathtt{ext}\,D\{..\} \qquad \mathtt{atts(void)} \triangleq \emptyset$$
$$\mathtt{atts}(C\mathtt{<}ar,v\mathtt{>}) \triangleq \mathtt{atts}(C) \cup \{ar\} \quad \mathtt{atts}(ea\,ty) \triangleq ea \cup \mathtt{atts}(ty) \quad \mathtt{atts}(o) \triangleq \mathtt{atts}(\mathtt{ty}(o))$$

We interpret expression attributes ea as subsets of $\{\mathtt{anon}, \mathtt{rdonly}, \mathtt{wrlocal}\}$ ordered by set inclusion.

Subtyping, $\Gamma \vdash T \preceq U$:

(Sub Rep)
$$\frac{\Gamma \vdash ar, v, v' : \mathsf{ok} \quad C <: C' \quad ea' \subseteq ea}{\Gamma \vdash ea\,C\mathtt{<}ar,v\mathtt{>} \preceq ea'\,C'\mathtt{<}ar,v\mathtt{>}}$$

(Sub World)
$$\frac{\Gamma \vdash ar, ar' : \mathsf{ok} \quad ea' \subseteq ea \quad C <: C'}{\Gamma \vdash ea\,C\mathtt{<}ar,\mathtt{world}\mathtt{>} \preceq ea'\,C'\mathtt{<}ar',\mathtt{world}\mathtt{>}}$$

(Sub Void)
$$\frac{ea' \subseteq ea}{\Gamma \vdash ea\,\mathtt{void} \preceq ea'\,\mathtt{void}}$$

(Sub Share)
$$\frac{ea' \subseteq ea \quad C <: C' \quad \Gamma \vdash v, v' : D, D' \text{ in } \mathtt{world} \quad \mathtt{immutable} \in \mathtt{atts}(D) \cap \mathtt{atts}(D')}{\Gamma \vdash ea\,C\mathtt{<rd},v\mathtt{>} \preceq ea'\,C'\mathtt{<rd},v'\mathtt{>}}$$

The interesting rules are (Sub Share) and (Sub World). The former allows flows of read-restricted objects with immutable owners into locations for read-restricted objects of other immutable owners. That is, our type system permits sharing representation objects among immutable objects as long as those are read-restricted. The rule (Sub World) expresses that ownerless objects do not have to follow access policies. It is needed to ensure that our type system is sound in an open world that includes clients that do not follow Jimuva-policies. Compared to type systems with read references, e.g., the Universe type system [MPH01], it is noteworthy that we do not allow upcasting read-write objects to read objects. Allowing this would lead to an unsoundness in our system. This means that read-restricted objects have to be created as read-restricted objects. Of course, we then must allow constructors of read-restricted objects to initialize their own state. This is safe, as long as constructors of read-restricted objects are `wrlocal`.

Sharing mutable representation objects. This example illustrates sharing of mutable representation objects. The subtyping rule (Sub Share) is used to upcast `o.m`'s type from `SharedRepObject<rd,o>` to `SharedRepObj<rd,this>` so that the assignment to `this.m` becomes possible.

```
immutable class SharedRepObject ext Object {
  Mutable<rd,this> m;
  rdonly int get(){ m.get() } }
  anon wrlocal SharedRepObject.k1(int i) {
      this.m = new Mutable<rd,this>.k(i); }
  anon wrlocal SharedRepObject.k2(SharedRepObject o) {
      this.m = o.m; } /* sharing of mutable representation object */ }
```

6 The Immutability Type System – Formally

A *type environment* $\Gamma = (\Gamma_{\mathsf{acc}}, \Gamma_{\mathsf{own}}, \Gamma_{\mathsf{val}})$ is a triple of partial functions $\Gamma_{\mathsf{acc}} \in \{\mathtt{myaccess}\} \to \{\bullet\}$, $\Gamma_{\mathsf{own}} \in \mathsf{Var} \cup \mathsf{ObjId} \to \{\bullet\}$ and $\Gamma_{\mathsf{val}} \in \mathsf{Var} \cup \mathsf{ObjId} \to \mathsf{ExpTy}$. If

$v \notin \mathsf{dom}(\Gamma_{\mathsf{val}}) \cup \{\mathtt{null}\}$, we define $\Gamma_{\mathsf{val}}, v : T \triangleq \Gamma_{\mathsf{val}} \cup \{(x,T)\}$. Similarly, for Γ_{acc} and Γ_{own}. We define $\Gamma, v : T \triangleq (\Gamma_{\mathsf{acc}}, \Gamma_{\mathsf{own}}, (\Gamma_{\mathsf{val}}, v : T))$. Similarly, for Γ_{acc} and Γ_{own}. We often write $\Gamma(v) = T$ as an abbreviation for $\Gamma_{\mathsf{val}}(v) = T$. Similarly, for Γ_{acc} and Γ_{own}. We define $\mathsf{dom}(\Gamma) \triangleq \mathsf{dom}(\Gamma_{\mathsf{acc}}) \cup \mathsf{dom}(\Gamma_{\mathsf{own}}) \cup \mathsf{dom}(\Gamma_{\mathsf{val}})$.

Substitution Application for Environments, $\Gamma[\sigma]$:

$\Gamma[\sigma] \triangleq (\Gamma_{\mathsf{acc}}[\sigma], \Gamma_{\mathsf{own}}[\sigma], \Gamma_{\mathsf{val}}[\sigma]) \qquad \Gamma_{\mathsf{val}}[\sigma] \triangleq \{(v, T[\sigma]) \mid (v,T) \in \Gamma_{\mathsf{val}}\}$
$\Gamma_{\mathsf{acc}}[\sigma] \triangleq \{(ar[\sigma], \bullet) \mid ar \in \mathsf{dom}(\Gamma_{\mathsf{acc}})\} \cap \{(\mathtt{myaccess}, \bullet)\}$
$\Gamma_{\mathsf{own}}[\sigma] \triangleq \{(v[\sigma], \bullet) \mid v \in \mathsf{dom}(\Gamma_{\mathsf{own}})\} \cap (\mathsf{Var} \cup \mathsf{ObjId}) \times \{\bullet\}$

In addition to subtyping, there are judgments of the following forms:

$\vdash c : \mathsf{ok}$	"c is a good class declaration"
$\Gamma \vdash e : T \text{ in } v, ar$	"if $\mathtt{this} = v$ and v has access rights ar, then e has type T"

In useful judgments ($\Gamma \vdash e : T \text{ in } v, ar$), the `this`-binding v is either `this` itself or an object identifier. For type-checking class declarations, it is sufficient to consider judgments where $\mathsf{dom}(\Gamma) \subseteq \mathsf{Var} \cup \{\mathtt{world}, \mathtt{myaccess}\}$ and $v = \mathtt{this}$. We allow arbitrary object identifiers in type environments and as `this`-binders, so that we can type runtime states, which is needed for proving type soundness.

The typing judgments are defined with respect to an underlying class table. This class table remains fixed in all typing rules and we leave it implicit. In contexts where we want to explicitly mention it, we subscript the turnstyle: ($\Gamma \vdash_{\bar{c}} e : T \text{ in } v, ar$). We use auxiliary functions $\mathsf{ctype}(C.k)$ and $\mathsf{mtype}(C,m)$ that compute the types of constructors and methods based on the underlying class table. These are essentially as in FJ [IPW01]. *Method subtyping* treats methods invariantly in the parameter types and covariantly in the result type. See [HPSS07] for more details.

Auxiliary Predicates and Judgments:

$ea\,C\langle ar, v\rangle \text{ legal} \triangleq (v = \mathtt{myowner} \Leftrightarrow ar = \mathtt{myaccess}) \qquad ea\,\mathtt{void} \text{ legal} \triangleq \text{true}$
$C\langle ar, v\rangle \text{ generative} \triangleq (\mathtt{immutable} \in \mathsf{atts}(C) \Rightarrow v = \mathtt{world},\ v = \mathtt{world} \Rightarrow ar = \mathtt{rdwr})$
$(ea, u, ar_u, v_u) \text{ wrloc in } v \triangleq (u = v, \mathtt{wrlocal} \in ea) \text{ or } (ar_u, v_u) = (\mathtt{rdwr}, v)$
$ar \text{ wrsafe in } ar' \triangleq (ar = \mathtt{rdwr} \text{ or } ar' = \mathtt{rd} \text{ or } ar = ar')$
$(\vdash \bar{c} : \mathsf{ok}) \triangleq (\forall c \in \bar{c})(\vdash c : \mathsf{ok}) \qquad (\Gamma \vdash e : T) \triangleq (\Gamma \vdash e : T \text{ in } \mathtt{myaccess})$
$(\Gamma \vdash e : T \text{ in } ar) \triangleq (\Gamma \vdash e : T \text{ in } \mathtt{this}, ar) \qquad (\Gamma \vdash e : T \text{ in } v) \triangleq (\Gamma \vdash e : T \text{ in } v, \mathtt{rdwr})$
$(\Gamma \vdash \bar{e}, e : \bar{T}, T \text{ in } v, ar) \triangleq (\Gamma \vdash \bar{e} : \bar{T} \text{ in } v, ar \text{ and } \Gamma \vdash e : T \text{ in } v, ar)$
$(\Gamma \vdash e : T \preceq U \text{ in } v, ar) \triangleq (\Gamma \vdash e : T \text{ in } v, ar \text{ and } \Gamma \vdash T \preceq U)$
$(\Gamma \vdash \diamond) \triangleq (\mathtt{world} \in \mathsf{dom}(\Gamma_{\mathsf{own}}) \text{ and } (\forall v \in \mathsf{dom}(\Gamma_{\mathsf{val}}))(v \neq \mathtt{world} \text{ and } \Gamma \vdash \Gamma_{\mathsf{val}}(v) : \mathsf{ok}))$
$(\Gamma \vdash v : \bullet) \triangleq (\Gamma \vdash \diamond \text{ and } \Gamma(v) = \bullet) \qquad (\Gamma \vdash v : \mathsf{ok}) \triangleq (\Gamma \vdash \diamond \text{ and } v \in \mathsf{dom}(\Gamma) \cup \{\mathtt{null}\})$
$(\Gamma \vdash ar : \mathsf{ok}) \triangleq (\Gamma \vdash \diamond \text{ and } ar \in \mathsf{dom}(\Gamma) \cup \{\mathtt{rdwr}, \mathtt{rd}\})$
$(\Gamma \vdash ea\,\mathtt{void} : \mathsf{ok}) \triangleq (\Gamma \vdash \diamond) \qquad (\Gamma \vdash ea\,C\langle ar, v\rangle : \mathsf{ok}) \triangleq (\Gamma \vdash ar : \mathsf{ok} \text{ and } \Gamma \vdash v : \mathsf{ok})$

Good Class Declarations, $\vdash c : \mathsf{ok}$:

(Cls Dcl)
$$\frac{D \text{ is not } \texttt{final} \quad \Gamma = (\texttt{world}, \texttt{myowner}, \texttt{myaccess}, \texttt{this} : \bullet) \quad ca \neq \emptyset \Rightarrow (\mathsf{atts}(D) \neq \emptyset \text{ or } D = \texttt{Object}) \quad \mathsf{atts}(D) \neq \emptyset \Rightarrow ca \neq \emptyset \quad \Gamma, \texttt{this} : \texttt{rdonly}\ \texttt{wrlocal}\, C\texttt{<myaccess,myowner>} \vdash \bar{F}, \bar{K}, \bar{M} : \mathsf{ok\ in}\ C}{\vdash fm\, ca\, \texttt{class}\, C\, \texttt{ext}\, D\{\bar{F}\ \bar{K}\ \bar{M}\} : \mathsf{ok}}$$

(Fld Dcl)
$$\frac{C\,\texttt{ext}\,D \Rightarrow f \notin \mathsf{fd}(D) \quad E\texttt{<}ar,v\texttt{>}\ \mathsf{legal} \quad \Gamma \vdash ar : \mathsf{ok} \quad \Gamma \vdash v : \bullet}{\Gamma \vdash E\texttt{<}ar,v\texttt{>} f : \mathsf{ok\ in}\ C}$$

(Cons Dcl)
$$\frac{\bar{ty}\ \mathsf{legal} \quad \texttt{this} \notin \mathsf{vars}(\bar{ty}) \quad \mathsf{atts}(C) \neq \emptyset \Rightarrow \texttt{anon}, \texttt{wrlocal} \in ea \quad \Gamma, \bar{x} : \texttt{anon}\ \texttt{rdonly}\ \texttt{wrlocal}\, \bar{ty} \vdash e : ea\, \texttt{void}}{\Gamma \vdash ea\, C.k(\bar{ty}\bar{x})\{e\} : \mathsf{ok\ in}\ C}$$

(Mth Dcl)
$$\frac{C\,\texttt{ext}\,D \Rightarrow \Gamma \vdash \mathsf{mtype}(m,C) \preceq \mathsf{mtype}(m,D) \quad \mathsf{atts}(C) \neq \emptyset \Rightarrow \texttt{rdonly} \in \mathsf{atts}(T) \quad ar = \texttt{myaccess} \text{ or } (\{\texttt{rdonly}, \texttt{wrlocal}\} \cap ea = \emptyset, ar = \texttt{rdwr}) \quad \sigma = (\texttt{myaccess} \leftarrow ar) \quad \Gamma[\sigma], \bar{y} : \bullet, \bar{x} : \texttt{anon}\ \texttt{rdonly}\ \texttt{wrlocal}\, \bar{ty}[\sigma] \vdash e[\sigma] : T[\sigma]\ \mathsf{in}\ ar \quad \bar{ty}, T\ \mathsf{legal} \quad \texttt{this} \notin \mathsf{vars}(\bar{ty}, T)}{\Gamma \vdash fm\texttt{<}\bar{y}\texttt{>}\, T\, m(\bar{ty}\bar{x})\{e\} : \mathsf{ok\ in}\ C}$$

Well-typed Expressions, $\Gamma \vdash e : T\ \mathsf{in}\ v, ar$:

(Var)
$$\frac{\Gamma(x) = T \quad \Gamma \vdash ar_v, v : \mathsf{ok}, \bullet}{\Gamma \vdash x : T\ \mathsf{in}\ v, ar_v}$$

(Obj)
$$\frac{\Gamma(o) = T \quad ea = \{\texttt{anon} \mid o \neq p\} \quad \Gamma \vdash ar_p, p : \mathsf{ok}, \bullet}{\Gamma \vdash o : ea\, T\ \mathsf{in}\ p, ar_p}$$

(Sub)
$$\frac{\Gamma \vdash e : T \preceq U\ \mathsf{in}\ v, ar_v}{\Gamma \vdash e : U\ \mathsf{in}\ v, ar_v}$$

(Null)
$$\frac{\Gamma \vdash T, ar_v, v : \mathsf{ok}, \mathsf{ok}, \bullet}{\Gamma \vdash \texttt{null} : T\ \mathsf{in}\ v, ar_v}$$

(Let)
$$\frac{\Gamma \vdash e : ea_e\, ty_e\ \mathsf{in}\ v, ar_v \quad x \notin \mathsf{vars}(ty_{e'}) \quad \Gamma, x : ea_e\, ty_e \vdash e' : ea_{e'}\, ty_{e'}\ \mathsf{in}\ v, ar_v \quad ea = \bigcap(ea_e, ea_{e'})}{\Gamma \vdash \texttt{let}\, x\texttt{=}e\, \texttt{in}\, e' : ea\, ty_{e'}\ \mathsf{in}\ v, ar_v}$$

(Cast)
$$\frac{C\ \text{declared} \quad \Gamma \vdash e : ea_e\, C_e\texttt{<}ar_e, v_e\texttt{>}\ \mathsf{in}\ v, ar_v}{\Gamma \vdash (C)e : ea_e\, C\texttt{<}ar_e, v_e\texttt{>}\ \mathsf{in}\ v, ar_v}$$

(Get)
$$\frac{ty\, f \in \mathsf{fd}(C_u) \quad \sigma = \mathsf{self}(u, ar_u, v_u) \quad \Gamma \vdash u, v : ea_u\, C_u\texttt{<}ar_u, v_u\texttt{>}, C_u\texttt{<}ar_v, w_v\texttt{>}\ \mathsf{in}\ v, ar_v}{\Gamma \vdash u.f : \texttt{anon}\ \texttt{rdonly}\ \texttt{wrlocal}\, ty[\sigma]\ \mathsf{in}\ v, ar_v}$$

(Set)
$$\frac{ty\, f \in \mathsf{fd}(C_u) \quad \Gamma \vdash v_u : \bullet \quad ea = \bigcap(\{x\ \mathsf{as}\ \texttt{wrlocal} \mid (\{x\}, u, ar_u, v_u)\ \mathsf{wrloc\ in}\ v\} \cup \{\texttt{anon}\}, ea_e) \quad ar_u\ \mathsf{wrsafe\ in}\ ar_v \quad \Gamma \vdash u, v, e : ea_u\, C_u\texttt{<}ar_u, v_u\texttt{>}, C_u\texttt{<}ar_v, w_v\texttt{>}, ea_e\, ty[\sigma]\ \mathsf{in}\ v, ar_v \quad \sigma = \mathsf{self}(u, ar_u, v_u)}{\Gamma \vdash u.f\texttt{=}e : ea\, ty[\sigma]\ \mathsf{in}\ v, ar_v}$$

(Call)
$$\frac{\begin{array}{l} \mathsf{mtype}(m, C_u) = fm\texttt{<}\bar{y}\texttt{>}\bar{ty} \rightarrow ea_m\, ty' \\ (\texttt{rdonly} \in ea_m) \text{ or } (ar_u\ \mathsf{wrsafe\ in}\ ar_v) \quad \sigma = \mathsf{self}(u, ar_u, v_u), \bar{y} \leftarrow \bar{w} \\ ea = \bigcap \bar{ea}_{\bar{e}} \cap \bigcup(\ \{\texttt{anon}\} \cap (ea_m \cup ea_u),\ \{x\ \mathsf{as}\ \texttt{rdonly} \mid x \in ea_m \text{ or } v_u, \bar{w} = \texttt{world}\}, \\ \quad \{\texttt{wrlocal} \mid (ea_m, u, ar_u, v_u)\ \mathsf{wrloc\ in}\ v \text{ or } \texttt{rdonly} \in ea_m \text{ or } v_u = \texttt{world}\}\ ) \\ \Gamma \vdash u, \bar{e} : ea_u\, C_u\texttt{<}ar_u, v_u\texttt{>}, \bar{ea}_{\bar{e}}\, \bar{ty}[\sigma]\ \mathsf{in}\ v, ar_v \quad \Gamma \vdash \bar{w} : \bullet \quad (ar_u = \texttt{rd} \text{ or } \Gamma \vdash v_u : \bullet) \end{array}}{\Gamma \vdash u.m\texttt{<}\bar{w}\texttt{>}(\bar{e}) : ea\, ty'[\sigma]\ \mathsf{in}\ v, ar_v}$$

(New)
$$\frac{\begin{array}{l} \mathsf{ctype}(C.k) = \bar{ty} \rightarrow ea_k\, \texttt{void} \quad (ar = \texttt{rdwr}) \text{ or } (\texttt{wrlocal}, \texttt{anon} \in ea_k) \\ ea = \bigcap(\{\texttt{rdonly} \mid w = \texttt{world}\} \cup \{\texttt{wrlocal}, \texttt{anon}\}, \bar{ea}_{\bar{e}}) \quad \Gamma \vdash ar, w : \mathsf{ok}, \bullet \\ \Gamma \vdash \bar{e} : \bar{ea}_{\bar{e}}\, \bar{ty}[\sigma]\ \mathsf{in}\ v, ar_v \quad \sigma = \mathsf{self}(\texttt{null}, ar, w) \quad C\texttt{<}ar, w\texttt{>}\ \mathsf{generative} \end{array}}{\Gamma \vdash \texttt{new}\, C\texttt{<}ar,w\texttt{>}.k(\bar{e}) : ea\, C\texttt{<}ar, w\texttt{>}\ \mathsf{in}\ v, ar_v}$$

(Cons)
$$\frac{\mathsf{ctype}(C.k) = \bar{ty} \rightarrow ea_k\, \texttt{void} \quad \sigma = \mathsf{self}(v, ar_v, w_v) \quad \Gamma \vdash \bar{e}, v : \bar{ea}_{\bar{e}}\, \bar{ty}[\sigma], C\texttt{<}ar_v, w_v\texttt{>}\ \mathsf{in}\ v, ar_v \quad ea = \bigcap(ea_k, \bar{ea}_{\bar{e}})}{\Gamma \vdash C.k(\bar{e}) : ea\, \texttt{void}\ \mathsf{in}\ v, ar_v}$$

7 Conclusion

More on related work. We have already referenced and compared to some related work throughout the text and have no space to repeat all of that. Ernst et al's Javari language [BE04, TE05] statically checks reference immutability, i.e., read-only references. They report an impressive implementation. They do not support object immutability in an open world, like we do. In particular, their system does not fully prevent representation exposure. Pechtchanski et al [PS05] and Porat et al [PBKM00] present immutability analyses for Java. Their analyses are implementation driven and are not designed against a formal semantics like ours. Parts of our formal type system are inspired by similar informal static rules from Jan Schäfer's masters thesis [Sch04]. Clarke and Drossopolous [CD02] and Lu and Potter [LP06b, LP06a] combine ownership type systems with systems to control write- and/or read-effects. In spirit, this is similar to our system which contains a write-effect analysis (for `rdonly` and `wrlocal`) on top of an ownership type system. In contrast to the above mentioned systems, our system supports an open world and treats object constructors. Our system does not control read-effects. However, a read-effect analysis would be desirable, because for many applications of immutability, e.g., thread safety, it is important that immutable objects do not read from mutable state. We expect that we could combine our system with a variant of [CD02]'s read effect analysis to achieve this.

Summary. We have presented a core Java language with statically checkable immutability specifications in the form of a type system, which has been proved sound w.r.t. a formal semantic definition of object immutability. The system is quite flexible and employs, for instance, owner-polymorphic methods to permit dynamic aliasing during object construction, and read-only objects to permit sharing of mutable representation objects among immutable objects of the same class. We view this paper as the careful design for a sound, type-based immutability analysis and plan to implement an immutability checker for Java based on this system.

References

[BE04] A. Birka and M. D. Ernst. A practical type system and language for reference immutability. In *OOPSLA'04*, pages 35–49, October 26–28, 2004.

[Blo01] J. Bloch. *Effective Java.* Addison-Wesley, 2001.

[BLS03] C. Boyapati, B. Liskov, and L. Shrira. Ownership types for object encapsulation. In *POPL'03*, pages 213–223, 2003.

[CD02] D. Clarke and S. Drossopoulou. Ownership, encapsulation and the disjointness of type and effect. In *OOPSLA'02*, pages 292–310, 2002.

[CPN98] D. Clarke, J. Potter, and J. Noble. Ownership types for flexible alias protection. In *OOPSLA'98*, pages 48–64, 1998.

[DM05] W. Dietl and P. Müller. Universes: Lightweight ownership for JML. *Journal of Object Technology (JOT)*, 4(8):5–32, October 2005.

[Goe02] Brian Goetz. Java theory and practice: Safe construction techniques–don't let the "this" reference escape during construction. *IBM DevelopersWork*, 2002.

[HPSS07] C. Haack, E. Poll, J. Schäfer, and A. Schubert. Immutable objects for a Java-like language. Technical report, Radboud University Nijmegen, 2007. Forthcoming.

[IPW01] A. Igarashi, B. Pierce, and P. Wadler. Featherweight Java: a minimal core calculus for Java and GJ. *ACM TOPLAS*, 23(3):396–450, 2001.

[LP06a] Y. Lu and J. Potter. On ownership and accessibility. In *ECOOP'06*, volume 4067 of *LNCS*, pages 99–123. Springer-Verlag, 2006.

[LP06b] Y. Lu and J. Potter. Protecting representation with effect encapsulation. In *POPL'06*, pages 359–371. ACM Press, 2006.

[MPH01] P. Müller and A. Poetzsch-Heffter. Universes: A type system for alias and dependency control. Technical Report 279, Fernuniversität Hagen, 2001.

[PBKM00] S. Porat, M. Biberstein, L. Koved, and B. Mendelson. Automatic detection of immutable fields in Java. In *CASCON'02*. IBM Press, 2000.

[PS05] I. Pechtchanski and V. Sarkar. Immutability specification and applications. *Concurrency and Computation: Practice and Experience*, 17:639–662, 2005.

[Sch04] J. Schäfer. Encapsulation and specification of object-oriented runtime components. Master's thesis, Technische Universität Kaiserslautern, 2004.

[SR05] A. Salcianu and M. C. Rinard. Purity and side effect analysis for Java programs. In *VMCAI'05*, pages 199–215, 2005.

[TE05] M. S. Tschantz and M. D. Ernst. Javari: Adding reference immutability to Java. In *OOPSLA'05*, pages 211–230, October 18–20, 2005.

[VB01] J. Vitek and B. Bokowski. Confined types in Java. *Softw. Pract. Exper.*, 31(6):507–532, 2001.

[WF94] A. K. Wright and M. Felleisen. A syntactic approach to type soundness. *Information and Computation*, 115(1):38–94, 1994.

[ZPV06] T. Zhao, J. Palsberg, and J. Vitek. Type-based confinement. *Journal of Functional Programming*, 16(1):83–128, January 2006.

Scalar Outcomes Suffice for Finitary Probabilistic Testing

Yuxin Deng[1,⋆], Rob van Glabbeek[1,2], Carroll Morgan[1,⋆], and Chenyi Zhang[1,2]

[1] School of Comp. Sci. and Eng., University of New South Wales, Sydney, Australia
[2] National ICT Australia, Locked Bag 6016, Sydney, NSW 1466, Australia

Abstract. The question of equivalence has long vexed research in concurrency, leading to many different denotational- and bisimulation-based approaches; a breakthrough occurred with the insight that tests expressed within the concurrent framework itself, based on a special "success action," yield equivalences that make only inarguable distinctions.

When probability was added, however, it seemed necessary to extend the testing framework beyond a direct probabilistic generalisation in order to remain useful. An attractive possibility was the extension to *multiple* success actions that yielded *vectors* of real-valued outcomes.

Here we prove that such vectors are unnecessary when processes are *finitary*, that is finitely branching and finite-state: single *scalar* outcomes are just as powerful. Thus for finitary processes we can retain the original, simpler testing approach and its direct connections to other naturally scalar-valued phenomena.

1 Introduction

The theory of testing of De Nicola & Hennessy [4] yields equivalences making only inarguable distinctions: two processes are may-testing inequivalent iff there is a context, built with parallel composition and hiding or restriction operators, in which one of them *might* do a visible action but the other definitely can not; they are must-testing inequivalent iff there is a context in which one *must* do a visible action, but the other might never do any. This reduces a complex phenomenon to a scalar- (in fact Boolean-) valued outcome.

Wang & Larsen [21] generalised this theory in a straightforward way to processes with probabilistic and nondeterministic choice, again yielding only distinctions that are hard to argue with: two processes are may-testing inequivalent iff there is a context in which, in the best case (when resolving nondeterministic choice), one of them might do a visible action with some probability p whereas the other falls short of that. They are must-testing inequivalent iff there is a context in which, in the worst case, one must do a visible action with probability p, whereas the other might fall short of that.

Wang & Larsen ended with the question of finding denotational characterisations of may- and must testing; for non-trivial examples this is necessary to

⋆ We acknowledge the support of the Australian Research Council Grant DP034557.

R. De Nicola (Ed.): ESOP 2007, LNCS 4421, pp. 363–378, 2007.

show the equivalence of two processes. The question is still open today, although Jonsson & Wang [9] have found a denotational characterisation in the special case of may-testing for processes without internal actions.

Meanwhile, progress has been made elsewhere for notions of testing that are seemingly more powerful than Wang & Larsen's. Most notably, Segala [17] found denotational characterisations of variants of may- and must testing that employ multiple success actions instead of a single one, and consequently yield vectors of real-valued outcomes instead of scalars. Earlier, Jonsson, Ho-Stuart & Wang [8] characterised variants that employ so-called "reward testing," and that consider non-probabilistic test processes only.

It follows immediately from the definitions that Segala's vector-based testing is *at least* as powerful as the scalar testing of Wang & Larsen, while reward testing sits in between. Unfortunately, the possibility that these extended notions of testing are strictly *more* powerful suggests that the argument above, that testing equivalences make no unwarranted distinctions, might not apply to them.[1]

In this paper we show that in fact the argument *does* apply, at least for finitary processes, where we prove all three notions to be equally powerful. This is a fundamental prerequisite for a stable notion of program equivalence, a core concept for rigorous software engineering.

2 Probabilistic Testing of Probabilistic Automata

2.1 Probabilistic Structures and Notational Conventions

We write $f.s$ instead of $f(s)$ for function application, with left association so that $f.g.x$ means $(f(g))(x)$.

- A *discrete probability distribution* over a set X is a function $\mu \in X \rightarrow [0,1]$ with $\mu.X = 1$, where for subset X' of X we define $\mu.X' := \sum_{x \in X'} \mu.x$. We write $\overline{X}$ for the set of all such distributions over X.
- The *point-* or *Dirac distribution* $\overline{x}$ assigns probability one to $x \in X$.
- The *support* $\lceil \mu \rceil$ of distribution μ is the set of elements x such that $\mu.x \neq 0$.
- Given $p \in [0,1]$ and distributions $\mu, \zeta \in \overline{X}$, the *weighted average* $\mu\ {}_p\!\oplus \zeta \in \overline{X}$ is the distribution defined $(\mu\ {}_p\!\oplus \zeta).x := p \times \mu.x + (1-p) \times \zeta.x$.
- Given some function $f \in X \rightarrow \mathbb{R}$ (a *random variable*), its *expected value* $\mu.f$ over distribution μ is the weighted average $\sum_{x \in X} (\mu.x \times f.x)$.[2]
- Given a function $f \in X \rightarrow Y$, we write $f.\mu$ for the *image distribution* in $\overline{Y}$ formed by applying f to a distribution $\mu \in \overline{X}$: for element $y \in Y$ we define $f.\mu.y := \mu.\{x \in X \mid f.x = y\}$.
- The *product* of two discrete probability distributions μ, μ' over X, X' is the distribution $\mu \times \mu'$ over $X \times X'$ defined $(\mu \times \mu').(x, x') := \mu.x \times \mu'.x'$.

[1] However, Stoelinga & Vaandrager [19] offer evidence that the distinctions of Segala's vector-based may-testing are observable by repeating experiments many times.

[2] This extends to any linear vector space, in particular to functions in $X \rightarrow \mathbb{R}^N$.

2.2 Probabilistic Automata and Their Resolutions

In this paper we employ probabilistic automata [18] as representatives of a class of models that treat both probabilistic and nondeterministic choice [20,5,21,6].

Definition 1. A *probabilistic automaton* is a tuple $\mathrm{M} = (M, m^\circ, E, I, \mathcal{T})$ where

- M is a set of *states*,
- $m^\circ \in \overline{M}$ is a distribution of *start states*,
- E and I are disjoint sets of *external-* and *internal actions* respectively and
- $\mathcal{T} \in M \to \mathcal{P}(\Sigma \times \overline{M})$ is the *transition relation*, where $\Sigma := E \cup I$.

Automaton M is *fully probabilistic* if from each state $m \in M$ there is at most one outgoing transition, *i.e.* if the set $\mathcal{T}.m$ contains at most one element. If $\mathcal{T}.m$ is finite for all $m \in M$, then M is said to be *finitely branching*. An *execution sequence* of M is an alternating sequence of states and actions $m_0, \alpha_1, m_1, \alpha_2, \cdots$, either infinite or ending in state m_n, such that $m_0 \in \lceil m^\circ \rceil$ and for all $i > 0$ (and $i \leq n$ if finite) we have $\exists(\alpha_i, \mu_i) \in \mathcal{T}.m_{i-1}$ with $m_i \in \lceil \mu_i \rceil$. The execution sequence is *maximal* if either it is infinite or $\mathcal{T}.m_n = \emptyset$. ¶

From here on we use "automaton" to mean "probabilistic automaton."

Any automaton can be "resolved" into fully probabilistic automata as follows.

Definition 2. A *resolution* of an automaton $\mathrm{M} = (M, m^\circ, E, I, \mathcal{T})$ is a fully probabilistic automaton $\mathrm{R} = (R, r^\circ, E, I, \mathcal{T}')$ such that there is a *resolving function* $f \in R \to M$ with

- $f.r^\circ = m^\circ$, *equivalent initialisations*
- if $\mathcal{T}'.r = \{(\alpha, \mu)\}$ then $(\alpha, f.\mu) \in \mathcal{T}.(f.r)$ and *compatible choice taken*
- if $\mathcal{T}'.r = \emptyset$ then $\mathcal{T}.(f.r) = \emptyset$ *liveness preserved*

for any $r \in R$.[3] ¶

A resolution has as its main effect the choosing in any state of a single outgoing transition from all available ones; but f can be non-injective, so that the choice can vary between different departures from that state, depending *e.g.* on the history of states and actions that led there. Further, since a single state of M can be "split" into a distribution over several states of R, all mapped to it by f, probabilistic *interpolation* between distinct choices is obtained automatically.[4]

Fig. 1 illustrates the history-dependent choice with states $r_{1,4}$ both mapped to m_1; it illustrates interpolation with states $r_{2,4}$ both mapped to m_1.

2.3 Probabilities of Action Occurrences in Resolutions

For a fully probabilistic automaton in which all execution sequences are finite, like R from Fig. 1, the probability of an action's occurrence is easily obtained: we calculate probabilities for the maximal execution sequences, given for each by

[3] We use this abstract definition because of its useful mathematical properties; it is equivalent to Segala's [17] in that it generates the same distributions over action sequences, as the following discussion illustrates.

[4] In this regard our resolutions strictly generalise the ones of Jonsson *et al.* [8].

We show that M is resolved by R in the following diagram. Enclosing circles and ovals represent distributions, the enclosed shapes' relative sizes within hinting at probabilities; on the left the shapes are associated 1-1 with the distinct states, but the right-hand states' shapes indicate the left-hand states *to which they are mapped.* Thus the resolving function f is given by $f.r_{1,2,3,4} := m_1$, $f.r_5 := m_2$ and $f.r_6 := m_3$.

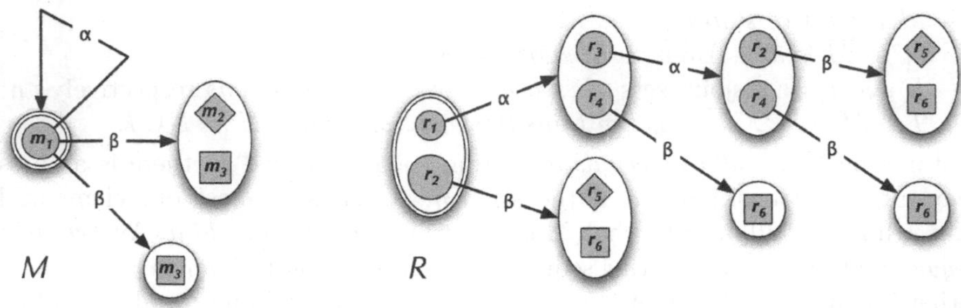

The left-hand automaton M has initial (Dirac) distribution $m^\circ = \overline{m_1}$ and transitions

$$\mathcal{T}.m_1 \;:=\; \{(\alpha, \overline{m_1}) \;,\; (\beta, \overline{m_2}\;{}_{\frac{1}{2}}\!\oplus \overline{m_3}) \;,\; (\beta, \overline{m_3})\} \;, \qquad \mathcal{T}.m_2 \;=\; \mathcal{T}.m_3 \;:=\; \emptyset \;.$$

The right-hand (fully probabilistic) resolution R has initial distribution $r^\circ = \overline{r_1}\;{}_{\frac{1}{3}}\!\oplus \overline{r_2}$; its non-$\emptyset$ transitions are

$$\begin{array}{lll} \mathcal{T}'.r_1 \;:=\; \{(\alpha, \overline{r_3}\;{}_{\frac{1}{2}}\!\oplus \overline{r_4})\} & & \mathcal{T}'.r_3 \;:=\; \{(\alpha, \overline{r_2}\;{}_{\frac{1}{2}}\!\oplus \overline{r_4})\} \\ \mathcal{T}'.r_2 \;:=\; \{(\beta, \overline{r_5}\;{}_{\frac{1}{2}}\!\oplus \overline{r_6})\} & & \mathcal{T}'.r_4 \;:=\; \{(\beta, \overline{r_6})\} \;. \end{array}$$

Fig. 1. Example of a fully probabilistic resolution

multiplication of the probabilities of the choices occurring along it; the probability of an action's occurrence is then the sum of the so-calculated probabilities for all maximal sequences containing it. For example, in R the maximal-execution-sequence probabilities are

$$\begin{array}{lll} \langle r_1, \alpha, r_3, \alpha, r_2, \beta, r_5\rangle \;@\,(1/3{\times}1/2{\times}1/2{\times}1/2) & \text{that is,} & \text{probability } 1/24 \\ \langle r_1, \alpha, r_3, \alpha, r_2, \beta, r_6\rangle \;@\,(1/3{\times}1/2{\times}1/2{\times}1/2) & & \text{probability } 1/24 \\ \langle r_1, \alpha, r_3, \alpha, r_4, \beta, r_6\rangle \;@\,(1/3{\times}1/2{\times}1/2{\times}1) & & \text{probability } 1/12 \\ \langle r_1, \alpha, r_4, \beta, r_6\rangle \;@\,(1/3{\times}1/2{\times}1) & & \text{probability } 1/6 \\ \langle r_2, \beta, r_5\rangle \;@\,2/3{\times}1/2 & & \text{probability } 1/3 \\ \langle r_2, \beta, r_6\rangle \;@\,2/3{\times}1/2 & & \text{probability } 1/3, \end{array}$$

with all other sequences being assigned probability zero. If we use f to map this distribution back to M, and aggregate, we get

$$\begin{array}{ll} \langle m_1, \alpha, m_1, \alpha, m_1, \beta, m_2\rangle & \text{probability } 1/24 \\ \langle m_1, \alpha, m_1, \alpha, m_1, \beta, m_3\rangle & \text{probability } 1/24 + 1/12 \\ \langle m_1, \alpha, m_1, \beta, m_3\rangle & \text{probability } 1/6 \\ \langle m_1, \beta, m_2\rangle & \text{probability } 1/3 \\ \langle m_1, \beta, m_3\rangle & \text{probability } 1/3, \end{array}$$

where we can see both history-dependence and interpolation at work. Finally, concentrating on just the actions gives us

$$\begin{array}{ll} \langle \alpha, \alpha, \beta \rangle & \text{probability } 1/24 + 1/24 + 1/12 \\ \langle \alpha, \beta \rangle & \text{probability } 1/6 \\ \langle \beta \rangle & \text{probability } 1/3 + 1/3. \end{array}$$

No matter which of the three views above we use, the probability that a particular action occurs is the probability assigned to the *set* of all sequences containing that action: thus the probability of α's occurrence is $1/24 + 1/24 + 1/12 + 1/6 = 1/3$; for β the probability is 1. (The sum exceeds one because both can occur.)

When our automata can generate infinite executions, however, there might be uncountably many of them: consider a looping automaton, choosing forever between bits 0 and 1, whose infinite sequences thus encode the whole unit interval $[0, 1]$ in binary. Simple summation within discrete distributions is then not appropriate;[5] in this case we apply the following more general definition.

Definition 3. Given a fully probabilistic automaton $\mathrm{R} = (R, r^\circ, E, I, \mathcal{T})$, the *probability that* R *starts with* a sequence of actions $\sigma \in \Sigma^*$, with $\Sigma := E \cup I$, is given by $r^\circ.(\mathrm{Pr}_{\mathrm{R}}.\sigma)$, where $\mathrm{Pr}_{\mathrm{R}} \in \Sigma^* \rightarrow R \rightarrow [0, 1]$ is defined inductively:

$$\mathrm{Pr}_{\mathrm{R}}.\varepsilon.r := 1 \quad \text{and} \quad \mathrm{Pr}_{\mathrm{R}}.(\alpha\sigma).r := \begin{cases} \mu.(\mathrm{Pr}_{\mathrm{R}}.\sigma) & \text{if } \mathcal{T}.r = \{(\alpha, \mu)\} \text{ for some } \mu \\ 0 & \text{otherwise} \end{cases}$$

Here ε denotes the empty sequence of actions and $\alpha\sigma$ the sequence starting with $\alpha \in \Sigma$ and continuing with $\sigma \in \Sigma^*$. Recall from Sec. 2.1 that $\mu.(\mathrm{Pr}_{\mathrm{R}}.\sigma)$ is the expected value over μ of the random variable $\mathrm{Pr}_{\mathrm{R}}.\sigma \in R \rightarrow [0, 1]$. The value $\mathrm{Pr}_{\mathrm{R}}.\sigma.r$ is the probability that R proceeds with sequence σ from state r.

Let $\Sigma^{*\alpha}$ be the set of finite sequences in Σ^* that contain α just once, namely at the end. Then the probability that a fully probabilistic automaton R ever performs an action α is given by $\sum_{\sigma \in \Sigma^{*\alpha}} r^\circ.(\mathrm{Pr}_{\mathrm{R}}.\sigma)$.[6] ¶

2.4 Probabilistic Testing

We now recall the testing framework of Segala [17] which, as we will see, differs from the testing framework of Wang and Larsen [21] in that a test may have countably many success actions rather than just one.[7]

---

[5] Discrete distributions' supports must be countable and so they cannot, for example, describe a situation in which the uncountably many infinite sequences are equally likely — unless they are all (equally) impossible.

[6] An alternative, but equivalent definition appeals to more general probabilistic measures: the probability of R's performing α is the measure of the set of sequences containing α at any point [17]. We have specialised here for simplicity.

[7] Another difference is that Segala's success actions must actually occur, whereas for Wang and Larsen (and earlier De Nicola and Hennessy [4]), it is sufficient that a state be reached from which the action is possible. Here we treat only the former.

We begin by defining the parallel composition of two automata in the CSP style [7], synchronising them on their common external actions.

Definition 4. Let $\mathrm{M}_1 = (M_1, m_1^\circ, E_1, I_1, \mathcal{T}_1)$ and $\mathrm{M}_2 = (M_2, m_2^\circ, E_2, I_2, \mathcal{T}_2)$ be two automata, and let $\Sigma_i := E_i \cup I_i$. They are *compatible* when the only actions they share are external, that is when $\Sigma_1 \cap \Sigma_2 \subseteq E_1 \cap E_2$. In that case their *parallel composition* $\mathrm{M}_1 \| \mathrm{M}_2$ is $(M_1 \times M_2, m_1^\circ \times m_2^\circ, E_1 \cup E_2, I_1 \cup I_2, \mathcal{T})$ where

$$\begin{aligned}\mathcal{T}.(m_1, m_2) := \{(\alpha,\ \mu_1 \times \mu_2) \mid \alpha \in \Sigma_1 \cup \Sigma_2 \quad \wedge \\ (\alpha, \mu_i) \in \mathcal{T}_i.m_i \text{ if } \alpha \in \Sigma_i \text{ else } \mu_i = \overline{m_i}, \text{for } i = 1, 2\}.\end{aligned}$$ ¶

Parallel composition is the basis of testing: it models the interaction of the observer with the process being tested; and it models the observer himself — as an automaton.

From here on, we fix some disjoint sets $\mathbb{E}$ and $\mathbb{I}$ of external and internal actions, and the automata we subject to testing —the ones for which testing preorders will be defined— are the ones whose components of external- and internal actions are subsets of $\mathbb{E}$ and $\mathbb{I}$. Now let $\Omega := \{\omega_1, \omega_2, \cdots\}$ be a countable set of *success actions*, disjoint from $\mathbb{E}$ and $\mathbb{I}$, and define a *test* to be an automaton $\mathrm{T} = (T, t^\circ, E, I, \mathcal{T})$ with $E \supseteq \mathbb{E} \cup \Omega$ and $I \cap \mathbb{I} = \emptyset$. Thus every such test T is automatically compatible with the automaton M that is to be tested, and in the parallel composition $\mathrm{M}\|\mathrm{T}$ *all* the external actions of M must synchronise with actions of T. Let $\mathbb{T}$ be the class of all such tests, and write $\mathbb{T}_N$ for the subclass of $\mathbb{T}$ that uses only N success actions; we write $\mathbb{T}_*$ for $\bigcup_{N \in \mathbb{N}} \mathbb{T}_N$ and, for convenience, allow $\mathbb{T}_{\mathbb{N}}$ as a synonym for $\mathbb{T}$ itself.

To *apply* test T to automaton M we first form the composition $\mathrm{M}\|\mathrm{T}$ and then consider all resolutions of that composition separately: in each one, any particular success action ω_i will have some probability of occurring; and those probabilities, taken together, give us a single *success tuple* for the whole resolution, so that if w is the tuple then w_i is the recorded probability of ω_i's occurrence. The set of all those tuples, *i.e.* over all resolutions of $\mathrm{M}\|\mathrm{T}$, is then the complete outcome of applying test T to automaton M: as such, it will be a subset of $\mathbb{W} := [0, 1]^{\mathbb{N}^+}$.

Definition 5. For a fully probabilistic automaton R, let its (single) success tuple $\mathbb{W}.\mathrm{R} \in [0, 1]^{\mathbb{N}^+}$ be such that $(\mathbb{W}.\mathrm{R})_i$ is the probability that R performs the action ω_i, as given in Def. 3.

Then for a (not necessarily fully probabilistic) automaton M we define the set of its success tuples to be those resulting as above from all its resolutions:

$$\mathbb{W}.\mathrm{M} \quad := \quad \{\mathbb{W}.\mathrm{R} \mid \mathrm{R} \text{ is a resolution of } \mathrm{M}\}.$$ ¶

We note that the success-tuple set $\mathbb{W}.\mathrm{M}$ is *convex* in the following sense:

Lemma 1. For any two tuples $w_1, w_2 \in \mathbb{W}.\mathrm{M}$, their weighted average $w_1\ {}_p\!\oplus w_2$ is also in $\mathbb{W}.\mathrm{M}$ for any $p \in [0, 1]$.

Proof. Let $\mathrm{R}_1, \mathrm{R}_2$ be the resolutions of M that gave rise to w_1, w_2. Form R as their disjoint union, except initially where we define $r^\circ := r_1^\circ\ {}_p\!\oplus r_2^\circ$. The new resolution R generates the interpolated tuple $w_1\ {}_p\!\oplus w_2$ as required. ¶

2.5 May- and Must Preorders

We now define various preorders $\sqsubseteq$ on testable automata; in general $\mathrm{M}_1 \sqsubseteq \mathrm{M}_2$ will mean that M_2 scores at least as well as M_1 does on certain tests.

For $w, w' \in \mathbb{W}$, we write $w \leq w'$ if $w_i \leq w'_i$ for all $i \in \mathbb{N}^+$. Given that Ω comprises "success" actions it is natural to regard $\leq$ on $\mathbb{W}$ as a (non-strict) "better than" order, *i.e.* that it is better to have higher probabilities for the occurrence of success actions. Since nondeterminism generates however *sets* of success tuples (Def. 5), rather than merely individuals, we are led to appeal to two complementary testing preorders on automata; they are based on the standard techniques for promoting an underlying order to a preorder on powersets.

Definition 6. Given two automata $\mathrm{M}_1, \mathrm{M}_2$ and a testing automaton T compatible with both, say that

$$\begin{array}{lll} \mathrm{M}_1 \sqsubseteq^{\mathrm{T}}_{\mathtt{may}} \mathrm{M}_2 & \text{iff} & \mathbb{W}.(\mathrm{M}_1\|\mathrm{T}) \leq_H \mathbb{W}.(\mathrm{M}_2\|\mathrm{T}) \\ \mathrm{M}_1 \sqsubseteq^{\mathrm{T}}_{\mathtt{must}} \mathrm{M}_2 & \text{iff} & \mathbb{W}.(\mathrm{M}_1\|\mathrm{T}) \leq_S \mathbb{W}.(\mathrm{M}_2\|\mathrm{T}), \end{array}$$

where $\leq_H, \leq_S$ are the Hoare, resp. Smyth preorders on $\mathcal{P}\,\mathbb{W}$ generated from the index-wise order $\leq$ on $\mathbb{W}$ itself.[8] Abstracting over all tests in $\mathbb{T}$ then gives us

$$\mathrm{M}_1 \sqsubseteq^{\mathbb{T}}_{-} \mathrm{M}_2 \quad \text{iff} \quad \forall \mathrm{T} \in \mathbb{T} : \mathrm{M}_1 \sqsubseteq^{\mathrm{T}}_{-} \mathrm{M}_2,$$

where within a single formula or phrase we use "–" for "`may`, `must` respectively" in the obvious way, and we define the preorders $\sqsubseteq^{\mathbb{T}*}_{-}$, and $\sqsubseteq^{\mathbb{T}_N}_{-}$ for $N{\geq}1$, by similar abstractions. Finally, *scalar testing* as employed by Wang & Larsen [21] is defined by taking suprema and infima, as follows:

$$\begin{array}{lll} \mathrm{M}_1 \sqsubseteq^{1}_{\mathtt{may}} \mathrm{M}_2 & \text{iff} & \forall \mathrm{T} \in \mathbb{T}_1 : \bigsqcup \mathbb{W}.(\mathrm{M}_1\|\mathrm{T}) \leq \bigsqcup \mathbb{W}.(\mathrm{M}_2\|\mathrm{T}) \\ \mathrm{M}_1 \sqsubseteq^{1}_{\mathtt{must}} \mathrm{M}_2 & \text{iff} & \forall \mathrm{T} \in \mathbb{T}_1 : \bigsqcap \mathbb{W}.(\mathrm{M}_1\|\mathrm{T}) \leq \bigsqcap \mathbb{W}.(\mathrm{M}_2\|\mathrm{T}). \end{array}$$ ¶

Thus, in vector-based testing $\sqsubseteq^{\mathbb{T}}_{-}$, for each test one compares sets of *tuples* of reals, whereas for $\sqsubseteq^{\mathbb{T}_1}_{-}$ one is merely comparing sets of (mono-tuple-, hence scalar) reals. Then, by taking extrema, scalar testing abstracts even further to a comparison of single scalars.

Clearly $(\sqsubseteq^{\mathbb{T}}_{-}) \Rightarrow (\sqsubseteq^{\mathbb{T}*}_{-}) \Rightarrow (\sqsubseteq^{\mathbb{T}_1}_{-}) \Rightarrow (\sqsubseteq^{1}_{-})$. Our principal interest is in determining the situations in which the last is as powerful as all the others, that is when the reverse implications also hold, giving equivalence: we ask

> Under what conditions are *scalar* tests on their own sufficient to distinguish probabilistic automata?

In Sec. 5 we identify general criteria which suffice for scalar testing; then in Secs. 6 and 7 we identify classes of automata on which we can achieve those criteria. Sections 3 and 4 introduce "reward testing" for that purpose.

---

[8] The Hoare order is defined by $X \leq_H Y$ iff $\forall x \in X : \exists y \in Y : x \leq y$; similarly the Smyth order is defined by $X \leq_S Y$ iff $\forall y \in Y : \exists x \in X : x \leq y$ [1].

3 Reward Testing of Finite-Dimensional Tuple Sets

Def. 5 gives tuple sets $\mathbb{W}.(\mathrm{M}\|\mathrm{T})$, coming from a testee M and test $\mathrm{T} \in \mathbb{T}_{\mathbb{N}}$; when in fact $\mathrm{T} \in \mathbb{T}_{*}$ they can be considered to lie in some N-dimensional unit cube $[0,1]^N$. We now abstract from automata, considering just those tuple sets; let N be fixed. This section shows it sufficient, under suitable conditions, to record only an "extremal expected reward" for each set of N-tuple outcomes, a single scalar rather than the whole tuple-set.

Definition 7. A *reward tuple* is an N-tuple $h \in [0,1]^N$ of real numbers; given such an h we define two forms of *extremal reward outcomes* with respect to any tuple set $W \subseteq [0,1]^N$:

- The *Hoare* outcome $h_H{\cdot}W$ is the supremum $\bigsqcup_{w \in W}(h \cdot w)$, and
- The *Smyth* outcome $h_S{\cdot}W$ is the infimum $\bigsqcap_{w \in W}(h \cdot w)$,

where within the extrema we write $h \cdot w$ for the dot-product of the two tuples.

Given a reward-tuple $h \in [0,1]^N$, the two forms of outcome give us two corresponding *reward orders* on tuple-sets $W_1, W_2 \subseteq [0,1]^N$:

$$\begin{array}{lcl} W_1 \leq^h_{\mathtt{may}} W_2 & \text{iff} & h_H{\cdot}W_1 \leq h_H{\cdot}W_2 \\ W_1 \leq^h_{\mathtt{must}} W_2 & \text{iff} & h_S{\cdot}W_1 \leq h_S{\cdot}W_2, \end{array}$$

where (note) the comparison $\leq$ on the right has now been reduced to simple scalars. As in Def. 6, this generalises so that we can define

$$W_1 \leq^N_{-} W_2 \qquad \text{iff} \qquad \forall h \in [0,1]^N : W_1 \leq^h_{-} W_2.$$ ¶

We will now show that these preorders coincide with $\leq_H$ and $\leq_S$, respectively, provided the tuple-sets have a certain form of closure, as follows:

Definition 8. We say that a subset W of the N-dimensional Euclidean space is *p-closed* (for *probabilistically* closed) iff

- It is *convex*, that is if $w_1, w_2 \in W$ and $p \in [0,1]$ then the weighted average $w_1\ {}_p{\oplus}\ w_2$ is also in W, and
- It is *Cauchy closed*, that is it contains all its limit points in the usual Euclidean metric, and it is *bounded.*[9] ¶

Our sets' being *p-closed* will allow us to appeal to the *Separating Hyperplane Lemma* from discrete geometry [11, Thm. 1.2.4 paraphrased]:[10]

Lemma 2. Let A and B be two convex- and Cauchy-closed subsets of Euclidean N-space; assume that they are disjoint and that at least one of them is bounded. Then there is a hyperplane that strictly separates them. ¶

Here a *hyperplane* is a set of the form $\{w \in \mathbb{R}^N \mid h{\cdot}w = c\}$ for certain $h \in \mathbb{R}^N$ (the *normal* of the hyperplane) and $c \in \mathbb{R}$, and such a hyperplane *strictly separates* A and B if for all $a \in A$ and $b \in B$ we have $h \cdot a < c < h \cdot b$ or $h \cdot a > c > h \cdot b$.

Our main theorem is then a direct application of Lem. 2: the normal h of the asserted hyperplane provides the rewards used in Def. 7.

---

[9] Cauchy closure and boundedness together amounts to *compactness*.

[10] The hyperplanes are motivated indirectly by a proof of McIver [14, Lem. 8.2].

Theorem 1. Let A, B be subsets of $[0,1]^N$; then we have

$$A \leq_H B \quad \text{iff} \quad A \leq^N_{\mathtt{may}} B \quad \text{if } B \text{ is } p\text{-closed, and}$$
$$A \leq_S B \quad \text{iff} \quad A \leq^N_{\mathtt{must}} B \quad \text{if } A \text{ is } p\text{-closed.}$$

Proof. We consider first the *only-if* -direction for the Smyth/must case:

$$\begin{array}{lll}
 & A \leq_S B & \\
\Leftrightarrow & \forall b \in B : \exists a \in A : a \leq b & \text{defn. } \leq_S \\
\Rightarrow & \forall h \in [0,1]^N : \forall b \in B : \exists a \in A : h \cdot a \leq h \cdot b & h \geq 0 \\
\Rightarrow & \forall h \in [0,1]^N : \forall b \in B : h_S{\cdot}A \leq h \cdot b & h_S{\cdot}A \leq h \cdot a \\
\Leftrightarrow & \forall h \in [0,1]^N : h_S{\cdot}A \leq h_S{\cdot}B & \text{defn. } (h_S\cdot)\text{; properties of } \sqcap \\
\Leftrightarrow & \forall h \in [0,1]^N : A \leq^h_{\mathtt{must}} B. & \text{defn. } \leq^h_{\mathtt{must}} \\
\Leftrightarrow & A \leq^N_{\mathtt{must}} B. & \text{defn. } \leq^N_{\mathtt{must}}
\end{array}$$

For the *if*-direction we use separating hyperplanes, proving the contrapositive:

$$\begin{array}{lll}
 & A \not\leq_S B & \\
\Leftrightarrow & \forall a \in A : \neg(a \leq b) & \text{defn. } \leq_S\text{; for some } b \in B \\
\Leftrightarrow & A \cap B' = \emptyset & \text{define } B' := \{b' \in \mathbb{R}^N \mid b' \leq b\} \\
\Leftrightarrow & \exists h \in \mathbb{R}^N, c \in \mathbb{R} : \; \forall a \in A, b' \in B' : \; h \cdot b' < c < h \cdot a, & \text{Lem. 2; } A \text{ is } p\text{-closed; } B' \text{ is convex and Cauchy-closed}
\end{array}$$

where *wlog* the inequality can be in the direction shown, else we simply multiply h, c by -1.

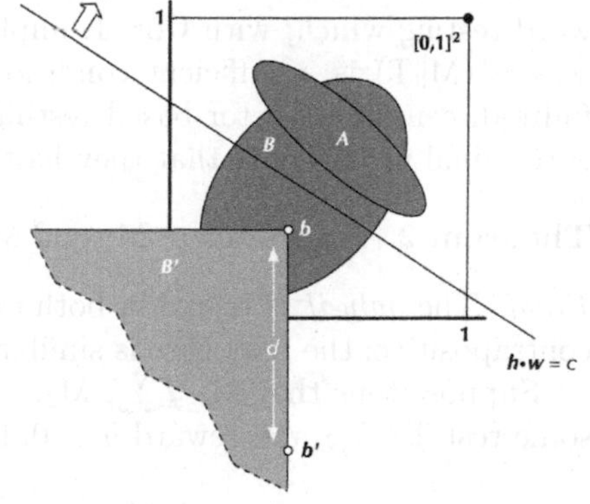

We now argue that h is non-negative, whence by scaling of h, c we obtain *wlog* that $h \in [0,1]^N$. Assume for a contradiction that $h_n < 0$. Choose scalar $d \geq 0$ large enough so that the point $b' := (b_1, \cdots, b_n{-}d, \cdots, b_N)$ falsifies $h \cdot b' < c$; since b' is still in B', however, that contradicts the separation. Thus we continue

$$\begin{array}{lll}
\Leftrightarrow & \exists h \in [0,1]^N, c \in \mathbb{R} : \; \forall a \in A, b' \in B' : \; h \cdot b' < c < h \cdot a, & \text{above comments concerning } d \\
\Leftrightarrow & \exists h \in [0,1]^N, c \in \mathbb{R} : \forall a \in A : h \cdot b < c < h \cdot a & \text{set } b' \text{ to } b\text{; note } b \in B' \\
\Rightarrow & \exists h \in [0,1]^N, c \in \mathbb{R} : h \cdot b < c \leq h_S{\cdot}A & \text{defn. } (h_S\cdot)\text{; properties of } \sqcap \\
\Rightarrow & \exists h \in [0,1]^N, c \in \mathbb{R} : h_S{\cdot}B < c \leq h_S{\cdot}A & b \in B\text{, hence } h_S{\cdot}B \leq h \cdot b \\
\Leftrightarrow & \exists h \in [0,1]^N : A \not\leq^h_{\mathtt{must}} B & \text{defn. } \leq^h_{\mathtt{must}} \\
\Leftrightarrow & A \not\leq^N_{\mathtt{must}} B. & \text{defn. } \leq^N_{\mathtt{must}}
\end{array}$$

The proof for the Hoare-case is analogous. ¶

4 Reward Testing of Automata

We now combine Secs. 2 and 3 by introducing preorders that use testing processes and rewards together: we define

$$\mathrm{M}_1 \sqsubseteq^N \mathrm{M}_2 \qquad \text{iff} \qquad \forall\, \mathrm{T} \in \mathbb{T}_N : \mathbb{W}.(\mathrm{M}_1 \| \mathrm{T}) \leq^N \mathbb{W}.(\mathrm{M}_2 \| \mathrm{T}).$$

We call the $\sqsubseteq^N$ relations —and $\sqsubseteq^*$, $\sqsubseteq^{\mathbb{N}}$ similarly— the *reward-testing* preorders for automata. When N=1 this definition of $\sqsubseteq^1$ is just scalar testing again (from Sec. 2.5) as, in this case, the reward "vectors" are just scalars themselves: thus the notations do not clash. The following is an immediate corollary of Thm. 1.

Corollary 1. If M_1 and M_2 are automata with the property that for any test $\mathrm{T} \in \mathbb{T}_*$ the sets $\mathbb{W}.(\mathrm{M}_1 \| \mathrm{T})$ and $\mathbb{W}.(\mathrm{M}_2 \| \mathrm{T})$ are *p-closed*, then finite-dimensional vector-based testing is equivalent to reward testing: from Thm. 1 we have

$$\mathrm{M}_1 \sqsubseteq^{\mathbb{T}_N} \mathrm{M}_2 \quad \text{iff} \quad \mathrm{M}_1 \sqsubseteq^N \mathrm{M}_2 \qquad\qquad \text{for all } N,$$

which in turn implies that $\mathrm{M}_1 \sqsubseteq^{\mathbb{T}*} \mathrm{M}_2$ iff $\mathrm{M}_1 \sqsubseteq^* \mathrm{M}_2$. ¶

5 Closure Suffices for Scalar Testing

We now show that scalar testing is equally powerful as finite-dimensional reward testing which, with Cor. 1, implies that *p-closure* of the generated tuple-sets $\mathbb{W}.(\mathrm{M} \| \mathrm{T})$ is a sufficient condition for scalar testing to be as powerful as finite-dimensional vector-based testing. In doing so, we assume that tests are ω-terminal in the sense that they halt after execution of any success action.[11]

Theorem 2. For automata M_1 and M_2 we have that $\mathrm{M}_1 \sqsubseteq^* \mathrm{M}_2$ iff $\mathrm{M}_1 \sqsubseteq^1 \mathrm{M}_2$.

Proof. The *only-if* is trivial in both cases. For *if* we prove the must-case in the contrapositive; the may-case is similar.

Suppose thus that $\mathrm{M}_1 \not\sqsubseteq^N_{\mathtt{must}} \mathrm{M}_2$, *i.e.* that $\mathrm{M}_1, \mathrm{M}_2$ are must-distinguished by some test $\mathrm{T} \in \mathbb{T}_N$ and reward $h \in [0,1]^N$, so that

$$\mathbb{W}.(\mathrm{M}_1 \| \mathrm{T}) \quad \not\leq^h_{\mathtt{must}} \quad \mathbb{W}.(\mathrm{M}_2 \| \mathrm{T}). \tag{1}$$

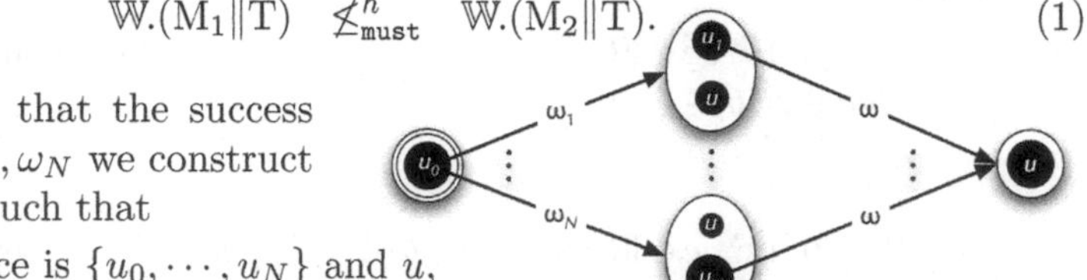

Assuming *wlog* that the success actions are $\omega_1, \cdots, \omega_N$ we construct an automaton U such that

- The state space is $\{u_0, \cdots, u_N\}$ and u,
- The actions are $\omega_1, \cdots \omega_N$ and ω, all external,
- The initial distribution u° is $\overline{u_0}$ and
- The transitions for $1 \leq i \leq N$ take u_0 via action ω_i to $(\overline{u_i}\ {}_{h_i}\!\oplus \overline{u})$, thence each u_i via ω to deadlock at $\overline{u}$.

[11] This assumption is justified in App. A.

We now consider the test T‖U with ω as its only success action. In T‖U an occurrence of ω_i is with probability h_i followed immediately by an occurrence of ω (and with probability $1-h_i$ by deadlock); and the overall probability of ω's occurrence, in any resolution of $M_{1,2}\|T\|U$, is therefore the h-weighted reward $h \cdot w$ for the tuple $w := (w_1, \cdots, w_N)$ in the corresponding resolution of $M_{1,2}\|T$.

Thus from (1) we have that M_1, M_2 can be distinguished using the scalar test T‖U with its single success action ω; that is, we achieve $M_1 \not\sqsubseteq^1_{\mathtt{must}} M_2$ as required. ¶

6 Very Finite Testing Is *p-closed*, Hence Scalar

Say that an automaton is *very finite* if it is finite-state, finitely branching and loop-free (no execution sequence repeats a state), so that there is a finite upper bound on the length of its execution sequences.

In Thm. 3 below we show that scalar outcomes suffice when dealing with very finite automata and tests, because the sets of success tuples are *p-closed* and thus Thm. 2 applies. We rely on the fact that when a test T is very finite, so are the composite automata T‖U and T‖V constructed in Sec. 5 and App. A.

Lemma 3. Let $W_{1,\ldots,N} \subseteq \mathbb{W}$ be *p-closed* success-tuple sets, and let $\mu \in \overline{\{1,\cdots,N\}}$ be a discrete distribution over their indices. Then we have[12]

1. The set $\{\mu.f \mid f \in \{1,\cdots,N\} \to \mathbb{W} \ \wedge \ \forall i : f.i \in W_i\}$ is *p-closed*, and
2. The set $\bigcup_{\mu \in \overline{\{1,\cdots,N\}}} \{\mu.f \mid f \in \{1,\cdots,N\} \to \mathbb{W} \ \wedge \ \forall i : f.i \in W_i\}$ is *p-closed.*

That is, a specific interpolation μ of *p-closed* sets is again *p-closed* (1), and the union of *all* such interpolations is also *p-closed* (2).

Proof. Standard results on convex hulls of compact sets [2, Sec. 5.3]. ¶

Lemma 4. If M and T are very finite automata, then the set $\mathbb{W}.(M\|T)$ of success tuples is *p-closed.*

Proof. (Sketch) Lem. 3 shows that *p-closure* is preserved in a fairly straightforward induction on the upper bound of the length of the execution sequences of the very finite automata M‖T. The details are omitted here, because Thm. 4 subsumes Thm. 3 anyway. ¶

Theorem 3. For very finite tests and automata, scalar testing suffices: we have

$$M_1 \sqsubseteq^{\mathbb{T}_{\mathbb{N}}}_{-} M_2 \quad \text{iff} \quad M_1 \sqsubseteq^{1}_{-} M_2.$$

Proof. Any very finite test has only finitely many success actions, and thus belongs to $\mathbb{T}_*$. Consequently, we have $M_1 \sqsubseteq^{\mathbb{T}_{\mathbb{N}}}_{-} M_2$ iff $M_1 \sqsubseteq^{\mathbb{T}_*}_{-} M_2$. Using this, the result follows from Lem. 4, Cor. 1 and Thm. 2. ¶

[12] Here we are taking the expected value of vectors: recall Footnote 2.

7 Also Finitary Testing Is Scalar

We now remove the no-looping restriction of Sec. 6, retaining however that the automata are finite-branching and have finitely many states:[13] this allows their execution sequences to become of infinite length. Such automata we call *finitary*.

The result depends on a connection with Markov Decision Processes (*MDP*'s) [16], abstracted here as a lemma implicitly using the more general probability measures mentioned in Def. 3 (Footnote 6).

Lemma 5. *Static resolutions suffice for finitary testing* Say that a resolution R of an automaton M is *static* if its associated resolving function $f \in R \to M$ is injective, so that on every visit to a state $m \in M$ any nondeterminism is resolved in the same way, and does not interpolate. Then, for all reward tuples $h \in [0,1]^N$,

- There is a static resolution R_h of M so that $h_S \cdot (\mathbb{W}.\mathrm{M}) = h_S \cdot (\mathbb{W}.\mathrm{R}_h)$ and
- There is a static resolution R'_h of M so that $h_H \cdot (\mathbb{W}.\mathrm{M}) = h_H \cdot (\mathbb{W}.\mathrm{R}'_h)$.

Thus in both cases the extremum over all resolutions is attained statically.[14]

Proof. An automaton $\mathrm{M} = (M, m^\circ, E, I, \mathcal{T})$ with a reward tuple $h \in [0,1]^{\mathbb{N}^+}$ constitutes isomorphically an *MDP* [16, Sec. 2.1]: in the tuple at the end of Sec. 2.1.3 take $T := \mathbb{N}^+$, $S := M$, $A_s := \mathcal{T}.s$ for $s \in S$, $p_t(\cdot \mid s, (\alpha, \mu)) := \mu$ and $r_t(s, (\alpha, \mu)) := h_i$ if $\alpha = \omega_i$, or 0 if $\alpha \notin \Omega$. The values of p and r are independent of t and s. Our resolutions are the (history-dependent, randomised) policies of Sec. 2.1.5, and our Smyth- and Hoare-outcomes (Def. 7) are the optimal outcomes accruing from such policies [Secs. 2.1.6, 4.1 and 5.2]; the Smyth-case is obtained by using negative rewards so that "optimal" is supremum either way.

Theorem 7.1.9 [Sec. 7.1.4] states (paraphrased) *Suppose that the state space and the set of actions available at each state are finite. Then there is a stationary deterministic optimal policy.* "Stationary deterministic" equates to "static" in our setting, and "optimal" means "attains the extremum." ¶

The crucial lever that Lem. 5 gives us in our treatment of testing is that a finitary automaton has only finitely many static resolutions (up to isomorphism), since neither variation-by-visit nor interpolation is allowed for them. With infinitely many resolutions in general, even for the finitary case, needing only finitely many is a significant advantage — as we now see in the following lemmas.

Lemma 6. Let $\mathbb{W}_f.\mathrm{M}$ be the convex closure of the statically generated success tuples of M; then $\mathbb{W}_f.\mathrm{M} \subseteq \mathbb{W}.\mathrm{M}$. If M is finitary, then $\mathbb{W}_f.\mathrm{M}$ is *p-closed.*

Proof. The first statement is trivial, since static resolutions are still resolutions and from Lem. 1 we know that $\mathbb{W}.\mathrm{M}$ is convex. For the second we note that as

[13] Having finitely many states and transitions is an equivalent restriction. Finitely many states does not on its own imply finite branching, however: there are infinitely many distributions possible over even a finite state space.

[14] More general work on games [12] led us to this; a similar result is argued directly by Philippou, Lee & Sokolsky [15] and Cattani and Segala [3], in both cases in the context of decision procedures for bisimulation.

M has only finitely many static resolutions, the set $\mathbb{W}_f.\mathrm{M}$ is the convex-closure of a finite number of points, and is thus *p-closed* by Lem. 3(2). ¶

Lemma 7. For all finitary automata M with N success actions, and reward tuples $h \in [0,1]^N$, we have

$$h_S{\cdot}(\mathbb{W}.\mathrm{M}) = h_S{\cdot}(\mathbb{W}_f.\mathrm{M}) \qquad \text{and} \qquad h_H{\cdot}(\mathbb{W}.\mathrm{M}) = h_H{\cdot}(\mathbb{W}_f.\mathrm{M}),$$

hence $\mathbb{W}.\mathrm{M}$ and $\mathbb{W}_f.\mathrm{M}$ are equivalent under $\leq^N_-$.

Proof. The $\leq$-case for Smyth is immediate from Lem. 6; from Lem. 5 there is some static resolution R_h of M with $h_S{\cdot}(\mathbb{W}.\mathrm{M}) = h_S{\cdot}(\mathbb{W}.\mathrm{R}_h) \geq h_S{\cdot}(\mathbb{W}_f.\mathrm{M})$.

The Hoare-case is similar; the equivalence then follows from Def. 7. ¶

Lemmas 6 and 7 allow us to strengthen Cor. 1, effectively requiring *p-closure* only of $\mathbb{W}_f.(\mathrm{M}_{1,2}\|\mathrm{T})$ rather than of $\mathbb{W}.(\mathrm{M}_{1,2}\|\mathrm{T})$.

Lemma 8. For finitary automata $\mathrm{M}_1, \mathrm{M}_2$ we have $\mathrm{M}_1 \sqsubseteq^{\mathbb{T}*}_- \mathrm{M}_2$ iff $\mathrm{M}_1 \sqsubseteq^*_- \mathrm{M}_2$.

Proof. For "only-if" apply Thm. 1 — this direction does not require *p*-closure. For *if* we prove the must-case in the contrapositive; the may-case is similar.

$$\begin{array}{lll}
 & \mathrm{M}_1 \not\sqsubseteq^{\mathbb{T}_N}_{\mathtt{must}} \mathrm{M}_2 & \text{for some } N \\
\Leftrightarrow & \mathbb{W}.(\mathrm{M}_1\|\mathrm{T}) \not\leq_S \mathbb{W}.(\mathrm{M}_2\|\mathrm{T}) & \text{Def. 6, for some } \mathrm{T} \in \mathbb{T}_N \\
\Rightarrow & \mathbb{W}_f.(\mathrm{M}_1\|\mathrm{T}) \not\leq_S \mathbb{W}.(\mathrm{M}_2\|\mathrm{T}) & \text{Lem. 6, } \mathbb{W}_f.(\mathrm{M}_1\|\mathrm{T}) \subseteq \mathbb{W}.(\mathrm{M}_1\|\mathrm{T}) \\
\Leftrightarrow & \mathbb{W}_f.(\mathrm{M}_1\|\mathrm{T}) \not\leq^N_{\mathtt{must}} \mathbb{W}.(\mathrm{M}_2\|\mathrm{T}) & \text{Lem. 6, } \mathbb{W}_f.(\mathrm{M}_1\|\mathrm{T}) \text{ is } \textit{p-closed}\text{; Thm. 1} \\
\Leftrightarrow & \mathbb{W}.(\mathrm{M}_1\|\mathrm{T}) \not\leq^N_{\mathtt{must}} \mathbb{W}.(\mathrm{M}_2\|\mathrm{T}) & \text{Lem. 7} \\
\Rightarrow & \mathrm{M}_1 \not\sqsubseteq^N_{\mathtt{must}} \mathrm{M}_2. & \text{Definition of reward testing.}
\end{array}$$ ¶

We can now establish the extension of Thm. 3 to finitary automata.

Theorem 4. For finitary tests and automata, scalar testing suffices.

Proof. As in the proof of Thm. 3 we observe that $\mathrm{M}_1 \sqsubseteq^{\mathbb{T}_{\mathbb{N}}}_- \mathrm{M}_2$ iff $\mathrm{M}_1 \sqsubseteq^{\mathbb{T}*}_- \mathrm{M}_2$ for (this time) finitary tests; we then apply Lem. 8 and Thm. 2. ¶

8 Beyond Finitary Testing

The principal technical ingredient of our results is *p-closure* of the result sets in $\mathbb{W}$, since that is what enables the hyperplane separation. Separation itself is not inherently finitary, since Lem. 2 extends to countably infinite dimensions [13, Lem. B.5.3 adapted], delivering a hyperplane whose normal is non-zero in only finitely many dimensions — just as required for our constructions above (although automaton V in App. A needs a slightly different approach).

It is the *p-closure* which (currently) depends essentially on finite dimensions (hence a finite state space). For countably infinite dimensions, its convexity component must be extended to infinite interpolations; but that happens automatically provided the sets are Cauchy closed. And it is again the closure that (within our bounded space) implies the compactness that separation requires. Thus Cauchy closure is the crucial property.

When the automata are finitely branching (up to interpolation), we believe a direct fixed-point construction of $\mathbb{W}.M$ (*i.e.* not indirectly via resolutions) gives, via intersection of a $\supseteq$-chain, a set whose up-closure (*wrt* $\leq$ over $\mathbb{W}$) is compact. Since must- (*i.e.* Smyth) testing is insensitive to up-closure, that would seem to extend our results to countably-infinite dimensional must-testing. For the may-testing case the analogous technique would be down-closure; but here, unfortunately, the limit is via union of a $\subseteq$-chain, and closure/compactness is not obviously preserved. As further evidence for this we note that the *MDP*-based results allow countably infinite state spaces in the infimum case (still however with finite branching) [16, Thm. 7.3.6], whereas the supremum case requires a finite state space.

Thus the key question is *What conditions are necessary to establish p-closure for infinitely many states?* At present, may- seems harder than must-.

9 Conclusion

Our reduction of vector- to scalar testing uses geometry (hyperplanes), elementary topology (compactness) and game theory (*MDP*'s); and it highlights the importance of *p-closure* and static resolutions. That those techniques contribute to probabilistic semantics is of independent theoretical interest; but our result ultimately is *practical* — any program calculus/algebra, a fundamental tool for rigorous software engineering, relies crucially on a tractable definition of equality.

A key feature is our use of *expected values of "rewards"* as outcomes for probabilistic tests; this approach subsumes the usual direct probabilities because an event's probability is just the expected value of its characteristic function.[15] It has been suggested before both for sequential [10] and concurrent [8] applications; and we believe it deserves greater attention, since it can lead to significant simplifications (of which this report provides an example).

We have shown that scalar testing suffices when requiring the *tests*, as well as their testees, to be finitary, and one may wonder whether the same holds if arbitrarily complex tests are allowed. We think this is indeed the case, for we conjecture that if two finitary automata can be distinguished by an arbitrary test, then they can be distinguished by a finitary test.

As stated in Sec. 2.4, Segala's testing framework [17] differs from others' [4,21] not only in the number of success actions, but also in how to report success. We claim that action- and state-based testing give rise to different must-testing preorders when the tested processes display divergence, because a success action ω may be delayed forever. Here we used action-based testing throughout, although we could have obtained the same results for state-based testing.

Finally, we note that our reduction via Thms. 2–4 of vector-based testing to extremal scalar testing has reduction to $\mathbb{T}_1$-testing as a corollary — thus showing that, under our assumptions, single success actions suffice for Segala's approach even if it is otherwise unchanged.

---

[15] For $\mu.X$ is the same whether X is taken as a set or as a characteristic function.

Acknowledgements

We thank Anna Philippou for corresponding with us about static resolutions, and Kim Border for a hyperplane-related counterexample.

References

1. S. Abramsky & A. Jung (1994): *Domain theory.* In S. Abramsky, D.M. Gabbay & T.S.E. Maibaum, editors: *Handbook of Logic and Computer Science*, volume 3, Clarendon Press, pp. 1–168.
2. C.D. Aliprantis & K.C. Border (1999): *Infinite Dimensional Analysis.* Springer, second edition.
3. S. Cattani & R. Segala (2002): *Decision algorithms for probabilistic bisimulation.* In Proc. *CONCUR 2002*, LNCS 2421, Springer, pp. 371–85.
4. R. De Nicola & M. Hennessy (1984): *Testing equivalences for processes. Theoretical Computer Science* 34, pp. 83–133.
5. H. Hansson & B. Jonsson (1990): *A calculus for communicating systems with time and probabilities.* In Proc. of the *Real-Time Systems Symposium* (RTSS '90), IEEE Computer Society Press, pp. 278–87.
6. He Jifeng, K. Seidel & A.K. McIver (1997): *Probabilistic models for the guarded command language. Science of Computer Programming* 28, pp. 171–92.
7. C.A.R. Hoare (1985): *Communicating Sequential Processes.* Prentice Hall.
8. B. Jonsson, C. Ho-Stuart & Wang Yi (1994): *Testing and refinement for nondeterministic and probabilistic processes.* In Proc. *Formal Techniques in Real-Time and Fault-Tolerant Systems*, LNCS 863, Springer, pp. 418–30.
9. B. Jonsson & Wang Yi (2002): *Testing preorders for probabilistic processes can be characterized by simulations. Theoretical Computer Science* 282(1), pp. 33–51.
10. D. Kozen (1985): *A probabilistic PDL. Jnl. Comp. Sys. Sciences* 30(2), pp. 162–78.
11. J. Matoušek (2002): *Lectures on Discrete Geometry.* Springer.
12. A.K. McIver & C.C. Morgan (2002): *Games, probability and the quantitative μ-calculus qMu.* In *Proc. LPAR*, LNAI 2514, Springer, pp. 292–310.
13. A.K. McIver & C.C. Morgan (2005): *Abstraction, Refinement and Proof for Probabilistic Systems.* Tech. Mono. Comp. Sci., Springer.
14. C.C. Morgan, A.K. McIver & K. Seidel (1996): *Probabilistic predicate transformers. ACM Trans. on Programming Languages and Systems* 18(3), pp. 325–53.
15. A. Philippou, I. Lee & O. Sokolsky (2000): *Weak bisimulation for probabilistic systems.* In Proc. *CONCUR 2000*, Springer, pp. 334–49.
16. M.L. Puterman (1994): *Markov Decision Processes.* Wiley.
17. R. Segala (1996): *Testing probabilistic automata.* In Proc. *CONCUR '96*, LNCS 1119, Springer, pp. 299–314.
18. R. Segala & N.A. Lynch (1994): *Probabilistic simulations for probabilistic processes.* In Proc. *CONCUR '94*, LNCS 836, Springer, pp. 481–96.
19. M.I.A. Stoelinga & F.W. Vaandrager (2003): A testing scenario for probabilistic automata. In Proc. *ICALP '03*, LNCS 2719, Springer, pp. 407–18.
20. M.Y. Vardi (1985): *Automatic verification of probabilistic concurrent finite state programs.* In Proc. *FOCS '85*, IEEE Computer Society Press, pp. 327–38.
21. Wang Yi & K.G. Larsen (1992): *Testing probabilistic and nondeterministic processes.* In Proc. IFIP TC6/WG6.1 Twelfth Intern. Symp. on *Protocol Specification, Testing and Verification*, *IFIP Transactions* C-8, North-Holland, pp. 47–61.

A One Success Never Leads to Another

Here we substantiate the claim made in Sec. 6 (Footnote 11) that *wlog* we can assume that our testing automata halt after engaging in any success action. The reward-testing construction requires this because the automaton U used in Thm. 2 implementing a particular reward-tuple h effectively causes the composite automaton T||U to halt after the reward is applied — hence for correctness of the construction we required that the automaton T must have halted anyway.

Below we show that the may- and must testing preorders do not change upon restricting the class of available tests to those that cannot perform multiple success actions in a single run. A second reduction to tests that actually halt after performing any success action is trivial: just change any transition of the form (s, ω_i, μ) into a transition $(s, \omega_i, \overline{0})$ leading to a deadlocked state 0.

Suppose our original testing automaton T has N success actions $\omega_1, \cdots, \omega_N$. By running it in parallel with another automaton V (below) we will convert it to an automaton with the required property and corresponding success actions $\omega'_1, \cdots, \omega'_N$, and with success N-tuples that are exactly $1/N$ times the success tuples of T; since testing is insensitive to scaling of the tuples, that will give us our result. Note that the $1/N$ factor is natural given that we are making our N success actions mutually exclusive: it ensures the tuple's elements' total does not exceed one.

We construct the automaton $\mathrm{V} := (V, v^\circ, E, I, \mathcal{T})$ as follows:

- The state space is $V := \mathcal{P}\{\omega_1, \ldots, \omega_n\} \cup (0, \ldots, N)$, where the powerset-states record which success actions have already occurred, the scalar states $1, \ldots, N$ are "about-to-terminate" states, and 0 is a deadlock state;
- The actions are $\omega_1, \ldots, \omega_N$ and $\omega'_1, \ldots, \omega'_N$, all external; and
- The initial distribution v° is the Dirac'd powerset-state $\overline{\emptyset}$.

The transitions of V are of three kinds:

- "Terminating" transitions take state n with probability one via action ω'_n to the deadlocked state 0;
- "Do-nothing" transitions, from state $v \in \mathcal{P}\{\omega_1, \cdots, \omega_N\}$, lead with probability one via action $\omega_n \in v$ back to v, implementing that second and subsequent occurrences of any success action in T can be ignored; and
- "Success" transitions, from state $v \in \mathcal{P}\{\omega_1, \cdots, \omega_N\}$ lead via action $\omega_n \notin v$ ... with probability $\frac{1}{N - \#v}$ to state n, whence the subsequent terminating transition will emit ω'_n;

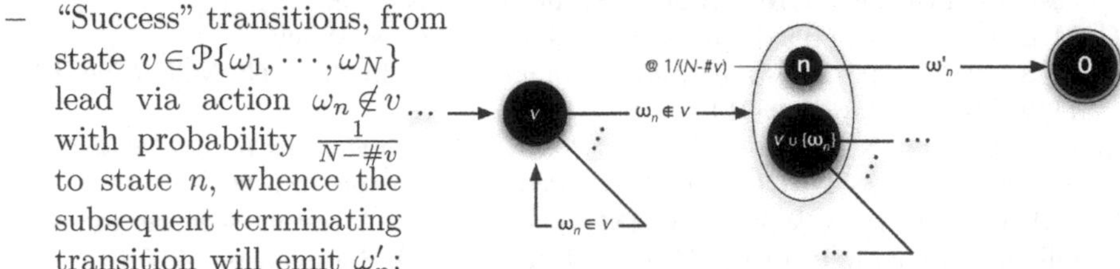

  the remaining probability at v leads to state $v \cup \{\omega_n\}$, recording silently that ω_n has now been taken care of.

When the original test T has finitely many states and transitions, so does the composite test T||V.

Probabilistic Anonymity Via Coalgebraic Simulations

Ichiro Hasuo[1,*] and Yoshinobu Kawabe[2]

[1] Radboud University Nijmegen, the Netherlands
http://www.cs.ru.nl/~ichiro
[2] NTT Communication Science Laboratories, NTT Corporation, Japan
http://www.brl.ntt.co.jp/people/kawabe

Abstract. There is a growing concern on anonymity and privacy on the Internet, resulting in lots of work on formalization and verification of anonymity. Especially, importance of probabilistic aspect of anonymity is claimed recently by many authors. Among them are Bhargava and Palamidessi who present the definition of *probabilistic anonymity* for which, however, proof methods are not yet elaborated. In this paper we introduce a simulation-based proof method for probabilistic anonymity. It is a probabilistic adaptation of the method by Kawabe et al. for non-deterministic anonymity: anonymity of a protocol is proved by finding out a forward/backward simulation between certain automata. For the jump from non-determinism to probability we fully exploit a generic, coalgebraic theory of traces and simulations developed by Hasuo and others. In particular, an appropriate notion of probabilistic simulations is obtained by instantiating a generic definition with suitable parameters.

1 Introduction

Nowadays most human activities rely on communication on the Internet, hence on communication protocols. This has made verification of communication protocols a trend in computer science. At the same time, the variety of purposes of communication protocols has identified new verification goals—or *security properties*—such as anonymity, in addition to rather traditional ones like secrecy or authentication.

Anonymity properties have attracted growing concern from the public. There are emerging threats as well: for example, the European Parliament in December 2005 approved rules forcing ISPs to retain access records. Consequently more and more research activities—especially from the formal methods community—are aiming at verification of anonymity properties (see [2]).

Formal verification of anonymity properties is at its relative youth compared to authentication or secrecy. The topic still allows for definitional work (such as [4,7,8,11,16]) pointing out many different aspects of anonymity notions. Notably many authors [4,8,20,21] claim the significant role of *probability* in anonymity notions. This is the focus of this paper.

Bhargava and Palamidessi [4] define the notion of *probabilistic anonymity* which is mathematically precise and which subsumes many competing notions of anonymity

* This work was done during the first author's stay at NTT Communication Science Laboratories in September–October 2006.

R. De Nicola (Ed.): ESOP 2007, LNCS 4421, pp. 379–394, 2007.

in probabilistic settings. However, it is not yet elaborated *how* we can verify if an anonymizing protocol satisfies this notion of probabilistic anonymity.

In this paper we introduce a simulation-based proof method for probabilistic anonymity as defined by Bhargava and Palamidessi. It is a probabilistic extension of the method by Kawabe et al. [13,12] for a non-deterministic (as opposed to probabilistic) setting. The basic scenario is common in both non-deterministic and probabilistic cases:

1. First we model an anonymizing protocol to be verified as a certain kind of automaton $\mathcal{X}$.
2. Second we construct the *anonymized* version $\mathsf{an}(\mathcal{X})$ of $\mathcal{X}$. The automaton $\mathsf{an}(\mathcal{X})$ satisfies the appropriate notion of anonymity because of the way it is constructed.
3. We prove that

$$\text{(trace semantics of } \mathcal{X}) = \text{(trace semantics of } \mathsf{an}(\mathcal{X})).$$

Then, since the notion of anonymity is defined in terms of traces, anonymity of $\mathsf{an}(\mathcal{X})$ yields anonymity of $\mathcal{X}$. The equality is proved by showing that the (appropriate notion of) inclusion order $\sqsubseteq$ holds in both directions.
   - $\sqsubseteq$ holds because of the construction of $\mathsf{an}(\mathcal{X})$.
   - $\sqsupseteq$ is proved by finding a (forward or backward) *simulation* from $\mathsf{an}(\mathcal{X})$ to $\mathcal{X}$. Here we appeal to soundness theorem of simulations—existence of a simulation yields trace inclusion.

Hence the anonymity proof of $\mathcal{X}$ is reduced to finding a suitable forward/backward simulation.

There is an obvious difficulty in conducting this scenario in a probabilistic setting. The theory of traces and simulations in a non-deterministic setting is well studied e.g. by [14]; however appropriate definitions of probabilistic traces and simulations are far from trivial.

For the jump from non-determinism to probability we exploit a generic, coalgebraic theory of traces and simulations developed by Hasuo, Jacobs and Sokolova [9,10]. In the generic theory, fundamental notions such as systems (or automata), trace semantics and forward/backward simulations are identified as certain kinds of coalgebraic constructs. On this level of abstraction the general soundness theorem—existence of a (coalgebraic) simulation yields (coalgebraic) trace inclusion—is proved by categorical arguments.

The theory is generic in that, by fixing two parameters appearing therein, it instantiates to a concrete theory for various kinds of systems. In particular, according to the choice of one parameter, systems can be non-deterministic or probabilistic.[1] In this work a complex definition of probabilistic simulations is obtained as an instance of the general, coalgebraic definition. Moreover, this definition is an *appropriate* one: soundness theorem comes for free from the general soundness theorem.

[1] Unfortunately the combination of both non-determinism and probability—which is e.g. in probabilistic automata [19]—is not covered in this paper. In fact this combination is a notorious one [6,23]: many mathematical tools that are useful in a purely non-deterministic or probabilistic setting cease to work in the presence of both.

The paper is organized as follows. In Section 2 we illustrate the probabilistic aspect of anonymity properties using the well-known example of Dining Cryptographers. We model anonymizing protocols as a special kind of automata called (probabilistic) *anonymity automata*. This notion is introduced in Section 3; the definition of probabilistic anonymity following [4] is also there. Finally in Section 4 we describe our simulation-based proof method for anonymity and prove its correctness. In Section 5 we conclude.

Notations. In the sequel the disjoint union of sets X and Y is denoted by $X + Y$.

The set of lists over an alphabet X with length ≥ 1 is denoted by X^*X in a regular-expression-like manner: obviously we have $X^* = X^*X + \{\langle\rangle\}$. This appears as a domain of trace semantics for anonymity automata.

2 Motivating Example: Dining Cryptographers (DC)

In this section—following [4]—we shall illustrate the probabilistic aspect of anonymity, using the well-known *dining cryptographers* (DC) protocol [5].

2.1 The DC Protocol

There are three cryptographers (or users) dining together. The payment will be made either by one of the cryptographers, or NSA (U.S. National Security Agency) which organizes the dinner. Who is paying is determined by NSA; if one of the cryptographers is paying, she has been told so beforehand.

The goal of the DC protocol is as follows. The three cryptographers announce whether one of them is paying or not; but if it is the case, the information on *which* cryptographer is paying should be disguised from the viewpoint of an observer (called the *adversary* in the sequel) and also from that of the cryptographers who are not paying. This is where anonymity is involved.

The protocol proceeds in the following way. Three cryptographers Crypt_i for $i = 0, 1, 2$ sit in a circle, each with a coin Coin_i. The coins are held in such a way that they can be seen by the owner and one of the other two: in the following figure $\rightarrow$ denotes the "able-to-see-her-coin" relation.

$$\begin{array}{ccc} & \swarrow \mathsf{Crypt}_0 \nwarrow & \\ \mathsf{Crypt}_1 & \longrightarrow & \mathsf{Crypt}_2 \end{array}$$

Then the coins are flipped; each cryptographer, comparing the two coins she can see, announces to the public whether they *agree* (showing the same side) or *disagree*. The trick is that the one who is paying—if there is—lies on the announcement. For example, given that Crypt_0 is paying, then the configuration of coins

$$(\mathsf{h}, \mathsf{t}, \mathsf{h}) \qquad \text{that is} \qquad \begin{array}{ccc} & \swarrow \mathsf{h} \nwarrow & \\ \mathsf{t} & \rightarrow & \mathsf{h} \end{array},$$

results in the announcement

$$(\mathsf{a}, \mathsf{d}, \mathsf{a}) \qquad \text{that is} \qquad \begin{array}{ccc} & \swarrow \mathsf{a} \nwarrow & \\ \mathsf{d} & \rightarrow & \mathsf{a} \end{array}.$$

This announcement is the only thing the adversary can observe; occurrence of an odd number of d's reveals the presence of a liar, hence the presence of a payer among the cryptographers.

Can the adversary say which cryptographer is paying? No. In fact, given an announcement with an odd number of d's and any payer Crypt_i, we can construct a coin configuration which yields the given announcement. For example, the announcement $(\mathsf{a}, \mathsf{d}, \mathsf{a})$ above can be yielded by any of the following configurations.

Crypt_0 pays, and coins are $(\mathsf{h}, \mathsf{t}, \mathsf{h})$ or $(\mathsf{t}, \mathsf{h}, \mathsf{t})$
Crypt_1 pays, and coins are $(\mathsf{h}, \mathsf{h}, \mathsf{h})$ or $(\mathsf{t}, \mathsf{t}, \mathsf{t})$
Crypt_2 pays, and coins are $(\mathsf{h}, \mathsf{h}, \mathsf{t})$ or $(\mathsf{t}, \mathsf{t}, \mathsf{h})$

2.2 Probabilistic Anonymity in DC

Up to now the arguments have been non-deterministic: now we shall explain how probabilistic aspects in DC emerge. Assume that the coins are biased: each of three Coin_i's gives head with the probability $9/10$. Provided that Crypt_0 is paying, the announcement $(\mathsf{a}, \mathsf{d}, \mathsf{a})$ occurs with the probability $(9 \cdot 1 \cdot 9 + 1 \cdot 9 \cdot 1)/10^3$, because it results from $(\mathsf{h}, \mathsf{t}, \mathsf{h})$ or $(\mathsf{t}, \mathsf{h}, \mathsf{t})$. Similar calculations lead to the following table of probabilities.

	$(\mathsf{d}, \mathsf{a}, \mathsf{a})$	$(\mathsf{a}, \mathsf{d}, \mathsf{a})$	$(\mathsf{a}, \mathsf{a}, \mathsf{d})$	$(\mathsf{d}, \mathsf{d}, \mathsf{d})$
Crypt_0 pays	0.73	0.09	0.09	0.09
Crypt_1 pays	0.09	0.73	0.09	0.09
Crypt_2 pays	0.09	0.09	0.73	0.09

Are the cryptographers still "anonymous"? We would not say so. For example, if the adversary observes an announcement $(\mathsf{d}, \mathsf{a}, \mathsf{a})$, it is reasonable for her to suspect Crypt_0 more than the other two.

Nevertheless, if the coins are not biased, we cannot find any symptom of broken anonymity. Therefore we want to obtain the following two things.

The first is an appropriate notion of "probabilistic anonymity" which holds with fair coins but is violated with biased coins—this is done in [4]. The intuition is quite similar to the one behind the notion of *conditional anonymity* [8]. The adversary has a priori knowledge on "who is likely to be blamed"; however, after observing a run of an anonymizing protocol, the adversary should not gain any additional information—each user looks as suspicious as it did before the actual execution.

The second is an effective proof method to verify this notion of anonymity: this is what we aim at in the current work.

3 Probabilistic Anonymity

3.1 Anonymity Automata: Models of Anonymizing Protocols

In this work anonymizing protocols are formalized as a specific kind of probabilistic systems which we shall call (probabilistic) *anonymity automata*. The notion is similar to probabilistic automata [19]: however, in anonymity automata branching is purely probabilistic without any non-determinism. This modification, together with other minor ones, is made so that the coalgebraic framework in [9] applies.

The features of an anonymity automaton are as follows.

- By making a transition it can either
  - execute an action and successfully terminate ($x \xrightarrow{a} \checkmark$), or
  - execute an action and move to another state ($x \xrightarrow{a} y$).

  Internal, silent actions are not explicitly present.
- An action a can be either
  - an *observable action* o which can be seen by the adversary, or
  - an *actor action* $\mathsf{blame}(i)$ which denotes that a user i has performed the action whose performer we want to disguise (such as payment in DC).
- Each state comes with a probability subdistribution over the set of possible transitions. By "sub"distribution it is meant that the sum of all the probabilities is ≤ 1 rather than $= 1$: the missing probability is understood as the probability for deadlock.

Here is a formal definition.

Definition 3.1 (Anonymity automata). An *anonymity automaton* is a 5-tuple $(X, \mathcal{U}, \mathcal{O}, c, s)$ where:

- X is a non-empty set called the *state space*.
- $\mathcal{U}$ is a non-empty set of *users*.[2]
- $\mathcal{O}$ is a non-empty set of *observable actions*.
- $c\colon X \to \mathcal{D}(\mathcal{A} \times \{\checkmark\} + \mathcal{A} \times X)$ is a function which assigns to each state $x \in X$ a probability subdistribution $c(x)$ over possible transitions. The set $\mathcal{A}$ is the set of *actions* and defined by

$$\mathcal{A} = \mathcal{O} + \{\, \mathsf{blame}(i) \mid i \in \mathcal{U}\}.$$

  The operation $\mathcal{D}$ gives the set of subdistributions: for a set Y,

$$\mathcal{D}Y = \{d : Y \to [0,1] \mid \sum_{y \in Y} d(y) \leq 1\}. \tag{1}$$

  This operation $\mathcal{D}$ canonically extends to a monad[3] which we shall call the *subdistribution monad*.

  For example, the value $c(x)(a, \checkmark)$[4] in $[0,1]$ is the probability with which a state x executes a and then successfully terminate (i.e. $x \xrightarrow{a} \checkmark$).
- s is a probability subdistribution over the state space X. This specifies which state would be a *starting* (or *initial*) one.

---

[2] A user is called an *anonymous user* in [4].

[3] *Monads* are a categorical notion. Interested readers are referred to [3] for the details.

[4] To be precise this should be written as $c(x)\big(\kappa_1(a, \checkmark)\big)$, where $\kappa_1 : \mathcal{A} \times \{\checkmark\} \to \mathcal{A} \times \{\checkmark\} + \mathcal{A} \times X$ is the inclusion map.

Example 3.2 (Anonymity automaton $\mathcal{X}_{\mathrm{DC}}$ for DC). To model the DC protocol, we take

$$\mathcal{U} = \{0, 1, 2\}, \qquad \mathcal{O} = \{\mathsf{a}, \mathsf{d}\} \times \{\mathsf{a}, \mathsf{d}\} \times \{\mathsf{a}, \mathsf{d}\} = \{(\mathsf{x}, \mathsf{y}, \mathsf{z}) \mid \mathsf{x}, \mathsf{y}, \mathsf{z} \in \{\mathsf{a}, \mathsf{d}\}\}.$$

We need to fix the a priori probability distribution on who will make a payment, in view of the conditional notion of probabilistic anonymity. Let us denote by p_i the probability with which a user i pays.

The DC protocol (with its a priori probability distribution given by p_i's) is naturally described as follows. Probability for each transition is presented in square brackets; otherwise the transition occurs with probability 1.

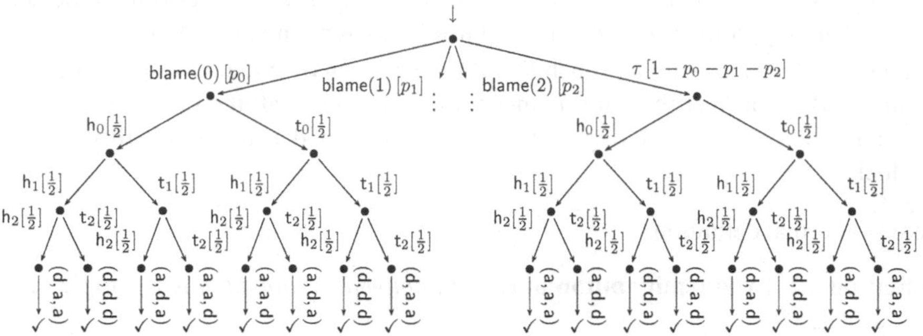

Here τ denotes an internal action with the intention of "NSA pays".

However, the actions h_i and t_i—with their obvious meanings—must not be present because they are not observable by the adversary. These actions are replaced by τ's. Moreover, for technical simplicity we do not allow τ's to appear in an anonymity automaton. Hence we take the "closure" of the above automaton in an obvious way, and obtain the following.

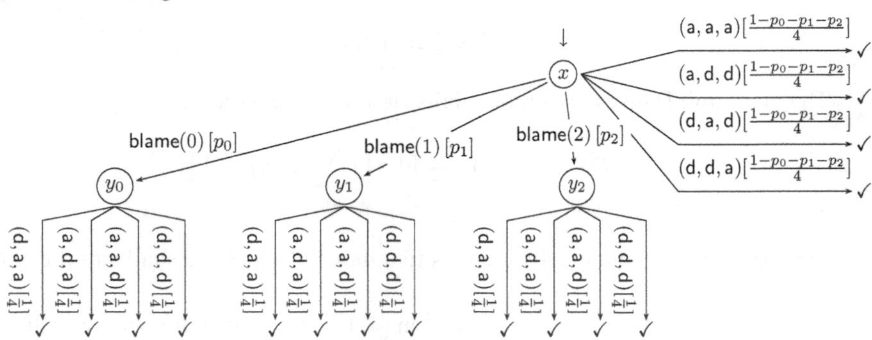

The start state distribution s is: $x \mapsto 1$. This anonymity automaton we shall refer to as $\mathcal{X}_{\mathrm{DC}}$.

3.2 Anonymity Automata Reconciled as Coalgebras

The generic, coalgebraic theory of traces and simulations in [9] applies to anonymity automata. The generic theory is developed with two parameters T and F:

- a monad T on **Sets** specifies the *branching-type*, such as non-determinism or probability;
- a functor F on **Sets** specifies the *transition-type*, i.e., what a system can do by making a transition.

Systems for which traces/simulations are defined are called *(T, F)-systems* in the generic theory, making the parameters explicit. The theory is coalgebraic because a (T, F)-system is essentially a coalgebra in a suitable category.

Anonymity automata fit in the generic theory. They are (T, F)-systems with the following choice of parameters T and F.

- T is the subdistribution monad $\mathcal{D}$, modeling purely probabilistic branching.
- $FX = \mathcal{A} \times \{\checkmark\} + \mathcal{A} \times X$, modeling the transition-type of "(action and terminate) or (action and next state)".

It is immediately seen that for this choice of F, the set $\mathcal{A}^*\mathcal{A}$ carries the following initial algebra in **Sets**. We denote its structure map by α.

$$\begin{array}{ccc} \mathcal{A} \times \{\checkmark\} + \mathcal{A} \times (\mathcal{A}^*\mathcal{A}) & \kappa_1(a, \checkmark) & \kappa_2(a, \boldsymbol{a}) \\ \alpha \downarrow \cong & \downarrow & \downarrow \\ \mathcal{A}^*\mathcal{A} & \langle a \rangle & a \cdot \boldsymbol{a} \end{array} ,$$

where $\langle a \rangle$ denotes a list of length 1, and $a \cdot \boldsymbol{a}$ is what would be written as (cons a $\boldsymbol{a}$) in LISP. Therefore [9, Corollary 5.2] suggests that the set $\mathcal{A}^*\mathcal{A}$ is the appropriate domain of (finite) trace semantics for anonymity automata: this is actually the case later in Definition 3.3.

3.3 Trace Semantics for Anonymity Automata

The trace semantics for anonymity automata is used in defining probabilistic anonymity. In a non-deterministic setting, trace semantics yields a *set* of lists of actions which can possibly occur. In contrast, trace semantics of a probabilistic system is a *probability subdistribution* over lists.

Definition 3.3 (Trace semantics for anonymity automata). Given an anonymity automaton $\mathcal{X} = (X, \mathcal{U}, \mathcal{O}, c, s)$, its *trace*

$$P_{\mathcal{X}} \in \mathcal{D}(\mathcal{A}^*\mathcal{A})$$

is defined as follows. For a list of actions $\langle a_0, a_1, \ldots, a_n \rangle$ with a finite length $n \geq 1$,

$$P_{\mathcal{X}}(\langle a_0, a_1, \ldots, a_n \rangle) = \sum_{x_0, x_1, \ldots, x_n \in X} P_{\mathcal{X}}(x_0 \stackrel{a_0}{\to} x_1 \stackrel{a_1}{\to} \cdots \stackrel{a_{n-1}}{\to} x_n \stackrel{a_n}{\to} \checkmark),$$

where the probability

$$\begin{aligned} & P_{\mathcal{X}}(x_0 \stackrel{a_0}{\to} x_1 \stackrel{a_1}{\to} \cdots \stackrel{a_{n-1}}{\to} x_n \stackrel{a_n}{\to} \checkmark) \\ &= s(x_0) \cdot c(x_0)(a_0, x_1) \cdot \cdots \cdot c(x_{n-1})(a_{n-1}, x_n) \cdot c(x_n)(a_n, \checkmark) \end{aligned}$$

is for the event that $\mathcal{X}$ starts at x_0, follows the path $\stackrel{a_0}{\to} x_1 \stackrel{a_1}{\to} \cdots \stackrel{a_{n-1}}{\to} x_n$ and finally terminates with $\stackrel{a_n}{\to} \checkmark$.

Intuitively the value $P_{\mathcal{X}}(\boldsymbol{a}) \in [0,1]$ for a list $\boldsymbol{a} \in \mathcal{A}^*\mathcal{A}$ is the probability with which the system $\mathcal{X}$ executes actions in $\boldsymbol{a}$ successively and then terminates. Our concern is on actions (observable actions or actor actions) the system makes but not on the states it exhibits.

The following alternative characterization allows us to apply the generic, coalgebraic theory of traces in [9,10].

Lemma 3.4 (Trace semantics via the generic theory). *Given an anonymity automaton $\mathcal{X}$, let (s, c) be a (T, F)-system identified with $\mathcal{X}$ as in Section 3.2.*

The trace $P_{\mathcal{X}}$ of $\mathcal{X}$ coincides with the coalgebraic trace $\mathsf{tr}_{(s,c)}$ defined in the generic theory [9, Definition 5.7] for (s, c). □

Example 3.5 (Dining cryptographers). For the anonymity automaton $\mathcal{X}_{\mathrm{DC}}$ in Example 3.2, its trace $P_{\mathcal{X}_{\mathrm{DC}}}$ is the following probability subdistribution.

$$\begin{array}{lll@{\qquad}lll}
\langle\, \mathsf{blame}(i), (\mathsf{d},\mathsf{a},\mathsf{a})\,\rangle & \mapsto & p_i/4 & \langle\, (\mathsf{a},\mathsf{a},\mathsf{a})\,\rangle & \mapsto & (1-p_0-p_1-p_2)/4 \\
\langle\, \mathsf{blame}(i), (\mathsf{a},\mathsf{d},\mathsf{a})\,\rangle & \mapsto & p_i/4 & \langle\, (\mathsf{a},\mathsf{d},\mathsf{d})\,\rangle & \mapsto & (1-p_0-p_1-p_2)/4 \\
\langle\, \mathsf{blame}(i), (\mathsf{a},\mathsf{a},\mathsf{d})\,\rangle & \mapsto & p_i/4 & \langle\, (\mathsf{d},\mathsf{a},\mathsf{d})\,\rangle & \mapsto & (1-p_0-p_1-p_2)/4 \\
\langle\, \mathsf{blame}(i), (\mathsf{d},\mathsf{d},\mathsf{d})\,\rangle & \mapsto & p_i/4 & \langle\, (\mathsf{d},\mathsf{d},\mathsf{a})\,\rangle & \mapsto & (1-p_0-p_1-p_2)/4 \\
 & \text{(for } i = 0,1,2) & & & &
\end{array}$$

The other lists in $\mathcal{A}^*\mathcal{A}$ have probability 0.

In this work we assume that in each execution of an anonymizing protocol there appears at most one actor action. This is the same assumption as [4, Assumption 1] and is true in all the examples in this paper.

Assumption 3.6 (At most one actor action). Let $\mathcal{X} = (X, \mathcal{U}, \mathcal{O}, c, s)$ be an anonymity automaton and $\boldsymbol{a} \in \mathcal{A}^*\mathcal{A}$. If $\boldsymbol{a}$ contains more than one actor actions, then

$$P_{\mathcal{X}}(\boldsymbol{a}) = 0.$$

3.4 Definition of Probabilistic Anonymity

In this section we formalize the notion of probabilistic anonymity following [4]. First, for the sake of simplicity of presentation, we shall introduce the following notations for predicates (i.e. subsets) on $\mathcal{A}^*\mathcal{A}$.

Definition 3.7 (Predicates $[\mathsf{blame}(i)]$ and $[o]$)

- For each $i \in \mathcal{U}$, a predicate $[\mathsf{blame}(i)]$ on $\mathcal{A}^*\mathcal{A}$ is defined as follows.

  $$[\mathsf{blame}(i)] = \{\boldsymbol{a} \in \mathcal{A}^*\mathcal{A} \mid \mathsf{blame}(i) \text{ appears in } \boldsymbol{a}\}$$

  By Assumption 3.6, it is the set of lists obtained by augmenting $\mathsf{blame}(i)$ with observable actions: in a regular-expression-like notation,

  $$[\mathsf{blame}(i)] = \mathcal{O}^*\, \mathsf{blame}(i)\, \mathcal{O}^*.$$

  Moreover, $[\mathsf{blame}(i)] \cap [\mathsf{blame}(j)] = \emptyset$ if $i \neq j$.

– For each $o \in \mathcal{O}^*$, a predicate $[o]$ on $\mathcal{A}^*\mathcal{A}$ is defined as follows.

$$[o] = \{a \in \mathcal{A}^*\mathcal{A} \mid \mathsf{removeActor}(a) = o\},$$

where the function $\mathsf{removeActor} : \mathcal{A}^*\mathcal{A} \to \mathcal{O}^*$—which is defined by a suitable induction—removes actor actions appearing in a list. The set $[o] \subseteq \mathcal{A}^*\mathcal{A}$ consists of those lists which yield o as the adversary's observation. It is emphasized that $[o]$ is *not* the set of lists which contain o as sublists: we remove only actor actions, but not observable actions.

Note that we are overriding the notation $[\_]$: no confusion would arise since the arguments are of different types. Values such as $P_{\mathcal{X}}(\,[\mathsf{blame}(i)]\,)$ are defined in a straightforward manner:

$$P_{\mathcal{X}}(\,[\mathsf{blame}(i)]\,) = \sum_{a \in [\mathsf{blame}(i)]} P_{\mathcal{X}}(a).$$

This is the probability with which $\mathcal{X}$ yields an execution in which a user i is to be blamed.

We follow [4] and adopt the following definition of anonymity.

Definition 3.8 (Probabilistic anonymity [4]). We say an anonymity automaton $\mathcal{X}$ is *anonymous* if for each $i, j \in \mathcal{U}$ and $o \in \mathcal{O}^*$,

$$\begin{aligned} & P_{\mathcal{X}}(\,[\mathsf{blame}(i)]\,) > 0 \quad \wedge \quad P_{\mathcal{X}}(\,[\mathsf{blame}(j)]\,) > 0 \\ \Longrightarrow \quad & P_{\mathcal{X}}(\,[o] \mid [\mathsf{blame}(i)]\,) = P_{\mathcal{X}}(\,[o] \mid [\mathsf{blame}(j)]\,). \end{aligned}$$

Here $P_{\mathcal{X}}(\,[o] \mid [\mathsf{blame}(i)]\,)$ is a conditional probability: it is given by

$$P_{\mathcal{X}}(\,[o] \mid [\mathsf{blame}(i)]\,) = \frac{P_{\mathcal{X}}(\,[o] \cap [\mathsf{blame}(i)]\,)}{P_{\mathcal{X}}(\,[\mathsf{blame}(i)]\,)}.$$

The intuition behind this notion—sketched in Section 2.2—is similar to the one behind conditional anonymity [8]. In fact, it is shown in [4] that under reasonable assumptions the two notions of anonymity coincide. For completeness the definition of conditional anonymity (adapted to the current setting) is also presented.

Definition 3.9 (Conditional anonimity [8]). An anonymity automaton $\mathcal{X}$ satisfies *conditional anonymity* if for each $i \in \mathcal{U}$ and $o, o' \in \mathcal{O}^*$,

$$\begin{aligned} & P_{\mathcal{X}}(\,[\mathsf{blame}(i)] \cap [o]\,) > 0 \\ \Longrightarrow \quad & P_{\mathcal{X}}(\,[\mathsf{blame}(i)] \mid [o]\,) = P_{\mathcal{X}}(\,[\mathsf{blame}(i)] \mid \bigcup_{j \in \mathcal{U}} [\mathsf{blame}(j)]\,). \end{aligned}$$

The notion in Definition 3.8 is (one possibility of) probabilistic extension of *trace anonymity* in [18]. It is emphasized that these anonymity notions are based on trace semantics which is at the coarsest end in the linear time-branching time spectrum [22]. Hence our adversary has less observation power than one in [1] for example where security notions are bisimulation-based. A justification for having such a weaker adversary is found in [13].

4 Anonymity Proof Via Probabilistic Simulations

In this section we extend the proof method [13,12] for anonymity to the probabilistic setting. In the introduction we have presented the basic scenario. Now we shall describe its details, with all the notions therein (traces, simulations, *etc.*) interpreted probabilistically.

4.1 Anonymized Automaton $\mathsf{an}(\mathcal{X})$

We start with the definition of $\mathsf{an}(\mathcal{X})$, the *anonymized version* of an anonymity automaton $\mathcal{X}$. Recall that our notion of anonymity is conditional: the adversary has a priori knowledge on who is more suspicious. In an anonymity automaton $\mathcal{X}$, the a priori probability with which a user i does wrong is given by $P_{\mathcal{X}}(\,[\mathsf{blame}(i)]\,)$. Its normalized, conditional version

$$r_i \stackrel{\text{def.}}{=} P_{\mathcal{X}}(\,[\mathsf{blame}(i)] \mid \bigcup_{j\in\mathcal{U}} [\mathsf{blame}(j)]\,) = \frac{P_{\mathcal{X}}(\,[\mathsf{blame}(i)] \cap \bigcup_{j\in\mathcal{U}} [\mathsf{blame}(j)]\,)}{P_{\mathcal{X}}(\bigcup_{j\in\mathcal{U}} [\mathsf{blame}(j)]\,)}$$
$$= \frac{P_{\mathcal{X}}(\,[\mathsf{blame}(i)]\,)}{\sum_{j\in\mathcal{U}} P_{\mathcal{X}}(\,[\mathsf{blame}(j)]\,)}$$

(the equalities are due to Assumption 3.6) plays an important role in the following definition of $\mathsf{an}(\mathcal{X})$. The value r_i is the conditional probability with which a user i is to be blamed, given that there is any user to be blamed; we have $\sum_{i\in\mathcal{U}} r_i = 1$. Of course, for the values r_i to be well-defined, the anonymity automaton $\mathcal{X}$ needs to satisfy the following reasonable assumption.

Assumption 4.1 (There is someone to blame). For an anonymity automaton $\mathcal{X}$,

$$\sum_{j\in\mathcal{U}} P_{\mathcal{X}}(\,[\mathsf{blame}(j)]\,) \neq 0.$$

Intuitively, $\mathsf{an}(\mathcal{X})$ is obtained from $\mathcal{X}$ by distributing an actor action $\mathsf{blame}(i)$ to each user j, with the probability distributed in proportion to r_j.

Definition 4.2 (Anonymized anonymity automaton $\mathsf{an}(\mathcal{X})$). Given an anonymity automaton $\mathcal{X} = (X, \mathcal{U}, \mathcal{O}, c, s)$, its *anonymized automaton* $\mathsf{an}(\mathcal{X})$ is a 5-tuple $(X, \mathcal{U}, \mathcal{O}, c^{\mathsf{an}}, s)$, where c^{an} is defined as follows. For each $x \in X$,

$$\begin{aligned} c^{\mathsf{an}}(x)(\mathsf{blame}(i), u) &= \textstyle\sum_{j\in\mathcal{U}} r_i \cdot c(x)(\mathsf{blame}(j), u) && \text{for } i \in \mathcal{U} \text{ and } u \in \{\checkmark\} + X, \\ c^{\mathsf{an}}(x)(o, u) &= c(x)(o, u) && \text{for } o \in \mathcal{O} \text{ and } u \in \{\checkmark\} + X. \end{aligned}$$

On the first equation, the summand $r_i \cdot c(x)(\mathsf{blame}(j), u)$ results from distributing the probability $c(x)(\mathsf{blame}(j), u)$ for a transition $x \xrightarrow{\mathsf{blame}(j)} u$, to a user i. This is illustrated in the following figure: here $\mathcal{U} = \{0, 1, \ldots, n\}$ and $q = c(x)(\mathsf{blame}(j), u)$.

 (2)

The automaton $\mathsf{an}(\mathcal{X})$ is "anonymized" in the sense of the following lemmas.

Lemma 4.3. *Let $\mathcal{X}$ be an anonymity automaton. In its anonymized version* $\mathsf{an}(\mathcal{X}) = (X, \mathcal{U}, \mathcal{O}, c^{\mathsf{an}}, s)$ *we have*

$$r_j \cdot c^{\mathsf{an}}(x)(\mathsf{blame}(i), u) = r_i \cdot c^{\mathsf{an}}(x)(\mathsf{blame}(j), u)$$

for any $i, j \in \mathcal{U}$, $x \in X$ *and* $u \in \{\checkmark\} + X$.

Proof. Obvious from the definition of c^{an}. □

Lemma 4.4 ($\mathsf{an}(\mathcal{X})$ **is anonymous).** *For an anonymity automaton* $\mathcal{X}$, $\mathsf{an}(\mathcal{X})$ *is anonymous in the sense of Definition 3.8.*

Proof. Let $\mathbf{o} = \langle o_1, o_2, \ldots, o_n \rangle \in \mathcal{O}^*$ and $i, j \in \mathcal{U}$. Moreover, assume

$$P_{\mathsf{an}(\mathcal{X})}(\,[\mathsf{blame}(i)]\,) \neq 0 \quad \text{and} \quad P_{\mathsf{an}(\mathcal{X})}(\,[\mathsf{blame}(j)]\,) \neq 0,$$

hence $r_i \neq 0$ and $r_j \neq 0$. Then

$$\begin{aligned}
&P_{\mathsf{an}(\mathcal{X})}(\,[\mathbf{o}] \cap [\mathsf{blame}(i)]\,)\\
&= P_{\mathsf{an}(\mathcal{X})}(\,\langle \mathsf{blame}(i), o_1, o_2, \ldots, o_n \rangle\,)\\
&\quad + P_{\mathsf{an}(\mathcal{X})}(\,\langle o_1, \mathsf{blame}(i), o_2, \ldots, o_n \rangle\,)\\
&\quad + \cdots + P_{\mathsf{an}(\mathcal{X})}(\,\langle o_1, o_2, \ldots, o_n, \mathsf{blame}(i) \rangle\,)\\
&= \sum_{x_0, x_1, \ldots, x_n \in X} s(x_0) \cdot c^{\mathsf{an}}(x_0)(\mathsf{blame}(i), x_1) \cdot c^{\mathsf{an}}(x_1)(o_1, x_2) \cdot \cdots \cdot c^{\mathsf{an}}(x_n)(o_n, \checkmark)\\
&\quad + \sum_{x_0, x_1, \ldots, x_n \in X} s(x_0) \cdot c^{\mathsf{an}}(x_0)(o_1, x_1) \cdot c^{\mathsf{an}}(x_1)(\mathsf{blame}(i), x_2) \cdot \cdots \cdot c^{\mathsf{an}}(x_n)(o_n, \checkmark)\\
&\quad + \cdots\\
&\quad + \sum_{x_0, x_1, \ldots, x_n \in X} s(x_0) \cdot c^{\mathsf{an}}(x_0)(o_1, x_1) \cdot c^{\mathsf{an}}(x_1)(o_2, x_2) \cdot \cdots \cdot c^{\mathsf{an}}(x_n)(\mathsf{blame}(i), \checkmark).
\end{aligned}$$

We have the same equation for j instead of i. Hence by Lemma 4.3 we have

$$r_j \cdot P_{\mathsf{an}(\mathcal{X})}(\,[\mathbf{o}] \cap [\mathsf{blame}(i)]\,) = r_i \cdot P_{\mathsf{an}(\mathcal{X})}(\,[\mathbf{o}] \cap [\mathsf{blame}(j)]\,). \tag{3}$$

This is used to show the equality of two conditional probabilities.

$$\begin{aligned}
P_{\mathsf{an}(\mathcal{X})}(\,[\mathbf{o}] \mid [\mathsf{blame}(i)]\,) &= \frac{P_{\mathsf{an}(\mathcal{X})}(\,[\mathbf{o}] \cap [\mathsf{blame}(i)]\,)}{P_{\mathsf{an}(\mathcal{X})}(\,[\mathsf{blame}(i)]\,)}\\
&= \frac{r_i}{r_j} \cdot \frac{P_{\mathsf{an}(\mathcal{X})}(\,[\mathbf{o}] \cap [\mathsf{blame}(j)]\,)}{P_{\mathsf{an}(\mathcal{X})}(\,[\mathsf{blame}(i)]\,)} && \text{By (3)}\\
&= \frac{P_{\mathsf{an}(\mathcal{X})}(\,[\mathbf{o}] \cap [\mathsf{blame}(j)]\,)}{P_{\mathsf{an}(\mathcal{X})}(\,[\mathsf{blame}(j)]\,)} && \text{By definition of } r_i, r_j\\
&= P_{\mathsf{an}(\mathcal{X})}(\,[\mathbf{o}] \mid [\mathsf{blame}(j)]\,).
\end{aligned}$$

□

4.2 Forward/Backward Simulations for Anonymity Automata

We proceed to introduce appropriate notions of forward and backward simulations. The (tedious) definition and soundness theorem—existence of a forward/backward simulation implies trace inclusion—come for free from the generic theory in [9]. This forms a crucial part of our simulation-based proof method.

Definition 4.5 (Forward/backward simulations for anonymity automata). Let $\mathcal{X} = (X, \mathcal{U}, \mathcal{O}, c, s)$ and $\mathcal{Y} = (Y, \mathcal{U}, \mathcal{O}, d, t)$ be anonymity automata which have the same sets of users and observable actions.

A *forward simulation* from $\mathcal{X}$ to $\mathcal{Y}$—through which $\mathcal{Y}$ *forward-simulates* $\mathcal{X}$—is a function

$$f : Y \longrightarrow \mathcal{D}X$$

which satisfies the following inequalities in $[0, 1]$.

$$\begin{array}{lll} s(x) & \le \sum_{y \in Y} t(y) \cdot f(y)(x) & \text{for any } x \in X, \\ \sum_{x \in X} f(y)(x) \cdot c(x)(e, \checkmark) & \le d(y)(e, \checkmark) & \text{for any } y \in Y \text{ and } e \in \mathcal{A}, \\ \sum_{x \in X} f(y)(x) \cdot c(x)(e, x') & \le \sum_{y' \in Y} d(y)(e, y') \cdot f(y')(x') & \\ & & \text{for any } y \in Y,\ e \in \mathcal{A} \text{ and } x' \in X. \end{array}$$

A *backward simulation* from $\mathcal{X}$ to $\mathcal{Y}$—through which $\mathcal{Y}$ *backward-simulates* $\mathcal{X}$—is a function

$$b : X \longrightarrow \mathcal{D}Y$$

which satisfies the following inequalities in $[0, 1]$.

$$\begin{array}{lll} \sum_{x \in X} s(x) \cdot b(x)(y) & \le t(y) & \text{for any } y \in Y, \\ c(x)(e, \checkmark) & \le \sum_{y \in Y} b(x)(y) \cdot d(y)(e, \checkmark) & \text{for any } x \in X \text{ and } e \in \mathcal{A}, \\ \sum_{x' \in X} c(x)(e, x') \cdot b(x')(y') & \le \sum_{y \in Y} b(x)(y) \cdot d(y)(e, y') & \\ & & \text{for any } x \in X,\ e \in \mathcal{A} \text{ and } y' \in Y. \end{array}$$

The definition definitely looks puzzling. Why does a forward simulation have the type $Y \to \mathcal{D}X$? Why is a backward simulation not of the same type? How come the complex inequalities? How do we know that the inequalities are in the correct direction?

In fact, this definition is an instantiation of the general, coalgebraic notions of forward/backward simulations [9, Definitions 4.1, 4.2]. More specifically, the two parameters T and F in the generic definition are instantiated as in Section 3.2.

Theorem 4.6 (Soundness of forward/backward simulations). *Assume there is a forward (or backward) simulation from one anonymity automaton $\mathcal{X}$ to another $\mathcal{Y}$. Then we have trace inclusion*

$$P_{\mathcal{X}} \sqsubseteq P_{\mathcal{Y}},$$

where the order $\sqsubseteq$ is defined to be the pointwise order: for each $\boldsymbol{a} \in \mathcal{A}^* \mathcal{A}$,

$$P_{\mathcal{X}}(\boldsymbol{a}) \le P_{\mathcal{Y}}(\boldsymbol{a}).$$

Proof. We know (Lemma 3.4) that the notions of traces and simulations for anonymity automata are instantiations of the general, coalgebraic notions in [9,10]. Therefore we can appeal to the general soundness theorem [9, Theorem 6.1]. □

4.3 Probabilistic Anonymity Via Simulations

We shall use the materials in Sections 4.1 and 4.2 to prove the validity of our simulation-based proof method (Theorem 4.11).

The following lemma—which essentially says $P_{\mathcal{X}} \sqsubseteq P_{\mathsf{an}(\mathcal{X})}$—relies on the way $\mathsf{an}(\mathcal{X})$ is constructed. The proof is a bit more complicated than in the non-deterministic setting [13,12].

Lemma 4.7. *Let $\mathcal{X}$ be an anonymity automaton. Assume there exists a forward or backward simulation from* $\mathsf{an}(\mathcal{X})$ *to $\mathcal{X}$—through which $\mathcal{X}$ simulates* $\mathsf{an}(\mathcal{X})$. *Then their trace semantics are equal:*

$$P_{\mathcal{X}} = P_{\mathsf{an}(\mathcal{X})}.$$

Proof. By the soundness theorem (Theorem 4.6) we have

$$P_{\mathcal{X}} \sqsupseteq P_{\mathsf{an}(\mathcal{X})}, \tag{4}$$

where $\sqsupseteq$ refers to the pointwise order between functions $\mathcal{A}^*\mathcal{A} \rightrightarrows [0,1]$. We shall show that this inequality is in fact an equality.

First we introduce an operation obs which acts on anonymity automata. Intuitively, $\mathsf{obs}(\mathcal{Y})$ is obtained from $\mathcal{Y}$ by replacing all the different actor actions $\mathsf{blame}(i)$ with single $\mathsf{blame}(\mathsf{sb})$—sb is for "somebody". This conceals actor actions in $\mathcal{Y}$; hence $\mathsf{obs}(\mathcal{Y})$ only carries information on the observable actions of $\mathcal{Y}$.

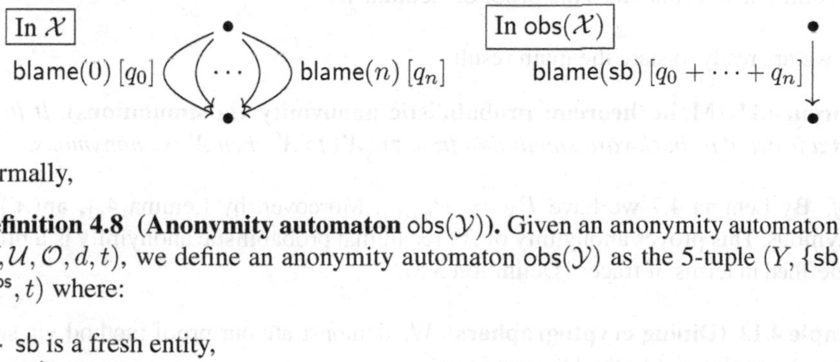

In $\mathcal{X}$: $\mathsf{blame}(0)\ [q_0]$ $(\cdots)$ $\mathsf{blame}(n)\ [q_n]$ — In $\mathsf{obs}(\mathcal{X})$: $\mathsf{blame}(\mathsf{sb})\ [q_0 + \cdots + q_n]$ (5)

Formally,

Definition 4.8 (Anonymity automaton $\mathsf{obs}(\mathcal{Y})$). Given an anonymity automaton $\mathcal{Y} = (Y, \mathcal{U}, \mathcal{O}, d, t)$, we define an anonymity automaton $\mathsf{obs}(\mathcal{Y})$ as the 5-tuple $(Y, \{\mathsf{sb}\}, \mathcal{O}, d^{\mathsf{obs}}, t)$ where:

- sb is a fresh entity,
- d^{obs} is a function

$$d^{\mathsf{obs}} : Y \longrightarrow \mathcal{D}\big(\mathcal{A}^{\mathsf{obs}} \times \{\checkmark\} + \mathcal{A}^{\mathsf{obs}} \times Y\big)$$

where $\mathcal{A}^{\mathsf{obs}} = \mathcal{O} + \{\mathsf{blame}(\mathsf{sb})\}$, defined by:

$$\begin{aligned} d^{\mathsf{obs}}(y)(\mathsf{blame}(\mathsf{sb}), u) &= \textstyle\sum_{i \in \mathcal{U}} d(y)(\mathsf{blame}(i), u) && \text{for } y \in Y \text{ and } u \in \{\checkmark\} + Y, \\ d^{\mathsf{obs}}(y)(o, u) &= d(y)(o, u) && \text{for } y \in Y, o \in \mathcal{O} \text{ and } u \in \{\checkmark\} + Y. \end{aligned}$$

The following fact is obvious.

Sublemma 4.9. *For an anonymity automaton $\mathcal{X}$,* $\mathsf{obs}(\mathcal{X})$ *and* $\mathsf{obs}(\mathsf{an}(\mathcal{X}))$ *are identical.* □

The following sublemma is crucial in the proof of Lemma 4.7. Two automata $\mathcal{Y}$ and $\mathsf{obs}(\mathcal{Y})$, although their trace semantics distributes over different sets, have the same sum of probabilities taken over all executions.

Sublemma 4.10. *For an anonymity automaton $\mathcal{Y}$,*

$$\sum_{\boldsymbol{a}\in\mathcal{A}^*\mathcal{A}} P_{\mathcal{Y}}(\boldsymbol{a}) = \sum_{\boldsymbol{a}'\in(\mathcal{A}^{\mathsf{obs}})^*\mathcal{A}^{\mathsf{obs}}} P_{\mathsf{obs}(\mathcal{Y})}(\boldsymbol{a}') .$$

Recall that $\mathcal{A} = \mathcal{O} + \{\mathsf{blame}(i) \mid i \in \mathcal{U}\}$ and $\mathcal{A}^{\mathsf{obs}} = \mathcal{O} + \{\mathsf{blame}(\mathsf{sb})\}$.

Proof. From the definition of trace semantics (Definition 3.3), the sublemma is proved by easy calculation. □

We turn back to the proof of Lemma 4.7. We argue by contradiction—assume that the inequality in (4) is strict. That is, there exists $\boldsymbol{a}_0 \in \mathcal{A}^*\mathcal{A}$ such that $P_{\mathcal{X}}(\boldsymbol{a}_0) \gneq P_{\mathsf{an}(\mathcal{X})}(\boldsymbol{a}_0)$. Then, by (4) we have $\sum_{\boldsymbol{a}\in\mathcal{A}^*\mathcal{A}} P_{\mathcal{X}}(\boldsymbol{a}) \gneq \sum_{\boldsymbol{a}\in\mathcal{A}^*\mathcal{A}} P_{\mathsf{an}(\mathcal{X})}(\boldsymbol{a})$. However,

$$\begin{aligned}
\textstyle\sum_{\boldsymbol{a}\in\mathcal{A}^*\mathcal{A}} P_{\mathcal{X}}(\boldsymbol{a}) &= \textstyle\sum_{\boldsymbol{a}'\in(\mathcal{A}^{\mathsf{obs}})^*\mathcal{A}^{\mathsf{obs}}} P_{\mathsf{obs}(\mathcal{X})}(\boldsymbol{a}') && \text{By Sublemma 4.10}\\
&= \textstyle\sum_{\boldsymbol{a}'\in(\mathcal{A}^{\mathsf{obs}})^*\mathcal{A}^{\mathsf{obs}}} P_{\mathsf{obs}(\mathsf{an}(\mathcal{X}))}(\boldsymbol{a}') && \text{By Sublemma 4.9}\\
&= \textstyle\sum_{\boldsymbol{a}\in\mathcal{A}^*\mathcal{A}} P_{\mathsf{an}(\mathcal{X})}(\boldsymbol{a}) \ . && \text{By Sublemma 4.10}
\end{aligned}$$

This contradiction concludes the proof of Lemma 4.7. □

Now we are ready to state the main result.

Theorem 4.11 (Main theorem: probabilistic anonymity via simulations). *If there exists a forward or backward simulation from $\mathsf{an}(\mathcal{X})$ to $\mathcal{X}$, then $\mathcal{X}$ is anonymous.*

Proof. By Lemma 4.7 we have $P_{\mathcal{X}} = P_{\mathsf{an}(\mathcal{X})}$. Moreover, by Lemma 4.4, $\mathsf{an}(\mathcal{X})$ is anonymous. This proves anonymity of $\mathcal{X}$: recall that probabilistic anonymity is a property defined in terms of traces (Definition 3.8). □

Example 4.12 (Dining cryptographers). We demonstrate our proof method via simulations by applying it to the DC protocol.

Let $X = \{x, y_0, y_1, y_2\}$ be the state space of $\mathcal{X}_{\mathrm{DC}}$. Its anonymized version $\mathsf{an}(\mathcal{X}_{\mathrm{DC}})$ has the same state space: for notational convenience the state space of $\mathsf{an}(\mathcal{X}_{\mathrm{DC}})$ is denoted by $X' = \{x', y_0{}', y_1{}', y_2{}'\}$. It is verified by easy calculation that the following function $f : X \to \mathcal{D}(X')$ is a forward simulation from $\mathsf{an}(\mathcal{X}_{\mathrm{DC}})$ to $\mathcal{X}_{\mathrm{DC}}$.

$$f(x) = [x' \mapsto 1] \qquad f(y_0) = f(y_1) = f(y_2) = \begin{bmatrix} y_0{}' \mapsto \frac{p_0}{p_0+p_1+p_2} \\ y_1{}' \mapsto \frac{p_1}{p_0+p_1+p_2} \\ y_2{}' \mapsto \frac{p_2}{p_0+p_1+p_2} \end{bmatrix}$$

By Theorem 4.11 this proves (probabilistic) anonymity of $\mathcal{X}_{\mathrm{DC}}$, hence of the DC protocol.

5 Conclusion and Future Work

We have extended the simulation-based proof method [13,12] for non-deterministic anonymity to apply to the notion of probabilistic anonymity defined in [4]. For the move we have exploited a generic theory of traces and simulations [9,10] in which the difference between non-determinism and probability is just a different choice of a parameter.

The DC example in this paper fails to demonstrate the usefulness of our proof method: for this small example direct calculation of trace distribution is not hard. A real benefit would arise in theorem-proving anonymity of an unboundedly large system (which we cannot model-check). In fact, the non-deterministic version of our proof method is used to theorem-prove anonymity of a voting protocol with arbitrary many voters [12]. A probabilistic case study of such kind is currently missing.

In [4] the probabilistic π-calculus is utilized as a specification language for automata. We have not yet elaborated which subset of the calculus is suitable for describing our notion of anonymity automata.

There is a well-established body of work on verification of probabilistic information-hiding properties such as non-interference [24,17]. Our proof method could be reconciled in this context by, for example, finding a translation of anonymity into a non-interference property.

The significance of having both non-deterministic and probabilistic branching in considering anonymity is claimed in [15]. However the current method cannot handle this combination due to the lack of suitable coalgebraic framework. Elaboration in this direction would also help better understanding of the nature of the (notorious) combination of non-determinism and probability.

Acknowledgments. Thanks are due to Ken Mano, Peter van Rossum, Hideki Sakurada, Ana Sokolova, Yasuaki Tsukada and the anonymous referees for helpful discussions and comments. The first author is grateful to his supervisor Bart Jacobs for encouragement.

References

1. M. Abadi and A. Gordon. A calculus for cryptographic protocols: The Spi calculus. In *Fourth ACM Conference on Computer and Communications Security*, pages 36–47. ACM Press, 1997.
2. Anonymity bibliography. `http://freehaven.net/anonbib/`.
3. M. Barr and C. Wells. *Toposes, Triples and Theories*. Springer, Berlin, 1985.
4. M. Bhargava and C. Palamidessi. Probabilistic anonymity. In M. Abadi and L. de Alfaro, editors, *CONCUR 2005*, volume 3653 of *Lect. Notes Comp. Sci.*, pages 171–185. Springer, 2005.
5. D. Chaum. The dining cryptographers problem: Unconditional sender and recipient untraceability. *Journ. of Cryptology*, 1(1):65–75, 1988.
6. L. Cheung. *Reconciling Nondeterministic and Probabilistic Choices*. PhD thesis, Radboud Univ. Nijmegen, 2006.

7. F.D. Garcia, I. Hasuo, W. Pieters, and P. van Rossum. Provable anonymity. In R. Küsters and J. Mitchell, editors, *3rd ACM Workshop on Formal Methods in Security Engineering (FMSE05)*, pages 63–72, Alexandria , VA, U.S.A., November 2005. ACM Press.
8. J.Y. Halpern and K.R. O'Neill. Anonymity and information hiding in multiagent systems. *Journal of Computer Security*, to appear.
9. I. Hasuo. Generic forward and backward simulations. In C. Baier and H. Hermanns, editors, *International Conference on Concurrency Theory (CONCUR 2006)*, volume 4137 of *Lect. Notes Comp. Sci.*, pages 406–420. Springer, Berlin, 2006.
10. I. Hasuo, B. Jacobs, and A. Sokolova. Generic trace theory. In N. Ghani and J. Power, editors, *International Workshop on Coalgebraic Methods in Computer Science (CMCS 2006)*, volume 164 of *Elect. Notes in Theor. Comp. Sci.*, pages 47–65. Elsevier, Amsterdam, 2006.
11. D. Hughes and V. Shmatikov. Information hiding, anonymity and privacy: A modular approach. *Journal of Computer Security*, 12(1):3–36, 2004.
12. Y. Kawabe, K. Mano, H. Sakurada, and Y. Tsukada. Backward simulations for anonymity. In *International Workshop on Issues in the Theory of Security (WITS '06)*, 2006.
13. Y. Kawabe, K. Mano, H. Sakurada, and Y. Tsukada. Theorem-proving anonymity of infinite state systems. *Information Processing Letters*, 101(1), 2007.
14. N. Lynch and F. Vaandrager. Forward and backward simulations. I. Untimed systems. *Inf. & Comp.*, 121(2):214–233, 1995.
15. C. Palamidessi. Probabilistic and nondeterministic aspects of anonymity. In *MFPS '05*, volume 155 of *Elect. Notes in Theor. Comp. Sci.*, pages 33–42. Elsevier, 2006.
16. A. Pfitzmann and M. Köhntopp. Anonymity, unobservability, and pseudonymity: A proposal for terminology. Draft, version 0.17, July 2000.
17. A. Sabelfeld and D. Sands. Probabilistic noninterference for multi-threaded programs. In *Proceedings of the 13th IEEE Computer Security Foundations Workshop (CSFW'00)*, pages 200–214, 2000.
18. S. Schneider and A. Sidiropoulos. CSP and anonymity. In *ESORICS '96: Proceedings of the 4th European Symposium on Research in Computer Security*, pages 198–218, London, UK, 1996. Springer-Verlag.
19. R. Segala and N. Lynch. Probabilistic simulations for probabilistic processes. *Nordic Journ. Comput.*, 2(2):250–273, 1995.
20. A. Serjantov. *On the Anonymity of Anonymity Systems*. PhD thesis, University of Cambridge, March 2004.
21. V. Shmatikov. Probabilistic model checking of an anonymity system. *Journ. of Computer Security*, 12(3):355–377, 2004.
22. R. van Glabbeek. The linear time-branching time spectrum (extended abstract). In J. Baeten and J. Klop, editors, Proceedings *CONCUR '90, Theories of Concurrency: Unification and Extension,* Amsterdam, August 1990, volume 458 of *Lect. Notes Comp. Sci.*, pages 278–297. Springer-Verlag, 1990.
23. D. Varacca and G. Winskel. Distributing probabililty over nondeterminism. *Math. Struct. in Comp. Sci.*, 16(1):87–113, 2006.
24. D.M. Volpano and G. Smith. Probabilistic noninterference in a concurrent language. *Journ. of Computer Security*, 7(1), 1999.

A Fault Tolerance Bisimulation Proof for Consensus (Extended Abstract)

Adrian Francalanza[1] and Matthew Hennessy[2]

[1] Imperial College, London SW7 2BZ, England
adrianf@doc.ic.ac.uk
[2] University of Sussex, Brighton BN1 9RH, England
matthewh@sussex.ac.uk

Abstract. The possibility of partial failure occuring at any stage of computation complicates rigorous formal treatment of distributed algorithms. We propose a methodology for formalising and proving the correctness of distributed algorithms which alleviates this complexity. The methodology uses fault-tolerance bisimulation proof techniques to split the analysis into two phases, that is a failure-free phase and a failure phase, permitting separation of concerns. We design a minimal partial-failure calculus, develop a corresponding bisimulation theory for it and express a consensus algorithm in the calculus. We then use the consensus example and the calculus theory to demonstrate the benefits of our methodology.

1 Introduction

The areas of Distributed Systems and Process Calculi are two (major) areas in Computer Science addressing the same problems but "speak(ing) different languages" [14]. In particular, seminal work in Distributed Systems, such as [2,11] present algorithms in semi-formal pseudo-code and correctness proofs of an informal algorithmic nature. The understandable reluctance to apply the rigorous theory of process calculi to formal proofs for standard distributed algorithms stems from the complexity and sheer size of the resulting formal descriptions and proofs. This problem is accentuated when failures are considered, which typically occur at any point during computation and can potentially affect execution. More specifically, in a process calculus with formal semantics based on labelled transition systems (lts), and a related bisimulation equivalence $\approx$, correctness proofs compare the behaviour of the distributed algorithm, described in the base calculus, to a correctness specification, also defined in the base calculus, using $\approx$; see Table 1(a). The required witness bisimulation relations resulting from this general approach turn out to be substantial, even for the simplest of algorithms and specifications. Even worse, partial failure tends to obfuscate the simplicity of the correctness specification while enlarging the state space of the bisimulations.

To tame such complexity, attempts at formalising distributed algorithm proofs have made use of mechanised theorem provers [8] or translations into tailor-made abstract interpretations [14]. In spite of their effectiveness, such tools and techniques tend to obscure the natural structure of the proofs of correctness, because they either still produce monolithic proofs, which are hard to digest, or else depart from the source formal language in which the algorithm is expressed.

We propose a prescriptive methodology to formally prove correctness of distributed algorithms which fine tunes well-studied bisimulation techniques to a partial failure

R. De Nicola (Ed.): ESOP 2007, LNCS 4421, pp. 395–410, 2007.

Table 1. Correctness proofs using fault-tolerant bisimulation techniques

system ≈ observables complex specification (a)

system wrapper observables ≈ simple specification (b)

system wrapper ≈ simple specification (c)

system wrapper ≈ system wrapper (d)

reliable faulty

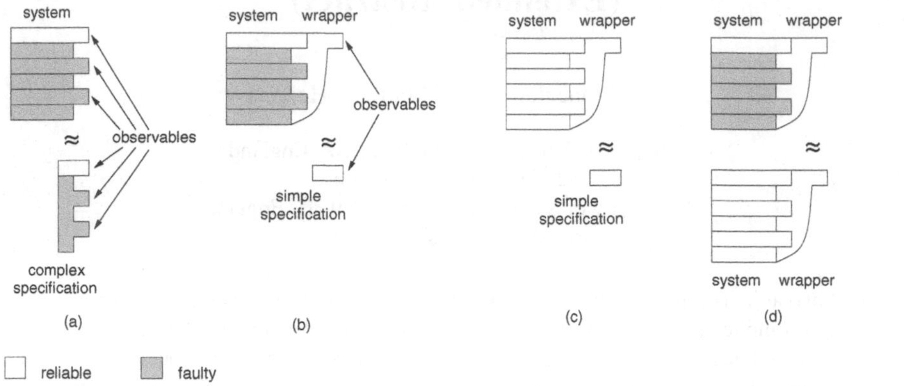

setting. The methodology is based on a common assumption that some processes are assumed to be reliable, thus immortal. Failure can affect behaviour in two ways: either *directly*, when the process itself fails, or *indirectly*, when a process depends on internal interaction with a secondary process which in turn fails. The methodology limits observations to reliable processes *only*, which are *only* indirectly affected by failure. Using wrapper code around the algorithm being analysed, we reformulate the equivalence described earlier into a comparison between the re-packaged algorithm and a *simpler* specification that does not include unreliable processes (Table 1(b)). The wrappers can be *dedicated*, testing for separate correctness criteria. We can therefore decompose generic catch-all specifications into separate simpler specifications, which are easier to formulate, understand and verify against the expected behaviour.

This reformulation carries more advantages than merely decomposing the specification and shifting the complexity of the equivalence from the specification side to the algorithm side in the form of wrappers. A specification that does not include unreliable processes permits *separation of concerns* through *fault-tolerance* bisimulation techniques [7]. These techniques allow us to decompose our reformulated equivalence statement into two sub-statements. In the first we temporarily ignore failures and test for *basic correctness*: we use "standard" bisimulations to compare the specification with the behaviour of the repackaged algorithm in a *failure-free* setting (Table 1(c)). In the second sub-statement we test for fault-tolerance and *correctness preservation*: we compare the behaviour of the repackaged algorithm in the failure-free setting with the repackaged algorithm itself in the failure setting (Table 1(d)). We argue that the fault-tolerance reformulation is a natural way to tackle such a proof, dividing it into two sub-proofs, which can be checked independently. The reformulation however carries further advantages. For a start, the first equivalence is considerably easier to prove, and can be treated as a vetting test before attempting the more involving second proof. Moreover, when proving the second equivalence statement, which compares the same code but under different conditions, we can exploit the common structure on both sides of the equivalence to construct the required witness bisimulation.

Our proposed methodology goes one step further and uses (permanent) failure to reduce the size of witness bisimulations in two ways. First, we note that while permanent failure may induce abnormal behaviour in the live code, it also *eliminates* transitions from dead code. Thus, by developing appropriate abstractions to represent dead code, we can greatly reduce the size of witness bisimulations. Second, we note that distributed algorithms tolerate failure (and preserve the expected behaviour) through the use of *redundancy* which is usually introduced in the form of *symmetrical replicated code*. As a result, correctness bisimulations for such algorithms are characterised by a considerable number of transitions that are similar in structure. This, in turn, gives us scope for identifying a subset of these transitions which are *confluent* and developing up-to techniques that abstract over these confluent moves. The number of replication patterns are arguably bounded and are reused throughout a substantial number of fault-tolerant algorithms, which means that we expect these up-to techniques to be applicable, at least in part, to a range of fault-tolerant distributed algorithm. More importantly however, they identify the (non-confluent) transitions that really matter, making the bisimulation proofs easier to describe and understand.

The remaining text is structured as follows. In Section 2 we introduce our language, a *partial-failure calculus*. In Section 3 we express a consensus algorithm in our calculus, realising the long considered view of consensus as a fault-tolerance problem [4]; we also show how to express the correctness of the algorithm in terms of basic correctness and correctness preservation equivalences. In Section 4 we develop up-to techniques for our algorithm and in Section 5 we give its proof of correctness.

2 Language

Our *partial-failure* calculus is inspired by [15] and consists of processes from a subset of CCS[12], distributed across a number of failing locations. We assume a set Act of communicating actions equipped with a bijective function $\bar{\cdot}$; for every name $a \in$ Act we have a complement $\bar{a} \in$ Act; α ranges over strong actions, defined as Act$\cup\{\tau\}$, including the distinguished silent action τ. We also assume a distinct set Locs of locations l, k which includes the immortal location $\star$.

Processes, defined in Table 2, can be guarded by an action, composed using choice, composed in parallel or scoped. As in [15], only actions can be scoped (not locations). By contrast to [15], we here simplify the calculus and disallow process constants and replication (thus no recursion and infinite computation) and migration of processes (thus no change in failure dependencies). Another important departure from [15] is that instead of *ping* we use a guarding construct susp $l.P$, already introduced in [5], which *tests* for the status of l and releases P once it (correctly) suspects that l is dead; the construct captures the intuition that failure detection is separate from the actual failure, and can be delayed. Systems, also defined in Table 2, are *located* processes composed in parallel with channel scoping. We view our calculus as a *partial-failure* calculus rather than a *distributed* calculus as it permits action synchronisations across locations. This implies a tighter synchronisation assumption between locations, which in our calculus merely embody *units of failure*. Nevertheless, distributed choices are still disallowed because their implementation is problematic in a dynamic partial-failure setting.

Table 2. Syntax

Processes

$P, Q ::= \alpha.P$ (guard) $\mid \mathbf{0}$ (inert) $\mid P + Q$ (choice) $\mid (\nu a)P$ (scoping) $\mid P|Q$ (fork) $\mid \mathsf{susp}\ k.P$ (failure detector)

Systems

$M, N ::= l[\![P]\!]$ (located) $\mid N|M$ (parallel) $\mid (\nu a)N$ (scoping)

Table 3. Reduction Rules

Assuming $l \in \mathcal{L}$, $n \geq 0$

(Act)
$$\frac{}{\langle \mathcal{L}, n\rangle \triangleright l[\![\alpha.P]\!] \xrightarrow{\alpha} l[\![P]\!]}$$

(Susp)
$$\frac{}{\langle \mathcal{L}, n\rangle \triangleright l[\![\mathsf{susp}\ k.P]\!] \xrightarrow{\tau} l[\![P]\!]}\ k \notin \mathcal{L}$$

(Halt)
$$\frac{}{\langle \mathcal{L}, n{+}1\rangle \triangleright M \xrightarrow{\tau} \langle \mathcal{L}{-}l, n\rangle \triangleright M}$$

(Fork)
$$\frac{}{\langle \mathcal{L}, n\rangle \triangleright l[\![P|Q]\!] \xrightarrow{\tau} l[\![P]\!]|l[\![Q]\!]}$$

(New)
$$\frac{}{\langle \mathcal{L}, n\rangle \triangleright l[\![(\nu a)P]\!] \xrightarrow{\tau} (\nu a)l[\![P]\!]}$$

(Sum)
$$\frac{\langle \mathcal{L}, n\rangle \triangleright l[\![P_i]\!] \xrightarrow{\alpha} l[\![P]\!]}{\langle \mathcal{L}, n\rangle \triangleright l[\![\sum_{i\in I} P_i]\!] \xrightarrow{\alpha} l[\![P]\!]}$$

(Rest)
$$\frac{\langle \mathcal{L}, n\rangle \triangleright M \xrightarrow{\alpha} \langle \mathcal{L}', n'\rangle \triangleright M'}{\langle \mathcal{L}, n\rangle \triangleright (\nu a)M \xrightarrow{\alpha} \langle \mathcal{L}', n'\rangle \triangleright (\nu a)M'}\ \alpha \notin \{a, \bar{a}\}$$

(Par)
$$\frac{\langle \mathcal{L}, n\rangle \triangleright M \xrightarrow{\alpha} \langle \mathcal{L}', n'\rangle \triangleright M'}{\begin{array}{l}\langle \mathcal{L}, n\rangle \triangleright M|N \xrightarrow{\alpha} \langle \mathcal{L}', n'\rangle \triangleright M'|N \\ \langle \mathcal{L}, n\rangle \triangleright N|M \xrightarrow{\alpha} \langle \mathcal{L}', n'\rangle \triangleright N|M'\end{array}}$$

(Com)
$$\frac{\langle \mathcal{L}, n\rangle \triangleright M \xrightarrow{\alpha} M' \qquad \langle \mathcal{L}, n\rangle \triangleright N \xrightarrow{\bar{\alpha}} N'}{\begin{array}{l}\langle \mathcal{L}, n\rangle \triangleright M|N \xrightarrow{\tau} M'|N' \\ \langle \mathcal{L}, n\rangle \triangleright N|M \xrightarrow{\tau} N'|M'\end{array}}$$

Notation: We denote a series of parallel processes $P_1|\ldots|P_n$ as $\prod_{i\in I} P_i$ and a series of choices $P_1 + \ldots + P_n$ as $\sum_{i\in I} P_i$ for $I = \{1, \ldots, n\}$. We omit the final $\mathbf{0}$ term in processes, writing $a.\mathbf{0}$ as a. We also denote the located inactive process $l[\![\mathbf{0}]\!]$ as simply $\mathbf{0}$ and omit location information for processes located at the immortal location. Thus, at system level, we write $M \mid P \mid \mathbf{0}$ to denote $M \mid \star\ [\![P]\!] \mid l[\![\mathbf{0}]\!]$.

Operational Semantics: We define a *liveset*, $\mathcal{L}$, as a set of locations, $\{l_1, \ldots, l_n\}$ denoting the locations that are alive; we usually omit mention of the special location $\star$, which is assumed to be in every $\mathcal{L}$. A system M subject to a liveset, $\mathcal{L}$, and a bounded number of dynamic failures, n, is called a configuration, and is denoted as $\langle \mathcal{L}, n\rangle \triangleright M$. Intuitively it denotes a system M that is running on the network (state) $\mathcal{L}$ where at most n locations from $\mathcal{L}$ may fail. Transitions are defined between tuples of configurations as

$$\langle \mathcal{L}, n\rangle \triangleright M \xrightarrow{\alpha} \langle \mathcal{L}', n'\rangle \triangleright M' \tag{1}$$

by the rules in Table 3. To improve readability, we abbreviate (1) to $\langle \mathcal{L}, n\rangle \triangleright M \xrightarrow{\alpha} M'$ whenever the state of the network $\langle \mathcal{L}, n\rangle$ does not change in the residual configuration. The rules in Table 3 are standard located CCS rules, with the exception of (Susp) describing perfect failure detection [2], and (Halt) describing dynamic failure [7]. All rules assume $l \in \mathcal{L}$ and $n \geq 0$.

Example 1. In (2) below, the system $\star[\![a.P + \mathsf{susp}\ l.P]\!]$ is in some sense *fault tolerant* up to 1 failure occuring in $\mathcal{L}$. Although $a.P$ depends on the liveness of l to proceed as P, the summand $\mathsf{susp}\ l.P$ also produces the same continuation P whenever l is dead. In order to verify this we have three cases to consider: (a) if $l \notin \mathcal{L}$ then $\mathsf{susp}\ l.P$ will trigger and produce $\star[\![P]\!]$; (b) if $l \in \mathcal{L}$ and $n = 0$, then l can never die and $a.P$ will always synchronise with $l[\![\bar{a}]\!]$ and continue as $\star[\![P]\!]$; (c) if $l \in \mathcal{L}$ and $n \neq 0$ then if l dies before the synchronisation on a occurs, we have case (a), otherwise we have case (b).

$$\langle \mathcal{L}, n \rangle \triangleright (\nu a)\ \ l[\![\bar{a}]\!] \mid \star\ [\![a.P + \mathsf{susp}\ l.P]\!] \qquad (2)$$

The equivalence relation chosen for our partial-failure calculus is *(weak) bisimulation equivalence*, based on weak matching moves $\overset{\hat{\alpha}}{\Longrightarrow}$ denoting $\overset{\tau}{\longrightarrow}^{*}\overset{\alpha}{\longrightarrow}\overset{\tau}{\longrightarrow}^{*}$ if $\alpha \in \{a, \bar{a}\}$ and $\overset{\tau}{\longrightarrow}^{*}$ if $\alpha = \tau$.

Definition 1 (Weak bisimulation equivalence). *Denoted as $\approx$, is the largest relation over configurations such that if $\langle \mathcal{L}_1, n_1 \rangle \triangleright M_1 \approx \langle \mathcal{L}_2, n_2 \rangle \triangleright M_2$ then*

- $\langle \mathcal{L}_1, n_1 \rangle \triangleright M_1 \overset{\alpha}{\longrightarrow} \langle \mathcal{L}'_1, n'_1 \rangle \triangleright M'_1$ *implies* $\langle \mathcal{L}_2, n_2 \rangle \triangleright M_2 \overset{\hat{\alpha}}{\Longrightarrow} \langle \mathcal{L}'_2, n'_2 \rangle \triangleright M'_2$ *such that* $\langle \mathcal{L}'_1, n'_1 \rangle \triangleright M'_1 \approx \langle \mathcal{L}'_2, n'_2 \rangle \triangleright M'_2$
- $\langle \mathcal{L}_2, n_2 \rangle \triangleright M_2 \overset{\alpha}{\longrightarrow} \langle \mathcal{L}'_2, n'_2 \rangle \triangleright M'_2$ *implies* $\langle \mathcal{L}_1, n_1 \rangle \triangleright M_1 \overset{\hat{\alpha}}{\Longrightarrow} \langle \mathcal{L}'_1, n'_1 \rangle \triangleright M'_1$ *such that* $\langle \mathcal{L}'_1, n'_1 \rangle \triangleright M'_1 \approx \langle \mathcal{L}'_2, n'_2 \rangle \triangleright N'_2$

Assuming that $\mathbf{loc}(M)$ is a function returning the set of all location names used in M (together with $\star$), then system M is said to be executing in a *failure-free* setting if it is subject to the network $\langle \mathbf{loc}(M), 0 \rangle$. Based on this intuition and our notion of equivalence, we can give a formal definition for fault-tolerant systems.

Definition 2 (Fault Tolerance). *A system M is fault tolerant up to n faults whenever*

$$\langle \mathbf{loc}(M), 0 \rangle \triangleright M \quad \approx \quad \langle \mathbf{loc}(M), n \rangle \triangleright M$$

Our chosen definitions are not arbitrary. Definition 1 is sound with respect to a standard contextual equivalence called reduction barbed congruence [10]. Definition 2 is sound with respect to dynamic fault-tolerance up-to n faults defined in [7], using fault inducing contexts. The adaptation of these definitions to our calculus and the proof of the corresponding soundness statements will appear in the full version of the paper.

Example 2. Using Definitions 1 and 2, we can now show that (2) above is fault tolerant up to 1 fault by giving a witness bisimulation relation satisfying

$$\langle \{l\}, 0 \rangle \triangleright (\nu a)\ l[\![\bar{a}]\!] \mid \star\ [\![a.P + \mathsf{susp}\ l.P]\!] \quad \approx \quad \langle \{l\}, 1 \rangle \triangleright (\nu a)\ l[\![\bar{a}]\!] \mid \star\ [\![a.P + \mathsf{susp}\ l.P]\!]$$

3 Consensus

Despite its limitations (no infinite computation), our calculus is expressive enough to describe a number of (non-recursive) standard distributed algorithms in the presence

Table 4. The Rotating Co-ordinator Algorithm for Participant i

```
1   xi := input;
2   for r := 1 to n do {  if r = i then broadcast xi;
3                         if alive(pr) then xi := input_from_broadcast };
4   output xi;
```

of dynamic failure. As an example we describe the rotating co-ordinator algorithm [16], solving a specific instance of consensus using *strong* failure detectors ($\mathcal{S}$ [2]); the pseudo-code description is reproduced in Table 4. The algorithm consists of n parallel, independently failing participants, ordered and named 1 to n, each *inputting* a value v from a set of values V and then *deciding* by outputting a value $v' \in V$. Each participant executes the code in Table 4, going through n rounds (the loop on lines 2 and 3) and changing the broadcasting co-ordinator to participant i for round $r = i$. The correctness criteria for *consensus* is defined by the following three conditions [11, pg. 101]:

Termination: All non-failing participants must eventually decide.

Agreement: No two participants decide on different values.

Validity: If all participants are given the same value $v \in V$ as input, then v is the only possible decision value.[1]

To attain consensus with $n-1$ dynamic failures, the algorithm needs to be fault-tolerant with respect to two error conditions, namely *Decision Blocking* (when a participant may be waiting forever for a value to be broadcast from a crashed co-ordinator) and *Corrupted Broadcast* (when co-ordinator may broadcast its values to a *subset* of the participants before crashing). The code in Table 4 overcomes decision blocking by using a failure detector to determine the state of the co-ordinator (`alive`(p_r)) and overcomes the possibility of $(n-1)$ corrupted broadcasts by repeating the broadcast for n rounds.

We give a precise description of the rotating co-ordinator algorithm as the system C, given in Table 5. Without loss of generality, we assume that the decision set is simply $V = \{true, false\}$ and have n participants located at *independently failing* locations $l_1 \ldots l_n$. The process $\mathsf{P}^x_{i,r}$, for $x \in \{true, false\}$, denotes the ith participant, at round r, with current estimate x. It is defined in terms of two parallel processes, $\mathsf{B}^x_{i,r}$ for *broadcasting* the current value at round r, and $\mathsf{R}^x_{i,r}$ for *receiving* the new value at round r. As in Table 4, broadcast is only allowed if $i = r$ and otherwise it acts as the inert process. On the other hand, the receiver at round r awaits synchronisation on $true_{i,r}$ or $false_{i,r}$ and updates the estimate for round $(r+1)$ accordingly. At the same time, the receiver guards this distributed synchronisation with $\mathsf{susp}\ l_r.\mathsf{P}^x_{i,r+1}$ to prevent decision blocking in case l_r, the location of the participant currently broadcasting, fails. Estimates for round r can only come from the participant at l_r and thus all actions $true_{i,r}$ and $false_{i,r}$ are scoped in C. Every participant can be arbitrarily initialised as $\mathsf{P}^{true}_{i,1}$ or $\mathsf{P}^{false}_{i,1}$ through the free actions $prop^{true}_i$ and $prop^{false}_i$ respectively. Finally every participant decides at round $(n+1)$ to either report true, executing dec^{true}_i, or report false, executing dec^{false}_i.

We can also give a precise description of the consensus correctness requirements in our calculus. As stated in the Introduction, we repackage our algorithm as a fault-tolerant

[1] When $|V| = 2$ this implies a stronger notion of validity: any decision value for any participant is the initial value of some process.

Table 5. Rotating Co-ordinator Algorithm in our Partial-Failure Calculus

(Consensus)

$$\mathsf{C} \stackrel{\text{def}}{=} \left(\nu^{n}_{i,r=1}\, \mathit{true}_{i,r}, \mathit{false}_{i,r}\right) \prod_{i=1}^{n} l_i[\![\mathit{prop}^{\mathit{true}}_i.\mathsf{P}^{\mathit{true}}_{i,1} + \mathit{prop}^{\mathit{false}}_i.\mathsf{P}^{\mathit{false}}_{i,1}]\!]$$

(Participant)

$$\mathsf{P}^x_{i,r} \stackrel{\text{def}}{=} \mathsf{R}^x_{i,r} \mid \mathsf{B}^x_{i,r} \quad x \in \{\mathit{true}, \mathit{false}\},\ r \le n$$

$$\mathsf{P}^x_{i,n+1} \stackrel{\text{def}}{=} \overline{\mathit{dec}^x_i} \quad x \in \{\mathit{true}, \mathit{false}\}$$

(Broadcast)

$$\mathsf{B}^x_{i,r} \stackrel{\text{def}}{=} \prod_{j=1}^{n} \overline{x_{j,r}} \quad x \in \{\mathit{true}, \mathit{false}\},\ r = i$$

$$\mathsf{B}^x_{i,r} \stackrel{\text{def}}{=} \mathbf{0} \quad x \in \{\mathit{true}, \mathit{false}\},\ r \ne i$$

(Recieve)

$$\mathsf{R}^x_{i,r} \stackrel{\text{def}}{=} \mathit{true}_{i,r}.\mathsf{P}^{\mathit{true}}_{i,r+1} + \mathit{false}_{i,r}.\mathsf{P}^{\mathit{false}}_{i,r+1} + \mathsf{susp}\ l_r.\mathsf{P}^x_{i,r+1}$$

system where any interactions with observers occur through wrapper code residing at the immortal location $\star$; this allows us to decompose our proof into the basic correctness and correctness preservation phases, as in Table 1(c) and (d).

Table 6 defines the *wrapper code* which, when put in parallel with C of Table 5, provides separate *testing scenarios* for the algorithm. We have two forms of initialization code: I^{gen} arbitrarily initialises every participant to either *true* or *false* after the action *start* whereas I^{true} and I^{false} initialise *all* participants to just *true*, or just *false* respectively. We also have two processes for evaluating the values decided upon: A^{gen}_1 checks that all the participants 1 to n agreed on a value (either *true* or *false*) or else crashed, producing the action $\overline{ok}$ if the test is successful; A^{true}_1 and A^{false}_1 check that all participants have agreed on the specific value *true*, and *false* respectively, or crashed.

Definition 3 (Consensus). *Let $\mathcal{L}_n$ denote $\{l_1, \dots, l_n, \star\}$, and $(\tilde{m})$ stand for the actions $prop^{true}_i$, $prop^{false}_i$, dec^{true}_i, dec^{false}_i for $1 \le i \le n$. Then C satisfies consensus whenever*

Strong Basic Agreement: $\langle \mathcal{L}_n, 0\rangle \triangleright (\nu\tilde{m})(C \mid \mathsf{I}^{gen} \mid \mathsf{A}^{gen}_1) \approx \langle \emptyset, 0\rangle \triangleright \mathit{start}.\overline{\mathit{ok}}$

Basic Validity:
$\langle \mathcal{L}_n, 0\rangle \triangleright (\nu\tilde{m})(C \mid \mathsf{I}^{true} \mid \mathsf{A}^{true}_1) \approx \langle \emptyset, 0\rangle \triangleright \mathit{start}.\overline{\mathit{ok}}$
$\langle \mathcal{L}_n, 0\rangle \triangleright (\nu\tilde{m})(C \mid \mathsf{I}^{false} \mid \mathsf{A}^{false}_1) \approx \langle \emptyset, 0\rangle \triangleright \mathit{start}.\overline{\mathit{ok}}$

and moreover

Strong ft-Agreement: $\langle \mathcal{L}_n, 0\rangle \triangleright (\nu\tilde{m})(C \mid \mathsf{I}^{gen} \mid \mathsf{A}^{gen}_1) \approx \langle \mathcal{L}_n, n-1\rangle \triangleright (\nu\tilde{m})(C \mid \mathsf{I}^{gen} \mid \mathsf{A}^{gen}_1)$

ft-Validity:
$\langle \mathcal{L}_n, 0\rangle \triangleright (\nu\tilde{m})(C \mid \mathsf{I}^{true} \mid \mathsf{A}^{true}_1) \approx \langle \mathcal{L}_n, n-1\rangle \triangleright (\nu\tilde{m})(C \mid \mathsf{I}^{true} \mid \mathsf{A}^{true}_1)$
$\langle \mathcal{L}_n, 0\rangle \triangleright (\nu\tilde{m})(C \mid \mathsf{I}^{false} \mid \mathsf{A}^{false}_1) \approx \langle \mathcal{L}_n, n-1\rangle \triangleright (\nu\tilde{m})(C \mid \mathsf{I}^{false} \mid \mathsf{A}^{false}_1)$

In Definition 3 *strong agreement* subsumes the agreement and termination conditions: it composes C with I^{gen} and A^{gen}_1. *Validity* uses more specific wrappers, and composes C first with $\mathsf{I}^{true} \mid \mathsf{A}^{true}_1$ and then with $\mathsf{I}^{false} \mid \mathsf{A}^{false}_1$. Scoping the actions $prop^{true}_i$, $prop^{false}_i$, dec^{true}_i and dec^{false}_i in each test case limits external interaction to the non-failing actions *start* and $\overline{ok}$ at $\star$, the immortal location. This allows Definition 3 to divide *consensus* conditions into basic correctness and correctness preservation conditions. For example

Strong Agreement: $\langle \mathcal{L}_n, (n-1)\rangle \triangleright (\nu\tilde{m})(C \mid \mathsf{I}^{gen} \mid \mathsf{A}^{gen}_1) \approx \langle \emptyset, 0\rangle \triangleright \mathit{start}.\overline{\mathit{ok}}$

follows from **Strong Basic Agreement**, **Strong ft-Agreement** and transitivity of $\approx$.

Table 6. Consensus Wrappers

(Initialisation)

$$\mathsf{I}^x \stackrel{\text{def}}{=} start.\prod_{i=1}^{n} \overline{prop_i^x} \qquad \mathsf{I}^{gen} \stackrel{\text{def}}{=} start.\prod_{i=1}^{n}(\overline{prop_i^{true}} + \overline{prop_i^{false}}) \qquad x \in \{true, false\}$$

(Agreement)

$$\mathsf{A}_i^x \stackrel{\text{def}}{=} dec_i^x.\mathsf{A}_{i+1}^x + \mathsf{susp}\ l_i.\mathsf{A}_{i+1}^x \qquad \mathsf{A}_{n+1}^x \stackrel{\text{def}}{=} \overline{ok} \qquad x \in \{true, false\},\ i \leq n$$

$$\mathsf{A}_i^{gen} \stackrel{\text{def}}{=} dec_i^{true}.\mathsf{A}_{i+1}^{true} + dec_i^{false}.\mathsf{A}_{i+1}^{false} + \mathsf{susp}\ l_i.\mathsf{A}_{i+1}^{gen} \qquad i \leq n$$

4 Up-to Techniques in the Presence of Failure

Definition 3 expresses consensus in terms of six bisimulations. The main complication in proving these bisimulations lies in the large amount of internal actions that need to be considered. A large number of these internal actions are regular in structure (processes executing symmetric transitions at different locations and at different rounds) and most of these transitions are *confluent*; they do not affect the set of transitions that can be taken, either now or in the future. In the fault-tolerance bisimulations, we also have an extensive amount of *dead code*, that is code at dead locations or code that is forever blocked because it can only be released by actions at dead locations. Here we develop up-to bisimulation techniques that abstract over confluent moves and dead code.

We define a structural equivalence relation over configurations as the least relation satisfying the rules in Table 7. Even though this equivalence is normally defined over systems, we exploit the state of the network $\langle \mathcal{L}, n \rangle$ to define a stronger relation. Apart from the first six rules and the last two (contextual) rules, all of which are fairly standard, we also have new rules such as (s-Dead), adopted from [7], equating any code at dead locations, irrespective of its form. The network information is also used to define the new structural rule (gc-Susp), identifying suspicions that can never trigger because the location tested for can never fail; it is alive and no more failures can be induced. Also new is (gc-Act) which identifies action branches that can never trigger because there is no corresponding co-action within the action scope.[2] Our structural equivalence is a strong bisimulation.

Lemma 1 **(≡ is a strong bisimulation)**

$$\begin{array}{ccccccc} \langle \mathcal{L}, n \rangle \triangleright N & \equiv & \langle \mathcal{L}, n \rangle \triangleright M & \textit{implies} & \langle \mathcal{L}, n \rangle \triangleright N & \equiv & \langle \mathcal{L}, n \rangle \triangleright M \\ \downarrow \alpha & & & & \downarrow \alpha & & \downarrow \alpha \\ \langle \mathcal{L}', m' \rangle \triangleright N' & & & & \langle \mathcal{L}', m' \rangle \triangleright N' & \equiv & \langle \mathcal{L}', m' \rangle \triangleright M' \end{array}$$

We now identify a number of τ-actions, referred to as β-actions or β-moves, and show that they are confluent. These silent β-actions are denoted as

$$\langle \mathcal{L}, n \rangle \triangleright N \stackrel{\tau}{\longmapsto}_{\beta} \langle \mathcal{L}, n \rangle \triangleright M$$

[2] We purposefully use the naming convention (gc-) for certain structural rules that are generally applied in one direction rather than the other to "garbage collect" redundant dead code.

Table 7. Structural Equivalence Rules

(s-Scomm)	$\langle\mathcal{L},n\rangle \triangleright l[\![P+Q]\!] \equiv \langle\mathcal{L},n\rangle \triangleright l[\![Q+P]\!]$	
(s-Sassoc)	$\langle\mathcal{L},n\rangle \triangleright l[\![(P+Q)+R]\!] \equiv \langle\mathcal{L},n\rangle \triangleright l[\![P+(Q+R)]\!]$	
(s-inert)	$\langle\mathcal{L},n\rangle \triangleright l[\![P+\mathbf{0}]\!] \equiv \langle\mathcal{L},n\rangle \triangleright l[\![P]\!]$	
(s-Pcomm)	$\langle\mathcal{L},n\rangle \triangleright N \mid M \equiv \langle\mathcal{L},n\rangle \triangleright M \mid N$	
(s-Passoc)	$\langle\mathcal{L},n\rangle \triangleright (N \mid M) \mid M' \equiv \langle\mathcal{L},n\rangle \triangleright N \mid (M \mid M')$	
(gc-Inert)	$\langle\mathcal{L},n\rangle \triangleright M \mid l[\![\mathbf{0}]\!] \equiv \langle\mathcal{L},n\rangle \triangleright M$	
(s-Extr)	$\langle\mathcal{L},n\rangle \triangleright (\nu a)(M \mid N) \equiv \langle\mathcal{L},n\rangle \triangleright M \mid (\nu a)N$	$a \notin \mathbf{fn}(M)$
(gc-Scope)	$\langle\mathcal{L},n\rangle \triangleright (\nu a)M \equiv \langle\mathcal{L},n\rangle \triangleright M$	$a \notin \mathbf{fn}(M)$
(gc-Act)	$\langle\mathcal{L},n\rangle \triangleright (\nu a)l[\![\alpha.P + \sum_i P_i]\!] \equiv \langle\mathcal{L},n\rangle \triangleright (\nu a)l[\![\sum_i P_i]\!]$	$\alpha \in \{a, \bar{a}\}$
(gc-Susp)	$\langle\mathcal{L},0\rangle \triangleright l[\![\text{susp } k.P + \sum_i P_i]\!] \equiv \langle\mathcal{L},0\rangle \triangleright l[\![\sum_i P_i]\!]$	$k \in \mathcal{L}$
(s-Dead)	$\langle\mathcal{L},n\rangle \triangleright l[\![P]\!] \equiv \langle\mathcal{L},n\rangle \triangleright l[\![Q]\!]$	$l \notin \mathcal{L}$

(s-Rest)
$$\frac{\langle\mathcal{L},n\rangle \triangleright M \equiv \langle\mathcal{L},n\rangle \triangleright N}{\langle\mathcal{L},n\rangle \triangleright (\nu a)M \equiv \langle\mathcal{L},n\rangle \triangleright (\nu a)N}$$

(Par)
$$\frac{\langle\mathcal{L},n\rangle \triangleright M \equiv \langle\mathcal{L},n\rangle \triangleright M'}{\begin{array}{c}\langle\mathcal{L},n\rangle \triangleright M|N \equiv \langle\mathcal{L},n\rangle \triangleright M'|N \\ \langle\mathcal{L},n\rangle \triangleright N|M \equiv \langle\mathcal{L},n\rangle \triangleright N|M'\end{array}}$$

and defined in Table 8. We then develop up-to bisimulation techniques that abstract from matching configurations related by β-moves. The details differ considerably from [7] because we use different constructs like choice and failure detection, and allow distributed synchronisation across locations. Apart from the standard local rules (BNew) and (BFork), and the context rules (BRest) and (BPar), Table 8 has three new rules dealing with synchronisations. (BLin) states that distribution does not interfere with a scoped linear synchronisation, as long as *we cannot induce more dynamic failures*, that is $n = 0$. (BLoc) states that a *local* scoped linear synchronisation is always a β-move. Finally, (BFTol) states that a distributed scoped linear synchronisation is a β-move if it is *asynchronous from one end* and the co-synchronisation at the other end is *guarded by a* susp *with the same continuation*; these conditions make τ-move in (BFTol), in a sense, *fault-tolerant* as we have already seen in (2). We prove a special form of confluence for our β-moves.

Lemma 2 (Confluence of β-moves). $\overset{\tau}{\longmapsto}_\beta$ *observes the diamond property:*

$$\begin{array}{ccccc}
\langle\mathcal{L},n\rangle \triangleright N \overset{\tau}{\longmapsto}_\beta \langle\mathcal{L},n\rangle \triangleright M & \textit{implies} & \langle\mathcal{L},n\rangle \triangleright N & \overset{\tau}{\longmapsto}_\beta & \langle\mathcal{L},n\rangle \triangleright M \\
\downarrow \alpha & & \downarrow \alpha & & \downarrow \alpha \\
\langle\mathcal{L}',n'\rangle \triangleright N' & & \langle\mathcal{L}',n'\rangle \triangleright N' & \mathcal{R} & \langle\mathcal{L}',n'\rangle \triangleright M'
\end{array}$$

where $\mathcal{R}$ *is* $\overset{\tau}{\longmapsto}_\beta$ *or* $\equiv$, *or else* $\alpha = \tau$ *and* $\langle\mathcal{L},n\rangle \triangleright M = \langle\mathcal{L}',n'\rangle \triangleright N'$

Note the use of the non-standard $\mathcal{R}$ to close the diamond instead of $\overset{\tau}{\longmapsto}_\beta$ in this Lemma. It allows for the special case when the code causing the β-move crashes. In this case, we only require that resulting pair are structurally equivalent, using (s-Dead).

Table 8. Transition Rules for β-moves

Assuming $l \in \mathcal{L}$, $n \geq 0$

(BLin)
$$\frac{}{\langle \mathcal{L}, 0\rangle \triangleright (\nu a)(l[\![\bar{a}.P]\!] \mid k[\![a.Q]\!]) \overset{\tau}{\longmapsto}_\beta \langle \mathcal{L}, 0\rangle \triangleright (\nu a)(l[\![P]\!] \mid k[\![Q]\!])}\; l,k \in \mathcal{L}$$

(BLoc)
$$\frac{}{\langle \mathcal{L}, n\rangle \triangleright (\nu a)(l[\![\bar{a}.P]\!] \mid l[\![a.Q]\!]) \overset{\tau}{\longmapsto}_\beta \langle \mathcal{L}, n\rangle \triangleright (\nu a)(l[\![P]\!] \mid l[\![Q]\!])}$$

(BFTol)
$$\frac{}{\langle \mathcal{L}, n\rangle \triangleright (\nu a)(l[\![\bar{a}]\!] \mid k[\![a.P + \mathsf{susp}\; l.P]\!]) \overset{\tau}{\longmapsto}_\beta \langle \mathcal{L}, n\rangle \triangleright (\nu a)k[\![P]\!]}\; l,k \in \mathcal{L}$$

(BNew)
$$\frac{}{\langle \mathcal{L}, n\rangle \triangleright l[\![(\nu a)P]\!] \overset{\tau}{\longmapsto}_\beta \langle \mathcal{L}, n\rangle \triangleright (\nu a)l[\![P]\!]}\; l \in \mathcal{L}$$

(BRest)
$$\frac{\langle \mathcal{L}, n\rangle \triangleright M \overset{\tau}{\longmapsto}_\beta \langle \mathcal{L}, n\rangle \triangleright M'}{\langle \mathcal{L}, n\rangle \triangleright (\nu a)M \overset{\tau}{\longmapsto}_\beta \langle \mathcal{L}, n\rangle \triangleright (\nu a)M'}$$

(BFork)
$$\frac{}{\langle \mathcal{L}, n\rangle \triangleright l[\![P|Q]\!] \overset{\tau}{\longmapsto}_\beta \langle \mathcal{L}, n\rangle \triangleright l[\![P]\!]|l[\![Q]\!]}\; l \in \mathcal{L}$$

(BPar)
$$\frac{\langle \mathcal{L}, n\rangle \triangleright M \overset{\tau}{\longmapsto}_\beta \langle \mathcal{L}, n\rangle \triangleright M'}{\begin{array}{c}\langle \mathcal{L}, n\rangle \triangleright M|N \overset{\tau}{\longmapsto}_\beta \langle \mathcal{L}, n\rangle \triangleright M'|N \\ \langle \mathcal{L}, n\rangle \triangleright N|M \overset{\tau}{\longmapsto}_\beta \langle \mathcal{L}, n\rangle \triangleright N|M'\end{array}}$$

We defined a modified bisimulation relation from Definition 1 where the conditions for the matching residuals are relaxed; instead of demanding that they are again related in $\approx$ we allow approximate matching through $\equiv$ and $\overset{\tau}{\longmapsto}{}^*_\beta$.

Definition 4 (β-transfer property). *A relation $\mathcal{R}$ over configurations satisfies the β-transfer property if*

$$\begin{array}{ccc} \langle \mathcal{L}, n\rangle \triangleright N \;\; \mathcal{R} \;\; \langle \mathcal{L}, n\rangle \triangleright M \\ \downarrow \alpha \\ \langle \mathcal{L}', n'\rangle \triangleright N' \end{array} \quad \textit{implies} \quad \begin{array}{ccc} \langle \mathcal{L}, n\rangle \triangleright N & \mathcal{R} & \langle \mathcal{L}, n\rangle \triangleright M \\ \downarrow \alpha & & \downarrow \alpha \\ \langle \mathcal{L}', n'\rangle \triangleright N' & \mathcal{A}_l \circ \mathcal{R} \circ \mathcal{A}_r & \langle \mathcal{L}', n'\rangle \triangleright M' \end{array}$$

where $\mathcal{A}_l$ *is* $\equiv \circ \overset{\tau}{\longmapsto}{}^*_\beta$ *and* $\mathcal{A}_r$ *is* $\approx$

Definition 5 (Bisimulation up-to-β). *A relation $\mathcal{R}$ over configurations is a bisimulation up-to-β if it and its inverse $\mathcal{R}^{-1}$ satisfy the β-transfer property.*

Before we can use bisimulations up-to-β, we need to show they are sound with respect to Definition 1. This soundness proof uses the results of Lemma 3.

Lemma 3 ($\overset{\tau}{\longmapsto}{}^*_\beta$ implies $\approx$). $\langle \mathcal{L}, n\rangle \triangleright N \overset{\tau}{\longmapsto}{}^*_\beta \langle \mathcal{L}, n\rangle \triangleright M$ *implies* $\langle \mathcal{L}, n\rangle \triangleright N \approx \langle \mathcal{L}, n\rangle \triangleright M$.

Theorem 1 (Soundness of bisimulations up-to-β). *If* $\langle \mathcal{L}, n\rangle \triangleright N \,\mathcal{R}\, \langle \mathcal{L}', m\rangle \triangleright M$, *where* $\mathcal{R}$ *is a bisimulation up-to-β, then* $\langle \mathcal{L}, n\rangle \triangleright N \approx \langle \mathcal{L}', m\rangle \triangleright M$.

Example 3. Suppose $l, k \in \mathcal{L}$. Then we can show that

$$\langle \mathcal{L}, n\rangle \triangleright (\nu a, b)\ l[\![\bar{a}]\!] \mid k[\![a.P + b.Q + \mathsf{susp}\ l.P]\!] \ \approx\ \langle \mathcal{L}, n\rangle \triangleright (\nu a, b) k[\![P]\!] \qquad (3)$$

To see this first note that using (s-Extr), (s-Scomm), (s-Sassoc), (gc-Act) and (s-Extr) again we can tighten the scope of νb, garbage collect the branch guarded by b and then scope extrude νb again to obtain

$$\langle \mathcal{L}, n\rangle \triangleright (\nu a, b)\ l[\![\bar{a}]\!] \mid k[\![a.P + b.Q + \mathsf{susp}\ l.P]\!] \equiv \langle \mathcal{L}, n\rangle \triangleright (\nu a, b)\ l[\![\bar{a}]\!] \mid k[\![a.P + \mathsf{susp}\ l.P]\!]$$

An application of (BFTol) gives

$$\langle \mathcal{L}, n\rangle \triangleright (\nu a, b)\ l[\![\bar{a}]\!] \mid k[\![a.P + \mathsf{susp}\ l.P]\!] \ \stackrel{\tau}{\longmapsto}_\beta\ \langle \mathcal{L}, n\rangle \triangleright (\nu a, b)\ k[\![P]\!]$$

and now (3) follows from Lemma 1 and Lemma 3.

5 Consensus Satisfaction Proof

Using Theorem 1, we just need to give witness bisimulations up-to β-moves satisfying the bisimulations set out in Definition 3. In the following witness bisimulations, we use the letters t, f, p and d for the action names *true*, *false*, *prop* and *dec*, respectively. Our presentation makes use of sets of integers I_i partitioning the set $\{1 \ldots n\}$; the partition predicate is:

$$\mathsf{part}_1^n(I_1, \ldots, I_k) \ \stackrel{\text{def}}{=}\ I_1 \cup \ldots \cup I_k = \{1 \ldots n\} \ \text{and}\ \forall i, j \in \{1 \ldots k\}\ I_i \cap I_j = \emptyset$$

We also denote the smallest number in a partition I_i as $I_{i\,min}$ and the largest number in a partition I_i that is smaller that any element in any other partition I_j as $I_{i\,min}^{+}$.

We first prove the basic (failure-free) equivalences. We here only give the witness bisimulation for Strong Basic Agreement; the two witness bisimulations required for Basic Validity are similar but simpler. We assume $\tilde{m} = \prod_{i,r=1}^{n} t_{i,r}, f_{i,r}, p_i^t, p_i^f, d_i^t, d_i^f$ and use A, I, $\mathcal{L}_n$ and $\emptyset$ as shorthand for A_1^{gen}, I^{gen}, $\langle\{1 \ldots n\}, 0\rangle$ and $\langle\emptyset, 0\rangle$ respectively. We also partition $\{1 \ldots n\}$ into three sets: I denotes the set of *uninitialised* participants, whereas J and H denote initialised participants with current estimates t and f respectively; when we do not use partition H, participants in J all have either estimate t or f. We also use the process definition $N_i \stackrel{\text{def}}{=} l_i[\![p_i^t.\mathsf{P}_{i,1}^t + p_i^f.\mathsf{P}_{i,1}^f]\!] \mid \overline{p_i^t} + \overline{p_i^f}$ for *non-initialised* participant i.

$$\left\{\begin{array}{ll}
1)\quad \left\langle \mathcal{L}_n \triangleright (\nu\tilde{m})\left(C \mid \mathsf{I}^{gen} \mid \mathsf{A}_1^{gen}\right),\ \emptyset \triangleright start.\overline{ok}\right\rangle & \\
2)\ \left\langle \mathcal{L}_n \triangleright (\nu\tilde{m})\left(\mathsf{A} \mid \prod_{i\in I} N_i \mid \prod_{j\in J} l_j[\![\mathsf{R}_{j,1}^t]\!] \mid \prod_{h\in H} l_h[\![\mathsf{R}_{h,1}^f]\!]\right),\ \emptyset \triangleright \overline{ok}\right\rangle & \left|\ \begin{array}{l}\mathsf{part}_1^n(I,J,H)\\ \text{and } I_{min} = 1\end{array}\right. \\
3)\ \left\langle \mathcal{L}_n \triangleright (\nu\tilde{m})\left(\mathsf{A} \mid \prod_{i\in I}\left(N_i \mid \prod_{r=1}^{I_{min}-1} l_r[\![\overline{x_{i,r}}]\!]\right) \mid \prod_{j\in J} l_j[\![\mathsf{R}_{j,I_{min}}^x]\!]\right),\ \emptyset \triangleright \overline{ok}\right\rangle & \left|\ \begin{array}{l}\mathsf{part}_1^n(I,J)\\ \text{and } I_{min} \neq 1\\ \text{and } x \in \{t, f\}\end{array}\right. \\
4)\quad \left\langle \mathcal{L}_n \triangleright \overline{ok},\ \emptyset \triangleright \overline{ok}\right\rangle &
\end{array}\right\}$$

In the above up-to β witness bisimulation case (2) represents the states where participants have different estimates at round $r = 1$ because the broadcaster at round 1 has not been initialised yet. Case (3) represents participants in agreement for rounds $r \geq 2$, but blocked because the co-ordinator participant for round r has not been initialised. We note that in case (3), uninitialised participants $i \in I$ include the broadcasted values from previous rounds that are yet to be consumed by them once they are initialised.

We highlight the salient aspect of the above bisimulation relation: apart from the initialisation τ-moves, *all* the remaining τ-transitions turn out to be β-moves; they are instances of (BLin) (modulo $\equiv$). We illustrate this through a walk-through of the main transitions:

- If we are in (2) and the jth participant in the left configuration is initialised (through a τ action) with $x \in \{t, f\}$ then
  - if $j \neq 1$ the participant proceeds to round 1 with estimate x and joins set J or H accordingly. We match this action by the empty move and remain in case (2).
  - if $j = 1$ the participant proceeds to round 1 and acts as the co-ordinator, broadcasting x. For all participants $j \in J$ or $h \in H$, broadcast synchronisation turns out to be a β-move using (BLin), and (gc-Act) and (gc-Susp), among other rules, to garbage collect inactive branches as in Example 3. At this point all initialised participants agree on the broadcasted value x at round 2, and proceed through the next rounds using β-moves, still agreeing on x, until they block again on the next I_{min}. We match this action with the empty action and progress to case (3).
- If we are in (3) and the ith participant is initialised then
  - if $i \neq I_{min}$ then the right configuration performs an empty move and we remain in case (3), abstracting away from the β-moves of participant i consuming all the broadcasts to reach round I_{min} with estimate x.
  - if $i = I_{min}$ then the matching move is similar but with two further sub-cases
    - If $I = \{i\}$ then all participant would have agreed on x, the first broadcasted value and we progress to case (4) through a series of β-moves.
    - If $|I| \geq 2$ then all participants $j \in J$ progress to the round of the next minimum uninitialised participant $(I/\{i\})_{min}$, and remain in case (3).

The witness bisimulation for Strong ft-Agreement up to $(n-1)$ faults is given below; we leave similar but simpler witness bisimulations for ft-Validity to the interested reader. We carry over all the shorthand notation used for the failure-free witness bisimulation together with some more: the operation $\ddot{x}$ denotes value inverse for $x \in \{t, f\}$, and is defined as $\ddot{t} = f$ and $\ddot{f} = t$; for $K \subset \{1 \ldots n\}$, $\mathcal{L}_n^K$ denotes the network state $\langle \mathcal{L}_n/\{l_k \mid k \in K\}, n - |K| \rangle$; $B(i,x)_j^{j+n}$ denotes the sequence of broadcasts of x for participant i from rounds j up to $j+n$, that is $\prod_{r=j}^{j+n} l_r[\![\bar{x}_{i,r}]\!]$.

The salient aspect of our correctness preservation witness bisimulations is that they automatically bring to the fore the mechanisms that enable the algorithm to overcome decision blocking and corrupted broadcast. Through the use of the β-moves (BLoc), in the case of participant initialisation in ft-Validity, and (BFTol), in the case of broadcast communications where a participant receives the same estimate it currently holds, our witness bisimulations abstract over superfluous transitions. This means that the only non-confluent τ-moves remaining are those for participant initialisation, in the case of Strong ft-Agreement, those that crash participants and those where the broadcasted value and the current participant estimate differ. The latter two kinds are the core transitions that embody corrupted broadcast, when the broadcaster crashes, and lead towards the eventual agreement, when not interfered with by failure. The up-to-β level of abstraction also makes the overall structure of the bisimulation proof reflect move closely the reasoning needed in a careful, informal proof of correctness.

$$
\left\{
\begin{array}{lll}
1) & \langle \mathcal{L}_n \triangleright (\nu\tilde{m})\mathsf{A} \mid \mid \mathsf{C},\ \mathcal{L}_n^K \triangleright (\nu\tilde{m})\mathsf{A} \mid \mid \mathsf{C}\rangle & \Big| K \subseteq \{1\ldots n\} \\[2ex]
2) & \begin{array}{l} \Big\langle \mathcal{L}_n \triangleright (\nu\tilde{m})\Big(\mathsf{A} \mid \prod_{i\in I} N_i \mid \prod_{j\in J} l_j\llbracket \mathsf{R}^t_{j,1}\rrbracket \mid \prod_{h\in H} l_h\llbracket \mathsf{R}^f_{h,1}\rrbracket \mid \prod_{k\in K} l_k\llbracket P_k\rrbracket\Big) \\ ,\ \mathcal{L}_n^K \triangleright (\nu\tilde{m})\Big(\mathsf{A} \mid \prod_{i\in I} N_i \mid \prod_{j\in J} l_j\llbracket \mathsf{R}^t_{j,1}\rrbracket \mid \prod_{h\in H} l_h\llbracket \mathsf{R}^f_{h,1}\rrbracket\Big)\Big\rangle \end{array} & \Bigg| \begin{array}{l} \mathsf{part}^n_1(I,J,H,K) \\ \text{and } I_{min} = 1 \end{array} \\[4ex]
3) & \begin{array}{l} \Big\langle \mathcal{L}_n \triangleright (\nu\tilde{m})\left(\begin{array}{l} \mathsf{A} \mid \prod_{i\in I}\Big(N_i \mid B(i,x)_1^{I_{min}-1}\Big) \mid \prod_{j\in J} l_j\llbracket \mathsf{R}^x_{j,I_{min}}\rrbracket \\ \mid \prod_{h\in H} l_h\llbracket \mathsf{R}^x_{h,I_{min}}\rrbracket \mid \prod_{k\in K} l_k\llbracket P_k\rrbracket \end{array}\right) \\ ,\ \mathcal{L}_n^K \triangleright (\nu\tilde{m})\Big(\mathsf{A} \mid \prod_{i\in I} N_i \mid \prod_{j\in J} l_j\llbracket \mathsf{R}^y_{j,I_{min}}\rrbracket \mid \prod_{h\in H} l_h\llbracket \mathsf{R}^y_{h,I_{min}}\rrbracket\Big)\Big\rangle \end{array} & \Bigg| \begin{array}{l} \mathsf{part}^n_1(I,J,H,K) \\ \text{and } 1 \neq I_{min} < J_{min} \\ \text{and } I_{min} < H_{min} \\ \text{and } x,y \in \{t,f\} \\ \text{and } \{1,\ldots,(I_{min}-1)\} \subseteq K \end{array} \\[6ex]
4) & \begin{array}{l} \Big\langle \mathcal{L}_n \triangleright (\nu\tilde{m})\left(\begin{array}{l} \mathsf{A} \mid \prod_{i\in I}\Big(N_i \mid B(i,x)_1^{I_{min}-1}\Big) \mid \prod_{j\in J} l_j\llbracket \mathsf{R}^x_{j,I_{min}}\rrbracket \\ \mid \prod_{h\in H} l_h\llbracket \mathsf{R}^x_{h,I_{min}}\rrbracket \mid \prod_{k\in K} l_k\llbracket P_k\rrbracket \end{array}\right) \\ ,\ \mathcal{L}_n^K \triangleright (\nu\tilde{m})\left(\begin{array}{l} \mathsf{A} \mid \prod_{i\in I}\Big(N_i \mid B(i,y)_{J_{min}}^{J^+_{min}}\Big) \mid \prod_{j\in J} l_j\llbracket \mathsf{R}^y_{j,I_{min}}\rrbracket \\ \mid \prod_{h\in H}\Big(l_h\llbracket \mathsf{R}^y_{h,J_{min}}\rrbracket \mid B(i,y)_{J_{min}}^{J^+_{min}}\Big) \end{array}\right)\Big\rangle \end{array} & \Bigg| \begin{array}{l} \mathsf{part}^n_1(I,J,H,K) \\ \text{and } J_{min} < I_{min} < H_{min} \\ \text{and } x,y \in \{t,f\} \\ \text{and } |J|, |I| \geq 1 \end{array} \\[6ex]
5) & \begin{array}{l} \Big\langle \mathcal{L}_n \triangleright (\nu\tilde{m})\left(\begin{array}{l} \mathsf{A} \mid \prod_{i\in I}\Big(N_i \mid B(i,x)_1^{I_{min}-1}\Big) \mid \prod_{j\in J} l_j\llbracket \mathsf{R}^x_{j,I_{min}}\rrbracket \\ \mid \prod_{h\in H} l_h\llbracket \mathsf{R}^x_{h,I_{min}}\rrbracket \mid \prod_{k\in K} l_k\llbracket P_k\rrbracket \end{array}\right) \\ ,\ \mathcal{L}_n^K \triangleright (\nu\tilde{m})\left(\begin{array}{l} \mathsf{A} \mid \prod_{i\in I}\Big(N_i \mid B(i,y)_{J_{min}}^{J^+_{min}}\Big) \mid \prod_{j\in J} l_j\llbracket \mathsf{R}^y_{j,H_{min}}\rrbracket \\ \mid \prod_{h\in H}\Big(l_h\llbracket \mathsf{R}^y_{h,J_{min}}\rrbracket \mid B(i,y)_{J_{min}}^{J^+_{min}}\Big) \end{array}\right)\Big\rangle \end{array} & \Bigg| \begin{array}{l} \mathsf{part}^n_1(I,J,H,K) \\ \text{and } J_{min} < H_{min} < I_{min} \\ \text{and } x,y \in \{t,f\} \\ \text{and } |J|, |H|, |I| \geq 1 \end{array} \\[6ex]
6) & \begin{array}{l} \Big\langle \mathcal{L}_n \triangleright (\nu\tilde{m})\Big(\mathsf{A} \mid \prod_{j\in J} l_j\llbracket \mathsf{R}^x_{j,I_{min}}\rrbracket \mid \prod_{h\in H} l_h\llbracket \mathsf{R}^x_{h,I_{min}}\rrbracket \mid \prod_{k\in K} l_k\llbracket P_k\rrbracket\Big) \\ ,\ \mathcal{L}_n^K \triangleright (\nu\tilde{m})\Big(\mathsf{A} \mid \prod_{j\in J} l_j\llbracket \mathsf{R}^y_{j,H_{min}}\rrbracket \mid \prod_{h\in H}\Big(l_h\llbracket \mathsf{R}^y_{h,J_{min}}\rrbracket \mid B(i,y)_{J_{min}}^{J^+_{min}}\Big)\Big)\Big\rangle \end{array} & \Bigg| \begin{array}{l} \mathsf{part}^n_1(J,H,K) \\ \text{and } J_{min} < H_{min} \\ \text{and } x,y \in \{t,f\} \\ \text{and } |J|, |H| \geq 1 \end{array} \\[4ex]
7) & \mathcal{L}_n \triangleright \overline{ok},\ \ \mathcal{L}_n^K \triangleright \overline{ok} &
\end{array}
\right\}
$$

Characterised by the non-confluent transitions (participant initialisation, participant crashing and broadcasts where the value broadcasted and the current participant estimate differ), the witness bisimulation partitions the n participants into 4 mutually exclusive sets: I denotes the participants that are yet *uninitialised*, K denotes the participants that have *crashed*, J denotes the participants with estimate x, the value being broadcasted at the current round and H denote the participants with current estimate $\ddot{x}$ differing from broadcasted value x at the current round.

Based on these participant partitions, the witness bisimulation describes the following cases for bisimilar pairs: in (2) no broadcast has yet occured because the first coordinator is still uninitialised; (3) is a similar case where the *live* participant with the lowest index i is uninitialised (all the participants $< i$ have crashed); (4) describes the case when the live participant with the lowest index j is initialised with x, and all initialised participants with estimate x are blocked because I_{min} is yet to be initialised; (5) is similar to case (4), only that participants with estimate x that is being broadcasted are blocked on an *initialised* participant from partition H with estimate $\ddot{y}$ which still needs to consume a broadcast (and change its estimate); (6) is a special case of (5) where there are no uninitialised participants. Thus, in this last case, (6), we map live blocked participants in a dynamic failure setting to unblocked participants in a failure free setting at the final round n.

We note that witness bisimulation shows that even though agreement is reached in both failure-free (left) and dynamic failure (right) sides, each side may agree on different values at round $(n + 1)$. More specifically in the failure-free setting agreement is reached on the value to which the first participant is initialised; this is not necessarily the case in dynamic failure setting. We also note that the witness bisimulation is uncluttered from crashed code through the structural rule (s-Dead). Thus, in every bisimilar pair, it maps the corresponding live code in a left (failure-free) configuration, irrespective of its state, to the inert process **0**, on the right. We overview the main transitions of the important (enumerated) stages in this relation, that is for stages (3), (4), (5) and (6):

Stage (3)**:** If participant $i \in I$ is initialised, then we go to stage (4) or (5), depending on the value y it is initialised to and whether $(I/\{i\})^+_{min} < J_{min}, H_{min}$. If participant $i \in I$ crashes, then if $(I/\{i\})^+_{min} < J_{min}, H_{min}$ we remain in (3) else go to stage (4) or (5).

Stage (4)**:** If participant $j \in J$ crashes, then if $J_{min} = J^+_{min}$ we go to stage (3), otherwise we remain in (4). If participant $i \in I$ is initialised we have a number of cases: if it is initialised to y or it is initialised to $\ddot{y}$ and $(i \neq I_{min})$ then

- we remain in (4) if $|I| \neq 1$.
- we go to (6) if $|I| = 1$.
- we go to (7) if $(|H| = 0 \wedge |I| = 1)$.

Else, if the I_{min} is initialised to $\ddot{y}$, then

- we go to (5) if $|I| \neq 1$, swapping J for H and vice-versa.
- we go to (6) if $|I| = 1$, again swapping J for H and vice-versa.
- we go to (7) if $(|H| = 0 \wedge |I| = 1)$

Similarly, if participant I_{min} crashes, then depending on the next smallest participant every $j \in J$ blocks on, we can either remain in (4) or transition to stage (5) if $|I| \neq 1$, stage (6) if $|I| = 1$ or stage (7) if $(|H| = 0 \wedge |I| = 1)$. Finally, if participant $h \in H$ consumes the broadcasts or crashes, we still remain in stage (4), potentially making $|H| = 0$.

Stage (5)**:** If participant $j \in J$ crashes, then if $J_{min} \neq J^+_{min}$ we remain in (5), otherwise we transition to stage (4) where H is swapped for J (and vice-versa). If participant $h \in H$ accepts the broadcast or crashes, we remain in (5) or transition back to (4), depending on whether $H_{min} = H^+_{min}$. If participant $i \in I$ is initialised, we still remain in (5) whereas if $i \in I$ crashes, we remain in (5) or transition to (6) if $|I| = 1$.

Stage (6)**:** If participant $j \in J$ crashes, then if $|J| = 1$ we reach agreement and go to stage (7), otherwise we remain in (6), possibly swapping participants $h \in H$ for participants $j \in J$. If participant $h \in H$ accepts the broadcast or crashes, we transition to stage (7) if $|H| = 1$ or remain in (6).

All the above transitions are matched by the empty transition on the failure-free side, except those transitions that involve initialising participants: In this case we match the transition by initialising the corresponding participant in the failure-free setting.

6 Conclusion

We have designed a *partial-failure* process calculus in which distributed algorithms can be formally described and analysed. We have also developed up-to techniques in this calculus by identifying novel confluent moves involving the choice and perfect failure detection operator, together with a stronger structural equivalence abstracting over dead code. Most importantly however, we have proposed a methodology for formally proving the correctness of distributed algorithms in the presence of failure using fault-tolerance bisimulation techniques. We have shown how this methodology can alleviate the burned of exhibiting such formal proofs by giving, what to our knowledge is, the first bisimulation-based proof of Consensus with perfect failure detectors. Moreover, the decomposition of the proof into basic correctness and correctness preservation equivalences permits separation of concerns and leads to a better understanding of the role and weight of each action in the studied algorithm.

Future Work: There are various possible extension to our calculus. We can weaken our failure detectors to $\diamond\mathcal{S}$, [2], by enhancing our network representation with two livesets, suspectable and non-suspectable, similar to the techniques used in [14,13]. We can also introduce recursive computation, which would allow us to study consensus solving algorithms with no static bounds on the number of rounds. Such a study would require more sophisticated reasoning about termination; work such as [3,17] should shed more light on this complication. Independent of the calculus, we plan to validate our proposed methodology by applying it to a range of fault-tolerant distributed algorithms expressed in various calculi; examples of such algorithms include those in [11,16].

Related Work: The confluence of certain τ-steps has long been known as a useful technique in the management of bisimulations, [9]. See [8] for particularly good examples of where they have significantly decreased the size of witness bisimulations. We have extended the concept, by considering confluence up to a particularly strong form of structural equivalence which enables useful garbage collections to be carried out in fault-tolerance proofs, by virtue of the presence of dead locations.

The closest to our work is [14], where the correctness of a consensus solving algorithm for a more complex setting which uses $\diamond\mathcal{S}$ failure detectors is formalised using a process calculus. However, their proof methods differ from ours: they give a translation from the calculus encoding of the algorithm into an abstract interpretation and then perform correctness analysis on the abstract interpretation. Results similar to ours are also presented in [1]; there the atomicity of the 2-phase commit protocol is encoded and proved correct using a process calculus with persistence and transient failure; bisimulations are used to obtain algebraic laws which are then used to prove atomicity.

Acknowledgments. We would like to thank the referees for their incisive comments on a preliminary version of this paper.

References

1. Martin Berger and Kohei Honda. The two-phase commitment protocol in an extended pi-calculus. *Electr. Notes Theor. Comput. Sci.*, 39(1), 2000.
2. Tushar Deepak Chandra and Sam Toueg. Unreliable failure detectors for reliable distributed systems. *Journal of the ACM*, 43(2):225–267, March 1996.
3. Yuxin Deng and Davide Sangiorgi. Ensuring termination by typability. In *IFIP TCS*, pages 619–632, 2004.
4. Michael J. Fischer. The consensus problem in unreliable distributed systems (a brief survey). In *Proceedings of the 1983 International FCT-Conference on Fundamentals of Computation Theory*, pages 127–140. Springer-Verlag, 1983.
5. Cedric Fournet, Georges Gonthier, Jean Jaques Levy, and Remy Didier. A calculus of mobile agents. *CONCUR 96*, LNCS 1119:406–421, August 1996.
6. Adrian Francalanza and Matthew Hennessy. A theory of system behaviour in the presence of node and link failures. In *CONCUR*, volume 3653 of *Lecture Notes in Computer Science*, pages 368–382. Springer, 2005.
7. Adrian Francalanza and Matthew Hennessy. A theory of system fault tolerance. In L. Aceto and A. Ingolfsdottir, editors, *Proc. of 9th Intern. Conf. on Foundations of Software Science and Computation Structures (FoSSaCS'06)*, volume 3921 of *LNCS*. Springer, 2006.
8. J. F. Groote and M. P. A. Sellink. Confluence for process verification. *Theor. Comput. Sci.*, 170(1-2):47–81, 1996.
9. Jan Friso Groote and Jaco van de Pol. State space reduction using partial tau-confluence. In *Mathematical Foundations of Computer Science*, pages 383–393, 2000.
10. K. Honda and N. Yoshida. On reduction-based process semantics. *Theoretical Computer Science*, 152(2):437–486, 1995.
11. Nancy A. Lynch. *Distributed Algorithms*. Morgan Kaufmann, 1996.
12. R. Milner. *Communication and Concurrency*. Prentice-Hall, 1989.
13. Uwe Nestmann and Rachele Fuzzati. Unreliable failure detectors via operational semantics. In *ASIAN*, pages 54–71, 2003.
14. Uwe Nestmann, Rachele Fuzzati, and Massimo Merro. Modeling consensus in a process calculus. In *CONCUR: 14th International Conference on Concurrency Theory*. LNCS, Springer-Verlag, 2003.
15. James Riely and Matthew Hennessy. Distributed processes and location failures. *Theoretical Computer Science*, 226:693–735, 2001.
16. Gerard Tel. *Introduction to distributed algorithms*. Cambridge University Press, New York, NY, USA, 1994.
17. Nobuko Yoshida, Martin Berger, and Kohei Honda. Strong normalisation in the pi-calculus. *Inf. Comput.*, 191(2):145–202, 2004.

A Core Calculus for a Comparative Analysis of Bio-inspired Calculi

Cristian Versari

Università di Bologna, Dipartimento di Scienze dell'Informazione
Mura Anteo Zamboni 7, 40127 Bologna, Italy
versari@cs.unibo.it

Abstract. The application of process calculi theory to the modeling and the analysis of biological phenomena has recently attracted the interests of the scientific community. To this aim several specialized, bio-inspired process calculi have been proposed, but a formal comparison of their expressivity is still lacking. In this paper we present π@, an extension of the π-Calculus with priorities and polyadic synchronisation that turns out to be suitable to act as a core platform for the comparison of other calculi. Here we show π@ at work by providing "reasonable" encodings of the two most popular calculi for modeling membrane interactions, namely, BioAmbients and Brane Calculi.

Keywords: pi-calculus, priority, polyadic synchronisation, BioAmbients, Brane Calculi.

1 Introduction

After the first use of π-Calculus for the modeling of biological processes [22], the applications of process calculi to Systems Biology attracted increasing research efforts. The direct employment of π-Calculus allowed the formalisation of several biological mechanism, its variants and extension [20,23,8] permitted the representation or analysis *in silico* of cellular processes [13,7]. To obtain higher abstraction level and biological faithfulness, more complex calculi have been proposed [4,24,21,10,11,12] which are based on or get inspiration from π-Calculus. Even if they present many common features, each calculus focuses its attention on particular biological entities or mechanisms. Their similarity induces the interest for a parallel analysis, but their specialisation does not allow a direct comparison.

The π@ language was designed to this aim: its simple but powerful extensions to π-Calculus – polyadic synchronisation and prioritised communication – allow to express the ideas shared by all these formalisms and flexibly adapt to represent the peculiarities of each one. Moreover, its simple syntax and semantics, very close to π-Calculus, allow a natural extension of many properties and results already stated for standard π-Calculus, thus facilitating π@ theoretical analysis.

In this paper we show π@ at work by encoding two of these formalisms: Brane Calculi and BioAmbients. Their straightforward embedding in the same language

R. De Nicola (Ed.): ESOP 2007, LNCS 4421, pp. 411–425, 2007.

allows to understand clearly their structural/semantical common points and differences and provides their ready-to-run implementation on top of a common platform.

The paper is structured as follows. Next section presents π@ language, first by introducing its extensions to π-Calculus, then by giving its syntax and semantics. Section 3 is devoted to the explanation of the central ideas behind the encodings, followed by their formalisation and analysis. For a detailed treatment of BioAmbients and Brane Calculi see [24,4].

2 The π@ Language

The π@ calculus – pronounced like the french "paillette" – consists in π-Calculus with the addition of two features: polyadic synchronisation and prioritised communication. The first one is used to model *localisation* of communication typical of the majority of bio-inspired calculi, which usually formalise it by the explicit introduction of compartments (i.e. ambients and membranes in the case of the two languages considered here). Priority is exploited as a powerful mechanism for achieving *atomicity*, that is the completion, without overlapping, of complex atomic operations by the execution of several simple steps.

Before presenting π@, we shortly recall π-Calculus syntax and semantics, on which π@ is strongly based.

2.1 The π-Calculus

Here we recall the syntax and the reduction semantics of π-Calculus, chosen as the basis for π@ because of the simplicity and closeness to the semantics used for the majority of bio-inspired calculi. For a full threatment of π-Calculus we refer to [14,15].

Definition 1. *Let*

$\mathcal{N}$ *be a set of names on a finite alphabet,* $x, y, z, \ldots \in \mathcal{N}$*;*
$\overline{\mathcal{N}} = \{\overline{x} \mid x \in \mathcal{N}\}$

The syntax of π*-Calculus is defined as*

$$P \;::=\; \mathbf{0} \;\Big|\; \sum_{i\in I} \pi_i.P_i \;\Big|\; P \mid Q \;\Big|\; !\,P \;\Big|\; (\nu x)P$$

$$\pi \;::=\; \tau \;\Big|\; x(y) \;\Big|\; \overline{x}\langle y\rangle$$

Definition 2. *The congruence relation* $\equiv$ *is defined as the least congruence satisfying alpha conversion, the commutative monoidal laws with respect to both* $(\mid, \mathbf{0})$ *and* $(+, \mathbf{0})$ *and the following axioms:*

$$\begin{aligned} (\nu x)P \mid Q &\equiv (\nu x)(P \mid Q) && \text{if } x \notin fn(Q) \\ (\nu x)P &\equiv P && \text{if } x \notin fn(P) \\ !\,P &\equiv\, !\,P \mid P \end{aligned}$$

where the function fn *is defined as*

$$
\begin{array}{rclrcl}
fn(\tau) & \stackrel{def}{=} & \emptyset & fn(x(y)) & \stackrel{def}{=} & \{x\} \\
fn(\overline{x}\langle y\rangle) & \stackrel{def}{=} & \{x, y\} & fn(\mathbf{0}) & \stackrel{def}{=} & \emptyset \\
fn(\pi.P) & \stackrel{def}{=} & fn(\pi) \cup fn(P) & fn(\sum_{i\in I} \pi_i.P_i) & \stackrel{def}{=} & \bigcup_i fn(\pi_i.P_i) \\
fn(P \mid Q) & \stackrel{def}{=} & fn(P) \cup fn(Q) & fn(!\,P) & \stackrel{def}{=} & fn(P) \\
fn((\nu x)P) & \stackrel{def}{=} & fn(P) \setminus \{x\} & & &
\end{array}
$$

Definition 3. *π-Calculus semantics is given in terms of the reduction system described by the following rules:*

$$
\frac{}{\tau.P \;\rightarrow\; P} \qquad \frac{}{(\mu(y).P + M) \mid (\overline{\mu}\langle z\rangle.Q + N) \;\rightarrow\; P\{z/y\} \mid Q}
$$

$$
\frac{P \;\rightarrow\; P'}{P \mid Q \;\rightarrow\; P' \mid Q} \qquad \frac{P \;\rightarrow\; P'}{(\nu\, x)P \;\rightarrow\; (\nu\, x)P'} \qquad \frac{P \equiv Q \quad P \;\rightarrow\; P' \quad P' \equiv Q'}{Q \;\rightarrow\; Q'}
$$

2.2 Polyadic Synchronisation

In π-Calculus channels and names are usually synonyms. Polyadic synchronisation (introduced in [3]) consists in giving *structure* to channels: each channel is composed of one or more names and identified by all of them in the exact sequence they occur. For example, an email address is usually written in the form *username@domain*, where *username* and *domain* are two strings – two names – both necessary to identify the given email address. Moreover, their order is crucial since *domain@username* specifies another, likely unexisting, address. Following this analogy, π@ channels are written in the form $name_1@name_2@\ldots@name_n$ without limit in the number of names, even if just two suffice for most of the applications. In other words, a channel is indicated by a vector of names $(name_1, name_2, \ldots, name_n), n \geq 1$, and communication between two processes may happen only if they are pursuing a synchronisation along channels composed of the same number of names, with the same multiplicity and appearing order.

Apart from this, communication in π@ happens in the same way as in π-Calculus. For example, the transition

$$
\overline{comm}\langle d\rangle.P \mid comm(x).Q \quad \rightarrow \quad P \mid Q\{d/x\}
$$

is still valid in π@. Output actions are overlined as usual, even in case of polyadic synchronisations:

$$
\overline{polyadic@comm}\langle d\rangle.P \mid polyadic@comm(x).Q \quad \rightarrow \quad P \mid Q\{d/x\}
$$

Communication produces the same renaming effect, but with one difference: in π-Calculus the transmission of a name always stands for the transmission of a channel, while in π@ the transmitted name may represent a channel or just one of its components, or both. For example, in the following expression the transmitted name d represents a channel in the first output action $\overline{d}\langle y\rangle$, while in $\overline{d@comm}\langle y\rangle$ it is just the first part of the channel $d@comm$.

$$\overline{polyadic@comm}\langle d\rangle.P \mid polyadic@comm(x).(\overline{x}\langle y\rangle \mid \overline{x@comm}\langle y\rangle) \quad \rightarrow$$
$$P \mid \overline{d}\langle y\rangle \mid \overline{d@comm}\langle y\rangle$$

For concision and readability, polyadic synchronisation is often used also in conjunction with polyadic communication:

$$\overline{polyadic@comm}\langle a,b,c\rangle.P \mid polyadic@comm(x,y,z).Q \quad \rightarrow$$
$$P \mid Q\{a/x, b/y, c/z\}$$

Finally, the following transitions are not allowed:

$$\overline{x@y}\langle\rangle.P \mid y@x().Q \quad \not\rightarrow \qquad\qquad (x \neq y)$$

$$\overline{x}\langle\rangle.P \mid x@x().Q \quad \not\rightarrow$$

In the first expression, the output and input channels are composed of the same names, but with different appearing order. In the second one, channels are represented by the same name but with different multiplicity. In both cases the vectors of names do not match.

2.3 Priority

Priority behaves as expected: a high-priority process holds the central processing unit and executes its job before any low priority process. In π@ high priority synchronisations or communications are executed before any other low priority action. Usually a high priority action is indicated by underlining the name of the channel one or more times. For example, the expression

$$\overline{stand}\langle x\rangle.P \mid \overline{\underline{walk}}\langle y\rangle.Q \mid \overline{\underline{\underline{run}}}\langle z\rangle$$

contains three processes with different, increasing priority. To express more than three levels of priority another notation is used, where the priority of the process is represented by a number following the channel names. The above expression may be rewritten as

$$\overline{stand:2}\langle x\rangle.P \mid \overline{walk:1}\langle y\rangle.Q \mid \overline{run:0}\langle z\rangle$$

where a lower priority action is labelled with a higher number (the highest priority is denoted by 0).

Interaction between processes may occur only if channels have the same priority. In this example

$$\overline{\underline{x}}\langle y\rangle.P \mid x(z).Q \quad \not\rightarrow$$

$$\overline{\underline{x}}\langle y\rangle.P \mid \underline{x}(z).Q \quad \rightarrow \quad P \mid Q\{y/z\}$$

only the second interaction is allowed, because the expressions x and $\underline{x}$ denote actually two different channels. Finally, as expected, low priority actions occur only if no higher priority action may occur:

$$\bar{l}\langle w\rangle \mid l(x).P \mid \overline{\underline{h}}\langle y\rangle \mid \underline{h}(z).Q \not\rightarrow \mathbf{0} \mid P\{w/x\} \mid \overline{\underline{h}}\langle y\rangle \mid \underline{h}(z).Q$$

$$\bar{l}\langle w\rangle \mid l(x).P \mid \overline{\underline{h}}\langle y\rangle \mid \underline{h}(z).Q \rightarrow \bar{l}\langle w\rangle \mid l(x).P \mid \mathbf{0} \mid Q\{y/z\} \rightarrow \mathbf{0} \mid P\{w/x\} \mid \mathbf{0} \mid Q\{y/z\}$$

The first of the two transitions is not allowed because interactions on low-priority channel l may happen only after the high-priority communication on channel $\underline{h}$. For a detailed survey of priority in process algebras, see [9].

2.4 The π@ Syntax and Semantics

The π@ language is very close to π-Calculus: from a syntactical point of view the only difference is the structure of channels, composed of multiple names followed by the priority of the action. We use μ to denote a vector of names $x_1, \ldots, x_n$ and $\mu : k$ to denote a channel, that is a vector of names μ followed by a colon and a natural number k specifying the priority. As usual, $\overline{\mu : k}$ represents an output operation along channel $\mu : k$, while $\alpha : k$ stands for a generic input, output or silent action τ of priority k.

Definition 4. *Let*

$\mathcal{N}$ be a set of names on finite alphabet, $x, y, z, \ldots \in \mathcal{N}$;
$\mathcal{N}^+ = \bigcup_{i>0} \mathcal{N}^i, \quad \mu \in \mathcal{N}^+$;
$\overline{\mathcal{N}}^+ = \{\bar{\mu} \mid \mu \in \mathcal{N}^+\}$;
$\alpha \in (\overline{\mathcal{N}}^+ \cup \mathcal{N}^+ \cup \{\tau\})$;

The syntax of π@ defined as

$$P ::= \mathbf{0} \;\Big|\; \sum_{i\in I} \pi_i.P_i \;\Big|\; P \mid Q \;\Big|\; !P \;\Big|\; (\nu x)P$$

$$\pi ::= \tau : k \;\Big|\; \mu : k(x) \;\Big|\; \overline{\mu : k}\langle x\rangle$$

As previously introduced, some abbreviations are very often used in this paper:

$$\mu(x) = \mu : 2(x) \qquad \bar{\mu}\langle x\rangle = \overline{\mu : 2}\langle x\rangle$$
$$\underline{\mu}(x) = \mu : 1(x) \qquad \overline{\underline{\mu}}\langle x\rangle = \overline{\mu : 1}\langle x\rangle$$
$$\underline{\underline{\mu}}(x) = \mu : 0(x) \qquad \overline{\underline{\underline{\mu}}}\langle x\rangle = \overline{\mu : 0}\langle x\rangle$$

The definition for structural congruence $\equiv$ is exactly the same as given for π-Calculus, where the function fn is naturally extended to the π@ syntax, that is

$$fn(\mu : k(y)) \stackrel{def}{=} \{\mu_1, \ldots, \mu_n\}$$
$$fn(\overline{\mu : k}\langle y\rangle) \stackrel{def}{=} \{\mu_1, \ldots, \mu_n, y\}$$

where $\mu = \mu_1@\cdots@\mu_n$. The reduction semantics is very similar, but defined in terms of an auxiliary function $I^k(P)$, representing the set of actions of priority k which the process P may immediately execute. For example, if

$$P = a.Q \mid \underline{b} \mid \underline{\underline{c}}.R \mid \overline{\underline{d}} + \underline{\underline{e}}.S \mid \overline{a}.T$$

then $I^0(P) = \{\overline{c}, e\}$, $I^1(P) = \{b, \overline{d}\}$, $I^2(P) = \{a, \overline{a}, \tau\}$, where the availability of τ action derives from the interaction of the first and last process.

Definition 5. *Let* $I^k(P)$ *be*

$$\begin{aligned}
I^k(\sum_i \alpha_i : l_i.P_i) &= \{\alpha_i \mid l_i = k\};\\
I^k((\nu\, y)\ P) &= I^k(P) \setminus \{\alpha \mid y \in \{x_1, \ldots, x_n\} \wedge \\
&\qquad (\alpha = x_1@\ldots@x_n \ \vee\ \alpha = \overline{x_1@\ldots@x_n})\};\\
I^k(!P) &= I^k(P \mid P);\\
I^k(P \mid Q) &= I^k(P) \cup I^k(Q) \cup \{\tau \mid I^k(P) \cap \overline{I^k(Q)} \neq \emptyset\},\\
&\quad \overline{I^k(Q)} = \{\overline{\alpha} \mid \alpha \in I^k(Q)\}
\end{aligned}$$

$\pi@$ semantics is given in terms of the following reduction system:

$$\frac{\tau \notin \bigcup_{i<k} I^i(M)}{\tau : k.P + M \ \rightarrow_k\ P} \qquad \frac{P \ \rightarrow_k\ P'}{(\nu\, x)P \ \rightarrow_k\ (\nu\, x)P'}$$

$$\frac{\tau \notin \bigcup_{i<k} I^i(M \mid N)}{(\mu : k(y).P + M) \mid (\overline{\mu} : k\langle z\rangle.Q + N) \ \rightarrow_k\ P\{z/y\} \mid Q}$$

$$\frac{cP \ \rightarrow_k\ P' \qquad \tau \notin \bigcup_{i<k} I^i(P \mid Q)}{P \mid Q \ \rightarrow_k\ P' \mid Q} \qquad \frac{P \equiv Q \quad P \ \rightarrow_k\ P' \quad P' \equiv Q'}{Q \ \rightarrow_k\ Q'}$$

$\pi@$ reduction rules are exactly the same of π-Calculus, except for the additional condition $\tau \notin \bigcup_{i<k} I^i(\ldots)$ which avoids the execution of low priority actions if higher priority communications (represented by τ actions) are immediately available.

2.5 Notation

In addition to standard reduction relation $\rightarrow_k$, some derived relations are used for the formulation of theorems. As usual, $\rightarrow_k^*$ is the reflective-transitive closure of $\rightarrow_k$, while $\rightarrow_k^{(n)}$ is used to evidence the length of the derivation, that is

$$P \rightarrow^{(n)} Q \quad \text{iff} \quad \exists\, P_1, \ldots, P_{n-1} : P \rightarrow P_1 \rightarrow \ldots \rightarrow P_{n-1} \rightarrow Q$$

Similar notation are used for the derived relations.

Definition 6. *Let P, Q, Q' be $\pi@$ processes. The reduction relations $\rightarrow$, $\rightarrowtail_k$, $\mapsto$, $\rightrightarrows_k$, are defined as follows:*

1. $P \rightarrow Q \quad \triangleq \quad P \rightarrow_k Q,\ k \in \mathbb{N};$
2. $P \rightarrowtail_k Q \quad \triangleq \quad P \rightarrow_h Q,\ h \leq k;$
3. $P \mapsto Q \quad \triangleq \quad P \rightarrow_k P' \wedge P' \rightarrowtail^*_{k-1} Q,\ \tau \notin \bigcup_{i<k} I^i(Q).$
4. $P \rightrightarrows_k Q \quad \triangleq \quad P \rightarrowtail^*_{k-1} Q,\ \tau \notin \bigcup_{i<k} I^i(Q) \ \wedge$
   $(P \rightarrowtail^*_{k-1} Q',\ \tau \notin \bigcup_{i<k} I^i(Q') \text{ implies } Q \equiv Q').$

$\rightarrow$ is the standard reduction relation, disregarding the priority of the reduction. $\rightarrowtail_k$ denotes the derivation through reduction with priority higher or equal to k. $\mapsto$ indicates that, after a reduction with a certain (low) priority and, in case, a sequence of higher priority actions, the process comes back to a state where it is ready to perform only low priority synchronisations. $\rightrightarrows_k$ states a confluence property of the process, meaning that all the states from which it is not possible to perform a reduction of priority higher than k and reachable only by reductions of priority higher than k, are congruent.

3 Encodings

The key feature which differentiates recent bio-inspired calculi from π-Calculus is the explicit formalisation of compartments. BioAmbients is a modified version of Ambient calculus [5], where compartments are represented by ambients, a sort of boxes containing processes or other nested boxes. In Brane compartments are bounded by membranes, on the surface of which processes compute. Both ambients and membranes are organised in a tree structure, both can dinamically modify this structure by performing for example *merge*, *enter/exit* or *exo* operations. The central issue is *how* they modify this structure: the most observable difference is the bitonality preserved by brane semantics and totally absent in BioAmbients. As remarked in [4], this peculiarity is enough to preclude an immediate embedding of one language into the other, thus not allowing a direct comparison of their expressivity. An alternative analysis can be performed by encoding both in a third formalism and compare their encoding functions. These functions must obviously satisfy some "reasonable" properties (as discussed in section 3.1) and they must also be as simple as possible by hiding irrelevant details. $\pi@$ features were chosen to meet these criteria: the lack of a predefined semantics for compartments together with the possibility of expressing localisation (by means of polyadic synchronisation) and complex atomic operations (by means of priority) place $\pi@$ one abstraction level lower, as a sort of *assembly* language for compartmentalised formalisms.

3.1 Requirements

The fundamental criterion guiding any encoding is the preservation of some addressed semantics. According to [16], this often means that the encoding function $[\![\cdot]\!]$ must at least fulfill the notion of *operational correspondence*, characterised by two complementary properties: completeness and soundness. The first means that every possible execution of the source language may be simulated by its translation, the second ensures that all the states reached by the translation correspond to some state of the source. Since all the languages we consider are Turing-complete (even Brane [2,6], despite of its simplicity), as usual for concurrent languages we require some additional criteria. As remarked in [17], a *reasonable* encoding should also preserve the degree of distribution of the source language (i.e. homomorphism w.r.t. parallel composition) and should not depend on the channel (or compartment) names of the term to be encoded. This also implies a very valuable property, that is modular compilation, as discussed in [1]. In addition to the cited criteria, we also require the encoding to preserve the termination or diverging behaviour of the translated term, in order to obtain a totally faithful encoding function. The following definition formalises the notion of *reasonable encoding* used in this paper.

Definition 7. *An encoding $[\![\, \cdot \,]\!]$ is reasonable if it enjoys the following properties:*

1. *homomorphism w.r.t. parallel composition:* $[\![\, P_1 \mid P_2 \,]\!] = [\![\, P_1 \,]\!] \mid [\![\, P_2 \,]\!]$;
2. *renaming preserving:* *for any permutation of the source names* θ, $[\![\, \theta(P) \,]\!] = \theta([\![\, P \,]\!])$;
3. *termination invariance:* $P \Downarrow$ *iff* $[\![\, P \,]\!] \Downarrow$, $P \Uparrow$ *iff* $[\![\, P \,]\!] \Uparrow$;
4. *operational correspondence:*
   (a) *if* $P \to P'$ *then* $[\![\, P \,]\!] \to^* [\![\, P' \,]\!]$,
   (b) *if* $[\![\, P \,]\!] \to^* Q$ *then* $\exists P' : P \to^* P' \wedge Q \to^* [\![\, P' \,]\!]$.

3.2 Basic Ideas

Compartment and their nesting are very intuitive abstractions: the simple statement that an object is enclosed in a box suggests that it is someway isolated from the external context; putting one box into another means that, after the operation, the inner box *with all its content* are located inside the outer one; merging the content of two boxes implies putting in the same box *all the enclosed objects*. To obtain this behaviour in $\pi@$ we must recognise the exact meaning of every operation on compartments and reproduce step by step the same semantics.

The first concept to unfold is nesting: compartments compose a dynamical tree structure which must be encoded in $\pi@$. As suggested in [15], these kind of structures can be represented as a set of processes linked by the share of private channels between parent and child nodes. Like in [22], the scoping of private names represents the boundaries of compartments, but thanks to polyadic synchronisation each private name may represent an unlimited number of private communication channels, as shown in section 2.2. If each node is supplied with one distinctive name, the simplest way to encode the tree is by ensuring that each node knows the name identifying its parent compartment.

Therefore, trivial changes in the tree structure may affect an unlimited number of processes: the simple disclosure of a compartment implies that all contained processes must be notified of their new parent compartment name. The same situation occurs when splitting or merging the content of two compartments, like in *merge+* /*merge–* and *exo*/$exo^{\perp}$ operations. In π@ this turns out to be a sort of *multicast* communication, where specifical groups of nodes – that is sibling and child processes – must receive on the proper channel a new compartment name. This result is achieved by a smart use of priority levels: a high priority loop notifies in turn all the interested processes and ends when such processes do not exist anymore. By a single line of code, we obtain in π@ the same mechanism typical of broadcast communication:

$$BCAST \quad \equiv \quad !\, \underline{\underline{bcast}}(x,y).(\underline{\tau} + \underline{\overline{x}}\langle y\rangle.\overline{\underline{\underline{bcast}}}\langle x,y\rangle)$$

The above process can be triggered by an output operation $\overline{\underline{\underline{bcast}}}\langle chn, newchn\rangle$ and terminate when no high priority synchronisations are available, leaving no residual terms. Obviously, a high priority complementary output loop $!\ \overline{\underline{\underline{bcast}}}\langle chn, newchn\rangle$ would cause the system to hang, since it prevents any other computation with normal priority. This is one of the reasons that do not allow a trivial translation of Brane and Bioambients replication operators and induce an explicit reproduction of their unfolding technique in both the encoding functions.

3.3 Encoding BioAmbients

Ambients are containers organised in a tree structure: running processes and nested sub-ambients are located inside them. If each node of the tree represents an ambient, nodes are complex structures: each node may contain zero or more parallel processes and may be linked zero or more nested sub-ambients. Consequently, for the implementation of the tree structure each encoded BioAmbients process must be aware of the name of its containing (immediate) ambient, but also of the name indicating the parent of its immediate ambient. This explains why the encoding function $[\![\ ]\!]^{\alpha}_{K,a,pa}$ requires the (bound) names a and ap, which represent the immediate ambient and the parent ambient, respectively. The free names oa, opa are placeholders standing for the immediate ambient and parent ambient of the outer processes, while bound names na and npa represent a new ambient or new parent ambient name received by the process. The first parameter K is the set of names used for the explicit unfolding of replicated processes when encoding the bang operator: the cardinality of K is the number of bangs in front of the process to encode.

Definition 8. *The function* $[\![\cdot]\!]^{\alpha}$ *from BioAmbients to* π@ *processes is defined as follows:*

$$\begin{aligned}
[\![\, \mathbf{0} \,]\!]^{\alpha} &\triangleq \mathbf{0} \\
[\![\, P \mid Q \,]\!]^{\alpha} &\triangleq [\![\, P \,]\!]^{\alpha} \mid [\![\, Q \,]\!]^{\alpha} \\
[\![\, (new\ n)P \,]\!]^{\alpha} &\triangleq [\![\, (new\ n)P \,]\!]^{\alpha}_{\emptyset,oa,opa} \\
[\![\, [\,P\,] \,]\!]^{\alpha} &\triangleq [\![\, [\,P\,] \,]\!]^{\alpha}_{\emptyset,oa,opa}
\end{aligned}$$

$$
\begin{array}{rcl}
[\![\, !P \,]\!]^{\alpha} & \triangleq & [\![\, !P \,]\!]^{\alpha}_{\emptyset,oa,opa} \\
[\![\, \mathbf{0} \,]\!]^{\alpha}_{K,a,pa} & \triangleq & \mathbf{0} \\
[\![\, P \mid Q \,]\!]^{\alpha}_{K,a,pa} & \triangleq & [\![\, P \,]\!]^{\alpha}_{K,a,pa} \mid [\![\, Q \,]\!]^{\alpha}_{K,a,pa} \\
[\![\, (new\ n)P \,]\!]^{\alpha}_{K,a,pa} & \triangleq & \nu n [\![\, P \,]\!]^{\alpha}_{K,a,pa} \\
[\![\, [\,P\,] \,]\!]^{\alpha}_{K,a,pa} & \triangleq & \nu c [\![\, P \,]\!]^{\alpha}_{K,c,a} \\
[\![\, !P \,]\!]^{\alpha}_{K,a,pa} & \triangleq & \nu b(BANG(b,a,pa) \mid [\![\, P \,]\!]^{\alpha}_{K\cup\{b\},a,pa} \mid \\
 & & !\,\underline{\underline{new@b}}(na,npa).[\![\, P \,]\!]^{\alpha}_{K\cup\{b\},na,npa}) \\
[\![\, \sum_{i\in I,\ I\neq\emptyset} \xi_i.P_i \,]\!]^{\alpha}_{K,a,pa} & \triangleq & BCAST \mid \nu s(!\,\underline{\underline{s}}(na,npa). \\
 & & ([\![\, \xi_i.P_i \,]\!]^{\alpha}_{K,na,npa} + TREE(s,na,npa)) \mid \\
 & & [\![\, \xi_i.P_i \,]\!]^{\alpha}_{K,a,pa} + TREE(s,a,pa)) \\
[\![\, enter\ n.P \,]\!]^{\alpha}_{K,a,pa} & \triangleq & enter@n@pa(x).\overline{\underline{\underline{bcast}}}\langle pa,a,x\rangle.([\![\, P \,]\!]^{\alpha}_{\emptyset,a,x} \mid \Pi_K) \\
[\![\, accept\ n.P \,]\!]^{\alpha}_{K,a,pa} & \triangleq & \overline{enter@n@pa}\langle a\rangle.([\![\, P \,]\!]^{\alpha}_{\emptyset,a,pa} \mid \Pi_K) \\
[\![\, exit\ n.P \,]\!]^{\alpha}_{K,a,pa} & \triangleq & expel@n@pa(x).\overline{\underline{\underline{bcast}}}\langle pa,a,x\rangle.([\![\, P \,]\!]^{\alpha}_{\emptyset,a,x} \mid \Pi_K) \\
[\![\, expel\ n.P \,]\!]^{\alpha}_{K,a,pa} & \triangleq & \overline{expel@n@a}\langle pa\rangle.([\![\, P \,]\!]^{\alpha}_{\emptyset,a,pa} \mid \Pi_K) \\
[\![\, merge-\ n.P \,]\!]^{\alpha}_{K,a,pa} & \triangleq & merge@n@pa(x). \\
 & & \quad \overline{\underline{\underline{bcast}}}\langle merge,a,x\rangle.([\![\, P \,]\!]^{\alpha}_{\emptyset,x,pa} \mid \Pi_K) \\
[\![\, merge+\ n.P \,]\!]^{\alpha}_{K,a,pa} & \triangleq & \overline{merge@n@pa}\langle a\rangle.([\![\, P \,]\!]^{\alpha}_{\emptyset,a,pa} \mid \Pi_K) \\
[\![\, local\ n!\{m\}.P \,]\!]^{\alpha}_{K,a,pa} & \triangleq & \overline{local@n@a}\langle m\rangle.([\![\, P \,]\!]^{\alpha}_{\emptyset,a,pa} \mid \Pi_K) \\
[\![\, local\ n?\{m\}.P \,]\!]^{\alpha}_{K,a,pa} & \triangleq & local@n@a(m).([\![\, P \,]\!]^{\alpha}_{\emptyset,a,pa} \mid \Pi_K) \\
[\![\, s2s\ n!\{m\}.P \,]\!]^{\alpha}_{K,a,pa} & \triangleq & \overline{s2s@n@pa}\langle m\rangle.([\![\, P \,]\!]^{\alpha}_{\emptyset,a,pa} \mid \Pi_K) \\
[\![\, s2s\ n?\{m\}.P \,]\!]^{\alpha}_{K,a,pa} & \triangleq & s2s@n@pa(m).([\![\, P \,]\!]^{\alpha}_{\emptyset,a,pa} \mid \Pi_K) \\
[\![\, p2c\ n!\{m\}.P \,]\!]^{\alpha}_{K,a,pa} & \triangleq & \overline{p2c@n@a}\langle m\rangle.([\![\, P \,]\!]^{\alpha}_{\emptyset,a,pa} \mid \Pi_K) \\
[\![\, c2p\ n?\{m\}.P \,]\!]^{\alpha}_{K,a,pa} & \triangleq & p2c@n@pa(m).([\![\, P \,]\!]^{\alpha}_{\emptyset,a,pa} \mid \Pi_K) \\
[\![\, c2p\ n!\{m\}.P \,]\!]^{\alpha}_{K,a,pa} & \triangleq & \overline{c2p@n@pa}\langle m\rangle.([\![\, P \,]\!]^{\alpha}_{\emptyset,a,pa} \mid \Pi_K) \\
[\![\, p2c\ n?\{m\}.P \,]\!]^{\alpha}_{K,a,pa} & \triangleq & c2p@n@a(m).([\![\, P \,]\!]^{\alpha}_{\emptyset,a,pa} \mid \Pi_K) \\
BANG(b,a,pa) & \equiv & !\,\underline{\underline{b}}(na,npa). \\
 & & \quad (\underline{\underline{unfold@b}}.\overline{\underline{\underline{new@b}}}\langle na,npa\rangle + TREE(b,na,npa)) \mid \\
 & & \underline{\underline{unfold@b}}.\overline{\underline{\underline{new@b}}}\langle a,pa\rangle + TREE(b,a,pa)) \\
TREE(b,na,npa) & \equiv & \underline{\underline{npa@na}}(x).\overline{\underline{\underline{b}}}\langle na,x\rangle + \underline{\underline{merge@npa}}(x).\overline{\underline{\underline{b}}}\langle na,x\rangle + \\
 & & \underline{\underline{merge@na}}(x).\overline{\underline{\underline{b}}}\langle x,npa\rangle \\
\Pi_K & \equiv & \overline{\underline{\underline{unfold@k_1}}} \mid \cdots \mid \overline{\underline{\underline{unfold@k_n}}}, \\
 & & K = \{k_1,\ldots,k_n\} \\
BCAST & \equiv & !\,\underline{\underline{bcast}}(x,y,z).(\overline{\underline{\underline{x@y}}}\langle z\rangle.\overline{\underline{\underline{bcast}}}\langle x,y,z\rangle + \underline{\tau})
\end{array}
$$

The strict relationship between BioAmbients and π-Calculus simplifies the encoding of base operators: parallel composition and restriction are homomorphically translated. Like for restriction, each ambient produces a private name, but in this case the new name is inserted in the tree structure by passing it to the subsequent encoding. Remarkably, the translation of each communication or capability choice requires a loop: in fact, each process ready to execute an action may be notified of an occurring change in the nesting tree structure, caused by other processes. Consequently, it should receive and replace the proper names representing its immediate and/or parent ambients before attempting to perform the desired actions: each $TREE$ subprocess is ready to handle this kind of events. Communications and capabilities are directly encoded by means of polyadic synchronisation: the possibility of using an unlimited number of names for each *pi@* channel (up to three, in this case) simplifies extremely the simultaneous expression of localisation inside ambients and synchronisation on different directions (*p2p*, *s2s*, ...) equipped with names. After the execution of each capability, the reorganisation of the tree structure and the eventual unfolding of replicated processes is obtained by a sequence of high priority actions consisting in the triggering of one $BCAST$ loop and a set of $unfold@k_i$ synchronisations.

Finally, the encoding function $[\![\cdot]\!]^{\alpha}$ enjoys the requirements discussed in section 3.1, as stated by the following theorem.

Theorem 1. $[\![\cdot]\!]^{\alpha}$ *is a reasonable encoding (modulo structural congruence), that is: let* P, P_1, P_2 *be BioAmbients processes, let* Q *be a* $\pi@$ *process, then*

1. $[\![P_1 \circ P_2]\!]^{\alpha} = [\![P_1]\!]^{\alpha} \mid [\![P_2]\!]^{\alpha}$;
2. *for any permutation of the source names* θ, $[\![\theta(P)]\!]^{\alpha} = \theta([\![P]\!]^{\alpha})$;
3. $P \Downarrow$ *iff* $[\![P]\!]^{\alpha} \Downarrow$, $P \Uparrow$ *iff* $[\![P]\!]^{\alpha} \Uparrow$;
4. (a) *if* $P \rightarrow P_1$ *then* $\exists P_2 : P_2 \equiv P_1 \wedge [\![P]\!]^{\alpha} \rightarrow^* [\![P_2]\!]^{\alpha}$;
   (b) *if* $[\![P]\!]^{\alpha} \rightarrow^* Q$ *then* $\exists P_1 : P \rightarrow^* P_1 \wedge Q \rightarrow^* [\![P_1]\!]^{\alpha}$.

3.4 Encoding Brane Calculi

Like ambients, membranes are organised in tree structures: each node of the tree may contain membrane processes or nested membranes. Unlike BioAmbients, Brane Calculi present two main entities: systems and branes. Their distinction implies slightly different translations, because the encoding function of systems needs only two parameters (K, the set corresponding to the bang operators in front of the system and *pc*, the name representing the parent compartment) while an additional parameter is needed for encoding branes (*c*, the name of the compartment where the brane process resides). Similarly to BioAmbients encoding, *oc* and *opc* are placeholders standing for the compartment and parent compartment of outer processes, while *nc* and *npc* are bound names representing the new compartment and new parent compartment received during the tree structure reorganisation.

Definition 9. *The function* $\llbracket \cdot \rrbracket^{\beta}$ *from Brane to* $\pi@$ *processes is defined as follows:*

$$
\begin{aligned}
\llbracket \diamond \rrbracket^{\beta} &\triangleq \mathbf{0} \\
\llbracket P \circ Q \rrbracket^{\beta} &\triangleq \llbracket P \rrbracket^{\beta} \mid \llbracket Q \rrbracket^{\beta} \\
\llbracket\, !\, P \rrbracket^{\beta} &\triangleq \llbracket\, !\, P \rrbracket^{\beta}_{\emptyset, oc} \\
\llbracket \sigma (\!| P |\!) \rrbracket^{\beta} &\triangleq \llbracket \sigma (\!| P |\!) \rrbracket^{\beta}_{\emptyset, oc} \\
\llbracket \diamond \rrbracket^{\beta}_{K,pc} &\triangleq \mathbf{0} \\
\llbracket P \circ Q \rrbracket^{\beta}_{K,pc} &\triangleq \llbracket P \rrbracket^{\beta}_{K,pc} \mid \llbracket Q \rrbracket^{\beta}_{K,pc} \\
\llbracket\, !\, P \rrbracket^{\beta}_{K,pc} &\triangleq \nu b(\llbracket P \rrbracket^{\beta}_{K \cup \{b\},pc} \mid\ !\, \underline{\underline{new@b}}(npc).\llbracket P \rrbracket^{\beta}_{K \cup \{b\},npc} \mid \\
&\qquad !\, \underline{\underline{b}}(npc). \\
&\qquad (\underline{\underline{unfold@b}}.\overline{\underline{\underline{new@b}}}\langle npc \rangle + \underline{\underline{exo@npc}}(x).\overline{\underline{\underline{b}}}\langle x \rangle) \mid \\
&\qquad \underline{\underline{unfold@b}}.\overline{\underline{\underline{new@b}}}\langle pc \rangle + \underline{\underline{exo@pc}}(x).\overline{\underline{\underline{b}}}\langle x \rangle) \\
\llbracket \sigma (\!| P |\!) \rrbracket^{\beta}_{K,pc} &\triangleq \nu c(\llbracket \sigma \rrbracket^{\beta}_{K,c,pc} \mid \llbracket P \rrbracket^{\beta}_{K,c}) \\
\llbracket \mathbf{0} \rrbracket^{\beta}_{K,c,pc} &\triangleq \mathbf{0} \\
\llbracket \sigma \mid \rho \rrbracket^{\beta}_{K,c,pc} &\triangleq \llbracket \sigma \rrbracket^{\beta}_{K,c,pc} \mid \llbracket \rho \rrbracket^{\beta}_{K,c,pc} \\
\llbracket\, !\, \sigma \rrbracket^{\beta}_{K,c,pc} &\triangleq \nu b(BANG(b,c,pc) \mid \llbracket \sigma \rrbracket^{\beta}_{K \cup \{b\},c,pc} \mid \\
&\qquad !\, \underline{\underline{new@b}}(nc,npc).\llbracket \sigma \rrbracket^{\beta}_{K \cup \{b\},nc,npc}) \\
\llbracket a.\sigma \rrbracket^{\beta}_{K,c,pc} &\triangleq BCAST \mid \nu s(!\, \underline{\underline{s}}(nc,npc). \\
&\qquad (\llbracket a.\sigma \rrbracket^{\beta}_{K,nc,npc} + TREE(s,nc,npc)) \mid \\
&\qquad \llbracket a.\sigma \rrbracket^{\beta}_{K,c,pc} + TREE(s,c,pc)) \\
\llbracket phago_n.\sigma \rrbracket^{\beta}_{K,c,pc} &\triangleq phago@n@pc(x).\overline{\underline{\underline{bcast}}}\langle pc,c,x \rangle.(\llbracket \sigma \rrbracket^{\beta}_{\emptyset,c,x} \mid \mathit{\Pi}_K) \\
\llbracket phago_n^{\perp}(\rho).\sigma \rrbracket^{\beta}_{K,c,pc} &\triangleq \nu x(\overline{phago@n@pc}\langle x \rangle.(\llbracket \sigma \rrbracket^{\beta}_{\emptyset,c,pc} \mid \llbracket \rho \rrbracket^{\beta}_{\emptyset,x,c} \mid \mathit{\Pi}_K)) \\
\llbracket exo_n.\sigma \rrbracket^{\beta}_{K,c,pc} &\triangleq exo@n@pc(x).\overline{\underline{\underline{bcast}}}\langle exo,c,x \rangle.(\llbracket \sigma \rrbracket^{\beta}_{\emptyset,pc,x} \mid \mathit{\Pi}_K) \\
\llbracket exo_n^{\perp}.\sigma \rrbracket^{\beta}_{K,c,pc} &\triangleq \overline{exo@n@c}\langle pc \rangle.(\llbracket \sigma \rrbracket^{\beta}_{\emptyset,c,pc} \mid \mathit{\Pi}_K) \\
\llbracket pino(\rho).\sigma \rrbracket^{\beta}_{K,c,pc} &\triangleq \nu x\, \tau.(\llbracket \sigma \rrbracket^{\beta}_{\emptyset,c,pc} \mid \llbracket \rho \rrbracket^{\beta}_{\emptyset,x,c} \mid \mathit{\Pi}_K) \\
BANG(b,c,pc) &\equiv\ !\, \underline{\underline{b}}(nc,npc). \\
&\qquad (\underline{\underline{unfold@b}}.\overline{\underline{\underline{new@b}}}\langle nc,npc \rangle + TREE(b,nc,npc)) \mid \\
&\qquad \underline{\underline{unfold@b}}.\overline{\underline{\underline{new@b}}}\langle c,pc \rangle + TREE(b,c,pc)) \\
TREE(b,nc,npc) &\equiv \underline{\underline{npc@nc}}(x).\overline{\underline{\underline{b}}}\langle nc,x \rangle + \underline{\underline{exo@npc}}(x).\overline{\underline{\underline{b}}}\langle nc,x \rangle + \\
&\qquad \underline{\underline{exo@nc}}(x).\overline{\underline{\underline{b}}}\langle npc,x \rangle \\
\mathit{\Pi}_K &\equiv \overline{\underline{\underline{unfold@k_1}}} \mid \cdots \mid \overline{\underline{\underline{unfold@k_n}}}, \\
&\qquad K = \{k_1, \ldots, k_n\} \\
BCAST &\equiv\ !\, \underline{\underline{bcast}}(x,y,z).(\overline{\underline{\underline{x@y}}}\langle z \rangle.\overline{\underline{\underline{bcast}}}\langle x,y,z \rangle + \underline{\tau})
\end{aligned}
$$

Like for BioAmbients encoding, each operation of the original language is translated with a synchronisation followed by a sequence of high priority actions which manage the reorganisation of the tree structure and the unfolding of replicated processes involved in the computation. The presence of two distinct replication operators leads to two slightly different encodings which reflect the fact that systems are only provided of parent compartment, while branes present also their immediate compartment.

Also the encoding function $[\![\cdot]\!]^{\beta}$ enjoys the requirements discussed in section 3.1.

Theorem 2. *$[\![\cdot]\!]^{\beta}$ is a reasonable encoding (modulo structural congruence), that is: let P, P_1, P_2 and ρ_1, ρ_2 be respectively Brane systems and processes, let Q be a $\pi @$ process, then*

1. $[\![P_1 \circ P_2]\!]^{\beta} = [\![P_1]\!]^{\beta} \mid [\![P_2]\!]^{\beta}$,
   $[\![\rho_1 \mid \rho_2]\!]^{\beta} = [\![\rho_1]\!]^{\beta} \mid [\![\rho_2]\!]^{\beta}$
2. *for any permutation of the source names* θ, $[\![\theta(P)]\!]^{\beta} = \theta([\![P]\!]^{\beta})$;
3. $P \Downarrow$ *iff* $[\![P]\!]^{\beta} \Downarrow$, $P \Uparrow$ *iff* $[\![P]\!]^{\beta} \Uparrow$;
4. (a) *if* $P \to P_1$ *then* $\exists P_2 : P_2 \equiv P_1 \wedge [\![P]\!]^{\beta} \to^{*} [\![P_2]\!]^{\beta}$;
   (b) *if* $[\![P]\!]^{\beta} \to^{*} Q$ *then* $\exists P_1 : P \to^{*} P_1 \wedge Q \to^{*} [\![P_1]\!]^{\beta}$.

3.5 Encodings Comparison

Brane and BioAmbients are different for several aspects. Brane has a very simple syntax, provided with only three base operations, lacks any restriction and choice operator, there is no explicit name communication mechanism. BioAmbients is provided with elaborate, multi-level communication primitives in addition to compartment operations. But in [4] all these operators are considered as possible Brane extensions and their encoding in $\pi @$ would be exactly the same of the original BioAmbients operators. Therefore, the crucial difference is not intended to be in the syntax, but in the semantics: Brane compartment operations have been designed to preserve *bitonality*, a concept totally absent in BioAmbients, furthermore processes are thought to be *on the surface* of membranes, not *inside* ambients.

By translating both languages in $\pi @$, we are able to discern at first sight where processes are exactly placed and what are the differences in the dynamical rearrangement of the tree structure. The encoding of *phago*, *exo*, *pino*, *enter/accept*, *exit/expel*, *merge*± operations clearly shows that both kind of processes own the same information about their localisation in the tree, therefore the tree structure is very similar: the only difference is in the scoping of the names of their parent ambients. In fact, unlike the encoding of ambients, the encoding function of a Brane system P does not need the parameter c representing the immediate compartment of the process. This difference justifies the assumption that Brane processes are located *on* membranes. Bitonality simply arises in the order of the parameters given to the last term of the $TREE$ subprocess and in the choice of the names broadcasted and recursively passed to the encoding function (this is particulary evident in the $exo^{\perp}$ operation, where the name of the parent compartment *pc*, instead of the immediate compartment *c*, is the object of communication).

In conclusion, the two analised languages present much more common points than differences: concurrency, interleaving semantics, compartments with tree nesting and very similar structure for nodes, implicit multicast communications within compartment boundaries. If we consider all the extensions proposed in [4], the two formalisms may be considered close variants of the same language.

4 Conclusions and Future Work

We presented a new calculus, π@, designed to be a core language for analysing formalisms which model localisation and compartmentalisation. We showed π@ at work by a formal comparison of the reasonable encodings of BioAmbients and Brane languages, which permitted to clarify their structural similarities and semantical differences.

This is the first part of a wide analysis towards a disparate variety of biologically inspired languages, like [21,11,12]. The generality of π@ features allow to extend its application not only to process calculi, but also to formalisms not pertaining to concurrency theory, like P systems [18,25].

Finally, thanks to the strong affinity with π-Calculus, we plan to implement a stochastic version of π@ as a direct extension of the SPIM simulator [19], hence providing a platform on top of which it is possible to immediately execute all the embedded formalisms.

Acknowledgements. we would like to thank Nadia Busi for the precious suggestions and support.

References

1. F. de Boer, C. Palamidessi. Embedding as a Tool for Language Comparison. In *Information and Computation 108(1)*, 1994.
2. N. Busi, R. Gorrieri. On the computational power of Brane Calculi. *Third Workshop on Computational Methods in Systems Biology.* Edinburgh, 2005.
3. M. Carbone, S. Maffeis. On the Expressive Power of Polyadic Synchronisation in pi-calculus. In *Nordic Journal of Computing* 10(2): 70-98, 2003.
4. L. Cardelli. Brane Calculi - Interactions of Biological Membranes. In *Computational Methods in Systems Biology*, 2004.
5. L. Cardelli, A. D. Gordon. Mobile Ambients. In *Foundations of Software Science and Computation Structures: First International Conference, FOSSACS '98.* Springer-Verlag, 1998.
6. L. Cardelli, G. Păun. An universality result for a (mem)brane calculus based on mate/drip operations. In *International Journal of Foundations of Computer Science.* World Scientific Publishing Company, 2005.
7. D. Chiarugi, M. Curti, P. Degano, R. Marangoni. VICE: A VIrtual CEll. *Computational Methods in Systems Biology.* 2004

8. M. Curti, P. Degano, C. T. Baldari. Causal π-Calculus for Biochemical Modelling In *Computational Methods in Systems Biology.* 2003.
9. R. Cleaveland, G. Lüttgen, V. Natarajan. Priority in Process Algebra. In J.A. Bergstra, A. Ponse, S. A. Smolka, editors, *Handbook of Process Algebra*, Elsevier, 2001.
10. V. Danos, C. Laneve. Formal Molecular Biology. In *Theoretical Computer Science 325 (1)*, 2004.
11. V. Danos, S. Pradalier. Projective Brane-calculus. *Computational Methods in Systems Biology: Second International Workshop, CMSB?04, 3082:134?148.* 2004.
12. C. Laneve, F. Tarissan. A simple calculus for proteins and cells In *Proc. of the Workshop on Membrane Computing and Biologically Inspired Process Calculi (MeCBIC'06).* 2006.
13. P. Lecca, C. Priami, C. Laudanna, G. Constantin. Predicting cell adhesion probability via the biochemical stochastic pi-calculus. In *Symposium on Applied Computing.* 2004
14. R. Milner. The Polyadic π-Calculus: a Tutorial. In F. L. Hamer, W. Brauer and H. Schwichtenberg, editors, *Logic and Algebra of Specification.* Springer-Verlag, 1993.
15. R. Milner. Communicating and Mobile Systems: The π-Calculus. Cambridge University Press, 1999.
16. U. Nestmann, B.C. Pierce. Decoding Choice Encodings. In *Proc. of the 7th International Conference on Concurrency Theory (CONCUR '96).* 1996.
17. C. Palamidessi. Comparing the expressive power of the synchronous and the asynchronous π-calculi. *Mathematical Structures in Computer Science 13(5): 685-719.* 2003.
18. G. Păun. Computing with membranes. *Journal of Computer and System Sciences*, 61(1):108–143, 2000.
19. A. Phillips, L. Cardelli. A correct abstract machine for the stochastic pi-calculus. *Transactions on Computational Systems Biology.* 2005.
20. C. Priami. Stochastic π-calculus. *The Computer Journal 38 (7).* 1995.
21. C. Priami, P. Quaglia. Beta binders for biological interactions. In *Computational Methods in Systems Biology*, 2004.
22. A. Regev, W. Silverman, E. Shapiro. Representation and simulation of biochemical processes using the π-Calculus process algebra. In *Proc. of the Pacific Symposium on Biocomputing (PSB '01).* World Scientific Press, 2001.
23. C. Priami, A. Regev, W. Silverman, E. Shapiro. Application of a stochastic passing-name calculus to representation and simulation of molecular processes. *Information Processing Letters 80.* 2001.
24. A. Regev, E. Panina, W. Silverman, L. Cardelli, E. Shapiro. BioAmbients: an abstraction for biological compartments. *Theoretical Computer Science*, 2004.
25. C. Versari. Encoding catalytic P systems in π@. In *Proc. of the Workshop on Membrane Computing and Biologically Inspired Process Calculi (MeCBIC'06).* 2006.

A Rewriting Semantics for Type Inference

George Kuan, David MacQueen, and Robert Bruce Findler

University of Chicago
1100 East 58th Street, Chicago, IL 60637
{gkuan,dbm,robby}@cs.uchicago.edu

Abstract. When students first learn programming, they often rely on a simple operational model of a program's behavior to explain how particular features work. Because such models build on their earlier training in algebra, students find them intuitive, even obvious. Students learning type systems, however, have to confront an entirely different notation with a different semantics that many find difficult to understand.

In this work, we begin to build the theoretical underpinnings for treating type checking in a manner like the operational semantics of execution. Intuitively, each term is incrementally rewritten to its type. For example, each basic constant rewrites directly to its type and each lambda expression rewrites to an arrow type whose domain is the type of the lambda's formal parameter and whose range is the body of the lambda expression which, in turn, rewrites to the range type.

When students first learn programming, they often rely on a simple operational model of a program's behavior to explain how particular features work. Because such models build on their earlier training in algebra, students find them intuitive, even obvious. Students learning type systems, however, have to confront an entirely different notation with a different semantics that many find difficult to understand.

In this work, we begin to build the theoretical underpinnings for treating type checking in a manner like the operational semantics of execution. Intuitively, each term is incrementally rewritten to its type. For example, each basic constant rewrites directly to its type and each lambda expression rewrites to an arrow type whose domain is the type of the lambda's formal parameter and whose range is the body of the lambda expression which, in turn, rewrites to the range type.

When students first learn programming, they often rely on a simple operational model of a program's behavior to explain how particular features work. Because such models build on their earlier training in algebra, students find them intuitive, even obvious. Students learning type systems, however, have to confront an entirely different notation with a different semantics that many find difficult to understand.

In this work, we begin to build the theoretical underpinnings for treating type checking in a manner like the operational semantics of execution. Intuitively, each term is incrementally rewritten to its type. For example, each basic constant rewrites directly to its type and each lambda expression rewrites to an arrow type whose domain is the type of the lambda's formal parameter and whose range is the body of the lambda expression which, in turn, rewrites to the range type.

When students first learn programming, they often rely on a simple operational model of a program's behavior to explain how particular features work. Because such

R. De Nicola (Ed.): ESOP 2007, LNCS 4421, pp. 426–440, 2007.

models build on their earlier training in algebra, students find them intuitive, even obvious. Students learning type systems, however, have to confront an entirely different notation with a different semantics that many find difficult to understand.

In this work, we begin to build the theoretical underpinnings for treating type checking in a manner like the operational semantics of execution. Intuitively, each term is incrementally rewritten to its type. For example, each basic constant rewrites directly to its type and each lambda expression rewrites to an arrow type whose domain is the type of the lambda's formal parameter and whose range is the body of the lambda expression which, in turn, rewrites to the range type.

When students first learn programming, they often rely on a simple operational model of a program's behavior to explain how particular features work. Because such models build on their earlier training in algebra, students find them intuitive, even obvious. Students learning type systems, however, have to confront an entirely different notation with a different semantics that many find difficult to understand.

In this work, we begin to build the theoretical underpinnings for treating type checking in a manner like the operational semantics of execution. Intuitively, each term is incrementally rewritten to its type. For example, each basic constant rewrites directly to its type and each lambda expression rewrites to an arrow type whose domain is the type of the lambda's formal parameter and whose range is the body of the lambda expression which, in turn, rewrites to the range type.

When students first learn programming, they often rely on a simple operational model of a program's behavior to explain how particular features work. Because such models build on their earlier training in algebra, students find them intuitive, even obvious. Students learning type systems, however, have to confront an entirely different notation with a different semantics that many find difficult to understand.

In this work, we begin to build the theoretical underpinnings for treating type checking in a manner like the operational semantics of execution. Intuitively, each term is incrementally rewritten to its type. For example, each basic constant rewrites directly to its type and each lambda expression rewrites to an arrow type whose domain is the type of the lambda's formal parameter and whose range is the body of the lambda expression which, in turn, rewrites to the range type.

When students first learn programming, they often rely on a simple operational model of a program's behavior to explain how particular features work. Because such models build on their earlier training in algebra, students find them intuitive, even obvious. Students learning type systems, however, have to confront an entirely different notation with a different semantics that many find difficult to understand.

In this work, we begin to build the theoretical underpinnings for treating type checking in a manner like the operational semantics of execution. Intuitively, each term is incrementally rewritten to its type. For example, each basic constant rewrites directly to its type and each lambda expression rewrites to an arrow type whose domain is the type of the lambda's formal parameter and whose range is the body of the lambda expression which, in turn, rewrites to the range type.

When students first learn programming, they often rely on a simple operational model of a program's behavior to explain how particular features work. Because such models build on their earlier training in algebra, students find them intuitive, even ob-

vious. Students learning type systems, however, have to confront an entirely different notation with a different semantics that many find difficult to understand.

In this work, we begin to build the theoretical underpinnings for treating type checking in a manner like the operational semantics of execution. Intuitively, each term is incrementally rewritten to its type. For example, each basic constant rewrites directly to its type and each lambda expression rewrites to an arrow type whose domain is the type of the lambda's formal parameter and whose range is the body of the lambda expression which, in turn, rewrites to the range type.

When students first learn programming, they often rely on a simple operational model of a program's behavior to explain how particular features work. Because such models build on their earlier training in algebra, students find them intuitive, even obvious. Students learning type systems, however, have to confront an entirely different notation with a different semantics that many find difficult to understand.

In this work, we begin to build the theoretical underpinnings for treating type checking in a manner like the operational semantics of execution. Intuitively, each term is incrementally rewritten to its type. For example, each basic constant rewrites directly to its type and each lambda expression rewrites to an arrow type whose domain is the type of the lambda's formal parameter and whose range is the body of the lambda expression which, in turn, rewrites to the range type.

When students first learn programming, they often rely on a simple operational model of a program's behavior to explain how particular features work. Because such models build on their earlier training in algebra, students find them intuitive, even obvious. Students learning type systems, however, have to confront an entirely different notation with a different semantics that many find difficult to understand.

In this work, we begin to build the theoretical underpinnings for treating type checking in a manner like the operational semantics of execution. Intuitively, each term is incrementally rewritten to its type. For example, each basic constant rewrites directly to its type and each lambda expression rewrites to an arrow type whose domain is the type of the lambda's formal parameter and whose range is the body of the lambda expression which, in turn, rewrites to the range type.

When students first learn programming, they often rely on a simple operational model of a program's behavior to explain how particular features work. Because such models build on their earlier training in algebra, students find them intuitive, even obvious. Students learning type systems, however, have to confront an entirely different notation with a different semantics that many find difficult to understand.

In this work, we begin to build the theoretical underpinnings for treating type checking in a manner like the operational semantics of execution. Intuitively, each term is incrementally rewritten to its type. For example, each basic constant rewrites directly to its type and each lambda expression rewrites to an arrow type whose domain is the type of the lambda's formal parameter and whose range is the body of the lambda expression which, in turn, rewrites to the range type.

When students first learn programming, they often rely on a simple operational model of a program's behavior to explain how particular features work. Because such models build on their earlier training in algebra, students find them intuitive, even ob-

vious. Students learning type systems, however, have to confront an entirely different notation with a different semantics that many find difficult to understand.

In this work, we begin to build the theoretical underpinnings for treating type checking in a manner like the operational semantics of execution. Intuitively, each term is incrementally rewritten to its type. For example, each basic constant rewrites directly to its type and each lambda expression rewrites to an arrow type whose domain is the type of the lambda's formal parameter and whose range is the body of the lambda expression which, in turn, rewrites to the range type.

When students first learn programming, they often rely on a simple operational model of a program's behavior to explain how particular features work. Because such models build on their earlier training in algebra, students find them intuitive, even obvious. Students learning type systems, however, have to confront an entirely different notation with a different semantics that many find difficult to understand.

In this work, we begin to build the theoretical underpinnings for treating type checking in a manner like the operational semantics of execution. Intuitively, each term is incrementally rewritten to its type. For example, each basic constant rewrites directly to its type and each lambda expression rewrites to an arrow type whose domain is the type of the lambda's formal parameter and whose range is the body of the lambda expression which, in turn, rewrites to the range type.

When students first learn programming, they often rely on a simple operational model of a program's behavior to explain how particular features work. Because such models build on their earlier training in algebra, students find them intuitive, even obvious. Students learning type systems, however, have to confront an entirely different notation with a different semantics that many find difficult to understand.

In this work, we begin to build the theoretical underpinnings for treating type checking in a manner like the operational semantics of execution. Intuitively, each term is incrementally rewritten to its type. For example, each basic constant rewrites directly to its type and each lambda expression rewrites to an arrow type whose domain is the type of the lambda's formal parameter and whose range is the body of the lambda expression which, in turn, rewrites to the range type.

When students first learn programming, they often rely on a simple operational model of a program's behavior to explain how particular features work. Because such models build on their earlier training in algebra, students find them intuitive, even ob-

vious. Students learning type systems, however, have to confront an entirely different notation with a different semantics that many find difficult to understand.

In this work, we begin to build the theoretical underpinnings for treating type checking in a manner like the operational semantics of execution. Intuitively, each term is incrementally rewritten to its type. For example, each basic constant rewrites directly to its type and each lambda expression rewrites to an arrow type whose domain is the type of the lambda's formal parameter and whose range is the body of the lambda expression which, in turn, rewrites to the range type.

When students first learn programming, they often rely on a simple operational model of a program's behavior to explain how particular features work. Because such models build on their earlier training in algebra, students find them intuitive, even obvious. Students learning type systems, however, have to confront an entirely different notation with a different semantics that many find difficult to understand.

In this work, we begin to build the theoretical underpinnings for treating type checking in a manner like the operational semantics of execution. Intuitively, each term is incrementally rewritten to its type. For example, each basic constant rewrites directly to its type and each lambda expression rewrites to an arrow type whose domain is the type of the lambda's formal parameter and whose range is the body of the lambda expression which, in turn, rewrites to the range type.

When students first learn programming, they often rely on a simple operational model of a program's behavior to explain how particular features work. Because such models build on their earlier training in algebra, students find them intuitive, even obvious. Students learning type systems, however, have to confront an entirely different notation with a different semantics that many find difficult to understand.

In this work, we begin to build the theoretical underpinnings for treating type checking in a manner like the operational semantics of execution. Intuitively, each term is incrementally rewritten to its type. For example, each basic constant rewrites directly to its type and each lambda expression rewrites to an arrow type whose domain is the type of the lambda's formal parameter and whose range is the body of the lambda expression which, in turn, rewrites to the range type.

When students first learn programming, they often rely on a simple operational model of a program's behavior to explain how particular features work. Because such models build on their earlier training in algebra, students find them intuitive, even obvious. Students learning type systems, however, have to confront an entirely different notation with a different semantics that many find difficult to understand.

In this work, we begin to build the theoretical underpinnings for treating type checking in a manner like the operational semantics of execution. Intuitively, each term is incrementally rewritten to its type. For example, each basic constant rewrites directly to its type and each lambda expression rewrites to an arrow type whose domain is the type of the lambda's formal parameter and whose range is the body of the lambda expression which, in turn, rewrites to the range type.

When students first learn programming, they often rely on a simple operational model of a program's behavior to explain how particular features work. Because such models build on their earlier training in algebra, students find them intuitive, even ob-

vious. Students learning type systems, however, have to confront an entirely different notation with a different semantics that many find difficult to understand.

In this work, we begin to build the theoretical underpinnings for treating type checking in a manner like the operational semantics of execution. Intuitively, each term is incrementally rewritten to its type. For example, each basic constant rewrites directly to its type and each lambda expression rewrites to an arrow type whose domain is the type of the lambda's formal parameter and whose range is the body of the lambda expression which, in turn, rewrites to the range type.

When students first learn programming, they often rely on a simple operational model of a program's behavior to explain how particular features work. Because such models build on their earlier training in algebra, students find them intuitive, even obvious. Students learning type systems, however, have to confront an entirely different notation with a different semantics that many find difficult to understand.

In this work, we begin to build the theoretical underpinnings for treating type checking in a manner like the operational semantics of execution. Intuitively, each term is incrementally rewritten to its type. For example, each basic constant rewrites directly to its type and each lambda expression rewrites to an arrow type whose domain is the type of the lambda's formal parameter and whose range is the body of the lambda expression which, in turn, rewrites to the range type.

When students first learn programming, they often rely on a simple operational model of a program's behavior to explain how particular features work. Because such models build on their earlier training in algebra, students find them intuitive, even obvious. Students learning type systems, however, have to confront an entirely different notation with a different semantics that many find difficult to understand.

In this work, we begin to build the theoretical underpinnings for treating type checking in a manner like the operational semantics of execution. Intuitively, each term is incrementally rewritten to its type. For example, each basic constant rewrites directly to its type and each lambda expression rewrites to an arrow type whose domain is the type of the lambda's formal parameter and whose range is the body of the lambda expression which, in turn, rewrites to the range type.

When students first learn programming, they often rely on a simple operational model of a program's behavior to explain how particular features work. Because such models build on their earlier training in algebra, students find them intuitive, even obvious. Students learning type systems, however, have to confront an entirely different notation with a different semantics that many find difficult to understand.

In this work, we begin to build the theoretical underpinnings for treating type checking in a manner like the operational semantics of execution. Intuitively, each term is incrementally rewritten to its type. For example, each basic constant rewrites directly to its type and each lambda expression rewrites to an arrow type whose domain is the type of the lambda's formal parameter and whose range is the body of the lambda expression which, in turn, rewrites to the range type.

When students first learn programming, they often rely on a simple operational model of a program's behavior to explain how particular features work. Because such models build on their earlier training in algebra, students find them intuitive, even ob-

vious. Students learning type systems, however, have to confront an entirely different notation with a different semantics that many find difficult to understand.

In this work, we begin to build the theoretical underpinnings for treating type checking in a manner like the operational semantics of execution. Intuitively, each term is incrementally rewritten to its type. For example, each basic constant rewrites directly to its type and each lambda expression rewrites to an arrow type whose domain is the type of the lambda's formal parameter and whose range is the body of the lambda expression which, in turn, rewrites to the range type.

When students first learn programming, they often rely on a simple operational model of a program's behavior to explain how particular features work. Because such models build on their earlier training in algebra, students find them intuitive, even obvious. Students learning type systems, however, have to confront an entirely different notation with a different semantics that many find difficult to understand.

In this work, we begin to build the theoretical underpinnings for treating type checking in a manner like the operational semantics of execution. Intuitively, each term is incrementally rewritten to its type. For example, each basic constant rewrites directly to its type and each lambda expression rewrites to an arrow type whose domain is the type of the lambda's formal parameter and whose range is the body of the lambda expression which, in turn, rewrites to the range type.

When students first learn programming, they often rely on a simple operational model of a program's behavior to explain how particular features work. Because such models build on their earlier training in algebra, students find them intuitive, even obvious. Students learning type systems, however, have to confront an entirely different notation with a different semantics that many find difficult to understand.

In this work, we begin to build the theoretical underpinnings for treating type checking in a manner like the operational semantics of execution. Intuitively, each term is incrementally rewritten to its type. For example, each basic constant rewrites directly to its type and each lambda expression rewrites to an arrow type whose domain is the type of the lambda's formal parameter and whose range is the body of the lambda expression which, in turn, rewrites to the range type.

When students first learn programming, they often rely on a simple operational model of a program's behavior to explain how particular features work. Because such models build on their earlier training in algebra, students find them intuitive, even ob-

vious. Students learning type systems, however, have to confront an entirely different notation with a different semantics that many find difficult to understand.

In this work, we begin to build the theoretical underpinnings for treating type checking in a manner like the operational semantics of execution. Intuitively, each term is incrementally rewritten to its type. For example, each basic constant rewrites directly to its type and each lambda expression rewrites to an arrow type whose domain is the type of the lambda's formal parameter and whose range is the body of the lambda expression which, in turn, rewrites to the range type.

When students first learn programming, they often rely on a simple operational model of a program's behavior to explain how particular features work. Because such models build on their earlier training in algebra, students find them intuitive, even obvious. Students learning type systems, however, have to confront an entirely different notation with a different semantics that many find difficult to understand.

In this work, we begin to build the theoretical underpinnings for treating type checking in a manner like the operational semantics of execution. Intuitively, each term is incrementally rewritten to its type. For example, each basic constant rewrites directly to its type and each lambda expression rewrites to an arrow type whose domain is the type of the lambda's formal parameter and whose range is the body of the lambda expression which, in turn, rewrites to the range type.

When students first learn programming, they often rely on a simple operational model of a program's behavior to explain how particular features work. Because such models build on their earlier training in algebra, students find them intuitive, even obvious. Students learning type systems, however, have to confront an entirely different notation with a different semantics that many find difficult to understand.

In this work, we begin to build the theoretical underpinnings for treating type checking in a manner like the operational semantics of execution. Intuitively, each term is incrementally rewritten to its type. For example, each basic constant rewrites directly to its type and each lambda expression rewrites to an arrow type whose domain is the type of the lambda's formal parameter and whose range is the body of the lambda expression which, in turn, rewrites to the range type.

When students first learn programming, they often rely on a simple operational model of a program's behavior to explain how particular features work. Because such models build on their earlier training in algebra, students find them intuitive, even obvious. Students learning type systems, however, have to confront an entirely different notation with a different semantics that many find difficult to understand.

In this work, we begin to build the theoretical underpinnings for treating type checking in a manner like the operational semantics of execution. Intuitively, each term is incrementally rewritten to its type. For example, each basic constant rewrites directly to its type and each lambda expression rewrites to an arrow type whose domain is the type of the lambda's formal parameter and whose range is the body of the lambda expression which, in turn, rewrites to the range type.

When students first learn programming, they often rely on a simple operational model of a program's behavior to explain how particular features work. Because such models build on their earlier training in algebra, students find them intuitive, even ob-

vious. Students learning type systems, however, have to confront an entirely different notation with a different semantics that many find difficult to understand.

In this work, we begin to build the theoretical underpinnings for treating type checking in a manner like the operational semantics of execution. Intuitively, each term is incrementally rewritten to its type. For example, each basic constant rewrites directly to its type and each lambda expression rewrites to an arrow type whose domain is the type of the lambda's formal parameter and whose range is the body of the lambda expression which, in turn, rewrites to the range type.

When students first learn programming, they often rely on a simple operational model of a program's behavior to explain how particular features work. Because such models build on their earlier training in algebra, students find them intuitive, even obvious. Students learning type systems, however, have to confront an entirely different notation with a different semantics that many find difficult to understand.

In this work, we begin to build the theoretical underpinnings for treating type checking in a manner like the operational semantics of execution. Intuitively, each term is incrementally rewritten to its type. For example, each basic constant rewrites directly to its type and each lambda expression rewrites to an arrow type whose domain is the type of the lambda's formal parameter and whose range is the body of the lambda expression which, in turn, rewrites to the range type.

When students first learn programming, they often rely on a simple operational model of a program's behavior to explain how particular features work. Because such models build on their earlier training in algebra, students find them intuitive, even obvious. Students learning type systems, however, have to confront an entirely different notation with a different semantics that many find difficult to understand.

In this work, we begin to build the theoretical underpinnings for treating type checking in a manner like the operational semantics of execution. Intuitively, each term is incrementally rewritten to its type. For example, each basic constant rewrites directly to its type and each lambda expression rewrites to an arrow type whose domain is the type of the lambda's formal parameter and whose range is the body of the lambda expression which, in turn, rewrites to the range type.

When students first learn programming, they often rely on a simple operational model of a program's behavior to explain how particular features work. Because such models build on their earlier training in algebra, students find them intuitive, even obvious. Students learning type systems, however, have to confront an entirely different notation with a different semantics that many find difficult to understand.

In this work, we begin to build the theoretical underpinnings for treating type checking in a manner like the operational semantics of execution. Intuitively, each term is incrementally rewritten to its type. For example, each basic constant rewrites directly to its type and each lambda expression rewrites to an arrow type whose domain is the type of the lambda's formal parameter and whose range is the body of the lambda expression which, in turn, rewrites to the range type.

When students first learn programming, they often rely on a simple operational model of a program's behavior to explain how particular features work. Because such models build on their earlier training in algebra, students find them intuitive, even ob-

vious. Students learning type systems, however, have to confront an entirely different notation with a different semantics that many find difficult to understand.

In this work, we begin to build the theoretical underpinnings for treating type checking in a manner like the operational semantics of execution. Intuitively, each term is incrementally rewritten to its type. For example, each basic constant rewrites directly to its type and each lambda expression rewrites to an arrow type whose domain is the type of the lambda's formal parameter and whose range is the body of the lambda expression which, in turn, rewrites to the range type.

When students first learn programming, they often rely on a simple operational model of a program's behavior to explain how particular features work. Because such models build on their earlier training in algebra, students find them intuitive, even obvious. Students learning type systems, however, have to confront an entirely different notation with a different semantics that many find difficult to understand.

In this work, we begin to build the theoretical underpinnings for treating type checking in a manner like the operational semantics of execution. Intuitively, each term is incrementally rewritten to its type. For example, each basic constant rewrites directly to its type and each lambda expression rewrites to an arrow type whose domain is the type of the lambda's formal parameter and whose range is the body of the lambda expression which, in turn, rewrites to the range type.

When students first learn programming, they often rely on a simple operational model of a program's behavior to explain how particular features work. Because such models build on their earlier training in algebra, students find them intuitive, even obvious. Students learning type systems, however, have to confront an entirely different notation with a different semantics that many find difficult to understand.

In this work, we begin to build the theoretical underpinnings for treating type checking in a manner like the operational semantics of execution. Intuitively, each term is incrementally rewritten to its type. For example, each basic constant rewrites directly to its type and each lambda expression rewrites to an arrow type whose domain is the type of the lambda's formal parameter and whose range is the body of the lambda expression which, in turn, rewrites to the range type.

When students first learn programming, they often rely on a simple operational model of a program's behavior to explain how particular features work. Because such models build on their earlier training in algebra, students find them intuitive, even obvious. Students learning type systems, however, have to confront an entirely different notation with a different semantics that many find difficult to understand.

In this work, we begin to build the theoretical underpinnings for treating type checking in a manner like the operational semantics of execution. Intuitively, each term is incrementally rewritten to its type. For example, each basic constant rewrites directly to its type and each lambda expression rewrites to an arrow type whose domain is the type of the lambda's formal parameter and whose range is the body of the lambda expression which, in turn, rewrites to the range type.

When students first learn programming, they often rely on a simple operational model of a program's behavior to explain how particular features work. Because such models build on their earlier training in algebra, students find them intuitive, even ob-

vious. Students learning type systems, however, have to confront an entirely different notation with a different semantics that many find difficult to understand.

In this work, we begin to build the theoretical underpinnings for treating type checking in a manner like the operational semantics of execution. Intuitively, each term is incrementally rewritten to its type. For example, each basic constant rewrites directly to its type and each lambda expression rewrites to an arrow type whose domain is the type of the lambda's formal parameter and whose range is the body of the lambda expression which, in turn, rewrites to the range type.

When students first learn programming, they often rely on a simple operational model of a program's behavior to explain how particular features work. Because such models build on their earlier training in algebra, students find them intuitive, even obvious. Students learning type systems, however, have to confront an entirely different notation with a different semantics that many find difficult to understand.

In this work, we begin to build the theoretical underpinnings for treating type checking in a manner like the operational semantics of execution. Intuitively, each term is incrementally rewritten to its type. For example, each basic constant rewrites directly to its type and each lambda expression rewrites to an arrow type whose domain is the type of the lambda's formal parameter and whose range is the body of the lambda expression which, in turn, rewrites to the range type.

When students first learn programming, they often rely on a simple operational model of a program's behavior to explain how particular features work. Because such models build on their earlier training in algebra, students find them intuitive, even obvious. Students learning type systems, however, have to confront an entirely different notation with a different semantics that many find difficult to understand.

In this work, we begin to build the theoretical underpinnings for treating type checking in a manner like the operational semantics of execution. Intuitively, each term is incrementally rewritten to its type. For example, each basic constant rewrites directly to its type and each lambda expression rewrites to an arrow type whose domain is the type of the lambda's formal parameter and whose range is the body of the lambda expression which, in turn, rewrites to the range type.

When students first learn programming, they often rely on a simple operational model of a program's behavior to explain how particular features work. Because such models build on their earlier training in algebra, students find them intuitive, even obvious. Students learning type systems, however, have to confront an entirely different notation with a different semantics that many find difficult to understand.

In this work, we begin to build the theoretical underpinnings for treating type checking in a manner like the operational semantics of execution. Intuitively, each term is incrementally rewritten to its type. For example, each basic constant rewrites directly to its type and each lambda expression rewrites to an arrow type whose domain is the type of the lambda's formal parameter and whose range is the body of the lambda expression which, in turn, rewrites to the range type.

When students first learn programming, they often rely on a simple operational model of a program's behavior to explain how particular features work. Because such models build on their earlier training in algebra, students find them intuitive, even ob-

vious. Students learning type systems, however, have to confront an entirely different notation with a different semantics that many find difficult to understand.

In this work, we begin to build the theoretical underpinnings for treating type checking in a manner like the operational semantics of execution. Intuitively, each term is incrementally rewritten to its type. For example, each basic constant rewrites directly to its type and each lambda expression rewrites to an arrow type whose domain is the type of the lambda's formal parameter and whose range is the body of the lambda expression which, in turn, rewrites to the range type.

When students first learn programming, they often rely on a simple operational model of a program's behavior to explain how particular features work. Because such models build on their earlier training in algebra, students find them intuitive, even obvious. Students learning type systems, however, have to confront an entirely different notation with a different semantics that many find difficult to understand.

In this work, we begin to build the theoretical underpinnings for treating type checking in a manner like the operational semantics of execution. Intuitively, each term is incrementally rewritten to its type. For example, each basic constant rewrites directly to its type and each lambda expression rewrites to an arrow type whose domain is the type of the lambda's formal parameter and whose range is the body of the lambda expression which, in turn, rewrites to the range type.

When students first learn programming, they often rely on a simple operational model of a program's behavior to explain how particular features work. Because such models build on their earlier training in algebra, students find them intuitive, even obvious. Students learning type systems, however, have to confront an entirely different notation with a different semantics that many find difficult to understand.

In this work, we begin to build the theoretical underpinnings for treating type checking in a manner like the operational semantics of execution. Intuitively, each term is incrementally rewritten to its type. For example, each basic constant rewrites directly to its type and each lambda expression rewrites to an arrow type whose domain is the type of the lambda's formal parameter and whose range is the body of the lambda expression which, in turn, rewrites to the range type.

When students first learn programming, they often rely on a simple operational model of a program's behavior to explain how particular features work. Because such models build on their earlier training in algebra, students find them intuitive, even obvious. Students learning type systems, however, have to confront an entirely different notation with a different semantics that many find difficult to understand.

In this work, we begin to build the theoretical underpinnings for treating type checking in a manner like the operational semantics of execution. Intuitively, each term is incrementally rewritten to its type. For example, each basic constant rewrites directly to its type and each lambda expression rewrites to an arrow type whose domain is the type of the lambda's formal parameter and whose range is the body of the lambda expression which, in turn, rewrites to the range type.

When students first learn programming, they often rely on a simple operational model of a program's behavior to explain how particular features work. Because such models build on their earlier training in algebra, students find them intuitive, even ob-

vious. Students learning type systems, however, have to confront an entirely different notation with a different semantics that many find difficult to understand.

In this work, we begin to build the theoretical underpinnings for treating type checking in a manner like the operational semantics of execution. Intuitively, each term is incrementally rewritten to its type. For example, each basic constant rewrites directly to its type and each lambda expression rewrites to an arrow type whose domain is the type of the lambda's formal parameter and whose range is the body of the lambda expression which, in turn, rewrites to the range type.

When students first learn programming, they often rely on a simple operational model of a program's behavior to explain how particular features work. Because such models build on their earlier training in algebra, students find them intuitive, even obvious. Students learning type systems, however, have to confront an entirely different notation with a different semantics that many find difficult to understand.

In this work, we begin to build the theoretical underpinnings for treating type checking in a manner like the operational semantics of execution. Intuitively, each term is incrementally rewritten to its type. For example, each basic constant rewrites directly to its type and each lambda expression rewrites to an arrow type whose domain is the type of the lambda's formal parameter and whose range is the body of the lambda expression which, in turn, rewrites to the range type.

When students first learn programming, they often rely on a simple operational model of a program's behavior to explain how particular features work. Because such models build on their earlier training in algebra, students find them intuitive, even obvious. Students learning type systems, however, have to confront an entirely different notation with a different semantics that many find difficult to understand.

In this work, we begin to build the theoretical underpinnings for treating type checking in a manner like the operational semantics of execution. Intuitively, each term is incrementally rewritten to its type. For example, each basic constant rewrites directly to its type and each lambda expression rewrites to an arrow type whose domain is the type of the lambda's formal parameter and whose range is the body of the lambda expression which, in turn, rewrites to the range type.

When students first learn programming, they often rely on a simple operational model of a program's behavior to explain how particular features work. Because such models build on their earlier training in algebra, students find them intuitive, even obvious. Students learning type systems, however, have to confront an entirely different notation with a different semantics that many find difficult to understand.

In this work, we begin to build the theoretical underpinnings for treating type checking in a manner like the operational semantics of execution. Intuitively, each term is incrementally rewritten to its type. For example, each basic constant rewrites directly to its type and each lambda expression rewrites to an arrow type whose domain is the type of the lambda's formal parameter and whose range is the body of the lambda expression which, in turn, rewrites to the range type.

When students first learn programming, they often rely on a simple operational model of a program's behavior to explain how particular features work. Because such models build on their earlier training in algebra, students find them intuitive, even ob-

vious. Students learning type systems, however, have to confront an entirely different notation with a different semantics that many find difficult to understand.

In this work, we begin to build the theoretical underpinnings for treating type checking in a manner like the operational semantics of execution. Intuitively, each term is incrementally rewritten to its type. For example, each basic constant rewrites directly to its type and each lambda expression rewrites to an arrow type whose domain is the type of the lambda's formal parameter and whose range is the body of the lambda expression which, in turn, rewrites to the range type.

When students first learn programming, they often rely on a simple operational model of a program's behavior to explain how particular features work. Because such models build on their earlier training in algebra, students find them intuitive, even obvious. Students learning type systems, however, have to confront an entirely different notation with a different semantics that many find difficult to understand.

In this work, we begin to build the theoretical underpinnings for treating type checking in a manner like the operational semantics of execution. Intuitively, each term is incrementally rewritten to its type. For example, each basic constant rewrites directly to its type and each lambda expression rewrites to an arrow type whose domain is the type of the lambda's formal parameter and whose range is the body of the lambda expression which, in turn, rewrites to the range type.

When students first learn programming, they often rely on a simple operational model of a program's behavior to explain how particular features work. Because such models build on their earlier training in algebra, students find them intuitive, even obvious. Students learning type systems, however, have to confront an entirely different notation with a different semantics that many find difficult to understand.

In this work, we begin to build the theoretical underpinnings for treating type checking in a manner like the operational semantics of execution. Intuitively, each term is incrementally rewritten to its type. For example, each basic constant rewrites directly to its type and each lambda expression rewrites to an arrow type whose domain is the type of the lambda's formal parameter and whose range is the body of the lambda expression which, in turn, rewrites to the range type.

When students first learn programming, they often rely on a simple operational model of a program's behavior to explain how particular features work. Because such models build on their earlier training in algebra, students find them intuitive, even obvious. Students learning type systems, however, have to confront an entirely different notation with a different semantics that many find difficult to understand.

In this work, we begin to build the theoretical underpinnings for treating type checking in a manner like the operational semantics of execution. Intuitively, each term is incrementally rewritten to its type. For example, each basic constant rewrites directly to its type and each lambda expression rewrites to an arrow type whose domain is the type of the lambda's formal parameter and whose range is the body of the lambda expression which, in turn, rewrites to the range type.

When students first learn programming, they often rely on a simple operational model of a program's behavior to explain how particular features work. Because such models build on their earlier training in algebra, students find them intuitive, even ob-

vious. Students learning type systems, however, have to confront an entirely different notation with a different semantics that many find difficult to understand.

In this work, we begin to build the theoretical underpinnings for treating type checking in a manner like the operational semantics of execution. Intuitively, each term is incrementally rewritten to its type. For example, each basic constant rewrites directly to its type and each lambda expression rewrites to an arrow type whose domain is the type of the lambda's formal parameter and whose range is the body of the lambda expression which, in turn, rewrites to the range type.

Principal Type Schemes for Modular Programs

Derek Dreyer and Matthias Blume

Toyota Technological Institute at Chicago
{dreyer,blume}@tti-c.org

Abstract. Two of the most prominent features of ML are its expressive module system and its support for Damas-Milner type inference. However, while the foundations of both these features have been studied extensively, their interaction has never received a proper type-theoretic treatment. One consequence is that both the official Definition and the alternative Harper-Stone semantics of Standard ML are difficult to implement correctly. To bolster this claim, we offer a series of short example programs on which no existing SML typechecker follows the behavior prescribed by either formal definition. It is unclear how to amend the implementations to match the definitions or vice versa. Instead, we propose a way of defining how type inference interacts with modules that is more liberal than any existing definition or implementation of SML and, moreover, admits a provably sound and complete typechecking algorithm via a straightforward generalization of Algorithm $\mathcal{W}$. In addition to being conceptually simple, our solution exhibits a novel hybrid of the Definition and Harper-Stone semantics of SML, and demonstrates the broader relevance of some type-theoretic techniques developed recently in the study of recursive modules.

1 Introduction

The standard way of defining the static semantics of languages with type inference is to give a set of *declarative* Curry-style typing rules that assign types to untyped terms. Since these rules are typically written in a nondeterministic fashion, it is not *prima facie* decidable whether a term can be assigned a type. The most canonical example of such a type system is that of Hindley and Milner (HM) [15], which is at the core of higher-order, typed languages like ML and Haskell. For HM, there exists a well-known type inference algorithm, Damas and Milner's Algorithm $\mathcal{W}$ [1], that is sound and complete with respect to it. Soundness means that if type inference succeeds, it returns a valid typing. Completeness means that if a valid typing exists, then type inference will succeed. To achieve completeness, Algorithm $\mathcal{W}$ relies on the fact that, in HM, all well-typed terms e have a *principal type scheme*, *i.e.*, a type τ that is in some sense more general than any other type that e could be assigned.

The Definition of Standard ML [16] (SML for short) provides a declarative semantics of the language, including both the core language and the module system. It is often assumed that this combination can be typechecked effectively via a straightforward extension of Algorithm $\mathcal{W}$. In this paper we observe that

R. De Nicola (Ed.): ESOP 2007, LNCS 4421, pp. 441–457, 2007.

```
functor F (X: sig type t end) = struct
    val f = id id
end
structure A = F (struct type t = int end)
structure B = F (struct type t = bool end)
```

Fig. 1. Common preamble for examples (a) and (b)

```
val _ = A.f 10
val _ = B.f false
```

Fig. 2. Example (a)

```
val _ = A.f 10
val _ = B.f "dude"
```

Fig. 3. Example (b)

this is not so. As we will explain, all existing implementations of SML differ from the Definition—and from one another—in rather subtle ways when it comes to the interaction of type inference and modules. In particular, this occurs when the *value restriction* forces certain module-level **val**-bindings to be monomorphic.

The value restriction [11,22], which is important for ensuring type safety, limits the set of **val**-bindings that may be assigned polymorphic types to those whose right-hand sides are *syntactic values*, i.e., terms that are syntactically known to be free of effects. For example, consider

```
val f = id id
```

where `id` is the identity function **fn** `x => x`. According to the declarative semantics of SML, `f` can be assigned any (monomorphic) type $\tau \to \tau$ where τ is a type that is well-formed at the point where `f` is defined. However, it *cannot* be given the polymorphic type $\forall\alpha.\alpha \to \alpha$ because `id id` is not a syntactic value.

Example (a). The situation changes if `f` is defined in the body of a functor. Consider the code in Figures 1 and 2. The value restriction forces the type of `f` in functor `F` to be monomorphic. Since `A` is an instantiation of `F`, and since `A.f` is applied to an integer, one might expect that the type of `f` must be `int` $\to$ `int`, in which case the application of `B.f` to `false` would be ill-typed. In fact, though, there exists another solution: `f` can also be given the type `X.t` $\to$ `X.t`, in which case the type of `A.f` is `int` $\to$ `int`, the type of `B.f` is `bool` $\to$ `bool`, and the program typechecks. In essence, by appearing in the body of a functor with an abstract type argument, `f` can turn into an (explicit) polymorphic function.

This example has profound implications for the use of Damas-Milner type inference in typechecking modular programs. When `f` is typechecked by Algorithm $\mathcal{W}$, the algorithm returns a principal type scheme $\boldsymbol{\alpha} \to \boldsymbol{\alpha}$, where $\boldsymbol{\alpha}$ is a *unification variable* (u-var) that may be instantiated to a particular type later on. However, when the typechecker leaves the body of functor `F`, the u-var $\boldsymbol{\alpha}$ must become a Skolem function parameterized over the abstract type components of `F`'s argument, in this case the type `t`. When `A.f` is applied to `int`, we learn *not* that $\boldsymbol{\alpha}$ = `int`, but rather that $\boldsymbol{\alpha}$(`int`) = `int`. Similarly, when `B.f` is applied to `false`, we learn that α(`bool`) = `bool`. Together, these two equations determine that the only possible instantiation of α is the identity function λ`t.t`.

In general, finding solutions to these kinds of constraints requires a form of higher-order unification. While it is possible that the fragment of higher-order unification required is decidable, no SML typechecker implements it. As a result, no existing SML implementation accepts Example (a)... that is, except MLton.

1.1 Generalized Functor Signatures

The MLton compiler for SML takes an unusual approach to the typechecking of programs with functors. Although it is well-known that MLton is a whole-program compiler that achieves great performance gains through defunctorization, it is perhaps less well-known that MLton performs defunctorization *during typechecking*. That is, after typechecking a functor such as `F` in Example (a), MLton inlines the definition of `F` at every point where `F` is applied before proceeding to typecheck the rest of the program. This has the effect that the definition of `F` is re-typechecked at every application, and each copy of `F` may be assigned a different signature. In the case of Example (a), this means that in the first copy of `F`, its binding for `f` may be assigned type `int` $\rightarrow$ `int`, and in the second copy of `F`, its binding for `f` may be assigned type `bool` $\rightarrow$ `bool`.

Example (b). While MLton's approach to typechecking functors results in the acceptance of Example (a), it also results in the acceptance of similar programs that are *not* well-typed according to the Definition. Consider Example (b) in Figures 1 and 3. Since `B.f` is now applied to a string instead of a boolean, there is no single type for `f` that would make the program typecheck. Put another way, there is no solution to the unification problem α(`int`) = `int` $\wedge$ α(`bool`) = `string`. However, since MLton inlines `F` prior to typechecking the definition of `B`, it is happy to assign `f` the type `string` $\rightarrow$ `string` in the second copy of `F`.

We prefer MLton's behavior to that prescribed by the Definition for several reasons. First, it does not require any higher-order unification and is therefore simpler and easier to implement. Second, it is more liberal than the Definition in a way that is perfectly type-safe. Third, it is arguably more intuitive. Given that the type `X.t` and the definition of `f` are completely unrelated, we feel it is very odd that Example (a) type-checks under the Definition but Example (b) does not. That said, the MLton approach has the serious drawback that it needs to know all uses of `F`, *i.e.*, it needs access to the whole program.

To overcome this limitation of MLton's approach, we observe that MLton's inlining of functors is analogous to the well-known explanation of **let**-polymorphism (*e.g.*, see Pierce's textbook [19]), in which **let** $x = e_1$ **in** e_2 is well-typed if and only if e_1 and $e_2[e_1/x]$ are. Inlining the definition of x has the same effect as binding x in the context with a generalized polymorphic type for e_1. Similarly, to mimic the inlining of a functor `F`, we need to bind `F` in the context with a *generalized functor signature*, *i.e.*, a signature that takes *implicit* type arguments in addition

```
functor G () = struct
    datatype t = V
    val f = id id
end
structure C = G()
val _ = C.f C.V
```

Fig. 4. Example (c)

```
functor G () = struct
    val f = id id
    datatype t = V
end
structure C = G()
val _ = C.f C.V
```

Fig. 5. Example (d)

to the usual explicit module arguments. In the case of Examples (a) and (b), we would like to assign F the signature

$$\texttt{(X: sig type t end)} \rightarrow \underline{\forall\alpha.}\ \textbf{sig val}\ \texttt{f} : \alpha \rightarrow \alpha\ \textbf{end}$$

At each application of F, the type argument α could then be implicitly instantiated with a new type τ, thus enabling both Examples (a) and (b) to typecheck. The reason that it is sound to permit this kind of implicit polymorphic generalization at the definition of F—*i.e.*, the reason it does not violate the value restriction—is that functor bindings *are* bindings of syntactic values.

1.2 Abstract Data Types and Dependencies

The idea of generalized functor signatures sketched above is at the heart of the type system we present in Sections 2 and 3. However, functors are not the only complication that modular ML programs introduce into the HM type system. Another such complication is ML's facility for defining abstract data types.

Example (c). Consider the code in Figure 4. In this case, the body of functor G defines an abstract data type t, as well as a value V of type t, prior to its binding for f. Consequently, the application of C.f to C.V is well-typed according to the Definition, since f could have been assigned the type t → t.

We run into an interesting problem, though, if we attempt to typecheck this example using a generalized functor signature for G. In particular, the obvious generalized signature that one would expect to assign to G is the following:

$$\texttt{()} \rightarrow \underline{\forall\alpha.}\ \textbf{sig datatype}\ \texttt{t = V}\ \textbf{val}\ \texttt{f} : \alpha \rightarrow \alpha\ \textbf{end}$$

In order to typecheck the definition of C in such a way that the subsequent application (C.f C.V) will be well-typed, the application of G must instantiate G's implicit parameter α with the type C.t. But C.t is not in scope until after G has been applied, so how can C.t be passed as an argument to G?!

One way to view this problem is as a variation on the original problem that we observed with typechecking Example (a). In parameterizing G's signature over α, we failed to account for the possibility that α might refer to t. In other words, one might argue, the parameter α should really be a Skolem function, and f's type should be $\alpha(\texttt{t}) \rightarrow \alpha(\texttt{t})$. This observation is not very encouraging, though, since it only seems to lead us back to the need for higher-order unification. Fortunately,

Example	Definition	Reject All	No-HOU/No-track	MLton	Our Approach
(a)	✓	×	×	✓	✓
(b)	×	×	×	✓	✓
(c)	✓	×	✓	✓	✓
(d)	×	×	✓	×	✓

Fig. 6. Comparison of behaviors of different semantics and implementations on Examples (a)-(d). *Definition:* This reflects the behavior of both the Definition and the Harper-Stone alternative semantics of SML [7]. *Reject All:* SML/NJ, the ML Kit, TILT, SML.NET, and Hamlet reject all examples. *No-HOU/No-track*: Poly/ML, Alice, and Moscow ML fail to accept Example (a) and fail to reject Example (d). (Actually, Moscow ML rejects (d) in batch mode but accepts it in interactive mode.) *MLton* fails to reject Example (b). *Our Approach* is more liberal than any of the existing definitions or implementations, and it is easy to implement correctly.

as we will explain shortly in Section 2, we have an alternative solution to this dilemma that does not require higher-order unification.

Example (d). Lastly, let us consider the code in Figure 5, which is the same as that in Figure 4 save that the order of the bindings of `t` and `f` has been switched. Because of this switch, Example (d) is not legal SML, for `t` is not in scope at the point where `f` is defined.

The fact that the Definition treats Examples (c) and (d) differently means that a faithful implementation of SML must track the potential dependencies between unification variables (u-vars) and the abstract types that are in scope when the u-vars are introduced. This tracking adds a layer of complexity to the type inference algorithm that, when combined with the problems we have observed concerning type inference and functors, seems to be tricky to get right. As evidence of this, we note that, with the exception of MLton (and Moscow ML when run in batch mode), no implementation of SML correctly handles both Examples (c) and (d) according to the Definition (see Figure 6). Furthermore, as the design we propose below will demonstrate, having a declarative semantics that permits Example (d) to typecheck is not only perfectly type-safe—it makes the typechecking algorithm much easier to specify.

1.3 The SML/NJ Approach

As we have seen, it is difficult to implement type inference for SML correctly. A number of existing implementations reject all four examples presented above—even though Examples (a) and (c) are legal SML—and for at least one compiler (namely, SML/NJ), the rejection of these examples is the result of a deliberate implementation decision [13]. Specifically, SML/NJ's policy is that no unification variables created during type inference are permitted to escape to the module level, even if subsequent code determines how they must be instantiated. This policy has the benefit of being consistent and predictable, and since programmers are not exactly clamoring for the rather contrived Examples (a)-(d) to be accepted anyway, one may wonder why it has not been adopted more widely.

In fact, there are several reasons why we find SML/NJ's *reject-all* approach unsatisfactory. First and foremost, a consequence of this policy that is well-known to be irritating to many programmers is that one cannot write a side-effecting module binding **val** `x = ref nil` and have the SML/NJ typechecker infer the specific type of `x` from later use within the module—one is forced to write a type annotation on `x`.

Second, SML/NJ's semantics is based on the *algorithmic* notion of unification variables escaping to the module level. In order to give a declarative account of SML/NJ's semantics, the typing rule for a module-level **val**-binding would have to demand that the expression being bound have a *unique* type in the case that it is not a syntactic value. Since uniqueness is a higher-order statement about the set of all possible typing derivations for a given term, formulating such a rule requires care in order to ensure that the typing judgment is well-founded.

We believe it is straightforward to show that such a higher-order rule makes sense, *provided* that the static semantics of the core language does not depend on that of the module language (*i.e.*, that module definitions cannot appear within core terms). This assumption is valid for Standard ML. It is also true for Extended ML [8], in whose formalization Kahrs *et al.* employ similar higher-order rules with different motivation. However, from a language design standpoint, this condition is unnecessarily limiting. Several implementations of Standard ML (*e.g.*, Moscow ML and Alice ML) extend the language with features such as first-class modules [21] and the ability to write module bindings within **let**-expressions, which introduce interdependencies between the core and module languages. It is unclear whether the natural declarative account of SML/NJ's semantics is well-founded in the presence of such extensions.

2 Our Approach

Instead of attempting to prohibit any interaction between core type inference and module type checking, we propose a way of understanding and defining the semantics of type inference in the presence of modules that is *more* liberal than any existing definition or implementation of SML. In fact, our formalization of type inference (Section 3) embraces the interaction with modules in the sense that polymorphic generalization and instantiation (typically viewed as strictly core-language notions) are treated as coercions between the core and module languages. Moreover, our approach admits a provably sound and complete type-checking algorithm via a straightforward generalization of Algorithm $\mathcal{W}$. This is the first (positive) result that we are aware of concerning the interaction of ML-style modules and Damas-Milner type inference.

One key element of our approach is the idea of classifying functors using *generalized functor signatures* (GFS's), which we sketched at the end of Section 1. We will characterize their semantics precisely in Section 3.

The second key element of our approach concerns the treatment of abstract data types. As explained in Section 1, the problem with Example (c) is that we need access to the abstract type `C.t`, generated by the functor application `G()`, *ahead of time* so that we can use it to instantiate `G`'s implicit type argument.

To make this possible, we use ideas and formal techniques from a type system developed recently by Dreyer [2] (in the study of recursive modules) that provides precisely the feature we are looking for: *forward references* to abstract types.

Traditionally, abstract data types are modeled by values of existential type ($\exists\alpha.\tau$), which must be "unpacked" in order to obtain a fresh abstract type α and a value x of type τ representing the (operations on) values of type α [17]. In Dreyer's system, the type name α may be created ahead of time, before the package defining α and the (operations on) values of type α is even available. This is motivated by the goal of modeling recursive module programming, in which the abstract type components of a module may be "forward-declared".

To see how Dreyer's approach is useful in typechecking Example (c), let us first consider the declarative module typing judgment that we will formalize in Section 3. This judgment has the form $\Delta\,;\Gamma \vdash \mathit{mod} : \Sigma \ \mathsf{with}\ \overline{\alpha}\downarrow$, and can be read: "In type context Δ and term/module context Γ, module *mod* can be assigned signature Σ and, when evaluated, will define the abstract types $\overline{\alpha}$."[1] (*Note:* We use $\overline{\alpha}$ as a semantic representation of the abstract types defined by *mod*—the $\overline{\alpha}$ are not permitted to appear syntactically in *mod* itself.) An invariant of this judgment is that the variables $\overline{\alpha}$ must be bound in the type context Δ—*i.e.,* they must already have been created prior to the evaluation of *mod*. In order to ensure that abstract types are defined *exactly* once, we follow Dreyer in employing techniques reminiscent of a linear type system. In particular, we have several different binding forms for type variables that indicate whether or not they have been defined. In the typing judgment given above, $\overline{\alpha}$ are assumed to be bound in Δ as *undefined* (written $\overline{\alpha \uparrow \mathrm{K}}$), and the evaluation of *mod* has the effect of changing the bindings of $\overline{\alpha}$ to *defined* (written $\overline{\alpha \downarrow \mathrm{K}}$).

As for Example (c): Under the approach to declarative module typing we have sketched above, since the binding **structure** `C = G()` results in the definition of an abstract type `C.t`, the typing of this binding must occur in a context where `C.t`, represented semantically by some α, is already bound (as undefined). Since α must appear in the context of the binding, it is no problem to instantiate `G`'s implicit argument using α, and thus Example (c) will be deemed well-typed.

Concerning Example (d): As we argued in Section 1, we believe it is perfectly legitimate for Example (d) to be accepted, and our declarative module typing judgment affirms this stance. Specifically, since the body of functor `G`—let's call it *mod*—defines an abstract type `t`, it must be that the semantic type variable α representing `t` is bound as undefined in the initial context under which *mod* is typechecked. As a result, α is in scope throughout all of *mod*, including the binding for `f`, regardless of the order in which `t` and `f` are bound. (Admittedly, this has the somewhat odd effect that `f` is assigned a type with which the programmer could not have annotated `f` explicitly. However, due to the so-called *avoidance problem* [12], this situation already arises in SML in other contexts.)

In summary, the main benefit of using this style of declarative typing judgment is that we are freed from worrying about the relative order in which unification variables and ADT's are introduced into scope during type inference.

---

[1] We adopt the notation $\overline{E}$ to mean a (possibly empty) ordered list $E_1, \ldots, E_n$.

Label Seq's	ℓs ::=	$\epsilon \mid \ell.\ell s$
Paths	P ::=	$X.\ell s$
Kinds	K, L ::=	$\mathbf{T} \mid \mathbf{T}^n \to \mathbf{T}$
Type Con's	con, typ ::=	$P \mid \alpha \mid typ \to typ \mid \lambda(\overline{\alpha}).typ \mid con(\overline{typ})$
Terms	exp ::=	$P \mid x \mid \lambda x.exp \mid exp_1(exp_2) \mid exp : typ \mid \texttt{let } X = mod \texttt{ in } exp$
Values	val ::=	$P \mid x \mid \lambda x.exp \mid val : typ$
Signatures	sig ::=	$[\![K]\!] \mid [\![= con : K]\!] \mid [\![\forall(\overline{\alpha}).typ]\!] \mid [\![\overline{\ell \triangleright X : sig}]\!] \mid (X : sig_1) \to sig_2$
Modules	mod ::=	$P \mid [con] \mid [exp] \mid [\overline{\ell \triangleright X = mod}] \mid \lambda(X : sig).mod \mid P_1(P_2) \mid$ $\texttt{let } X = mod_1 \texttt{ in } mod_2 \mid mod :> sig \mid mod : sig$

Fig. 7. External language syntax

Finally, since our approach to module typing is based on a *type system*, which has been proven type-safe by Dreyer using standard syntactic methods, it is quite easy to show that our approach is type-safe. Following Harper and Stone [7], we do not give a dynamic semantics directly for our ML-style module language, but rather by *elaboration* (aka *evidence translation*) into an internal language type system (IL). In the case of the Harper-Stone alternative formalization of SML, that IL is a variant of Harper-Lillibridge/Leroy's module type system [6,10]. The IL we employ here is a variant of Dreyer's type system for recursive modules (minus the recursion) [3]. The details of this translation are given in a companion technical report [4]. We omit further discussion due to space limitations.

Our ability to prove type safety in a straightforward manner is a clear advantage of our approach over the *ad hoc* formal approach adopted by the Definition [16], as well as improvements to the Definition style such as Russo's [20]. As we will see in the next section, however, there are several aspects of our declarative typing judgment that are more reminiscent of the Definition than they are of the Harper-Stone semantics. Our design thus exhibits a viable hybrid of two approaches to defining SML that are often viewed as incompatible.

3 Declarative Semantics

Figure 7 presents the syntax of our *external* (*i.e.*, source-level) SML-like language. In order to provide a clean formal account of the essential issues, our formalism pares away some of the syntactic complexities of real SML programs.

First, we model type and value bindings in modules as a special case of module bindings, in which the module being bound is an *atomic* type or term module, *i.e.*, a module containing a single type or term component. The signature $[\![K]\!]$ models an *opaque specification* of an atomic type module $[con]$ whose type (constructor) component con has kind K. The signature $[\![= con : K]\!]$ models a *transparent specification* of an atomic type module whose type component is manifestly equal to con of kind K. The signature $[\![\forall(\overline{\alpha}).typ]\!]$ models a *value specification*, classifying atomic term modules $[exp]$ whose term component exp has

IL Type Con's	$A, \tau ::= \alpha \mid \tau_1 \to \tau_2 \mid \lambda(\overline{\alpha}).\tau \mid A(\overline{\tau})$
IL Signatures	$\Sigma ::= [\![= A : K]\!] \mid [\![\tau]\!] \mid [\![\overline{\ell : \Sigma}]\!] \mid \Sigma_1 \to \Sigma_2 \mid \forall(\overline{\alpha}).\Sigma \mid \forall(\overline{\alpha \downarrow K}).\Sigma \mid \exists(\overline{\alpha \downarrow K}).\Sigma$
Type Contexts	$\Delta ::= \emptyset \mid \Delta, \alpha \uparrow K \mid \Delta, \alpha \downarrow K \mid \Delta, \alpha$
Term/Module Contexts	$\Gamma ::= \emptyset \mid \Gamma, x : \tau \mid \Gamma, X : \Sigma$

Interpretation of type constructors: $\Delta ; \Gamma \vdash con \rightsquigarrow A : K$

$$\frac{\Delta ; \Gamma \vdash P : [\![= A : K]\!]}{\Delta ; \Gamma \vdash P \rightsquigarrow A : K}\ (1)$$

Other rules in technical report [4]...

Interpretation of signatures: $\Delta ; \Gamma \vdash sig \rightsquigarrow \exists(\overline{\alpha \downarrow K}).\Sigma$

$$\frac{}{\Delta ; \Gamma \vdash [\![K]\!] \rightsquigarrow \exists(\alpha \downarrow K).[\![= \alpha : K]\!]}\ (2) \qquad \frac{\Delta ; \Gamma \vdash con \rightsquigarrow A : K}{\Delta ; \Gamma \vdash [\![= con : K]\!] \rightsquigarrow \exists().[\![= A : K]\!]}\ (3)$$

$$\frac{\Delta ; \Gamma \vdash typ \rightsquigarrow \tau : \mathbf{T}}{\Delta ; \Gamma \vdash [\![\forall().typ]\!] \rightsquigarrow \exists().[\![\tau]\!]}\ (4) \qquad \frac{\Delta, \overline{\alpha} ; \Gamma \vdash typ \rightsquigarrow \tau : \mathbf{T}}{\Delta ; \Gamma \vdash [\![\forall(\overline{\alpha}).typ]\!] \rightsquigarrow \exists().\forall(\overline{\alpha}).[\![\tau]\!]}\ (5)$$

$$\frac{}{\Delta ; \Gamma \vdash [\![]\!] \rightsquigarrow \exists().[\![]\!]}\ (6) \qquad \frac{\Delta ; \Gamma \vdash sig_1 \rightsquigarrow \exists(\overline{\alpha_1 \downarrow K_1}).\Sigma_1 \quad \Delta, \overline{\alpha_1 \downarrow K_1} ; \Gamma, X_1 : \Sigma_1 \vdash [\![\overline{\ell \triangleright X : sig}]\!] \rightsquigarrow \exists(\overline{\alpha \downarrow K}).[\![\overline{\ell : \Sigma}]\!]}{\Delta ; \Gamma \vdash [\![\ell_1 \triangleright X_1 : sig_1, \overline{\ell \triangleright X : sig}]\!] \rightsquigarrow \exists(\overline{\alpha_1 \downarrow K_1}, \overline{\alpha \downarrow K}).[\![\ell_1 : \Sigma_1, \overline{\ell : \Sigma}]\!]}\ (7)$$

$$\frac{\Delta ; \Gamma \vdash sig_1 \rightsquigarrow \exists(\overline{\alpha_1 \downarrow K_1}).\Sigma_1 \quad \Delta, \overline{\alpha_1 \downarrow K_1} ; \Gamma, X : \Sigma_1 \vdash sig_2 \rightsquigarrow \exists(\overline{\alpha_2 \downarrow K_2}).\Sigma_2}{\Delta ; \Gamma \vdash (X : sig_1) \to sig_2 \rightsquigarrow \exists().\forall(\overline{\alpha_1 \downarrow K_1}).\Sigma_1 \to \forall().\exists(\overline{\alpha_2 \downarrow K_2}).\Sigma_2}\ (8)$$

Fig. 8. Interpretation of signatures

type $\forall(\overline{\alpha}).typ$. (Note that if $\overline{\alpha} = \emptyset$, this degenerates from a polymorphic type to a monomorphic type.)

Second, we follow Harper and Lillibridge [6] and model structures as records $[\overline{\ell \triangleright X = mod}]$, each of whose components has both a distinct external name (a label ℓ) and a distinct internal name (a variable X). The label is used to refer to the component from the outside of the module, whereas the variable is used to refer to the component in subsequent bindings within the structure. Thus, each X is bound in the context of the subsequent bindings and may be alpha-varied. For simplicity, we adopt the ML convention that projections are not permitted from arbitrary modules. The only projection form is the path P, which consists of zero or more projections from a module variable X. (Note: We will usually drop the trailing "$.\epsilon$" from a path, *e.g.*, writing X instead of X.ϵ.)

Third, we model the classic distinction between "polytypes" and "monotypes" as a special case of the distinction between signatures and types. In other words, polymorphic generalization occurs when a core-level value *val* is encapsulated in

Declarative typing for terms: $\Delta\,;\Gamma \vdash \mathit{exp} : \tau$

$$\frac{\Delta\,;\Gamma \vdash \mathrm{P} : [\![\tau]\!]}{\Delta\,;\Gamma \vdash \mathrm{P} : \tau}\ (9) \qquad \frac{\Delta\,;\Gamma \vdash \mathrm{P} : \forall(\overline{\alpha}).[\![\tau]\!] \quad \Delta \vdash \delta : \overline{\alpha}}{\Delta\,;\Gamma \vdash \mathrm{P} : \delta\tau}\ (10) \qquad \frac{x:\tau \in \Gamma}{\Delta\,;\Gamma \vdash x : \tau}\ (11)$$

$$\frac{\Delta \vdash \tau_1 : \mathbf{T} \quad \Delta\,;\Gamma, x:\tau_1 \vdash \mathit{exp} : \tau_2}{\Delta\,;\Gamma \vdash \lambda x.\mathit{exp} : \tau_1 \to \tau_2}\ (12) \qquad \frac{\Delta\,;\Gamma \vdash \mathit{exp}_1 : \tau_2 \to \tau \quad \Delta\,;\Gamma \vdash \mathit{exp}_2 : \tau_2}{\Delta\,;\Gamma \vdash \mathit{exp}_1(\mathit{exp}_2) : \tau}\ (13)$$

$$\frac{\Delta\,;\Gamma \vdash \mathit{exp} : \tau \quad \Delta\,;\Gamma \vdash \mathit{typ} \leadsto \tau : \mathbf{T}}{\Delta\,;\Gamma \vdash \mathit{exp} : \mathit{typ} : \tau}\ (14) \qquad \frac{\Delta, \overline{\alpha \uparrow \mathrm{K}}\,;\Gamma \vdash \mathit{mod} : \Sigma \text{ with } \overline{\alpha}\downarrow \quad \Delta, \overline{\alpha \downarrow \mathrm{K}}\,;\Gamma, \mathrm{X}:\Sigma \vdash \mathit{exp} : \tau \quad \overline{\alpha} \# \mathsf{FTV}(\tau)}{\Delta\,;\Gamma \vdash \mathtt{let}\ \mathrm{X} = \mathit{mod}\ \mathtt{in}\ \mathit{exp} : \tau}\ (15)$$

Declarative typing for modules: $\Delta\,;\Gamma \vdash \mathit{mod} : \Sigma \text{ with } \overline{\alpha}\downarrow$

We omit "with $\overline{\alpha}\downarrow$" if $\overline{\alpha} = \emptyset$ (*i.e.*, if *mod* does not define any abstract types).

$$\frac{\mathrm{X}:\Sigma \in \Gamma}{\Delta\,;\Gamma \vdash \mathrm{X} : \Sigma}\ (16) \qquad \frac{\Delta\,;\Gamma \vdash \mathrm{P} : [\![\ldots, \ell:\Sigma, \ldots]\!]}{\Delta\,;\Gamma \vdash \mathrm{P}.\ell : \Sigma}\ (17) \qquad \frac{\Delta\,;\Gamma \vdash \mathit{con} \leadsto \mathrm{A} : \mathrm{K}}{\Delta\,;\Gamma \vdash [\mathit{con}] : [\![= \mathrm{A} : \mathrm{K}]\!]}\ (18)$$

$$\frac{\Delta\,;\Gamma \vdash \mathit{exp} : \tau}{\Delta\,;\Gamma \vdash [\mathit{exp}] : [\![\tau]\!]}\ (19) \qquad \frac{\Delta, \overline{\alpha}\,;\Gamma \vdash \mathit{val} : \tau}{\Delta\,;\Gamma \vdash [\mathit{val}] : \forall(\overline{\alpha}).[\![\tau]\!]}\ (20) \qquad \frac{}{\Delta\,;\Gamma \vdash [] : [\![]\!]}\ (21)$$

$$\frac{\Delta\,;\Gamma \vdash \mathit{mod}_1 : \Sigma_1 \text{ with } \overline{\alpha_1}\downarrow \quad \Delta \,@\, \overline{\alpha_1}\downarrow\,;\Gamma, \mathrm{X}_1:\Sigma_1 \vdash [\overline{\ell \rhd \mathrm{X} = \mathit{mod}}] : [\![\overline{\ell : \Sigma}]\!] \text{ with } \overline{\alpha}\downarrow}{\Delta\,;\Gamma \vdash [\ell_1 \rhd \mathrm{X}_1 = \mathit{mod}_1, \overline{\ell \rhd \mathrm{X} = \mathit{mod}}] : [\![\ell_1 : \Sigma_1, \overline{\ell : \Sigma}]\!] \text{ with } \overline{\alpha_1}, \overline{\alpha}\downarrow}\ (22)$$

$$\frac{\Delta\,;\Gamma \vdash \mathit{sig} \leadsto \exists(\overline{\alpha_1 \downarrow \mathrm{K}_1}).\Sigma_1 \quad \Delta, \overline{\alpha_1 \downarrow \mathrm{K}_1}, \overline{\beta}, \overline{\alpha_2 \uparrow \mathrm{K}_2}\,;\Gamma, \mathrm{X}:\Sigma_1 \vdash \mathit{mod} : \Sigma_2 \text{ with } \overline{\alpha_2}\downarrow}{\Delta\,;\Gamma \vdash \lambda(\mathrm{X}:\mathit{sig}).\mathit{mod} : \forall(\overline{\alpha_1 \downarrow \mathrm{K}_1}).\Sigma_1 \to \forall(\overline{\beta}).\exists(\overline{\alpha_2 \downarrow \mathrm{K}_2}).\Sigma_2}\ (23)$$

$$\frac{\begin{array}{c}\Delta\,;\Gamma \vdash \mathrm{P}_1 : \forall(\overline{\alpha_1 \downarrow \mathrm{K}_1}).\Sigma_1 \to \forall(\overline{\beta}).\exists(\overline{\alpha_2 \downarrow \mathrm{K}_2}).\Sigma_2 \quad \Delta\,;\Gamma \vdash \mathrm{P}_2 : \Sigma \\ \Delta \vdash \Sigma \preceq \exists(\overline{\alpha_1 \downarrow \mathrm{K}_1}).\Sigma_1 \leadsto \delta_1 \quad \Delta \vdash \delta : \overline{\beta} \quad \Delta \vdash \delta_2 : \overline{\alpha_2 \uparrow \mathrm{K}_2}\end{array}}{\Delta\,;\Gamma \vdash \mathrm{P}_1(\mathrm{P}_2) : \delta\delta_1\delta_2\Sigma_2 \text{ with } \overline{\delta_2\alpha_2}\downarrow}\ (24)$$

$$\frac{\Delta\,;\Gamma \vdash \mathit{mod}_1 : \Sigma_1 \text{ with } \overline{\alpha_1}\downarrow \quad \Delta \,@\, \overline{\alpha_1}\downarrow\,;\Gamma, \mathrm{X}:\Sigma_1 \vdash \mathit{mod}_2 : \Sigma_2 \text{ with } \overline{\alpha_2}\downarrow}{\Delta\,;\Gamma \vdash \mathtt{let}\ \mathrm{X} = \mathit{mod}_1\ \mathtt{in}\ \mathit{mod}_2 : \Sigma_2 \text{ with } \overline{\alpha_1}, \overline{\alpha_2}\downarrow}\ (25)$$

$$\frac{\begin{array}{c}\Delta\,;\Gamma \vdash \mathit{sig} \leadsto \exists(\overline{\alpha \downarrow \mathrm{K}}).\Sigma \quad \Delta, \overline{\beta \uparrow \mathrm{L}}\,;\Gamma \vdash \mathit{mod} : \Sigma' \text{ with } \overline{\beta}\downarrow \\ \Delta, \overline{\beta \downarrow \mathrm{L}} \vdash \Sigma' \preceq \exists(\overline{\alpha \downarrow \mathrm{K}}).\Sigma \leadsto \delta' \quad \Delta \vdash \delta : \overline{\alpha \uparrow \mathrm{K}}\end{array}}{\Delta\,;\Gamma \vdash \mathit{mod} :> \mathit{sig} : \delta\Sigma \text{ with } \overline{\delta\alpha}\downarrow}\ (26)$$

$$\frac{\begin{array}{c}\Delta\,;\Gamma \vdash \mathit{sig} \leadsto \exists(\overline{\alpha \downarrow \mathrm{K}}).\Sigma \quad \Delta\,;\Gamma \vdash \mathit{mod} : \Sigma' \text{ with } \overline{\beta}\downarrow \\ \Delta \,@\, \overline{\beta}\downarrow \vdash \Sigma' \preceq \exists(\overline{\alpha \downarrow \mathrm{K}}).\Sigma \leadsto \delta'\end{array}}{\Delta\,;\Gamma \vdash \mathit{mod} : \mathit{sig} : \delta'\Sigma \text{ with } \overline{\beta}\downarrow}\ (27)$$

Fig. 9. Declarative typing rules for terms and modules

an atomic term module [*val*], and polymorphic instantiation happens implicitly when a module path P is used as a core-level expression. This approach deconstructs so-called "let-polymorphism" into its orthogonal component parts. The classic let-polymorphic construct, `let` $x = exp_1$ `in` exp_2, is encodable in our language as "`let` $\mathrm{X} = [exp_1]$ `in` $\{x \mapsto \mathrm{X}\}exp_2$".[2]

Concerning the remaining constructs: Functors are modeled as λ-abstractions. Functor applications restrict the functor and its argument to be paths, but the more general SML-style "P(*mod*)" can be encoded using module-level `let` as "`let` X = *mod* `in` P(X)". The two sealing constructs, *mod* :> *sig* and *mod* : *sig*, model SML's *opaque* and *transparent* signature ascription, respectively.

Figure 8 defines the semantic interpretation of external-language (EL) signatures in terms of internal-language (IL) signatures. The IL is a variant of Dreyer's type system for recursive modules [3], but it is not necessary to be familiar with the whole IL in order to understand how IL signatures are used to interpret EL signatures. The basic idea is that, in IL signatures, abstract type components are modeled as type variables, and their scope is made explicit through the use of universal and existential quantifiers. In fact, IL signatures are very close, both conceptually and formally, to the *semantic objects* employed by the Definition.

As we explained in Section 2, type variables α that represent abstract type components of modules may be bound in type contexts Δ as *undefined* ($\alpha \uparrow \mathrm{K}$) or as *defined* ($\alpha \downarrow \mathrm{K}$). Type contexts provide an additional binding form (written just α), which is used to represent the implicit type arguments to polymorphic functions (and generalized functors). This third binding form is necessary because implicit type arguments may be instantiated with types that are either defined or undefined (see Example (c)). All type variables of this third kind are assumed to have base kind $\mathbf{T}$. Term/module contexts, as one would expect, bind term variables x to types τ, and module variables X to signatures Σ. We adopt the convention that contexts are unordered and that commas join together contexts whose domains are disjoint.

The signature interpretation judgment has the form $\Delta ; \Gamma \vdash sig \rightsquigarrow \exists(\overline{\alpha \downarrow \mathrm{K}}).\Sigma$, which means that $\overline{\alpha}$ (of kinds $\overline{\mathrm{K}}$) represent the opaque type components of EL signature *sig*, and Σ is essentially *sig* with its opaque components defined transparently in terms of $\overline{\alpha}$. For example, **sig type** `t` **val** `v : t` **end** would be interpreted as $\exists(\alpha \downarrow \mathbf{T}).[\![\mathtt{t} : [\![= \alpha : \mathbf{T}]\!], \mathtt{v} : [\![\alpha]\!]]\!]$.

Most of the rules for interpreting signatures are straightforward. One point of note is in Rule 8 for functor signatures. While the $\forall\!\rightarrow\!\exists$ interpretation of SML's generative functors is entirely standard (see Russo's thesis [20]), the "$\forall()$." that precedes the existential in the result signature is unusual. In fact, this is simply a degenerate instance of a *generalized functor signature* (GFS), which may in the general case use the universal quantifier preceding the existential to bind a set of implicit type variables. (For example, see Rule 23, discussed below.)

Figure 9 shows the declarative typing rules for terms and modules. In Section 2 we explained the interpretation of the module typing judgment, and the interpretation of the term typing judgment is the standard one. Before considering the inference rules in detail, let us first define some notation:

We say that A is *defined* in Δ, written $\Delta \vdash \mathrm{A} \downarrow \mathrm{K}$, if $\Delta \vdash \mathrm{A} : \mathrm{K}$ and $\mathsf{FTV}(\mathrm{A}) \subseteq \{\alpha \mid \alpha \downarrow \mathrm{K} \in \Delta\}$. We will write $\Delta @ \overline{\alpha}\downarrow$ to mean $\Delta \backslash \{\alpha \uparrow \mathrm{K} \mid \alpha \in \overline{\alpha}\} \uplus \{\alpha \downarrow \mathrm{K} \mid \alpha \in$

[2] We use $\{x \mapsto \mathrm{X}\}$ to denote the capture-avoiding substitution of X for x.

$\overline{\alpha}\}$. We assume and maintain the invariant that all types are kept in β-normal form. (Thus, type substitutions are assumed to implicitly β-normalize.)

Definition 3.1 (Well-Formed Type Substitution)
A type substitution δ mapping Δ to Δ' is *well-formed*, written $\Delta' \vdash \delta : \Delta$, if:

1. $\mathsf{dom}(\delta) \subseteq \mathsf{dom}(\Delta)$
2. $\forall \alpha \uparrow \mathrm{K} \in \Delta.\ \exists \beta \uparrow \mathrm{K} \in \Delta'.\ \beta = \delta\alpha$
3. $\forall \alpha_1 \uparrow \mathrm{K}_1 \in \Delta.\ \forall \alpha_2 \uparrow \mathrm{K}_2 \in \Delta.\ (\delta\alpha_1 = \delta\alpha_2) \Rightarrow (\alpha_1 = \alpha_2)$
4. $\forall \alpha \downarrow \mathrm{K} \in \Delta.\ \Delta' \vdash \delta\alpha \downarrow \mathrm{K}$
5. $\forall \alpha \in \Delta.\ \Delta \vdash \delta\alpha : \mathbf{T}$

Conditions (2) and (4) ensure that substitutions preserve the (un-)definedness of type variables, and condition (3) ensures that undefined variables do not become aliased under substitution. Condition (5) ensures that no restrictions are placed on the types that can be substituted for implicit variables.

Rule 10 performs polymorphic instantiation when coercing a module path P to the term level. Given a path P of *polytype* signature $\forall(\overline{\alpha}).[\![\tau]\!]$, the second premise of the rule nondeterministically guesses a substitution δ for the implicit type arguments $\overline{\alpha}$, which is then applied to the type τ. Rule 20 performs polymorphic generalization when coercing a value *val* to the module level. It acts as a dual to Rule 10 in that it nondeterministically guesses a set of implicit $\overline{\alpha}$ to be added to the context during the typing of *val*.

Rules 21 and 22 define typing for structures. Regarding the latter, there are two points of note. First, all the abstract types defined by the structure (namely, $\overline{\alpha_1}$ and $\overline{\alpha}$) are assumed to be bound as undefined in the initial typing context Δ. Thus, they are in scope throughout the whole structure. Second, note that once the first module binding (mod_1) is typechecked, the remainder of the structure is typechecked in a context where $\overline{\alpha_1}$ are considered defined (namely, $\Delta @ \overline{\alpha_1 \downarrow}$). This ensures that the remainder of the structure will not attempt to redefine $\overline{\alpha_1}$. The typing of module-level `let` (Rule 25) is nearly identical.

Rule 23 defines typing for functors $\lambda(\mathrm{X} : sig).mod$. The second premise adds three sets of type variables to the context when typing the functor body. The $\overline{\alpha_1}$ represent the abstract type components of the functor argument, which are assumed to be defined. The $\overline{\beta}$ represent the implicit type variables over which the functor is polymorphically generalized (in much the same way as the $\overline{\alpha}$ in Rule 20). The $\overline{\alpha_2}$ represent the undefined abstract type components that the functor body *mod* will define itself. Although the choice of $\overline{\alpha_2}$ to add to the context appears to be nondeterministic, the completeness theorem for type inference will show that there is only one way to choose them.

Rule 24 defines typing for functor applications $\mathrm{P}_1(\mathrm{P}_2)$. After checking that P_1 has a valid GFS and that P_2 has some signature Σ, it uses the signature matching judgment $\Delta \vdash \Sigma \preceq \exists(\overline{\alpha_1 \downarrow \mathrm{K}_1}).\Sigma_1 \rightsquigarrow \delta_1$ to determine whether Σ is coercible to P_1's argument signature. The signature matching judgment, which is defined formally in the technical report [4], returns a substitution δ_1 representing the manifest definitions that Σ provides for the abstract type components $\overline{\alpha_1}$ of P_1's argument signature. This δ_1 has the property that $\Delta \vdash \delta_1 : \overline{\alpha_1 \downarrow K_1}$. The details of signature matching are largely similar to those in existing accounts of SML.

The fourth premise of Rule 24 nondeterministically guesses a substitution for P_1's implicit type arguments $\overline{\beta}$ (in much the same way as the polymorphic instantiation in Rule 10). Since the functor application will result in the definition of a set of abstract types of the shape specified in P_1's result signature (*i.e.,* in the shape of $\overline{\alpha_2 \downarrow K_2}$), the last premise of Rule 24 requires that such a set of abstract types already exist, undefined, in the context Δ. These abstract types are denoted by $\overline{\delta_2\alpha_2}$.

Finally, Rules 26 and 27 define typing for opaque and transparent sealing, respectively. In both rules, the signature Σ' of the module *mod* is matched against the interpretation $\exists(\overline{\alpha \downarrow K}).\Sigma$ of the ascribed signature *sig*. This results in a substitution δ', which conveys how *mod* implements the abstract type components $\overline{\alpha}$ of *sig*. In the case of opaque sealing, this information is irrelevant, since the signature of the sealed module keeps the $\overline{\alpha}$ abstract (albeit renamed by δ, whose role is similar to that of δ_2 in Rule 24). In the case of transparent sealing, the substitution δ' obtained from signature matching is applied to Σ in the signature of the sealed module, thus allowing *mod*'s definitions for the $\overline{\alpha}$ to leak out.

In both sealing rules, *mod* is permitted to define a set of abstract types $\overline{\beta}$. However, Rule 26 adds $\overline{\beta}$ to the context Δ when typechecking *mod*, whereas Rule 27 assumes $\overline{\beta}$ are already present in Δ. The reason for this is as follows. If *mod* is opaquely sealed, then $\overline{\beta}$ cannot escape the scope of the sealed module—*i.e.,* $\overline{\beta}$ are *local* abstract types, which are thus introduced into scope locally by Rule 26. If *mod* is transparently sealed, then $\overline{\beta}$ can leak out into the signature of the sealed module, and must therefore be bound in the surrounding context Δ.

4 Type Inference Algorithm

The type inference algorithm for our language is based closely on Algorithm $\mathcal{W}$. We employ unification variables (u-vars), written $\boldsymbol{\alpha}$, in the usual way. In particular, we do not explicitly bind u-vars in the context Δ. The u-vars appearing free in an expression E, which we write as $\mathsf{UV}(E)$, are all taken to have kind $\mathbf{T}$.

The inference judgment for terms has the familiar form $\Delta ; \Gamma \vdash exp \Rightarrow (\tau; \theta)$. Here, Δ, Γ, and *exp* are considered inputs. τ is the *principal type scheme* of *exp*, meaning that any other type that one can assign to *exp* declaratively must be a u-var substitution instance of τ. Lastly, θ is an idempotent u-var substitution whose domain is a subset of $\mathsf{UV}(\Gamma)$. (In some rules, this is enforced by explicitly writing $\theta|_\Gamma$, which denotes θ with its domain restricted to $\mathsf{UV}(\Gamma)$.) It represents the minimal substitution that must be applied to Γ in order to make *exp* well-typed. The rules for this judgment are standard (see the technical report [4]).

Figure 10 defines the inference judgment for modules, which has the form $\Delta ; \Gamma \vdash mod \Rightarrow \exists(\overline{\alpha \downarrow K}).(\Sigma; \theta)$. Here, Δ, Γ, and *mod* are considered inputs. The $\overline{\alpha \downarrow K}$ represent the abstract types that *mod* wants to define. Unlike the declarative judgment, inference does not make any assumption that $\overline{\alpha}$ are bound (as undefined) in the input context Δ.

Signature inference for modules: $\Delta\,;\Gamma \vdash mod \Rightarrow \exists(\overline{\alpha\downarrow\mathrm{K}}).(\Sigma;\theta)$

We omit "$\exists(\overline{\alpha\downarrow\mathrm{K}})$." if $\overline{\alpha\downarrow\mathrm{K}} = \emptyset$ (*i.e.*, if *mod* does not define any abstract types).

$$\frac{\Delta\,;\Gamma \vdash \mathrm{P} : \Sigma}{\Delta\,;\Gamma \vdash \mathrm{P} \Rightarrow (\Sigma;\mathsf{id})}\;(28) \qquad \frac{\Delta\,;\Gamma \vdash con \rightsquigarrow \mathrm{A} : \mathrm{K}}{\Delta\,;\Gamma \vdash [con] \Rightarrow ([\![=\mathrm{A}:\mathrm{K}]\!];\mathsf{id})}\;(29) \qquad \frac{}{\Delta\,;\Gamma \vdash [] \Rightarrow ([\![]\!];\mathsf{id})}\;(30)$$

$$\frac{\Delta\,;\Gamma \vdash exp \Rightarrow (\tau;\theta) \quad exp \text{ not a } val}{\Delta\,;\Gamma \vdash [exp] \Rightarrow ([\![\tau]\!];\theta)}\;(31) \qquad \frac{\Delta\,;\Gamma \vdash val \Rightarrow (\tau;\theta) \quad \overline{\alpha} = \mathsf{UV}(\tau)\backslash\mathsf{UV}(\theta\Gamma)}{\Delta\,;\Gamma \vdash [val] \Rightarrow (\forall(\overline{\alpha}).[\![\tau]\!];\theta)}\;(32)$$

$$\frac{\Delta\,;\Gamma \vdash mod_1 \Rightarrow \exists(\overline{\alpha_1\downarrow\mathrm{K}_1}).(\Sigma_1;\theta_1) \qquad \Delta,\overline{\alpha_1\downarrow\mathrm{K}_1}\,;\theta_1\Gamma,\mathrm{X}_1:\Sigma_1 \vdash [\overline{\ell \triangleright \mathrm{X} = mod}] \Rightarrow \exists(\overline{\alpha\downarrow\mathrm{K}}).([\![\overline{\ell:\Sigma}]\!];\theta_2)}{\Delta\,;\Gamma \vdash [\ell_1 \triangleright \mathrm{X}_1 = mod_1, \overline{\ell \triangleright \mathrm{X} = mod}] \Rightarrow \exists(\overline{\alpha_1\downarrow\mathrm{K}_1},\overline{\alpha\downarrow\mathrm{K}}).([\![\ell_1:\theta_2\Sigma_1,\overline{\ell:\Sigma}]\!];\theta_2\theta_1|_\Gamma)}\;(33)$$

$$\frac{\Delta\,;\Gamma \vdash sig \rightsquigarrow \exists(\overline{\alpha_1\downarrow\mathrm{K}_1}).\Sigma_1 \quad \Delta,\overline{\alpha_1\downarrow\mathrm{K}_1}\,;\Gamma,\mathrm{X}:\Sigma_1 \vdash mod \Rightarrow \exists(\overline{\alpha_2\downarrow\mathrm{K}_2}).(\Sigma_2;\theta) \qquad \overline{\alpha} = \mathsf{UV}(\Sigma_2)\backslash\mathsf{UV}(\theta\Gamma) \quad \overline{\alpha_1},\overline{\alpha_2}\,\#\,\mathsf{FTV}(\theta)}{\Delta\,;\Gamma \vdash \lambda(\mathrm{X}:sig).mod \Rightarrow (\forall(\overline{\alpha_1\downarrow\mathrm{K}_1}).\Sigma_1 \to \forall(\overline{\alpha}).\exists(\overline{\alpha_2\downarrow\mathrm{K}_2}).\Sigma_2;\theta)}\;(34)$$

$$\frac{\Delta\,;\Gamma \vdash \mathrm{P}_1 : \forall(\overline{\alpha_1\downarrow\mathrm{K}_1}).\Sigma_1 \to \forall(\overline{\beta}).\exists(\overline{\alpha_2\downarrow\mathrm{K}_2}).\Sigma_2 \quad \Delta\,;\Gamma \vdash \mathrm{P}_2 : \Sigma \qquad \Delta \vdash \Sigma \preceq \exists(\overline{\alpha_1\downarrow\mathrm{K}_1}).\Sigma_1 \Rightarrow (\delta;\theta) \quad \overline{\alpha} \text{ fresh}}{\Delta\,;\Gamma \vdash \mathrm{P}_1(\mathrm{P}_2) \Rightarrow \exists(\overline{\alpha_2\downarrow\mathrm{K}_2}).(\{\overline{\beta\mapsto\alpha}\}\theta\delta\Sigma_2;\theta)}\;(35)$$

$$\frac{\Delta\,;\Gamma \vdash mod_1 \Rightarrow \exists(\overline{\alpha_1\downarrow\mathrm{K}_1}).(\Sigma_1;\theta_1) \qquad \Delta,\overline{\alpha_1\downarrow\mathrm{K}_1}\,;\theta_1\Gamma,\mathrm{X}:\Sigma_1 \vdash mod_2 \Rightarrow \exists(\overline{\alpha_2\downarrow\mathrm{K}_2}).(\Sigma_2;\theta_2)}{\Delta\,;\Gamma \vdash \mathtt{let}\ \mathrm{X} = mod_1\ \mathtt{in}\ mod_2 \Rightarrow \exists(\overline{\alpha_1\downarrow\mathrm{K}_1},\overline{\alpha_2\downarrow\mathrm{K}_2}).(\Sigma_2;\theta_2\theta_1|_\Gamma)}\;(36)$$

$$\frac{\Delta\,;\Gamma \vdash sig \rightsquigarrow \exists(\overline{\alpha\downarrow\mathrm{K}}).\Sigma \quad \Delta\,;\Gamma \vdash mod \Rightarrow \exists(\overline{\beta\downarrow\mathrm{L}}).(\Sigma_1;\theta_1) \qquad \Delta,\overline{\beta\downarrow\mathrm{L}} \vdash \Sigma_1 \preceq \exists(\overline{\alpha\downarrow\mathrm{K}}).\Sigma \Rightarrow (\delta;\theta_2) \quad \overline{\beta}\,\#\,\mathsf{FTV}(\theta_2\theta_1|_\Gamma)}{\Delta\,;\Gamma \vdash mod :> sig \Rightarrow \exists(\overline{\alpha\downarrow\mathrm{K}}).(\Sigma;\theta_2\theta_1|_\Gamma)}\;(37)$$

$$\frac{\Delta\,;\Gamma \vdash sig \rightsquigarrow \exists(\overline{\alpha\downarrow\mathrm{K}}).\Sigma \quad \Delta\,;\Gamma \vdash mod \Rightarrow \exists(\overline{\beta\downarrow\mathrm{L}}).(\Sigma_1;\theta_1) \qquad \Delta,\overline{\beta\downarrow\mathrm{L}} \vdash \Sigma_1 \preceq \exists(\overline{\alpha\downarrow\mathrm{K}}).\Sigma \Rightarrow (\delta;\theta_2)}{\Delta\,;\Gamma \vdash mod : sig \Rightarrow \exists(\overline{\beta\downarrow\mathrm{L}}).(\delta\Sigma;\theta_2\theta_1|_\Gamma)}\;(38)$$

Fig. 10. Inference rules for modules

Σ is the *principal signature scheme* of *mod*, meaning that any other signature that one can assign to *mod* declaratively must be "less general" than some u-var substitution instance of Σ. In traditional presentations of HM, "less general" is characterized by means of a *subsumption* relation on polytypes. Since polytypes in our language are just a special case of signatures, we generalize subsumption to be a relation on signatures. Defined in Figure 11, the judgment $\Delta \vdash \Sigma_1 \sqsubseteq \Sigma_2$ says that Σ_1 is more general than Σ_2. Note that Rules 40 and 41 exploit the polymorphic instantiation offered by the declarative Rules 9 and 10.

As in the inference judgment for terms, θ is the minimal substitution to be applied to Γ in order to make *mod* well-typed. An important point is that the free variables of θ may include the abstract types $\overline{\alpha}$ defined by *mod*. This is critical because it enables forward references to abstract types. For example, suppose

Signature subsumption: $\Delta \vdash \Sigma_1 \sqsubseteq \Sigma_2$

$$\frac{}{\Delta \vdash [\![=A:K]\!] \sqsubseteq [\![=A:K]\!]}\ (39) \qquad \frac{\Delta\,;X:\Sigma \vdash X:\tau}{\Delta \vdash \Sigma \sqsubseteq [\![\tau]\!]}\ (40) \qquad \frac{\Delta,\overline{\alpha}\,;X:\Sigma \vdash X:\tau}{\Delta \vdash \Sigma \sqsubseteq \forall(\overline{\alpha}).[\![\tau]\!]}\ (41)$$

$$\frac{}{\Delta \vdash [\![]\!] \sqsubseteq [\![]\!]}\ (42) \qquad \frac{\Delta \vdash \Sigma_1 \sqsubseteq \Sigma_1' \quad \Delta \vdash [\![\overline{\ell:\Sigma}]\!] \sqsubseteq [\![\overline{\ell:\Sigma'}]\!]}{\Delta \vdash [\![\ell_1:\Sigma_1,\overline{\ell:\Sigma}]\!] \sqsubseteq [\![\ell_1:\Sigma_1',\overline{\ell:\Sigma'}]\!]}\ (43)$$

$$\frac{\Delta,\overline{\alpha_1\downarrow K_1},\overline{\beta'},\overline{\alpha_2\downarrow K_2} \vdash \delta:\overline{\beta} \quad \Delta,\overline{\alpha_1\downarrow K_1},\overline{\beta'},\overline{\alpha_2\downarrow K_2} \vdash \delta\Sigma_2 \sqsubseteq \Sigma_2'}{\Delta \vdash \forall(\overline{\alpha_1\downarrow K_1}).\Sigma_1 \to \forall(\overline{\beta}).\exists(\overline{\alpha_2\downarrow K_2}).\Sigma_2 \sqsubseteq \forall(\overline{\alpha_1\downarrow K_1}).\Sigma_1 \to \forall(\overline{\beta'}).\exists(\overline{\alpha_2\downarrow K_2}).\Sigma_2'}\ (44)$$

Fig. 11. Signature subsumption

that, as a result of inference for an earlier binding in the program, a variable X is bound in Γ with $[\![\boldsymbol{\beta} \to \boldsymbol{\beta}]\!]$. If during inference for *mod* the u-var $\boldsymbol{\beta}$ is unified with one of the $\overline{\alpha}$ defined by *mod*, then that constitutes a forward reference from the signature of X to an abstract type defined later in the program, and we want it in general to be accepted (for the reasons explained in Section 2).

That said, there are instances in which forward references must be prohibited in order to ensure soundness of type inference. One such instance is the inference rule for functors (Rule 34), which includes a side condition stipulating that the abstract type components of the argument and result ($\overline{\alpha_1}$ and $\overline{\alpha_2}$, respectively) do not appear in the free variables of the output substitution θ. This restriction is necessitated by the fact that $\overline{\alpha_1}$ and $\overline{\alpha_2}$ are *local* abstract types that are only in scope within the body of the functor. Indeed, the declarative rule for functors (Rule 23) imposes the same restriction—when typechecking the functor body it adds $\overline{\alpha_1}$ and $\overline{\alpha_2}$ to Δ instead of assuming that they were already bound in it to begin with. This has the effect that the typing of earlier bindings in the program cannot make forward references to $\overline{\alpha_1}$ and $\overline{\alpha_2}$.

We have verified manually that the type inference algorithm is sound and complete with respect to the declarative semantics. Here we state the soundness and completeness theorems in abbreviated form (only giving the cases concerning modules, and with some of the side conditions elided). The full theorem statements, together with relevant auxiliary judgments, are given in [4].

Theorem 4.1 (Soundness)
Assuming certain side conditions on Γ and *mod*,
if $\Delta\,;\Gamma \vdash mod \Rightarrow \exists(\overline{\alpha\downarrow K}).(\Sigma;\theta)$, then $\Delta,\overline{\alpha\uparrow K}\,;\theta\Gamma \vdash mod : \Sigma$ with $\overline{\alpha}\downarrow$.

Theorem 4.2 (Completeness)
Assuming certain side conditions on Γ, Γ', θ, and *mod*,
if $\Delta' \supseteq \Delta,\overline{\alpha\uparrow K}$ and $\Delta' \vdash \theta\Gamma \sqsubseteq \Gamma'$ and $\Delta'\,;\Gamma' \vdash mod : \Sigma$ with $\overline{\alpha}\downarrow$,
then $\Delta\,;\Gamma \vdash mod \Rightarrow \exists(\overline{\alpha\downarrow K}).(\Sigma';\theta')$
and there exists θ'' such that $\theta''\theta'\Gamma = \theta\Gamma$ and $\Delta' \vdash \theta''\Sigma' \sqsubseteq \Sigma$.

The premise $\Delta' \vdash \theta\Gamma \sqsubseteq \Gamma'$ in the completeness statement refers to the natural generalization of signature subsumption to context subsumption. We use it here to build a weakening property of declarative derivations directly into the induction hypothesis, so as to avoid having to prove it separately.

5 Related and Future Work

Russo describes a type inference algorithm for ML with higher-order and first-class modules, in which he uses alternating $\exists\forall$-quantification to track the scoping restrictions on abstract types imposed by The Definition [20]. This technique is also known as *unification under a mixed prefix* [14]. Although Russo states soundness and completeness conjectures, he does not attempt to prove them, and the implementation of his algorithm in Moscow ML rejects Example (a).

Many researchers have investigated the problem of type inference for a wide spectrum of languages in the design space between Hindley-Milner and System F. For example, Odersky and Läufer consider the problem of type inference in the presence of abstract data types and higher-order polymorphism [18]. Their type system relies on programmer-provided type annotations for handling polymorphic function arguments and existentials. It does not, however, include explicit type abstractions, and thus cannot directly model ML functors. Due to the presence of programmer-declared existential types, their inference algorithm, like Russo's, has to perform unification under a mixed prefix.

For future work, we are interested in extending our type system and its inference algorithm to more complete languages, in particular to full SML, as well as to languages with *applicative functors* [9]. The most prominent example of such a language is OCaml. Currently, the OCaml compiler rejects all four of our examples with error messages similar to TILT's. This comes as no surprise since, applicative functors aside, the typecheckers of both compilers are based closely on the Harper-Lillibridge/Leroy type system [6,10].

The problems concerning type inference and modules that we have explored in this work were originally discovered during the development of a modular account of Haskell-style type classes in ML [5]. Therefore, we hope to be able to adapt the techniques developed in this paper in order to obtain a similar soundness and completeness result for modular type classes.

References

1. Luis Damas and Robin Milner. Principal type schemes for functional programs. In *POPL '82*.
2. Derek Dreyer. Recursive type generativity. To appear in Journal of Functional Programming. Original version appeared in *ICFP '05*.
3. Derek Dreyer. Practical type theory for recursive modules. Technical Report TR-2006-07, University of Chicago, Department of Computer Science, August 2006.
4. Derek Dreyer and Matthias Blume. Principal type schemes for modular programs. Technical Report TR-2007-02, Univ. of Chicago Comp. Sci. Dept., January 2007.
5. Derek Dreyer, Robert Harper, and Manuel M. T. Chakravarty. Modular type classes. In *POPL '07*.

6. Robert Harper and Mark Lillibridge. A type-theoretic approach to higher-order modules with sharing. In *POPL '94*.
7. Robert Harper and Chris Stone. A type-theoretic interpretation of Standard ML. In G. Plotkin, C. Stirling, and M. Tofte, editors, *Proof, Language, and Interaction: Essays in Honor of Robin Milner*. MIT Press, 2000.
8. Stefan Kahrs, Donald Sannella, and Andrzej Tarlecki. The definition of Extended ML: A gentle introduction. *Theoretical Computer Science*, 173(2):445–484, 1997.
9. Xavier Leroy. Applicative functors and fully transparent higher-order modules. In *POPL 95*.
10. Xavier Leroy. Manifest types, modules, and separate compilation. In *POPL '94*.
11. Xavier Leroy. *Polymorphic Typing of an Algorithmic Language*. PhD thesis, Université Paris 7, 1992.
12. Mark Lillibridge. *Translucent Sums: A Foundation for Higher-Order Module Systems*. PhD thesis, Carnegie Mellon University, May 1997.
13. David MacQueen, 2006. Private communication.
14. Dale Miller. Unification under a mixed prefix. *Journal of Symbolic Computation*, 14:321–358, 1992.
15. Robin Milner. A theory of type polymorphism in programming. *Journal of Computer and System Sciences*, 17:348–75, 1978.
16. Robin Milner, Mads Tofte, Robert Harper, and David MacQueen. *The Definition of Standard ML (Revised)*. MIT Press, 1997.
17. John C. Mitchell and Gordon D. Plotkin. Abstract types have existential type. *Transactions on Programming Languages and Systems*, 10(3):470–502, 1988.
18. Martin Odersky and Konstantin Läufer. Putting type annotations to work. In *POPL '96*, pages 54–67.
19. Benjamin C. Pierce. *Types and Programming Languages*. MIT Press, 2002.
20. Claudio V. Russo. *Types for Modules*. PhD thesis, University of Edinburgh, 1998.
21. Claudio V. Russo. First-class structures for Standard ML. *Nordic Journal of Computing*, 7(4):348–374, 2000.
22. Andrew K. Wright. Polymorphic references for mere mortals. In *ESOP '92*.

A Consistent Semantics of Self-adjusting Computation

Umut A. Acar[1], Matthias Blume[1], and Jacob Donham[2]

[1] Toyota Technological Institute
[2] Carnegie Mellon University

Abstract. This paper presents a semantics of self-adjusting computation and proves that the semantics is correct and consistent. The semantics integrates change propagation with the classic idea of memoization to enable reuse of computations under mutation to memory. During evaluation, reuse of a computation via memoization triggers a change propagation that adjusts the reused computation to reflect the mutated memory. Since the semantics combines memoization and change-propagation, it involves both non-determinism and mutation. Our consistency theorem states that the non-determinism is not harmful: any two evaluations of the same program starting at the same state yield the same result. Our correctness theorem states that mutation is not harmful: self-adjusting programs are consistent with purely functional programming. We formalized the semantics and its meta-theory in the LF logical framework and machine-checked the proofs in Twelf.

1 Introduction

Self-adjusting computation is a technique for enabling programs to respond to changes to their data (e.g., inputs/arguments, external state, or outcome of tests). By automating the process of adjusting to any data change, self-adjusting computation generalizes incremental computation (e.g., [10,18,19,12,11,17]). Previous work shows that the technique can speed up response time by orders of magnitude over recomputing from scratch [3,7], closely match best-known (problem-specific) algorithms both in theory [2,6] and in practice [7,8].

The approach achieves its efficiency by combining two previously proposed techniques: change propagation [4], and memoization [5,1,17,15]. Due to an interesting duality between memoization and change propagation, combining them is crucial for efficiency. Using each technique alone yields results that are far from optimal [3,2]. The semantics of the combination, however, is complicated because the techniques are not orthogonal: conventional memoization requires purely functional programming, whereas change propagation crucially relies on mutation for efficiency. For this reason, no semantics of the combination existed previously, even though the semantics of change propagation [4] and memoization (e.g., [5,17]) has been well understood separately.

This paper gives a general semantic framework that combines memoization and change propagation. By modeling memoization as a non-deterministic oracle,

R. De Nicola (Ed.): ESOP 2007, LNCS 4421, pp. 458–474, 2007.

we ensure that the semantics applies to many different ways in which memoization, and thus the combination, can be realized. We prove two main theorems stating that the semantics is *consistent* and *correct* (Section 3). The consistency theorem states that the non-determinism (due to memoization) is harmless by showing that any two evaluations of the same program in the same store yield the same result. The correctness theorem states that self-adjusting computation is consistent with purely functional programming by showing that evaluation returns the (observationally) same value as a purely functional evaluation. Our proofs do not make any assumptions about typing. Our results therefore apply in both typed and untyped settings. (All previous work on self-adjusting computation assumed strongly typed languages.)

To study the semantics we extend the *adaptive functional language* AFL [4] with a `memo` construct for memoization. We call this language AML (Section 2). The dynamic semantics of AML is store-based. Mutation to the store between successive evaluations models incremental changes to the input. The evaluation of an AML program also allocates store locations and updates existing locations. A `memo` expression is evaluated by first consulting the *memo-oracle*, which non-deterministically returns either a *miss* or a *hit*. Unlike in conventional memoization, hit returns a trace of the evaluation of the memoized expression, not just its result. To adjust the computation to the mutated memory, the semantics performs a change propagation on the returned trace. Change propagation and ordinary evaluation are, therefore, intertwined in a mutually recursive fashion to enable computation reuse under mutation.

The proofs for the correctness and consistency theorems (Section 3) are made challenging because the semantics consists of a complex set of judgments (where change propagation and ordinary evaluation are mutually recursive), and because the semantics involves mutation and two kinds of non-determinism: non-determinism in memory allocation, and non-determinism due to memoization. Due to mutation, we are required to prove that evaluation preserves certain well-formedness properties (e.g., absence of cycles and dangling pointers). Due to non-deterministic memory allocation, we cannot compare the results from different evaluations directly. Instead, we compare values structurally by comparing the contents of locations. To address non-determinism due to memoization, we allow evaluation to recycle existing memory locations. Based on these techniques, we first prove that memoization is harmless: for any evaluation there exists a memoization-free counterpart that yields the same result without reusing any computations. Based on structural equality, we then show that memoization-free evaluations and fully deterministic evaluations are equivalent. These proof techniques may be of independent interest.

To increase confidence in our results, we encoded the syntax and semantics of AML and its meta-theory in the LF logical framework [13] and machine-checked the proofs using Twelf [16] (Section 4). The Twelf formalization consist of 7800 lines of code. The Twelf code is fully foundational: it encodes all background structures required by the proof and proves all lemmas from first principles. The Twelf code is available at `http://www.cs.cmu.edu/~jdonham/aml-proof/`. We note that checking the proofs in Twelf was not a merely an encoding exercise. In fact, our initial paper-and-pencil proof was not correct. In the process of making Twelf accept the proof, we simplified the rule systems, fixed the proof, and even generalized it. In retrospect, we feel that the use of Twelf was critical in obtaining the result.

Since the semantics models memoization as a non-deterministic oracle, and since it does not specify how the memory should be allocated while allowing pre-existing locations to be recycled, the dynamic semantics of AML does not translate to an algorithm directly. In Section 5, we describe some implementation strategies for realizing the AML semantics. One of these strategies has been implemented and discussed elsewhere [3]. We note that this implementation is somewhat broader than the semantics described here because it allows re-use of memoized computations even when they match partially, via the so called `lift` construct. We expect that the techniques described here can be extended for the `lift` construct.

2 The Language

We describe a language, called AML, that combines the features of an adaptive functional language (AFL) [4] with memoization. The syntax of the language extends that of AFL with **memo** constructs for memoizing expressions. The dynamic semantics integrates change propagation and evaluation to ensure correct reuse of computations under mutations. As explained before, our results do not rely on typing properties of AML. We therefore omit a type system but identify a minimal set of conditions under which evaluation is consistent. In addition to the memoizing and change-propagating dynamic semantics, we give a pure interpretation of AML that provides no reuse of computations.

2.1 Abstract Syntax

The abstract syntax of AML is given in Figure 1. We use meta-variables x, y, and z (and variants) to range over an unspecified set of variables, and meta-variable l (and variants) to range over a separate, unspecified set of locations—the locations are modifiable references. The syntax of AML is restricted to "2/3-cps", or "named form", to streamline the presentation of the dynamic semantics.

Expressions are classified into three categories: values, *stable* expressions, and *changeable* expressions. Values are constants, variables, locations, and the introduction forms for sums, products, and functions. The value of a stable expression is not sensitive to modifications to the inputs, whereas the value of a changeable expression may directly or indirectly be affected by them.

The familiar mechanisms of functional programming are embedded in AML as stable expressions. Stable expressions include the `let` construct, the elimination forms for products and sums, stable-function applications, and the creation of new modifiables. A *stable function* is a function whose body is a stable expression. The application of a stable function is a stable expression. The expression `mod` e_c allocates a modifiable reference and initializes it by executing the changeable

Values	$v ::= \texttt{()} \mid n \mid x \mid l \mid (v_1, v_2) \mid \texttt{inl}\ v \mid \texttt{inr}\ v \mid$ $\texttt{funs}\ f(x)\ \texttt{is}\ e_s \mid \texttt{func}\ f(x)\ \texttt{is}\ e_c$
Prim. Op.	$o ::= \texttt{not} \mid \texttt{+} \mid \texttt{-} \mid \texttt{=} \mid \texttt{<} \mid \ldots$
Exp.	$e ::= e_s \mid e_c$
St. Exp.	$e_s ::= v \mid o(v_1, \ldots, v_n) \mid \texttt{mod}\ e_c \mid \texttt{memos}\ e_s \mid \texttt{apply}_\texttt{S}(v_1, v_2) \mid$ $\texttt{let}\ x = e_s\ \texttt{in}\ e'_s \mid \texttt{let}\ x_1 \times x_2 = v\ \texttt{in}\ e_s \mid$ $\texttt{case}\ v\ \texttt{of}\ \texttt{inl}\ (x_1) \Rightarrow e_s \mid \texttt{inr}\ (x_2) \Rightarrow e'_s\ \texttt{end}$
Ch. Exp.	$e_c ::= \texttt{write}(v) \mid \texttt{read}\ v\ \texttt{as}\ x\ \texttt{in}\ e_c \mid \texttt{memo}_\texttt{C}\ e_c \mid \texttt{apply}_\texttt{C}(v_1, v_2) \mid$ $\texttt{let}\ x = e_s\ \texttt{in}\ e_c \mid \texttt{let}\ x_1 \times x_2 = v\ \texttt{in}\ e_c \mid$ $\texttt{case}\ v\ \texttt{of}\ \texttt{inl}\ (x_1) \Rightarrow e_c \mid \texttt{inr}\ (x_2) \Rightarrow e'_c\ \texttt{end}$
Program	$p ::= e_s$

Fig. 1. The abstract syntax of AML

expression e_c. Note that the modifiable itself is stable, even though its contents is subject to change. A memoized stable expression is written $\texttt{memo}_\texttt{S}\ e_s$.

Changeable expressions always execute in the context of an enclosing `mod`-expression that provides the implicit target location that every changeable expression writes to. The changeable expression `write(`v`)` writes the value v into the target. The expression `read` v `as` x `in` e_c binds the contents of the modifiable v to the variable x, then continues evaluation of e_c. A `read` is considered changeable because the contents of the modifiable on which it depends is subject to change. A *changeable function* is a function whose body is a changeable expression. A changeable function is stable as a value. The application of a changeable function is a changeable expression. A memoized changeable expression is written $\texttt{memo}_\texttt{C}\ e_c$. The changeable expressions include the `let` expression for ordering evaluation and the elimination forms for sums and products. These differ from their stable counterparts because their bodies consists of changeable expressions.

2.2 Stores, Well-Formed Expressions, and Lifting

Evaluation of an AML expression takes place in the context of a store, written σ (and variants), defined as a finite map from locations l to values v. We write $\texttt{dom}(\sigma)$ for the domain of a store, and $\sigma(l)$ for the value at location l, provided $l \in \texttt{dom}(\sigma)$. We write $\sigma[l \leftarrow v]$ to denote the extension of σ with a mapping of l to v. If l is already in the domain of σ, then the extension replaces the previous mapping.

$$\sigma[l \leftarrow v](l') = \begin{cases} v & \text{if } l = l' \\ \sigma(l') & \text{if } l \neq l' \text{ and } l' \in \texttt{dom}(\sigma) \end{cases}$$
$$\texttt{dom}(\sigma[l \leftarrow v]) = \texttt{dom}(\sigma) \cup \{l\}$$

We say that an expression e is *well-formed* in store σ if 1) all locations reachable from e in σ are in $\texttt{dom}(\sigma)$ ("no dangling pointers"), and 2) the portion of σ reachable from e is free of cycles. If e is well-formed in σ, then we can obtain a "lifted" expression e' by recursively replacing every reachable location l with its

$$\frac{v \in \{(), n, x\}}{v, \sigma \xrightarrow{\texttt{wf}} v, \emptyset} \quad \frac{l \in \texttt{dom}(\sigma) \quad \sigma(l), \sigma \xrightarrow{\texttt{wf}} v, L}{l, \sigma \xrightarrow{\texttt{wf}} v, \{l\} \cup L} \quad \frac{v_1, \sigma \xrightarrow{\texttt{wf}} v_1', L_1 \quad v_2, \sigma \xrightarrow{\texttt{wf}} v_2', L_2}{(v_1, v_2), \sigma \xrightarrow{\texttt{wf}} (v_1', v_2'), L_1 \cup L_2}$$

$$\frac{e_c, \sigma \xrightarrow{\texttt{wf}} e_c', L}{\texttt{mod}\ e_c, \sigma \xrightarrow{\texttt{wf}} \texttt{mod}\ e_c', L} \quad \frac{v, \sigma \xrightarrow{\texttt{wf}} v', L}{\texttt{in}_{\{\texttt{l},\texttt{r}\}}\ v, \sigma \xrightarrow{\texttt{wf}} \texttt{in}_{\{\texttt{l},\texttt{r}\}}\ v', L} \quad \frac{v, \sigma \xrightarrow{\texttt{wf}} v', L}{\texttt{write}(v), \sigma \xrightarrow{\texttt{wf}} \texttt{write}(v'), L}$$

$$\frac{e, \sigma \xrightarrow{\texttt{wf}} e', L}{\texttt{fun}_{\{\texttt{s},\texttt{c}\}}\ f(x)\ \texttt{is}\ e, \sigma \xrightarrow{\texttt{wf}} \texttt{fun}_{\{\texttt{s},\texttt{c}\}}\ f(x)\ \texttt{is}\ e', L}$$

$$\frac{v_1, \sigma \xrightarrow{\texttt{wf}} v_1', L_1 \quad \cdots \quad v_n, \sigma \xrightarrow{\texttt{wf}} v_n', L_n}{o(v_1, \ldots, v_n), \sigma \xrightarrow{\texttt{wf}} o(v_1', \ldots, v_n'), L_1 \cup \cdots \cup L_n}$$

$$\frac{v_1, \sigma \xrightarrow{\texttt{wf}} v_1', L_1 \quad v_2, \sigma \xrightarrow{\texttt{wf}} v_2', L_2}{\texttt{apply}_{\{\texttt{s},\texttt{c}\}}(v_1, v_2), \sigma \xrightarrow{\texttt{wf}} \texttt{apply}_{\{\texttt{s},\texttt{c}\}}(v_1', v_2'), L_1 \cup L_2}$$

$$\frac{e_1, \sigma \xrightarrow{\texttt{wf}} e_1', L \quad e_2, \sigma \xrightarrow{\texttt{wf}} e_2', L'}{\texttt{let}\ x = e_1\ \texttt{in}\ e_2, \sigma \xrightarrow{\texttt{wf}} \texttt{let}\ x = e_1'\ \texttt{in}\ e_2', L \cup L'}$$

$$\frac{v, \sigma \xrightarrow{\texttt{wf}} v', L \quad e, \sigma \xrightarrow{\texttt{wf}} e', L'}{\texttt{let}\ x_1 \times x_2 = v\ \texttt{in}\ e, \sigma \xrightarrow{\texttt{wf}} \texttt{let}\ x_1 \times x_2 = v'\ \texttt{in}\ e', L \cup L'}$$

$$\frac{v, \sigma \xrightarrow{\texttt{wf}} v', L \quad e_1, \sigma \xrightarrow{\texttt{wf}} e_1', L_1 \quad e_2, \sigma \xrightarrow{\texttt{wf}} e_2', L_2}{\begin{array}{l}(\texttt{case}\ v\ \texttt{of}\ \texttt{in}_\texttt{l}\ (x_1) \Rightarrow e_1 \mid \texttt{in}_\texttt{r}\ (x_2) \Rightarrow e_2\ \texttt{end}), \sigma \xrightarrow{\texttt{wf}} \\ \quad (\texttt{case}\ v'\ \texttt{of}\ \texttt{in}_\texttt{l}\ (x_1) \Rightarrow e_1' \mid \texttt{in}_\texttt{r}\ (x_2) \Rightarrow e_2'\ \texttt{end}), L \cup L_1 \cup L_2\end{array}}$$

$$\frac{e, \sigma \xrightarrow{\texttt{wf}} e', L}{\texttt{memo}_{\{\texttt{s},\texttt{c}\}}\ e, \sigma \xrightarrow{\texttt{wf}} \texttt{memo}_{\{\texttt{s},\texttt{c}\}}\ e', L}$$

$$\frac{v, \sigma \xrightarrow{\texttt{wf}} v', L \quad e_c, \sigma \xrightarrow{\texttt{wf}} e_c', L'}{\texttt{read}\ v\ \texttt{as}\ x\ \texttt{in}\ e_c, \sigma \xrightarrow{\texttt{wf}} \texttt{read}\ v'\ \texttt{as}\ x\ \texttt{in}\ e_c', L \cup L'}$$

Fig. 2. Well-formed expressions and lifts

stored value $\sigma(l)$. The notion of lifting will be useful in the formal statement of our main theorems (Section 3).

We use the judgment $e, \sigma \xrightarrow{\texttt{wf}} e', L$ to say that e is well-formed in σ, that e' is e lifted in σ, and that L is the set of locations reachable from e in σ. The rules for deriving such judgments are shown in Figure 2. Any finite derivation of such a judgment implies well-formedness of e in σ.

We will use two notational shorthands for the rest of the paper: by writing $e \uparrow \sigma$ or $\texttt{reach}\,(e, \sigma)$ we implicitly assert that there exist a location-free expression e' and a set of locations L such that $e, \sigma \xrightarrow{\texttt{wf}} e', L$. The notation $e \uparrow \sigma$ itself stands for the lifted expression e', and $\texttt{reach}\,(e, \sigma)$ stands for the set of reachable locations L. It is easy to see that e and σ uniquely determine $e \uparrow \sigma$ and $\texttt{reach}\,(e, \sigma)$ (if they exist).

2.3 Dynamic Semantics

The evaluation judgments of AML (Figures 5 and 6) consist of separate judgments for stable and changeable expressions. The judgment $\sigma, e \Downarrow^{\mathsf{S}} v, \sigma', \mathtt{T}_s$ states that evaluation of the stable expression e relative to the input store σ yields the value v, the trace $\mathtt{T}_s$, and the updated store σ'. Similarly, the judgment $\sigma, l \leftarrow e \Downarrow^{\mathsf{C}} \sigma', \mathtt{T}_c$ states that evaluation of the changeable expression e relative to the input store σ writes its value to the target l, and yields the trace $\mathtt{T}_c$ together with the updated store σ'.

A *trace* records the adaptive aspects of evaluation. Like the expressions whose evaluations they describe, traces come in stable and changeable varieties. The abstract syntax of traces is given by the following grammar:

$$\begin{array}{ll} \textit{Stable} & \mathtt{T}_s ::= \epsilon \mid \mathtt{mod}\ l \leftarrow \mathtt{T}_c \mid \mathtt{let}\ \mathtt{T}_s\ \mathtt{T}_s \\ \textit{Changeable} & \mathtt{T}_c ::= \mathtt{write}\ v \mid \mathtt{let}\ \mathtt{T}_s\ \mathtt{T}_c \mid \mathtt{read}_{l \to x = v.e}\ \mathtt{T}_c \end{array}$$

A stable trace records the sequence of allocations of modifiables that arise during the evaluation of a stable expression. The trace $\mathtt{mod}\ l \leftarrow \mathtt{T}_c$ records the allocation of the modifiable l and the trace of the initialization code for l. The trace $\mathtt{let}\ \mathtt{T}_s\ \mathtt{T}'_s$ results from evaluating a `let` expression in stable mode, the first trace resulting from the bound expression, the second from its body.

A changeable trace has one of three forms. A write, $\mathtt{write}\ v$, records the storage of the value v in the target. A sequence $\mathtt{let}\ \mathtt{T}_s\ \mathtt{T}_c$ records the evaluation of a `let` expression in changeable mode, with $\mathtt{T}_s$ corresponding to the bound stable expression, and $\mathtt{T}_c$ corresponding to its body. A read $\mathtt{read}_{l \to x = v.e}\ \mathtt{T}_c$ specifies the location read (l), the value read (v), the context of use of its value ($x.e$) and the trace ($\mathtt{T}_c$) of the remainder of the evaluation within the scope of that read. This records the dependency of the target on the value of the location read.

The set of locations allocated (via `mod`) during the evaluation that produced a trace $\mathtt{T}$ is denoted $\mathtt{alloc}\,(\mathtt{T})$ (the full definition is given in the accompanying technical report [9]). For example, if $\mathtt{T}_{\text{sample}} = \mathtt{let}\ (\mathtt{mod}\ l_1 \leftarrow \mathtt{write}\ 2)\ (\mathtt{read}_{l_1 \to x = 2.e}\ \mathtt{write}\ 3)$, then $\mathtt{alloc}\,(\mathtt{T}_{\text{sample}}) = \{l_1\}$.

Well-formedness, lifts, and primitive operations. We require that primitive operations preserve well-formedness. In other words, when a primitive operation is applied to some arguments, it does not create dangling pointers or cycles in the store, nor does it extend the set of locations reachable from the argument. Formally, this property can be states as follows.

$$\begin{array}{l} \text{If } \forall i.v_i, \sigma \xrightarrow{\mathtt{wf}} v'_i, L_i \text{ and } v = o(v_1, \ldots, v_n), \\ \text{then } v, \sigma \xrightarrow{\mathtt{wf}} v', L \text{ such that } L \subseteq \bigcup_{i=1}^{n} L_i. \end{array}$$

Moreover, no AML operation is permitted to be sensitive to the identity of locations. In the case of primitive operations we formalize this by postulating that they commute with lifts:

$$\begin{array}{l} \text{If } \forall i.v_i, \sigma \xrightarrow{\mathtt{wf}} v'_i, L_i \text{ and } v = o(v_1, \ldots, v_n), \\ \text{then } v, \sigma \xrightarrow{\mathtt{wf}} v', L \text{ such that } v' = o(v'_1, \ldots, v'_n). \end{array}$$

In short this can be stated as $o(v_1 \uparrow \sigma, \ldots, v_n \uparrow \sigma) = (o(v_1, \ldots, v_n)) \uparrow \sigma$.

$$\frac{\sigma, e_s \Downarrow^{\mathsf{S}} v, \sigma', \mathtt{T} \qquad \mathtt{alloc}\,(\mathtt{T}) \cap \mathtt{reach}\,(e_s, \sigma) = \emptyset}{\sigma, e_s \Downarrow^{\mathsf{S}}_{\text{ok}} v, \sigma', \mathtt{T}} \textbf{(valid/s)} \qquad \frac{\sigma, l \leftarrow e_c \Downarrow^{\mathsf{C}} \sigma', \mathtt{T} \qquad \mathtt{alloc}\,(\mathtt{T}) \cap \mathtt{reach}\,(e_c, \sigma) = \emptyset \qquad l \notin \mathtt{reach}\,(e_c, \sigma) \cup \mathtt{alloc}\,(\mathtt{T})}{\sigma, l \leftarrow e_c \Downarrow^{\mathsf{C}}_{\text{ok}} \sigma', \mathtt{T}} \textbf{(valid/c)}$$

Fig. 3. Valid evaluations

For example, all primitive operations that operate only on non-location values preserve well formedness and commute with lifts.

Valid evaluations. We consider only evaluations of well-formed expressions e in stores σ, i.e., those e and σ where $e \uparrow \sigma$ and $\mathtt{reach}\,(e, \sigma)$ are defined. Well-formedness is critical for proving correctness: the requirement that the reachable portion of the store is acyclic ensures that the approach is consistent with purely functional programming, the requirement that all reachable locations are in the store ensures that evaluations do not cause disaster by allocating a "fresh" location that happens to be reachable. We note that it is possible to omit the well-formedness requirement by giving a type system and a type safety proof. This approach limits the applicability of the theorem only to type-safe programs. Because of the imperative nature of the dynamic semantics, a type safety proof for AML is also complicated. We therefore choose to formalize well-formedness separately.

Our approach requires showing that evaluation preserves well-formedness. To establish well-formedness inductively, we define *valid evaluations.* We say that an evaluation of an expression e in the context of a store σ is *valid*, if

1. e is well-formed in σ,
2. the locations allocated during evaluation are disjoint from locations that are initially reachable from e (i.e., those that are in $\mathtt{reach}\,(e, \sigma)$), and
3. the target location of a changeable evaluation is contained neither in $\mathtt{reach}\,(e, \sigma)$ nor the locations allocated during evaluation.

We use $\Downarrow^{\mathsf{S}}_{\text{ok}}$ instead of $\Downarrow^{\mathsf{S}}$ and $\Downarrow^{\mathsf{C}}_{\text{ok}}$ instead of $\Downarrow^{\mathsf{C}}$ to indicate valid stable and changeable evaluations, respectively. The rules for deriving valid evaluation judgments are shown in Figure 3.

The Oracle. The dynamic semantics for AML uses an oracle to model memoization. Figure 4 shows the evaluation rules for the oracle. For a stable or a changeable expression e, we write an oracle miss as $\sigma, e \uparrow^{\mathsf{S}}$ or $\sigma, l \leftarrow e_c \uparrow^{\mathsf{C}}$, respectively. The treatment of oracle hits depend on whether the expression is stable or changeable. For a stable expression, it returns the value and the trace of a valid evaluation of the expression in some store. For a changeable expression, the oracle returns a trace of a valid evaluation of the expression in some store with some destination.

The key difference between the oracle and conventional approaches to memoization is that the oracle is free to return the trace (and the value, for stable

$$\frac{}{\sigma, e_s \uparrow^{\mathsf{S}}}\ (\textbf{miss/s}) \qquad \frac{\sigma_0, e_s \Downarrow^{\mathsf{S}}_{\text{ok}} v, \sigma_0', \mathrm{T}}{\sigma, e_s \downarrow^{\mathsf{S}} v, \mathrm{T}}\ (\textbf{hit/s})$$

$$\frac{}{\sigma, e_c \uparrow^{\mathsf{C}}}\ (\textbf{miss/c}) \qquad \frac{\sigma_0, l \leftarrow e_c \Downarrow^{\mathsf{C}}_{\text{ok}} \sigma_0', \mathrm{T}}{\sigma, e_c \downarrow^{\mathsf{C}} \mathrm{T}}\ (\textbf{hit/c})$$

Fig. 4. The oracle

$$\frac{}{\sigma, v \Downarrow^{\mathsf{S}} v, \sigma, \varepsilon}\ (\textbf{value}) \qquad \frac{v = \mathsf{app}(o, (v_1, \ldots, v_n))}{\sigma, o(v_1, \ldots, v_n) \Downarrow^{\mathsf{S}} v, \sigma, \varepsilon}\ (\textbf{prim.'s})$$

$$\frac{l \notin \mathtt{alloc}\,(\mathrm{T}) \qquad \sigma, l \leftarrow e \Downarrow^{\mathsf{C}} \sigma', \mathrm{T}}{\sigma, \mathtt{mod}\ e \Downarrow^{\mathsf{S}} l, \sigma', \mathtt{mod}\ l \leftarrow \mathrm{T}}\ (\textbf{mod})$$

$$\frac{\begin{array}{c}\sigma, e \uparrow^{\mathsf{S}} \\ \sigma, e \Downarrow^{\mathsf{S}} v, \sigma', \mathrm{T}\end{array}}{\sigma, \mathtt{memo_S}\ e \Downarrow^{\mathsf{S}} v, \sigma', \mathrm{T}}\ (\textbf{memo/miss}) \qquad \frac{\begin{array}{c}\sigma, e \downarrow^{\mathsf{S}} v, \mathrm{T} \\ \sigma, \mathrm{T} \overset{\mathsf{S}}{\curvearrowright} \sigma', \mathrm{T}'\end{array}}{\sigma, \mathtt{memo_S}\ e \Downarrow^{\mathsf{S}} v, \sigma', \mathrm{T}'}\ (\textbf{memo/hit})$$

$$\frac{v_1 = \mathtt{fun_S}\ f(x)\ \mathtt{is}\ e \qquad \sigma, [v_1/f, v_2/x]\ e \Downarrow^{\mathsf{S}} v, \sigma', \mathrm{T}}{\sigma, \mathtt{apply_S}\,(v_1, v_2) \Downarrow^{\mathsf{S}} v, \sigma', \mathrm{T}}\ (\textbf{apply})$$

$$\frac{\sigma, e_1 \Downarrow^{\mathsf{S}} v_1, \sigma_1, \mathrm{T}_1 \quad \sigma_1, [v_1/x]\ e_2 \Downarrow^{\mathsf{S}} v_2, \sigma_2, \mathrm{T}_2 \quad \mathtt{alloc}\,(\mathrm{T}_1) \cap \mathtt{alloc}\,(\mathrm{T}_2) = \emptyset}{\sigma, \mathtt{let}\ x = e_1\ \mathtt{in}\ e_2 \Downarrow^{\mathsf{S}} v_2, \sigma_2, \mathtt{let}\ \mathrm{T}_1\ \mathrm{T}_2}\ (\textbf{let})$$

$$\frac{\sigma, [v_1/x_1, v_2/x_2]\ e \quad \Downarrow^{\mathsf{S}} \quad v, \sigma', \mathrm{T}}{\sigma, \mathtt{let}\, x_1{\times}x_2 = (v_1, v_2)\, \mathtt{in}\, e \Downarrow^{\mathsf{S}} v, \sigma', \mathrm{T}}\ (\textbf{let}{\times})$$

$$\frac{\sigma, [v/x_1]\ e_1 \Downarrow^{\mathsf{S}} v', \sigma', \mathrm{T}}{\sigma, \mathtt{case}\ \mathtt{in_l}\ v\ \mathtt{of}\ \mathtt{in_l}\ (x_1) \Rightarrow e_1 \mid \mathtt{in_r}\ (x_2) \Rightarrow e_2\ \mathtt{end} \Downarrow^{\mathsf{S}} v', \sigma', \mathrm{T}}\ (\textbf{case/inl})$$

$$\frac{\sigma, [v/x_2]\ e_2 \Downarrow^{\mathsf{S}} v', \sigma', \mathrm{T}}{\sigma, \mathtt{case}\ \mathtt{in_r}\ v\ \mathtt{of}\ \mathtt{in_l}\ (x_1) \Rightarrow e_1 \mid \mathtt{in_r}\ (x_2) \Rightarrow e_2\ \mathtt{end} \Downarrow^{\mathsf{S}} v', \sigma', \mathrm{T}}\ (\textbf{case/inr})$$

Fig. 5. Evaluation of stable expressions

expressions) of a computation that is consistent with any store—not necessarily with the current store. Since the evaluation whose results are being returned by the oracle can take place in a different store than the current store, the trace and the value (if any) returned by the oracle cannot be incorporated into the evaluation directly. Instead, the dynamic semantics performs a change propagation on the trace returned by the oracle before incorporating it into the current evaluation (this is described below).

Stable Evaluation. Figure 5 shows the evaluation rules for stable expressions. Most rules are standard for a store-passing semantics except that they also return traces. The interesting rules are those for `let`, `mod`, and `memo`.

$$\frac{}{\sigma, l \leftarrow \texttt{write}(v) \Downarrow^{\mathsf{C}} \sigma[l \leftarrow v], \texttt{write}\ v}\ \textbf{(write)}$$

$$\frac{\sigma, l \leftarrow [\sigma(l')/x]\ e \Downarrow^{\mathsf{C}} \sigma', \mathtt{T}}{\sigma, l \leftarrow \texttt{read}\ l'\ \texttt{as}\ x\ \texttt{in}\ e \Downarrow^{\mathsf{C}} \sigma', \texttt{read}_{l' \to x = \sigma(l').e}\ \mathtt{T}}\ \textbf{(read)}$$

$$\frac{\sigma, e \uparrow^{\mathsf{C}} \quad \sigma, e \Downarrow^{\mathsf{C}} \sigma', \mathtt{T}}{\sigma, l \leftarrow \texttt{memo}_{\mathsf{C}}\ e \Downarrow^{\mathsf{C}} \sigma', \mathtt{T}}\ \textbf{(memo/miss)} \qquad \frac{\sigma, e \downarrow^{\mathsf{C}} \mathtt{T} \quad \sigma, l \leftarrow \mathtt{T} \overset{\mathsf{C}}{\curvearrowright} \sigma', \mathtt{T}'}{\sigma, l \leftarrow \texttt{memo}_{\mathsf{C}}\ e \Downarrow^{\mathsf{C}} \sigma', \mathtt{T}'}\ \textbf{(memo/hit)}$$

$$\frac{v_1 = \texttt{func}_{\mathsf{C}}\ f(x)\ \texttt{is}\ e \qquad \sigma, l \leftarrow [v_1/f, v_2/x]\ e \Downarrow^{\mathsf{C}} \sigma', \mathtt{T}}{\sigma, l \leftarrow \texttt{apply}_{\mathsf{C}}(v_1, v_2) \Downarrow^{\mathsf{C}} \sigma', \mathtt{T}}\ \textbf{(apply)}$$

$$\frac{\sigma, e_1 \Downarrow^{\mathsf{S}} v, \sigma_1, \mathtt{T}_1 \quad \sigma_1, l \leftarrow [v/x]\ e_2 \Downarrow^{\mathsf{C}} \sigma_2, \mathtt{T}_2 \quad \texttt{alloc}(\mathtt{T}_1) \cap \texttt{alloc}(\mathtt{T}_2) = \emptyset}{\sigma, l \leftarrow \texttt{let}\ x = e_1\ \texttt{in}\ e_2 \Downarrow^{\mathsf{C}} \sigma_2, \texttt{let}\ \mathtt{T}_1\ \mathtt{T}_2}\ \textbf{(let)}$$

$$\frac{\sigma, l \leftarrow [v_1/x_1, v_2/x_2]\ e \Downarrow^{\mathsf{C}} \sigma', \mathtt{T}}{\sigma, l \leftarrow \texttt{let}\ x_1 \times x_2 = (v_1, v_2)\ \texttt{in}\ e \Downarrow^{\mathsf{C}} \sigma', \mathtt{T}}\ \textbf{(let}\times\textbf{)}$$

$$\frac{\sigma, l \leftarrow [v/x_1]\ e_1 \Downarrow^{\mathsf{C}} \sigma', \mathtt{T}}{\sigma, l \leftarrow \texttt{case}\ \texttt{inl}\ v\ \texttt{of}\ \texttt{inl}\ (x_1) \Rightarrow e_1 \mid \texttt{inr}\ (x_2) \Rightarrow e_2\ \texttt{end} \Downarrow^{\mathsf{C}} \sigma', \mathtt{T}}\ \textbf{(case/inl)}$$

$$\frac{\sigma, l \leftarrow [v/x_2]\ e_2 \Downarrow^{\mathsf{C}} \sigma', \mathtt{T}}{\sigma, \texttt{case}\ \texttt{inr}\ v\ \texttt{of}\ \texttt{inl}\ (x_1) \Rightarrow e_1 \mid \texttt{inr}\ (x_2) \Rightarrow e_2\ \texttt{end} \Downarrow^{\mathsf{C}} \sigma', \mathtt{T}}\ \textbf{(case/inr)}$$

Fig. 6. Evaluation of changeable expressions

The `let` rule sequences evaluation of its two expressions, performs binding by substitution, and yields a trace consisting of the sequential composition of the traces of its sub-expressions. For the traces to be well-formed, the rule requires that they allocate disjoint sets of locations. The `mod` rule allocates a location l, adds it to the store, and evaluates its body (a changeable expression) with l as the target. To ensure that l is not allocated multiple times, the rule requires that l is not allocated in the trace of the body. Note that the allocated location does not need to be fresh—it can already be in the store, i.e., $l \in \texttt{dom}(\sigma)$. Since every changeable expression ends with a `write`, it is guaranteed that an allocated location is written before it can be read.

The `memo` rule consults an oracle to determine if its body should be evaluated or not. If the oracle returns a miss, then the body is evaluated as usual and the value, the store, and the trace obtained via evaluation is returned. If the oracle returns a hit, then it returns a value v and a trace $\mathtt{T}$. To adapt the trace to the current store σ, the evaluation performs a change propagation on $\mathtt{T}$ in σ and returns the value v returned by the oracle, and the trace and the store returned by change propagation. Note that since change propagation can change the contents of the store, it can also indirectly change the (lifted) contents of v.

Changeable Evaluation. Figure 6 shows the evaluation rules for changeable expressions. Evaluations in changeable mode perform *destination passing.* The

$$\frac{}{\sigma, \varepsilon \overset{\mathsf{S}}{\curvearrowright} \sigma, \varepsilon}\ (\textbf{empty})$$

$$\frac{l \notin \mathtt{alloc}(\mathtt{T}') \qquad \sigma, l \leftarrow \mathtt{T} \overset{\mathsf{C}}{\curvearrowright} \sigma', \mathtt{T}'}{\sigma, \mathtt{mod}\ l \leftarrow \mathtt{T} \overset{\mathsf{S}}{\curvearrowright} \sigma', \mathtt{mod}\ l \leftarrow \mathtt{T}'}\ (\textbf{mod}) \qquad \frac{}{\sigma, l \leftarrow \mathtt{write}\ v \overset{\mathsf{C}}{\curvearrowright} \sigma[l \leftarrow v], \mathtt{write}\ v}\ (\textbf{write})$$

$$\frac{\sigma, \mathtt{T}_1 \overset{\mathsf{S}}{\curvearrowright} \sigma', \mathtt{T}_1' \qquad \sigma', \mathtt{T}_2 \overset{\mathsf{S}}{\curvearrowright} \sigma'', \mathtt{T}_2' \qquad \mathtt{alloc}(\mathtt{T}_1') \cap \mathtt{alloc}(\mathtt{T}_2') = \emptyset}{\sigma, \mathtt{let}\ \mathtt{T}_1\ \mathtt{T}_2 \overset{\mathsf{S}}{\curvearrowright} \sigma'', \mathtt{let}\ \mathtt{T}_1'\ \mathtt{T}_2'}\ (\textbf{let/s})$$

$$\frac{\sigma, \mathtt{T}_1 \overset{\mathsf{C}}{\curvearrowright} \sigma', \mathtt{T}_1' \qquad \sigma', l \leftarrow \mathtt{T}_2 \overset{\mathsf{C}}{\curvearrowright} \sigma'', \mathtt{T}_2' \qquad \mathtt{alloc}(\mathtt{T}_1') \cap \mathtt{alloc}(\mathtt{T}_2') = \emptyset}{\sigma, l \leftarrow (\mathtt{let}\ \mathtt{T}_1\ \mathtt{T}_2) \overset{\mathsf{C}}{\curvearrowright} \sigma'', (\mathtt{let}\ \mathtt{T}_1'\ \mathtt{T}_2')}\ (\textbf{let/c})$$

$$\frac{\sigma(l') = v \qquad \sigma, l \leftarrow \mathtt{T} \overset{\mathsf{C}}{\curvearrowright} \sigma', \mathtt{T}'}{\sigma, l \leftarrow \mathtt{read}_{l' \rightarrow v = x.e}\ \mathtt{T} \overset{\mathsf{C}}{\curvearrowright} \sigma', \mathtt{read}_{l' \rightarrow v = x.e}\ \mathtt{T}'}\ (\textbf{read/no ch.})$$

$$\frac{\sigma(l') \neq v \qquad \sigma, l \leftarrow [\sigma(l')/x]e \Downarrow^{\mathsf{C}} \sigma', \mathtt{T}'}{\sigma, l \leftarrow \mathtt{read}_{l' \rightarrow x = v.e}\ \mathtt{T} \overset{\mathsf{C}}{\curvearrowright} \sigma', \mathtt{read}_{l' \rightarrow x = \sigma(l').e}\ \mathtt{T}'}\ (\textbf{read/ch.})$$

Fig. 7. Change propagation judgments

`let`, `memo`, `apply` rules are similar to the corresponding rules in stable mode except that the body of each expression is evaluated in changeable mode. The `read` expression substitutes the value stored in σ at the location being read l' for the bound variable x in e and continues evaluation in changeable mode. A `read` is recorded in the trace, along with the value read, the variable bound, and the body of the read. A `write` simply assigns its argument to the target in the store. The evaluation of memoized changeable expressions is similar to that of stable expressions.

Change propagation. Figure 7 shows the rules for change propagation. As with evaluation rules, change-propagation rules are partitioned into stable and changeable, depending on the kind of the trace being processed. The stable change-propagation judgment $\sigma, \mathtt{T}_s \overset{\mathsf{S}}{\curvearrowright} \sigma', \mathtt{T}_s'$ states that change propagating into the stable trace $\mathtt{T}_s$ in the context of the store σ yields the store σ' and the stable trace $\mathtt{T}_s'$. The changeable change-propagation judgment $\sigma, l \leftarrow \mathtt{T}_c \overset{\mathsf{C}}{\curvearrowright} \sigma', \mathtt{T}_c'$ states that change propagation into the changeable trace $\mathtt{T}_c$ with target l in the context of the store σ yields the changeable trace $\mathtt{T}_c'$ and the store σ'. The change propagation rules mimic evaluation by either skipping over the parts of the trace that remain the same in the given store or by re-evaluating the `read`s that read locations whose values are different in the given store. The rules are labeled with the expression forms they mimic.

If the trace is empty, change propagation returns an empty trace and the same store. The `mod` rule recursively propagates into the trace $\mathtt{T}$ for the body to obtain a new trace $\mathtt{T}'$ and returns a trace where $\mathtt{T}$ is substituted by $\mathtt{T}'$ under the condition that the target l is not allocated in $\mathtt{T}'$. This condition is necessary to ensure the allocation integrity of the returned trace. The stable `let` rule propagates into its two parts $\mathtt{T}_1$ and $\mathtt{T}_2$ recursively and returns a trace by combining the resulting traces $\mathtt{T}'_1$ and $\mathtt{T}'_2$ provided that the resulting trace ensures allocation integrity. The `write` rule performs the recorded write in the given store by extending the target with the value recorded in the trace. This is necessary to ensure that the result of a re-used changeable computation is recorded in the new store. The `read` rule depends on whether the contents of the location l' being read is the same in the store as the value v recorded in the trace. If the contents is the same as in the trace, then change propagation proceeds into the body T of the read and the resulting trace is substituted for T. Otherwise, the body of the `read` is evaluated with the specified target. Note that this makes evaluation and change-propagation mutually recursive—evaluation calls change-propagation in the case of an oracle hit. The changeable `let` rule is similar to the stable `let`.

Most change-propagation judgments perform some consistency checks and otherwise propagate forward. Only when a `read` finds that the location in question has changed, it re-runs the changeable computation that is in its body and replaces the corresponding trace.

Evaluation invariants. Valid evaluations of stable and changeable expressions satisfy the following invariants:

1. All locations allocated in the trace are also allocated in the result store, i.e., if $\sigma, e \Downarrow^{\mathsf{S}}_{\mathrm{ok}} v, \sigma', \mathtt{T}$ or $\sigma, l \leftarrow e \Downarrow^{\mathsf{C}}_{\mathrm{ok}} \sigma', \mathtt{T}$, then $\mathtt{dom}(\sigma') = \mathtt{dom}(\sigma) \cup \mathtt{alloc}\,(\mathtt{T})$.
2. For stable evaluations, any location whose content changes is allocated during that evaluation, i.e., if $\sigma, e \Downarrow^{\mathsf{S}}_{\mathrm{ok}} v, \sigma', \mathtt{T}$ and $\sigma'(l) \neq \sigma(l)$, then $l \in \mathtt{alloc}\,(\mathtt{T})$.
3. For changeable evaluations, a location whose content changes is either the target or gets allocated during evaluation, i.e, if $\sigma, l' \leftarrow e \Downarrow^{\mathsf{C}}_{\mathrm{ok}} \sigma', \mathtt{T}$ and $\sigma'(l) \neq \sigma(l)$, then $l \in \mathtt{alloc}\,(\mathtt{T}) \cup \{l'\}$.

Memo-free evaluations. The oracle rules introduce non-determinism into the dynamic semantics. Lemmas 3 and 4 in Section 3 express the fact that this non-determinism is harmless: change propagation will correctly update all answers returned by the oracle and make everything look as if the oracle never produced any answer at all (meaning that only **memo/miss** rules were used).

We write $\sigma, e \Downarrow^{\mathsf{S}}_{\emptyset} v, \sigma', \mathtt{T}$ or $\sigma, l \leftarrow e \Downarrow^{\mathsf{C}}_{\emptyset} \sigma', \mathtt{T}$ if there is a derivation for $\sigma, e \Downarrow^{\mathsf{S}} v, \sigma', \mathtt{T}$ or $\sigma, l \leftarrow e \Downarrow^{\mathsf{C}} \sigma', \mathtt{T}$, respectively, that does not use any **memo/hit** rule. We call such an evaluation *memo-free*. We use $\Downarrow^{\mathsf{S}}_{\emptyset,\mathrm{ok}}$ in place of $\Downarrow^{\mathsf{S}}_{\mathrm{ok}}$ and $\Downarrow^{\mathsf{C}}_{\emptyset,\mathrm{ok}}$ in place of $\Downarrow^{\mathsf{C}}_{\mathrm{ok}}$ to indicate that a valid evaluation is also memo-free.

2.4 Deterministic, Purely Functional Semantics

By ignoring memoization and change-propagation, we can give an alternative, purely functional, semantics for location-free AML programs [9]. This semantics gives a store-free, pure, deterministic interpretation of AML that provides for no computation reuse. Under this semantics, both stable and changeable expressions evaluate to values, `memo`, `mod` and `write` are simply identities, and `read` acts as another binding construct. Our correctness result states that the pure interpretation of AML yields results that are the same (up to lifting) as those obtained by AML's dynamic semantics (Section 3).

3 Consistency and Correctness

We now state consistency and correctness theorems for AML and outline their proofs in terms of several main lemmas. As depicted in Figure 8, consistency (Theorem 1) is a consequence of correctness (Theorem 2).

3.1 Main Theorems

Consistency uses *structural equality* based on the notion of *lifts* (see Section 2.2) to compare the results of two potentially different evaluations of the same AML program under its non-deterministic semantics. Correctness, on the other hand, compares one such evaluation to a pure, functional evaluation. It justifies saying that even with stores, memoization and change propagation, AML is essentially a purely functional language.

Theorem 1 (Consistency). *If* $\sigma, e \Downarrow^{\mathsf{s}}_{\mathrm{ok}} v_1, \sigma_1, T_1$ *and* $\sigma, e \Downarrow^{\mathsf{s}}_{\mathrm{ok}} v_2, \sigma_2, T_2$*, then* $v_1 \uparrow \sigma_1 = v_2 \uparrow \sigma_2$.

Theorem 2 (Correctness). *If* $\sigma, e \Downarrow^{\mathsf{s}}_{\mathrm{ok}} v, \sigma', T$*, then* $(e \uparrow \sigma) \Downarrow^{\mathsf{s}}_{\mathrm{det}} (v \uparrow \sigma')$.

Recall that by our convention the use of the notation $v \uparrow \sigma$ implies well-formedness of v in σ. Therefore, part of the statement of consistency is the preservation of well-formedness during evaluation, and the inability of AML programs to create cyclic memory graphs.

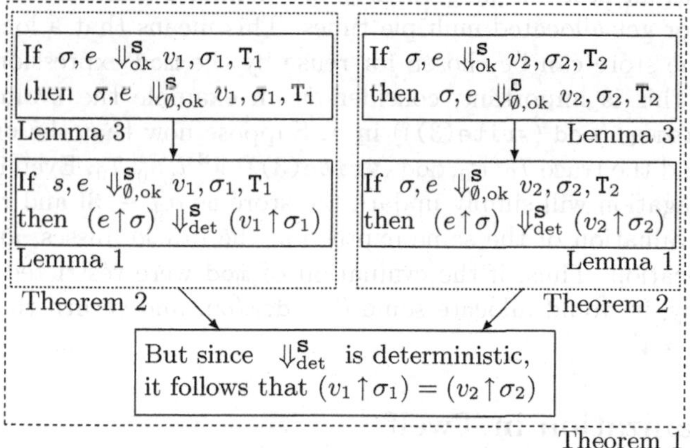

Fig. 8. The structure of the proofs

3.2 Proof Outline

The consistency theorem is proved in two steps. First, Lemmas 1 and 2 state that consistency is true in the restricted setting where all evaluations are memo-free.

Lemma 1 (purity/st.). *If* $\sigma, e \Downarrow^{\mathsf{S}}_{\emptyset,\mathrm{ok}} v, \sigma', T$, *then* $(e \uparrow \sigma) \Downarrow^{\mathsf{S}}_{\mathrm{det}} (v \uparrow \sigma')$.

Lemma 2 (purity/ch.). *If* $\sigma, l \leftarrow e \Downarrow^{\mathsf{C}}_{\emptyset,\mathrm{ok}} \sigma', T$, *then* $(e \uparrow \sigma) \Downarrow^{\mathsf{C}}_{\mathrm{det}} (l \uparrow \sigma')$.

Second, Lemmas 3 and 4 state that for any evaluation there is a memo-free counterpart that yields an *identical* result and has *identical* effects on the store. Notice that this is stronger than saying that the memo-free evaluation is "equivalent" in some sense (e.g., under lifts). The statements of these lemmas are actually even stronger since they include a "preservation of well-formedness" statement. Preservation of well-formedness is required in the inductive proof.

Lemma 3 (memo-freedom/st.). *If* $\sigma, e \Downarrow^{\mathsf{S}}_{\mathrm{ok}} v, \sigma', T$, *then* $\sigma, e \Downarrow^{\mathsf{S}}_{\emptyset} v, \sigma', T$ *where* $\mathtt{reach}(v, \sigma') \subseteq \mathtt{reach}(e, \sigma) \cup \mathtt{alloc}(T)$.

Lemma 4 (memo-freedom/ch.). *If* $\sigma, l \leftarrow e \Downarrow^{\mathsf{C}}_{\mathrm{ok}} \sigma', T$, *then* $\sigma, l \leftarrow e \Downarrow^{\mathsf{C}}_{\emptyset} \sigma', T$ *where* $\mathtt{reach}(\sigma'(l), \sigma') \subseteq \mathtt{reach}(e, \sigma) \cup \mathtt{alloc}(T)$.

The proof for Lemmas 3 and 4 proceeds by simultaneous induction over the expression e. It is outlined in far more detail in the accompanying technical report [9]. Both lemmas state that if there is a well-formed evaluation leading to a store, a trace, and a result (the value v in the stable lemma, or the target l in the changeable lemma), the same result (which will be well-formed itself) is obtainable by a memo-free run. Moreover, all locations reachable from the result were either reachable from the initial expression or were allocated during the evaluation. These conditions help to re-establish well-formedness in inductive steps.

The lemmas are true thanks to a key property of the dynamic semantics: allocated locations need not be completely "fresh" in the sense that they may be in the current store as long as they are neither reachable from the initial expression nor get allocated multiple times. This means that a location that is already in the store can be chosen for reuse by the `mod` expression (Figure 5). To see why this is important, consider as an example the evaluating of the expression: $\mathtt{memo}_{\mathsf{S}}$ (`mod (write(3))`) in σ. Suppose now that the oracle returns the value l and the trace T_0: $\sigma_0, \mathtt{mod}\ (\mathtt{write(3)}) \Downarrow^{\mathsf{S}} l, \sigma_0', \mathtt{T}_0$. Even if $l \in \mathtt{dom}(\sigma)$, change propagation will simply update the store as $\sigma[l \leftarrow 3]$ and return l. In a memo-free evaluation of the same expression the oracle misses, and `mod` must allocate a location. Thus, if the evaluation of `mod` were restricted to use fresh locations only, it would allocate some $l' \notin \mathtt{dom}(\sigma)$, and return that. But since $l \in \mathtt{dom}(\sigma)$, $l \neq l'$.

4 Mechanization in Twelf

To increase our confidence in the proofs for the correctness and the consistency theorems, we have encoded the AML language and the proofs in Twelf [16] and machine-checked the proofs. We follow the standard *judgments as types* methodology [13], and check our theorems using the Twelf metatheorem checker. For full details on using Twelf in this way for proofs about programming languages, see Harper and Licata's manuscript [14].

The LF encoding of the syntax and semantics of AML corresponds very closely to the paper judgments (in an informal sense; we have not proved formally that the LF encoding is *adequate*, and take adequacy to be evident). However, in a few cases we have altered the judgments, driven by the needs of the mechanized proof. For example, on paper we write memo-free and general evaluations as different judgments, and silently coerce memo-free to general evaluations in the proof. We could represent the two judgments by separate LF type families, but the proof would then require a lemma to convert one judgment to the other. Instead, we define a type family to represent general evaluations, and a separate type family, indexed by evaluation derivations, to represent the judgment that an evaluation derivation is memo-free.

The proof of consistency (a metatheorem in Twelf) corresponds closely to the paper proof (see [9] for details) in overall structure. The proof of memo-freedom consists of four mutually-inductive lemmas: memo-freedom for stable and changeable expressions (Lemma 3 and Lemma 4), and versions of these with an additional change propagation following the evaluation (needed for the hit cases). In the hit cases for these latter lemmas, we must eliminate two change propagations: we call the lemma once to eliminate the first, then a second time on the output of the first call to eliminate the second. Since the evaluation in the second call is not a subderivation of the input, we must give a separate termination metric. The metric is defined on evaluation derivations and simply counts the number of evaluations in the derivations, including those inside of change propagations. In an evaluation which contains change propagations, there are "garbage" evaluations which are removed during hit-elimination. Therefore, hit-elimination reduces this metric (or keeps it the same, if there were no change propagations to remove). We add arguments to the lemmas to account for the metric, and simultaneously prove that the metric is smaller in each inductive call, in order for Twelf to check termination.

Aside from this structural difference due to termination checking, the main difference from the paper proof is that the Twelf proof must of course spell out all the details which the paper proof leaves to the reader to verify. In particular, we must encode "background" structures such as finite sets of locations, and prove relevant properties of such structures. While we are not the first to use these structures in Twelf, Twelf has poor support for reusable libraries at present. Moreover, our needs are somewhat specialized: because we need to prove properties about stores which differ only on a set of locations, it is convenient to encode stores and location sets in a slightly unusual way: location sets are represented as lists of bits, and stores are represented as lists of value options; in both representations the nth list element corresponds to the nth location. This makes it easy to prove the necessary lemmas by parallel induction over the lists. The Twelf code can be found at `http://www.cs.cmu.edu/~jdonham/aml-proof/`

5 Implementation Strategies

The dynamic semantics of AML (Section 2) does not translate directly to an algorithm, not to mention an efficient one.[1] In particular, an algorithm consistent with the semantics must specify an oracle and a way to allocate locations to ensure that all locations allocated in a trace are unique. We briefly describe a conservative strategy for implementing the semantics. The strategy ensures that

1. each allocated location is fresh (i.e., is not contained in the memory)
2. the oracle returns only traces currently residing in the memory,
3. the oracle never returns a trace more than once, and
4. the oracle performs function comparisons by using tag equality.

The first two conditions together ensure that each allocated location is unique. The third condition guarantees that no location can appear in the execution trace more than once. This condition is conservative, because it is possible that the parts of a trace returned by the oracle are thrown away (become unused) during change propagation. This strategy can be relaxed by allowing the change-propagation algorithm to return unused traces to the oracle. The last condition enables implementing oracle queries by comparing functions and their arguments by using tag equality. Since in the semantics, the oracle is non-deterministic, this implementation strategy is consistent with the semantics.

The conservative strategy can be implemented in such a way that the total space consumption is no more than that of a from-scratch run. Such an implementation has been completed and shown to be effective for a reasonably broad range applications [3,7]. The implementation, however, places further restrictions on the oracle that are not required by the proof (e.g., computations must always be re-used in the same order).Our results shows that these restrictions are not necessary for correctness and can potentially be relaxed—such an implementation can be more broadly applicable.

We note that the described conservative implementation does not guarantee correctness, because it requires the programmer to supply all the free variables of memoized expressions. When the programmer misspecifies the free variables, the correctness guarantee fails. This problem can be addressed by a type system or detecting the free variables of memoized expressions automatically with a static analyzer.

6 Conclusion

Recent experimental results show that it is possible to adjust computations to changes to their data (e.g., inputs, outcomes of comparisons) efficiently by using a combination of change propagation and memoization. This paper formalizes a general semantics for combining memoization and change propagation where

[1] This does not constitute a problem for our results, since our theorems and lemmas concern given derivations (not the problem finding them).

memoization is modeled as a non-deterministic oracle, and computation re-use is possible in the presence of mutation. Our main theorem shows that the semantics is consistent with deterministic, purely functional programming.

By giving a general semantics for combining memoization and change propagation, we cover a variety of possible techniques for implementing self-adjusting-computation. By proving the semantics correct with minimal assumptions, we identify the properties that correct implementations must satisfy. In particular, the results show that some assumptions made by existing implementations are not necessary for correctness and that they may be further improved.

References

1. M. Abadi, B. W. Lampson, and J.-J. Levy. Analysis and caching of dependencies. In *International Conference on Functional Programming*, pages 83–91, 1996.
2. U. A. Acar. *Self-Adjusting Computation.* PhD thesis, Department of Computer Science, Carnegie Mellon University, May 2005.
3. U. A. Acar, G. E. Blelloch, M. Blume, and K. Tangwongsan. An experimental analysis of self-adjusting computation. In *Proceedings of the ACM SIGPLAN Conference on Programming Language Design and Implementation*, 2006.
4. U. A. Acar, G. E. Blelloch, and R. Harper. Adaptive functional programming. In *Proc. of the 29th Ann. ACM Symp. on POPL*, pages 247–259, 2002.
5. U. A. Acar, G. E. Blelloch, and R. Harper. Selective memoization. In *Proc. of the 30th Annual ACM Symposium on Principles of Programming Languages*, 2003.
6. U. A. Acar, G. E. Blelloch, R. Harper, J. L. Vittes, and M. Woo. Dynamizing static algorithms with applications to dynamic trees and history independence. In *ACM-SIAM Symposium on Discrete Algorithms (SODA)*, 2004.
7. U. A. Acar, G. E. Blelloch, K. Tangwongsan, and J. L. Vittes. Kinetic algorithms via self-adjusting computation. Technical Report CMU-CS-06-115, Department of Computer Science, Carnegie Mellon University, March 2006.
8. U. A. Acar, G. E. Blelloch, and J. L. Vittes. An experimental analysis of change propagation in dynamic trees. In *Workshop on Algorithm Engineering and Experimentation*, 2005.
9. U. A. Acar, M. Blume, and J. Donham. A consistent semantics of self-adjusting computation. Technical Report CMU-CS-06-168, Department of Computer Science, Carnegie Mellon University, 2006.
10. M. Carlsson. Monads for incremental computing. In *Proc. of the 7th ACM SIGPLAN Intl. Conf. on Funct. Prog.*, pages 26–35. ACM Press, 2002.
11. A. Demers, T. Reps, and T. Teitelbaum. Incremental evaluation of attribute grammars with application to syntax directed editors. In *Proceedings of the 8th Annual ACM Symposium on Principles of Programming Languages*, pages 105–116, 1981.
12. J. Field and T. Teitelbaum. Incremental reduction in the lambda calculus. In *Proceedings of the ACM '90 Conference on LISP and Functional Programming*, pages 307–322, June 1990.
13. R. Harper, F. Honsell, and G. Plotkin. A framework for defining logics. *Journal of the Association for Computing Machinery*, 40(1):143–184, January 1993.
14. R. Harper and D. Licata. Mechanizing language definitions. (Submitted for publication.), April 2006.

15. D. Michie. 'memo' functions and machine learning. *Nature*, 218:19–22, 1968.
16. F. Pfenning and C. Schürmann. System description: Twelf — a meta-logical framework for deductive systems. In H. Ganzinger, editor, *Proceedings of the 16th International Conference on Automated Deduction (CADE-16)*, pages 202–206, Trento, Italy, July 1999. Springer-Verlag LNAI 1632.
17. W. Pugh and T. Teitelbaum. Incremental computation via function caching. In *Proceedings of the 16th Annual ACM Symposium on Principles of Programming Languages*, pages 315–328, 1989.
18. G. Ramalingam and T. Reps. A categorized bibliography on incremental computation. In *Conference Record of the 20th Annual ACM Symposium on POPL*, pages 502–510, Jan. 1993.
19. R. S. Sundaresh and P. Hudak. Incremental compilation via partial evaluation. In *Conf. Record of the 18th Ann. ACM Symp. on POPL*, pages 1–13, Jan. 1991.

Multi-language Synchronization

Robert Ennals and David Gay

Intel Research Berkeley,
2150 Shattuck Avenue, Berkeley,
CA 94704, USA
robert.ennals@intel.com
david.e.gay@intel.com

Abstract. We propose *multi-language synchronization*, a novel approach to the problem of migrating code from a legacy language (such as C) to a new language. We maintain two parallel versions of every source file, one in the legacy language, and one in the new language. Both of these files are fully editable, and the two files are kept automatically in sync so that they have the same semantic meaning and, where possible, have the same comments and layout.

We propose *non-deterministic language translation* as a means to implement multi-language synchronization. If a file is modified in language A, we produce a new version in language B by translating the file into a non-deterministic description of many ways that it could be encoded in language B and then choosing the version that is closest to the old file in language B.

To demonstrate the feasibility of this approach, we have implemented a translator that can synchronize files written in a straw-man language, Jekyll, with files written in C. Jekyll is a high level functional programming language that has many of the features found in modern programming languages.

1 Introduction

The programming language community has produced many programming languages that improve on legacy languages such as C in useful ways. They have produced languages that are easier to use, easier to understand, safer, more portable, more reusable, etc. But, despite all these advantages, a large proportion of important software projects continue to use legacy languages.

Why is this? Prior work suggests that one of the principal reasons why programmers continue to use legacy languages is that they have built up such a strong ecosystem around them that the switching costs associated with moving to a new language are prohibitive [28,17]. In particular:

– Much software is already written in legacy languages.
– Many libraries are written in legacy languages.
– Many programmers only understand legacy languages.
– Many tools only understand legacy languages.

R. De Nicola (Ed.): ESOP 2007, LNCS 4421, pp. 475–489, 2007.

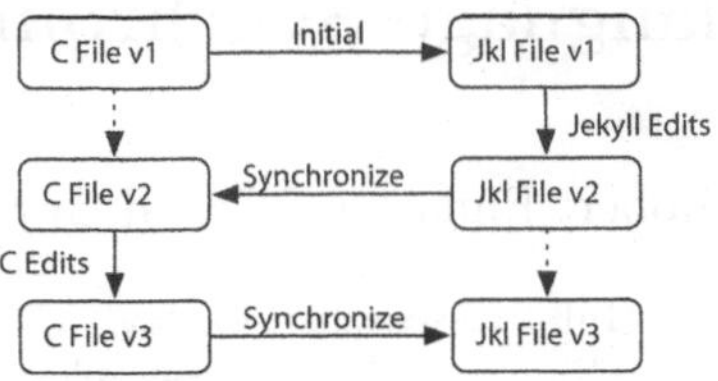

Fig. 1. *JT* keeps the Jekyll and C versions of a file synchronized

- Developers are wary of trusting a language that might not be maintained in 10 years time.
- For existing projects, developers are unwilling to port large code bases to new languages, both because of the effort involved and the risk of introducing new bugs.

Historically, one way that new languages have achieved success is by having some degree of compatibility with an existing language, allowing them to exploit its ecosystem (e.g. C++ [27] and Objective C [24], which are supersets of C). In this paper, we propose a novel way for a new language to exploit the ecosystem of legacy languages such as C. Our approach is to maintain two parallel versions of each source file, one in the legacy language and one in the new language. Both of these files are human readable, un-annotated, and fully editable. A synchronizer program propagates updates between the two files, ensuring that they remain semantically equivalent, and, as much as possible, have the same comments and layout (Figure 1). We call this technique *multi-language synchronization.*

The hope is that, by providing an editable version of a file in the legacy language, it becomes easier for a project to adopt a new language, since greater use can be made of the ecosystem of the legacy language. In particular, programmers who do not know the new language can edit the legacy file, legacy language tools can be applied to the legacy file, legacy programs can transition to a new language without having to abandon the legacy language, and if the new language ceases to be maintained development can fall back to the legacy language. When legacy programmers and new-language programmers work on the same program, edits made by one group can be seen as minimal edits by the other group - preserving language-specific structure and layout.

While the task of translating between two languages without losing language-specific information might seem daunting, we show that it can be done using *non-deterministic language translation.* To translate a file from language A to language B, we produce a description of many encodings of the file in language B, and then select the version that is closest to the old file in language B (Section 3).

To demonstrate the feasibility of multi-language synchronization, we have implemented a translator, *JT*, which can synchronize files written in C with files written in a new language, called Jekyll. The design of Jekyll is not a goal in itself; rather it is intended to show that multi-language translation is possible between two fairly different languages: Jekyll is a modern functional programming language which has many of the features present in languages such as

Haskell [25], ML [21], and Cyclone [15], including generic types, lambda expressions, pattern matching, algebraic datatypes, and type classes. Jekyll also has all of the features of C, although potentially unsafe features such as pointer arithmetic require use of a explicit **unsafe** keyword in order to avoid a warning (in common with C# [5]). A more complete description of Jekyll can be found in a companion tech report [8]; JT is available on SourceForge at:

`http://sourceforge.net/projects/jekyllc`

The main contributions of this paper are the concept of multi-language synchronization, presented in more detail in Section 2, and the algorithms and techniques that make multi-language synchronization possible (Section 3). In Section 4 we present a preliminary evaluation of multi-language synchronization based on our experiences with JT. This evaluation shows that multi-language synchronization does work in practice. In the future, we hope to conduct a full evaluation based on a realistic successor to C used on a large-scale software project, as part of the Ivy project [2]. We discuss related work in Section 5 and conclude in Section 6.

2 Multi-language Synchronization

We start by outlining the basic model for, and usability requirements on, multi-language synchronization (Section 2.1), followed by a discussion of the requirements on the languages being translated (Section 2.2), For concreteness, in this section and the rest of the paper, we discuss multi-language synchronization in terms of C, Jekyll and JT. However, except when referring to language-specific features, our comments apply to multi-language synchronization in general.

2.1 Model and Usability Requirements

Our basic model for multi-language synchronization, shown earlier in Figure 1, is that at all times each source file S exists in C (S_{C}) and Jekyll forms (S_{J}). After a programmer edits the C file $\mathrm{X_C}$, the system regenerates ("synchronizes") the corresponding Jekyll file $\mathrm{X_J}$, based on the **new** contents of the C file and the **old** contents of the Jekyll file; edits to Jekyll files are handled in an analogous fashion. This regeneration is expected to happen frequently (e.g., after every successful build or before every commit to a source-code control system).

It is of course also possible to translate a C file to Jekyll without any previous Jekyll version (e.g., when importing an existing project). However, the presence of a previous version allows for a better translation preserving the use of Jekyll-specific features not explicitly present in the C version of the source code, as discussed in Section 3 and shown in the examples of Section 4.

Multi-language synchronization is an inexact science. A C file generated from a Jekyll file is typically not as readable as a C file written by a C programmer, and there are limits on the degree to which a C programmer can edit C code that represents a higher-level Jekyll feature before JT is unable to produce a good corresponding update to the Jekyll file.

The goal however is not to be perfect, but to be good enough to be useful. In particular, the translation should be good enough that a C programmer unfamiliar with Jekyll would find it easier to edit the C file than to edit the Jekyll file, and a developer would find it easier to use an existing C tool on the C file than to work without that tool using the Jekyll file. More generally, the translation has the following goals:

- **Semantics are preserved:** C code translated into Jekyll has unchanged behavior, and vice-versa.
- **Edits are translated naturally:** The result of making a change to a C file and then translating it to Jekyll is close to the result of translating the original C file to Jekyll and logically making the same change, and vice-versa.
- **C programmers can understand C code produced by JT:** Generated C code is readable, fully commented, and does not contain additional annotations.
- **JT can understand code produced by C programmers:** JT is sufficiently tolerant of edits to C code encoding Jekyll features that it can produce reasonable Jekyll updates for a large proportion of C updates.
- **No special infrastructure needed:** JT works from the text files containing the C and Jekyll source code. It does not require, for example, that all code modifications be performed by a special editor. We do however use, as outlined above, the previous version of the **target** of the translation.

Note that some of these goals may be in conflict: for instance, as we discuss in more detail in Section 3.7, the desire to produce a translation from C which preserves the use of some Jekyll feature — in support of the natural edit translation goal — may lead JT to change the semantics during translation. Such behavior is acceptable in a translator as long as it always warns the programmer in an appropriate way, and only does it in well-justified cases (e.g., JT believes the code it was translating was buggy).

2.2 Language Requirements

We do not believe that multi-language synchronization between arbitrary pairs of languages is practical. We do believe the following properties of Jekyll and C (especially the first two) are what makes JT practical, and suggest that these should serve as guidelines in the design of other multi-language translation systems:

- **All C features can be translated reasonably easily into Jekyll.** In particular, Jekyll supports all unsafe features of C (although their use is discouraged, and warnings are produced unless the **unsafe** keyword is used).
- **All Jekyll features can be translated into reasonably readable C.** In particular, Jekyll does not support lazy evaluation or tail recursion elimination, and several features (e.g., the implementation of closures) are designed with a C encoding in mind.
- **Jekyll uses the same data-layout as C.** This is particularly important in a language such as C where low-level features expose the data layout.

3 Non-deterministic Language Translation

One approach to maintaining two consistent versions of the same file in different languages would be to apply the actions performed on one file (e.g., rename this function, insert this code) to the other, in a fashion similar to database view updates [14,6]. However, this approach is not practical as editors do not record such information, and deducing what actions have been performed can be difficult.

Instead, our approach to implementing multi-language synchronization is *non-deterministic language translation.* A modified C file can be encoded into Jekyll in many different ways. Rather than picking one of these encodings, JT translates a C file into a non-deterministic description of many of the ways that the file might be encoded as Jekyll. JT then resolves this non-determinism by attempting to choose the Jekyll file that is the closest textual match to the previous Jekyll version of the file (Figure 2). Similarly, there are many different ways that a Jekyll file might be translated to C. JT attempts to choose the decoding that most closely resembles the previous C file.

This non-deterministic approach avoids the need for JT to enforce any canonical encoding of Jekyll into C, and thus allows JT to be reasonably tolerant of edits to C code while still ensuring that round-tripping through Jekyll is lossless. The non-deterministic approach also allows the implementation to be simple and elegant. The translator need merely describe the various ways in which C and Jekyll can be encoded into each other, and the details of how to choose the correct encoding are left to a generic matching algorithm. There is no need for special-purpose code to recognize particular kinds of updates or preserve particular kinds of information, and new encodings and new language features can be added easily.

Figure 2 illustrates the structure of the translation system used by JT. In the following sections, we will discuss this translation process in more detail.

3.1 Non-deterministic Abstract Syntax Trees (ASTs)

When an AST is translated from one language into another, some of the nodes in the target syntax tree may be special *choice* nodes that represent a non-deterministic choice of encoding/decoding. A choice node takes three arguments:

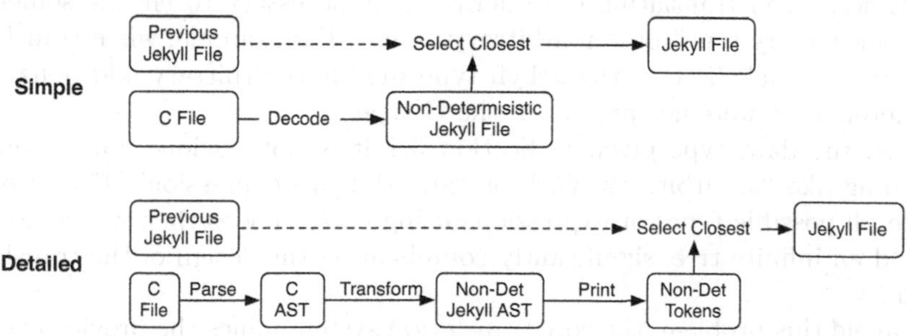

Fig. 2. The structure of the JT translation system (other direction is the same)

- The **decision variable** v (*true* or *false*).
- The **options** a_t and a_f are the different nodes that the choice node can resolve to. If v is *true* then the node resolves to a_t, otherwise it resolves to a_f. Although only two options are specified, an arbitrarily long list of options can be encoded using several nested choice nodes.
  Different alternatives will often have substantial similarities. To avoid blow-up in the size of our AST, different choices can share sub-nodes.

Decision variables allow specification of dependencies between choices made in different parts of the tree. This is useful since a single encoding/decoding decision may have effects in a number of places throughout the file. For example a C function that is never called directly and has its address taken once could be decoded either as a Jekyll function or as a lambda expression. Since a decision needs to be made, a decision variable is allocated. This variable will be *true* if the function is a lambda expression and *false* if the C function is just a Jekyll function. This decision variable is then used to parameterize each point in the AST at which this decision would cause the Jekyll program to be different, including the function definition and the function use.

The a_f option is the *default* option, and is the option that the *select closest* stage (Figure 2) will choose if neither of the two options is a close match to the previous file. The default option should always be the most conservative choice. For example, when decoding C as Jekyll, the default is to produce Jekyll code that is identical to the original C code. Amongst other things, the default option will typically be used when new code is added to a file, or no current version exists in the other language.

The transform phase (Figure 2) is written directly as ML code. A series of functions use pattern matching to find AST features of interest and then translate them into the equivalent features in the other language, using choice nodes when there are several ways that the feature can be translated. Unlike some other bi-directional translation systems [10,16], the two translation directions are written separately, rather than being generated from a common description. We leave a combined approach for future work.

3.2 Encoding Arbitrary Elements

Sometimes, when translating C to Jekyll, it is necessary to encode something like "an arbitrary type" or "an arbitrary name". For example, when translating a C type to a Jekyll type, the Jekyll type may have arbitrary additional type parameters that were not present in the C type.

Given the data type given in Section 3.1 it is not obvious how to encode something like "an arbitrary type" or "an arbitrary expression". If we were to encode all possible types or expressions using choice nodes then we would have to build an infinite tree, significantly complicating the design of the translation system.

To avoid this problem, the core translation system mines the previous version of the file for instances of particular syntax elements. If the translate stage wants to encode "an arbitrary type" then rather than describing all types possible in the language, it lists all the types present in the previous version.[1]

At first it might seem that this technique would artificially restrict the choice of types and prevent the *select closest* stage from selecting the encoding that most closely matches the previous version. However, since the *select closest* stage aims to minimize the textual distance from the previous version, it will always choose types that appear in the previous version in preference to types that do not. Thus there is no need to list types that do not appear in the previous version, and no need for JT to support infinite ASTs. This approach would need to be changed if non-determinism was resolved based on a smarter metric than textual difference — for example if type correctness was taken into account (Section 3.4).

3.3 Non-deterministic Token Sequences

Rather than resolving non-determinism directly at the AST level, we instead translate the AST into a *non-deterministic token sequence* and resolve the non-determinism at the token level. Alternatively we could resolving the non-determinism directly at the tree level, however, we leave such approaches for future work.

This non-deterministic token sequence preserves all of the non-determinism that was present in the non-deterministic AST, but reduces the abstraction level down to a sequence of strings, described as follows:

$$\begin{array}{ll} t \leftarrow v \;?\; t_f : t_t & \text{non-deterministic choice} \\ \quad \mid\; t_0 \bullet t_1 \mid \text{“}s\text{”} \mid \emptyset & \text{sequence, literal, empty} \end{array}$$

The *pretty print* stage produces a non-deterministic token sequence by applying a pretty printing function to each node in the non-deterministic AST. A choice node in the AST is translated into a choice node in the token sequence with the same decision var and with choices that are produced by pretty printing the choices from the AST node. All other nodes in the AST are pretty printed by sequencing literal tokens together with token sequences from subtrees. As with ASTs, non-deterministic token sequences use sharing to avoid blow-up.

3.4 Distance Between Two Files

The *select closest* stage resolves a non-deterministic token sequence t into a deterministic token sequence t'. In so doing it attempts to minimize the *distance* between t' and previous tokens from the previous version of the file (Figure 2).

The distance metric we have chosen is the number of distinct *spans* needed to construct the target file from the previous file, where a span is defined to be either a single token, or a consecutive sequence of tokens from the previous file. For example, the distance from "`int x = 3; int j`" to "`int j = 3; int z`" is 3, since the new string can be constructed from the following three spans:

[1] The actual implementation is a little cleverer than this, leaving some of the list expansion until match time.

(i) "`int j`", *(ii)* "`= 3; int`", *(iii)* "`z`". We believe this metric fits a programmers intuitive model of what it means for files to be similar.

This metric is different from the edit distance. Edit distance only considers insertion, deletion, and substitution of a single character; it does not consider copyings and reorderings of large blocks of text. If the order of two functions was swapped, then the edit distance would be twice the number of characters in the smaller of the two functions, while the number of spans would be 2.

It is likely that better results could be achieved with a smarter metric. For example a metric that favored Jekyll files that type checked (in the style of Mycroft's type-based decompilation [22]), or a metric that biased against using the same span more than once. We leave such ideas for future work.

3.5 Optimal Translation Is NP-Hard

Ideally, we would like the *select closest* stage to guarantee that it resolves a non-deterministic token sequence to the token sequence that is closest to the previous token sequence — we refer to this problem as *optimal matching*. Unfortunately, optimal matching turns out to be NP-hard. This result is not surprising, given a similar result is known for synchronizing database views [3].

We can demonstrate that optimal matching is NP-hard by showing that it takes only a polynomial number of steps to translate any problem in 3-SAT (known to be NP-hard) into an optimal-matching problem. The encoding $[\![A]\!]$ of a 3-SAT expression A as a non-deterministic token sequence is quite simple:

$$\begin{array}{rlrl} [\![v]\!] &= v \ ?\ \text{"true"} : \text{"false"} & [\![\neg v]\!] &= v \ ?\ \text{"false"} : \text{"true"} \\ [\![A \wedge A']\!] &= [\![A]\!] \bullet [\![A']\!] & [\![A \vee A']\!] &= x \ ?\ [\![A]\!] : [\![A']\!] \quad \text{where } x \text{ is fresh} \end{array}$$

The previous file is an infinite sequence of *"true"* tokens. Provided the 3-SAT formula A has more than one disjunction[2], the formula is satisfiable if and only if the optimal matching of $[\![A]\!]$ has distance of 1 (a single span of *"true"* tokens).

Fortunately, like many NP-hard problems, we have found that it is possible to produce an approximate algorithm that behaves well in practice. Our current algorithm is a simple greedy search that walks sequentially through the token sequence, choosing variable assignments such as to maximize the length of the longest matching span[3]. While the worst case performance of this algorithm is still exponential, we have found that this algorithm runs in reasonable time and produces good results on reasonable-size source files (Section 4). This is partly an artifact of the kind of non-deterministic ASTs produced by JT, in which the options at a choice node tend to be quite different, and partly a result of the structure of C and Jekyll programs, which tend to have fairly little textual self-similarity. This algorithm is only a first stab — we believe it should be possible to produce an algorithm with a non-exponential upper bound that works even better.

---

[2] Since a single "false" token would also have distance 1.

[3] See our tech report [8] for details.

3.6 Synchronizing Comments and Whitespace

It is important that any comments present in one view of a file be also present in the other file. Similarly it is important that synchronization not make gratuitous changes to the whitespace of a file. JT divides whitespace into *common* and *private* whitespace. Common whitespace is considered to be part of the program representation and is carried across during translation. The other whitespace is considered private and is inferred non-deterministically to match the previous version of the target file.

The rules for distinguishing common and private whitespace are language-specific. The intention is that common whitespace be used in places where comments are typically placed, and private whitespace be used in cases where there is no obvious corresponding location in the other language, or where the correct whitespace is likely to be language-specific. A warning is generated if comments are found in private whitespace.

3.7 Checking Correctness

Sometimes a C programmer will edit C code implementing a Jekyll feature such that it is no longer a valid implementation of that Jekyll feature. For example JT requires that if a C function is implementing a Jekyll lambda expression then the first argument of that function must be the lambda expression's environment. If a C programmer changes the argument order then the function will no longer be a correctly encoded lambda expression. While we could just translate the C code to equivalent low-level Jekyll code, ignoring the Jekyll feature, it is likely that this result is not what the programmer intended.

To deal with such cases, Jekyll will attempt to decode any code as a Jekyll feature if it looks like the code *intended* to encode a Jekyll feature, even if the code does not encode that feature correctly. Once JT has translated a C file to a Jekyll file, it checks that the Jekyll file can be translated back to the original C file. If it cannot then the programmer is warned that the result of the transformation may be incorrect, and is encouraged to look at the differences between their file and the correctly encoded C file.

4 Evaluating JT

In this section, we present a preliminary evaluation of JT. We start by showing JT's behavior on simple snippets of code (Section 4.1), then evaluate its use on edits of source files from the GNU C Compiler [26] (Section 4.2). We conclude with a discussion of the limitations of our prototype (Section 4.3).

4.1 Feature Translation

We show here how JT handles the translation between two higher-level Jekyll features not found in C: generic types and closures. The output code is a very slightly cleaned-up version of the results of the JT tool, and is similar to real examples we encountered when modifying GCC (Section 4.2).

Jekyll has generic types similar to those found in ML [21], Haskell [25], and Cyclone [15]. Type variables are written as %a, rather than the more conventional 'a, to allow Jekyll files to be easily processed using the standard C preprocessor. When generic types are translated into C, all generic type information is thrown away. When translating back to Jekyll this information is reconstructed from the previous file (Section 3.2). For example:

Jekyll	C
`struct<%a> Node{`	`struct Node{`
`  %a *element;`	`  void *element;`
`  List<%a> tail;`	`  List tail;`
`};`	`};`
`%a* get_element(Node<%a>* x){`	`void* get_element(Node* x){`
`  return x->element;`	`  return x->element;`
`}`	`}`

When translating from C to Jekyll, type parameters are chosen based purely on textual similarity to the previous version, without regard to the meaning of the program. This can chose incorrect type parameters if C edits introduce previously unmentioned types that should have parameters, or make complex changes to functions that use the same type constructor with multiple types. It is likely that better choices would be made if JT prioritized files that type checked.

Jekyll supports closures and lambda expressions, as found in functional programming languages such as ML. Closures are written with syntax similar to Smalltalk [13], with arguments separated from their body by a colon. A lambda expression is translated into a function with an environment argument.[4]

By default, Jekyll uses ff, fe and ft prefixes for lambda functions, closure environment types, and closure values, however the programmer is free to change these names to whatever they prefer, since JT allows arbitrary names to be used (Section 3.2).

Jekyll

```
int dbl(int z){
  return twice(3,
    {x: ret x+z;});
}
```

C

```
struct fe_dbl{
  int *z;
};
int ff_dbl(struct fe_dbl *_env, int x){
  return x+*(_env->z);
}
int dbl(int z){
  struct fe_dbl ft = {&z};
  return twice(3,(void*)&ff_dbl,&ft);
}
```

[4] Free variables are passed by reference since they may be modified. In this case JT could have passed z by value since `ff_dbl` does not modify it.

4.2 Edit Translation

To demonstrate the behavior of edits, we took the `hashtab.c`, `hashtab.h`, and `ssa.c` files from the SPEC2006 version of GCC (3,070 lines total), and performed a sequence of edits on them. For each edit, we note the language the edit was made in (L), what the edit was and the effect it had in the other language, and the number of lines that changed in C and Jekyll, as measured by diff[5] (DC and DJ respectively). All file versions are available in the Jekyll source distribution.

L	Description	DC	DJ
C	Remove the use of macros that Jekyll does not understand.	55	new
C	Convert to Jekyll – Jekyll is a near-superset of C, so only change is `#including` "hashtab.jkh" in place of `"hashtab.h"`	0	2
J	Make the hashtable generic and make the visitor callback a closure — leaves the C file largely unchanged. Most differences due to callback arguments changing order, GCC source using `PTR` in place of `void*`, Jekyll code replacing a typedef with a literal generic type	18	40
J	Update ssa.c to use lambda expressions. Generated C file is correct.	376	358
C	Rename generated lambda functions. Jekyll unchanged.	22	0
C	Rename functions, reorder functions, and insert and delete code – all mapping into correct Jekyll updates	42	43
C	Reorder arguments to the closure type – No longer recognized as a closure. Reverts back to being a basic function	2	2

4.3 Where It Works, and Where It Doesn't Work

JT has two significant limitations. First, it does not support the C preprocessor very well. Jekyll currently uses an ad-hoc series of annotations that tell JT how to treat particular macros (e.g., treat like a function of this type, or ignore). We believe that the results of the Macroscope project [18] could be used to design a better approach.

Secondly, as we saw in the last edit in Section 4.2, JT does not cope well with some kinds of edits. In particular:

- Breaking encoding rules: Some encodings of Jekyll features into C have rules that must be followed. For example closures must take their environment as their first argument and features that expand to several statements require that those statements not be re-ordered. If C edits break these rules then the translation will either revert to the raw C, or generate non-equivalent Jekyll code (Section 3.7). In some cases these rules could be relaxed (e.g., reordering non-side-effecting statements), but in other cases they are necessary in order to allow meaningful translation.
- Moving Between files: JT only looks at the current file. If code is moved between files then the translation will revert to the defaults.

[5] Less accurate than our distance metric, but something people are familiar with.

– Large updates: If an update has caused many separate changes to a file then JT will find it harder to find the correct decoding, since the new version will correlate less well with the old version. Synchronizing often is a good idea.

However our limited personal experience is that many kinds of update work well. In particular, any C update that does not affect code implementing a Jekyll feature is highly likely to work correctly, since the translate stage will find few things that look like Jekyll features and the select-closest phase will be unlikely to find close matches to Jekyll features. Similarly, we have found that simple transformations such as renaming variables, reordering definitions, and adding and deleting code work reliably. Ideally, a synchronizer would be used with an interactive tool that allowed the user to pick the correct translation in cases where the correct result is unclear.

5 Related Work

Much previous work has looked at connections between different languages: bidirectional translation between different data formats, languages that are designed to extend C, languages that are translatable to C, and tools that preserve program formatting while editing. As far as we are aware, no previous work has performed bi-directional synchronization between programming languages.

5.1 Bidirectional Translation

The Harmony project [9] uses a set of tree-based combinators [10] to transform data structures between different data representations, with the aim of allowing easy synchronization of data between different programs and devices. BiXJ [16] uses a similar set of combinators for XML transformation. Like JT, Harmony and BiXJ use information from the previous file during translation. Unlike JT, they do all matching on local subtrees rather than doing a global analysis based on textual comparisons. While this approach works well for the domain that these tools are designed for, it is not clear whether this approach would perform well in the domain of programming language translation, where transformations are complex and edits can move expressions to arbitrary positions in a program.

XSugar [1] provides bi-directional translation between XML documents and alternative syntaxes. Unlike JT, XSugar only preserves information that is present in both representations and otherwise normalizes documents to a canonical form.

Meertens [20] applies the concept of bi-directional translation to the world of user interfaces. The idea here is that a user interface provides a view onto some underlying data, and constraints are established that ensure that the user interface remains an accurate representation of the data, even when the data or the user interface is manipulated. This approach is constraint based, and it is not clear whether it could be applied to something as complex as translating between programming languages.

In the database community, there has been a lot of work on "the view update problem", in which one tries to translate an update to a view into an appropriate update to the underlying database [14,6]. As with JT, a view update is able to see the previous version of a database when applying an update to it, and will try to minimize the extent of the change made. Unlike JT, a view update operation has the privilege of being able to see the exact update commands used, rather than simply being presented with a changed file and trying to work out what was intended.

Martin Fowler proposes the idea of a Language Workbench [11], which is an IDE in which users write programs using multiple user-defined DSLs. In some cases it may be possible to represent the same AST using different DSLs (e.g., graphical and Java representations of a GUI). As with database view updates, the IDE translates operations rather than programs.

5.2 Inter-language Translation

Many people have implemented language translators that translate one language into another. For example FOR_C [4] translates FORTRAN to C, and p2c [12] translates Pascal to C. While the resulting program is human-readable, there is no means to keep the files in sync if they are modified.

5.3 Languages That Extend Other Languages

Many languages have extended C with new features. Cyclone [15], Vault [7], C++ [27], Objective C [24] and many others all add useful new features to the core C language. While existing C code is often valid in these languages, any use of new features will prevent the program being a valid C program. In principle it should be possible for us to apply the transformation techniques used by JT to translate one of these languages to and from C.

Several authors have designed systems that use macros, templates, and naming conventions to embed extra features into C programs. CCured [23] allows a programmer to annotate their C programs with safety annotations, which are used by the CCured compiler, but ignored by a C compiler. FC++ [19] is a template library that makes it easy to express common functional programming idioms. These languages benefit from the ability to retain full C/C++ compatibility without translation, but are forced to use non-optimal syntax in order to do so — as with our encoding of Jekyll into C.

6 Conclusions

While it would be necessary to perform detailed evaluations with real programming teams to determine conclusively that multi-language synchronization works in practice, our experience so far has been very positive. Those C programmers that we have shown JT to have been impressed by its ability to cope with changes to code updates and have claimed that they would be able to edit C code generated from JT.

As part of the Ivy project [2], which aims to produce a system's programming language to replace C, we intend to apply multi-language synchronization to Ivy and C, and use it to make modifications to large legacy systems. Ultimately, we aim to convince external developers to use this system.

JT, the Jekyll Translator, is available on SourceForge at: `http://sourceforge.net/projects/jekyllc`

Acknowledgements

The design of Jekyll has been influenced by discussions with many people. Particular thanks must go to Michael Dales, Minos Garofalakis, Simon Peyton Jones, Bill McCloskey, Greg Morrisett, Alan Mycroft, Matthew Parkinson, Claus Reinke, Richard Sharp, Simon Thompson, and everyone in the Kent Theory group, Cambridge Systems Research Group, and Berkeley Ivy group.

References

1. Brabrand, C., Møller, A., and Schwartzbach, M. I. Dual syntax for XML languages. In *Proc. 10th International Workshop on Database Programming Languages, DBPL '05* (August 2005), vol. 3774 of *LNCS*, Springer-Verlag, pp. 27–41.
2. Brewer, E., Condit, J., McClosky, B., and Zhou, F. Thirty years is long enough: Getting beyond C. In *Proceedings of the USENIX workshop on Hot topics in Operating Systems* (2005).
3. Buneman, P., Khanna, S., and Tan, W. C. On propagation of deletions and annotations through views. In *PODS'02* (2002).
4. FOR_C: Converts FORTRAN into readable, maintainable C code. http://www.cobalt-blue.com.
5. *C# Language Specification.* ECMA, June 2005.
6. Dayal, U., and Bernstein, P. A. On the correct translation of update operations on relational views. *ACM Transactions on Database Systems 8* (Sept. 1982).
7. DeLine, R., and Fahndrich, M. Enforcing high-level protocols in low-level software. In *Proceedings of the ACM conference on Programming Language Design and Implementation* (2001).
8. Ennals, R. Dr Jekyll and Mr C. Tech. Rep. IR-TR-2005-104, Intel Research, 2005.
9. Foster, J. N., Greenwald, M. B., Kirkegaard, C., Pierce, B. C., and Schmitt, A. Exploiting schemas in data synchronization. In *Database Programming Languages (DBLP)* (2005).
10. Foster, J. N., Greenwald, M. B., Moore, J. T., Pierce, B. C., and Schmitt, A. Combinators for bi-directional tree transformations: A linguistic approach to the view update problem. In *Proceedings of the ACM SIGPLAN-SIGACT Symposium on Principles of Programming Languages (POPL'05)* (2005).
11. Fowler, M. Language workbenches: The killer-app for domain specific languages. `http://www.martinfowler.com/articles/languageWorkbench.html`, June 2005.
12. Gillespie, D. p2c. http://www.synaptics.com/people/daveg/.
13. Goldberg, A., and Robson, D. *Smalltalk-80: The Language.* Addison-Welsey, 1989.
14. Gottlob, G., Paolini, P., and Zicari, R. Properties and update semantics of consistent views. *ACM Transactions on Database Systems 13* (Dec. 1988).

15. JIM, T., MORRISETT, G., GROSSMAN, D., HICKS, M., CHENEY, J., AND WANG, Y. Cyclone: A safe dialect of C. In *Proceedings of the USENIX annual technical conference* (2002).
16. LIU, D., KAKEHI, K., HU, Z., TAKEICHI, M., AND WANG, H. A Java library for bidirectional XML transformation. In *JSSST annual conference* (2005).
17. MASHEY, J. R. Languages, levels, libraries, and longevity. *ACM Queue 2*, 9 (Dec. 2004).
18. MCCLOSKEY, B., AND BREWER, E. ASTEC: A new approach to refactoring c. In *Proceedings of the 10th European Software Engineering Conference* (Sept. 2005).
19. MCNAMARA, B., AND SMARAGDAKIS, Y. Functional programming in C++. In *Proceedings of the ACM SIGPLAN International Conference on Functional Programming (ICFP'00)* (Sept. 2000).
20. MEERTENS, L. Designing constraint maintainers for user interaction. http://www.kestrel.edu/home/people/meertens/, 1998.
21. MILNER, R., TOFTE, M., HARPER, R., AND MACQUEEN, D. *The Definition of Standard ML (Revised).* The MIT Press, 1997.
22. MYCROFT, A. Type-based decompilation. *Lecture Notes in Computer Science 1576* (1999).
23. NECULA, G. C., CONDIT, J., HARREN, M., MCPEAK, S., AND WEIMER, W. CCured: type-safe retrofitting of legacy software. *ACM Transactions on Programming Languages and Systems* (2004).
24. *The Objective C Programming Language.* Apple, Oct. 2005.
25. PEYTON JONES, S., Ed. *Haskell 98 Language and Libraries.* Cambridge University Press, 2003.
26. STALLMAN, R. M. *Using and Porting GNU CC (Version 2.0).* Free Software Foundation, Feb. 1992.
27. STROUSTRUP, B. *The C++ Programming Language.* Addison Wesley, 1997.
28. WADLER, P. Why no-one uses functional languages. *SIGPLAN Notices 33* (Aug. 1998).

Type-Based Analysis of Deadlock for a Concurrent Calculus with Interrupts

Kohei Suenaga[1] and Naoki Kobayashi[2]

[1] University of Tokyo
[2] Tohoku University

Abstract. The goal of our research project is to establish a type-based method for verification of certain critical properties (such as deadlock- and race-freedom) of operating system kernels. As operating system kernels make heavy use of threads and interrupts, it is important that the method can properly deal with both of the two features. As a first step towards the goal, we formalize a concurrent calculus equipped with primitives for threads and interrupts handling. We also propose a type system that guarantees deadlock-freedom in the presence of interrupts. To our knowledge, ours is the first type system for deadlock-freedom that can deal with both thread and interrupt primitives.

1 Introduction

The goal of our research project is to establish a type-based method for verification of certain critical properties (such as deadlock- and race-freedom) of operating system kernels. As operating system kernels make heavy use of threads and interrupts, it is important that the method can properly deal with both of the two features. Though several calculi that deal with either interrupts [3,14] or concurrency [12,13] have been proposed, none of them deal with both.

Combination of those two features can actually cause errors which are very difficult to find manually. For example, consider the program in Figure 1. The example is taken from an implementation of a protocol stack used in an ongoing research project on cluster computing [11]. Though the original source code is written in C, the example is shown in an ML-style language. The function `flush_buffer` flushes the local buffer and sends pending packets to appropriate destinations. The function `receive_data` is called when a packet arrives. That function works as an interrupt handler (as specified in the main expression) and is asynchronously called whenever a packet arrives. Since `receive_data` calls `flush_buffer` in order for the local buffer to be flushed as soon as the function knows there is a room in the remote buffer (a similar mechanism called *congestion control* is used in TCP), the following control flow causes deadlock:

Call to `flush_buffer` → `lock(devlock)`
→ an interrupt (call to `receive_data`)
→ call to `flush_buffer` → `lock(devlock)`

R. De Nicola (Ed.): ESOP 2007, LNCS 4421, pp. 490–504, 2007.

```
let flush_buffer devlock =
  let data = dequeue () in
  while !data != NULL do
    (* Interrupts should be forbidden before this lock operation *)
    lock(devlock);
    ... (* send data to the device *) ...
    unlock(devlock);
    data := dequeue ()
  done

(* interrupt handler *)
let receive_data packettype data devlock =
  ...
  (* If there is room in the remote buffer, flush the local buffer *)
  if packettype = RoomInBuffer then
    flush_buffer devlock
  ...

(* main *)
let _ =
  (* set receive_data as an interrupt handler *)
  request_irq(receive_data);
  flush_buffer (get_devlock ())
```

Fig. 1. An example of program which cause deadlock

Note that an interrupt handler does not voluntarily yield. To prevent the deadlock, `flush_buffer` has to forbid interrupts before it acquires the device lock as shown in Figure 2.

In order to statically detect such a deadlock, we propose (1) a calculus which is equipped with both interrupts and concurrency and (2) a type system for verifying deadlock-freedom. To our knowledge, ours is the first type system for deadlock-freedom that can deal with both thread and interrupt primitives.

Our type system associates a totally-ordered *lock level* to each lock and guarantees that locks are acquired in an increasing order of the levels even if interrupts occur. To achieve this, the type system tracks (1) a lower bound of the levels of locks acquired during evaluation and (2) an upper bound of the levels of locks acquired while interrupts are enabled. With our type system, the example in Figure 1 is rejected. On the other hand, if `flush_buffer` forbids interrupts before it acquires the device lock (as in Figure 2), our type system accepts the program.

The outline of this paper is as follows. Section 2 introduces the syntax and the semantics of our calculus. Section 3 shows our type system and states the type soundness theorem. After discussing related work in Section 4, we conclude in Section 5.

```
let flush_buffer devlock =
  let data = dequeue () in
  while !data != NULL do
    disable_interrupt(); lock(devlock);
    ... (* send data to the device *) ...
    unlock(devlock); enable_interrupt(); data := dequeue ()
  done
```

Fig. 2. A correct version of `flush_buffer`

2 Target Language

2.1 Syntax

The syntax of our target language is defined in Figure 3. Our language is an imperative language which is equipped with concurrency and interrupt handling.

A program P consists of a sequence of function definitions $\widetilde{D}$ and a main expression M. A function definition is constructed from a function name x, a sequence of formal arguments $\widetilde{y}$ and a function body. Function definitions can be mutually recursive. Note that a function name belongs to the class of variables, so that one can use a function name as a first-class value.

Expressions are ranged over by a meta-variable M. $\triangleright$ and $\blacktriangleleft$ are left-associative. For the sake of simplicity, we have only block-structured primitives (**sync** x **in** M and **disable_int** M) for acquiring/releasing locks and disabling/enabling interrupts. We explain intuition of several non-standard primitives below.

$$
\begin{array}{rcl}
x, y, z, f \ldots & \in & \mathit{Var} \\
\mathit{lck} & ::= & \textbf{acquired} \mid \textbf{released} \\
P & ::= & \widetilde{D}M \\
D & ::= & x(\widetilde{y}) = M \\
M & ::= & () \mid n \mid x \mid \textbf{true} \mid \textbf{false} \\
 & \mid & x(\widetilde{v}) \mid \textbf{let}\ x = M_1\ \textbf{in}\ M_2 \mid \textbf{if}\ v\ \textbf{then}\ M_1\ \textbf{else}\ M_2 \\
 & \mid & \textbf{let}\ x = \textbf{ref}\ v\ \textbf{in}\ M \mid x := v \mid !v \\
 & \mid & (M_1 \mid M_2) \mid \textbf{let}\ x = \textbf{newlock}\ ()\ \textbf{in}\ M \\
 & \mid & \textbf{sync}\ x\ \textbf{in}\ M \mid \textbf{in\_sync}\ x\ \textbf{in}\ M \\
 & \mid & M_1 \triangleright M_2 \mid M_1 \blacktriangleleft_M M_2 \mid \textbf{disable\_int}\ M \mid \textbf{in\_disable\_int}\ M \\
v & ::= & () \mid \textbf{true} \mid \textbf{false} \mid n \mid x \\
E & ::= & [\,] \mid \textbf{let}\ x = E\ \textbf{in}\ M \\
 & \mid & (E \mid M) \mid (M \mid E) \\
 & \mid & \textbf{in\_sync}\ x\ \textbf{in}\ E \mid \textbf{in\_disable\_int}\ E \\
 & \mid & E \triangleright M \mid M_1 \blacktriangleleft_M E \\
I & ::= & \textbf{enabled} \mid \textbf{disabled}
\end{array}
$$

Fig. 3. The Syntax of Our Language

```
flush_buffer_iter(devlock, data) =
if !data = Null then () else
(sync devlock in ()); flush_buffer_iter(devlock, dequeue())
flush_buffer(devlock) = flush_buffer_iter(devlock, dequeue())
receive_data(packettype, data, devlock) =
if packettype = Room then flush_buffer(devlock) else ()
(* Main expression *)
let devlock = newlock() in
let data = ref Null in
flush_buffer(devlock) ▷ receive_data(Room, data, devlock)
```

Fig. 4. An Encoding of the Program in Figure 1

- **let** x = **ref** v **in** M creates a fresh reference to v, binds x to the reference and evaluates M.
- $M_1 \mid M_2$ is concurrent evaluation of M_1 and M_2. Both of M_1 and M_2 should evaluate to ().
- **let** x = **newlock** () **in** M generates a new lock, binds x to the lock and evaluates M.
- **sync** x **in** M attempts to acquire the lock x and evaluates M after the lock is acquired. After M is evaluated to a value, the lock x is released.
- $M_1 \rhd M_2$ installs an interrupt handler M_2 and evaluates M_1. Once an interrupt occurs, M_1 is suspended until M_2 evaluates to a value. When M_1 evaluates to a value v, $M_1 \rhd M_2$ evaluates to v.
- **disable_int** M disables interrupts during an evaluation of M.

The following three primitives only occur during evaluation and should not be included in programs.

- **in_sync** x **in** M represents the state in which M is being evaluated with the lock x acquired. After M evaluates to a value, the lock x is released.
- $M_1 \blacktriangleleft_M M_2$ represents the state in which the interrupt handler M_2 is being evaluated. After M_2 evaluates to a value, the interrupted expression M_1 and the initial state of interrupt handler M are recovered.
- **in_disable_int** M represents the state in which M is being evaluated with interrupts disabled. After M evaluates to a value, interrupts are enabled.

We write $M_1; M_2$ for **let** $x = M_1$ **in** M_2 where x is not free in M_2.

Figure 4 shows how the example in Figure 1 is encoded in our language. Though that encoding does not strictly conform to the syntax of our language (e.g., *flush_buffer_iter* is applied to an expression *dequeue*(), not to a value), one can easily translate the program into one that respects our syntax.

Our interrupt calculus is very expressive and can model various interrupt mechanisms, as discussed in Examples 1–4 below.

Example 1. In various kinds of CPUs, there is a priority among interrupts. In such a situation, if an interrupt with a higher priority occurs, interrupts with lower priorities do not occur. We can express such priorities by connecting several expressions with $\rhd$ as follows.

$$\mathit{do\_something}(\ldots) \rhd \mathit{interrupt\_low}(\ldots) \rhd \mathit{interrupt\_high}(\ldots)$$

If an interrupt occurs in $\mathit{do\_something}(\ldots) \rhd \mathit{interrupt\_low}(\ldots)$ (note that $\rhd$ is left-associative), the example above is reduced to

$$(\mathit{do\_something}(\ldots) \blacktriangleleft_{\mathit{interrupt\_low}(\ldots)} \mathit{interrupt\_low}(\ldots)) \rhd \mathit{interrupt\_high}(\ldots).$$

That state represents that *interrupt_low* interrupted *do_something*. From that state, *interrupt_high* can still interrupt.

$$(\mathit{do\_something}(\ldots) \blacktriangleleft_{\mathit{interrupt\_low}(\ldots)} \mathit{interrupt\_low}(\ldots)) \blacktriangleleft_{\mathit{interrupt\_high}(\ldots)} \mathit{interrupt\_high}(\ldots).$$

interrupt_high can interrupt also from the initial state.

$$(\mathit{do\_something}(\ldots) \rhd \mathit{interrupt\_low}(\ldots)) \blacktriangleleft_{\mathit{interrupt\_high}(\ldots)} \mathit{interrupt\_high}(\ldots)$$

From the state above, *interrupt_low* cannot interrupt until $\mathit{interrupt\_high}(\ldots)$ evaluates to a value.

Example 2. In our calculus, we can locally install interrupt handlers. Thus, we can express a multi-threaded program in which an interrupt handler is installed on each thread.

$$(\mathit{thread1}(\ldots) \rhd \mathit{handler1}(\ldots)) \mid (\mathit{thread2}(\ldots) \rhd \mathit{handler2}(\ldots)) \ldots$$

This feature is useful for modeling a multi-CPU system in which even if an interrupt occurs in one CPU, the other CPUs continue to work in non-interrupt mode.

Example 3. In the example in Figure 4, we assume that no interrupt occur in the body of *receive_data*. One can express that an interrupt may occur during an execution of *receive_data* by re-installing an interrupt handler as follows.

$$\begin{array}{l}\mathit{receive\_data}(\mathit{packettype}, \mathit{data}, \mathit{devlock}) = \\ \quad (\mathbf{if}\ \mathit{packettype} = \mathit{Room}\ \mathbf{then}\ \mathit{flush\_buffer}(\mathit{devlock})\ \mathbf{else}\ ()) \rhd \\ \hfill \mathit{receive\_data}(\mathit{Room}, \mathit{data}, \mathit{devlock})\end{array}$$

Example 4. Since many operating system kernels are written in C, we make design decisions of our language based on that of C. For example, names of functions are first-class values in our language because C allows one to use a function name as a function pointer and because operating system kernels heavily use function pointers. With this feature, we can express a runtime change of interrupt handler as follows:

$$\mathbf{let}\ x = \mathbf{ref}\ f\ \mathbf{in}\ ((\ldots; x := g; \ldots) \rhd (!x)())$$

Until g is assigned to the reference x, the installed interrupt handler is f. After the assignment, the interrupt handler is g. This characteristic is useful for modeling operating system kernels in which interrupt handlers are changed when, for example, device drivers are installed.

$$\frac{x(\widetilde{y}) = M' \in \widetilde{D}}{(\widetilde{D}, H, L, I, E[x(\widetilde{v})]) \rightarrow (\widetilde{D}, H, L, I, E[[\widetilde{v}/\widetilde{y}]M'])} \quad \text{(E-APP)}$$

$$(\widetilde{D}, H, L, I, E[\mathbf{let}\ x = v\ \mathbf{in}\ M]) \rightarrow (\widetilde{D}, H, L, I, E[[v/x]M]) \quad \text{(E-LET)}$$

$$(\widetilde{D}, H, L, I, E[\mathbf{if\ true\ then}\ M_1\ \mathbf{else}\ M_2]) \rightarrow (\widetilde{D}, H, L, I, E[M_1]) \quad \text{(E-IFTRUE)}$$

$$(\widetilde{D}, H, L, I, E[\mathbf{if\ false\ then}\ M_1\ \mathbf{else}\ M_2]) \rightarrow (\widetilde{D}, H, L, I, E[M_2]) \quad \text{(E-IFFALSE)}$$

$$\frac{x' \text{ is fresh}}{(\widetilde{D}, H, L, I, E[\mathbf{let}\ x = \mathbf{ref}\ v\ \mathbf{in}\ M]) \rightarrow (\widetilde{D}, H[x' \mapsto v], L, I, E[[x'/x]M])} \quad \text{(E-REF)}$$

$$(\widetilde{D}, H[x \mapsto v'], L, I, E[x := v]) \rightarrow (\widetilde{D}, H[x \mapsto v], L, I, E[()]) \quad \text{(E-ASSIGN)}$$

$$(\widetilde{D}, H[x \mapsto v], L, I, E[!x]) \rightarrow (\widetilde{D}, H[x \mapsto v], L, I, E[v]) \quad \text{(E-DEREF)}$$

$$\frac{x' \text{ is fresh}}{\begin{array}{l}(\widetilde{D}, H, L, I, E[\mathbf{let}\ x = \mathbf{newlock}\ ()\ \mathbf{in}\ M]) \rightarrow \\ \qquad (\widetilde{D}, H, L[x' \mapsto \mathbf{released}], I, E[[x'/x]M])\end{array}} \quad \text{(E-LETNEWLOCK)}$$

$$(\widetilde{D}, H, L, I, E[() \mid ()]) \rightarrow (\widetilde{D}, H, L, I, E[()]) \quad \text{(E-PAREND)}$$

$$\begin{array}{l}(\widetilde{D}, H, L[x \mapsto \mathbf{released}], I, E[\mathbf{sync}\ x\ \mathbf{in}\ M]) \rightarrow \\ \qquad (\widetilde{D}, H, L[x \mapsto \mathbf{acquired}], I, E[\mathbf{in\_sync}\ x\ \mathbf{in}\ M])\end{array} \quad \text{(E-LOCK)}$$

$$(\widetilde{D}, H, L[x \mapsto \mathbf{acquired}], I, E[\mathbf{in\_sync}\ x\ \mathbf{in}\ v]) \rightarrow (\widetilde{D}, H, L[x \mapsto \mathbf{released}], I, E[v]) \quad \text{(E-UNLOCK)}$$

$$(\widetilde{D}, H, L, \mathbf{enabled}, E[M_1 \rhd M_2]) \rightarrow (\widetilde{D}, H, L, \mathbf{enabled}, E[M_1 \blacktriangleleft_{M_2} M_2]) \quad \text{(E-INTERRUPT)}$$

$$(\widetilde{D}, H, L, I, E[M_1 \blacktriangleleft_{M_2} v]) \rightarrow (\widetilde{D}, H, L, I, E[M_1 \rhd M_2]) \quad \text{(E-EXITINTERRUPT)}$$

$$(\widetilde{D}, H, L, I, E[v \rhd M]) \rightarrow (\widetilde{D}, H, L, I, E[v]) \quad \text{(E-NOINTERRUPTVALUE)}$$

$$(\widetilde{D}, H, L, \mathbf{enabled}, E[\mathbf{disable\_int}\ M]) \rightarrow (\widetilde{D}, H, L, \mathbf{disabled}, E[\mathbf{in\_disable\_int}\ M]) \quad \text{(E-DISABLEINTERRUPT1)}$$

$$(\widetilde{D}, H, L, \mathbf{disabled}, E[\mathbf{disable\_int}\ M]) \rightarrow (\widetilde{D}, H, L, \mathbf{disabled}, E[M]) \quad \text{(E-DISABLEINTERRUPT2)}$$

$$(\widetilde{D}, H, L, I, E[\mathbf{in\_disable\_int}\ v]) \rightarrow (\widetilde{D}, H, L, \mathbf{enabled}, E[v]) \quad \text{(E-ENABLEINTERRUPT)}$$

Fig. 5. The Operational Semantics of Our Language

2.2 Operational Semantics

The semantics is defined as rewriting of a configuration $(\widetilde{D}, H, L, I, M)$. H is a heap, which is a map from variables to values. (Note that references are represented by variables.) L is a map from variables to $\{\mathbf{acquired}, \mathbf{released}\}$. I is an interrupt flag, which is either **enabled** or **disabled**.[1]

[1] We do not assign an interrupt flag to each interrupt handler in order to keep the semantics simple. Even if we do so, the type system introduced in Section 3 can be used with only small changes.

Figure 5 shows the operational semantics of our language. We explain several important rules.

- In (E-REF) and (E-LETNEWLOCK), newly generated references and locks are represented by fresh variables.
- Reduction with the rule (E-LOCK) succeeds only if the lock being acquired is not held. (E-UNLOCK) is similar.
- **disable_int** changes the interrupt flag only when the flag was **enabled** (rule (E-DISABLEINTERRUPT1)). Otherwise, **disable_int** does nothing (rule (E-DISABLEINTERRUPT2)).
- If the interrupt flag is **enabled**, then a handler M_2 can interrupt M_1 anytime with the rule (E-INTERRUPT). When the interrupt occurs, the initial expression of interrupt handler M_2 is saved. After the handler terminates, the saved expression is recovered with (E-EXITINTERRUPT).

The following example shows how the program in Figure 4 leads to a deadlocked state. We write L_u for $\{devlock' \mapsto \mathbf{released}\}$ and L_l for $\{devlock' \mapsto \mathbf{acquired}\}$. We omit $\widetilde{D}, H$ and I components of configurations.

$$\begin{array}{l}
(L_u, \mathit{flush_buffer}(devlock') \rhd \mathit{receive_data}(Room, data, devlock')) \\
\rightarrow^* (L_u, \mathbf{sync}\ devlock'\ \mathbf{in}\ () \rhd \mathit{receive_data}(Room, data, devlock)) \\
\rightarrow (L_l, \mathbf{in_sync}\ devlock'\ \mathbf{in}\ () \rhd \mathit{receive_data}(Room, data, devlock)) \\
\rightarrow (L_l, \mathbf{in_sync}\ devlock'\ \mathbf{in}\ () \blacktriangleleft_{\mathit{receive_data}(\ldots)} \mathit{receive_data}(Room, data, devlock)) \\
\rightarrow^* (L_l, \mathbf{in_sync}\ devlock'\ \mathbf{in}\ () \blacktriangleleft_{\mathit{receive_data}(\ldots)} \mathit{flush_buffer}(devlock')) \\
\rightarrow^* (L_l, \mathbf{in_sync}\ devlock'\ \mathbf{in}\ () \blacktriangleleft_{\mathit{receive_data}(\ldots)} \mathbf{sync}\ devlock'\ \mathbf{in}\ ())
\end{array}$$

The last configuration is in a deadlock because the attempt to acquire *devlock'*, which is already acquired in L_l, never succeeds and because the interrupt handler **sync** *devlock'* **in** () does not voluntarily yield.

3 Type System

3.1 Lock Levels

In our type system, every lock type is associated with a *lock level*, which is represented by a meta-variable *lev*. The set of lock levels is $\{-\infty, \infty\} \cup \mathbb{N}$, where $\mathbb{N}$ is the set of natural numbers. We extend the standard partial order $\leq$ on $\mathbb{N}$ to that on $\{-\infty, \infty\} \cup \mathbb{N}$ by $\forall lev \in \{-\infty, \infty\} \cup \mathbb{N}. -\infty \leq lev \leq \infty$. We write $lev_1 < lev_2$ for $lev_1 \leq lev_2 \wedge lev_1 \neq lev_2$.

3.2 Effects

Our type system guarantees that a program acquires locks in a strict increasing order of lock levels. To achieve this, we introduce *effects* which describe how a program acquires locks during evaluation.

An effect, represented by a meta-variable φ, is a pair of lock levels (lev_1, lev_2). The meaning of each component is as follows.

$$\begin{array}{l} \tau ::= \textbf{unit} \mid \textbf{int} \mid \textbf{bool} \mid \widetilde{\tau_1} \xrightarrow{\varphi} \tau_2 \mid \tau\ \textbf{ref} \mid \textbf{lock}(lev) \\ lev \ \in \ \{-\infty, \infty\} \cup \mathbb{N} \\ \varphi ::= (lev_1, lev_2) \end{array}$$

Fig. 6. Syntax of types

- lev_1 is a lower bound of the lock levels of locks that may be acquired.
- lev_2 is an upper bound of the lock levels of locks that may be acquired or have been acquired while interrupts are enabled.

For example, an effect $(0, -\infty)$ means that locks whose levels are more than or equal to 0 may be acquired and that no locks are acquired while interrupts are enabled. An effect $(0, 1)$ means that locks whose levels are more than or equal to 0 may be acquired and that a lock of level 1 may be acquired or has already been acquired while interrupts are enabled. We write $\emptyset$ for $(\infty, -\infty)$.

We define the subeffect relation and the join operator for effects as follows.

Definition 1 (Subeffect Relation). *$(lev_1, lev_2) \leq (lev'_1, lev'_2)$ holds if and only if $lev'_1 \leq lev_1$ and $lev_2 \leq lev'_2$.*

$(lev_1, lev_2) \leq (lev'_1, lev'_2)$ means that an expression that acquires locks according to the effect (lev_1, lev_2) can be seen as an expression with the effect (lev'_1, lev'_2). For example, $(1, 2) \leq (0, 3)$ holds. $\emptyset$ is the bottom of $\leq$.

Definition 2 (Join). $(lev_1, lev_2) \sqcup (lev'_1, lev'_2) = (min(lev_1, lev'_1), max(lev_2, lev'_2))$

For example, $(1, 2) \sqcup (0, 1) = (0, 2)$ and $(0, -\infty) \sqcup (1, 2) = (0, 2)$ hold. $\emptyset$ is an identity of $\sqcup$.

3.3 Syntax of Types

Figure 6 shows the syntax of types and effects. A type, represented by a meta-variable τ, is either **unit, int, bool,** $\widetilde{\tau_1} \xrightarrow{\varphi} \tau_2$, τ **ref** or $\textbf{lock}(lev)$. We write $\widetilde{\tau}$ for a sequence of types. τ **ref** is the type of a reference to a value of type τ. $\widetilde{\tau_1} \xrightarrow{\varphi} \tau_2$ is the type of functions which take a tuple of values of type $\widetilde{\tau_1}$ and return a value of type τ_2. φ is the latent effect of the functions.

3.4 Type Judgment

The type judgment form of our type system is $\Gamma \vdash M : \tau \;\&\; \varphi$ where Γ is a map from variables to types. The judgment means that the resulting value of the evaluation of M has type τ if an evaluation of M under an environment described by Γ terminates, and that locks are acquired in a strict increasing order of lock levels during the evaluation. The minimum and maximum lock levels acquired are constrained by φ. For example, $x : \textbf{lock}(0), y : \textbf{lock}(1) \vdash \textbf{sync}\ x\ \textbf{in}\ \textbf{sync}\ y\ \textbf{in}\ () : \textbf{unit}\ \&\ (0, 1)$ and $x : \textbf{lock}(0), y : \textbf{lock}(1) \vdash \textbf{sync}\ x\ \textbf{in}\ (\textbf{disable\_int}\ \textbf{sync}\ y\ \textbf{in}\ ()) : \textbf{unit}\ \&\ (0, 0)$ hold.

Definition 3. *The relation $\Gamma \vdash M : \tau \ \& \ \varphi$ is the smallest relation closed under the rules in Figures 7 and 8. The predicate noIntermediate*(M) *in Figure 8 holds if and only if M does not contain* **in_sync** x **in** M', **in_disable_int** M' *or* $M_1 \blacktriangleleft_{M'} M_2$ *as subterms.*

We explain several important rules.

- (T-SYNC): If the level of x is *lev*, then M can acquire only locks whose levels are more than *lev*. That is guaranteed by the condition $lev < lev_1$ where lev_1 is a lower bound of the levels of locks that may be acquired by M.
- (T-DISABLEINTERRUPT): The second component of the effect of **disable_int** M is changed to $-\infty$ because no interrupt occurs in M, so that no locks are acquired by interrupt handlers.
- (T-INSTHANDLER): The second component of the effect of M_1 should be less than the first component of the effect of M_2 because M_2 can interrupt M_1 at any time. This is why we need to include the maximum level in effects.
- (T-FUNDEF): The condition $\varphi' \leq \varphi_i$ guarantees that the latent effect of the type of the function being defined soundly approximates the runtime locking behavior.

We show how the program in Figure 4 is rejected in our type system. From the derivation tree in Figure 9, *flush_buffer_iter* has a type $(\mathbf{lock}(1), \tau_d\ \mathbf{ref}) \xrightarrow{(1,1)} \mathbf{unit}$, where τ_d is the type of the contents of the reference *data*. Thus, *flush_buffer* has a type $\mathbf{lock}(1) \xrightarrow{(1,1)} \mathbf{unit}$ and *receive_data* has a type $(\tau_p, \tau_d, \mathbf{lock}(1)) \xrightarrow{(1,1)} \mathbf{unit}$, where τ_p is the type of *packettype*.

Consider the main expression of the example. Let Γ be *devlock* : **lock**(1), *data*: τ_d **ref**. Then, we have

- $\Gamma \vdash$ *flush_buffer*(*devlock*) : **unit** & $(1, 1)$ and
- $\Gamma \vdash$ *receive_data*(*Room*, *data*, *devlock*) : **unit** & $(1, 1)$.

However, the condition $lev_2 < lev'_1$ of the rule (T-INSTHANDLER) prevents the main expression to be well-typed ($1 < 1$ does not hold).

Suppose that **sync** *devlock* **in** () in the body of *flush_buffer_iter* is replaced by **disable_int sync** *devlock* **in** (). Then, *flush_buffer_iter* has a type $(\mathbf{lock}(1), \tau_d\ \mathbf{ref}) \xrightarrow{(1,-\infty)} \mathbf{unit}$ Thus, because $\Gamma \vdash$ *flush_buffer*(*devlock*) : **unit** & $(1, -\infty)$ and $-\infty < 1$ hold, the program is well-typed.

3.5 Type Soundness

We prove the soundness of our type system. Here, type soundness means that a well-typed program does not get deadlocked if one begins an evaluation of the program under an initial configuration (i.e., under an empty heap, an empty lock environment and enabled interrupt flag).

We first define deadlock. The predicate *deadlocked*(L, M) defined below means that M is in a deadlocked state under L.

$$\Gamma \vdash () : \mathbf{unit} \ \& \ \emptyset \quad \text{(T-Unit)} \qquad \Gamma \vdash n : \mathbf{int} \ \& \ \emptyset \quad \text{(T-Int)}$$

$$\Gamma \vdash \mathbf{true} : \mathbf{bool} \ \& \ \emptyset \quad \text{(T-True)} \qquad \Gamma \vdash \mathbf{false} : \mathbf{bool} \ \& \ \emptyset \quad \text{(T-False)}$$

$$\frac{\Gamma(x) = \tau}{\Gamma \vdash x : \tau \ \& \ \emptyset} \ \text{(T-Var)} \qquad \frac{x : (\tau_1, \ldots, \tau_n) \xrightarrow{\varphi'} \tau \in \Gamma \quad \Gamma \vdash v_i : \tau_i \ \& \ \emptyset \ (i = 1, \ldots, n)}{\Gamma \vdash x(v_1, \ldots, v_n) : \tau \ \& \ \varphi'} \ \text{(T-App)}$$

$$\frac{\Gamma \vdash M_1 : \tau_1 \ \& \ \varphi_1 \quad \Gamma, x : \tau_1 \vdash M_2 : \tau \ \& \ \varphi_2}{\Gamma \vdash \mathbf{let} \ x = M_1 \ \mathbf{in} \ M_2 : \tau \ \& \ \varphi_1 \sqcup \varphi_2} \ \text{(T-Let)} \qquad \frac{\Gamma \vdash v : \mathbf{bool} \ \& \ \emptyset \quad \Gamma \vdash M_1 : \tau \ \& \ \varphi_1 \quad \Gamma \vdash M_2 : \tau \ \& \ \varphi_2}{\Gamma \vdash \mathbf{if} \ v \ \mathbf{then} \ M_1 \ \mathbf{else} \ M_2 : \tau \ \& \ \varphi_1 \sqcup \varphi_2} \ \text{(T-If)}$$

$$\frac{\Gamma \vdash v : \tau \ \& \ \emptyset \quad x : \tau \ \mathbf{ref}, \Gamma \vdash M : \tau' \ \& \ \varphi}{\Gamma \vdash \mathbf{let} \ x = \mathbf{ref} \ v \ \mathbf{in} \ M : \tau' \ \& \ \varphi} \ \text{(T-Ref)} \qquad \frac{x : \tau \ \mathbf{ref} \in \Gamma \quad \Gamma \vdash v : \tau \ \& \ \emptyset}{\Gamma \vdash x := v : \mathbf{unit} \ \& \ \emptyset} \ \text{(T-Assign)}$$

$$x : \tau \ \mathbf{ref}, \Gamma \vdash !x : \tau \ \& \ \emptyset \ \text{(T-Deref)} \qquad \frac{\Gamma \vdash M_1 : \mathbf{unit} \ \& \ \varphi_1 \quad \Gamma \vdash M_2 : \mathbf{unit} \ \& \ \varphi_2}{\Gamma \vdash M_1 \mid M_2 : \mathbf{unit} \ \& \ \varphi_1 \sqcup \varphi_2} \ \text{(T-Par)}$$

$$\frac{x : \mathbf{lock}(lev), \Gamma \vdash M : \tau \ \& \ (lev_1, lev_2)}{\Gamma \vdash \mathbf{let} \ x = \mathbf{newlock} \ () \ \mathbf{in} \ M : \tau \ \& \ (lev_1, lev_2)} \ \text{(T-Newlock)}$$

$$\frac{x : \mathbf{lock}(lev) \in \Gamma \quad \Gamma \vdash M : \tau \ \& \ (lev_1, lev_2) \quad lev < lev_1 \quad \varphi = (lev, lev) \sqcup (lev_1, lev_2)}{\Gamma \vdash \mathbf{sync} \ x \ \mathbf{in} \ M : \tau \ \& \ \varphi} \ \text{(T-Sync)}$$

$$\frac{x : \mathbf{lock}(lev) \in \Gamma \quad \Gamma \vdash M : \tau \ \& \ (lev_1, lev_2) \quad lev < lev_1 \quad \varphi = (\infty, lev) \sqcup (lev_1, lev_2)}{\Gamma \vdash \mathbf{in\_sync} \ x \ \mathbf{in} \ M : \tau \ \& \ \varphi} \ \text{(T-Insync)}$$

$$\frac{\Gamma \vdash M : \tau \ \& \ (lev_1, lev_2)}{\Gamma \vdash \mathbf{disable\_int} \ M : \tau \ \& \ (lev_1, -\infty)} \ \text{(T-DisableInterrupt)} \qquad \frac{\Gamma \vdash M : \tau \ \& \ (lev_1, lev_2)}{\Gamma \vdash \mathbf{in\_disable\_int} \ M : \tau \ \& \ (lev_1, -\infty)} \ \text{(T-InDisableInterrupt)}$$

$$\frac{\Gamma \vdash M_1 : \tau \ \& \ (lev_1, lev_2) \quad \Gamma \vdash M_2 : \mathbf{unit} \ \& \ (lev_1', lev_2') \quad lev_2 < lev_1' \quad \varphi = (lev_1, lev_2) \sqcup (lev_1', lev_2')}{\Gamma \vdash M_1 \rhd M_2 : \tau \ \& \ \varphi} \ \text{(T-InstHandler)}$$

$$\frac{\Gamma \vdash M_1 : \tau \ \& \ (lev_1, lev_2) \quad \Gamma \vdash M_2 : \mathbf{unit} \ \& \ (lev_1', lev_2') \quad \Gamma \vdash M : \mathbf{unit} \ \& \ (lev_1'', lev_2'') \quad lev_2 < lev_1' \quad lev_2 < lev_1'' \quad \varphi' = \varphi \sqcup (lev_1, lev_2) \sqcup (lev_1', lev_2')}{\Gamma \vdash M_1 \blacktriangleleft_M M_2 : \tau \ \& \ \varphi'} \ \text{(T-InInterrupt)}$$

Fig. 7. Typing rules

Definition 4 (Deadlock). *The predicate deadlocked*(L, M) *holds if and only if for all* E *and* i, $M = E[i]$ *implies that there exist* x *and* M' *such that* $i =$ **sync** x **in** $M' \wedge L(x) =$ **acquired**. *Here,* i *is defined by the following syntax.*

$$\frac{\begin{array}{c}\Gamma \supseteq f_1 : (\tau_{1,1}, \ldots, \tau_{1,m_1}) \xrightarrow{\varphi_1} \tau_1, \ldots, f_n : (\tau_{n,1}, \ldots, \tau_{n,m_n}) \xrightarrow{\varphi_n} \tau_n \\ \Gamma, x_{i,1} : \tau_{i,1}, \ldots, x_{i,m_i} : \tau_{i,m_i} \vdash M_i : \tau_i \,\&\, \varphi' \\ \varphi' \leq \varphi_i \qquad \mathit{noIntermediate}(M_i)\end{array}}{\Gamma \vdash_D f_i(x_{i,1}, \ldots, x_{i,m_i}) = M_i : (\tau_{i,1}, \ldots, \tau_{i,m_i}) \xrightarrow{\varphi_i} \tau_i} \quad \text{(T-FUNDEF)}$$

$$\frac{\begin{array}{c}\{f_1, \ldots, f_n\} \text{ is the set of names of functions declared in } \widetilde{D} \\ \Gamma \supseteq \{f_1 : (\tau_{1,1}, \ldots, \tau_{1,m_1}) \xrightarrow{\varphi_1} \tau_1, \ldots, f_n : (\tau_{n,1}, \ldots, \tau_{n,m_n}) \xrightarrow{\varphi_n} \tau_n\} \\ \Gamma \vdash_D D_i : (\tau_{i,1}, \ldots, \tau_{i,m_i}) \xrightarrow{\varphi_i} \tau_i \quad (1 \leq i \leq n) \\ \Gamma \vdash M : \mathbf{unit} \,\&\, \varphi \qquad \mathit{noIntermediate}(M)\end{array}}{\vdash_P \widetilde{D}M} \quad \text{(T-PROG)}$$

$$\frac{\begin{array}{c}\widetilde{D} = \{f_1(x_{1,1}, \ldots, x_{1,m_1}) = M_1, \ldots, f_l(x_{l,1}, \ldots, x_{l,m_l}) = M_l\} \\ H = \{y_1 \mapsto v_1, \ldots, y_k \mapsto v_k\} \\ L = \{z_1 \mapsto \mathit{lck}_1, \ldots, z_n \mapsto \mathit{lck}_n\} \\ \Gamma \vdash_D (f_i(x_{i,1}, \ldots, x_{i,m_i}) = M_i) : (\tau_{i,1}, \ldots, \tau_{i,m_i}) \xrightarrow{\varphi_i} \tau_i \quad (1 \leq i \leq l) \\ \Gamma \vdash v_i : \tau_i' \,\&\, \emptyset \quad (1 \leq i \leq k) \\ \Gamma = f_1 : (\tau_{1,1}, \ldots, \tau_{1,m_1}) \xrightarrow{\varphi_1} \tau_1, \ldots, f_l : (\tau_{l,1}, \ldots, \tau_{l,m_l}) \xrightarrow{\varphi_l} \tau_l, \\ y_1 : \tau_1' \,\mathbf{ref}, \ldots, y_k : \tau_k' \,\mathbf{ref}, \\ z_1 : \mathbf{lock}(\mathit{lev}_1), \ldots, z_n : \mathbf{lock}(\mathit{lev}_n)\end{array}}{\vdash_{\mathit{Env}} (\widetilde{D}, H, L) : \Gamma} \quad \text{(T-ENV)}$$

$$\frac{\vdash_{\mathit{Env}} (\widetilde{D}, H, L) : \Gamma \qquad \Gamma \vdash M : \tau \,\&\, (\mathit{lev}_1, \mathit{lev}_2)}{\vdash_C (\widetilde{D}, H, L, I, M) : \tau} \quad \text{(T-CONFIG)}$$

Fig. 8. Typing Rules for Program and Configuration

$$\begin{array}{rl} i ::= & x(\widetilde{v}) \mid \mathbf{let}\ x = v\ \mathbf{in}\ M \\ \mid & \mathbf{if\ true\ then}\ M_1\ \mathbf{else}\ M_2 \mid \mathbf{if\ false\ then}\ M_1\ \mathbf{else}\ M_2 \\ \mid & \mathbf{let}\ x = \mathbf{ref}\ v\ \mathbf{in}\ M \mid x := v \mid !x \\ \mid & \mathbf{let}\ x = \mathbf{newlock}\ ()\ \mathbf{in}\ M \mid (() | ()) \mid \mathbf{sync}\ x\ \mathbf{in}\ M \mid \mathbf{in\_sync}\ x\ \mathbf{in}\ v \\ \mid & M_1 \blacktriangleleft_{M_2} v \mid v \rhd M \mid \mathbf{disable\_int}\ M \mid \mathbf{in\_disable\_int}\ v \end{array}$$

In the definition above, i is a term that can be reduced by the rules in Figure 5. Thus, *deadlocked*(L, M) means that every reducible subterm in M is a blocked lock-acquiring instruction. For example,

$$\mathit{deadlocked}(L, (\mathbf{in\_sync}\ x\ \mathbf{in}\ (\mathbf{sync}\ y\ \mathbf{in}\ 0)) \mid (\mathbf{in\_sync}\ y\ \mathbf{in}\ (\mathbf{sync}\ x\ \mathbf{in}\ 0)))$$

holds where $L = \{x \mapsto \mathbf{acquired}, y \mapsto \mathbf{acquired}\}$.

Note that $M_1 \rhd M_2$ is not included in the definition of i because, in the real world, whether $M_1 \rhd M_2$ is reducible or not depends on the external environment which is not modeled in our calculus. For example, $(\mathbf{sync}\ x\ \mathbf{in}\ ()) \rhd ()$ is deadlocked under the environment in which x is acquired.

Theorem 1 (Type Soundness). *If* $\vdash_P \widetilde{D}M$ *and* $(\widetilde{D}, \emptyset, \emptyset, \mathbf{enabled}, M) \to^* (\widetilde{D}', H', L', I', M')$, *then* $\neg \mathit{deadlocked}(L', M')$.

$$\frac{\vdots \quad \mathcal{T}_1 \quad \mathcal{T}_2}{\Gamma \vdash \textbf{if} \ldots \textbf{then} \; () \; \textbf{else} \; (\textbf{sync} \; \mathit{devlock} \; \textbf{in} \; ()); \mathit{flush\_buffer\_iter}(\ldots) : \textbf{unit} \;\&\; (1,1)}$$

$$\vdots$$

where

$$\mathcal{T}_1 = \frac{\Gamma \vdash () : \textbf{unit} \;\&\; \emptyset \quad 1 < \infty}{\Gamma \vdash \textbf{sync} \; \mathit{devlock} \; \textbf{in} \; () : \textbf{unit} \;\&\; (1,1)}$$

$$\mathcal{T}_2 = \frac{\Gamma \vdash \mathit{flush\_buffer\_iter} : (\textbf{lock}(1), \tau_d) \stackrel{(1,1)}{\rightarrow} \textbf{unit} \;\&\; \emptyset \quad \vdots}{\Gamma \vdash \mathit{flush\_buffer\_iter}(\mathit{devlock}, \mathit{dequeue}()) : \textbf{unit} \;\&\; (1,1)}$$

Fig. 9. Derivation Tree of the body of *flush_buffer_iter*. $\Gamma = \mathit{flush\_buffer\_iter} : (\textbf{lock}(1), \tau_d \; \textbf{ref}) \stackrel{(1,1)}{\rightarrow} \textbf{unit}, \mathit{flush\_buffer} : \textbf{lock}(1) \stackrel{(1,1)}{\rightarrow} \textbf{unit}, \mathit{receive\_data} : (\tau_p, \tau_d \; \textbf{ref}, \textbf{lock}(1)) \stackrel{(1,1)}{\rightarrow} \textbf{unit}, \mathit{devlock} : \textbf{lock}(1), \mathit{data} : \tau_d$.

The theorem above follows from Lemmas 1–4 below. In those lemmas, we use a predicate $\mathit{wellformed}(L, I, M)$ which means that L, I and the shape of M are consistent.

Definition 5. *$\mathit{wellformed}(L, I, M)$ holds if and only if*

- *$L(x) =$ **released** or $x \notin$ **Dom**(L) implies that M does not contain **in_sync** x,*
- *$L(x) =$ **acquired** implies $\mathit{AckIn}(x, M)$,*
- *$I =$ **enabled** implies that M does not contain **in_disable_int**.*
- *$I =$ **disabled** implies that there exist E and M' such that $M = E[$**in_disable_int** $M']$ and both E and M' do not contain **in_disable_int**.*

Here, $\mathit{AckIn}(x, M)$ is the least predicate that satisfies the following rules.

$$\frac{E \text{ and } M' \text{ do not contain } \textbf{in\_sync} \; x \; \textbf{in}}{\mathit{AckIn}(x, E[\textbf{in\_sync} \; x \; \textbf{in} \; M'])} \; (\text{AckIn-Base})$$

$$\frac{\mathit{AckIn}(x, M_1) \quad E, M' \text{ and } M_2 \text{ do not contain } \textbf{in\_sync} \; x \; \textbf{in}}{\mathit{AckIn}(x, E[M_1 \blacktriangleleft_{M'} M_2])} \; (\text{AckIn-Interrupt})$$

Lemma 1. *If $\vdash_P \widetilde{D}M$, then $\mathit{wellformed}(\emptyset, \textbf{enabled}, M)$ and $\vdash_C (D, \emptyset, \emptyset, \textbf{enabled}, M)$.*

Lemma 2. *If $\mathit{wellformed}(L, I, M)$ and $(\widetilde{D}, H, L, I, M) \rightarrow (\widetilde{D}', H', L', I', M')$, then $\mathit{wellformed}(L', I', M')$.*

Lemma 3 (Preservation). *If $\vdash_C (\widetilde{D}, H, L, I, M) : \tau$ and $(\widetilde{D}, H, L, I, M) \rightarrow (\widetilde{D}', H', L', I', M')$, then $\vdash_C (\widetilde{D}', H', L', I', M') : \tau$.*

Lemma 4 (Deadlock-Freedom). *If $\vdash_C (\widetilde{D}, H, L, I, M) : \tau$ and wellformed (L,I,M), then $\neg \mathit{deadlocked}(L, M)$.*

Proofs of those lemmas are in the full version of this paper.

3.6 Type Inference

We can construct a standard constraint-based type inference algorithm as follows. The algorithm takes a program as an input, prepares variables for unknown types and lock levels, and extracts constraints on them based on the typing rules. By the standard unification algorithm and the definition of the subeffect relation, the extracted constraints can then be reduced to a set of constraints of the form $\{\rho_1 \geq \xi_1, \ldots, \rho_n \geq \xi_n\}$ where the grammar for $\xi_1, \ldots, \xi_n$ is given by

$$\begin{aligned} \xi ::= &\ \rho \text{ (lock level variables)} \\ | &\ -\infty \mid \infty \mid min(\xi_1, \xi_2) \mid max(\xi_1, \xi_2) \mid \xi + 1. \end{aligned}$$

Note that $lev < lev_1$ in (T-SYNC) can be replaced by $lev + 1 \leq lev_1$. The constraints above can be solved as in Kobayashi's type-based deadlock analysis for the π-calculus [7]. We will formalize the algorithm in the full version of the current paper.

4 Related Work

Chatterjee et al. have proposed a calculus that is equipped with interrupts [3,14]. They also proposed a static analysis of stack boundedness (i.e., interrupt chains cannot be infinite) of programs. The main differences between our calculus and their calculus are as follows. (1) Their calculus is not equipped with concurrency primitives. (2) Each handler has its own interrupt flag in their calculus. (3) Our calculus can express an install, a change and a detach of interrupt handlers. Due to (1), we cannot use their calculus to discuss deadlock-freedom analysis. As for (2), their calculus has an interrupt mask register (imr) to control which handlers are allowed to interrupt and which are not. This feature is indispensable in the verification of operating system kernels. We can extend our calculus to incorporate this feature by adding a tag to each interrupt handler ($M \rhd \{t_1 : M_1, \ldots, t_n : M_n\}$) and by specifying a tag on interrupt disabling primitives (**disable_int** t **in** M). A handler with tag t cannot interrupt inside **disable_int** t **in**. We also extend effects like (lev, $taglevel$), where $taglevel$ is a map from tags to lock levels. $taglevel(t)$ is an upper bound of the lock levels of locks that may be acquired or have been acquired while interrupts specified by t is enabled. Typing rules need to be modified accordingly. Concerning (3), our calculus can express a change of interrupt handlers as shown in Section 2.

Much work [2,7,8,9] on deadlock-freedom analysis of concurrent programs has been done. However, none of them deal with interrupts. Kobayashi et al. [7,8,9] have proposed type systems for deadlock-freedom of π-calculus processes. Their idea is (1) to express how each channel is used as a *usage expression* and (2) to add *capability levels* and *obligation levels* to the inferred usage expression in order to detect circular dependency among input/output operations to channels. Their capability/obligation levels correspond to our lock levels. Their usage expressions are unnecessary in the present framework because our synchronization primitive is block-structured. That notion would be useful if we allow non-block-structured lock primitives. Flanagan and Abadi [1,4] have proposed a type-based deadlock-freedom and race-freedom analysis for a Java-like language. Though their type system also uses lock levels, they need to track only a lower bound of acquired level as an effect because they do not deal with interrupts. In our type system, we need to track lower and upper bounds of levels as an effect in order to guarantee deadlock-freedom in the presence of interrupts.

Asynchronous exceptions [5,10] in Java and Haskell are similar to interrupts in that both cause an asynchronous jump to an exception/interrupt handler. Asynchronous exceptions are the exceptions that may be unexpectedly thrown during an execution of a program as a result of some events such as timeouts or stack overflows. Marlow et al. [10] extended Concurrent Haskell [6] with support for handling asynchronous exceptions. However, an asynchronous exception does not require the context in which the exception is thrown to be resumed after an exception handler returns, while an interrupt requires the context to be resumed.

5 Conclusion

We have proposed a calculus which is equipped with concurrency and interrupts. We have also proposed a type system for verification of deadlock-freedom for the calculus.

There remain much work to be done to make our framework applicable to verification of real operating system kernels. Since many operating system kernels are written in C, we need to include records, arrays and pointer arithmetics in our calculus. For those extensions, we may also need to refine the type system. In the current lock-level-based approach, a lock level is statically assigned to each *syntactic* occurence of a lock, so that the same lock level may be assigned to different locks. To prevent that problem, we may need to introduce lock-level polymorphism and run-time ordering of lock levels as proposed in [2].

We also plan to develop type systems for verifying other crucial safety properties such as race-freedom and atomicity.

Acknowledgement

We are grateful to Eijiro Sumii, Hiroya Matsuba, Toshiyuki Maeda and Yutaka Ishikawa for the comment on this research. We are also grateful to the anonymous reviewers for their fruitful comments.

References

1. Martín Abadi, Cormac Flanagan, and Stephen N. Freund. Types for safe locking: Static race detection for java. *ACM Transactions on Programming Languages and Systems*, 28(2):207–255, March 2006.

2. Chandrasekhar Boyapati, Robert Lee, and Martin Rinard. Ownership types for safe programming: Preventing data races and deadlocks. In *Proceedings of the 2002 ACM SIGPLAN Conference on Object-Oriented Programming Systems, Languages and Applications, (OOPSLA 2002)*, volume 37 of *SIGPLAN Notices*, pages 211–230, November 2002.
3. Krishnendu Chatterjee, Di Ma, Rupak Majumdar, Tian Zhao, Thomas A. Henzinger, and Jens Palsberg. Stack size analysis for interrupt-driven programs. *Information and Computation*, 194(2):144–174, 2004.
4. Cormac Flanagan and Martín Abadi. Types for safe locking. In *Proceedings of 8the European Symposium on Programming (ESOP'99)*, volume 1576 of *Lecture Notes in Computer Science*, pages 91–108, March 1999.
5. James Gosling, Bill Joy, Guy Steele, and Gilad Bracha. *The Java Language Specification, Third Edition.* Addison-Wesley Professional, June 2005.
6. Simon Peyton Jones, Andrew Gordon, and Sigbjorn Finne. Concurrent haskell. In *Proceedings of the 23rd ACM SIGPLAN-SIGACT Symposium on Principles of Programming Languages (POPL 1996)*, pages 295–308, January 1996.
7. Naoki Kobayashi. Type-based information flow analysis for the pi-calculus. *Acta Informatica*, 42(4–5):291–347, 2005.
8. Naoki Kobayashi. A new type system for deadlock-free processes. In *Proceedings of the 17th International Conference on Concurrency Theory*, volume 4137 of *Lecture Notes in Computer Science*, pages 233–247, August 2006.
9. Naoki Kobayashi, Shin Saito, and Eijiro Sumii. An implicitly-typed deadlock-free process calculus. In *Proceedings of CONCUR 2000*, volume 1877 of *Lecture Notes in Computer Science*, pages 489–503, August 2000.
10. Simon Marlow, Simon Peyton Jones, and Andrew Moran. Asynchronous exceptions in haskell. In *Proceedings of ACM SIGPLAN 2001 Conference on Programming Language Design and Implementation (PLDI 2001)*, June 2001.
11. Hiroya Matsuba and Yutaka Ishikawa. Single IP address cluster for internet servers. In *Proceedings of 21st IEEE International Parallel and Distributed Processing Symposium (IPDPS2007)*, March 2007.
12. Robin Milner. *Communication and Concurrency.* Prentice Hall, September 1995.
13. Robin Milner. *Communicating and Mobile Systems: the Pi-Calculus.* Cambridge University Press, 1999.
14. Jens Palsberg and Di Ma. A typed interrupt calculus. In *Proceedings of 7th International Symposium on Formal Techniques in Real-Time and Fault Tolerant Systems*, volume 2469 of *Lecture Notes in Computer Science*, pages 291–310, September 2002.

Type Reconstruction for General Refinement Types

Kenneth Knowles and Cormac Flanagan

University of California, Santa Cruz

Abstract. *General refinement types* allow types to be refined by predicates written in a general-purpose programming language, and can express function pre- and postconditions and data structure invariants. In this setting, with expressive and possibly verbose types, type reconstruction is particularly valuable, yet typeability is undecidable because it subsumes type checking. Using a generalized notion of type reconstruction, we present the first type reconstruction algorithm for a type system with base types refined by abitrary program terms. Our algorithm is a typeability-*preserving* transformation and defers type checking to a subsequent phase. The algorithm generates and solves a collection of implication constraints over refinement predicates, inferring maximally precise refinement predicates in a largely syntactic manner that is reminiscent of strongest postcondition calculation. Perhaps surprisingly, our notion of type reconstruction is decidable even though type checking is not.

1 Introduction

A *refinement type*, such as $\{x\colon \texttt{Int} \mid x \geq 0\}$, describes the set of terms of type `Int` satisfying the *refinement predicate* $x \geq 0$. Refinement types [13] significantly extend the expressive power of traditional type systems and, when combined with dependent function types, can document expressive function pre- and postconditions, as well as data structure invariants.

In the language λ^H [10], refinement predicates are unrestricted boolean expressions, and so, for example, any computable set of integers can be described by a λ^H type. Type checking requires proving implications between refinement predicates, such as that the postcondition of one function implies the precondition of another. Since the language of refinement predicates is λ^H itself, implication is undecidable, and hence so is type checking.

Hybrid type checking [10] circumvents this decidability limitation by passing each implication to a theorem prover that tries to prove or refute the implication, but also may give up and return "maybe," resulting in an inserted run-time check. The SAGE language implementation demonstrates that hybrid type checking interacts comfortably with a variety of typing constructs, including first-class types, polymorphism, recursive data structures, as well as the type `Dynamic`, and that the number of inserted casts for some example programs is low or none [15].

R. De Nicola (Ed.): ESOP 2007, LNCS 4421, pp. 505–519, 2007.

But even for small examples, writing explicitly typed terms can be tedious, and would become truly onerous for larger programs. To reduce the annotation burden, many typed languages – such as ML, Haskell, and their variants – perform type reconstruction, often stated as: *Given a program containing type variables, find a replacement for those variables such that the resulting program is well-typed.* If there exists such a replacement, the program is said to be *typeable*. Under this definition, type reconstruction subsumes type checking. Hence, for expressive and undecidable type systems, such as that of λ^H, type reconstruction is clearly undecidable.

Instead of surrendering to undecidability, we separate type reconstruction from type checking, and define the type reconstruction problem as: *Given a program containing type variables, find a replacement for those variables such that typeability is preserved.* In a decidable type system, this definition coincides with the previous one, since the type checker can decide if the resulting explicitly-typed program is well-typed. The generalized definition also extends to undecidable type systems, since alternative techniques, such as hybrid type checking, can be applied to the resulting program. In particular, type reconstruction for λ^H is now decidable!

Our approach to inferring refinement predicates is inspired by techniques from axiomatic semantics, most notably the strongest postcondition (SP) transformation [2]. This transformation supports arbitrary predicates in some specification logic, and computes the most precise correctness predicate for each program point. It is essentially syntactic in nature, deferring all semantic reasoning to a subsequent theorem-proving phase. For example, looping constructs in the program are expressed simply as fixpoint operations in the specification logic.

In the richer setting of λ^H, which includes higher-order functions with dependent types, we must infer both the structural shape of types and also any refinement predicates they contain. We solve the former using traditional type reconstruction techniques, and the latter using a syntactic, SP-like, transformation. Like SP, our algorithm infers the most precise predicates possible.

The resulting, explicitly-typed program can then be checked by the λ^H compilation algorithm [10], which reasons about local implications between refinement predicates. If the compilation algorithm cannot prove or refute a particular implication, it dynamically enforces the desired property via a run-time check. These dynamic checks are only ever necessary for user-specified predicates; inferred predicates (which may include existential quantification and fixpoint operations) are correct by construction.

The following section reviews the syntax, semantics, and type system of λ^H. Section 3 formalizes and discusses the type reconstruction problem, which we reduce to satisfiability of a set of subtyping constraints in Section 4. Sections 5 and 6 then explain how we solve these constraints via shape reconstruction followed by predicate inference. Section 7 states and proves correctness of the reconstruction algorithm. The remaining sections are dedicated to related work and concluding remarks.

2 A Review of λ^H

The language λ^H [10] is an extension of the lambda-calculus with dependent function types and refined base types; see Figure 1 for the complete syntax and operational semantics. In the dependent function type $x\!:\!S \rightarrow T$, the argument x is bound in the return type T. (This notation is preferred to the equivalent $\Pi x : S.T$). In a refined base type $\{x\!:\!B \mid t\}$, B is a base type such as `Int` or `Bool`, and t is a boolean predicate over x. Informally, $\{x\!:\!B \mid t\}$ is the subset of B for which the predicate t holds

Types have an operational interpretation via run-time casts: The term $\langle S \triangleright T \rangle\, t$ attempts to cast t from type S to type T. A cast to a refined base type is checked by evaluating the refinement predicate, while a cast to a function type is split into a delayed cast on the function's input and another on the function's output.

We assume some countable alphabet of constants c, each with an associated semantic function $[\![c]\!]$ that is applied when c is in the function position of an application. These constants include, for each type T, a fixpoint operator $\mathtt{fix}_T$ that computes the least fixed point of a function $t : T \rightarrow T$, enabling unrestricted recursion:

$$[\![\mathtt{fix}_T]\!](t) \quad = \quad t\ (\mathtt{fix}_T\ t)$$

$$\begin{array}{rcl} s, t \in \mathit{Term} & ::= & x \\ & | & c \\ & | & \lambda x\!:\!S.\,t \\ & | & (t\ t) \\ & | & \langle S \triangleright T \rangle\, t \end{array} \qquad \begin{array}{rcl} S, T \in \mathit{Type} & ::= & x\!:\!S \rightarrow T \ \mid\ \{x\!:\!B \mid t\} \\ B & ::= & \mathtt{Bool} \mid \mathtt{Int} \mid \cdots \\ E & ::= & \varnothing \mid E, x : T \end{array}$$

Evaluation $\boxed{s \longrightarrow t}$

$$\begin{array}{rll} (\lambda x\!:\!S.\,t)\ s \longrightarrow t[x := s] & & [\text{E-}\beta] \\ c\ t \longrightarrow [\![c]\!](t) & & [\text{E-Prim}] \\ \langle (x\!:\!S_1 \rightarrow S_2) \triangleright (x\!:\!T_1 \rightarrow T_2) \rangle\, t \longrightarrow \lambda x\!:\!T_1.\, \langle S_2 \triangleright T_2 \rangle\, (t\ (\langle T_1 \triangleright S_1 \rangle\, x)) & & [\text{E-Cast-F}] \\ \langle \{x\!:\!B \mid s\} \triangleright \{x\!:\!B \mid t\} \rangle\ c \longrightarrow c & \text{if } t[x := c] \longrightarrow^* \mathtt{true} & [\text{E-Cast-C}] \\ \mathcal{E}[s] \longrightarrow \mathcal{E}[t] & \text{if } s \longrightarrow t & [\text{E-Compat}] \end{array}$$

Contexts $\boxed{\mathcal{E}}$

$$\mathcal{E} \ ::= \ \bullet \mid \bullet\ t \mid t\ \bullet \mid \langle S \triangleright T \rangle\, \bullet$$

Fig. 1. Syntax and Semantics

Type rules $\boxed{E \vdash t : T}$

[T-VAR]
$$\frac{(x : T) \in E}{E \vdash x : T}$$

[T-CONST]
$$\frac{}{E \vdash c : ty(c)}$$

[T-FUN]
$$\frac{E \vdash S \qquad E, x : S \vdash t : T}{E \vdash (\lambda x : S.\, t) : (x : S \to T)}$$

[T-CAST]
$$\frac{E \vdash t : S \qquad E \vdash T}{E \vdash \langle S \rhd T \rangle\ t : T}$$

[T-APP]
$$\frac{E \vdash t_1 : (x : S \to T) \qquad E \vdash t_2 : S}{E \vdash t_1\ t_2 : T[x := t_2 : S]}$$

[T-SUB]
$$\frac{E \vdash t : S \qquad E \vdash S <: T \qquad E \vdash T}{E \vdash t : T}$$

Well-formed types $\boxed{E \vdash T}$

[WT-ARROW]
$$\frac{E \vdash S \qquad E, x : S \vdash T}{E \vdash x : S \to T}$$

[WT-BASE]
$$\frac{E, x : B \vdash t : \texttt{Bool}}{E \vdash \{x : B \mid t\}}$$

Subtyping $\boxed{E \vdash S <: T}$

[S-ARROW]
$$\frac{E \vdash T_1 <: S_1 \qquad E, x : T_1 \vdash S_2 <: T_2}{E \vdash (x : S_1 \to S_2) <: (x : T_1 \to T_2)}$$

[S-BASE]
$$\frac{E, x : B \vdash s \Rightarrow t}{E \vdash \{x : B \mid s\} <: \{x : B \mid t\}}$$

Implication $\boxed{E \vdash s \Rightarrow t}$

[IMP]
$$\frac{\forall \sigma.\, (E \models \sigma \text{ and } \sigma(s) \longrightarrow^* \texttt{true} \text{ implies } \sigma(t) \longrightarrow^* \texttt{true})}{E \vdash s \Rightarrow t}$$

Consistent Substitutions $\boxed{E \models \sigma}$

[CS-EMPTY]
$$\frac{}{\emptyset \models \emptyset}$$

[CS-EXT]
$$\frac{\emptyset \vdash t : T \qquad (x := t)E \models \sigma}{x : T, E \models (x := t, \sigma)}$$

Fig. 2. Type Rules

The typing rules for λ^H are reproduced in Figure 2. Each constant c is assigned a type $ty(c)$ by rule [T-CONST]; the axioms on constants, detailed in [10], ensure that $ty(c)$ and $[\![c]\!]$ uphold type soundness. The type of a variable is extracted from the environment by rule [T-VAR] and functions are assigned dependent function types by rule [T-FUN]. For an application $t_1\ t_2$, the rule [T-APP] checks that t_1 has a dependent function type $x : S \to T$ and that t_2 has type S. The application is then assigned the type $T[x := t_2 : S]$, which is T with the concrete argument t_2 substituted for the argument variable x. The substitution is annotated with the argument type S to aid type reconstruction.

Typing of λ^H is based on subtyping, which utilizes an implication judgement between refinement predicates, rendering subtyping undecidable. The implication judgement $E \vdash s \Rightarrow t$ is defined by rule [IMP], which reads: term s implies term t in environment E if, for any substitution σ on the variables bound in E that is consistent with the types of those variables in E, $\sigma(p) \longrightarrow^* \texttt{true}$ implies $\sigma(q) \longrightarrow^* \texttt{true}$. For example, $x : \texttt{Int} \vdash (x > 1) \Rightarrow (x > 0)$, because for any integer i chosen to substitute for x, whenever $(i > 1)$ evaluates to $\texttt{true}$, so does $(i > 0)$.

3 Type Reconstruction

For the type reconstruction problem, we extend the type language with type variables $\alpha \in \mathit{TyVar}$. Type reconstruction yields a function $\pi : \mathit{TyVar} \rightarrow \mathit{Type}$, here called a *type replacement*. Application of a type replacement is lifted compatibly to all syntactic sorts, and is not capture avoiding.

The three phases of type reconstruction proceed as follows:

1. The input program is processed to yield a set C of subtyping constraints of the form $E \vdash S <: T$ (the same as the subtyping judgement).
2. The shape reconstruction phase then reduces C into a set P of implication constraints, each of the form $E \vdash p \Rightarrow q$ (the same as the implication judgement).
3. The last phase of type reconstruction solves P.

3.1 Delayed Substitutions

To facilitate our development, we require that the language be closed under substitution. But a substitution cannot immediately be applied to a type variable, so each type variable α has an associated delayed substitution θ (which may be empty).

$$\begin{array}{rcl} T & ::= & \cdots \mid \theta \cdot \alpha \\ \theta & ::= & [\,] \mid [x := t : T], \theta \end{array}$$

The usual definition of capture-avoiding substitution is extended to type variables, which simply delay that substitution:

$$(\theta \cdot \alpha)[x := s : T] \;=\; ([x := s : T], \theta) \cdot \alpha$$

When a type replacement is applied to a type variable α with a delayed substitution θ, the substitution $\pi(\theta)$ is immediately applied to $\pi(\alpha)$:

$$\pi(\theta \cdot \alpha) \;=\; \pi(\theta)(\pi(\alpha))$$

4 Constraint Generation

The constraint generation judgement $E \vdash t : T \;\&\; C$ is defined in Figure 3 and reads: term t has type T in environment E, subject to the constraint set C. Each rule is derived from the corresponding type rule, with subsumption distributed throughout the derivation to make the rules syntax-directed.

Constraint Generation rules $\boxed{E \vdash t : T \,\&\, C}$

[CG-VAR]
$$\frac{(x:T) \in E}{E \vdash x : T \,\&\, \emptyset}$$

[CG-CONST]
$$\frac{}{E \vdash c : ty(c) \,\&\, \emptyset}$$

[CG-FUN]
$$\frac{E \vdash S \,\&\, C_1 \qquad E, x : S \vdash t : T \,\&\, C_2}{E \vdash (\lambda x{:}S.\, t) : (x{:}S \to T) \,\&\, C_1 \cup C_2}$$

[CG-APP]
$$\frac{E \vdash t_1 : T \,\&\, C_1 \qquad E \vdash t_2 : S \,\&\, C_2 \qquad \alpha \text{ fresh}}{E \vdash t_1\, t_2 : [x := t_2 : S] \cdot \alpha \,\&\, C_1 \cup C_2 \cup \{E \vdash T <: (x{:}S \to \alpha)\}}$$

[CG-CAST]
$$\frac{E \vdash t : S' \,\&\, C_1 \qquad E \vdash T \,\&\, C_2}{E \vdash \langle S \rhd T \rangle\, t : T \,\&\, C_1 \cup C_2 \cup \{E \vdash S' <: S\}}$$

Well-formed Type Constraint Generation $\boxed{E \vdash T \,\&\, C}$

[WTC-ARROW]
$$\frac{E \vdash S \,\&\, C_1 \qquad E, x : S \vdash T \,\&\, C_2}{E \vdash x{:}S \to T \,\&\, C_1 \cup C_2}$$

[WTC-BASE]
$$\frac{E, x : B \vdash t : \texttt{Bool} \,\&\, C}{E \vdash \{x{:}B \mid t\} \,\&\, C}$$

[WTC-VAR]
$$\frac{}{E \vdash \theta \cdot \alpha \,\&\, \emptyset}$$

Fig. 3. Constraint Generation Rules

For a type replacement π, if $\pi(C)$ contains only valid subtyping relationships, then π *satisfies* C. When applied to a typeable λ^H program, the constraint generation rules emit a satisfiable constraint set. Conversely, if the constraint set derived from a program is satisfiable, then that program is typeable.

Lemma 1. *For any environment E and term t:*

$$\exists \pi, T.\ \pi(E) \vdash \pi(t) : \pi(T) \quad \iff \quad \exists \pi', S, C. \begin{cases} E \vdash t : S \,\&\, C \\ \pi' \text{ satisfies } C \end{cases}$$

Proof outline: Each direction proceeds by induction on the respective derivation. (All complete proofs are included in the extended technical report [19].) $\square$

Consider the following λ^H term t (the expression $\texttt{let}\ x : T = s\ \texttt{in}\ t$ is syntactic sugar for $(\lambda x{:}T.\, t)\ s$).

$$\begin{array}{l} \texttt{let}\ id : (x{:}\alpha_1 \to \alpha_2) = \lambda x{:}\alpha_3.\, x\ \texttt{in} \\ \texttt{let}\ w : \{n{:}\texttt{Int} \mid n = 0\} = 0\ \texttt{in} \\ \texttt{let}\ y : \{n{:}\texttt{Int} \mid n > w\} = 3\ \texttt{in} \\ id\ (id\ y) \end{array}$$

Eliding some generated type variables for clarity, the corresponding constraint generation judgement is

$$\varnothing \vdash t : [x := (id\ y) : \alpha_1] \cdot \alpha_2 \,\&\, C$$

where C contains the following constraints, in which $T_{id} \equiv (x:\alpha_1 \to \alpha_2)$ and $T_y \equiv \{n:\texttt{Int} \mid n > w\}$:

$$\begin{array}{rcrcl}
\varnothing & \vdash & x:\alpha_3 \to \alpha_3 & <: & x:\alpha_1 \to \alpha_2 \\
id : T_{id} & \vdash & \{n:\texttt{Int} \mid n = 0\} & <: & \{n:\texttt{Int} \mid n = 0\} \\
id : T_{id},\ w : \{n:\texttt{Int} \mid n = 0\} & \vdash & \{n:\texttt{Int} \mid n = 3\} & <: & \{n:\texttt{Int} \mid n > w\} \\
id : T_{id},\ w : \{n:\texttt{Int} \mid n = 0\}, y : T_y & \vdash & \{n:\texttt{Int} \mid n > w\} & <: & \alpha_1 \\
id : T_{id},\ w : \{n:\texttt{Int} \mid n = 0\}, y : T_y & \vdash & [x := y : \alpha_1] \cdot \alpha_2 & <: & \alpha_1
\end{array}$$

5 Shape Reconstruction

The second step of reconstruction is to infer a type's basic shape, ignoring refinement predicates. To defer reconstruction of refinements, we introduce placeholders $\gamma \in Placeholder$ to represent unknown refinement predicates (in the same way that type variables represent unknown types) Like type variables, each placeholder has an associated delayed substitution.

$$t \ ::= \ \cdots \mid \theta \cdot \gamma$$

A placeholder replacement is a function $\rho : Placeholder \to Term$ and is lifted compatibly to all syntactic structures. As with type replacements, applying placeholder replacement allows any delayed substitutions also to be applied.

$$\begin{array}{c}
[x := t : T](\theta \cdot \gamma) = ([x := t : T], \theta) \cdot \gamma \\
\rho(\theta \cdot \gamma) = \rho(\theta)(\rho(\gamma))
\end{array}$$

The shape reconstruction algorithm, detailed in figure 4 takes as input a subtyping constraint set C and processes the constraints in C nondeterministically according to the rules in Figure 4. When the conditions on the left-hand side of a rule are satisfied, the updates described on the right-hand side are performed. The set P of implication constraints, each of the form $E \vdash p \Rightarrow q$, and the type replacement π are outputs of the algorithm. For a placeholder replacement ρ, if $\rho(P)$ contains only valid implications, then ρ *satisfies* P.

Each rule in Figure 4 resembles a step of traditional type reconstruction. When a type variable α must have the shape of a function type, it is replaced by $x:\alpha_1 \to \alpha_2$, where α_1 and α_2 are fresh type variables. The function *occurs* checks that α has a finite solution, since λ^H does not have recursive types. Occurences of α which appear in refinement predicates or in the range of a delayed substitution are ignored – these occurences do not require a solution involving recursive types.

$$\begin{array}{rcl}
occurs(\alpha, \{x:B \mid t\}) & = & false \\
occurs(\alpha, \theta \cdot \alpha') & = & false \quad (\alpha \neq \alpha') \\
occurs(\alpha, \theta \cdot \alpha) & = & true \\
occurs(\alpha, x:S \to T) & = & occurs(\alpha, S) \vee occurs(\alpha, T)
\end{array}$$

When a type variable must be a refinement of a base type B, the type variable is replaced by $\{x:B \mid \gamma\}$ where γ is a fresh placeholder. A subtyping constraint

Input: C
Output: π, P
Initially: $P = \emptyset$ and $\pi = [\,]$
match some constraint in C until quiescent:

$$\begin{array}{rcl}
E \vdash \theta \cdot \alpha <: x{:}T_1 \to T_2 & \Longrightarrow & \text{if } \mathit{occurs}(\alpha, x{:}T_1 \to T_2) \text{ then } \mathit{fail} \\
\text{or } E \vdash x{:}T_1 \to T_2 <: \theta \cdot \alpha & & \text{otherwise for fresh } \alpha_1, \alpha_2 \\
& & \pi := [\alpha := x{:}\alpha_1 \to \alpha_2] \circ \pi \\
& & C := \pi(C) \\
& & P := \pi(P) \\
E \vdash \theta \cdot \alpha <: \{x{:}B \mid t\} & \Longrightarrow & \text{for fresh } \gamma \\
\text{or } E \vdash \{x{:}B \mid t\} <: \theta \cdot \alpha & & \pi := [\alpha := \{x{:}B \mid \gamma\}] \circ \pi \\
& & C := \pi(C) \\
& & P := \pi(P) \\
E \vdash (x{:}S_1 \to S_2) <: (x{:}T_1 \to T_2) & \Longrightarrow & C := C \cup \left\{ \begin{array}{l} E \vdash T_1 <: S_1, \\ E, x : T_1 \vdash S_2 <: T_2 \end{array} \right\} \\
E \vdash \{x{:}B \mid p\} <: \{x{:}B \mid q\} & \Longrightarrow & P := P \cup \{E \vdash p \Rightarrow q\} \\
E \vdash \{x{:}B \mid p\} <: x{:}S \to T & & \\
\text{or } E \vdash x{:}S \to T <: \{x{:}B \mid p\} & \Longrightarrow & \mathit{fail}
\end{array}$$

Fig. 4. Shape Reconstruction Algorithm

between two function types induces additional constraints between the domains and codomains of the function types. When two refined base types are constrained to be subtypes, a corresponding implication constraint between their refinements is added to P.

The algorithm terminates once no more progress can be made. At this stage, any type variables remaining in $\pi(C)$ are not constrained to be subtypes of any concrete type but may be subtypes of each other. We set these type variables equal to an arbitrary concrete type to eliminate them (the resulting subtyping judgements are trivial by reflexivity).

Lemma 2. *For a set of subtyping constraints C, one of the following occurs:*

1. *Shape reconstruction fails, in which case C is unsatisfiable, or*
2. *Shape reconstruction succeeds, yielding π and P. Then P is satisfiable if and only if C is satisfiable. Furthermore, if ρ satisfies P then $\rho \circ \pi$ satisfies C.*

Proof outline: Each step maintains the invariant that C is satisfiable if and only if $\exists \pi', \rho$ such that ρ satisfies P and $\rho \circ \pi' \circ \pi$ satisfies C. □

Returning to our example, shape reconstruction returns the type replacement

$$\pi = [\ \alpha_1 := \{n{:}\mathtt{Int} \mid \gamma_1\},\ \alpha_2 := \{n{:}\mathtt{Int} \mid \gamma_2\},\ \alpha_3 := \{n{:}\mathtt{Int} \mid \gamma_3\}\ ]$$

and the following implication constraint set P, in which $T_{id} = x:\{n:\texttt{Int} \mid \gamma_2\} \to \{n:\texttt{Int} \mid \gamma_3\}$ and $T_y = \{n:\texttt{Int} \mid n > w\}$:

$$\begin{array}{rcl} n : \texttt{Int} \vdash & \gamma_1 \Rightarrow \gamma_3 \\ x : \{n:\texttt{Int} \mid \gamma_1\},\ n : \texttt{Int} \vdash & \gamma_3 \Rightarrow \gamma_2 \\ id : T_{id},\ n : \texttt{Int} \vdash & (n = 0) \Rightarrow (n = 0) \\ id : T_{id},\ w : \{n:\texttt{Int} \mid n = 0\},\ n : \texttt{Int} \vdash & (n = 3) \Rightarrow (n > w) \\ id : T_{id}, w : \{n:\texttt{Int} \mid n = 0\},\ y : T_y,\ n : \texttt{Int} \vdash & (n > w) \Rightarrow \gamma_1 \\ id : T_{id}, w : \{n:\texttt{Int} \mid n = 0\},\ y : T_y,\ n : \texttt{Int} \vdash & [x := y : \{n:\texttt{Int} \mid \gamma_1\}] \cdot \gamma_2 \Rightarrow \gamma_1 \end{array}$$

6 Satisfiability

The final phase of type reconstruction solves the residual implication constraint set P by finding a placeholder replacement that preserves satisfiability.

Our approach is based on the intuition that implications are essentially data-flow paths that carry the specifications of data sources (constants and function post-conditions) to the requirements of data sinks (function pre-conditions), with placeholders functioning as intermediate nodes in the data-flow graph. Thus, if a placeholder γ appears on the right-hand side of two implication constraints $E \vdash p \Rightarrow \gamma$ and $E \vdash q \Rightarrow \gamma$, then our replacement for γ is simply the disjunction $p \vee q$ (the strongest consequence) of these two lower bounds. Our algorithm repeatedly applies this transformation until no placeholders remain, but several difficulties arise:

1. p or q may contain variables that cannot appear in a solution for γ
2. γ may have a delayed substitution
3. γ may appear in p or q

To help resolve these issues, we extend the language with the following terms.

$$s, t \in \mathit{Term} \quad ::= \quad \cdots \ \mid \ t \vee t \ \mid \ t \wedge t \ \mid \ \exists x : T.\ t$$

The parallel disjunction $t_1 \vee t_2$ (respectively conjunction $t_1 \wedge t_2$) evaluates t_1 and t_2 nondeterministically, reducing to `true` (resp. `false`) if either of them reduces to `true` (resp. `false`). The existential term $\exists x : T.\ t$ binds x in t, and evaluates by nondeterministically replacing x with a closed term of type T. The evaluation rules are summarized in Figure 5.

6.1 Free Variable Elimination

In our example program, the type variable α_1 appeared in the empty environment and $\pi(\alpha_1) = \{n:\texttt{Int} \mid \gamma_1\}$, so the solution for γ_1 should be a well-formed boolean expression in the environment $n : \texttt{Int}$. The only variable that can appear in a solution for γ_1 is therefore n. But consider the following constraint over γ_1:

$$id : T_{id},\ w : \{n:\texttt{Int} \mid n = 0\},\ y : T_y,\ n : \texttt{Int} \vdash (n > w) \Rightarrow \gamma_1$$

Since id, w, and y cannot appear in a solution for γ_1, we rewrite this constraint as

$$n : \texttt{Int} \vdash (\exists id : T_{id}.\ \exists w : \{n:\texttt{Int} \mid n = 0\}.\ \exists y : T_y.\ n > w) \Rightarrow \gamma_1$$

$$\begin{array}{rcll} \texttt{true} \vee t & \longrightarrow & \texttt{true} & \text{[E-OR-L]} \\ t \vee \texttt{true} & \longrightarrow & \texttt{true} & \text{[E-OR-R]} \\ \texttt{false} \vee \texttt{false} & \longrightarrow & \texttt{false} & \text{[E-OR-F]} \end{array} \qquad \begin{array}{rcll} \texttt{false} \wedge t & \longrightarrow & \texttt{false} & \text{[E-AND-L]} \\ t \wedge \texttt{false} & \longrightarrow & \texttt{false} & \text{[E-AND-R]} \\ \texttt{true} \wedge \texttt{true} & \longrightarrow & \texttt{true} & \text{[E-AND-T]} \end{array}$$

$$\exists x : T.\, t \longrightarrow t[x := s : T] \quad \text{if } \varnothing \vdash s : T \qquad \text{[E-EXISTS]}$$

$$\mathcal{E} ::= \cdots \mid t \vee \bullet \mid \bullet \vee t \mid \bullet \wedge t \mid t \wedge \bullet$$

Fig. 5. Additional Evaluation Rules

In general, each placeholder γ introduced by shape reconstruction has an associated environment E_γ in which it must have type `Bool`. This gives us a reasonable definition for the free variables of a placeholder (with its associated delayed subtitution):

$$fv(\theta \cdot \gamma) = (dom(E_\gamma) \setminus dom(\theta)) \cup fv(rng(\theta))$$

We then rewrite each implication constraint $E, y : T \vdash p \Rightarrow q$ where $y \notin fv(q)$ into the constraint $E \vdash (\exists y : T.\ p) \Rightarrow q$. This transformation is semantics-preserving:

Lemma 3. *For $y \notin fv(q)$, $E, y : T \vdash p \Rightarrow q$ if and only if $E \vdash (\exists y : T.\ p) \Rightarrow q$*

Proof outline: The single-step evaluations of the existential term are in one-to-one correspondence with the possible values of $y : T$ in a closing substitution. □

Repeatedly applying this transformation, we rewrite each implication constraint until the domain of the environment (and hence the free variables of the left-hand side) is a subset of the free variables of the right-hand side.

6.2 Delayed Substitution Elimination

The next issue is the presence of delayed substitutions in constraints of the form $E \vdash p \Rightarrow \theta \cdot \gamma$. To eliminate the delayed substitution θ we first split it into an environment $env(\theta)$ and a term $[\![\theta]\!]$:

$$\begin{array}{rl} env([\,]) &= \varnothing \\ env([x := t : T], \theta) &= x : T, env(\theta) \end{array} \qquad \begin{array}{rl} [\![\, [\,] \,]\!] &= \texttt{true} \\ [\![\, [x := t : T], \theta \,]\!] &= (x = t) \wedge [\![\theta]\!] \end{array}$$

The environment $env(\theta)$ binds all the variables in $dom(\theta)$ while the term $[\![\theta]\!]$ represents the semantic content of θ.

We then transform the constraint $E \vdash p \Rightarrow \theta \cdot \gamma$ into $E, env(\theta) \vdash [\![\theta]\!] \wedge p \Rightarrow \gamma$. But we can rewrite the constraint even more cleanly: E must be some prefix of E_γ since by the previous transformation $dom(E) \subseteq fv(\theta \cdot \gamma) \subseteq dom(E_\gamma)$. Any $x \in dom(\theta)$ such that $x \notin dom(E_\gamma)$ can be dropped from θ and we see that $E, env(\theta)$ is then exactly E_γ. So our constraint is

$$E_\gamma \vdash [\![\theta]\!] \wedge p \Rightarrow \gamma$$

To prove this transformation correct, we use the following well-formedness judgement $E \vdash_{\text{wf}} \theta$ which distinguishes those delayed substitutions that may actually occur in context E.

$$\text{[WF-EMPY]}\quad \frac{}{E \vdash_{\text{wf}} [\,]} \qquad \text{[WF-EXT]}\quad \frac{E \vdash t : T \qquad E, x : T \vdash_{\text{wf}} \theta'}{E \vdash_{\text{wf}} [x := t : T], \theta'}$$

Lemma 4. *Suppose ρ is a placeholder replacement such that $\rho(E) \vdash_{\text{wf}} \rho(\theta)$. Then ρ satisfies $E \vdash p \Rightarrow \theta \cdot \gamma$ if and only if ρ satisfies $E, env(\theta) \vdash [\![\theta]\!] \wedge p \Rightarrow \gamma$*

Proof outline: The evaluations of the antecedents of each judgement can be mapped into the evaluations of the other. □

6.3 Placeholder Solution

After the previous transformations, all lower bounds of a placeholder γ appear in constraints of the form

$$E_\gamma \vdash p_i \Rightarrow \gamma$$

for $i \in \{1..n\}$, assuming γ has n lower bounds. We want to set γ equal to the parallel disjunction $p_1 \vee p_2 \vee \cdots \vee p_n$ of all its lower bounds (the disjunction must be parallel because some subterms may be nonterminating). However, γ may appear in some p_i due to recursion or self-composition of a function. In this case we use a least fixed point operator, conveniently already available in our language, to find a solution to the equation $\gamma = p_1 \vee \cdots \vee p_n$.

More formally, suppose $E_\gamma = x_1 : T_1, \cdots, x_k : T_k$. Then γ is a predicate over $x_1 \cdots x_k$ and we can interpret it as a function $\mathcal{F}_\gamma : T_1 \to \cdots \to T_k \to \texttt{Bool}$. We use the following notation for clarity:

$$\bar{T} \to \texttt{Bool} \equiv T_1 \to T_2 \to \cdots \to T_k \to \texttt{Bool}$$
$$\lambda \bar{x} : \bar{T}.\, t \equiv \lambda x_1 : T_1.\, \lambda x_2 : T_2.\, \cdots \lambda x_k : T_k.\, t$$
$$f\, \bar{x} \equiv f\; x_1\; x_2\; \cdots\; x_k$$

The function $\mathcal{F}_\gamma$ can then be defined as the following least fixed point computation:

$$\mathcal{F}_\gamma \;=\; \texttt{fix}_{\bar{T} \to \texttt{Bool}}\, (\lambda f : \bar{T} \to \texttt{Bool}.\, \lambda \bar{x} : \bar{T}.\, (p_1 \vee \cdots \vee p_n)[\gamma := f\, \bar{x}])$$

Our solution for γ is $LB(\gamma) = \mathcal{F}_\gamma\, \bar{x}$. This is the strongest consequence that is implied by all lower bounds of γ and is in some sense canonical, analogously to the strongest postcondition of a code block.

Lemma 5. *If a placeholder replacement ρ satisfies P, then ρ satisfies $E_\gamma \vdash LB(\gamma) \Rightarrow \gamma$.*

Proof outline: For any σ such that $\rho(E_\gamma) \models \sigma$, the lemma follows by induction on the length of the reduction sequence of $\sigma(\rho(LB(\gamma))) \longrightarrow^* \texttt{true}$. □

The result of equisatisfiability follows from the fact that we have chosen the strongest possible solution for γ.

Lemma 6. *P is satisfiable if and only if $P[\gamma := LB(\gamma)]$ is satisfiable.*

Proof outline: ($\Rightarrow$): Consider any $\rho : PlaceHolders \to Terms$ that satisfies P. By Lemma 5 if $\rho(\gamma) \Rrightarrow p$ occurs in P, then $LB(\gamma) \Rrightarrow \rho(\gamma) \Rrightarrow p$; covariant occurences of γ in environments are analogous. If $p \Rrightarrow \rho(\gamma)$ occurs in P, then $p \Rrightarrow LB(\gamma)$ by construction of $LB(\gamma)$; contravariant occurences of types in environments do not affect satisfiability. □

In our example, the only lower bound of γ_3 is γ_1 and the only lower bound of γ_2 is γ_3, so let us set $\gamma_3 := \gamma_1$ and $\gamma_2 := \gamma_3$ in order to discuss the more interesting solution for γ_1. The resulting unsatisfied constraints (simplified for clarity) are:

$$n : \mathtt{Int} \vdash \exists w : \{n{:}\mathtt{Int} \mid n = 0\}.\ (n > w) \ \Rrightarrow\ \gamma_1$$
$$n : \mathtt{Int} \vdash \exists w : \{n{:}\mathtt{Int} \mid n = 0\}.\ \exists y : \{n{:}\mathtt{Int} \mid n > w\}.\ [x := y] \cdot \gamma_1 \Rrightarrow \gamma_1$$

The exact text of $LB(\gamma_1)$ is too large to print here, but it is equivalent to $\exists w : \{n{:}\mathtt{Int} \mid n = 0\}.\ (n > w)$ and thus equivalent to $(n > 0)$. The resulting explicitly-typed program (simplified according to the previous sentence's discussion) is:

$$\mathtt{let}\ id : (x{:}\{n{:}\mathtt{Int} \mid n > 0\} \to \{n{:}\mathtt{Int} \mid n > 0\}) = \lambda x{:}\{n{:}\mathtt{Int} \mid n > 0\}.x\ \mathtt{in}$$
$$\mathtt{let}\ w : \{n{:}\mathtt{Int} \mid n = 0\} = 0\ \mathtt{in}$$
$$\mathtt{let}\ y : \{n{:}\mathtt{Int} \mid n > w\} = 3\ \mathtt{in}$$
$$id\ (id\ y)$$

7 Correctness

The output of our algorithm is the composition of the type replacement returned by shape reconstruction and the placeholder replacement returned by the satisfiability routine. Application of this composed replacement is a typeability-preserving transformation. Moreover, for any typeable program, the algorithm succeeds in producing such a replacement.

Theorem 1. *For any λ^H program t, one of the following occurs:*

1. *Type reconstruction fails, in which case t is untypeable, or*
2. *Type reconstruction returns a type replacement π such that t is typeable if and only if $\pi(t)$ is well-typed.*

Proof

Case 1: Only shape reconstruction can fail. If it does, then by Lemma 2 the subtyping constraints are unsatisfiable. Then by Lemma 1, t is not typeable.
Case 2: Type reconstruction solved constraints that were faithful, by Lemma 1. Thus by Lemma 2 we have π and by Lemma 6 we have ρ such that $(\rho \circ \pi)(t)$ is typeable (well-typed) if and only if t is typeable. □

8 Related Work

Freeman and Pfenning introduced *datasort refinements*, which express restrictions on the recursive structure of algebraic datatypes [13]. Type reconstruction for the finite set of programmer-specified datasort refinements is decided by abstract interpretation. Hayashi [16] and Denney [6] explored various logics for refinement predicates, while Davies and Pfenning [5], and Mandelbaum *et al* [22] combined refinements with computational effects. All of these systems require type annotations, though many perform some manner of local type inference [27].

Xi and Pfenning [29] developed Dependent ML, which uses dependent types along with *index types* to express invariants for complex data structures such as red-black trees. Dependent ML solves systems of linear inequalities to infer a restricted class of type indices. Dunfield [8] combined index types and datasort refinements in a system with decidable type checking, but the programmer is required to provide sufficient type annotations to guide the type checking process.

Recently, Ou *et al* [26] developed a system with dependent types and refinement types where a section of code may be dynamically typed in order to reduce the annotation burden. For the static dependently-typed portion of a program, they forbid recursive functions in refinement predicates to ensure decidability of type checking, and perform no type reconstruction.

Constraint-based type reconstruction for systems with subtyping is a tremendously broad topic, and we cannot fully review it here. The problem is studied in some generality by Mitchell [23], Fuh and Mishra [14], Lincoln and Mitchell [21], Aiken and Wimmers [1], and Hoang and Mitchell [18]. Type inference systems parameterized by a subtyping constraint system are developed by Pottier [28] and Odersky *et al* [25]. This paper is complimentary to generalized systems in that it focuses on the solution of our particular instantiation of subtyping constraints; we also do not investigate parametric polymorphism, which is included in the mentioned frameworks. Set-based analysis presents many similar ideas, and we draw inspiration from the works of Heintze [17], Cousot and Cousot [4], Fähndrich and Aiken [9], and Flanagan and Felleisen [11].

The precondition/postcondition discipline for imperative programs dates back to the work of Floyd [12], Hoare [3], and Dijkstra [7]. General refinement types apply similar ideas to functional, higher-order, programs. Our transformation of predicates to infer refinements resembles and is inspired by Dijkstra's weakest precondition calculation but is most closely related to the related strongest postcondition defined by Back [2]. Nanevski *et al* [24] have introduced another relationship between axiomatic semantics and type systems with their Hoare Type Theory, which adds pre- and postconditions to the types of effectful monadic computation.

9 Conclusions and Future Work

Refinement type systems are a promising method for expressing precise program specifications, but many such specifications are not decidable at compile time.

Hybrid type checking offers a practical strategy to enforce undecidable refinement types. This work demonstrates that while typeability for such systems is undecidable, a generalized notion of type reconstruction *is* decidable and resembles a natural application of specification techniques for imperative programs in a declarative context.

The connection with predicate transformations used in the analysis of imperative programs deserves further attention, and one clear avenue of future work is propagating information "backwards" as in a weakest precondition calculation, and combining this information with the information we propagate "forwards", in order to infer the least type for any term. We infer the strongest possible refinement predicates, but in the most precise type for a function, the contravariant domain has the *weakest* possible refinement.

Inferred refinement predicates may be large and unsuitable for use in error messages, much like the verification conditions of axiomatic semantics. Instead of simply presenting the user with a counterexample to the verification condition, ESC/Java illustrates each warning message with a partial trace of the program [20]; it may be possible to present similar traces for untypable programs.

References

1. A. Aiken and E. Wimmers. Type inclusion constraints and type inference. In *Proceedings of the Conference on Functional Programming Languages and Computer Architecture*, pages 31–41, 1993.
2. R. J. R. Back. A calculus of refinements for program derivations. *Acta Informatica*, 25(6):593–624, 1988.
3. C. A. R. Hoare. An axiomatic basis for computer programming. *Communications of the ACM*, 12:576–580, 1969.
4. P. Cousot and R. Cousot. Formal language, grammar, and set-constraint-based program analysis by abstract interpretation. In *Proceedings of the International Conference on Functional Programming and Computer Architecture*, pages 170–181, 1995.
5. R. Davies and F. Pfenning. Intersection types and computational effects. In *Proceedings of the ACM International Conference on Functional Programming*, pages 198–208, 2000.
6. E. Denney. Refinement types for specification. In *Proceedings of the IFIP International Conference on Programming Concepts and Methods*, volume 125, pages 148–166. Chapman & Hall, 1998.
7. E. W. Dijkstra. *A Discipline of Programming*. Prentice-Hall, 1976.
8. J. Dunfield. Combining two forms of type refinements. Technical Report CMU-CS-02-182, CMU School of Computer Science, Pittsburgh, Penn., 2002.
9. M. Fähndrich and A. Aiken. Making set-constraint based program analyses scale. Technical Report UCB/CSD-96-917, University of California at Berkeley, 1996.
10. C. Flanagan. Hybrid type checking. In *Proceedings of the ACM Symposium on Principles of Programming Languages*, pages 245 – 256, 2006.
11. C. Flanagan and M. Felleisen. Componential set-based analysis. In *Proceedings of the ACM Conference on Programming Language Design and Implementation*, pages 235–248, 1997.

12. R. W. Floyd. Assigning meaning to programs. In *Proceedings of the Symposium in Applied Mathematics: Mathematical Aspects of Computer Science*, pages 19–32, 1967.
13. T. Freeman and F. Pfenning. Refinement types for ML. In *Proceedings of the ACM Conference on Programming Language Design and Implementation*, pages 268–277, 1991.
14. Y. Fuh and P. Mishra. Type inference with subtypes. In *Proceedings of the European Symposium on Programming*, pages 155–175, 1988.
15. J. Gronski, K. Knowles, A. Tomb, S. N. Freund, and C. Flanagan. Sage: Practical hybrid checking for expressive types and specifications. In *Proceedings of the Workshop on Scheme and Functional Programming*, pages 93–104, 2006.
16. S. Hayashi. Logic of refinement types. In *Proceedings of the Workshop on Types for Proofs and Programs*, pages 157–172, 1993.
17. N. Heintze. *Set Based Program Analysis*. PhD thesis, Carnegie Mellon University, 1992.
18. M. Hoang and J. C. Mitchell. Lower bounds on type inference with subtypes. In *Proceedings of the ACM Symposium on Principles of Programming Languages*, pages 176 – 185, 1995.
19. K. Knowles and C. Flanagan. Type reconstruction for general refinement types. `http://www.soe.ucsc.edu/~cormac/papers/htr-full.pdf`, 2007.
20. K. R. M. Leino, T. Millstein, and J. B. Saxe. Generating error traces from verification-condition counterexamples. *Science of Computer Programming*, 55(1-3): 209–226, 2005.
21. P. Lincoln and J. C. Mitchell. Algorithmic aspects of type inference with subtypes. In *Proceedings of the ACM Symposium on Principles of Programming Languages*, pages 293 – 304, 1992.
22. Y. Mandelbaum, D. Walker, and R. Harper. An effective theory of type refinements. In *Proceedings of the ACM International Conference on Functional Programming*, pages 213–225, 2003.
23. J. C. Mitchell. Coercion and type inference. In *Proceedings of the ACM Symposium on Principles of Programming Languages*, pages 175 – 185, 1983.
24. A. Nanevski, G. Morrisett, and L. Birkedal. Polymorphism and separation in hoare type theory. In *Proceedings of the International Conference on Functional Programming*, pages 62–73, 2006.
25. M. Odersky, M. Sulzmann, and M. Wehr. Type inference with constrained types. *Theory and Practice of Object Systems*, 5(1):35–55, 1999.
26. X. Ou, G. Tan, Y. Mandelbaum, and D. Walker. Dynamic typing with dependent types. In *Proceedings of the IFIP International Conference on Theoretical Computer Science*, pages 437–450, 2004.
27. B. C. Pierce and D. N. Turner. Local type inference. In *Proceedings of the ACM Symposium on Principles of Programming Languages*, pages 252–265, 1998.
28. F. Pottier. Simplifying subtyping constraints. In *Proceedings of the ACM International Conference on Functional Programming*, pages 122–133, 1996.
29. H. Xi and F. Pfenning. Dependent types in practical programming. In *Proceedings of the ACM Symposium on Principles of Programming Languages*, pages 214–227, 1999.

Dependent Types for Low-Level Programming

Jeremy Condit[1], Matthew Harren[1], Zachary Anderson[1], David Gay[2], and George C. Necula[1]

[1] University of California, Berkeley
[2] Intel Research, Berkeley

Abstract. In this paper, we describe the key principles of a dependent type system for low-level imperative languages. The major contributions of this work are (1) a sound type system that combines dependent types and mutation for variables and for heap-allocated structures in a more flexible way than before and (2) a technique for automatically inferring dependent types for local variables. We have applied these general principles to design Deputy, a dependent type system for C that allows the user to describe bounded pointers and tagged unions. Deputy has been used to annotate and check a number of real-world C programs.

1 Introduction

Types provide a convenient and accessible mechanism for specifying program invariants. Dependent types extend simple types with the ability to express invariants relating multiple state elements. While such dependencies likely exist in all programs, they play a fundamental role in low-level programming. The following widespread low-level programming practices all involve dependencies: an array represented as a count of elements along with a pointer to the start of the buffer; a pointer to an element inside an array along with the array bounds; and a variant type (as in a Pascal variant, or a C union) along with a tag that identifies the active variant. If we cannot describe such dependencies we cannot prove even the memory safety of most low-level programs.

In this paper, we consider the main obstacles that limit the convenient use of dependent types in low-level programs:

- *Soundness:* Mutation of variables or heap locations, used heavily in low-level programs, might invalidate the types of some state elements. Previous dependent type systems are of limited usefulness because they contain restrictions that preclude the use of mutable variables in dependent types [2,19,20]. Instead, we show that it is possible to combine mutation and dependencies in a more flexible manner by using a type rule inspired by Hoare's rule for assignment. This approach can be used for dependencies between variables and between fields of heap-allocated structures.
- *Decidability:* Dependent type checking involves reasoning about the run-time values of expressions. In most previous dependent type systems, dependencies are restricted to the point where all checking can be done statically.

R. De Nicola (Ed.): ESOP 2007, LNCS 4421, pp. 520–535, 2007.

Instead, we propose the use of run-time checks where static checking is not sufficient. This hybrid type-checking strategy, which has also been used recently by Flanagan [7], is essential for handling real-world code.

– *Usability:* Writing complete dependent type declarations can be a considerable burden. We describe a technique for automatic dependency inference for local variables, starting from existing declarations for global variables, data structures, and functions.

We have applied these general principles for low-level dependent types to create the Deputy type system for the C programming language. Deputy's dependent types allow programmers to specify common C programming idioms involving pointer arithmetic and union types. Previous approaches to safe C involved significant changes in the program's data representation in order to add metadata for checking purposes: certain pointers were given a "fat" representation that includes the pointer and its bounds, and tags were added to union values [11,14]. Instead, Deputy allows programmers to specify relationships between existing data elements, which in turn allows the compiler to check the safety of most pointer and union operations without changing program data structures. This approach enables users to apply Deputy modularly and incrementally to system components, which is especially important for very large systems or in the presence of external libraries.

In Section 2, we present a high-level preview of the main stages in the Deputy system for safe low-level programming, using a simple example. Section 3 contains the technical core of the paper, describing our dependent types for a core imperative language with references and structures, and Section 4 presents our automatic dependency inference technique. Then, Section 5 shows how this dependent type framework can be instantiated to provide safe handling of pointer arithmetic and union types in C. Finally, we discuss related work in Section 6.

2 Overview

In order to provide an intuition for the general principles described in this paper, we discuss here how these principles are instantiated for enforcing memory safety with the Deputy type system. Consider the sample code shown in Figure 1 without any of the underlined or italicized statements. This program is standard C, with one programmer-supplied annotation for the type of the `buf` formal argument. The annotated type "`int * count(end - buf)`" describes a pointer to an array of at least `end - buf` integers.

Deputy processes this program in three passes:

Pass 1: Inference of missing annotations. For each pointer type without bounds annotations (e.g., `tmp`), Deputy introduces a fresh local variable to hold the bounds, along with appropriate assignments for this variable whenever the pointer is assigned. In Figure 1, this inference pass adds the underlined code; specifically, it introduces the variable `tmplen`, which is updated to store the length of the array pointed to by `tmp`. We describe this algorithm in Section 4.

```
1 int sum (int * count(end - buf) buf, int * end) {
2   int sum = 0;
3   while (buf < end) {
4     assert(0 < end - buf);
5     sum += * buf;
6     int tmplen = (end - buf) - 1;
7     assert(0 <= 1 <= end - buf);
8     int * count(tmplen) tmp = buf + 1;
9     assert(0 <= end - tmp <= tmplen);
10    buf = tmp;
11  }
12  return sum;
13 }
```

Fig. 1. A Deputy program, along with the code added during automatic dependency inference (underlined) and the assertions added during type checking (in italics). The temporary variable is shown to better demonstrate Deputy features but is not required.

Pass 2: Flow-insensitive type checking and instrumentation. Next, Deputy type checks the program using a flow-insensitive type system. Any checks that involve reasoning about run-time values of expressions are emitted as run-time assertions. In Figure 1, the italicized code shows the assertions that have been added in this stage. For example, the assertion in line 4 ensures that the `buf` array is nonempty and can therefore be safely dereferenced.

The check on line 9 is particularly interesting because it shows the power of Deputy's handling of mutation in presence of dependent types. Previous dependent type systems would disallow any assignments to `buf` because there exist types in the program that depend on it. Instead, Deputy inserts checks that ensure that `buf`'s type invariant will still hold after the assignment. Here, we ensure that `tmp` has at least `end - tmp` elements and thus will satisfy `buf`'s type invariant when assigned to `buf`. Such self-dependencies are particularly useful when designing flexible types for low-level code. The rules for type checking and for inserting run-time checks are described in Section 3.

Pass 3: Flow-sensitive optimization of checks. Because our flow-insensitive type checker has limited ability to recognize redundant checks, we follow type checking with a flow-sensitive optimization phase. Using standard data-flow techniques, we can eliminate a large number of the unnecessary checks in the program, and we can also identify checks that are guaranteed to fail. In Figure 1, all checks could reasonably be eliminated by the optimizer. By separating the flow-insensitive type checker from the flow-sensitive optimizer, we simplify both the implementation and the programmer's view of the type system. Our current optimizer uses standard data-flow techniques and is discussed in detail in a separate technical report [1]. However, it is worth pointing out that the amount of static memory safety enforcement depends directly on the quality of the optimizer.

We can use this example to contrast our approach with safe C type systems that use fat pointers [11,14]. With these systems, the pointer `buf` might be

Ctors	$C ::= \text{int} \mid \text{ref} \mid \ldots$	Cmds	$c ::= \text{skip} \mid c_1; c_2 \mid$
Types	$\tau ::= C \mid \tau_1\ \tau_2 \mid \tau\ e$		$\ell := e \mid \text{assert}(\gamma) \mid$
Kinds	$\kappa ::= \text{type} \mid \text{type} \to \kappa \mid \tau \to \kappa$		$\text{let } x : \tau = e \text{ in } c \mid$
L-exprs	$\ell ::= x \mid * e$		$\text{let } x = \text{new } \tau(e) \text{ in } c$
Exprs	$e ::= n \mid \ell \mid e_1 \text{ op } e_2$	Preds	$\gamma ::= e_1 \text{ comp } e_2 \mid \text{true} \mid \gamma_1 \wedge \gamma_2$

$x, y \in$ Variables $\qquad n \in$ Integer constants
op $\in$ Binary operators $\qquad$ comp $\in$ Comparison operators

Fig. 2. The grammar for a simple dependently-typed imperative language

stored as a two-word pointer, which means that all callers of this function must be instrumented as well. In contrast, Deputy's annotations require no changes outside this function, which is a crucial advantage over existing tools. Also, since Deputy's checks refer to existing program data, our optimizer can take advantage of existing checks such as the conditional in line 3. These benefits have allowed us to apply Deputy incrementally to modular software such as Linux device drivers and TinyOS components, as described in Section 5.3.

3 Dependent Type Framework

This section presents the key components of our dependent type framework. Our full type system supports dependencies between, and mutation of, local variables, formal parameters, global variables, and structure fields. In this section, we start with a system that includes only local variables, and then we extend it with heap-allocated structures. The remaining features are not discussed in this paper, but further details are available in a companion technical report [5].

3.1 Language

Although our implementation uses the concrete syntax of C, as shown in the previous section, for the purposes of our formalism we use the simpler language shown in Figure 2. In this language, types are specified using type constructors, which represent type families indexed by types or by expressions. The built-in constructors are the nullary type constructor "int" (a prototypical base type) and the unary type constructor "ref". The "ref" constructor allows the creation of types such as "ref int", which is an ML-style reference to an integer; this reference type is introduced here so that we can show how our type system works in the presence of memory reads and writes. In later sections, we will introduce additional type constructors, such as more expressive pointer types. The built-in constructors do not yield dependent types, but the additional constructors will.

Types are classified into kinds. The kind "type" characterizes complete types, whereas the functional kinds characterize type families that have to be applied to other complete types, or to expressions of a certain type, to eventually form complete types. For the two constructors we have seen so far, the kind of "int" is "type", and the kind of "ref" is "type $\to$ type".

To show how this system can be extended with additional type constructors, consider the `count` annotation used in Figure 1. To represent this annotated pointer type, we can introduce the constructor "array" with kind "type → int → type", such that "array τ e_{len}" is the type of arrays of elements of type τ and length at least e_{len}. In the concrete syntax this type is written as "τ * count(e_{len})".

The remainder of this language is standard. Note that $*$ represents pointer dereference, as in C. Also note that assertions are present only for compilation purposes and do not appear in the input program. Finally, note that we omit loops and conditionals, which are irrelevant to our flow-insensitive type system, and we omit function calls, which can be added later as an extension [5].

3.2 Type Rules

In this section, we present the type rules for the core language. Figure 3 shows these rules and summarizes the judgment forms involved.

Our strategy for handling mutation in the presence of dependent types relies on two important components. First, we use a typing rule inspired by the Hoare axiom for assignment to ensure that each mutation operation preserves well-typedness of the state. Second, dependencies in types are restricted such that we can always tell statically which types can be affected by each mutation operation. For this purpose, we restrict types to contain only expressions formed using constants, local variables, and arbitrary arithmetic operators. In other words, we do not allow memory dereferences in types. We refer to these restricted notions of expressions and types as *local expressions* and *local types*. Our type rules will require that all types written by the programmer be local types. Note that when we add structures to the language in the next section, we will extend this notion to allow field types to refer to other fields of the same structure.[1]

We now consider the well-formedness rules for types, shown at the top of Figure 3. If Γ is a mapping from variables to their types, we say that a type τ is well-formed in Γ if τ depends only on the variables in Γ. Note that type arguments must be well-formed in the empty environment, as shown in rule (TYPE TYPE), whereas expression arguments must be well-typed in Γ, as shown in rule (TYPE EXP). This conservative restriction is essential for the "ref" constructor. If we allowed variables in Γ to appear in the base type of a reference, then we would need perfect aliasing information to ensure that we can find all references to a certain location when its type is invalidated through mutation.

We have two judgments for checking expressions: one for local expressions and one for non-local expressions. The rules for local expressions are standard, but the rules for non-local expressions produce a condition γ that must hold in order for the judgment to be valid. This condition is generated during type checking and will be emitted as a run-time check unless it is discharged statically by the optimizer.

---

[1] In the full version of Deputy for C, local expressions exclude function calls, references to fields of other structures, and variables whose address is taken.

$\Gamma \vdash_L \tau :: \kappa$	In type environment Γ, τ is a local, well-formed type with kind κ.

$$\frac{}{\Gamma \vdash_L C :: \mathrm{kind}(C)}\ (\textsc{type ctor}) \qquad \frac{\Gamma \vdash_L \tau :: (\tau' \to \kappa) \quad \Gamma \vdash_L e : \tau'}{\Gamma \vdash_L \tau\ e :: \kappa}\ (\textsc{type exp}) \qquad \frac{\Gamma \vdash_L \tau_1 :: (\mathrm{type} \to \kappa) \quad \emptyset \vdash_L \tau_2 :: \mathrm{type}}{\Gamma \vdash_L \tau_1\ \tau_2 :: \kappa}\ (\textsc{type type})$$

$\Gamma \vdash_L e : \tau$	In type environment Γ, e is a local, well-typed expression with type τ.

$$\frac{\Gamma(x) = \tau}{\Gamma \vdash_L x : \tau}\ (\textsc{local name}) \qquad \frac{}{\Gamma \vdash_L n : \mathrm{int}}\ (\textsc{local num}) \qquad \frac{\Gamma \vdash_L e_1 : \mathrm{int} \quad \Gamma \vdash_L e_2 : \mathrm{int}}{\Gamma \vdash_L e_1\ \mathrm{op}\ e_2 : \mathrm{int}}\ (\textsc{local int arith})$$

$\Gamma \vdash e : \tau \Rightarrow \gamma$	In type environment Γ, e is a well-typed expression with type τ, if γ is satisfied.

$$\frac{\Gamma(x) = \tau}{\Gamma \vdash x : \tau \Rightarrow \mathrm{true}}\ (\textsc{var}) \qquad \frac{}{\Gamma \vdash n : \mathrm{int} \Rightarrow \mathrm{true}}\ (\textsc{num}) \qquad \frac{\Gamma \vdash e_1 : \mathrm{int} \Rightarrow \gamma_1 \quad \Gamma \vdash e_2 : \mathrm{int} \Rightarrow \gamma_2}{\Gamma \vdash e_1\ \mathrm{op}\ e_2 : \mathrm{int} \Rightarrow \gamma_1 \wedge \gamma_2}\ (\textsc{int arith}) \qquad \frac{\Gamma \vdash e : \mathrm{ref}\ \tau \Rightarrow \gamma}{\Gamma \vdash *e : \tau \Rightarrow \gamma}\ (\textsc{deref})$$

$\Gamma \vdash c \Rightarrow c'$	In type environment Γ, command c compiles to c', where c' is identical to c except for added assertions.

$$\frac{}{\Gamma \vdash \mathrm{skip} \Rightarrow \mathrm{skip}}\ (\textsc{skip}) \qquad \frac{\Gamma \vdash c_1 \Rightarrow c_1' \quad \Gamma \vdash c_2 \Rightarrow c_2'}{\Gamma \vdash c_1; c_2 \Rightarrow c_1'; c_2'}\ (\textsc{seq})$$

$$\frac{x \in \mathrm{Dom}(\Gamma) \quad \text{for all } (y : \tau_y) \in \Gamma,\ \ \Gamma \vdash y[^e/_x] : \tau_y[^e/_x] \Rightarrow \gamma_y}{\Gamma \vdash x := e \ \Rightarrow\ \mathrm{assert}(\bigwedge_{y \in \mathrm{Dom}(\Gamma)} \gamma_y);\ x := e}\ (\textsc{var write})$$

$$\frac{\Gamma \vdash e_1 : \mathrm{ref}\ \tau \Rightarrow \gamma_1 \quad \Gamma \vdash e_2 : \tau \Rightarrow \gamma_2}{\Gamma \vdash *e_1 := e_2 \ \Rightarrow\ \mathrm{assert}(\gamma_1 \wedge \gamma_2);\ *e_1 := e_2}\ (\textsc{mem write})$$

$$\frac{x \notin \mathrm{Dom}(\Gamma) \quad \Gamma, x : \tau \vdash_L \tau :: \mathrm{type} \quad \Gamma \vdash e : \tau[^e/_x] \Rightarrow \gamma \quad \Gamma, x : \tau \vdash c \Rightarrow c'}{\Gamma \vdash \mathrm{let}\ x : \tau = e\ \mathrm{in}\ c \ \Rightarrow\ \mathrm{assert}(\gamma);\ \mathrm{let}\ x : \tau = e\ \mathrm{in}\ c'}\ (\textsc{let})$$

$$\frac{x \notin \mathrm{Dom}(\Gamma) \quad \emptyset \vdash_L \tau :: \mathrm{type} \quad \Gamma \vdash e : \tau \Rightarrow \gamma \quad \Gamma, x : \mathrm{ref}\ \tau \vdash c \Rightarrow c'}{\Gamma \vdash \mathrm{let}\ x = \mathrm{new}\ \tau(e)\ \mathrm{in}\ c \ \Rightarrow\ \mathrm{assert}(\gamma);\ \mathrm{let}\ x = \mathrm{new}\ \tau(e)\ \mathrm{in}\ c'}\ (\textsc{alloc})$$

Fig. 3. The four judgments used by our type system and the core type checking rules for each. Additional rules (with nontrivial γ predicates) will be added later.

The rules presented in Figure 3 do not generate any interesting guard conditions themselves. Our intent is that an instantiation of this type system will provide additional type constructors whose typing rules include non-trivial guards. For example, to access arrays using the array constructor introduced earlier, we might add new typing rules for pointer arithmetic and dereference:

$$\text{(ARRAY DEREF)}\quad \frac{\Gamma \vdash e : \text{array}\ \tau\ e_{len} \Rightarrow \gamma_e}{\Gamma \vdash *e : \tau \Rightarrow \gamma_e \wedge (0 < e_{len})}$$

$$\text{(ARRAY ARITH)}\quad \frac{\Gamma \vdash e : \text{array}\ \tau\ e_{len} \Rightarrow \gamma_e \qquad \Gamma \vdash e' : \text{int} \Rightarrow \gamma_{e'}}{\Gamma \vdash e + e' : \text{array}\ \tau\ (e_{len} - e') \Rightarrow \gamma_e \wedge \gamma_{e'} \wedge (0 \leq e' \leq e_{len})}$$

These rules are responsible for the assertions generated in line 4 and line 7 in Figure 1. Note that we allow zero-length arrays to be constructed, but we check for this case at dereference; this approach is useful in programs that construct pointers to the end of an array, as allowed by ANSI C. We might also add a coercion rule, allowing long arrays to be used where shorter arrays are expected:

$$\text{(ARRAY COERCE)}\quad \frac{\Gamma \vdash e : \text{array}\ \tau\ e_{len} \Rightarrow \gamma_e \qquad \Gamma \vdash e'_{len} : \text{int} \Rightarrow \gamma_{e'_{len}}}{\Gamma \vdash e : \text{array}\ \tau\ e'_{len} \Rightarrow \gamma_e \wedge \gamma_{e'_{len}} \wedge (0 \leq e'_{len} \leq e_{len})}$$

In our implementation, we ensure that type checking is syntax-directed by invoking coercion rules only from the rules for commands.

The judgment for checking commands, written $\Gamma \vdash c \Rightarrow c'$, says that in environment Γ, command c is compiled to command c' by adding assertions with the necessary guard conditions. These two commands have identical semantics if no assertion in c' fails.

The (VAR WRITE) rule is responsible for updates to variables in the presence of dependent types and is a key contribution of our type system. This rule says that when updating a variable x with the value of expression e, we check all variables y in the current environment to see that their types still hold after substituting e for x. This rule essentially verifies that the assignment does not break any dependencies in the current scope.

The intuition for this rule is based on the Hoare axiom for assignment, which says that an assignment $x := e$ preserves an invariant ϕ if and only if one can prove that $\phi \implies \phi[{}^{e}\!/\!_{x}]$. If we view the type environment Γ as an invariant predicate on the state of the program, the (VAR WRITE) rule states that assignments maintain the invariant. Section 3.4 makes this intuition more precise.

To understand this rule in more detail, consider the following code:

$$\begin{array}{l} \text{let } n : \text{int} = \ldots \text{ in} \\ \text{let } a : \text{array int } n = \ldots \text{ in} \\ n := n - 1 \end{array}$$

In this example, decrementing n should be safe as long as $n \geq 1$, because if a is an array of length n, it is also an array of length $n-1$. When we apply the (VAR WRITE) rule to this assignment, the premises are $\Gamma \vdash n[^{n-1}/_n] : \text{int}[^{n-1}/_n] \Rightarrow \gamma_n$ and $\Gamma \vdash a[^{n-1}/_n] : (\text{array int } n)[^{n-1}/_n] \Rightarrow \gamma_a$. The first premise is trivial, with $\gamma_n = \text{true}$. The second premise is more interesting. After substitution, it becomes $\Gamma \vdash a : \text{array int } (n-1) \Rightarrow \gamma_a$. If we apply the (ARRAY COERCE) rule shown above, we can derive this judgment with $\gamma_a = 0 \leq n-1 \leq n$. After static optimization, this check can be reduced to $0 \leq n-1$, which is precisely the check we expected.[2]

Generally speaking, the (VAR WRITE) rule allows us to verify that dependencies in the local environment have not been broken, and the local-type restriction on base types of pointers ensures that there are no dependencies from the heap. In short, a combination of the Hoare-inspired assignment rule and the local type restriction have allowed us to verify mutation in the presence of dependent types.

The remainder of the rules for commands are largely straightforward. Note that the (MEM WRITE) rule requires no reasoning about dependencies because the well-formedness rule for reference types requires that the contents of a reference be independent of its environment. The (LET) and (ALLOC) rules require a substitution when checking e; however, since we are introducing a new variable, we need not check the rest of the environment as in the (VAR WRITE) rule.

3.3 Structures

We now extend our presentation to allow mutable C-like structures as a natural extension of our dependent types for local variables. We allow field types to depend on other fields of the same structure, which enables us to express common idioms such as a structure containing a pointer to an array along with its length.

To add structures to our language, we add several new syntactic constructs. We add the type "struct $\{f_1 : \tau_1; \ \ldots \ f_n : \tau_n\}$", which defines a mutable record type in which the ith field has label f_i and type τ_i, and we add the l-expression $\ell.f$, which accesses a field with name f. We also add the expression $\{f_1 = e_1; \ldots; f_n = e_n\}$, which is a structure literal that initializes field f_i to expression e_i. For example, we could declare a structure with two fields such that field f_1 is an array whose length is one greater than the value in field f_2:

$$y \ : \ \text{struct}\ \{f_1 : \text{array int } (f_2 + 1);\ f_2 : \text{int}\}$$

Note that it is legal to apply the "ref" constructor to a structure type whose fields depend on one another, because all of the structure type's dependencies are self-contained. Pointers to structures with internal dependencies are quite common in C programs.

Figure 4 shows the rules for type checking structures. The (TYPE STRUCT) rule ensures that field types depend only on other fields in the *same* structure. The (STRUCT READ) rule substitutes these field names with the appropriate

[2] We take care to account for possible overflow of machine arithmetic, which is simple when reasoning about array indices that must be bound by the length of an array.

$$\frac{\text{for all } 1 \le i \le n, \quad (f_1 : \tau_1, \ \ldots \ f_n : \tau_n) \vdash_L \tau_i :: \text{type}}{\Gamma \vdash_L \text{struct } \{f_1 : \tau_1; \ \ldots \ f_n : \tau_n\} :: \text{type}} \ (\text{TYPE STRUCT})$$

$$\frac{\text{for all } 1 \le i \le n, \quad \Gamma \vdash e_i : \tau_i \left[{}^{e_j}/_{f_j}\right]_{1 \le j \le n} \Rightarrow \gamma_i \qquad \gamma = \bigwedge_{1 \le j \le n} \gamma_i}{\Gamma \vdash \{f_1 = e_1; \ldots; f_n = e_n\} : \text{struct } \{f_1 : \tau_1; \ \ldots \ f_n : \tau_n\} \Rightarrow \gamma} \ (\text{STRUCT LITERAL})$$

$$\frac{\Gamma \vdash \ell : \text{struct } \{f_1 : \tau_1; \ \ldots \ f_n : \tau_n\} \Rightarrow \gamma_\ell}{\Gamma \vdash \ell.f_i : \tau_i \left[{}^{\ell.f_j}/_{f_j}\right]_{1 \le j \le n} \Rightarrow \gamma_\ell} \ (\text{STRUCT READ})$$

$$\frac{\begin{array}{l}\Gamma \vdash \ell : \text{struct } \{f_1 : \tau_1; \ \ldots \ f_n : \tau_n\} \Rightarrow \gamma_\ell \\ \text{for all } 1 \le j \le n, \quad \Gamma \vdash \rho(f_j) : \rho(\tau_j) \Rightarrow \gamma_j \\ \text{where } \rho(e') = e' \left[{}^{e}/_{f_i}, {}^{\ell.f_j}/_{f_j}\right]_{1 \le j \le n, j \ne i}\end{array}}{\Gamma \vdash \ell.f_i := e \ \Rightarrow \ \text{assert}(\gamma_\ell \wedge \bigwedge_{1 \le j \le n} \gamma_j); \ \ell.f_i := e} \ (\text{STRUCT WRITE})$$

Fig. 4. Structure type checking rules

expressions; for example, using the declaration above, a read from $y.f_1$ would have type "array int $(y.f_2 + 1)$". The (STRUCT WRITE) rule is analogous to the (VAR WRITE) rule; when a field is changed, we check all of the other fields in the current environment to make sure that any dependencies are satisfied.

In the technical report [5], we present a similar extension that allows us to type check calls to functions whose arguments depend on one another.

3.4 Soundness

We have proved the soundness of the core type system of Section 3.2. We omit the details of this proof for space reasons, but we present here the formal requirements on the framework for ensuring sound handling of mutation in presence of dependent types. Full details can be found in the technical report [5].

We define the state of execution, ρ, to be a tuple containing, among other things, a mapping ρ_A from addresses to types representing the allocation state. We define $[\![e]\!]\rho$ to be the value $v \in \text{Val}$ of expression e in state ρ.

An essential element of the formalization is that for each type τ we can define the set of values of that type in state ρ as $[\![\tau]\!]\rho$, as follows:

$$[\![\text{int}]\!]\rho = \text{Val} \qquad [\![\tau_1 \ \tau_2]\!]\rho = ([\![\tau_1]\!]\rho)([\![\tau_2]\!]\rho)$$
$$[\![\text{ref}]\!]\rho = \lambda t.\{a \in \text{Dom}(\rho_A) | t = [\![\rho_A(a)]\!]\rho\} \qquad [\![\tau \ e]\!]\rho = ([\![\tau]\!]\rho)([\![e]\!]\rho)$$

In particular, each constructor C must have some meaning given by $[\![C]\!]\rho$. If additional constructors are added, the proof requires that their meanings be given as well, and in some cases, these definitions may require an augmented notion of state (e.g., a constructor characterizing lock state may require a history of locking operations). The fact that types have state-based meanings allows us to view the type environment as a predicate on the state of the program, which is essential for the adequacy of using Hoare's assignment axiom for type checking.

3.5 Limitations

One limitation of this type system is its flow-insensitivity. For example, incrementing an array before decrementing its length would result in an error even though these two operations are safe when taken together. One way to overcome this limitation is to use automatic dependencies to generate fresh dependencies for local variables, as discussed in Section 4. Another alternative is to use an extended (VAR WRITE) rule that handles several statements at once.

A second limitation is the use of local expressions. Although many dependencies can be annotated correctly using local expressions, there are a number of dependencies that cannot be directly expressed in this way. In these cases, the programmer must rewrite the code or mark it as trusted. We believe that such rewrites are good practice even in the absence of a verifier such as Deputy.

4 Automatic Dependencies

Until now, we have presented our type checker under the assumption that all dependent types were fully specified. To reduce the programmer burden, our type system includes a feature called *automatic dependencies*, which automatically adds missing dependencies of local variables. As described in Section 2, this feature operates as a preprocessing step before type checking.

We allow local variables to omit expressions in their dependent types. For example, a variable might be declared to have type "array int", where the length of the array is unspecified. For every missing expression in a dependent type of a local variable, we introduce a new local variable that is updated along with the original variable. For example, in Figure 1, we added `tmplen` to track the length of `tmp`, updating it as appropriate.

Formally, we maintain a mapping Δ from variables to the list of new variables that were added to track their dependencies. If a variable x had a complete type in the original program, $\Delta(x)$ is the empty list. We describe the automatic dependency inference as a judgment $\Gamma; \Delta \vdash c \rightsquigarrow c'$, which says that in the context $\Gamma; \Delta$, the command c can be transformed into command c' such that all types in c' are complete and such that c' computes the same result as c.

The interesting rules for deriving this judgment are given in Figure 5. In the (AUTO LET) rule, we add new variables to track any missing dependencies for x. These variables are initialized using expressions from the type of e (by using the type checking judgment). Note that γ is unused in this rule; however, it will be checked appropriately during the type checking phase. In the (AUTO VAR WRITE) rule, we update all of the automatic variables associated with x using a similar approach. For the purposes of this rule, we add syntax for parallel assignment, written $x_1, \ldots, x_n := e_1, \ldots, e_n$, where all expressions e_i are evaluated before assignments take place. The type checking rule for parallel assignment is

$$\frac{\begin{array}{c}(\text{AUTO LET})\\ \Gamma \vdash_L \tau :: \tau_1 \to \ldots \to \tau_n \to \text{type} \qquad \Gamma \vdash e : \tau\ e_1 \ldots e_n \Rightarrow \gamma \\ \tau' = \tau\ x_1 \ldots x_n \qquad x_1, \ldots, x_n \text{ fresh} \\ (\Gamma, x_1 : \tau_1, \ldots, x_n : \tau_n, x : \tau); (\Delta, x \mapsto (x_1, \ldots, x_n)) \vdash c \rightsquigarrow c'\end{array}}{\begin{array}{c}\Gamma; \Delta \vdash \text{let } x : \tau = e \text{ in } c \rightsquigarrow \\ \text{let } x_1 : \tau_1 = e_1 \text{ in } \ldots \text{let } x_n : \tau_n = e_n \text{ in let } x : \tau' = e \text{ in } c'\end{array}}$$

$$\frac{\begin{array}{c}(\text{AUTO VAR WRITE})\\ \Gamma(x) = \tau\ x_1 \ldots x_n \qquad \Delta(x) = (x_1, \ldots, x_n) \\ \Gamma \vdash e : \tau\ e_1 \ldots e_n \Rightarrow \gamma\end{array}}{\Gamma; \Delta \vdash x := e \ \rightsquigarrow\ x,\ x_1, \ldots, x_n := e,\ e_1, \ldots, e_n}$$

Fig. 5. Rules for automatic dependencies

a straightforward extension of the (VAR WRITE) rule. Note that this technique is independent of the actual dependent types in use.

In the following example, the underlined code can be inferred using this technique:

$$\begin{array}{l}\text{let } a1 : \text{array int } n1 = \ldots \text{ in} \\ \text{let } a2 : \text{array int } n2 = \ldots \text{ in} \\ \underline{\text{let } nx : \text{int} = n1 \text{ in}} \\ \text{let } x : \text{array int } \underline{nx} = a1 \text{ in} \\ \text{if } (\ldots) \text{ then } x,\ \underline{nx} := a2,\ \underline{n2}; \\ *(x+3) := 0;\end{array}$$

By using automatic dependencies, we ensure that nx contains the number of elements in x regardless of which branch of the conditional was taken. Inferring a similar result with a purely static analysis would be much more difficult. Note, however, that in cases where static analysis would suffice, our optimizer can eliminate variables and assignments that were introduced by this transformation.

This transformation recovers some of the flow-sensitivity that is absent in the core type system. In many cases, it is difficult to annotate a variable with a single dependent type that is valid throughout a function. By adding fresh variables that are automatically updated with the appropriate values, we provide the programmer with a form of flow-sensitive dependent type. As with the optimizer, we have found that separating this feature from the core type system simplifies both the implementation and the user's view of the type system.

5 Dependent Types for C

We now show how our dependent type framework can be instantiated to support pointer bounds and tagged unions in C programs. Further details can be found in the SafeDrive paper [21] (see related work) and in the technical report [5].

5.1 Pointer Bounds

Our type constructor for bounded pointers is a generalization of the array constructor presented earlier. This new type, written "ptr τ lo hi", represents a possibly-null pointer to an array of elements of type τ, where lo and hi are expressions that indicate the bounds of this array. Specifically, lo is the address of the first accessible element of the array, and hi is the address of the first inaccessible element after the end of the area. We also add to the language an operator $\oplus$ for C-style pointer arithmetic, which moves a pointer forwards or backwards by a certain number of elements rather than bytes. The $\oplus$ operator may be used in local expressions. Finally, we add typing rules for all relevant operations on this type (e.g., dereference and arithmetic), the details of which can be found in the technical report [5]. Examples of the ptr type are as follows:

$$x : \text{ptr int } b\ (b \oplus 8) \quad \text{// 8 integer area starting at } b$$
$$x : \text{ptr int } x\ (x \oplus n) \quad \text{// } n \text{ integer area starting at } x$$
$$x : \text{ptr int } x\ e \quad \text{// from } x \text{ to } e$$

These declarations (with syntactic sugar for common cases) offer C programmers a tractable but expressive way to declare pointer bounds without modifying existing data structures. Note that many of the uses of this type involve self-dependencies, which are made tractable by our support for mutation.

5.2 Dependent Union Types

To ensure that C unions are used correctly, programmers often provide a "tag" that indicates which union field is currently in use; however, the conventions for how this tag is used vary from program to program. Our type system provides dependent type annotations that allow the programmer to specify for each union field the condition that must hold when that field is in use.

To introduce unions, we add a family of new type constructors called "union$_n$", where n indicates the number of fields in the union. This constructor takes n type arguments indicating the types of each field of the union as well as n integer arguments indicating whether the corresponding field of the union is currently active. Thus, we write a union type as "union$_n$ τ_1 $\dots$ τ_n e_1 $\dots$ e_n", where τ_i are the field types and e_i are *selector expressions*. If selector e_j is nonzero, then the corresponding field with type τ_j is the active field of the union. As usual, the selectors are local expressions, so they can depend on other values in the current environment just as pointer bounds do. As with bounded pointers, we add type rules for the relevant operations on this new type constructor. For example:

$$x : \text{struct } \{\ tag : \text{int};\ u : \text{union}_2 \text{ int (ref int) } (tag \geq 2)\ (tag = 1)\ \}$$

Here, we have a structure containing a union and its associated tag, which is a common idiom found in C programs. The union $x.u$ contains two fields: an integer and a reference to an integer. The selector expressions indicate that the union contains an integer when $tag \geq 2$ and that it contains an integer reference when $tag = 1$. Note that these selector expressions must be mutually exclusive.

5.3 Experiments

We implemented Deputy using the CIL infrastructure [15].[3] Our implementation is 18,000 lines of OCaml code in addition to the CIL front-end itself. Given an annotated C program, our implementation adds automatic bounds variables, type checks the program (which inserts run-time checks), optimizes the inserted checks, and then emits the program as C code for compilation with `gcc`. The flow-sensitive optimizer tracks facts such as which pointers are null, and it uses forward substitution of locals plus basic arithmetic facts to eliminate inserted checks and to detect checks that will always fail [1]. To use Deputy, programmers run `deputy` in place of `gcc` as their compiler, and then they modify code or type annotations in order to eliminate the resulting compile-time and run-time errors.

Our implementation covers most of C's features, many of which are not discussed in this paper. However, we do not check inline assembly, some variable-argument functions, and code explicitly marked as trusted by the programmer. In addition, Deputy does not check memory deallocation, which is an orthogonal problem; for now, the user can choose to trust deallocations or to run a garbage collector. Aside from these caveats, Deputy ensures that the program is free of type and memory errors, including bounds violations and misuse of unions.

To test Deputy, we annotated a number of standard benchmarks, including Olden [4], Ptrdist [3], and selected tests from the SPEC CPU [18] and MediaBench [12] suites. We also used Deputy to enforce type safety in version 2 of the TinyOS [10] sensor network operating system, including three simple demo applications: periodic LED blinking (Blink), forwarding radio packets to and from a PC (BaseStation), and simple periodic data acquisition (Oscilloscope). Finally, we have applied Deputy to a number of Linux device drivers for use with the SafeDrive driver recovery system [21].

Results for these experiments are shown in Table 1. In all experiments, we changed less than 11% of the lines of code in the program; in most cases, we changed about 2-4%. We added a total of 27 trusted annotations that tell Deputy to ignore bad code. The slowdown exhibited by these benchmarks was within 25% in at least half of the tests, with 98% overhead in the worst case. With the sole exception of `yacr2` (on the Ptrdist benchmarks), Deputy's performance improves on the performance reported for CCured on the SPEC, Olden, and Ptrdist benchmarks [14]. However, CCured is checking stack overflow and uses a garbage collector, whereas Deputy is not. Nevertheless, these numbers show that Deputy's run-time checks have a relatively low performance penalty that is competitive with other memory safety tools. Further details can be found in the accompanying technical report [5] and in the SafeDrive paper [21].

During these tests Deputy found several bugs. A run-time failure in a Deputy-inserted check exposed a bug in TinyOS's radio stack (some packets with invalid lengths were not being properly filtered). In `epic` we found an array bounds violation and a call to `close` that should have been a call to `fclose`. We also caught several bugs that we were previously aware of: `ks` has two type errors in arguments to `fprintf`, and `go` has six array bounds violations.

[3] This implementation is available at `http://deputy.cs.berkeley.edu/`

Table 1. Deputy benchmarks. For each test, we show the size of the benchmark including comments, the number of lines we changed in order to use Deputy, and the ratio of the execution time under Deputy to the original execution time. "OS components" are the parts of TinyOS used by the three TinyOS programs.

Suite	Benchmark	Lines	Lines Changed	Exec. Time Ratio
SPEC	`go`	29722	80 (0.3%)	1.11
	`gzip`	8673	149 (1.7%)	1.23
	`li`	9636	319 (3.3%)	1.50
Olden	`bh`	1907	139 (7.3%)	1.21
	`bisort`	684	24 (3.5%)	1.01
	`em3d`	585	45 (7.7%)	1.56
	`health`	717	15 (2.1%)	1.02
	`mst`	606	66 (10.9%)	1.02
	`perimeter`	395	3 (0.8%)	0.98
	`power`	768	20 (2.6%)	1.00
	`treeadd`	377	40 (10.6%)	0.94
	`tsp`	565	4 (0.7%)	1.02
Ptrdist	`anagram`	635	36 (5.7%)	1.40
	`bc`	7395	191 (2.6%)	1.30
	`ft`	1904	58 (3.0%)	1.03
	`ks`	792	16 (2.0%)	1.10
	`yacr2`	3976	181 (4.6%)	1.98
MediaBench I	`adpcm`	387	15 (3.9%)	1.02
	`epic`	3469	240 (6.9%)	1.79
TinyOS	`Blink`	74	0 (0%)	1.04
	`BaseStation`	282	0 (0%)	1.17
	`Oscilloscope`	149	3 (2.0%)	1.13
	OS components	11698	48 (0.4%)	–

6 Related Work

SafeDrive. In a companion paper, we present SafeDrive [21], a system for safe and recoverable Linux device drivers that uses Deputy to detect faults. The SafeDrive paper contains a high-level description of Deputy from the C programmer's perspective, whereas this paper presents in detail the principles behind our type system, including our techniques for handling mutation and automatic dependencies.

Dependent types. DML [20], Xanadu [19], and Cayenne [2] are previous languages that use dependent types. In DML and Xanadu, expressions appearing in dependent types are different from program expressions and must be decidable at compile time. In Cayenne, arbitrary expressions from the same language are allowed, and thus the type system may be undecidable. We attempt to find a middle ground, allowing expressive annotations in the source language while using run-time checks to keep the type checker simple and decidable. We also allow mutation of expressions in dependent types, unlike these other systems.

Hoare Type Theory [13] uses a monadic type constructor based on Hoare triples to isolate and reason about mutation in dependently-typed imperative programs. In contrast, we assign flow-insensitive types to each program variable, using run-time checks for decidability and automatic dependencies for usability.

Harren and Necula [9] developed a dependent type system for verifying the assembly-level output of CCured. Their system allows dependencies on mutable data, but it requires programs to be statically verifiable.

Microsoft's SAL annotation language [8] provides interface annotations similar to those of Deputy. These annotations are viewed as preconditions and postconditions as opposed to Deputy's simpler flow-insensitive types. Microsoft's ESPX checker attempts to check all code statically, whereas Deputy is designed to emit run-time checks for additional flexibility.

Hybrid type checking. Our type system uses a form of hybrid type checking [7] with a flow-insensitive type system and automatic dependency generation. We demonstrate the effectiveness of this approach for low-level code.

Ou et al. [16] present a type system that splits a program into portions that are either dependently or simply typed, using run-time checks at the boundaries. Our type system uses run-time checks for safety everywhere and relies on an optimizer to handle statically verifiable cases. Ou et al. allow coercions between simply- and dependently-typed mutable references at the cost of a complex run-time representation for such references. In contrast, we focus on handling mutation of local variables and structure fields in the presence of dependencies.

Gradual typing [17] allows static and dynamic types to coexist using run-time checks, but it does not use dependent types.

Safety for imperative programs. CCured [14] analyzes a whole program in order to instrument pointers with checkable bounds information, and Cyclone [11] is a type-safe variant of C that incorporates many modern language features. Both use "fat" pointers, which make the resulting programs incompatible with existing libraries; Deputy's dependent types solve this crucial problem. Cyclone allows some dependent type annotations; for example, the programmer can annotate a pointer with the number of elements it points to. Deputy provides more general pointer bound support as well as support for dependent union types.

Dhurjati and Adve [6] use run-time checks to ensure that C programs access objects within their allocated bounds. Their system has low overhead on a set of small to medium-size programs but does not ensure full type safety.

7 Conclusion

We have described a series of techniques that allow dependent types to be used in existing low-level imperative programs. Inspired by the handling of assignment in axiomatic semantics, we have designed a type rule for assignment that is simple yet powerful, allowing us to handle mutation in the presence of dependent types. We address decidability with run-time checks, and we address usability with a technique for automatic dependency generation. The result is a practical type system for annotating and checking low-level code.

Acknowledgments. Thanks to Feng Zhou, Ilya Bagrak, Bill McCloskey, Rob Ennals, and Eric Brewer for their contributions. This material is based upon work supported by the National Science Foundation under Grant Nos. CCR-0326577, CCF-0524784, and CNS-0509544, as well as gifts from Intel Corporation.

References

1. ANDERSON, Z. R. Static analysis of C for hybrid type checking. Tech. Rep. EECS-2007-1, UC Berkeley, 2007.
2. AUGUSTSSON, L. Cayenne—a language with dependent types. In *ICFP'98*.
3. AUSTIN, T. M., BREACH, S. E., AND SOHI, G. S. Efficient detection of all pointer and array access errors. In *PLDI'94*.
4. CARLISLE, M. C. *Olden: Parallelizing Programs with Dynamic Data Structures on Distributed-Memory Machines.* PhD thesis, Princeton University, June 1996.
5. CONDIT, J., HARREN, M., ANDERSON, Z., GAY, D., AND NECULA, G. Dependent types for low-level programming. Tech. Rep. EECS-2006-129, UC Berkeley, 2006.
6. DHURJATI, D., AND ADVE, V. Backwards-compatible array bounds checking for C with very low overhead. In *ICSE'06*.
7. FLANAGAN, C. Hybrid type checking. In *POPL'06*.
8. HACKETT, B., DAS, M., WANG, D., AND YANG, Z. Modular checking for buffer overflows in the large. In *ICSE'06*.
9. HARREN, M., AND NECULA, G. C. Using dependent types to certify the safety of assembly code. In *SAS'05*.
10. HILL, J., SZEWCZYK, R., WOO, A., HOLLAR, S., CULLER, D. E., AND PISTER, K. S. J. System architecture directions for networked sensors. In *ASPLOS'00*.
11. JIM, T., MORRISETT, G., GROSSMAN, D., HICKS, M., CHENEY, J., AND WANG, Y. Cyclone: A safe dialect of C. In *USENIX Annual Technical Conference* (2002).
12. LEE, C., POTKONJAK, M., AND MANGIONE-SMITH, W. H. MediaBench: A tool for evaluating and synthesizing multimedia and communicatons systems. In *International Symposium on Microarchitecture* (1997).
13. NANEVSKI, A., AND MORRISETT, G. Dependent type theory of stateful higher-order functions. Tech. Rep. TR-24-05, Harvard University.
14. NECULA, G. C., CONDIT, J., HARREN, M., MCPEAK, S., AND WEIMER, W. CCured: Type-safe retrofitting of legacy software. *TOPLAS 27*, 3 (May 2005).
15. NECULA, G. C., MCPEAK, S., AND WEIMER, W. CIL: Intermediate language and tools for the analysis of C programs. In *CC'02*, Grenoble, France.
16. OU, X., TAN, G., MANDELBAUM, Y., AND WALKER, D. Dynamic typing with dependent types. In *IFIP Conference on Theoretical Computer Science* (2004).
17. SIEK, J. G., AND TAHA, W. Gradual typing for functional languages. In *Scheme and Functional Programming* (2006).
18. SPEC. Standard Performance Evaluation Corporation Benchmarks. *http://www.spec.org/osg/cpu95/CINT95* (July 1995).
19. XI, H. Imperative programming with dependent types. In *LICS'00*.
20. XI, H., AND PFENNING, F. Dependent types in practical programming. In *POPL'99*.
21. ZHOU, F., CONDIT, J., ANDERSON, Z., BAGRAK, I., ENNALS, R., HARREN, M., NECULA, G., AND BREWER, E. SafeDrive: Safe and recoverable extensions using language-based techniques. In *OSDI'06*.

Author Index

Lecture Notes in Computer Science

For information about Vols. 1–4312

please contact your bookseller or Springer

Vol. 4429: R. Lu, J.H. Siekmann, C. Ullrich (Eds.), Cognitive Systems. X, 161 pages. 2007. (Sublibrary LNAI).

Vol. 4424: O. Grumberg, M. Huth (Eds.), Tools and Algorithms for the Construction and Analysis of Systems. XX, 738 pages. 2007.

Vol. 4422: M.B. Dwyer, A. Lopes (Eds.), Fundamental Approaches to Software Engineering. XV, 440 pages. 2007.

Vol. 4421: R. De Nicola (Ed.), Programming Languages and Systems. XVII, 538 pages. 2007.

Vol. 4420: S. Krishnamurthi, M. Odersky (Eds.), Compiler Construction. XIV, 233 pages. 2007.

Vol. 4415: P. Lukowicz, L. Thiele, G. Tröster (Eds.), Architecture of Computing Systems - ARCS 2007. X, 297 pages. 2007.

Vol. 4414: S. Hochreiter, R. Wagner (Eds.), Bioinformatics Research and Development. XVI, 482 pages. 2007. (Sublibrary LNBI).

Vol. 4405: L. Padgham, F. Zambonelli (Eds.), Agent-Oriented Software Engineering VII. XII, 225 pages. 2007.

Vol. 4403: S. Obayashi, K. Deb, C. Poloni, T. Hiroyasu, T. Murata (Eds.), Evolutionary Multi-Criterion Optimization. XIX, 954 pages. 2007.

Vol. 4397: C. Stephanidis, M. Pieper (Eds.), Universal Access in Ambient Intelligence Environments. XV, 467 pages. 2007.

Vol. 4396: J. García-Vidal, L. Cerdà-Alabern (Eds.), Wireless Systems and Mobility in Next Generation Internet. IX, 271 pages. 2007.

Vol. 4394: A. Gelbukh (Ed.), Computational Linguistics and Intelligent Text Processing. XVI, 648 pages. 2007.

Vol. 4393: W. Thomas, P. Weil (Eds.), STACS 2007. XVIII, 708 pages. 2007.

Vol. 4392: S.P. Vadhan (Ed.), Theory of Cryptography. XI, 595 pages. 2007.

Vol. 4390: S.O. Kuznetsov, S. Schmidt (Eds.), Formal Concept Analysis. X, 329 pages. 2007. (Sublibrary LNAI).

Vol. 4389: D. Weyns, H.V.D. Parunak, F. Michel (Eds.), Environments for Multi-Agent Systems III. X, 273 pages. 2007. (Sublibrary LNAI).

Vol. 4385: K. Coninx, K. Luyten, K.A. Schneider (Eds.), Task Models and Diagrams for Users Interface Design. XI, 355 pages. 2007.

Vol. 4384: T. Washio, K. Satoh, H. Takeda, A. Inokuchi (Eds.), New Frontiers in Artificial Intelligence. IX, 401 pages. 2007. (Sublibrary LNAI).

Vol. 4383: E. Bin, A. Ziv, S. Ur (Eds.), Hardware and Software, Verification and Testing. XII, 235 pages. 2007.

Vol. 4381: J. Akiyama, W.Y.C. Chen, M. Kano, X. Li, Q. Yu (Eds.), Discrete Geometry, Combinatorics and Graph Theory. XI, 289 pages. 2007.

Vol. 4380: S. Spaccapietra, P. Atzeni, F. Fages, M.-S. Hacid, M. Kifer, J. Mylopoulos, B. Pernici, P. Shvaiko, J. Trujillo, I. Zaihrayeu (Eds.), Journal on Data Semantics VIII. XV, 219 pages. 2007.

Vol. 4378: I. Virbitskaite, A. Voronkov (Eds.), Perspectives of Systems Informatics. XIV, 496 pages. 2007.

Vol. 4377: M. Abe (Ed.), Topics in Cryptology – CT-RSA 2007. XI, 403 pages. 2006.

Vol. 4376: E. Frachtenberg, U. Schwiegelshohn (Eds.), Job Scheduling Strategies for Parallel Processing. VII, 257 pages. 2007.

Vol. 4374: J.F. Peters, A. Skowron, I. Düntsch, J. Grzymała-Busse, E. Orłowska, L. Polkowski (Eds.), Transactions on Rough Sets VI, Part I. XII, 499 pages. 2007.

Vol. 4373: K. Langendoen, T. Voigt (Eds.), Wireless Sensor Networks. XIII, 358 pages. 2007.

Vol. 4372: M. Kaufmann, D. Wagner (Eds.), Graph Drawing. XIV, 454 pages. 2007.

Vol. 4371: K. Inoue, K. Satoh, F. Toni (Eds.), Computational Logic in Multi-Agent Systems. X, 315 pages. 2007. (Sublibrary LNAI).

Vol. 4370: P.P Lévy, B. Le Grand, F. Poulet, M. Soto, L. Darago, L. Toubiana, J.-F. Vibert (Eds.), Pixelization Paradigm. XV, 279 pages. 2007.

Vol. 4369: M. Umeda, A. Wolf, O. Bartenstein, U. Geske, D. Seipel, O. Takata (Eds.), Declarative Programming for Knowledge Management. X, 229 pages. 2006. (Sublibrary LNAI).

Vol. 4368: T. Erlebach, C. Kaklamanis (Eds.), Approximation and Online Algorithms. X, 345 pages. 2007.

Vol. 4367: K. De Bosschere, D. Kaeli, P. Stenström, D. Whalley, T. Ungerer (Eds.), High Performance Embedded Architectures and Compilers. XI, 307 pages. 2007.

Vol. 4366: K. Tuyls, R. Westra, Y. Saeys, A. Nowé (Eds.), Knowledge Discovery and Emergent Complexity in Bioinformatics. IX, 183 pages. 2007. (Sublibrary LNBI).

Vol. 4364: T. Kühne (Ed.), Models in Software Engineering. XI, 332 pages. 2007.

Vol. 4362: J. van Leeuwen, G.F. Italiano, W. van der Hoek, C. Meinel, H. Sack, F. Plášil (Eds.), SOFSEM 2007: Theory and Practice of Computer Science. XXI, 937 pages. 2007.

Vol. 4361: H.J. Hoogeboom, G. Păun, G. Rozenberg, A. Salomaa (Eds.), Membrane Computing. IX, 555 pages. 2006.

Vol. 4360: W. Dubitzky, A. Schuster, P.M.A. Sloot, M. Schroeder, M. Romberg (Eds.), Distributed, High-Performance and Grid Computing in Computational Biology. X, 192 pages. 2007. (Sublibrary LNBI).

Vol. 4358: R. Vidal, A. Heyden, Y. Ma (Eds.), Dynamical Vision. IX, 329 pages. 2007.

Vol. 4357: L. Buttyán, V. Gligor, D. Westhoff (Eds.), Security and Privacy in Ad-Hoc and Sensor Networks. X, 193 pages. 2006.

Vol. 4355: J. Julliand, O. Kouchnarenko (Eds.), B 2007: Formal Specification and Development in B. XIII, 293 pages. 2006.

Vol. 4354: M. Hanus (Ed.), Practical Aspects of Declarative Languages. X, 335 pages. 2006.

Vol. 4353: T. Schwentick, D. Suciu (Eds.), Database Theory - ICDT 2007. XI, 419 pages. 2006.

Vol. 4352: T.-J. Cham, J. Cai, C. Dorai, D. Rajan, T.-S. Chua, L.-T. Chia (Eds.), Advances in Multimedia Modeling, Part II. XVIII, 743 pages. 2006.

Vol. 4351: T.-J. Cham, J. Cai, C. Dorai, D. Rajan, T.-S. Chua, L.-T. Chia (Eds.), Advances in Multimedia Modeling, Part I. XIX, 797 pages. 2006.

Vol. 4349: B. Cook, A. Podelski (Eds.), Verification, Model Checking, and Abstract Interpretation. XI, 395 pages. 2007.

Vol. 4348: S.T. Taft, R.A. Duff, R.L. Brukardt, E. Ploedereder, P. Leroy (Eds.), Ada 2005 Reference Manual. XXII, 765 pages. 2006.

Vol. 4347: J. Lopez (Ed.), Critical Information Infrastructures Security. X, 286 pages. 2006.

Vol. 4346: L. Brim, B. Haverkort, M. Leucker, J. van de Pol (Eds.), Formal Methods: Applications and Technology. X, 363 pages. 2007.

Vol. 4345: N. Maglaveras, I. Chouvarda, V. Koutkias, R. Brause (Eds.), Biological and Medical Data Analysis. XIII, 496 pages. 2006. (Sublibrary LNBI).

Vol. 4344: V. Gruhn, F. Oquendo (Eds.), Software Architecture. X, 245 pages. 2006.

Vol. 4342: H. de Swart, E. Orłowska, G. Schmidt, M. Roubens (Eds.), Theory and Applications of Relational Structures as Knowledge Instruments II. X, 373 pages. 2006. (Sublibrary LNAI).

Vol. 4341: P.Q. Nguyen (Ed.), Progress in Cryptology - VIETCRYPT 2006. XI, 385 pages. 2006.

Vol. 4340: R. Prodan, T. Fahringer, Grid Computing. XXIII, 317 pages. 2007.

Vol. 4339: E. Ayguadé, G. Baumgartner, J. Ramanujam, P. Sadayappan (Eds.), Languages and Compilers for Parallel Computing. XI, 476 pages. 2006.

Vol. 4338: P. Kalra, S. Peleg (Eds.), Computer Vision, Graphics and Image Processing. XV, 965 pages. 2006.

Vol. 4337: S. Arun-Kumar, N. Garg (Eds.), FSTTCS 2006: Foundations of Software Technology and Theoretical Computer Science. XIII, 430 pages. 2006.

Vol. 4336: V.R. Basili, H.D. Rombach, K. Schneider, B. Kitchenham, D. Pfahl, R.W. Selby, Empirical Software Engineering Issues. XVII, 194 pages. 2007.

Vol. 4335: S.A. Brueckner, S. Hassas, M. Jelasity, D. Yamins (Eds.), Engineering Self-Organising Systems. XII, 212 pages. 2007. (Sublibrary LNAI).

Vol. 4334: B. Beckert, R. Hähnle, P.H. Schmitt (Eds.), Verification of Object-Oriented Software. XXIX, 658 pages. 2007. (Sublibrary LNAI).

Vol. 4333: U. Reimer, D. Karagiannis (Eds.), Practical Aspects of Knowledge Management. XII, 338 pages. 2006. (Sublibrary LNAI).

Vol. 4332: A. Bagchi, V. Atluri (Eds.), Information Systems Security. XV, 382 pages. 2006.

Vol. 4331: G. Min, B. Di Martino, L.T. Yang, M. Guo, G. Ruenger (Eds.), Frontiers of High Performance Computing and Networking – ISPA 2006 Workshops. XXXVII, 1141 pages. 2006.

Vol. 4330: M. Guo, L.T. Yang, B. Di Martino, H.P. Zima, J. Dongarra, F. Tang (Eds.), Parallel and Distributed Processing and Applications. XVIII, 953 pages. 2006.

Vol. 4329: R. Barua, T. Lange (Eds.), Progress in Cryptology - INDOCRYPT 2006. X, 454 pages. 2006.

Vol. 4328: D. Penkler, M. Reitenspiess, F. Tam (Eds.), Service Availability. X, 289 pages. 2006.

Vol. 4327: M. Baldoni, U. Endriss (Eds.), Declarative Agent Languages and Technologies IV. VIII, 257 pages. 2006. (Sublibrary LNAI).

Vol. 4326: S. Göbel, R. Malkewitz, I. Iurgel (Eds.), Technologies for Interactive Digital Storytelling and Entertainment. X, 384 pages. 2006.

Vol. 4325: J. Cao, I. Stojmenovic, X. Jia, S.K. Das (Eds.), Mobile Ad-hoc and Sensor Networks. XIX, 887 pages. 2006.

Vol. 4323: G. Doherty, A. Blandford (Eds.), Interactive Systems. XI, 269 pages. 2007.

Vol. 4322: F. Kordon, J. Sztipanovits (Eds.), Reliable Systems on Unreliable Networked Platforms. XIV, 317 pages. 2007.

Vol. 4320: R. Gotzhein, R. Reed (Eds.), System Analysis and Modeling: Language Profiles. X, 229 pages. 2006.

Vol. 4319: L.-W. Chang, W.-N. Lie (Eds.), Advances in Image and Video Technology. XXVI, 1347 pages. 2006.

Vol. 4318: H. Lipmaa, M. Yung, D. Lin (Eds.), Information Security and Cryptology. XI, 305 pages. 2006.

Vol. 4317: S.K. Madria, K.T. Claypool, R. Kannan, P. Uppuluri, M.M. Gore (Eds.), Distributed Computing and Internet Technology. XIX, 466 pages. 2006.

Vol. 4316: M.M. Dalkilic, S. Kim, J. Yang (Eds.), Data Mining and Bioinformatics. VIII, 197 pages. 2006. (Sublibrary LNBI).

Vol. 4314: C. Freksa, M. Kohlhase, K. Schill (Eds.), KI 2006: Advances in Artificial Intelligence. XII, 458 pages. 2007. (Sublibrary LNAI).

Vol. 4313: T. Margaria, B. Steffen (Eds.), Leveraging Applications of Formal Methods. IX, 197 pages. 2006.